THE O

THE
O

THE OXFORD HANDBOOK OF

THE SOCIOLOGY OF RELIGION

Edited by

PETER B. CLARKE

OXFORD
UNIVERSITY PRESS

Great Clarendon Street, Oxford OX2 6DP

Oxford University Press is a department of the University of Oxford.
It furthers the University's objective of excellence in research, scholarship,
and education by publishing worldwide in

Oxford New York

Auckland Cape Town Dar es Salaam Hong Kong Karachi
Kuala Lumpur Madrid Melbourne Mexico City Nairobi
New Delhi Shanghai Taipei Toronto

With offices in

Argentina Austria Brazil Chile Czech Republic France Greece
Guatemala Hungary Italy Japan Poland Portugal Singapore
South Korea Switzerland Thailand Turkey Ukraine Vietnam

Oxford is a registered trade mark of Oxford University Press
in the UK and in certain other countries

Published in the United States
by Oxford University Press Inc., New York

First published 2009
First published in paperback 2011

British Library Cataloguing in Publication Data
Data available

Library of Congress Cataloging in Publication Data
Data available

Typeset by SPI Publisher Services, Pondicherry, India
Printed in Great Britain
on acid-free paper by
CPI Antony Rowe
Chippenham, Wilts.

ISBN 978–0–19–927979–1 (Hbk.)
ISBN 978–0–19–958896–1 (Pbk.)

1 3 5 7 9 10 8 6 4 2

Acknowledgements

Editing a volume or writing a book would be impossible without the help of others. I wish to thank those at Oxford University Press who were an important part of this Handbook. They include Jenny Wagstaffe, whose co-operation was most helpful and very readily given.

David Bromley gave me invaluable help with the structure and content of the volume, and others, including Robert Bellah, suggested possible contributors. To both of them and to everyone else who contributed in these and other ways I am most grateful.

Works like this take a considerable length of time to create, and family and friends, however uninterested they may be in the subject, tend to become sounding boards. In this case this happened to the extent that they began to ask not, 'How are you?', but 'How's the Handbook going?' That gives some idea of how much they were obliged to share in its creation, and I thank them all for their forbearance, kindness, and support.

There are fifty-six contributions to this Handbook and every single contributor co-operated in a friendly and helpful way, and I sincerely wish to extend my thanks to each and every one of them, and from all of them I learnt much.

The Handbook is not free of errors, but what mistakes there are, are my responsibility and mine alone.

Contents

PART II METHOD

PART III RELIGION AND BOUNDARIES: MORALITY, SCIENCE, IRRELIGION, ART, AND EMBODIMENT (TRANCE)

PART IV RELIGION AND THE STATE, THE NATION, THE LAW

PART V GLOBALIZATION, FUNDAMENTALISM, MIGRATION, AND RELIGIOUS DIVERSITY

PART VI RELIGIOUS COLLECTIVITIES AND THE STATUS AND ROLE OF THE RELIGIOUS PROFESSIONALS (THE CLERGY)

PART VII SECULARIZATION AND THE REPRODUCTION AND TRANSMISSION OF RELIGION

PART VIII RELIGIOUS CHANGE: NEW RELIGIONS AND NEW SPIRITUALITIES, ESOTERICISM AND IMPLICIT RELIGION

PART IX RELIGION AND ECOLOGY, HEALTH, SOCIAL ISSUES, AND VIOLENCE

PART X TEACHING THE SOCIOLOGY OF RELIGION

Contributors

Nancy T. Ammerman is Professor of Sociology of Religion, Boston University, USA.

Edward Bailey was Rector of the Parish of Winterbourne, Bristol from 1970 to 2006, is Founding Director of the Centre for the Study of Implicit Religion and Contemporary Spirituality, and Visiting Professor at Middlesex and Staffordshire Universities, UK.

William Sims Bainbridge is Co-Director of Human-Centred Computing at the National Science Foundation, Virginia, USA, and part-time Professor of Sociology at George Mason University, Washington, DC, USA.

Meerten ter Borg is a sociologist of religion and Professor of Non-Institutional Religion at Leiden University, the Netherlands.

Gary D. Bouma is Professor of Sociology and UNESCO Chair in Inter-Religious and Intercultural Relations—Asia Pacific Region, at Monash University, Melbourne, Australia.

David G. Bromley is Professor of Religious Studies and Sociology in the School of World Studies at Virginia Commonwealth University, Richmond, Va., USA.

Gary R. Bunt is Senior Lecturer in Islamic Studies, University of Wales Trinity Saint David, Lampeter, UK.

Wendy Cadge is an Associate Professor of Sociology at Brandeis University, Waltham, Mass., USA.

Peter B. Clarke is Professor Emeritus of the History and Sociology of Religion, King's College, University of London, and currently Professor in the Faculty of Theology, University of Oxford, UK.

Peter Collins is Senior Lecturer in the Department of Anthropology at the University of Durham, UK.

Lorne L. Dawson is Professor of Sociology and Religious Studies at the University of Waterloo, Ontario, Canada.

Karel Dobbelaere is Professor Emeritus of Sociology, Catholic University of Leuven and University of Antwerp, Belgium.

André Droogers is Professor Emeritus of Cultural Anthropology, with special reference to the Anthropology of Religion and Symbolic Anthropology, at VU University, Amsterdam, the Netherlands.

Penny Edgell is Professor and Director of Graduate Studies in the Sociology Department at the University of Minnesota, USA.

Inger Furseth is Professor and Research Associate at KIFO Center for Church Research, Oslo, Norway.

David N. Gellner is Professor of Social Anthropology and Fellow of All Souls, University of Oxford, UK.

Kennet Granholm is Assistant Professor in History of Religions at Stockholm University, and Docent in comparative religion at the Åbo Akademi University, Turku, Finland.

Mathew Guest is Senior Lecturer in Theology and Religion at the University of Durham, UK.

Eva M. Hamberg is Docent in Sociology of Religion and Professor of Migration Studies at the Center for Theology and Religious Studies, Lund University, Sweden.

Malcolm Hamilton is Senior Lecturer in Sociology in the School of Sociology, Politics and International Relations, University of Reading, UK.

Phillip E. Hammond† was D. MacKenzie Brown Professor Emeritus of Religious Studies at the University of California, Santa Barbara, USA.

Sîan Hawthorne is Lecturer in Critical Theory and the Study of Religions and Chair of the Centre for Gender and Religions Research at the School of Oriental and African Studies, University of London, UK.

Paul Heelas is Professor in Religion and Modernity in the Department of Religious Studies, Lancaster University, UK.

Robert W. Hefner is Professor of Anthropology and Director of the Institute of Culture, Religion, and World Affairs, Boston University, USA, where he also directs the program on Islam and Civil Society.

Titus Hjelm is Lecturer in Finnish Society and Culture at the School of Slavonic and East European Studies, University College London, UK.

Dean R. Hoge† was Professor Emeritus of Sociology at the Catholic University of America, Washington, DC, USA.

Stewart M. Hoover is Professor and Director, Center for Media, Religion, and Culture, School of Journalism and Mass Communications, University of Colorado, Boulder, USA.

Keishin Inaba is Associate Professor in the Graduate School of Human Development, Kobe University, Japan.

Christophe Jaffrelot is Senior Research Fellow of the Centre d'Études et de Recherches (CERI) at the Sciences-Po, Paris, France.

Jeppe Sinding Jensen is Associate Professor in the Department for the Study of Religion, University of Aarhus, Denmark.

Byron R. Johnson is Distinguished Professor of Sociology, Director of the Institute for Studies of Religion, and Director of the Program on Prosocial Behavior, Baylor University, Waco, Texas, and Senior Fellow at the Witherspoon Institute, Princeton, USA.

Mark Juergensmeyer is Professor of Sociology and Global Studies and Director of the Orfalea Center for Global and International Studies at the University of California, Santa Barbara, USA.

Hans G. Kippenberg is Fellow at the Max-Weber-Kolleg, Universität Erfurt, Germany.

Michael Kirwan, SJ, is a Jesuit priest and Lecturer in Theology at Heythrop College, University of London, UK.

Ioan M. Lewis is a Fellow of the British Academy and Professor Emeritus of Anthropology at the London School of Economics, UK.

Rod Ling is a Post-Doctoral Fellow in the School of Political and Social Inquiry at Monash University, Melbourne, Australia.

Kate Loewenthal is Professor Emeritus, Department of Psychology, Royal Holloway College, University of London, UK.

David W. Machacek is Chief Operating Officer at Humanity in Action, New York, USA.

Eleanor Nesbitt is Professor of Religions and Education, University of Warwick, UK.

Enzo Pace is Professor of Sociology, Sociology of Religion, and Human Rights, Faculty of Political Sciences, University of Padua, Italy.

William E. Paden is Professor Emeritus of Religion at the University of Vermont, Burlington, USA.

Anne Birgitta Pessi is Academy Research Fellow and Adjunct Professor at the Collegium for Advanced Studies at the University of Helsinki, Finland.

Caroline Plüss is Assistant Professor in the Division of Sociology School of Humanities and Social Sciences, Nanyang Technical University, Singapore.

John Reeder is Professor Emeritus of Religious Studies at Brown University, Providence, RI, USA.

K. Helmut Reich is Professor Emeritus of the former Rutherford University School of Consciousness Studies and Sacred Traditions and Senior Research Fellow Emeritus at Fribourg University School of Education, Switzerland.

James T. Richardson is Professor in the Department of Sociology and Judicial Studies and Director of the Judicial Studies Program at the University of Nevada, Reno, USA.

Ole Preben Riis is Professor of Sociology of Religion at Agder University, Kristiansand, Norway.

Roland Robertson is Professor Emeritus of the University of Aberdeen, Scotland, UK, and Distinguished Service Professor Emeritus of Sociology, University of Pittsburgh, USA.

Wade Clark Roof is J. F. Rowny Professor Emeritus and Director of the Walter H. Capps Center for the Study of Ethics, Religion, and Public Life at the University of California, Santa Barbara, USA.

Anson Shupe is Professor in the Department of Sociology, Indiana University–Purdue University, Indiana, USA.

James V. Spickard is Professor of Sociology, University of Redlands, California, USA.

Mary Evelyn Tucker is Senior Lecturer and Research Scholar at Yale University, New Haven, USA and Director of the Yale Forum on Religion and Ecology.

Bryan S. Turner is Professor of Sociology at the Asia Research Institute, National University of Singapore.

Matt Waggoner is Associate Professor of Philosophy at Albertus Magnus College, New Haven, USA.

Nikolai G. Wenzel is Wallace and Marion Reemelin Chair in Free-Market Economics and Assistant Professor of Economics at Hillsdale College, Michigan, USA.

Robert Wuthnow is Andlinger Professor of Sociology and Director of the Center for the Study of Religion at Princeton University, USA.

Sami Zubaida is Professor Emeritus of Politics and Sociology, Birkbeck College, University of London, UK.

INTRODUCTION

TOWARDS A MORE ORGANIC UNDERSTANDING OF RELIGION WITHIN A GLOBAL FRAMEWORK

PETER B. CLARKE

In the present age, engaging effectively in identifying, articulating, and elucidating the dynamics of religion involves the development of a less institutional and more organic concept of religion, and the use of a more global framework. This is the main challenge for contemporary sociology of religion, the effect of which will be to transform the approach to the study of religion from a discipline largely informed by Western notions of religion derived from the study of Christianity, and Western interests, into one driven by a more rounded cross-culturally relevant understanding of the phenomenon.

It is of pressing concern that the sociology of religion embraces a wider range of issues, including cognitive science's understanding of religious development, the changing character of secularization, the emergence of new forms of religious transmission and of religious pluralism and diversity and their impact on social harmony—not necessarily by any means a zero-sum situation—and on the formulation and public expression of truth claims. Increasingly relevant to an understanding of the dynamics of religion in society is research on the contest between governments and radicals to control religion, and the strategies put in place by the former to ensure that disaffected second and later generations of immigrants do not succumb to what are described as the extreme ideas and philosophies of the latter. Such political management and shaping of religion rely heavily on various 'voluntary' initiatives and programmes for the purpose of constructing particular forms of moderate religion whose potential can then be harnessed to generate social capital and undermine the control of religion by militant extremism.

Relatively recently, sociology of religion has turned its attention, with considerable benefit to the subdiscipline, to new areas of research, to which an organic understanding of religion is best suited, such as the phenomenon of unchurched spirituality, and to the new religious vitality which is widespread and which would appear to owe much of its strength to both local and global trends, including economic migration and the revolution in communications evidenced in the explosion in the use of cyberspace, an innovation that has contributed as much as any other technological innovation to the democratization and the de-objectification of religious knowledge and its transmission.

Among research topics equally relevant and important to a sociology of religion for this generation, but which have on the whole been neglected, are those of religion and ecology, religion and science, and the subject of irreligion. The last mentioned if taken country by country may appear highly marginal, but when looked at globally is in fact a substantial topic. In the case of all of these, as well as others mentioned above, the use of a global perspective and framework of analysis will serve research best, although the social roots or causes will never be exclusively global.

Many of these issues are addressed with expertise in the Handbook. So here I will confine myself to a few observations on some of the questions raised for the sociology of religion by such developments as the rise of the new religious vitality evident in contemporary society, the new forms of religious pluralism and diversity, and the political management of religion, and will end this section of the Introduction with a brief definition of what is meant here by the concept of organic religion. I suggest that this concept be used to overcome some of the serious limitations of the institutionalized understanding of religion and in particular its tendency to create an impression of religion as fixed and static, doctrinally focused, and of processes such as syncretism as aberrations. I also suggest that taking a more organic view of religion has implications for methodology in the sociology of religion, necessitating, as I believe it does, a greater use of ethnography and qualitative methods generally.

The New Religious Vitality

A generation ago, mainstream sociology of religion concerned itself almost exclusively with Western society, leaving the rest of the world to anthropology, and within that framework with Christianity. The dominant paradigm of the sociology of religion was religion's loss of significance at the institutional level and at the level of consciousness. The discourse in broad terms centred on the historical and sociological processes of differentiation whereby religion, once the dominant and overarching societal institution, was decoupled from other spheres of public life. A collective amnesia regarding religious history, beliefs, and practices followed. Now would seem to be the moment to refocus and place the emphasis on religious vitality and processes of 're-coupling', 'de-differentiation' and 'de-secularization'.

This change in focus should not, however, mean an end to research and debate on such standard topics as secularization and sectarianism, for these have by no means been exhausted. As Charles Taylor's *A Secular Age* (2007) shows, new dimensions of secularization remain to be explored, and we have hardly begun to understand sectarianism outside the Christian context. Studies of this kind of well-established topics will doubtless breathe new life into the debate on these and other standard questions, as a number of the contributions to this Handbook show, including those that discuss issues such as the relationships between religion and evolutionary biology, religion and cognitive science, religious diversity, religious pluralism, the orientation of religions toward the world with special reference to modernization and the environment, religion and culture, religion and delinquency, and irreligion, among others.

It is not the point, therefore, of this Introduction to suggest that the past of sociology of religion has no future and that it be abandoned in favour of a totally new agenda; nor does it seek to discourage the further study of the classical sociological literature on religion. The subdiscipline can only benefit from this being better known and more widely read.

While sociological interest in the issue of religious vitality began some time ago (see Stark and Bainbridge 1985; Martin 1990; Berger *et al.* 1999), it has increased markedly since 9/11, when religion in its extreme forms came to be seen as a major social problem and in its 'moderate' forms as particularly useful for generating social capital, promoting pro-social behaviour, and protecting the most materially and socially vulnerable against crime.

The renewed religious vitality that we are at present witnessing is a worldwide phenomenon, the reasons for which vary from place to place, as do the forms it takes. In Western Europe it is sometimes misleadingly seen as resulting from the arrival of unprecedented numbers of believing and practising economic migrants from Asia, Africa, and parts of Eastern Europe such as Poland and Lithuania. It cannot, however, be attributed solely to these developments, any more than the growth and dynamism of new forms of evangelical Protestantism in Latin America, the resurgence of Islam across the Middle East and South and Southeast Asia, and the rise in China, Japan, and elsewhere in Asia of countless New Religious Movements (NRMs), some of them with millions of followers (Clarke 2006), can be attributed solely and directly to the forces of modernization and Westernization. In every incidence of religious vitality, both local and global social, economic, religious, and political forces are at work. The migration westwards of Muslims or Hindus or Buddhists from the Middle East and Asia has undoubtedly contributed to the vitality of religion in Western Europe, and in some cases has acted as a catalyst in this regard, giving rise to a Christianity that is more self-aware and self-assertive. But it has also to be kept in mind that there has been much lapsing and/or backsliding among immigrants, including among Muslim youth, and this has had repercussions on *daw'a*, or mission, and on the quality of education provided by the madrasahs (Muslim schools), which in many parts of the world have become stricter about such matters as the effective teaching of Islamic knowledge. Backsliding is usually attributed to Western influence, and it has become the first priority of large, well-organized Islamic missionary movements such as Tablighi Jama'at to reconvert those who lapse.

The religious dynamism and vitality and the ever increasing interest in spirituality, wherever they are found, need to be observed from within an internal–external, or a local and a global, framework. The expansion of Evangelical Christianity in Latin America, as Martin (1990) points out, can be best understood if seen from this perspective. It makes little sense to attribute it to CIA sponsorship of North American evangelists whom it is paying to brainwash the peoples of Latin America by spreading pacific forms of pro-American propaganda. The popular association of Catholicism with many of the political and economic ills of the continent has been crucial to the success of Evangelicalism. Likewise in the Muslim world, the Ikhwan or Muslim Brothers movement founded in 1929 by Hassan al Banna (1906–48)—perhaps the most influential of all the Islamist movements of modern times—cannot be fully understood, as Gibb (1978) and Mitchell (1969) point out, if seen purely as a response to Western influence in the Muslim world. The Brotherhood was concerned as much as anything else with rescuing Islam from local forms of corruption. The renewed religious vitality, then, whether we are discussing two of its main centres, Latin America and the Muslim world, clearly has its origins in both local and global conditions.

At this juncture I would like to describe briefly what is meant here by religious vitality. I want to stress that it is not to be understood primarily in terms of numerical growth, but concerns rather the dynamism, or 'force', and the 'scope' of religion in the contemporary world.

Religious Vitality Unpacked

Although he saw them as related, as they clearly are, the American anthropologist Clifford Geertz (1968: 111–12) made a useful distinction between the 'force' and the 'scope' of religion. His idea of force was not unlike Durkheim's (1915: 209) and referred to the degree of determination with which believers hold and are held by their faith. By scope he meant the range of social contexts within which religious views are considered as being either more or less relevant. Both of these aspects of religion have become more pronounced in recent times—as, it is worth noting, political ideologies have come to differ more in form than in substance. It could be said that religions too, at the lay level and the level of practice, are becoming increasingly like each other, and hence the concern of official religion to define more clearly the boundaries.

The increases in force and scope of religious belief have aroused considerable concern among humanists and even among devout and practising politicians, some of them Muslim, others Christian, and others Hindu. Among the Christian politicians who have expressed concern in this regard is the former United States President Jimmy Carter, who is persuaded that religion is striving to acquire too great an influence over the public realm, to the disadvantage of both the public and the religious spheres. By contrast, some secularization theorists continue to be persuaded that religion's influence over the public sphere has decreased, is decreasing, and will continue to decrease, for they argue that an ever more diverse and pluralist world that increasingly relativizes religious truth claims makes it virtually impossible for religion to regain a firm hold over the public arena. The present growth in individual religiosity and spirituality, it is claimed, affords proof of this.

It might be argued that secularization theory, on account of its institutional focus and its static concept of the phenomenon, has lost sight of religion's organic qualities, its potential dynamism, its capacity to reinvent itself and to combine with many other forms of life while retaining its own distinctiveness and conserving its own identity. Perhaps it has also underestimated religion's intellectual role, considering it to have been replaced by scientific explanation. However, for so many in the West as elsewhere, religious explanations of such persistent and intractable problems as the problem of evil and suffering remain as attractive as other, secular kinds of explanation. Moreover, religion's capacity to engender hope that the world can be transformed through such messianic beliefs as belief in the Second Advent of Jesus or in the case of Muslims in the coming of the Mahdi (God-guided one) who will, it is thought, ensure the triumph of Islam and restore equality and justice to the earth, or in the appearance every 100 years of the *mujaddid* or renewer, whose role is similar to that of the Mahdi, would appear to be undiminished. Beliefs of this kind continue to be strongly held almost everywhere in the modern world, even in places where one would least expect to find them, including in the world of Japanese Buddhism, particularly in its more recent expressions such as Soka Gakkai, in neo-Hindu movements such as the Brahma Kumaris (daughters of Brahma) movement, in the Korean Won Buddhist movement, and in such Chinese movements as Falun Gong (Chang 2004) and the Chinese Christian-derived Eastern Lightning and/or Church of Almighty God.

There is hardly a single example of religious innovation in the contemporary world in which these beliefs have not figured prominently. Yet only very few sociological treatises have examined their potential to generate powerful religious commitment and ideological fervour. Until recently, it was common for sociologists of religion to view all such religious enthusiasm, commitment, and fervour as features of traditional societies as Weber defined them. And even where religion fails to explain, and faith tends to waver, many adopt Pascal's position that it would be wiser to act as if God does exist rather than if she or he doesn't.

The social impact of the new religious vitality takes many forms. In modern, late modern, and/or postmodern society, it gives rise to the previously mentioned contest over public space in which religions are now engaged with secular society. The contest is highlighted by the modes of social insertion that certain religions tend to adopt as they become established in new territories. Today most religion is global, and the ending of religious regionalism has come rapidly. When I began researching Islam in Western Europe in the early 1970s, that religion was no more than an exotic appendage to the rest of Western European religious culture, whereas now it makes sociological sense to speak of European Islam as it does of European and, in the United States, American Buddhism (Queen 2000; Cadge 2005). These new religious formations give rise to new forms of what was referred to above as social insertion as they begin to challenge publicly mainstream society's arrangements in relation to religion and society, religion and law, health, education, politics, employment legislation, and worship.

In contemporary Western society and in predominantly Muslim countries such as Turkey, the contest over public space between the secular and the religious, rather than being resolved, is intensifying and engages both those who regard religion as a private matter and those who are so gripped by their religious beliefs—not necessarily in an intellectual sense—that they refuse to accept limitations on their application, cases in point being certain forms of Islamism that pursue the establishment of an Islamic state which, they argue, is a Muslim imperative. The obligation to establish an Islamic state is not only not accepted by all Islamists, but is one that, it has been argued by specialists in both Islamic and Western jurisprudence, is incompatible not only with democracy but also with theocracy (El Fadl 2004).

That religion has come to be seen once again as an influential force in contemporary society presents it with opportunities to engage more actively in the debate in the public domain on issues of education, delinquency, ethics and morality, politics, the environment, race, immigration, and health. This is a noticeable change, in that until relatively recently the voice of religion, while it was on occasion listened to with respect, is now considered to be a necessary element in the decision-making process. In this sense there is already under way an informal process of desecularization in which the relationship between the sacred and the secular is undergoing realignment and can no longer be described as one of separation. Recent discussions in France over the status of degrees offered by

Catholic universities and other tertiary-level religious institutions is but one example of this realignment.

A sociology of religion agenda for the present generation might usefully be constructed around the issues touched on above within the framework of a discourse on religious vitality worldwide, a vitality whose force and scope in many parts of the world is on a scale equal to that of any religious revival in history. Moreover, where the degree and extent of religious innovation are concerned, the present age might well be described as an axial age. There can be little doubt that Buddhism, Islam, Hinduism, and Christianity, to name but these four religions, have undergone in the past fifty to a hundred years or so changes as profound as any in their previous history, and are continuing to experience change on an unprecedented scale. Even the misleadingly labelled Traditional religions such as those of Africa, Oceania, the Americas, and Asia are radically changing, some of them changing even their very character and orientation as ethnically based, non-proselytizing religions, to universal religions with a salvific mission.

While the force and scope of religion have increased, as we have seen, no one religious orientation predominates with the exception of a few parts of the world; nor does religion or any one religion communicate an uncontested ideological message. For example, in North America and in the West generally, while there has been an explosive rise over the past fifty years of theologically, morally, and socially conservative religion, liberal religion has also been on the increase, as has involvement in unchurched spirituality (Stark *et al.* 2005; Heelas and Woodhead 2005). The new kind of religious pluralism everywhere in evidence has contributed to this diversity of religious opinion, particularly in the West. At the same time it has introduced new styles of being religious and new ways of believing and belonging, and has also enlarged and diversified the 'spiritual marketplace' (Roof 1993), raising for further discussion important questions that preoccupied classical sociology, including the question of the relationship between religion and social cohesion.

It could of course be argued that the religious vitality and spirituality driving the process of desecularization are transient phenomena, their transience resulting in large measure from their lack of adequate institutional structures. While further comments will be made on this issue below, this seems an appropriate place to make the point that solid structures can create as many dilemmas for the survival of religion as can their absence. This was seen in the decline of Anglicanism and the rise of Methodism in eighteenth-century England, when the Anglican Church's structures wedged it firmly in the rural areas, while Methodism's lack of structure gave it the flexibility necessary to evangelize the emerging industrial towns.

Religion, then, does not survive only when it is institutionalized. Although they have become highly complex structures of a kind, there is no church of Buddhism, or of Hinduism or Islam. Furthermore, given the profound transformation in communications now under way, it might well prove to be the case once again that solid structures impede growth, while movements with fragile structures that are easily dismantled and that depend on networking may be better prepared to reorganize and meet new demands as types and styles of religion and spirituality change, for, as studies of New Religious Movements (NRMs) have shown, they do tend to change almost every decade, if not more often.

The New Religious Pluralism and Social Harmony

The new types of religious pluralism and diversity which have emerged during the past fifty years have never before been encountered in the West or anywhere else in the form and on the scale which they have now assumed. While previously it was mostly branches of the same religion that provided pluralism and diversity, now it is different religions each of which contains within itself a variety of expressions. This is the new feature of religious pluralism and diversity that needs addressing in relation to social harmony and integration.

Religious diversity is not new to sociological enquiry. It was an important part of the original agenda of sociology, which sought to understand the challenges to social cohesion posed by differences, cultural and religious. Sociologists from the outset asked fundamental questions of a hermeneutical kind regarding the meaning of different ways of life and how these impacted on society. One weakness of the classical sociological approach to interpreting the meaning of different ways of life, including different ways of being religious, was its tendency to think of societies as singular entities or integrated units and its apparent blindness to the many different worlds that members of these societies might be inhabiting simultaneously.

Thus, while it must continue to meet the challenge of interpreting religious difference, contemporary sociology of religion must also consider, whatever the unit of analysis, integration as an empirical variable. Outside and within religions, beliefs, moral and theological, are contested, and boundaries porous, providing fertile soil for the revitalization of religion. As indicated previously, such pluralism and diversity fed mainly by economic migration do not and need not create a zero-sum situation where social harmony and integration are jeopardized, but may well prove to be a strength in this respect. What is further of great interest about this topic is how religious pluralism and diversity are handled in public places such as school and college assemblies, how the approach and understanding of those who teach religion in these and similar institutions, and of those who interpret and execute the law have been affected, and the contribution all this might make to social cohesion and the related sphere of human rights.

The Political Management of Religion

The question of the political management of religion touched upon above takes different forms depending on constitutional arrangements, the ideology of the governments in question, the nature of the legitimacy, if any, that governments enjoy, and the kind of political control they seek or have a mandate to exercise. These factors in turn determine governments' attitudes toward, and the measures they are prepared to adopt to uphold, order and stability.

As previously noted, in Europe governments are engaged more or less directly, depending on the context, in creating 'moderate' religion and in particular 'moderate' Islam, a highly controversial term. In China the search goes on for a neo-Confucianism that will assist in dealing with the moral and social issues raised by rapid economic expansion; in Thailand Buddhism continues to be used to 'civilize' the so-called Hill Tribe peoples such as the Akha; and in Japan scholars and government are assessing the contribution that the teaching of religion in schools might make to lowering suicide rates among the young and tackling behavioural problems such as bullying.

Virtually everywhere, governments are engaged in the management and even the production of religion and spirituality through education and other means, and in certain contexts one of the indirect and mostly unintended consequences of this has been to allow greater space to religion in the public sphere. However, government initiatives to construct moderate and socially purposeful religion do not always have the desired effect, and can contribute to the spread among opponents of the existing political regime of what is presented as 'authentic' politically uncontaminated religion. Both of these situations give strength to the idea of religion as an ideology, a perception that religious leaders are at pains to discount.

Conclusions

One of the main intellectual implications of what has been said about contemporary forms of religious vitality is that thinking about religion in the same way and with the same habits of mind as in the past is no longer sustainable. Using, as has been suggested above, a global framework and a more organic model of religion would allow the sociology of religion to develop a more refined and sophisticated understanding and approach to religion in the contemporary world, where the de-objectification of religious knowledge and the teaching and practice of spirituality through the media and cyberspace have reached an advanced stage, and where tool kits for constructing both religions and spiritualities are readily available and in plentiful supply. An organic understanding of religion would transfer the emphasis from belief and institutions to religion as life, to the implications of what is lived out as religion, often in a personal sense, to an idea of religion as open to change and as having the power to change society. Indeed, it remains for millions the only instrument available with this power and their only language of political discourse. For this reason it is in certain political contexts tightly controlled.

While research on vertical, institutional forms and standard types of religion remains an important ingredient of the agenda of the sociology of religion—for, as was previously mentioned with reference to secularization, these issues have not been exhausted, nor could they ever be—at the same time it would seem to make sense to place greater emphasis on research into the more creative and horizontal forms of religion and spirituality. Researching this kind of religion, which receives much of its stimulus from the new kinds of pluralism and diversity that are taking shape across the world, necessitates the use of mixed methods and, in particular, a greater reliance on qualitative and ethnographic methods. Moreover, its success will depend on the development of both a more organic understanding of religion and a new perspective, a global perspective, both of which should enable research to appreciate more fully the complexities of the somewhat baffling contemporary phenomenon of the revival of religion, the explosion of religious vitality, and the future of the religious past, in modernizing, modern, and postmodern or late modern contexts.

The Handbook

The remit of this volume has been to provide scholars with the opportunity to reflect critically on issues long discussed by sociology of religion, to introduce others long relevant but little researched, and to consider the implications for the subdiscipline of the sociology of religion of others that have begun to emerge only relatively recently. It has also been kept in mind that the so-called established or standard issues that have preoccupied sociologists of religion have undergone change and are no longer precisely the same kinds of issues as they were when first discussed, as the chapters on secularization and related topics clearly indicate (see among other contributions the chapters by Dobbelaere and Turner).

The structure of the Handbook is somewhat arbitrary. In a number of instances chapters placed in one part could well fit in another, an example being Paden's (see Part I) creative and thought-provoking reappraisal of Durkheim in the light of research in evolutionary biology on *Homo sapiens*. This counters the tendency to take a static view of the classics of the sociology of religion such as Durkheim's *Elementary Forms* (1915) and Weber's *Protestant Ethic* thesis (1965), and often to rule out any possibility of reconciling their theories on religious belief and practice with more modern and postmodern scientific world views.

While even an uncommonly lengthy volume such as this could not hope to address all of the issues with which sociologists of religion might wish to engage, it is worth mentioning that some topics apparently missing appear in a hidden, implicit form, and some that are treated directly are also taken up in contribution after contribution. The all too brief summary that follows of the content of the chapters cannot hope to do justice to their quality.

Part I: Theory: Classical, Modern, and Postmodern

As the above discussion of the importance of an organic understanding and a global framework for the sociology of religion for the present age makes clear, classical theory remains a core element of the subdiscipline. The contributions to Part I offer critical reflection on several aspects of classical sociological theory, including its capacity to meet the needs of contemporary sociology of religion, on how the classical sources have been interpreted, and on the uses to which they have been put (see chapters by Gellner, Kippenberg, Turner, and Paden).

This critical revisiting of classical sociology suggests—and this point is strongly made by Kippenberg and Paden in particular—that, if understood as intended, it remains a useful hermeneutical resource. As Kippenberg, for example, points out, Weber's sociology of religion has been mostly read as a theory of secularization, when what Weber assumed was a different relationship between religion and modernization than this reading suggests. A strong emphasis in Weber, Kippenberg argues, was on how the process of disenchantment when establishing secular orders as autonomous spheres becomes a catalyst for new types of religiosity rather than the decline of religion. The themes of secularization/disenchantment and enchantment emerge again in Turner's chapter on Weber's sociology of comparative religion and his Kantian notion of secularization. In this chapter Turner argues that whatever the tradition—Christian, Islamic, or Confucian—the life and authority of the educated and elite carriers of religion are undergoing a serious challenge from the popular 'spiritual supermarkets' (see Roof 1999 and Chapter 34 below). This form of re-enchantment of the world, Turner suggests, would appear to contradict Weber's general secularization thesis.

Gellner's presentation also focuses on Weber, and mainly on the selective and variable use and/or lack of use of Max Weber in anthropological discourse on Buddhism and Hinduism. Gellner also draws some insightful parallels between classical and contemporary social-scientific discourse and in particular between the ideas of Weber and those of Foucault.

Furseth suggests that Foucault's and Bourdieu's ideas are important to the study of religion, particularly for the insights they provide into the links between religion and power, a theme taken up by ter Borg, who develops a model of religious power based on the human need for ontological security. Furseth further suggests that there is much theoretical potential in Habermas's ideas on religion in the public sphere and on the rights of religious minorities, a topic of increasing relevance.

Hamilton's chapter critiques one of the most widely discussed and controversial of modern sociological theories of religion, rational choice theory (RCT), a theory also discussed by Hefner among others. Following Spickard (1998), Hamilton suggests that RCT is best seen not as a theory that explains individual actions and choices, but as a heuristic device for understanding religious provision and consumption.

That globalization makes it impossible for the sociology of religion to continue in the same vein as in the past is one of the main emphases of Hefner's wide-ranging contribution on religion and modernity worldwide. This chapter also contains a critique of rational choice theory, classical thinking on secularization, and key postmodern concepts concerning religion. Regardless of the answer to the thorny question of whether objectively there is a postmodern culture and philosophy, Wenzel's approach is to insist that subjectively such a phenomenon exists, and that its consequences for standard or traditional church-based religion entail further secularization (see also Dobbelaere's chapter), the emergence of new styles of expressive, personal styles of religion (see the contributions by Bailey, Hamberg, Heelas, and Granholm), and the growth of fundamentalism as a backlash (see Shupe's chapter).

The location of religion in modern and postmodern society is also a theme in Waggoner's wide-ranging chapter which examines the thinking of Durkheim, Marx, Foucault, and Derrida on culture and religion. This chapter also provides a historical and sociological critique of the notion of religion as a state of affairs, rather than a state of mind, a debate which in the social sciences goes back to Durkheim and Marx.

The study of religion in general, and not just the sociology of religion, often tends to be slower than other branches of the social sciences and humanities to take up and test new sociological thinking and theory, and this slowness is evident, Hawthorne points out, in relation to feminist and gender theory, which had already become a meta-critical tool in the social sciences and humanities before the study of religion sought to engage with it. As to the future, Hawthorne suggests a move away from universalist pretensions of the study of religion and a greater readiness on the part of gender-critical approaches to the study of religion to engage in more constructive dialogue with post-colonialist theory.

PART II: METHOD

Debate over sociological method (see Riis's chapter) has been one of a number of constant themes in sociology of religion, as has debate over the use of the term religion itself and its definition (see Droogers's chapter) and the related questions of the boundaries between religion and other areas of life—for example, morality (see Reeder's chapter), art (see Wuthnow's chapter), and science (see Bainbridge's chapter on science and religion). This debate has more recently been extended to cover the subject of the role of cognition in relation to the origins and development of religion (see Reich's chapter). These issues have been made ever more complex by the all-pervasive pluralist and global character of contemporary society and by the profound transformations already referred to, which religions are presently undergoing. Finding adequate methods for the sociological study of religion in this context is a difficult challenge, but one nevertheless taken up by Riis, who discusses the relative value of quantitative and qualitative approaches and offers compelling reasons for a methodological combination which makes use of both. This does not, however, mean closure where the debate on method is concerned, for as Riis warns, his proposal brings with it its own difficulties.

Jensen's chapter on the nature and role of conceptual models—which also involves an analysis of the nature and role of ideal types—makes a bold attempt in the direction of further refinement of methods widely used in the sociology of religion, while Droogers tackles the vexed question of defining religion by looking at a map of the landscape through which definers travel. He highlights the merits of a social-constructionist approach to the issue, maintaining that definitions cannot be isolated from the position of the definer in global society, or from the religion and science and the secularization debates (see Bainbridge's chapters and Dobbelaere's chapter).

Unlike anthropology of religion, sociology of religion has paid little attention to date to the contribution that cognitive science might make to our understanding of the origins and development of religion. Reich looks at the concept of religion as used in cognitive science, by which he means evolutionary neurobiological cognitive science, over against psychological studies of cognition and its ontogenic development. He critiques the work of Boyer (2001) among others in this area, whose idea of religion, he suggests, is too narrow. In its place Reich offers a model which he believes serves to describe the dynamics of religious and spiritual development, which, he maintains, can be triggered by events either outside or inside the multiple self. Reich divides this multiple self into a central, striving, social, and religious self, a concept and definition of self that will be of interest to scholars in the fields of contemporary spirituality (see the chapters by Hamberg and Heelas), Oriental religions and certain of the so-called Traditional religions.

Part III: Religion and Boundaries: Morality, Science, Irreligion, Art, and Embodiment (Trance)

As several of the contributors to Parts I and II make clear, there is no fixed, ongoing relationship between religion and other spheres of thinking and behaviour. This notwithstanding, religion and other spheres can become differentiated, and Reeder examines in this section of the Handbook the processes whereby morality has been decoupled from religion, not only in the world of academia but throughout society. In doing so he questions the hermeneutic value of the cosmicization thesis as applied to morality, principally because it obscures the attempt to relate norms and values to the perceived environment. The sense in which these two systems of ideas and behaviour can be understood as distinctive relates, he suggests, to their focus, morality being concerned primarily with interhuman issues, in contrast with religion, which fixes its attention on the fundamental causes of well-being and suffering.

The relationship between religion and science was a prominent theme in the formative period of sociology as a discipline, and Bainbridge examines recent attempts by scientists and religious scholars to delineate the potential for a relationship between the two in the vastly different context of modern society, and what kind of relationship might be a fitting one. While maintaining that there are strong grounds for thinking that the relationship will inevitably be hostile—regardless of whether the type of religion in question is fundamentalist or conservative or liberal—Bainbridge notes that recent research has identified a tendency among the young to believe that an accommodation between the two is a possibility.

The question of the relationship between religion and science emerges again in Bainbridge's contribution on the relationship between religion and irreligion and/or atheism, a much neglected theme, as was previously noted, in the sociology of religion. In this second contribution he argues that the study of atheism, although a minority viewpoint, is indispensable to the study of religion in that, among other things, it poses several complex and difficult questions for all theories of religion. Interestingly, Bainbridge suggests that the future of this minority position often considered unworthy of serious attention by scholars and dismissed as merely froth on the beer—the beer being belief in God—might lie in developments of cognitive science (see Reich's contribution).

As Wuthnow's presentation shows, perhaps surprisingly for many, religion and art, while they overlap at certain points, do not easily accommodate each other. The relationship spans a continuum, the oppositional end of which would include Islam, which prohibits all forms of representational art; types of Buddhism, including such modern movements as Korean Won Buddhism and the Thai Santi Asoke movement, both of which oppose the use of images of the Buddha; forms of Christian asceticism, including elements of the Western monastic tradition and Puritanism; and at the more accommodating end one could place types of Hinduism such as devotional Hinduism, Shinto, and many African and African-derived religions such as Umbanda and Candomble. Wuthnow's main focus is the United States, where he sees overlap in several domains, including dance and rock music in the liturgy. However, he is also aware that this relationship is a much neglected theme in the sociology of religion, where there is little or no research available on what further bridging between the two spheres might be possible.

Sociology of religion has made little effort to understand the sociological dimensions of ecstatic forms of religion, including trance and/or possession, forms which are central to the religion and spirituality of peoples worldwide. Lewis, a social anthropologist, has long been concerned with the question of the social roots and meaning of trance and possession (see his book *Ecstatic Religion*, 1971), and in his contribution to this Handbook he explores, through an examination of altered states of consciousness most frequently externalized in behaviour through trance, the correspondence between religious and sexual experience which is as yet little studied.

Part IV: Religion and the State, the Nation, the Law

Until recently it was widely taken for granted in the Western world that clearly defined boundaries existed between church and state. But, as we saw in the first part of this Introduction, such thinking has begun to be challenged as world views increasingly compete with each other and with humanist and secular philosophies in the same public arena and demand greater space and a voice on all matters of life, from health to education, to politics, economics, law, and religion. This is not an exclusively Western issue, but has also flared up in recent times in Indonesia, India, and Nigeria. In Nigeria the demand for a federal Shari'a court during the debate on the constitution for the Second Republic in the late 1970s almost tore the nation apart.

The relationship between religion and the state has never been easy or harmonious for long. Moreover, it has taken a variety of forms, as Hammond and Machacek show in their historical overview of the variable relations that have existed between religions and the state with reference to several countries, including China, Brazil, and Poland. These two contributors to the Handbook also note the difference often overlooked between the relationship of politics and religion and that of religion and the state. While there is increasing focus on the relations between religion and the state, few topics can be as relevant today as the ever tighter link between religion and nationalism. This is not so surprising in many parts of the world where the only effective language of political discourse, as was previously mentioned, is religious language. Jaffrelot highlights the ambiguous nature of the relationship between religion and nationalism, illustrating his argument with reference primarily to India, but also examining other cases.

Although present in the classical sociological writings of Durkheim and Weber, the relationship between law and religion has largely been ignored in the sociology of religion. This topic is central to Richardson's contribution, which focuses on the impact that religion has had on legal systems, and how religious groups, especially dominant ones, can make use of such systems and even contribute to the process of their construction. He also considers how law and legal systems can be used to exert control over religions and religious practitioners, especially over minority faiths, an issue that scholars of New Religious Movements (NRMs) have frequently addressed (Richardson 2004).

It is sometimes assumed that once enshrined in a Constitution or Bill of Rights or United Nations Declaration, human rights will be protected. Pace, in a contribution that ranges widely across different religious traditions and branches within those traditions—Hindu, Islamic, and Christian—focuses in particular on the lack of fit that can exist between state law that guarantees human rights and religious law or custom, examples being freedom of belief and worship and the right to choose one's partner. The importance of this field of research increases with the emergence on the back of globalization of ever more religiously diverse societies and new forms of religious pluralism.

Part V: Globalization, Fundamentalism, Migration, and Religious Diversity

Every entry in this Handbook treats to a greater or lesser extent the question of the impact of globalization and its effects on contemporary and historic forms of religion and spirituality. There can be little doubt about the considerable impact that Oriental religions have had in recent times on Western forms of religion and spirituality and of that exercised by Western Christianity over a longer period on Oriental religions.

As Robertson's chapter points out, there has been a reaction from humanists among others to global developments in religion. Robertson argues that one of the core features of the contemporary global situation as it impacts on religion is the rapidly developing tension between the widespread and disputed quest for explicitly formulated national identities, on the one hand, and the problematic increase in the intra-societal valorization of religious faiths, on the other. The reasons for this include the aggressive promotion of ostensibly atheistic and secularistic ideas by prominent intellectuals in the UK and the USA, and he cites as examples Dawkins 2006 and Hitchens 2007. This and related tensions have their roots, Robertson maintains, in global connectivity and increasing global awareness. Drawing on Durkheim's notion of society and religion as inextricably bound together, Robertson sees emerging in the United States a politicized civil religion with a strong theocratic flavour, a strange paradox given the post 9/11 war on Islamist extremists whose goal is the creation of an Islamic state.

Shupe's chapter relates extremist forms of religious orientation directly to globalization; indeed, Shupe sees it as the other side of the same coin. By contrast, Plüss's account of migration and the globalization of religion speaks of the multipolar processes of belief and practice that result as migrants of the same religious tradition, on finding themselves in different contexts, use their beliefs to address important existential questions that arise from their new experiences. Religion, however, does not always act as a social glue binding migrants together. The extent of the religious involvement of immigrants should not be exaggerated, for there are those among them, in some cases a sizeable minority, who use their new status to 'liberate' themselves from religion, or at least the religion of their birth and upbringing. As was already noted, it is this turning away, viewed by religious authorities as lapsing or in Islamic terms as backsliding, that provides the catalyst for the growth and expansion worldwide of missionary movements such as Tablighi Jama'at. First-generation immigrants tend to live in quarantine in relation to the host society, and this stage is followed by a process of mixing, in which there tends to be a decline in religious practice, and following on this stage reform, a stage which is a marked feature of Muslim communities in the Western world.

In their chapter on religious diversity Bouma and Ling question the utility of the nation-state as a primary focus of analysis of contemporary forms of this phenomenon, which is mostly global. Notwithstanding its increasingly complex nature, Bouma and Ling maintain that religious diversity offers the researcher a useful conceptual tool for examining how changes in religion impact on social life, and the converse.

Part VI: Religious Collectivities and the Status and Role of the Religious Professionals (the Clergy)

Dawson in his chapter attempts to refine the classification of religious collectivities into churches, denominations, sects, and cults; while convinced that it remains a useful typology, he recognizes that its ethnocentric character largely limits it use to the Western context. However, rather than abandoning the ideas of Weber and Troeltsch on which this typology is based, Dawson suggests that researchers revisit their writings to gain a better-informed understanding of their ideas, which will, he believes, provide them with a universally applicable way of categorizing religious organizations, based essentially on the variable of mode of membership.

Zubaida examines the divide between the Sunni or mainstream Islam and the Shi'i branches of Islam. There are many types of Shi'ism, the largest being the Imami or Twelver Branch of Shi'ism, which is the religion of the majority of Muslims in Iran, southern Iraq, Azerbaijan, and Lebanon. Zubaida provides a historical overview of the divide between Sunnis and Shi'ites before raising the question of the renewed political thrust of the once politically quiescent Shi'ism in modern times, beginning with its construction as a radical ideology in Iran in 1979. Zubaida's view is that the Sunni–Shi'ite divide is effectively more a political and sociological category than a theological one, as it becomes significant only at times of political and social upheaval.

Ammerman looks at what, from the perspective of the sociology of religion although not historically, is a relatively new kind of religious collectivity, the congregation. This form of religious association consists of a locally situated, multi-generational, voluntary group of people who see themselves as distinct and engage jointly in religious activities. While closely associated with contemporary religious practice in the United States, where there are well over 3,000 such congregations, 80 per cent of which are Protestant in persuasion, this form of gathering may have had its origins among the Jews in exile in Babylon in 586 BCE and would appear to be a particularly appropriate forum for worship among religious communities in diaspora whose culture goes unsupported by the wider society. Ammerman sees the congregation becoming ever more important as a point of communal identification as global migration increases in scale (see Plüss's chapter).

The clergy have come under more scrutiny in recent times than perhaps any other profession, and the social and religious issues that have given rise to such intense scrutiny—paedophilia, the ordination of women, and homosexuality, among others—are addressed by Hoge, who also writes of the declining authority and status of this profession. Among the more important reasons for this decline, he suggests, are increasing differentiation and greater egalitarianism in the relationships between clergy and laity. Hoge is persuaded that there is a need for more relevant and appropriate training for the clergy if they are to perform an effective role in a world that is turning ever more religiously diverse, and suggests that new research be started in a number of areas with which scholars are familiar but about which little of substance is known, including those of women clergy, homosexual clergy, and clergy outside any denomination.

Part VII: Secularization and the Reproduction and Transmission of Religion

It is worth repeating here the point made above, that standard religion is experiencing change and challenges on an unprecedented scale, both from without and within. Addressing mainly the situation in the West, and more specifically the European Union, Dobbelaere argues that there are clear indications that what he refers to as 'manifest secularization' or 'laicization' as it is known in France will increase in the years to come. He is at the same time careful to point out that this process, since it is 'man-made', is not irreversible. Dobbelaere also takes up the question of the continuing sensitivity to religion displayed by individuals under the label of 'individual secularization', which he sees as the loss of control by religious authorities over the form and content of what people believe and how they practise. Defined thus, Dobbelaere contends that the continuation of religious belief and practice at the individual level confirms rather than refutes the theory of secularization. Among the most complex and serious challenges confronting standard and other forms of religion such as Pentecostalist and Evangelical forms of religion in Korea and New Religious Movements (NRMs) (see Bromley's chapter) is the challenge of intergenerational transmission. Roof's presentation stresses the importance of the nexus between generations and religion, and calls for more research on every aspect of the intergenerational question and in particular on 'second-generation' immigrants across countries, about whom very little is known.

Edgell, who has carried out extensive and in-depth research on religion and the family, concentrates in her contribution to this Handbook on such questions as the ways in which religion shapes family life and how families sustain—and change—religious institutions, which she describes as social locations for the production and transmission of religious familism or ideology about what constitutes a family and what a good family should be like. Edgell also asks a set of pertinent questions that seek to understand the fit—or lack of fit—between religion and the family today. This already complex topic is made ever more complex by the increasingly diverse and pluralistic character of modern society.

Guest critiques theories of transmission and reproduction of religion from Comte through Marx and Durkheim to contemporary sociologists of religion, including Berger, engaging as he does so with positivist and sociology of knowledge approaches to the question, among others. He also deals with the issues of transmission and reproduction in the context of secularization theory in its various guises and against the background of the McDonaldization of religion, one form of which, Guest maintains, is the Alpha Course. Guest further considers Hervieu-Léger's (2000 [1993]) views on the phenomenon of 'cultural amnesia', the effects of which gravely undermine the passing on of religious beliefs and values. Transmission and reproduction, as Guest points out, do not necessarily depend on the mainstream churches, which are increasingly less effective in this regard. The emergence of small-scale, alternative community structures (see Ammerman's contribution) could possibly, he suggests, perform the role of sustaining and passing on core values. Building on the thinking of Bourdieu, Guest offers the suggestion that a fruitful approach to understanding future processes of transmission and reproduction might come through adopting 'a resource mobilization perspective' which would focus on those resources associated with religion and pay less attention to factors such as institutions.

Ritual, with its expressive, performative, symbolic, and rational dimensions, has always been assumed to be a key element in the dynamic of transmission and reproduction of religion, and in his chapter on this topic Collins illustrates how it builds and consolidates Quaker community.

The mediation of religion in both the global and the local context is, as Hoover's presentation on the media points out, one of a number of emerging new research areas in media studies. Scholars are examining the representation of religions in various contexts, including the Internet and the Web, and how such mediation of religion might contribute to religious ferment. However, Hoover is keen to stress the serious shortcomings of a purely instrumentalist understanding of the relationship between the media and religion. Bunt's discussion of the Internet and religion emphasizes the capacity of the former to transform religion in the areas of representation and adherent networking as a proselytizing tool. This is happening to such an extent that some belief systems and practices may already be dependent on search engine ratings and placement 'to acquire and maintain an impact or profile'. For this reason and others—motivations can vary—religious organizations are increasingly becoming keen media and service providers.

Fieldwork on religion in cyberspace poses its own particular difficulties, the most important of which are highlighted in Bunt's presentation which, like Hoover's, not only makes an important contribution to the debate on the transmission and reproduction of religion, but also complements Riis's and Jensen's chapters on method.

Part VIII: Religious Change: New Religions and New Spiritualities, Esotericism and Implicit Religion

One's sense of the level of impact made by New Religious Movements (NRMs) and New Spirituality Movements (NSMs) on contemporary thinking about and practice of religion and spirituality will differ depending on the angle from which one views them. Seen from the perspective of South Asia and parts of East Asia, it is clear that so called neo-Hindu movements and lay Buddhist movements have greatly influenced these regions (Clarke 2006).

NRMs and NSMs have also impacted on the study and teaching of Religion (Bromley 2007), and these are some of the issues addressed by Bromley in his contribution to the Handbook. Limiting himself to the West, Bromley traces the development of the emerging specialization of New Religious Studies (NRS), which offers a multi-disciplinary approach to the phenomenon of New Religion and Spirituality. One of the scholarly merits of this discipline, he maintains, is that it provides space in research and teaching for topics which have hitherto been marginalized, the focus having been on the more dominant forms of religion and spirituality.

The important question of the interaction between dominant forms of religion and spirituality and less dominant forms is one of the subjects addressed by Heelas and Woodhead (2005). And it is considered again by both Hamberg and Heelas in this Handbook. Hamberg questions the assumption that the present decline in church-based religion in Europe is part of a long-term process of decline. She also raises the question for further research of the extent to which the decline in standard religion has contributed to the growth of spirituality outside the churches, and the apparently problematic relationship of that spirituality to science. Overall, Hamberg is cautious in her conclusions regarding the relationship of church-based religion and spirituality, as well as on the question of the origins and strength of the social and cultural forces driving the phenomenon of unchurched spirituality. She also expresses methodological concerns relating to definition (see Droogers's chapter). These are but some of the issues to which research, Hamberg believes, needs to turn its attention in a more systematic and sustained manner.

Setting aside the discussion of the possibility of a causal relationship of whatever kind between secularization and the rise of unchurched spirituality, the contemporary interest and involvement in spiritualities of all kinds is indisputable and on such a scale as to prompt Heelas in his contribution to this Handbook to suggest that the Sociology of Religion be renamed the Sociology of Religion and Spirituality. This idea could find favour with, among others, Roof (1998), who points out that one of the weaknesses of the sociology of religion is that it suffers from an overly rationalized, narrowly defined, institutionalized conception of the religious. One might also add a criticism of sociology of religion's geographical narrowness whereby with some notable exceptions, including Hefner (1999) and Martin (1999), it has confined its focus to the West and then largely to one or two forms of Christianity in the West, while aiming to construct a set of general principles of religious behaviour.

Heelas in his discussion of 'Spiritualities of Life' is anxious, among other things, to counter the argument that present-day spirituality is simply a tool of consumer capitalism, pointing out that it is often bound up 'with humanistic and expressivistic values' such as equality and authenticity. Regarding the persistence of the Spiritualities of Life, Heelas, in contrast to Bruce (2002), is persuaded that the evidence of their continuing growth and their capacity to handle the dilemmas of contemporary life should assure Spiritualities of Life a 'rosy future'. In relation to the type of analysis of the secularization process and its fundamental elements which Bruce's position seems to represent, it can be said that it hides a Weberian positivistic understanding of the relationship between religion and modernization and implies that what is said to be happening and/or to have happened in the West by way of the decline of religious influence over society and individual consciousness will almost inevitably be the case elsewhere. The contemporary global situation is, however, a much different environment in relation to the communication and transmission of religious ideas and practices, among others, than that of the modern world in which Weber attempted to assess the future of religion.

Among spiritual developments that overlap with Spiritualities of Life and are of growing interest is that of esotericism. Granholm's chapter on this topic is not limited to a discussion of its core elements, but also examines the changing relationship between esotericism and Christianity from the nineteenth century. Under the impact of secularization, this relationship changed from one in which esotericists identified themselves as Christians and made use of Christian symbolism and terminology to one in which many esotericists influenced by secular modes of thinking and eventually free to express themselves as they saw fit sought to expound their philosophy and beliefs in 'scientific' language, thus bringing to an end the idea of esotericism as 'deviant' knowledge.

The significance of implicit religion is another example of a topic that, while on the agenda since the late 1960s, has not so far been treated with any great seriousness by the sociology of religion. Yet, as Bailey contends in his contribution to this Handbook, without an understanding of the role of implicit religion, it is impossible to understand people's secular lives. In his historical overview of the development of the concept and its meaning, he also indicates how implicit religion overlaps with and differs from spirituality. In addition, Bailey points to its relevance to questions concerning group solidarities, organizational institutions, and ritual behaviour, among others.

Part IX: Religion and Ecology, Health, Social Issues, and Violence

The environmental crisis, perhaps more than any other concern of contemporary society, is turning attention to religion not primarily as a means of salvation in a transcendental, other-worldly sphere, but increasingly, as Tucker points out in her chapter, as the provider of 'a broad road to the cosmos and human roles in it'.

The role of religion in relation to the environmental crisis remains highly controversial, several religions endorsing an exclusively anthropocentric view of moral rights and obligations, while others uphold beliefs which are seen as undermining attempts to control the world's population, whose present rate of increase is believed to be detrimental to the survival of the planet. Aware of these difficulties, Tucker in her contribution in part circumvents them by considering religions in broader terms than the institutional and denominational forms they take. They are for her purposes world views which, despite the problems associated with some of their teachings on such matters as domination of nature by humans and certain kinds of birth control, can help to construct a much needed global ethical perspective in relation to environmental issues and help inculcate qualities such as truth telling, trust, and visioning that are indispensable to ecological sustainability.

The relationship between religion, spirituality, and health is addressed by Cadge in her presentation from an institutional perspective. She adopts this standpoint principally for the reason that, as she points out, most research on this relationship ignores the institutional aspects of health provision and care. From a sociological perspective this is self-defeating, Cadge argues, for if research agendas included institutional dimensions, they could greatly enhance our knowledge of the specific relationship in itself and at the same time provide an appropriate contextual frame for discussing and debating a host of other issues relating religion, spirituality, and health, such as health-care workers' religious and moral obligations, spiritually oriented alternative medical approaches, and spiritual and medical intervention at the end of life.

Johnson's presentation focuses on the relationship between religion and delinquency and finds that religious commitment helps protect youth, whatever their socio-economic conditions, from delinquent behaviour and deviant activities, including the use of illegal drugs. There is also a more constructive side to the relationship between religion and behaviour, in the sense that religious belief and practice not only protect against delinquent behaviour but, according to Johnson's findings, also foster positive and/or normative behaviour.

Inaba and Loewenthal explore the relationship between religion and altruism, a research concern identified and pursued by classical sociologists including Max Weber, and one of interest and concern today, especially in societies where the building of social capital encounters serious obstacles. Inaba and Loewenthal point out that while early research was rather muddled about the correlation between religion and altruism, research since the 1980s is less ambiguous in suggesting that religion is likely to play a causal role in promoting altruism.

More time has been spent on discussing the correlation between religion and violence than on any other aspect of religion since 9/11. This was doubtless a defining moment in modern thinking about religion. Prior to 9/11, many were reluctant to believe that there were any close links between religion and violence (see Bruce 1986 on the conflict in Northern Ireland). The violence of 9/11 challenged that certainty. And while politicians and religious leaders are inclined to emphasize that good religion is moderate and peaceful, some researchers think differently. While Juergensmeyer is anxious to stress that religions are not only about violence, he nonetheless in his discussion of the concept of cosmic war argues that religion is driven by a fundamental impulse in the form of a quest for order, and from this starting point it introduces the concept and reality of violence as the pathway to harmony and peace.

Kirwan frames his analysis of religion and violence with special reference to modern martyrdom in terms of a critique of Girard's theory of religion and violence which speaks of the annulment of the violent sacred. Kirwan sees this account which is robustly Christian as being highly problematic for many in a religiously pluralistic society. However, it is Kirwan's view that, if understood correctly, the Girardian idea of religion and the annulment of violence need not offend non-Christians. From this starting point he introduces an interesting discussion of ways in which militant *jihad* and *shahid* or Islamic martyrdom may possibly be interpreted in a way similar to the Girardian intepretation that speaks of the 'abrogation' of the false and violent sacred. This is not simply wishful thinking, for Islam is not as bereft of hermeneutical tools as is widely thought.

While the relationship between religion and social issues has begun to attract a good deal of interest from researchers in recent years, it is without much theoretical guidance in the way of social problem theory. This is a gap that Hjelm's contribution attempts to fill. His presentation focuses the following issues: on social problems as a claims-making activity, on how religions construct solutions to social problems, on how religion itself is constructed as a social problem, and on how this impacts on the way religion is perceived.

While Pessi's contribution covers some of the same ground as Hjelm's, it is essentially an empirically based discussion of the topic of religion and social issues. She offers several interesting critiques of empirical research on this relationship between religion and social problems in Europe and in particular in Finland. Like Hjelm, she poses a number of important questions for religions, including that of how they may come over time to be perceived as social welfare institutions rather than bearers of a transcendental message. Pessi argues that religions that seek to resolve social problems come to be perceived as providing 'institutions of authenticity' in the sense of providing those meaningful horizons that individual choice always requires.

Part X: Teaching the Sociology of Religion

Increasing religious pluralism clearly impacts directly on the teaching of the sociology of religion, and with this in mind Nesbitt looks at the contexts in which religion is taught, including Sunday school, state school, university, and so on—each one making its own demands and raising its own questions. She also identifies the variety of types of teacher of religion—for example, the insider and the outsider to the faith community in question, the salaried school teacher, and the volunteer Sunday school teacher. In Nesbitt's view one of the more important demands that modern, ethnically diverse, religiously pluralistic society makes of teachers is that they acquire ethnographic skills. If they fail to do so, she argues, they will not adequately recognize and appreciate diversity, and as a result will be unable to engage in citizenship education, which is integral to the role of the teacher of religion, at least in the United Kingdom. To be ethnographically aware is to make explicit to oneself what one's view of religion is, and this will involve as a consequence, Nesbitt contends, challenging the taken-for-granted equation of religion with belief and practice. The teacher of religion's task extends not only to acquiring ethnographic skills for the better performance of their own role but also training students in ethnography, seeing in them potential co-ethnographers.

Spickard takes up the topic of teacher- or student-centred teaching in the context of American tertiary education. He begins with an account of the sea-change in ethnography during the past thirty years which began by questioning the quality and value of teacher-directed education and went on to suggest that a student-centred approach to learning was the more effective in training people to reflect, analyse, and internalize knowledge. It was also seen as a more effective means of transmitting knowledge. Not all institutions of higher education favour this kind of equality approach in teaching and research, and the result is a bimodal system of learning. The situation in the churches regarding the transmission of religious faith and practice, as Spickard points out, is also bimodal, some institutions favouring a top-down clergy-directed approach, while others are disposed to follow the participant-centred approach which makes a fit with the voluntarism which now characterizes the approach of increasing numbers of believers to religious beliefs and practice.

The Handbook, then, has been about creating new insights and breaking boundaries in the sociology of religion. Its intention has also been to encourage further debate about the methods, theoretical orientations, teaching, and objectives of the discipline of the sociology of religion. In looking forward, the past has not been neglected. Moreover, some of the major issues which it has addressed historically, including the new forms that some of these issues, such as secularization, religious pluralism, social integration and harmony, and religious violence, have been revisited, with creativity and insight.

References

Berger, Peter L., *et al.* (eds.) (1999). *The De-secularization of the World.* Grand Rapids, Mich., and Cambridge: Wm. B. Eerdmans Publishing Co.

Boyer, Pascal (2001). *Religion Explained: The Evolutionary Origins of Religious Thought.* New York: Basic Books.

Bromley, David (2007). *Teaching New Religious Movements.* Oxford: Oxford University Press.

Bruce, Steve (1986). *God Save Ulster: The Religion and Politics of Paisleyism.* Oxford: Oxford University Press.

—— (2002). *God is Dead: Secularization in the West.* Oxford: Blackwell.

Cadge, Wendy (2005). *Heartwood: The First Generation of Theravada Buddhism in America.* Chicago: University of Chicago Press.

Chang, Maria Hsia (2004). *Falun Gong.* New Haven and London: Yale University Press.

Clarke, Peter (2006). *New Religions in Global Perspective.* London: Routledge.

Dawkins, Richard (2006). *The God Delusion.* London: Bantam.

Durkheim, Émile (1915). *The Elementary Forms of Religious Life.* London: George Allen & Unwin.

El Fadl, Khalid Abou (2004). 'Islam and the Challenge of Democracy'. In *idem* (ed.), *Islam and the Challenge of Democracy*, Oxford: Oxford University Press, 3–49.

Geertz, Clifford (1968). *Islam Observed.* Chicago: University of Chicago Press.

Gibb, H. A. R. (1978). *Islam.* Oxford: Oxford University Press.

Heelas, Paul, and Woodhead, Linda (2005). *The Spiritual Revolution: Why Religion is Giving Way to Spirituality.* Oxford: Blackwell.

Hefner, Robert W. (1999). 'Multiple Modernities: Christianity, Islam, and Hinduism in a Globalizing Age'. *Annual Review of Anthropology*, 27: 83–104.

Hervieu-Léger, D. (2000[1993]). *Religion as a Chain of Memory*, trans. Simon Lee. Cambridge: Polity Press.

Hitchens, Christopher (2007). *God is Not Great: How Religion Poisons Everything.* New York: Hatchette.

Lewis, Ioan M. (1971). *Ecstatic Religion.* Harmondsworth: Penguin Books.

Martin, David (1990). *Tongues of Fire.* Oxford: Blackwell.

Mitchell, Richard P. (1969). *The Muslim Brothers.* London: Oxford University Press.

Queen, Christopher (ed.) (2000). *Engaged Buddhism in the West.* Boston: Wisdom.

Richardson, James T. (2004). *Regulating Religion: Case Studies from around the Globe.* New York: Kluwer.

Roof, Wade Clark (1993). *A Generation of Seekers: The Spiritual Journeys of the Baby Boom Generation.* San Francisco: Harper.

—— (1998). 'Religious Borderlands: Challenge for Future Study'. *Journal for the Scientific Study of Religion*, 37/1: 1–15.

—— (1999). *Spiritual Marketplace: Baby Boomers and the Remaking of American Religion.* Princeton and Oxford: Princeton University Press.

Spickard, James V. (1998). 'Rethinking Religious Social Action: What is "Rational" about Rational Choice Theory?'. *Sociology of Religion*, 59/2: 99–115.

Stark, Rodney, and Bainbridge, William Sims (1985). *The Future of Religion.* Berkeley and Los Angeles: University of California Press.

—— Hamberg, Eva, and Miller, Alan S. (2005). 'Exploring Spirituality and Unchurched Religion in America, Sweden and Japan'. *Journal of Contemporary Religion*, 20/1: 3–25.

Taylor, Charles (2007). *A Secular Age*. Cambridge, Mass.: Harvard University Press.

Weber, Max (1965). *The Protestant Ethic and the Spirit of Capitalism*. London: Allen & Unwin.

PART I

THEORY: CLASSICAL, MODERN, AND POSTMODERN

CHAPTER 1

REAPPRAISING DURKHEIM FOR THE STUDY AND TEACHING OF RELIGION

WILLIAM E. PADEN

INTEREST in Durkheim has undergone something of a revival through the publications of the British Centre for Durkheimian Studies in Oxford (Pickering 2001), and, following Pickering's comprehensive work *Durkheim's Sociology of Religion* (1984), the study of Durkheim's views on religion in particular has proceeded apace (Allen, Pickering, and Watts Miller 1998; Idinopulos and Wilson 2002; Godlove 2005; Strenski 2006).

Yet a previous generation of religion scholars had faulted Durkheim's reductionism, just as anthropologists had challenged his ethnographic categories. Joachim Wach's classic, titled *Sociology of Religion*, mentioned Durkheim but twice time in passing—only to issue a warning against the positivism of confusing religious and social values (Wach 1949: 5, 95). Even a later textbook on the history of comparative religion republished in 1986 concluded its telling portrayal of Durkheim with these words:

> Although widely read, Durkheim was so dominated by the desire to explain away the phenomenon of religion that his theories about the origins of religion are of little

consequence. His failure to accept mankind's belief in the actual existence of an unseen supernatural order—a failure in which he was to have many followers—led him into serious errors of interpretation. . . . The student of comparative religion will, perhaps, read him less in order to acquire a knowledge of either the nature of religion or the thorny problem of the origins of religion, than to learn something of the standing of these theories in turn-of-the-century France. (Sharpe 1986: 86)

At the same time, social theory was starting to take hold. In the late 1960s came the influence of the neo-Durkheimians Mary Douglas, Victor Turner, Peter Berger, Louis Dumont, Clifford Geertz, Robert Bellah, and Claude Lévi-Strauss, all of whom contributed theoretical and interpretive frames that religion scholars found academically legitimizing—and perhaps, as a benefit, religiously unthreatening. Through and after the 1980s, the "History of Religions" field—usually the methodological flagship of religious studies—was becoming "socialized" and anthropologized. *The Elementary Forms of Religious Life* was transitioning in classrooms from being an instance of dated nineteenth-century-style speculation to being recognized as something of a gold mine of theoretic capital, and found its secure place on the reading lists of courses on theory and method. Historian of religion Jonathan Z. Smith was continuing the Durkheimian trajectory in fresh, critical directions (1978; 1987; 2005), and could write that while one may not accept "the answers Durkheim set forth to the questions he posed", nevertheless his questions and sociological vision continue to "establish our agendum" (1987: 36).

The acceptability of the neo-Durkheimians was not only because they provided theory where theory had been lacking in religious studies, but because on the whole their conceptualizations were not dismissively anti-religious or offensively reductive. Thus, from the point of view of the academic study of religion, the question of the ultimate referential reality of religion could conveniently be deferred or bracketed, and the social construction of phenomenological reality could be adopted as a working matrix. Durkheim could therefore be read with a new slant: had he not stressed the enduring, effective nature of religious forces, albeit socially originated, over against rationalist views that dismissed them as mere illusions? This motif even became a major theme in the lengthy introduction of Karen Fields to her new translation of *Elementary Forms* (Fields 1995). Durkheim's thesis, moreover, could be construed not as a reduction of religion to society, in the commonsense meaning of "society", but rather as a special enlargement of the notion of society that focused on its intrinsically religious nature, including the irreducible, *sui generis* structuring and functioning of "the sacred". Concurrent with the appropriation of sociological frames in religious studies was general acceptance of the methodological point that all thought and interpretation, religious or scientific, is necessarily reductive, selecting some features of the world for purposes of baseline analysis, while ignoring others.

This chapter focuses primarily on ways in which some of Durkheim's ideas on religion have been, and can be, appropriated and developed, particularly his central category of sacrality—which is more heterogeneous than most observers take it to be, and a subject benefiting from differentiation, modification, and aspectual analysis. Not just a nineteenth-century or primitive archaism, the factor of the "sacred" continues to be observable wherever group identities are challenged and put at stake, as in conflicts over ethnic and national autonomy, in loyalty to tribes and sects, in human-rights issues, and in domestic wars over such things as the inviolability of human embryos, marriage, and traditional gendered classifications. While post-structuralist thought has tried to replace ideal types and the language of universal patterns by turning attention to micro-social behaviors of strategizing "habits", the role of cross-cultural modeling does not cease to lose its value, particularly as studies of religion explore connections with the human sciences. Whereas Durkheim thought that his elementary forms encompassed the whole of religion, today one is more methodologically circumspect and one is more likely to take structural types as addressing "aspects" of a phenomenon and not whole or total entities. The essay concludes with a discussion of the relevance of the sciences of evolutionary sociality for reappraising Durkheimian ideas of the social formations of religious behavior.

Differentiating the Category of the Sacred

A key criticism of the phenomenology of religion tradition was that its grounding concept, "the sacred", or "the holy", was explicitly or implicitly theological and metaphysical, and thus completely inappropriate as an academic category. Here religious phenomena were often presented as "manifestations" of that transcendent power—a power that resembled divinity. The sacred, as a term, was essentialized and reified as an a priori religious reality—a reality experienced in countless ways and cultural forms. In sharp contrast, Durkheim's *le sacré* was a social representation, rather than a superhuman presence, and thus functioned in an altogether different, unidealized theoretical universe. The sacred in this frame is a value placed *on* objects, rather than a power that shines through them because of their extraordinary qualities. Much of the analytic potential of Durkheim's theory of religion is linked to the applicability of the bedrock idea of the social generation of "sacred things".

Yet in Durkheim's work this key concept seemed to vary in context and contain a variety of conceptual influences and levels. Thus, sacredness for Durkheim had one clear ritual prototype in the anthropological notion of taboo, following J. G. Frazer and W. Robertson Smith; yet this needed to be wedded to the discourse of the sociological binary of collective and individual realms of life—and, in turn, that representational level had to be connected with the origin of the sacred in the emotional experience of effervescent group gatherings. As well, all of this, in Durkheim's mind, was linked with his sociological version of a neo-Kantian idea of obligatory, categorical morality. It follows that this repertoire of aspects of sacrality contains a range of possibilities. Is "the sacred" a prohibited object, not to be violated by any contact, or is it—as we learn halfway through *Elementary Forms*—discovered in a state of emotional, communal ecstasy, if not pandemonium? Is it a cult of imperative morality and sacrifice inspired by the constraints of social authority, or is it a totemically "signed", semiotic emblem representing differential identities among groups? Is it a realm of ideals, or is it a status to be achieved through a deliberate process of self-transformation? Is it the prestige attributed to any object at any point in culture, or is it a zone of culture always and everywhere found to be marked off from ordinary life? Is it a "force", a kind of mana, that conveys itself by contagious association, or is it an embodiment of a social norm? To make it even more complex, Durkheim accepted W. Robertson Smith's idea that the sacred contains its own binary of pure–impure (1995: 412–17). In *Elementary Forms* the sacred is all these things, according to sequence or context. To be sure, while identifying each aspect separately, one must grant their interdependence on a circle of relationships—for example, the sacred is a mark of group experience and identity, and thus acquires prestige, which means in turn that it contains a certain experienced force, which is a force that must in turn be managed through proper ritual protocols. The following sections sort out and discuss some of the key features of this process.

The Sacred/Profane Binary as Principle of Religious Conduct

Durkheim's vocabulary about the "sacred and profane" as exclusive realms that repel and contradict each other has been thoroughly criticized, and for many became grounds for rejecting the category of the sacred entirely. It is natural to address this issue first. Criticisms of the binary have been reviewed in detail by Pickering (1984: 115–49). The main charge is that so many cultures and religions do not keep these worlds separate, as Durkheim's theory seems to require. Clearly Durkheim's language about all religion forming a "bipartite" universe of sacred and profane (1995: 38) led to this problem, and seems to be indefensible if by "profane" is meant an actual realm of life different from the sacred realm. But it can be shown that Durkheim's binary refers to ritual relationships that regulate incompatible states, not static areas on the map of the world. That the sacred/profane is a class not of things, but of relationships *to* things, is a distinction that Durkheim should have made clearer (Lukes 1972: 27).

The sacred/profane binary can be understood as a cultic distinction referring to protocols of ritualized negotiation between two kinds of status. Notably,

Durkheim's prototypes of the binary refer to rites of passage where there is a costly process of transitioning from one state to another: initiation rites, the requirements for entering monastic life, the practices of ascetics in achieving sanctity, and even the phenomenon of religious suicide (1995: 37). There are two actions going on here: (1) keeping a boundary between things with more powerful status and things with less status, and (2) engaging in processes by which the latter can gain access to the former—as in the ordeals of initiation, in taking off one's shoes before entering a shrine, or in having to bow before a king. This is a social, not a metaphysical, duality.

Durkheim's use of the sacred/profane binary—the sacred thing "is, par excellence, that which the profane must not and cannot touch with impunity" (1995: 38)—was profoundly shaped by the notion of taboo, a category that Robertson Smith and Frazer were linking with the term "sacred", taking the latter to mean forbidden or restricted from common use (much as with the Latin *sacer*, forbidden). From this came the idea of the ambiguity of the sacred object as having a positive or a negative force. But Durkheim's theory of religion progressed well beyond the idea of the prohibitions of primitive thought, showing how separation could be conceived as "abstention", and how abstentions could be shown to be the gate of access to achieving sanctity through such things as costly renunciations of the world of attachments. That "man cannot approach his god intimately while still bearing the marks of his profane life" (1995: 312) takes the idea of interdiction far beyond the notion of primitive taboo. Robertson Smith, too, had shown that the conception of holiness evolved from primitive connotations of danger to notions of purity of life (W.R. Smith 1956: 140–1).

The Sacred versus "the Divine" as General Organizing Category for Studying Religion

It is possible simply to take the notion of sacredness in a less dynamic sense and refer to a class of objects that have been made sacred. Pickering thus argues (1984: 149–62) that Durkheim's basic concept of the sacred is useful beyond its encasement in the dichotomous and controversially phrased sacred/profane binary stated early on in *Elementary Forms*. For Durkheim religion is a vast set of "sacred things", the content of which is infinitely varied over time. One has to be careful here about just slipping into an equation of the sacred and the religious, where the former simply connotes some transcendental dimension of life that all religions have in common. Still, assuming that "sacred" here means objects constructed by social prestige rather than being just a placeholder term for "the nonempirical", this would indeed be an alternative way of reading the history of religion—alternative, in the case of religious studies, to seeing history as just a succession of varying beliefs or ideas about the nature of divinity or reality. The compelling nature of those objects, which may or may not include gods, is a reflection of their status within a system; protectedness and inviolability are concomitants. Such an anthropologized history, among other things, would include attention to the emergence of certain secular values, understood as sacred, including the history of the sacralization of the idea of a human "person", or other notions of a secular sacrality (Carrithers, Collins, and Lukes 1985; Watts Miller 2002).

A methodological assumption in this sociological model is that the "objective" world is what it is through collective representations, rather than construed as an a priori, existing reality which all religions and cultures aspire to describe with their symbols. As will be addressed below, such an approach would also converge ultimately with studies of the evolution of human sociality.

The Sacred as a Marker of Shared Identity

Sacredness is not just an attribute of objects as such, but has a semiotic nature signaling the shared identity capital of a particular group. Thus, "things are classified as sacred and profane by reference to the totem. It is the very archetype of sacred things" (Durkheim 1995: 118). Whatever its original ethnographic viability, Durkheim's model was that a "clan" is a group that has a unity based on its members sharing the same "name", the same emblems of identity, and the same ritual relations with the same sacred objects—but it is not necessarily consanguineous or territorially based. The members then share the same "essence" by way of participating in what the totemic emblem represents—that is, their "kind". The emblems are ways in which a group becomes conscious of itself and "perpetuates" that consciousness (1995: 233). As soon as one clan or group is differentiated from another, elements of this totemic identity come into play. Group-specific histories and rites follow suit. In Mary Douglas's phrase, "the sacred for Durkheim and Mauss was nothing more mysterious or occult than shared classifications, deeply cherished and violently defended" (1987: 97).

This concept has not lost its value, and continues to describe the signature formations of new and traditional groups—where "group" here does not mean social environments in general, but rather the self-representations of specifically differentiated collective units or subunits. A group is a kind of linguistic construct that functions as an essentialized representation of aggregates of individuals, and thus comes to have the effect of a "thing" or an objectivity. Benedict Anderson's (1991) popular term, "imagined communities", though referring to modern ethnic and anti-colonial national movements, would just as well describe any group; indeed, it is Durkheim's term, too: "the clan was possible only on condition of being imaginable"; "take away the name and the symbol that gives it tangible form, and the clan can no longer even be imagined" (1995: 235). J. Z. Smith's work connected to Durkheim through this linguistic, classificatory feature of sacrality

(2005: 102–8; 1987), a feature implicit in the notion of the totemic emblem—where the abstract "mark" on the *churinga* was the one factor that gave it its sacred character.

Markers, or stereotypic signatures, of group definition come in many forms. One might think of the role of patron saints like the Mexican Virgin of Guadalupe in constructing a national identity; the role of female circumcision as a strategic community membership sign in African communities; allusions to "remember Kosovo" for Serbian nationalists or to the iconic Western Wall for Jews; the identifying sign of headscarves for Muslim women or the differences between the way in which Sunnis and Shi'ites hold their arms in performing daily prayers. The notion of "axiomatic" community markers has been productively applied to the discursive formulations of evangelical groups that base themselves on biblical authority (Malley 2004). Durkheim's clan "signs" can be endlessly ramified in the communicative displays of any historical social formations.

Sacred Order and its Violation

With sign differentiation come boundaries and defending boundaries from violation. Sacredness can then refer not just to an object, but to the whole order or system on which the object depends and to which it refers. Here sacrality is what keeps a world of representations in place—the representations of the group being at the same time the representations of its world. Social classifications and their ideological representations become a kind of property, and maintaining such territory against violation or compromise draws upon the deepest instincts for self-preservation or survival.

The "profane", here, if one is to employ the term at all, is what violates or offends the system; it is not simply the mundane or what is outside the system. It is oppositional. The sacred is not set apart because dangerous (*sacer*), but, as the Latin term *sanctus* conveyed, because ordained or secured as inviolable. Emic terms pointing to this aspect of the sacred order include Hindu *dharma*, Islamic *sharia*, and Confucian notions of *Li* (propriety), *T'ien* (order of heaven), and *Hsiao* (filial piety). In biblical tradition, "covenants" with God determine the order of the moral universe.

The binary of order and its violation was developed in several ways. For example, Mary Douglas's (2002) model of cognitive boundaries dropped the distinction of primitive and modern systems of order, showing how any group will have its own versions of pollution, danger, or anomaly. In her terms, where there is an order of things, there will be the prospect of impurity—famously, "where there is dirt there is system" (2002: 36). Order generates boundaries between and within groups, and the boundaries will be consequential according to whether groups are "strong" or "weak" relative to the outside world, and according to whether the internal classifications ("grids") of those groups emphasize strict internal role gradations or not. Strong groups, for example, will have the most highly defined purity rules for maintaining membership.

Other neo-Durkheimian models have added to the theme. Louis Dumont's *Homo Hierarchicus* (1980) joined notions of purity with social hierarchy. J. Z. Smith built a typology distinguishing "locative", bounded religious systems—where sacrality is a function of things being in their proper place—and those which are "utopic", non-worldly and a-spatial (1978: 129–71). Others have pointed to additional facets of symbolic order, such as *nomos* (Berger 1967), the sacralization of identity (Mol 1975; Rappaport 1999), hierarchy (Isambert 1982), systemic order (Paden 1996), and symbolic classification related to space (Anttonen 2000; J. Z. Smith 1987). The relation of sacred order to the notion of honor should be a productive research area.

Effervescence, Regeneration, Anti-Structure

Yet another salient dimension of the Durkheimian "sacred" is the effervescence of group gatherings, in contrast with routine life. Durkheim tried to include this in his sacred/profane binary (the individual gives up his ordinary feelings and identity to participate in the group festivity), but its duality goes in another direction from those described above. It plays on the contrast of collective high arousal and ordinary habit. The sacred is generated through the feelings activated in ecstatic collective events. Others have shown that the festival moment contains the seeds of anti-structure behaviors that could potentially subvert the otherwise regulated, boundaried structure of the sacred. Breaking taboos, rather than keeping them, then becomes the gate of access to the sacred.

The anti-structural but life-renewing aspect of the sacred was elaborated by Roger Caillois (1913–78) and Georges Bataille (1897–1962), representatives of the so-called left-wing Durkheimian school and its Collège de Sociologie. This work extended the notion of the unrestrained "festival" or "expenditure" mode of the sacred, and has had a revival of influence (Richman 2002; Taussig 1998). In Caillois's synthesis, *Man and the Sacred* (1959; first pub. 1939), the sacred is ambivalent in the sense of being both a constraining, containing, inhibiting force of order *and* a creative, transgressive, liberating, sacrificial force which breaks through old forms and rigidities. It is both the "tabooed" and that which destroys the congealed conformities of law and normativity—both what is to be protected and what violates protected order when the latter wears out or becomes resistant. In Caillois's view, war has taken over the function of festival paroxysm in modern society—"a total phenomenon that exalts and transforms modern society in its entirety, cutting with terrible contrast into the calm routine of peacetime" (1959: 165). "The festival", he proposes, "is in the same relationship to the time of labor, as war is to peace. They are both phases of movement and excess, as against the phases of stability and moderation" (1959: 166). Bataille expanded upon the paroxysmal, even violent, nature of the sacred, as well as its relation to erotic effusion and ecstatic mysticism, festival reversals, the emptying of order, wealth-destroying potlatch, and "expenditure" (*dépense*) generally (Bataille 1985). For Bataille, the "right hand" of social conservation thus contrasts with the "left hand" of social expenditure.

Michèle Richman's major work (2002) on the concept of effervescence in theories of social dynamics explores the theoretical issues in the notion of regenerative upheavals and explosive contestations, events that contrast with the socialization of maintaining status quo civility and thus static notions of structure. Durkheimians argue that this "socio-logic of effervescence" can be distinguished from psychological notions of crowd psychology in its simply irrational, regressive aspects. Victor Turner's (1969) concept of unstructured *communitas* had previously addressed aspects of this concept. Not just archaic and exotic, these regenerative moments become a permanent feature of social history. Thus Karen Fields notes "the tumultuous arrival in 1979 of Ruhollah Khomeini at Tehran airport", and the "birth of a nation" in 1989 when Lithuanians returned the bones of St Casimir to the People's House of Culture, then reconsecrated as the cathedral of Vilnius—or even Nazi and Ku Klux Klan rallies, "with individuals led to impute to themselves shared inborn essences and fabulous collective identities" (1995: pp. xliv–xlv, xlii). One could also point to stadium-filled gatherings of sports fans or evangelicals, a million-man march on Washington, the national rites of mourning following the events of September 11, 2001, rave culture (St John 2003), and even the shared emotion, community, and "sociomental bonds" between those who have never met face to face but who experience common events through common media events (Chakyo 2002). Michel Maffesoli (1996) has examined the notion of "postmodern tribes", temporary social identifications and identities—distinct from institutional structures—which, despite their impermanence, still have a collective feeling or enthusiasm, a certain sympathy and power, an "immanent" transcendence.

Yet the same "regeneration" prototype indeed raises questions about how group violence, or social pathologies—lynch mobs, ethnic cleansing campaigns—fit the template. The anthropologist Stanley Tambiah therefore asks of the Durkheimian model "how in the context of ethnic riots, participants accede to the call of violating and victimizing the enemy as a moral imperative, socially induced and legitimated" (1997: 303).

It remains the fact that periodic festivals, ceremonies, or collective observances also have a conserving, integrative, mnemonic function and as such comprise an infrastructure of most religious systems. One can find the effervescence factor either in connection with high-stimulus sensory pageantry, recurrently choreographed, or in anti-formal groups that generate emotional ecstasy in formats expressing more personal involvement, or in marked periods, such as Ramadan, where strong social displays of non-ordinary observances intensify motivation and collective commitment. In each of these the totemic sacred is being kept "alive" and in memory, over against the forces of its diminution and neglect. Studies of the dynamics and cognitive bases of memory and emotion in relation to ritual frequency and sensory stimulus add new interest and complexity to this theme (Whitehouse 2004; Connerton 1989; Hervieu-Léger 2000).

After Durkheim: Some Trajectories

Durkheim and Religious Studies

The eclectic work of Mircea Eliade (1907–86)—the major, classical figure in comparative religion who extended the range and modalities of data concerning the sacred as none other had—straddled the phenomenological and neo-Durkheimian worlds. Eliade explicitly recognized the influence of Caillois, and in widely read works such as *The Sacred and the Profane* (1959) kept the language of the heterogeneity of sacred/profane realms while at the same describing the ways in which religious cultures reunite them in time, space, myth, and ritual. As well, he developed Durkheimian notions of festivals as "openings" onto an eternal, "Great Time".

For Eliade, the sacred and the profane represent a simpler duality than Durkheim's: they are respectively the cosmological realm of myth and the ordinary life world. Otherwise put, these are the realms of supernatural archetypes and of nature. Whereas Durkheim was focusing on the exclusivity of two realms that required ritual transformation, Eliade elaborated more on the connectivity and integration of dualities—that is, the various ways in which the mythic realm gave value to aspects of the human world. "Some of the highest religious experiences", he wrote, "identify the sacred with the whole universe. To many a mystic the integrated quality of the cosmos is itself a hierophany" (1963: 459). While Eliade objected to sociological reductions, preferring to reconstruct the patterned "worlds" of religious insiders more at the level of existential phenomenology, both men imagined religion as plural systems of mythically and ritually constructed worlds—worlds understood not as objectivities but as symbolic schemas with a life of their own. Both believed that the study of religious worlds was relevant for contemporary people in the search for moral and spiritual values. A Durkheimian reading of Eliade, and vice versa, would be mutually illuminating and a helpful way of re-understanding the French connection in religious studies—a connection that has been implicit rather than overt in Eliade's work (Paden 1994; 2002).

At the same time, a post-Eliadean generation of religion scholars connects with Durkheim more in terms of the way in which collective classifications contain and authorize socio-political agendas and practices. "In keeping with the Durkheimian tradition of sociological studies on religion and myth", writes Russell McCutcheon, "we could say that a social formation is the activity of experimenting with, authorizing or combating, and reconstituting widely circulated ideal types, idealizations or, better put, mythifications that function to control the means of and sites where social significance is selected, symbolized and communicated" (2000: 203). The Durkheimian/Maussian notion of mythology as containing classifications and hierarchies, and thus ideology in narrative form, is central to the work of scholars, like Chicago historian of religion Bruce Lincoln, who take Durkheim as basic, but add the critical, political edges of cultural theorists "from Antonio Gramsci to Roland Barthes and Pierre Bourdieu" (1999: 147).

Evolutionary Sociality: A New Linkage with Durkheimian Ideas?

Recent developments have raised the prospect of narrowing the traditional gulf between Durkheimian sociology of religion and evolutionary biology (Dunbar, Knight, and Power 1999; D. S. Wilson 2002). Insofar as Durkheim postulates universal social forms, and insofar as evolutionary thought has now provided extensive research on the evolution of human sociality and social cognition, it is an area worth investigating (Schmaus 2004).

Of course Durkheim's task, in context, was to propose and defend the autonomy and irreducibility of a sociological level of facts. Here the distinctiveness of humans, in contrast to nonhuman species, was their social life and representations; it would be a "vain quest", Durkheim thought, to infer human sociality from animal life (1995: 62). Yet he also admits that a theory of religion must rest on the sciences, including "the sciences of nature... since man and society are linked to the universe and can be abstracted from it only artificially" (1995: 432). Today the formerly hallowed dichotomy of culture and nature is much less clear, and the picture of hominid sociality evolving through life in small groups and forming group-related cognitive and behavioral adaptations has widely replaced Durkheim's late nineteenth-century world view. Thus, the intrinsic, inherited sociality of the human species includes dispositions for accepting group representations, biases for loyalty, coalition making, and conformity, capacities for reciprocity, cooperation, and altruism, and—relevant to the Durkheimian notion of collective or totemic representations—responsiveness to signals of kin associations.

All of this suggests new prospects for reading Durkheim. For example, in his ambitious work *Darwin's Cathedral* (2002), the biologist D. S. Wilson drew on

Durkheim to help explain how group selection might operate in some religious groups, particularly through the unifying power of moral commitment to sacred symbols.

> Recall Durkheim's statement that "in all its aspects and at every moment of history, social life is only possible thanks to a vast symbolism".... This statement may be ninety years old and well worn in various branches of the social sciences, but it is brand new against the background of modern evolutionary theories of social behavior, including human social behavior. It often seems as if the integration of biology and the social sciences is a one-way street, more a conquest by biology than a fertile interchange. Here is a case where the influence needs to flow the other way. (2002: 226)

In Wilson's model, sacred symbols command respect and affect behavior, which is to say, phenotypic variation, which in turn can influence survival and reproduction.

Anthropologist Roy Rappaport (1999) gave a sustained account of the factor of sacrality in social evolution, focusing on the function of inviolability in ritual and language as an adaptive necessity by which groups preserve their identities while also responding to change. "Sacred postulates" and invariable rites are posited as beyond any falsifiability, giving a trans-empirical quality that attempts to guarantee constancy. Sacred language, for its part, is an antidote to the subversive plasticity of language. "Sanctity's role in human evolution", Rappaport writes, "has been profound" (1999: 416); it is "a functional replacement for genetic determination of patterns of behavior" (1999: 418).

Kinship behavior suggests another potential point of connection with Durkheim and evolutionary theory. For example, at the genetic level, "kin selection" and "inclusive fitness" theory means that individual animals—the first stage of research was on social insects—will be willing to sacrifice themselves for the greater good of their gene pool to the relative extent that their genes are the same as those in the group cohort. While human group affiliation is not limited to close biological families, any group can function as kin equivalent, and it is possible that the social dispositions evolved in small group living can also be triggered by the circumstances of *constructed* group identities. "Kin" here becomes a cultural formation, and this was Durkheim's point about clans. A disposition that evolved for in-group defense—whether of resources or reproductive line—or for favoring and trusting one's "kind", is then applied to "one's group", however defined: country, fraternity, club, clan, team, street gang, military unit, labor union, political party, school, family ancestry, ethnic tradition, or religion.

As well, the markers of totemic identity, within an evolutionary world view, might be understood as continuous with kin or in-group communication systems. In the natural world, animals sense affiliation by any number of pheromonal, visual, or behavioral "indicators"—and kin recognition cues, or phenotypic matching as a way of detecting relatedness, may be involved with the stereotypic identity signals and codes of human groups. The totemic principle and cult, with its patron gods and progenitors, might then be thought to activate kin mechanisms—amounting, as some evolutionists have put it, to a "hypertrophied kin recognition process" (Kirkpatrick 2005: 248–51). Likewise, ritually enhanced or "exaggerated" displays will stimulate extra feelings of respect, just as certain animals will respond more fully to an exaggerated representation of a sexual object—for example, made of cardboard or a painting—than to the real thing (E. O. Wilson 1999: 252). Mythic histories, then, would be the enhanced lineages of one's "kind", understood in both a sociological and a biological sense, and ritual would be the "cult" of reproducing its signals. As well, some evolutionary theory has shown that behavioral signals that are demonstrably costly or hard to fake (self-sacrifice, strict moral observance), advertise an individual's high commitment to the group, thus enhancing the commitment of others (Sosis and Alcorta 2003: 266–7).

Another area of possible mutual interest between evolutionists and Durkheimians is the notion of prestige goods as social capital. Durkheim's sacred objects are made of the stuff of social prestige. But the "prestige" is also understood as an evolutionary social adaptation (Henrich and Gil-White 2001). Persons of rank and status, and objects that represent rank and status, will compel attention; individuals in an in-group will tend to acknowledge the values placed by superiors on prestige objects. Such objects are sources of salient social information. Evolutionists have also pointed out the transition from primate dominance complexes to the coming of "human symbolic prestige" (Barkow 1989: 6, 183), and with the emergence of human artifact cultures, the extension of prestige to objects (Dissanayake 1992; Mithen, 1999). An economy of prestige goods would allow tribal leaders to attract respect and gain hierarchical relations with competing groups. Religious systems would become the epitome of "symbolic culture" understood as an emergent evolutionary environment (Chase 1999: 42). Thus, the religious history of the species would emerge as a history of the attaching of prestige to various kinds of objects and institutions, ultimately producing the thousands of holy objects sitting side by side on the planet, each a priceless currency for its community, yet each irrelevant in other social landscapes. In large-scale groups, these "cult objects" (scriptures, hierarchies, sacred institutions and objects, gods) would become hypertrophied forms of prestige, taking on a life of their own—prestige generates prestige. The relationship to Durkheim's views on the sacred as a construction of social prestige (1995: 209–11), and to his lectures on the sacred character of property and property rights (1958: 121–220), is there to develop. Likewise, Murray Milner Jr (1994) has given a sustained argument—though not in an evolutionary context—that brings status relationships and sacral relationships into a common, integrated, theoretical model.

At the same time, evolutionary psychologists often refer to Durkheim as an exemplar of a social-science model that ignores the inherited, adapted mechanisms of individual minds. This "Standard Social Science Model", in their view, erroneously pictures the mind as a blank slate into which social norms are downloaded and reproduced. Yet in Durkheim's case, at least, this is questionable (Schmaus 2004). Thus, in the *Elementary Forms* we read: "The whole social world seems populated with forces that in reality exist only in our minds" (p. 228); "ideas can only release emotive forces that are already within us" (p. 419); the totemic principle itself "exists only in our minds" (p. 349); "society can only exist in and by means of individual minds, it must enter into us and become organized within us" (p. 211); sacred/profane representations are not in nature, but are based on "psychic antagonism" (p. 321), or "psychic mechanisms" (p. 325). One could argue that the edifice of social symbolism, for Durkheim, is maintained by the strength of "countless individual representations" (p. 210).

Where evolutionary psychologists deny that culture and cultural world views are "things" that are just internalized in individuals, their point is important; yet a distinction should be made between amorphous culture in general and group-specific representations/identities in particular. While groups are indeed made up of individual, self-interested components, those individual components have dispositions to respond to representations of group identities and accept or trust group or "kin" ideas as objectivities (Plotkin 2003: 248–90). "Groups" may be continuously reconstructed "output fictions" of individual minds, and thus epiphenomena; but among those fictions are powerful ideologies that constrain behaviors and can have deadly motivation and causal force. In short, insofar as imagined communities, norms, totemic symbols, or essentialized identities are *believed in* by aggregates of individuals, the collective factor then comes back into play as a functioning social "ontology". The notion of the construction of a social "reality" that *functions* as an objectivity is therefore not conceptually at odds with the point that it is individual brains which "select" for it and make decisions about its input information.

The Durkheimian project of explaining the elementary forms of religious behavior as elementary forms of social behavior could therefore find a complementary project with evolutionary research on the social dispositions of *Homo sapiens.*

References

Allen, N. J., Pickering, W. S. F., and Watts Miller, W. (eds.) (1998). *On Durkheim's Elementary Forms of Religious Life.* London: Routledge.

Anderson, Benedict (1991). *Imagined Communities: Reflections on the Origin and Spread of Nationalism,* rev. edn. London: Verso.

Anttonen, Veikko (2000). "Sacred", In Willi Braun and Russell T. McCutcheon (eds.), *Guide to the Study of Religion,* London: Cassell, 271–82.

Barkow, Jerome H. (1989). *Darwin, Sex, and Status: Biological Approaches to Mind and Culture.* Toronto: University of Toronto Press.

Bataille, Georges (1985). *Visions of Excess: Selected Writings, 1927–1939*, trans. and ed. Allan Stoekl. Minneapolis: University of Minnesota Press.

Berger, Peter (1967). *The Sacred Canopy: Elements of a Sociological Theory of Religion.* Garden City, NY: Doubleday.

Caillois, Roger (1959). *Man and the Sacred*, trans. Meyer Barash. Glencoe, Ill.: Free Press.

Carrithers, Michael, Collins, Steven, and Lukes, Steven (eds.) (1985). *The Category of the Person: Anthropology, Philosophy, History.* Cambridge: Cambridge University Press.

Chakyo, Mary (2002). *Connecting: How We Form Social Bonds and Communities in the Internet Age.* Albany, NY: SUNY Press.

Chase, Philip G. (1999). "Symbolism as Reference and Symbolism as Culture". In Robin Dunbar, Chris Knight, and Camilla Power (eds.), *The Evolution of Culture.* New Brunswick, NJ: Rutgers University Press, 34–49.

Connerton, Paul (1989). *How Societies Remember.* Cambridge: Cambridge University Press.

Dissanayake, Ellen (1992). *Homo Aestheticus: Where Art Comes From and Why.* New York: Free Press.

Douglas, Mary (1987). *How Institutions Think.* London: Routledge & Kegan Paul.

—— (2002). *Purity and Danger: An Analysis of Concepts of Pollution and Taboo.* London: Routledge.

Dumont, Louis (1980). *Homo Hierarchicus: The Caste System and Its Implications*, rev. edn., trans. Mark Sainsbury, Louis Dumont, and Basia Gulati. Chicago: University of Chicago Press.

Dunbar, Robin, Knight, Chris, and Power, Camilla (eds.) (1999). *The Evolution of Culture: An Interdisciplinary View.* New Brunswick, NJ: Rutgers University Press.

Durkheim, Émile (1958). *Professional Ethics and Civic Morals*, trans. Cornelia Brookfield. Glencoe, Ill.: Free Press.

—— (1995). *The Elementary Forms of Religious Life*, trans. Karen Fields. New York: Free Press.

Eliade, Mircea (1959). *The Sacred and the Profane: The Nature of Religion*, trans. Willard R. Trask. New York: Harcourt Brace Jovanovich.

—— (1963). *Patterns in Comparative Religion*, trans. Rosemary Sheed. New York: World Publishing Co.

Fields, Karen (1995). "Religion as an Eminently Social Thing", translator's introduction. In Émile Durkheim, *The Elementary Forms of Religious Life*, trans. Karen Fields, New York: Free Press, pp. xvii–lxxiii.

Godlove, Terry F. Jr. (ed.) (2005), *Teaching Durkheim.* New York: Oxford University Press.

Henrich, Joseph, and Gil-White, Francisco J. (2001). "The Evolution of Prestige: Freely Conferred Deference as a Mechanism for Enhancing the Benefits of Cultural Transmission". *Evolution and Human Behavior*, 22: 165–96.

Hervieu-Léger, Danièle (2000). *Religion as a Chain of Memory*, trans. Simon Lee. New Brunswick, NJ: Rutgers University Press.

Idinopulos, Thomas A., and Wilson, Brian C. (eds.) (2002). *Reappraising Durkheim for the Study and Teaching of Religion Today.* Leiden: Brill.

Isambert, François-André (1982). *Le Sens du Sacré: Fête et Religion Populaire.* Paris: Les Éditions de Minuit.

Kirkpatrick, Lee A. (2005). *Attachment, Evolution, and the Psychology of Religion.* New York: Guilford Press.

Lincoln, Bruce (1999). *Theorizing Myth: Narrative, Ideology, and Scholarship.* Chicago: University of Chicago Press.

Lukes, Steven (1972). *Emile Durkheim: His Life and Work.* New York: Harper & Row.

Maffesoli, Michel (1996). *The Time of the Tribes.* London: Sage.

Malley, Brian (2004). *How the Bible Works: An Anthropological Study of Evangelical Biblicism.* Walnut Creek, Calif.: Altamira Press.

McCutcheon, Russell T. (2000). "Myth". In Willi Braun and Russell T. McCutcheon (eds.), *Guide to the Study of Religion.* London: Cassell, 190–208.

Milner, Murray Jr. (1994). *Status and Sacredness: A General Theory of Status Relations and an Analysis of Indian Culture.* New York: Oxford University Press.

Mithen, Stephen (1999). "Symbolism and the Supernatural". In Dunbar *et al.* (1999), 147–72.

Mol, Hans (1975). *Identity and the Sacred: A Sketch for a New Social-Scientific Theory of Religion.* Oxford: Basil Blackwell.

Paden, William E. (1994). "Before 'The Sacred' Became Theological: Rereading the Durkheimian Legacy". In Thomas A. Idinopulos and Edward A. Yonan, (eds.), *Religion and Reductionism: Essays on Eliade, Segal and the Challenge of the Social Sciences for the Study of Religion.* Leiden: E. J. Brill, 198–210.

—— (1996). "Sacrality as Integrity: 'Sacred Order' as a Model for Describing Religious Worlds". In Thomas A. Idinopulos and Edward A. Yonan, (eds.), *The Sacred and its Scholars: Comparative Methodologies for the Study of Primary Religious Data.* Leiden: E. J. Brill, 3–18.

—— (2002). "The Creation of Human Behavior: Reconciling Durkheim and the Study of Religion". In Idinopulos and Wilson (2002), 15–26.

Pickering, W. S. F. (1984). *Durkheim's Sociology of Religion.* London: Routledge & Kegan Paul.

—— (ed.) (2001). *Emile Durkheim: Critical Assessments of Leading Sociologists,* Third Series, 1–4. London: Routledge.

Plotkin, Henry (2003). *The Imagined World Made Real: Toward a Natural Science of Culture.* New Brunswick, NJ: Rutgers University Press.

Rappaport, Roy (1999). *Ritual and Religion in the Making of Humanity.* Cambridge: Cambridge University Press.

Richman, Michèle H. (2002). *Sacred Revolutions: Durkheim and the Collège de Sociologie,* Contradictions, 14. Minneapolis: University of Minnesota Press.

Schmaus, Warren (2004). *Rethinking Durkheim and his Tradition.* Cambridge: Cambridge University Press.

Sharpe, Eric (1986). *Comparative Religion: A History,* 2nd edn. La Salle, Ill.: Open Court.

Smith, Jonathan Z. (1978). *Map is Not Territory: Studies in the History of Religions.* Chicago: University of Chicago Press.

—— (1987). *To Take Place: Toward Theory in Ritual.* Chicago: University of Chicago Press.

—— (2005). *Relating Religion: Essays in the Study of Religion.* Chicago: University of Chicago Press.

Smith, W. Robertson (1956). *The Religion of the Semites: The Fundamental Institutions.* New York: Meridian Books.

Sosis, Richard, and Alcorta, Candace (2003). "Signaling, Solidarity, and the Sacred: The Evolution of Religious Behavior". *Evolutionary Anthropology,* 12: 264–74.

St. John, Graham (ed.) (2003). *Rave Culture and Religion.* London: Routledge.

Strenski, Ivan (2006). *The New Durkheim.* New Brunswick, NJ: Rutgers University Press.

Tambiah, Stanley Jeyaraja (1997). *Leveling Crowds: Ethnonationalist Conflicts and Collective Violence in South Asia.* Berkeley: University of California Press.

Taussig, Michael (1998). "Transgression". In Mark C. Taylor (ed.), *Critical Terms for Religious Studies.* Chicago: University of Chicago Press, 349–64.

Turner, Victor (1969). *The Ritual Process: Structure and Anti-structure.* Ithaca, NY: Cornell University Press.

Wach, Joachim (1949). *Sociology of Religion.* Chicago: University of Chicago Press.

Watts Miller, W. (2002). "Secularism and the Sacred: Is There Really Something Called 'Secular Religion'?". In Idinopulos and Wilson (2002), 27–44.

Whitehouse, Harvey (2004). *Modes of Religiosity: A Cognitive Theory of Religious Transmission.* Walnut Creek, Calif.: Altamira Press.

Wilson, David Sloan (2002). *Darwin's Cathedral: Evolution, Religion, and the Nature of Society.* Chicago: University of Chicago Press.

Wilson, Edward O. (1999). *Consilience: The Unity of Knowledge.* New York: Random House.

Suggested Reading

The annual journal of the British Centre for Durkheimian Studies, *Durkheimian Studies,* is recommended; also Allen *et al.* (1998); Godlove (2005); Idinopulos and Wilson (2002); Pickering (1984 and 2001); and Strenski (2006).

CHAPTER 2

THE USES OF MAX WEBER

LEGITIMATION AND AMNESIA IN BUDDHOLOGY, SOUTH ASIAN HISTORY, AND ANTHROPOLOGICAL PRACTICE THEORY

DAVID N. GELLNER

In this essay I ask what we can learn by looking at the different ways in which Weber has been used or not used in the study of South Asian religion and in social anthropology more generally. There is an interesting contrast in the reception of Weber: what he wrote on Hinduism and Indian history has been largely ignored, whereas scholars of Buddhism have frequently drawn upon his writings on Buddhism for inspiration. The fact that Weber's influence is largely absent from works on

I would like to thank Lola Martinez, Ralph Schroeder, and David Chalcraft for helpful comments on earlier drafts of this essay.

Hinduism is parallelled by the way his name has dropped out of discussions of 'practice theory', at least in so far as its anthropological incarnations are concerned.

Weber's Fundamental Question

As is well known, Weber undertook his long study of the economic ethics of Hinduism and Buddhism as part of a global survey of world religions. Originally published in German in 1916–17 as 'The Economics of the World Religions: Hinduism and Buddhism' (Weber 1916–17), it came out in English in the USA in 1958 as *The Religion of India: The Sociology of Hinduism and Buddhism* (henceforth *ROI*). As Kantowsky (1986: 214–16) has described, the translation is based on a draft that Don Martindale, then a graduate student, had done in order to practise his German. It is evident that Hans Gerth, the senior co-editor, did not, as he promised Martindale he would, check the translation. The text as published contains many infelicities and downright inaccuracies, not to mention the fact that no one checked the bibliography or the South Asian terms used, so that it is riddled with inappropriate—because Germanic or simply incorrect—transliterations of technical terms. Clearly, a re-translation, ideally by a South Asian specialist, would be highly desirable. None the less, enough of Weber's original survives in *ROI* for the sheer daring of Weber's synthesis of South Asian specialists' work, and the acuity of many of his sociological interpretations, to come through loud and clear.[1]

It is often not appreciated, especially by regional specialists, that Weber had a very particular question in mind. In search of the answer, he devoted some evidently very intense periods of study to the best sources he could lay his hands on.[2] What he wanted to know was whether, at any point in their history, non-European civilizational traditions had within them the religious and cultural resources to give rise to a capitalist spirit, as had happened with forms of Protestantism in Europe and North America. His studies of China, South Asia, and the Islamic world were a counterpart to his famous Protestant ethic thesis in the European context. He thereby launched enormous numbers of research programmes, many of them, from the strictly Weberian viewpoint, misguided. For

[1] For assessments of Weber's work, see Gellner (1982; 1988), Kantowsky (1986), Schroeder (1992). For the 2001 revised version of Gellner (1982), I checked quoted passages against the original German and, where necessary, re-worked them.

[2] It is astonishing that at the very time when he was studying these sources on Hinduism and Buddhism so closely, he was also much taken up with following and attempting to influence the course of the First World War (Marianne Weber 1988: 552).

Weber was not seeking to establish whether particular religions were or were not suited to capitalistic activity, once the practices and benefits of capitalism were widespread and well known. Rather, he was interested only in the emergence of a capitalist spirit where the 'substance' of capitalism was lacking—where, in other words, the spirit operated as its own reward in a hostile and unfavourable environment. The practical and political problems of transferring the benefits of industrialization and modernization to the places which lacked them, once this new form of society was established 'on mechanical foundations', was not of Weber's time and was not one that he faced.

This has not prevented many authors from seeing Weber's studies as relevant to 'development' and 'modernization'. Hence there are studies that attempt to identify something about Hinduism as the key to India's backwardness, or Confucianism as the key to the success of Taiwan, South Korea, and Japan. (No doubt some are even now seeking the key to India's success in computer programming in some aspect of the 'Hindu spirit'.) Even the translators of Weber's work on Hinduism and Buddhism, Hans Gerth and Don Martindale, wrote in their prefatory note that 'the central concern of this and other of Weber's studies of countries we today describe as "developing" was with the obstacles to industrialization and modernization' (*ROI*, p. v).

This mistake is perhaps understandable—and must be understood—in the context of the simple-minded, evolutionist developmentalism of the immediate post-Second World War period and of the Cold War in the 1950s. North American sociologists sought an emblematic and foundational sociological thinker to oppose to Marx; they were also trying to theorize about development, and to explain why some countries developed faster than others. It was no doubt natural to press Weber into service on both counts. It was attractive, if simplistic, to be able to blame a lack of development on a single factor or 'cause', a mode of thinking that still flourishes in countries attempting to develop.

Such confusions about Weber have perhaps died away in the Western academy, but not because they are universally understood. Rather, Weber scholars, who nowadays have a much more nuanced understanding of their subject, have become denizens of a specialized subdiscipline. And the large themes that Weber tackled have become identified with other thinkers—Giddens, Foucault, Bourdieu, and others—whose influence means that most working sociologists and anthropologists do not go beyond their brief undergraduate acquaintance with the classics. Sociology has become a fragmented discipline, with one wing believing that only humanistic, non-cumulative subjects waste their time reading the classics, and the other wing, while still believing that the classics matter, tending to leave the interpretation of them to intellectual historians or other specialists.

Weber's Answer

So what was Weber arguing in *The Protestant Ethic and the Spirit of Capitalism* and in his studies of Hinduism, Buddhism, Confucianism, Judaism, and Islam?[3] In the first place, as I have argued elsewhere (Gellner 1982), it is a great mistake to take Weber's argument to be that the Protestant ethic (infused by the Calvinist predestination doctrine) was 'the' cause of capitalism (as exemplified by Benjamin Franklin and his motto 'time is money'), in any strong sense of 'whenever A, then B'. However, there is another, much more sophisticated (yet paradoxically closer to everyday usage) sense in which the Protestant ethic *may* be said to be a cause of capitalism. This very specific sense of cause has been analysed by J. L. Mackie (1965), who argued that in much everyday reasoning what we mean by 'cause' is an INUS condition. An INUS condition is an insufficient but necessary part of a set of conditions which, taken together, are unnecessary but sufficient to produce the result.[4]

The way in which this applies to the first appearance of capitalism may be seen as follows. There was a set of conditions (C_1, C_2, C_3, ... C_n) which, taken together, were sufficient to produce the first, unplanned appearance of capitalist, industrial society. C_1 may be taken to be a reliable banking system, C_2 double-entry book-keeping, C_3 a given level of technology, C_4 a balance of power (both within states and between neighbouring states) such that merchants could not easily be appropriated by sovereigns, and so on.[5] The central point of Weber's theory was that the existence of these technical and economic conditions was not enough. China made many advances in banking and in science long before Europe. Marco Polo (assuming that he did in fact go there) was clear that in China he was visiting a much more advanced and impressive power than what he had left behind in Europe.

The key condition lacking in China, according to Weber, was the 'spiritual' factor, some equivalent of the Protestant ethic capable of inducing entrepreneurs to live austerely, endlessly (and from one point of view irrationally) reinvesting their profits in further capitalistic activity, rather than turning themselves (or their progeny) into gentlemen. Weber's survey of world religions isolated four key aspects of Protestantism: it was *active*, *rational*, *this-worldly*, and *ascetic*.[6] Protestantism thus

[3] On these, and on more recent interpretations of Weber's entire œuvre, see Turner (Ch. 4, this volume). Weber did not live to produce a book-length essay on Islam, but what it would have contained is discussed by Turner (1974). The literature on Weber is gigantic. For a recent, very short introduction to Weber, see Chalcraft (2006). For the debate over the Protestant ethic, see Marshall (1982) and Chalcraft and Harrison (2001).

[4] More detail of this argument is given in the 2001 version of Gellner (1982). Mackie points out that in everyday life we name 'cause' that condition (of many) over which we have some control or are able to fix.

[5] A good summary of these conditions is to be found in Collins (1986: 23–4, 28).

[6] 'Rational' is here to be understood as systematic, relating all aspects of life to the given ethic and world view. See Brubaker (1984) for an excellent introduction to Weber on rationality. For a massive reconstruction of Weber's thought in terms of rationalization, see Schluchter (1989).

produced a very specific kind of personality—one driven to endless accumulation. In his examination of other religious systems, he was particularly interested to enquire what kinds of 'self-making' were encouraged or enabled for those who took their messages seriously.

Other religious currents often displayed several of these characteristics, but rarely all four. Confucianism, for example, was rational and this-worldly, but it was not ascetic; mercantile activity was tolerated, but the successful merchant would always want his son to become a scholar. Islam was active and this-worldly. But the influence of a warrior ethic prevented it from applying full rationality to its admittedly ascetic personal creed.

Buddhism was rational, but not very ascetic (it was specifically hostile to extreme asceticism); it did not encourage an active, this-worldly orientation on the part of its most dedicated followers. In traditional contexts its lay ethic was always inferior to the path of the monastic. Hinduism cannot be seen as a single religion, but in so far as it was ascetic, it was other-worldly. In Jainism, Weber found a major parallel to Protestantism. Despite the fact that, as in Buddhism, the hierarchical division between monastic and lay was fundamental to the organization of the religion, the laity were much more closely bound to monastic discipline than in Buddhism, so that the lay ethic was indeed active, rational, ascetic, and yet—by virtue of remaining in the world and often in commercial activities—this-worldly. Jains were, and often are, highly successful merchants. In this case, Weber's explanation of the lack of appearance of capitalism in India shifted to the absence other conditions (C_1, C_2, etc.). In effect, his conclusion was that in pockets a capitalist spirit may have appeared, but that the overall extreme division of ethical, economic, and religious labour in South Asia militated against its being taken up or having an independent effect.

Weber's fundamental point was that the appearance of a new form of society—industrial capitalism—was anything but inevitable. It was not the 'natural' outcome of processes inherent in pre-modern forms of society, but rather the surprising and unintended consequence of a combination of conditions, one of which was a peculiar and extreme form of 'self-making'. Weber concludes *ROI* by reiterating that the 'rationally formed missionary prophecy'—that is, the fully worked out and systematized versions of South Asian religions—had no consequences for the 'ethic of everyday life' of ordinary people:

> The appearance of such [consequences] in the Occident, however—above all, in the Near East—with the extensive consequences borne with it, was conditioned by highly particular historical constellations without which, despite differences of natural conditions, development there could easily have taken the course typical of Asia, particularly of India. (*ROI*, 343)

As others have noted, Foucault's interest in the 'self-making' project of Puritanism is but a reformulation of Weber's fundamental question about the emergence of a new kind of person at that particular period in history.[7]

[7] e.g. van Krieken (1990); Keyes (2002: 249–50).

Weber on Hinduism and India

Specialists on South Asia are rarely motivated by a desire to answer such ambitiously large comparative questions about the origins of modernity. So it is perhaps not surprising that they do not engage with Weber's fundamental question. None the less, it is interesting that some find inspiration in aspects of his work, and others do not.

Few serious scholars of India or of Hinduism have concerned themselves with Weber's theories. Weber offered an overall picture of the development of Hinduism. He made many acute observations about the way in which Brahmans had transformed the bases of their religious pre-eminence over the centuries. He had a good understanding of the way in which Hinduism spreads into tribal areas and the role of Brahman priests in that process (*ROI*, 9–21, 43–4). He also grasped intuitively the fact that Islamic dominance removed the Kshatriyas as a counterbalance and enabled Brahman claims, till then often confined to the law books, to be enforced and put into practice (*ROI*, 125). He understood how priests were the bearers of Hinduism throughout South Asia (*ROI*, 153). All these are themes which have received attention in recent years, but this has not led to any noticeable revival of interest in Weber. Weber also had interesting insights into the ways in which Brahmanical teachings presupposed the individual (*ROI*, 169), a point which may anticipate the arguments of Louis Dumont.[8] Dumont, however, did not care to acknowledge Weber as a major influence.

Symptomatic of studies of the history of India is the recent *magnum opus* by Sheldon Pollock, *The Language of the Gods in the World of Men* (2006). This 684-page work takes in the whole sweep of South Asian history from the point of view of language use and the relation of language to power at different periods. It is highly sophisticated, both in its use of indigenous sources and in its handling of 'metropolitan' theory, thereby itself exemplifying the Sanskritic self-awareness, learning, and grasp of different idioms that is its own subject matter. Pollock's aim is ambitious: to understand the role of Sanskrit at different periods and to explain its relationship to power. The book offers a new periodization, or at least an entirely new way of thinking about the periodization of South Asian history. Furthermore, it is genuinely and skilfully comparative, invoking evidence from different periods of European history in comparison with South Asia. The richness of Pollock's documentation and the sheer number of diverse theoretical arguments being made may well limit the book's impact. Lesser mortals can only marvel at Pollock's skill in keeping so many balls in the air at the same time.

For present purposes the important point is that Pollock ignores Weber on South Asia and on South Asian religion completely. It seems to go without saying

[8] For other ways in which Weber anticipated Dumont, see Gellner (1988: 86, 90).

(in a book where almost nothing goes without saying and every possible theoretical digression is pursued in a footnote somewhere) that nothing in *ROI* is worth discussing. On the other hand, Weber, the sociological theorist of the state, of ethnicity, and—above all—of legitimation, most certainly is worth engaging with. Pollock is particularly concerned to attack the—as he sees it—crass way in which historians have explained the proliferation of high Hindu cults and rituals sponsored by Hinduizing kings, whether in the subcontinent or in Southeast Asia (what Geertz called 'the theatre state'), as driven by the need for legitimation. Weber is here rejected in the name of a relationship between culture and power that is neither functionalist nor yet Marxist—but what exactly it is, is hard to specify. Though Pollock rejects Weber's stress on legitimation, at least on these questions of sociological theory Weber is taken sufficiently seriously to be considered worth arguing with.

The Influence of Weber on Buddhist Studies

While Max Weber's observations about Hinduism have been largely neglected,[9] what he wrote about Buddhism has often been an inspiration to later scholars.[10] In so far as his writings on Buddhism have been used, it has rarely been in a context of his wider oeuvre.[11]

The anthropology of Theravada Buddhism is rich in excellent, theoretically sophisticated studies. In the first place, there is the psychoanalytically inspired study of Burmese Buddhism by Spiro (1970); then there is the textually learned and Popperian historical study of Sri Lanka by Gombrich (1971), and the structuralist anthropological work on north-east Thailand of Tambiah (1970). Alongside these are many others, including the numerous early articles by Obeyesekere on Sri Lankan Buddhism, which in their search for meaning might indeed be characterized as Weberian; Obeyesekere had not yet gone in for the person-centred, psychoanalytic style of interpretive anthropology that was later to make him famous.

In different ways, all of these works might be said to have been influenced, broadly and generally, by Weber. It is Tambiah's works that could be said to be fully Weberian in scope, expanding, as they do, from a single-village study to include the

[9] At least in major reassessments of the field; but see the contributions to Schluchter (1984) and Kantowsky (1986).

[10] This point has been made well by Keyes (2002: 246–7).

[11] For an assessment of Weber's specific assertions about Buddhism in *ROI*, see Gellner (1988).

whole history of Buddhism 'as a civilizational phenomenon', the history of Thai kingship and the relation of the Buddhist monastic community to it, and the ways in which charisma was routinized by monks in the form of amulets and relics (Tambiah 1976; 1984).

It was Obeyesekere who first coined the term 'Protestant Buddhism' to refer to the kind of modernist, rationalizing, and political Buddhism propagated by the reformer Anagarika Dharmapala.[12] The term has been used in subsequent analyses by him and Gombrich (Gombrich and Obeyesekere 1988; Gombrich 1988) as well as by H. L. Seneviratne (1999). Although Seneviratne couches his argument as a criticism of Weber—for failing to see the modernizing and rationalizing potentials in Buddhism—this rather misses the point that Sri Lankan Protestant Buddhism arose only *after* influences from Christianity and Western anti-Christian trends like Theosophy. To count as a criticism of 'the Weber thesis', he would have to show that Theravada Buddhism—with its worship of relics, spiritual hierarchy, and scriptures preserved in a sacred language not available to the laity—had this potential before colonial influences.

As Keyes (2002: 246) points out, there are also many American students of Buddhism who absorbed a lively interest in Weber through their contact with Parsons's Harvard school of sociology: Keyes himself (1978; 1983; 1993), Kirsch (1975), Spiro (1970), and Nash (1966). Coming from an interest in Weber first kindled by discussions with Steven Lukes and Mark Elvin, I myself attempted to apply Weberian framing ideas to a description of Mahayana Buddhism in Nepal (Gellner 1992; 2001*a*).

The Case of the Missing Theorist: Weber, Ortner, and Practice Theory

I turn now to a different kind of influence, or lack of influence. Of course, Weber most certainly did influence Anthony Giddens and Pierre Bourdieu. But by the time they came to influence Sherry Ortner, one of the most widely read cultural anthropologists in North America, Weberian influence had, it would appear, been almost completely bleached out. Weber was identified with Geertz, and Geertz was seen to be the problem.

[12] The spread of this 'Protestant Buddhism' to Nepal is discussed in LeVine and Gellner (2005). Outside Sri Lanka, however, scholars have been reluctant to use the term 'Protestant Buddhism', preferring the more neutral 'Buddhist modernism'.

Now Geertz was a more interesting thinker and anthropologist than many assume.[13] His own anthropological work was by no means limited to the analysis of 'discourse', as his interpretive theory might imply (the *locus classicus* being his introduction to *The Interpretation of Cultures* (1973)). But—and Geertz himself must perhaps take part of the blame for this, because he downplayed his earlier interests in development, politics, and so on—Geertz was identified, even by those such as Ortner who were taught by him, with a straightforward interpretivist position. And since Geertz himself invoked Weber to justify his position, it was assumed that Weber too was a Geertzian.

It is interesting to contrast Geertz with Louis Dumont in this regard. Geertz and Dumont appear as mirror images of each other, in so far as they are related to Weber. Geertz nails Weber's flag to his mast (Geertz 1973: 5)—but he is actually very much more Durkheimian than he would have admitted at that stage, particularly in the key role he gives to collective ritual in producing the 'uniquely realistic' 'moods and motivations' that characterize religious experience on his definition (1973: 90). Dumont, on the other hand, more or less erased Weber from his genealogy, but—given his interest in the rise of the West, the religious origins of individualism, and the India versus the West contrast that dominates his thinking—he is in fact deeply Weberian. Exaggerating only slightly for effect, it is possible to say that Geertz claimed to be Weberian, but was actually far more Durkheimian than he cared to admit (no doubt due to his education at Harvard with Talcott Parsons), whereas Dumont claimed to be a true descendant of the French school of Durkheim and Mauss (which indeed he was), but was just as much, and arguably even more so, a follower of Max Weber.

Ortner began her academic career with a Ph.D. at Chicago under Geertz. His influence was clear in her first monograph, *Sherpas through their Rituals* (1978, and still in print). It was published in a series called 'Cambridge Studies in Cultural Systems', of which Geertz was the general editor; few titles were published in the series, and it is now defunct. Ortner's book was a classic ethnographic study, in the sense that it provided a straightforward account of Sherpa life and Sherpa rituals. It was extremely well written and accessible. History was introduced only as part of the scene setting or in the notes. Ortner pointed out that Sherpa society was relatively open to immigrants, such that many Sherpas had relatives in other ethnic groups or castes; but the permeability or problematic nature of the category Sherpa was not a central part of the analysis. None the less, the book cannot be put into a straitjacket of stereotypical functionalist monograph. Unlike in Fürer-Haimendorf's book, *The Sherpas of Nepal* (1964), the stress was not on the cheerfulness and good spirits of the Sherpas. Instead, Ortner provided a very detailed and subtle ethnography and analysis of hospitality, which brought out its highly problematic, coercive underside. She drew attention to the parallels with worship of the gods, which also attempts to

[13] A point made by both Ortner (1999*a*; 1999*b*: 138) and Keyes (2002: 242–3).

coerce them through offerings. In short, she focused on tensions within Sherpa society (including differences between 'big people' and 'little people') and on expelling evils, a major theme in Tibetan Buddhist ritual. The Sherpas are famous for their monastic exorcism ritual, Mani Rimdu, which has been much filmed and photographed. It is mentioned a few times in *Sherpas through their Rituals.* What is not discussed is the fact that, far from being a traditional part of 'ancient Sherpa custom', it was introduced from Tibet only in the first half of the twentieth century and was part of a conscious attempt on the part of the monks to 'clean up' Sherpa popular religion. This was a theme that Ortner was to turn to later. She did so as part of her discovery of 'practice theory', which formed part of a move away from a purely Geertzian theoretical stance.

Ortner's position is best approached through her well-known article 'Theory in Anthropology since the Sixties' (1984). She begins by identifying Weber with Geertz, as so many anthropologists do, and as Geertz encouraged them to do, as described above. Early on in the essay, she remarks that 'much of the later practice-centered work builds on a Geertzian (or Geertzo-Weberian) base' (Ortner 1984: 130, 1994: 375). Now this essay was an attempt both to define a field and to push it in the direction she herself favoured; the history it offered was not dispassionate or objectivist, but, by her own admission, was a mythical charter.

What did it mean to be a 'practice theorist'? She allowed that the term 'practice' was extremely vague, so broad as to include anything human beings did. As with so many theories, it is best described in terms of what it was and is against, which was no doubt the point of constructing a historical dialectic from which it could emerge. It was, in the first place, against the pursuit of abstract social, historical, conceptual, or any other kind of structures divorced from the people who produce and reproduce them. In other words, there was an emphasis on *agency*—that is, the actor's point of view, and and attempt to capture what particular actors are striving to achieve. Second, it was against the notion that there is *the* Sherpa or Bongo-Bongo view of anything: rather, it insisted that all conceptual schemes are, if you like, ideologies: they are held more firmly by some people than by others, and serve some people's interests better than those of others. In other words, issues of *power* are an integral part of the analysis. We have seen that in her own ethnography this was already the case, though she had not explicitly theorized it in that way. Thirdly, there is *history.* Ortner's practice approach insists that the cultures studied not be seen as static or unchanging.

These concerns were meant to be illustrated and worked out in *High Religion: A Cultural and Political History of Sherpa Buddhism* (1989). While the theoretical aim of the book was to be an exemplar of 'practice theory', the main ethnographic problem was to explain the founding of celibate monasteries in the Sherpa area in the first half of the twentieth century. Sherpas are supposed to have migrated to the area just below (on the south side of) Mt Everest in what is now the state of Nepal around the end of the fifteenth century. For 400 years their priests were non-celibate, i.e. married lamas, based in temples, attached to the Nyingmapa sect, and sometimes going for training in Tibet. Only in the twentieth century did Sherpas found celibate monasteries. Ortner begins by going back to the stories of temple foundings. She argues that underlying them is a *cultural schema*—a model, if you like—that is widely understood by Sherpas, and that presents a solution to the problems that they face. This schema has to do with the competition for prestige and position between rivals, often brothers, who do not inherit equally. Many Sherpa oral histories and stories relate events of opposition, both physical and ritual; the loser departs, and gains a powerful protector or patron; returns and defeats his opponent, wins over his followers, and founds a temple; the previous winner is now the loser, and has to cede the field.

Ortner attempts to show not only that the early temple foundings of the seventeenth and eighteenth centuries followed this schema, but that in the twentieth century the founders of the new celibate monasteries seem to have been following it too. The first two monasteries in Solu-Khumbu were founded by two rich brothers who were rival tax-collectors and headmen. Both, at different periods, had to depart and then returned. But why did they found celibate monasteries? This was a period of increasing centralization. The Sherpas were increasingly becoming incorporated within the state of Nepal. The Tibetan monks over the border who provided the spiritual leaders of the Sherpas were keen to expand their domain. The lay sponsors sought prestige. At the same time other Sherpas had increasing economic opportunities outside the Sherpa area, particularly in Darjeeling. Ortner claims that the small people who migrated to Darjeeling, earned money, and returned empowered to participate in monastery foundings could also be seen to be following the cultural schema in their relations with the big people, 'at least in a metaphoric sense' (1989: 167).

Sherry Ortner is, as she herself has described, engaged in the 'serious game' of convincing academic colleagues (1996: 217–18, 226–7); she is of course a highly skilful player, one of the best. In 'Theory in Anthropology since the Sixties' she recognizes, briefly, Weber's importance. Discussing the Marxist influence on 'the newer practice theory', she remarks:

> Yet to speak of a Marxist influence in all of this is actually to obscure an important aspect of what is going on: an interpenetration, almost a merger, between Marxist and Weberian frameworks. In the sixties, the opposition between Marx and Weber, as 'materialist' and 'idealist', had been emphasized. The practice theorists, in contrast, draw on a set of writers who interpret the Marxist corpus in such a way as to render it quite compatible with Weber's views. As Weber put the actor at the centre of his model, so these writers emphasize issues of human praxis in Marx. As Weber subsumed the economic within the political, so these writers encompass economic exploitation within political domination. And as Weber was centrally concerned with ethos and consciousness, so these writers stress similar issues within Marx's work. Choosing Marx over Weber as one's theorist of reference is a tactical move of a certain sort. In reality, the theoretical framework involved [i.e. the 'new practice' position of which Ortner approves] is about equally indebted to both. (Ortner 1984: 147; 1994[1984]: 391)

Having said this, Ortner moves briskly on.[14] One might remark that *not* making Weber one's theorist of reference 'is a tactical move of a certain sort' on her part: better, far, to cite Williams, Foucault, and Bourdieu. Dumont also was less than fulsome in his acknowledgement of Weber, though he did not write him out so completely. Now it would seem that what Ortner is thinking of here is still Geertzo-Weber. This is despite the fact that two of the theorists she frequently cites, Giddens and Bourdieu, have a much deeper knowledge of Weber, both of them being well aware that the idealist Geertzo-Weber is a wholly inadequate view of Weber's position; however, Ortner does not follow them in this. In fact, all the theoretical advances she claims for 'practice theory' are already there in Weber.

Conclusion

The probable reason why social and cultural anthropologists tend to ignore Weber is that he is too closely identified with sociology, and in particular with the complacent, developmentalist, worthy, but ultimately rather dull, sociology of Talcott Parsons. In so far as anthropologists ponder the inappropriateness of this view of Weber, they identify him with Geertzian interpretivism, which is now deemed out of date and inadequate. It is even possible to hold these two contradictory images of Weber—as Parsonian positivist and Geertzian interpretivist—simultaneously, primarily because anthropologists simply do not think about Weber very much.

Despite the fact that, from a purely intellectual point of view, Weber would serve anthropological purposes very well, there are too many sociologists engaged in the task of reclaiming Weber as an intellectual ancestor, of 'de-Parsonizing Weber'. Viewed in terms of ideological survival or product differentiation, Weber would be an unlikely choice for anthropologists. Allegiance to Weber would only muddy the boundary between social anthropology and sociology—a boundary fence that in most of the institutional contexts in which anthropologists find themselves, whether in Europe or in North America (South Asia is different), it would be most unwise for them to pull down, since sociologists are always far more numerous than anthropologists, and always have a more plausible claim on the public purse than anthropologists.

[14] The only other reference to Weber of comparable length that I am aware of in Ortner's œuvre is in her essay 'Gender Hegemonies' (1996: 143–5), originally published in 1990. Here she begins from Weber's key analytical distinction between prestige and power, notes the relation to Dumont, and recognizes that Weber's typologies have to be seen as processual and dynamic, that it is necessary to return to the 'historical dynamism' of his argument, to avoid the theoretical impasses of the past.

In so far as anthropologists have come to Weberian themes, they have acquired them, unbeknown to themselves, from Foucault. Above all, Foucault's term 'governmentality', for governmental rationality, might have come straight out of Weber (as others have noted: Gordon 1987: 297). The connection between power and particular schemes (or discourses) of personal conduct, the origins of the particularly Western and modern 'techniques of the self', and the way in which the new Protestant view of the self emerges precisely at the time when a new form of statecraft is being evolved—these fundamental themes can be found in Weber before they were ever explored by Foucault.[15] Bryan Turner points out that Weber's philosophy of history suffers from exactly the same weaknesses as Foucault's (Turner 1992: 129). This is in fact an indication of how much they share.[16]

A similar story of constructed and neglected intellectual antecedents could be told about the academic study of Buddhism and Hinduism, though it is less plausible to relate the difference to questions of disciplinary self-definition and survival. Whereas students of Buddhism have been happy to mine Weber for insights and inspiration, and some have also been happy to see him as a sophisticated forebear capable of bearing the weight of their theoretical ambitions, in the study of Hinduism and in the history of South Asia, Weber is ignored or dismissed. He is identified with outdated Orientalizing tendencies. The fact that with unrivalled scholarship and sophistication he addressed the same issues of power, culture, history, and agency that are being tackled by currently fashionable figures is forgotten.

References

Brubaker, R. (1984). *The Limits of Rationality: An Essay on the Social and Moral Thought of Max Weber.* London: George Allen & Unwin.

Chalcraft, D. J. (2006). 'Max Weber'. In J. Scott (ed.), *Fifty Key Sociologists: The Formative Theorists.* London: Routledge, 203–9.

—— and Harrington, A. (eds.) (2001). *The Protestant Ethic Debate: Max Weber's Replies to His Critics, 1907–1910.* Liverpool: Liverpool University Press.

Collins, R. (1986). *Weberian Social Theory.* Cambridge: Cambridge University Press.

Fürer-Haimendorf, C. von (1964). *The Sherpas of Nepal: Buddhist Highlanders.* London: John Murray.

Geertz, C. (1973). *The Interpretation of Cultures: Selected Essays.* New York: Basic Books.

[15] This connection has been brilliantly explored by Gorski in *The Disciplinary Revolution* (2001), an attempt—in his own words—'to combine Weber's sociology of religion with Foucault's theory of micropolitics' (2001: 28).

[16] Turner (1992: 138) concludes: 'Neither Weber nor Foucault provided a phenomology of the active body as an essential component of human knowledgeable agency.' Whether such a theory or phenomenology is indeed essential to an account of agency cannot be addressed here.

Gellner, D. N. (1982). 'Max Weber, Capitalism, and the Religion of India'. *Sociology*, 16/4. Repr. with revisions in Gellner (2001*a*), 19–44.

—— (1988). 'Priesthood and Possession: Newar Religion in the Light of some Weberian Concepts'. *Pacific Viewpoint*, 29/2. Repr. in Gellner (2001*a*), 85–105.

—— (1992). *Monk, Householder, and Tantric Priest: Newar Buddhism and its Hierarchy of Ritual.* Cambridge: Cambridge University Press.

—— (2001*a*). *The Anthropology of Buddhism and Hinduism: Weberian Themes.* Delhi: Oxford University Press.

—— (2001*b*). 'Introduction'. In Gellner (2001*a*), 1–16.

Gombrich, R. F. (1971). *Precept and Practice: Traditional Buddhism in the Rural Highlands of Ceylon.* Oxford: Oxford University Press. Reissued in 1991 as *Buddhist Precept and Practice.* Delhi: Motilal Banarsidass.

—— (1988). *Theravada Buddhism: A Social History from Ancient Benares to Modern Colombo.* London and New York: Routledge.

—— and Obeyesekere, G. (1988). *Buddhism Transformed: Religious Change in Sri Lanka.* Princeton: Princeton University Press.

Gordon, C. (1987). 'The Soul of the Citizen: Max Weber and Michel Foucault on Rationality and Government'. In S. Whimster and S. Lash (eds.), *Max Weber, Rationality and Modernity.* London: Allen & Unwin, 293–316.

Gorski, P. S. (2001). *The Disciplinary Revolution: Calvinism and the Rise of the Modern State in Early Modern Europe.* Chicago and London: University of Chicago Press.

Kantowsky, D. (ed.) (1986). *Recent Research on Max Weber's Studies of Hinduism.* Munich: Weltforum Verlag.

Keyes, C. F. (1978). 'Structure and History in the Study of the Relationship between Theravāda Buddhism and Political Order'. *Numen*, 25/2: 156–70.

—— (1983). 'Economic Action and Buddhist Morality in a Thai Village'. *Journal of Asian Studies*, 42/3: 851–68.

—— (1993). 'Buddhist Economics and Buddhist Fundamentalism in Burma and Thailand'. In M. Marty and S. Appleby (eds.), *Remaking the World: Fundamentalist Impact.* Chicago: University of Chicago Press, 367–409.

—— (2002). 'Weber and Anthropology'. *Annual Review of Anthropology*, 31: 233–55.

Kirsch, A. T. (1975). 'Economy, Polity, and Religion in Thailand'. In V. W. Skinner and A. T. Kirsch (eds.), *Change and Persistence in Thai Society: Homage to Lauristan Sharp*, Ithaca, NY: Cornell University Press, 172–96.

Krieken, R. van (1990). 'The Organisation of the Soul: Elias and Foucault on Discipline and the Self'. *European Journal of Sociology*, 31/2: 353–71.

LeVine, S., and Gellner, D. N. (2005). *Rebuilding Buddhism: The Theravada Movement in Twentieth-Century Nepal.* Cambridge, Mass.: Harvard University Press.

Mackie, J. L. (1965). 'Causes and Conditions'. *American Philosophical Quarterly*, 2: 245–64.

Marshall, G. (1982). *In Search of the Spirit of Capitalism.* London: Hutchinson.

Nash, M. (ed.) (1966). *Anthropological Studies in Theravada Buddhism.* SE Asia Studies. New Haven: Yale University Press.

Ortner, S. B. (1978). *Sherpas through their Rituals.* Cambridge: Cambridge University Press.

—— (1994[1984]). 'Theory in Anthropology since the Sixties'. *Comparative Studies in Society and History*, 26: 126–66. Repr. in N. B. Dirks, G. Eley, and S. B. Ortner (eds.), *A Reader in Contemporary Social Theory.* Princeton: Princeton University Press, 372–411.

Ortner, S. B. (1989). *High Religion: A Cultural and Political History of Sherpa Buddhism.* Princeton: Princeton University Press.
—— (1996). *Making Gender: The Politics and Erotics of Culture.* Boston: Beacon Press.
—— (1999*a*). 'Introduction'. In S.B. Ortner (ed.), *The Fate of 'Culture': Geertz and Beyond.* Berkeley: University of California Press, 1–29.
—— (1999*b*). 'Thick Resistance: Death and the Cultural Construction of Agency in Himalayan Mountaineering'. In S.B. Ortner (ed.) *The Fate of 'Culture': Geertz and Beyond.* Berkeley: University of California Press, 136–63.
Pollock, S. (2006). *The Language of the Gods in the World of Men.* Berkeley: University of California Press.
Schluchter, W. (ed.) (1984). *Max Webers Studie über Hinduismus und Buddhismus.* Frankfurt: Suhrkamp.
—— (1989). *Religion, Rationalism, and Domination: A Weberian Perspective,* trans. N. Solomon. Berkeley: University of California Press.
Schroeder, R. (1992). *Max Weber and the Sociology of Culture.* London: Sage.
Seneviratne, H. L. (1999). *The Work of Kings: The New Buddhism in Sri Lanka.* Chicago: University of Chicago Press.
Spiro, M. E. (1970). *Buddhism and Society: A Great Tradition and its Burmese Vicissitudes.* Berkeley: University of California Press; 2nd edn. 1982.
Tambiah, S. J. (1970). *Buddhism and the Spirit Cults in North-east Thailand.* Cambridge: Cambridge University Press.
—— (1976). *World Conqueror and World Renouncer.* Cambridge: Cambridge University Press.
—— (1984). *The Buddhist Saints of the Forest and the Cult of Amulets: A Study in Charisma, Hagiography, Sectarianism, and Millennial Buddhism.* Cambridge: Cambridge University Press.
Turner, B. L. (1974). *Weber and Islam: A Critical Study.* London: Routledge & Kegan Paul.
—— (1992). *Max Weber: From History to Modernity.* London and New York: Routledge.
Weber, Marianne (1988). *Max Weber: A Biography,* ed. and trans. H. Zohn. New Brunswick, NJ, and London: Transaction Publishers.
Weber, Max. (1916–17). 'Die Wirtschaftsethik der Weltreligionen (Dritter Artikel): Hinduismus und Buddhismus'. *Archiv für Sozialwissenschaft und Sozialpolitik,* 41/3: 313–744; 42/2: 345–461; 42/3: 687–814. Repr. in M. Weber, *Gesammelte Aufsätze zur Religionssoziologie,* ii. Tübingen: J. C. B. Mohr, 1921. Reissued 1996 and 1998 in standard edition of Weber's works, ed. H. Schmidt-Glinzter, Mohr-Siebeck.
—— (1958). *The Religion of India: The Sociology of Buddhism and Hinduism,* ed. and trans. H. H. Gerth and D. Martindale. New York: Free Press.
—— (1976). *The Protestant Ethic and the Spirit of Capitalism,* trans. T. Parsons, 2nd edn. London: Allen & Unwin.

Suggested Reading

The following are recommended: Gellner (2001*a*); Gorski (2001); Kantowsky (1986); Keyes (2002); Ortner (1984); and Weber (1958).

CHAPTER 3

MAX WEBER

RELIGION AND MODERNIZATION

HANS G. KIPPENBERG

Max Weber, born in Erfurt (Germany) in 1864, enrolled in 1882 in Heidelberg in jurisprudence; in 1884 he carried on his study in Berlin, where he received a doctorate for a work on trading societies in Italian cities. In 1891 he did a post-doctoral essay on the importance of Roman agrarian history for government and private law. In 1893 Weber was appointed as professor of economics at Freiburg (Germany), and three years later he got a similar chair in Heidelberg, where he lived until 1918—since 1903 retired from his professorial duties for health reasons. In 1919 he accepted an appointment at the University of Munich, where he died in 1920.

Conditions for the Rise of Capitalism

In 1891/2 Weber did an empirical survey of the situation of farm-workers on estates in East Prussia. In analyzing the data he recognized a dilemma of the noble owners: in becoming modern entrepreneurs producing for the market and hiring cheap Polish laborers, they undermine inadvertently the German presence in that region. But when sticking to their traditional way of life, they are in danger of descending to the status of simple farmers (Weber 1892[1984]: 903). The dilemma, as Weber described it, bears witness to his keen interest in the condition and consequence of a change to a capitalist economy.

Weber did not see the emergence of a capitalist economy as self-evident, as he argued in a lecture on the "The Social Causes of the Decay of Ancient Civilization" in 1896. Most scholars ascribed the fall of Rome to catastrophic mass migrations; Weber, by contrast, saw it as an outcome of a gradual social change inside the Empire itself. Initially, ancient civic communities were based economically on slave labor. Because of their advantageous position on the coast, they engaged heavily in industry and trade. After the second century CE, because of the *Pax Romana*, when the supply of slaves dried up and the economic focus shifted inland, a self-sufficient estate economy gradually displaced the urban economy. When government officials and soldiers could no longer cover their needs through taxes, but had recourse to barter, little remained of the ancient capitalistic economy. The cities disintegrated into villages, the culture once again became rural. It was this reversal of development that allowed the dramatic devastation of the mass migrations.

It was Weber's credo that it is the kind of social integration that determines the fate of capitalism. An intensely expanding political power, either in antiquity or in the modern age, seemed especially dangerous to him: "The bureaucratization of society will overcome capitalism in our society too, just as it did in Antiquity" (1909 [1976]: 277–8). This problem continued to bother Weber: "Faced with this superiority of the tendency of bureaucratization, how is it still possible to rescue some remnant of 'individualist' freedom of movement in any sense?", he asked in 1917 (1914–18[1984]: 465).

Religious Ethics and the Spirit of Capitalism

For a capitalist economy political conditions alone are not sufficient. What else had to be added is the subject of Weber's famous essay, *The Protestant Ethic and the Spirit of Capitalism* (1904/5 [1930] and [2002]). Weber was not the first to notice a connection between Protestant regions and capitalism; but he was the first to attempt a serious explanation. Impending capitalism needed the support of an internal power, an ethos, because it first had to bring down a powerful opponent: *traditionalism.*

> A person does not 'by nature' want to make more and more money, but simply to live—to live in the manner in which he is accustomed to live, and to earn as much as is necessary for this. Wherever capitalism has begun its work of increasing the 'productivity' of human labor by increasing its intensity, it has run up against the infinitely persistent resistance of this leitmotiv of pre-capitalist economic labor. (1904/5[2002]: 16)

This dogged resistance, which Weber almost ascribed to human nature, did not fade away by itself. It was broken by Puritanism, since it required from believers a methodical pattern of working and abstention from consumption. It was this manner of life that inadvertently pushed forward the development of capitalism. Weber's thesis elicited a heated debate. Though a couple of scholars were critical, in the end Weber was convinced that his argument about the Puritan origins of a methodical pattern of life conduct, fostering the development of Western capitalism, has withstood all objections (Weber 1910[1978]). Now he wanted "to correct the isolation of this study and to place it in relation to the whole of cultural development" (1904/5[1930]: 284). In her biography, Marianne Weber gives some valuable particulars about this shift in Weber's thought.

> When around 1911 he resumed his studies on the sociology of religion, he was attracted to the Orient—to China, Japan, and India, then to Judaism and Islam. He now wanted to investigate the relationship of the five great world religions to economic ethics. His study was to come full circle with an analysis of early Christianity. And while in his first treatise on the spirit of capitalism Weber expressly set out to illuminate only one causal sequence, namely, the influence of religious elements of consciousness upon everyday economic life, he now undertook the larger task as well—namely, the investigation of the influence of the material, economic, and geographical conditions of the various spheres of culture with a view to their religious and ethical ideas. (Marianne Weber 1926 [1988]: 331)

The segment on "Religious Communities" in *Economy and Society* that was written 1913 but only published after his death in 1921/2 was an early outcome of this effort. Though Weber published his studies on *The Economic Ethic of the World Religions* separately, he did not see them as standing alone; he conceived of them, rather, as "preliminary studies and annotations to the *systematic* sociology of religions" (letter to the publisher Paul Siebeck, 22 June 1915). When the first of these studies appeared—*The Religion of China*—Weber pointed out that it was designed to be published at the same time as *Economy and Society* and "to interpret and complement the section on the sociology of religion (and, however, to be interpreted by it in many points)" (1915–20 [1989]: 236). Likewise, in 1919, when Weber reworked the text of *The Protestant Ethic and the Spirit of Capitalism* for inclusion in his *Collected Papers on the Sociology of Religions*, he added that he hoped to treat ethnographic material, when systematically revising "the sociology of religion" (1904/5 [1930]: 30). Weber repeatedly emphasized the systematic nature of his sociology of religion. But how do we have to characterize it?

Disenchantment as a Particular Religious Path to Modernity

During his study of Confucianism, Hinduism, Buddhism, Judaism, and Islam, and their relationship to economic ethics, Weber made an exciting discovery. It is recounted by Marianne Weber:

> As soon as a man thinks ahead, he begins to feel that the structure of the world should be, or could become, a meaningfully ordered cosmos. He inquires about the relationship between good fortune and merit, seeks a justification for suffering, sin and death that satisfies his reason, and creates a 'theodicee'. In other words, religious feelings and experiences are treated intellectually, the process of *rationalization* dissolves the magical notions and increasingly 'disenchants' the world and renders it godless. Religion changes from magic to doctrine. And now, after the disintegration of the primitive image of the world, there appear two tendencies: a tendency towards the *rational* mastery of the world and one toward *mystical* experience. But not only the religions receive their stamp from the increasing development of thought; the process of rationalization moves on several tracks, and its autonomous development encompasses all creations of civilization—the economy, the state, law, science, and art. All forms of Western civilization in particular are decisively determined by a methodological *way of thinking* that was first developed by the Greeks, and this way of thinking was joined in the Age of Reformation by a methodological *conduct of life*. [...]. Weber regarded this recognition of the special character of [occidental] *rationalism* and the role it was given to play for Western culture as one of his most important discoveries. As a result, his original inquiry into the relationship between religion and economics expanded into an even more comprehensive inquiry into the *special nature of all of Western culture*. (Marianne Weber 1926[1988]: 333)

From this point onward, the process of "disenchantment" figured centrally in Weber's thinking about religion.

The notion "disenchantment" surfaced for the first time in 1913, in an essay in which Weber explained the fundamentals of his theory of action: "Some Categories of Interpretive Sociology". At the same time he worked on the section on "Religious Communities" and constructed it around this concept. Decisive passages effectively encapsulate Weber's view of its development. At the beginning of the process, according to Weber, "only the things or events that actually exist or take place played a role in life", though this situation changed early on with the rise of the magician: "Now certain experiences, of a different order in that they only signify something, also play a role. Thus magic is transformed from a direct manipulation of forces into a *symbolic activity*" (1978: 403). Regarding the outcome of the process, Weber concludes: "intellectualism suppresses belief in magic, the world's processes become disenchanted, lose their magical significance, and henceforth simply 'are' and 'happen' but no longer signify anything" (1978: 506). It was this development that, in Weber's view, divested the world of inherent meanings and ultimately transformed religion into a separate realm of its own.

For Weber the concept of disenchantment indicates the reciprocal relationship between religion and modernization. It is clearly distinct from the concept of secularization, which he also uses, but as a legal one. The concept of disenchantment does not indicate the rise of a godless world (as Marianne Weber seems to suggest), but the transformation of religion into a theoretical and practical sphere of its own, related to the unavoidable experience of a world devoid of meaning.

Constructing Religious History

Weber's thesis, that the rise of modern culture cannot be explained without taking into account religious history, was enabled by two new paradigms that had gained acceptance in religious studies since 1900. In Great Britain 'pre-animism' replaced the scheme of a continuous religious evolution, and in Germany a new type of historiography arose that focused on religious attitudes to the world. Both reconstructions of religious data were extremely helpful to Max Weber's attempt to conceive of modernization in terms of religious history, and the other way round.

It was a paper on "Pre-animistic Religion" (1900) by Robert Ranulph Marett (1866–1943) that established in a short time a powerful new paradigm in religious studies. According to Marett, an explanation of primitive religion as a belief in souls and as explaining unexpected natural processes, as E. B. Tylor had argued, was too intellectualistic. The origins of religion do not derive from an intellectual need for explanation, but from a primordial experience of uncertainty and dependence, an experience that persists in the modern world. Max Weber embraced Marett's approach as most other scholars of religions at that time did.

A second scholarly paradigm derived from German scholarship. German Orientalists were not tied to the politics of colonialism, as their British colleagues were, but engaged with religious meanings and their subjective appropriation. Their public forum became a series edited by Paul Hinneberg under the title *Die Kultur der Gegenwart* (*Contemporary Culture*). In 1906, two important volumes were issued, one on Oriental religions, another on Christianity as well as Israel and Judaism. Some of the most eminent scholars who contributed to these volumes also became authorities for Weber's *Religious Communities*: Julius Wellhausen on Israel and Judaism, Ignaz Goldziher on Islam, and Hermann Oldenberg on Hinduism and Buddhism.

These German Orientalists imagined religions as driving forces in establishing positive or negative attitudes toward the world. In his contribution Julius Wellhausen (1844–1918) presented a new account of the history of ancient Israel and Judaism. Critical analysis of the Bible had revealed that the fifth book of Moses,

Deuteronomy, was the book found in 621 BCE in the Temple in Jerusalem; this book required the worship of Yahweh exclusively in Jerusalem, and demanded the destruction of all other places of cultic worship outside Jerusalem. Before this time, biblical prophets like Amos had already proclaimed that these idolatrous practices were the reason for Yahweh's anger against Israel, and that pleasing Yahweh required loyalty and obedience to his commandments. Only when Judah was threatened with military defeat, however, was this message accepted by king and priests, since it offered an explanation for Israel's suffering. Henceforth, ethics defined the true Jew. But a new issue arose. Faithful believers obeyed God's laws yet still experienced suffering. This paradoxical situation stimulated the rise of a theodicy. This account of Wellhausen had an important bearing on Weber: ethics as means of salvation and the problem of theodicy are major concepts in his construction of the stages of disenchantment.

When Weber addressed Islamic history, he relied on Ignaz Goldziher (1850–1921). In his contribution to Hinneberg's series, Goldziher sketched a series of developments by means of similar concepts. Islam, when rising, was surrounded by Christian ideas of asceticism and world denial. Subsequently, however, these ideas were rejected, as Islam became a religion of war and conquest, aimed at ruling the world. But the one-sided emphasis on conquest provoked opposition from Sufis, who resisted a purely legal and political Islam and established world denial as a highly respected form of voluntary piety.

With regard to India, Weber relied on the researches of Hermann Oldenberg (1854–1920). According to Oldenberg, the gods in early India were simply personified powers of nature. This primordial view ceased, however, when the necessities of social life required gods who would protect law and morals. Moreover, these gods were approachable not only through sacrifice and prayer, but also through magic—a force that was expected to intervene directly in the course of events. From cosmological speculation about the efficacy of sacrifice and magic arose the notion of Brahman, understood as the unchanging essence of the universe, an essence that is also present in the individual (as Atman). Combined with the belief that the transmigration of the soul is dependent upon its karma, these notions formed the matrix on which Jainism and Buddhism emerged as religions of world denial.

The contributions to the manual of Paul Hinneberg reveal a particular point of view in reconstructing religious history. These Orientalists retrieved from their sources world views and ethics constitutive of human subjects and their practices. Similar considerations informed philosophers. Hermann Siebeck in a textbook divided historical religions into three categories: natural religions, which considered gods as saviors from external evil; morality religions, which viewed gods as guarantors of social norms and upheld a positive attitude toward the world; and salvation religions, which postulated a contradiction between the existence of God and the reality of evil in the world, and fostered an attitude of world denial (1893: 49). Siebeck's entire concept depended on an understanding of religious history terminating in "world denial".

Religious Genealogies of Modern Institutions and Attitudes

This approach proved particularly attractive to German scholars, who, for the most part, rejected the idea that history was governed by objective natural laws, and preferred to focus on its subjective, cultural dimension. From their point of view, not only capitalism, but other modern institutions and practices alike, required explanations based on actors and their beliefs. Accordingly, they incorporated religious history into their analyses of modernization, minimizing the impact of the Enlightenment.

There is no better opportunity to observe the relevance of this approach than to read the minutes of the first official meeting of German social scientists, which was held in Frankfurt in 1910 (Troeltsch 1911). At this event, Ernst Troeltsch argued that Christianity had generated three social forms: first, the church, an organization administering the means of salvation (for Troeltsch, the most powerful type); second, the voluntary sect, a community of truly committed believers; and third, mysticism, the embodiment of radical individualism. According to Troeltsch, this plurality of social forms was a consequence of the fact that the Christian "church", confronted with the challenge of a life according to the realities of this world while upholding faith in the coming kingdom of God, had adopted Stoicism, distinguishing a perfect natural law embodied in man ruled by reason from a relative natural law requiring merely ethical control of emotions and passions. In contrast to the church, "sects" rejected the relative view of natural law and recognized nothing other than the severe ethical requirements of Jesus in his Sermon on the Mount. Finally, "mysticism" denied the inherent validity of the natural order on principle and relied on an interior divine light. By means of these distinctions, Troeltsch sought to make sense of the different practical attitudes to the world that Christianity had generated in the course of Western history and that had an impact on modern culture.

At the meeting, Troeltsch's presentation immediately set off a heated debate among Ferdinand Tönnies, Georg Simmel, Eberhard Gothein, Martin Buber, Hermann Kantorowicz, and Max Weber. In this debate Weber clarified issues that were fundamental for his section on *Religious Communities.* First he opposed Tönnies, who argued that the various social forms of Christianity had been caused by their dependence on different economic classes. Weber rejected this explanation, holding that religious antagonisms were never caused by economic antagonisms. Second, he accepted the three types of social forms of Christianity that Troeltsch had outlined, but emphasized that, in reality, these three generally occurred in mixed forms. He also disputed Troeltsch's assertion that the church had had a greater cultural impact than sects. Here, he cited the example of the United

States—the country Weber considered most religious in terms of numbers of believers and their level of commitment—where Christianity became strong and popular because it was organized by sects and not churches. Finally he reacted to Georg Simmel, who expressed doubt that Christianity could assume an effective *social* form at all due to its indifference to mundane issues and claimed that it has its genuine place only inside the intimate relation between the soul and God. Martin Buber urged a similar point, rejecting mysticism as a social form and identifying it as a purely psychological form. Responding to both, Weber remarked that even a world-rejecting religion involves practices necessary to prove one's convictions; these practices infuse all kinds of religion with a social dimension. Weber's remarks anticipate his later work that emphasizes the tremendous impact that world-rejecting religions had on the rise of modern institutions and attitudes.

Dissecting "Action": Motivation versus Meaning, Rationality versus Correctness

In order to incorporate the new paradigms of history of religions into his project, Weber dissected the category of action. In 1913, he published an essay on "Some Categories of Interpretive Sociology", which—as he explained in a footnote—he hoped would provide "a systematic basis for substantive investigations", including those in *Economy and Society* (1913[1981]: 179 n. 1). In the very same footnote, Weber declared that he intended "to separate sharply subjectively intended meaning from objectively valid meaning (thereby deviating somewhat from Simmel's method)". Years later, in the first part of *Economy and Society*, he repeated his point: "The present work departs from Simmel's method... in drawing a sharp distinction between subjectively intended and objectively valid 'meanings', two different things which Simmel not only fails to distinguish but often deliberately treats as belonging together" (1978: 4). Weber posits this distinction in regard to his notion of action: "Action (including intentional omission and acquiescence) is always intelligible behavior towards objects, behavior whose 'actual' or 'intended' *subjective meaning* may be more or less clear to the actor, whether consciously noted or not" (1913 [1981]: 152). Weber recognized well that Simmel too had distinguished understanding the meaning of an action from understanding an actor's motives; but Simmel had not adhered to this distinction, he objected. Simmel indeed, like other representatives of vitalism, assumed that religions have their roots in an irrational dimension of human life—a claim central to what later became known as "Phenomenology of Religion", one of the master paradigms in twentieth-century religious studies. This was, however, a view to which Weber was opposed. According to him, religions provide actors with concepts of meaning. Even if an actor is unable to explicate these meanings, they nonetheless remain part of his or her social interactions. Weber insisted, therefore, that meaning differs from personal motivations, and that it must be retrieved by observation, not by empathy. Only when one appreciates this argument can one understand Weber's interest in looking for meanings governing social interactions. Such meanings are generated in religious communities.

Closely connected with the first distinction is another one that Weber draws between rational and correct action:

> Subjectively rational instrumental action and action 'correctly' oriented toward objectively valid goals ('correctly rational') are two very different things. An action which the researcher is seeking to explain may appear to him to be instrumentally rational in the highest degree and yet be oriented to assumptions of the actor that are totally invalid to the researcher. Action oriented toward conceptions of magic, for example, is often subjectively of a far more instrumentally rational character than any non-magical 'religious' behavior, for precisely in a world increasingly disenchanted [or divested of magic], religiosity must take on increasingly (subjective) irrational meaning relationships (ethical or mystical, for instance). (1913[1981]: 154–5).

This distinction became the point of departure for analyzing religion in the section "Religious Communities":

> Religiously or magically motivated behavior is relatively rational behavior, especially in its earliest manifestations.... Only we, judging from our modern views of nature, can distinguish objectively in such behavior those attributions of causality which are 'correct' from those which are 'fallacious', and then designate the fallacious attributions of causality as irrational, and the corresponding acts as 'magic. (1978: 400)

That is to say, while 'rationality' of life conduct is independent of falsification or verification by empirical proof, it is, on the other hand, dependent on a religious disenchantment of the world. This disenchantment is caused not by an increasing body of knowledge but by acknowledging ethics and mysticism as subjective means of securing meaning in one's life. The primary place of disenchantment of the world is in the area not of knowledge but of religiously constituted meaning.

Religion as Communal Action

Weber conceived of religion as a "particular type of communal action (*Gemeinschaftshandeln*)" (1978: 399). What Weber means by "community" (*Gemeinschaft*) and its opposite, "society" (*Gesellschaft*), has been clarified by Klaus Lichtblau (2000). Weber was in need of a notion that explained the validity of rationality without referring either to correctness or to personal psychological motivations. Here he introduced the notion of communal action. Communal actions have a structure and laws of their own (*Eigengesetzlichkeit*); they are attached to social interactions as an "overarching relationship" and affect the exchange of goods and the obedience to rules and persons. The process of rationalization, Weber's main concern, penetrates primarily the sphere of communal action, and only by this detour becomes an essential factor in supporting or obstructing certain types of social interactions. Although economic conditions are often of decisive causal importance for communities and communal actions, conversely, the economy is usually also influenced by the autonomous structure of communal action. Weber conceived of this interrelationship in terms of "elective affinity" between concrete communal structures and concrete forms of economic organization: whether they further or impede or exclude one another—whether they are 'adequate' or 'inadequate' in relation to one another. This perspective explains Weber's abiding interest in religious communities as the matrix for practical attitudes to the world. The entire structure of *Economy and Society,* with its cross-references back and forth between different topical sections, rests on a model that traces interrelationships between types of communal actions and social orders.

Avoiding the difficult task of defining religion in general, Weber posits that an understanding of religious behavior "can only be achieved from the viewpoint of the subjective experiences, ideas, and purposes of the individuals concerned, in short from the viewpoint of the religious behavior's 'meaning'. The most elementary forms of behavior motivated by religious or magical factors are oriented to *this* world." Clarifying the last point, Weber quotes the Bible: "That it may go well with thee… and that thou mayest prolong thy days upon earth" (Deut. 4: 40; Eph. 6: 2 ff.) (1978: 399). It is most important to realize that, in contrast to cultural anthropologists, who use the category "meaning" epistemologically, Weber conceives of it as an expectation transcending the realities of the world. Weber's entire exposition depends on this loaded understanding of "meaning"; the difference between religious and non-religious behavior lies, for him, solely in the subjective expectations of the actor, not in the type of action itself.

Weber was interested not in isolating religion, but in detecting its social effects on the constitution of social orders. This required a different approach from defining religion. Already in his essay on *The Protestant Ethic and the Spirit of Capitalism* he argued that any historical concept cannot be determined by way of definition. "It must be composed from its individual elements taken from historical reality." "This is in the nature of 'historical concept-formation', which for its methodological purposes does not seek to embody historical reality in abstract generic concepts but endeavors to integrate them in concrete configurations which are always and inevitably individual in character" (1904/5 [2002]: 8–9). To attain that goal, Weber forged the instrument of the ideal type. Ideal types are not generic terms, under which reality is subsumed; they are notions, by means of which an observable reality can be analyzed in terms of the 'meaning' encoded in an action. The instrument of the ideal type enables the scholar to recognize subjective 'meaning' even in actions that appear dominated by mundane interests. From Weber's perspective, via the exchange of practical meaning between individuals and classes, world views and ethics of religious communities are permeating the social orders of law, politics, and, not least, economics.

Types of Religious Communities

In order to bring the various types of religious communal actions into sharper focus, Weber drew, upon the concept of "symbolic representation" that Hermann Usener had introduced in 1896. The choice was well-founded. Usener developed an approach to religion that did not privilege unmediated human experience at the expense of human symbolic expression. The earliest human experience of the unfathomable powers as "mana", "orenda", "maga", or "charisma" constituted practical attitudes towards the world; by means of a process of symbolic abstraction, they crystallized into distinct spiritual beings who answered to the human quest to live in a "meaningful world".

In Weber's view, that quest went hand in hand with the emergence of various types of religious specialists, which Weber specified according to their manner of mediating. He identified the magician, the priest, the prophet, and the intellectual as divergent types concerned with conceiving and controlling the mysterious powers and evoking highly different expectations among their followings. Though he continually speaks about development, he does not present the historical data as cases of a linear evolution, but as evidence for a differentiation, as his examples drawn from the past as well as the present demonstrate.

The starting point is the magician, a figure whose charisma is represented by ecstasy. "For the laymen this psychological state is accessible only in occasional actions.... [It] occurs in a social form, the *orgy*, which is the primordial form of religious community (*Vergemeinschaftung*)" (Weber 1978: 401). Urged on by political necessities, this occasional form of association was replaced by more regular ones. In this context, Weber points to the interdependence of community and society: "There is no concerted [communal] action (*Gemeinschaftshandeln*), as there is no individual action, without its special god. Indeed, if a [social] association is to be permanently guaranteed, it must have such a god" (1978: 411). By this route, the gods of religious communities became "guardians of the legal order", a development accompanied by the emergence of priests and stable cults that, together, ensured the permanence of social association, while believers, in their practical lives, began conceiving of the entire world as an "enduringly and meaningfully ordered cosmos" (1978: 430). Historically, acceptance of this postulate stimulated the spread of legal orders and ethical requirements, while simultaneously eliciting an awareness of the rift between expectation and the inevitable experience of a reality devoid of meaning. In this circumstance, according to Weber, prophets arose to furnish an explanation for this experience and to address the increasing ethical demands that the gods seemed unable to answer. In order to specify different types of prophecy, Weber adopted from the scholarship of his time the distinction between a strict, transcendent God who demands loyalty, and a divine being that is immanent in man and can be approached by contemplation. The former conception dominated in the Middle East and was at the origin of Western rational life conduct, while the latter conception prevailed in India and China. The two types correspond, respectively, to Weber's "ethical" and "exemplary" forms of prophecy. Finally, turning to intellectuals, Weber presented this group as driven by "metaphysical needs", by the urge to reflect on ethical and religious questions and to "understand the world as a meaningful cosmos and to take up a position toward it" (1978: 499). These intellectuals play a crucial part in suppressing belief in magic and promoting the world's disenchantment.

When communities around these specialists included laymen, their needs had to be met; accordingly, religions showed variations according to "what religion must provide for the various social strata" (1978: 491). Different social strata ideal-typically adopted world views and ethical doctrines that conformed to their economic and political position. Thus, the religious preferences of peasants, a stratum dependent on the unpredictability of nature, were mostly for tradition and magic, while warrior nobles inclined toward a religion of conquest, and bureaucrats toward a manipulation of religion as a means to domesticate the masses. The religious preferences of bourgeois strata were less uniform, dependent on the bourgeoisie's economic situation and its access to political privileges.

Religions Operating in the Disenchanted World

Weber directed his comparison to religions that developed a fully fledged congregational religiosity, rather than only occasional gatherings. Such congregations faced a major challenge, however, when religion took the direction of world rejection as the means to salvation. For, in Weber's account, the more a religion of salvation developed and became systematized and internalized as an *ethic of commitment*, in contrast to an ethic of compliance with laws, the more its adherents experienced 'tensions' with the world—tensions that elicited new forms of religiosity.

Weber for the first time sketched this truly revolutionary analysis of religion in the modern world in the section on Religious Communities in *Economy and Society* (1978: 576–610). He later revised and expanded that outline in his "Intermediate Reflections" (*Zwischenbetrachtung*) 1915 [1946]). Necessarily, tensions a rise between ethics requiring brotherly love and the ethically neutral autonomous spheres of economics, politics, sexuality, and art; the "Zwischenbetrachtung" added science. These tensions are resolved by either fleeing the world or mastering it, by either mysticism or ascetism. These new religious practices are typical and fundamental to religions operating in the disenchanted world.

Weber conceived of modern culture not as godless culture, as Marianne Weber suggests in her account. The rational culture, with its awareness of the unethical character of the social orders and powers, unleashes new kinds of religiosity. Weber's exposition abounds in examples. When Calvinism abandoned the prohibition of usury, due to the inherent forces of economics, it organized charity for the poor and needy. Mystical religions chose the opposite path and practiced—at least in principle—a loving self-surrender: not for the sake of the poor, but for the sake of surrender itself. Likewise, in the sphere of politics, congregational religiosity did not merely oppose the use of violence by the state; it favored either a world-fleeing pacifism or an active employment of force to fight the powers of sin. In the case of sexuality and art, practices of a re-enchantment of the world surfaced that rivaled world rejection: eroticism and art became means of escaping "the cold skeleton hands of rational orders" (1915 [1946]: 347).

The less the inhabitants of modern culture are able to find meaning in nature and history, the more the quest for meaning is thrown back onto the individual. In this context, the religions handed down from the past are turned into sources of conduct of life, based on subjective individual decisions. In this guise, the gods are still alive, as Weber declared in his famous speech "Science as Vocation" (1917): "Today the routines of everyday life challenge religion. Many old gods ascend from their graves; they are disenchanted and hence take the form of impersonal forces. They strive to gain power over our lives and again they resume their eternal struggle with one another" (1917: 149)

For years, Weber's sociology of religion was read as a theory of secularization: With the rise of modernity, social institutions are separated from religious ones, and religious beliefs and practices are declining and marginalized to the private sphere. But this reading does not correspond to the relationship that Weber assumed between religion and modernization. According to him, the process of disenchantment when establishing secular orders as autonomous spheres becomes a propelling force for new types of religiosity; "meaning" is moving from the objective side of history and nature to the side of subjective conviction; institutional religion yields to individual religiosity. Recent studies of the contemporary rise and spread of apocalypticism and esotericism would benefit from Weber's sociology of religion, if they would take notice of his concept of disenchantment.

References

Works of Max Weber

—— (1892[1984]). *Die Lage der Landarbeiter im ostelbischen Deutschland.* In *Max Weber Gesamtausgabe* (MWG), ed. Martin Riesebrodt, I/3, 2 vols. Tübingen: Mohr Siebeck. 1984.

—— (1896[1924]). "Die sozialen Gründe des Untergangs der antiken Kultur". In *Gesammelte Aufsätze zur Sozial- und Wirtschaftsgeschichte.* Tübingen: Mohr Siebeck. 289–311. Trans. as "The Social Causes of the Decay of Ancient Civilization" by Christian Mackauer, in Richard Swedberg (ed.), *Max Weber, Essays in Economic Sociology.* Princeton: Princeton University Press, 1999, 138–53.

—— (1904/5[1930]). *The Protestant Ethic and the Spirit of Capitalism*, trans. and introduced by Talcott Parsons. London: G. Allen & Unwin: repr. Routledge, 1992 (Weber's 2nd edn.).

—— (1904/5[2002]). *The Protestant Ethic and the "Spirit" of Capitalism and other Writings*, trans. and introduced by Peter Baehr and Gordon C. Wells. Harmondsworth: Penguin, (Weber's 1st edn).

—— (1909[1976]). *The Agrarian Sociology of Ancient Civilizations*, trans. I. R. Frank. London: New Left Books.

—— (1910[1978]). "Anti-critical Last Word on The Spirit of Capitalism", trans. Wallace M. Davis. *American Journal of Sociology*, 83: 1105–31.

—— (1913[1981]). "Some Categories of Interpretive Sociology", trans. Edith Graber. *Sociological Quarterly*, 22: 151–80.

—— (1913[2001]). *Wirtschaft und Gesellschaft*, ii: *Religiöse Gemeinschaften*, ed. Hans G. Kippenberg in cooperation with Petra Schilm and Jutta Niemeier, MWG I/22–2. Tübingen: Mohr Siebeck.

—— (1915[1946]). *Zwischenbetrachtung.* Trans. as "Religious Rejections of the World and their Directions" by Hans H. Gerth and C. Wright Mills, in *From Max Weber: Essays in Sociology.* Oxford: Oxford University Press, 323–59.

—— (1915–20[1989]). *Die Wirtschaftsethik der Weltreligionen: Konfuzianismus und Taoismus*, ed. Helwig Schmidt-Glintzer in cooperation with Petra Kolonko, MWG I/19. Tübingen: Mohr Siebeck.

—— (1916–20[1996]). *Die Wirtschaftsethik der Weltreligionen: Hinduismus und Buddhismus*, ed. Helwig Schmidt-Glintzer in cooperation with Karl Heinz Golzio, MWG I/20. Tübingen: Mohr Siebeck.

—— (1917/19[1992]). *Wissenschaft als Beruf*; *Politik als Beruf*, ed. Wolfgang J. Mommsen and Wolfgang Schluchter in cooperation with Brigitte Morgenbrod, MWG I/17. Tübingen: Mohr Siebeck. Trans as "Politics as Vocation" and "Science as Vocation" by Hans H. Gerth and C. Wright Mills, in *From Max Weber: Essays in Sociology.* Oxford: Oxford University Press, 1946, 77–128 and 129–56.

—— (1920). *Gesammelte Aufsätze zur Religionssoziologie*, 3 vols. Tübingen: Mohr Siebeck.

—— (1921/2). *Wirtschaft und Gesellschaft*, Teil i: *Die Wirtschaft und die gesellschaftlichen Ordnungen und Mächte*; Teil ii: *Typen der Vergemeinschaftung und Vergesellschaftung*, ed. Marianne Weber, Grundriß der Sozialökonomik III Abtlg., Tübingen.

—— (1978). *Economy and Society: An Outline of Interpretive Sociology*, ed. Günther Roth and Claus Wittich. Berkeley: University of California Press.

—— 1914–18[1984]. *Zur Politik im Weltkrieg: Schriften und Reden 1914–1918*, ed. Wolfgang J. Mommsen in cooperation with Gangolf Hübinger, MWG I/15. Tübingen: Mohr Siebeck.

—— (2002). *Schriften 1894–1922*, ed. Dirk Kaesler. Stuttgart: Kröner, 2002.

Weber's Authorities in Religious History

Hinneberg, Paul (ed.) (1906*a*). *Christliche Religion mit Einschluss der israelitisch-jüdischen Religion*, Die Kultur der Gegenwart, ihre Entwicklung und ihre Ziele, Teil 1, Abt. 4. Berlin and Leipzig: B. G. Teubner.

—— (ed.) (1906*b*). *Die orientalischen Religionen*, Die Kultur der Gegenwart, ihre Entwicklung und ihre Ziele, Teil 1, Abt. 3,1. Berlin and Leipzig: B. G. Teubner.

Marett, Robert Ranulph, (1900[1909]). "Pre-animistic Religion". In *idem*, *The Threshold of Religion*. London: Methuen & Co. Ltd., 1–28.

Siebeck, Hermann (1893). *Lehrbuch der Religionsphilosophie*. Freiburg and Leipzig: Mohr Siebeck.

Troeltsch, Ernst (1911). "Das stoisch-christliche Naturrecht und das moderne profane Naturrecht". In *Verhandlungen der Deutschen Soziologentage*, I. Band: *Verhandlungen des Ersten Deutschen Soziologentages vom 19.–22. Oktober 1910 in Frankfurt am Main. Reden und Vorträge [...] und Debatten*. Tübingen: Mohr Siebeck, 166–92; minutes of the debate, pp. 192–214.

Usener, Hermann (1896). *Götternamen: Versuch einer Lehre von der religiösen Begriffsbildung*. Bonn: Friedrich Cohen.

Secondary Literature

Lichtblau, Klaus (2000). "'Vergemeinschaftung' und 'Vergesellschaftung' bei Max Weber: eine Rekonstruktion seines Sprachgebrauchs". *Zeitschrift für Soziologie*, 29: 423–43.

Weber, Marianne, (1926[1988]). *Max Weber: A Biography*, ed. and trans. H. Zohn. New Brunswick, NJ, and Oxford: Transaction Publishers 1988.

Suggested Reading

Bellah, Robert, (1999). "Max Weber and World-Denying Love: A Look at the Historical Sociology of Religion". *Journal of the American Academy of Religion* 67: 277–304.

Camic, Charles, Gorski, Philip, and Trubek, David (eds.) (2005). *Max Weber's Economy and Society: A Critical Companion*. Stanford, Calif.: Stanford University Press.

Gauchet, Marcel (1999). *The Disenchantment of the World: A Political History of Religion*. Princeton: Princeton University Press.

Kippenberg, Hans G. (2005). "Religious Communities and the Path to Disenchantment: The Origins, Sources, and Theoretical Core of the Religion Section". In Charles Camic,

Philip Gorski, and David Trubek (eds.), *Max Weber's Economy and Society: A Critical Companion*, Stanford, Calif.: Stanford University Press, 164–82.

Kippenberg, Hans G. and Riesebrodt, Martin (eds.) (2001). *Max Webers 'Religionssystematik'.* Tübingen: Mohr Siebeck.

Lehmann, Hartmut, and Roth, Günther (eds.) (1993). *Weber's Protestant Ethic: Origins, Evidence, Contexts.* Cambridge: Cambridge University Press.

Oexle, Otto Gerhard (2001). "Max Weber—Geschichte als Problemgeschichte". In *idem* (ed.), *Das Problem der Problemgeschichte 1880–1932*, Göttingen: Wallstein, 9–37.

Radkau, Joachim (2005). *Max Weber: die Leidenschaft des Denkens.* Munich: Hanser.

Roth, Guenther (2001). *Max Webers deutsch-englische Familiengeschichte 1800–1950 mit Briefen und Dokumenten.* Tübingen: Mohr Siebeck.

Schluchter, Wolfgang (1989). *Rationalism, Religion, and Domination: A Weberian Perspective.* Berkeley: University of California Press.

—— and Graf, Friedrich Wilhelm (eds.) (2005). *Asketischer Protestantismus und der 'Geist' des modernen Kapitalismus: Max Weber und Ernst Troeltsch.* Tübingen: Mohr Siebeck.

Swedberg, Richard (2005). *The Max Weber Dictionary: Key Words and Central Concepts.* Stanford, Calif.: Stanford University Press, 2005.

Tenbruck, Friedrich H. (1999). *Das Werk Max Webers: Gesammelte Aufsätze zu Max Weber*, ed. Harald Homann. Tübingen: Mohr Siebeck.

CHAPTER 4

MAX WEBER ON ISLAM AND CONFUCIANISM

THE KANTIAN THEORY OF SECULARIZATION

BRYAN S. TURNER

Introduction: Religion as a 'Moralizing Faith'

There has been considerable academic debate about the coherence or otherwise of Max Weber's sociology as a whole. Much of the analysis has focused on the notion of rationalization as the master theme of his sociological work. By rationalization, Weber referred to a set of interrelated social processes by which the modern world had been systematically transformed into a rational system. Among these various processes, rationalization included the systematic application of scientific reason to the everyday world and the intellectualization of mundane activities through the application of systematic knowledge to practice. Rationalization was also associated with the disenchantment of reality that is the secularization of values and attitudes. The sociology of religion was therefore a central aspect of Weber's sociological interests as a whole. An influential interpretation of this theme of religion and rationalization was developed by Friedrich Tenbruck (1975; 1980) in his essays on the thematic unity of Weber's work.

Tenbruck questioned Marianne Weber's description of the posthumous two-volume *Economy and Society* as Weber's principal work (*Hauptwerk*). In directing attention away from *Economy and Society*, Tenbruck argued that there is no particular key to the interpretation of *Economy and Society*, precisely because that text is a conglomerate of disparate elements which do not constitute a recognizable major work. Instead, Tenbruck identified the underlying anthropological dimension of Weber's sociology: namely, his account of humans as 'cultural beings'. This cultural activity involved the construction of the meaningfulness of the everyday world, especially with respect to the brute necessity to satisfy economic needs. Tenbruck thus emphasized the centrality of the idea of 'the Economic Ethic of World Religions': namely, Weber's interest in the sociology of religion with respect to the rationalization process. The various studies of Judaism (1952), Confucianism and Taoism (1951), Hinduism and Buddhism (1958*b*), and the incomplete studies of Islam and Islamic law, or Shari'a (Turner 1974), represent a series of empirical applications of the theme of religious prescriptions for economic behaviour. These works on the economic ethics represent the principal consolidation of the initial argument of the essays on the Protestant ethic. The Protestant ethic thesis was simply a component of the central analysis of religion and economics which occupied the *Gesammelte Aufsätze zur Religions soziologie* (Weber 1921). Tenbruck also underlined the special importance of the 'Author's Introduction' (*Vorbemerkung*) to the sociology of religion as a whole, which was included by Talcott Parsons in his 1930 translation of *The Protestant Ethic and the Spirit of Capitalism* (Weber 1976). Weber wrote an additional introduction in 1913, which was published in 1915 with the title 'Intermediate Reflections' (*Zwischenbetrachtung*) and which was conceived after the 'Author's Introduction' was already in print. The *Zwischenbetrachtung* was translated by Hans Gerth and C. Wright Mills in *From Max Weber* (Gerth and Mills 1961: 323–62) as 'Religious Rejections of the World and their Directions'. Tenbruck's thesis is thus that the analysis of 'the Economic Ethic of the World Religions' dominated Weber's intellectual activities from around 1904 to 1920. Because his publications on religion occupied this creative period of Weber's life, it is these texts on religion and economics that should be regarded as his principal work, rather than *Economy and Society*.

In this exegetical framework, the thematic unity of these texts in the comparative sociology of religion is a study of the ways in which religious orientations towards the world did or did not lead to an ethic of world mastery: that is, to a process of rationalization. In the 'Introduction', the 'Intermediate Reflections', and 'the Author's Introduction', Weber developed a universal and historical conceptualization of these rationalization processes. This development is wholly compatible with Weber's notion of interpretative sociology, because it was these meaning systems within religion that generated specific world views that acted as the motivations for action. This interpretation is also consistent with the idea of the fatefulness of world images in Weber's meta-theory, because it was the irrational quest for salvation which generated a rational solution to our being in the world (Turner 1981).

Weber's interest in the religious quest for salvation resulted in an anthropology of the rules which govern the practical conduct of life (*Lebensführung*). In this anthropology of conduct Weber distinguished between a theodicy of good fortune (*Glück*) and a theodicy of suffering (*Leid*). In coming to terms with fortune and suffering, human beings extend their conception of their personal experience beyond the everyday material world. It is these experiences of fortune and suffering which undermine the rational or purposive categories of pragmatic orientation to reality. However, it was primarily within the monotheistic and ascetic religions that the rationalization of the problem of theodicy reached its ultimate fruition. The development of the concept of a universal God in a framework of history and salvation, demanding a human quest for salvation, produced a rational theodicy of reality as such. In short, it was the legacy of the Judaeo-Christian world, based upon the notions of ethical prophecy and monotheism, which was crucial to the development of a radical solution to theodicy in terms of highly intellectual, rational soteriologies. For example, the intellectual rationalism of the Protestant sects was critical in pushing European civilization towards a pattern of religious individualism involving strict norms of personal discipline and salvation. In short, Weber was in the process of developing a comprehensive sociology of piety as the core issue of his sociology of religion.

Many of these issues were taken up and further elaborated by Wilhelm Hennis (1988) in his important study of Weber in his essays in reconstruction. For Hennis the central question in Weber's sociology concerns the issues of personality and life orders. Hennis argued that it was the historical development of *Menschentum* that was the central issue in Weber's sociology: namely, how certain cultural developments produced a particular type of personality and a particular rational conduct of life (*Lebensführung*), particularly in the idea of a calling as part of the constitutive question of modernity (Stauth and Turner 1986). In more precise terms, Weber's sociology addressed the historical origins of life regulation as rational conduct in the development of modern vocations in the social world. Weber's analysis of the ascetic regulation of life is therefore simply one dimension of this analysis of *Lebensführung*, or the study of the personality effects arising from particular kinds of religious activity. The rationalization theme to which Weber draws attention in the Protestant ethic thesis involved a transformation of discipline and methodology relevant to particular forms of economic life regulation. Weber's analysis of capitalism was concerned not so much to explain its economic structure and functions as to understand the ways in which forms of capitalist economic activity had an 'elective affinity' with forms of personality and life order.

By 'personality' Weber did not have in mind what we would now call 'the personality system' within an empirical social psychology, but rather what kind of ontology would be produced by different life orders; that is, Weber asked an existential question from the perspective of German cultural values.

The intellectual motivation behind the exegesis of Hennis and others such as Keith Tribe (1989) was to re-establish Weber as a figure in classical political philosophy, thereby emphasizing his wish to understand the political order of society as the basis of ethics and ontology. In this respect Weber belongs to a tradition of political philosophy that started with Aristotle, in the sense that Weber's sociology of religion sought to contrast the virtues and habitus behind the various world religions, since out of these different personality constructs there evolved the virtues (or pieties) of different religions.

These exegetical issues, particularly as they impinge upon questions of liberalism and democracy, have dominated much of the philosophical debate about the implications of Weber's work in contemporary Germany. This critical (re)interpretation of Weber was specifically directed against Talcott Parsons's interpretation of Weber as one of the founding fathers of the sociology of action. By contrast, Hennis has been explicit in attempting to re-establish Weber as contributing to a German tradition of political and philosophical enquiry. According to Hennis, Weber's central question was about the ethical character of human existence, not the narrower one of the cultural foundations of Western capitalism in the theology of the Protestant sects. As a result, we can better understand the claim that 'Weber was a *German* thinker, from the land of "Dr Faustus"' (Hennis 1988: 195). The tragic problem of Weberian sociology is that the heroic personality of Protestant asceticism is no longer compatible with the secular world of capitalism—'Today the spirit of religious asceticism—whether finally who knows?—has escaped from the cage'—as he declared at the end of *The Protestant Ethic and the Spirit of Capitalism* (Weber 1976: 181).

This interpretation of Weber is in fact compatible with an article by Karl Löwith that first appeared in the *Archiv für Sozialwissenschaft und Sozialpolitik* in 1932, and was translated in 1982 as *Max Weber and Karl Marx* and was recently reprinted in a new edition in 1993. Löwith sought to demonstrate that, regardless of the very real differences between Karl Marx and Weber, their sociological perspectives were joined by a common philosophical anthropology, as a result of which there is an important convergence in their attitudes towards to the destructive features of bourgeois civilization which Marx developed through the idea of alienation and Weber through the theme of rationalization. In terms of their ontology, both Weber and Marx saw capitalism as a destructive economic system, but one which also opened up new possibilities through the transformation of tradition.

The common theme in these accounts is the recognition of the profoundly ethical character of Weber's social theory and its underpinning in an anthropological theory of personality and life orders. Both Tenbruck and Löwith share this interest in the religious theme within Weber's life and work, particularly the focus on questions relating to theodicy in which the rationalization theme was a product of the existential question of meaning. One can conclude that, first, the differences between Tenbruck and Hennis (between seeing Weber as either a sociologist or a political philosopher) are not significant. Both insist on the ethical character of Weber's work. We can argue that Weber was working towards a sociology of piety: namely, the rules of pious activity in the everyday world. Piety eventually produces 'character' as a result of such training. Secondly, we can better understand Weber's concern for the interconnections between piety and ethics by recognizing the long-lasting impact of Immanuel Kant's philosophy of religion on Weber's sociology as a whole.

In his comparative studies, Weber sought to preserve the view that the radical message of Protestant Christianity involves a heroic struggle for self-mastery or piety, the consequence of which is the radical transformation of the traditional world. For Weber, there were two related issues here. In order for the radical ethic of Christianity to function, religion had to be clearly separated from the state, otherwise the religious ethic was subordinated to the secular interests of power. This fusion of religion and politics constituted the problem of 'caesaro-papism', the authoritarian domination of society by the confusion of sacred and secular power. Weber's view of the necessary separation of religion and politics is a core aspect of liberal philosophy, but in the German case it also reflected Weber's experience of the political legacy of Bismarck and the *Kulturcampf* in which the German chancellor had successfully manipulated anti-Catholic liberal sentiment to political advantage, in simultaneously attacking clerical control of education and traditionalists within the Reich. Weber's views on political power reflected his experiences of Bismarck's statecraft, which had destroyed many of the institutions that could have kept the state accountable to parliament. Bismarck had destroyed liberalism and reinforced the political passivity in Germany that was also the legacy of Lutheranism, which defended law and order over liberty of conscience.

As a liberal, Weber was not sympathetic to Catholicism, and he was in any case deeply influenced by his mother's Protestant piety, specifically by the moral teaching of William Ellery Channing, who emphasized rational control over the instincts rather than emotional experiences of divinity (Mitzman 1971: 29). Catholicism remained an issue in Weber's sociology of religion. While he did not devote much explicit attention to the social consequences of Catholicism in Europe, devoting most of his intellectual energies to Protestantism, we can assume that he regarded Catholic piety as a conservative social force.

Furthermore, religion as an ethical activity of self-creation had to be distinct from popular religion as merely a set of rituals for bringing good fortune and good health. Religion as a radical faith of self-transformation had to be concerned not with *Gluck* but with *Leid*. This was the problem of routinization, in which a radical religion of inner conviction became merely a therapeutic practice of folk religiosity.

In adopting these moral issues from Kant, Weber also had to, as it were, look over his shoulder to Friedrich Nietzsche, and especially to the questions: Are these Christian morals in fact merely driven by resentment, in which case they are not a self-reflexive moral world view. And secondly, is a warrior religion somehow 'healthier' than the religion of slaves—namely, early Christianity? To what extent is Islam, which does not privilege suffering and repentance, healthier (a life-affirming doctrine) than the religion of the crucified Jesus?

Given Weber's ethical concerns, both Islam and Confucianism offered him two useful case studies, since, as far as Weber was concerned, neither wholly rejected caesaropapism. First, Weber's treatment of Confucianism is somewhat ambiguous because, while he classified it as a world religion, in practice he interpreted it as the ethics of the literati within the Chinese court system. Secondly, while Weber was forced to recognize Islam as a member of the monotheistic, Abrahamic tradition, in practice he interpreted it as a warrior religion in which there was no fundamental separation of secular and sacred power. Confucianism was simply a court ethics whose principal value was filial piety. For Weber, Islam was a warrior religion whose soteriological doctrines were transformed by a history of imperial power. Christian ethics were also corrupted by the history of the medieval Catholic Church; but the radical message of the primitive church was constantly revived by the Protestant sects whose ethical demands produced a reformation of personality.

The Kantian Legacy

The word 'religion' (*religio*) has two distinctive roots. First, *relegere* from *legere* means to bring together, to harvest, or to gather (in). Secondly, *religare* from *ligare* means to tie or to bind together. The first meaning indicates the religious foundations of any social group that is gathered together, while the second points to the disciplines or morality that are necessary for controlling human beings and creating a regulated mentality. The first meaning describes the role of the cult in forming human membership, while the second indicates the regulatory framework of religious practices and doctrine that discipline the passions. This dichotomy formed the basis of Kant's philosophical analysis of religion and morality. In *Religion within the Boundaries of Mere Reason* Kant (1998) distinguished between religion as cult (*des blossen Cultus*), which seeks favours from God through prayer and offerings to bring healing and wealth to its followers, and religion as moral action (*die Religion des guten Lebenswandels*), which commands human beings to change their behaviour in order to lead a better life. Kant further elaborated this argument through an examination of 'reflecting faith', compelling human beings to strive for salvation through faith rather than the possession of religious knowledge. The implication of this distinction was that (Protestant) Christianity was the only true 'reflecting faith', and in a sense, therefore, the model of all authentic religious intentions. Kant's distinction was fundamentally about those religious injunctions that call human beings to (moral) action and hence demand that humans assert their autonomy and responsibility. These authentic moral demands in true religions contrast sharply with those folk practices that are essentially magical in seeking a technology to manipulate the world. In order to have autonomy, human beings need to act independently of God. True religion is a technology of the self; false religions are a magical technology of manipulation. The real psychological tension in radical Christian soteriology was that the faithful could not influence God by prayer or magic, and hence divinity was hidden from the eyes of the believer. In a paradoxical fashion, Christianity implies the tragic 'death of God' because it calls people to freedom, and hence the Christian faith is ultimately self-defeating.

Alongside these concepts of life orders and personality, Weber developed the idea of various spheres of life into which the world is divided. These different spheres make demands on both the individual and social levels, and can combine or conflict with each other. This analysis of the spheres of life in the two lectures on 'politics as a vocation' and 'science as a vocation' found a more elaborate classification in the 'Intermediate Reflections', where Weber identified a wider range of life spheres or value spheres: economics, politics, aesthetics, the erotic, the intellectual, and the religious. The different world religions represent different resolutions of the various levels of contradiction between religion and 'the world'. One central question for Weber was whether religion is simply a sphere of values or in fact the principle that guarantees or determines the other spheres. Is religion a component of life spheres ('the world') or that source of values that determines the life spheres of the world? If religion is in tension with the other spheres (as in the notion of religious orientations and their rejection of the world), then Weber's sociology implies a special status for religion. If religion is simply one institution, then there is no essential conflict. The problem of historicism implied that through the differentiation of the spheres of life with secularization, religion had become a separate institution alongside the other life spheres. The differentiation of the spheres meant that no single coherent meaningful life was possible, hence this polytheism of values was the 'fate' of modern people (Gerth and Mills 1991: 357). The attempt to preserve charisma through the cultivation of 'a cosmic brotherhood' could only be an aristocratic religious response, unlikely to succeed in an age of mass democracies and rationalized bureaucratization of politics. In this Weberian sense, therefore, religious studies are a product of the differentiation of the life spheres, the disenchantment of reality, and the assimilation of religion by culture.

Weber adhered to the assumption that it is possible to create a hierarchy of religions in terms of their inner consistency to a radical this-worldly asceticism. Weber may therefore have accepted a hierarchy of values mapped on to a hierarchy of religions, with Calvinism and Lutheranism at the top of this chain of radical engagement with the world, through the emotional and pietist sects, to the Old Testament prophets of Judaism. Islamic prophecy fell below that of Christianity and Judaism, but was more significant than the religions of the Orient: namely, Confucianism and Buddhism. Weber's study of the economic ethics of the world religions implied a hierarchical order of the ethical contents of religious rejections of the world and their consequences. This 'intellectual solution' has been frequently criticized, and any hierarchical arrangement of religion has in recent scholarship been rejected as a species of Orientalism (Said 1978). The notion of a clear hierarchy of religious orientations to the world does not fit easily into a global context of religious studies. Weber's attempts to create a value-free science of society left him poorly equipped to offer specific advice or guidance with respect to desirable ends of action, and the values that underpin the idea of a secular vocation appear to be arbitrary. Weber's secular science of society has been rejected by philosophers such as Leo Strauss (1953), who did not accept Weber's sociology as an adequate grounding for politics or the modern study of religions. In defence of Weber, although his views may be unfashionable, they raise a number of challenging questions that continue to influence modern analysis: Is something equivalent to the ascetic piety of Puritanism necessary as a challenge to the secular spheres, especially the spheres of politics and economics?

These Kantian principles were translated into Weber's distinction between mass and virtuoso religion in his *Sociology of Religion* (1966). While the mass of the population seeks comfort from religion, especially healing, the virtuosi fulfil the ethical demands of religion in search of spiritual salvation or enlightenment. The religion of the masses requires saints and holy men to satisfy their needs; hence charisma is in the long run corrupted by the demand for miracles and spectacles. More importantly, Weber distinguished between those religions that reject the world by challenging its traditions (such as inner-worldly asceticism) and religions that seek to escape from the world through mystical flight (such as other-worldly mysticism). The former religions (primarily the Calvinistic radical sects) have had revolutionary consequences for human society in the formation of rational capitalism. The implication of this tradition is paradoxical. First, Christianity (or at least Puritanism) is the only true religion (as a reflecting faith), and secondly, Christianity gives rise to a process of secularization that spells out its own self-overcoming (*Aufhebung*).

The most influential account of this 'moralizing faith' of course was presented in Weber's *The Protestant Ethic and the Spirit of Capitalism*, in which he argued that the religious practices of the virtuosi had been taken out of the monastery and into the ordinary household, and from there piety, or 'this-worldly asceticism', had undertaken 'to penetrate just that daily routine of life with its methodicalness, to fashion it into a life in the world' (Weber 1976: 154). Perhaps the most celebrated version of this penetration of the world in Britain was undertaken by John Wesley (1703–91) and the Methodist chapels. The Wesleyan sect took its name 'Methodism' from the methods by which the laity came to regulate their lives, such as modesty in dress, regularity of prayer, and acts of charity towards the poor. The sociological consequences are well known (Thompson 1963). Pious practice and biblical study produced a disciplined and literate Methodist laity, which came to exercise some degree of political and cultural leadership among the British working class. As a result, Methodists came to be predominantly a comfortable bourgeoisie, moving gradually away from their original piety. The experience of Methodists came to be identified by sociologists of religion as a key feature of a more general process of secularization.

In summary, a true religion is one which is motivated by moral dispositions, and it has been noted that in Kant's account there is no real need for revelation, because religion involves inward commitment to a moral order. Hence Kant argued that most of humanity were in fact committed to adherence to what he called 'faith'—that is, the institutional structures of religion. The various faiths were merely popular manifestations of a more serious religious vocation, which was available to the elite (Kant 1998: 116–17). When we describe somebody as a Protestant, a Muslim, or a Buddhist, we are in reality describing their faith, rather than the true religion. Weber's ethical sociology appears to accept this view at least implicitly: for example, in the discussion of the routinization of charisma, and the distinction between the mass and the religious virtuosi.

The Sociology of Islam

Weber did not produce a complete study of Islam, and his view of Islam has to be reconstructed from a variety of sources, most notably his sociology of law and his classification of types of prophecy. By comparison with his work on Protestantism and the 'religions of Asia', Weber's sociology of Islam has been somewhat neglected. The principal exceptions have been Maxime Rodinson's *Islam and Capitalism* (1978), which appeared originally in 1966, my own *Weber and Islam* (Turner 1974), and Wolfgang Schluchter's edition on Islam (1987), which has been translated as *Max Weber and Islam* (Huff and Schluchter 1999). These works interpret Weber's commentary on Islam as an aspect of his more general project: namely, to show why modern, rational capitalism appeared uniquely in the Christian West.

In retrospect, I now see Weber's intention within both a broader and a narrower framework. Let us start with his more general set of questions. First, Weber sought to understand the status of Muhammad as an ethical prophet, and how the Prophet articulated a set of revelations in the Qur'an to challenge the traditional values of Arab society. In this respect, we can see the commentary on early Islam as a contribution to the more general study of authority, of which charismatic authority was a major dimension. Weber's view of the Prophet, by comparison with his analysis of the Old Testament prophets in *Ancient Judaism*, was not complimentary, and Weber was more impressed by the Prophet as a military leader who creates a state. On this basis, Weber developed a set of significant contrasts between Christianity and Islam. For example, Islam has no church as such, and no sacerdotal priesthood. The *ulema* do not exercise authority over institutionalized grace, and their authority is not derived directly from the Prophet but from their training and the consensual recognition they receive from the community; whereas in the Roman Catholic Church, religious authority is ultimately inscribed in papal authority and the bishops, such that the 'keys of grace' are located in a centralized, hierarchical, and ultimately bureaucratic structure.

In the case of Islam, Weber was aware of an important difference between Shi'ism and Sunni Islam. While the Shi'ites identified authority with the descendants of the Prophet and anticipated the eventual return of a spiritual leader (the *Imam*), the Sunni tradition recognized the caliphate as the legitimate system of authority. The pre-Islamic Iranian priestly model of despotism was imitated by later Islamic regimes, whose aristocratic power was legitimized by the *'ulama*. For example, the works of al-Mawardi (974–1058) described a rigid social world composed of aristocratic horsemen, priests, peasants, and merchants. The model was both functional and hierarchical. In response to these despotic institutions, political conflict in Islam has subsequently been organized around utopian criticism of the urban hierarchy, a utopian opposition that often appeals nostalgically to the egalitarian solidarity (*asabiyya*) of the foundation community. For example, in the Iranian revolution of 1977–9, Ayatollah Khomeini mobilized the oppressed and the innocent in the name of a radical Islamic state against the urban elite, who were the principal agents of the Shah's authoritarian programme of economic modernization. The revolution involved a successful alliance between the clergy behind Khomeini, sections of urban working class, and the dispossessed (*Mostaz'afin*) who were typically landless rural migrants. In radical Islamism, the voice of the people became an expression of divine will against the inequalities of the secular state. Authority in Sunni Islam is communal, devolved, and localized; hence there is considerable dispute over the correct interpretation of law and tradition in a religious system in which legal decisions (*fatwas*) can be posted on the Internet by any teacher who claims to represent a religious community. In this respect, the *ulema* have, sociologically, a much closer relationship to the Jewish rabbis as respected religious teachers and scholars. Neither Judaism nor Islam has a social role that approximates to the sacerdotal priesthood of Western Christendom.

Secondly, Weber was interested in a related set of relationships between state and church, which we can summarize under the sociological concept that was implicit in the structure of *Economy and Society*: namely, the issue of caesaropapism. As prophetic, Abrahamic religions of revelation, both Christianity and Islam stand in opposition to the empirical world in which violence, inequality, and cruelty reign supreme. The problem with all revealed religions is the establishment of religious authority over secular processes of political power, economics, and social structures. This endless struggle between the ideal world of the brotherly community of love and the brutal reality of everyday life has been the principal religious leverage towards social change in human societies (Parsons 1966: p. xlvii). The core components of worldliness in the Abrahamic religions have been sexuality and money, which represent the corruption of power and selfishness. The religious orientations of asceticism, mysticism, and 'legal-mindedness' represent the historically dominant religious rejections of the fallen world. This sacred–profane dynamic is particularly important in Islam. Its first theological premiss is the affirmation in the Qur'an (the *sura* of unity, cxii): He is God alone, God the Eternal. Islamic doctrine is radically egalitarian, because its monotheistic fundamentalism precludes any ontological hierarchy in either human society or nature; but there is a permanent contradiction between theology and the history of hierarchy and inequality in actual societies (Marlow 1997). While the divine purpose is to establish peace between human beings, the early history of the Islamic caliphs was violent: 'Umar, 'Uthman, and 'Ali , the successors or caliphs of the Prophet, were assassinated.

Thirdly, Weber provided a comprehensive analysis of Islamic law which contributed an additional illustration to his study of charismatic authority (in the form of revelation) and rationalization. Islam is a revealed religion that came to mankind through the prophetic agency of Muhammad. This revelation is contained within a sacred text, the Qur'an, which was assembled after the death of the Prophet. Once this process of collection was complete, the Qur'an as the word of God was closed and transformed into a canon of revelation (*mushaf*). This closure of orthodoxy was known as the closing of *ijtihad* (intellectual effort or legal judgement). Western sociologists such as Max Weber argued subsequently that the rigidity of Islamic cultures was a consequence of the attempt to contain legal and theological speculation within a narrow framework (Turner 1974). In addition to the Qur'an, Muslims have the tradition (*sunna*) of the Prophet known through a chain of authority of witnesses (*isnad*). This tradition is the *hadith*. We might say, therefore, that the law, the book, and the Prophet constitute Islam. More precisely, Islam as a religion is the beaten path (*sunna*) of the Prophet.

Fourthly, Weber was interested in the sociology of the city as either a military camp or a site of democratic institutions. In *The City* (1958*a*) Weber argued that the city in the West had distinctive features that promoted the rise of citizenship and democratic civil institutions. The European city was not based on tribal affiliation; it was not simply a military base; and finally, it was relatively autonomous as a self-governing set of institutions. Christianity had contributed to these developments by creating a social bond that was based on a religious fellowship rather than on blood. Weber argued that, by contrast, the city in the Middle East was essentially a military camp, and that tribal and familial allegiance had never been totally broken down by the idea of religious belonging. The city in the history of Islam had not emerged as a basis for civil institutions to limit the power of the state.

At its inception Islam was an egalitarian brotherhood that assumed the equality of free (male) believers, developing neither church nor priesthood. This religious egalitarian monotheism was reinforced by Arabic tribalism, which also had an egalitarian ethic. These religious doctrines were compromised, however, by the success of Islamic military expansion, which encouraged the growth of a more status-conscious and hierarchical social order. The prominent religious role that was played by the wives of the Prophet (in particular Khadija and 'Aisha) was eventually overshadowed by the patriarchical cultures of the Islamicate societies in which women, outside the elite, became socially invisible (Ahmed 1992). These tendencies were increasingly legitimized by the Islamic incorporation of Greek political thought, which conceptualized the city as a hierarchical political formation. In the polis, social order required the harmony that was produced by a wise but despotic leader. In Iraq and Iran in the Sassanian period, social inequality became progressively hereditary, and the dominant class was recruited from the landed nobility.

Finally, Weber's narrower concern was with piety. This concern suggests that sociology should examine fundamental differences between religious traditions in terms of the emergence of the self. At the core of Christianity was a world view based on the notions of personal responsiveness to the redemptive love and historical actions of a personal God, operating in a corrupt world through a series of sacrificial acts (Hodgson 1960). The crucifixion of Jesus was the foundational event in this cosmic history of salvation. By contrast, the core of Islam was the demand for personal responsibility towards God, who has established a framework for moral order through the revelation of the law. The ethical concerns of Irano-Semitic monotheism, as expressed through its ethical prophets, were embodied in the law, on the one hand, and by the quest for mystical understanding of God, on the other. The unity of Islamicate culture was developed through 'Sharia-mindedness'—a moral code which constituted the inner conscience of Islam, and which expressed an opposition to the hierarchical and despotic systems of power that often characterized the Mughal, Safavi, and Ottoman empires (Hodgson 1974: i. 238). The community of the pious and learned (*'ulama*) developed the religious activities that cultivated this Sharia-mindedness as a major religious orientation in Islam.

Sharia-mindedness, which was carried down the centuries by *'ulama* and Sufis, was founded on a sense of justice, and thus stood in opposition to the culture of the emerging military states of Islamicate empires. The practices that developed

Sharia-mindedness are an equivalent religious orientation to what Weber (1966: 166) had in mind by his distinction between ascetic inner-worldly religion and mystical other-worldly orientations in *The Sociology of Religion.* It is also the equivalent of the idea of a 'technology of the self' (Foucault 1997: 224), since Sharia-mindedness requires discipline to produce a special type of personality; Sharia-consciousness is a technology of self-understanding. The notion that Sharia-conscience functioned as a religious critique of traditional pre-Islamic society is important, in order to emphasize the idea of Islam in opposition to folk religions, to the Sufi orders of ordinary society. This puritanical view of religious consciousness was thus sharply contrasted with the magical practices and popular rituals of the Sufi brotherhoods. Sharia-mindedness was the core of the Islamicate legal tradition, and a major issue in the resurgence of Islam in the modern world.

The critical literature on Weber's sociology of religion is considerable. Suffice it to say that Weber's vision of 'Asian religions' has been condemned as an example of Orientalism in which a dynamic West is contrasted with a stagnant East (Said 1978; Turner 1978). Taking the more substantive features of Weber's analysis of Islam, research suggests that the city was a context within which civil institutions such as charitable associations (*waqf*) flourished, and that in many Islamic urban centres civil society flourished around the mosque and the madrasah. There is also the argument that Weber overstated the impact of imperial military institutions and values on Islam, and at the same time neglected the role of the Sufi brotherhoods as conduits of trade, especially between the Middle East and Southeast Asia. Although these criticisms are substantial, Weber's sociological perspective continues to influence more debates, often implicitly, around the compatibility between Islam and democratic institutions. Indeed, the 'clash of civilizations' can be regarded as a revival of Weber's own civilizational analysis.

The Sociology of Confucianism

Weber's study of Confucianism and Taoism has received considerable scholarly attention, and his argument is relatively well known of China (Bellah 1963; Eisenstadt, 1985; Schluchter 1983; Sprenkel 1964). In Weber's typology of religious orientations to the world, Islam and Confucianism stand at opposite ends. In fact, it is not clear that Confucianism is a religion at all in Weber's terms. Weber (1951: 152) observed that 'Confucianism, like Buddhism, consisted only of ethics and in this *Tao* corresponds to the Indian *dharma*.... Confucianism meant adjustment to the world, to its orders and conventions. Ultimately it represented just a tremendous code of political maxims and rules of social propriety for the cultured men of the world.'

Weber observed that Confucianism tolerated a range of popular cults and did attempt to systematize them into a coherent religious doctrine. Confucianism did not represent a challenge to the world, and was content to teach an adjustment to the secular sphere. The morally superior man of the educated literati would stay away from any pursuit of wealth in this world, and as a consequence, the educated bureaucrat of the imperial civil service was honoured far more than the business man.

In general, Weber did not believe that happiness was a genuine goal of ethics; hence he attacked utilitarianism. He was equally scornful of Freudianism, which he regarded as a form of mental hygiene which sought to make men happy. In this respect, Weber may have followed Nietzsche, who had condemned what he called the 'Happiness of the Last Man'. This may in part explain his criticism of Confucianism, in which the deities of the Chinese heavens 'obviously desired only the happiness of the world and especially the happiness of man' (Weber 1951: 153).

By comparison with the Abrahamic religions, is Confucianism a religion at all? Chinese civilization has no tradition of prophecy, and did not develop a sacerdotal stratum of priests with control over sacraments. In one sense, the emperor was the high priest of the state religion. The worship of deities was a matter of state business, while ancestor worship was required of all social classes. There was no soteriology as such, and the 'Confucian had no desire to be "saved" either from the migration of souls or from punishment in the beyond' (Weber 1951: 156). In this sense Confucianism was a state theory which institutionalized filial piety as the core duty of religious activity. Confucianism tolerated both magic and mysticism, provided they were useful instruments for controlling the masses. From the perspective of the elite, 'magic was powerless in the face of virtue. He who loved the classical way of life need not fear the spirits; only lack of virtue in high places gave power to the spirits' (Weber 1951: 155). Both Buddhism and Christianity were opposed at various stages by the emperor, because they were a threat to both social order and devotion to the emperor cult. We can reasonably regard Confucianism as the state religion of the literati, and Taoism as the popular religion of the masses.

In Weber's sociology of religion, Confucianism and Puritanism both represented significant, but alternative, types of rationalization, in that they offered pious frameworks for the regulation of the everyday world. Both promoted self-regulation and restraint, but Confucianism sought to preserve and defend a status hierarchy based on the ideal of the educated gentleman, filial piety, and civilized behaviour as conservative life orientations. Puritanism promoted piety as a technique for a 'revolution of the saints'. Paradoxically, Puritan vocations also contributed to the fashioning of rational capitalism in the West. By contrast, Weber identified a variety of conditions that inhibited capitalism in China. These included the fact that many technical innovations were opposed by conservative religious groups. The very strength of the kinship system and ancestor worship protected its members from adversity and discouraged a work discipline and the rationalization of work processes. These same kinship groups prevented the development of modern legal institutions, the codification of laws, and the rise of a class of professional lawyers.

Weber's analysis of Confucianism has of course been much disputed. He did not consider the widespread influence of Confucianism outside China, for example in Vietnam and Japan. In the Japanese case, Confucianism often played a more radical political role in opposition to Shinto. Despite these criticisms, Weber's view of Chinese capitalism continues to influence research, for example with respect to the entrepreneurial role of overseas Chinese communities in the global economy (Redding 1993). Weber was deeply influential in the development of Robert Bellah's sociological research on Asia. For example, Bellah (2003) came to the conclusion that what he called 'bureaucratic individualism' was characteristic of both Japan and Confucian China, and this form of individualism was itself the outcome of a process of rationalization.

Weber's views have also been attacked by philosophers who have promoted neo-Confucianism as an ethical system that can simultaneously fill the moral gap left by the collapse of secular communism and compete with Western individualism as an account of personal development. In the Cultural Revolution (1966–76), Mao Zedong encouraged students to denounce the traditions of their elders as feudal and counter-revolutionary. This experience was profoundly shocking for this generation, because it flew completely in the face of the Confucian tradition of filial piety. Contemporary neo-Confucianism has been supported by some scholars as an important defence of the cultural standing of education in many Asian societies, as an effective political theory of good governance, and as a valuable framework for self-realization (Bell and Chaibong 2003). A prominent figure in this development of neo-Confucianism is Professor Tu Wei-Ming, Director of the Harvard–Yenching Institute, who has emphasized the importance of the social relations within which the self emerges in continuous dialogue with others, thereby rejecting the traditional Western view of the isolated, sovereign self. He is also critical of interpretations of the Confucian *Analects*, including Weber's reading of Confucian political theory, in which the individual is forced into submission in the interests of social order. Tu Wei-Ming (1985) has categorically rejected Weber's view that Confucianism required the individual to undertake an 'adjustment to the world' (Weber 1951: 235).

These criticisms of Weber point at one level to the limitations of Weber's notion of the ideal type, which extracts from a complex array of empirical data an interpretation for the purpose of comparative and historical research. Tu Wei-Ming and others are presenting a more complex historical picture of Confucianism, noting, among other things, the subtle but important variations in Confucian influences in China, Vietnam, Korea, and Japan (Oldstone-Moore 2005). In defence of Weber, we might note that Tu Wei-Ming is himself constructing a particular interpretation of Confucian thought, stressing the centrality of the idea of personal virtue or piety in Confucian ethics. Clearly Confucian piety and Protestant piety were very different, given the different concepts of the self in these contrasting traditions.

Conclusion: Religion, Economics, and Politics

Weber's analysis of Christian radicalism in relation to Islam has become an implicit dimension of the clash of civilizations thesis (Huntington 1997), and his analysis of Christian dynamism in relation to Confucianism continues to form the principal foundation of theories of the rise of capitalism in modern Asia (Bellah 1963). Whereas sociologists have often neglected the social role of religion in advanced capitalism, accepting the secularization thesis, Weber placed religion at the centre of the social world. Indeed, religion was a core-defining sphere of meaning. Although social scientists have been critical of the Huntington thesis, from a Weberian perspective the struggle between religions must be an inevitable outcome of the process of globalization. Weber's vision of world cultures presupposes a Darwinian struggle for survival, or 'elbow room', as he claimed in his Freiburg inaugural lecture in May 1895 (Weber 1989). Despite their normative commitment to the principles of 'brotherly love', even Islam and Christianity must participate in this global struggle. At the same time, Confucianism as the ethic of civic stability has been drawn into the ideological justification of the Asian capitalist tigers.

Finally, we should return to the central issues of secularization that were important in Weber's sociology, but which we must now conceptualize in the context of globalization. In retrospect, the twentieth century witnessed two forms of secularization. First there was the intensification of individualism that was associated with neo-liberalism and the commodity boom of the 1970s. The global deregulation of financial and labour markets transformed the economies of the world and installed hedonism as the ethic of a consumer society, as foretold in an article written in the winter of 1969 and 1970 by Daniel Bell and later published as *The Cultural Contradictions of Capitalism* (1976). The second form of secularization—and one strangely ignored by sociologists—was the spread of atheist ideology through communism in Russia, eastern Europe, Asia, and Latin America. In Russia, Vietnam, and China this movement involved the active suppression of religion. Both forms of secularism—liberal and Communist—appear for the time being to have stalled. There is for many sociologists a 'desecularization' of the world (Berger 1999), and again this development was partly foreseen by Bell (1980: 353), who spoke of the 'exhaustion of Modernism' and the 'aridity of Communism' in his Hobhouse lecture of 1977 on 'the return of the sacred'. We might say that 'resacralization' has also taken two forms. First there is a worldwide resurgence of evangelical fundamentalism in Christianity, Islam, and Judaism; but similar global transformations have been taking place in Buddhism and Hinduism. These movements involve various levels of 'pietization': namely, the spread of personal discipline. Second, there is the spread of 'new spiritualism': namely, personal, syncretistic, commodified, and de-institutionalized religiosity (Hunt 2005). Revivalism in both Islam and Christianity are overtly hostile to the commercialization of popular New Age spirituality, offering instead a highly disciplined piety. Neo-Confucianism also offers a subjectivity that requires training and discipline rather than experience and emotion as orientations to the everyday world. However, what is true in all religions is that the life and authority of the educated, elite carriers of religion is challenged by popular 'spiritual markets' (Roof 1999) that cater to the masses. In this sense the traditional relationship between the virtuosi and the mass has been inverted by global commercialism. While Weber's Kantian view of the self-limiting nature of Protestant rationalism may have been valid, the paradoxical re-enchantment of the world through a global spiritual marketplace appears to contradict Weber's general secularization thesis.

References

Ahmed, Leila (1992). *Women and Gender in Islam: Historical Roots of a Modern Debate.* New Haven and London: Yale University Press.

Bell, Daniel (1976). *The Cultural Contradictions of Capitalism.* London: Heinemann.

—— (1980). *The Winding Passage: Essays and Sociological Journeys 1960–1980.* New York: Basic Books.

—— and Chaibong, Hahm (eds.) (2003). *Confucianism for the Modern World.* Cambridge: Cambridge University Press.

Bellah, Robert N. (1963). 'Reflections on the Protestant Ethic Analogy in Asia'. *Journal of Social Issues,* 19/1: 52–61.

—— (2003). *Imagining Japan: The Japanese Tradition and its Modern Interpretations.* Berkeley: University of California Press.

Berger, Peter L. (ed.) (1999). *The Desecularization of the World: Resurgent Religion and World Politics.* Grand Rapids, Mich.: William B. Eerdmans.

Eisenstadt, Shmuel N. (1985). 'This-Worldly Transcendentalism and the Structuring of the World: Weber's *Religion of China* and the Format of Chinese History and Civilization'. *Journal of Developing Societies,* 1–2: 168–86.

Foucault, Michel (1997). 'Technologies of the Self'. In *Ethics: The Essential Works,* i. London: Allen Lane, 223–51.

Gerth, Hans, and Mills, C. Wright (eds.) (1991). *From Max Weber.* London: Routledge.

Hennis, Wilhelm (1988). *Max Weber: Essays in Reconstruction.* London: Allen and Unwin.

Hodgson, Marshall G. S. (1960). 'A Comparison of Islam and Christianity as Frameworks for Religious Life'. *Diogenes,* 32: 49–74.

—— (1974). *The Venture of Islam: Conscience and History in a World Civilization.* Chicago and London: University of Chicago Press.

Huff, Toby, and Schulchter, Wolfgang (eds.) (1999). *Max Weber and Islam.* New Brunswick, NJ: Transaction Publishers.

Hunt, Stephen (2005). *Religion and Everyday Life.* London and New York: Routledge.

Huntington, Samuel (1997). *The Clash of Civilizations: Remaking of World Order.* New York: Touchstone.

Kamali, M. (2001). 'Civil Society and Islam: A Sociological Perspective'. *European Journal of Social Theory*, 4/2: 131–52.

Kant, Immanuel (1998). *Religion within the Boundaries of Mere Reason*. Cambridge: Cambridge University Press.

Löwith, Karl (1993). *Max Weber and Karl Marx*. London: Routledge.

Marlow, Louise (1997). *Hierarchy and Egalitarianism in Islamic Thought*. Cambridge: Cambridge University Press.

Mitzman, Arthur (1971). *The Iron Cage: An Historical Interpretation of Max Weber*. New York: Universal Library.

Oldstone-Moore, Jennifer (2005). 'Confucianism'. In Michael D. Coogan (ed.), *Eastern Religions*. London: Duncan Baird, 314–415.

Parsons, Talcott (1966). 'Introduction'. In Weber (1966), pp. xix–lxvii.

Redding, Gordon (1993). *The Spirit of Chinese Capitalism*. Berlin: De Gruyter.

Rodinson, Maxime (1978). *Islam and Capitalism*. Austin, Tex.: University of Texas Press.

Roof, Wade Clark (1999). *Spiritual Marketplace: Baby Boomers and the Remaking of American Religion*. Princeton and Oxford: Princeton University Press.

Roy, Olivier (1994). *The Failure of Political Islam*. Cambridge, Mass.: Harvard University Press.

Said, Edward W. (1978). *Orientalism*. London: Routledge.

Schluchter, Wolfgang (ed.) (1983). *Max Webers Studie über das Konfuzianismus und Taoismus: Interpretation und Kritik*. Frankfurt: Suhrkamp.

—— (ed.) (1987). *Max Webers Sicht des Islams: Interpretation und Kritik*. Frankfurt: Suhrkamp.

Sprenkel, O. B. van der (1964). 'Max Weber on China'. *History and Theory*, 3/3: 348–70.

Stauth, Georg, and Turner, Bryan S. (1986). 'Nietzsche in Weber oder die Geburt des modernen Genius im professionellen Menschen'. *Zeitschrift für Soziologie*, 15/2: 81–94.

Strauss, Leo (1953). *Natural Right and History*. Chicago: University of Chicago Press.

Tenbruck, Friedrich (1975). 'Das Werk. Max Webers'. *Kölner Zeitschrift für Soziologie und Sozialpsychologie*, 27: 663–702.

—— (1980). 'The Problem of the Thematic Unity in the Works of Max Weber'. *British Journal of Sociology*, 31/3: 316–51.

Thompson, Edward Palmer (1963). *The Making of the English Working Class*, 2nd edn. London: Victor Gollancz.

Tribe, Keith (ed.) (1989). *Reading Weber*. London and New York: Routledge.

Tu Wei-Ming (1985). *Confucian Thought: Selfhood as Creative Transformation*. New York: State University of New York Press.

Turner, Bryan S. (1974). *Weber and Islam: A Critical Study*. London: Routledge & Kegan Paul.

—— (1978). *Marx and the End of Orientalism*. London: Allen & Unwin.

—— (1983). *Religion and Social Theory*. London: Heinemann.

—— (1993). 'Preface'. In Löwith (1993), 1–32.

—— (1994). *Orientalism, Postmodernism and Globalism*. London: Routledge.

Weber, Max (1921). *Gesammelte Aufsätze zur Religions soziologie*. Tübingen: J. C. B. Mohr.

—— (1951). *The Religion of China: Confucianism and Taoism*. New York: Macmillan.

—— (1952). *Ancient Judaism*. Glencoe, Ill.: Free Press.

—— (1958*a*). *The City*. New York: Free Press.

—— (1958*b*). *The Religion of India, the Sociology of Hinduism and Buddhism*. New York: Free Press.

—— (1965). *The Protestant Ethic and the Spirit of Capitalism*. London: Allen & Unwin.

—— (1966). *The Sociology of Religion*. London: Methuen.

—— (1968). *Economy and Society*. New York: Bedminster Press.

—— (1976). *The Protestant Ethic and the Spirit of Capitalism*, 2nd edn. with an introduction by Anthony Giddens. London: Allen & Unwin.

—— (1989). 'The National State and Economic Policy'. In Keith Tribe (ed.), *Reading Weber*, London and New York: Routledge, 188–209.

Suggested Reading

Gilsenan, Michael (1990). *Recognizing Islam: Religion and Society in the Modern Middle East*. London: I. B. Tauris.

Hodgson, Marshall G. S. (1993). *Rethinking World History*. Cambridge: Cambridge University Press.

Ikels, Charlotte (ed.) (2004). *Filial Piety: Practice and Discourse in Contemporary China*. Stanford, Calif.: Stanford University Press.

Lehmann, Hartmut, and Ouedraogo, Jean Martin (eds.) (2003). *Max Webers Religionssoziologie in interkultureller Perspektive*. Göttingen: Vandenhoeck & Ruprecht.

Sharot, Stephen (2001). *A Comparative Sociology of World Religions: Virtuosos, Priests and Popular Religion*. New York: New York University Press.

Turner, Bryan S. (ed.) (2003). *Islam: Critical Concepts in Sociology*, 4 vols. London and New York: Routledge.

Waley, Arthur (1988). *The Analects of Confucius*. London: Unwin Hyman.

Yang, Fenggang, and Tamney, Joseph B. (eds.) (2005). *State, Market and Religions in Chinese Societies*. Leiden: Brill.

CHAPTER 5

RELIGION IN THE WORKS OF HABERMAS, BOURDIEU, AND FOUCAULT

INGER FURSETH

THIS chapter discusses how the theoretical perspectives of Jürgen Habermas, Pierre Bourdieu, and Michel Foucault may illuminate studies of religion. Although these contemporary social and cultural theorists have not written extensively on religion, it does appear as a theme in their work. Their conceptual tools are also used more generally in studies of religion, which call for attention to these theorists by sociologists of religion. Here, I will first give a brief presentation of Habermas's, Bourdieu's, and Foucault's critiques of religion, before looking at the possible implications that their theories may have for understanding religion in present-day society.

Thanks to Peter Clarke and Ole Riis for their helpful comments and suggestions for changes.

Jürgen Habermas: Religion in the Public Sphere

In his earlier work, Jürgen Habermas (1929–) largely follows Weber's theory of rationalization and secularization. His theory of religion is related to his understanding of the dual structure of society comprised of system and life world. He sees the life world as a "finite province of meaning" and as a public sphere of communicative action (Habermas 1980[1973]: 117–18). Traditions, values, and religion constitute part of the life world, on which communicative competence is based.

For Habermas, religion is integral to social evolution, even if it is not abolished by evolution (Mendieta 2005: 8). In *Legitimation Crisis* (1980[1973]: 119–20) he argues that modernization has resulted in an independent sphere of secular knowledge and the limitation of religion to questions of meaning and purpose. The life world is threatened by reification due to trespassing by the non-communicative media of money and power. The rational potential of the life world is realized when formal processes of communicative action, *discourses*, are institutionalized. For Habermas, the emergence of undistorted communication is a fulfillment of the Enlightenment ideal. Religion is bound to lose its relevance in modern, differentiated society, where "the authority of the holy is gradually replaced by the authority of an achieved consensus" (1987[1981]: 77). Religious discourse is also "limited in the degree of its freedom of communication" (1992: 233). However, there is one exception, where religion may have a function, and this is in the communication process of the life world. In some theological debates, the idea of God is transformed into an abstraction that shares those characteristic traits that Habermas believes describe the ideal form of communication (Habermas 1980 [1973]: 121).

In *The Theory of Communicative Action* (1981), Habermas develops his sociology of religion further. Here, his view on religion is based on a theory of the "linguistification of the sacred", a developmental process whereby that which has been perceived as a referent set apart, God, comes to be known immanently as a communicative structure (Habermas 1987[1981]: 77–111). Mythical views of the world involve little or no differentiation between culture and nature, or between language and world. Since mythical world views hinder a clear demarcation of a domain of subjectivity, full communication is not possible under the conditions of religion (1984[1981]: 49–52). Thus, discourses can include talk about the truth and rightfulness of religion, but religion will not serve emancipated communicative action in any fundamental way (1982: 251).

Scholars have objected to Habermas's theory of the public sphere by pointing out that his ideal speech community assumes a singular public sphere rather than a multiplicity of public spheres (Calhoun 1992: 34–5; 1995; Herbert 1996; 2003). He also tends to overemphasize the importance of consensus as the outcome of rational discourse rather than consider the relationship between different and competing public spheres. In addition, arguments have been raised against his view of religion as anathema to rational critical discourse. He interprets religion as "a monolithic and reified phenomenon", and ignores the various philosophical influences upon it (Dillon 1999: 290–1). Thereby, he overlooks the fact that contemporary religion and theology "bring the critical principles of the Enlightenment into religion itself and into theological reflection" (Fiorenza 1992: 74). Habermas's polarization of reason and religion prevents an understanding of reasoned debates within various religious traditions of doctrine, interpretations, and scripture.

Other scholars claim that while Habermas is a secularist, it is a misconception that he is anti-religion (Mendieta 2002). He acknowledges the role that religion has played in the identity of the West, and views religion as a fundamental part of the life world. Religion also provides societies with common languages they use to address hopes and discontents (Mendieta 2005: 8). Indeed, Habermas has opened up for discussion the idea that religion can contribute in a positive way to social development. Although he still thinks that religious statements made in the public sphere must be transformed into a general language, he emphasizes that secular actors must also be willing to understand religion (Habermas 2006; Habermas and Ratzinger 2007). Religion has a role in the public sphere in the West, and Western societies are now what he calls "post-secular". Habermas has become a spokesperson for post-metaphysical thought. He continues to build on a sharp division between faith and knowledge, but he argues against the use of "a scientifically limited conception of reason" and the idea that religious doctrines must be excluded from "the genealogy of rationality" (Habermas 2006: 16). Habermas concludes that "post-metaphysical thought is prepared to learn from religion, but remains agnostic in the process" (2006: 17).

Nevertheless, Habermas's idea of "the totalizing trait of a mode of believing that infuses the very pores of daily life" (2006: 8) shows that he sees religion as a phenomenon severed from practical reason, social context, and everyday experiences. He also fails to see that religious identity can be one of multiple identities (along with gender, sexuality, and ethnicity) that in some instances are in contradiction to each other, as, for example, the identity of being lesbian or gay and evangelical Christian (Thumma and Gray 2005; Wilcox 2003).

European and American theologians have included Habermas in their discussions for decades (Adams 2006; Arens 1989; Browning and Fiorenza 1992; de Roest 1998; Garrigan 2004; Geyer, Janowski, and Schmidt 1970; Siebert 1985), a fact that puzzles Habermas (1992: 226). Some have suggested that the affinity theologians have for Habermas is related to their need to demonstrate dialogue with contemporary society (Lindhardt 2006: 66–7). Nevertheless, Habermas's theories are relevant for sociological analyses of the role of religion in liberal democratic societies. The contemporary United States experiences conflicting values regarding the political role of religion in the state and the public sphere (Demerath 2001). Most European countries are attempting to adjust to a growing religious diversity and its implications for the role of religion in the public sphere (Byrnes and Katzenstein 2006; Cesari and McLoughlin 2005). Habermas's theories suggest that embedded in modern liberal institutions there is a place for reason, emancipation, and rational-critical communication. Thus, they offer an optimistic view of the human capacity to communicate and function together, even in situations of different secular and religious world views and traditions. In many ways, the shifting focus of religion in Habermas's thinking reflects a thinker who interprets the changing role of religion in the world.

Pierre Bourdieu: Religious Field and Habitus

Pierre Bourdieu's (1930–2002) view of religion has been termed "paradoxical" (Dianteill 2003: 529; Kühle 2004: 37). Although his direct contributions to the field are relatively modest, some of his most important concepts such as "belief" (*croyance*) and "field" (*champ*) were developed from the social-scientific study of religion (Bourdieu 1994*a*[1982–7]: 22, 49).

Bourdieu's most thorough sociological discussions of religion were originally published in 1971 (1971*a*, *b*), and preceded *Outline of a Theory of Practice* (1977 [1972]). In these early articles, Bourdieu draws heavily on classical sociology, in particular Marx and Weber (Dianteill 2003; Kühle 2004; Swartz 1996; 1997: 41–5; Verter 2003). His aim is to detect the strategies used by the dominant classes to sustain their power and prestige. Bourdieu analyzes Weber's theory of religious power by using the notion of "field", which refers to "the set of all the possible objective relations between positions" (Bourdieu 1987[1971]: 121). Urbanization and division of labor led to the constitution of a relatively autonomous "religious field" characterized by the structure of relations among different categories of laypersons and religious agents, such as prophets and priests (1971*a*: 301). The symbolic interactions that take place in the religious field are results of the religious interests in play (1987[1971]: 122).

Competition for religious power has to do with competition for religious legitimacy: that is, the legitimate power of the specialists to modify the practice and world view of lay people by imposing on them "a religious habitus" (Bourdieu 1971*b*: 11; 1971*a*: 319; 1991[1971]: 22). The notion of habitus refers to the "matrix of perceptions" or "the basis of perception and appreciation of all subsequent experiences" (1977[1972]: 78). The dynamics of the religious field are characterized by the relations of competition between specialists and the exchange relations between specialists and laypersons.

Drawing on Weber's idea of charisma and legitimacy, Bourdieu develops a theory of symbolic power. The term "symbolic" is related to the construction of reality, which establishes order and meaning in the social world (Bourdieu 1994*b*[1982]: 166). Religions can only produce the legitimation they produce by simultaneously producing what Bourdieu terms "misrecognition" (*méconnaissance*) of the real conditions (1971*a*: 310). "Misrecognition" refers to "false consciousness" or "denial" of the fundamental interests at play in a set of practices (Rey 2004: 334; Swartz 1996: 76–7). One example is religious specialists who conceal that their struggles have political interests at stake (Bourdieu 1971*a*: 316–17; Bourdieu and Saint-Martin 1982).

Religious legitimacy reflects the religious power relations at the time, and is related to the degree to which an agent has control over what Bourdieu terms "material and symbolic weapons of religious violence" (1987[1971]: 128). An example of such a weapon is the excommunication of a priest. For Bourdieu, power and domination have to do with the domination of the categories of perception (1971*a*: 328), in the sense that the dominant culture establishes distinctions and categories of "true religion" versus "heresy", for example, which always favor those who are in power. This means that those who are dominated tend to diminish themselves and their own religious perceptions. This is a condition that Bourdieu describes as "symbolic violence" (1971*a*: 322). Thus, religious violence is another form of symbolic violence.

Bourdieu's early sociology of religion is strongly colored by his situatedness in French society, with its dominating Roman Catholic Church (Dianteill 2003: 534; Robertson 1992: 154). His definition of religion, for example, centers on "the goods of salvation" (*les biens de salud*) (Bourdieu 1971*a*: 299, 318–19), which refers to sacraments and membership in a church that is regarded as requisite to salvation (Rey 2004: 337). Others have suggested that Bourdieu has a relatively "unidimensional" view of religion, interpreting it almost entirely in organizational terms (Verter 2003: 151). Therefore, he fails to address relevant issues in contemporary religious life, such as individual "bricolage" of beliefs that operate more or less outside institutions (Engler 2003: 455, 457; Verter 2003: 151).

In the 1970s Bourdieu presented religion as one of many symbolic systems of classification (Bourdieu 1971*a*: 308). In the 1990s he seemed to have subsumed his work on religion under that of culture, stating that "the sociology of culture is the sociology of the religion of our day" (Bourdieu 1993: 132). Several scholars find central concepts such as habitus, capital, and field useful in understanding the interaction between the individual and social dimensions of religion (Rey 2007). The concept of habitus, for example, has, been used to analyze the interactions and relations between Muslim women of different ethnic and national backgrounds. A study of predominantly Asian Muslim women in their early teaching careers in England showed that the differences in social habitus affected their relations with other teachers (Benn 2003).

The women felt isolated when interacting with secular teachers because conversations about lifestyle choices, food, holidays, and entertainment were antithetical to their Muslim lifestyles. On some level, they could relate to white Christian teachers, because they were both outsiders, and to other non-Muslim Asian women, but they would connect at the deepest level only with other Asian Muslim women (Benn 2003). The concepts of habitus, capital, and field have also been used in studies of competition in the religious field in societies characterized by sharp social class and/or ethnic divisions (Rey 2004), religio-political ethnic movements (Yadgar 2003), as well as broader issues of struggle over religion in the United States (Swartz 1996: 83).

In 1979 Bourdieu's most influential work, *Distinction*, was published. Here, he analyzes differences in taste between various social classes (1986[1979]: 111). Bourdieu develops the notion that cultural capital is a matter of disposition, not just acquisition. Religion and spirituality can function as "distinctions" in the sense that one seeks out "that which is rare, distinguished and separate" (1994*a*[1982–7]: 150). One study interprets spiritual capital, such as piety, as a form of cultural capital and a matter of taste. In this context, the religious taste and practice of high-status individuals have had a broad impact on religious diffusion. Examples are celebrities such as Aldous Huxley (Vedanta), Jack Kerouac (Zen), the Beatles (Transcendental Meditation), Shirley MacLaine (channeling), Richard Gere (Tibetan Buddhism), and Madonna (Kabbalah) (Verter 2003). Another study inspired by Bourdieu is a comprehensive study of social space and the space of lifestyles, including religious lifestyles, in the Norwegian town of Stavanger (Rosenlund 2000). Thus, Bourdieu's distinctions between cultural, economic, social, and symbolic capital can be fruitful in analyses of social class and religion.

Bourdieu addresses different ways in which religion is an instrument of knowledge and communication, a theme addressed by Habermas, as well as by Berger and Luckmann (1981). The contribution of Bourdieu is that he relates religion to power and domination, themes that Berger and Luckmann neglect (Beckford 1987: 16). His conceptual tools are fruitful in understanding how formation of meaning and identity can be constituted by power, and how religion can function as a "distinction" in contemporary society.

Michel Foucault: Religion, Governmentality, and the Body

Although Michel Foucault (1926–84) does not offer any systematic examination of religious themes, he looks at Christianity as an important shaping force in Western history, and there are underlying religious questions hidden in much of his work

1999; 2000; Pinto 2002). For the most part, Foucault's critique of religion it in negative terms. Nevertheless, his work also reveals a more positive or ious view on religious discourse (McCall 2004: 7).

cault delivers a critique of religion in several different ways. In his early work produced in the 1950s and 1960s, he focused on the repressive nature of religion, and engaged in the "death of God" discourse (Foucault 1999: 85–6). *Madness and Civilization* (1967[1961]) and *The Birth of the Clinic* (1973[1963]) present religion as a part of the culture that influences and determines how madness and medicine have been understood in the West. In his examination of how knowledge is reconstituted in different historical periods in *The Order of Things* (1970[1966]), he calls these particular knowledge forms *epistēmē*, by which he means sets of presuppositions that organize what counts as knowledge, reality, and truth, and indicate how these matters can be discussed. Later, Foucault began to explore how a discourse is formed. In *Discipline and Punish: The Birth of the Prison* (1977[1975]) he examines how power and knowledge are bound up in a complex "network of relations" and demonstrates how different models of punishment have a religious basis, especially in developing a concern for the soul and its improvement.

Foucault's critique of religion also focuses on religious authority. In the multi-volume *History of Sexuality* (1976–84), he engages in an explicit discussion of Christianity by examining confession and the ethics of self. Like Bourdieu, Foucault's French Catholic heritage influences his work, which he also admits (Schuld 2003: 1). According to Foucault, sexuality is not a given, but is historically constructed (1986 [1976]). Early notions in the Greco-Roman world of sexuality were modified by Christianity through its ideas about "finitude, the Fall and evil" (Foucault 1988 [1984]: 239). The sexual discourse during the eighteenth and nineteenth centuries was largely established by the Christian practice of confession and was later adopted by secular practices, such as medicine, psychiatry, and pedagogy (Schuld 2003: 145, 148).

In texts such as "Omnes et Singulatim" (2000*a*[1994]) Foucault shows how the Christian "pastoral modality of power" leads to practices in modern society that seek to govern all aspects of life. In "What is Critique?" (1996) he points out that the Christian pastoral practice developed the idea that every individual "ought to be governed and ought to let himself be governed" by being directed toward his salvation by someone (God) to whom he is bound in total obedience (Foucault 1996: 383). In this way, religion is a set of discourses and practices that seek to govern individuals and groups of individuals.

According to Jeremy R. Carrette (2000: 143–51), Foucault's critique of religion operates on the basis of five interrelated factors. First, religion and culture are integrated in Foucault's work. Second, Foucault believes that religious discourse is framed and positioned in and through the human process of power/knowledge. Third, discourses on religious faith and practice center on the body—as, for example, by regulating sexuality through discourses on sin and salvation. Furthermore, and fourth, religion is a system of power, as it orders life through a set of forced relations. Finally, religion attempts to govern the self. In modern society, people discipline themselves as good citizens and diligent workers. Foucault does not envision a future of increasing liberation, even if religion is left behind (Herbert 2003: 87). His critique of religion implies a critique of all regimes of knowledge.

In spite of this relatively negative view of religion, there is simultaneously a more positive view of it present in Foucault's work. This view focuses on the capacity of religion to foster a critique of, and contest, governmentality and state control (McCall 2004: 8). In "What is Critique?" he traces the idea of "how not to be governed" or "not accepting it as true because an authority tells you that it is true" (1996: 384). For him, critiquing can be a means for the individual to practice autonomy (Foucault 1997[1994]: 323). The Protestant Reformation is the first movement in the way of the art of not being governed, because it represents a refusal of, and challenge to, ecclesiastical discourse and practice. The second example is found in Foucault's analysis of the Iranian revolution (Leezenberg 2004; McCall 2004: 8). In "Useless to Revolt?" (2000*b*[1994]) he argues that revolutions can be religious and provide a basis for social change. Nevertheless, these two religious movements differ in important ways, as the Reformation implies a turn to individuality, whereas the Iranian revolution expresses a form of general will. The questioning of authority in the Reformation eventually led to questioning all forms of authority, which made it an important example of critique, and thus an example of individual autonomy.

Altogether, reflections on the role of religious movements are important because they affect thinking about the role of religion in society and the relations between religion and the state. Foucault's skepticism about the various devices for governing people can provide insights into studies of religious movements, as these tend to challenge current ideas of what are acceptable and unacceptable symbols and expressions. His analytical tools can be used to study conversion and recruitment processes to religious movements, where confession is central in affecting human subjectivity and action. Yet, his approach can also shed light on specific explanatory categories deployed in anti-cult discourse, such as the medicalization of the "cult" problem (Beckford 2003: 184).

Foucault is established as an important figure in debates on the body and sexuality, and thus on religion, sexuality, and the body (Carrette 2004; Jordan 2004; Mahon 2004). His work is useful in understanding how religious practices have been applied to discipline the body and how these practices are related to power. Inspired by Foucault, some scholars have also called for "a theology of the body" that incorporates the insights of feminist and Foucauldian scholarship (Bernauer and Carrette 2004; Carrette and King 1998: 131).

Foucault has been criticized for focusing on a white, male, Western tradition and failing to address the effect that power has on dominated groups, such as women and ethnic minorities (Bartky 1999). His analysis of discourses of power, truth, sexuality, and religion is viewed as a masculine analysis. In addition, Foucault's notion of power is too diffuse, and it makes resistance impossible (Sandmo 1999: 88). Nevertheless, Foucault's work continues to be relevant to analyses of religion and power, religion and culture, and religion and the body.

Power and Religion

A common theme in the theories of Habermas, Bourdieu, and Foucault is power. Here, we will attempt to detect their different understandings of power, and the implications that these differences have for their views on religion. To illustrate, we will discuss the Muslim headscarf, which is a contested religious symbol often debated in terms of power in contemporary Western and some Muslim societies.

One of the most fundamental concepts in Habermas's theory of power is the concept of communicative power (Høibraaten 1999). Communicative power arises between actors who in fellowship search for correct norms for social interaction and act accordingly, because they have been freely convinced of their validity. In Habermas's early work, religion has little or no relevance in the public sphere of modern, differentiated society, as religious discourse will not serve the emancipated communicative action or the free everyday communicative practices. If we apply these notions to the issue of the Muslim headscarf, the hijab has a place only in the private sphere of the lives of Muslim women. It could be a hindrance to rational communication in the public sphere, because this sphere is characterized by secular knowledge.

However, one of the key aspects in the contemporary public sphere is what may be called "identity politics" (Warner 1992: 378). Social and religious movements increasingly focus on the personal identity formation of minority groups and make appeals for respect for their difference. In the early 1990s, Charles Taylor (1992; 2003) addressed the claims made by ethnic groups to maintain a distinctive identity and engage in "the politics of recognition". Habermas conceded that the "politics of recognition" has become a chief concern of public culture. The question Taylor raised was whether it was possible to organize a society around a strong collective definition without limiting the basic rights of people who did not share this definition. Habermas's reply to Taylor was that the social glue in complex societies was based on consensus about procedures for legality and exercise of political power (Habermas 1994: 139). Even in religiously diverse societies, it is the burden of the faithful to "endure the secularization of knowledge and the pluralism of world pictures regardless of the religious truths they hold" (Habermas 2002: 151).

In Habermas's later work, religion has a place in discourse, but only on the premises of rationality. When religious statements are made in the public sphere, they must be transformed into a general language, using rational arguments. Based on this premise, religious statements are legitimate in the public sphere, and religion can become a legitimate partner in the democratic discourse (Habermas 2006). Thereby, the hijab can be used as a religious symbol and statement in the public sphere, but only if the women who wear it argue for their use of this symbol according to universal norms for rational debate. Habermas admits that "secular citizens or those of other religious persuasions can under certain circumstances learn something from religious contributions" (Habermas 2006: 10), which must include statements made by covered Muslim women. In this way, the hijab can be brought out into the public sphere.

Habermas tends to discuss legitimate domination as a question of references to laws, norms, and principles that make people accept authority. Although Bourdieu agrees with Habermas that these forms of legitimation can be important, he views the most effective form of domination as the ones that are not justified at all, but are taken for granted and perceived as "natural". Thus, Bourdieu and Foucault represent a shift in focus, as they emphasize power as something that is part of the most trivial practices, thoughts, and discourses (Danielsen and Hansen 1999: 53–4, 63–4).

An overall aim in Bourdieu's sociology is to detect hidden power relations and mechanisms that create social inequality. Religious power is connected to positions in the religious field, to the structure of relations among different categories of religious agents and laypersons. If we return to the example of the hijab, Muslim authoritative leaders can be interpreted as those who produce and reproduce "secret knowledge" (and therefore rare knowledge) (Bourdieu 1971*a*: 304)—that is, true interpretations according to the Qur'an and the *hadiths* (the literature on the Prophet's statements and actions). These religious leaders also possess cultural capital in the form of education and scriptural knowledge. Traditionally, Muslim women have, as laypersons, been excluded from this knowledge, and therefore they have been dependent upon the interpretations and instructions of male religious authorities. The recent growth in numbers of women Muslim scholars means that they are able to acquire "secret knowledge" hitherto reserved for men, and thus possess cultural and religious capital, even if women Muslim scholars still do not have the same authority and inhabit the same positions as male Muslim leaders do.

Many religious leaders want to impose on the Muslim women "a religious habitus", or a disposition to cover and the practices that go along with it. This "habitus" is not necessarily conscious, but it is taken for granted and perceived as common in the group as a demonstration of "good" taste for proper Muslim women. In return, the women who comply with the religious ideal of covering will receive legitimations of their place in public and private and of their privileges as true Muslim women. The hijab provides the women with a sense of honor and dignity, which creates moral obligations in men to treat them with respect. In this way, there is an exchange in this religious field built on a shared understanding of field and habitus.

Nevertheless, the distinctions between the women who cover and those who do not are political in nature, because they justify social class or group domination. In Bourdieu's terms, the hijab can be seen as a symbol of misrecognition, where the real and worldly conditions are hidden: namely, that male religious authorities (even if there are some female scholars) exercise power and domination over women. The idea that women must cover favors men who are in power, whereas the women who are dominated diminish themselves and their perceptions by going along with this idea. To use Bourdieu's terms, the hijab becomes a form of symbolic violence.

Since Habermas has such a strong focus on communication, he does not emphasize the body as important in secular or religious understanding. However, perspectives offered by Bourdieu and Foucault can be used to recognize that religious knowledge and practices are embodied. Indeed, both theorists have affected contemporary studies in sociology and anthropology on the body (Ulland 2007: 51). In the concept of "habitus", Bourdieu points to bodily dispositions. He focuses on practices of dress, physical bearing, and styles of comportment, which are signs of a more fundamental reality of social structures. When Bourdieu considers the different practices that characterize various groups, such as their styles of eating and socializing, he focuses on the embodiment of these practices. Clearly, it would be of interest to have more research on the links between embodied religious expressions, such as the hijab, and social, cultural, and economic capital. To what degree is the use of the hijab connected to other forms of cultural and educational capital? Are conflicts over the hijab as much connected to conflicts over distinctions of cultural capital as they are over religious difference? Is the hijab perceived to be offensive in Europe because it is connected with non-white women of lower socio-economic status?

Bourdieu also analyzes different ways in which power is exercised through classifications and name giving, which may take place in more or less formalized rituals (Bourdieu 1977[1972]; 1994*b*[1982]). His view on ritual implies that it is a social practice, and here he emphasizes the body. Social practices structure the body and construct social individuals through the internalization of classifications and values. His approach has been important in studies of ritual, which also include religious rituals and ritual practice (Bell 1990; 1992; 1997: 77–9). It could be of interest to use Bourdieu's perspective in a study in which covered Muslim women speak about the significance that the hijab has as a bodily ritual practice in their lives and in their faith.

Foucault never developed an explicit theory of power, but power is a fundamental theme in most of his work (Sandmo 1999). He focuses on the power of language and religious discourse in governing individuals. Although Foucault has been accused of reproducing sexism because he treats the body as if it were a uniform entity and does not distinguish between the different bodily experiences of women and men, his theory has been used to analyze the disciplinary practices that produce the feminine body (Bartky 1999; Butler 1993). Foucault offers a description of power that some feminist scholars have embraced as potentially useful when reflecting upon how control over women's bodies functions to control women as such. Using Foucault's perspective, Islamic notions of women's chastity, modesty, and the hijab can be interpreted as attempts at regulating women's behavior within a patriarchal culture. The purpose of the headscarf is to discipline the female Muslim body, and by wearing the hijab, Muslim women contribute to reproducing their own domination. This perspective assumes that Muslim women are oppressed by religious clothing.

Nevertheless, it is also possible to use a Foucauldian perspective on power to argue that much of the political discourse opposing the hijab (especially when directed at Muslim women living in the West who choose to cover) constitutes a discourse of domination in which Muslim women are rendered "docile bodies" rather than active agents (Sheik 2004). Feminism has tended to interpret conservative religious women in patriarchal traditions either as passive victims of "false consciousness" or as agents who resist and set limits to male domination. This idea is contested by Mahmood (2005) in her analysis of the women's mosque movement in Egypt, a conservative Islamic revival that enables women both to teach and to learn Islamic practices of virtue. Mahmood draws on two aspects of Foucault's theory of power: namely, that power is understood as a strategic relation of force that permeates life, and that the subject does not precede power relations in the form of individual consciousness, but is produced through these relations (2005: 17–18). In her analysis of conservative women in the Egyptian mosque movement, she looks at the power configurations within which these movements navigate to the kinds of subjects they create. Her argument is that the agency of the pious Muslim women cannot be seen simply as a synonym for resistance to relations of domination. Their bodily practices carried out according to traditional norms do not necessarily represent thoughtless submission to oppressive norms either. Instead, she attempts to show that there are several forms of agency that meaningfully shape women's lives.

Furthermore, Foucault's perspective on the role of religion in disciplining the body can be useful in studies of "body politics". The experience of the body is undergoing change, as religious groups continue to engage in "body politics" and debate what legitimately should be done with the body (abortion, *in vitro* fertilization, same-sex marriages). The issue of Muslim dress for women also constitutes part of "body politics" that has relevance and consequences for key political issues in multicultural societies, such as freedom of religion and the role of religion in the public sphere.

Conclusion

By looking at the view of religion and power in the works of the early Habermas, Bourdieu, and Foucault, we find that they share a relatively negative view of religion. In the early work of Habermas, emancipation is found in secularity, and religion has no significant role in the public sphere in modern democratic societies. For Foucault, religion means primarily a discipline of the self and the body, whereas Bourdieu views religious power as power over perception, so that religion constitutes one aspect of symbolic violence.

There are some similarities between Bourdieu and Foucault in their view of religion and power. Foucault attempts to uncover how power is not just an oppressing force that "comes from outside", but something that is part of trivial practices, thoughts, and discourse. Bourdieu also focuses on local contexts for power and claims that power is an aspect of practices that are often considered spheres of leisure (art, culture, consumption, religion). Therefore, their theories tend to focus on the different hidden ways in which religious statements and symbolism, including bodily religious symbolism such as the hijab, can be oppressive. In contrast, Habermas discusses power in reference to laws, norms, and principles, which leads him to focus on the rights of Muslim women and other religious minorities to religious practices in the public sphere as well as their contribution to public debate. As a result, Habermas takes seriously the claims made by some Muslim women that wearing the hijab is a conscious free choice, and that it harbors a multiplicity of meanings. In this way, covered Muslim women have a role in the public sphere.

Nevertheless, there are also differences between Bourdieu and Foucault in this area. In Bourdieu's work, power is connected to positions in the field. Therefore, his analytical apparatus is useful in analyzing the oppressive aspects of religious symbolism and statements within the religious field. For Foucault, all discourses are loaded with power, which is manifested in numerous asymmetrical relations that form the ways in which knowledge is established. In this way, Foucault's approach can be useful in analyzing not just how the hijab can be used to dominate Muslim women, but also how Western feminist discourse can be oppressive towards Muslim women.

Furthermore, Habermas gives little attention to the different ways in which religions are embodied, a theme found in the work of Bourdieu and Foucault. Whereas James A. Beckford states that "studies of the social and cultural significance of the human body have much to gain from taking religion seriously" (Beckford 2003: 206), David Lyon (2006: 207) claims that "studies of religion have much to gain from taking the body seriously". There is a need to continue to place embodiment of religion high on the research agenda in the sociology of religion, as religious actors, including Muslim women, engage in negotiations with their embodied experiences, with leaders in religious communities, and with religious symbols, traditions, and theology.

Foucault's and Bourdieu's perspectives represent important contributions to the sociology of religion, as they give insights into the link between religion and power, the different ways in which religion can be used as means of oppression, and the bodily aspects of religion. Sociologists of religion must also take Habermas into account and consider his views on the complex role of religion in the public sphere, the normative basis for liberal democracies, and the rights of religious minorities. All three theorists offer understanding of the dynamics of religiously diverse contemporary societies.

References

ADAMS, N. (2006). *Habermas and Theology.* Cambridge: Cambridge University Press.

ARENS, E. (ed.) (1989). *Habermas und die Theologie: Beiträge zur theologischen Rezeption, Diskussion und Kritik der Theorie kommunikativen Handelns.* Düsseldorf: Patmos.

BARTKY, S. (1999). "Foucault, Femininity and the Modernization of Patriarchal Power". In M. Pearsall (ed.), *Women and Values: Readings in Recent Feminist Philosophy.* Belmont, Calif.: Wadsworth, 160–73.

BECKFORD, J. A. (1987). "The Restoration of Power to the Sociology of Religion". In T. Robbins and R. Robertson (eds.), *Church–State Relations.* New Brunswick, NJ, and Oxford: Transaction Books, 13–37.

—— (2003). *Social Theory and Religion.* Cambridge: Cambridge University Press.

BELL, C. (1990). "The Ritual Body and the Dynamics of Ritual Power". *Journal of Ritual Studies*, 4/2: 299–313.

—— (1992). *Ritual Theory, Ritual Practice.* New York: Oxford University Press.

—— (1997). *Ritual: Perspectives and Dimensions.* New York: Oxford University Press.

BENN, T. (2003). "Muslim Women Talking: Experiences of their Early Teaching Careers". In H. Jawad and T. Benn (eds.), *Muslim Women in the United Kingdom and Beyond*, Leiden: Brill, 131–50.

BERGER, P. L., and LUCKMANN, T. (1981). *The Social Construction of Reality.* Harmondsworth: Penguin.

BERNAUER, J., and CARRETTE, J. (eds.) (2004). *Michel Foucault and Theology: The Politics of Religious Experience.* Aldershot: Ashgate.

BOURDIEU, P. (1971*a*). "Genèse et structure du champ religieux". *Revue française de sociologie*, 12/3: 295–334.

—— (1971*b*). "Un interprétation de la théorie de la religion selon Max Weber". *Archives européennes de sociologie*, 12: 3–21.

—— (1977[1972]). *Outline of a Theory of Practice*, trans. R. Nice. Cambridge: Cambridge University Press.

—— (1986[1979]). *Distinction: A Social Critique of the Judgement of Taste*, trans. R. Nice. London and New York: Routledge & Kegan Paul.

BOURDIEU, P. (1987[1971]). "Legitimation and Structured Interests in Weber's Sociology of Religion". In S. Lash and S. Whimster (eds.), *Max Weber, Rationality and Modernity*, London: Allen & Unwin, 119–36.

—— (1991[1971]). "Genesis and Structure of the Religious Field". *Comparative Social Research*, 13: 1–44.

—— (1993). *Sociology in Question*, trans. R. Nice. London: Sage.

—— (1994*a*[1982–7]). *In Other Words: Essays Towards a Reflexive Sociology*, trans. M. Adamson. Cambridge: Polity Press.

—— (1994*b*[1982]). *Language and Symbolic Power*, trans. G. Raymond and M. Adamson. Cambridge: Polity Press.

—— (2000/1997). *Pascalian Meditations*, trans. R. Nice. Cambridge: Polity Press.

—— and SAINT MARTIN, M. DE (1982). "La sainte famille: L'épiscopat français dans le champ du pouvoir". *Actes de la recherche en sciences socials*, 44–5: 2–53.

BROWNING, D. S., and FIORENZA, F. S. (eds.) (1992). *Habermas, Modernity, and Public Theology*. New York: Crossroad.

BUTLER, J. (1993). *Bodies that Matter: On the Discursive Limits of "Sex"*. New York: Routledge.

BYRNES, T. A., and KATZENSTEIN, P. J. (eds.) (2006). *Religion in an Expanding Europe*. Cambridge: Cambridge University Press.

CALHOUN, C. (1992). "Introduction: Habermas and the Public Sphere". In *Habermas and the Public Sphere*. Cambridge, Mass.: MIT Press, 1–48.

—— (1995). *Critical Social Theory: Culture, History, and the Challenge of Difference*. Cambridge, Mass.: Blackwell.

CARRETTE, J. R. (1999). "Prologue to a Confession of the Flesh". In Foucault (1999), 1–47.

—— (2000). *Foucault and Religion: Spiritual Corporality and Political Spirituality*. London and New York: Routledge.

—— (2004). "Beyond Theology and Sexuality: Foucault, the Self and the Que(e)rying of Monotheistic Truth". In Bernauer and Carrette (2004), 217–32.

—— and KING, R. (1998). "Giving Birth to Theory: Critical Perspectives on Religion and the Body". *Scottish Journal of Religious Studies* (special edition), 19/1: 123–43.

CESARI, J., and MCLOUGHLIN, S. (eds.) (2005). *European Muslims and the Secular State*. Aldershot: Ashgate.

DANIELSEN, A., and HANSEN, M. NORDLI (1999). "Makt i Pierre Bourdieus sosiologi" ([Power in Pierre Bourdieu's sociology]). In F. Engelstad (ed.), *Om makt: Teori og kritikk*. Oslo: Gyldendal, 43–78.

DEMERATH, N. J. III, (2001). *Crossing the Gods: World Religions and Worldly Politics*. New Brunswick, NJ, and London: Rutgers University Press.

DE ROEST, H. (1998). *Communicative Identity: Habermas' Perspectives of Discourse as a Support for Practical Theology*. Kampen: Kok.

DIANTEILL, E. (2003). "Pierre Bourdieu and the Sociology of Religion: A Central and Peripheral Concern". *Theory and Society*, 32/5–6: 529–49.

DILLON, M. (1999). "The Authority of the Holy Revisited: Habermas, Religion, and Emancipatory Possibilities". *Sociological Theory*, 17/3: 290–306.

ENGLER, S. (2003). "Modern Times: Religion, Consecration and the State in Bourdieu". *Cultural Studies*, 17/3–4: 445–67.

FIORENZA, F. S. (1992). "The Church as a Community of Interpretation: Political Theology between Discourse Ethics and Hermeneutical Reconstruction". In Browning and Fiorenza (1992), 66–91.

FOUCAULT, M. (1967[1961]). *Madness and Civilization: A History of Insanity in the Age of Reason*, trans. R. Howard. London: Tavistock.

—— (1970[1966]). *The Order of Things*. London: Tavistock.

—— (1973[1963]). *The Birth of the Clinic: An Archeology of Medical Perception*, trans. A. M. Sheridan Smith. London: Tavistock.

—— (1977[1975]). *Discipline and Punish: The Birth of the Prison*, trans. A. Sheridan. London: Allen Lane.

—— (1986[1976]). *The History of Sexuality*, i. *An Introduction*, trans. R. Hurley. New York: Viking.

—— (1988[1984]). *The History of Sexuality*, iii. *The Care of the Self*, trans. R. Hurley. New York: Vintage.

—— (1996). "What is Critique?" In J. Schmidt (ed.), *What Is Enlightenment? Eighteenth-Century Answers and Twentieth-Century Questions*. Berkeley: University of California Press, 382–98.

—— (1997[1994]). "The Masked Philosopher". In *The Essential Works of Foucault, 1954–1984*, i: *Ethics*, ed. P. Rabinow, trans. R. Hurley *et al.* London: Penguin, 320–8.

—— (1999). *Religion and Culture*, selected and ed. J. R. Carrette. Manchester: Manchester University Press.

—— (2000*a*[1994]). "Omnes et Singulatim": Toward a Critique of Political Reason". In *The Essential Works of Foucault, 1954–1984*, iii. *Power*, ed. J. D. Fabuion, trans. R. Hurley *et al.* New York: New Press, 298–325.

—— (2000*b*[1994]). "Useless to Revolt?" In *The Essential Works of Foucault, 1954–1984*, iii. *Power*, ed. J. D. Fabuion, trans. R. Hurley *et al.* New York: New Press, 449–53.

GARRIGAN, S. (2004). *Beyond Ritual: Sacramental Theology after Habermas*. Aldershot: Ashgate.

GEYER, H.-G., JANOWSKI, H.-N., and SCHMIDT, A. (1970). *Theologie und Soziologie*. Stuttgart: Kohlhammer.

HABERMAS, J. (1980[1973]). *Legitimation Crisis*, trans. T. McCarthy. London: Heinemann.

—— (1982). "A Reply to my Critics". In J. B. Thompson and D. Held (eds.), *Habermas: Critical Debates*. London: Macmillan, 219–83.

—— (1984[1981]). *The Theory of Communicative Action*, i. *Reason and the Rationalization of Society*, trans. T. McCarthy. London: Heinemann.

—— (1987[1981]). *The Theory of Communicative Action*, ii. *Lifeworld and System: A Critique of Functionalist Reason*, trans. T. McCarthy. Boston: Beacon Press.

—— (1992). "Transcendence from Within, Transcendence in This World". In Browning and Fiorenza (1992), 226–50.

—— (1994). "Struggles for Recognition in the Democratic Constitutional State". In C. Taylor, *Multiculturalism: Examining the Politics of Difference*, ed. with an introduction by A. Gutman, Princeton: Princeton University Press, 107–48.

—— (2002). *Religion and Rationality: Essays on Reason, God, and Modernity*, ed. with an introduction by E. Mendieta. Cambridge: Polity Press.

—— (2006). "Religion in the Public Sphere". *European Journal of Philosophy*, 14/1: 1–25.

—— and RATZINGER, J. (2007). *The Dialectic of Secularization: On Reason and Religion*. San Francisco: Ignatius Press.

HERBERT, D. (1996). "Religious Traditions in the Public Sphere: Habermas, MacIntyre and the Representation of Religious Minorities". In W. A. R. Shadid and P. S. van Kongingsveld (eds.), *Muslims in the Margin*. Kampen: Kok Pharos, 66–79.

HERBERT, D. (2003). *Religion and Civil Society: Rethinking Public Religion in the Contemporary World.* Aldershot: Ashgate.

HØIBRAATEN, H. (1999). "Kommunikativ makt og sanksjonsbasert makt hos Jürgen Habermas" [Communicative Power and Power Based Sanctions in Jürgen Habermas]. In F. Engelstad (ed.), *Om makt: Teori og kritikk.* Oslo: Gyldendal, 223–61.

JORDAN, M. D. (2004). "Sodomites and Churchmen: The Theological Invention of Homosexuality". In Bernauer and Carrette (2004), 233–44.

KÜHLE, L. (2004). "Bourdieu og religionssociologien" [Bourdieu and the Sociology of Religion]. In A. Geertz, H. J. Lundager Jensen, and J. P. Schjødt (eds.), *Det brede og det skarpe.* Fredriksberg: Anis, 37–45.

LEEZENBERG, M. (2004). "Power and Political Spirituality: Michel Foucault on the Islamic Revolution in Iran". In Bernauer and Carette (2004), 99–115.

LINDHARDT, J. (2006). "Efterord" [Postscript]. In J. Habermas and J. Ratzinger, *Fornuft og religion: Sekulariseringens dialektik.* Højbjerg: Hovedland, 63–70.

LYON, D. (2006). "New Media, Niche Markets, and the Body: Excarnate and Hypercarnate Challenges for Theory and Theology". In J. A. Beckford and J. Walliss (eds.), *Theorising Religion: Classical and Contemporary Debates.* Aldershot: Ashgate, 197–210.

MAHMOOD, S. (2005). *Politics of Piety: The Islamic Revival and the Feminist Subject.* Princeton and Oxford: Princeton University Press.

MAHON, M. (2004). "Catholic Sex". In Bernauer and Carrette (2004), 245–66.

MCCALL, C. (2004). "Autonomy, Religion, & Revolt in Foucault". *Journal of Philosophy & Scripture,* 2/1: 7–14.

MENDIETA, E. (2002). "Introduction". In Habermas (2002), 1–36.

—— (2005). "Introduction: Religion as Critique: Theology as Social Critique and Enlightened Reason". In *idem* (ed.), *The Frankfurt School on Religion: Key Writings by the Major Thinkers.* New York: Routledge, 1–17.

PINTO, H. (2002). *Foucault, Christianity and Interfaith Dialogue.* London and New York: Routledge.

REY, T. (2004). "Marketing the Goods of Salvation: Bourdieu on Religion". *Religion,* 34: 331–43.

—— (2007). *Bourdieu on Religion: Imposing Faith and Legitimacy.* London: Equinox Publishing.

ROBERTSON, R. (1992). "The Economization of Religion? Reflections on the Promise and Limitations of the Economic Approach". *Social Compass,* 39/1: 147–57.

ROSENLUND, L. (2000). *Social Structures and Change: Applying Pierre Bourdieu's Approach and Analytic Framework,* Working Papers 85. Stavanger: Stavanger University College.

SANDMO, E. (1999). "Michel Foucault som maktteoretiker" [Michel Foucault as a Theorist on Power]. In F. Engelstad (ed.), *Om makt: Teori og kritikk.* Oslo: Gyldendal, 79–96.

SCHULD, J. J. (2003). *Foucault and Augustine: Reconsidering Power and Love.* Notre Dame, Ind.: University of Notre Dame Press.

SHEIK, C. S. (2004). "Dress and Discipline: A Foucauldian Analysis of the Hijab Controversy". Paper read at Association for the Sociology of Religion's 66th Annual Meeting, San Francisco.

SIEBERT, R. J. (1985). *The Critical Theory of Religion: The Frankfurt School.* Berlin, New York, and Amsterdam: Mouton.

SWARTZ, D. (1996). "Bridging the Study of Culture and Religion: Pierre Bourdieu's Political Economy of Symbolic Power". *Sociology of Religion,* 57/1: 71–85.

—— (1997). *Culture & Power: The Sociology of Pierre Bourdieu.* Chicago and London: University of Chicago Press.

TAYLOR, C. (1992). *Multiculturalism and "The Politics of Recognition".* Princeton: Princeton University Press.

—— (2003). "The Politics of Recognition". In J. Stone and R. Dennis (eds.), *Race and Ethnicity: Comparative and Theoretical Approaches.* Oxford: Blackwell, 373–81.

THUMMA, S., and GRAY, E. R. (eds.) (2005). *Gay Religion.* Walnut Creek, Calif.: AltaMira Press.

ULLAND, D. (2007). *Guds karneval: En religionspsykologisk studie av Toronto-vekkelsens ekstatiske spiritualitet* [God's Carnival: A Study in the Psychology of Religion of the Ecstatic Spirituality in the Toronto Revival]. Lund Studies in Psychology of Religion, 9. Lund: Lunds Universitet.

VERTER, B. (2003). "Spiritual Capital: Theorizing Religion with Bourdieu Against Bourdieu". *Sociological Theory,* 21/2: 150–74.

WARNER, M. (1992). "The Mass Public and the Mass Subject". In C. Calhoun (ed.), *Habermas and the Public Sphere.* Cambridge, Mass.: MIT Press, 377–401.

WILCOX, M. M. (2003). *Coming Out in Christianity: Religion, Identity, & Community.* Bloomington and Indianapolis: Indiana University Press.

YADGAR, Y. (2003). "SHAS as a Struggle to Create a New Field: A Bourdieuan Perspective of an Israeli Phenomenon". *Sociology of Religion,* 64/2: 223–46.

SUGGESTED READING

The following are recommended: Bernauer and Carrette (2004); Bourdieu (1971*a*; 1987 [1971]); Carrette (2000); Dianteill (2003); Foucault (1999); Habermas (2002; 2006); Habermas and Ratzinger (2007); and Rey, T. (2007).

CHAPTER 6

RATIONAL CHOICE THEORY

A CRITIQUE

MALCOLM HAMILTON

Introduction

Of all the applications of rational choice theory (RCT), it is the application to religious belief and practice that has been most controversial. Religion, many would argue, is that sphere of human activity least susceptible to the application of rational choice. Allegiance to a particular form of religion is simply not something that is chosen on the basis of a cost–benefit schedule.

Derived ultimately from economic theory, RCT argues that many aspects of human behaviour can best be understood as motivated by the desire to maximize benefits at least cost (Becker 1986). In other words, behaviour is fundamentally rational in the same way as it is in the case of economic behaviour. So, for example, in choosing a marriage partner or friends with whom to associate and socialize, it is the net excess of benefits over costs involved that will determine the outcome. In this way, patterns of marriage and friendship alliances can be analysed and understood.

Often strenuously disputed in sociology, RCT applied to the sociology of religion has become an issue of intense debate. It claims to put the subdiscipline on a new basis, has led to a fundamental reassessment of the secularization thesis, and claims to offer new insights into the study of sectarianism and religious movements.

The Tenets of Rational Choice Theory of Religion

The Foundations

RCT was first systematically applied to religion by Rodney Stark and William Sims Bainbridge (1980; 1985; 1987), and has since been modified, developed, and refined by them, especially Stark, and a number of associates and followers, most notably Laurence Iannaccone and Roger Finke (Finke 1997; Finke and Iannaccone 1993; Iannaccone 1992*a*; 1992*b*; 1997; Stark and Finke 2000). This section will set out the main tenets of the most current version of the rational choice theory of religion (henceforth RCTR), while the next will present the key arguments of its leading critics.

Stark and Bainbridge originally presented what they considered to be a deductive theory of religion (1980; 1987), and this has very much been retained in recent formulations (Stark 1999*a*; Stark and Finke 2000). They derive their theory of religion from a general theory of human nature and action described by a limited number of fundamental axioms together with a series of propositions which either follow from these axioms or the truth of which has been established in other contexts. The approach relies heavily on exchange theory, which is based on the principle that all, or nearly all, human interaction can be treated as a form of exchange. Exchange theory itself may be regarded as a special case of RCT, in that the latter holds that in exchanges actors always seek to maximize net benefits.

The proposition which initiates the argument in the most recent statement of RCTR states that 'within the limits of their information and understanding, restricted by available options, guided by their preferences and tastes, humans attempt to make rational choices' (Stark and Finke 2000: 65). In doing so, they weigh anticipated rewards against costs, including the opportunity cost of not taking some other course of action. They also formulate explanations of how rewards can be obtained and costs minimized. Explanations are evaluated on the basis of the results they yield, those that prove most effective being retained, and others discarded.

Rewards are defined as anything which human beings desire and are willing to incur some cost to obtain. They include very specific as well as very general things, such as peace and happiness. Whether specific or general, rewards are always limited in supply. Some, and often those most intensely desired, such as immortality, are unobtainable in this world. Humans will tend to accept explanations of how such general and difficult-to-obtain rewards may be obtained which state that this is possible in an afterlife or in some non-verifiable context. This is where religion comes into the picture.

Religion is the attempt to secure desired rewards in the absence of more everyday means. It is essentially an unverifiable system of explanations of how the most general of rewards may be obtained which must be taken on trust. It is a system of explanations which promises other-worldly rewards which can be obtained only by reference to the supernatural—forces believed to be beyond or outside nature which are able to overrule natural physical forces.[1] Systems of explanations which do not refer to the supernatural are not considered to be religions. The atheism of canonical Theravada Buddhism, for example, is distinguished from popular Buddhism, which postulates the existence of various supernatural beings and is considered, therefore, to be truly religious.

Furthermore, systems of explanations are not fully religious according to Stark and Finke's version of RCTR unless they postulate the existence of gods, which are defined as beings having consciousness and desires. Vague and abstract concepts of divinity do not count as truly religious according to this view. Notions such as the Tao or the 'ground of being' do not qualify as true gods.

At this point the element of exchange theory is introduced. In pursuit of rewards humans enter into exchange relations with a god or gods, but only when everyday means of attaining rewards are not available, as they generally are not in the case of very general rewards.[2] Having assembled the essential elements, Stark and Finke (2000: 91) can now formulate a definition of religion. 'Religion consists of very general explanations of existence, including terms of exchange with a god or gods.' Religious explanations state what the gods want from humans and what humans can get from the gods in return. In addition, religious explanations answer the fundamental questions concerning the meaning of life, how humans came to exist, why we are here, what happens to us after death, and so on. RCTR thus rests upon quite strong intellectualist foundations, in that it considers religion to be largely explanatory and rejects analysis of it in functionalist terms or in terms of symbolic systems which integrate, promote social solidarity, or maintain social order, etc. The extent to and circumstances in which it may or may not do such things is considered to be an empirical matter, to be established by investigation.

The characteristics attributed to gods vary greatly. Gods are seen as more or less powerful, benevolent, malevolent, reliable, consistent, and so on. The terms of exchange between humans and gods depend upon these variable characteristics.

[1] In the original formulation, Stark and Bainbridge (1985; 1987) spoke of such rewards as 'compensators', an ill-chosen term by these authors' own later admission, since it suggested the idea of something being promised instead of the desired reward, rather than a promise of the reward in some future state of being, life, or mode of existence. This caused much misunderstanding and misplaced criticism, and the term has been entirely discarded in more recent formulations.

[2] Highly specific, mundane rewards are those which magic delivers, rather than religion. Magic is not concerned with gods, but with impersonal conceptions of the supernatural. Nor is it concerned with explanations and rewards of a very general kind. As Durkheim argued, and because of these characteristics, it does not lead to religious organization but involves only practitioners and individual clients.

Exchanges may be short-term, relatively trivial, and non-exclusive, or long-term, deeply significant, and exclusive.

In more complex societies which manifest some degree of division of labour, dealings with the gods become the responsibility of specific cultural specialists, and this evolves into a specific cultural system constituted by organizations concerned with religious matters.

Placing trust in religious explanations is a risky affair, Stark and Finke (2000) explain. Such explanations are difficult, if not impossible, to evaluate and assess. Confidence in them will be greater to the extent that many others also place their trust in them. For this reason religion is always a collective and community affair. The collective reinforcement of trust in religious propositions is usually expressed in the form of communal ritual and ceremony. Ritual also instils confidence. One aspect of prayer, a form of private ritual, is that it generates reassurance that religious entities are real, as does belief in miracles and mystical experiences.

A number of religious organizations may emerge in a society offering a variety of explanations. Here RCTR takes on its most stridently 'economic' character. Religious organizations are seen as firms in competition with one another, offering products at various prices (costs) to consumers, who choose between them according to how well the products meet their particular preferences and their estimation of the net benefit to be gained when rewards are assessed against costs of participation.

Because the propositions of religion are very often not susceptible to verification, once religious specialists emerge, they will tend to combine in organizations which are exclusive in nature. Exclusive organizations offer rewards that appear less uncertain, according to Stark and Finke (2000). For this reason, exclusive religious organizations tend to drive out those that allow multiple allegiances.

People's preferences, however, vary considerably with regard to what religious organizations have to offer, just as they do with regard to any other kind of activity or pattern of consumption. What suits one will not suit another. Some prefer, for example, a style of worship which emphasizes expressive excitement, while others find satisfaction in calm contemplation. It is a tenet of RCT that underlying preferences are relatively stable. Human beings generally want the same things: security, comfort, material well-being, entertainment, and so on. RCT tends to ignore how such preferences are determined, since in its eyes this is largely down to biology and universal aspects of human nature. In the case of religion, it is assumed that there is a universal need for some system of beliefs which offers rewards otherwise unobtainable. Religious answers to the eternal problems of human life are always needed.

Individual leanings towards one or an other type of answer are also relatively fixed. There will thus be a range of potential market niches which religious organizations can seek to occupy. These will range from those which are closely in tune with predominant social values and those which deviate markedly in this respect; or, as rational choice theorists express it, those in either a low or a high state of tension with the society. In a free religious market religious organizations will emerge which cater to the whole of this range. Stark and Finke (2000) see this range as also reflecting degrees of liberality and strictness, with high-tension religious organizations being ultra-strict and low-tension organizations being ultra-liberal. Religious organizations will tend to be normally distributed, with most being neither very strict nor very liberal, but located towards the centre, where most individual preferences lie.

RCTR strongly emphasizes the supply side of the religious market. Given that religious preferences are relatively fixed, religious change, the emergence of new 'firms' offering novel religious 'products', is not driven by changing demand. Rather, it is the activities of religious entrepreneurs that seek to cater to varying religious preferences that shape the religious marketplace. The religious needs of potential 'customers' lie dormant until religious entrepreneurs come forward offering something that appeals to them.

The more pluralistic the religious market, the greater is the probability that there will be something on offer that will appeal to any given potential consumer. In other words, a wide choice of religious products and competition between suppliers ensure that most consumers' preferences will be met. Competition means that suppliers must actively seek to recruit members, adopting a range of strategies to attract them.

In taking this position, RCTR turns conventional theory on its head. It had long been assumed that pluralism and competition in the case of religion undermine its authority, foster indifference, and promote secularization. Conversely, the robust plausibility structure provided by a single, unchallenged church and set of doctrines ensures that dissent and deviance are extremely difficult and uncommon (Berger 1973).

RCTR, in contrast, holds that monopolistic supply and regulation of the religious market leave most preferences unmet and latent. Also, religious specialists and functionaries are secure in their positions whether or not they attract popular participation. Little effort need be expended in attempting to meet the religious needs of the population, which simply has to take or leave what is on offer. In such a religious market religion tends to lose its vitality; there is at best only nominal allegiance to the religious organization, and at worst widespread indifference. Pluralism ensures that all preferences are catered for, and that religion is zealously promoted and marketed, since success depends upon it. Remove monopoly and regulation, and the result will be a flourishing religious market, religious vitality, and high levels of active participation in a wide range of religious organizations.

A number of empirical studies have sought to test these claims in a variety of contexts. Some have found in favour of them, but others have produced contrary findings, or have found flaws in the methods used by rational choice theorists, as will be examined below.[3]

[3] For a review of this empirical work see Chavez and Gorski (2001).

Choice of religious affiliation, rational choice theorists are aware, is not quite like choosing an everyday product. There are very specific factors which tend to constrain such choice. Many people are brought up in a religious faith. Once committed, either through upbringing or by a choice made at some point in their lives, most people do not easily change their affiliation. This is explained by rational choice theorists in terms of social and religious capital. Social capital (Stark and Finke 2000) is the network of personal relationships that an individual has with other members of their religious organization. This network is not relinquished lightly, by joining a new religious organization. Religious capital (Iannaccone 1990; Stark and Finke 2000) is the accumulated stock of religious knowledge and competencies in which considerable investment has usually been made. The greater this stock of capital, Iannaccone suggests, the greater will be the satisfaction an individual derives from subsequent religious activity. From this one can predict that converts will be disproportionately from younger age-groups, since the young have less religious capital to lose. A second prediction is that the old will tend to participate more in their religious group than the young. Iannaccone (1990) supports these predictions with analysis of empirical data.

Empirical Application

Secularization and Pluralism

The long accepted thesis that modernity means secularity and the marginalization or even demise of religion has been dramatically challenged by rational choice theorists. For them, secularization as an inevitable process in modern societies is a myth induced by the assumption that modernity is incompatible with religion. Traditional secularization theory has, in their view, grossly overstated the extent of secularization, discounted or overlooked contrary evidence, and wrongly assumed that the process, where it has occurred, is irreversible (Stark 1996).

Loss of religious vitality, indifference to religion, low rates of church membership and participation, as we have seen, are the result, rational choice theorists argue, of monopoly, regulation, and lack of competition in the religious marketplace. Where there is a free market, pluralism, and competition, religion flourishes. The clearest example of this is the United States. Dismissed by traditional theorists in the sociology of religion as anomalous, rational choice theorists see it as lending strong support to their position. The United States, one of the most advanced countries technologically yet one of the most religious, was always a problem for traditional secularization theory. Again turning long accepted ideas on their head, it is actually Europe, according to RCTR, that is anomalous, and for particular historical reasons relating to the conditions of the religious market. Much of Europe, until quite recently, did not have a free religious market but was characterized by monopoly or regulation.

Rational choice theorists have sought to support these claims by marshalling historical and comparative empirical data in their favour. Finke and Stark (1992) examined data for the United States between 1776 and 1990, arguing that the progressive emergence of a free competitive religious market over that period was accompanied by a continuous and substantial rise in religious affiliation and church attendance from unremarkable and modest to contemporary high levels.

Iannaccone (1991) analysed data for eighteen countries, fourteen of them in Europe, and found a strong correlation between competition and religious participation. Competition accounted for in excess of 90 per cent of attendance. In contrast to the United States, Scandinavia offers one of the clearest examples of the stifling of religious vitality by monopoly and state regulation. In Sweden the subsidizing of the established Lutheran Church by the state has, according to Finke (1997), impeded the emergence of other religious organizations, since it greatly increases their start-up costs. Legislative and administrative interference in church affairs is also common, Stark and Finke (2000) argue, with the result that these indicators of religious vitality in those countries show it to be very weak. Similarly, bureaucratic hindrance of new religions in Germany, they argue, has inhibited their growth and development.

Sects, Cults, and Movements

RCT claims to be able to integrate many findings of earlier work on religious sects and cults within the framework in a more systematic way. Stark and Bainbridge (1979; 1985; 1987) and Stark and Finke (2000) define sects and cults as deviant religious organizations. They use the term 'sect' to refer to a deviant religious organization that breaks away from an established religious organization, while the term 'cult' is used to refer to a deviant religious organization that is entirely new, rather than a schismatic movement. Both stand in a relationship of relatively high tension with the surrounding socio-cultural environment.

The tendency towards sectarian schism is derived by rational choice theorists from the fact that the membership of any religious organization is bound to be internally differentiated (Stark and Bainbridge 1987; Stark and Finke 2000). Especially important in this respect are divisions between the better- and worse-off, and between the more and the less powerful. Thus there is always potential for conflict within religious organizations. Sect movements stem from such conflict, and occur when certain conditions favour it. Broadly speaking, schismatic sect movements tend to occur when the relatively deprived members perceive that the potential gains from breaking away outweigh the potential costs. The greater the degree of stratification within religious organizations, the more likely this is to be the case.

There are four possible outcomes of the conflicts, and varying expectations within religious organizations, according to Stark and Bainbridge (1987). First, forces may balance one another, and the group will maintain unity and cohesion at an equilibrium level of tension with the society. Secondly, the group may split in two, each moving in an opposite direction, one churchward and one sectward. Third, the relatively powerful may prevail, and the whole group will move churchward—a very common pattern. Finally, a relatively dissatisfied majority may be successful in moving the whole group sectward, a relatively rare occurrence requiring rather special circumstances.

Rational choice theorists, particularly Stark and Bainbridge (1987) and Stark and Finke (2000) have paid much attention to these processes. Much of this work is not closely dependent upon the principles of RCTR per se, so will not be discussed in detail here. RCTR, however, has had a good deal to say about the specific characteristics of schismatic sectarian movements which stem directly from the application of its essentially economic theoretical foundations.

Iannaccone (1988; 1992*a*; 1992*b*; 1995) in particular has contributed in this respect, and his work has been largely incorporated into RCTR (Stark 1996; Stark and Finke 2000). Iannaccone extends the approach to the understanding of such typical features of sects as their strictness, conservatism, high levels of participation, relatively low socio-economic social base, and why these characteristics tend to go together.

Central to this work is an emphasis on the perennial problem that faces all voluntary organizations: namely, that of the free-rider. The collective provision of benefits to all members regardless of contribution carries the danger that some of those who enjoy them can do so while leaving others to contribute the effort, resources, and time that make the generation of the benefits possible. In order to prevent this, sectarian groups tend to make costly demands upon members, which deter those whose commitment is limited. Such demands often involve costs of a gratuitous kind, such as wearing distinctive dress, dietary and other prohibitions, segregated lifestyles, and strictly regulated behavioural standards—in other words, things which differentiate sect members from others and the surrounding society. Only those who value the religious benefits offered by the sect sufficiently highly will be prepared to accept these demands. They will be highly committed, and less likely to attempt to free-ride.

Since such requirements lead to the sect becoming a relatively segregated group, it will seek to provide those gratifications that would otherwise come from integration within the broader society, such as socialization and friendships. There tends, therefore, to be a high level of participation in the life of the sect on the part of its members.

Criticisms of Rational Choice Theory of Religion

Foundations

Critiques of RCTR are many and various. Every aspect of it is contentious, from its fundamental tenets to its application to secularization and sectarian movements.

Beginning with the fundamental tenets, numerous critics question the core notion that religious affiliation is a matter of choice at all, or that the activities that constitute religion can adequately be described in terms of the language of exchange and rational choice. Bruce (1993) stresses the essential difference between religion and consumer products. One does not change one's religion according to what is on offer in the market as one changes the make of car one drives. In fact, religion is often the sort of thing that, ideally, one does not change at all, since a central aspect of it is precisely commitment. Believers are precisely *believers*, rather than consumers. In believing they espouse what they consider to be the truth, and the truth is not something one has any choice about accepting (Bankston 2002).

What people take to be true is determined to a large extent, of course, by what others around them take to be true. Their beliefs are determined by socialization and the cultural environment in which they find themselves. RCTR, its critics point out, neglects such social and cultural as well as traditional and historical factors. The focus is on individual decision making, without regard to any social and cultural context (Ellison 1995). Sherkat (1997) points out that markets are always embedded in social relations, and religious markets particularly so. Sherkat reminds us also that choices cannot simply be equated with preferences. We do not always choose what we prefer; our choices are shaped also by the attitudes and actions of significant others around us and our anticipations of their reactions to our behaviour and the consequences it has for them.

Furthermore, RCTR's emphasis on religion as a set of explanations about how rewards can be obtained is open to question. Truth encompasses many propositions other than those which deal with the means by which concrete ends can be achieved. Truth can simply be about why things are the way they are, about what this means for us, and how we can relate to it. This is, of course, especially the case with religion, which, as Weber argued, is as much about making sense of things as it is about achieving benefits. RCTR tends to equate rational action with action calculated to achieve concrete goals by the most appropriate means, with instrumental, or what Weber termed *zweck* rationality. There is, however, a form of rationality which is more concerned with meaning and making sense of things, which Jerolmack and Porpora (2004) term 'epistemic rationality'. Epistemic rationality applies to beliefs, rather than to actions. Beliefs are rationally held if they are warranted, rather than if they lead to desired outcomes. Jerolmack and Porpora consider that beliefs about spiritual entities may be warranted and, therefore, rational, if they are based upon some kind of actual experience. Rational choice theory, in focusing entirely on instrumental rationality, neglects that aspect of religion which stems from certain kinds of experience and feelings of conviction. Religion eminently entails epistemic rationality in this sense, and not simply or even primarily instrumental rationality.

In making sense of things, religion, as Weber stresses, confronts the problems of evil and of ethics. RCTR has little to say about this aspect of religion (Collins 1997). Ethics and moral sentiments are about community and solidarity, as Durkheim taught us. Again, RCTR neglects this whole dimension of religion which is, consequently, about punishment as well as reward. This is why it postulates threatening entities such as devils and why its gods are often as punitive as they are benevolent (Guthrie 1996).

Yet another form of rational behaviour is oriented to the pursuit of values: namely, that which Weber termed *wertrational* action. Here the commitment to the realization of the value overrides considerations of personal advantage, cost, or convenience. Again much religious behaviour belongs to this type and cannot, therefore, be understood in terms of calculation of costs and benefits (Spickard 1998).

A second fundamental tenet of RCTR which critics have found problematic is its equation of religion with belief in the supernatural. It is a remarkably ethnocentric conception, as many discussions of the definition of religion have argued (Goody 1961; Horton 1967; Spiro 1966), and fails to include religions such as Buddhism.[4] RCTR is, in general, not easily applied to non-Western religions such as Buddhism. For this reason an ethnocentric bias is often perceived to characterize it, undermining the claimed universalism of its propositions (Carroll 1996; Sharot 2002). Sharot reminds us also that RCTR from the outset confined its claims to the exclusivist congregational religious forms typical of the West, and cannot be applied to societies and cultures in which religion is embedded in local communities and non-exclusivist in character. Neither can it have much to say about popular or folk religious belief and behaviour, which have historically persisted in Western as well as other cultures, which is non-congregational, diffuse, and unorganized. Since most religious cultures are of the non-exclusivist and non-congregational type, RCTR can be applied only to a limited range of types of religion.

Leaving aside the emphasis on gods, RCTR still fails to account for why people come to think that they can get the rewards they desire from supernatural sources in the first place. It fails to 'explain how wishful fantasies become plausible enough to satisfy us' (Guthrie 1996: 413). Guthrie also points out that it fails to explain why

[4] Stark and Finke (2000) mount a spirited defence of their position, but one which is highly contentious. Space does not allow the debated to be explored here.

religious belief postulates not just gods but fearful aspects such as demons, devils, and hells that threaten, rather than reward. One might add that gods themselves are not always benevolent, but often punitive.

The emphasis of RCTR on the supply side and the assumption that demand is relatively fixed and preferences relatively stable is a third fundamental proposition with which critics have taken issue. This neglects the social and cultural influences that shape preferences. In particular, critics have pointed out that religious preferences are determined by such factors as class and status. In societies where substantial social mobility is possible, change of class or status position often leads to change in religious preference, an observation that RCTR itself acknowledges in its analysis of denominationalization and sect-to-church movements. To the extent that we can speak of religious markets, it should be recognized that they are always embedded in specific social contexts and subject to social processes that influence religious preferences, and thereby play a crucial role in determining choices (Sherkat and Wilson 1995; Bankston 2002). Religious affiliations are, consequently, not easily changed, and may attract strong disapproval of significant others or be seen as disloyal or as rejection of family and community (Ellison 1995).

Finally, even if one were to accept the notion of a religious market comprised of organizations offering benefits in competition for members, there are severe limitations upon the capacity of such organizations to behave as rational maximizers, since it is difficult, if not impossible, to measure costs and benefits in the absence of any accounting unit or currency of the sort which allows economic markets to operate effectively (Bryant 2000).

Empirical Applications

Secularization and Pluralism

The application of RCTR to specific substantive issues is as intensely debated as its theoretical basis, not least its reversal of the long-accepted relationship between pluralism and religious vitality. Empirical studies which support the RCTR position on this were cited above. Many others have found instead in favour of the traditional hypothesis that pluralism undermines religious participation.[5] Both sides of the debate have questioned the methods and interpretations of the other with regard to how diversity, vitality, or participation are measured, the units of analysis used, and so on.

Many attempts to test the hypothesis that pluralism strengthens religious vitality, whether they find in favour or against it have been shown to rest upon dubious methodological foundations. Voas, Olson, and Crockett (2002) demonstrate that both positive and negative correlations between measures of religious participation

[5] See Chavez and Gorski (2001).

and the index used to measure pluralism, the Herfindahl index, are largely mathematical artefacts rendering the conclusions of almost all these studies fallacious. The correlations are the consequence of the relative sizes of the religious organizations and the way they are distributed in the area under investigation. This leave the whole issue of the relationship between pluralism and religious vitality uncertain.[6]

The only conclusion that can wisely be drawn about the issue of whether pluralism is positively associated with religious vitality is, perhaps, that of Bruce: 'sometimes it is and sometimes it isn't' (1995: 520), depending upon the circumstances. It may in certain circumstances even be the case that growth of religious competition brings about relaxation of state regulation, as Beyer (1997) found in the case of Canada. The same point is argued by Bruce in the cases of Britain, Australia, and the United States (1999) and for the Nordic states (2000). And, significantly, deregulation in the Nordic area has not produced a religious revival. The rational choice response to this point, that there is always a considerable time lag after deregulation before the market develops sufficiently to stimulate religious revival, is not very persuasive, given the time that has passed since deregulation. The critics perceive this argument as a rather too convenient alibi used to protect the theory against disconfirmation.

Whatever the case in this respect, it is hard to deny that such things as ethnic or national identity and theology, emphasized by Bruce (1999), play a significant role. Many other factors, such as historical circumstances, political structures, systems of class and status, must also be taken into account, as they are by Martin (1978) and Bruce (1992; 1993). Some rational choice theorists treat such influences as extraneous variables which produce market distortions (Stark, Finke, and Iannaccone 1995),[7] while others acknowledge the key significance of prevailing social and political factors (Chavez and Cann 1992). The sluggishness of Europe to produce a vibrant religious market may well be due to such factors. The social, cultural, and historical factors that determine what people seek from religion, how or whether they seek to participate in organized religion, the forces which have shaped religious markets, and so on, are highly variable, and must be taken into account in trying to understand different patterns of religious activity across communities and nations (Ammerman 1997; Neitz and Mueser 1997).

Among such factors are those which may prevent a monopolistic situation from depressing religious vitality. In circumstances in which non-religious benefits such as solidarity and integration are provided by monopolistic or dominant religious

[6] One recent study of US counties, however, which uses a method which does not suffer from the problems of the Herfindahl index, finds against the 'pluralism promotes vitality' thesis (Montgomery 2003). The author points out that his findings could be compatible with the thesis, but that this would require recognition of the importance of the demand side in determining preferences, as well as the supply side.

[7] For a more extensive discussion of how social factors introduce market imperfections which can, in his view, nevertheless be analysed in terms of economic theory, see Sherkat (1997).

organizations, participation can be high. Northern and southern Ireland, Poland, Catholics in North America, and Mormons in Utah are examples of this (Sherkat 1997). As a result of such arguments, rational choice theorists have had to refine some of their claims, resorting to factors which are outside the theoretical framework of RCTR. Finke and Stark (1988; 1989), for example, acknowledge that in circumstances where a religiously homogeneous, geographically concentrated, minority group is surrounded by a majority of different and essentially hostile religious persuasion, it often becomes the focal point for integration and solidarity, and receives, consequently, strong support. Stark and Iannaccone (1994) account for traditionally high religious participation in Catholic Ireland in terms of nationalism and conflict.

A further concession of RCTR has been to qualify the proposition that diversity produces religious vitality, by acknowledging that this is not so when there are high levels of pluralism, when an increase in diversity does not increase competition, and has little effect on vitality.

Beyer (1997) points out that if conventional secularization theory falsely universalizes the European experience, then the RCTR runs the risk of replacing it merely with an American provincialism. It is, he points out (Beyer 1998), quoting Simpson (1990: 371), not just American, but 'gloriously American'. Understanding can best be furthered in Beyer's view by using each perspective to correct the other. His analysis of the situation in Canada shows that in some respects the market model works, but not in others. The debate about pluralism and other aspects of RCTR is thus proving highly stimulating and fruitful, and promises to further our understanding considerably as more studies are carried out.

Sects, Cults, and Movements

One of the most striking things about religious affiliation is the extent to which it is passed on from generation to generation and the result of socialization and the acquisition of a culture and an identity. Change of religious affiliation is, consequently, unusual and untypical in most social contexts. How, then, can religion be a matter of choice? Critics point out that the assumption that a pluralistic religious situation means the possibility of choice is often unrealistic. Diversity does not necessarily mean choice, but rather reflects ethnic and cultural diversity. Polish Catholicism is not an alternative for someone of Swedish Lutheran background. RCTR takes diversity as an indicator of competition, but this is not necessarily the case, leaving it without an adequate measure of competition (Beyer 1999).

This challenge to RCTR has stimulated refinements which rest upon the notions of religious and social capital. Such defences of RCTR run up against the criticism mentioned above that it neglects the fact that religious beliefs are accepted because they are seen to be the truth, and not because of the benefits they provide. Social bonds and links may indeed be important factors which prevent switching affiliation, but not so much because potential loss of them is weighed against the benefits of alternatives but because they act to reinforce the credibility of the belief system. They are part of the plausibility structure (Berger 1973; Bankston 2002) which upholds a system of beliefs. It is true, also, that social bonds are often benefits that come from membership of a church or denomination over and above judgements of the truth of doctrines, and that it may be costly to relinquish them; but it is difficult to accept that they will not be relinquished if those doctrines appear false or no longer credible. In other words, social capital is a bonus that may come with affiliation to a religious organization fundamentally grounded in conviction, and one does not choose to be convinced that something is true. Religious capital is not a matter of costs and benefits. It is thus not capital at all, and choice of religious affiliation is not an exercise in accountancy. We are not dealing here with investments that might be sacrificed for a greater gain. The truth is beyond value. Falsehood is worthless.

The rational choice approach to the study of sects and movements has, perhaps, been the most fruitful of its applications, and has generated considerable insight into their characteristics. Here again, however, there are those who would take issue with its characterization of the sect member as a calculating consumer attempting to maximize the benefits obtained while incurring as little cost as possible. Objections are voiced to the activities of members, such as prayer, ritual involvement, observance of rules of behaviour, and so on, as costs, rather than gratifying in themselves as expressions of piety, commitment, spirituality, evidence of being chosen, or progress towards salvation (Bryant 2000).To put this another way, the distinction between costs and rewards made by RCTR is somewhat dubious (Neitz and Mueser 1997; Johnson 2003).

Conclusion

RCTR has clearly had a major impact in the sociology of religion. It has done so because it offers a number of advantages over previous paradigms. It has shown us that religion involves active agency, and is not simply the product of socialization. It involves behaviour no less rational in many ways than any other form of human behaviour motivated by desires and needs and pursued by the use of appropriate means. In doing so it avoids the pitfalls of functionalist approaches and those that equate religion with irrationality, delusion, or false consciousness.

On the other hand, it goes, perhaps, rather too far in this direction, ignoring structural variables and social constraints. It works best when applied to the congregational style of Western religiosity, but less well outside this tradition. While it may overstress the market metaphor and be guilty of the 'economization' of religion (Robertson 1992), it reminds us that there is, nevertheless, competition between religious organizations and that potential followers can and do change their religious affiliations as their circumstances change and as more attractive alternatives are offered to them.

It has mounted a serious challenge to the long-established thesis that pluralism undermines religion, yet the matter remains unresolved as a consequence of inadequate measures of competition and diversity. It promises revealing insights into sectarian religious behaviour, but at the expense of neglecting the fact that while religion may be thought of as to some extent a product which is consumed, its consumers are also the producers of what they consume through their participation in religious activities. In the process it has given us some counterintuitive insights. Costly conservative and sectarian religion, for example, does not necessarily disappear in contemporary societies.

RCTR is, perhaps, best seen as a fruitful model of aggregate processes which helps us understand systems of religious provision and consumption, rather than a theory which explains individual actions and choices (Spickard 1998). It generates considerable insight into the overall patterns that result from many individual actions by treating people *as if* they were consumers of religious products in the way that economic theory treats them, deliberately unrealistically, as rational maximizers of utility, as economic men and women.

References

Ammerman, N. T. (1997). 'Religious Choice and Religious Vitality: The Market and Beyond'. In Young (1997), 119–32.

Bankston, C. L. III (2002). 'Rationality, Choice and the Religious Economy: The Problem of Belief'. *Review of Religious Research*, 43/4: 311–25.

Becker, G. (1986). 'The Economic Approach to Human Behaviour'. In J. Elster (ed.), *Rational Choice*. Oxford: Blackwell, 108–22.

Berger, P. (1973). *The Social Reality of Religion*. Harmondsworth: Penguin.

Beyer, P. (1997). 'Religious Vitality in Canada: The Complementarity of Religious Market and Secularization Perspectives'. *Journal for the Scientific Study of Religion*, 36/2: 272–88.

—— (1998). 'Sociological Theory of Religion between Description and Prediction: A Weberian Question Revisited'. In R. Laermans, B. R. Wilson, and J. Billiet (eds.), *Secularisation and Social Integration: Papers in Honour of Karel Dobbelaere*. Leuven: Leuven University Press, 83–105.

—— (1999). 'Secularization from the Perspective of Globalization: A Response to Dobbelaere'. *Sociology of Religion*, 60/3: 289–301.

Bruce, S. (1992). 'Pluralism and Religious Vitality'. In *idem* (ed.), *Religion and Modernisation: Sociologists and Historians Debate the Secularization Thesis*. Oxford: Clarendon Press, 170–94.

—— (1993). 'Religion and Rational Choice: A Critique of Economic Explanations of Religious Behaviour'. *Sociology of Religion*, 54: 193–205.

—— (1995). 'A Novel Reading of Nineteenth Century Wales: A Reply to Stark, Finke and Iannaccone'. *Journal for the Scientific Study of Religion*, 34/4: 520–2.

—— (1999). *Choice and Religion: A Critique of Rational Choice Theory*. Oxford: Oxford University Press.

—— (2000). 'The Supply-Side Model of Religion: The Nordic and Baltic States'. *Journal for the Scientific Study of Religion*, 39/1: 32–40.

Bryant, J. (2000). 'Cost–Benefit Accounting and the Piety Business: Is *homo religiosus*, at Bottom, a *homo economicus*?' *Method and Theory in the Study of Religion*, 12: 520–48.

Carroll, M. P. (1996). 'Stark Realities and Androcentric/Eurocentric Bias in the Sociology of Religion'. *Sociology of Religion*, 57/3: 225–39.

Chavez, M., and Cann, D. E. (1992). 'Regulation, Pluralism and Religious Market Structure: Explaining Religious Vitality'. *Rationality and Society*, 4/3: 272–90.

—— and Gorski, P. S. (2001). 'Religious Pluralism and Religious Participation'. *Annual Review of Sociology*, 27: 261–81.

Collins, R. (1997). 'Stark and Bainbridge, Durkheim and Weber: Theoretical Comparisons'. In Young (1997), 161–80.

Ellison, C. G. (1995). 'Rational Choice Explanations of Individual Religious Behaviour: Notes on the Problem of Social Embeddedness'. *Journal for the Scientific Study of Religion*, 34/1: 89–97.

Finke, R. (1997). 'The Consequences of Religious Competition: Supply Side Explanations for Religious Change'. In L. A. Young (ed.), *Rational Choice Theory and Religion*. London: Routledge, 46–65.

—— and Iannaccone, L. R. (1993). 'The Illusion of Shifting Demand: Supply-Side Explanations for Trends and Change in the American Religious Market Place'. *Annals of the American Association of Political and Social Science*, 527 (May): 27–39.

—— and Stark, R. (1988). 'Religious Economies and Sacred Canopies: Religious Mobilisation in American Cities'. *American Sociological Review*, 53: 41–9.

—— —— (1989). 'Evaluating the Evidence: Religious Economics and Sacred Canopies'. *American Sociological Review*, 54: 1054–6.

—— —— (1992). *The Churching of America, 1776–1990: Winners and Losers in Our Religious Economy*. New Brunswick, NJ: Rutgers University Press.

Goody, J. (1961). 'Religion and Ritual: The Definitional Problem'. *British Journal of Sociology*, 12: 142–64.

Guthrie, S. E. (1996). 'Religion: What Is It?' *Journal for the Scientific Study of Religion*, 35/4: 412–19.

Horton, R. (1967). 'African Traditional Thought and Western Science'. *Africa*, 37/1: 50–71, 2: 155–87. Repr. in B. R. Wilson (ed.), *Rationality*. Oxford: Blackwell, 1970, 131–71.

Iannaccone, L. R. (1988). 'A Formal Model of Church and Sect'. *American Journal of Sociology*, 94 suppl.: 5241–68.

—— (1990). 'Religious Participation: A Human Capital Approach'. *Journal for the Scientific Study of Religion*, 29/3: 297–314.

—— (1991). 'The Consequences of Religious Market Structure'. *Rationality and Society*, 3/2: 156–77.

—— (1992*a*). 'Religious Markets and the Economics of Religion'. *Social Compass*, 39/1: 123–31.

—— (1992*b*). 'Sacrifice and Stigma: Reducing Free-Riding in Cults, Communes, and Other Collectives'. *Journal of Political Economy*, 100/2: 271–91.

Iannaccone, L. R. (1995). 'Voodoo Economics?: Reviewing the Rational Choice Approach to Religion'. *Journal for the Scientific Study of Religion*, 29/3: 297–314.

—— (1997). 'Rational Choice: Framework for the Scientific Study of Religion'. In Young (1997), 26–45.

Jerolmack, C., and Porpora, D. (2004). 'Religion, Rationality, and Experience: A Response to the New Rational Choice Theory of Religion'. *Sociological Theory*, 22/1: 140–60.

Johnson, D. P. (2003). 'From Religious Markets to Religious Communities: Contrasting Implications for Applied Research'. *Review of Religious Research*, 44/4: 325–40.

Martin, D. A. (1978). *A General Theory of Secularisation*. Oxford: Blackwell.

Montgomery, J. (2003). 'A Formalization and Test of the Religious Economies Model'. *American Sociological Review*, 68: 782–809.

Neitz, M. J., and Mueser, P. R. (1997). 'Economic Man and the Sociology of Religion: A Critique of the Rational Choice Approach'. In Young (1997), 105–17.

Robertson, R. (1992). 'The Economisation of Religion? Reflections on the Promise and Limitations of the Economic Approach'. *Social Compass*, 39: 147–57.

Sharot, S. (2002). 'Beyond Christianity: A Critique of the Rational Choice Theory of Religion from a Weberian and Comparative Religions Perspective'. *Sociology of Religion*, 63/4: 427–54.

Sherkat, D. E. (1997). 'Embedding Religious Choices: Integrating Preferences and Social Constraints into Rational Choice Theories of Religious Behaviour'. In Young (1997), 66–86.

—— and Wilson, J. (1995). 'Preferences, Constraints, and Choices in Religious Markets: An Examination of Religious Switching and Apostasy'. *Social Forces*, 73/3: 993–1026.

Simpson, J. H. (1990). 'The Stark–Bainbridge Theory of Religion in "The Work of Rodney Stark: A Review Panel"'. *Journal for the Scientific Study of Religion*, 29: 367–71.

Spickard, J. V. (1998). 'Rethinking Religious Social Action: What is "Rational" about Rational Choice Theory?' *Sociology of Religion*, 59/2: 99–115.

Spiro, M. E. (1966). 'Religion: Problems of Definition and Explanation'. In M. Banton (ed.), *Anthropological Approaches to the Study of Religion*, A.S.A. Monograph no. 3. London: Tavistock, 85–126.

Stark, R. (1996). 'Why Religious Movements Succeed or Fail: A Revised General Model'. *Journal of Contemporary Religion*, 11: 133–46.

—— (1999*a*). 'Microfoundations of Religion: A Revised Theory'. *Sociological Theory*, 17: 264–89.

—— (1999*b*). 'Secularization: R.I.P.' *Sociology of Religion*, 60/3: 249–73.

—— and Bainbridge, W. S. (1979). 'Of Churches, Sects and Cults: Preliminary Concepts for a Theory of Religious Movements'. *Journal for the Scientific Study of Religion*, 18/2: 117–33.

—— —— (1980). 'Secularisation, Revival and Cult Formation'. *Annual Review of the Social Sciences of Religion*, 4: 85–119.

—— —— (1985). *The Future of Religion*. Berkeley: University of California Press.

—— —— (1987). *A Theory of Religion*. New York: Lang.

—— and Finke, R. (2000). *Acts of Faith: Explaining the Human Side of Religion*. Berkeley: University of California Press.

—— —— and Iannaccone, L. R. (1995). 'Pluralism and Piety: England and Wales 1851'. *Journal for the Scientific Study of Religion*, 34/4: 431–44.

—— and Iannaccone, L. R. (1994). 'A Supply Side Reinterpretation of the "Secularization" of Europe'. *Journal for the Scientific Study of Religion*, 33/3: 230–52.

Voas, D., Olson, D. V. A., and Crockett, A. (2002). 'Religious Pluralism and Participation: Why Previous Research is Wrong'. *American Sociological Review*, 67: 212–30.

Young, L. A. (ed.) (1997). *Rational Choice Theory and Religion*. London: Routledge.

Suggested Reading

The following are recommended: Bruce (1999); Stark, and Finke (2000); and Young (1997).

CHAPTER 7

RELIGION AND GENDER

SÎAN HAWTHORNE

'Contentious Traditions': The Study of Religions and the Gender-Theoretical Critique

Very few academic fields have been unaffected by the emergence of feminist and gender theory as a meta-critical tool in the social sciences and humanities. The study of religions in all its various guises is no exception, although it has been slower to respond to and incorporate gender-critical work. One reason for the relative inertia of religious studies in this regard has been its commitment to phenomenological principles of empathy with religious world views which, however laudable against the background of the colonial disparagement of non-Christian traditions, has led to a reluctance to critique the ways in which most religions persistently justify inequitable social arrangements. In contrast, feminist and gender theory within the study of religions has called attention to the forms of misogyny that are produced and legitimated by religious discourses, the subsequent marginalization or subordination of women within religious traditions, and the distorted accounts of religious phenomena that result from the failure of religious studies scholars to attend both to gender differences and to the broader ideological dimensions of its own history. The result has been an ongoing tension between the objectives of the study of religions as an academic field and gender-critical scholarship.[1]

Gender-critical approaches to the study of religions engage in explicitly political discursive practices, and this stance places them at odds with the declared neutrality of the study of religions. This is perhaps even more the case with feminist scholarship, because it intervenes in hegemonic discourses in order to oppose and resist the universalizing tendencies of 'scientific' bodies of knowledge in so far as they ignore the specificities of gender. The differences between a feminist and a gender-theoretical approach are important to note here. While both are politically committed, in so far as they identify sources of gender inequality and work to analyse its causes and alleviate its symptoms, their units of analysis are subtly different. Feminists have tended to use the category 'woman' as a universal trope; gender-critical scholarship, on the other hand, leaves categories like 'women', 'men', 'gender', 'sexuality', and 'identity' open to interrogation, or, in Judith Butler's terms 'troubled' (1990), and, further, acknowledges the intersectionality of identification (in terms of race, class, gender, physical ability, nationality, and so on), refusing essences in favour of theorizing contextual positionality. Butler's work has proved to be of critical importance for many gender theorists, as it has expanded inquiry beyond the analysis of women's subordination and the analytical operation of the category of 'woman' as the common ground upon which the political programme of feminism is organized, in order to challenge the binarized nature of gender categories. Butler has suggested the need to deconstruct these hierarchical arrangements in order to question the 'political construction and regulation of identity itself' (1990: p. xxix), and it is this aspect of her work that has marked both a departure from the liberal feminist adherence to the category 'woman' and an alignment with the intersectionalist tenor of post-colonial theories.

Another reason for the tension between the study of religions and gender-critical scholarship thus concerns the dualist framework within which many conceptualizations of the form and structure of religions are organized, most paradigmatically those of subject/object, sacred/secular, private/public, centre/margin, insider/outsider. Here the field is again at odds with gender-critical approaches, which have offered a sustained and programmatic critique of the ways in which these kinds of binaries build on, and imply, a primary structural division of male/female, with its attendant positive/negative or normative/particular valuations (for an early example, see Cixous and Clément 1996: 63 ff.). The sociology of religion, at least as far as elements of the field remain obdurately committed to the classical sociological frameworks established by Durkheim, Weber, Troeltsch, and Mauss, amongst others, or maintain a strict division between sociological, phenomenological, and

[1] Throughout this chapter I will use the term 'gender-critical' to refer to scholarship that is explicitly informed by those feminist discourses that are inscribed within, or conducted with reference to, the post-Enlightenment, liberalist rhetoric of human rights.

text-historical research methods, has often replicated this binary framework. There has consequently been little work in mainstream religious studies examining the political implications of the continued reliance on this dualistic framework, with its encoding of structurally conservative gender valuations (see Warne 2000; 2001*b*).

However, feminist and gender-critical approaches to the study of religions are themselves not without serious weaknesses and ethical lacunae, particularly with regard to their own complicity in the social, political, and epistemic violence that has been exercised by the West towards non-Western cultures historically. Because the field was formed out of a feminist theory, its politically motivated critique of the androcentric tenor of the study of religions has resulted in a variety of reconstructions of the history of religions in order to retrieve non-patriarchal sites of religiosity in their formative contexts. However, this has resulted in the production, against the grain of its own critical stance, of what Hewitt suggests is 'another ideological interest', to the extent that 'ideology critique devolves into ideology formation' (1999: 50, 51). The problem here, as I will discuss in more detail below, is not simply the elevation of its own ideological position over those of more mainstream religious studies, but that the reconstructions undertaken operate a kind of discursive colonization in the service of feminist political goals at the expense of rigorous scholarly practice. Finally, despite a sophisticated recognition of the problems with dualist frameworks, feminist and gender-critical approaches to the study of religion have nonetheless persistently operated with alternative dualist models that imply the divisions male/female, or masculine/feminine experiences of religion, and androcentric/gynocentric scholarly modes of inquiry.

With these problems in mind, the task of this chapter will be to trace what has generally been characterized by a number of scholars as, at best, a contentious relationship between the two (see, e.g., Christ 1991; 1992; Gross 1996; Plaskow 1993; Shaw 1995; Warne 1991: 353–5; 1995: 97–9; 2001*a*). Indeed, Shaw states that the 'relationship between feminism and mainstream history of religions is not merely awkward; it is mutually toxic' (1995: 70). I will examine core approaches and concerns articulated in gender-critical scholarship: namely, the invisibility of women within religious traditions and in the intellectual frameworks that seek to understand them, and the need to challenge the androcentric assumptions of religious studies. I will do so in order to question the extent to which mainstream religious studies and gender-critical approaches have, in fact, been at odds, and will suggest, rather, that the two fields have much in common, in that they share attitudes and intellectual trajectories that require a series of critical adjustments. Although much of the debate inaugurated by gender-critical and feminist scholarship has offered a wide-ranging critique of the methodological and empirical content of the study of religions, I will suggest that both the study of religions and gender-critical approaches have failed to respond to the significant challenges posed by post-colonial criticism, particularly as related to their roles in maintaining and policing inequitable power relations across a variety of binarized axes. The implications of the post-colonial debate for the field of religion and gender cannot be ignored, either in good conscience or if scholars in the field remain committed to what Morny Joy refers to as 'intellectual adequacy in a postcolonial world' (2001: 183). I will thus argue that both need to attend to their ethical positionings along these axes, and to be vigilant about their implication in colonialist power relations. I conclude by suggesting a number of ways in which the study of religions and gender-critical approaches might pursue a more adequate and ethically attuned course with regard to practices of representation.

Rationality, Gender, and the Colonial Legacy of *Religionswissenschaft*

In 1995 Walter Capps located the primary intellectual paradigm of religious studies as developing from 'the comprehensive approach to human knowledge that was constructed and fashioned at the time of the Enlightenment'. He then suggested the ways in which

> methodological approaches designed under the influence of the scientific method have functioned to parse the subject, to break it down into its constituent elements.... The overall intent was to make the subject of religion intelligible.... Enlightenment philosophy was made congruent with religion's demonstrable intelligibility, and both of these were made congruent with a modified understanding of the teachings of Christianity (to which was sometimes appended Judaism, and, perhaps, the other religions of the world). (1995: 345–6)

In locating the intellectual foundations of the field in the nineteenth-century consolidation of Enlightenment thought, Capps indicates how the scientific study of religions (*Religionswissenschaft*) first understood its task as a field of discrete scholarship, and how it came, historically, to categorize its objects of study under the classificatory norms and procedures of the dominant scientific method of rational inquiry. In pursuing the 'intelligibility' of religion, any examination of the truth claims or soteriological projections of a tradition was to be suspended—these were in doubt in any case—in favour of a methodical cataloguing of varieties of religious phenomena, which were then to be interpreted in accordance with universal (trans-cultural) principles. The political and intellectual utility of adopting the scientific model should not be underestimated, although Capps certainly underplays this aspect. The study of religions as a field of knowledge was legitimized by its alignment with Enlightenment values, and was consequently able to articulate its purpose in terms of an objective approach to religious phenomena, achieved by employing scientific methods of disinterested observation and the creation of universal categories of analysis such as religion itself, *Homo religiosus*, and the universal *sui generis* nature of religion.

Crucially, the 'narrative' of universality characteristic of Enlightenment thought coincided with, and enabled, European colonial expansion. The vision of social and intellectual progress elaborated by the Enlightenment *philosophes* provided the ideological justification—the condition of possibility—for imperialist ambitions (or what became euphemized as the 'civilizing mission'). It enabled the elaboration of a discourse which privileged an élitist European subjectivity and produced a corresponding formulation (with spatial and temporal significance) of abject Otherness, seen to be embodied by the colonized peoples. Enlightenment knowledge production placed local narratives (simultaneously inscribing them as inferior) in the singular context of 'World History' that served to confirm the Enlightenment version of history as one of inevitable and irresistible progress (see Stocking 1987: 8–45). Temporality in this mode was reconfigured as naturally sequential and inexorable, a movement from a primitive origin in antiquity to the civilized and civilizing present. A logical corollary of this rationalist conception of history was the tendency of Enlightenment thinkers to demean or deride those cultures and peoples, past and present, which lacked consciousness of the principles of enlightened reason and who persisted in slavish adherence to superstition, myth, and religion.

The study of religions, in its adoption of Enlightenment principles of reason and emancipated individuality, was certainly implicated in the broader political topography of the colonialist project, reflecting its values and enacting its politics. As McCutcheon has suggested, correctly in my view:

> We need to inquire into the relations between the rise of our field in the mid-nineteenth century and the state-sponsored colonialism that was at that time taking over from the private-enterprise colonialism of the previous age. Is it a coincidence that scholars working in Britain (Müller) and the Netherlands (Tiele) are so prominent in our histories, or has it something to do with the growing need those countries had for developing more efficient ways to describe, categorize, contain, control, and profit from diverse customs and populations? We need to investigate the intellectual as well as the cultural and material capital that the field accrues. We might learn that the origin of the field lies more in the realm of global politics than in the insights of the disengaged mind. (1999*b*: 529)

McCutcheon's point is well made, but it is important to note that the motivation for the production of a methodological framework particular to the study of religious traditions was prompted in part as a way of avoiding a cavalier attitude to religious practices and beliefs that were alien to a Christian paradigm. However, affiliation with the rationalist paradigm of the Enlightenment also helped to establish the study of religions as a field of study distinct from theology, with its seemingly 'contaminating' allegiance to confessional modes of inquiry, in order to make more secure its institutional position.

The dominant methodological approach that enabled this task was the phenomenology of religion. In its classical manifestation, underlying the practice of phenomenology was an assumption that one could enumerate universal patterns of human religiosity (if not the meanings assigned to them) and retrieve the essence of diverse religious practices and orientations through procedures of detached empathy, eidetic vision, comparison, and anti-reductionist observation. Here the position of the investigator was 'bracketed out', as were his or her own ideological commitments, so that subject and object relations remain intact, clearly separate. The classical sociology of religion, although much more cognizant than the history of religions of the need to relate religion to particular societal formations and to challenge the universality of Western models of rationality (see, e.g., Weber 2002: 149) also operated within universalist parameters, using the history and contemporary nineteenth-century forms of Christian Protestantism as a model upon which to theorize about religion more generally (see Lechner 2006).

Gender-critical theorists have long challenged the claim of the study of religions historically to undertake disinterested observation of religious phenomena and to replicate scientific empiricism at the methodological level. Their challenge to the androcentric nature of the study of religions (explored below), coupled with a recognition of the residue of its colonialist legacy, certainly renders the claim of methodological disinterestedness not only demonstrably false, but theoretically naive. The resistance met by feminist scholars when suggesting the need for the field to transform its discursive frameworks to take into account female difference is explicable on the basis that challenging the androcentric perspective of religious studies called into question the objectivity and credibility of accumulated knowledge in the field. In so doing, gender-critical scholarship threatened the reliability of the foundational categories and structures upon which the field was built, and the opposition it encountered is similar to the way in which the field has tended to resist postcolonial critique.

The complicity of the study of religions in colonialist intellectual schemas has only recently come under scrutiny, and from a variety of directions (see Asad and Dixon 1985; Radhakrishnan 1996; Young 1990), although it should be noted that scholars within the field have been lamentably slow in undertaking the kind of critical reflection on European intellectual ethnocentrism that has guided internal debate in the neighbouring fields of anthropology and history (notable exceptions are Fitzgerald 2000; Flood 1999; R. King 1999; Joy 2001). This is partly due to an entrenched and, in my view, shameful resistance to a sustained internal examination of the ways in which the field's colonialist history continues to play itself out in the classificatory practices and underlying assumptions of contemporary scholarship.

One of the ways this occurs is with regard to the category 'religion' itself. Richard King has argued forcefully that Christianity has served as the primogenitive model in the identification and analysis of those traditions we now understand as religious and that, as a result, 'the comparative study of religion remains founded on a conceptual framework that is unmistakably theological and Christian in orientation' (1999: 40). He goes on to suggest that the 'debates about the precise denotation of the term "religion"... do not question the fundamental assumption that there are things called "religions" that are easily identifiable and classified in terms of specific names such as Christianity, Islam, Hinduism, etc.' (1999: 41). Thus, to question the basic Christian model as an adequate means of identifying whether or not a tradition is 'religious' is perhaps to suggest that the study of religions may merely be in the business of constructing straw dolls, a conclusion to which many in the field are not receptive.

Another point of resistance to postcolonial critique emerges out of the alignment of the study of religions with the secularist values of the Enlightenment legacy. Such a practice has encoded a system of hierarchical valuations, where secularism is assumed to be a neutral stance in comparison with, and in preference to, the confessional, and thus less 'objective', commitments that characterize traditional theology. However, as King points out, 'the modern study of religions is not unaffected by the Christian heritage of western culture and by the development of theology as an academic discipline in the west, nor is the apparently secular nature of study of religions a view from nowhere' (1999: 41). More troublingly, however, the secular framework upon which the field is founded extends well beyond the need to contrast itself with theology in order to establish its neutral status by implying the devaluation of all religious beliefs and explanations in what is arguably a colonial move that validates the civilized, objective, and knowing self against the primitive, unreliable, and known other. This, together with the elevation of Christianity as a prototype of religion, mobilizes diverse 'religious' objects of inquiry in order to establish the epistemological superiority of a set of ideological paradigms that have arisen from, and been formed by, very dissimilar contexts to those of the religions themselves.

Gender-critical scholarship has been well placed to inaugurate the debate regarding the need to interrogate the colonialist legacy of the study of religion, given that, as Suchocki argues:

> Absolutizing one religion such that it becomes normative for all others is a dynamic with clear parallels to sexism, whereby one gender is established as the norm for human existence. Therefore the critique of gender can be extended as a critique of religious imperialism. (1989: 150)

Moreover, as Joy has argued, 'the process of "othering" that has been inflicted by dominant Western values is similar to the way women... have been judged and found wanting according to prevailing standards of masculinity and/or rationality' (2001: 178). However, the metaphorical extension of concepts related to the historical fact of European colonization in order to refer to the othering and exploitation of women employs a series of problematic assumptions—not least that all colonialism operates in the same way and towards the same ends—which not only result in the elision of the specific historicity of the European colonial period but suggest that all women share a similar experience of gender oppression assessed predominantly in the terms prescribed by Anglo-American feminism (Mohanty 1991: 52). Indeed, feminism, by appropriating for all women the dubious privilege of colonized victim status, engages in a form of discursive colonization that places under erasure the significant differences between women across national, religious, political, and ethnic divides, and excuses itself from having to acknowledge its own complicity in colonialist schemes of domination (see Lewis 1996; Yegonoglu 1998). There should be no mistaking the kind of intellectual sleight of hand that this tactic enables or the rhetorical advantages it secures. I do not mean to suggest here that Joy herself (con)fuses the position of woman with that of the colonized subject—she in fact takes pains to listen to those postcolonial voices which challenge the feminist appropriation of the experiences of non-Western women—but rather to draw attention to the broader tendency in some feminist scholarship to ignore the specificity of the colonial era in order to draw on its rhetorical power.

At the same time, Western feminist scholarship,[2] in particular, still operates according to a binary logic of differentiation, re-enacting the colonialist imposition of a subject/object division (between, in this instance, white women and women of colour, or emancipated feminist/oppressed 'Third-World'[3] women). The function of this binarization operates according to a logic of the self-same, wherein the construction of a distinct and impermeable identity can be achieved only through the exclusion of the 'other' in order to secure the coherence, autonomy, and singularity of the self (see Hawthorne 2006: 272–82). However, the process of excluding alterity in order to secure selfhood is complicated, and indeed contradicted, by a simultaneous logic of inclusion whereby homogenizing signifiers such as 'woman' (instead of the more multivalent 'women'), for example, cover over significant differences. Chandra Talpade Mohanty has suggested that some Western feminist writing on the 'Third World' enacts this contradictory procedure in maintaining self and other in a simultaneously dialectical and mutual relationship when she argues that the elevation of the category 'woman' in feminist discourse

[2] In using the term 'Western feminism' I want to acknowledge the particularity of its discourse and history, in order to resist the totalizing tendencies of feminism historically to ignore differences of context, culture, political orientation, and national allegiances when framing the meaning and purpose of its political agendas. At the more localized level, however, the term is generally unsatisfactory, inasmuch as it obscures the huge regional and political differences between the feminisms that operate in the countries that make up what is, at least in popular discourse, understood to be the 'West'. Moreover, it appropriates those forms of feminism that are critical of the ethnocentrism of 'Western feminism' and which may not want to be identified as 'Western' but which are nonetheless produced within the context of the Western intellectual and political environment.

[3] I would acknowledge here that the terms 'Third World', 'Western', and 'non-Western' are profoundly embedded in precisely the kind of colonialist logic that I am opposing. Thus, when I employ them, I am doing so either in acknowledgement of the historical (but essentially imaginative) contexts in which they have been constituted as opposed realities or in contexts where the postcolonialist writers whose work I am referencing are using them. Even then, it is important to note that these writers do so critically and reflexively. See Joy 2001: 182 n. 5 for a similar stance.

> Discursively colonize[s] the material and historical heterogeneities of the lives of women in the third world, thereby producing/re-presenting a composite, singular, 'third world woman'—an image which appears arbitrarily constructed, but nevertheless carries with it the authorizing signature of Western humanist discourse. (1991: 53)

Without this composite image of the 'Third World woman', the specific conception of Western feminists as emancipated from patriarchal oppression becomes difficult. Thus, as Mohanty makes clear, Western feminists are reliant on a representation of their 'third world' others as victimized and in need of the liberatory power of feminism in so far as 'by contrasting the representation of women in the third world with western feminisms' self-presentation... western feminists alone become the true "subjects".... Third world women, on the other hand, never rise above the debilitating generality of their "object status"' (1991: 71). This production has thus enabled some Western feminists to view their apparently benevolent efforts to ameliorate the oppressive conditions of 'Third World' women in ways that are similar to those of the British 'civilizing mission' in India, where the colonial move to abolish the practice of sati could be characterized, in Gayatri Spivak's famous phrase, as 'White men saving brown women from brown men' (1988: 297). While I will return below to consider one way in which gender-critical scholarship in the study of religions stands guilty of perpetuating colonialist practices, here I would suggest that we might begin to see that the study of religion and gender-critical perspectives in the field (in so far as they are informed by a feminist sensibility) share some considerable common ground. Both employ the subject/object framework of the Enlightenment rationalist emancipatory project, and this results in an oppressive enactment of (neo)colonialist intellectual practices. Moreover, the dualist framework of the study of religions is replicated by some gender-critical scholars in two ways: first, there is slippage between the analytical category 'woman' and the material and heterogeneous category 'women'; secondly, a sharp distinction is drawn between male and female religiosity and modes of scholarship. Nowhere is this clearer than in the gender-critical assessment of the androcentrism of the study of religions and the corollary efforts by some scholars to reconstruct women-centred histories of religion.

Androcentrism, Feminist Reconstructions, and the Colonialist Move

Perhaps more than any other area of gender-critical analysis in the field, the critique of core disciplinary questions historically formulated from the perspective of predominantly white, educated men has preoccupied gender-critical work in the field. Thus, feminist scholars have criticized the textual bias of historical studies for replicating élite male perspectives and rendering the participation of women in religious traditions either invisible or defined only in male terms. Moreover, categories like *Homo religiosus* and the insider/outsider formula have been censured for further enacting the marginalization of women. Rosalind Shaw has correctly argued, for example, that the *Homo religiosus*, as representative of a religious collective, is generally 'undifferentiated by gender, race, class or age, or defined explicitly as male' (1995: 67). The insider/outsider trope has failed to account for the 'outsider' status of women within at least orthodox forms of religion, and builds in a rather stark distinction between observer and observed (see McCutcheon 1999*a*). From the perspective of feminist analyses, the main consequence of biased, androcentric scholarship has been the production of distorted, partial scholarly accounts that contain serious deficiencies at the level of data collection and interpretation, as well as in the subsequent development of theoretical paradigms (Gross 1974: 7).

Consequently, much pioneering gender-critical scholarship in the 1960s and 1970s was concerned with mapping women's lives and experiences within religious traditions in order to render them analytically visible. June O'Connor has summarized their efforts as 'rereading, reconceiving, and reconstructing', informed by questions regarding 'women as subject', 'sensitivity to and criticism of the manner in which [religious] traditions ... have been studied and ... formulated', and a concern with 'our scholarly angles of vision, our research methods and approaches' (1989: 101–2). Accordingly, four main preoccupations have characterized work in the field: first, scholars have exposed the androcentrism and misogyny of a variety of religions; secondly, women have been identified as a legitimate category of analysis, with women's experiences being promoted as a corrective tool; thirdly, new forms of female-centred religiosity have been explored; and fourthly, epistemological and methodological tools have been developed in order to challenge the androcentric bias of mainstream scholarship in theology and religious studies (see Hawthorne 2005 for a general survey of literature reflecting these trends). Focus has also been extended, however, to women as active agents and religious innovators in their own right (see Ruether and McLaughlin 1979). Cross-cultural studies in the field of feminist religious studies have demonstrated women's strategies of resistance and innovation within a multitude of religions, and have assessed the ambiguity of gendered symbolism within many religious systems (see, e.g., Christ and Plaskow 1979; Plaskow and Christ 1989; Falk and Gross 1980; Haddad and Banks Findly 1985; Atkinson, Buchanan, and Miles 1985; U. King 1989). However, as Randi Warne has suggested, the partiality of mainstream religious studies is not solved simply by adding the study of women to existing scholarship, for the reason that 'Women were not simply "omitted" through a[n] ... act of scholarly absent-mindedness; women were excluded from ... scholarship, as from "significant" subject matter, as from positions of authority and power, when the basic ideas, definitions, principles and facts were being formulated' (2001*a*: 150). Thus the foundational suppositions of religious studies have been in need of radical reformulation, and this has lead to the suggestion that gender-critical studies offer the study of religions a 'paradigm shift' (see King 1995: 1–38).

Another solution that has been proposed to counter women's exclusion is the undertaking of historical reconstructions in order to identify the apparently non-patriarchal elements of religions' formative years, thus making them more compatible with feminist politics. However, while an emphasis on women has been crucial for identifying the unique place of female expression, it has nonetheless often operated according to a set of assumed commonalities in female experience and female religiosity across geographic and historical divides. More worryingly, the trend towards reconstruction has reflected a nostalgia for a pristine golden age of religion uncontaminated by sexist agendas, and here again we might both see the colonialist move enacted in gender-critical scholarship and draw out further some of the common ground shared by the study of religions and gender-critical approaches.

Rita Gross's *Buddhism after Patriarchy: A Feminist History, Analysis, and Reconstruction of Buddhism* (1993) stands as an exemplar of recent reconstructive efforts in gender-critical studies of religion. She attempts to show how a reconstructed authentic core of Buddhism reflects and supports feminist values, in so far as it 'is without gender bias, whatever the practical record may reveal, and that sexist practices are in actual contradiction with the essential core teachings of the tradition' (1993: 210). She argues that her work constitutes a 'feminist revalorization of Buddhism' (1993: 305), and extrapolates from this to suggest that many religions may originally have possessed an egalitarian, non-sexist central vision uncontaminated by later patriarchal distortions introduced by an exclusively male hierocracy intent on asserting male privilege and power. However, Marsha Hewitt has strongly criticized Gross's and others' efforts in this regard, demonstrating the ways in which they cultivate 'subterranean discourses of liberation and egalitarianism which hold the promise of refiguring religion in terms of values that are judged to be more authentic and faithful to the tradition itself' (1999: 51). As she quite correctly points out,

> it is illegitimate for scholars in religion to import an external, foreign, modern ideology into an ancient religious tradition in order to proclaim this ideology as the underlying center of authenticity of that religion.... [In so doing] the scholar... sets up a new authoritative voice [and] engages in forms of intellectual imperialism that feminist theory has painstakingly worked to identify and overcome. (Hewitt 1999: 54–5)

Thus, according to Hewitt, Gross makes herself the arbiter of the Buddhist tradition, imposing on an alien context a historically specific, ethnocentric, and ideological vision of appropriate religiosity (informed by liberal feminist values), and simultaneously endorses the universality of feminist insights against evidence to the contrary. Gross, in contradiction to her claim that early Buddhism contained the elements of a feminist sensibility, argues that a revalorized Buddhism will be achieved by learning from the prophetic traditions of Christianity and Judaism, with which she sees Christian feminist theology 'in direct continuity' (1993: 134). Hewitt points out that in attempting to 'transform Buddhism into a modern Western feminist philosophy', Gross subjects Buddhism to 'ideological colonization', and that in deciding what constitutes the irreducible feminist core of the religion, 'the question is decided in terms of the primacy of feminism, not tradition' (Hewitt 1999: 57, 58). One of the most serious problems with the approach adopted by Gross is the way in which it compromises the principles of scholarly rigour by assuming that ideology can take the place of careful argumentation, to the detriment of the reputation of those gender-critical (and other) scholars who are far less cavalier with their sources. This is not to suggest, however, that there are scholarly approaches that are non-ideological, but that to detach those ideologies from the contexts in which they emerged and to impose them retrospectively on material wholly different historically, philosophically, and geographically is to indulge in a form of discursive imperialism.

Hewitt's critique is a persuasively formulated and timely intervention in the sometimes unreflexive ways in which gender-critical scholarship has pursued its course. She thus demonstrates another way in which some of the practices of gender-critical scholarship and the mainstream study of religions share some common ground. The study of religions, in a way similar to feminist reconstructive efforts, as I noted above, has historically imposed what is in effect an ideological itinerary upon its objects of inquiry, classifying them according to values and constructs that are the products of a very particular philosophical trajectory.

Acknowledging Common Ground

Although long characterized as contentious, perhaps the study of religions and gender-critical approaches have instead been unwitting 'partners in crime', in so far as both are in need of reform, for similar reasons, from a postcolonial perspective. What postcolonial theories and those gender theories that are informed by the postcolonial critique (most notably those of Judith Butler) show is that the central analytical categories of both the study of religions and feminist theory—the common ground of each—are universalist and essentialist, at the expense of an ethical recognition of, and relation to, difference or otherness as more than just an oppositional category constrained and bound to a hierarchical binary system within Western metaphysics historically.[4] Both can be criticized for disguising or failing to recognize their own political investment in maintaining a division between self and other, however that is expressed. In Western feminist theory it seems to be a division between the universal category 'woman' and the materiality of actual 'women'. This division has implications for another form of othering between the Western woman and the 'Third World woman'. In the context of religion it manifests itself in a variety of ways. The rubric of insider/outsider that has recently been so popular in the study of religions is a particular example which, for all its attempts to elevate an 'insider' point of view, enables scholars of religion too easily to distance themselves from their objects of study by uncritically situating the non-Christian religious practitioner as an authentic 'insider'. By naming ourselves as 'outsiders' to the world views of religious practitioners, we avoid our complicity in North–South politics, hiding behind naiveté, lack of expertise, or methodological disinterest when the 'insider' becomes another word for 'other'. Further, the formulation encodes a form of idealization of the religious point of view which either helps to contain and depoliticize difference in terms of ethnicity, gender, race, class, physical ability, or puts the onus for representation exclusively on the 'native informant' as a representative of otherness.

It is risky to assume that otherness can be encountered on a level playing field. Our interactions with, and representations of, others are inevitably overdetermined by the West's privileged historical and geographic position with regard to the material and cultural advantages resulting from imperialism. When we as 'knowing subjects' ignore our complicity in this history, pretend to be unaffected by wider geo-political determinations, or claim to be detached and disinterested, in order to ensure the reliability of the scientific method, we do the opposite of removing ourselves from the scene of analysis: we privilege and protect ourselves from valid political critique by bracketing off our own ideological investments as incidental—rather than central—to our scholarly interests, all in the name of the 'Other'. Our apparently noble and altruistic attempts to represent our objects of knowledge carefully are never just that: knowledge, as Michel Foucault so persuasively demonstrated, is always imbricated with power, so that, if the history of colonial scholarship can tell us anything, working to know the other is usually also about placing it under surveillance and disciplining it in order to have a more manageable Other. Moreover, our scholarly discourses and methods are often predetermined by

[4] Generally speaking, the metaphysics that has proposed an ethical orientation towards others has postulated an autonomous agent, routinely inscribed as normatively masculine, whose obligations to the other come from 'his' realization that the other must be the same, or at least equivalent to, 'himself'. The autonomous subject of this ethics does not have a relation to any other; rather, it always and only has a relationship to the self-same—that is, a selfhood posited as the same against an other as representative of difference. Ethics in a postcolonial or gender-theoretical frame conceives of relations of difference that do not operate according to a dualist logic of opposition, but rather work on an assumption of the other as inherent within oneself instead of as exterior. See Gottschall 2002 for a helpful analysis of ethics, moral agency, and deconstructive gender theory.

our geo-political and institutional positioning. Thus there can be no such thing as a non-institutional environment or a wholly detached and disinterested perspective: our representative practices are constructed, at least in part, based on the values and aspirations of such an environment. However, I do believe that although we cannot escape the history of the discourses in which we work, we can still undertake the necessary critique of those hegemonic representations that force us into dialectical encounters between self and other. I want to conclude, therefore, by very briefly suggesting a number of ways, based on the work of Gayatri Spivak, in which our field might pursue its future.[5]

The first step is to recognize that, although we can never act from an 'outside', we should also see that our situatedness is the place from which our work can start. As Spivak states, 'let us become vigilant about our own practice and use it as much as we can rather than make the totally counter-productive gesture of repudiating it' (1990: 11). Thus the problematic history of the study of religions and its continuing legacy do not preclude the possibility of salvaging from within it an ethical orientation towards the Other; so we need to redouble our efforts to find within the theoretical frameworks of the study of religion those elements that are directed towards respecting difference. Secondly, Spivak's work calls upon us to recognize our complicity in the maintenance of a series of inequitable arrangements, in so far as she demonstrates how all scholars in the business of representation are inevitably positioned in a variety of discourses, such that our personal and institutional desires and interests are unavoidably reflected in our work. Thus we need to acknowledge that empathetic orientations, disinterested scholarship, and critique are always already inscribed in relations of power. As Ilan Kapoor suggests, 'acknowledging one's contamination... helps to temper and contextualize one's claims, reduces the risk of personal arrogance or geoinstitutional imperialism, and moves one toward a non-hierarchical encounter with the Third World/subaltern' (2004: 641). A related step is the task of what Spivak refers to as 'un-learning our privilege as our loss' (1990: 9). For Spivak, one should not undertake 'fieldwork' elsewhere without first doing one's 'homework'. Representation of the Other 'over there' requires a deep analysis of the 'here', in order to re-imagine 'what we mean by the "field" or the "there"' (Kapoor 2004: 641). As such, we need to revisit the history of our prejudices (whether racism, sexism, and classism, to academic elitism and ethnocentrism) in order to 'unlearn' hegemonic systems of knowledge and representation (Kapoor 2004: 641). Finally, Spivak suggests that we should learn to work 'with no guarantees' (2001: 15), which means that we should be willing to acknowledge the operational and systemic limits of our field of knowledge and to resist the totalizing imperative to provide wholly accurate and complete representational models. This is because, as Spivak argues, the Other is 'irretrievably heterogenous' (1988: 284). And here she echoes Jonathan Z. Smith's argument against the universalist pretensions of the study of

[5] My reading of Spivak is adapted here from Kapoor's argument (2004) for the utility of Spivak's work in adjusting the representational practices of international development scholarship.

religions when he states that: 'Any enumeration of the... persistent and allegedly unique features of [humanity] ... must record a set of traits so numerous and diverse as to result in a motley list rather than a persuasive demonstration of "truth" or of an "essence"' (1982: 38).

Recent work in both the study of religions and gender-critical approaches does offer a testament to a new willingness to engage in dialogue of the kind promoted by Spivak, to challenge core assumptions, and to learn from the perspectives of post-colonial theory (see, e.g., King and Beattie 2004). It is clear, however, that much work remains to be done. All scholars of religion, regardless of their broader ideological investments are faced, first, with recognizing their own privileged positions as producers of knowledge about religion, and secondly, with the daunting task of dismantling and reforming the foundational certainties of both the study of religion and that of gender-critical thought in order to ensure that the call to ethical engagement by post-colonial theorists, in particular, is heard and acted upon. In this regard both scholars of religion and gender-critical theorists have much 'homework' to do together—not as adversaries, or partners in crime, but through acknowledging our common ground and committing ourselves to 'intellectual adequacy in a postcolonial world'.

References

ASAD, TALAL, and DIXON, J. (1985). 'Translating Europe's Others'. In Francis Barker *et al.* (eds.), *Europe and its Others: Proceedings of the Essex Conference on the Sociology of Literature, July 1984*. Colchester: Essex University Press, 170–7.

ATKINSON, CLARISSA W., BUCHANAN, CONSTANCE H., and MILES, MARGARET R. (eds.) (1985). *Immaculate and Powerful: The Female Sacred Image and Social Reality.* Boston: Beacon Press.

BUTLER, JUDITH (1990). *Gender Trouble: Feminism and the Subversion of Identity.* New York and London: Routledge.

CAPPS, WALTER (1995). *Religious Studies: The Making of a Discipline.* Minneapolis: Fortress Press.

CHRIST, CAROL (1991). 'Mircea Eliade and the Feminist Paradigm Shift'. *Journal of Feminist Studies in Religion*, 7: 75–94.

—— (1992). 'Feminists—Sojourners in the Field of Religious Studies'. In Cheris Kramarae and Dale Spender (eds.), *The Knowledge Explosion: Generations of Feminist Scholarship*, New York: Teacher's College, 82–8.

—— and PLASKOW, JUDITH (eds.) (1979). *Womanspirit Rising: A Feminist Reader in Religion.* New York: Harper & Row.

CIXOUS, HÉLÈNE, and CLÉMENT, CATHERINE (1996). *The Newly Born Woman.* London: I. B. Tauris.

FALK, NANCY, and GROSS, RITA (eds.) (1980). *Unspoken Worlds: Women's Religious Lives in Non-Western Cultures.* San Francisco: Harper & Row.

FITZGERALD, TIMOTHY (2000). *The Ideology of Religious Studies.* New York and Oxford: Oxford University Press.

FLOOD, GAVIN D. (1999) *Beyond Phenomenology: Rethinking the Study of Religion*. London and New York: Cassell.

GOTTSCHALL, MARILYN (2002). 'The Ethical Implications of the Deconstruction of Gender'. *Journal of the American Academy of Religion*, 70/2: 279–99.

GROSS, RITA (ed.) (1974). *Beyond Androcentrism: New Essays on Women and Religion*. Missoula, Mont.: Scholars Press for the American Academy of Religion.

—— (1993). *Buddhism after Patriarchy: A Feminist History, Analysis, and Reconstruction of Buddhism*. Albany, NY: State University of New York Press.

—— (1996). *Feminism and Religion: An Introduction*. Boston: Beacon Press.

HADDAD, YVONNE YAZBECK, and BANKS FINDLY, ELLISON (eds.) (1985). *Women, Religion and Social Change*. Albany, NY: State University of New York Press.

HAWTHORNE, SÎAN (2005). 'Gender & Religion: History of Study'. In Lindsay Jones *et al.* (eds.), *Encyclopedia of Religions*, 2nd edn. Farrington Hills, Mich.: Thompson Gale, v. 3310–18.

—— (2006). 'Origins, Genealogies, and the Politics of Identity: Towards a Feminist Philosophy of Myth' (Ph.D. thesis, London). Stable URL: <http://eprints.soas.ac.uk/archive/00000144/01/Origins,_Genealogies,_and_the_Politics_of_Identity.pdf.>

HEWITT, MARSHA AILEEN (1999). 'Ideology Critique, Feminism, and the Study of Religion'. *Method and Theory in the Study of Religion*, 11: 47–63.

JOY, MORNY (2001). 'Postcolonial Reflections: Challenges for Religious Studies'. *Method and Theory in the Study of Religions*, 13: 177–95.

KAPOOR, ILAN (2004). 'Hyper-Self-Reflexive Development? Spivak on Representing the Third World "Other"'. *Third World Quarterly*, 25/4: 627–47.

KING, RICHARD (1999). *Orientalism and Religion: Post-Colonial Theory, India and the Mystic East*. New York: Routledge.

KING, URSULA (1989). *Women and Spirituality: Voices of Protest and Promise*. Basingstoke and London: Macmillan.

—— (ed.) (1995). *Religion & Gender*. Oxford and Cambridge, Mass.: Blackwell.

—— and BEATTIE, TINA (eds.) (2004). *Gender, Religion and Diversity: Cross-Cultural Perspectives*. London and New York: Continuum.

LECHNER, FRANK J. (2006). 'Trajectories of Faith in the Global Age: Classical Theory and Contemporary Evidence'. In James A. Beckford and John Walliss (eds.), *Theorising Religion: Classical and Contemporary Debates*. Aldershot and Burlington, Ont.: Ashgate, 44–59.

LEWIS, REINA (1996). *Gendering Orientalism: Race, Femininity, and Representation*. London: Routledge.

MCCUTCHEON, RUSSELL, (ed.) (1999*a*). *The Insider/Outsider Problem in the Study of Religions: A Reader*. London and New York: Cassell.

—— (1999*b*). 'Review of Walter Capps' *Religious Studies: The Making of a Discipline*', *Zygon*, 34/3: 527–30.

MOHANTY, CHANDRA TALPADE (1991). 'Under Western Eyes: Feminist Scholarship and Colonial Discourses'. In Chandra Talpade Mohanty, Ann Russo, and Lourdes Torres (eds.), *Third World Women and the Politics of Feminism*, Bloomington, Ind.: Indiana University Press, 51–80.

O'CONNOR, JUNE (1989). 'Rereading, Reconceiving and Reconstructing Traditions: Feminist Research in Religion'. *Women's Studies*, 17: 101–23.

PLASKOW, JUDITH (1993). 'We Are Also Your Sisters: The Development of Women's Studies in Religion'. *Women's Studies Quarterly*, 21/1: 9–21.

Plaskow, Judith and Christ, Carol P. (eds.) (1989). *Weaving the Vision: New Patterns in Feminist Spirituality.* San Francisco: Harper & Row.

Radhakrishnan, R. (1996). *Diasporic Mediations: Between Home and Location.* Minneapolis: University of Minnesota Press.

Ruether, Rosemary Radford, and McLaughlin, Eleanor (eds.) (1979). *Women of Spirit: Female Leadership in the Jewish and Christian Traditions.* New York: Simon & Schuster.

Shaw, Rosalind (1995). 'Feminist Anthropology and the Gendering of Religious Studies'. In Ursula King (1995), 65–76.

Smith, Jonathan Z. (1982). *Imagining Religion: From Babylon to Jonestown.* Chicago: University of Chicago Press.

Spivak, Gayatri Chakravorty (1988). 'Can the Subaltern Speak?' In C. Nelson and L. Grossberg (eds.), *Marxism and Interpretation of Culture.* Chicago: University of Illinois Press, 271–313.

—— (1990). *The Post-Colonial Critic: Interviews, Strategies, Dialogues.* New York and London: Routledge.

—— (2001). 'A Note on the New International'. *Parallax* 7/3: 12–16.

Stocking, George W. (1987). *Victorian Anthropology.* New York: Free Press.

Suchocki, Marjorie Hewitt (1989). 'In Search of Justice'. In John Hick and Paul F. Knitter (eds.), *The Myth of Christian Uniqueness: Toward a Pluralistic Theology of Religions.* Maryknoll, NY: Orbis, 149–61.

Warne, Randi (1991). 'Women's Studies and Religious Studies: Reactions, Resonances, and Future Possibilities'. In Larry Hurtado and Klaus Klostermaier (eds.), *Religious Studies: Issues, Prospects, and Proposals*, ii. Atlanta: Scholars Press, 347–60.

—— (1995). 'Further Reflections on the "Unacknowledged Quarantine": Feminism and Religious Studies'. In Lorraine Code and Sandra Burt (eds.), *Changing Methods: Feminists Transforming Practice.* Peterborough, Ont.: Broadview, 75–103.

—— (2000). 'Gender'. In Willi Braun and Russell T. McCutcheon (eds.), *Guide to the Study of Religion.* London and New York: Cassell, 140–54.

—— (2001*a*). '(En)gendering Religious Studies'. In Darlene Juschka (ed.), *Feminism in the Study of Religions: A Reader.* London and New York: Continuum, 147–56.

—— (2001*b*). 'Gender and the Study of Religion'. *Method and Theory in the Study of Religion*, 13/3: 141–52.

Weber, Max (2002). *The Protestant Ethic and the Spirit of Capitalism* (with other essays), trans. Stephen Kalberg. Los Angeles: Roxbury.

Yegonoglu, Meyda (1998). *Colonial Fantasies: Towards a Feminist Reading of Orientalism.* Cambridge: Cambridge University Press.

Young, Robert (1990). *White Mythologies: Writing History and the West.* New York and London: Routledge.

Suggested Reading

Ahmed, Durre S. (ed.) (2002). *Gendering the Spirit: Women, Religion & the Post-Colonial Response.* London: Zed Books.

Hewitt, Marsha (1995). *Critical Theory of Religion: A Feminist Analysis.* Minneapolis: Fortress Press.

Joy, Morny, and Neumaier-Dargyay, Eva K. (eds.) (1995). *Gender, genre, and religion: Feminist reflections.* Waterloo, Ont.: Wilfrid Laurier University Press for the Calgary Institute for the Humanities.

Mohanty, Chandra Talpade, Russo, Ann, and Torres, Lourdes (eds.) (1991). *Third World Women and the Politics of Feminism.* Bloomington: Indiana University Press.

Narayan, Uma, and Harding, Sandra (eds.) (2000). *Decentering the Center: Philosophy for a Multicultural, Postcolonial, and Feminist World.* Bloomington, Ind.: Indiana University Press.

Taylor, Mark C. (ed.) (1998). *Critical Terms for Religious Studies.* Chicago and London: University of Chicago Press.

Also King (1995) and King and Beattie (2004).

CHAPTER 8

RELIGION AND MODERNITY WORLDWIDE

ROBERT W. HEFNER

FEW of classical sociology's founding claims achieved greater currency in the twentieth century than the assertion that, under conditions of modernity, religion is destined to decline until it "shall disappear altogether except, possibly, in the private realm" (Mills 1959: 33). Today, few of our forebears' convictions seem more misplaced than this one. Recent years have seen an upsurge in religious activity around the world, in phenomena as diverse as Hindu nationalism, Islamic resurgence, Pentecostal conversion, and America's culture wars. These trends suggest that rumors of religion's demise are, to say the least, exaggerated.

Although sociologists now agree that religion has proved more resilient than once forecast, there is less agreement as to why this is so, and just what this means for modern religions and the concept of modernity itself. In part, the lack of theoretical consensus reflects the dizzying pace of contemporary religious change. But the disagreement also reflects the fact that, "as sociologists of religion, we know a great deal about the twentieth-century West, but relatively little about anything else" (Gorski 2003: 110). The Eurocentric slant to the sociology of religion is fast changing, however, as sociologists join with scholars in other disciplines to examine religion and modernity worldwide.

In this chapter I present reflections on religion and modernity in three religious traditions, the centers of gravity of which lie in the non-Western world. The three traditions are Pentecostal Christianity, resurgent Islam, and Hindu nationalism. Several things stand out from this overview. The first is that religious change worldwide bears the imprint of, not a unitary secularization, but each tradition's engagement with the world-building powers of our age. The historic, or "world", religions are the most long-lasting of civilizational institutions (Eisenstadt 2002; Hefner 1993). But the key to these religions' evolutionary achievement lies not in their staying the same, but in their ability to respond with moral imagination and organizational vigor to the ascendant powers of each age. Among the world-building powers shaping the course of modern religious change are capitalism, the nation-state, new modes of knowledge and communications, and non-religious ideologies like liberalism and secular nationalism.

The second point is that, contrary to some earlier forecasts, the impact of these world-building forces on religion has been heterogeneous rather than homogenizing. In Western Europe and a few other societies, the public role of religion, at least for non-immigrants, has declined (Davie 2000; McLeod 2003). In other areas of the world, however, the influence of religion on public and private affairs is as strong as ever. Religious development in these regions has been marked by the emergence of an alert and more participatory public, with its attendant fragmentation of religious authority, challenges to established elites, and debates over the common good (Casanova 1994; Hefner 2000; Meyer and Moors 2006; Salvatore and Eickelman 2004; van der Veer 2002). The "publicization" of religion is often conservative in cultural content, however, and its political effects are by no means inherently democratic.

Even as cultural and economic globalization advance, then, their impact on religious life varies, because it is mediated by embedded interactions among states, markets, religious actors, and non-religious forces (see Casanova 1994; 2001; Gorski 2003; Martin 1978). The complexity of this interaction insures that, even as they respond to similar global events, religions and modernity will remain "multiple" in their developmental streams for many years to come.

Gifts of the Spirit Globalized

Few modern religious developments compare in scale and social energy with the global expansion of Pentecostal Christianity. Having begun a century ago in a few impoverished neighborhoods in the western United States, Pentecostal Christianity today is a worldwide religious industry. Estimates put the global Pentecostal population at between 300 and 500 million people, most of whom reside in Latin America, Africa, East Asia, and the Pacific Oceania (Barrett and Johnson 2002: 284;

Martin 2002: p. xvii). Seventy-five percent of Latin America's 60 million Protestants are Pentecostal, and in the largest Latin American country, Brazil, the number of Pentecostals attending church each Sunday exceeds that of the Catholic population (Chesnut 2003: 40, 63). Africa has 120 million Pentecostals (Barrett *et al.* 2001).

Pentecostalism's roots reach back to the eighteenth century's Great Awakening in England and the USA and its Methodist successor in the nineteenth century (Noll 2001; Martin 1990: 28). In the early years of the twentieth century, Pentecostalism's North American founders took the evangelical recipe of millennial hope, scriptural truth, and baptism by the Holy Spirit and spiced it with ecstatic weeping, dancing, and speaking in tongues. Unlike the Christian fundamentalists with whom they are sometimes confused, Pentecostal Christians place greater emphasis on enthusiastic experience of the divine than on "the correct grammar of belief" (Martin 1990: 52; cf. Corten 1997: 312). Although Pentecostal politics varies (Freston 2001), the mainstream differs from its fundamentalist brethren in its acceptance of the separation of church and state and its preference for quietist worship over militant activism.

Pentecostalism's vibrancy owes much to its populist, decentralized, and networked social organization. Although in some countries North American preachers have served as midwives to local churches, most congregations quickly become indigenous and self-governing. Once in operation, however, churches take advantage of modern media and communications technologies to maintain contact with a "far-flung network of people held together by their publications and other media productions, conferences, revival meetings, and constant travel" (Robbins 2004: 125; cf. Coleman 2000; Martin 1990: 52; Meyer 2006).

Pentecostalism's diffusion has also been facilitated by the low start-up costs for clerical training and church facilities. Unlike their Roman Catholic and mainline Protestant rivals, Pentecostals insist that the primary qualification for founding a church is not seminary training but gifts of the Spirit (Stoll 1990: 13). Although some churches, like Brazil's Assemblies of God, have developed a more hierarchical organization, and may even require a few years of seminary, even in these churches rates of lay participation are high (Chesnut 1997: 135). Although men monopolize most positions of formal leadership, women are active as lay preachers, teachers, and healers. Indeed, in male-dominated Latin America, two-thirds of the Pentecostal congregation is estimated to be female (Chesnut 2003; Corten 1999: 27). The Pentecostal emphasis on tithing also serves to reinforce local participation and institutional autonomy.

Pentecostalism's flexible networks, vigorous sociability, and egalitarian disregard of race, class, ethnicity, and, within limits, gender explains much of the tradition's appeal among the displaced and impoverished of the developing world (Burdick 1998: 123). But the islands of solidarity offered by Pentecostal churches do not nurture a casual attitude on matters of doctrine. Pentecostals subscribe to a strict cosmological dualism that pits the post-conversion present against the pre-conversion past, and the world of the saved against the forces of Satan. For individual believers, the two worlds are separated by the baptism of the Spirit and "rituals of rupture" that establish morally charged boundaries between believers and unbelievers (Robbins 2003: 224; Meyer 1998). The rituals are accompanied by requirements for equally consequential changes in social behavior. These typically weigh most heavily on men, prohibiting gambling, drugs, alcohol, dancing, and extramarital sex. Spiritual cosmology is handled in an equally clear-cut manner. Rather than, as with mainline Protestantism, denying the existence of witches and spirits, Pentecostals acknowledge their reality. Consistent with their dualistic cosmology, however, Pentecostals redefine these beings as minions of Satan (Barker 2001: 107–8; DeBernardi 1999: 77). This accommodation and repositioning of indigenous spirit beliefs is part of the formula whereby a globalized Pentecostalism is able to speak to local concerns (see Casanova 2001: 438).

In Latin America, the Pentecostal surge has led some analysts to speak of the "Pentecostalization of Latin American Christianity" (Chesnut 2003: 15). Pentecostalism's influence can be seen in, among other things, the fact that its most important rival today is no longer mainstream Catholicism, but Catholic Charismatic Renewal (CCR). Established in the 1980s by educated middle-class Catholics determined to counter the Pentecostal surge, CCR maintains Catholicism's emphasis on the clergy, sacraments, and veneration of the Virgin Mary. For prayer services, however, CCR borrows Pentecostalism's emphasis on ritual enthusiasm, gifts of the Holy Spirit, and battling Satan (Gill 1998). Many CCR devotees adhere to a less ascetic moral code than Pentecostals, allowing men to smoke and drink.

In Africa and the Pacific, Pentecostalism has made equally dramatic inroads into the religious landscape (Barker 2001; Hayward 1997; Meyer 1999). As in Latin America, Pentecostal churches recruit most heavily among the poor and displaced; churches show a gendered profile similar to that of Latin America as well. In Africa, as in Latin America, Pentecostalism's advance has spurred the formation of charismatic prayer groups among mainline Protestants and Roman Catholics (Martin 2002; Meyer 1999; 2004; Gifford 1998). African Pentecostalism has made some of its most unexpected inroads, however, into the continent's once-powerful African Independent Churches (AICs). The AICs are self-governing congregations that blend African styles of healing and worship with aspects of Christian cosmology and worship. Recent studies suggest that, at more than 120 million followers, the number of Pentecostal Christians now exceeds the once more numerous AIC congregations by some 50 percent (Barrett *et al.* 2001).

Few religions in modern times can ignore the looming presence of capitalist consumption and circulation. Some have responded by attempting to erect moral dams against the capitalist cultural flow. Other religious movements, however, have developed new streams, which, rather than going against the economistic current, swim with it, developing a public face that is "happily commercializing, celebrating individuality, and encouraging profit" (Weller 1999: 18). Recently an important stream in global Pentecostalism has developed a market-friendly version of the faith (cf. Coleman 1995; Hackett 1995). Neo-Pentecostals preach a "Prosperity Gospel" which declares that health and wealth are divine gifts delivered to all who are suitably faithful (Coleman 2000; Martin 2002; Maxwell 1998). The expensive cars and clothing flaunted by some prosperity pastors disturb Catholics, mainline Protestants, and even many traditional Pentecostals (D. J. Smith 2001). Although the Prosperity Gospel appeals to urban youth and the upwardly mobile, African Independent Churches and, in Latin America, African diaspora religions offer alternative spiritual vehicles for bounty and enrichment. These have the additional advantage of placing fewer ethical demands on their adherents than does Pentecostalism (Chesnut 2003: 109).

Pentecostals operate in a landscape whose commanding heights are dominated by the modern state as well as capitalism. Notwithstanding the activities of a few churches, most Pentecostals prefer a low-profile politics of family and neighborhood to the high-stakes maneuvers of national politics. Discursively speaking, too, Pentecostal pronouncements on politics tend to lack empirical depth and theological rigor. As David Martin has observed (1990: 108), "being a religion of the poor (rather than a religion for the poor) [Pentecostalism] lacks sophisticated structural views of society and of political change"; this disposition often results in a "truncated understanding of the social world" (1990: 266). The same impulse can lead to suspicion of science and humanist learning. Misgivings as regards formal education distinguish today's Pentecostals from Weber's Protestant-ethic Calvinists. A key question for the long term will be whether their anti-intellectualism softens as Pentecostals experience upward mobility.

The fact that many of its practitioners live in politically dangerous environments also serves to curb ordinary Pentecostals' interest in a systematic theology of politics. This benign neglect distinguishes Pentecostals from the Roman Catholic clergy, North America's Protestant fundamentalists, and, not least of all, the modern world's second largest religious movement, resurgent Islam.

God's Law, Re-Engaged

The Islamic resurgence is the second of the modern world's most vibrant religious movements, and is arguably the most politically engaged. All of the world's 1.4 billion Muslims have felt the effects of the resurgence in piety, religious education, and proselytization (*da'wa*) that has swept Muslim countries since the 1970s.

Some analysts have mistakenly equated the resurgence with fundamentalism and terrorist violence. However, ethnographic studies and national polling have repeatedly shown that, although Muslims today are more religiously observant than their parents' generation, only a small minority support radical Islamist programs; an even smaller number support terrorist violence. Rather than radicalism, the really striking change in Muslim political culture over the past generation has been the growing support among ordinary Muslims for political democracy (Inglehart and Norris 2004; Fattah 2006; cf. Moaddel 2002).

Putting these democratic aspirations into practice, however, has often proved difficult. A well-organized minority among the Islamists has shown a gift for socializing its cadres into pluralism-denying political projects. "Rather than simply... appealing to the self-interests of potential recruits", the cadres are taught "a new ethic of civic obligation demanding that every Muslim participate in the Islamic reform of society and state, regardless of the benefits and costs incurred" (Wickham 2003: 15). Where successful, these programs of identity reformation allow militant activists to achieve a political influence greatly disproportionate to their numbers in society (Hefner 2005).

As with the Pentecostal advance in Latin America, Africa, and the Pacific, the Islamic resurgence has taken place against a backdrop of migration, sprawling urban growth, and rampant de-traditionalization. After their parents moved to urban neighborhoods in the 1950s and 1960s, the younger generation of Muslims became the target of state-directed campaigns of citizen making; the process was typically more coercive than its counterpart in non-Muslim Latin America, Africa, and Asia. Sponsored by socialist and secular nationalist leaders, these nation-building programs obliterated "much of the traditional centuries-old synthesis of the Muslim religion in its relation to the state" (C. Brown 2000: 129; Starrett 1998). Contrary to the claims of clash-of-civilizations analysts (Huntington 1996), the central stream in Muslim politics had long been quietist rather than militant, sanctioning in practice if not in jurisprudential principle a separation of religious and state authority (Lapidus 1975; Schacht 1964: 71; but cf. Zaman 1997). Ironically, secular nationalist meddling in religious affairs provoked an étatization of religion from which the Islamist opposition eventually benefited (Hefner 2000; Starrett 1998: 77–82; Wickham 2003).

Other influences, however, worked to give the Islamic resurgence a distinctive social form. State-sponsored schooling brought literacy to much of the newly mobile population (Eickelman 1992; Hefner and Zaman 2007; Starrett 1998). Contrary to its sponsors' expectations, however, many among the newly educated used their learning to develop an independent perspective on their faith. Their efforts were buoyed by the growth of a print-capitalist market in inexpensively produced Islamic books and pamphlets, as well as, more recently, the arrival of new electronic media and the Internet (Anderson 2003; Eickelman and Anderson 2003; Gonzalez-Quijono 1998; Hefner 2003). Herein lies another difference with Pentecostalism. Whereas Pentecostalism first spread among the poor and uneducated, the center of gravity for the Islamic resurgence has long been educated segments of the middle and lower middle class. In this regard, the resurgence's social profile resembles early modern Protestantism more than it does today's poor Pentecostals.

With the help of mass education and new print media, the Islamic resurgence has shattered the centuries-old divide between classically trained religious scholars, the *'ulama*, and unlettered Muslims (C. Brown 2000: 137). The development has heightened the public's interest in normative Islam, undermined long-cherished folk-Islamic traditions, and enhanced many believers' conviction that Islam's jurisprudential injunctions must be implemented by all believers. At the same time, by undermining the *'ulama*'s monopoly on religious knowledge, this "direct and broader access to the printed word" (Eickelman and Piscatori 1996: 43) has contributed to a significant pluralization of religious authority. Today, television preachers, secularly educated "new Muslim intellectuals" (Meeker 1991), and government-appointed Muslim advisors compete with classically trained religious scholars for public influence. The competition centers not only on the mobilization of followers, but also on the question of how to define Islam and realize God's law (Shari'a) (Eickelman and Piscatori 1996: 5–8).

Some years ago Western analysts had predicted that the *'ulama* would slowly lose ground to secularly educated new Muslim intellectuals, and that this change would open the way for a less traditionalist and more liberal Islam. In much of the Muslim world, however, the *'ulama* have adapted to the competitive religious market with impressive skill, and have reasserted their religious influence (Arjomand 1988; Zaman 2002). Many *'ulama* today aim their message at a mass market, writing popular religious tracts, appearing on television, and even posting legal judgements (*fatawa*) on the Internet (Anderson 2003; Mandaville 2005).

Religious scholars have also benefited from the Muslim public's awareness that Islam is a religion of law, and that the first duty of the pious is to implement God's commands in personal and public life. Although the idea that God has provided guidance for believers has long been central to Islam, ordinary Muslims' familiarity with the Shari'a was limited (Peletz 1997; Zubaida 2003). Unlettered Muslims often assumed that their customs were consistent with the Shari'a, and left the matter there. Some even mocked the *'ulama* for their allegedly arid approach to the divine (Berkey 1992: 244). Faced with this truculent plurality, scholars often resigned themselves to the idea that God's law is so perfect that its comprehensive realization is impossible. With mass education and the growth of scripturalist piety, however, many resurgents have refused this traditionalist accommodation. The new believers have rallied to a program which identifies Islam as an objective "system" (*minhaj*) that contains specific, positive, and practical prescriptions intended to cover all aspects of life (Eickelman and Piscatori 1996: 42; Shamsul 1997).

The fact that growing numbers of Muslims have developed this positive sense has not always made it easier for believers to agree on the law's practical entailments. The new awareness has freighted the law with a greater political charge, however, as some believers insist that the state should assume responsibility for implementing the law, and that its varied jurisprudential streams should be condensed into a unitary canon (Bowen 2003: 189–99; Brinkley 1993). During most of its historic development, the law lacked a central legislative agency, and judgments as to just what the law entailed were made by diverse legal specialists (*fuqaha'*), not the state. There was no canon, and on many key questions different rulings were reached (Weiss 1998: 113–32). Today, however, conservative resurgents take Western positive law as their model, conflating a Western tradition with the Islamic. In a few countries, some go further, accusing fellow Muslims of apostasy, a crime that, under classical Islamic law, is grounds for capital punishment (El Fadl 2002; 2004). The threat of this accusation has a chilling effect on the Islamic public sphere, but it has also stimulated efforts by pluralist Muslims to strengthen citizen freedoms (Hefner 2005; Soroush 2000).

With its competitive pluralization of religious authority, the Islamic resurgence bears a partial resemblance to the rise of Methodism in nineteenth-century England or the spread of Pentecostalism in contemporary Latin America. All three developments took place against the backdrop of the "erosion of organic unities" (Martin 1990: 3) and the breakup of a monopolistic religious "marketplace" (cf. Chesnut 2003; Finke and Stark 2003). However, in the case of Islam, the emergence of a more competitive religious sphere has not been accompanied by broad agreement that believers should be free "to choose among the hundreds of religious products that best suit their spiritual and material needs" (Chesnut 2003: 3). Because many believers see Islam as a religion of divine law, and the law as systemic and all-embracing, many are reluctant to concede that religion can ever be made a matter of individual choice.

This is not to say that recipes for surrendering authority for God's law to state officials will become the preferred option of most Muslims. There is a long history of *'ulama* suspicion of the state and of proposals that would give the state authority over religious affairs (Munson 1993: 27; cf. Schacht 1964). Survey and ethnographic studies today indicate that Muslims in most countries see constitutional democracy as compatible with Islam. In many countries, however, there appears as yet to be no "overlapping consensus" (Rawls 1999: 144) on just how such a system of government should accommodate God's law (Hallaq 1997: 207–54; Vikor 2005: 257–79).

What does all this mean for the future of the Muslim world? For some time to come, culture wars over the relationship of Islam and the state are likely to flare in many settings. The primary dividing line in the contest will not pit secular liberals against conservative fundamentalists. The more widespread cleavage will pit formalists who insist that God's law is unchanging and all-encompassing against ethical substantivists who insist that the purpose of the law is to promote general welfare based on the universal values of justice and human dignity (Barton 1995; El Fadl 2002; Soroush 2000). Substantivists also believe that democracy is the most effective political instrument for achieving these ends. Concentrating religious authority in the hands of state officials, they add, risks subordinating Islam's high ideals to low political intrigues, corrupting Islam itself (see Madjid 1994; Tamimi 2001).

Where they occur, then, pressures for democracy and the rule of law will be based primarily, not on Enlightenment notions of the autonomy of the individual, but on the desire to develop procedures for protecting religion and public ethics from abuse at the hands of self-appointed stewards of Islam. Concerns over the étatization of religion are, of course, something that Muslim pluralists share with believers in other modern faith traditions.

Hinduism as Nation

Although Kant, Hegel, and other Enlightenment philosophers viewed it as the very antithesis of the modern (D. Smith 2003: 8–16), Hinduism in modern times has undergone doctrinal and organizational permutations even greater than those of Christianity and Islam. During its Middle Ages, Hinduism lacked the centralized hierarchy of medieval Christianity, as well as the jurists and scholars who stabilized classical Islam over time and space. Hinduism had many books rather than *the* Book, and its priests and ascetics sustained disparate oral and literate traditions rather than the modularized orthopraxis of its Abrahamic counterparts. Contrary to some claims, however, Hinduism was not just invented in the nineteenth century for the purposes of colonial rule. Rather, in the course of the colonial encounter, the tradition's tributaries were repackaged and elevated to the status of a world religion comparable to Christianity and Islam (Pennington 2005: 5).

Even before the arrival of British colonialism in South Asia, Hinduism had begun to show signs of "long-term processes of centralization and homogenization" (van der Veer 1994: 46). Shrines and pilgrimage centers created a continent-wide network of transport and communication, over which people, goods, and ideas continuously flowed (Assayag 1995; Babb 1975; Cohn 1964; van der Veer 1988). Princes, merchants, and religious orders established devotional centers, often at preexisting cultic sites. Although, historically, Christianity also accommodated indigenous cults (P. Brown 1981; Christian 1989), over time reform movements tended to redefine these pre-Christian inheritances as heretical (see also Badone 1990; Brandes 1990; Merrill 1988; Schneider 1990). Pre-modern Hindus allowed non-Hindu cults to operate alongside or within the confines of Hindu devotionalism. This pattern of coexistence and integration allowed elements of the local tradition to be cycled up into a high-cosmological superstructure, which gradually spread over the subcontinent (Babb 1975; van der Veer 1994: 47; cf. Hefner 1985).

Although confessional boundaries have hardened since the nineteenth century (particularly as regards Muslims), this process of integration and Hinduization has continued to this day.

The Muslim advance into India stimulated efforts by Hindus to create more effectively coordinated networks for devotion, pilgrimage, and military defense. The rationalization of Hindu tradition took an even more decisive turn under British rule, which began on a large scale in Bengal in 1757. The British systematized native legal traditions, subordinating them to British law, while creating a stark divide between "Hindu" and "Muhammadan" law (Hansen 1999: 34). In the late nineteenth century, British censuses formalized borders between the two communities even further, creating the appearance of a unitary Hindu majority distinct from the once dominant Muslim minority. Although the British helped to introduce concepts of rights and equality into Indian political discourse, then, the notions were applied in an illiberal manner, categorizing collectivities for the purposes of control, rather than strengthening individual rights (Dirks 1989; Hansen 1999: 40). Through processes like these, colonial rule reified the distinction between Muslims and Hindus, and laid the foundation for the twentieth century's struggle between Islamic, Hindu, and secular nationalisms (Hansen 1999: 33–8; van der Veer 1994: 20).

In the postcolonial period, Hindu reformists have intensified their efforts to encourage congregational worship, develop a scriptural canon, and standardize ritual and belief (Jaffrelot 1996: 201). Although many of their initiatives are modeled on reformist versions of Islam and Christianity, reformed Hinduism's exuberant polytheism and devotionalism remain distinctive. Some among India's Hindu nationalist reformers have also insisted on the need to establish a nation-state grounded on *Hindutva*, or "Hinduness", presented as the authentic culture of the majority. The dominant understanding of secularism in Indian politics never mandated the removal of religion from the public sphere, but the secular nationalist elite did encourage religion's depoliticization (Hansen 1999: 11; Madan 1987). Responding to what they regard as Western cultural globalization, historical abuses at the hands of Muslim rulers, and status uncertainties in Indian society, Hindu nationalists have rejected this formula and sought to make *Hindutva* the bedrock for a new religious nationalism.

The *Hindutva* movement's majoritarian appeals to national honor resonate with some of the urban poor, and its militant wing recruits fighters from the ranks of boss-led gangs (Brass 2003). The movement's leadership and most active membership, however, come from the educated middle class (Hansen 1999: 7). Although Hinduism continues to be characterized by a high degree of ritual and doctrinal diversity, the *Hindutva* movement's efforts to impose uniformity on a diverse tradition threaten Hindu non-conformists as well as India's religious minorities (van der Veer 1994: 105; Wright 2001).

From a comparative perspective, then, Hindu nationalism shows the imprint of colonialism and the modern state to an arguably greater degree than Pentecostal Christianity or many varieties of resurgent Islam. As in early modern Western Europe and contemporary East Asia, many non-Pentecostal variants of Christianity contributed symbols to the nation-building cause (McLeod 2003; Wells 1990). More recently, a few African politicians have wrapped themselves in a Pentecostal flag (Meyer 1999). However, most ordinary Pentecostals seem preoccupied more with the ravages of poverty, illness, alcoholism, and machismo than with the politics of the nation-state. In the case of resurgent Islam, nation making has had a more pervasive influence, but its consequences have also been ambiguous, because some of the Muslim public seem reluctant to embrace a too étatized understanding of their faith.

Hindu nationalism shows less such reluctance. Yet many ordinary Hindus continue to have doubts about the wisdom of tethering religion so tightly to the nation-state. Although startled by its Hindu nationalist upstart, a neo-Gandhian nationalism, vaguely Hindu in inspiration, continues to appeal to broad portions of the Indian public. Other Indians continue to look to secular nationalism and socialism as models for modern citizenship (see Carroll 2001; Hansen 1999: 45). Meanwhile, large numbers of Hindus in India and the diaspora continue to be drawn to movements of devotional piety organized around charismatic gurus. Although some gurus have rallied to the cause of Hindu nationalism (McKean 1996), many are politically quietist. Most of their devotees are concerned less with capturing the state than with achieving consonance between their emotions, conscience, and thoughts, "in a manner which recalls Protestant values" (Kent 2000: 12).

Conclusion

This brief overview of the contemporary restructuring of Pentecostalism, Islam, and Hinduism offers insights into religion and modernity beyond these three traditions. First, and most familiarly, the examples illustrate that, contrary to the claims of mainstream secularization theory, religion in modern times has not everywhere declined or been sequestered in private life (Berger 1999; Casanova 1994). Indeed, rather than declining, religion in many societies has gained greater public urgency.

A second point follows from this first. It is that the most successful of today's religious currents are those that put aside the pattern of establishment religion, with its learned virtuosos and done deals with rulers, and open the religious field to public participation. Although sometimes understood as religion's "democratization", this shift is typically ambiguous in its political and ethical effects. The publicization of religion has fragmented religious authority, intensified debates over the common good, and ushered heretofore marginal believers into the public religious sphere. But not all new religious publics have been tolerant of religious minorities and non-conformists, and the forms of political participation to which they have given rise have not always been procedurally democratic.

Scholars of religion associated with the "religious economy" or "supply side" model in the sociology of religion often use a market analogy to describe modern religions' reorganization. These writers note that rates of religious participation are likely to be higher in "unregulated religious economies" than in monopolistic ones, where the state grants one religion an exclusive position (Finke and Stark 1992: 18). In a competitive religious market, success will go to those "firms" that craft religious goods and services that meet the needs of masses of religious consumers.

At first all this seems reasonable enough, and empirical studies using religious market models have shed a bright light on developments in many parts of the world (Chesnut 2003). However, one of the blind spots in neoclassical theories of market behavior has always centered on the origins and evolution of consumer tastes. Some economists have pretended to resolve this problem by defining preference formation as an "irrational" phenomenon not amenable to scientific analysis (Samuelson 1955: 90). Others have pushed the problem aside by claiming that human preferences do not really change over time (Becker 1976: 133; Becker and Stiglitz 1977; cf. MacPherson 1980). Unfortunately, some religious market analysts have incorporated these sociologically implausible assumptions into their models. They suggest that religious preferences are stable over time and space, and that the really critical issue in the sociology of modern religion is the question of state regulation and producer "supply".

In the cases examined in this chapter, however, religious preferences have been anything but stable, and the forces shaping them are more varied than the religious economy model implies. After all, it is not just the state that attempts to impose controls on the religious marketplace. Families, neighborhoods, and religious communities do as well. Hindu nationalists have at times taken violent action against Muslims and Christian missionaries, in defiance of official state policies (Brass 2003; Wright 2001). In parts of the Muslim world, too, radical Islamists have mobilized against religious minorities and Muslim non-conformists, often again in defiance of state regulations (Hefner 2005; Malik 1996; Zaman 2002: 112–24). Even among Pentecostals, individuals who defy parents, neighbors, and community guardians risk ostracism. The assumption that the removal of state monopolies allows free consumer choice, then, unwittingly obscures one of the most pressing questions in the sociology of religion: namely, how and why, not only the state, but diverse societal groupings, inspire, discipline, and suppress religious preference.

A third point follows from this second. It is that, as religions move out into late modern society, many feel obliged to develop strategies for dealing with the agencies and powers that prevail there, including the state, the capitalist market, and the proponents of rival religious and non-religious ideologies. As they confront the plurality of modernity's powers, however, different communities train their attention on different agencies and different moral concerns. Their choice of target reflects both the nature of the external challenge and the discursive concerns intrinsic to the religious tradition itself. For example, of the three religious movements discussed in this chapter, mainstream Pentecostals appear least interested (as yet) in developing a theologically comprehensive program for engaging the nation-state, notwithstanding a few contrary examples in Brazil, Africa, and the United States. In this, Pentecostalism differs from Hindu nationalism, Christian fundamentalism, and the more politicized variants of resurgent Islam. The irony in the Pentecostal attitude is that, in many countries, Pentecostalism's rise has been deeply dependent on state protections. A free religious market is not sociologically free, but requires expensive legal guarantees and state enforcements, like those in modern Latin America that did away with the Roman Catholic monopoly and legalized Protestant professions of the faith (Chesnut 2003: 10).

By comparison with Pentecostals, Hindu nationalists and politicized variants of resurgent Islam have committed greater cultural resources to the task of devising strategies for wooing or capturing the state. Both movements have internalized a modernist model of governance, with its interventionist ambitions and pretension to "omnicompetence" (Martin 1990: 294; cf. Nasr 1996: 80–106). The model owes more to the modern example of Western state corporatism than it does to Muslim or Hindu traditions. Inasmuch as activists in these religious movements come to "see like a state" (Scott 1999), most hope to use its powers to compel conformity to their idea of the common good. Movements of this sort are not likely to regard liberal or libertarian understandings of religious freedom as consonant with God's commands.

A final point flows from this overview. It is that, notwithstanding the errors of classical secularization theory, secularization is a real social phenomenon, and research on its genealogy and locations should remain an important part of the sociology of religion and modernity. All around the modern world, religious discourses have been marginalized or repositioned in fields like bio-medicine, engineering, military training, and mass communications. In these technical fields, modern Muslims, Hindus, and Christians have embraced discourses the internal logic of which is predominantly secular. If by secularization we mean the reorganization of a once religious field without direct reference to religious authorities or meanings, then secularization has indeed taken place in many modern social fields, even in societies otherwise in the throes of religious resurgence. In fact, over the long term, one of the most vexing challenges to citizenship and public culture will be how to facilitate civil coexistence across organizations and arenas animated by divergent ideas on religion and secularity (see Bowen 2003: 253–8; Hunter 1991; Rosenblum 2000; Wuthnow 2004: 12–17).

To be analytically useful, the concept of secularization has to be separated once and for all from modernization theory and modernist teleologies that assume that religions' decline is inevitable. Secularization can occur, but not as a force that sweeps uniformly across the social landscape. Rather, as David Martin (1978) recognized a generation ago, secularization and sacralization proceed in domain-specific ways, reflecting the temporary accommodations reached by different social groupings committed to diverse social discourses (cf. Casanova 1994; Gorski 2003; McLeod 2003). Classical secularization theory's tendency to see secularization as a unitary and society-wide force was based on the confidence that a growing differentiation of structures, roles, and meanings is intrinsic to modern social life. Social differentiation generates cultural and cognitive pluralization, and this pluralization undermines shared belief systems, while favoring the autonomy of the individual. "Unless we can imagine a reversal of the increasing cultural autonomy of the individual, secularization must be seen as irreversible" (Bruce 2001: 262).

When religion and modernity are viewed from a global perspective, however, it is easy to find many examples of such "reversals". As the case studies in this chapter have illustrated, modern social differentiation unleashes, not just individualization, but vigorous contests to create new publics and new terms of admissions to and exclusion from cultural citizenship. Contests of this sort will likely continue to have a transformative impact on religions around the world.

Modernity has not ushered in, then, the global decline of religion. It has instead drawn growing numbers of people into public contests over citizenship and the uses and meanings of religion itself. This moment in the sociology of modern religions appears to be in its early, rather than final, phases.

References

ANDERSON, JON W. (2003). "The Internet and Islam's New Interpreters". In Eickelman and Anderson (2003), 45–60.

ARJOMAND, SAID AMIR (1988). *The Turban for the Crown: The Islamic Revolution in Iran.* New York: Oxford University Press.

ASSAYAG, J. (1995). *Au Confluent de Deux Rivières: Musulmans et hindous dan le Sud de l'Inde.* Paris: Presses de l'École Française d'Extrême-Orient.

BABB, LAWRENCE A. (1975). *The Divine Hierarchy: Popular Hinduism in Central India.* New York: Columbia University Press.

BADONE, ELLEN (ed.) (1990). *Religious Orthodoxy and Popular Faith in European Society.* Princeton: Princeton University Press.

BARKER, JOHN (2001). "Afterword". *Journal of Ritual Studies*, 15/2: 105–8.

Barret, David B., and Johnson, Todd M. (2002). "Global Statistics". In S. M. Burgess and E. M. van der Maas (eds.), *The New International Dictionary of Pentecostal and Charismatic Movements*. Grand Rapids, Mich.: Zondervan Publishing, 283–302.

—— Kurian, George T., and Johnson, Todd M. (eds.) (2001). *World Christian Encylopedia: A Comparative Study of Churches and Religions in the Modern World*, 2 vols. Oxford: Oxford University Press.

Barton, Greg (1995). "Neo-Modernism: A Vital Synthesis of Traditionalist and Modernist Islamic Thought in Indonesia". *Studia Islamika: Indonesian Journal for Islamic Studies*, 2/3: 1–71.

Becker, Gary S. (1976). *The Economic Approach to Human Behavior*. Chicago: University of Chicago Press.

—— and Stigler, George J. (1977). "De Gustibus non est disputandum". *American Economic Review*, 67: 76–90.

Berger, Peter L. (ed.) (1999). *The Desecularization of the World: Resurgent Religion and World Politics*. Grand Rapids, Mich.: Eerdmans Publishing.

Berkey, Jonathan (1992). *The Transmission of Knowledge in Medieval Cairo: A Social History of Islamic Education*. Princeton: Princeton University Press.

Bowen, John R. (2003). *Islam, Law and Equality in Indonesia: An Anthropology of Public Reasoning*. Cambridge: Cambridge University Press.

Brandes, Stanley (1990). "Conclusion: Reflections on the Study of Religious Orthodoxy and Popular Faith in Europe". In Badone (1990), 185–99.

Brass, Paul R. (2003). *The Production of Hindu Muslim Violence in Contemporary India*. Seattle: University of Washington Press.

Brinkley, Messick (1993). *The Calligraphic State: Textual Domination and History in a Muslim Society*. Berkeley: University of California Press.

Brown, Carl (2000). *Religion and State: The Muslim Approach to Politics*. New York: Columbia University Press.

Brown, Peter (1981). *The Cult of the Saints: Its Rise and Function in Latin Christianity*. Chicago: University of Chicago Press.

Bruce, Steve (2001). "The Social Process of Secularization". In Richard K. Fenn (ed.), *The Blackwell Companion to Sociology of Religion*. Oxford: Blackwell Publishing, 249–63.

Burdick, John (1998). *Blessed Anastácia: Women, Race, and Popular Christianity in Brazil*. New York: Routledge.

Carroll, John J. (2001). "In the Shadow of Ayodhya: Secularism in India". In Arvind Sharma (ed.), *Hinduism and Secularism after Ayodhya*. New York: Palgrave, 25–39.

Casanova, José (1994). *Public Religions in the Modern World*. Chicago: University of Chicago Press.

—— (2001). "Religion, the New Millennium, and Globalization". *Sociology of Religion*, 62/4: 415–41.

Chesnut, R. Andrew (1997). *Born Again in Brazil: The Pentecostal Boom and the Pathogens of Poverty*. New Brunswick: Rutgers University Press.

—— (2003). *Competitive Spirits: Latin America's New Religious Economy*. Oxford: Oxford University Press.

Christian, William A. (1989). *Person and God in a Spanish Valley*. Princeton: Princeton University Press.

Cohn, Bernard S. (1964). "The Role of Gosains in the Economy of the Eighteenth- and Nineteenth-Century Upper India". *Indian Economic and Social History Review*, 1: 175–82.

COLEMAN, SIMON (1995). "America Loves Sweden: Prosperity Theology and the Cultures of Capitalism". In Richard H. Roberts (ed.), *Religion and the Transformations of Capitalism: Comparative Approaches.* London: Routledge, 161–79.

—— (2000). *The Globalisation of Charismatic Christianity: Spreading the Gospel of Prosperity.* Cambridge: Cambridge University Press.

CORTEN, ANDRÉ (1997). "The Growth of the Literature on Afro-American, Latin American and African Pentecostalism". *Journal of Contemporary Religion*, 12/3: 311–34.

—— (1999). *Pentecostalism in Brazil: Emotion of the Poor and Theological Romanticism.* New York: St Martin's Press.

DAVIE, GRACE (2000). *Religion in Modern Europe: A Memory Mutates.* Oxford: Oxford University Press.

DEBERNARDI, JEAN (1999). "Spiritual Warfare and Territorial Spirits: The Globalization and Localization of a 'Practical Theology' ". *Religious Studies and Theology*, 18/1: 66–96.

DIRKS, NICHOLAS (1989). "The Invention of Caste: Civil Society in Colonial India". *Social Analysis*, 25: 42–51.

EICKELMAN, DALE F. (1992). "Mass Higher Education and the Religious Imagination in Contemporary Arab Societies". *American Ethnologist*, 19/4: 1–13.

—— and ANDERSON, JON W. (eds.) (2003). *New Media in the Muslim World: The Emerging Public Sphere.* Bloomington, Ind.: Indiana University Press.

—— and PISCATORI, JAMES (1996). *Muslim Politics.* Princeton: Princeton University Press.

EISENSTADT, SHMUEL N. (2002). *Multiple Modernities.* New Brunswick, NJ: Transaction Publishers.

EL FADL, KHALED ABOU (2002). *The Place of Tolerance in Islam.* Boston: Beacon Press.

—— (2004). *Islam and the Challenge of Democracy.* Princeton: Princeton University Press.

FATTAH, MOATAZ A. (2006). *Democratic Values in the Muslim World.* Boulder, Col.: Lynne Rienner.

FINKE, ROGER, and STARKE, RODNEY (1992). *The Churching of America, 1776–1990: Winners and Losers in our Religious Economy.* New Brunswick, NJ: Rutgers University Press.

—— —— (2003). "The Dynamics of Religious Economies". In Michele Dixon (ed.), *The Handbook of the Sociology of Religion.* Cambridge: Cambridge University Press, 96–109.

FRESTON, PAUL (2001). *Evangelicals and Politics in Asia, Africa and Latin America.* Cambridge: Cambridge University Press.

GIFFORD, PAUL (1998). *African Christianity: Its Public Role.* Bloomington, Ind.: Indiana University Press.

GILL, ANTHONY J. (1998). *Rendering Unto Caesar: The Roman Catholic Church and the State in Latin America.* Chicago: University of Chicago Press.

GONZALEZ-QUIJONO, YVES (1998). *Les Gens du livre: Édition et champ intellectuel dans l'Égypte républicaine.* Paris: CNRS Éditions.

GORSKI, PHILIP S. (2003). "Historicizing the Secularization Debate: An Agenda for Research". In Michele Dillon (ed.), *Handbook of the Sociology of Religion.* Cambridge: Cambridge University Press, 110–23.

HACKETT, ROSALIND I. J. (1995). "The Gospel of Prosperity in West Africa". In Richard H. Roberts (ed.), *Religion and the Transformations of Capitalism: Comparative Approaches.* London: Routledge, 199–214.

HALLAQ, WAEL B. (1997). *A History of Islamic Legal Theories: An Introduction to Sunnî usul al fiqh.* Cambridge: Cambridge University Press.

Hansen, Thomas Blom (1999). *The Saffron Wave: Democracy and Hindu Nationalism in Modern India.* Princeton: Princeton University Press.

Hayward, Douglas James (1997). *Vernacular Christianity among the Mulia Dani.* Lanham, Md.: University Press of America.

Hefner, Robert W. (1985). *Hindu Javanese: Tengger Tradition and Islam.* Princeton: Princeton University Press.

—— (1993). "World Building and the Rationality of Conversion". In Robert W. Hefner (ed.), *Conversion to Christianity: Historical and Anthropological Perspectives on a Great Transformation.* Berkeley: University of California Press, 3–44.

—— (2000). *Civil Islam: Muslims and Democratization in Indonesia.* Princeton: Princeton University Press.

—— (2003). "Civic Pluralism Denied? The New Media and *Jihadi* Violence in Indonesia". In Dale F. Eickelman and Jon W. Anderson (eds.), *New Media in the Muslim World: The Emerging Public Sphere.* Bloomington, Ind.: Indiana University Press, 158–79.

—— (2005). "Muslim Democrats and Islamist Violence in Post-Soeharto Indonesia". In *idem* (ed.), *Remaking Muslim Politics: Pluralism, Contestation, Democratization.* Princeton: Princeton University Press, 273–301.

—— and Zaman, Muhammad Qasim (2007). *Schooling Islam: The Culture and Politics of Modern Muslim Education.* Princeton: Princeton University Press.

Hunter, James Davison (1991). *Culture Wars: The Struggle to Define America.* New York: Basic Books.

Huntington, Samuel P. (1996). *The Clash of Civilizations and the Remaking of the World Order.* New York: Simon & Schuster.

Inglehart, Ronald, and Norris, Pippa, (2004). *Sacred and Secular: Religion and Politics Worldwide.* Cambridge: Cambridge University Press.

Jaffrelot, C. (1996). *The Hindu Nationalist Movement in India.* New York: Columbia University Press.

Kent, A. (2000). "Creating Divine Unity: Chinese Recruitment in the Sathya Sai Baba Movement of Malaysia". *Crossroads,* 13: 29–51.

Lapidus, Ira (1975). "The Separation of State and Religion in the Development of Early Islamic Society". *International Journal of Middle East Studies,* 6/4: 363–85.

MacPherson, Michael S. (1980). "Want Formation, Morality, and the Interpretive Dimension of Economic Inquiry". Research Paper 33. Willamstown, Mass.: Williams College.

McKean, Lise (1996). *Spiritual Enterprise: Gurus and the Hindu Nationalist Movement.* Chicago: University of Chicago Press.

McLeod, Hugh (2003). "Introduction". In Hugh McLeod and Werner Utsorf (eds.), *The Decline of Christendom in Western Europe, 1750–2000.* Cambridge: Cambridge University Press, 1–26.

Madan, T. N. (1987). "Secularism in its Place". *Journal of Asian Studies,* 46/4: 747–59.

Madjid, Nurcholish (1994). "Islamic Roots of Modern Pluralism: Indonesian Experience". *Studia Islamika: Indonesian Journal for Islamic Studies,* 1/1: 55–77.

Malik, Jamal (1996). *Colonialization of Islam: Dissolution of Traditional Institututions in Pakistan.* New Delhi: Monahar Press.

Mandaville, Peter (2005). "Sufis and Salafis: The Political Discourse of Transnational Islam". In Robert W. Hefner (ed.), *Remaking Muslim Politics: Pluralism, Contestation, Democratization.* Princeton: Princeton University Press, 302–25.

MARTIN, DAVID (1978). *A General Theory of Secularization.* Oxford: Blackwell Publishing.

—— (1990). *Tongues of Fire: The Explosion of Protestantism in Latin America.* Oxford: Blackwell Publishing.

—— (2002). *Pentecostalism: The World their Parish.* Oxford: Blackwell Publishing.

MAXWELL, DAVID (1998). "Delivered from the Spirit of Poverty? Pentecostalism, Prosperity and Modernity in Zimbabwe". *Journal of Religion in Africa*, 28: 350–73.

MEEKER, MICHAEL E. (1991). "The New Muslim Intellectuals in the Republic of Turkey". In Richard Tapper (ed.), *Islam in Modern Turkey: Religion, Politics and Literature in a Secular State.* London: I. B. TAURIS & Co., 189–219.

MERRILL, WILLIAM L. (1988). *Raramuri Souls: Knowledge and Social Process in Northern Mexico.* Washington: Smithsonian Institution Press.

MEYER, BIRGIT (1998). "'Make a Complete Break with the Past': Memory and Post-Colonial Modernity in Ghanaian Pentecostalist Discourse". *Journal of Religion in Africa*, 27/3: 316–49.

—— (1999). *Translating the Devil: Religion and Modernity among the Ewe in Ghana*, IAL-Series. Trenton, NJ: Africa World Press.

—— (2004) 'Christianity in Africa: From African Independence to Pentecostal–Charismatic Churches'. *Annual Review of Anthropology*, 33: 447–74.

—— (2006). "Impossible Representations: Pentecostalism, Vision, and Video Technology in Ghana". In Meyer and Moors (2006), 290–312.

—— and MOORS, ANNELIES (eds.) (2006). *Religion, Media, and the Public Sphere.* Bloomington, Ind.: Indiana University Press.

MILLS, C. WRIGHT (1959). *The Sociological Imagination.* Oxford: Oxford University Press.

MOADDEL, MANSOOR (2002). *Jordanian Exceptionalism: A Comparative Analysis of State–Religion Relationships in Egypt, Iran, Jordan, and Syria.* New York: Palgrave.

MUNSON, H. JR (1993). *Religion and Power in Morocco.* New Haven: Yale University Press.

NASR, SEYYED VALI REZA (1996). *Mawdudi and the Making of Islamic Revivalism.* Oxford: Oxford University Press.

NOLL, MARK A. (2001). *American Evangelical Christianity: An Introduction.* Oxford: Blackwell Publishers.

PELETZ, MICHAEL P. (1997). "'Ordinary Muslims' and Muslim Resurgents in Contemporary Malaysia: Notes on an Ambivalent Relationship". In Robert W. Hefner and Patricia W. Horvatich (eds.), *Islam in an Era of Nation-States: Politics and Religious Renewal in Muslim Southeast Asia.* Honolulu: University of Hawaii Press, 231–73.

PENNINGTON, BRIAN K. (2005). *Was Hinduism Invented? Britons, Indians, and the Colonial Construction of Religion.* Oxford: Oxford University Press.

RAWLS, JOHN (1999). *The Law of Peoples, with "The Idea of Public Reason Revisited".* Cambridge, Mass.: Harvard University Press.

ROBBINS, JOEL (2003). "On the Paradoxes of Global Pentecostalism and the Perils of Continuity Thinking". *Religion*, 33: 221–31.

—— (2004). "The Globalization of Pentecostal and Charismatic Christianity". *Annual Review of Anthropology*, 33: 117–43.

ROSENBLUM, NANCY L. (ed.) (2000). *Obligations of Citizenship and Demands of Faith: Religious Accommodation in Pluralist Democracies.* Princeton: Princeton University Press.

SALVATORE, ARMONDO, and EICKELMAN, DALE F. (eds.) (2004). *Public Islam and the Common Good.* Leiden: Brill.

Samuelson, Paul A. (1955). *The Foundation of Economics.* Cambridge, Mass.: Harvard University Press.

Schacht, Joseph (1964). *An Introduction to Islamic Law.* Oxford: Oxford University Press.

Schneider, Jane (1990). "Spirits and the Spirit of Capitalism". In Badone (1990), 24–54.

Scott, James (1999). *Seeing Like a State: How Certain Schemes to Improve the Human Condition Have Failed.* New Haven: Yale University Press.

Shamsul, A. B. (1997). "Identity Construction, Nation Formation, and Islamic Revivalism in Malalaysia". In Robert W. Hefner and Patricia W. Horvatich (eds.), *Islam in an Era of Nation-States: Politics and Religious Renewal in Muslim Southeast Asia.* Honolulu: University of Hawaii Press, 207–27.

Smith, David (2003). *Hinduism and Modernity.* Oxford: Blackwell Publishing.

Smith, D. J. (2001). "'The Arrow of God': Pentecostalism, Inequality, and the Supernatural in South-Eastern Nigeria". *Africa,* 71/4: 587–613.

Soroush, Abdolkarim (2000). *Reason, Freedom, and Democracy in Islam.* Oxford: Oxford University Press.

Starrett, Gregory (1998). *Putting Islam to Work: Education, Politics, and Religious Transformation in Egypt.* Berkeley: University of California Press.

Stoll, David (1990). *Is Latin America Turning Protestant? The Politics of Evangelical Growth.* Berkeley: University of California Press.

Tamimi, Azzam S. (2001). *Rachid Ghannouchi: A Democrat within Islamism.* Oxford: Oxford University Press.

van der Veer, Peter (1988). *Gods on Earth: The Management of Religious Experience and Identity in a North Indian Pilgrimage Centre.* London: Athlone.

—— (1994). *Religious Nationalism: Hindus and Muslims in India.* Berkeley: University of California Press.

—— (2002). "Religion in South Asia". *Annual Review of Anthropology,* 31: 173–87.

Vikor, Knut S. (2005). *Between God and the Sultan: A History of Islamic Law.* Oxford: Oxford University Press.

Weiss, Bernard G. (1998). *The Spirit of Islamic Law.* Athens, Ga.: University of Georgia Press.

Weller, Robert P. (1999). *Alternate Civilities: Democracy and Culture in China and Taiwan.* Boulder, Col.: Westview Press.

Wells, K. M. (1990). *New God, New Nation: Protestants and Self-Reconstruction Nationalism in Korea, 1896–1937.* Honolulu: University of Hawaii Press.

Wickham, Carrie Rosefsky (2003). *Mobilizing Islam: Religion, Activism, and Political Change in Egypt.* New York: Columbia University Press.

Wright, Theodore P. (2001). "The Muslim Minority Before and After Ayodhya". In Arvind Sharma (ed.), *Hinduism and Secularism after Ayodhya.* New York: Palgrave, 1–24.

Wuthnow, Robert (2004). *Saving America? Faith-Based Services and the Future of Civil Society.* Princeton: Princeton University Press.

Zaman, Muhammad Qasim (1997). "The Caliphs, the 'Ulama', and the Law: Defining the Role and Function of the Caliph in the Early 'Abbasid Period'". *Islamic Law and Society,* 4/1: 1–36.

—— (2002). *The 'Ulama in Contemporary Islam: Custodians of Change.* Princeton: Princeton University Press.

Zubaida, Sami (2003). *Law and Power in the Islamic World.* London: I. B. Tauris.

Suggested Reading

Hefner, Robert W. (ed.) (2005). *Remaking Muslim Politics: Pluralism, Contestation, Democratization.* Princeton: Princeton University Press.

McLeod, Hugh, and Ustorf, Werner (eds.) (2003). *The Decline of Christendom in Western Europe, 1750–2000.* Cambridge: Cambridge University Press.

Also Casanova (1994); Chesnut (2003); Fickelman and Piscatori (1996); Fresten (2001); Meyer and Moors (2006); and van der Veer (1994).

CHAPTER 9

POSTMODERNISM AND RELIGION

NIKOLAI G. WENZEL

Introduction

The contemporary religious scene is somewhat bewildering for social scientists, as we observe apparently contradictory trends. Is the situation best captured by secularization theory, or by the notion of a resurgence of spirituality? By the decline in traditional religiosity, or by the upsurge of fundamentalism? Current religious trends make better sense when viewed through the frame of larger, more-encompassing shifts in mental models, and specifically postmodernism—a term often used, but even more often misunderstood.

The first section defines postmodernism, an alternative to modernity's enthusiasm. The second section surveys the literature on three contemporary religious trends—a decline in traditional religion, a resurgence in alternative forms of religiosity, and a fundamentalist backlash—through the analytical lens of postmodernism. The third section sketches more difficult and controversial debates on postmodernism and religion. The final section is a conclusion.

For insights, review, and discussion, thanks to Richard Wagner, Peter Boettke, Donald Colleton, John Sheridan, Christopher Martin, the Reverend Andrea Martin, Nathaniel Paxson, the Henry C. Simons Circle at George Mason University, Stacy Mueller, and participants in the 2005 and 2006 annual meetings of the Public Choice Society, the Summer 2005 Mercatus–Earhart workshop at George Mason University, and the Fall 2005 workshop on religion, economics, and culture at George Mason University. Thanks to Jenny Bowser for research assistance. The usual caveat applies.

What is Postmodernism?

Starting roughly in the seventeenth century, modernism (the Enlightenment) replaced the pre-modern appeal to faith with an appeal to reason (note that I intentionally conflate different, and often contradictory, schools of modernism—sacrificing, with some trepidation, accuracy for simplicity. I return to this point in the third section below). Without lapsing into the details of philosophical theory (for such details, see Yack 1986; Harvey 1989; Pippin 1999), the implications of modernism ring familiar, as they are still with us today: the modern nation-state, with legitimacy derived from the people rather than from the monarch's divine right; the supreme authority of reason (over tradition or faith); human rights; free markets; and the mastery of nature through science and technology (Pippin 1999: 4–5). Harvey (1989: 12) explains how the purpose of the modern project was

> to use the accumulation of knowledge generated by many individuals working freely and creatively in the pursuit of human emancipation and the enrichment of daily life. The scientific domination of nature promised freedom from scarcity, want, and the arbitrariness of natural calamity. The development of rational forms of social organization and rational modes of thought promised liberation from the irrationalities of myth, and religious superstition, and release from the arbitrary use of power, as well as from the dark side of our human natures. Only through such a project could the universal, eternal, and the immutable qualities of all humanity be revealed.

Habermas (1983: 9) adds that the early moderns had 'the extravagant expectation that the arts and sciences would promote not only the control of natural forces but also understanding of the world and of the self, moral progress, the justice of institutions and even the happiness of human beings'. Modernism was a hopeful, excited project, an optimistic unleashing of the human spirit and previously untapped human creativity, after earlier stifling by the bonds of tradition and faith.

Modernism offered a new epistemological appeal, detached from earlier religious confines. Harvey (1989: 13) explains that modernity was 'a secular movement that sought the demystification and desacralization of knowledge and social organization in order to liberate human beings from their chains'. Even as it broke from the earlier religious monopoly, Modernity did not shed transcendent foundations entirely; for example, Kurtz (1986: 12) writes that 'the issue of Modernity was fundamentally a conflict between ecclesiastical authority and the authority of independent scholars', i.e. a new approach to religion, rather than a total jettisoning of faith—what Daly (1985) refers to as 'the Kantian ideal of religion within the limits of reason'.

But the modern project was not without its doubters. As early as the nineteenth century, the very premises of modernism began to be called into question (beyond more traditional philosophy, as discussed below, some see early hints of anti-modern and post-modern dissent in the nineteenth-century movements of Romanticism and

Transcendentalism; see, e.g., Clarke 2006: ch. 5 on the Transcendentalist roots of the New Age movement, which exhibits many of the same traits as postmodernism). What began as doubts about the limitations of reason (initially brushed aside by modernism's confident optimism) evolved into a fuller critique. Modernism was seen to be spiritually weakening at best, and downright destructive at worst. Pippin (1999: p. xii) describes 'the widespread nineteenth century suspicions (at least on the European continent) that . . . the two greatest accomplishments of world civilization, modern natural science and technology, and a progressive, liberal democratic culture, were . . . slowly and inexorably enervating and spiritually destroying that very culture'. In many ways, such early grumblings foreshadowed much of the twentieth century's ugliness and many of its problems. The scale and horror of two World Wars galvanized the theoretical concerns. Pippin (1999: 7) explains that:

> The great self-confidence and progressivism characteristic of the modern enterprise, and especially what seemed its nineteenth-century fruition, all looked even more difficult to accept after the historical horrors of the twentieth century. The fact that art, intellectual pursuits, the development of the natural sciences, many branches of scholarship flourished in close spatial, temporal proximity to massacre and the death camps has raised for many doubts about not only Modernity's self-assurances, but about all of Western culture, has raised the issue: Why did humanistic traditions and models of conduct prove so fragile a barrier against political bestiality?

Harvey (1989: 13) echoes this thought, explaining that 'whether or not the Enlightenment project was doomed from the start to plunge us into a Kafkaesque world, whether or not it was bound to lead to Auschwitz and Hiroshima, and whether it has any power left to inform and inspire contemporary thought and action, are crucial questions'.

According to the alternative school of *post*modernism, the modern project, 'laudable though it may have been at one time, has in its turn come to oppress humankind, and to force it into certain set ways of action' (Sim 2001: p. vii). Zuckert (1996: 1) traces the concerns back to the 'conviction that modern rationalism ha[d] exhausted its promise and possibilities', starting with Nietzsche. Where some saw aberrations or challenges within the modern project, postmodernism saw unavoidable and logical consequences: colonialism; fascism/communism and industrially planned genocide; the destruction of the natural environment in the name of unfettered progress and technology; the North's 'exploitation' of the South; the horrors of modern warfare, compounded by methodical application of the very science and technology initially meant to liberate humanity; and the spiritual poverty and alienation of mass consumerism. Harvey (1989: 13) explains that 'there are those—and this is . . . the core of post-modernist philosophical thought—who insist that we should, in the name of human emancipation, abandon the Enlightenment project entirely'. The postmodern rejection of the modern project is thus both (a) theoretical and methodological, and (b) applied and political.

On the theoretical and methodological side, we see a 'rejection of many, if not most, of the cultural certainties in which life in the West has been structured over the last couple of centuries' (Sim 2001: p. vii). Specifically, postmodernism attacks the very core of the modern project, questioning the existence of any truth (universal or otherwise) and the ability of human reason to find it. As a radical alternative, postmodernism holds that knowledge and belief are products of the environment, and that we should thus speak of contingent 'narratives' rather than absolute truths. Naturally, different people will have different narratives, as they have different cultural, intellectual, economic, and sociological backgrounds. Thus, a postmodern comparison of narratives replaces the modern search for truth. On the applied and political side, two principal consequences follow from this radical relativism.

First, postmodernism rejects any claim of absolute truth as an attempt to impose one world view over others. No individual narrative has a legitimate right to exclude any other; everything is contingent on context and background, so there is no 'inside track' to truth (see Natoli 1997). In the vocabulary of postmodernism, claims of superiority or truth are referred to as attempts to impose a 'master voice' or 'meta-narrative' (see Lyotard 1981). 'Postmodern politics then becomes a continuous negotiating of various compromises as to what meanings and values are to be represented in the social order and to what degree. Outcomes here are relative to time and place and the already established dispositions of power' (Natoli 1997: 18). There follows a suspicion of certainty and philosophical foundations, and the replacement of absolute 'meaning' with relative 'interpretation'. Pippin (1999: 41) explains that 'for many so-called postmodernists, modernism represents the last game played by Western bourgeois high culture, an elitist code designed only to preserve and celebrate the . . . point of view of an exhausted but still immensely powerful middle class'.

Second, postmodernism challenges the main tenets of modern political economy. Thus, the modern nation-state becomes an instrument of centralized repression of minority voices; the supreme authority of reason ends up being but the 'voice' of those in power attempting to impose their personal views as 'the master voice' over all other narratives; natural rights are not universal values, but a Western concept, imposed on the rest of the world by 'cultural imperialism' or even brute force; free markets are seen as the freezing of one particular institutional arrangement that benefits those who have the power to expand their wealth through addictive, exploitative, and spiritually hollow mass consumerism; and the mastery of nature through science and technology becomes an excuse for 'ecocide' in the empty name of progress.

Postmodernism is not just a cute way of interpreting literature, to the delight of sadistic faculty and the terror of students; it has slowly crept into the Western world view (see Huyssens 1984).

This paper is intended to provide an overview of the literature on and trends in postmodernism and religion, rather than a detailed explanation of postmodern theory. Terms such as 'simulacra', '*différance*', 'the Other', and '(k)nots' are thus eschewed, as are such technical subtleties as described by Connor (2004: 4): 'How one capitalized or hyphenated—"post-modern," "Post-Modern," "postmodern," or "Postmodern"—seemed to many to matter a great deal, along with whether one chose to refer to "Postmodernism," "postmodernity," or simply "the postmodern".' Such details are beyond the present scope, and the interested reader is invited to visit the literature for greater depth (see, e.g., Lyotard 1981; Habermas 1983; Huyssens 1984; Harvey 1989; Bauman 1992; 1995; 1997; Bertens 1995; Natoli 1997; Sim 2001; Connor 2004).

Postmodernism and Religion

Borrowing from economics (see Friedman 1953), the following analysis does not assume that individuals and religious groups have explicitly or intentionally adopted postmodernism as a personal philosophy, or are even aware that they are acting in a postmodern world (or reacting to it). But they are most certainly acting 'as if' this were the case—and contemporary religious trends certainly fit neatly into an optic of postmodernism (and its discontents). The trends are three.

Twilight of the Churches

First, postmodernism has entailed secularization and a drop in traditional religiosity (this trend started with modernity, and was compounded by postmodernism; whereas the former rejected the tyranny of tradition and faith (and thus the absolute authority of religious institutions) in favor of reason, the latter rejects truth itself—with much more staggering consequences for religion). Secularization is the most obvious implication of postmodernism. While early secularization theories may have been technically incorrect (as discussed in the next section), they have certainly been accurate in predicting a drop in mainstream religious participation and traditional belief, and a retreat of religion from the public square. Indeed, the literature points to a decline in mainstream religion over the past half century (Repstad 1996*b*; Roof and Aagedal 1996; Greeley 1989; Iannaccone 1998).

This is especially the case in Western Europe, where, as Roberts (1998) points out, mainstream Christian Churches are in decline. In a recent survey, 51 percent of French respondents declared themselves to be Catholic, down from 67 percent in 1994 and 80 percent in the late 1970s (Donegani 2007). In general, Weigel (2005: 27) refers to Europe as 'Christophobic', having rejected religion in favor of an 'exclusive humanism' that claims to be 'neutral toward worldviews' (p. 61; see also Owen 2003), while lacking any 'transcendent allegiance' (pp. 49–51). Europeans, he writes, have 'convinced [themselves] that in order to be modern and free, [they] must be radically secular' (p. 53).

Viewed through the optic of postmodernism, this should come as no surprise. Lyotard (1981) summarizes postmodernism as 'incredulity towards all meta-narratives'. And what is traditional religion if not a 'meta-narrative', claiming for itself the one truth and one true meaning, along with an associated institutional monopoly on interpretation and salvation? Modernity had already weakened the grip of institutional religion by supplanting faith's exclusivity with reason grounded in faith; postmodernism offered the knell. Not only is reason now under suspicion, but so is truth—along with any attempt to impose one's personal narrative on others in the guise of a 'meta-narrative' cloaked as truth. The implications are obvious, and we should not be surprised to read of the drop in religious participation and the weakened role of traditional religion. If there are no absolutes, why worship an absolute, and submit oneself to the authority of those who have the power to claim possession of the truth? Neuhaus (1986), for example, asserts that 'the hostility to religion in law, education and public policy today is part of a larger hostility to normative culture'.

From Authority to Expression: A Religious Revival (of Sorts)

Postmodernism has not entailed a decline in religiosity, *tout court*, but a decline in *traditional* religiosity, as new forms of religious expression emerge. Roberts (1998: 188) speaks of 'new religious growths spurt[ing] fungi-like on the stumps and trunks of the fallen trees of tradition'. While a postmodern questioning of 'meta-narratives' and authority has indeed meant a drop in participation in *institutional* and *traditional* religion, it has not meant a complete drop in religiosity or religious participation. Lyon (2000: 75) explains that 'believing subjects show no particular loss of interest in matters that once were the concern of religious institutions (indeed, in many countries, religious interest indices show an up-swing), but seek to satisfy that interest in ways that sideline the old institutions'. In sum, 'who needs the authority of religious specialists when the autonomous individual can choose for herself [*sic*]?'

The terms have changed, as consumers of religion—and that is indeed what they now are, consuming ideas in the religious marketplace as they might in the market for goods and services—find new ways of expressing and feeling their religiosity. Lyon (2000: 39) further explains that 'in this world [of contemporary capitalism], political legitimation, central values, and dominant ideologies are no longer needed.... Unlimited consumer choice and a variety of tastes integrate everyone into a spending utopia. It is these factors that are behind the decline of certainty, and of authority.' There is thus an *appearance* of secularization today, rather than actual secularization (see Berry 2004), accompanied by a general return to religion, in what Bauman (in Berry 2004: 172) has called 'the re-enchantment of the world'. B. Martin (1998: 106) explains that 'far from fading away as Modernity bit, religion has acquired a new lease on life in the postmodern era, sprouting vigorous revival movements in Islam and a vast, worldwide expansion of... Christianity'. In fact, Berger (1992) opines that the secularization and 'post-material values' of Western Europe now constitute the exception rather than the trend.

Postmodernism has thus seen a rise in more personal, alternative forms of religion. In a recent survey (Donegani 2007), a scant 7 percent of French Catholics expressed a belief that Catholicism is the one true religion (down from more than 50 percent in 1952); 52 percent of respondents agreed that it is possible to find truth in other religions. This is particularly striking for a religion that, as recently as 1864, listed in its Syllabus of Errors the belief that 'every man is free to embrace and profess that religion which, guided by the light of reason, he shall consider true' (Woodhead *et al.* 2002). Furthermore, a full 39 percent of French respondents believe that all religions are equivalent (Donegani 2007). Donegani concludes (translation my own) that 'it is now up to the individual to appreciate the relative value of a religion, independent of the institution'. Lyon (2000: 23) echoes this, explaining that 'religion can easily be understood as merely customary behavior (like church-going) or as cognitive activity (logical beliefs), whereas in fact it also—more profoundly—has to do with faith, identity, and non-cognitive aspects of life, such as emotion'. See also Bellah *et al.*'s (1985) description of religion as 'habits of the heart... essential cultural elements of life that connect the abstract structural sphere with the motives and actions of human agents'—rather than more formalistic definitions. Langley (1999) summarizes how 'people have moved away from "religion" as something anchored in organized worship and systematic beliefs within an institution, to a self-made "spirituality," outside formal structures, which is based on experience, has no doctrine, and makes no claim to philosophical coherence'.

Contemporary religious practice increasingly involves syncretism, as religious consumers borrow from different faiths and denominations to find their own comfort blend, increasingly approaching the religious market as a cafeteria menu (see Roberts 1995; Roof and Aagedal 1996; Greeley 1989; and Lyon 2000). The work of Ammerman (1994) reveals that Christians increasingly use the services of several churches and religious organizations without necessarily offering primary allegiance to any. Berger (1967) sees the contemporary religious world as a supermarket in which customers are shopping for suitable commodities that address their individual needs. Likewise, Bibby (1987) sees religion as a set of consumer items that are available *à la carte*. Heelas (1998: 3) writes of the loss of boundaries between the religious and the sacred in postmodernism. In general terms, this observed practice fits with postmodernism's theoretical rejection of the strict dichotomies of modernity, e.g. between rationalism and faith (see Derrida 1998; 2002).

Heelas (1998: 5) explains how postmodern religion, like postmodernism, has featured a move from institutions to individuals: 'people no longer feel obliged to heed the boundaries of the religions of Modernity.' This attitude matches postmodernism's rejection of meta-narratives; Bauman (1995) has described the postmodern condition as 'life in fragments', without a need for overarching explanations, institutions, or belief systems. The contemporary question of religiosity has changed from 'How do I conform?' to 'How do I choose?' (Lyon 2000: 43), a question echoed by Bibby's (1987) view that religion has been increasingly moving from religious *commitment* to religious *consumption.* Roof (1993) refers to religious consumers as 'seekers', moving from religion to religion to find their own meaning and satisfaction, in a movement characterized by the catch-phrase, 'I'm not religious, but I'm very spiritual' (see Wuthnow 1998).

New Age and 'spirituality' are increasingly replacing traditional religion, with an emphasis on individual religious experience over institutional teaching, authority, discipline, obedience, the super-individual, and other hallmarks of traditional, institutional religion (on New Age movements, see Clarke 2006). Heelas (1998: 5) explains how, in postmodern religion, 'spiritual experience' is more important than belief, just as 'what works for me' is more important than dogma or truth. The 1996 study on 'God and Society in North America', as described in Lyon (2000: p. xii), 'showed very clearly how much religious activity—often relating to orthodox belief—goes on outside conventional settings of churches, and for that matter, mosques and synagogues. This is a tremendously important aspect of contemporary religiosity, central to religion in postmodern times' (see also Lemieux 1996). As Taylor (1991: 14) explains, the general cultural trend is now premised on the view that 'everyone has a right to develop their [*sic*] own form of life, grounded on their [*sic*] own sense of what is important or of value' (see also Wuthnow 1991). In sum, Nolen (1999, A1) explains, people do want a personal relationship with God, but they also want 'an easier, faster, no-fuss, microwavable God'.

A Fundamentalist Backlash

Third, there has been a backlash against the perceived spiritual emptiness of modernity, as exacerbated by the fuzzy relativism of postmodernism, in the form of a fundamentalist revival in all of the world's religions. As an aside, the very term 'fundamentalism' generates controversy in the literature, as it applies, literally, only to US Protestant movements at the dawn of the twentieth century. However, it is a convenient catch-all phrase for literalist, ultra-orthodox movements that derive their 'identity primarily from a posture of resistance to the modern world order' (Hunter 1990: 58). Generally, see Cohen (1990); Kaplan (1992); Nielsen (1993); and

Marty and Appleby (1991; 1993*a*; 1993*b*; 1994; 1995); for a historical and theological overview of the US phenomenon, see Pelikan (1990); Marsden (1990); Pinnock (1990); and Nielsen (1993). See also the dissatisfaction expressed in Wieseltier (1990); Nasr (1984); and Lewis (1988) on the use of the word 'fundamentalism', a concern more strongly expressed in Hassan's (1990) outright rejection of the word as applied to Islam. For the present purposes, I beg the indulgence of readers who may object to this deliberate simplification.

Roberts (1998: 187) explains that 'traditional religious discourse, forced by secularization to the margins of social life [has been] problematically rebirthed in the subcultures of fundamentalism and New Age'. To be sure, fundamentalism is not, per se, a postmodern phenomenon—quite the contrary, it rejects modernism's secularism and postmodernism's rejection of truth; in fact, fundamentalism could best be described as pre-modern, as it returns to an appeal to faith and authority over reason. But fundamentalism is, in many ways, a reaction to postmodernism, and thus bears mention in this review—not for the details of fundamentalism, which are best left to other essays, but to demonstrate how fundamentalism emerged, in large part, as a reaction to the radical relativism of postmodernism.

Armstrong (2000: p. ix) writes that 'one of the most startling developments of the late 20th century has been the emergence within every major religious tradition of a militant piety popularly known as "fundamentalism"'. As reason displaced religion and the search for meaning, many started seeking comfort in stricter religion, which filled the spiritual void left by the Enlightenment's enthusiasm for logic, reason, and technology, and postmodernism's subsequent rejection thereof. Armstrong (2000: p. x) further explains that, with modernity, 'it was assumed that as human beings became more rational, they either would have no further need for religion or would be content to confine it to the immediate personal and private areas of their life. But in the late 1970s, fundamentalists began to rebel against this secularist hegemony and started to wrest religion out of its marginal position and back to center stage.' Giddens (1990) and Bauman (1992; 1997) see fundamentalism as an answer to the moral questions thrown up by modernity and postmodernism. When postmodernism challenged the very possibility of truth itself, and those seeking religious meaning started finding it outside the confines of traditional religion, those who stayed within the traditional institutions reacted against the relativistic fuzziness of 'cafeteria religion' by strengthening dogma.

Although not a postmodern phenomenon, the contemporary fundamentalist backlash is exactly that—a reaction to postmodernism, and a fight of absolutes against relativism. Thus did Pope John Paul II (1988) worry, in his encyclical on faith and reason, about 'the widespread mentality which claims that a definitive commitment should no longer be made, because everything is fleeting and provisional' (incidentally, Pope John Paul II was not himself a fundamentalist, but led a battle against postmodernism's radical relativism that is still a *cheval de bataille* of today's Catholic Church, and especially the new pontificate). Lyon (2000) sees fundamentalism as a reaction to the decline in institutional and doctrinal authority, and the parallel rise in individual interpretation (see also Bauman 1998 and Smart 1998). Heelas (1998: 1) explains that 'for some, the disintegration of the certainties of Modernity has left a situation in which postmodern religion ... can develop. For others, the distressing certainties of modernity have resulted in the valorization of a pre-modern past.' Bauman (1998: 74) reminds us that 'the allure of fundamentalism stems from its promise to emancipate the converted from the agonies of choice. Here one finds, finally, the indubitably supreme authority, an authority to end all other authorities'—no doubt appealing in a postmodern world that has dismissed all authorities (and thus metaphysical certainties) as mere 'meta-narrative' power plays.

In an apparent contradiction, the literature points to a decline in mainstream religion (Roof and Aagedal 1996; Repstad 1996*a*), with a parallel rise in fundamentalism (Johnson 1986; Neuhaus 1986; Roof and McKinney 1987). Iannaccone (1998: 1471) summarizes, that 'throughout the world, fast growing religions tend to be strict, sectarian and theologically conservative. In the United States, such groups continue to gain members, even as theologically liberal Protestant denominations... struggle with relative and absolute losses' (see also Greeley 1989). For general trends on religious development, and especially the mainstream–fundamentalist divide, see Stark and Bainbridge (1985) and Berger (1999).

The apparent contradiction makes more sense when viewed through the optic of postmodernism's rejection of truth and the corresponding backlash: fundamentalism is the reverse of the postmodern medal. Just as postmodernism questioned, then rejected, the modern project, so the rise in religious fundamentalism can be seen as a reaction to both modernism and postmodernism. If the horrors of the twentieth century are seen as fundamental failures of modernism (and inevitable), a pre-modern rejection makes just as much sense as a postmodern one. The direction of the counter-claim is just that—a question of direction (see Johnson 1986).

In a specific geographical example, some authors even speak of a Fourth Great Awakening in the USA (see Johnson 1986). Considering that the first three awakenings were major factors in the American Revolution, the Civil War, and twentieth-century progressivism, respectively, the Fourth Great Awakening—if it is indeed that—promises to be of no minor consequence. Interestingly, this trend includes not only traditional religious groups, but also others concerned with the overall decline in American values and morality (see Marty and Appleby's multi-volume Fundamentalism Project (1991; 1993*a*; 1993*b*; 1994; 1995)). Neuhaus (1986) explains that the current rise in fundamentalism goes beyond traditional religious forces, to incorporate many who are troubled by a perceived decline in American values.

Speculation and Futures

The preceding sketch is just that—a sketch. It outlines the major trends and contributions to the literature on postmodernism and religion. Beyond the three fairly straightforward trends—decline in mainstream religiosity, personal religious experience supplanting institutional dogma and participation, and a fundamentalist backlash—other questions are more difficult. Here are three, outlined for consideration.

Making Sense of Islam

The discussion hitherto has focused (intentionally) on general trends, with an admitted (and probably inevitable) emphasis on the West, and thus Christianity, as the home of both modernity and postmodernism. Space considerations prevent a thorough review of the world's religions other than major trends; such a review is, in any event, beyond the scope of this essay.

The case of Islam, however, merits a pause. How does Islam fit into postmodernity (or modernity, for that matter)? Which country is representative of contemporary Islam: Turkey with its nationalist secularism or Iran with its theocracy? Islam and Welty (1996: 159–61) caution us that 'most Muslims take positions that do not lie at either of these extremes'.

The recent trend of radical Islamism would certainly appear to place Islam in parallel with other fundamentalisms. Gellner (1992: 4) comments that 'in our age, fundamentalism is at its strongest in Islam', and remarks that, whereas other religions have declined in the past century, Islam is as strong—or stronger—than a century ago (1992: 5). Dekmejian (1985) sees fundamentalism as a core attribute of the Islamic mind-set. Likewise, Ajami (2004) reports the teaching of radical Islamist Sayyid Qutb, that 'a Muslim has no nationality except his belief'—a clear rejection of modernity's nation-state, just as attempts to impose Shari'a law contradict modern freedom of religion and the separation of church and state. Tibi (1988) opines that Islam is, by definition, incompatible with the scientific-technological culture of the modern world. In more fundamental terms, Mawdudi (1979: 37) expresses Islam's repudiation of modernity—a repudiation along *pre*-modern, rather than *post*modern lines:

> It is neither for us to decide the aim and purpose of our existence nor to prescribe the limits of our worldly authority, nor is anyone else entitled to make these decisions for us... Nothing can claim sovereignty, be it a human being, a family, a class, a group of people, or even the human race in the world as a whole. God alone is the Sovereign, and His commandments the Law of Islam.

See also Adams (1983); Mawdudi (1976); Choueiri (1990); and Armstrong (2000), as well as Hefner (1998) and Gellner (1992) on Islam and secularization.

Surely such a world view clashes with modernity. Yet, one must be cautious about applying Western paradigms to the Islamic situation, as the latter is so intertwined with colonialism and the forceful imposition of modernity. Ahmed (2004: pp. xii, 28–9) explains that the Islamic world is still wrestling with modernity, let alone postmodernism. What might easily be dismissed as fundamentalism could just as easily be a return to pre-colonial traditions, or a post-colonial search for identity (see Lundin and Lundin 1996; Armstrong 2000). With such different historical experiences, the reaction to modernity will, of course, be different, as the Islamic world has reacted as much to Western colonialism as to Western ideas. Ahmed (2004: 31), reminds us that, for much of the Muslim World 'modernization' amounted to emulation of British ways; and today 'the few Muslim comments on postmodernism are tentative and sweeping; they dismiss it as a continuation of Western modernism, as destructive and doomed...equated to "Americanization," "nihilism," "anarchy" and "devastation" .... Indeed, [they] equate postmodernism broadly with American civilization'. Generally, see Gellner (1992: 10–20) for a commentary on Islam's reaction to modernism. Thus does Clarke (2006: 166) enjoin us that 'such changes as are occurring in [the Islamic world] cannot be fully understood and explained if seen solely as responses to Westernization and modernization'. Moreover, as Abou El Fadl (2004: 15–16) points out, elements of modernization (such as the nation-state, communications and technology, and 'the instrusive modern state') have altered traditional balances in Islam; in essence, the 'modern praetorian state [has] become the maker and enforcer of divine law'. This is further complicated by the politicization of fundamentalist Islam (see Sivan 1992; Abrahamian 1992; Waines 2002; see also Hunter 1990; Hassan 1990 for further cautionary notes).

In addition, dissent, theological evolution, and the debates over interpretation and authority that are so central to the modern–postmodern clash are nothing new in Islam. Clarke (2006: 165) explains that 'although often seen as a response to modernization and globalization, several of the core issues that engage Islamist groups, who are defined essentially by their demand for an Islamic state, have a long history'. Likewise, Abou el Fadl (2004: 15) explains how 'concerns about the reach of the government's power under Shariah law have antecedents in Islamic history, and so, by the standards of the modern age, this is not an entirely novel issue'. In fact, Clarke (2006: 165) continues, the central 'debate on the relationship of revelation and reason did not begin in the Muslim world with the rise of modern science and the impact of Enlightenment thinking from the West, but can be traced back to earlier times'—even if (2006: 166) modernization and Westernization have 'widened and complicated the issues that Muslims have had to grapple with for centuries'. For a history of the various Muslim intellectual revolutions and their intended targets, see Clarke (2006: 184). In Islam, this question of interpretation revolves around the conflict (and not a new one, at that) between *ijtihad* (personal interpretation) and the community or scholarly consensus, as led by *'ulama* scholars (see Clarke 2006: 165 and ch. 7 generally, as well as Abou el Fadl 2004: esp. 7–9). In fact, Clarke (2006: 168) sees an '*ijithad* revolution' in modern Islam—not at all unlike the Protestant Reformation that triggered modernity in the first place.

In light of both the methodological pitfall (of the Islamic world's particular exposure to modernity) and the fact that the interpretation debate is not new in Islam, there exists the possibility that Islam will come to terms with modernity—as have significant segments of Christianity—or other peaceful alternatives to the fundamentalist scenarios presented above. Abou el Fadl (2004: 51), citing Nader A. Hashmi, offers an optimistic perspective, opining that 'like other religious traditions whose origins lie in the pre-modern era and are scripturally based, Islam is neither more nor less compatible with modern democracy than Christianity or Judaism' (generally, see Abou El Fadl 2004 on the possible—and indeed historical—coexistence of Islam with very modern concepts such as rule of law and separation of powers). Nielsen (1993: 89) asks rhetorically (if pleadingly) 'how is it that a religion of the historical richness and strength of Islam has now come to be associated with a one-dimensional reactionary integralism?' (See also Smart 1998 and Ahmed 2004: esp. ch. 4, on the three trends in contemporary Islam: traditional, modernizing, and radical). Nielsen (1993: 102) concludes that 'the historical evidence is that the Islamic paradigm is not intrinsically (and has not always been) fundamentalist'. Generally, see Lawrence (1998); Hefner (1998); Waines (2002); and Armstrong (2000).

Static Creeds, Dynamic Beliefs: The Challenge of Study and Self-Reporting

Changing mental models imply changing methodologies. What if we are studying postmodern phenomena with inadequate modern tools? Lyon (2000: 21) cautions us that 'many contemporary accounts of religion in the modern world are charmingly simple but profoundly misleading. This state of affairs can be traced to a single social one-idea-fits-all theory, called secularization. The theory suggests that the growth of science and technology, of urban industrial social patterns, and of the nation state, has deleterious effects on religious life. Modern society, so the story goes, runs on non-religious principles, churches lose social influence, and people stop attending them.' As discussed above, secularization theory was accurate to an extent—but provided only half the story.

Furthermore, the decline in mainstream religion is probably much more dramatic than the literature indicates. For example, there are methodologically confusing problems, such as the possibility of 'belonging without believing'—that is, belonging to a church for social, spiritual, or other reasons, without believing its teachings (Repstad 1996*a*; Botvar 1996)—or the tension between static (official) creeds and dynamic (individual) beliefs, which will create huge difficulties in distinguishing between stated and actual preferences. For example, Donegani (2007) reports that only 51 percent of French respondents describe themselves as Catholics; but he further reports that only 52 percent of French Catholics believe in God, and only 18 percent define God according to the teachings of the Catholic Church. What does it really mean to be a Catholic any more? Conversely, what does it mean to claim that religious participation is dwindling—without looking beyond institutional participation? Lyon (2000: p. ix) complains that '"religion" smacks of conventional, organized religiosity, inappropriate to today's world of spiritualities and seekers'. Social scientists will have to consider such problems when asking questions and studying religiosity.

Assessing Postmodernism

Finally, the question ought to be asked: what are we to make of postmodernism and its effect on religion?

The critiques

The religious fundamentalists, obviously, have offered their answer, if we consider the fundamentalist backlash to be largely a response to the squishiness of postmodern forms of belief and religious participation. But, moving from the religious to the philosophical, what of scholarly responses to postmodern thought and postmodern attitudes?

The two main critiques of postmodernism are, first, healthy concern about postmodernism's relativism (and the language in which it is conveyed), and, second, a simultaneous sympathy for postmodernism's healthy concern about the limits of reason (and some of the consequences that blind worship of reason has brought to humanity); in sum, postmodernism raises important questions about the modern project, but the answers are found wanting.

Gellner (1992: 41, 48) expresses a worry about postmodernism's twin sins of relativism and obscurantist language when he complains that 'there is no end to this metatwaddle', and 'that relativism leads to sloppy research, appalling prose, much pretentious obscurity, and in any case constitutes a highly ephemeral phenomenon, destined for oblivion when the next fad arrives'; alas, that 'is not all there is to say' about postmodernism and its accompanying relativism. Indeed, he continues (1992: 71) with the assessment that 'Postmodernism as such doesn't matter too much. It is a fad which owes its appeal to its seeming novelty and genuine obscurity, and it will pass soon enough, as such fashions do. But it is a specimen of relativism, and relativism does matter. It is objectionable because it leads to cognitive nihilism, which is simply false.' Giddens (1990: 46) likewise points to a fundamental inconsistency within postmodernism: how can postmodernism supersede modernism if there are no legitimate foundations (or, for that matter, no foundations at all)?

In spite of his concerns about postmodernism, Giddens (1990: 48–9) recognizes the fundamental dilemma of modernity—'How can we justify a commitment to reason in the name of reason?'—as an honest question that is asked, if not answered, by postmodernism. As an alternative, Giddens (1990: ch. 5) suggests a rethinking of modernity to overcome its shortcomings, rather than a proverbial discarding of the baby with the bathwater. Similarly, Gellner (1992: 75–84) offers a third way—beyond the modern–postmodern divide, and beyond the fundamentalist–postmodern schism—of 'rationalist fundamentalism'. This position 'retains the faith in the uniqueness of truth, but does not believe we can ever possess it definitively, and . . . uses, as the foundation for practical conduct and inquiry, not any substantive conviction, but only a loyalty to certain procedural rules [of logic], scientific procedure, and opening of all hypotheses to inquiry' (Gellner 1992: pp. vii, 80–3). In a similar vein, Kermode (1968) and Foster (1983) see postmodernism as an extension and self-understanding of modernity, rather than a complete break; see also Bellah (1969) on 'modern religion'.

Critiques on the critiques

For all their merits, there are two fundamental problems with the existing critiques of postmodernism and religion. First, a scholarly critique of postmodernism and religion is, in a sense, irrelevant. Indeed, lapsing for a moment into pop culture, the simplest analysis of postmodernism and religion is that 'it is what it is'. Gellner (1992: 72), for example, writes of postmodernism that it is a 'tortuous, somewhat affected fad' of academics. That it is, for sure; but this is only part of the picture. Regardless of its merits, postmodernism has crept into popular consciousness, as a deeper manifestation of what Clarke (2006: 25–6) describes as New Age's move from elite fad to worldwide mass movement. Regardless of philosophical merits, postmodernism exists and is prevalent; but it is too limiting to critique it exclusively from a scholarly perspective. Indeed, it is a safe assumption that most Europeans and North Americans have not read Derrida, Rorty, Habermas, Nietzsche, and the other high priests of postmodernism in any detail—if at all. It is also safe to assume that most people (whether drawn from the general population, from postmodern Christian denominations, or New Age movements) would fail a test on the basics of postmodernism. Yet more and more people seem to embrace the postmodern ideology, as reflected in institutions (see Petroni 2003, 2004; Wenzel 2007*c*; 2008), religious practice, and general *Weltanschauung*—again, 'as if' they had studied postmodernism and embraced it (see Friedman 1953). Where, then, did postmodernism come from? Is it taught in the schools? Has it made its way somehow into the popular culture, without being identified as such by the very people who embrace it? And if the ideology's main tenets do not explicitly exist in people's mind, where do they reside, and how are they transmitted? In and through conventions, language, standards, and ever elusive 'culture'? Such answers will come from a deeper integration of theology, philosophy, sociology, anthropology, and even economics, with its insights regarding mental models and institutions (see, e.g., North 1978; 1990; 1994; Pejovich 2003; Wenzel 2007*a*; 2007*b*; 2007*c*; 2008).

Second, it is a dangerous conflation and sleight of hand to speak of 'the' Enlightenment. Out of simplicity, I have conflated here two very different (and often contradictory) schools of Enlightenment thought: namely, the Scottish and Continental Enlightenments. This is a dangerous—if far too common—conflation, as the Scots (Locke, Hume, Ferguson, etc.) emphasized humility, reason grounded in faith, and a healthy acceptance of human nature, whereas the Continentals (Rousseau, Hegel, Comte, etc.) lapsed into a hubristic cult of reason, leading to social engineering, a complete negation of the individual in favor of some putative 'greater' or 'common' good—and, to put it bluntly, Auschwitz and the Gulag. For details on the two Enlightenments, see Hayek (1967; 1978; 1979); Hampson (1991); Boettke (2000); Porter (2001); Himmelfarb (2004); and Wenzel (2007*b*). As much as I shudder to conflate the two lines of thought, I must resign myself to the fact that they are indeed conflated in the popular—and intellectual—mind. Even such serious thinkers as Gellner (1992), Giddens (1990), Bauman (1989), and Ahmed (2004) conflate the two Enlightenments. Most strikingly, Giddens (1990: 172) writes that 'totalitarianism and modernity are not just contingently, but inherently, connected, as Zygmunt Bauman in particular has made clear'—totalitarianism is certainly a consequence of the Continental Enlightenment; of the Scottish Enlightenment, unequivocally not. The postmodern reaction, then—if it is indeed a reaction to Auschwitz, the Gulag, the growth of the state at the expense of individual autonomy, the destruction of the environment through ill-defined property rights, and the industrialization of war, all of which are necessary and inevitable consequences of the Continental Enlightenment—makes perfect sense. If we return to the humility of the Scottish Enlightenment, grounded in self-inquiry, doubt, and a foundation of 'faith within reason', then there is room to question the shortcomings of (prevalent/conflated/Continental) modernity, without lapsing into the nihilism and linguistic obscurantism of postmodernism. In fact, I suspect that this is what many thinkers are indeed trying to do, without making the appeal to the Scots explicit.

Conclusion

The above patterns—modernization and secularization, postmodernism, fundamentalism—and the struggles and questions associated with them, exist in all of the world's religions (see Armstrong 2000). Kaplan (1992: p. vii) reminds us that 'examples of real fanaticism, usually accompanied by violence, continue throughout the world with unceasing regularity. Whether the struggles occur among Sikhs, Muslims and Hindus in India, or between Jews and Muslims in Jerusalem, there are enough instances to remind the informed public that fundamentalism and its ramifications are an ongoing phenomenon.' Likewise, the world's religions are affected by the changes of postmodernism.

Space considerations prevent a detailed discussion of all religions. For general trends in the world's religions, see Lundin and Lundin (1996) and Woodhead *et al.* (2002). On Judaism, see Wieseltier (1990); Hertzberg (1992); Friedman (1992); Lundin and Lundin (1996); Haas (1996); Woodhead *et al.* (2002); Kunin (2002); and Armstrong (2000). On Hinduism, see Rudolph and Rudolph (1967; 1987); Nielsen (1993); Lundin and Lundin (1996); Smith (2002; 2003); and Woodhead *et al.* (2002). On Sikhism, see Nielsen (1993); Lundin and Lundin (1996); Shackle (2002); and Woodhead *et al.* (2002). On Buddhism, see Nielsen (1993); Cantwell and Kawanami (2002).

The debate is far from settled, as we are merely observing the ongoing effects of radical shifts in mental models and their effects on religion and religiosity. Concluding with the words of Lyon (2000: 148), we find both a warning and a harbinger of exciting scholarship in the future: 'how faith finds new forms, how spirituality finds new modes of expression, within postmodern conditions, cannot be predicted. The point is not prediction (even if it was for some modernist sociologies), but the tracing of trends, the mapping of everyday experiences.' And, lest we fall victims to our own cleverness, we should not seek to find all answers in scholarship and explicit philosophies, but also in observed actions, participation, and implicit beliefs.

References

Abou El Fadl, K. (2004). *Islam and the Challenge of Democracy.* Princeton: Princeton University Press.

Abrahamian, E. (1992). 'Khomeini: A Fundamentalist?' In Kaplan (1992), 109–25.

Adams, C. (1983). 'Mawdudi and the Islamic State'. In J. Esposito, (ed.), *Voices of Resurgent Islam.* New York and Oxford: Oxford University Press, 99–133.

Ahmed, A. (2004). *Postmodernism and Islam: Predicament and Promise.* New York: Routledge.

Ajami, F. (2004). 'The Moor's Last Laugh'. *Wall Street Journal,* 22 Mar.

Ammerman, N. (1994). 'Telling Congregational Stories'. *Review of Religious Research,* 35: 4.

Armstrong, K. (2000). *The Battle for God.* New York: Alfred A. Knopf.

Bauman, Z. (1989). *Modernity and the Holocaust.* Cambridge: Polity Press.

—— (1992). *Intimations of Postmodernity.* London and New York: Routledge.

—— (1995). *Life in Fragments.* Oxford and Malden, Mass.: Blackwell.

—— (1997). *Postmodernity and its Discontents.* Cambridge: Polity Press.

—— (1998). 'Postmodern Religion'. In Heelas *et al.* (1998), 58–78.

BELLAH, R. (1969). 'Religious Evolution'. In R. Robertson (ed.), *The Sociology of Religion: Selected Readings*. Baltimore: Penguin Books, 262–92.

—— MADSEN, R., SULLIVAN, W., SWIDLER, A., and TIPTON, S. (1985). *Habits of the Heart: Individualism and Commitment in American Life*. Berkeley: University of California Press.

BERGER, P. (1967). *The Sacred Canopy*. New York: Anchorage–Doubleday.

—— (1992). *A Far Glory*. New York: Anchor/Doubleday.

—— (ed.) (1999). *The Desecularization of the World: Resurgent Religion and World Politics*. Grand Rapids, Mich.: Wm. B. Eerdmans Publishing Co.

BERRY, P. (2004). 'Postmodernism and Post-religion'. In Connor (2004), 168–81.

BERTENS, H. (1995). *The Idea of the Postmodern: A History*. London: Routledge.

BIBBY, R. (1987). *Fragmented Gods*. Toronto: Irwin.

BOETTKE, P. (2000). 'Which Enlightenment and Whose Liberalism?: Hayek's Research Program for Understanding the Liberal Society'. In *idem* (ed.), *The Legacy of F. A. Hayek*. Aldershot: Edward Elgar, i. pp. xi–iv.

BOTVAR, P. K. (1996). 'Belonging without Believing? The Norwegian Religious Profile Compared with the British One'. In Repstad (1996*b*), 119–34.

CANTWELL, C., and KAWANAMI, H. (2002). 'Buddhism'. In Woodhead *et al.* (2002), 41–69.

CHOUEIRI, Y. (1990). *Islamic Fundamentalism*. Boston: Twayne Publishers.

CLARKE, P. (2006). *New Religions in Global Perspective*. New York: Routledge.

COHEN, N. (ed.) (1990). *The Fundamentalist Phenomenon: A View from Within, a Response from Without*. Grand Rapids, Mich.: William B. Eerdmans Publishing Co.

CONNOR, S. (ed.) (2004). *The Cambridge Companion to Postmodernism*. Cambridge: Cambridge University Press.

DALY, G. (1985). 'Catholicism and Modernity'. *Journal of the American Academy of Religion*, 53/4: 773–96.

DEKMEJIAN, R. (1985). *Islam in Revolution: Fundamentalism in the Arab World*. Syracuse, NY: Syracuse University Press.

DERRIDA, J. (1998). 'Faith and Knowledge: The Two Sources of "Religion" at the Limits of Reason Alone'. In J. Derrida and G. Vattimo (eds.), *Religion*. Stanford, Calif.: Stanford University Press, 1–78.

DONEGANI, J. M. (2007). 'L'Église sera vaincue par le libéralisme'. *Le Monde*, at <www.lemonde.fr, January 20, 2007>.

FOSTER, H. (ed.) (1983). *Postmodern Culture*. London: Pluto.

FRIEDMAN, M. (1953). 'The Methodology of Positive Economics'. In *idem* (ed.), *Essays in Positive Economics*. Chicago: University of Chicago Press, 3–43.

—— (1992). 'Jewish Zealots: Conservative versus Innovative'. In Kaplan (1992), 159–76.

GELLNER, E. (1992). *Postmodernism, Reason and Religion*. London: Routledge.

GIDDENS, A. (1990). *The Consequences of Modernity*. Stanford, Calif.: Stanford University Press.

—— (1991). *Modernity and Self-Identity*. Stanford, Calif.: Stanford University Press.

GREELEY, A. (1989). *Religious Change in America*. Cambridge, Mass.: Harvard University Press.

HAAS, P. (1996). 'Trends in Contemporary Jewish Literature'. In Lundin and Lundin (1996), 57–130.

Habermas, J. (1983). 'Modernity: An Incomplete Project'. In H. Foster (ed.) (1983), *The Anti-Aesthetic: Essays on Postmodern Culture.* Seattle: Bay Press, 3–15.

Hampson, N. (1991). *The Enlightenment: An Evaluation of its Assumptions, Attitudes and Values.* New York: Penguin.

Harvey, D. (1989). *The Condition of Postmodernity: An Enquiry into the Origins of Cultural Change.* Oxford: Basil Blackwell.

Hassan, R. (1990). 'The Burgeoning of Islamic Fundamentalism: Toward an Understanding of the Phenomenon'. In Cohen (1990), 151–71.

Hayek, F. A. (1967). *Studies in Philosophy, Politics and Economics.* Chicago: University of Chicago Press.

—— (1978). *New Studies in Philosophy, Politics and Economics and the History of Ideas.* London: Routledge & Kegan Paul.

—— (1979). *The Counter-Revolution of Science: Studies in the Abuse of Reason.* Indianapolis: Liberty Fund.

Heelas, P. (ed.) (1998) with the assistance of D. Martin and P. Morris. *Religion, Modernity and Postmodernity.* Oxford: Blackwell Publishers.

Hefner, R. (1998). 'Secularization and Citizenship in Muslim Indonesia'. In Heelas (1998), 147–68.

Hertzberg, A. (1992). 'Jewish Fundamentalism'. In Kaplan (1992), 152–8.

Himmelfarb, G. (2004). *The Road to Modernity: The British, French and American Enlightenments.* New York: Knopf.

Hunter, J. (1990). 'Fundamentalism in its Global Contours'. In Cohen (1990), 56–72.

Huyssens, A. (1984). 'Mapping the Post-Modern'. *New German Critique,* 33: 5–52.

Iannaccone, L. (1998). 'Introduction to the Economics of Religion'. *Journal of Economic Literature,* (Sept.): 1465–96.

Islam, A., and Welty, G. (1996). 'The Religion of Islam'. In Lundin and Lundin (1996), 181–68.

John Paul II (1998). *Fides et Ratio: Encyclical Letter of the Supreme Pontiff John Paul II to the Bishops of the Catholic Church on the Relationship between Faith and Reason.* Vatican: Libreria Editrice Vaticana.

Johnson, P. (1986). 'The Almost Chosen People: Why America is Different'. In R. Neuhaus (ed.), *Unsecular America.* Grand Rapids, Mich.: Wm. B. Eerdmans Publishing Co. in cooperation with The Rockford Institute Center on Religion & Society.

Kaplan, L. (ed.) (1992). *Fundamentalism in Comparative Perspective.* Amherst, Mass.: University of Massachusetts Press.

Kermode, F. (1968). 'Modernisms'. In *idem* (ed.), *Continuities.* London: Routledge & Kegan Paul, 1–27.

Kunin, S. (2002). 'Judaism'. In Woodhead *et al.* (2002), 128–52.

Kurtz, L. (1986). *The Politics of Heresy.* Berkeley: University of California Press.

Langley, C. (1999). 'A Spiritual Land with Little Time for Church'. *Daily Telegraph,* (17 Dec.), 31.

Lawrence, B. (1998). 'From Fundamentalism to Fundamentalisms: A Religious Ideology in Multiple Forms'. In Heelas (1998), 88–101.

Lemieux, R. (1996). 'La Religion au Canada: Synthèse et Problématiques'. *Social Compass,* 43/1: 135–58.

Lewis, B. (1988). *The Political Language of Islam.* Chicago: University of Chicago Press.

LUNDIN, G. E., and LUNDIN, A. H. (eds.) (1996). *Contemporary Religious Ideas: Bibliographic Essays*. Englewood, Col.: Libraries Unlimited.

LYON, D. (2000). *Jesus in Disneyland: Religion in Postmodern Times*. Cambridge: Polity Press in association with Blackwell Publishers Ltd.

LYOTARD, F. (1981). *The Postmodern Condition*. Minneapolis: University of Minnesota Press.

MARSDEN, G. (1990). 'Defining American Fundamentalism'. In Cohen (1990). 22–37.

MARTIN, B. (1998). 'From Pre- to Postmodernity in Latin America: The Case of Pentecostalism'. In Heelas (1998), 102–46.

MARTIN, D. (1996). 'Religion, Secularization, and Post-Modernity: Lessons from the Latin-American Case'. In Repstad (1996*b*), 35–43.

MARTY, M. and APPLEBY, R. S. (eds.) (1991). *Fundamentalisms Observed*. Chicago: University of Chicago Press..

—— —— (eds.) (1993*a*). *Fundamentalisms and Society*. Chicago: University of Chicago Press.

—— —— (eds.) (1993*b*). *Fundamentalisms and the State*. Chicago: University of Chicago Press.

—— —— (eds.) (1994). *Accounting for Fundamentalisms*. Chicago: University of Chicago Press.

—— —— (eds.) (1995). *Fundamentalisms Comprehended*. Chicago: University of Chicago Press.

MAWDUDI, A. (1976). *Jihad in Islam*. Lahore: Islamic Publications, Ltd.

—— (1979). *Islamic Way of Life*. Lahore: Islamic Foundation.

NASR, S. (1984). 'Present Tendencies, Future Trends'. In M. Kelly (ed.), *Islam: The Religious and Political Life of a World Community*. New York: Praeger, 275–92.

NATOLI, J. (1997). *A Primer to Postmodernity*. Oxford: Blackwell Publishers.

NEUHAUS, R. (1986). 'From Providence to Privacy: Religion and the Redefinition of America'. In *idem* (ed.), *Unsecular America*. Grand Rapids, Mich.: Wm. B. Eerdmans Publishing Co. in cooperation with The Rockford Institute Center on Religion & Society, 52–66.

NIELSEN, N. (1993). *Fundamentalism, Mythos and World Religion*. Albany, NY: SUNY Press.

NOLEN, S. (1999). 'Give them Jesus, but Hold the Theology'. *Globe and Mail*, (2, Jan.), A1, A6.

NORTH, D. (1978). 'Structure and Performance: The Task of Economic History'. *Journal of Economic Literature*, 16/3 (Sept.): 963–78.

—— (1990). *Institutions, Institutional Change, and Economic Performance*. Cambridge: Cambridge University Press.

—— (1994). 'Economic Performance Through Time'. *American Economic Review*, 84/3 (June): 359–68.

OWEN, G. (2003). 'Habermas + Derrida: Modernism as a Beneficiary of War in Iraq'. *National Post*, (2 Aug).

PEJOVICH, S. (2003). 'Understanding the Transaction Costs of Transition: It's the Culture, Stupid'. Forum Series on the Role of Institutions in Promoting Economic Growth, Directed by the Mercatus Center at George Mason University and the IRIS Center, Washington, DC, 4 April, 2003.

PELIKAN, J. (1990). 'Fundamentalism and/or Orthodoxy? Toward an Understanding of the Fundamentalist Phenomenon'. In Cohen (1990), 3–21.

PETRONI, A. (2003). 'A Constitution for the European Union?' Lecture given at the XXVIth Summer University of the New Economy, Aix-en-Provence, 2 Sept.

—— (2004). 'Perspectives for Freedom of Choice in Bioethics and Health Care in Europe'. Paper prepared for Liberty Fund, January.

PINNOCK, C. (1990). 'Defining American Fundamentalism: A Response'. In Cohen (1990), 38–55.

PIPPIN, R. (1999). *Modernism as a Philosophical Problem: On the Dissatisfactions of European High Culture.* Oxford: Blackwell Publishers.

PORTER, R. (2001). *The Enlightenment: Studies in European History.* New York: Palgrave Macmillan.

REPSTAD, P. (1996*a*). 'Introduction: A Paradigm Shift in the Sociology of Religion?'. In Repstad (1996*b*). (ed.),

—— (ed.) (1996*b*). *Religion and Modernity: Modes of Co-existence.* Oslo: Scandinavian University Press, 1–10.

ROBERTS, R. (ed). (1995). *Religion in Sociological Perspective.* Belmont, Calif.: Wadsworth Publishing Company.

—— (1998). 'The Construals of "Europe": Religion, Theology and the Problematics of Modernity'. In Heelas (1998), 186–217.

ROOF, W. C. (1993). *A Generation of Seekers: The Spiritual Journeys of the Baby Boom Generation.* New York: HarperCollins.

—— and AAGEDAL, O. (1996). 'The Same Generation, the Same Religion? The Religiosity of the Norwegian and American Baby-Boomers'. In Repstad (1996*b*), 135–58.

—— and MCKINNEY, W. (1987). *American Mainline Religion.* New Brunswick, NJ: Rutgers University Press.

RUDOLPH, L., and RUDOLPH, S. (1967). *The Modernity of Tradition.* Chicago: University of Chicago Press.

—— —— (1987). *In Pursuit of Lakshmi: The Political Economy of the Indian State.* Chicago: University of Chicago Press.

SHACKLE, C. (2002). 'Sikhism'. In Woodhead *et al.* (2002), 70–85.

SIM, S. (ed.) (2001). *The Routledge Companion to Postmodernism.* London and New York: Routledge.

SIVAN, E. (1992). 'The Islamic Resurgence: Civil Society Strikes Back'. In Kaplan (1992), 96–108.

SMART, N. (1998). 'Tradition, Retrospective Perception, Nationalism and Modernism'. In Heelas (1998), 79–87.

SMITH, D. (2002). 'Hinduism'. In Woodhead *et al.* (2002), 15–40.

—— (2003). *Hinduism and Modernity.* Oxford: Blackwell Publishing.

STARK, R., and BAINBRIDGE, W. (1985). *The Future of Religion: Secularization, Revival, and Cult Formation.* Berkeley: University of California Press.

TAYLOR, C. (1991). *The Malaise of Modernity.* Toronto: Anasi.

TIBI, B. (1988). *The Crisis of Modern Islam: A Preindustrial Culture in the Scientific-Technological Age.* Salt Lake City: University of Utah Press.

WAINES, D. (2002). 'Islam'. In Woodhead *et al.* (2002), 182–203.

WEIGEL, G. (2005). *The Cube and the Cathedral: Europe, America and Politics without God.* New York: Basic Books.

WENZEL, N. (2007*a*). 'Beyond Parchment, Beyond Formal Rules: Constitutional Culture and Constitutional Political Economy'. *Ama-Gi, Journal of the Hayeh Society of the London School of Economics,* 8/1.

—— (2007*b*). 'Which Enlightenment, Which Modernity? Humble Scots and Hubristic Continentals'. Hilsdale College, Working Paper.

—— (2007*c*). 'Ideology and Institutional Change: The EU Constitution as Reflection of Europe's Emergent Postmodern Ideology'. *Romanian Economic and Business Review,* 2/3.

—— (2008). 'Postmodernism and its Discontents: Whither Constitutionalism after God and Reason?' *New Perspectives on Political Economy* (forthcoming).
WIESELTIER, L. (1990). 'The Jewish Face of Fundamentalism'. In Cohen (1990), 192–6.
WOODHEAD, L., FLETCHER, P., KAWANAMI, H., and SMITH, D. (eds.) (2002). *Religions in the Modern World.* London and New York: Routledge.
WUTHNOW, R. (1991). *The Struggle for America's Soul.* Grand Rapids, Mich.: William B. Eerdmans Publishing Co.
—— (1998). *After Heaven: Spirituality in America since the 1950s.* Berkeley: University of California Press.
YACK, B. (1986). *The Longing for Total Revolution: Philosophical Sources of Social Discontent from Rousseau to Marx and Nietzsche.* Princeton: Princeton University Press.
ZUCKERT, C. (1996). *Postmodern Platos.* Chicago: University of Chicago Press.

SUGGESTED READING

The following are recommended: Berger (1999); Gellner (1992); Harvey (1989); Hayek (1979); Heelas (1998); Natoli (1997); Pippin (1999); and Repstad (1996*b*).

CHAPTER 10

RELIGION AND POWER

MEERTEN B. TER BORG

Introduction

In this essay, I will investigate the workings of religious power. How is it possible that people exert power over each other by means of 'religion', by reference to matters of which the existence cannot be proved (or indeed falsified) by scientific means?

I will first describe the terms 'power' and 'religion', no easy task to begin with, and then merge the two into 'religious power'. A clear distinction must be made between religious power, on the one hand, and the power of religious leaders and institutions, on the other. Once a certain degree of conceptual clarity has been attained, I will introduce a hypothesis about the functioning of religious power. I will demonstrate this with a rather curious example of religious power known as pillarization in the Netherlands in the first half of the twentieth century, and its relevance for the situation in the world today.

A Matter of Definition

As terms, 'power' and 'religion' have at least this much in common, that to reach conceptual agreement about their precise meaning seems next to impossible.

This is due to the fact that we are dealing here with basic elements of human existence. Power and religion are both cornerstones of human life. Not only are power and religion almost too precarious to be analysed, they are also well-nigh unidentifiable. They are always present, one way or another, integrated with everything human beings are and do. They are almost impervious to objective analysis, which demands that we isolate them from their context. Consequently, these terms need to be redefined all the time, depending on the situation, and no single definition is truly satisfying. If we are to define religion or power, we must disentangle them from life, and that is always unsatisfactory. But it can provide us with concepts that help our understanding of human life.

Religion provides an answer to the human condition. It helps human beings to come to terms with and cope with their vulnerability, fallibility, and mortality. It lends human existence meaning in spite of our finiteness. It gives people the hope and courage to continue, in spite of the overwhelming evidence of hopelessness. I do not limit the term 'religion' to belief in a god. Belief in political doctrines, such as communism or fascism, can also be religious in nature, as can *ad hoc* religious movements focusing on football stars, pop stars, etc. I will not dwell on such 'implicit religion' because it is dealt with elsewhere in this volume (Chapter 44). It can, however, be subject to the same dynamics in relation to power as is religion in the more traditional sense.

When I speak about religion, I am referring to *powers, meanings, or realities that transcend what is ordinarily thought of as human.* With this broad approach I avoid many of the difficulties that are discussed in the extensive literature on this topic. I avoid questions of belief and disbelief, on the one hand, and ritual, on the other, as well as the relationship between feeling and thought. With the phrase 'to transcend what is ordinarily thought of as human', the definition is substantial (rather than formal or functional), while having ample scope.

'Power' is a quality inherent in all human relationships, at least partly determining the character of a society. The significance of power to every individual makes it into something that is desirable, intimidating, and dangerous. One might say that this alone gives power something of the sacred.

In this essay, I will make no distinction between power and social power. From this point on, I will use the term 'power' as shorthand for 'social power'. *Social power is the chance of getting people to do things.*[1] This definition is simple and abstract. It abstracts from the preconditions many experts set to be able to really speak about power: for instance, that it should involve confrontation, inequality, conflicting interests, coercion, or even violence. In my view, social power can include persuasion, consensus, and consent. With religious power this is often the case.

[1] Here I use the term 'chance' rather than 'capacity', because social power depends on a social process of which the outcome is dependent not only on the capacity of the actors, but also on the dynamics of the process itself (cf. Weber 1980: 28).

My concept also abstracts from the scope of power; in my view, it has a role to play in face-to-face relations, on a global scale, and anywhere in between. Power does not necessarily require explicit decision making or action. With religious power, decisions are often implicit or non-existent, and passivity certainly has a role to play.[2] But it still remains necessary to define the combination: religious power. Here we must distinguish between the 'power of a religion' and 'religious power'. The power of religion is a power *of*: of religious functionaries, of religious organizations, and of institutions. Those who discuss the power of a religion usually refer to institutionalized religion, without explicating the sources of power. These need not be religious in character. Indeed, the power of religious functionaries or institutions can derive from anything. The power of the Roman Catholic Church in the early Middle Ages was based as much on its monopoly of the art of writing as on its monopoly in providing the sacraments. The power of Cardinal de Richelieu in seventeenth-century France rested on a combination of tradition and political competence, rather than on his piety.

The power of religion is not the focal point of this essay. It is religious power, referring to the source of power. It is 'power from' rather than 'power of'. I can now define 'religious power' as follows: *the chance of getting people to do things, by making reference to 'realities' or meanings that transcend what is ordinarily thought of as human.* This working definition will suffice for the purposes of this essay.

Power and Barter, Capabilities and Desires

To understand the exercise of power, it is useful to view it as a kind of barter. From this perspective, the exercise of social power can be seen to depend on the relationship between capabilities, on the one hand, and desires, on the other. Someone's power obviously depends on his own capacities to provide what the other party desires. But it also depends on the intensity of those desires. If that intensity is low, if the other party hardly cares whether or not his desires are fulfilled, the resulting power based on a capacity to provide for those desires is not very great. If the desires are intense, if the other party feels hardly able to cope without their fulfilment, the resulting power is very great. Examples from the erotic sphere immediately spring to mind. The mistress whose lover will do anything for one glance, one kind word, loses this power as the latter's love diminishes. The economic power over an ascetic monk is a good example of what I mean. By

[2] A good general overview of the problems relating to power remains that by Clegg (1989).

mitigating his material desires, the hermit can practically shake off economic power. Another relevant example is the suicide terrorist, whose lack of desire to live gives him power over his opponent, whose only hope is to get back home safely. If power depends on both capability and desire, in the physical, economic, and erotic fields, what about religious sources of power?

A Function for Religion in the Survival of the Human Species

Religion derives from the human capacity for transcendence. Here I do not understand 'transcendence' as a divine attribute, a characteristic of a god or a godly place, but as a human capability.[3] The capacity to transcend is the imagination to look beyond the here and now. It enables human beings to shift the limits of their world beyond the immediate horizons of space and time. They can imagine worlds imperceptible to their senses. They are also able to transcend their own physicality. They are able to imagine places or ways in which they will continue to live on after death.

This human capacity has advantages and disadvantages. One of the advantages is that human beings are capable of creating their own world view, implying that they are partly capable of creating their own world. Hence the great variety of world views and cultures greatly exceeds what has been determined biologically. This increases the species' chances of survival. It helps human beings to fight the threats posed by the physical world. For instance, it is transcendence which enables human beings to build dykes against a possible rise in sea-level or to irrigate the desert. Both on the societal and on the individual level, the capacity to transcend the here and now makes it possible to plan for the future, and thus increase the chance of survival.

But the human urge to transcend the here and now also has significant disadvantages: human beings can become awkwardly—indeed, terrifyingly—aware of the ultimate hopelessness of their situation. They know they will die, they fear they might suffer, they are anxious that they might fail. They sense that the cultural 'reality' they live in is shadowy, and that 'reality' and 'truth' are continually being tampered with. Such insights can lead to a paralysing fear, cancelling out the advantages of this capacity to transcend. Ultimately, people can survive, physically and emotionally, in a state of such *ontological insecurity*[4] only for a limited period

[3] This anthropological perspective on transcendence is inspired by Luckmann (1967), although it is not identical to it.

[4] The term 'ontological insecurity' is a counterpart to Giddens's *ontological security* (Giddens 1984: 50). This term refers to the philosophical impact that we are talking about: what is at stake here is the grip on reality.

of time. They have a strong desire for anything that can liberate them from this paralysing condition.

Luckily, the capacity for transcendence that is the source of this lurking anxiety can also provide its solution. The ability to doubt, to the point of total despair, also implies the ability to imagine 'realities' or develop meanings that can limit the damage, that can give a purpose to any state of misery, or compensate for it. These realities can, but need not, be gods, or spirits. Any reality, specific or abstract, that is conceived of as outlasting, overcoming, or surpassing human frailty can perform the job.

Religion, then, is a player in the contest between human frailty and transcendence. It lies in the alternation between an awareness of finiteness and vulnerability, on the one hand, and faith in 'realities' or meanings that can mitigate this paralysing fear, on the other. Victory is when fear is turned into its opposite: hope. What people need, therefore, is perhaps not religion as such, but ontological security. They need to feel that their world view, the meanings they attach to the world around them, will hold.

Wherever and whenever ontological security becomes shaky, or shows serious defects, a desire arises to repair it. A wide variety of strategies have been developed to maintain a state of ontological security.[5] Human beings are thus occupied in repairing and strengthening their world view and boosting their ontological security or a substantial part of their lives.

Ultimately, however, this reparation and strengthening of a world view cannot be done in human terms. An anchor is needed, which can be thrown out to steady the ship, and allow it to weather the storm. There is a fundamental need for a superhuman 'reality', an ultimate guarantee against the undermining of a world view and the fear and despair that ensue. Religion meets this need. It offers 'salvation' from human fallibility and the fallibility of the humanly constructed world view. It is the final antidote against the negative effects of man's capability to transcend. From this perspective, religious meanings that manage to guarantee steadfast ontological security are essential to the continued existence of the human species.

Symbolic and Religious Power

In order to gain a better understanding of religious power, it is important to investigate its relation to symbolic power. Whoever is capable of satisfying the desire for ontological security possesses symbolic power.[6]

[5] Compare Berger and Luckmann (1967: 104, 147). They provide only a few strategies, which can be supplemented and varied on.

[6] The term '*symbolic power*', but not the definition, derives from Bourdieu (1991).

People are continually helping each other to maintain or restore their ontological security by confirming commonly understood meanings. In this sense, everybody possesses a certain amount of symbolic power over everybody else. Everybody can to some degree give or withhold what others desire to have: confirmation of meaning and, ultimately, ontological security. This bartering process takes place on many different levels, from the interior monologue of the individual to ordinary conversation to the mass media. Of course, inequality plays a role here, as in any other sphere of power. Some are more in need of confirmation, and others are better equipped to give it.

This exchange of reassurances is highly complicated, particularly in our ever more complicated society. Confirmation of meaning has a temporal dimension: people can appeal to ancient texts or to fragments of a forgotten movie, but also to expectations for the future. Anyone who loses his way and fails to maintain his sense of ontological security can call upon experts: from clerics to personal coaches.

Here the religious dimension enters in. Anyone who is unable to solve the problem by normal means—that is, by mutual confirmation of meaning—may crave a stronger antidote. This desire for ultimate security creates the opportunity and scope for religious power. When ordinary, human participants in the interaction fail to uphold ontological security, superhuman 'realities' which surpass human shortcomings still can. This is the domain of religion. Whoever has the capacities to affirm, strengthen, or restore ontological security by means of superhuman realities and meanings can wield religious power.[7] Here, as in other spheres of power, capability meets desire.

The need for religious confirmation of a world view, of the definition of a situation, of the aspirations people might have, of the role they perceive for themselves, and so forth, occurs more frequently than one might expect. Whenever a crisis looms, a world view comes under pressure, and religious reinforcement becomes a welcome and even indispensable supplement to other means of symbolic power. Most people will, however, seek and find a superhuman or religious confirmation of their world view well before the first cracks appear.

Religious Empowerment

So how do superhuman realities or meanings guarantee ontological security?

People imagine that something or someone who surpasses the limitations of human beings, human bodies and minds, can guarantee the adequacy of their

[7] Religious power, as defined here, is a subcategory of symbolic power.

world view. The way in which Descartes managed to anchor his world view is an example of this in its most naked form. God, Descartes claimed, is perfect, and a perfect being would not lie to him (Descartes 1996[1637]). In this way, God guarantees ontological security for Descartes, providing him with a foundation for his thoughts and actions. Thus, Descartes left doubt behind, boosted his world view, and found new energy in his notion of divinity.

Other people have similar experiences, though they express them in a more emotional way: 'I had the feeling that God approved of what I thought or did or wanted.' Or, a more subjective, secular variant: 'Something inside me told me it was right.'

This is one of the functions of prayer: to evoke ontological security by the assumed contact with a superhuman reality, to empower the believer to continue with his or her life. Prayer is empowerment, in so far as it gives people the reassurance they need to act. Such empowerment is made possible by the human imagination. It can be considered as self-empowerment, as power people exercise over themselves.

It becomes social power once other people become involved: witnesses, who confirm the existence of a superhuman entity or principle. Because people are social beings, who depend on others for their ontological security, society always plays a role. This is even the case for self-empowerment, based on imagination. Imagination works within the bounds of tradition, or at least uses tradition as a springboard. The god who confirmed the world view for Descartes was the traditional, Christian God. The strength of that tradition made it very easy for this god to escape from the philosopher's radical doubt.

So what appears to be a solitary experience is in fact a social act. Religious self-empowerment depends on interactions that have taken place in the past, of common meanings that the believer has internalized. People praying often simply do what they have been taught. They are using their 'religious capital' acquired through years of training, to boost their world view and ontological security. The same holds for Descartes. In regaining ontological security, people make good use of a well-tested way of thinking, a ripe set of meanings and rules, even when acting in utmost privacy.

What Descartes and praying believers do is use their religious capital to give their world view an unassailable certainty. This capital is institutionalized religious power, in so far as it provides for the individual's desire or need to anchor his ontological security. Through the individual, the world view could be said to reaffirm itself.

Bearers of Religious Power

Even though self-empowerment is social, its social nature can remain well hidden. People experience it as a private activity, and only a few hermits feel that it fully satisfies their needs. Humans are social creatures, and this means that they require confirmation which is explicitly social in nature. This is what is enacted in religious, social ritual. In this setting people can help each other achieve a state which Durkheim calls *effervescence* (Durkheim 1915: 210f.), in which emotions and intellect join forces to raise one's world view beyond doubt. This common experience can be recalled later, in interactions or in memory. The very memory of *effervescence* can lead to self-empowerment, both individual and collective, in other situations. But not only that. By cherishing this collective memory, by repeating parts of it, or by adjusting one's behaviour to it, people have time and time again been able to reaffirm the reality of the divine anchor of their world view. Because people depend upon each other to fulfil their desire for anchorage and their need for collective ritual, they can be said to wield religious power over each other. Collective religious empowerment implies mutual religious power. This collective self-empowerment can lead to peace of mind and provide self-confidence, and sometimes more than that.

But collective enhancement of ontological security has its drawbacks. Memories are not very precise; living together is always ambiguous; and others can undermine self-confidence or punish arrogance. Conflict threatens. People may seek to use the religious power they have over others to pursue certain agendas or to organize collective ritual or reaffirm religious memories in exchange for other advantages and privileges. Thus religious power becomes yet another weapon in the power struggle that constitutes human society.

The need arises eventually for persons with religious authority, to impose decisions with regard to religious conflicts or dilemmas. Generally, the preference is for someone in a special position, which means someone (a) devoid of personal interest and (b) closer than most to the unassailable divinity. In family conflicts, this could be the head of the family, in tribes the head of the tribe. In the self-empowerment of a New Age adherent, it could be an Indian guru. What people are actually doing when they submit their dilemmas and doubts to religious authority is to delegate their own religious power to somebody else, hoping for a higher return. In their quest for a superhuman guarantee for their world view, they realize that the efficacy of their own self-empowerment or mutual exchange is insufficient. The task of religious empowerment is now transferred to somebody who is seen to wield sufficient religious power to be able to fulfil the desire for a guarantee.

This, in my view, is the source of power of religious specialists. I would call such a specialist a *priest* in so far as the religious power delegated to him is institutionalized in such a way as to grant him a near monopoly. The functionary is invested with a special dignity, and his position is marked with special attributes, which place him somewhere in between the believers and the divinity. He will wear special clothing, and display special behaviour, and even his lifestyle may be distinctive and special, and may include such practices as celibacy—all of this to underline his special status.

Religious questions will be submitted to such a person, whose answers will be seen as beyond doubt, given his special position and knowledge. There are ways in which he can achieve a further expansion of his power—for instance, by means of canonization.[8] Through this process, certain 'holy' texts are characterized as being absolutely reliable, and the word, or the recorded tradition that is contained in it, as the only option. This strengthens the position of the priest who is linked to these texts, at the expense of other would-be specialists. But it turns out that even such clear-cut holy texts need constant reinterpretation. The ensuing uncertainty offers new avenues for power; whoever gives the most plausible and appealing interpretations gains in power. Just as the establishment of a canon represents a seizing of power, so can making an end to further interpretation make for a consolidation of power.

Priests come in different sizes and shapes, from vicars to gurus, and from monks to shamans. Basically, the source of their power is the same. The institution of priesthood undergoes a development, and becomes a part of religious capital. The interpretation of institutionalized religion is entrusted to these religious specialists. A priest is a religious dignitary who exercises his religious authority on behalf of the community, and hence the power a priest possesses ultimately is, and remains, delegated power. Such power can, in time, be removed, if the priest's performance in terms of ontological reassurance is not satisfactory. He can be opposed by a competing specialist and, with the support of the believers, be cast aside.

Interim Summary

The model I have used so far explains why people need religious reassurance and how this need draws them subsequently to obey religious commandments and dignitaries. Religion offers the fulfilment of a basic need: for ontological security. Religion can confirm and guarantee the world view on which life depends in a way that no other system of belief and practice can. This is because it connects the world view to something or somebody who is unassailable in that it transcends human frailty. People may try to maintain their ontological security by other means, but in the end these prove insufficient in themselves.

The model outlined above tries to make clear why religious power is such a strong power. It attempts to explain why people are willing to sacrifice themselves for religion. It is not so much the virgins in paradise that inspire suicide terrorists,

[8] For canonization as a means of power, see Borg, ter (1998).

it is the conviction of the final and indubitable triumph of their world view over all else.[9] Compared to that, individual survival becomes relativity insignificant.

The model also tries to clarify the motives and reasons for obedience to religious specialists. Their power derives from a (delegated) capacity to anchor ontological security, and thus fulfil the desire for ontological reassurance. In principle, people empower themselves and each other. The empowerment by the specialist is delegated by them. The rules and regulations, the sanctions, positive and negative, with which priests exercise their power, are ultimately accepted only because they confirm the omnipotence of the divinity, who provides the ultimate legitimacy of the world view, and is thus the guarantor of ontological security.

Religious Power: Its Effect on Culture

The importance of religious power for the development of a culture can hardly be overestimated. Because religious power is fundamental to the development and consolidation of world views, its significance for culture, its *Kulturbedeutung*, to use Weber's term, is decisive (Weber 1920: 30, 205). There is extensive literature in which the significance of religious power for culture and society is elaborated and discussed. The most well-known example is the debate on Weber's *Die protestantische Ethik und die Geist des Kapitalismus* (*The Protestant Ethic and the Spirit of Capitalism*). Weber's position is, briefly, that there is a *Wahlverwandtschaft*, an elective affinity between the ethics flowing from Protestantism, on the one hand, and the mind-set of Western capitalism, on the other. The two are supposed to have reinforced each other.[10]

In terms of the model developed in this article, more can be said about this affinity between religion and mind-set. It is not merely a case of mutual reinforcement between religion and economic practice. Protestantism did more than reinforce the capitalist world view. It sanctioned it by giving it superhuman connotations. The ultimate legitimacy of making a profit was a divine one. Whereas the medieval God forbade lending or investment for interest, the Protestant God positively required it. It was to attain inner peace that Protestant believers acted according to the requirement of maximizing profit, as Catholic believers had done before them by abstaining from money lending for profit. In both cases believers wielded power over themselves via their religious institutions.

[9] This is how Juergensmeyer's evidence (2001) should be interpreted.

[10] For a concise overview of the never ending discussion of the so-called Weber thesis, see Hamilton (1995: 165f.); Poggi (1983).

A second discussion with regard to the cultural importance of religious power is less focused: that on the genesis of the nuclear family.[11] The power of the clergy over the family began with their control of the institution of marriage. The church managed to gain jurisdiction over marriage, by monopolizing the sanctifying of the tie between a man and a woman. One of the most unstable and precarious relationships was given divine sanction. It is a particularly good example of what religious power means: what threatens to be unstable is put on a firmer foundation by means of reference to a higher power. People are willing to discipline their sexual desires in order to honour and obey this higher power, and the priests representing it on earth, because their need for ontological security is paramount. As other sources of ontological security become available, the divine sanction of marriage loosens, and instability returns.

To gain and consolidate their ontological security, people bestow power on priests and their organizations, and this power is used to generate even greater power. For instance, the powerful Catholic priesthood used its power to introduce confession and, subsequently, to make it obligatory. This greatly increased the grip the Church had on individuals, which it used to further enforce sexual and conjugal ethics.

Consequently, strict family ethics which were divinely sanctioned, were imposed and controlled by God's representatives on earth. Here again, people, believers, were ultimately exercising power over themselves, via the priesthood. The increasing availability of other options for boosting ontological security, coinciding with the arrival of contraceptives, led people to withdraw from the priests the power over sexual conduct and keep it in their own hands.

Religious Power: Constellation and Convertibility

The foregoing provides an overview of what religious power consists of in theory, and I now move on to discuss what role it can play in practice, in the everyday world. One thing that becomes apparent from these examples of religious power is that it is fairly diffuse, and connected to other forms of power. In daily life, we mainly see mixed forms of power. Religious power in its pure form is rare. It is always connected to other forms of power.

I have argued that religious power exists thanks to the ability to sanction a world view and thus fulfil the need for ontological security. This implies that it is not limited to a special sphere. Religious power is rooted in, and is relevant to, everyday life. That means religious power, like power from other sources, appears in

[11] The next two paragraphs are based on the work of Flandrin (1984) and Foucault (1979).

complex constellations. Religious power is intermingled with economic, sexual, and political power, and so on.

This merging of different kinds of power in power constellations presupposes power convertibility. All power is convertible. This means that religious power, based on the capability to guarantee a world view by means of an appeal to the authority of a superhuman reality, can generate other forms of power. The priest can demand from his followers that they invest him with political and economic power. On the other hand, religious power is often delegated to somebody who already possesses much social power. This is where the distinction between religious power and the power of religion is to be located.[12] Religious dignitaries can wield power coming from all kinds of sources. But also other persons, such as pop stars, military heroes, or statesmen, can be given religious power by a multitude craving for ontological security. If warring popes are an example of the first, Joan of Arc and Hitler surely are examples of the second. In short, religious powers always appears mixed with other kinds of power, and conversion between different sources of power is constant and continuous.

The most conspicuous form of power with which religious power connected is political power. The key role of religion in society means that it is usually connected, in one way or another, with the existing societal elites. Or again, those awarded religious power become members perhaps of a new societal elite. Such constellations can result in a theocracy (in which the priests hold political power) or in caesaropapism (in which politicians hold religious power).

The Christian religion, and particularly the Western variant, shows a wide range of different power constellations. It must be added that dignitaries of the various streams in the Christian religion have been exceptionally adept at the game of power convertibility.

Religious Regimes and Modernization

When religion plays a dominant role in power constellations, we can speak of religious regimes.[13] Religious regimes give us another insight into the functioning

[12] They key issue is the distinction that Robertson Smith makes between 'community cults' and 'religious communities' (Casanova 1994: 45). In the first instance, social power has been converted into religious power, and in the second, religious power has been converted into social power. The distinction is parallel to that between caesaropapism, on the one hand, and theocracy, on the other.

[13] In Dutch sociology, the term was first used by M. Bax, who defines it as follows: 'A religious regime can be described as a more or less formalised and institutionalised constellation of dependency relationships, legitimised by a thought process propagated by religious specialists' (Bax 1985: 25).

of religious power. Pillarization in the Netherlands in the nineteenth and twentieth centuries can serve as an example.

In the Netherlands, religion has traditionally been connected to society in a special, conflict-ridden way. The history of what would later be called the Netherlands was defined as religious history, however complex it might have been in reality. In the sixteenth century, the Protestant Dutch rebelled against the Catholic oppressors from Spain. The Protestants emerged victorious from this battle, and, as they believed, God rewarded them with a wealth that had no parallel at that time, turning Holland into the new Promised Land.

Religion was therefore part and parcel of the political power struggles. Exercising power was legitimized in religious terms; social mobilization was inspired by religion. This special place of religion in Dutch society lasted well into the twentieth century. Its importance was reflected in the social prestige and political power of Protestant vicars. The Netherlands was a country of vicars.

It is not surprising, therefore, that in the Netherlands, the social and cultural unrest, which are now referred to as 'the process of modernization', would be given a religious interpretation. People attempted to use religious meanings to find their way in the insecurities caused by this turbulence. If they opposed the ideas of the French Revolution, it was in the name of the Gospel. In the early nineteenth century, Protestant leaders, among whom Groen van Prinsterer (1801–76) was the most important, called upon their followers to resist 'the spirit of this century'. According to them, the French Revolution had unleashed a wave of anti-religious hostility over Europe, and this had to be opposed. It was essential to react, not only against that part of the Enlightenment thinking that openly rejected God, but also against so-called modern theology, which attempted to combine Enlightenment values with religion.

This 'anti-Revolutionary' movement was successful. It was the theologian Abraham Kuyper (1837–1920) who had the deepest understanding of this success. He gradually came to realize that his supporters were not opposed to modernization as such, and were even willing to grasp the opportunities that modern society offered. What they were afraid of, and what they resisted, was the moral desperation to which modernization could lead. What they were afraid of were the existential insecurities of modern life. They feared the collapse of a world view within which they felt ontologically secure and at peace. Kuyper's answer was: modernization, but within the secure boundaries of faith.

It was on the basis of this understanding of the importance of a religiously guaranteed context for the modernization process that Abraham Kuyper rose to power, becoming one of the most influential politicians in the nation's history ever. Modernization was, in his view, in his policy, to be fitted within the framework of a strong Calvinist faith. It was to be supported by a sharply defined community of believers. To this end all sorts of religiously defined organizations were created: schools, mass media, housing corporations, an employers' union, a workers' union, a university, and a political party: all working within the framework of the orthodox Protestant faith, led by Protestants on every level, and with an all Protestant membership.

The example of the orthodox Protestant group was followed by Catholics, and even organizations without a religious background had little option but to do likewise, explicitly labelling themselves as neutral. Thus the system known as 'pillarization' was developed. Its dividing lines were not horizontal, as in so many other countries, but vertical. The dominant structure was not a class structure, but a structure of 'pillars'. A 'pillar' was a conglomerate of organizations, defined in terms of a particular world view or religion. Typically it included persons of that world view, from low to high. Catholic workers were joined in the pillar to Catholic entrepreneurs, and separated from their fellow workers of Protestant conviction, with whom they were severely encouraged not to mix. Every type of organization, from school to broadcasting corporation, had a Protestant, Catholic, and non-denominational variant, allowing the Dutch to live their lives from cradle to grave without really getting to know their neighbours from another denomination. But they did feel that much closer to persons of their own belief system, from whatever walk of life. Thus social organization supported the consolidation of the world view. As the country modernized, so ontological security was guaranteed.

This, briefly, is the process of pillarization. It came to pass peacefully, but not amicably. Group solidarity was maintained and reinforced, by service to God and, if necessary, by demonizing other groups. Kuyper in particular invoked strong feelings against 'enemies' from other denominations. But at the top, the pillars co-operated, reaching a consensus which prevented violence.

Pillarization is an example of a religious regime offering a context for a peaceful process of modernization. The religiously defined pillars, which organized practically all aspects of daily life in a religious way, helped many Dutch people to enter modernity without losing their sense of ontological security. This example offers a perspective to people undergoing and experiencing the seismic changes produced by present-day processes of modernization and globalization.

Generally, the side effects of modernization, in terms of the loss of ontological security, cannot be overestimated. The ensuing anxiety can stimulate people to delegate religious power to 'specialists' or persons with a potential for charisma who will rise to the occasion, and increase the religious power offered them by conversion to other types of power. The Dutch example shows that if this process is understood, it need not lead to extremism and violence. Modernization within a religious context can provide for the ontological security which modernization coupled with secularization may undermine.

Conclusion

In this essay I have tried to develop and apply a model of religious power that is based on the human need for ontological security. Whoever is able to fulfil this need by religious means that transcend ordinary human shortcomings possesses this kind of power.

Religious power has characteristics that are identical to those of other kinds of power. It is very unstable and unpredictable, like any form of power. It can be converted in other kinds of power—for instance, financial power. It can be part of power constellations. When it dominates these, we might speak of religious regimes. The significance of religious power for the development of society cannot be orerestimated, and is studied intensively.

References

Bax, M. (1985). 'Religienze regimes en staatsontwikkeling: Notities voor een figuraties benadening' [Religious Regimes and State Formations: Note for a Figurational Approach]. *Sociologisch tijdschrift*, 1: 22–49.

—— (1987). 'Religious Regimes and State Formation: Towards a Research Perspective'. *Anthropological Quarterly*, 60/1: 1–11.

—— (1995). *Medjugorje: Religion, Politics and Violence in Rural Bosnia.* Amsterdam: VU-uitgeverij.

Berger, P. L. and Luckmann, T. (1967). *The Social Construction of Reality.* New York: Doubleday.

Borg, M. B. ter (1998). 'Canon and Social Control'. In A. van der Kooij and K. van der Toorn (eds.), *Canonization and Decanonization.* Leiden, Boston, and Cologne: Brill, 411–24.

Bourdieu, P. (1991). *Language and Symbolic Power.* Cambridge: Polity Press.

Casanova, J. (1994). *Public Religions in the Modern World.* Chicago and London: University of Chicago Press.

Clegg, S. R. (1989). *Frameworks of Power.* London: Sage.

Descartes, R. (1996[1637]). *Discourse on the Method and Meditations on First Philosophy.* New Haven: Yale University Press.

Durkheim, E. (1915). *The Elementary Forms of Religious Life.* London: Allen & Unwin.

Flandrin, J. L. (1984). *Familles, parenté, maison sexualité dans l'ancienne societé.* Paris: Seuill.

Foucault, M. (1979). *The History of Sexuality*, i. Harmondsworth: Allen Lane.

—— (1980). *Power/Knowledge: Selected Interviews and Other Writings 1972–1977*, ed. Colin Gordon. New York: Pantheon Books.

Giddens, A. (1984). *The Constitution of Society.* Cambridge: Polity Press.

—— (1991). *Modernity and Self-Identity.* Cambridge: Polity Press.

Goody, J. (1983). *The Development of the Family and Marriage in Europe.* Cambridge: Cambridge University Press.

Hamilton, M. B. (1995). *The Sociology of Religion: Theoretical and Comparative Perspectives.* London: Routledge.

Juergensmeyer, M. (2001). *Terror in the Mind of God: The Global Rise of Religious Violence.* Berkeley: University of California Press.

Kossmann, E. H. (1987). *The Low Countries 1780 – 1940.* Oxford: Clarendon Press.

Luckmann, T. (1967). *The Invisible Religion.* New York: Macmillan.

Platvoet, J. G., and Molendijk, A. L. (eds.) (1999). *The Pragmatics of Defining Religion: Contexts, Concepts and Contests.* Leiden: Brill.

Poggi, G. (1983). *Calvinism and the Capitalist Spirit: Max Weber's Protestant Ethic.* London: Macmillan.

Weber, M. (1920). 'Die protestantische Ethik und der Geist des Kapitalismus'. In *Gesammelte Aufsätze zur Religionssoziologie*, i, Tübingen: J. C. B. Mohr, 30–205.

—— (1963). *The Sociology of Religion.* Boston: Beacon Press.

—— (1980). *Wirtschaft und Gesellschaft: Grundriss der Verstehenden Socziologie.* Tübingen: J. C. B. Mohr.

Wrong, D. (1979). *Power: Its Forms, Bases and Uses.* Oxford: Blackwell.

Suggested Reading

Still useful overviews of the theorizing about power are Clegg (1989) and Wrong (1979). For the defining of religion, see Platvoet and Molendijk (1999) and Hamilton (1995). For the anthropological relevance of concept of transcendence, see Luckmann (1967). For ontological security, see Giddens (1984; 1991). For another view on symbolic and religious power, see Bourdieu (1991) and Foucault (1979; 1980). For a modern, empirical study of religious empowerment, see, e.g., Juergensmeyer (2001).

For the role of the collectivity in religion, see Durkheim (1915: 422). The classic on the power of priests is Weber (1963). On the *Kulturbedeutung* of religion according to Weber, Poggi (1983) is useful. For the influence of religion on the making of the family, see Goody (1983) and Flandrin (1984). On religious regimes, see Bax (1987; 1995). For the history of pillarization, see Kossmann (1987).

CHAPTER 11

CULTURE AND RELIGION

MATT WAGGONER

INTRODUCTION

Like other disciplines in the humanities, over the course of the last couple of decades, religious studies has fashioned itself in relation to the discourses of 'culture' and, indirectly, cultural studies. In practical terms this entailed the importation of new avenues of inquiry, with new vocabularies, enlisting headings like postcolonial theory, feminist theory, gender theory (women's studies as well as masculinity studies), gay and lesbian studies (or queer theory), critical race studies, diaspora studies, media studies, and more. This new face of the discipline shapes the conference programs of groups like the American Academy of Religion (AAR), the International Association of the History of Religions (IAHR), the Society of Biblical Literature (SBL), and related organizations. It also prompted the creation of new journals like *Culture and Religion*, the *Journal of Cultural and Religious Theory*, the *Journal of Religion and Popular Culture*, and others. Peruse the table of contents of an anthology such as *Critical Terms for Religious Studies* and notice the virtual absence of entries with explicitly 'religious' connotations; they include, instead, standard categories in the lexicon of cultural studies: body, gender, modernity, conflict, culture, experience, image, liberation, transformation, transgression, performance, person, territory, writing (M. C. Taylor 1998).

In entries similar to the current one that appear in recent anthologies in religious studies, historians of religion Bruce Lincoln and Tomoko Masuzawa approached the subject of culture by surveying the history of the term and theories that emphasize conflict, power, negotiation, and fluidity (Lincoln 2000; Masuzawa 1998). Their essays model a study of religion *as* culture: that is, a human social production in which the rhetoric of gods and transcendence encodes social preoccupations with power, privilege, and identity formation. The reader is strongly encouraged to seek out these essays as indispensable resources for any attempt to consider the relationship between religion and culture. The present contribution differs slightly. It regards the association of religion and culture as a signifier for certain methodological and theoretical innovations. Here the question is not, *What is culture and how might we study religion as culture?*, but instead, *How has 'culture' become emblematic of certain orientations toward agency and structure, ideology and system, subjective experience and subject formation?* How have these intervening orientations informed the study of religion, challenging which rubrics of analysis? What fruitful lines of inquiry remain open to studies of religion situated at the intersection of 'religion and culture'?

In what follows I survey trajectories of religious inquiry whose antecedents commonly stem from the classical sociological tradition, but whose outcomes vary with respect to the way they deal with reductive tendencies in the social sciences. To whatever extent contemporary studies of religion remain divided, as has been suggested by Russell T. McCutcheon, between essentialist theories (with roots in the phenomenological tradition) and social-constructivist theories (with roots in the social sciences), it will be argued here that the key contribution of cultural analyses of religion consists in the way it has problematized this well-worn impasse by positing the possibility of a non-reductive yet thoroughly sociological study of religion (McCutcheon 2003).

The Marxist Tradition: Culture, Cultural Studies, and Ideology Critique

Historically, 'culture' evoked the accoutrements of bourgeois life, intimating standards of taste, the greatest products that civilizations had to offer, the best books, musical compositions, and works of art. It implied a notion of *canon* as inclusion within what a given class in society privileged as uniquely emblematic of a culture. As such, 'culture' sanctioned a sphere of art and ideas which would preserve a dominant faction's definitions of the good, the true, and the beautiful (Williams 1977; 1983; 1985).

Marginal currents of twentieth-century Marxism later radicalized the concept and political significance of culture, the result of a specific history of reflection on the significance of culture dating back to the Enlightenment. Expanding Jean-Jacques Rousseau's Romantic ideal of the 'voice within' as a guide for remaining true to oneself or authentic, Johann Gottfried Herder considered the way in which *nations* coalesced around essential value sets, structures of feeling, and ways of being, unifying members into coherent communities with shared, authentic life ways. For G. W. F. Hegel, culture expressed more than the pure particularity of national life ways; the specificity of historical communities and their cultural practices participated in the epic realization of the Absolute (Spirit, Reason, or *Geist*) in history. Hegel invested culture with the significance of history's movement toward concrete forms of reason *in* history, its endpoint the achievement of societies attaining freedom no longer as an abstract concept (as he maintained Immanuel Kant's was) but as an embodied experience mediated by the cultures and polities of modern republican states (Taylor 2003).

In the shadow of Hegelian philosophy, German and, later, British Marxism resuscitated a new form of ambivalence towards culture, this time as either the domain of ruling-class ideology or the terrain in which the struggle for freedom occurs. In Britain especially, the New Left and cultural studies emerged in the 1960s as attempts to interrogate this ambiguity by working with and against traditional Marxian–Hegelian paradigms. A founding figure within that tradition, Raymond Williams's late twentieth-century work concentrated largely on the question of culture's place in histories of Marxist thought, wresting Marx's texts from the way in which orthodox, scientific Marxism interpreted them. Distancing himself from a mechanical style of Marxist theory and practice, Williams noted that Marx's early philosophical writings, which had suffered obscurity for many years after Marx's death, conveyed rather different attitudes toward the relation between structural and cultural formations. He argued that Marx rarely, and unsystematically, employed many of the concepts commonly associated with him, such as false consciousness and base/superstructure. And many of the early texts, as well as Engels's clarifications after Marx's death, flatly contradicted the spirit of those earlier readings. Instead of economic determinism, a view of ideology as an active and equally determining sphere in its own right (rather than the passive product of more substantive processes) emerged from close readings of the early Marx (Williams 1977).

Williams, and the kind of rereading of Marx that he popularized, helped engineer the rise of modern cultural studies and the revaluation of culture's relation to the political. With Richard Hoggart and E. P. Thompson he founded the Centre for Contemporary Cultural Studies at the University of Birmingham. The CCCS took as its point of departure its disillusionment with orthodox Marxism and its political outcomes (Lave *et al.* 1992; Hall 1996*a*). Among the early works produced by the Birmingham School, we can consider more closely two, in order to reflect on the early significance of the conjunction of religion and culture and what it opposed in traditional Marxist orientations to religion and ideology: E. P. Thompson's *The Making of the English Working Class* (1963)—especially the chapter 'The Transforming Power of the Cross', a lengthy study of the relation of revival Methodism to Britain's stifled revolution—and Stuart Hall's early essay 'The Problem of Ideology: Marxism without Guarantees' (1996*c*).

E. P. Thompson

A lesser-known feature of the history of Marxist thought consists in its long-held preoccupation with religion, not just in the form of a critique of religious ideology, but through its attempts to comprehend religious movements that in some ways mirrored Marxism's own desire to mobilize the working classes to spontaneous outbursts. One example of Marxism's complex engagement with religion is the case of English Methodism. The combination of working-class support systems and collective eruptions led Marxists and other historians of Britain's failed revolution to want to understand in political terms the social significance of revivalism.

This debate became closely associated with Elie Halevy, Eric Hobsbawm, and Thompson. At mid-century, Hobsbawm and Thompson responded to Halevy's early twentieth-century thesis that Methodist revivalism frustrated revolution in England, thwarting the proletarianization of the working classes by distracting them with other-worldly concerns. Halevy (1961 [1911]) maintained that revivalism compensated for its political quietism with ritual histrionics. In the 1950s, Hobsbawm (1957) challenged Halevy's thesis by pointing to evidence that the correspondence between church membership and radical society rosters seemed to indicate that revival-goers were no less politically engaged than others, and that, in fact, Methodism seemed to support working-class agitations. Six years later, in *The Making of the English Working Class* (1963) Thompson introduced a complex account of the way in which Methodist revivalism ebbed and flowed in tandem with swings in radical political activity, concluding that religious spontaneity provided outlets for pent-up political frustrations. Thompson labeled this cathartic function of revival religions 'psychic masturbation'; Methodism's revival tendencies were emotional surrogates for unexpressed political grievances.

Arguably, Thompson's conclusions advanced very little beyond orthodox Marxism's ideology critique of religion as a dead-end distraction, if not a smokescreen benefiting and perhaps even propagated by the ruling classes. In the end he viewed Methodism as an impotent and misdirected response to political conflict, a 'reactive dialectic'. In any case, the seriousness with which Thompson contemplated Methodism's place in the making of English class consciousness improved upon the mechanistic model in other ways. In particular, Thompson rethought class, no longer in rigid economic terms, where one's class identity mirrors one's position in dominant modes of production, but instead in terms of 'class consciousness' (citing Georg Lukács's use of that term earlier in the century, cf. *History and Class Consciousness*). Thompson argued in the introduction to *The Making of the English Working Class* for an experiential understanding of class consciousness, reliant upon modes of feeling and perception shaped not only by structural conditions but by cultural practices as well, including religious ones.

Whatever their limitations were, Thompson's arguments about English Methodism affirmed that the cultural and the political are linked inextricably. Even if Thompson toed the Marxist line by reducing cultural processes to underlying structural realities, he did at least unsettle the formulaic shape it usually assumed. The radicalization of what remained implicit in Thompson's argument eventually constituted the central claim of cultural studies in Britain, both in the works of Raymond Williams and under the intellectual leadership of Jamaican-born British sociologist Stuart Hall.

Stuart Hall

Stuart Hall's writing demonstrates how influential the claims of Raymond Williams were that Marx was susceptible to plausible, alternative readings which militated against the reductionism normally attributed to him. In 'The Problem of Ideology: Marxism without Guarantees', Hall performed his own exegesis of Marx's texts, concluding, with Williams, that only a narrow reading of Marx sustains the view of culture as secondary and epiphenomenal. Hall argued that for Marx culture instead exists in a 'co-determining' relation to productive forces in society. Moreover, Marx appeared to regard culture as part of a process whereby societies (or factions within them) do not simply deceive themselves and others; rather, culture comprises the 'processes by which new forms of consciousness, new conceptions of the world, arise, which move the masses of the people into historical action against the prevailing system' (Hall 1996*c*: 27).

Hall's work added to Williams's contribution the insights of the Italian Marxist Antonio Gramsci, whose early twentieth-century writings from prison had only recently been recovered after a period of obscurity, much like Marx's. Hall was largely responsible for bringing Gramsci to a wider audience and distilling from his texts implications for the study of class, culture, race, and ethnicity, as well as his critique of economic reductionism and his more optimistic view of the role that ideologies play in what Gramsci called the 'hegemonic' process (Hall 1996*b*). In short, Gramsci imagined a position marginal to the orthodox Marxism of his day by considering how non-metropolitan, 'subaltern' classes do not follow the trajectory of normative proletarianization that both Marx and Marxists predicted on the basis of their analyses of productive processes in the centers of industrial Europe.

Gramsci's *Prison Notebooks* criticized and undermined analyses of economic determinism that relegate culture to the status of a derivative reflection of more determinate processes. He considered the role that popular religion (as well as street theater, music, and other things) played in facilitating among subaltern masses a sense of identity and opposition to dominant social forces (Gramsci 1971). Hall wielded Gramsci's notes as an affirmation of ideology in the process of subject formation in ways that could not simply be regarded along traditional lines as duping, but instead as critical engagements with hegemony, or what he and others began to call *counter-hegemonic* discourses. In the spirit of Gramsci, Hall's phrase 'Marxism without guarantees' continues to serve as a kind of slogan for the anti-reductive claims upon which cultural studies was founded (Hall *et al.* 2000).

These recollections of the emergence of cultural studies suggest that the intersection culture–religion carries with it an implicit theoretical rejection of reductive approaches, retaining, however, the claim that one can study religion methodologically as a social phenomenon. In other words, they suggest the compatibility of sociological with non-reductive studies of religion. To whatever extent this narrative of the relationship between a cultural turn in religious studies and the history of Marxist cultural studies is anything like correct, we should not overlook an important irony with respect to other traditions of cultural and religious study. That is to say, while the influence of Marxist cultural studies on religious studies consists primarily of a shift *away* from reductive theories, the general pattern elsewhere among scientific approaches to the study of religion has been less consistent.

Social-Scientific Studies of Culture and Religion

The study of religion as just one among many cultural formations (with no more privileged status than any other) characterizes much of the social-science tradition since at least the nineteenth century. Yet these traditions yield no consensus with respect to the question of reduction. In this section I briefly survey how a few key contributions to the sociological study of religion outside the Marxist tradition imagined religion's relation to culture; secondly, I comment on how these classical approaches in the sociology of religion inform contemporary work in religious studies, where questions of culture and reductionism prevail.

The Classical Tradition

Whereas according to traditional readings Marx reduced religion to socio-economic causes, according to an equally traditional reading Max Weber reversed the order by arguing that one religion—namely, Protestantism—significantly contributed to the formation and success of socio-economic patterns in Europe such as capitalism. In fact, however, Weber proceeded with indefatigable caution in order not to suggest that Protestantism acted as a determining cause; he claimed only to show that Protestantism enabled the ideological atmosphere in which capitalism could and did thrive in Europe. In any case, Weber's legacy in subsequent sociology and religious studies runs counter to explicitly reductive approaches by considering how ideologies are not simply by-products of underlying processes but also play determining roles in the construction of society.

Alongside Marx and Weber, Émile Durkheim introduced a third classical source of sociological inquiry in the study of religion. Durkheim's thesis in *Elementary Forms of Religious Life* that collective consciousnesses project the sacred—that societies *construct* religion, and that religious formations enact social formation through a kind of group transference—represents another version of the claim about religion's essential sociality. Like Marx, Durkheim treated religion as a product of the imagination—'religious society is only human society stretched ideally to beyond the stars' (1972: 220)—but, unlike Marx, he regarded the function of an imaginary locus of group identity as indispensable to the construction of societies; there can be no society without this collective identification with an external object which simultaneously transcends and congeals the group. To simplify, we might say: for Durkheim religion *occasions* the social; for Weber religion *shapes* the social; and for Marx religion *symptomatizes* the social.

The Contemporary Tradition

One might identify three landmark interventions in the contemporary study of religion that advanced a certain kind of sociological claim by insisting *not only* that religions are cultural phenomena, but that the very *concept* of religion is a cultural construction. First, Wilfred Cantwell Smith's *The Meaning and End of Religion* (1959) posited that 'religion', viewed as a discrete realm of human experience, is both a *new* and a *culturally specific* concept—a modern, Western invention. Prior to the modern era, and beyond the boundaries of Western discourse, religion (where an equivalent term appears, which he showed is not always the case) did not carry the connotation of a realm separable from other aspects of cultural life; nor was it conceivable that one could enumerate some number of discrete religions (e.g., 'Hinduism'). That is to say, he argued that modern, Western habits of imagining religion as a discrete realm of experience, and religions as coherent entities, mistake social conventions for phenomenological realities. Although he maintained that how we conceive of religion involves a kind of culturally inherited mental mistake, Smith did not go so far as to deny religion a reality of any sort (W. C. Smith 1959). He ultimately proposed the recovery of a pre-modern conception of religion as something like faith, betraying, we might say, his own inability to extricate himself from the predispositions of Protestantism (cf. Asad 2001).

Secondly, W. C. Smith's view of 'religion' as a modern, Western concept resurfaced a few decades later in one of the most frequently cited remarks in Religious Studies: Jonathan Z. Smith's argument in the introduction to *Imagining Religion* that 'while there is a staggering amount of data, of phenomena, of human experiences and expressions that might be characterized in one culture or another, by one criterion or another, as religious—*there is no data for religion.* Religion is solely the creation of the scholar's study. It is created for the scholar's analytic purposes by his imaginative acts of comparison and generalization. Religion has no independent existence apart from the academy' (J. Z. Smith 1982). J. Z. Smith's thesis has been debated and commented on at length, in part because of its susceptibility to so many interpretations. Did he mean that religion 'in itself' eludes our grasp, and that we are left with no other recourse than to imagine it? Did he mean, alternatively (and most probably), that religion has no existence apart from our fabrications of it? In another register, did he mean to suggest that the history of the production of 'religion' as an object of study was the result merely of *academic* reification, and not of a certain cultural politics beyond the academy? Did the invention of religion and religions not also take place within the context of the colonial imagination and those other settings in which comparisons of peoples and their cultures informed the self-fashioning of Europe and its justification for dominating and conquering non-European others?

These questions highlight similarities between Smith's thesis and Edward Said's only three years before in a seminal text of post-colonial theory, *Orientalism*: that the 'Orient' as such does not exist, but is instead a reified product of the Western imperial imagination (Said 1979). One might also compare J. Z. Smith's claim, in 'Map is Not Territory' (1978), that within the framework of the history of religion, primitive peoples literally do not exist, because they fail to register within the discourses of 'religion' codified by the academy, to Gayatri Spivak's (1987) provocative suggestion (in another seminal work in postcolonial theory) that 'the subaltern cannot speak' because her speech is incomprehensible to dominant discourses of meaning, speech, agency, and recognition.

In any case, J. Z. Smith's remark seems at least to acknowledge, as W. C. Smith's had, that the contemporary habit of imagining religion as a discrete object, embodied by a number of discrete entities ('religions'), indicates less *the way things are* and more *the way we imagine them to be*—a social-constructivist thesis (Smith identified it with Kant, presumably with the idea that we do not grasp things themselves but must instead represent them to ourselves, a process involving imaginative acts of cognition and classification). But, unlike W. C. Smith, J. Z. Smith refused to subscribe to a notion of religion as 'faith' or anything like it. Religion, for J. Z. Smith, can be grasped only as a fiction, even if, as he was not at all reluctant to state, a necessary fiction. In other words, while we must study 'religion' and 'religions', we must do so cognizant of the fact that these reifications simply assist us in the taxonomic effort of studying the ways in which humans construct worlds and world views (J. Z. Smith 1996). The requirement of the scholar of world-construction processes is that she not naively imitate religious participants' mental errors by mistaking the discourse of 'religion' for a real object. Although Smith likened his approach to Kant's, I would argue that his 'imagining religion' thesis fits better with the empiricism of David Hume, who similarly maintained that while we cannot live without the inferences we routinely make (e.g., about causation), we must remain cognizant of the real limits, even impoverishment, of our knowledge.

Thirdly, Bruce Lincoln's work raises several objections to the *status quo* of scholarly inquiry into things religious, influenced by basic sociological suppositions about the social determinations of religion, and by those histories of post-Marxist thought recited above. In early works, particularly his very important *Discourse and the Construction of Society* (1992), Lincoln did two things. First, he developed a theory of religion as a set of rhetorical strategies that societies employ in the normal processes of social formation. In this sense, Lincoln posited a routine feature of the Durkheimian tradition. On the other hand, he moved away from that tradition in his emphasis on themes of conflict, authority, and power, all muted in Durkeim's account of the social.

Particularly in his very important *Discourse*, Lincoln aligned himself with Marxists like Roland Barthes, Louis Althusser, and Antonio Gramsci as someone interested in relations of power as they permeate culture. He argued that culture, especially religion, serves as a site for ongoing negotiations for power and privilege in society, or the 'hegemonic struggle' (Lincoln 1992). In retrospect, Lincoln's nearly three decades of writing tend to emphasize only one side of culture's role in the hegemonic struggle: its *ideological* role, e.g., its effort to cloak its own historicity through transcendental claims meant to authorize one position and de-legitimize others. That is to say, he does not examine the way in which the hegemonic struggle for Gramsci and those he influenced (Stuart Hall and the Birmingham School, Ernesto Laclau and Chantal Mouffe, cf. *Hegemony and Socialist Strategy* (Laclau and Mouffe 1986)) referred not simply to constructions of power and authority (by those *in* power), e.g., co-opting and appropriating dissent, fabricating authority and so forth; the hegemonic struggle also referred to efforts to challenge and de-legitimize those fictitious claims to authority, power, and privilege, precisely by rendering visible the arbitrariness of their claims.

Lincoln's most concise contribution to conceptualizing 'culture and religion' as a critical model in the study of religion appeared in the form of his very short 'Theses on Method' (1996), a text patterned on Marx's 'Theses on Feuerbach' (1978) and Walter Benjamin's 'Theses on the Philosophy of History' (1969). In the first place, Lincoln argued that religion, like all culture, should be approached as a negotiation of power through rhetoric, by paying attention to questions like 'Who speaks ... to what audience ... who wins what, and how much? Who, conversely, loses?' Second, he raised the issue of the scholar's relation to cultural objects, or the question of situatedness: 'Many who would not think of insulating their own or their parents' religion against critical inquiry still afford such protection to other people's faith.' In other words, Lincoln observed beneath the façade of tolerance and multiculturalism in the study of religion traces of a lingering imperial posture, i.e., 'the guilty conscience of Western imperialism'. Third, Lincoln reiterated one of the important contributions of the cultural studies tradition: namely, the critique of cultural essentialism: the 'dubious—not to say fetishistic—construction of "cultures" as if they were stable and discrete groups of people defined by stable and discrete values, symbols, and practices'. Lincoln suggested that cultural essentialism errs by conflating a dominant faction's representations of cultural meaning with cultures as such, obscuring the contentions through which those representations signal a struggle for the privilege of defining groups against the backdrop of otherwise competing narratives, value sets, identity claims, and so forth. In a related point, he observed scholars' difficulties in recognizing systems of ideology operational in their own societies because (a) 'one's consciousness is itself a product of that society' and (b) 'the system's very success renders its operation invisible' (Lincoln 1996).

Thus, Lincoln's combination of neo-Durkheimian and neo-Marxist orientations to the study of religion and culture consists of three main features. First, he proceeds from the supposition that societies construct religion, and that this construction lies near the heart of the process of social formation. Second, he stresses that religion comprises a rhetoric of power, and that, as in all cultural instances, one has to view religion within the context of operations of hegemonic struggles. Third, he makes a methodological suggestion: in the study of religion one must regard with suspicion religion's own claims, rather than treat them as first-hand evidence, since religious rhetoric functions by concealing its own culturally and historically specific origins, claiming instead the authorship and authority of transcendent, supra-historical origins.

These, then, illustrate some of the important recent interventions in the social-scientific study of religion which take seriously the role of culture, by (1) viewing religion as a subset of culture rather than something *sui generis* (see further McCutcheon 2005); by (2) stressing the ways that religion, too, participates in the hegemonic struggle; and by (3) marking the way in which the very *category* of religion already betrays the cultural specificity of the modern West. In the final portion of this essay I reflect on the problem of reductionism in religious studies by exploring some of the ways that the cultural turn has resulted in a shift from consciousness-based orientations to one that emphasizes the way in which something like religion may reside not within consciousness but instead within culture itself. I conclude by summarizing the argument put forward here that one of the most productive contributions of the 'culture and religion' intersection may be the shift towards an analysis of religion as it is inscribed within cultural formations, rather than within the hearts, minds, or bodies of participants. I take this to be one of sociology's promising contributions to the study of religion, even if sociology remains often enough just as susceptible to belief-centered approaches.

Religion as a State of Affairs (Not a State of Mind)

Notwithstanding the importance of Jonathan Z. Smith's contribution to the scholarly study of religion, would it be possible to acknowledge that religion is more than subjectively 'imagined' by conceding that religion's existence has its locus beyond brains and bodies, beyond myth and performance, i.e., in something like a culture or a social system, in technologies of representation and of the self, in discourses of truth and subjectivity? I conclude by proposing the need for the study of religion to consider what it would mean to disarticulate religion from individual and group consciousness as the primary unit of analysis, to imagine instead how 'religion' resides in another locus exterior to one or more subjects. If the general trend within Marxism and the social sciences was to reduce religion to a subjective construction, how might we rethink religion as an objective social phenomenon in order to grasp how it continues to structure late modern society?

This approach complies with what sometimes goes by the name of discourse theory, but can be traced to elements within the thinking of Marx. To begin with, Marx showed that insofar as social realities may be ideological, they arise from objective conditions. Even the subject with 'consciousness' and beliefs emerges out of determinate conditions in Marx's analysis. While the religiousness of believers is to be expected, given their estrangement from the mechanisms that actually govern their lives, the real site of mystical phenomena and theological sleight of hand, for Marx, occurs at the structural level of the political-economic organization of society.

To illustrate this, notice how Marx's well-known comments in *Capital* on the 'fetishism of the commodity and its secret' did two things (Marx 1977: 163–77). First, it satirized 'Enlightened', demythologized society, which looked condescendingly at African and New World fetishism. Western society regarded these things as superstitious attributions of value to inanimate objects, while Europe, at the height of its highly advanced and civilized social development, constructed a socio-economic system with attendant political formations on the basis of an equally mystical transformation of human processes and raw materials into special objects with inexplicable values, which is to say, commodities (see further Mulvey 1996;

Taussig 1983). Secondly, Marx's critique of commodity fetishism broke with the common sense that regarded religion as a state of mind. If religiousness exists in the minds of individuals, it is because the conditions that give rise to those beliefs are already mystical in nature. The most ideological thing of all would be to look no further than cognition for an account of religion, for that would foreclose an analysis of the circumstances which engender religion as their cultural consciousness.

The problem, historically, is that sociology has tended to rely almost as much as psychology on the framework of consciousness; it merely provides a different account of its formation, as illustrated by a particular moment in Durkheim's *The Elementary Forms of Religious Life.* In the following excerpt, Durkheim specified what can qualify as sacred, and in doing so excluded, *contra* Marx, anything which could not be explained in terms of projections of individuals or group consciousness:

> It is not enough that one thing be subordinated to another for the second to be sacred in regard to the first. Slaves are inferior to their masters, subjects to their king, soldiers to their leader, the miser to his gold, the man ambitious for power to the hands which keep it from him; but if it is sometimes said of a man that he makes a religion of those beings or things whose eminent value and superiority to himself he thus recognizes, it is clear that in any case the word is taken in a metaphorical sense, and that there is nothing in these relations which is really religious. (Durkheim 1976: 37)

As if to challenge Marx's claims about the religiousness of social systems, Durkheim differentiated religion from relations of exchange, domination, and valuation in society stemming from structures of power and political economy. In doing so he avoided reference to anything identifiably modern, limiting himself to generic relations between slaves and masters, subjects and kings, soldiers and commandants, the power-seeking and the power-keeping. Interesting in this is the inclusion of gold fetishism, as if to say that while pre-capitalist fetishism may be religious, its capitalist counterpart surely is not.

Durkheim's effort to justify this distinction requires him to reduce all those examples of structurally derived relations of power and alienation to subjective phenomena: 'if it is sometimes said of a man that he makes a religion of those beings or things....'. The reduction from structural to subjective conceptualizations of value enables Durkheim to disqualify political economy as 'religious' for the same reason as he later disqualified magic; magic and commodity fetishism are, notwithstanding their secondary associations with collective supports (e.g., priesthoods or modes of production), fundamentally individual activities. The man who 'makes a religion' of gold apparently does so independently of historical circumstances in which gold is revered as an inexplicably valuable object; his fetishism is therefore cognitive in nature, a mental mistake, and is to be distinguished from 'really religious' instances in which societies collectively regard beings and objects as inherently valuable.

By assigning metaphorical status to the colloquial ascription of 'religion' to class structures and commodity fetishism, Durkheim clings to the code of regarding the products of Western culture, such as capitalism, as just what they claim to be: that is, rational and secular. Excluding the designation 'religious' from anything which cannot represent itself in the form of a consciousness, Durkheim effectively foreclosed the possibility of analyzing the religiousness of the cultures, discourses, apparatuses, technologies, rules, and systems that coordinate the conditions in which attributions and perceptions of value take place. Durkheim upholds the supposition rejected by Marx, who recognized religion in objective states of affairs and not just in states of mind.

Among recent theories of discourse and the subject, an alternative to the persistent subjectivism of both essentialism and anti-essentialist constructivism has taken the form of a turn to the exteriority of the subject, conceding that the locus of the self is in something like language or discourse. This axial turn emerged in the twentieth century primarily by way of Freud and Lacan, on the one hand, and Foucault, on the other. It is thus curious that Freud and Foucault continue to be regarded as polarized figureheads for the essentialist–constructivist controversy.

Responding to that situation, Theresa de Lauretis has argued that Freud's 'stubborn drive' and Foucault's 'relations of power' 'are not as incompatible or mutually exclusive as they are generally taken to be' (de Lauretis 1998: 858). In Foucault's depiction of the process of subjectivization, power produces the subject as an effect of discourse 'without depending even on the mediation of the subject's own representations… [without] having first to be interiorised in people's consciousnesses' (de Lauretis 1998: 858). Freud's construction of sexualization, meanwhile, relied on a notion of something which is partly innate and partly not. That is, in sexuality there is nothing innate; nothing psychically or biologically predetermines the formation of the subject sexually. But what does preexist the possible articulations of sexual fantasy is the drive (*Sexualtrieb*). For Freud, the drive exists in the body, but it is to be distinguished from the modes of phantasmatic representation (signs) which are taken up and articulated by the drive as sexuality. 'And if the drive is not to be equated with sexuality', de Lauretis continued, 'even less can it be equated with consciousness' (1998: 858).

She suggested that Foucault's concept of 'relations of power', which took shape in the late 1970s, depicted a notion of power working on and in the body, but independent of consciousness, and in that case must be read in the context of (Lacanian) constructions of the subject constituted 'in the field of the Other'—that is, through a linguistically organized unconscious. My point is not to agree that Foucault achieved no more than what psychoanalysis had by then already asserted; it is to identify the emergence of models of subjectivation which locate the origin of subjectivity in modes of discourse and representation that exist outside and independent of the subject's 'imagination', consciousness, cognition, or whatever other metaphors for the locus of subjectivity one employs. By implication, neither the object 'religion' nor the processes of 'imagining religion' are adequately viewed as housed within the heads and hearts of folks. Heads and hearts, minds and bodies, fail to exhaust the operation of culture and discourse.

The linguistic turn challenged the model of a connection between individual and society which presupposed mechanical processes between discretely organic entities: on the one hand, individuals, bounded by their bodies, and on the other hand, societies, as mere complexes of individuals. With a theory of signification, what emerged was the possibility of saying, as Foucault did, that 'something like a language, even if it is not in the form of explicit discourse, even if it has not been deployed for a consciousness, can in general be given to representation' (Foucault 1970: 361). To the extent that Foucault's history of the human sciences in *The Order of Things* stemmed from his critique of psychoanalysis, what remains evident is that the error of Freud was not to have posited a behind-the-back determination of the subject by the unconscious; it was his failure to follow through with a conception of the subject and of the unconscious as an effect of language, and therefore to conceive of them as entities whose locus is not in themselves but in something external to them. De Lauretis may be right that Freud did so in his theory of the drive; in another way, this was Lacan's achievement when he redescribed the unconscious as something structured like a language: the subject's locus is in the other, and the locus of the other is in language.

The future study of religion, I argue, will find it increasingly necessary to take seriously the exteriority of religion to the subject in ways that make the 'imagining religion' thesis less pertinent than it has been regarded in the past. Such a study may find models in the work of someone like Jacques Derrida, who contributed a number of books and essays on the topic of religion during the last decade and a half of his life. Derrida analyzed television, telecommunication, jet travel, and other components of globalization as instances of what he referred to as the 'afterlife of religion' following the so-called 'death of religion'. His argument, seminal to what has come to be called philosophy's 'religious turn', was that religion is hardly dead in the midst of secularization. This is because there is a kind of rebirth, or perhaps intensification, of the religious within the structures of the global engineered by the process of expansionist capital, by the instantaneous proliferation of the word (through communication) and presence (through travel), and by juridical discourses of the global such as human rights (Derrida 1996; 2001). There is not space here fully to explicate Derrida's argument; suffice it to say that in Derrida's view we do not see religion today as much in the beliefs of individuals as in the cultural logics of the late modern world. I suggest that a sociology of religion relevant to the developments of late modernity will be one capable of attending to this model of religion as a state of affairs rather than a state of mind, and that to do so will require the field of study to relinquish long-held predispositions toward 'reducing' religion from a perceived objective reality to something merely imagined. The question may instead be: In what ways is the world we inhabit structured religiously even as it clings to the guise of secularization?

References

Asad, Talal (2001). 'Reading a Modern Classic: W. C. Smith's *The Meaning and End of Religion*'. In H. De Vries and S. Weber, (eds.), *Media and Religion*. Stanford, Calif.: Stanford University Press, 131–47.

Benjamin, Walter (1969). 'Theses on the Philosophy of History'. In *Illuminations: Essays and Reflections*. New York: Schocken Books, 253–64.

Braun, Willi, and McCutcheon, Russell T. (2000). *Guide to the Study of Religion*. London: Cassell and Co.

de Lauretis, Theresa (1998). 'The Stubborn Drive'. *Critical Inquiry*, 24: 360–72.

Derrida, Jacques (1996). 'Faith and Knowledge: The Two Sources of "Religion" at the Limits of Reason Alone'. In J. Derrida and G. Vattimo, (eds.), *Religion*. Stanford, Calif.: Stanford University Press, 1–78.

—— (2001). 'Above All, No Journalists!' In H. De Vries and S. Weber (eds.), *Media and Religion*. Stanford, Calif.: Stanford University Press, 56–93.

Durkheim, Émile (1972). *Selected Writings*, ed. A. Giddens. Cambridge: Cambridge University Press.

—— (1976). *The Elementary Forms of the Religious Life*, trans. Joseph Ward Swain. London: George Allen & Unwin.

Foucault, Michel (1970). *The Order of Things: An Archaeology of the Human Sciences*. New York: Vintage Press.

Gramsci, Antonio (1971). *Selections from the Prisons Notebooks*, ed. Quinton Hoare and Geoffrey Nowell Smith. London: Lawrence and Wishart.

Halevy, Elie (1961 [1911]). *England in 1815: Halevy's History of the English People in the Nineteenth Century*, i. London: Ernest Benn Ltd.

Hall, Stuart (1996*a*). 'Cultural Studies and its Theoretical Legacies'. In *Critical Dialogues in Cultural Studies*. New York: Routledge, 262–75.

—— (1996*b*). 'Gramsci's Relevance to the Study of Race and Ethnicity'. In *Critical Dialogues in Cultural Studies*. New York: Routledge, 411–40.

—— (1996*c*). 'The Problem of Ideology: Marxism without Guarantees'. In *Critical Dialogues in Cultural Studies*. New York: Routledge, 25–46.

—— Gilroy, P., Grossberg, L., and McRobbie, A. (2000). *Without Guarantees: In Honor of Stuart Hall*. New York: Verso.

Hobsbawm, Eric (1957). 'Methodism and the Threat of Revolution in Britain'. *History Today*, 7/2: 115–24.

Laclau, Ernesto, and Mouffe, Chantal (1986). *Hegemony and Socialist Strategy*. New York: Verso.

Lave, Jean, Duguid, P., and Fernandez, N. (1992). 'Coming of Age in Birmingham: Cultural Studies and Conceptions of Subjectivity'. *Annual Review of Anthropology*, 21: 257–82.

Lincoln, Bruce (1992). *Discourse and the Construction of Society: Comparative Studies of Myth, Ritual, and Classification*. Oxford: Oxford University Press.

—— (1996). 'Theses on Method'. *Method and Theory in the Study of Religion*, 8/3: 225–7.

—— (2000). 'Culture'. In Braun and McCutcheon (2000), 409–22.

Lukács, Georg (1971). *History and Class Consciousness: Studies in Marxist Dialectics*, trans. Rodney Livingstone. Cambridge, Mass.: MIT Press.

Marx, Karl (1977). *Capital*, i. *A Critique of Political Economy*. New York: Vintage Books.

—— (1978). 'Theses on Feuerbach'. In *The Marx–Engels Reader.* ed. R. Tucker, New York: Norton and Norton, 143–5.

Masuzawa, Tomoko (1998). 'Culture'. In Mark C. Taylor (ed.), *Critical Terms for Religious Studies.* Chicago: University of Chicago Press, 70–93.

McCutcheon, Russell T. (2003). *The Discipline of Religion: Structure, Meaning, Rhetoric.* New York: Routledge.

—— (2005). *Manufacturing Religion: The Discourse on sui generis Religion and the Politics of Nostalgia.* Oxford: Oxford University Press.

Mulvey, Laura (1996). *Fetishism and Curiosity.* Bloomington, Ind.: Indiana University Press.

Said, Edward (1979). *Orientalism.* New York: Vintage Books.

Smith, Jonathan Z. (1978). 'Map is Not Territory'. In *Map is Not Territory.* Chicago: University of Chicago Press, 289–309.

—— (1982). *Imaging Religion: From Babylon to Jonestown.* Chicago: University of Chicago Press.

—— (1996). 'A Matter of Class'. *Harvard Theological Review,* 89/4: 387–40.

Smith, Wilfred Cantwell (1959). *The Meaning and End of Religion.* Minneapolis: Augsburg Fortress Press.

Spivak, Gayatri Chakravorty (1987). 'Can the Subaltern Speak?' In C. Nelson and L. Grossberg, (eds.), *Marxism and the Interpretation of Culture.* Champaign, Ill.: University of Illinois Press, 271–313.

Taussig, Michael (1983). *The Devil and Commodity Fetishism in South America.* Chapel Hill, NC: University of North Carolina Press.

Taylor, Charles (2003). *Hegel and Modern Society.* Cambridge: Cambridge University Press.

Taylor, Mark C. (ed.) (1998). *Critical Terms for Religious Studies.* Chicago: University of Chicago Press.

Thompson, E. P. (1963). *The Making of the English Working Class.* New York: Vintage Books.

Williams, Raymond (1977). *Marxism and Literature.* Oxford: Oxford University Press.

—— (1983). *Culture and Society, 1780–1950.* New York: Columbia University Press.

—— (1985). *Keywords: A Vocabulary of Culture and Society.* Oxford: Oxford University Press.

Suggested Reading

Asad, Talal (1993). *Genealogies of Religion: Discipline and Reasons of Power in Christianity and Islam.* Baltimore: John Hopkins University Press.

Lincoln, Bruce (2003). *Holy Terrors: Thinking about Religion after September 11.* Chicago: University of Chicago Press.

Mahmood, Saba (2004). *Politics of Piety: The Islamic Revival and the Feminist Subject.* Princeton: Princeton University Press.

Masuzawa, Tomoko (2005). *The Invention of World Religions: Or, How European Universalism Was Preserved in the Language of Pluralism.* Chicago: University of Chicago Press.

Smith, Jonathan Z. (2004). *Relating Religion: Essays in the Study of Religion.* Chicago: University of Chicago Press.

Also Derrida (2001); McCutcheon (2003); and W.C. Smith (1959).

PART II

METHOD

CHAPTER 12

METHODOLOGY IN THE SOCIOLOGY OF RELIGION

OLE PREBEN RIIS

The Methodological Challenge

There is little discussion on methodology in the sociology of religion. Empirical sociology of religion relies on quantitative textbook standards or qualitative studies which follow exemplary studies. However, there is a drastic development in social scientific methodology due to post-positivist philosophy of science and to computerized assistance. This opens up new possibilities. It is the aim of this chapter to discuss the limits of the standard methods, to present some new possibilities, and to argue for combined methods as a fruitful approach.

Textbooks on methodology tend to simplify the schools of philosophy of science, and thereby hinder approaches that build on more nuanced or complex views. The basic critique of both positivism and its counter-position of subjectivism has led to reflections on how to get beyond a subject–object dualism, and thus a gap between epistemology and ontology. These reflections have inspired methodologists in the social sciences to suggest new approaches, some of which will be outlined below.

The term 'methods' refers to practical research techniques for selecting, collecting, and analyzing information. Methods must be usable for illuminating the problem raised in a project and relevant to its theoretical framework. Methods are tools for bridging the gap between theories and their empirical foundation.

A divorce between theory and method leads to grand ideas without empirical grounding, on the one hand, and banal findings without theoretical significance, on the other.

In specifying the research problem by referring to certain theories, a specific range of methods become relevant. For example, Berger's and Luckmann's phenomenological theories point to reconstructing peoples' world views from written sources, field observations, or in-depth interviews. Rational choice theory points to methods derived from market research. Giddens's structuration theory is closely connected to his methodology (1993), and thus an approach of double hermeneutics. By applying Bourdieu's (1979) concepts, it logically follows to use his method of field study, and to find patterns of qualitative indicators by correspondence analysis. A study based on critical realist theory must look for appropriate methods for identifying latent causal mechanisms by a 'retroductive analysis' utilizing mixed methods. This leads to such methods as those presented by Andrew Sayer (1992).

The term 'methodology' refers to questions which reach beyond the aim of a specific project. Methodology reflects on the adequacy of research designs and the validity of research findings from the perspective of philosophy of science. The problems raised by sociology of religion are complex, and thus demand a combination of several types of information, which have to be obtained by different methods.

Operationalizing Religion

Sociology of religion has obtained some consensus about what may come under the term 'religion' as researchable by social-scientific methods. There is also an agreement that many interesting religious questions fall outside its competence. A project in the sociology of religion has to narrow its scope and focus on certain aspects. This means proposing both a nominal definition, which provides a theoretical anchorage, as well as an operational definition, which provides an empirical grounding.

It has implications for the choice of methods, whether religion is defined at a macro-level, a micro-level, or as a dialectical relation between structure and agency. It also has methodological implications for which aspects of religion are focused on. Religion may be characterized as a world view, an ideology, an organization, an attitude, a set of values, as moods and motivations, or as an ethical disposition—and each operative definition points to a certain methodological approach. Sociologists may study religion as situated in a context of ordinary life or situated in a context of individual or collective crisis. The former leads to focusing on religious habits, while the latter raises the issue of theodicy. Religion may be studied by referring to its established, official mode; it may be studied in its manifold popular varieties; or it may be defined functionally and studied in implicit forms which have religious parallels.

Each of these definitions calls for a range of relevant methods. In an empirical investigation, the nominal definition is followed by an operational definition which provides the key to the choice of method. Different scientific perspectives lead to divergent understandings of the act of operationalization. It can, for instance, be regarded as a measurement of a latent dimension, an observation grasping a phenomenon, or as a double hermeneutic reconstruction of a world view. Each single empirical project has to select a particular perspective. This leaves general sociology of religion with the challenge of assembling and systematizing the findings. The advancement of sociology of religion in general thus depends on combining information derived from studies which utilize a broad spectrum of methods.

Studying religions in social contexts is a complex venture, also because religion is a complex phenomenon. It is questionable to assume that we can identify religions as discrete entities. It is untenable to assume that people are affiliated with 'a religion'. Societies may be characterized by polytheism, syncretism, eclecticism, or bricolage. Such religious complexity calls for a combination of several indicators. If commitment to the established religions is used as the main indicator in a social process of increasing religious complexity, the new modes of religiosity seem marginal.

The complexity of religion can be clarified by pointing out major characteristics or dimensions. Ninian Smart (1996) has proposed a multi-dimensional approach for comparative religion. It includes a ritual or practical dimension, a doctrinal or philosophical one, a mythic or narrative one, an experiential or emotional one, an ethical or legal one, an organizational or social one, a material or artistic one, and, finally, the political and economic dimensions of religion. This framework aims at comparative studies of religions. Several sociologists of religion have divided religion into believing and belonging, and some add a practical dimension. By adding more dimensions, more nuances can be drawn. However, each of these dimensions calls for a specific operationalization.

Each dimension can be subdivided further. Charles Glock (in Glock and Stark 1965) has thus proposed distinguishing between five dimensions of religious commitment: experiential, ritualistic, ideological, intellectual, and consequential. An adequate operationalization should be balanced. Thus, it should indicate both attachment to religion and distance from it. For instance, a scale measuring degrees of religiosity should be supplemented by a scale measuring gradual approaches to a strict atheism.

Possibilities and Problems of Quantitative Methods

Quantitative studies are characterized by seeing social characteristics as variables, which are subject to standardized measurement and assigned numbers. A measurement depends on a criterion of correspondence with reality. Religion is thus regarded as a phenomenon which consists of one or more dimensions, each of which can be operationalized and described by a meaningful attribution of numbers. To determine the dimensions of religion is both a theoretical and an empirical challenge. A variable is not necessarily a changeable property. It can just indicate a comparative reference. Measurements vary in degree of specificity from dichotomizing, nominal classification, rank ordering, or interval scaling. Sociology of religion refers to all these types of measurements. However, the statistical models often presume continuous quota measurements, and sociologists of religion must consider whether a certain statistical model fits the available data.

Although logical empiricism had a preference for quantitative studies, these are not necessarily deductive or positivistic. Quantitative designs normally call for meticulous planning, precise and reliable measurements, and strict procedures for analysis. These characteristics point to a deductive approach, but it may be modified during the analysis.

Quantitative studies may be longitudinal, such as panel studies. However, surveys are often used as a substitute. Special problems arise when cross-sectional studies are used in order to obtain causal explanations. The first aim of a survey is to obtain an overview of the distribution of specific characteristics in a sample drawn from the population. Normally, the characteristics refer to attitudes. Surveys are based on analysing items, or standardized response options for standardized questions. Items are subject to pilot tests in order to control whether respondents interpret the wording according to its intention and whether they can respond by using the presented categories. By simplifying and standardizing the measurements, surveys enable comparisons among a large set of cases.

As each item of measurement is subject to error, quantified studies often combine several items into a scale, in order to enhance reliability and provide an internal control for validity. A valid scale should ideally be unidimensional, as all items relate to the same topic. If the items are measured as dichotomies, reference to a Guttman scale provides control for their unidimensional character. If the items are rank-ordered, it is possible to assess whether they may form a Likert scale, and to use Kronbach's alpha to measure their reliability, while the correlation coefficient between an item and the remaining scale indicate its unidimensionality.

Many survey studies use factor analyses in order to identify a set of items which can be combined into a single measure. Factor analysis is based on testing whether a set of items are closely correlated, and whether the correlations can be attributed to a common background factor. If the factors seem to be interrelated, a rotation can be used to identify which items can be ascribed to each factor. This procedure is often presented as inductive, although confirmatory factor analysis is also possible. Factor analysis is in principle based on interval-scaled measurements, and it must be used with caution when the data are rank-ordered.

Quantitative designs generally aim at identifying stable patterns of co-variation between the characteristics in order to identify causal relations. The procedures presuppose that all relevant variables are included. Otherwise, the analysis will either point at 'false correlations', where a co-variation can be identified without a causal relation, or 'Simpson's paradox', where co-variation is not found due to divergent causal processes. Provided that the relevant variables have been entered, a graphic correlation model—such as Digram—is able to identify causal chains among rank-ordered data. Such models have also been used by sociologists of religion, for instance, on data from the European Values Study.

Surveys are based on cross-sectional information, and causal hypotheses are therefore tested by conditional co-variations. Regression analysis relates to hypotheses about the causal influence of one or more 'independent' variables on a 'dependent' variable. A regression coefficient expresses the degree of change in the dependent variable following from a unit change in an independent variable.

Lenski's (1961) study is a classic example of a quantitative survey. Its aim was to find out whether people's religious commitments influence their everyday actions. The study was devised as a substitute for direct observations based on standardized, personal interviews with a sample of persons from Detroit. Religion was identified by two dimensions: doctrinal orthodoxy and devotionalism—or communion with God. The social context was identified by economy, politics, and the family. Causation was determined by patterns of association, which were theoretically reasonable and logical and shared no contradictory evidence, according to Lenski. The study concluded that religion is 'constantly influencing daily lives of the masses of men and women in modern America metropolis', and that 'religion makes an impact on all the other institutional systems of the community' (1961: 320). The study has become paradigmatic for quantitative surveys, but also a prime target for criticism of quantitative methods.

A more recent textbook example can be found in DeVaus (1996: ch. 18). It demonstrates the standard procedure of operationalization of religion, determination of dimensions, and regression models as explanatory tools. However, it fails to take measurement errors into consideration, and the regression model omits interaction terms.

Surveys inspired by behaviourism tend to ask questions about religious behaviour or attitudes. However, it is possible to raise other types of questions. The questionnaire for the European project on religious and moral pluralism (Dobbelaere and Riis 2002) raised questions about reasons behind an act and conditions for taking an attitude. Thereby, the study came closer to providing the respondent's manner of reasoning than do analyses of correlations between attitudes. The Religious and Moral Pluralism (RAMP) study provided an analysis which weighted alternative determinants for religious commitment. It was done by a multiple regression analysis with interaction terms (Billiet *et al.* 2003). The analysis confronted a series of theoretical explanations—including modernization–secularization theory—with the empirical indicators. Such a 'goodness-of-fit' analysis points to the relative correspondence between a theoretical model and the empirical data. Several models may fit the data more or less well. This procedure does not identify a single explanation as true, but it gradually excludes improbable explanations.

Statistical modelling is advancing so fast that textbook examples soon become outdated. A first step is to allow for interaction between the independent variables. This implies that they may have a combined effect, in addition to their individual effects. A further step is to allow for dichotomous independent variables by using 'dummy variables' in regression analysis. Recent advances have also been made towards entering rank-ordered data. Logistic regression models allow for a dichotomous dependent variable, and thus demonstrate the probability that it changes its characteristics through the influence of the independent variables.

Regression analyses normally illustrate a relatively simple set of causal issues: namely, the stable, probabilistic outcome of a one-sided process in which all the influencing factors are included. They may identify stable stimulus–response patterns, but they cannot identify the causal mechanism in the process.

LISREL analysis represents a somewhat different approach, which considers covariations between the factors. This allows for models which contain feedback mechanisms. It also allows for measurement errors. Thereby, LISREL models are much closer to theoretical explanations. LISREL models were at first designed for interval-scaled data. However, recently attempts have been made to allow for rank-ordered data.

Due to these developments, the statistical models come closer to the theoretical presuppositions of sociology of religion. However, the output from advanced statistical models can be difficult to interpret. For instance, it is quite complicated to read the output from a logistical regression analysis with several interacting variables. In order to make the analysis manageable, the number of variables has to be reduced. So, despite their statistical sophistication, they can be too simple from a theoretical point of view. Finally, by using too sophisticated statistical models, the researcher may confuse him- or herself as well as the readers.

Possibilities and Problems of Qualitative Methods

Qualitative methods refer to a heterogeneous category of approaches. Types of qualitative methods differ in scientific views, aims, and practical procedures. Among common features is a focus on hermeneutic interpretation of complex, contextualized cultural phenomena. Interpretations depend on a criterion of coherence or consistency. This can mean either that the expressions are not contradictory or that each of the expressions can be derived from a more comprehensive system of meaning, a world view. By aiming at an internal integration of a case study, it may become difficult to relate it to other cases and further to integrate all the cases into a general sociology of religion.

Qualitative information is not characterized by being 'softer' than quantitative data. Rather, it is characterized by studying human meanings which are to be interpreted by the researcher. Qualitative designs are often used in order to give a 'thick description' of a single case or a few cases based on observation of humans in their 'natural environment', or by attempts to understand the internal world view of human agents through in-depth interviews. Such case studies often contain an implicit comparison between the studied case and 'normal society'.

Several varieties of qualitative methods depend on a single researcher, such as fieldwork or a series of in-depth interviews. Thereby, the perspective of the researcher becomes a methodological issue. Some see such subjectivism as positive, and allow personal opinions in the description and analysis, such as Brown (1991). The presentation weaves a narrative with the voices of both priestess and author. The author becomes a close friend of the priestess and participates in rites of initiation into voodoo. The presentation is coloured by the author's own participation, and this is openly admitted by the author. The personal approach is defended by a counter-critique: 'Omniscient but invisible ethnographers leave their readers with little idea of authorial authority or how the authors interacted with the people they represented' (Spickard *et al.* 2002: 132). A field study may also lead to a critical distance on the part of the researcher and thus lead to an ethical dilemma, as documented by Roy Wallis's (1987) study of Scientology.

The dilemma of subjectivism can be reduced by involving several fieldworkers in a project and letting their corrections control for subjective bias. McGuire (1988) demonstrated this approach in her study of healing groups. The aim of the study was 'to understand adherents' framework of knowledge', 'to understand believers' actions from their own point of view'. It called for a 'methodological empathy'. Even strange behaviour is considered meaningful within the believer's frame of reference. This leads to seeking a balance between establishing empathy and trust and keeping a scientific subject–object distance. The study began with participant observation. All members of the research group had to clarify their personal stance. In order to participate, the observer would show genuine interest and respect. Some groups held views which differed basically from that of the observer. In such cases a supplementary observer was brought into the group. The fact that each observer participated in more groups helped to keep a scientific distance. The study was followed up by a series of intensive interviews. As the interviews contained emotionally moving accounts of suffering, the interviewers responded as fellow human beings. One major methodological challenge was to locate experiences and ideas in term of the respondent's larger belief system, including their ideas about causality, moral responsibility, theodicies of illness, and cosmology. The study was admittedly limited by being merely exploratory. However, its findings point to hypotheses which could be tested by further research.

Many qualitative designs allow for flexibility, and the analytical interpretation is formed by the researcher. In order to avoid subjectivism, the information is often made subject to a systematic and well-documented analysis. There are many ways of analysing qualitative information, and the same set of data can be analysed in many ways. Very often, the focus is directed on expressions concerning a certain theme in the material. However, it is equally possible to focus on hidden or implicit themes, or on the line of argument, or on the style of rhetoric, or on the semiotic usage of signs, or on the type of discourse to which the arguments refer. The focus can be either on certain themes or on individual biographies. Each of these perspectives leads to a specific analytical approach.

The classical way of thematic analysis consists of writing out reports, rejecting irrelevant passages, sorting passages into broad categories, systematizing them into main categories, and relating the main categories to each other in a consistent theoretical presentation. This can be done in a more or less systematic way. Grounded Theory (Glaser and Strauss 1967) represents a qualitative methodology which aims to be theoretically open and flexible, on the one hand, and systematic, precise, stringent, and replicable, on the other. It is based on a systematic, stepwise comparative coding of the empirical evidence, first as a thematic coding, and secondly as a coding of unifying themes and relations between themes.

If the material is large, the process is cumbersome. Inspired by Grounded Theory, a set of computer-assisted tools has been developed in order to obtain a higher degree of reliability and control, such as NUD*IST and InVivo. They allow the researcher to identify relevant passages in a document and attribute passages which contain the same meaning with a code. The criteria for inclusion in a category must be clear. If the coding is too mechanistic, the contextual meaning of the passage can be lost. It is possible to secure an intersubjective control by cross-coding. Some projects develop the codes inductively from the data, while others utilize codes which refer to theoretical categories. A programmatic coding can be a great assistance for collecting all the expressions which relate to a theme in empirical material. However, it is still the analyst who has to produce the interpretation.

The use of qualitative methods in sociology of religion is rather conservative. There are, for instance, few examples of trying out ethnomethodology or conversation analysis, despite the fact that religion provides a rich source of examples of 'indexicality', 'situated accounts', and 'artful practices', in which actors assign meaning to their use of religious symbols and rituals.

It is notoriously difficult to compare a large set of qualitative cases. Such comparisons necessitate reducing the complexity of the cases and focusing on a few, basic dimensions. One new approach to comparative qualitative studies is correspondence analysis (Greenacre and Blasius 1994). It was developed as a tool for summarizing information based on a set of nominal indicators. It aims at presenting an overview of closeness between different characteristics analysed in graphic format. The point of departure is a cross-tabulation matrix of data. The analysis aims at finding patterns of correspondence between row criteria—for instance, religious membership—and column criteria—such as employment. It is relevant for a large data matrix in which distances between rows and columns can be meaningfully interpreted, and in which the structure is not known beforehand. The analysis points to correspondences between criteria, but it does not tell how and why they are associated.

Qualitative comparative analysis (QCA) of case studies leaves room for causal complexity. Causality is seen as a constellation of conditions which are necessary and sufficient for a certain outcome. Causality is sensitive to the context and conjunction of conditions. QCA points not to 'the best' explanation, but to a series of causal conjunctions which may lead to the outcome. It is based on Boolean algebra, and thus to a replicable logic of 'if–then' statements which are either true or false. The analysis leads to specification of constellations of conditions for the outcome, and then reduces the Boolean expression to a minimum that unveils the regular patterns in the data. It is up to the researcher to interpret such a minimal expression theoretically. The approach allows one to compare a relatively small number of cases, provided that the number of characteristics (variables) is relatively small. The number of possible constellations increases exponentially with the number of characteristics. Furthermore, in principle, information is required about all characteristics in all cases.

One of the alleged problems of QCA is its foundation on dichotomous data. This is, of course, due to the usage of Boolean logic. For some problems, where relevant conditions are continuous, dichotomization leads to loss of information. Furthermore, the classification of cases is not always certain in practice, and a single contradictory case can logically contradict a firm conclusion from the remaining cases. Charles Ragin (2000) has therefore proposed to overcome the problem of dichotomizing by applying fuzzy-set logic. This implies that one can allow membership of a category to be considered as a continuum between 0—not a member—to 1—a full member. In cases of uncertainty, this allows one to specify probable degrees of membership. By taking a probabilistic approach and using programs for fuzzy logic, it is possible to identify necessary and sufficient conditions for the outcome to be explained. Another way of approaching the problem of dichotomies is by using multi-value logical synthesis, which does not include probabilistic criteria. Special software has been developed for this type of analysis (Tosmana). However, this type of analysis depends inherently on the choice of thresholds.

All these types of qualitative comparative analyses have been widely used by practitioners of several branches of social science, especially by political scientists. However, despite a strong tradition of comparative studies in the sociology of religion, there are very few examples in the discipline of the usage of the novel systematic approaches to qualitative comparative studies. However, David Smilde (2005) has demonstrated the potentials of this approach for sociology of religion by using QCA analysis on religion in Latin America. The causal mechanism is not identified by the above-mentioned type of qualitative comparative studies. Other types of qualitative studies may provide this, such as analyses presenting a historical process, or observations of a sequence of actions.

The Core Problem of Validity

The concluding inferences from an empirical project raise the basic methodological issue of validity. This relates both to procedures for controlling methods and to meta-reflections on the method in the perspective of theory of science. A well-documented, rigid, standardized procedure seems more convincing than a flexible, *ad hoc* approach which is rendered by memorial notes. Accordingly, quantitative approaches seem better able to answer the issue of validity than many qualitative ones. However, procedural clarity and rigidity do not ensure validity of the construct. Some qualitative studies sidestep the problem or immunize the conclusion with vague provisos. Proponents of qualitative or quantitative approaches may disagree on some basic points regarding philosophy of science. However, they cannot insulate themselves. They are challenged with the task of convincing other sections of academia, and society in general, of the validity of their chosen approach. Instead of confronting other approaches as incommensurable, they could be seen as providing possibilities for controlling validity.

The 'measurements' of social indicators become theoretically meaningful through a hermeneutic interpretation of their meaning. This problem is often solved by referring to common sense. However, such assisting hypotheses regarding the interpretation of acts or expressions can be controlled by cross-reference to qualitative studies of how respondents interpret questions and answer categories, or how certain acts are related to intentions and limitations. Quantitative studies are based on analyses of a small number of variables which are measured by a narrow set of indicators. Therefore, they are confronted with a basic problem regarding the adequacy of the measurement. Whereas it may be argued that the indicators relate to the theoretical theme, it is less easy to demonstrate that they cover all relevant aspects of it. One way of producing evidence for adequacy was by cross-reference to qualitative studies, which include a wider spectrum of indicators. Another problem relates to causal explanations based on studies of co-variation. The causal mechanism which links the independent variables to the dependent one is merely hypothesized. This problem could be solved by cross-references to processual studies.

Qualitative studies do not aim at measurement in an objective sense. Nevertheless, they are still subject to self-critical reflection on the issue of validity in an intersubjective sense. It is an issue whether double hermeneutic interpretations are correct regarding informants' views, the researcher's immediate interpretation, and the theoretical analysis of the information. Within the framework of qualitative studies, the issue of validity tends to focus on bias, whether due to selection of information, an impression of the observations, or prejudices of the researcher. At the core of this is the trustworthiness of the researcher. However, qualitative methodologists have also initiated an extended discussion on validity (Kvale 1989; Denzin and Lincoln 2003). This discussion raises the issues of authenticity and intersubjectivity. In order to be convincing, an interpretative and explanatory study must provide reasons which can convince others. In order to ensure an intersubjective consensus, the methodological procedure has to be well-documented and convincing. Some schools would add a criterion of praxis: that the inquiry should also provide usable guidelines for action.

One way of validating the conclusions from a qualitative study is to confront it with findings from other studies. In many cases, qualitative studies refer to a limited case. It is therefore necessary to specify its range and level of generalization. In order to tie it together with general sociology of religion, it is furthermore valuable to point at possible comparisons, both as similar and as contrasting cases.

Betwixt and Between: Possibilities of Combined Methods

The methodological split originated in the great classics of sociology of religion. Max Weber's methodology was inspired by neo-Kantian philosophy. Weber (1976: 1) proposed a methodology oriented towards comprehending (*deutend verstehen*) social acts and thereby causally explaining (*ursachlich erklären*) their outcomes and effects (*Ablaufen und Wirkungen*). Weber saw sociology as a generalizing extension of history, which based its analyses on ideal types of social actors. Émile Durkheim's (1964[1912]) methodology was inspired by positivism. He proposed studying social facts as if they were things, defined by common, external characteristics, considered from an aspect independent of their individual manifestations. Normal or average phenomena should be distinguished from pathological phenomena. The analysis should classify social types ('social morphology'), and for each one explain its efficient causes and the function it fulfils ('social physiology'). However, Weber's principles did not make him refrain from using statistical data in *The Protestant Ethic*, and Durkheim's study on the function of religion among an Australian Aborigine tribe was based on ethnographic reports.

Max Weber and Émile Durkheim agreed on the need for cross-cultural comparisons, and they both found inspiration in John Stuart Mills's methodology. Comparative studies are still a source of inspiration for sociology of religion. Nevertheless, systematic comparisons are not widespread in sociological studies of religion. A series of cross-national survey studies have provided valuable insights. However, they typically omit discussion of the cultural embeddedness. There are also several interesting comparative studies based on qualitative indicators. However, they often omit methodological reflections.

One major methodological challenge is to make systematic comparisons which can specify similarities and differences and identify explanations. Drawing a religious group into a comparative scheme implies going beyond its self-description and self-understanding. A comparison is based on forming an abstract standard which in some sense reduces and changes the perspectives of the groups studied. It can be formed as a transcendental hermeneutic, a comprehensive interpretation based on the specific interpretations of the internal perspectives of the groups involved.

One of the hidden points of disagreement between qualitative and quantitative approaches relates to the issue of causality. Quantitative studies generally aim at explaining recurrent events through analysis of co-variation, and recurrent effects through regression analysis. Qualitative studies generally aim at comprehending the meaning behind the act through in-depth interviews, or mechanisms which trigger a process through processual analysis, or the conditions which determine its outcome through comparative analysis. Qualitative and quantitative methods thus take up different aspects of the complex of causal analysis, but neither approach covers it in its entirety.

Causality studies of human acts in a social setting relate to both structural determinants and individual intentions, both to recurrent patterns and specific events, both to conditions and mechanisms, both to potential changing powers and observable behaviours. A comprehensive explanation of a complex socio-religious process, such as the secularization of Northwestern Europe, calls for all these aspects, and thus for a combination of methods.

Instead of regarding qualitative and quantitative methods as mutually exclusive, they ought to be seen as complementary (Bryman 1988; Riis 2001). A combination of methods can have more purposes. It may provide supplementary information. Furthermore, by combining methods, it is possible to check their validity. Finally, the scope of a generalized conclusion may be specified by combining more methods.

Some quantitative studies are still characterized by an implicit search for objective facts, while several qualitative studies are presented as a quest for subjective insight. However, objectivism is impossible, and subjectivism insufficient as a foundation for such disciplines as the sociology of religion. Scientific research begins with a discourse in a community, and it is temporarily concluded by its evaluation of the information considered relevant. Whereas the community may not follow a specific paradigm, it generally agrees on certain standards of craftsmanship. As a reaction against positivist domination, the qualitative urge is understandable. However, this does not mean that all quantifications are to be censured and that all forms of non-positivist discourse are laudable. Just because we cannot expect an account of the world to have a unique match with reality does not imply that all accounts are on a par. Some accounts are more convincing than others. Methods form an important clue for this continuing assessment.

Seen in the perspective of a general sociology of religion, both quantitative and qualitative information is needed in order to illuminate the subject. In order to assess church commitment, we need to know the rules for membership, the membership rates, and the agents' reasons for being members. Qualitative and quantitative information is mutually illuminating. In order to interpret membership rates, we must know the rules; and in order to see the extension of the rules, we need to know the proportions. As different methods can illustrate different aspects of a phenomenon, methodological combinations give a more complete, multi-faceted picture.

Moreover, the big methodological issue of validity calls for cross-methodological control. It does not suffice to check a series of measurements with one instrument by referring to measurements which come from a similar instrument. Both series of measurements may be flawed. Furthermore, it does not suffice to refer to a specific indicator or to common sense. The indicator rests on measurement procedures which can be contested, and common sense is often less common than is supposed. If the same conclusion can be drawn from studies using different methodological approaches, then it is more convincing. If different approaches lead to divergent conclusions, then we have to consider whether they contradict each other, and thus whether some of the methods lead to invalid results, or whether they supplement each other by illuminating different levels, aspects, or dimensions of the phenomenon. A methodological combination can therefore be used to control whether conclusions are valid.

Finally, a methodological combination can lead to specification of the extension of an empirical conclusion. Quantitative studies often aim at obtaining representativity for the population, while using a few standardized measurements, whereas qualitative studies often aim at covering all aspects of the phenomenon by obtaining information from a few cases. While such quantitative studies have a problem with extending the scope of the measurements, such qualitative studies have a problem with generalizing the findings from the cases investigated. A combination of both types of methods makes it possible to specify the extension of the conclusions, regarding both population and theme. By supplementing a qualitative case study with a survey, it becomes possible to formulate clearer generalizations which go beyond the case material. By supplementing a survey study with an in-depth case study, it becomes possible to specify the thematic scope of the measurements. This also implies the need to specify what the study does not cover. It thus becomes possible to formulate conclusions which are clearer, regarding both their representativity and their thematic scope.

One example of a study in the sociology of religion based on a planned combination of methods is Barker (1984). The study aims at explaining conversion to a controversial religion. It presents the perspectives of both believers and outsiders. Furthermore, it covers the personal perspective of an individual Moonie, the interpersonal level between Moonies internally and between Moonies and those outside the movement, and an impersonal level locating the movement within society. This task calls for a combination of several methods. An initial participant observation prepared the researcher for in-depth interviews. Preliminary analysis led to formulating hypotheses, which were operationalized in questionnaires and pilot-tested. The final questionnaires were either handed out or sent through the post. Answers were either pre-coded or post-coded by assistants. The resulting answers were compared with answers to similar questions by other groups. Special comparisons were made with respondents who had access to the sorts of social contexts from which Moonies might be recruited. The following analysis was thus based on a complex set of information from a varied spectrum of sources utilizing statistical analysis in order to support a *Verstehen* of converts to the Unification Church.

Methodological combinations raise a new set of challenges. In order to unite results obtained from different methods, the design must include several specific links. With combined approaches, the number of possible designs increases dramatically. A methodological variety does not indicate a paradigm crisis. It can express a mature reflection on the methodological challenge of studying complex religion in a dynamic social context.

References

Barker, Eileen (1984). *The Making of a Moonie.* Oxford: Blackwell.

Billiet, Jaak, *et al.* (2003). 'Church Commitment and Some Consequences in Western and Central Europe'. *Research in the Social Scientific Study of Religion*, 14: 129–60.

Bourdieu, Pierre (1979). *La Distinction.* Paris: Le Seuil.

Bryman, Alan (1988). *Quantity and Quality in Social Research.* London: Routledge.

Brown Karen M. (1991). *Mama Lola: A Vodou Priestess in Brooklyn.* Berkeley: University of California Press.

Denzin, Norman K., and Lincoln, Yvonne S. (eds.) (2003). *The Landscape of Qualitative Research.* London: Sage Publications.

DeVaus, David (1996). *Surveys in Social Research.* London: UCL Press.

Dobbelaere, Karel, and Riis, Ole (2002). 'Religious Pluralism'. *Research in the Social Scientific Study of Religion,* 13: 159–72.

Durkheim, Émile (1964[1912]). *The Rules of Sociological Method.* New York: Free Press.

Giddens, Anthony (1993). *New Rules of Sociological Method.* Cambridge: Polity Press.

Glaser, Barney, and Strauss, Anselm (1967). *The Discovery of Grounded Theory.* Chicago: Aldine.

Glock, Charles, and Stark, Rodney (1965). *Religion and Society in Tension.* Chicago: Rand McNally.

Greenacre, Michael J., and Blasius, Jorg (1994). *Correspondence Analysis in the Social Sciences.* London: Academic Press.

Kvale, Steinar (ed.) (1989). *Issues of Validity in Qualitative Research.* Lund: Studentlittertur.

Lenski, Gerhard (1961). *The Religious Factor.* New York: Doubleday.

McGuire, Meredith (1988). *Ritual Healing in Suburban America.* New Brunswick, NJ: Rutgers University Press.

Ragin, Charles (2000). *Fuzzy-Set Social Science.* Chicago: University of Chicago Press.

Riis, Ole (2001). *Metoder på tværs.* Copenhagen: DJØF Forlag.

Sayer, Andrew (1992). *Method in Social Science: A Realist Approach.* London: Routledge.

Smart, Ninian (1996). *Dimensions of the Sacred: An Anatomy of the World's Beliefs.* London: Fontana Press.

Smilde, David (2005). 'A Qualitative Comparative Analysis of Conversion to Venezuelan Evangelicanism: How Networks Matter'. *American Journal of Sociology,* 111/3: 757–96.

Spickard, Jim V., *et al.* (2002). *Personal Knowledge and Beyond.* New York: New York University Press.

Wallis, Roy (1987). 'My Secret Life: Dilemmas of Integrity in the Conduct of Field Research'. In R. Kristensen and O. Riis (eds.), *Religiøse Minoriteter.* Århus: Aarhus Universitetsforlag, 101–20.

Weber, Max (1976). *Wirtschaft und Gesellschaft.* Tübingen: Mohr Siebeck.

Suggested Reading

Bryman, Alan (1992). *Mixed Methods: Qualitative and Quantitative Research.* Aldershot: Avebury.

Cicourel, Aaron (1964). *Method and Measurement in Sociology.* New York: Free Press.

Creswell, John W., and Plano, Clark Vicki L. (2007). *Designing and Conducting Mixed Methods Research.* London: Sage.

Danermark, Berth, *et al.* (2002). *Explaining Society: Critical Realism in the Social Sciences.* London: Routledge.

Denzin, Norman K., and Lincoln, Yvonne S. (eds.) (2005). *The Sage Handbook of Qualitative Research.* Thousand Oaks, Calif.: Sage.

DeVaus, David (2001). *Research Design in Social Sciences.* London: Sage.

Kaplan, David (ed.) (2004). *The Sage Handboook of Quantitative Methodology for the Social Sciences.* Thousand Oaks, Calif.: Sage.

Little, Daniel (1991). *Varieties of Social Explanation.* Oxford: Westview.

Ragin, Charles (1987). *The Comparative Method: Moving Beyond Qualitative and Quantitative Strategies.* Berkeley: University of California Press.

CHAPTER 13

CONCEPTUAL MODELS IN THE STUDY OF RELIGION

JEPPE SINDING JENSEN

This chapter surveys the nature and role of conceptual models in the study of religion, be it, e.g., historical, ethnographic, psychological, or sociological. My aim is to replace prior ideas of religious 'phenomena' as given, self-evident 'data', whether conceived either as metaphysical 'givens' or as human existential 'experiences'. In the general and comparative study of religion, a revised view of conceptual models should replace those older notions denoting the 'stuff' that we work with. The argument presented here deliberately goes against the intuitive, positivist idea that we work with obvious and immediately accessible 'facts' and 'data' presented on the serving trays of history and society. Using a culinary metaphor, you might say that it takes a lot of cooking before the raw materials can be served as scholarly delicacies. The 'plain facts' do not cook—or present—themselves.

Now, whereas facts and data may appear to us *just* as facts and data, models are clearly something that *we* work with. We often suppose that we find them, but obviously we also quite often make them. When we sometimes forget that we are working with models, it does turn out, upon closer inspection, that we work with unacknowledged or hidden models that shape our cognition of the worlds (material, mental, and symbolic) in which we navigate as humans. So, the term 'model' has a 'manufactured' ring to it, and it also points to the fact that we are not working with immediate 'reality', but with selected features of such reality, as we may be able to perceive it. Also, what we perceive depends on how and with what conceptual tools we perceive. For instance, if we had no conceptual model of religion at all, it would be difficult to perceive anything as being 'religious'. Without specific ideas of 'ritual', or 'myth', or 'sacrifice', none of these 'phenomena' would appear to us as informative. The information they yield, then, further depends on the theoretical grounding or formation of the conceptual model, the 'ideas' we have of, say, 'sacrifice', where it is obvious that the model and what we gain by applying it is directly dependent upon the theory. By consciously working with models, we are reminded of the active role that scholarship plays in the production of its data and insights. A relevant example here is the conceptual model of religion itself.

It has been said that there 'is no data for religion' (Smith 1982: 19), but that statement is apt to be misinterpreted as 'religion does not exist', which would be a silly statement, considering the state of affairs in this world. 'Religion' is a term, a concept, that circulates in the world of media, politics, etc. and one that is not likely to disappear shortly. The validity of the statement of course depends on what is meant by 'exist'—for surely religion does not exist as does hydrogen or gold—but as a designation used to cover a conventionally selected spectrum of human behaviour, 'religion' exists as much as does economics, art, or sport. One should not confuse map with territory, nor concept with phenomenon; it is obvious that the concept of gold is not gold, and nor is the concept of religion identical with religion 'as such'. That being said, a sensible account of the existence of religion also requires a theoretical clarification of the conceptual model involved, so a sensible definition could run thus: The term 'religion' can be applied to sets of human practices and ideas which involve communication with superhuman agents. In order to clarify matters, it can be stated that these superhuman agents generally have counterintuitive properties. The concept of religion exists and belongs to our epistemic tool-box—that is, to our means and ways of acquiring knowledge. The entities which make up the behavioural complex 'religion' belong to our ontology: that is, they exist as something in the world; the ideas, representations, actions, and institutions, etc. that go into what we call 'religion' *do* exist. Religion may be a construction as a concept and a construction as modes of social practice, but this does not make religion one bit less real than other human forms of life. Thus, it is sensible to use the term 'religion' and also to ponder the role played by conceptual models in the construction of religion, by practitioners (first order) as well as by scholars (second order) in the analysis of matters best characterized by the term 'religion'.

The substance of this essay consists in the appraisal of the nature and function of conceptual models in religion and in the study of religion. The situation concerning models does appear somewhat confusing, recalling many of the former methodological debates, not least those exhibited in the self-doubts expressed by critical deconstructive voices who have claimed that many things 'do not exist'. It has been a reasonable pursuit to purge the study of religion of the most unusable or infelicitous terms; but the drive towards what might be labelled 'conceptual eliminativism' is not always constructive.

Obviously, then, one could turn from the state of affairs concerning the state of model construction and model use in the study of religion and take a look at some neighbouring disciplines to see how and what they do. The interested reader will find very little on models in the study of religion literature (as might have been intuited), but a little more in other 'places' such as anthropology and linguistics which can be considered 'model sciences' for the study of religion (Jensen 2003). On the other hand, a quick search will ascertain that the philosophy of science is replete with 'model talk'; but much of what can be found is not readily transposable to the study of religion. Considerable work remains to be done on these issues, and this essay is but a modest contribution to such an undertaking.

One of the main effects of working with models is that they enable an expansion of our cognitive scale, as our range of concepts can be given more concrete form when instantiated in models. We are thus able to get a better handle on, or come to grips with, complicated or ephemeral matters. The approach utilized here is a pragmatic one: I do not consider it very useful to spend too much time and effort on the truth-value of models, i.e. their 'fit with reality'; rather, one should consider their utility. Consider models as 'tools for thought', as when explaining complicated things via simpler and more familiar things. Models are inextricably related to, or intertwined with, concepts, and in order to stress that point, I shall stay with the term 'conceptual model'. Conceptual models can be in minds, and they can be between minds, thus uniting the socio-cultural and the mental 'worlds'.[1]

Examples of the use of conceptual models underscore their ubiquity and their salience for human understanding. Consider, for example, how the familiar is used (quite literally) to understand the alien from the ways in which most nations use family or 'neighbour' models for foreign relations. Consider also how we anthropomorphize nature, the 'marketplace', or the economy as a superhuman entity, albeit one with many human properties. In the established range of conceptual models of religion, the following stand out. The functionalist 'organic model' emphasizes how organs work together in maintaining a physiological or homeostatic equilibrium in a social 'body'. The 'architectural model' elaborates on the structures of life worlds, ideologies, cultural systems, etc. and the relations between parts and wholes. The 'patriarchal model' or 'police model' focuses on political aspects of religion, such as social control or the exercise of power in religious traditions (or the use of them). The 'highway code model' may view religion as 'bookish' and with a lot of rules manifested in ideas about a preferred 'way of life';

[1] 'Mental' covers cognitive as well as emotional-affective, and models are more than 'cool reason', and some may be chosen *precisely* because of their potential emotional trigger effects.

this may be seen as beneficial to the individual (or group) in the 'comfort-model', where religion almost assumes the role of 'parental guidance'. The 'salvific model' is one which stresses how religion (as 'meaning provision') helps a person to realize their true human, or even cosmic, potential in a less than perfect world. In an extreme form that idea can be seen as a model of 'communication from the beyond'. By contrast, on the critical side are, for example, anthropological and sociological models of conflict or struggle. Philosophical or cognitive science critics of religion may use models of 'cognitive virus infections' which invade human minds and inoculate them against reality. The list is long.

The important point is to recognize how our cognitive competence and interpretive understanding depend on what we already 'have in mind' and the sociocultural explanatory repertoires at our disposal—that is, not least the conceptual models we have and which we employ in order to make meaning, either to ourselves or to others. Thus, I shall concentrate on the semantic aspects of models—because of the emphasis on the intersubjective and communicative properties of the models we employ in our research. First, however, a brief look at the philosophy of science.

Models in the Philosophy of Science

In many sciences models are mostly mathematical (e.g. as 'model theory')—population genetics, rocket ballistics, market behaviour—and it is evident that models are central to understanding and 'manipulating' in the natural sciences—'manipulation' because in many complicated scientific analyses the wealth of data is so immense that it is impossible to realize anything meaningful without arranging the date according to models. Computational modelling in neuro-psychology is an example of high-level complexity, where scientists construct models that produce insights. On the state of the art of the discussion in the philosophy of science and continuing more classic works by Arbib and Hesse (1986) are such works as *Models as Mediators* (Morgan and Morrison 1999). Other specialists in the field include Nancy Cartwright (1999) and Emma Ruttkamp (2002, discussing Cartwright 1999: 119–34). A common-sense perspective is represented in Simon Blackburn's *Oxford Dictionary of Philosophy* article:

—**model** (science). A representation of one system by another, usually more familiar, whose workings are supposed analogous to that of the first. Thus one might model the behaviour of sound waves upon that of waves in water, or the behaviour of a gas upon that of a volume containing moving billiard balls. Whilst nobody doubts that models have a useful heuristic role in science, there has been intense debate over whether a good explanation of some phenomenon needs a model, or whether an organized structure of laws from which it can be deduced suffices for scientific explanation. (1996: 246–7)

It should be noted—as a curious fact—that the term 'model' is not an entry in Blackwell's *A Companion to Epistemology*—or in its *Companion to Metaphysics*. So, where do models belong?

The term 'model' is used in several ways. Simple and popular forms are those displayed, for example, in molecular models, in models of DNA or of the solar system, where the model is merely an isomorphic illustration, on a smaller or larger scale, of the physical properties of the 'thing' represented by the models—as in a 'model railway'. However 'simple' such models are, they are interesting for the reason that they bring otherwise invisible or unimaginable dimensions into the realm of 'medium-sized objects' (in philosophical parlance) that may be handled by our evolved perceptual and cognitive systems. In a similar vein, by making inaccessible entities accessible, computerized modelling is very important in many fields: for example, DNA models in genetics or complex climate models in meteorology. For the most part, such models are simplifications that focus on certain aspects, so a model is basically an amplification of some aspects over others. Conceptual models are constructed, used, and tested for specific purposes. It is evident, then, that models are closely related to theories and to definitions, which are theories made as succinct as possible. Models are instantiations of theories and their explanatory potentials. And, because you cannot explain all of reality (physical, social, mental, etc.) at one time, a selection of entities, properties, and functions is called for. Thus, scientific models are selective, as are maps of specific shapes of reality: highways, metros, sewers, etc.

Models are models *of* reality, and to a certain extent they are also models *for* reality, because they always include a measure of theoretical normativity concerning the ways in which we should use the models; thereby they help us create our understanding of the world and act according to our intentions. Models are in that sense intervention-oriented: that is, they point to where and how we may alter the world. If this sounds overstated, consider an example of how an altered understanding of the world is driven by a normative concern: namely, that of increased cognitive control over the environment. And that is, in itself, a normative quest. The models and theories of religion that have been devised over time have been so created as to make it possible to understand one specific realm of human activity, that which now passes for religion. Also, it is quite evident that the making and using of models involve a degree of creativity (Laschyk 1986). In that connection it is interesting to investigate just how and about what scientists actually think when making and using models (Bailer-Jones 2002).

The relations between models, theories, and data, over against reality and the 'factual' world, are the subjects of a great deal of philosophical debate, especially concerning their modes of reference (Devitt 1996) and their ways of 'representation'

(Tallis 1999, with a critique of Johnson-Laird 1983). One of the main questions is whether models are (1) representational, that is, they re-present or re-state matters of fact; or are (2) interpretative, that is, that they have a semantic content so that we may understand matters in a certain way; or are (3) explanatory, in the sense of explaining either the origin and cause, or function and effects, of reality. The most inclusive observation one can make about them is that models come in various kinds, and that they do various jobs: tell us about reality, how we should understand it, and what we can do about it.

The following are a few observations of importance to our appropriation of a more sophisticated theory of what models do in 'our field'—the study of religion—as consciously elaborated scholarly models. First, models are subject to the conditions of the 'universals' problem (this is somewhat overlooked), so they should be generally applicable. Second, models are as much social facts as are definitions and theories; thus they are historically contingent, with all the problems that this entails for their validity and function. And third, a related point, models are as much 'cultural posits' (Quine 1953) as are scientific theories and most (if not all) of our human knowledge.[2]

Reflections from the History of the Study of Religion: 'Sacrifice'

Social-science models and models in the humanities are normally quite complex constructs that are highly dependent upon a theoretical outlook and given developments in the formation of theory. Thus, it is a matter of course that our conceptions of phenomena change with our knowledge, with our theories *and* with our models. So, a model of, say, 'sacrifice' will depend on how and why we detect some practice or some event as a 'sacrifice'. In ancient Greece we would have had the indigenous notion of '*thusia*'—a gift to the gods as stipulated in Homer. With William Robertson Smith our model of sacrifice changed into one of community building and cultural reproduction activity. With Marcel Mauss it becomes symbolic exchange; with Stanley Tambiah it is viewed as performative action, with René Girard a kind of violence-aversive undertaking; with Pierre Bourdieu we see it as a transaction in a symbolic economy, etc. The point is that no data are model-free,

[2] They are not 'simply' cognitive representations ('inner pictures') of realities; see e.g. McDowell 1996: 185–6; Putnam 1995: 414–15. In Quine's example, physical objects and Homer's gods equally enter our conception 'only as cultural posits' (1953: 44), because physical objects are conceptually imported into our knowledge of things. When I think of rocks, I do not have rocks in my head, but conceptions of rocks.

no model is theory-free, and conversely, no theory is without models. They come and go together. The ancient Greek conception of sacrifice was also a theory, albeit a folk one and an indigenous cultural model.

Any scholarly work on anything, however specific, is possible only through the deployment of theories and models, and its nature or 'essence' may change radically with new theory building. The phenomenon 'sacrifice' is, as we see, underdetermined by the empirical evidence, as the piecing together of the materials that 'compose a sacrifice' is directly theory-dependent. Precisely the same goes for other models, because they are involved in the manufacture of the 'facts'. The 'facts' would not be facts at all if they were unrelated to our models. There would still be certain kinds of behaviour—but we would not know it as 'sacrifice'.

Thus, it comes as a rather plain fact that the inventory or the catalogue of the general and comparative study of religion does not consist of facts; it consists of models, which instantiate the 'facts'—the available evidential materials—as something that becomes comparable and scholarly interesting. This is why 'ideal types'—a subcategory of conceptual models—that are tied to theories are much more interesting than purported 'real types' (as some have called them) that should supposedly be unrelated to theorizing and emerge, instead, out of pure empirical subject matter. Ideal types are types that are ideas, or ideational. And—that is it. Just to push the idea a bit: it is quite common to 'imagine' (ideas again), in a religious universe, this mundane world over against the 'other world' of superhuman agents and powers, communication with which is the business of religious practice. Examples of this cosmological situation and relation are usually illustrated by the use of Venn diagrams—the 'two world model'—as drawn, for example, by Edmund Leach (1976). Obviously, no one living inside a religious cosmology ever saw such a diagram. It is purely ideational—an ideal type. The type as such has no reality apart from being an idea. But, if we share it, it, is very useful.

There has been a lot of criticism of 'old models'; but, to be quite blunt, nothing was really wrong with the old models—only with the way they were used. The metaphorical quality of models was not duly recognized, and the impression was that a model should be a 'photo' or an iconic rendition of 'reality', so that what was perceived as model was a token of identity and essence. Sir James G. Frazer—and many others at that time—could thus collapse form and content—all things that looked similar had the same reference and the same 'meaning'. For Gerardus van der Leeuw, the references of phenomenological models were to real ontological and sacred entities. Similarly, for Mircea Eliade, references pointed to universal symbolic deep structures (meta-psychoanalysis) and a specific human existential level of experiential reality. The list of potential examples is long, but these should suffice and demonstrate that many of the critical features of the models were intuited or reached by impressionistic form criteria.

Models Graphic—and Not Graphic—and Knowledge Organization

Models often come in graphic form, and thus one could easily think also of models in relation to maps and metaphors. So, are models simply maps or images that depict or look like their references? Or are models metaphors? That is, are they conceptual images that convey information about something by (re-)presenting something else?[3] With an inspiration from Charles S. Peirce's (1839–1914) classification of signs, we may see graphic models as coming in three kinds. First, models can be *iconic* and analogical: toy cars, scale-model airplanes, or simply a 'model railway'. Second, models come as *indexical*: that is, as referential and metonymic, pointing to things 'in the world'—a map of your local neighbourhood or a representation of the Paris metro. The same goes for most other maps that show the way to organize things: for instance, 'mind maps' and models that show functions, such as, for example, wiring diagrams in a TV set. Also, we may consider models of authority and hierarchy, for example, flow charts, in business and government.

Symbolic and metaphoric models are like 'geographies of concepts', where matters in one domain ('target') are being mapped by entities from another ('source') domain that is cognitively suitable and culturally acceptable for organizing complex information, so that it may achieve a degree of stability. Other than this, symbolic models have evocational potential, in that they have construction potential for working up socially relevant models that contribute to cultural reproduction. An example from Christianity: the cross is an iconic representation of a cross as an instrument of torture; on a road-map it is an indexical representation of where there is a church; and as a symbol it may represent the whole story of the suffering of Jesus Christ. Thus models are not only graphic or mathematical; many of them come in the form of narratives, and as such they organize human knowledge, expectations, and representations. Models may also be thought of as mind-external devices that anchor metaphors, abstract conceptual blends. Models *in* religious traditions and practices, such as rules of conduct and purity systems, are also conceptual, and mostly come in narrated format or formats that may be given a narrative exegesis. This suggests that models are mostly symbolically and linguistically mediated. Thus there is potential in looking at models as stories; for without the stories, most models would be incomprehensible and would not work. They would also be very difficult to communicate and transmit, between and

[3] In an influential and important article, Fitz John Porter Poole (1986) worked with maps and metaphors—but not explicitly with models, although many of his hypotheses would fit there as well.

across generations. This 'narrative turn' in a theory of conceptual models is not simply a redefinition ploy in order to emphasize one specific aspect in the nature of models. Models are semantic entities (in the social and human sciences at least), and they do not work without the stories. By 'semantic', I do not imply that they are so in the traditional philosophical truth-conditional sense, but that they contain information and support and/or modify intentionality. If that is so, this means that similar conditions hold for conceptual models as for propositions. Then it is a fundamental question to ask whether correspondence or coherence function as the grounding of the validity of models?

This issue is largely a matter also of whether the models we operate with in the study of religion are discovered (emic) or constructed (etic), as the study of religion contains both kinds. An example of an emic model is 'taboo', which is a certain kind of organizing principle that has been discovered in a specific socio-cultural setting and then used as a model in an other. An etic model could be 'religious world', the theoretician's 'shorthand' for the comprehensive whole of a religious tradition (itself a model, derived from Latin, meaning 'handing over'). So, emic models are found in traditions, whereas etic models are manufactured by the analyst, scholar, scientist, etc. Part of the confusion surrounding models can be traced to a neglect of the difference between these two levels, especially when emic models are used etically in and about traditions other than those in which they were found; examples would be shaman, mana, and nagual.

In the meta-level, construction of models intended to cover the entire span of the objects of the study of religion, the models developed will be largely etic; and, as noted, some emic models may be used as etic models, so that coherence more than correspondence may be the decisive or defining factor: that is, how well a given model relates to and functions with other models and theories. That is what I would call 'model holism'. Thus, the 'meaning' of the model lies not in its direct correspondence with the world, but in its coherence with other models, concepts, and theories. Models are relational.

What Models Are Made Of

There are many kinds of models made of various 'materials'; some are physical, some are images, some are mathematical symbolic or linguistic reproductions of certain aspects of the object(s) that the models are applied to shed light on, or in virtue of which the data 'appear'. Models represent because they generate a measure of analogical similarity between object(s), on the one hand, and models and theories, on the other. There is an intricate interaction between (1) models in the mind, (2) the socio-cultural models and theories in the intersubjective world of knowledge, and (3) the entities, functions, relations, and structures in the world that they (re)present to us.

Beginning with mental models, these are the stuff that cognitive psychology is made of, in that they are typically seen as psychological representations of real, hypothetical, or imaginary situations. Salient mental models include those of selfhood and personhood. The notion 'mental model' was introduced by psychologist Kenneth Craik in 1943, as 'small-scale models' of reality constructed in working memory and used in reasoning, in explanation, and to anticipate events—in perception, in imagination, and in discourse. An essential characteristic is that they correspond to what they represent, and are in that sense 'image-like' or iconic. A further development in theory arrived in the 1970s with 'ideal cognitive models' (Rosch and Lloyd 1978), which are prototypes in a cognitive sense, as when we cognitively distinguish between, say, birds and fruits, where a sparrow is more 'typically' a bird than a penguin, and an orange is more typically a fruit than a melon (as experimental evidence demonstrates). 'Template' is a term sometimes used for model, as when we 'intuitively' seem to know how various species of animals are composed: four legs, heart, and blood, etc. Some of our models of the world's furniture we seem to have intuitively. Whether the models are psychologically 'given' through our evolved capacities or more consciously constructed it is an important point that models come with certain affordances ('what they are good for') as well as with constraints and limits. We are born with some intuitions about things in the world, but, most things we need to learn about. Then, when we apply models (mental or cultural), we experience their 'usability', how well they perform their job.

Turning to cultural models, this is a field that has attracted interest among anthropologists because of the frequent conflict between the scientific models of the analyst and the folk models utilized by the 'natives' (Quinn and Holland 1987). Whatever kind of model may be applied, all models, scientific as well as local folk models, are all (1) social facts and (2) 'cultural posits', as they were termed by the philosopher William van Orman Quine (1953: 44). Any model, however local, exotic, or strange, shares with even the most stringent scientific model the feature of being made by humans in some system of description that belongs to a given tradition. When it comes to a comparison, current scientific models are (hopefully) more theoretically adequate and more philosophically justified. Models in the natural sciences may be abstract, descriptive, predictive, or causal; but they are all made by humans, as are maps in general—'map is not territory'. So, even the strictest of scientific procedures are involved in some degree of 'making up' things. However accurate the model may appear to us now, it will probably be supplanted by something else in the future. The 'exact sciences' are only as exact as we can make them for the time being. That, however, does not mean that models (of whatever kind) are made and used according to taste—models in the exact sciences are rigorously and continuously tested, verified or falsified, modified or rejected. Medical diagnoses are a case in point; medical history as well as medical anthropology confirms this (e.g. Kamppinen 1989).

In the human and social sciences something more is at stake, because the models employed are 'isomorphic' with (of the same nature as) the stuff they 'represent'. This argument is grounded in the nature of human intentionality and the linguistic nature of our shared knowledge. We study society and culture with the same tools as we make society and culture: intentionality, language, conventions, reflexivity, and criticism. The strange achievement is that we are able to make human constructions so that they seem to be as natural and compelling as the facts of the physical world. The ontology of the social world has been dealt with by scholars in the humanities, social scientists, and philosophers. There is reason to refer explicitly to John Searle for an account of the construction and nature of social and institutional reality (1999: 122 ff.). The idea that humans construct their social, cultural, religious (etc.) worlds is not new; but when considered in relation to models, this recognition has some interesting consequences. A catalogue of the possible properties of models may again resemble one of concepts. Thus, we can ask whether models are primarily metaphoric: that is, are they stories 'about' something? Or are they metonymic, in the sense that there is a similarity between them and their reference? Are the models based on resemblances made, or are there inherent or essential qualities and identities that relate models and their references? In brief, are models, or any one specific model, a nominalist conventional construction, or is it a real ontological feature of the world? Again, is a model a cognitive image (representation), or is it more of a cultural narrative? Are models descriptive in relation to their object, or are they constructive?

Models Descriptive and Performative

It is the hypothesis here that models can be seen as analogous to sentences or propositions in the sense that they fall in two main classes that are well known from the history of philosophy: analytic sentences and synthetic sentences. The first are true by their own definition—for example, 'Bachelors are unmarried males'—and the second may or may not be true according to the state of the world—'Bachelors are untidy' or 'Bachelors have more fun'. The same seems to hold for models—at least in the study of such social affairs as religion. Consider this example (borrowed from Mircea Eliade) of an analytic statement: '"Axis mundi" is the centre of a religious world.' Now the statement also creates some kind of knowledge, and this demonstrates the performativity of conceptual models. Another way of explaining some of the properties of models is to equate their status with that of 'speech acts'. Speech act theory concerns the role of language in relation to action. When I say 'I promise', I not only say it, but I also make a promise; and so it is with many other propositions, as, for example, when a priest pronounces two persons 'husband and wife', and then they *are* a married couple, because it is a wedding ceremony. Thus, there is action in the locution, and the term 'illocutionary' is used to identify such propositions. The interesting aspect is that such propositions cannot simply be said to be true or false; they must be judged in terms of what is called their 'felicity conditions': they must be used by the right person, in the right circumstances, etc. (as in the example of the wedding) for the outcome of the illocutionary action to be 'felicitous'. Similarly, I suggest that we judge conceptual models by their applicability: that is, their 'felicity conditions'. Sometimes it makes good sense to use the 'axis mundi' model, at other times not. The conceptual models of sacrifice or wedding ceremonies exhibit similar characteristics. You cannot judge them by their fit with the world; rather, it is the other way round: whether things in the world actually fit the model—for example, are the entities and their features such that what goes on 'qualifies' as a sacrifice? An analytic model is true in virtue of being defined the way it is. Thus, an interesting point about analytic models is that they (being tautological like theories) are illocutionary, in that they create what they name.

Now, other models are obviously of a more synthetic kind, and their value *can* be judged by their correspondence with the states of affairs in the world. An example from the cognitive study of religion might be the model of mind–brain modularity, because the model is tied to the hypothesis that the mind is composed of modules with specific cognitive functions. Although there is not yet unanimous agreement on this, there is no doubt that the model can (somewhere down the line) be subjected to empirical testing. The falsifiability of the model hinges on sophisticated neuro investigations, and time will tell whether the hypothesis inherent in the model will be validated.

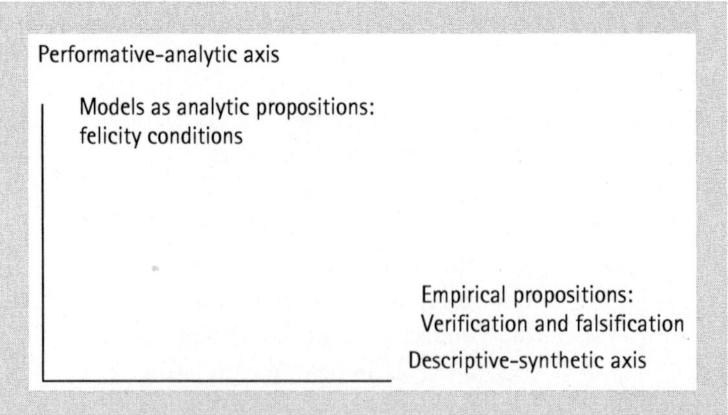

Fig. 13.1. Truth or felicily.

The nature and function of models are illustrated in Figure 13.1. Some models can be considered entirely analytic and performative, to be judged solely on their felicity conditions, while others take on the character of empirical propositions to be verified or falsified. However, a substantial number of models will fall in various places in the quadrant between the performative, analytic axis and the descriptive, synthetic axis, because they are what we may term 'composite models'. The diagram is no arbiter of truth but a means of conceptualizing the relations between the different aspects of the work of models.

Typological Reflections

The philosopher Peter Caws has put forward a functional typology and classification of models into a threefold division, which he has termed 'representational', 'operational', and 'explanatory'. As for the first two, 'the representational model corresponds to the way the individual thinks things are, the operational model to the way he practically responds or acts' (1997: 224). The third, the 'explanatory model', is to be found in the scholars' or scientists' mind and work (1997: 226). Caws's typology and classification has been used by some anthropologists (see also his model 1997: 228).[4] In an elaboration on Caws's model (Fig. 13.2), I have added another triadic set of parameters, so that we get a grid that also refers to three different levels, the 'mental', 'socio-cultural', and 'analytic':

An explanatory note: the 'mental' level indicates that the models are to be found in individual minds; the 'socio-cultural' level covers shared, publicly accessible and available models; and 'analytic' refers to the models consciously created and employed in research. The critical exercise is to take a model and plot it into the grid. A mental representational model has very different properties and functions

Levels:	mental	socio-cultural	analytic
Models:			
representational			
operational			
explanatory			

Fig. 13.2. A typology of models and levels.

[4] Caws (1997: 220–30) also discusses Lévi-Strauss's notion of models.

from, say, an operational socio-cultural one. Consequently, the grid allows us to spot errors or confusions between types of models and their respective level of reference: that is, what they are about or refer to.

The Narrative Nature of Models

An underestimated aspect of models (briefly noted above) is that they are stories about something less known by way or means of the more well known; that is, they are like parables. When Clifford Geertz presented his complex definition of religion in 1966, he stressed his distinction between models 'of' and 'for': descriptive models of the world tell us what it is (relative to our interpretation), and normative models for the world tell us about how it should be (relative to our philosophy, religion, ideology, etc.). These models depend on there being stories to be told; for they would not function if they could not be presented in narrative format. Later, in 1996, Mark Turner introduced the notion of the 'Literary mind'—an image of our mental world in which the story-telling and parable-making capacities of humans occupy centre stage: it is through our ability to make stories that we are able to imagine and understand. When we apply and unfold the workings of models in our materials, we seem doomed to do so in the form of stories. Make a simple experiment, and tell the story of what a ritual, for instance, does—soon the story will unfold with something that resembles subjects, actions, objects, projects, intentions, etc. No wonder that we as humans tend both to anthropomorphize the non-human and essentialize the abstract. Perhaps we simply cannot understand anything unless we make a story of it? This assumption might overstate the point, but there is definitely something to it, for it is evident from the literature that each and every book on 'something', say sacrifice (again), contains lengthy expositions, stories, about the doings, not only of humans, but also of the models that transform the events recorded into meaningful human actions.

Cognitive and cultural models are related and depend on each other in human behaviour—which includes mental operations such as explaining and understanding. It is not even clear that they are simply to be seen as inside and outside the individual. Cognitive models emanate from minds, and enter the world as ideas, symbols, words, stories, images, etc.—in fact, anything that the human brain produces (including religion). On the other hand, cultural models are internalized by minds as programmes for actions and models of and for the world. They come in formats akin to stories, and very often in bits and pieces, in scripts and frames. Cultural models are fundamental to social life; they format and reproduce the conventions of a given society, and they are the 'bricks' that social institutions are built of, whether they concern such issues as politics, morals, economics, marriage, education, dress, food, and proprieties in general. Cultural models override or overrule cognition and emotion, and govern the ways in which we behave. History tells us that these things change, albeit sometimes slowly and unconsciously.

Makers of models (cognitive or cultural) are creative, and were it not for interpersonal constraints on imagination and invention, individual model making could go in all directions. The invention of religious traditions is a case in point, but also shows that for this to succeed, there must be forces of 'intention converging'. This is also the case when religious reformers make substantial use of former traditional material. Even the most radical reformer must make use of the materials provided by the tradition to be reformed. Cultures and societies have certain stocks of 'templates', and 'schemata' as form patterns for making copies, for comparisons with others and as the bases for change. Models stabilize representations in cultures and societies. Models come in all formats and materials, from material and mechanical to the purely imaginary and even counterintuitive; but they are necessary in order to transmit information of all kinds, from myths to scientific theories. Models function as 'attractors'; that is, when we receive information, we attempt to decode it in accordance with the models we have.

Models and Normativity

Conceptual models and ideal types are tied to our ideas about things. The word 'ideal' always has a normative component, as the models are inevitably judged against their utility; but the 'ideal' does not imply that things ought to be as the models indicate. That is, however, a human default assumption, as we tend to want 'reality' or 'data' to correspond with the ideals we already have, for models and ideal types are made by humans, and they bear the imprint of human construction. The construction of human social worlds—that is, the construction of social facts—depends on the unique human cognitive ability to let some things 'count as' other things: symbols stand for power, some green paper slips count as money, a wedding indicates that one is married, etc. (Searle 1999). Now, what 'counts as' what will always be a normative judgement; but only rigid positivists need worry about that, for the rest of us this is just as good as it gets. But this also means that models are flexible and open-ended (cf. 'sacrifice' above). The threat of strong relativism seems apparent here, but there are (of course) constraints on what can count as probable and reasonable, because there are constraints either by convention or by resistance from the materials to which models refer. Poetry is also constrained—by convention and intelligibility—but scientific models are even more constrained, partly by the world and partly by our cognitive capacities. 'Idealized cognitive models' are apparently just 'normal' operations of the human physiological mental mechanisms; but they are in a sense also normative, because some features of the world are more attention attracting and salient—we do not perceive the world in a flat two-dimensional representation devoid of interest. Even at the level of our evolved capacities, there are degrees of involvement and interest.

With the construction and use of models, we enter the arena of ideological fabrication, for the social world of knowledge is made of models, so there is no way we can dismiss them or disregard their necessity. Almost anything in the world may be used for good or for bad. As with so many other things, models should be used responsibly, reflexively, and with a measure of common sense and rationality (Jensen 2003). For the sociology of religion, this means that long (sometimes even tedious) debates about the validity of say, Max Weber's ideas about ideal types or similar model distinctions could be treated more easily and applied more flexibly. Ideal types are models, as are most other of the concepts that we employ; and as such, they exist primarily in the scholar's universes. Models are the tools that both participants and scholars use to make sense of the affairs of the world (cf. Figs. 13.1 and 13.2 above), and the 'models' (and concepts) we use in sociological research thus belong to *our* cognitive apparatus. They are not features of the material world 'as such'; they are themselves the products of social acts, part and parcel of our social construction of the world(s) as we best happen to know them for the time being. And that only makes them so much more interesting sociologically.

References

Arbib, Michael, and Hesse, Mary B. (1986). *The Construction of Reality.* Cambridge: Cambridge University Press.

Bailer-Jones, Daniela M. (2002). 'Scientists' Thoughts on Scientific Models'. *Perspectives on Science,* 10/3: 275–301.

Blackburn, Simon (1996). Article in *Oxford Dictionary of Philosophy.* Oxford: Oxford University Press, 246–7.

Bourdieu, Pierre (1990). *The Logic of Practice.* Cambridge: Polity Press.

Cartwright, Nancy (1999). *The Dappled World: A Study of the Boundaries of Science.* Cambridge: Cambridge University Press.

Caws, Peter (1997). *Structuralism: A Philosophy for the Human Sciences.* Atlantic Highlands, NJ: Humanities Press.

Clark, Andy (2001). *Being There: Putting Brain, Body, and World Together Again.* Cambridge, Mass.: MIT Press.

Cooper, Richard P. (2002). *Modelling High-Level Cognitive Processes.* Mahwah, NJ, and London: Lawrence Erlbaum Associates, Publishers.

Craik, K. J. W. (1943). *The Nature of Explanation*. Cambridge: Cambridge University Press.

Devitt, Michael (1996). *Coming to Our Senses: A Naturalistic Program for Semantic Localism*. Cambridge: Cambridge University Press.

Fauconnier, Gilles (1997). *Mappings in Thought and Language*. Cambridge: Cambridge University Press.

Garnham, Alan (1987). *Mental Models as Representations of Discourse and Text*. Chichester: Elis Horwood Ltd.

Geertz, Clifford (1966). 'Religion as a Cultural System'. In M. Banton (ed.), *Anthropological Approaches to the Study of Religion*. London: Tavistock, 1–46.

Giere, Ronald (1988). *Explaining Science: A Cognitive Approach*. Chicago: University of Chicago Press.

Girard, René (1977). *Violence and the Sacred*. Baltimore: Johns Hopkins University Press.

Hubert, Henri, and Mauss, Marcel (1964). *Sacrifice: Its Nature and Function*. Chicago: University of Chicago Press.

Jensen, Jeppe Sinding (2003). *The Study of Religion in a New Key: Theoretical and Philosophical Soundings in the Comparative and General Study of Religion*. Aarhus: Aarhus University Press.

—— and Martin, Luther H. (eds.) (2003). *Rationality and the Study of Religion*. London: Routledge.

Johnson-Laird, P. N. (1983). *Mental Models: Towards a Cognitive Science of Language, Inference and Consciousness*. Cambridge: Cambridge University Press.

Kamppinen, Matti (1989). *Cognitive Systems and Cultural Models of Illness*. FF Communications no. 244. Helsinki: Academia Scientiarum Fennica. 1989.

Lakoff, George, and Johnson, Mark (1987). *Metaphors We Live By*. Chicago: University of Chicago Press.

Laschyk, Eugene (1986). 'Heuristics for Scientific and Literary Creativity: The Role of Models, Analogies, and Metaphors'. In J. Margolis, M. Krausz, and R. M. Burian (eds.), *Rationality, Relativism and the Human Sciences*. Dordrecht: Martinus Nijhoff Publishers, 151–85).

Leach, Edmund (1976). *Culture and Communication: The Logic by which Symbols are Connected*. Cambridge: Cambridge University Press.

Magnani, Lorenzo, Nersessian, Nancy, and Thagard, Paul (eds.) (1999). *Model-Based Reasoning in Scientific Discovery*. New York: Kluwer Academic/Plenum Publishers.

Mauss, Marcel (1967). *The Gift: Forms and Functions of Exchange in Archaic Societies*. New York: W. W. Norton.

McDowell, John (1996). *Mind and World*. Cambridge, Mass.: Harvard University Press.

Morgan, Mary S., and Morrison, Margaret (eds.) (1999). *Models as Mediators: Perspectives on Natural and Social Science*. Cambridge: Cambridge University Press.

Oakhill, Jane, and Garnham, Alan (eds.) (1996). *Mental Models in Cognitive Science: Essays in Honour of Phil Johnson-Laird*. Hove: Psychology Press.

Poole, John Fitz Porter (1986). 'Metaphors and Maps: Towards Comparison in the Anthropology of Religion'. *Journal of the American Academy of Religion*, 54/3: 411–57.

Putnam, Hilary (1995). *Words & Life*. Cambridge, Mass.: Harvard University Press.

Quine, W. V. O. (1953). *From a Logical Point of View*. Cambridge, Mass.: Harvard University Press.

Quinn, Naomi, and Holland, Dorothy (eds.) (1987). *Cultural Models in Language and Thought*. Cambridge: Cambridge University Press.

Rosch, Eleanor, and Lloyd, Barbara B. (eds.) (1978). *Cognition and Categorization.* Hillsdale, NJ: Lawrence Erlbaum.

Ruttkamp, Emma (2002). *A Model-Theoretic Realist Interpretation of Science.* Dordrecht: Kluwer Academic Publishers.

Searle, John R. (1999). *Mind, Language and Society: Philosophy in the Real World.* London: Phoenix.

Smith, Jonathan Z. (1982). 'In Comparison a Magic Dwells'. In *Imagining Religion: From Babylon to Jonestown.* Chicago: University of Chicago Press, 19–35.

Tallis, Raymond (1999). *On the Edge of Certainty.* London: Macmillan.

Tambiah, Stanley J. (1990). *Magic, Science, Religion, and the Scope of Rationality.* Cambridge: Cambridge University Press.

Turner, Mark (1996). *The Literary Mind.* New York: Oxford University Press.

Suggested Reading

The following are recommended: Arbib and Hesse (1986); Cartwright (1999); Holland and Quinn (1987); Jensen (2003); Johnson-Laird (1983); Morgan and Morrison (1999); Oakhill and Garnham (1996); and Quinn and Holland (1987).

CHAPTER 14

DEFINING RELIGION

A SOCIAL SCIENCE APPROACH

ANDRÉ DROOGERS

> Definitions of religion, in a sense, remind one of the fable of the blind men attempting to define an elephant. One touches its trunk and describes it as a snake; another touches its ear and describes it as a winnowing-fan; another touches its leg and describes it as a tree; another its tail and describes it as a broom.
>
> (Sharpe 1983: 46)

Introduction: Drawing the Map

In the social sciences of religion the task of defining religion can be characterized as a necessary, exploratory, and useful task, but also as a superfluous, impossible, and ethnocentric activity. In this chapter the landscape is mapped through which definers of religion travel, including its T-junctions and crossroads. Mapping is discussed in two ways: first, focusing on some of the results that are put forward by the cartographers of religion, especially their definitions of the field as a map for others to orientate themselves by; but second, and a bit more distant, also discussing the art of cartography, making an inventory of the varied ways in which to present and represent the religious landscape in the form of a definition.

At both levels, much depends on the specific focus chosen, the questions that are raised, and the characteristics that are selected. Introductory books on the social sciences' approach to religion nearly always carry a first or second chapter or section on the question of the definition of religion (e.g., Aldridge 2007: 17–41; Bowie 2006: 18–22; Budd 1973: 5–11; Child and Child 1993: 2–4; Hargrove 1979: 3–13; Klass 1995: 17–24; Pandian 1991: 9–13; Wulff, 1991: 3–5). The topic has also led to a few special volumes (e.g. Clarke and Byrne 1993; Platvoet and Molendijk 1999).

To bring some order into the complex variety of views on defining religion, I follow Guba (1990: 18), who distinguishes three dimensions in any scientific activity. Tried and tested as this classic subdivision is, it should help us to cover and uncover, as completely as is possible in this short chapter, the various aspects of defining religion.

- The first dimension regards the *ontological* aspects of defining religion: 'What can be said about the nature of religion?' This is the heart of the matter. What are the parameters for deciding on the nature of religion?
- The second dimension is *epistemological*, and the corresponding question is: 'What is the relation of the definer with religion as the phenomenon to be defined?' This question regards questions of distance and closeness, observation and participation, objectivity and subjectivity.
- The third dimension is *methodological* in nature, regarding the way in which the definer should technically proceed when defining religion. It concerns what a definition is meant to do, and how the elements that are exclusively religious are selected.

In describing the three dimensions, both the maps and the cartographers must be considered. As will immediately be evident, the three dimensions cannot be viewed in strict isolation, because they influence each other, and in fact form a triangle. The definer's views on religion cannot be separated from the way in which religion is represented and from the form the definition is given. Even those who refuse to define religion position themselves within the parameters of these three dimensions.

In the final section the picture that appears when the three dimensions are considered is summarized. The net result of the efforts to define religion will reveal an impasse that tells us more about the definers as blind men around the elephant than about religion. I will suggest that if religion is a construct, the constructors should be viewed as part of the phenomenon, and therefore also of the definition.

The Ontology of Defining Religion: What Can Be Said about the Nature of Religion?

Defining religion is nothing less than telling, as precisely and completely as possible, what the nature of religion is and was, at all times and in all places. In technical terms: A set of definientia must be selected to define the definiendum, in this case religion. A definiens is the typical characteristic that is included in the definition of a particular class of identical—or at least similar—phenomena. The presupposition is that the term, in whatever way defined, refers to a part of universal human reality that is bounded, and as such can be distinguished from other spheres. It can be categorized, thus being separated from other sectors of reality—that are in turn defined regarding their essential nature. Often this type of categorization works with contrasts and dichotomies. Thus the opposite of the religious is the secular or the profane, but science also appears as the counter term.

In view of the latter opposition, the fruity detail in the case of religion is that the scientific activity of defining is not done just from an objective outsider's position, as the positivist tradition of science wants it, but that as a consequence of the dichotomist way of thinking, science is part of the secular reality that is the opposite of religion. Defining religion therefore resembles the type of situation in which two opposing parties seek the intervention of an objective judge, unaware of the fact that one of the two parties is disguised as that judge. The result is that religion is said to refer to a reality that from an empirical perspective—that is, in the way science produces correct knowledge—is denied existence. Thus Van Baal and Van Beek (1985: 3) emphasize this non-empirical nature of religious knowledge when they define religion as 'all explicit and implicit notions and ideas, accepted as true, which relate to a reality which cannot be verified empirically'. Another example is Robertson's inclusion of an acknowledgement of the empirical/super-empirical dimension in his definitions of religious culture and religious action (Robertson 1970: 47).

In compensation, the objective attitude of the scholar can of course inspire an impartial rendering of the religious, formulated in a definition that could even be acceptable to believers, abstaining from a scientific judgement on these believers' convictions and experiences. The reference to their experience of the sacred could act as a substitute for a direct reference to the sacred itself, although even in that case there would be a difficulty of fully understanding that experience. It would demand that the researcher succeed in sharing adequately what the believers experience. Though the sacred reality cannot be shown to have an empirical basis, the believers' praxis can at least be observed empirically and described accordingly—for example, showing the social or psychological functions of their belief. A definition of religion that does not pass judgement on the degree of reality of the sacred then becomes possible. The basic question is to what degree scholars are able to define the nature of religion without including a scientific critique of religious views, let alone without a reference to the sacred. In other words: how to define religion in a scientific way if one of the elements that is a candidate for inclusion in a definition is not considered real and is for that reason consciously left out of the definition.

To complicate things, there is a problem with the term 'reality' that is not limited to religion or the sacred reality that believers claim to experience and that science denies. The constructivist and postmodern waves have inculcated the neat impression that what once had been called solid reality, legitimated by positivist science's authority, has melted into thin air—to use Berman's interpretation of a phrase taken from 'The Communist Manifesto' by Marx and Engels (Berman 1982). If reality consists of constructs that can easily evaporate, apparently more relevant but equally temporal newcomers will substitute for these. Therefore reality is no longer what it used to be. The ultimate consequence of this rather extreme and cynical position is that any definition goes—so none goes. One result of the debate, however, is that the term 'reality' has come to be viewed with more care, and so has the art of defining. With regard to the scientific critique of religion, the ironic effect is that not only religious reality can be denied existence, but that the same fate also befalls the realities formerly grounded by positivist science. Thus reality is not 'by definition' knowable. An interesting consequence of this trend has been that the distance between scholar and her or his object of study has shortened, and that so-called objectivity has come under severe criticism. Once reality becomes fragmented into realities that 'exist in the form of multiple mental constructions, socially and experientially based, local and specific, dependent for their form and content on the persons who hold them' (Guba 1990: 27), the very process of discovering the nature of this object and expressing it in trustworthy knowledge, such as in a definition, has become an issue for debate. The scholar is drawn into the field, and the believer as an object becomes a subject in the construction of knowledge.

So in terms of ontology the problem that religion presented, especially to hard-core positivist scholars, was deepened after the positivist rock became subject to erosion. Depending on the paradigm that is adopted with regard to the mission of science, the nature of the knowable will vary. The possibility of producing a definition that survives times and fashions has met with scepticism. Even when a correct definition is considered viable, the definer of religion will have to face the question of whether to engage in the debate about the foundations of the religious knowledge. In sum: the difficulty of establishing the nature of religious reality was aggravated once reality and realities lost their absolute character. Absolute believers in either religious or scientific truths have ultimately met the same fate.

From what has been observed so far, it is obvious that one cannot discuss the nature of the knowable without touching on epistemological and methodological questions. The basic ideas presented in this section will therefore be elaborated in the following sections.

The Epistemology of Defining Religion: What is the Relation of the Definer with Religion as the Phenomenon needing Definition?

From the previous section it has become clear that the definer's position, whether distant or to some degree involved, is of importance. The involvement could include a critical attitude, just as it may imply sympathy. Marx's famous characterization of religion is an example of the critical representation of religion, emphasizing a function it is thought to have in the class struggle: 'Religion is the sigh of the oppressed creature, the heart of a heartless world, and the soul of soulless conditions. It is the opium of the people' (Marx 1844). Moreover, as we saw, the definer's view of the mission of science will influence form and content of the definition. It may even lead to the conclusion that to define is an impossible task, a way of proposing essential labels that sooner or later prove to be arbitrary characterizations or even illusions.

Despite these obstacles, scholars have consciously faced up to the difficulties of definition and made an effort to come to terms with them. They were motivated by the need for some agreement among scholars in the same field regarding the boundaries of that field. Without some form of consensus, normal academic activities in terms of publications, journals, professorial chairs, conferences, etc. could not be organized. The sociology of academia points to the need to agree, with a bit more consensus than the minimum of agreeing to disagree. One way to do this is to make an inventory of the possible positions that can be distinguished in the debate.

Berger (1967) suggested one such typology of positions. The three positions carry the adjective 'methodological', suggesting that they are concerned with the professional attitude, and not the scholar's private position. Thus methodological theism, atheism, and agnosticism are distinguished. In the first position the scholar accepts the religious truth as an essential element in scholarly discourse. The second position rejects such a way of including religious truth in the scientific study and—more particularly—explanation of religion. The agnostic position is characterized by neutrality with regard to the matter of religious truth. Concerning the definition of religion the three positions may result in striking differences. Even though these three methodological attitudes have not necessarily resulted in representative definitions, the typology can be extended to the defining of religion. Definitions of a methodological theist type include a reference to a revealed divine truth. Methodological atheist definitions do not include such a reference, unless to deny such a truth. Instead there is a view of religion and the religious that possibly includes a reference to the functions that religion may have and as a consequence to the secular elements in the social and personal order to which it may be reduced. The third type certainly does not include a truth claim; neither does it refer to a denial. Possibly the uncertain nature of the sacred will be mentioned.

Another way of distinguishing between types of definitions is by reference to the different disciplines that engage in the study of religion (see Clarke and Byrne 1993: part II). Within the social sciences the disciplinary background of the scholar will influence his or her way of defining religion. The division of labour within the social sciences results in differences in focus, each discipline having its own emphasis on a particular aspect of religion. This will reflect on the definitions that are produced within a discipline. An example is the difference in approach in the sociology of religion and the anthropology of religion. Whereas sociologists will probably look for the social dimension of religion, characterizing religion by the way it is organized and practised, anthropologists tend to draw attention to religion as a cultural phenomenon, and to a certain degree connected with other aspects of culture such as politics, economics, and of course the social. Thus Geertz's well-known article on the definition of religion is entitled 'Religion as a Cultural System' (Geertz 1966). If we add the disciplines outside the social sciences that study religion, more diversity appears. Thus, the science of religion, religious studies, history of religions, phenomenology of religion, all have their own brand of studying religion and will accordingly produce their own definitions. Interdisciplinary contacts may have a cumulative effect, in that elements from different disciplines are brought together in the task of defining religion. And where theology is viewed as another discipline that studies religion, even more elements may be included, probably of a methodologically theist kind.

When theoretical approaches are added to this constellation of disciplines that study religion, more diversity in defining religion appears (cf. Clarke and Byrne 1993: part II; Cunningham 1999; Morris 1987; Thrower 1999). Though a particular theoretical perspective may dominate a discipline, theoretical trends usually work across boundaries, often being applied in an interdisciplinary manner. Some form of functionalist paradigm may be applied in a variety of disciplines. Functionalism is a way of avoiding references to the sacred, focusing instead on the use that religion may have. More concretely, religion may be characterized by its contribution to order in society, or in the believer's psyche. Even the Marxist view of religion as opium of the people is of a functionalist nature. Another example of a theoretically inspired definition comes from rational choice theory, also applied in more than one discipline (see Chapter 6 above). The believer, as a rational agent, is put at the centre, and this influences the way in which religion is understood and defined:

'Religion consists of very general explanations of existence, including the terms of exchange with a god or gods' (Stark and Finke 2000: 91). Within this approach magic is even closer to the heart of the believer, and is accordingly distinguished from religion: 'Magic refers to all efforts to manipulate supernatural forces to gain rewards (or avoid costs) without reference to a god or gods or to general explanations of existence' (Stark and Finke 2000: 105).

Evidently disciplines and theories change in the course of time, and therefore every era will produce its particular definitions of religion. These will reflect what was considered normal and accepted at the time. Thus nineteenth-century definitions may have evolutionist undertones. These are part of modernization, the process that at a later stage led to the secularization thesis. Religion was supposed to disappear under the influence of modernizing influences. If modernization is defined as the ever increasing dominance of the influence of science and technology on the organization and outlook of society, the contrast between religious and secular, as referred to above, can be seen as a spin off of that process. Consequently, the debate on the secularization thesis has relevance for the social sciences' definition of religion and may influence that definition (see Chapter 33 below).

This is most clearly visible in the distinction between substantive and functional definitions (Berger 1967; Beyer 2003: 422; Hamilton 2001: 14–20; McGuire 1992: 10–15; Robertson 1970: 34–42; Yinger 1970: 4, 5). Whereas substantive definitions contain a reference to the sacred, a functional definition moves the focus to the uses that religion can be put to, consciously or unconsciously. A substantive definition informs us of what the sacred is, a functional one of what religion does. Tylor's classical definition of religion (1871) as 'the belief in Spiritual Beings' (Tylor 1958: i. 8) is of the substantive type. Geertz's much quoted definition is functionalist, religion being a provider of meaningful order. Religion, he states, is

> a system of symbols which acts to establish powerful, pervasive, and long-lasting moods and motivations in men by formulating conceptions of a general order of existence and clothing these conceptions with such an aura of factuality that the moods and motivations seem uniquely realistic. (Geertz 1966: 4)

Durkheim's famous definition combines both elements:

> A religion is a unified system of beliefs and practices relative to sacred things, that is to say, things set apart and forbidden—beliefs and practices which unite into one single moral community called a Church, all those who adhere to them. (Durkheim 1976: 47)

Depending on the definition of secularization that is used (cf. Casanova 1994: 211), especially when combined with either a substantive or a functional definition of religion, the verdict on the future of religion varies. Where secularization is thought to refer to the erosion of notions of the sacred, from the perspective of a substantive definition, it is much more present than when a functional view of secularization is combined with a functional definition of religion. This latter perspective allows for the label 'religion' to be used of such phenomena as ideology, psychology, music, or even soccer, which, while they do not refer to the sacred, serve similar functions. Of course, the secularization thesis has recently been criticized even by some of its authors (e.g. Berger 2002). Though de-churching has occurred, religiosity is still very much present. In the secularization debate, those defending the thesis that modernization will lead to the erosion and disappearance of religion will, by logical necessity, use a substantive definition; whereas those who criticize the thesis will speak of a transformation of religion, defining it in a functional way, and pointing to continuity instead of rupture.

One way out of this impasse is to change definitions, as Heelas and Woodhead (2005) have proposed. They introduce a distinction between religion and spirituality, religion being associated with behaviour that is steered by an external authority and modelled as 'life-as'—that is, living a particular social role—while in the case of spirituality the authority stems from the authenticity of what the authors call 'subjective-life': 'life lived in deep connection with the unique experiences of my self-in-relation'. In both, the social dimension is present, but the source of the authority differs. With regard to the secularization debate, the reference to an external authority points to a substantive definition of religion. Although the new form is no longer labelled religion, but spirituality, the attractive side of this way of looking at religious change is that it allows for some form of continuity while at the same time acknowledging changes in the religious field. These authors predict a spiritual revolution within the next half-century, religion being substituted by spirituality. This is the 'subjective turn', responsible for both secularization (the erosion of substantive religion) and sacralization (the transformation of religion into 'subjective-life' spirituality).

The Methodology of Defining Religion: How Should the Definer Proceed when Defining Religion?

The art of defining is the concern of all scientific activity. Accordingly, expertise has been developed regarding the methodology of defining. One important issue is the use that is to be made of a definition. Examples of the functions of a definition are:

- It helps to categorize reality, distinguishing between phenomena: for example, those that are religious and those that belong to the secular domain.
- Definitions may also deepen insight into the essence of a phenomenon, expressing its most characteristic elements or processes.

- A definition also helps us discover some form of order in a particular domain by identifying phenomena with similar characteristics—for example, making it possible to speak of 'world religions', presupposing common elements despite the immense diversity. Weber (1966: 1) was critical of developing a definition of religion as long as not all religions had been studied sufficiently (cf. Aldridge 2007: 30–1; Robertson 1970: 34–5). To him a definition of religion comes at the end, not at the beginning. This raises the question of how the phenomena that need to be studied are to be selected if there is not already some idea of what religion is.
- In organizing academic work, a definition helps to circumscribe the field of study and its boundaries, marking off one academic territory from an other and giving a discipline its identity and some degree of consensus.
- Defining is also necessary when a phenomenon is to be measured, either in a descriptive sense (such as religious affiliation in a census) or in an explanatory sense, looking for hypothetical causal relations (e.g. the more educated are less religious). Any testing of hypotheses presupposes a way of measuring the variables involved—which therefore must be defined to become operational concepts. But also in qualitative studies, when describing a concrete situation, definitions serve to avoid vague, 'indefinite' affirmations.
- As a tool, a definition creates some consensus on terms, allowing for scholarly discussion. In the secularization debate, for example, the exchange of ideas has been frustrated by the lack of consensus on the definition of religion, some using a substantive and others a functional definition. When those who defend the secularization thesis do not make explicit that they use a substantive definition of religion, while simultaneously their critics do not indicate that they are defining religion in a functional way, a Babel-like confusion results.

More functions could be added, but this short list suffices to transmit the basic idea. Just as in geography a road-map is different from a map of waterways or of footpaths, so there is much diversity in the definitions and functions of religions and other phenomena.

In all these applications of a definition the difficulty remains that it consists of words that may in turn be subject to definition. Synonyms may help to clarify, but they refer to each other, just as the words used in the lemmas of a dictionary need explanation in the same dictionary. Any term is '*sous rature*', as Derrida suggested, inadequate but necessary (Sarup 1988: 35). This means that the value of a definition is not as absolute as might be thought by those who put much effort in seeking the perfect definition.

The variety of definitions is also a reason not to reify them too much, as if the landscape is supposed to obey the map. The more a phenomenon, such as religion, exists as a construct for academic use, the greater the risk of such a reification occurring. When different definitions are given, the constructed nature of the concept is obvious. These definitions may vary not only because they serve different functions, but also because they choose different definientia. The more varied the religious reality is, even within one religion, the more the differences must be ignored in order to arrive at a class of phenomena that can be summarized in one definition. The consequence is that idiosyncratic elements are treated as if they were not there, and this is a good reason to be critical of any definition.

Here the difference between monothetic and polythetic definitions becomes relevant (Hamilton 2001: 20–3). In the case of monothetic definitions, the elements that are included are deemed to be both sufficient and necessary. In other words, all the exemplars of a class, e.g. religions or world religions, show all the characteristics that the definition stipulates. Since in practice the monothetic definition often proves to be over-exclusive, limiting not only the range of phenomena that belong to a class but also the number of defining characteristics, the polythetic definition offers a better alternative. In such a definition a rather large number of definientia is included that are neither necessary nor sufficient. In other words, not all the exemplars of the class need to have all the definientia. A polythetic definition is also known—drawing on Wittgenstein's insight—as a family resemblance definition: not all members of a family show all the typical characteristics that are thought to characterize that family (Aldridge 2007: 38–41). Polythetic definitions provide a list of possible traits (cf. Whaling 1986: 38; Smart 1992: 12–21). The value of the distinction between monothetic and polythetic definitions can be seen in relation to, for example, Buddhism and whether or not it can be termed a religion. If the definiens 'god' or 'gods' is included in the monothetic definition of religion, some forms of Buddhism would have to be excluded from the class 'religions'. If the definition is made polythetic, the problem is resolved. Monothetic and polythetic definitions differ in as far as the members of the class are either identical or similar. In the latter case, the variety remains visible, despite the use of a common definition.

The notion of 'ideal type' constructs, introduced in the social sciences by Weber, is comparable to the polythetic definition. Not all the characteristics of a member of a class will be included in the ideal type that describes this class. An ideal type contains a one-sided emphasis on certain characteristics. This accentuation serves analytical and classificatory purposes, especially in comparative studies, when a particularly striking aspect is uncovered. Weber's analysis of the Protestant ethic is an example. Like a definition, an ideal type helps to uncover the order and the processes that characterize a domain.

When discussing the methodology of defining religion, another theme is worth mentioning, and that is the way in which the definer moves from the particular to the general. Before formulating a definition, some form of general knowledge of the variety of religions and religious forms is presupposed. A certain degree of arbitrariness may then influence the overview one has of religious reality. An example would be a focus on world religions, neglecting so-called tribal religions. Or one might consider, consciously or not, only the official versions of a religion, without bringing popular forms into the frame.

Bias may also stem from the expert knowledge a scholar may have of a particular religion. The characteristics of that religion may be extrapolated to religion in general. The same may occur when a scholar is also an adept of a religion, and classifies other religions by the categories that are common in her or his own. A similar subjective influence may come from the scholar's cultural context and its religious constellation. Thus Fitzgerald suggests that religion is an ideological category influenced by Christian theism: 'the so-called study of religion... is a disguised form of liberal ecumenical theology' (2000: 6). McCutcheon (1997; 2001) is critical of the reification of religion that elevates it to a category *sui generis*: 'religious behaviors are ordinary social behaviors—and not extraordinary private experiences' (2001: 14–15). Asad (1993) also pointed to the influence of Christianity on the categories used in the study of religion. To him this ethnocentric perspective is a reason to abstain from a definition of religion. Taking Geertz's definition as an example, he shows how the Western Christian experience after the Reformation has led Geertz, despite looking at religion as a cultural system, to neglect the power dimension in the religious field, taking a differentiation of the political and religious aspects as normal. Looking for an essence in religion is a way of complying with this differentiation, and therefore of ignoring power. Accordingly,

> what the anthropologist is confronted with is not merely an arbitrary collection of elements and processes that we happen to call 'religion'. For the entire phenomenon is to be seen in large measure in the context of Christian attempts to achieve a coherence in doctrines and practices, rules and regulations, even if that was a state never fully attained. My argument is that there cannot be a universal definition of religion, not only because its constituent elements and relationships are historically specific, but because that definition is itself the historical product of discursive processes... a transhistorical definition of religion is not viable. (Asad 1993: 29–30)

In other words, in defining religion there is no Archimedean point. Unlike the Baron of Münchhausen, one cannot draw oneself from the marsh by pulling at one's hair.

New Pathways?

This overview of the ontological, epistemological, and methodological dimensions of defining religion must appear rather discouraging to those who would hope to find therein a precise and unambiguous definition that points clearly to a universally identifiable essence of religion and enables it to be seen as a common phenomenon despite all of its variations. By summarizing the main difficulties encountered in describing both the state of the cartography and the maps that it has produced, one might well lose one's way in the morass. To explore possible new pathways, one should face the difficulties that have emerged. So let us first summarize them.

When considering the ontological dimension, or what can be said about the nature of religion, we met several of the core problems. By treating religion as a form of knowledge that is the opposite of secular knowledge, and from a positivist perspective, the question arises as to whether it receives unbiased treatment. On the other hand, a constructivist approach that emphasizes the relative nature of all forms of knowledge is no guarantee of this either. Moreover, people's experience of the sacred is not easily accessible to the researcher. Is reality 'really' more than the labels people put on it, whether scientific or religious? The possible existence of an essence of religion becomes as doubtful as the idea of a god. A definition of religion is by definition of a very contested, and thereby arbitrary, nature.

Looking at the epistemological dimension—that is, exploring the relation of the definer with religion as the phenomenon to be defined—this relative character of a definition becomes even more obvious. The definer's attitude with regard to believers' truth claims makes for different types of definition. A limitation of the definientia to functional elements offers a short-term solution, but at the same time it makes religious reality much broader and thus more vague. The influence of the secularization debate on the way in which religion is redefined in a functional way also revealed the subjective nature of definitions, and how they are influenced by the debates of a particular epoch. The juxtaposition of different disciplines also reinforces the relative value of the definitions they propose. Some form of inter-disciplinary synthesis may bring improvement, but even this does not alter the limited nature of a definition.

The methodological dimension proved to be no more promising. Definitions depend on the function they are supposed to serve. Words are not really optimal tools in rendering the essence of religion. Reification is a real danger, a construct being blown up to a universal supra-historical phenomenon. One price paid for defining religion is the sacrificing of the rich variety of religious forms. A polythetic definition offers some benefits, but not a solution. The influence of both the dominant science paradigm and the Western Christian cultural context on the practice of defining religion makes the search for the perfect definition even more intractable.

Are we to conclude, then, that the pursuit of a definition is an enterprise doomed to fail? Did positivism put us on a track that ended in a marsh? Much energy appears to have been spent on an illusion.

If the perfect definition does not exist, then a pragmatic definition is possible. We might look for a practical procedure that at least fulfils the need to facilitate scholarly debate, one of the functions of definitions mentioned above. One such practical solution might be to continue discussing the concept of religion, but treat it with less ambition and take into consideration the pros and cons of the accumulative debate of which the preceding paragraphs offer a summary. Another option is to move according to the least contested, and therefore most minimal, map; but that does not help in improving the art of cartography. A third practical and rather eclectic solution would be to use substantive and functional definitions in alternation, showing what becomes visible—or remains invisible—in each case. This would show both the rupture and the continuity in the secularization process. A fourth practical option is to choose a definition that fits the concrete project that one is working on—in fact, a working definition that makes research possible and effective, especially when quantitative methods are being used.

Yet, beyond the practical way out, and instead of a continued debate about each other's definitions, scholars ought perhaps to consider the practice of defining itself. It is not just the maps that must be discussed, but also, and primarily, the place of cartography in our times. The conditions under which scholars execute and discuss such a task as the definition of religion must be included in the debate. It would be misleading to limit the perspective to the more or less technical problem of the definition itself. We need to look at our scholarly discussion as a product of a very particular, and even unique, period in human history, characterized by modernization. The debate tells us as much about ourselves as about the nature of religion—and for that matter of science. If we address the environment in which we work—for example, when seeking to define religion—the debate should first of all be situated in the current context of our globalized world. Second, the development of science and the variety of views on its mission should be included in the debate as well. Both are symptoms of modernization. Let us take a closer look at each of these two conditions.

The last two centuries have brought immense change to the world. In comparison to what the world looked like during the millions of years before these changes occurred, the dramatic character of this transformation can hardly be exaggerated. 'Globalization' is only the most recent label to be put on this process, to express the point that modernization affects every part of the planet. Other processes—such as colonialism, the media revolution, and mass migration—preceded globalization, preparing it and introducing a new view of the world. More than ever, the global perspective has brought other religions to the attention of scholars—and of the world's believers. What has come to be called religion is of course older than the modernization process. But the need for a label, and therewith for a definition, is a result of the current constellation. Having its roots in the centre of world power, Christianity has been the prime frame of reference when religion was discussed, also because the above-mentioned processes facilitated its worldwide expansion. Asad's analysis is relevant in this sense, also because he shows how views must be contextualized instead of being taken *per se* or at face value. Though globalization produces homogenization in certain respects, it also has shown difference and variety. Cultural anthropology is one of the disciplines that study this immense variation, just as sociology focuses on the changes that modernization has brought to society. Within this context religion has become a theme. When a definition is proposed, the intention is to discover what is common to all the different forms that have nowadays become so visible. Obviously the 9/11 event has added to the interest in this field, but long before that, religion was attracting attention. This was partly due to the second context mentioned, the development of science.

Science has contributed greatly to the disagreement on the definition of religion. The wish to produce unequivocal knowledge, as proposed by the positivist and natural sciences implementation of academic work, introduced the idea that it would be possible to formulate the final and perfect definition of religion, just as the natural sciences have their generally accepted definitions of units used for measurement. What may work in the laboratory is not necessarily applicable to human beings. The constructivist critique of this paradigm has made scholars more modest in their ambitions. Most of them have become aware of the limits of the production of academic knowledge. The vicissitudes of the definition of religion reflect this insight. The goal of finding the essence of a phenomenon such as religion has become less attractive and compelling. Essentialism has met with strong criticism. Scholars have to position themselves with regard to the mission of science and the identity of their discipline. The history of the search for a definition of religion teaches us as much about the academic enterprise as about religion. The contrast between science and religion, as stimulated by positivist science and to a lesser degree by constructivist science, has introduced an extra problem into the quest for a definition of religion. This is even more the case when the secularization debate is drawn into the discussion. Since Western Europe seemed to confirm the secularization thesis, the prospects for religion were evaluated in connection with the rise of a scientific world view.

The inevitable conclusion is that the definition of religion cannot be isolated from the position of the definer in the context of global society, the science paradigm, and the secularization debate. As Beckford (2003: 3) has put it: 'I seek to analyse the processes whereby the meaning of the category of religion is, in various situations, intuited, asserted, doubted, challenged, rejected, substituted, recast, and so on.' He concludes that '"religion" is a social and cultural construct with highly variable meaning' (2003: 5). To assess the characteristics of religion, one must include the perspective of the scholar. The definition of religion is hardly objective—an old positivist ideal—without an appraisal of the presuppositions and hidden options. What was kept implicit or considered irrelevant needs to be made explicit, showing how definers behave at the crossroads and T-junctions, and why they act as they do. This means that scholars should look not only at the object of study but also at their own role. This is the consequence of a constructivist insight that can be said to contribute to the goal that scholars be as objective as possible. Instead of locating themselves outside their field, students of religion should view themselves, if only for a short time of self-examination, as actors in that field. Research can then be understood as a form of serious play, as a way of using simultaneously two ways of classifying reality, just as believers have their realities they play with, often applying the same dichotomies that scholars use: individuality and participation, distance and closeness, inexpressibility and representation, variety and unity.

This is the ultimate consequence of viewing the concept of religion as a recent construct, a product of a world that has become one place, but also an outcome of the also recent opposition between religion and secular science. This one-field approach could be the expressed in the following definition:

Religion is the field of experiencing the sacred—a field in which both believers and scholars act, each category applying the human capacity for play, within the constraints of power mechanisms, to the articulation of basic human dichotomies, thus adding an extra dimension to their construction and view of reality. (Slightly adapted from Droogers 1999: 310)

References

ALDRIDGE, ALAN (2007). *Religion in the Contemporary World: A Sociological Introduction*, 2nd edn. Cambridge: Polity.

ASAD, TALAL (1993). *Genealogies of Religion: Discipline and Reasons of Power in Christianity and Islam.* Baltimore and London: Johns Hopkins University Press.

BECKFORD, JAMES A. (2003). *Social Theory and Religion.* Cambridge: Cambridge University Press.

BERGER, PETER L. (1967). *The Sacred Canopy: Elements of a Sociological Theory of Religion.* Garden City, NY: Doubleday.

—— (2002). 'Secularization and De-secularization'. In Linda Woodhead *et al.* (eds.), *Religions in the Modern World.* London and New York: Routledge, 291–8.

BERMAN, MARSHALL (1982). *All That is Solid Melts into Air: The Experience of Modernity.* New York: Penguin Books.

BEYER, PETER (2003). 'Contemporary Social Theory as it Applies to the Understanding of Religion in Cross-cultural Perspective'. In Richard K. Fenn (ed.), *The Blackwell Companion to Sociology of Religion.* Malden, Mass.: Blackwell, 418–31.

BOWIE, FIONA (2006). *The Anthropology of Religion: An Introduction.* Malden, Mass.: Blackwell.

BUDD, SUSAN (1973). *Sociologists and Religion.* London: Collier-Macmillan.

CASANOVA, JOSÉ (1994). *Public Religions in the Modern World.* Chicago and London: University of Chicago Press.

CHILD, ALICE B., and CHILD, IRVIN L. (1993). *Religion and Magic in the Life of Traditional Peoples.* Englewood Cliffs, NJ: Prentice-Hall.

CLARKE, PETER B., and BYRNE, PETER (1993). *Religion Defined and Explained.* London and New York: Collier-Macmillan and St Martin's Press.

CUNNINGHAM, GRAHAM (1999). *Religion and Magic: Approaches and Theories.* Edinburgh: Edinburgh University Press.

DROOGERS, ANDRÉ (1999). 'The Third Bank of the River: Play, Methodological Ludism and the Definition of Religion'. In Platvoet and Molendijk (1999), 285–312.

DURKHEIM, ÉMILE (1976). *The Elementary Forms of the Religious Life*. London: George Allen & Unwin.

FITZGERALD, TIMOTHY (2000). *The Ideology of Religious Studies*. New York and Oxford: Oxford University Press.

GEERTZ, CLIFFORD (1966). 'Religion as a Cultural System'. In Michael Banton (ed.), *Anthropological Approaches to the Study of Religion*. London: Tavistock, 1–46.

GUBA, EGON G. (ed.) (1990). *The Paradigm Dialog*. Newbury Park, Calif.: Sage.

HAMILTON, MALCOLM B. (2001). *The Sociology of Religion: Theoretical and Comparative Perspectives*. London and New York: Routledge.

HARGROVE, BARBARA (1979). *The Sociology of Religion: Classical and Contemporary Approaches*. Arlington Heights, Ill.: AHM Publishing Corporation.

HEELAS, PAUL, and WOODHEAD, LINDA (2005). *The Spiritual Revolution: Why Religion is Giving Way to Spirituality*. Oxford and Malden, Mass.: Blackwell.

KLASS, MORTON (1995). *Ordered Universes: Approaches to the Anthropology of Religion*. Boulder, Col.: Westview Press.

MARX, KARL (1844). 'A Contribution to the Critique of Hegel's Philosophy of Right'. *Deutsch-Französische Jahrbücher*, Feb. <http://www.marxists.org/archive/marx/works/1843/critique-hpr/intro.htm>, consulted 21 Feb. 2007.

MCCUTCHEON, RUSSELL T. (1997). *Manufacturing Religion: The Discourse on Sui Generis Religion and the Politics of Nostalgia*. New York and Oxford: Oxford University Press.

—— (2001). *Critics Not Caretakers: Redescribing the Public Study of Religion*. Albany, NY: State University of New York Press.

MCGUIRE, MEREDITH B. (1992). *Religion: The Social Context*. Belmont, Calif.: Wadsworth.

MORRIS, BRIAN (1987). *Anthropological Studies of Religion: An Introductory Text*. Cambridge: Cambridge University Press.

PANDIAN, JACOB (1991). *Culture, Religion, and the Sacred Self: A Critical Introduction to the Anthropological Study of Religion*. Englewood Cliffs, NJ: Prentice-Hall, 1991.

PLATVOET, JAN G., and MOLENDIJK, ARIE L. (eds.) (1999). *The Pragmatics of Defining Religion*. Leiden: Brill.

ROBERTSON, ROLAND (1970). *The Sociological Interpretation of Religion*. Oxford: Blackwell.

SARUP, MADAN (1988). *An Introductory Guide to Post-Structuralism and Postmodernism*. New York: Harvester Wheatsheaf.

SHARPE, ERIC (1983). *Understanding Religion*. London: Duckworth.

SMART, NINIAN (1992). *The World's Religions: Old Traditions and Modern Transformations*. Cambridge: Cambridge University Press.

STARK, RODNEY, and FINKE, ROGER (2000). *Acts of Faith: Explaining the Human Side of Religion*. Berkeley: University of California Press.

THROWER, JAMES (1999). *Religion: The Classical Theories*. Edinburgh: Edinburgh University Press.

TYLOR, EDWARD BURNETT (1958). *Primitive Culture: Researches into the Development of Mythology, Philosophy, Religion, Language, Art and Custom*, 2 vols. London: John Murray.

VAN BAAL, J., and VAN BEEK, W. E. A. (1985). *Symbols for Communication: An Introduction to the Anthropological Study of Religion*. Assen: Van Gorcum.

WEBER, MAX (1966). *The Sociology of Religion*. London: Methuen.

WHALING, FRANK (1986). *Christian Theology and World Religions: A Global Approach*. London: Marshall, Morgan and Scott.

WULFF, DAVID M. (1991). *Psychology of Religion: Classic and Contemporary Views*. New York: John Wiley.

YINGER, MILTON J. (1970). *The Scientific Study of Religion*. New York and London: Macmillan.

SUGGESTED READING

The following are recommended: Clarke Byrne (1993); Platvoet and Molendijk (1999).

CHAPTER 15

A CRITICAL VIEW OF COGNITIVE SCIENCE'S ATTEMPT TO EXPLAIN RELIGION AND ITS DEVELOPMENT

K. HELMUT REICH

Introduction

In this chapter—after briefly recalling the concepts of cognition and cognitive science—I shall argue (a) that the concept of religion referred to in cognitive science is too narrow; (b) that even within that narrow concept some of its claims are questionable; (c) that it is persons in the full sense of that concept, embedded in human groups, that generate insight and social movements, not lone brain structures; (d) that studying the role of cognition in religion and its development did not start with the cognitive turn of 1956 (Miller 2003), but decades earlier, and covers a wider field than made out by cognitive science of religion (e.g., James 1902; Pratt 1920). To help make clear the distinction between what cognitive science refers to as religion and what others have referred to as religion, *cognitive science* is here taken to mean evolutionary neurobiological cognitive science over against *psychological studies* of cognition and its ontogenetic development. Pascal Boyer provides an opening example of how cognitive science has been referring to religion.

What makes notions of supernatural agency intuitively plausible? According to Boyer (2003: 119), 'religious concepts activate various functionally distinct mental systems, present also in non-religious contexts, and "tweak" the usual inferences of these systems'. And Boyer continues to explain that the mechanism invoked consists in the joint, co-ordinated activation of the mental systems dealing with detection and representation of animacy and agency, social exchange, moral intuitions, precaution against natural hazards and understanding of misfortune. 'In each of these systems religious thoughts are not a dramatic departure from, but a predictable byproduct of, ordinary cognitive function.' Boyer opposes his view to the 'common temptation to search for the origin of religion in general human urges, for instance in people's wish to escape misfortune or mortality or their desire to understand the universe'.

To put these quotations and paraphrases into a simpler, acuminating language: Boyer (2003) broadly claims that by concentrating on mental systems based on the functioning of neural systems in the brain, cognitive science can explain exhaustively the origin and persistence of religion and believers' acceptance.

While aware of relevant work of other researchers in cognitive science (e.g., Atran 2002; Pyysiäinen 2001; 2004), and of Boyer's (2001) more comprehensive publication, I here concentrate on Boyer's (2003) work in the spirit of *pars pro toto*, referring, for example, to Barrett (2007), Bulkeley (2006), Nynäs (2008), Oviedo (2008), and Ozarak (2005) for a fuller discussion of various aspects of cognitive scientists' dealing with religion. My main concern will be to add to what has already been said by others on the title theme, not so much to reformulate what they have already worked out and formulated well. On this account, and because of space restrictions, the discussion of some topics may unfortunately be expanded less than some readers might have wished. I hope that the indication of numerous references will a meliorate this state of affairs.

In recent years, cognitive science has experienced a marked upswing and has gained wider acceptance, and its voice is heard in the study of religion and its development. But are its claims fully justified? The position I argue here is that cognitive science takes too simplistic an approach to religion and religious development. I base my arguments partly on empirical research in the psychology of religion and on the capacity of relational and contextual reasoning (RCR) for reaching more encompassing insights (Reich 2002).

Just to avoid a misunderstanding: There is nothing wrong with the roaring progress of cognitive neuroscience *per se* (e.g., Gazzaniga 2004); quite the contrary, it is to be encouraged to cast its net wider (Walach and Reich 2005). Clearly, any explanation of human cognition has to take into account the findings of cognitive science: for instance, that even during 'willing suspension of disbelief' our imagination is constrained by our mental structuring of the ontological categories and their relations (Kelly and Keil 1985; Reich 2002: 28–9). What is questioned here are claims (characteristic of successful upcoming approaches, e.g., by behaviourism in its heyday) to be the explanation of all issues studied. A successful theory of the origins, the nature, and the phylogenetic and ontogenetic development of religion (and spirituality) in all likelihood will have to include elements perceived from various perspectives in addition to that of cognitive science. Some of these additional perspectives are brought in here.

Nicholas Gibson and Justin Barrett (2008) take up several of the topics dealt with here and come mostly to comparable conclusions. Moreover, they suggest remedial measures involving more professionally trained psychologists.

Cognition and Cognitive Science

Cognition

The concept of *cognition* is complex (e.g., Holyoak and Morrison 2005), being related to such topics as perceiving, apprehending, analysing, reflecting, reasoning, and problem solving.

In psychology and in artificial intelligence, 'cognition' refers to the mental functions, mental processes and states of intelligent entities (humans, human organizations, highly autonomous robots), such as comprehending, decision making, making inferences, learning, and planning. Advanced cognition is capable of abstracting, generalizing, and meta-reasoning; these may involve beliefs and sophisticated declarative and procedural knowledge.

Cognition and emotions do not necessarily exclude each other (but see Azari and Slors 2007); often emotions stimulate cognition, yet sometimes passions overrule cognition. Jonathan Haidt (2001) discusses their complex relationship, and argues notably that emotions can also be a form of cognition.

Subdividing the field, one may distinguish, for instance, general cognition (e.g., the capacity to argue coherently), social cognition (concerning social behaviour and relationships), moral cognition (dealing with moral principles, moral argumentation, and action), and epistemic cognition (domain-dependent systematic approaches to verifiable robust knowledge).

Cognitive Science

Cognitive science (e.g., Friedenberg and Silberman 2006; Gazzaniga 2004; Sobel 2001) is usually taken to have begun in earnest after the cognitive turn in 1956

(Miller 2003), and is said to represent the scientific interdisciplinary study of the mind. Disciplines involved include the science of artificial intelligence, linguistics, neuroscience, robotics, philosophy, and psychology. 'Cognitive science' does not refer to the sum of the results from research by these disciplines, but to their interaction on specific issues such as problem solving or even consciousness. Cognitive scientists mostly view the mind as an information processor, comparing it to a computer that represents and transforms information. Main research areas are attention, imagery, memory, pattern recognition, and problem solving. For the diversity and richness of corresponding models and theories, the reader is referred to the quoted literature.

Religion

Definition

As is well known, there exist many definitions of religion (cf. André Droogers, Ch. 14 above), but there is no consensus as to which one covers fully this multi-faceted, multi-variate phenomenon. In fact, it seems next to impossible to arrive at a satisfactory universal substantive definition. However, some definitions have worked better than others—or at least have led to fruitful research and understanding. A comparison of definitions indicates that a rather narrow concept of religion underlies (evolutionary neurobiological) cognitive science, which weakens some of its claims.

Among more functional definitions, Ninian Smart's (1989: 12–21) seven dimensions of religion stand out (slightly simplified here): (1) the Practical (rituals and practices, including praying); (2) the Experiential (religious experience and emotions); (3) the Narrative (the story side of religion including myths); (4) the Doctrinal (formal teachings which underpin the narrative/mythic parts of religion); (5) the Ethical (formal and moral laws); (6) the Social (institutional organization of the religious community); (7) the Material (buildings, instruments of ritual, sacred places, works of religious art).

Concentrating more on individuals, Charles Glock (1962) posited five dimensions: (1) the Ideological (belief); (2) the Ritualistic (religious practice); (3) the Intellectual (religious knowledge); (4) the Experiential (religious feeling); (5) the Consequential (effects of being religious). The empirical verification of Glock's dimensions does not yield undisputed results. The five dimensions are more evident when the persons studied belong to a religiously homogeneous sophisticated group rather than a heterogeneous group of religious and non-religious individuals (Wulff 1997: 212–19). Nevertheless, these dimensions are used in the present discussion as sufficiently representative. This all the more, as comparable five dimensions also figure in the quite different religious views of Loyal Rue (2005). Rue draws a picture of religion which is essentially a circle inside a pentagon. Inside the circle is his core theory of religion: namely, that it is a story which finds a way to create a credible cosmology, out of which grows a compelling morality, employing root metaphors and other devices of story. But the pentagon is important too, because each of its five points represents a 'supporting strategy' which helps make the basic story work; the five points are much like Smart's and Glock's, being (1) Intellectual strategies; (2) Ritual strategies; (3) Experiential strategies; (4) Aesthetic strategies; and (5) Institutional strategies.

Comparing Smart's and Glock's dimensions, one sees that Smart's dimension 1 (the Practical) corresponds to Glock's dimension 2, and Smart's 2 (the Experiential) to Glock's 4. Smart's dimension 3 (the Narrative) presumably shares features with Glock's 3, his 4 (the Doctrinal) with Glock's 1, and hopefully 5 (the Ethical) with Glock's 5.

The Perspective of Cognitive Science

How does Boyer's (2003) approach—his focusing on the centrality of supernatural agency, social exchange, moral sense, and misfortune as the core concepts of religion—score within this dimensional grid? The least one can say is that the experiential/emotional dimension does not get its full due; nor does the consequential/effect dimension. In a way, this is not too surprising, given that cognitive science is mainly about functional aspects, not about phenomenological aspects (what it feels like to lead a religious life within a religious community; cf. Nagel 1974). Similarly, religious insight and intuitive knowing (Watts and Williams 1988) get short shrift.

Elisabeth Ozarak (2005) provides a quite detailed critical overview of cognitive scientific approaches to religion, including perception; memory; knowledge structure and framing; judgement, decision making, and problem solving; implicit knowing; counterintuitive ideas; social cognition; social perception; language and narrative. She points out a number of lacunae yet to be filled. For Ozarak (2005: 229), 'understanding the ways in which religious cognition shapes human action is overdue to become a top priority for psychological research'.

Kelley Bulkeley (2006) faults the cognitive science of religion for paying insufficient attention to religiously significant phenomena such as vision, imagery, empathy, healing, sexuality, gender, reproduction, meditation, prayer, and dreaming (and for the absence of any reference to the past several decades of research in the psychology of religion).

Peter Nynäs (2008) queries the hypothesis proposed by some cognitive researchers that the attraction of counterintuitive representations provides an explanation of religion. Nynäs writes: 'All counter-intuitive representations are not religious and the specific character of religious ones is difficult to explain. How can we distinguish between the cognitive foundations of a religious belief, a limited psychotic experience, and a playful identification with Spiderman? This is a critical question and it indicates that some central aspects are missing in the explanation [by cognitive scientists].' He relies on cognitive-analytic perspectives based on a broader theoretical foundation. This provides a more complete picture, which also connects to the tradition built on Otto's (1923[1922]) idea of the 'wholly other'. From this perspective it is more plausible to assume that religious representations are trajectories of the early evolving tripartite sense of self, other, and world. In Nynäs's words: 'From a cognitive-analytic perspective we can learn that such processes are parts of complex patterns that are developed, formed and maintained within a matrix of relatedness. This means that the nature, character and quality of early forms of relatedness, as these are known and described in e.g. object relations theory and attachment theory form a central background to—or the spine of—human cognitive information processing.'

Justin Barrett (2007) argues in detail that none of the arguments advanced by bio-psychological explanations of religion prove formidable challenges for belief in gods. From an analysis of neuro-theology, evolutionary group selection theory, and cognitive science of religion, Barrett constructs five arguments against theism: (1) It is only a product of its neural substrate; (2), it is merely an evolutionary by-product; (3) it involves only utility, not truth; (4) it is simply inherited belief; (5) it is produced or accepted by error-prone minds. He then goes on to demonstrate weaknesses in each argument.

While agreeing largely with Ozarak, Bulkeley, Nynäs, and Barrett, I would add that cognitive science tends to collapse religion and faith (Smith 1979). Faith is not centred primarily on believing (or not) in supernatural agents with certain characteristics. Rather, faith manifests itself as the deep core of the individual, the centre of values, involving both conscious and unconscious motivation. It expresses itself through being involved and responding by faith-motivated actions: that is, whole persons performing in a certain way even in complex and ever changing circumstances. Examples are Mother Teresa devoting her life to help Calcutta's poor, in whom she saw Christ; Martin Luther King 'having a dream' and acting to make it come true; or more ordinary individuals living their religious faith by helping others despite their own difficulties in life (Kwilecki and Kwilecki 1999).

What Cognitive Science Misses within its Purview

Boyer (2003: 5) writes: 'People do not generally have religious beliefs because they have pondered the evidence for or against the actual existence of particular supernatural agents. Rather, they grow into finding a culturally acquired description of such agents intuitively plausible. How does that happen?' He then advances the explanations summarized above and critiqued by Barrett (2007), Bulkeley (2006), Nynäs (2008), Oviedo (2008), and Ozarak (2005). In my view, Boyer's statement translates a (too) restricted view of *ontogenetic religious (and spiritual) development*, and specifically of epistemic cognition's role in this connection. In particular, his statement does not sufficiently take into account human curiosity, creativity, ingenuity, and self-reliance (cf. Reich 2003*c*)—as is nicely illustrated in longitudinal studies of children's changing ways of thinking about religion and religious issues.

First, I recall the interview excerpts from an empirical longitudinal study in Switzerland (Fetz, Reich, and Valentin 2001: 183–96), translated and commented upon by me (Reich 2003*a*: 23–4, reproduced by kind permission of Koninklijke Brill N.V., likewise for the other excerpts from that publication). Over a span of ten years, respondents were interviewed three times, basically using the same twenty-eight questions about the origin, the evolution, and the characteristics of the universe, and God's role in it. Using Grounded Theory, four developmental stages were discerned. These stages are distinguished by (1) God's decreasing and changing role in the originating and evolving of the universe, and (2) increased cognitive competence in (re)constructing the interviewee's world view (Fetz *et al.* 2001: 156–8, 171–6).

Here is what Nina answered at age 5 years and 5 months (5, 5) to some of the standardized questions: ['Has all that you see in nature always existed, or did it come into being at some point in time?'] 'It came.' ['How do you know?'] 'Because I was born into the world, and the same with my mummy. God has made it that way.' ['Tell me about God!'] 'God is a kind man. If something happens, he helps us. He provides our food.' ['What else does God do?'] 'He has built the houses, except a few which people have built themselves.' ['Which were built by God?'] 'The high-rise buildings, because people couldn't make high-enough ladders.... And God has made cars before people knew how to do it. God gives and makes things we can't do.' ['What else can you tell me?'] 'First God has made the houses with tables and chairs, then the water, then the plants, and then people. This, because people couldn't wait for getting houses to live in, and something to drink and eat.' Nina has a long list of what else God has made, including peoples' eyes, noses, and mouths.

What are the characteristic features, observed equally with other children (cf. Piaget 1929 [1926])? Above all, Nina's capacity to construct her own world view in tune with her egocentrism and according to her anthropocentric artificialistic image of God. She projects her personal experiences on to everything else, and construes God's creation as the work of an artisan aimed at humanity's existence and well-being. Unsurprisingly, there is not a trace of questioning her own world view: in her mind everything simply is exactly as she says.

At the second interview, Nina (9, 2) partly maintains her views, and partly has changed them. 'The Earth, light, rain, and a warm climate needed to be there first so that plants could grow, and animals had something to eat. Then came humans. Now God sees to it that all works well, he provides the strength to live, knowledge, and materials to make things. But all things we need and use are made by humans.' Nina's object-related reasoning begins to show: the early human beings now build their own shelters, and humans make all artefacts. Also, God works through nature (although in curious ways), no longer with his own hands, for instance to build mountains: 'God lets stones grow.'

At the third interview (15, 9), Nina's world view clearly shows more changes; she no longer espouses a traditional Christian view, and artificiality has almost disappeared. 'The world has come into being of its own. Maybe God then has helped behind the scene so that it became what we have today. However, you can't really understand all that. Therefore, people look for an explanation they find plausible.... I don't believe that God has made humans in God's image, God is quite different, and we can't picture God.... I only know what God is not.'

Nina does not yet know how to deal effectively with conflicts between a religious and a scientific world view: 'In the beginning there was religion, and therefore we have the Genesis narrative, but then all evolved on its own, as explained by science' (cf. Martin 2007 and Hefner 2007 on this very issue). She describes her changed image of God as follows: 'As a child, I pictured God as an old man on a cloud, with a beard... probably, I have heard that from others, and never reflected on it. [Now I know better].'

What is to be retained from these excerpts? Nina (like other children) has a creative independent mind, and to some considerable extent constructs her religious world view from her own observations, analogies, imaginations, and reflections. Clearly, it is unlikely that its idiosyncratic features originated from socialization by adults. As her cognitive competence grew, she analysed her views more critically, and amended them where judged necessary.

We observed a similar process with the task of drawing the 'world' as seen by children: From a flat Earth (supported by a stony foundation) with a fixed firmament above from which sun, moon, and stars are hung (and divinities live beyond) to a spherical Earth held from above (by God's anchor) to a free-floating spherical Earth (cf. Vosniadou and Brewer 1992). Clearly, (younger) children's conceptualization of the world shares features with that of antiquity (Reich 1997).

Did they hear about those earlier views and adopt them, or did they themselves 'discover' them? I favour the latter explanation (cf. Gelman 2003; Mandler 2004; Rakison and Oakes 2003).

Human Development: Individuals and their Interactions

To grow up, both physically and mentally, babies and infants need not only to drink, sleep, and be kept warm, but also to be taken up, cuddled, smiled at, and played with, to receive scaffolding (Berk 2004), mirroring, and echoing (Nehaniv and Dautenhahn 2007). It is the child–caretaker dyad that largely determines the development of the newborn, not just his or her genes and neurons. And this holds, *mutatis mutandis*, even for a robot–caretaker dyad (Breazeal and Scassellati 2000).

In fact, human behaviour interacts with and affects genetic expression (Sabatini *et al.* 2007), and (stimulated) activities reinforce neuron connections in the brain, even create new ones. For instance—contrary to speaking competence (Broca's area, Wernicke's area)—there does not exist a brain area 'prewired' for reading competence—that is, decoding text and translating it into a speech form—it has to be developed (Wolfe and Nevills 2004). Broadly speaking, the brain translates social relations into biological signals that influence both the functioning of the body and the brain's microstructure (Eisenberg 1995; Bauer 2007).

Bernard Spilka (2003: 71) suggests that 'there is no direct connection between religion and genetics. An indirect connection may be found because of the various functions religion performs in life. Our suggestion is that people's religious faith satisfies people's needs for meaning, control, and social relationships'. Many persons want to reduce stressing conditions and pursue this objective actively.

In this context, an important yet often underrated point concerns the importance of an appropriate equilibrium between the individual and society. In earlier times, individuals usually simply had to 'fall into line' if they wanted to survive. At the present time, the tendency, at least in developed countries, is to overemphasize individual entitlements, freedoms, and rights. Apart from this *Zeitgeist*, the multicultural nature of many societies and globalization do not make it simple to achieve the desirable equilibrium (e.g., Kegan 1994; Riccardi 2007). However, survival demands that *all* members of the human society adhere to certain standards, hopefully worked out by a rational democratic process.

On the basis of the preceding analysis, an encompassing theory of ontogenetic religious (and spiritual) development needs to include the following features (Reich 1992: 151): (1) explication of relevant psychical (emotional, intellectual, volitional) processes that take place within the organism, including those aspects of such processes referred to as meaning making; (2) analysis of development as the gradual co-ordination of individual psyche and biophysical, socio-cultural, and perceived spiritual reality; (3) delineating social contexts in which development occurs and the ways in which those contexts relate to individual religious development; (4) accounting for the universal characteristics of religious development as well as for individual differences; (5) elucidating the mechanisms effecting developmental change and the workings of factors that favour or hinder religious development.

I am not aware of any single theory, which fulfils all five desiderata. For the time being, several theories have to be brought in to understand and explain a given religious development (e.g., Reich 1992: 173–4), including, of course, empirically tested parts of cognitive science theories.

The importance of these issues, bears underlining, given the confrontations in today's world, in which religion not infrequently plays a role. This raises the question of whether the human species can really survive. A better understanding of religion and its development would probably help bring about an improved peaceful 'living together' (Riccardi 2007).

Religious and Spiritual Development

Introduction

Religious and spiritual development is a complex, controversial issue, as presented notably by George Scarlett (2005). He discusses development (movement toward perfection) versus change with time; domains (related to overall religious and spiritual development) versus persons (development toward spiritual exemplars); perception and reason versus religious and spiritual imagining; structural versus content analysis; faith versus belief; the Kwileckis' substantive-functional approach; the spiritual child movement; cognitive-cultural theories; developmental systems theories (transactions between individuals and their various embedding contexts). While Scarlett (and others) find much fault with Piaget and his stage-structural accounts, he sees the need 'to combine the strength of stage-structural approaches with the strengths of current approaches' (Scarlett 2005: 31). Already at this stage one might suspect, and it will become increasingly clear, that the cognitive science of religion covers less ground.

Before coming to stage-structural approaches, a word needs to be said about Piaget's work (and similar work by other researchers). In my view the critique is overdone, probably due to insufficient knowledge of Piaget's work on religious development (Reich 2003*a*: 5–6; 2004) and on children's views of the world (Piaget 1929 [1926]), which unfortunately seems largely forgotten. His studies of the development of logico-mathematical thinking refer to idealized *epistemic* subjects. His sequence of developmental stages of this kind of thinking (sensorimotor stage, pre-operational stage, concrete operations, and formal operations) was not meant to elucidate the actual cognitive developmental path of each and every individual. And who, when knowledgeable about the social and societal environment of the 1920s and 1930s (when Piaget made his basic empirical studies) can be surprised that today's children and adolescents, embedded as they are in a world of television, computers, and electronic games, develop faster in some respects than many decades ago? Piaget's concept of universal developmental stages (versus domain-specific developments) has not been confirmed incontrovertibly, and he did not study development in adult age. Nevertheless, at least two of Piaget's important basic insights remain valid (see, e.g., Reich 2003*a*: 2–4): (i) psychic *structures* do exist which lead to a certain developmental logic: namely, from simple, more spontaneous, unreflected pragmatic thinking to more systematic object-oriented thinking, and on to complex, abstract reflective thinking (the reverse simply does not happen with healthy persons; socialization can influence the speed of development, but not its logical order); and (ii) individuals are not conscious of their ongoing intellectual development and its mechanisms; therefore these cannot be elucidated by means of standard questionnaires, etc., but can only be inferred from task performance or problem solving (e.g., Reich 2002: 191–8).

Stage-Structural Theories of Religious and Faith Development

Elsewhere, I have dealt extensively with these theories (Reich 1990; 1992; 1993; 2003*a*; 2005; 2008), specifically with the Faith Development Theory of James Fowler (1981), and the Theory of Religious Judgement of Fritz Oser and Paul Gmünder (1991 [1984]; see also Fowler, Nipkow, and Schweitzer 1991 for a critical review of the latter two theories). In these writings, the categorical and individual strengths and weaknesses of stage-structural theories of religious and faith development are discussed extensively. Fowler's theory is particularly helpful in pastoral counselling, and that of Oser and Gmünder in religious education.

Cognitive development is incorporated in both theories, although in different ways. Fowler's (1981: 243–57) pre-stage and his six stages of faith are labelled: (0) undifferentiated primal faith; (1) intuitive-projective faith; (2) mythic-literal faith; (3) synthetic-conventional faith; (4) individuative-reflective faith; (5) conjunctive faith; and (6) universalizing faith. The original seven dimensions incorporated into all of Fowler's stages are (i) form of logic; (ii) perspective taking; (iii) form of moral judgement; (iv) bounds of social awareness; (v) locus of authority; (vi) form of world's coherence; (vii) symbolic function; to which (viii) stages of self were added later (Fowler 1987). Clearly, all original dimensions have cognitive content to varying degrees; dimension (i), form of logic, is strictly cognitive. Fowler sees the development of logical thought initially along Piagetian lines and then (at stage 5) being based on what he calls 'dialectic logic' (which I call the logic of relational and contextual reasoning, Reich 2002: 43–6). The development of epistemic cognition is implicit in his theory.

However, Fowler's theory of faith development extends far beyond cognitive development. It also involves images and realities of power, myths, and issues of control.

The theory of Oser and Gmünder (1991 [1984]) deals with the evolving person–God relationship as construed from experiencing reality and relating it to God, especially in times of crisis. This relationship develops qualitatively over the life cycle. The five experimentally observed stages are labelled: (1) *deus ex machina*; (2) *Do ut des* (give so that you may receive); (3) deism; (4) divine plan; and (5) universal solidarity.

These stages characterize the subjects' developing capacity for a religious reconstruction of the events under discussion. This capacity is analysed in terms of the evolution of the subject's dealing with eight polar dimensional pairs: transcendence versus immanence, the holy versus the profane, eternity versus ephemerity, divine providence versus luck, faith (trust) versus fear (mistrust), hope versus absurdity, functional transparency versus opacity, freedom versus dependence. Religious development is conceived as discrete changes in the relationship between the two poles of each pair—for instance, transcendence versus immanence. 'Psychologically, this means that persons produce stage-specific equilibria between the immanent and the transcendent' (Oser and Gmünder 1991 [1984]: 27). With development, the two poles of a given pair are no longer seen as mutually exclusive, but are perceived as limiting as well as enabling each other: the *freedom* of religious believers comes about through their *dependence* on God. Relational and contextual reasoning (RCR), with its logic that overcomes blocking restrictions of classical binary logic, is helpful in making this change (Oser and Reich 1996; 2002; Reich 2002: 130–2).

Epistemic Cognition

In my view, students of religious development, especially cognitive scientists, do not take sufficient notice of epistemic cognition: that is, (a) ontological development; (b) stages of epistemic reflection; (c) matching the form of thought used (and its built-in logic) and the structure of the given task or problem. These points will now be dealt with briefly.

Ontological Development

'Do fairies, quarks, or unicorns exist or not?' 'Is that person who gives me presents really my uncle or not?' 'Are clouds alive or dead?' For various reasons (e.g., Reich

2002: 28–9), young children may take many years to become fully clear about the answers to such questions. Ontological development concerns the existence or non-existence of various entities and their predicates—more precisely, the material categories needed to discuss those predicates (Fetz *et al.* 2001: 145–7; Reich 2003*a*: 22). The problem is exacerbated by the fact that in religion the transcendent comes in, with which adults also have problems (e.g., Wulff 1997: 634–41).

The stage of reflecting on epistemic issues and the degree of mastering various thought forms (with their inherent logic) will co-determine the level of ontological development. That in turn (together with other factors, specifically religious experiences, interaction with the physical and human surroundings, special life events and their impact) co-determines religious development and the depth or importance accorded to one's religiousness.

Stages of Reflection on Epistemic Issues

The interviews with Nina show a developing reflection on epistemic issues. Is this true or not? How certain is my knowledge? Can we know this at all? Our studies indicate a pre-stage and three stages of this type of development, with stages 2 and 3 being closely related (Fetz *et al.* 2001: 140–5, 159–62; Reich 2002: 29–32; 2003*a*: 17–19).

In stage 0 (up to about 9 years in this study), the child is not really aware of epistemic issues, and hence does not reflect critically on them ('Eve was the first woman . . . Her mother . . .'). In fact, children up to about that age basically believe that (apart from matters of taste) all persons come to the same conclusions if they have the same information available. This state of affairs is independent of understanding the difference between making a factual statement, pulling somebody's leg, lying, making a mistake, etc., which 4-year-olds can do.

Stage 1 is that of *object* reflection: 'Is that really so?' For instance, a girl at the end of childhood explained to us that with so many people in this world, God couldn't watch over each and every person. Therefore God sends to each of us a guardian angel that can and will do that in God's stead. While progress with respect to stage 0, the main point is that individuals at this stage remain prisoners of their own ideas and representations; they essentially discuss the 'that' of God, that which concerns God as such, including God's very existence, and do not analyse critically the 'what' concerning God: namely, God's nature and attributes, or, more importantly, how one can know this reliably. In actual practice, they collapse their unquestioned personal view with the explanandum itself. An issue, if not *the* main issue, then becomes whether the explanandum, specifically God, 'really' exists. At one point of developing object reflection, fairies, Father Christmas, Santa Claus, the Easter Bunny, etc. are recognized one by one as figures out of the children's world, not from the 'real' world of adults. There is a likely possibility that God is jettisoned along with these figures.

At stage 2 the reflection turns to one's *means* of knowing specific 'facts'. For instance, an adolescent will become aware that analogical reasoning is not necessarily yielding 'true' knowledge about God. If humans need to eat and drink, that does not imply that God eats and drinks. Or, if humans build their houses with building materials and according to a blueprint, that does not imply that God creates the universe from some existing material such as stones, water, and air (as interviewed children argued). Thus, reflection on means permits children to disentangle the personal God idea from the question of who and what God really is. The result is a kind of negative theology: God is *not* the artisan who built the universe from some raw material according to a blueprint (or simply from nothing, by magic).

Reaching stage 3 involves an understanding of more general epistemic issues such as basic options: Am I a realist, and if so which version ('naïve', critical, hypothetical, etc.); a constructivist (a radical constructivist, a social constructivist, etc.); a relativist, a postmodernist, or what else? And why? Accordingly, among other things, the limits of what humans can know will be thematized. The answers may be different, yet are basically of the following type: 'As adults, our mind has difficulty visualizing that something could come from nothing.'

Summing up: Apart from learning new facts and, above all, facts of a different nature, it is the development of epistemic cognition that makes for a change of one's world view and religious outlook: 'I have thought about how it all fits together [and changed my beliefs accordingly].' 'Later on you are more critical about yourself and your beliefs [and so you change]' (Reich, Oser, and Valentin 1994: 164).

Matching Thought Form and Problem Structure

A thought form is understood here as a specific structure of the elements of thinking (and reasoning) whose relational organization ensures the functioning of the whole. Examples are (1) Piagetian operations, (2) dialectical thought, (3) analogical thought, (4) relational and contextual reasoning (RCR), and (5) cognitively complex thinking. Each time a different thought form is required—namely, that holding the same rank in the earlier and the later list of examples—to solve optimally the following tasks/problems: (i) crossword puzzle, (ii) wage negotiation between unions and employer, (iii) explaining the unknown by the known, (iv) explaining the particle-like and the wave-like behaviour of light (<http://www.colorado.edu/physics/2000/applets/twoslitsa.html>), (v) filling a well-defined post (Reich 2002: 88–97). For example, filling optimally the post needs cognitive complex thinking (differentiating various aspects and integrating in a partial conclusion).

RCR involves a trivalent logic with 'truth-values' *compatible*, *incompatible*, and *non-compatible*. If RCR is applicable, two competing theories (such as Nature and Nurture as explanation of skills) are seen not to be mutually incompatible, but

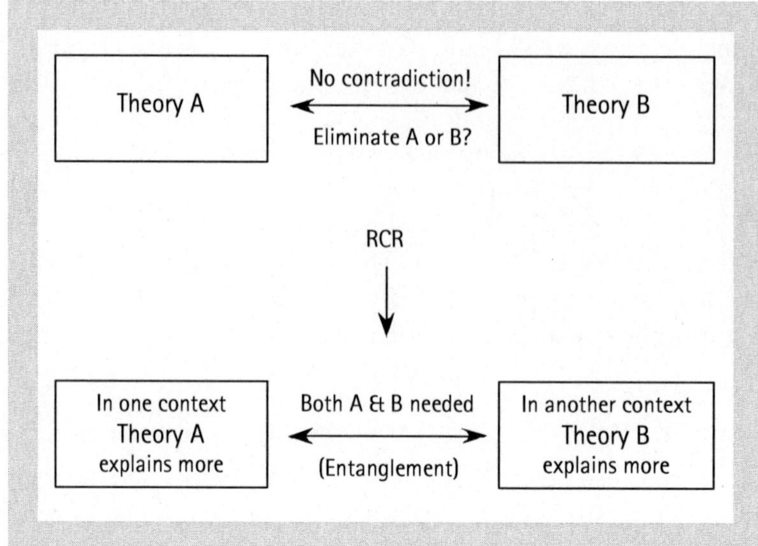

Fig. 15.1. Upper part: Using classsical binary logic, no contradiction between Theory A and Theory B is admitted, and this may lead us to exclude A or B. Lower part: In appropriate cases, applying the trivalent RCR logic resolves this problem.

(Source: Reich 2008; figure and explanatory text reproduced by kind permission of Koninklijke Brill N.V.)

non-compatible, i.e. in one context one theory explains more, in another the other; yet both are needed for a full understanding (fig. 15.1). RCR also helps us to understand religious doctrines, and how individuals develop religiously (Reich 2002: 116–32) by taking away the hurdle of binary logic: 'Only either A or non-A can be right, not both' no longer holds without limit. With RCR, this prescription is perceived as being a domain-specific, not a universally valid, approach.

Concluding Remarks

While cognitive science is an important ingredient in the process of understanding religion and spirituality, and their development during life, other ingredients are also needed for a more complete understanding, as pointed out in this and other chapters of the Handbook. To illustrate this, I refer to my own tentative model of religious and spiritual change (Reich 2003*b*). Conceived as action-based, this model incorporates feedback loops between the self and its environment as well as various loops inside the self (fig. 15.2).

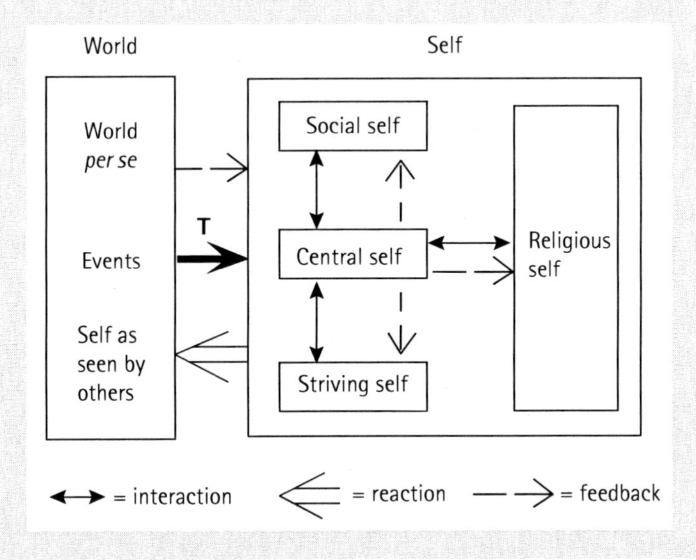

Fig. 15.2. Dynamic model of religious change. Schematic representation of a specific dynamic change: trigger T, interaction, reaction, and feedback.

(Source: Reich 2008; figure and explanatory text reproduced by kind permission of Koninklijke Brill N.V.)

The psychological construct of the *self* is understood as being of *one* piece; the subdivisions shown serve mainly to make it easier to implement the model fully. In the present state it serves to *describe* dynamic changes involving religiousness and spirituality, not yet to *simulate* them. Changes can be triggered either by outside events (deep religious experience, birth of a child, personal loss, etc.) or from inside the self (growing up, dreams, deep meditation, etc.). An outside trigger (the bold faced T in fig. 15.2) affects directly the *central self*. This is the human body, including the brain, cognition, emotions, volition/motivation, memory, and the subconscious. The *central self* then interacts with the *striving self* (short-term objectives, long-term life aims, world view), the *social self* (significant others, culture = socio-cultural symbolic environment), and the *religious self* (the relationship with what is considered the transcendent or ultimate, and its consequences for one's life). The interaction between these multiple partial selves produces a reaction toward the triggering event. In turn, this provides a feedback to the self: If the cycle is beneficial, the religious world view and attitude are reinforced; in the opposite case, changes may occur.

I have introduced this model here mainly on account of its heuristic value. It permits me to introduce the findings of the various multidisciplinary efforts to elucidate religion and its development without prior constraints as to which approach is the best (Reich 2003*b*). Of course, once fully evolved, the model may be quite different, especially if the efforts to simulate human functioning by advanced humanoid robots or supercomputers is successful. The main point is that approaches which are too simplistic, however valuable their contribution to a more encompassing view, when standing alone, cannot lead to a full understanding of religious and spiritual development and to a future-oriented insight into it.

References

Atran, Scott (2002). *In Gods We Trust: The Evolutionary Origins of Religious Thoughts.* Oxford: Oxford University Press.

Azari, Nina P., and Slors, Marc (2007). 'From Brain Imagining Religious Experience to Explaining Religion: A Critique'. *Archive for the Psychology of Religion*, 29: 67–85.

Barrett, Justin L. (2007). 'Is the Spell Really Broken? Bio-psychological Explanation of Religion and Theistic Belief'. *Theology and Science*, 5/1: 57–72.

Bauer, Joachim (2007). *Das Gedächtnis des Körpers: Wie Beziehungen und Lebensstile unsere Gene steuern*, 11th enlarged edn. Munich: Piper.

Berk, Laura (2004). *Awakening Children's Minds: How Parents and Teachers Can Make a Difference.* New York and Oxford: Oxford University Press.

Boyer, Pascal (2001). *Religion Explained: The Evolutionary Origins of Religious Thought.* London: Random House; New York: Basic Books.

—— (2003). 'Religious Thought and Behaviour as Byproducts of Brain Function'. *Trends in Cognitive Sciences*, 7/3: 119–24; accessed 28 Aug. 2007 from URL <http://artsci.wustl.edu/~anthro/blurb/b_boyer.html>

Breazeal, Cynthia, and Scassellati, Brian (2000). 'Infant-like Social Interactions between a Robot and a Human Caregiver'. *Adaptive Behavior*, 8/1: 49–74.

Bulkeley, K. (2006). Review of the 2004 volumes by H. Whitehouse, I. Pyysiainen, and J. L. Barrett on the Cognitive Science of Religion. *International Journal for the Psychology of Religion*, 16: 239–43.

Eisenberg, Leon (1995). 'The Social Construction of the Human Brain'. *American Journal of Psychiatry*, 152: 1563–75.

Fetz, Reto L., Reich, K. Helmut, and Valentin, Peter (2001). *Weltbildentwicklung und Schöpfungsverständnis. Eine strukturgenetische Untersuchung bei Kindern und Jugendlichen.* Stuttgart: Kohlhammer.

Fowler, James W. (1981). *Stages of Faith: The Psychology of Human Development and the Quest for Meaning.* San Francisco: Harper & Row.

—— (1987). *Faith Development and Pastoral Care.* Philadelphia: Fortress Press.

—— Nipkow, Karl Ernst, and Schweitzer, Friedrich (eds.) (1991[1988]). *Stages of Faith and Religious Development: Implications for Church, Education, and Society.* New York: Crossroad.

Friedenberg, Jay, and Silberman, Gordon (2006). *Cognitive Science: An Introduction to the Study of Mind.* Thousand Oaks, Calif., and London: Sage.

Gazzaniga, Michael S. (2004). *The Cognitive Neuroscience*, iii. Cambridge, Mass.: MIT Press.

Gelman, Susan A. (2003). *The Essential Child: Origins of Essentialism in Everyday Thought.* New York and Oxford: Oxford University Press.

Gibson, Nicholas J. S., and Barrett, Justin L. (2008). 'On Psychology and Evolution of Religion: Five Types of Contribution Needed from Psychologist'. In J. Bulbulia, R. Sosis, E. Harris, R. Genet, C. Genet, and K. Wyman (eds.), *The Evolution of Religion: Studies, Theories, and Critiques*. Santa Margarita, Calif.: Collins Foundation Press, 333–8.

Glock, Charles Y. (1962). 'On the Study of Religious Commitment'. *Religious Education*, research supplement, 57/4: S98–S110.

Haidt, Jonathan (2001). 'The Emotional Dog and its Rational Tail: A Social Intuitionist Approach to Moral Judgment'. *Psychological Review*, 108: 814–34.

Hefner, Philip (2007). 'Science and Well-Winnowed Wisdom: The Grand Quest' (editorial). *Zygon: Journal of Religion and Science*, 42/4: 799–802.

Holyoak, Keith J., and Morrison, Robert G. (eds.) (2005). *The Cambridge Handbook of Thinking and Reasoning*. Cambridge and New York: Cambridge University Press.

James, William (1902). *The Varieties of Religious Experience: A Study in Human Nature*. London and New York: Longmans, Green, and Co.

Kegan, Robert (1994). *In Over Our Heads: The Mental Demands of Modern Life*. Cambridge, Mass. and London: Harvard University Press.

Kelly, Michael H., and Keil, Frank C. (1985). 'The More Things Change...: Metamorphoses and Conceptual Structure'. *Cognitive Science*, 9: 403–16.

Kwilecki, Susan, with Kwilecki, Paul (1999). *Becoming Religious: Understanding Devotion to the Unseen*. Cranbury, NJ: Bucknell University Press.

Mandler, Jean Matter (2004). *The Foundations of Mind: Origins of Conceptual Thought*. New York and Oxford: Oxford University Press.

Martin, Louis (2007). 'Mundus Mendax, The Global Spiral: A Publication of the Metanexus Institute', 24 Aug. 2007; accessed 28 Aug. 2007 from URL <http://www.metanexus.net/Magazine/Default.aspx?TabId = 68&id = 7091&SkinSrc = %5bG%5dSkins%2f_default%2fNo + Skin&ContainerSrc = %5bG%5dContainers%2f_default%2fNo + Container>.

Miller, George A. (2003). 'The Cognitive Revolution: A Historical Perspective'. *Trends in Cognitive Sciences*, 7/3: 141–4; accessed 28 Aug. 2007 from URL <http://www.cogsci.princeton.edu/~geo/Miller.pdf>.

Nagel, Thomas (1974). 'What it is Like to Be a Bat'. *Philosophical Review*, 83: 435–50.

Nehaniv, Chrystopher L., and Dautenhahn, Kerstin (eds.) (2007). *Imitation and Social Learning in Robots, Humans and Animals: Behavioural, Social and Communicative Dimensions*. Cambridge and New York: Cambridge University Press.

Nynäs, Peter (2008). 'Religious Counter-Intuitive Representations from a Perspective of Early Intersubjective Development and Complex Representational Constellations—A Methodological Reflection'. *Archive for the Psychology of Religion*, 30: 37–55.

Oser, Fritz K., and Gmünder, Paul (1991[1984]). *Religious Judgement. A Developmental Approach*, trans. and enlarged by N. F. Hahn. Birmingham, Ala.: Religious Education Press.

—— and Reich, K. Helmut (1996). 'Religious Development from a Psychological Perspective'. *World Psychology*, 2/3–4: 365–96.

Otto, Rudolf (1923[1922]). *The Idea of the Holy*. Oxford: Oxford University Press.

Oviedo, Lluis (2008). 'Is a Complete Biogenetic Account of Religion Feasible?' *Zygon: Journal of Religion and Sciences*, 43/1: 103–26.

Ozarak, Elisabeth Weiss (2005). 'Cognitive Approaches to Religion'. In R. F. Paloutzian and C. L. Park (eds.), *Handbook of the Psychology of Religion and Spirituality*, New York and London: Guilford Press, 216–34.

Piaget, Jean (1929[1926]). *The Child's Conception of the World*. London: Kegan Paul Trench Trubner; several later English editions.

Pratt, James Bissett (1920). *The Religious Consciousness: A Psychological Study*. New York: Macmillan.

Pyysiäinen, Ilkka (2001). *How Religion Works: Towards a New Cognitive Science of Religion*. Leiden and Boston: Brill.

—— (2004). *Magic, Miracles, and Religion: A Scientist's Perspective*. Walnut Creek, Calif.: Altamira Press.

Rakison, David H., and Oakes, Lisa M. (eds.) (2003). *Early Category and Concept Development: Making Sense of the Blooming, Buzzing Confusion*. New York and Oxford: Oxford University Press.

Reich, K. Helmut (1990). 'The Relation between Science and Theology: The Case for Complementarity Revisited'. *Zygon: Journal of Religion and Science*, 25/4: 369–90.

—— (1992). 'Religious Development across the Life Span: Conventional and Cognitive Developmental Approaches'. In D. L. Featherman, R. M. Lerner, and M. Perlmutter (eds.), *Life Span Development and Behavior*, xi. Hillsdale, NJ: L. Erlbaum, 145–88.

—— (1993). 'Cognitive-Developmental Approaches to Religiousness: Which Version for Which Purpose?' *International Journal for the Psychology of Religion*, 3: 145–71.

—— (1997). 'Empirical Evidence for Parallelisms between Scientific Developments from their Origins to Galileo and the World View of Children'. Preprints des MPI für Wissenschaftsgeschichte (Berlin), no. 70.

—— (2002). *Developing the Horizons of the Mind: Relational and Contextual Reasoning and the Resolution of Cognitive Conflict*. Cambridge and New York: Cambridge University Press.

—— (2003*a*). 'Cognitive Preconditions for Religious Development'. *Research in the Social Scientific Study of Religion*, 14: 1–32.

—— (2003*b*). 'The Person–God Relationship: A Dynamic Model'. *International Journal for the Psychology of Religion*, 13: 229–47.

—— (2003*c*). 'Some German (Pre-)adolescents' Views on the Importance of Friends and God: A Pilot Study'. *Journal of Christian Education*, 46/3: 47–61.

—— (2004). 'Jean Piagets Vorstellungen von Religion und Entwicklung'. In A. A. Bucher with M. Brumlik and K. H. Reich, *Psychobiographien religiöser Entwicklung: Glaubensprofile zwischen Individualität und Universalität*, Stuttgart: Kohlhammer, 123–37.

—— (2005). 'Stage-Structural Approach to Religious Development'. In E. M. Dowling and W. G. Scarlett (eds.), *Encyclopedia of Spiritual and Religious Development in Childhood and Adolescence*. Thousand Oaks, Calif.: Sage, 431–7.

—— (2008). 'Extending the Psychology of Religion: A Call for Exploration of Psychological Universals, More Inclusive Approaches, and Comprehensive Models'. *Archive for the Psychology of Religion*, 30: 115–34.

—— (in press). 'The Oser–Gmünder Model of Religious Development'. In D. M. Wulff (ed.), *Handbook of Psychology of Religion*. New York and Oxford: Oxford University Press.

—— and Oser, Fritz K. (2002). 'Eine reifere Mensch-"Gott"-Beziehung und komplexeres Denken: Zwei ungleiche Seiten der selben Entwicklung'. In E. Beckers, H.-J. Hahn, H. A. Kick, and H. Schlosser (eds.), *Die Programmierung des kindlichen und jugendlichen*

Gehirns. 3. Symposium des Professorenforums, Gießen. Germany: Verlag des Professorenforums, (updated version of Oser and Reich 1996.) 77–96.

—— —— and VALENTIN, PETER (1994). 'Knowing Why I Now Know Better: Children's and Youth's Explanations of Their World View Changes'. *Journal of Research on Adolescence*, 4: 151–73.

RICCARDI, ANDREA (2007). *Vivre Ensemble*. Paris: Desclée de Brouwer.

RUE, LOYAL D. (2005). *Religion Is Not About God: How Spiritual Traditions Nurture our Biological Nature and What to Expect When They Fail*. New Brunswick, NJ, and London: Rutgers University Press.

SABATINI, MICHAEL J., EBERT, PHILIP, LEWIS, DAVID A., LEVITT, PAT, CAMERON, JUDY L., and MIRNICS, KÁROLY (2007). 'Amygdala Gene Expression Correlates of Social Behavior in Monkeys Experiencing Maternal Separation'. *Journal of Neuroscience*, 27/12: 3295–3304.

SCARLETT, W. GEORGE (2005). 'Toward a Developmental Analysis of Religious and Spiritual Development'. In E. C. Roehlkepartain, P. E. King, L. M. Wagener, and P. L. Benson (eds.), *The Handbook of Spiritual Development in Childhood and Adolescence*. Thousand Oaks, Calif.: Sage Publications, 21–33.

SMART, NINIAN (1989). *The World's Religions: Old Traditions and Modern Transformation*. Cambridge: Cambridge University Press.

SMITH, W. CANTWELL (1979). *Faith and Belief*. Princeton: Princeton University Press.

SOBEL, CAROLYN P. (2001). *The Cognitive Sciences: An Interdisciplinary Approach*. Mountain View, Calif.: Mayfield.

SPILKA, BERNARD (2003). 'Religion and Biology'. In B. Spilka, R. W. Hood Jr., B. Hunsberger, and R. Gorsuch, *The Psychology of Religion: An Empirical Approach*, 3rd edn. New York and London: Guilford Press, 54–72.

VOSNIADOU, STELLA, and BREWER, WILLIAM P. (1992). 'Mental Models of the Earth: A Study of Conceptual Change in Childhood'. *Cognitive Psychology*, 24: 535–85.

WALACH, HARALD, and REICH, K. HELMUT (2005). 'Reconnecting Science and Religion: Toward Overcoming a Taboo'. *Zygon: Journal of Religion and Science*, 40: 423–41.

WATTS, FRASER N., and WILLIAMS, MARK (1988). *The Psychology of Religious Knowing*. Cambridge: Cambridge University Press.

WOLFE, PATRICIA, and NEVILLS, PAMELA (2004). *Building The Reading Brain, PreK–3*. Thousand Oaks, Calif., and London: Corwin.

WULFF, DAVID M. (1997). *Psychology of Religion: Classsic and Contemporary Views*. New York: Wiley.

SUGGESTED READING

DOWLING, ELISABETH M., and SCARLETT, W. GEORGE (eds.) (2005). *Encyclopedia of Religious and Spiritual Development*. Thousand Oaks, Calif.: Sage.

OSER, FRITZ K., SCARLETT, W. GEORGE, and BUCHER, ANTON (2006). 'Religious and Spiritual Development throughout the Life Span'. In W. Damon and R. M. Lemer (eds.-in-chief), *Handbook of Child Psychology*, 6th edn., i: *Theoretical Models of Human Development*, ed. R. M. Lerner. Hoboken, NJ: Wiley, 942–98.

Paloutzian, Raymond F., and Park, Crystal L. (eds.) (2005). *Handbook of the Psychology of Religion and Spirituality.* New York and London: Guilford Press.

Roehlkepartain, Eugene C., King, Pamela Ebstyne, Wagener, Linda, and Benson, Peter L. (eds.) (2005). *The Handbook of Spiritual Development in Childhood and Adolescence.* Thousand Oaks, Calif.: Sage.

Russell, Robert J., Murphy, Nancey, Meyering, Theo C., and Arbib, Michael E. (eds.) (1999). *Scientific Perspectives on Divine Action*, iv: *Neuroscience and the Person.* Vatican City State: Vatican Observatory Publications; Berkeley, Calif.: Center for Theology and Natural Science (CNTS).

Spilka, Bernard, Hood, Ralph W. Jr., Hunsberger, Bruce, and Gorsuch, Richard (2003). *The Psychology of Religion: An Empirical Approach*, 3rd edn. New York and London: Guilford Press.

Wulff, David W. (ed.) (in press). *Handbook of Psychology of Religion.* New York and Oxford: Oxford University Press.

PART III

RELIGION AND BOUNDARIES

MORALITY, SCIENCE, IRRELIGION, ART, AND EMBODIMENT (TRANCE)

CHAPTER 16

SCIENCE AND RELIGION

WILLIAM SIMS BAINBRIDGE

In recent years, many scientists and religious scholars have sought to delineate the possible and proper relations between science and religion. Their views have been rooted in the historical realities of the latter part of the twentieth century, and thus may not apply equally well to either earlier or later periods. This era has been marked by increasing significance of science-based technologies, but in a highly fragmentary manner. Both science and engineering have divided into ever narrower specialties, and thus science does not speak with a single voice on issues that relate to religion. In parallel fashion, religion also has been fragmented, and its different factions relate in different ways to many of the domains of science. Highly educated, relatively secularized mainstream denominations have less to quarrel with science about than do conservative denominations, sects, or the Evangelical Movement. Yet there are good reasons to expect that the fundamental relationship between science and religion is one of mutual hostility.

Scholarly Perspectives

Historically, some religions seem to have encouraged science, and certain religions appear to have affinities with certain branches of science even today. Robert K. Merton

(1970) and Richard Westfall (1958) independently argued that the Protestantism of seventeenth-century England stimulated scientific and technological progress. As with Max Weber's case that the Protestant ethic had an elective affinity with capitalism, religion was not by any means the only cause, and it may have played no role after science had become well established.

There are several threads to the broader argument. Religion may sometimes encourage values, like austerity and rationality, that are conducive to the practice of science. Specific beliefs may encourage scientific thinking. For example, monotheism may imply that the universe follows a single set of laws rather than being chaotically unknowable. Science can even become a religious activity, if it is seen as a way of gaining further revelations about God and the world of nature he created. Finally, the influence can be indirect, as when a state-established religion suppresses witchcraft, thus driving sick people to conventional doctors for cures (Larner 1984). Because the reputations of doctors who hold respectable positions in society are valuable to them, they will seek to find empirically effective cures, thereby supporting medical science.

Popular writers Fritjof Capra (1975) and Gary Zukav (1979) argued that some concepts of modern physics have close affinities to Asian religious or mystical movements. Conversely, their arguments could be read as the claim that modern physics is especially incompatible with Judeo-Christian-Islamic monotheism. The list of discordant concepts may include general relativity, quantum theory, inconsistency and incompleteness in mathematics, models of reality based on chaos and complexity, and perhaps also cybernetic models of the mind, and the expansion of the universe accelerated by dark energy. The question then might become whether some new science-oriented religious tradition could arise, helping people come to terms with the new perceptions of reality proposed by scientists. Some novel religious movements like Scientology have even asserted that they themselves are sciences possessing spiritual technologies.

Perhaps the most influential scholarly typology of relations between science and religion was proposed by Ian Barbour (1990), who suggested that science and religion could relate in any of four different ways: independence, dialogue, integration, and conflict. Scientist Stephen Jay Gould was the most eloquent proponent of the independence view. A popularizer of science, as well as a scientist, he had battled against religion when it attacked the evolutionary principles of his own realm, paleontology. It is possible that his two-decade battle with cancer made him take religion more seriously, but he never himself became religious. In one of his last books, *Rocks of Ages* (Gould 1999), he enunciated a principle he called NOMA, Non-Overlapping Magisteria. The magisterium of science satisfies the human drive to understand the factual character of nature, and the magisterium of religion satisfies the drive to find meaning in our lives and a firm basis for morality.

Dialogue can take many forms, but one of great significance has been the discussion involving hundreds of scientists, religious scholars, and religious scientists on the preservation of the natural environment. For example, at the National Press Club in Washington DC, 17 January 2007, scientists connected with Harvard University's Center for Health and the Global Environment, in partnership with evangelical leaders, issued "An Urgent Call to Action: Scientists and Evangelicals Unite to Protect Creation". A prime scholarly example is the work done by Bron Taylor (2005) and many colleagues in creating *The Encyclopedia of Religion and Nature.* Among the most interesting questions in this area are the possible connections between specific religious traditions and environmental protection. Does the environmental movement have the effect of encouraging the rebirth of pre-Christian nature religions, including nature-oriented neo-pagan groups? Does evangelical Protestantism implicitly discourage environmentalism by promoting the beliefs that God gave the world to humanity for our use, and that God will preserve the environment so long as we keep faith? Whatever the correct answer to such questions might be, they illustrate the fact that dialogue may be most fruitful when it brings together not science and religion in general, but a particular branch of science that has something important to discuss with a particular religious tradition.

The potential for conflict varies across space and time, increasing when there is something specific to fight about and under socio-cultural conditions when it is difficult to disengage from combat. An argument can be made that the latter part of the twentieth century was a time unusually conducive to peace between science and religion, coming after a period in which religion progressively disengaged from public life, losing its established relationship with the state, and science had established formal relations with the state. It is instructive to consider the history of government support for science in the United States. With a few exceptions, like the US Geological Survey, little government money went to science in the nineteenth century. In something like their modern form, the National Institutes for Health were organized in 1930 on the basis of earlier public hygiene work; the National Science Foundation was established in 1950, and the National Aeronautics and Space Administration in 1958. Thus the institutional setting has changed dramatically from earlier centuries, in which overt conflict between science and religion occurred in public settings; but this does not mean that conflict in all forms has ended, or that further historical changes may not establish new potential battlefields.

Philip Hefner (1997) has offered a typology of six options in which religion may dialogue with, and be influenced by, science. He is the long-term editor of *Zygon: Journal of Religion and Science.* As of January 2007, the journal's website described its perspective thus: "Zygon's hypothesis is that, when long-evolved religious wisdom is yoked with significant, recent scientific discoveries about the world and human nature, there results credible expression of basic meaning, values, and moral convictions that provides valid and effective guidance for enhancing human life." Hefner calls the options: modern, postmodern New Age, critical post-Enlightenment, postmodern constructivist, constructivist traditional, and Christian evangelical.

The modern option seeks to translate the accumulated wisdom of the great world religions into scientific terms. Scientists should recognize that religion is the result of a process of evolution that shaped it to serve human survival and well-being. They should also recognize that science has been party to the secularizing process that has eroded the traditional institutions, beliefs, and moral codes that served humanity well over the centuries. If we are to overcome anomie and manage technology wisely, the time-tested wisdom embodied in religious metaphors needs to be translated into terms effective in a scientific age, to promote altruism, restraint, and discipline. Hefner's postmodern New Age option doubts the continuing ability of traditional religion to provide guidance, and looks instead to new mythologies to synthesize a pluralistic consensus.

The critical post-Enlightenment option rejects the idea that religion should be a central authority for the society, but rather inhabits the "obscure margin" of science, transcending what we can know rationally and thus representing human tendencies that science seeks to subjugate. The postmodern constructivist option wants to liberate religion from orthodox assumptions, which may reflect power differentials in society more than universal truths, without wanting either to banish religion from the public sphere or to establish a new orthodoxy. The constructivist traditional option is a theological attempt to reinterpret scientific concepts in terms of traditional religion—for example, saying that the Big Bang postulated by astrophysicists was the event in the Bible when God said, "Let there be light!" Finally, the Christian evangelical option reaffirms that traditional beliefs are not merely true in some metaphoric sense, but also factual and rational, in no way inferior to scientific theories.

Both Barbour and Hefner are sympathetic to religion, and Hefner's categories say much more about how religions should respond to science than about how science should respond to religion. They recognize that science and religion may come into conflict, but they hope for a peaceful and mutually beneficial accommodation. Consideration of some specific areas of dispute, past and present, can put these hopes in perspective.

Geocentrism

Humans are by nature anthropocentric. They are interested in things that affect their own lives, and the pursuit of knowledge is identical to the pursuit of personal benefit. Thus, when they first looked to the heavens with inquiring eyes, they assumed connections to their own lives. The sun provides warmth and light, so what function do the Moon, stars, and planets serve? Ancient peoples derived some minor benefits from astronomy, chiefly in navigation and the calendar, but they sought more. The Babylonians came to believe that their gods dwelled in the planets and developed the tradition of astrology that is still somewhat popular in Western civilization, as a way of anticipating the fate that these deities would give them. This work stimulated their progress in mathematics, and modern scientists still use their division of a circle into 360 degrees (Toulmin and Goodfield 1961).

Greek astronomy and astrology built upon the Babylonian. Mithraism, one of the most successful religious movements that competed with Christianity in the early years of the Roman Empire, incorporated astrological symbolism at the very heart of its creed, and found revolutionary spiritual meaning in the precession of the equinoxes (Ulansey 1989). The discovery of precession, an apparent shifting of the stars caused by a gradual movement of the Earth's axis, was one of the triumphs of ancient astronomy. In the first century BCE, the position of the Sun at the spring equinox moved from the constellation Aries to Pisces, inaugurating the "Age of Pisces", and in our own future it will pass into Aquarius and give us the much-celebrated "Age of Aquarius". It is interesting to speculate how the history of science might have been different, had Mithraism rather than Christianity triumphed.

Unlike Mithraism, Christianity is not saturated with astrological symbolism, and the stars play very minor roles in the Bible. The word "planet" appears only once in the King James Version, in 2 Kings 23: 5 when Josiah suppresses idolatrous priests and those who "burned incense unto Baal, to the sun, and to the moon, and to the planets, and to all the host of heaven". The Bible accepts the pre-scientific notion that heavenly bodies move above a stationary Earth. For example, Ecclesiastes 1: 5 says: "The sun also ariseth, and the sun goeth down, and hasteth to his place where he arose." Two passages describe the miracle of the Sun and the Moon standing still (Joshua 10: 12–13; Habakkuk 3: 11), without awareness of the catastrophe that would come from a sudden halt to the Earth's rotation. Precisely because it rejected the astrology of the Babylonians, the Judeo-Christian tradition was possibly better prepared than Mithraism would have been to accept the rise of modern astronomy, simply because astronomy was largely irrelevant to its central religious beliefs.

However, as we all know, in the early seventeenth century Galileo suffered house arrest and was threatened with torture and death because he taught that the Earth moved around the Sun after the church had condemned this theory. The history of the period is complex, and Galileo's misadventure may have been a mere side effect of the political machinations triggered by the competition between Catholicism and Protestantism. Astronomy was just beginning to emerge as an independent science, and many leading astronomers (notably Tycho Brahe and Johannes Kepler) were professional astrologers.

Social historian Thomas Kuhn (1957) has argued that this period saw a major revolution for science, quite apart from its religious implications. By means of a telescope, Galileo discovered the four largest moons of Jupiter, the first astronomical objects that could be seen to orbit around something other than the Earth. Nicolaus Copernicus and Kepler developed rigorous, mathematical models of the movements of planets around the Sun, including the Earth, and Isaac Newton provided a mathematical theory of gravity to explain the forces at work, developing calculus in the process. Three points are important for the present discussion. First, the new astronomy correctly recognized that heavenly bodies were physical objects, rather than spiritual beings. Second, it disconnected the stars and planets from the fears and desires of everyday life. Third, it displaced humanity from the center of the universe. All three of these developments promoted secularization by denying that the universe is a spiritual realm centered on human beings.

Since the days of Galileo, this process of demystification and estrangement has continued. An almost immediate corollary of the heliocentric model of the solar system is the discovery that the stars are very far away, because their relative position does not change appreciably over the course of six months as the Earth moves more than 180,000,000 miles from one side of its orbit to the opposite side. In the twentieth century, careful measurement showed that this parallax did actually exist, but was very tiny even for the closest stars. The nearest stars other than the Sun appear to move against the background of more distant stars less than one 4,000th of a degree, implying a distance of fully 25,000,000,000,000 miles. Further discoveries revealed that the Sun is a very ordinary star far from the center of a galaxy that is only one of a myriad of galaxies filling a space vastly larger than that encompassing our galaxy.

This modern astronomical awareness is humbling and might seem to reinforce Psalm 8, when it asks, "What is man, that thou art mindful of him?" However, it does not merely erode the feeling that we are God's special creatures. It also undercuts some traditional arguments for the very existence of God, notably the argument from design. This is the theory that the world must have been created by a benevolent God for our use, because it is so well suited to our existence. The argument from design pre-dates Christianity, and it features prominently in the tenth book of *The Laws* by Plato.

Sociologist and biochemist Lawrence Joseph Henderson (1913; 1917) expressed a sophisticated version of this argument in two books early in the twentieth century, offering a detailed chemical analysis to support the view that the properties of hydrogen, oxygen, carbon, and other elements are so improbably well suited to the evolution of life that no mere "mechanism" can be responsible, and the universe shows the hand of "teleology" or God.

The argument from design weakens once we realize that the universe contains an uncountably vast number of planets, having a wide range of conditions, such that intelligent life could have emerged on some of them purely by chance. This counter argument is often called the Anthropic Principle: The conditions we observe in our environment are favorable to our existence because only in such an environment could we have come into existence (Barrow and Tipler 1986; Bainbridge 1997). You are not reading this essay on the planet Venus, because its oppressive, burning hot, acid atmosphere would kill you in an instant. Thus, our existence in a propitious environment is merely a selection effect. Creating such a vast universe would seem to be the most inefficient way for God to create us, which raises the suspicion that we do not matter much to God at all, if indeed he even exists.

Science has not yet told us how the entire universe came into being; so any further discussion must be somewhat speculative. One possibility is that the entire universe is a quantum event, an uncaused, random fluctuation in space. Related is the observation that the sum total of all the positive and negative forces in the universe seems remarkably close to zero, and if the sum really is zero, then no creative effort at all was required to bring the universe into existence. The currently respected inflationary theory of the early history of the universe says that the universe we observe is only an immeasurably tiny portion of a multiverse divided into an infinite number of regions having every possible combination of physical characteristics, including different properties of chemical elements, thus providing further scope for the Anthropic Principle to explain the fundamental constants of physics. The very notions of space and time may merely reflect how we have evolved to perceive the relations between forces and entities within our world, and they may have no objective meaning for the cosmos as a whole.

Sociologically, the alienation of contemporary physics and cosmology from the dominant human cultures is a remarkable fact. Suffice it to say for now that few humans have a clue what cosmologists are talking about, and many ideas in physics and astronomy are highly counterintuitive. People go about their everyday lives as if the Earth were the center of the universe, and they still say that the Sun rises and sets, even if most know on some level that the Earth really spins on its axis. Thus, after Galileo's revolution, the effect of astronomical progress on religion has been slight. For their part, astronomers have been working away without benefit of religious guidance. Before recent concepts in cosmology and astrophysics could conflict with religion in a sociologically significant manner, other changes would need to again establish a close connection between the distant stars and our ordinary lives.

Evolution

Every major religion or traditional culture possesses at least one myth about the origins of living things, but it is the Judeo-Christian tradition that especially came into conflict with the theory of evolution by natural selection in the nineteenth century, because it was in Christian nations that this perspective was invented and first spread. Before the work of Charles Darwin, religion influenced geology and paleontology in a grand debate between catastrophists and gradualists (Gillispie 1951). Catastrophists were influenced by the legend of Noah's flood, and believed that the geological record of strata and fossils was laid down in a series of relatively brief episodes of catastrophic change. Gradualists believed that the Earth changed very slowly over many millions of years. The gradualist view that the Earth is very ancient is a necessary assumption for evolution by natural selection, because selection cannot occur rapidly.

Today, gradualism is not only dominant within geology, but well supported by ample empirical evidence, including proof of the antiquity of the Earth from radioactive dating methods. However, in recent years, a role has also been found for a kind of neo-catastrophism, in which asteroid impacts on our planet are thought to have ended the era of the dinosaurs, and other discontinuities in the fossil record are hypothesized to be the result of relatively brief geological, climatic, or even evolutionary episodes. The idea that essentially random asteroid impacts could kill off the dinosaurs, perhaps thereby giving mammals more chance to evolve into human beings, does not harmonize with traditional religion, as early nineteenth-century catastrophism did.

For philosopher Daniel C. Dennett, evolution by natural selection is a fundamentally revolutionary idea, which is incompatible not only with religion but with many other traditional human notions. He suggests that the theory is composed of three fundamental ideas (Dennett 1995: 343):

1. Variation: there is a continuing abundance of different elements.
2. Heredity or replication: the elements have the capacity to create copies or replicas of themselves.
3. Differential "fitness": the number of copies of an element that are created in a given time varies, depending on interactions between the features of that element and features of the environment in which it persists.

The elements could be the genes of mice, for a hypothetical example. Mutations in their genetic codes, caused by accidental damage by viruses or radiation, ensure that there will exist a range of genetic variations, alleles of every gene. Let us imagine that some genes affect how attractive the scent of cheese is for the mouse, and others influence the mouse's reaction to small rectangular objects. Mice that love cheese but are not worried by small rectangular objects will be killed by mousetraps, thereby removing their genes from the gene pool. Mice lacking these characteristics will survive, have many children, and dominate the population. While humans will respond by consciously inventing new mousetraps, no conscious action designed the mice to avoid the traps. God did not make them trap-averse; nor did the tiny rodents debate empirical studies of mysterious mouse deaths and decide to avoid traps. Evolution is an entirely mechanical process, lacking purpose or awareness, based on biased sampling from random variation.

Porter Abbott (2003) suggests that human thought organizes things in terms of narratives—stories in which protagonists face obstacles and take actions in pursuit of goals—and thus the scientific theory of evolution cannot compete with religious stories, because it is unnarratable. Religion offers "the greatest story ever told". Further, Western religions offer stories that relate directly to the life of the average person, offering narrative expressions of hope and comfort. Who could be so heartless as to explain to the mother of a dying child that the death will be a good thing, because it removes inferior genes from the gene pool?

However, increasingly prominent features of modern life harmonize with evolution by natural selection and even require it. Infectious disease is now commonly discussed in terms of mutation of diseases—like AIDS and bird flu—that become more contagious, triggering epidemics. The economic success of particular products or corporations can be modeled in terms of natural selection. Religion itself was described in evolutionary terms by sociologist Talcott Parsons in 1964. Importantly, effective computer methods for solving problems and designing technologies have employed evolution ever since genetic algorithms were first introduced into computer science decades ago (Holland 1975). The success of the theory of evolution by natural selection is becoming increasingly apparent, in a widening circle of practical fields, potentially outweighing its counterintuitiveness and unpleasant implications.

Especially in the United States, religious opposition to the theory of evolution has sometimes taken pseudo-scientific form, under terms like "creation science", or the "theory of intelligent design". Given the diversity of people who become scientists, and the relative openness of scientific debates, one would think that a few great geologists and paleontologists would endorse these ideas, if only for personal reasons. Research by Ronald Numbers (2006) reveals, however, that almost without exception the creationist propagandists are incompetent scientists with few if any accomplishments to their credit.

Psychology

It could be said that the crucial question about religion is not whether God exists, but whether the soul exists. Yale cognitive psychologist Paul Bloom (2004) has predicted that science and religion will battle to define the human mind in the twenty-first century. Already, many cognitive scientists have sought to explain religion as the natural result of human biological evolution, and in so doing to explain it away. Bloom himself argues that we falsely believe that we possess souls, because we are not conscious of the way our brains operate.

Historically speaking, however, the relationship between religion and the sciences of the mind has been tense at least since the middle of the nineteenth century, when psychiatry first established itself on a professional basis. As doctors documented how injury or illness could rob a patient of his mental or moral faculties, they struggled to assure the clergy that (somehow) their discoveries did not contradict religious notions of the immortal soul (Ray 1863; 1871). In the middle of the nineteenth century, psychiatrists in Britain, France, and the USA believed that religious insanity could be caused by excessive excitement, as generated by revival meetings, but they were careful to absolve the mainstream denominations to which most of their paying customers belonged (Bainbridge 1984). The issues raised by psychiatry with respect to moral responsibility and the nature of the soul still bother not only the churches but the legal system today.

The tensions became acute with the rise of the psychoanalytic movement, as illustrated by the title of one's of Freud's (1927) books about religion, *The Future of an Illusion*. Freud's disciple Geza Roheim (1955) went so far as to brand religion a shared psychosis. Ironically, several authors have argued that psychoanalysis was predicated upon Freud's Jewish heritage. John Cuddihy (1974) derived it from the culturally rich but socially marginal status of educated Jews in Western Europe. David Bakan (1958) and Nandor Fodor (1971) argued that psychoanalysis was the expression of Jewish mysticism. Other authors, like Peter Breggin (1971), suggested that psychoanalytically oriented psychotherapy was a form of applied ethics, rather than being a science-based psychological technology. Taken to the logical extreme, this analysis would argue that psychoanalysis was at heart religious, either a mystical cult or some hard-to-categorize new form of spiritual ethics. As such, it would naturally be in direct competition with the traditional Christian religion of the surrounding society, and thus biased toward diagnosing that established religion as pathological. Interestingly, when contemporary cognitive scientist Steven Pinker (1997) writes for a non-technical audience, he feels the need to attack both Freud and conventional religion.

In principle, "cognitive science" covers all systematic studies of human, animal, or machine intelligence, including perception and emotion as well as cognition. The website of the Cognitive Science Society and the front page of its journal, *Cognitive Science*, list seven fields: artificial intelligence, linguistics, psychology, philosophy, neuroscience, anthropology, and education. It is perhaps a tragic accident of history that sociology and political science have not been actively involved in the development of "cog-sci", omissions that future generations will need to correct. In such research areas as attitudes, beliefs, social influence, and ideology, these two sciences are certainly as cognitive as any other.

The exchange theory of religion proposed by Stark and Bainbridge (1987), sometimes too-narrowly called the "rational choice approach", is firmly sociological; yet it is also cognitive. The theory begins with a set of axioms, noting that human perception and action take place through time, from the past into the future. The past consists of the universe of conditions which can be known but not influenced. The future consists of the universe of conditions which can be influenced but not known. Human action is directed by a complex but finite information-processing system that functions to identify problems and attempt solutions to them. Some desired rewards are limited in supply, including some that simply do not exist. In the absence of a strongly desired reward, humans will seek information, often through social exchanges, that will tell them how to obtain the reward. As people exchange rewards of many kinds, they enter into obligations toward each other. When one person cannot provide the reward an exchange partner needs, there is a tendency to provide instead a "compensator", a belief that the reward can be obtained in the future. The more difficult and desired the reward, the more distant the future, until it becomes the supernatural. Supernatural beings are social-constructed, imaginary beings that offer rewards no human can give. Over the course of history, as formal organizations began to emerge, the exchange of supernaturally based compensators gave rise to the institution of religion.

Notice two things about this solidly sociological theory of religion. First, it is highly cognitive. Humans plan for the future, exchange information, and analyze problems under the control of minds that are information-processing systems. Second, it is highly damaging to religion. Unlike Parsons and other functionalists, it does not assume that religion serves positive functions. The implication is that compensators are false beliefs, although exchange theory publications often note that compensators are like IOUs that might possibly be redeemed for the actual rewards under conceivable future circumstances. In the absence of convincing empirical evidence that religion is beneficial in some indirect way, this theory debunks religion as a structure of illusions and deceptions.

Better known within the cognitive science community is a network of ideas proposed by many writers that might be called the "social inference" theory of religion. Pascal Boyer (2001), Scott Atran (2002), Justin L. Barrett (2004), and several other psychologists or anthropologists have argued that belief in the existence of supernatural beings comes from a specific function that evolution programmed into our brains, whether it is lodged in particular brain structures or encoded in some more subtle way. Over the hundreds of thousands or even millions of years during which human intelligence evolved, we lived under conditions in which we needed to deal with the animals and humans in our environment. As I like to put it, we learned to understand our predators, prey, and partners. We needed to predict the behavior of both dangerous animals that wanted to eat us and the animals that we ourselves wanted to eat. In exchange with other humans, we needed to know how to motivate them to help us, and to distinguish trustworthy from untrustworthy exchange partners.

With all these evolutionary pressures, the human brain developed an "inference system" that interprets the perceptions and intentions of other intelligent beings.

It was so important to our well-being and survival that it automatically takes charge under a great variety of circumstances. Thus, whenever we encounter a set of phenomena exhibiting complex behavior, we invoke our social inference system. We could do this with the weather, for example, or a flowing stream, or the entire universe. Religion, according to this theory, is the result of a hyperactive social inference system that sees intelligent beings where none actually exist.

Presumably, it would not be difficult to integrate exchange theory with social inference theory, as a step toward closer relations between sociology and cognitive science. Both theories describe an ironic situation. Religion is an expression of fundamental human nature, especially of some of the most valuable functions of the human mind; yet religious belief is a collection of cognitive errors. Needless to say, these theories could turn out to be wrong, or to be true to a great extent but incomplete. In neither case are the basic theoretical assumptions hostile to religion, but the conclusions are. Thus, if cognitive science grows in social influence, perhaps on the basis of solid scientific successes in a variety of areas, there is a good chance, as Bloom says, that it will come into direct conflict with faith.

Convergence

Sociobiologist Edward O. Wilson (1998) has argued that the many sciences are rapidly unifying into one science, a process he calls "consilience". Engineer Mihail Roco and sociologist William Bainbridge (2003) have edited a series of books whose authors argue that the various branches of technology are likewise converging, notably nanotechnology, biotechnology, information technology, and new technologies based on cognitive science. Wilson and Bainbridge are quite explicit in suggesting that religion probably cannot participate in this unification, with the result that conflict between the realms of faith and research is likely to increase.

If there are no longer any major gaps in knowledge, any God of the gaps will of necessity be small. When science was fragmented, most scientists did not directly experience any contradiction between the work they did and their family's traditional religious beliefs. But when evolution by natural selection and artificial intelligence are applied across all fields, it will be hard for scientists themselves to sustain religious faith. Unified science has the potential to become the universal world culture, because the technological might of any nation must be based upon it. Thus, one might theorize that the hostility between science and religion will spill over into the world at large.

This scenario is predicated on the assumption that science actually is influential in modern society, and this may not be the case. The technological products of science are fundamental to economic well-being, but scientists do not control them. Rather, entrepreneurs, corporate executives, and government policymakers hold the power, and make use of science only when it suits them. For many years, the US National Science Foundation conducted questionnaire studies of the attitudes and awareness of the American public. By and large, only about 15 percent even claimed to be very aware of what was happening in science (Division of Science Resources Statistics 2002).

The gulf of understanding between scientists and the general public is well illustrated by two of the items in a science test that was included in the General Social Survey, as 2,434 American adults responded to them. Respondents were asked to say whether these two statements were true or not true: "Astrology—the study of star signs—has some scientific truth"; "Human beings developed from earlier species of animals." Science would say that the astrology statement is false, and the second (an evolution statement that avoids using this word) is true. About 25 percent believe both statements are true, and another 25 percent believe both are false. Thus, half the population disagrees with scientists half the time. About 26 percent say astrology may have some truth, but evolution does not, completely disagreeing with scientists. The position that science would endorse—astrology is false, but evolution is true—is held by only 24 percent of American adults.

The facts that science is not yet really unified, and most people understand very little about science, means that religious conservatives who reject the theory of evolution are not hostile toward scientists in general. In the United States, however, some commentators have identified a worrisome trend in which the two main political parties are becoming religiously polarized, with Evangelicals identified with the Republicans.

Chris Mooney (2005) argues that the Republican Party has become an enemy of science, because many big corporations that support it wish to suppress troublesome findings about the health and environmental harm caused by their products, and the party has grown stronger by attracting religious conservatives who reject science because it threatens their ideological and moral system. Much earlier, Otto Larsen (1992) showed that the Reagan administration had tried to abolish social science at the National Science Foundation around 1982, presumably because they believed it supported left-wing ideologies. Sociologists Rodney Stark and Roger Finke (2000) have complained that secular social scientists have exhibited a bias against religion that was based on ideological secularism rather than objective analysis. If they are correct, then some future accommodation is possible, if sociology yields to religion; if not, perhaps not.

Such grand questions aside, there is much to be said for well-focused, down-to-earth empirical research on the complex relationship between science and religion, such as that carried out by Robert A. Campbell (2005; Campbell and Curtis 1996). His research tends to find that young people think religion and science can coexist, that their views are heavily shaped by friends and family, and that there are substantial national differences. Changes in public attitudes and beliefs tend to be slow, but not glacially so, and it is reasonable to expect that they reflect concrete changes in people's own lives, more than abstract intellectual trends among the intelligentsia.

Conclusion

Many pious intellectuals, religious social scientists, and other opinion leaders have sought to strengthen harmony between religion and science. For example, the John Templeton Foundation has a vigorous Science and Religion Program, described on its website thus: "In pursuing research at the boundary between science and religion, the Foundation seeks to unite credible and rigorous science with the exploration of humanity's basic spiritual and religious quests." *Zygon*'s website says: "The journal's contributors seek to keep united what may often become disconnected: values with knowledge, goodness with truth, religion with science." The historical and sociological literature implies that accomplishing all this will be difficult.

References

Abbott, H. Porter (2003). "Unnarratable Knowledge: The Difficulty of Understanding Evolution by Natural Selection". In David Herman (ed.), *Narrative Theory and the Cognitive Sciences*. Stanford, Calif.: Center for the Study of Language and Information, 143–62.

Atran, Scott (2002). *In Gods We Trust*. Oxford: Oxford University Press.

Bainbridge, William Sims (1984). "Religious Insanity in America: The Official Nineteenth-Century Theory". *Sociological Analysis*, 45: 223–40.

—— (1997). "The Omicron Point: Sociological Application of the Anthropic Theory". In Raymond A. Eve, Sara Horsfall, and Mary E. Lee (eds.), *Chaos and Complexity in Sociology: Myths, Models and Theory*. Thousand Oaks, Calif.: Sage, 91–101.

Bakan, David (1958). *Sigmund Freud and the Jewish Mystical Tradition*. Princeton: Van Nostrand.

Barbour, Ian G. (1990). *Religion in an Age of Science*. San Francisco: Harper & Row.

Barrett, Justin L. (2004). *Why Would Anyone Believe in God?* Walnut Creek, Calif.: Altamira Press.

Barrow, John D., and Tipler, Frank J. (1986). *The Anthropic Cosmological Principle*. New York: Oxford University Press.

Bloom, Paul (2004). *Descartes' Baby: How the Science of Child Development Explains what Makes Us Human*. New York: Basic Books.

Boyer, Pascal (2001). *Religion Explained: The Evolutionary Origins of Religious Thought.* New York: Basic Books.

Breggin, Peter Roger (1971). "Psychotherapy as Applied Ethics". *Psychiatry,* 34: 59–74.

Campbell, Robert A. (2005). "Students' Views on the Relationship between Religion and Science: Analyses of Results from a Comparative Survey". *Canadian Review of Sociology and Anthropology,* 42/3: 249–65.

—— and Curtis, James E. (1996). "The Public's Views on the Future of Religion and Science: Cross-National Survey Results". *Review of Religious Research,* 37/3: 164–71.

Capra, Fritjof (1975). *The Tao of Physics: An Exploration of the Parallels between Modern Physics and Eastern Mysticism.* New York: Random House.

Cuddihy, John Murray (1974). *The Ordeal of Civility: Freud, Marx, Lévi-Strauss, and the Jewish Struggle with Modernity.* New York: Basic Books.

Dennett, Daniel C. (1995). *Darwin's Dangerous Idea: Evolution and the Meanings of Life.* New York: Simon & Schuster.

Division of Science Resources Statistics (2002). *Science and Engineering Indicators—2002.* Arlington, Va.: National Science Foundation.

Fodor, Nandor (1971). *Freud, Jung and Occultism.* New Hyde Park, NY: International Universities Press.

Freud, Sigmund (1961[1927]). *The Future of an Illusion.* Garden City, NY: Doubleday.

Gillispie, Charles Coulston (1951). *Genesis and Geology: A Study in the Relations of Scientific Thought, Natural Theology, and Social Opinion in Great Britain, 1790–1850.* Cambridge, Mass.: Harvard University Press.

Gould, Stephen Jay (1999). *Rocks of Ages: Science and Religion in the Fullness of Life.* New York: Ballantine.

Hefner, Philip (1997). "The Science–Religion Relation: Controversy, Convergence, and Search for Meaning". *International Journal for the Psychology of Religion,* 7/3: 143–57.

Henderson, Lawrence Joseph (1913). *The Fitness of the Environment.* New York: Macmillan.

—— (1917). *The Order of Nature.* Cambridge, Mass.: Harvard University Press.

Holland, John H. (1975). *Natural and Artificial Systems.* Ann Arbor: University of Michigan Press.

Kuhn, Thomas S. (1957). *The Copernican Revolution: Planetary Astronomy in the Development of Western Thought.* Cambridge, Mass.: Harvard University Press.

Larner, Christina (1984). *Witchcraft and Religion: The Politics of Popular Belief.* New York: Blackwell.

Larsen, Otto N. (1992). *Milestones and Millstones: Social Science at the National Science Foundation, 1945–1991.* New Brunswick, NJ: Transaction Publishers.

Merton, Robert K. (1970). *Science, Technology and Society in Seventeenth-Century England.* New York: H. Fertig.

Mooney, Chris (2005). *The Republican War on Science.* New York: Basic Books.

Numbers, Ronald L. (2006). *The Creationists: From Scientific Creationism to Intelligent Design.* Cambridge, Mass.: Harvard University Press.

Parsons, Talcott (1964). "Evolutionary Universals in Society". *American Sociological Review,* 29: 339–57.

Pinker, Steven (1997). *How the Mind Works.* New York: Norton.

Ray, Isaac (1863). *Mental Hygiene.* Boston: Ticknor & Fields.

—— (1871). *A Treatise on the Medical Jurisprudence of Insanity.* Boston: Little Brown.

Roco, Mihail C., and Bainbridge, William Sims (2003). *Converging Technologies for Improving Human Performance.* Dordrecht: Kluwer.

Roheim, Geza (1955). *Magic and Schizophrenia.* Bloomington, Ind.: Indiana University Press.

Stark, Rodney, and Bainbridge, William Sims (1987). *A Theory of Religion.* New York: Peter Lang for the University of Toronto.

—— and Finke, Roger (2000). *Acts of Faith: Explaining the Human Side of Religion.* Berkeley: University of California Press.

Taylor, Bron R. (ed.) (2005). *The Encyclopedia of Religion and Nature.* New York: Thoemmes Continuum.

Toulmin, Stephen E., and Goodfield, June (1961). *The Fabric of the Heavens.* New York: Harper.

Ulansey, David (1989). *The Origins of the Mithraic Mysteries: Cosmology and Salvation in the Ancient World.* New York: Oxford University Press.

Westfall, Richard S. (1958). *Science and Religion in Seventeenth-Century England.* New Haven: Yale University Press.

Wilson, Edward O. (1998). *Consilience: The Unity of Knowledge.* New York: Knopf.

Zukav, Gary (1979). *The Dancing Wu Li Masters: An Overview of the New Physics.* New York: Morrow.

Suggested Reading

Bainbridge, William Sims (2007). *Across the Secular Abyss.* Lanham, Md.: Lexington.

Also Taylor (2005).

CHAPTER 17

ATHEISM

WILLIAM SIMS BAINBRIDGE

WHILE the research literature in the social science of religion is vast, the study of irreligion remains meager, fragmentary, and unappreciated. However, the fact that some individuals are able to get along without religious faith poses challenging questions for all theories of religion. We cannot understand faith without taking account of its absence, and we cannot fully understand the history of religion without imagining its disappearance. In any case, Atheists are an understudied group in society with great relevance to religion, and many of them complain that they are the victims of it.

DEFINING AND MEASURING ATHEISM

"Atheism" can be defined in many different ways, depending upon one's purpose, the surrounding social context, and one's own beliefs about divinity. For example, one may say that Atheists are people who do not believe in the existence of God, or that they are people who in some active way reject the possibility of God's existence. This distinction immediately raises the problem of defining "belief", which in turn is dependent upon the standards for belief in the surrounding society. In a traditional Christian or Islamic society, people are expected to proclaim faith in God, with a strong commitment to a well-defined belief system. Under such circumstances, an Atheist may merely be someone who harbors serious doubts. Arguably, in a polytheistic society an Atheist may be someone who does not believe in enough gods, such that a monotheist could be accused of Atheism.

Even such details as the question of whether one should capitalize the word depend upon one's decisions about such issues. Perhaps a mere atheist lacks belief, whereas an Atheist actively professes the conviction that gods do not exist, capitalized to show comparability with a professing Christian. Alternatively, one could argue that the word should not be capitalized unless the people belong to specific Atheist organizations, which, frankly, are few and far between. This essay chooses to capitalize the term in recognition that Atheists are a minority group experiencing some measure of discrimination in many societies, certainly including the United States. In the terminology of George H. Smith (1979), "implicit atheism" is mere lack of belief, whereas "explicit atheism" is the conscious (and perhaps public) rejection of the existence of gods.

Atheism is often contrasted with Agnosticism. The distinction is not entirely clear conceptually, but presumably Agnostics disagree less strenuously with those who possess religious faith, and receive less hostility from them in return. As J. G. Schurman (1895) observed over a century ago, agnosticism can be defined in two different ways. First, an agnostic may be an individual who does not personally know whether or not God exists. Second, an agnostic may be someone holding the philosophical position that it is impossible to know. This second, philosophical variety of Agnosticism is actually very similar to Atheism, in that it clearly rejects the kind of knowable God that most religious people believe in.

When social scientists began asking people about their religion in questionnaire surveys, it became readily apparent that there was a third group lacking religious faith, at least as large as the other two, but not associated with any well-developed philosophical position. These are often disrespectfully called the "nones", a pun on "nuns", because when asked what religion they belong to, they say "none" (Vernon 1968). Some of these nones may really be Atheists who conceal their beliefs in fear of reprisal from the religious people in their environment. Others may be Agnostics who are ignorant of the term or of the philosophical arguments associated with it. Others may simply be uninterested in religion, having no opinions about it. A small fraction turn out to be members of extreme religious sects who connect "religion" with the mainstream or liberal denominations they reject, thus inadvertently telling the poll-taker that they are irreligious when they really mean to say that they are hyper-religious. Some may be unchurched believers who think the question was about whether they belong to an organized religion. Finally, others are what scholars call "freethinkers", possessing unique views that are not identical to those of any particular religious denomination, although this term seems to have dropped out of popular usage in recent decades.

With distinctions like these in mind, social scientists have written questionnaire items to try to distinguish different categories of belief. Especially influential is the question about God included in the General Social Survey (GSS), a repeated questionnaire study of American adults, which is available online in an excellent statistical analysis system.[1] Asked in six years from 1988 through 2000, this question presented respondents with six statements and asked them to select the one that comes closest to expressing what they believe about God. Fully 64.4 percent said, "I know God really exists and I have no doubts about it." An additional 16.6 percent said, "While I have doubts, I feel that I do believe in God." Another 4.1 percent selected the following awkwardly worded statement: "I find myself believing in God some of the time, but not at others." Thus, a total of about 85 percent of Americans profess some degree of faith in God as conventionally defined.

The largest remaining group, 8.4 percent, could be described as Deists, because they selected: "I don't believe in a personal God, but I do believe in a Higher Power of some kind." Just 4.0 percent were Agnostics, saying, "I don't know whether there is a God and I don't believe there is any way to find out." This leaves just 2.5 percent who are Atheists, proclaiming: "I don't believe in God." A total of 8,027 people answered the questions, but only 203 picked this Atheistic option. Given that most survey datasets have far fewer respondents than does the General Social Survey, we have very little data about sufficient numbers of Atheists to carry out ambitious statistical analysis. This is one reason why there does not exist an extensive social-scientific literature on Atheism, although once we conceptualize Atheists as a disadvantaged minority group, we may find both scientific and humanitarian reasons to make a special effort to study them.

Factors Associated with Atheism

Following a suggestion by Richard Dawkins (2006), a scientist and vehement critic of religion, some Atheists have begun calling themselves "Brights", implying both that they are unusually intelligent and that the future for humanity would be bright if we were to abandon religious superstitions. However brilliant some critics of faith may be, we do not have evidence that Atheists on average are more intelligent than other people. Indeed, data from the General Social Survey suggest something quite different.

The survey contains a set of word-meaning questions, and the sum of correct answers—a variable appropriately called WORDSUM—functions reasonably well as a short-form intelligence test. I calculated the average scores for people giving different answers to the question about God's existence. There was little difference between people who are certain God exists (5.83) and those vacillators who believe

[1] <http://sda.berkeley.edu/archive.htm>.

in God part of the time (5.84). Those who harbor doubts but still believe achieved a much higher score (6.29). The Deist position scored considerably higher (6.82), and the highest score was earned by Agnostics (7.05). Atheists scored on average rather low (6.13), higher than dogmatic believers and vacillators, but lower than the more sophisticated brands of faith and far below Agnostics.

Another way to examine the intellectual status of Atheists, using GSS data, is to look at different education levels. Among those 6,207 American adults answering the questions who have not completed four years of college, 2.1 percent are Atheists, compared with 4.0 percent among 1,794 who are college graduates. The comparable figures for Agnostics are 3.1 percent and 7.4 percent. Apparently, college education does not quite double the fraction who are Atheists, but it more than doubles the proportion who are Agnostics. Of the 1,794 respondents who graduated from college, 549 achieved graduate degrees. Atheists are about 4.1 percent of ordinary college graduates, but only 3.8 percent of those with graduate degrees. The trend is quite different for Agnostics, 5.8 percent among mere graduates, and 10.9 percent among those with graduate degrees.

Thus, Agnosticism may be a more sophisticated way of being irreligious than Atheism. Alternatively, one may say that it is more polite. An Agnostic avoids debating the existence of God with believers, whereas an Atheist challenges their faith directly. When Snell Putney and Russell Middleton (1961) surveyed religious rebellion among youth decades ago, they used a question about God comparable to the one in the GGS, but coding two of the responses as Atheist: "I am sure there is no God." "Although one can never be certain, I believe there is no God." Their Agnostic response focused on personal doubts rather than philosophical undecidability: "I find it impossible to decide whether or not I believe in God." Their Deist response was also somewhat different from the GSS choice: "I believe in God, but as an impersonal force not concerned with individuals." Two points are worth noting here. First, questionnaire studies have included a variety of statements about God that indicated varying degrees of rejection of traditional faith in a personal deity. Second, we can never be sure how closely a respondent's personal views really fit the exact wording of the response he or she selected. In particular, it is hazardous to guess the difference in meaning that questionnaire respondents give to choices that the researcher codes as Atheist versus Agnostic.

The social context undoubtedly matters in how people define their own options. Putney and Middleton found that many of their respondents had moved away from their parents' religious views, and these predominantly moved toward the modal response among their own generation. Given that the respondents were college students, not surprisingly they tended to move toward a more secular perspective. However, some young people become more religious than their parents, and many such people may not have been included in the study because they did not attend college. There was also some evidence that young people whose parents disagreed with each other about religion tended to be closer to the view of their mothers. If college is an especially hospitable environment for irreligion, then whole cultures may differ, perhaps on the basis of their distinctive histories.

In a multi-nation study, Bernadette Hayes (2000) examined factors associated with being a "religious independent", sometimes describing Atheists as a separate category. Notably, men were more likely to fit these descriptions than women. The General Social Survey reveals the following: of 1,939 men answering the God question described above, 3.7 percent were Atheists, and 6.0 percent were Agnostics. The figures for 3,227 women were 1.7 percent and 2.5 percent.

As a member of a team headed by James Witte (2003), I was able to include religion-related items in *Survey2001*, a major online questionnaire study sponsored by the National Geographic Society. A series of items first asked respondents what religious tradition they belong to, then asked those answering "none" to say explicitly whether they were Atheists, Agnostics, or simply had "no religion". In this study, the gender differences were not huge. Atheists were 6.4 percent of 5,744 males, and 5.0 percent of 5,272 females. The figures for Agnostics were 6.7 percent versus 6.1 percent, and 11.0 percent versus 10.4 percent for "no religion". This suggests to me that while sex differences on faith in God are real, they are at least partly a result of education and cultural variables that are minimized by taking a sample of web-users and National Geographic readers.

Acknowledging that *Survey2001* is at best suggestive, because it did not employ a random sample, this international study affords the opportunity to compare cultures, because it was administered in four languages: English, Spanish, German, and Italian. Combining the three irreligious categories (Non-religious, Agnostic, Atheist) we find that the linguistic groups differ somewhat in rejection of religion: English (22.8 percent), Spanish (18.3 percent), German (26.7 percent), and Italian (23.5 percent). Given that they were recruited online by the National Geographic Society and various educational institutions, the respondents are better educated than the average. However, we can hope that this bias does not greatly distort cross-national comparisons. The fraction of the irreligious professing Atheism varies greatly across these four groups: English (22.4 percent), Spanish (22.4 percent), German (43.8 percent), and Italian (37.4 percent).

We may conjecture that the strength of Atheism among German-speakers partly reflects the historical residue of state-sponsored Atheism in East Germany, and that the Italian strength of Atheism may reflect historical debates about the role of the Roman Catholic Church in Italian politics. The more general point is that Atheism is only one of several forms of estrangement from religion, and social conditions will affect how often individuals express that particular position.

Colin Campbell (1972) noted that social scientists might tend to conceptualize Atheism in terms of estrangement from society, especially if they adhere to the tradition established by Émile Durkheim (1915) that considers religion to be an expression of social society. In the most simplified version, Durkheimian sociology says that when a person worships God, he or she is really worshiping society.

People who refuse for whatever reason to submit to society's religious demands are Atheists. With this in mind, I analyzed the connection between Atheism and responses to several questions that other researchers had placed in *Survey2001*, having to do with social obligations.

A number of comparisons suggested that Atheists are not fundamentally anti-social, but tend to be weak as regards enduring social bonds. Just 5.0 percent of 4,396 married individuals were Atheists, compared with 9.1 percent of 806 respondents who were part of a couple that is cohabiting without benefit of formal marriage. Among those with two or more children, 3.9 percent were Atheists, compared with 5.8 percent of those with one child, and 6.2 percent of those with no children. One of the more remarkable questions asked how much the respondent would enjoy a family reunion. The percent who were Atheists varied greatly across the responses: like it very much (3.4 percent), would like (5.7 percent), mixed feelings (9.1 percent), not really (9.8 percent), and not at all (15.9 percent). Apparently Atheists resist social obligations, and we can wonder if society returns the favor.

Hostility toward Atheists

In ways often subtle or covert, Atheists suffer prejudice and discrimination in the United States and in varying degrees in other nations as well. One of the offenders is the Bible, notably the beginning of Psalm 14.

- King James Version: "The fool hath said in his heart, There is no God. They are corrupt, they have done abominable works, there is none that doeth good."
- Contemporary English Version: "Only a fool would say, 'There is no God!' People like that are worthless; they are heartless and cruel and never do right."

Some secular dictionaries report that one traditional meaning of "atheism" is "wickedness". To be sure, more than one widespread view of religion casts Atheists in a negative light. If one believes in a God who demands worship and obedience, then Atheists are wicked for rejecting God. But even if one merely believes that religion helps people live moral lives, one would be reluctant to trust an Atheist. In 2002, the Religion in Public Life Survey found that 44.5 percent of American adults believe, "It is necessary to believe in God in order to be moral and have good values." Notice that this says necessary, not merely helpful. The original data can be downloaded from the Association of Religion Data Archives,[2] and when analyzed show that 65.0 percent of people who attend church more often than once a week feel this way, but even 25.7 percent of people who never attend also do so.

[2] <http://www.TheARDA.com>.

Atheists may suffer mistreatment even if a majority are tolerant of them. An example often mentioned by Atheists themselves is the complaint that an avowed Atheist cannot realistically hope to win high political office in the United States. As other minority groups have experienced, there may also be subtle discrimination against them in business or community organizations. The one area that has been the focus of extensive social-scientific research has been public policies about Atheism in education and public communication.

Over the years, three questions in the General Social Survey have asked peoples' views about "somebody who is against all churches and religion". Although they do not use the word "atheist", the GSS code-book explicitly calls these Atheism items. One asked: "If such a person wanted to make a speech in your (city/town/community) against churches and religion, should he be allowed to speak, or not?" On the basis of fully 29,818 respondents, 30.4 percent said such a person should not be allowed to speak. Atheists can take heart that the fraction of the public who feel this way has declined over the years, from 33.4 percent in 1972 to 22.8 percent in 2004. The second question was: "Should such a person be allowed to teach in a college or university, or not?" In this case nearly half, 49.8 percent, would not allow such a person to teach. From 1972 to 2004, this anti-Atheist response declined from 58.1 percent to 33.9 percent. The third question asked: "If some people in your community suggested that a book he wrote against churches and religion should be taken out of your public library, would you favor removing this book, or not?" Altogether 33.6 percent would remove the book, and the number declined from 37.2 percent in 1972 to 26.2 percent in 2004.

In 1991, the General Social Survey also asked: "Should books and films that attack religions be prohibited by law or should they be allowed?" Of 1,177 respondents, 15.6 percent said they definitely should be banned, and another 17.9 percent said they probably should. Thus, more than a third of the American public was ready to suppress criticism of religion, such as an Atheist might express. As reported by the Association of Religion Data Archives, in 2005 the Baylor Religion Survey found that 33.3 percent of respondents disagreed with this statement: "An atheist should be allowed to teach at a high school." Note that this item does not say the Atheist will teach against religion. Given that the better-educated members of the public have some sophistication about polls and opinion studies, and may favor freedom of speech, many respondents may feel negatively about Atheists but avoid taking the extreme positions presented in these anti-Atheist questionnaire items.

Historical Background

It is widely believed that Atheism is a modern phenomenon, but it is not at all certain that this is true. Rodney Stark and Roger Finke (2000) suggest that all societies contain Atheists, but only liberal, cosmopolitan societies give them the freedom to speak out and thus be counted. However, in a recent encyclopedia article about Atheism, John Henry (2000) asserts that religion was a "characterizing aspect" of Western culture until perhaps the seventeenth century. Furthermore, Henry expresses doubts that Anaxagoras, Socrates, or any other ancient Greeks really were Atheists, with the implication that religion may have been a characterizing aspect of earlier societies as well. This point immediately raises three linked social-scientific questions that we cannot answer here. To what extent is individual belief dominated by the ambient culture? To what extent are cultures unified wholes, rather than loosely structured collections of often incompatible elements? To what extent do surviving written documents and publications represent the full scope of their cultures, rather than expressing merely the narrow views of a literate subculture?

In his historical study *Without God, Without Creed*, James Turner (1985) offered a number of valuable ideas about the socio-cultural origins of Atheism, although he did not apply any of the social-science research methods needed to test his hypotheses. He argues rather forcefully that Atheism was not possible until the nineteenth century, when the rise of science and certain cultural changes within religion itself made it possible for a few intellectuals to conceptualize the world without recourse to the concept of God. According to Turner, in Western Europe and North America, a new framework for thinking about the world arose about two centuries ago. It was marked by four primary characteristics. (1) It trusted claims that had been tested against experience, more than it did supposed knowledge transmitted from earlier generations. (2) It relied upon empirical facts more than upon beliefs that transcended the physical world. (3) It preferred precision in the statement of facts and logical formulation of ideas. (4) It assumed, and even hoped, that knowledge would improve over time, with modern people knowing more than the ancients did.

Working within religious institutions, as well as within institutions of commerce, science, and government, these four factors combined, Turner said, to create a new world view that was not dependent upon God. Other related factors also helped prepare the way for Atheism among educated elites. Language about spiritual realities came to be seen as different from ordinary description, became metaphoric, and thus became less true. Religion became a matter of mere emotion. Then theodicy raised the question of how a modern person should feel about a God who allows evil and suffering in the world. Democratic ideals eroded the legitimacy of religious authorities, and perhaps even of God; citizens of democracies do not bow down to lords. Individuals came to feel that they had a duty to seek the truth, which implied that they did not already have it, and that this duty trumped the comforts afforded by faith. Religion came to be seen not infrequently as a barrier to human social and intellectual progress, and some reformers learned to derive hope from identification with the advancement of humanity, even in the face of personal death. All these factors may not have been powerful enough to impel the majority to become Atheists, but they did move educated people in the direction of disbelief, according to Turner.

Turner's data are limited to the religious and philosophical publications of earlier centuries, so strictly speaking, his key idea rests on assumptions about empirical reality that could conceivably be false. While we cannot voyage by time machine to the twelfth century to interview common people and determine if any of them were Atheists, or grill intellectuals to see what they really thought behind their respectable façades, it would be possible to survey people in developing nations to see how many were Atheists. Globalization may have progressed too far to find "pristine natives" unaffected by secular ideas from industrialized nations. However, I am reminded of a survey of four nearly pristine East African societies carried out in the 1960s that offers some insights. As reported by Robert B. Edgerton (1966), the four societies differed very much in their explanations for mental illness. Members of the Hehe and Kamba tended to think it was the result of supernatural factors, and people among the Pokot and Sebei either did not know or attributed psychosis to physical disease. This suggests to me that pre-modern people were capable of being Atheists.

Turner's theory is not quite the same as secularization theory, which in its simplest form holds that social and intellectual progress is rendering religion obsolete. Rather, his argument says that Atheism has become possible in recent centuries, but perhaps not necessary. Non-religious perspectives on human life and the surrounding universe exist now, but that fact says little about the proportion of people who will adopt them. Many social scientists have written recently about the ambiguous status of secularization, among them William H. Swatos Jr. and Kevin J. Christiano (1999). The best one can say of the state of the literature on this topic is that evidence is mixed. Religion has lost some of its earlier influence in society, and by some measures faith appears to be weakening in some societies. However, religious revival is widespread in modern society, markedly so in many supposedly developing societies.

In his massive work *Social and Cultural Dynamics*, Pitirim A. Sorokin (1937) argued that every successful civilization goes through a cycle of cultural change comparable to secularization and revival. A civilization is founded in bloodshed, when a particular group develops a powerful culture based on transcendent ideas and conquers or converts its neighbors. Sorokin called this early phase "ideational", and said that people in an ideational culture consider truth to be spiritual in nature. If one defines *religion* broadly, then every new civilization is founded with a distinctive, powerful religious vision that gives it the confidence and the drive to undertake difficult and dangerous actions. As time passes, and the civilization consolidates its conquests, faith in the original cultural vision erodes. The society becomes "sensate", a very different cultural complex that seeks truth in material reality and the world of experience. After the passage of time, usually several centuries, the civilization turns completely away from supernatural faith, its resolve weakens, and it becomes incapable of defending itself. Civilization comes near to collapse, but may be saved by a renewed faith and become ideational again. However, establishment of the ideational phase is carried out brutally, and religion in Sorokin's theory is connected with barbarism. When a warlord talks about faith, he is really demanding loyalty. It is worth noting that one of the main meanings of "true" is "loyal".

The Question of Truth

Practically all of the social-scientific literature on religion avoids addressing the central question: Is it true? This question cannot be avoided in the case of Atheism, if we really want to understand the profound social-scientific issues illuminated by it. One might be called the nature of "social cognition".

"*Quid est veritas? Est vir qui adest.*" These enigmatic Latin sentences, which remarkably are formed from the same letters of the alphabet, are often translated: "What is truth? It is the man who stands before you." This conjures up images of Jesus standing before Pilate, but can be read in many different ways. For example, the answers to the most profound questions are inseparable from the questions themselves. Truth may be embodied in human beings, rather than in words or other abstractions. Ultimate truth may be a mystery approachable only through metaphors, perhaps because the human species evolved to thrive, not to philosophize. Yet, the fact that this poetic word puzzle may assign such meanings to truth does not imply that they are indeed the truth about truth.

A good starting point is the work of the philosopher and psychologist William James. Throughout his life, James struggled with two opposite tendencies: on the one hand, a commitment to rational empiricism that seeks truth in phenomena that can be observed, and on the other hand, a deep attraction to the possibility of transcending the mundane world. His early research on supposed psychic phenomena, conducted at a time when psychology had not yet rejected the existence of such things as telepathy and precognition, is one example of his attempt to reconcile these two practically opposite tendencies (James 1986). Another example is his short essay "The Will to Believe", which successfully identifies the key issues, whether or not one is willing to judge that it addressed them successfully (James 1979).

James was writing about those situations in which a person is forced to make a choice between alternatives in the absence of good evidence with which to evaluate them. His substantive topic is religious belief, and part of his argument asserts that

Agnosticism is not really a viable option. He reminds the reader of the famous "wager" of French mathematician and philosopher Blaise Pascal. Quite apart from its religious quality, this argument is a classic statement of social-science decision theory. You have two choices: to believe in the Christian God, or not. The universe, as it were, also has two choices: to have the God of the Christians, or not to have it. This simple model of two dichotomous choices is a standard tool of modern game theory, giving four possible outcomes. By comparing the relative values of these outcomes, the person can decide whether to believe in God or not.

If you believe in the Christian God, and he actually exists, then you go to heaven and experience infinite rewards. If you believe in the Christian God, but he does not exist, you lose little, and may even experience some secondary gains from a life of faith. If you reject the Christian God, but he exists, you lose the chance to go to heaven, and may even be cast into hell (depending upon theological details that we will not consider here). If you reject the Christian God, and he does not in fact exist, you gain nothing. Analysis of this payoff matrix implies that you should believe in the Christian God.

Pascal's wager does not look so conclusive once one begins to admit other possibilities, such as the existence of multiple gods, the conjecture that God loves honest skeptics and has welcomed all the Stoic philosophers and adamant Atheists into heaven in appreciation of their courage and integrity, or a range of reasons why accepting a false belief could cascade throughout one's life decisions to an ultimately negative effect. In considering this problem, James was forced to reject alternative belief systems merely on the basis that his particular audience, having grown up in a largely Christian society, would not find them emotionally attractive. Although in itself a secondary point, it comes close to one of two key points made by James: when faced by uncertain alternatives in an important area of life, we have the right to choose without being accused of arbitrariness or bad faith.

The other point made by James, and fundamental to his entire philosophical approach, is this: religious faith of the conventional sort is beneficial to the individual. It provides a basis for morality, enhances human interaction, and serves our immediate psychological needs while also factoring in a better life in the future. James was an avowed pragmatist, holding that true ideas are useful ideas. He was aware that this position could be harmonized with biological theories of evolution: the human species evolved language and complex brains, because improvement in our abilities to communicate and calculate aided survival and reproduction. Setting aside the century-old essay by James, how might religion benefit people? There are really at least four different ways in which an "objectively false" belief in God might be beneficial for the individual:

1. It immediately provides subjective rewards, including hope for the future and relaxation of emotional tensions concerning practical problems that cannot be solved.

2. It leads indirectly to personal actions that are beneficial for the individual—for example, following a healthy lifestyle because it is prescribed by the particular religion.
3. It facilitates good results in interaction with other human beings who share the belief, even sustaining a positive definition of the relationship when one individual may on balance in fact be exploiting the other.
4. It establishes a moral community in society with many positive secondary and tertiary benefits, such as support for charities to help people during times of misfortune.

In my recent book, *Across the Secular Abyss* (Bainbridge 2007*a*), I examined a range of evidence and concluded that religion does have some of these benefits, although they have often been exaggerated and appear to be declining in modern society, quite apart from any weakening in religious faith. For example, we have fairly solid evidence that religion deters minor crimes like theft, but primarily through supporting a moral community, rather than through the psychology of individual believers. However, no evidence seems to exist that religion deters homicide. For another example, the ability of religion to deter suicide seems to have declined during the twentieth century, even though church membership has not. We really do not possess a solid, well-organized scientific literature on the possible harms that religion may cause, or the benefits of disbelief, although a survey of what has been published would undoubtedly turn up a few valuable works. Some conjectures in this direction include:

1. Religion legitimates, indirectly encourages, and even sometimes directly causes inter-group hostilities that lead to war and senseless killing.
2. In a religious economy of varied denominations and movements, many of the more extreme groups will exploit members, put both members and non-members in physical or psychological danger, and degrade the social consensus needed to adjudicate disagreements between groups in society.
3. Religious faith works against the social and behavioral sciences by promulgating fixed and unrealistic views about the nature of human individuals and society, and by working through political institutions to discourage support for these sciences.
4. By falsely convincing people that major problems of both knowledge and human welfare have been solved, religion discourages creative experimentation with alternatives and steers talented people away from careers dedicated to gaining improved knowledge and capabilities to find real solutions.

In "The Will to Believe", James implicitly discounted the last of these issues, in part because the diluted brand of religion he favored was not hostile to the science of his day. He explicitly argued that empirical knowledge of the world was so fragmentary that a decision to believe in the Christian God would not detract from our ability to continue scientific progress. Without wanting to exaggerate the progress that has been made over the past 111 years, I suggest that the scientific situation has changed fundamentally since when James wrote. The rapid unification of all the sciences—and of nanotechnology, with technologies based in biology, computer science, and cognitive science—has been amply documented by Edward O. Wilson (1998), Mihail C. Roco and myself (Roco and Bainbridge 2003; Bainbridge 2007*b*). One very recent result has been a new Atheist social movement (Bainbridge 2007*a*).

The New Atheism

It would be premature to say that science had achieved a unified picture of the world, let alone the maximum power to influence the world and thus the ability to render religion superfluous. At the most fundamental level, much of science today analyzes phenomena in terms of an increasingly integrated set of principles operating on input that is at least largely random. Already a quarter century ago, P. C. W. Davies (1982) described *The Accidental Universe*. Rather than imagining that the universe was created by an intelligent being to achieve some admirable purpose, science documents a number of processes of natural selection that can build order out of chaos without divine supervision. To the extent that science can find order in our lives and environment, then technology can control it. To the extent that science discovers that a particular phenomenon is the result of a vast number of random events—for example, as old age may be—then perhaps nothing can be done about it, and we must learn to accept it. In either case, religion ceases to have a role to play. Especially in the overlapping fields of evolutionary biology and cognitive science, a number of leading intellectuals seem bent on taking human life out of the domain of the sacred.

In the November 2006 issue of *Wired* magazine, Gary Wolf announced "the New Atheism", and a number of other news media carried similar stories around the same time. Wolf's story was based on interviewing researchers and science writers who have come to the conclusion that religion does not deserve respect. They argue that the central Western religious beliefs are not only false but harmful. They make a strong case that such doctrines as the existence of God and the soul contradict the increasingly profound findings of science, notably concerning biological evolution and human cognition. As scientists, they naturally feel that this is evil, both because it discourages public investments in scientific research along these lines, and also because it denies many ordinary people a full understanding of what science is discovering about ourselves. But some of these New Atheists also argue that on balance religion is socially harmful. They may be wrong about some of these points, but they are certainly right that fundamental contradictions exist and appear to be growing between religious faith and cognitive science.

Given that the social sciences have been largely absent from the development of cognitive science, it is worth noting that the theory of religion offered by sociologists Rodney Stark and myself (Stark and Bainbridge 1987) is both cognitive in nature and fundamentally Atheistic. The theory noted that the human mind is an information-processing system that evolved in order to serve the security and well-being of the species, and its defining feature is the ability to use language for cognition and communication. Humans seek rewards and attempt to avoid costs. In so doing, they frame explanations, plans, recipes, algorithms about how to proceed, and they exchange these with each other by means of language. In the absence of a desired reward, people seek exchanges with other people who may be able to provide it, and they pursue other exchanges to get information about where to find the reward. In the case of highly desired rewards that are difficult to obtain, such as health for the chronically ill and life for the dying, their plans for how to obtain the reward become progressively more desperate and unrealistic. They adopt beliefs technically called "compensators", postulations of reward according to non-empirical beliefs that in the more extreme cases are supernatural.

As I further developed the theory, I thought it worth distinguishing primary from secondary compensation. "Primary compensators" are non-empirical beliefs that satisfy the momentary psychological needs of the individual. A person confronted with death imagines living again in an afterlife, for example, thereby feeling at least somewhat less afraid. "Secondary compensators" are non-empirical beliefs that satisfy the social obligation that one person has to provide a reward to another. The parent of a dying child needs something to say to avoid guilt for letting their child die—something to tell the child and to tell other members of the family and community. Even if there is nothing practically they can do for the child, they must be seen to be doing their best, or others will lose confidence and expect the parents to renege on other obligations they have undertaken. A priest giving last rites is not only comforting the dying, but also announcing that the people with obligations to the dying person have fulfilled those obligations. Thus religious faith has much do to with sustaining faith between people, through helping secondary compensators function to fulfill defaulted obligations. On the other hand, from this perspective religious faith is bad faith, because it is behaviorally indistinguishable from lying intended to curry favor with one's exchange partners. Atheism threatens this entire system of wishful thinking and white lies, especially when a priesthood is also exploiting the system for its own advantage.

If the Stark–Bainbridge sociological theory placed motivation and communication at the heart of a cognitive theory, a more recent network of psychologists and anthropologists has independently focused on the tendency of humans to believe in supernatural beings. Notably, Paul Bloom (2004) has drawn on a variety of studies, including research on child development, to show that the instinctive human self-image is wrong. Our brains do not directly sense their own operation, so people feel they are somehow separate from their bodies. For the brain to be constantly monitoring its own behavior would waste a tremendous fraction of its computing power, especially because it consists of a diverse set of distinct modules dedicated to different functions. True self-awareness would interfere with the sensitive neural mechanisms that integrate different kinds of information. Furthermore, it is clear from the study of brain injuries and cognitively disabled people, that almost any brain function can be lost, yet modern medicine can keep the person alive for a considerable time. Combined, all these lines of research indicate that humans do not possess unitary, supernatural, immortal souls.

A number of writers, such as Scott Atran (2002), Pascal Boyer (2002), and Justin Barrett (2004)—offer a compatible evolutionary argument about why humans tend to imagine supernatural beings that have feelings, thoughts, and desires. Much of our cognition concerns other conscious beings, not only because language is by its very nature social, but also because the species evolved in an environment where we were both hunters and hunted. That is, the human mind evolved to handle relations between partners, predators, and prey. Thus, our brains have a powerful "mind-reading" inference system, that aggressively seeks to understand the goals of the beings we interact with. Indeed, it is so important to us that it is hyperactive, encouraging people to interpret all complex phenomena as the result of conscious action taken by another being. Justin Barrett considers this fact so important that he explicitly cautions Atheists that they should not expect the majority of people to abandon belief in God, because it is practically built into the structure of their brains. This raises the tantalizing but untested hypothesis that Atheists might be people with unusually weak mind-reading inference systems, which would square with the fact that they seem to be low in social obligations.

Conclusion

This leads to the interesting question, raised by Colin Campbell (1972) long ago, about what kinds of organizations Atheists can create. If they are not going to exchange supernaturally based compensators, and are not able to dispense spiritual services to lay believers, then they can hardly compete directly with the churches. Perhaps Atheists may sometimes organize for self-defense, but in a society that punishes Atheism, this only makes them visible targets for oppression. Daniel Dennett (2006) has argued that religion is a cultural parasite, which evolved to exploit human beings rather than to serve them. Yet, so long as large numbers of citizens in a democracy are religious, Atheist organizations will not be given the public mental health responsibility for eradicating religion. Thus, at this moment in human evolution Atheism is a minority viewpoint, possibly expressed by those skeptics who have less to lose socially than other skeptics, with little traction to change its position in society. Its future history may depend very heavily upon the degree of success achieved by cognitive science and other fields contributing to the very recent New Atheism movement.

References

Atran, Scott (2002). *In Gods We Trust.* Oxford: Oxford University Press.

Bainbridge, William Sims (2007*a*). *Across the Secular Abyss.* Lanham, Md.: Lexington Boohs.

—— (2007*b*). *Nanoconvergence.* Upper Saddle River, NJ: Prentice-Hall.

Barrett, Justin L. (2004). *Why Would Anyone Believe in God?* Walnut Creek, Calif.: AltaMira Press.

Bloom, Paul (2004). *Descartes' Baby.* New York: Basic Books.

Boyer, Pascal (2002). *Religion Explained.* New York: Basic Books.

Campbell, Colin (1972). *Toward a Sociology of Irreligion.* New York: Herder & Herder.

Davies, P. C. W. (1982). *The Accidental Universe.* Cambridge: Cambridge University Press.

Dawkins, Richard (2006). *The God Delusion.* Boston: Houghton Mifflin.

Dennett, Daniel C. (2006). *Breaking the Spell: Religion as a Natural Phenomenon.* New York: Viking.

Durkheim, Émile (1915). *The Elementary Forms of Religious Life.* London: G. Allen & Unwin.

Edgerton, Robert B. (1966). "Conceptions of Psychosis in Four East African Societies". *American Anthropologist,* 68: 408–24.

Hayes, Bernadette C. (2000). "Religious Independents within Western Industrialized Nations: A Socio-Demographic Profile". *Sociology of Religion,* 61: 191–207.

Henry, John (2000). "Atheism". In Darrel W. Amundsen, Gary B. Ferngren, Edward J. Larson, and Anne-Marie E. Nakhla (eds.), *The History of Science and Religion in the Western Tradition: An Encyclopedia.* New York: Garland, 182–8.

James, William (1979). *The Will to Believe and Other Essays in Popular Philosophy.* Cambridge, Mass.: Harvard University Press.

—— (1986). *Essays in Psychical Research.* Cambridge, Mass.: Harvard University Press.

Putney, Snell, and Middleton, Russell (1961). "Rebellion, Conformity, and Parental Ideologies". *Sociometry,* 24/2: 125–35.

Roco, Mihail C., and Bainbridge, William Sims (eds.) (2003). *Converging Technologies for Improving Human Performance.* Dordrecht: Kluwer.

Schurman, J. G. (1895). "Agnosticism". *Philosophical Review,* 4/3: 241–63.

Smith, George H. (1979). *Atheism: The Case against God.* Buffalo: Prometheus.

Sorokin, Pitirim A. (1937). *Social and Cultural Dynamics.* New York: American Book Company.

Stark, Rodney, and Finke, Roger (2000). *Acts of Faith.* Berkeley: University of California Press.

—— and Bainbridge, William Sims (1987). *A Theory of Religion.* New York: Lang.

Swatos, William H. Jr., and Christiano, Kevin J. (1999). "Secularization Theory: The Course of a Concept". *Sociology of Religion*, 60/3: 209–28.

Turner, James (1985). *Without God, Without Creed.* Baltimore: Johns Hopkins University Press.

Vernon, G. M. (1968). "The Religious 'Nones': A Neglected Category". *Journal for the Scientific Study of Religion*, 7: 219–29.

Wilson, Edward O. (1998). *Consilience: The Unity of Knowledge.* New York: Knopf.

Witte, James C. (2003). "The Case for Multimethod Design". In Philip N. Howard and Steve Jones, (eds.), *Society Online.* Thousand Oaks, Calif.: Sage, pp. xv–xxxiv.

Wolf, Gary (2006). "The Church of the Non-Believers". *Wired* (Nov.): 182–93.

Suggested Reading

The following are recommended: Bainbridge (2007); Campbell (1972); Dennett (2006); and Turner (1985).

CHAPTER 18

RELIGION AND MORALITY

JOHN REEDER

Differentiation of Spheres and the Autonomy of Morality

General notions of morality and religion are part of the legacy of modernity. They have taken shape in response to political and scholarly imperatives.[1] A familiar part of the narrative casts religion and morality as distinct spheres of culture and experience. José Casanova puts the general theory of differentiation as follows:

> The core component of the theory of secularization was the conceptualization of societal modernization as a process of functional differentiation and emancipation of the secular spheres—primarily the modern state, the capitalist market economy, and modern science—from the religious sphere, and the concomitant differentiation and specialization of religion within its own newly found religious sphere. (2006: 12–13)[2]

Many thanks to Wes Erdelack, Curtis Hutt, Andrew Flescher, Jung Lee, Thomas Lewis, David Little, Charles Lockwood, Gene Outka, Melissa Proctor, Michael Slater, Kevin Schilbrack, Jonathan Schofer, Brian Sorrells, Jeffrey Stout, and Sumner Twiss.

[1] See Chidester (1996) on stages of colonialization related to early definitions of religion. The process of differentiation has also been linked to the needs of the early modern nation-state for a public order independent of religious authority. Stout (1981: 3, 14) gives a historical account of the "differentiation of morality as an autonomous cultural domain", and in particular of the idea of the "logical autonomy" of morality as a "timeless characteristic of moral discourse as such". See also MacIntyre (1990: 26–8 ff., 174 ff.). On notions of religion, see Clarke and Byrne (1993).

[2] Casanova (2006: 13 ff.) defends this general thesis (Casanova 1994) against Asad's objections (2003: ch. 6; see also Asad 2006). Casanova (1994) argues, however, that some religious traditions

Just as the other "spheres" are differentiated from religion, so morality also comes to be widely conceived as an autonomous "secular sphere". The differentiation is said to have occurred not only in the work of intellectuals, but in society generally.

I will look at three senses of the autonomy of morality (cosmization as alienation, depth grammar, and practices).[3] I will present common objections (*concesso non dato*) against cosmization and depth grammar, but defend the idea of autonomous (sometimes overlapping) practices.

Cosmization as Alienation

"Cosmization" (Berger 1969[1967]) is the process in which a humanly constructed moral order is projected and reified as a wider reality (e.g., a god or a cosmic principle). Once projected and reified, the wider reality is then regarded as the metaphysical source and legitimating ground of the moral order. What is wholly human is pictured as transhuman reality. I will look at variations on this theme in Peter Berger, Clifford Geertz, and Catherine Bell.

Berger (1969[1967]), who cites Feuerbach[4] and Durkheim,[5] argued that human beings produce or "externalize" a *nomos*; the pattern then has an "objective" reality of its own as a tradition; new generations "internalize" the pattern through the process of socialization.[6] We experience deep anxiety, however, about the precariousness of the *nomos* (1969[1967]: 89). In the course of human evolution, as a way of quelling anxiety, the *nomos* comes to be seen as a wider reality; i.e., it is "cosmized" (1969[1967]: 24–8).[7] The *nomos* is first externalized, objectivized, and internalized simply as a human process of meaning-creation. Cosmization then writes the *nomos* into the nature of cosmic reality, and reinternalizies it as a structure to which humans must conform.[8]

which accept the modern differentiation of church and state nonetheless resist privatization and play a role in the public square. I will not try to deal here with notions and criticisms of the autonomy of religion. See Lindbeck (1984); Proudfoot (1985); McCutcheon (1997*b*); and Dubuisson (2003).

[3] Autonomy as differentiation refers to modes of belief and practice independent of religion; a morality of autonomy—the self-legislation of a rational being—is one version of the autonomy of morality in the broader sense. See Adams (1987*a*) and Schneewind (1988).

[4] On Feuerbach, see Harvey (1997[1995]).

[5] To criticize projection and reification as a theory of the imagination is not to deny that religions often shape and sustain moral identity. See Cladis on Durkheim (Cladis 1992; 2001: pp. xix–xx).

[6] *Nomos* signifies "society" as moral-political order (Berger 1969[1967]: 6–7, 19–21).

[7] Berger also says that when the *nomos* is taken for granted, it is cosmized (1969[1967]: 24–5).

[8] Berger (1969[1967]: 85–7) says that alienation is an "overextension of objectivation"; but I take him to mean that this overextension is the distinct process of cosmization.

To cosmize—to project and reify the *nomos*—is to forget that the social order is a changeable human invention. It is to attribute to the nature of things what is really only our creation or construction. Cosmization makes the *nomos* appear to be dependent on a transhuman source and ground, while in reality it is an independent or autonomous human product. Thus cosmization is "alienation": "The humanly made world is explained in terms that deny its human production.... The essence of all alienation is the imposition of a fictitious inexorability upon the humanly constructed world" (1969[1967]: 89, 95). Moreover, cosmization in a sacred mode, religious cosmization, is the earliest and most important form of cosmization. Sacred cosmization occurs when the wider reality that requires the *nomos* is said to be a sacred reality.[9] Later there are secular forms of cosmization, but the prototype is religious: "The fundamental 'recipe' of religious legitimation is the transformation of human products into supra- or non-human facticities" (1969 [1967]: 89).[10]

One also finds a version of cosmization in Geertz (1973*b*: 89–90, 112; 1973*a*: 126–7): The "ethos" is "implicit in", "imposed" by, or "ideally adapted to" the "'really real'":[11] "In itself, either side, the normative or the metaphysical is arbitrary, but taken together they form a gestalt with a particular kind of inevitability" (1973*a*: 130, 131). When worldview and ethos are ritually fused in the synthesis of sacred symbols they have a "congruence" which acts to "sustain each with the borrowed authority of the other" (1973*b*: 89–90; 1973*a*: 129).

Thus the "authoritative experience which justifies, even compels" masks the arbitrariness of the ethos; the justification is only apparent, not real: "In myths and rituals values are portrayed not as subjective human preferences but as the imposed conditions for life in a world with a particular structure" (1973*a*: 131).[12] Traditions depict a particular ethos as implicit in or imposed by the nature of things and the nature of things as adapted to that sort of ethos (1973*b*: 89–90).

[9] Berger adopts the "substantive" notion of the sacred as a "mysterious and awesome" power beyond, yet related to, humanity, which he discusses in Appendix I (1969[1967]: 175–7). See also Berger 1974. See also Clarke and Byrne (1993: 6–7) and Hervieu-Léger (2000) on substantive over against functional definitions of religion. See also Alles (2000: 112), who contrasts Spiro (1968[1966]) and Geertz (1973*b*).

[10] Berger could be saying that religion just is a form of cosmization: "religion is cosmization in a sacred mode" (1969[1967]: 25). But I think he posits an independent experience of sacred reality onto which the *nomos* is projected and reified. See Harvey's early essays (1973; 1979) and his recent remarks on ways of reading Berger (1997[1995]: 275 ff.). Harvey (1997[1995]: 264–8) says that Berger holds a view of "projection as socially constituted grid", in contrast to the "beam" theory of the early Feuerbach; but the idea of reification remains: religions "transform human products into superhuman facticities" (p. 268). In addition, religions serve as theodicies which respond to marginal situations (pp. 266, 270–1). On Harvey, see G. Green (1997).

[11] "Ethos" for Geertz also includes "aesthetic style", but I focus here on the moral-political sense.

[12] See Geertz (1999: 12), where he denies that "religion is but mask and mystification, an ideological cover-up for thoroughly secular, more or less selfish ambitions". I take him to say that the "model of"–"model for" synthesis is not merely an instrumental or manipulative use of religious symbols.

The idea that religions transform what is a purely human (and arbitrary) construction into a transhuman source and ground survives also in Bell (1992). Bell (1992: 108) attempts to avoid either the "mystifications" of "theological perspectives", or the claim that mystification is "essential to what ritual does", as "social scientific perspectives tend" to assert. Nonetheless, her view of ritualization seems to involve the idea of masking: "Ritualization does not see how it actively creates place, force, event, and tradition, how it redefines or generates the circumstances to which it is responding... in seeing itself as responding to an environment, ritualization interprets its own schemes as impressed upon the actors from a more authoritative source, usually from well beyond the immediate human community itself" (Bell 1992: 109–10).

Thus what are in reality purely human processes and distinctions are given an extra-human source and legitimization. The "efficacy" of ritual depends on participants not grasping what is actually happening (1992: 108, 140–1): "the production and objectification of structured and structuring schemes in the environment involve a misrecognition of the source and arbitrariness of these schemes. These schemes tend to be experienced as deriving from powers or realities beyond the community and its activities, such as god or tradition, thereby depicting and testifying to the ultimate organization of the cosmos."[13]

But what of objections to the cosmization as alienation thesis? Geertz actually seems to have been of two minds in his classic essays (1973*a*; 1973*b*). On the one hand, he seems to claim that the process of ritual synthesis produces the falsifying conviction that the ethos has its source and ground in the really real. What ought to be is made to appear as a requirement of what is (1973*a*: 126–7). On the other hand, he seems to suggest that the traditions exhibit a proper mode of justification: "Like bees who fly despite theories of aeronautics which deny them the right to do so, probably the overwhelming majority of mankind are continually drawing normative conclusions from factual premises (and factual conclusions from normative premises, for the relation between ethos and world view is circular) despite refined, and in their own terms impeccable, reflections by professional philosophers on the 'naturalistic fallacy'" (1973*a*: 141).

Thus Geertz seems to suggest that there *can* be a "reasonable way to live" (1973a: 130), a "way of life ideally adapted" (1973*b*: 90) to a particular view of the nature of things, and vice versa. The process of justification found in religious traditions is not a process of projection which results in misrecognition and alienation;[14] world

[13] Bell stresses nonetheless that the participant is empowered through processes of "consent, resistance, and negotiated appropriation" (1992: 116, 206–8; see pp. 81–4 on "redemptive hegemony"). Interestingly, in 1997 Bell seems sometimes to reaffirm the misrecognition theme (pp. 81–2, 169); but she also says that participants often have conscious purposes and are not deceived about what is really happening (pp. 224–5, 306, 332). On Bell see Schilbrack 2004: 85 ff.

[14] McCutcheon (1997*a*: 459), as part of his view of the role of the scholar as one who unmasks ahistorical and universal claims as "mechanisms of power and control" (p. 461), thinks that Geertz was right to say that religions furnish a spurious appearance of inevitability. But some religions acknowledge their finitude and revisability; moreover, to acknowledge that religions "defend and contest issues of social power" (p. 452) is not equivalent to the view that religious claims mask the real forces at work.

view and ethos legitimate each other in their webs of belief, just as the traditions take them to.[15]

More broadly, let us continue, if we understand how the process of justification works, if our understanding of the religious imagination is properly holistic,[16] we should say that humans look for reasons in how things are to support how they ought to live; this is one way they bring coherence to their webs of belief.[17] What vary across cultures are the views, metaphysical and moral, and the various sorts of links that traditions envisage. As Geertz urged, we should try to gain "insight into what values are and how they work" by looking at "actual people in actual societies living in terms of actual cultures" (1973*a*: 141).

But if there are—in various cultural contexts—internal links between *is* and *ought*, fact and value, what are some of them?[18] Robert P. George (1992: 32–3, 35–7, 41 n. 20) argues that one need not claim to derive moral conclusions that contain "reasons for action" from premises that do not contain any such reasons in order to hold that moral norms express ends that are "intrinsically perfective of human beings" (1992: 35). The premises themselves refer to such ends (see also MacIntyre 1984; 1988). No *is–ought* fallacy is committed. One need not claim that moral conclusions are logically derived from wholly non-moral premises in order to hold that religious world views (and secular surrogates) often contain notions of the ends perfective of human beings; thus in this sense the world view grounds the ethos.[19]

Another pattern (which links *is* and *ought*) is the idea of a transhuman author of the moral law. The moral law is a function of the command of a legislator or sovereign. There need be no suggestion of arbitrariness, for even if the law is rooted in "will" alone, rather than "reason", it can be said that the legislator commands in accordance with a certain character or nature (Adams 1987*c*). We see this pattern in the idea that the moral law simply confronts us as a demand which constrains our desires and emotions.

An additional pattern is the idea that we respond or relate ourselves to the character of reality. Our views of the good and the right are adjusted to the conditions of the wider environment (Geertz 1973*a*: 130). Given how things are,

[15] Cf. Frankenberry and Penner (1999: 621 and n. 5) and Schilbrack (2005*b*: 446–7 on religious conceptions as fictions. Schilbrack (2005*b*) argues that Geertz does not propound or assume a scheme–content dualism, the idea of belief as a private mental state, or a particular theory of truth. See also Schilbrack 2002; 2004; 2005*a*.

[16] See Stout (1981 *passim*; 1983: 310) on "epistemological holism". One tests a view against some set of wider beliefs, but not against one's beliefs as a whole (Stout 1981: 274 n. 9); nor does holism entail the semantic thesis that cultures are "self-contained wholes." (See also Moody-Adams 1997 and Tanner 1997). See Stout (1993; 2001[1988]; 2004: ch. 10) on "justification relative to context" and on "inferential commitment" (2004: chs. 8, 12).

[17] See Byrne (1998: 90–1): for Geertz, religions affirm that "the deepest human values and the most fundamental ontological structures cohere". Lovin and Reynolds make this point (1985: 30–1; 1986; 1992; Lovin 1985). See also Gustafson (1973; 1981; 1984; 1996); Schilbrack (2005*b*: 432–3).

[18] I am adapting here H. R. Niebuhr's (1999) categories.

[19] See Keown (1992) on "parameters of perfectability" in Buddhist traditions.

some goods may not be available to us, while others are attainable.[20] We find forces in the wider environment which are hostile to or supportive of our struggle to flourish and seek justice. As agents, we necessarily respond to how we construe the nature of things. Thus we do not need to find the notion of ends perfective of human nature or the idea of a transhuman legislator in order to recognize that a world view establishes possibilities and limits (Lovin and Reynolds 1985; 1986; 1992). Traditions which distinguish virtue from happiness still operate with visions of the moral and non-moral goods available to human beings. A parallel in contemporary discourse is the widespread idea that our biological, psychological, and social nature—indeed, our location within nature as a whole—establishes the basic elements and boundaries of human flourishing and justice (Nussbaum 2000).

In sum, instead of theorizing an inherently falsifying process of projection and reification, we can say that the religious imagination links world view and ethos in a variety of ways, with a variety of metaphors and models.[21] The metaphysical question remains open: There may or may not be a wider moral reality which transcends social constructions.[22]

Depth Grammar

Another sense of the autonomy of morality argues that it has its own distinctive content and justification, which are available to human beings independent of wider religious or quasi-religious world views. There is a moral depth grammar, as it were, that underlies all the moral languages.[23] Even if there is no wider reality,[24]

[20] See Stout (2001[1988]: 48–9).

[21] G. Green (1998; 2002); McFague (1987). My sense of the religious imagination is informed by Harvey's view of the later Feuerbach: "religion is an interpretative response to the constellation of forces that impinge upon the self" driven by a "rage-to-live and to flourish" (1997[1995]: 231, 263; see also pp. 271, 280). Cf. Guthrie (1993: 19–20, 191 ff., 212 n. 137; 2000), who makes the religious imagination part of a general anthropomorphizing attempt to interpret and influence the world. Many religions have been anthropomorphic, of course, but it seems unhelpful to exclude from the category of religion (and to regard as "philosophy") those traditions which regard personifying imagery as what must be transcended in order to grasp reality and achieve liberation. See Harvey (1997[1995]) and Saler (2000[1993]: 131–7) on Guthrie.

[22] See Clarke and Byrne (1993: 170–1, 204–5); Levine (1992: 390 n. 6). I am not suggesting that there is a "genetic fallacy" in the claim that projection and reification *ipso facto* produce an alienating illusion; I take the truth claim to be part of the explanatory hypothesis. The question is whether the explanation is convincing. Berger (1969[1967]: Preface, Appendix II, *passim*) suggested that his sociological theory bracketed questions of religious truth, but I read cosmization as an inherently falsifying process.

[23] On the "deep structure" metaphor, see Levine (1992).

[24] The alienation thesis only rules out a transhuman source and ground: it does not necessarily assert that values or norms are only a matter of actual desire or preference (Byrne 1999[1992]: 140–1, *passim*).

there is still a source and ground somehow within human nature itself.[25] The thesis that cosmization is alienation purportedly revealed that morality is not dependent on a transhuman source and ground; finding a source and ground in human nature as such reveals that morality, albeit a wholly human construction, is not arbitrary. The idea that the substantive shape of morality is provided by such a depth grammar takes a number of different forms.

Ronald M. Green (1978; 1988) formulated, for example, a neo-Kantian account. For Green, reason is instrumental and impartial; when applied in the basic circumstances of social life, it yields moral imperatives. It is in everyone's interest (within a social group) to adopt an agreed-upon system for resolving conflicts of interest without resort to violence.[26] Green also argues that religious assumptions are necessary to make the system work. For Green, moral duties may not turn out in an exceptional case to be in a particular individual's interest. In some cases, when one is the victim of morally evil forces, one's loss can be restored and the victims punished; but in other situations, one's loss is irrevocable, and the victims go free. Thus Green argues that we must assume some form of reparation and punishment beyond human powers.[27] Green also argues that morality needs a transhuman agent who can forgive and pardon in a way that humans cannot—that is, without relaxing the moral law.

In sum, Green finds across cultures some version of a moral system, and some set of beliefs and practices in regard to retribution and mitigation. He realizes that some critics of religion would argue that these postulates are not required for moral commitment, but are illusions invented to reinforce fallible and incomplete human institutions. The critic could keep Green's model of morality, but argue that we must make do with human institutions to provide reparation, punishment, and reconciliation.[28]

David Little (1986; 1993) has argued for a neo-Lockean notion of natural or human rights based on a self-evident principle available to reason. This supreme principle is not innate; it requires nurture and education (Little 1986: 94, 116–17 n. 87). Once grasped, however, it does not admit or require any further justification,

[25] Rorty (2006) argues in effect that any such notion is simply an echo of cosmization. Berger (1969 [1967]: 25) himself suggested that the *nomos* could be grounded in "'the nature of things'" either "cosmologically *or* anthropologically".

[26] It is important to note that self-interest can mean the interests of a self, self-regarding or other-regarding.

[27] Cf. Stark and Bainbridge (1985: 8) on the idea of religions providing "general compensators based on supernatural assumptions". Religious actors employ rational choice in the sense of weighing "anticipated rewards against anticipated costs", in light of "information", "options", and "preferences and tastes" (Stark 2000: 247–8). Stark (2000: 249) rejects altruism as "negative cost/benefit ratio purely for the benefit of others", but interprets self-sacrifice as "more rewarding than . . . survival". Cf. Euben (1999: ch. 1) on rational actor theories.

[28] R. M. Green himself says that we could fail to carry through the full rational enterprise in its religious expression (1988: 16–17). See Byrne (1998; 1999[1992]); Levine (1992); and Stout (1981) on Green.

and on reflection it cannot be revised; for it is presupposed in any moral judgments we make (1986: 92–4, 116–17 n. 87, 119 n. 97). The principle stipulates that it would be wrong, merely for our pleasure or for some other self-regarding interest, if "we restricted the liberty of [others], inflicted severe pain upon them, disabled or disfigured them, took their possessions, destroyed them, or refused them aid at minimal cost to ourselves" (1986: 93–4, 90, 91, 97, 98, 100–1, 102, 103, 104; see also 1993). The principle finds expression in rights to non-interference and to aid.

Thus the principle is an "unalterable and universal foundation of human life" (Little 1986: 81). The principle both applies to and is justifiable within all cultures, unless basic capacities have been eroded by biological or social conditions. Little does not say that everyone will reflectively grasp the principle. Moreover, different cultures will express the principle and interpret cases differently. Nonetheless, Little argues that we not only grasp the moral law independent of revelation, but that its content and justification are independent of religious beliefs. The moral law is autonomous, differentiated from religion. Believers can put such a moral law under a religious canopy when they attribute human nature to the creator; but morality as humans know it has its own content and justification.

Moreover, for this version of depth grammar, the moral demand is self-evident or self-justifying in the sense that it is not grounded on any further facts about human nature.[29] It is a feature *of* human experience, but although it may presuppose and require other beliefs for specification—e.g., that humans can be harmed in various ways—it does not depend for its justification on other beliefs *about* human nature (George 2004[1999]; Larmore 2005). In contrast to Little's single principle expressed in terms of natural or human rights, but with a similar notion of a self-evident starting-point(s), Grizez, Boyle, and Finnis (1987; George 2004 [1999]: 37–54, 68–9) argue for a modern natural law consisting of a first principle of practical reason ("good is to be done"), a set of self-evident goods, a "first principle of morality" ("choose ... only those possibilities ... compatible with integral human fulfilment") and derived "modes of responsibility".[30]

Still another form of depth grammar appeals to the nature of moral language, or "communicative" discourse. Even if one does not affirm religious beliefs, one's moral presuppositions would remain intact; morality is thus independent of religion. For example, Jürgen Habermas (1991[1983]; 1995[1993]) has argued that there is a basic ideal—uncoerced acceptability by all affected—inherent in

[29] See Porter (2005), who distinguishes *per se nota* from a priori principles.

[30] See Porter's critique (2005: 37–9, 127–31, 236–7). Other versions of natural law independent of revelation still have theological content and justification, e.g., the moral law as the relations of creatures of God. Some insist that natural law must be corrected and supplemented through scripture and tradition, or even that it involves such interpretation inherently (Porter 1999; 2005). See Herdt's (1997: 17–8 ff.) distinction between "classical" and "modern" notions of natural law. See also Stout (1992).

communicative moral discourse.[31] R. M. Hare argued (1952; 1963; 1981) that universalizability is a requirement of moral language; assuming certain basic human interests, "reason" constrains "freedom".[32] Views which purport to rely on moral discourse as such often make a distinction between basic moral rules and a separate realm of ideals or visions of the good (see Mitchell 1980; Yearley 1993; J. E. Hare 2007). Another related set of views does not look to moral discourse as such, but grounds a universal norm or norms—e.g., some set of human rights—in shared beliefs about human agency (e.g., Gewirth 1978). These beliefs—explicit or implicit—are putatively accessible and justifiable in principle across cultures; they are *independent* of wider religious or quasi-religious differences.[33]

The basic objection to depth grammar in its various forms is that we simply do not find a cross-cultural basis for morality in reason, language, or agency as such (Stout 1981; 1993; 2001[1988]; MacIntyre 1984; 1990). There is no self-evident or "transcendental" foundation of any sort, or a basis for morality in beliefs about human nature independent of wider views. As opposed to the idea of a depth grammar, Jeffrey Stout (2001[1988]: 90; 1993) and others argue that "justification is relative to context"; that is, to particular webs of belief in particular historical locations.[34] What any agent will find "acceptable", Stout argues, will depend on other presupposed beliefs, and these vary according to cultural context and tradition.[35] A representative view is Nicholas Wolterstorff on Locke: we do not possess a generically hard-wired moral law, for "I do not and cannot operate as a generic human being.... What I come to believe is a function of my experience plus what I already believe.... The traditions into which we have been inducted... have become part of ourselves as belief-forming agents: components of our programming. We live *inside* our traditions, not *alongside*" (Wolterstorff with Audi 1997: 89).

If there is no framework in reason, language, or agency as such, one must look at particular moral languages or traditions to see how they use concepts of moral rightness and goodness. One can then argue, for example, as Robert Adams once

[31] See McCarthy (1991[1978]: 279; 1995[1991]: 130–6) on Habermas. Habermas argues for an empirical reconstruction of communicative practice, rather than a transcendental structure of consciousness. See Habermas (2002: 162–4; Mendietta in Habermas 2002: 23–4) on the idea that religions remain useful in the sense that the insights carried within them have not been fully retrieved. Gamwell (1990), in contrast, combines a view of morality as transcendental demand with the thesis that one must necessarily make metaphysical assumptions. See F. S. Fiorenza (1992).

[32] See Habermas (1991[1983]: 62 ff.) on the "principle of universalization" and (1991[1983]: 55, 64) on Hare. See also (1995[1993]: chs. 1 and 2). See J. E. Hare (2007) on R. M. Hare.

[33] These beliefs could be read as transcendental presuppositions, or simply as widespread empirical convictions. They could also be linked to an explanation from evolutionary biology or neuroscience.

[34] See Outka (1996) on "all the way down". Stout thinks that overlaps can be explained without appealing to a universal pattern of reasoning (1993: 223–6). See Stout (2001[1988]) on Donagan (1977).

[35] Stout 1981: 223–5; 2001[1988]: 20, 132–5). As Stout (1993: 217–8, 219–20) cautiously says, a ground in "rational agency" as such is *probably* not available, for it has not been demonstrated satisfactorily to date.

did (1987*c*), that in the language of many Jewish and Christian believers the command of God is the criterion of right and wrong.[36] Adams insisted, however, that the use of this criterion presupposes a *loving* God (1987*c*: 101–2, 108–9).[37] Only if God is loving would the divine will count as the criterion; the believer's criterion is unworkable—it "breaks down"—unless God is loving (1987*c*: 107, 110, 120–1). Thus Adams grants that his believer presupposes a *valuation*—the value of love—but insists that such a believer does not presuppose a criterion of *moral* rightness that is independent of the divine will. The believer need not employ a non-theological criterion of moral right and wrong in order to judge whether to obey God (1987*c*: 109).[38]

Stout (1978: 11, *passim*) proposed that Adams's view should be restated in terms of a "linguistic holism" which "emphasizes the extent to which meanings are embedded in the web of belief". And Stout later (2001[1988]) proposed (to Kai Nielsen 1973) that love or some other consideration could function for the believer as a criterion or rightness along with the revealed divine will: instead of love as a presupposition, or even part of the criterion as a quality of the divine will, love and the divine will are now independent criteria which the believer affirms.[39] Should the believer become an atheist, then love, the criterion independent of the divine will, would remain. We should look in various moral languages for multiple criteria of right and wrong.[40]

Moreover, for Stout there is no gap of *is* and *ought*: we always hold in place some part of the raft of our beliefs even when we repair another, and the part of the raft we hold in place contains already established "connections" between "descriptive and evaluative terms" (1978: 14; 1981: 193–5; 1983: 311). Thus one could accept the thesis that "theism itself presupposes a moral vocabulary which can be independently

[36] Adams speaks for convenience of the criterion of "ethical wrongness".

[37] A divine command view of this sort is to be contrasted, says Adams, with the view that "what is right and wrong is independent of the divine will" (1987*c*: 99). See Quinn (1990); Sagi and Statman (1995: part I); Byrne (1999[1992]: ch. 8); Wainwright (2005: part II); J. E. Hare (2007: ch. 2).

[38] Adams grants that the criterion of rightness for his believer could be expressed simply as the command of a loving God (1987*c*: 101–2).

[39] The believer's reliance on scriptural revelation, however, may not signify an additional criterion of rightness, but a belief about a moral authority whose judgement transcends fallible human awareness; God's revealed will or legislation determines human judgements only in this secondary sense. See Sagi and Statman (1995) on "epistemic dependence" (ch. 4), which they also distinguish from "the dependence of activity" or motivation (ch. 5).

[40] Adams (1987*b*) later argued for an explanatory theory of the property of rightness and wrongness as such, in contrast to a "conceptual analysis... relative to a religious subcommunity". Wainwright (2005), in discussing Adams (1987*b*; 1999), distinguishes moral epistemology—i.e., how we "discover" our moral obligations through reason, etc.—and a metaphysical or constitutive explanation in terms of divine commands (Wainwright 2005: 84 ff.). See also J. E. Hare (2007: 100–1, 272) who notes (2007: 264) that if God is not the source of obligation, the alternatives are society or the individual. See Hare on the thesis that the idea of the will of God as the source of obligation is compatible with the idea of necessary moral truths. See Adams (1987*b*) on Stout's linguistic holism and Adams (1999) on divine command theory. See Stout (2004: 259–69) on Adams (1999).

understood"; but what one means is that theists presuppose some criteria which are not "purely theological", criteria which play an important role even for theists, e.g., distinguishing God from Satan (2001[1988]: 195). The moral language of the theist then depends for some of its content on theological beliefs, but other parts "can be independently understood". When this unity breaks up, then we have new and distinct moral languages at work (2001[1988]: 200).

Traditions can and do make universal truth claims, but they do so on the basis of particular webs of belief in particular historical contexts; no universal justifying ground seems available. Claims about human nature or moral agency are not ruled out, but they are taken as justified only within a wider set of religious or quasi-religious beliefs, not as a sphere of independent knowledge. Criteria such as justice and love, whether they serve merely as valuational presuppositions or as criteria of moral rightness and goodness, are affirmed in wider webs of belief.

The Autonomy of Moral Practice(s)

There is a third notion of the autonomy of religion and morality which does not presuppose cosmization as alienation or depth grammar. This view claims that we can differentiate religion and morality as elements of culture because they do different jobs, have different functions, in human experience.[41] Religious and moral practices, which include, but are more than, beliefs, often overlap in various ways, but we can distinguish their roles, even if they are not distinguished as such in a particular culture. We can think of moralities and religions as practices or sets of practices which have characteristic purposes or goals.[42]

David Little and Sumner Twiss (1978: 26, 32), for example, propose "reconstructive definitions" related to ordinary usage, but based on a variety of theoretical considerations.[43] These are stipulative, heuristic constructions which are more definite than family-resemblance concepts.[44] On the basis of these initial definitions, which are subject to revision, they propose to proceed, following Weber, to

[41] Little and Twiss (1978: 46 n. 2) argue that to say that a set of practices have a function in this sense is not to offer a functional explanation. See Penner (1971; 1988; 1999; 2003) on a logically fallacious functionalist argument; see also Frankenberry and Penner (1999) on Geertz. See also Emmet (1958).

[42] See Stout (2004: chs. 11, 12).

[43] For my purposes here, I will not distinguish between a definition, a concept, and a theory. Each is different, of course: one defines terms, uses concepts, develops theories. I will assume that when we are talking about religion and religions, we are engaging in these related activities.

[44] See Saler (2000[1993]: pp. ix–xvi, *passim*) on family resemblance and prototype.

describe patterns of meaning through which agents interpret their actions (1978: 12–17).

While Little and Twiss say that "the autonomy of a moral action-guide rests on the logical requirement that no moral conclusions can be derived from premises that do not themselves contain a moral element" (1978: 29, 46 n. 1), my sense is that for them the autonomy of morality as an "institution" or practice rests principally on the hypothesis that it functions to solve a particular social problem.[45] Moral action-guides are accepted by agents as a systemic solution to the "'problem of cooperation' among self-interested, competing, and conflicting persons and groups" (pp. 26–9).[46]

Morality is thus an "institution or a shared set of expectations" which promotes and protects basic human welfare—e.g., life, health, and security (pp. 28, 37–8). Moral action-guides are prescriptive; that is, they regulate human interactions. They are general; that is, they apply to agents in the same or similar circumstances (pp. 34–6). They usually, but not always, are thought to trump other sorts of considerations, e.g., religious ones (pp. 31–2). They give some normative weight to how others are affected as well as self (pp. 40–1), e.g., moralities of enlightened self-interest which take into account the good of others "indirectly", as well as moralities which give independent weight to the good of others (pp. 40–1). Moralities also often include norms for the treatment of strangers (48 n. 12).

Little and Twiss (following Weber and Geertz) also formulate a definition of religion as a practice with certain goals. Religions cope with "problems of interpretability": namely, "anxieties" about how to understand the natural and social environment, how to deal with suffering and death, and how to manage "puzzles" about moral conduct (pp. 54, 70 n. 1). Religions deal with these anxieties "conceptually" by developing world views or cosmologies, "emotionally" by reducing anxiety, and "practically" through ritual and other practices (pp. 55–6). Little and Twiss do not deny that other forms of culture can address these problems, but religions, they stipulate, do so in characteristic ways.

A religious world view thus involves a "sacred authority" (personal or impersonal, transcendent or immanent), which has a "special distinctiveness" (is different from anything else and is in some way beyond human control, though not necessarily a "superhuman being") (p. 61), a "special prominence" (bears on important matters, but is not necessarily "more important" than anything else) (pp. 56–61), and is "properly determinative" of "beliefs, attitudes, and practices" (p. 60). The religious subject "respects" the sacred authority, and fashions a way of life as an "appropriate" response (pp. 62–5). The authoritative impact of the sacred

[45] What Little and Twiss refer to as an "institution", I will speak of as a practice. As I note ahead, they include "practices" in the category of "action-guide" to refer to, say, promising or ritual. Cf. MacIntyre's (1984) distinction between practices and institutions.

[46] Little and Twiss (1978: 97–8) say that one cannot derive prescriptive conclusions from entirely non-prescriptive premises, but they insist that a prescriptive premise can be either moral or religious.

can be imaged, for example, as a charismatic divine command, as a role duty, as an evaluative standard, or as anthropological or cosmological truths in myth or narrative (pp. 66–7).

Thus Little and Twiss distinguish moral and religious patterns of belief and action on the basis of the jobs they do: "the distinctive emphasis of religious action-guides is on resolving problems of interpretability rather than problems of cooperation" (p. 63). Sometimes the same concept or set of concepts can do both jobs (see Geertz 1973*b* on symbols as "model of" and "model for"). Religious action-guides, which express a proper response to the religious object, in some traditions incorporate moral content: e.g., we should obey God out of gratitude, or out of respect for the creator's right over creation (pp. 98, 102–3, 104–5). Religious action-guides in turn often give religious legitimations for moral (and political) norms, e.g., to love God, love one's neighbor. But in other traditions, the "properly determinative" authority of the sacred is non-moral, and a proper response to the religious object can conflict with, and even trump, moral action-guides which promote and protect human welfare (pp. 31–2, 68–70, 97–8, 117–18).

Some objections to the idea of a distinction between religion and morality as forms of practice, and some replies: (1) One should not try to formulate definitions if these are conceived as relatively fixed notions which structure inquiry; rather, one should probably generalize only after empirical-historical inquiries (cf. Stout 1981; 1983; Little 1981; cf. also Bell 1998: 211).[47] In some kinds of inquiries, however, it seems useful to have heuristic definitions in hand, which already reflect empirical and theoretical assumptions, but which can be revised as one goes along. One will in any case use *some* notions as one proceeds (Little 1981; Clarke and Byrne 1993: 4 ff.; Saler 2000[1993]: ch. 2). A complete methodological particularism, of course, is impossible: one must assume some general concept of religion, even in a family resemblance sense, to speak of it taking shape in particular contexts; otherwise religion would be unrecognizable.

(2) One cannot propose a universally applicable concept of religion from a particular historical location; all one can do is to describe traditions in a particular context (Asad 1993: 29; King 1999: 10). Bruce Lincoln (2003: 1–3) reads Talal Asad to say that one cannot define anything that is not already a "discrete object". Since "religion" is purportedly not created until the Western Enlightenment—elsewhere it is not distinguished as a dimension of culture—one cannot offer a universal definition. But even if a particular culture does not distinguish religion as a distinct domain or sphere, a theorist can utilize heuristic categories. As Lincoln (2003: 5–8) argues, we can engage in "provisional attempts to clarify our thought", so long as we do not falsely universalize a notion of religion as a private sphere.

[47] Stout also (1981; 1983) objects to the notion of "conceptual analysis", and urges instead a "semantic holism" which focuses on webs of interconnected beliefs.

(3) The sort of definitions that Little and Twiss offer give a false unity and fixity to moral and religious dimensions of cultures; cultures, rather, are contested within and porous without; moreover, indeterminate moral and religious ideas are shaped by agents (Tanner 1997). Little and Twiss, however, can happily admit that religious and moral beliefs, which are often indeterminate, contested, and fluid, are given a determinate use in particular contexts.

(4) A focus on definitions gives an undue importance to ideation, and ignores a range of disciplinary practices. Asad charges (1993: 43, 32–6) that Geertz, for example, "appears, inadvertently, to be taking up the standpoint of theology when he insists on the primacy of meaning without regard to the processes by which meaning is constructed". Asad argues (1993: 35, 53–4) that "it is not mere symbols that implant true Christian dispositions, but power-ranging all the way from laws and other sanctions to the disciplinary activities of social institutions, and of human bodies". But for Geertz in his early essays it is not symbols as such that implant dispositions; it is in "ritual" that model *of* and model *for* are fused and the dispositions of agents shaped. Little and Twiss for their part include "practices" under the heading of action-guides. But one can grant that more needs to be said about social practices, how they include, yet are more than belief, and how they are related to power (Asad 2003: 50, 130–1; Schilbrack 2005*a*: 47, 51–2; 2005*b*: 435 ff.).

(5) The definitions do not reflect strands of belief and practice always and everywhere, but in fact mirror the situation of religion in the modern West. Asad (1993) argues that Geertz's putatively universal definition of religion, which focuses on "meaning" or "interpretability" (as does Little and Twiss's) reflects the privatized situation of religion in the modern world. Geertz's definition is in fact an heir of early modern Christian conceptions of natural religion: "From a set of practical rules attached to specific processes of power and knowledge, religion has come to be abstracted and universalized" (1993: 40–3, at 42).[48] Thus, "Geertz's treatment of religious belief, which lies at the core of his conception of religion, is a modern privatized one because and to the extent that it emphasizes the priority of belief as a state of mind rather than as a constituting activity in the world" (p. 47). Geertz's view falsely universalizes a historical situation where religion is no longer socially engendered or engendering, but consists merely in individual, privatized, solutions to the problem(s) of meaning (pp. 34–5).[49]

In response, one could reply that in his stress on the problems of "meaning" Geertz was trying to correct an emphasis in anthropology which made religion just a part of some other process, such as social integration. Moreover, Geertz argued that the world view–ethos synthesis occurs in ritual, which covers a variety of

[48] Cf. Byrne (1989: 207), who argues that the natural religion tradition contributed to an emphasis on the "historical, natural, and universal character of religion".

[49] See Peterson and Walhoff (2002: 6, 16 n. 18); see also Saler on Geertz and Asad (2000[1993]: 93–104).

experiences from the more individual to the collective; he also said clearly that religions shape ordinary life in different ways in different traditions. Neither Geertz's nor Little and Twiss's definition of religion suggests that religion is a *sui generis* phenomenon separate from other spheres such as politics (cf. King 1999: 12–14, 210). Nonetheless, it is true that Geertz (but not Little and Twiss) radically separates religious and scientific knowledge, and while he stressed the impact of religion on other aspects of culture, he did not focus in the early essays at least on how social and psychological structures have an impact on religion (Frankenberry and Penner 1999; Schilbrack 2005*b*).

(6) Are definitions in the tradition of Geertz—for instance, those of Little and Twiss—ethnocentric? That is, do they impose Western concepts on other traditions generally? Are they part of a process of cultural colonialism (Asad 1993; Chidester 1996; King 1999; Sands 2002; Masuzawa 2005)?[50] Little and Twiss work hard to avoid this charge. The category of sacred authority, or "religious object", is not necessarily a superhuman being, or separate reality; it includes Nirvana as well as the God of monotheism. They do not suggest, moreover, that all religions emphasize right belief. Nor do they make religion a matter of interior experience which is outwardly expressed in belief and ritual (see Lindbeck 1984 on the "experiential-expressive" conception of religion). They also tried to fashion a concept of morality which went beyond the idea of a set of rules or obligations; their moral "action-guides" pertain not just to acts in a narrow sense, but to "intentions, attitudes, motives, practices, and character" (1978: 27; see Williams 1985; MacIntyre 1990; Taylor 1995; Porter 2006). In any case, the general answer to the charge of ethnocentrism is that heuristic definitions are hermeneutical bridges that serve inquiry (Lewis *et al.* 2005). One simply keeps revising as one listens to the other.

Even if these sorts of definitions are feasible and valuable, one can always suggest improvements. First, for example, there is the question of the problem with which moralities are said to cope—cooperation among self-interested individuals and groups. One can argue that while this is one sort of problem that societies face, an adequate notion of the features of moralities should include, in Sandel's (1984; 1997 [1982]) phrase, "aims and attachments" which already connect agents in other ways (see Stout 1981: 235–41; 1983: 313). Second, one can question the problem(s) that

[50] Dubuisson (2003) criticizes "religion" as a product of Christian traditions: a notion of an interior and individual relation to the sacred or transcendent which comprises a "distinct domain" of culture and society. He proposes instead a broader theory of "cosmographic formations" and "prescriptions", "descriptions of the world and how to live in it" (pp. 16–18, 53, 64, 69, 95, 100, 116, 120, 128, 164, 184–6, 192, 194, 233 n. 23, ch. 9). The two are inseparable, for "a conception of humanity does not preexist" practice or "activity"; yet activity "seems to be informed by that conception at the same time as it in turn defines it" (pp. 177–8). His overall proposal, except for the idea of getting rid of the idea of religion, is very similar to that of Geertz (1973*a*; 1973*b*; see Dubuisson 2003: 288 n. 14). He even suggests that various cosmographies are "equally arbitrary" (pp. 11, 21), that they are a " projection of created social reality" (pp. 177–8), and that they function to give experience "a significance, a finality, or value" (pp. 49–51).

religions cope with. One could argue, against the emphasis on meaning or interpretability (Weber to Geertz to Little and Twiss), that the problem is more directly eudaimonistic: religions are about resources for, and threats to, flourishing posed by fundamental processes and powers (Harvey 1997[1995] on Feuerbach's later theory and Schweiker 1992: 281–2, 290 n. 36; see also McGill 1970). The anxiety about "interpretability", where it exists, follows on this more fundamental anxiety. We can say, then, that while moral norms of conduct and character focus principally on human interactions which bear on basic welfare, religious conceptions and norms have principally to do with processes and powers that bear on human life; religious conceptions locate morality in a wider view of the human condition (Schweiker 2005). Some traditions, in addition, link moral striving to a broader view of flourishing which includes ultimate well-being. Accordingly, we need to distinguish religious norms which rank ultimate well-being over earthly welfare, but are other-regarding in some sense and meet other criteria for serving as moral action-guides, from religious action-guides which purportedly transcend moral categories altogether (cf. Little and Twiss 1978: 37–42, 68–9 Schilbrack 2005*b*: 448). Moreover, processes and powers are not necessarily authoritative or "properly determinative"; they may serve only as limits grudgingly acknowledged in the struggle to live and flourish. Third, while Little and Twiss acknowledged that justification moves from the specific to the general, as well as from the general to the specific,[51] one can propose a notion of "reflective equilibrium" which emphasizes the revisability of general norms, as Little (1981: 219) grants, but which also dispenses with the notion of a basic or superior principle (Stout 1981; 1983; 2004: 285).[52]

Conclusion

Cosmization as alienation expressed a "hermeneutic of suspicion" (Ricoeur 1970; Harvey 1997[1995]): notions of a wider moral reality are nothing more than a projection and reification of humanly constructed moral-political arrangements. But the cosmization thesis—taken as a view of the cognitive process of the religious imagination—obscures the historically contextualized, contingent attempt to relate norms and values to the perceived environment. The wholly human thesis

[51] Little and Twiss, in addition to the "appellate" model (1978: 98, 102–3, 109), sketch a mode of "interpretation" which requires discretion, and a mode of "selection" in which one chooses which norm to apply (pp. 110–11; 120 n. 6).

[52] Stout (2001[1988]: 18–20; 1983: 308) argues that meanings depend on beliefs, and that it is fruitless to search for putatively basic beliefs, since even these will presuppose other beliefs. But he does not deny that in some contexts we arrange beliefs in a deductive pattern.

should be recast simply as one view in a long-standing metaphysical debate: The parameters of human existence do or do not include a transhuman source and ground.

In a similar way, the modern attempt to find a source and ground within human experience as such is said to founder on the shores of holistic historicism. Our moralities are not grounded in a depth grammar of any sort, but consist in a congeries of considerations justified relative to wider webs of belief in particular times and places. But we can communicate across traditions and find areas of moral agreement (MacIntyre 1988; 1990; Moody-Adams 1997; Stout 2001[1988]; 2004).

We can seek, moreover, as part of the process of inquiry, to improve our notions of the jobs that religious and moral patterns of practice do, and the complexities of their interrelationships in various traditions (Stout 1981; Little 1981). The heuristic value of our definitions is to help us elucidate the "topics" (Stout 1998; 1993; 2004) or concerns which moral and religious traditions address. Both religion and morality as patterns of practice (belief, but more than belief) have to do with how we try to flourish within the parameters of our environment, but while moralities focus principally on interhuman relations, religions focus principally on the fundamental sources of suffering and well-being.

References

Adams, R. M. (1987*a*). "Autonomy and Theological Ethics". In *The Virtue of Faith and Other Essays in Philosophical Theology*. New York: Oxford University Press, 123–7.

—— (1987*b*). "Divine Command Ethics Modified Again". In *The Virtue of Faith and Other Essays in Philosophical Theology*. New York: Oxford University Press, 128–43.

—— (1987*c*). "A Modified Divine Command Theory of Ethical Wrongness". In Outka and Reeder (1973), 318–47. Repr. in Adams, *The Virtue of Faith and Other Essays in Philosophical Theology*. New York: Oxford University Press, 97–122.

—— (1999). *Finite and Infinite Good: A Framework for Ethics*. New York: Oxford University Press.

Alles, G. D. (2000). "Exchange". In Willi Braun and Russell T. McCutcheon (eds.), *Critical Guide to the Study of Religion*. London: Cassell, 110–24.

—— (2001). "Toward a Genealogy of the Holy: Rudolf Otto and the Apologetics of Religion". *Journal of the American Academy of Religion*, 69/2 (June): 323–41.

Asad, T. (1993). *Genealogies of Religion: Discipline and Reasons of Power in Christianity and Islam*. Baltimore: Johns Hopkins University Press.

—— (2003). *Formations of the Secular: Christianity, Islam, Modernity*. Stanford, Calif.: Stanford University Press.

—— (2006). "Responses". In Scott and Hirshkind (2006), 206–41.

Bell, C. (1992). *Ritual Theory, Ritual Practice*. New York: Oxford University Press.

—— (1997). *Ritual: Perspectives and Dimensions*. New York: Oxford University Press.

—— (1998). "Performance". In Mark C. Taylor (ed.), *Critical Terms for Religious Studies.* Chicago: University of Chicago Press, 205–24.

BERGER, P. L. (1969[1967]). *The Sacred Canopy: Elements of a Sociological Theory of Religion.* Garden City, NY: Anchor Books.

—— (1974). "Some Second Thoughts on Substantive vs. Functional Definitions of Religion". *Journal for the Scientific Study of Religion*, 13/2: 125–33.

BYRNE, P. (1989). *Natural Religion and the Nature of Religion: The Legacy of Deism.* London: Routledge.

—— (1998). *The Moral Interpretation of Religion.* Grand Rapids, Mich., and Cambridge: William B. Eerdmans Publishing Co.

—— (1999[1992]). *The Philosophical and Theological Foundations of Ethics*, 2nd edn. London and New York: Macmillan Press Ltd. and St Martin's Press.

CASANOVA, J. (1994). *Public Religions in the Modern World.* Chicago: University of Chicago Press.

—— (2006). "Secularization Revisited: A Reply to Talal Asad". In Scott and Hirschkind (2006), 12–30.

CHIDESTER, D. (1996). *Savage Systems: Colonialism and Comparative Religion in Southern Africa.* Charlottesville, Va., and London: University Press of America.

CLADIS, M. S. (1992). *A Communitarian Defense of Liberalism: Emile Durkheim and Contemporary Social Theory.* Stanford, Calif.: Stanford University Press.

—— (2001). Introduction and Notes. In Émile Durkheim, *The Elementary Forms of the Religious Life*, trans. Carol Cosman. New York: Oxford University Press.

CLARKE, P. B., and BYRNE, P. (1993). *Religion Defined and Explained.* New York: St Martin's Press.

DONAGAN, A. (1977). *The Theory of Morality.* Chicago and London: University of Chicago Press.

DUBUISSON, D. (2003). *The Western Construction of Religion: Myths, Knowledge, and Ideology*, trans. William Sayers. Baltimore: Johns Hopkins University Press.

EMMET, DOROTHY (1958). *Function, Purpose, and Powers: Some Concepts in the Study of Individuals and Society.* London: Macmillan and Co. Ltd.

EUBEN, R. (1999). *Enemy in the Mirror: Islamic Fundamentalism and the Limits of Modern Rationalism.* Princeton: Princeton University Press.

FIORENZA, F. S. (1992). "The Church as Community of Interpretation: Political Theology between Discourse Ethics and Hermeneutical Reconstruction". In Don S. Browning and Francis Schüssler Fiorenza (eds.), *Habermas, Modernity, and Political Theology*, New York: Crossroads, 69–91.

FRANKENBERRY, N. K., and PENNER, H. H. (1999). "Clifford Geertz's Long-Lasting Moods, Motivations, and Metaphysical Conceptions". *Journal of Religion*, 79: 617–40. Repr. in Frankenberry and Penner (eds.), *Language, Truth, and Religious Belief: Studies in Twentieth-Century Theory and Method in Religion.* Atlanta, Ga.: Scholars Press, 1999, 218–45.

GAMWELL, F. I. (1990). *The Divine Good: Modern Moral Theory and the Necessity of God.* San Francisco: Harper San Francisco.

GEERTZ, C. (1973*a*). "Ethos, Worldview, and the Analysis of Sacred Symbols". In *The Interpretation of Cultures: Selected Essays.* New York: Basic Books, 126–41.

—— (1973*b*). "Religion as a Cultural System". In *The Interpretation of Cultures: Selected Essays.* New York: Basic Books, 87–125.

—— (1999). "'The Pinch of Destiny': Religion as Experience, Meaning, Identity, Power". *Raritan: A Quarterly Review*, 18/3: 1–19.

George, R. P. (1992). "Natural Law and Human Nature". In Robert P. George (ed.), *Natural Law Theory: Contemporary Essays*. Oxford: Clarendon Press, 31–41.

—— (2004[1999]). *In Defense of Natural Law*. Oxford: Oxford University Press.

Gewirth, A. (1978). *Reason and Morality*. Chicago: University of Chicago Press.

Green, G. (1997). "Who's Afraid of Ludwig Feuerbach? Suspicion and the Religious Imagination". In James O. Duke and Anthony L. Dunnavant (eds.), *Christian Faith Seeking Historical Understanding: Essays in Honor of H. Jack Forstman*. Macon, Ga.: Mercer University Press, 44–65.

—— (1998). *Imagining God: Theology and the Religious Imagination*. Grand Rapids, Mich.: Eerdmans.

—— (2002). *Theology, Hermeneutics and Imagination: The Crisis of Interpretation at the End of Modernity*. Cambridge: Cambridge University Press.

Green, R. M. (1978). *Religious Reason: The Rational and Moral Basis of Religious Belief*. New York: Oxford University Press.

—— (1988). *Religion and Moral Reason: A New Method for Comparative Study*. New York: Oxford University Press.

Grizez, G., Boyle, J., and Finnis, J. (1987). "Practical Principles, Moral Truth, and Ultimate Ends". *American Journal of Jurisprudence*, 32: 99–151.

Gustafson, J. M. (1973). "Religion and Morality from the Perspective of Theology". In Outka and Reeder (1973), 125–54.

—— (1981, 1984). *Ethics from a Theocentric Perspective*, i and ii. Chicago: University of Chicago Press.

—— (1996). *Intersections: Science, Theology, and Ethics*. Cleveland, Oh.: The Pilgrim Press.

Guthrie, S. E. (1993). *Faces in the Cloud: A New Theory of Religion*. New York: Oxford University Press.

—— (2000). "Projection". In W. Braun and R. T. McCutcheon, (eds.), *Guide to the Study of Religion*. London and New York: Cassell, 225–38.

Habermas, J. (1991[1983]). *Moral Consciousness and Communicative Action*, trans. Christian Lenhardt and Shierry Weber Nicholson, Introduction by Thomas McCarthy. Cambridge, Mass.: MIT Press.

—— (1995[1993]). *Justification and Application: Remarks on Discourse Ethics*, trans. Ciaran Cronin. Cambridge, Mass., and London: MIT Press.

—— (2002). *Religion and Rationality: Essays on Reason, God, and Modernity*, ed. with an introduction by Eduardo Mendietta. Cambridge, Mass.: MIT Press.

Hare, J. E. (2007). *God and Morality: A Philosophical History*. Oxford: Blackwell Publishing.

Hare, R. M. (1952). *The Language of Morals*. Oxford: Oxford University Press.

—— (1963). *Freedom and Reason*. Oxford: Oxford University Press.

—— (1981). *Moral Thinking: Its Levels, Method, and Point*. Oxford: Clarendon Press.

Harvey, V. A. (1973). "Some Problematical Aspects of Peter Berger's Theory of Religion". *Journal of the American Academy of Religion*, 41/1: 75–93.

—— (1979). "Religious Faith and the Sociology of Knowledge: The Unburdening of Peter Berger". *Religious Studies Review*, 5/1: 1–10.

—— (1997[1995]). *Feuerbach and the Interpretation of Religion*. Cambridge: Cambridge University Press.

Herdt, J. A. (1997). *Religion and Faction in Hume's Moral Philosophy*. Cambridge: Cambridge University Press.

HERVIEU-LÉGER, D. (2000). *Religion as a Chain of Memory*, trans. Simon Lee. New Brunswick, NJ: Rutgers University Press.

KEOWN, D. (1992). *The Nature of Buddhist Ethics*. New York: St Martin's Press.

KING, RICHARD (1999). *Orientalism and Religion: Postcolonial Theory, India, and 'the Mystic East'.* London and New York: Routledge.

LARMORE, C. (2005). "The Autonomy of Morality". <www.Law.nyu.edu/clppt/program 2005/readings/autonomy-of-morality.pdf>.

LEVINE, M. P. (1992). "Deep Structure and the Comparative Philosophy of Religion". *Religious Studies*, 28/3: 387–99.

LEWIS, T. A. , SCHOFER, J. W., STALNAKER, A., and BERSON, M. A. (2005). "Anthropos and Ethos: Categories of Inquiry and Procedures of Comparison". *Journal of Religious Ethics*, 33/2: 177–85.

LINCOLN, BRUCE (2003). *Holy Terrors: Thinking about Religion after September 11*. Chicago: University of Chicago Press.

LINDBECK, GEORGE A. (1984). *The Nature of Doctrine: Religion and Theology in the Post-liberal Age*. Philadephia: Westminster Press.

LITTLE, D. (1981). "The Present State of the Comparative Study of Religious Ethics". *Journal of Religious Ethics*, 9/2: 210–27.

—— (1986). "Natural Rights and Human Rights: The International Imperative". In Robert P. Davidow (ed.), *Natural Rights and Natural Law: The Legacy of George Mason*. Fairfax, Va.: George Mason University Press, 67–122.

—— (1993). "The Nature and Basis of Human Rights". In Outka and Reeder (1993), 73–92.

—— and TWISS, S. B. (1978). *Comparative Religious Ethics: A New Method*. New York: Harper & Row.

LOVIN, R. W. (1985). "Cosmogony, Contrivance, and Ethical Order". In Lovin and Reynolds (1985), 328–49.

—— and REYNOLDS, F. E. (eds.) (1985). *Cosmogony and Ethical Order: New Studies in Comparative Ethics*. Chicago: University of Chicago Press.

—— —— (1986). "Cosmogony and Religious Ethics: Focus Introduction". *Journal of Religious Ethics*, 14/1: 48–60.

—— —— (1992). "Ethical Naturalism and Indigenous Cultures: Introduction". *Journal of Religious Ethics*, 20/2: 267–8.

MASUZAWA, T. (2005). *The Invention of World Religions, or, How European Universalism Was Preserved in the Language of Pluralism*. Chicago: University of Chicago Press.

MCCARTHY, T. (1991[1978]). *The Critical Theory of Jürgen Habermas*. Cambridge, Mass., and London: MIT Press.

—— (1995[1991]). *Ideals and Illusions: On Reconstruction and Deconstruction in Contemporary Critical Theory*. Cambridge, Mass., and London: MIT Press.

MCCUTCHEON, R. T. (1997*a*). "A Default of Critical Intelligence? The Scholar of Religion as Public Intellectual". *Journal of the American Academy of Religion*, 65/2: 443–68.

—— (1997*b*). *Manufacturing Religion: The Discourse on Sui Generis Religion and the Politics of Nostalgia*. New York: Oxford University Press.

MCFAGUE, S. (1987). *Models of God: Theology for an Ecological, Nuclear Age*. Philadephia: Fortress Press.

MCGILL, A. C. (1970). "The Ambiguous Position of Christian Theology". In P. Ramsey and J. F. Wilson (eds.), *The Study of Religion in Colleges and Universities*. Princeton: Princeton University Press, 105–38.

MacIntyre, A. (1984). *After Virtue: A Study in Moral Theory*, 2nd edn. Notre Dame, Ind.: Notre Dame University Press.

—— (1988). *Whose Justice? Which Rationality?* Notre Dame, Ind.: University of Notre Dame Press.

—— (1990). *Three Rival Versions of Moral Enquiry: Encyclopaedia, Genealogy, and Tradition.* Notre Dame, Ind.: University of Notre Dame Press.

Mitchell, B. (1980). *Morality: Religious and Secular: The Dilemma of the Traditional Conscience.* Oxford: Clarendon Press.

Moody-Adams, M. (1997). *Fieldwork in Familiar Places: Morality, Culture, and Philosophy.* Cambridge, Mass.: Harvard University Press.

Niebuhr, H. R. (1999). *The Responsible Self: An Essay in Christian Moral Philosophy*, Foreword by William Schweiker, Introduction by James M. Gustafson. Philadephia: Westminster/John Knox Press.

Nielsen, K. (1973). *Ethics without God.* London: Pemberton Books; Buffalo:Prometheus Books; rev. edn. Amherst, NY: Prometheus Books, 1990.

Nussbaum, M. C. (2000). *Women and Human Development.* Cambridge: Cambridge University Press.

Outka, G. (1996). "The Particularist Turn in Theological and Philosophical Ethics". In Lisa Sowle Cahill and James F. Childress (eds.), *Christian Ethics: Problems and Prospects.* Cleveland, Oh.: The Pilgrim Press, 93–118.

—— and Reeder, J. P. Jr. (eds.) (1973). *Religion and Morality: A Collection of Essays.* Garden City, NY: Anchor Press/Doubleday.

—— —— (eds.) (1993). *Prospects for a Common Morality.* Princeton: Princeton University Press.

Penner, H. H. (1971). "The Poverty of Functionalism". *History of Religions*, 11 (Aug.): 91–7.

—— (1988). *Impasse and Resolution: A Critique of the Study of Religion.* New York: Peter Lang.

—— (1999). "What's Wrong with Functional Explanations". In N. K. Frankenberry and H. H. Penner (eds.), *Language, Truth, and Religious Belief: Studies in Twentieth-Century Theory and Method in Religion.* Atlanta, Ga.: Scholars Press, 246–72.

—— (2003). "On Self-Regulating Systems, Cannibals, and Cogs that Turn no Wheels: A Response to Joel Sweek". *Method and Theory in the Study of Religion*, 15: 390–408.

Peterson, D., and Walhof, D. (eds.) (2002). *The Invention of Religion: Rethinking Belief in Politics and History.* New Brunswick, NJ: Rutgers University Press.

Porter, J. (1999). *Natural and Divine Law: Reclaiming the Tradition for Christian Ethics*, Foreword by Nicholas Wolterstorff. Grand Rapids, Mich., and Cambridge: William B. Eerdmans Publishing Company.

—— (2005). *Nature as Reason: A Thomistic Theory of the Natural Law.* Grand Rapids, Mich., and Cambridge: William B. Eerdmans Publishing Company.

—— (2006). "Christian Ethics and the Concept of Morality: A Historical Inquiry". *Journal of the Society of Christian Ethics*, 26 (Fall–Winter): 3–22.

Proudfoot, W. (1985). *Religious Experience.* Berkeley: University of California Press.

Quinn, P. L. (1990). "The Recent Revival of Divine Command Ethics". *Philosophy and Phenomenological Research*, 50, suppl. (Autumn): 345–65.

Ricoeur, P. (1970). *Freud and Philosophy: An Essay on Interpretation*, trans. D. Savage. New Haven: Yale University Press.

RORTY, R. (2006). *Take Care of Freedom and Truth Will Take Care of Itself*, ed. and with an Introduction by Eduardo Mendietta. Stanford, Calif.: Stanford University Press.

SAGI, A., and STATMAN, D. (1995). *Religion and Morality*, trans. Batya Stein. Rodopi: Amsterdam-Atlanta.

SALER, BENSON (2000[1993]). *Conceptualizing Religion: Immanent Anthropologists, Transcendent Natives, and Unbounded Categories*. New York and Oxford: Berghahn Books.

SANDEL, MICHAEL J. (1984). "The Procedural Republic and the Unencumbered Self". *Political Theory*, 12/1: 81–96.

—— (1997[1982]). *Liberalism and the Limits of Justice*, 2nd edn. Cambridge: Cambridge University Press.

SANDS, K. M. (2002). "Tracking Religion: Religion Through the Lens of Critical and Cultural Studies". *The Council of Societies for the Study of Religion Bulletin*, 31/3: 68–74.

SCHILBRACK, K. (2002). "The Study of Religious Belief after Davidson". *Method and Theory in the Study of Religion*, 3–4: 335–49.

—— (2004). "Ritual Metaphysics". *Journal of Ritual Studies*, 18/1: 77–90.

—— (2005*a*). "Bruce Lincoln's Philosophy". *Method and Theory in the Study of Religion*, 17/1: 44–58.

—— (2005*b*). "Religion, Models of, and Reality: Are We Through with Geertz?" *Journal of the American Academy of Religion*, 73/2 (June): 429–52.

SCHNEEWIND, J. B. (1998). *The Invention of Autonomy: A History of Modern Moral Philosophy*. New York: Cambridge University Press.

SCHWEIKER, W. (1992). "The Drama of Interpretation and the Philosophy of Religions: An Essay on Understanding Comparative Religious Ethics". In Frank Reynolds and David Tracy (eds.), *Discourse and Practice*, Albany, NY: State University of New York Press, 263–94.

—— (2005). "On Religious Ethics". In W. Schweiker (ed.), *The Blackwell Companion to Religious Ethics*. Malden, Mass.: Blackwell Publishing, 1–15.

SCOTT, D., and HIRSCHKIND, C. (eds.) (2006). *Powers of the Secular Modern: Talal Asad and His Interlocutors*. Stanford, Calif.: Stanford University Press.

SPIRO, M. E. (1968[1966]). "Religion: Problems of Definition and Explanation". In Michael Banton (ed.), *Anthropological Approaches to the Study of Religion*. London: Tavistock Publications Limited, 85–126.

STARK, R. (2000). "Rationality". In W. Braun and R. T. McCutcheon, *Guide to the Study of Religion*. London and New York: Cassell, 239–58.

—— and BAINBRIDGE, W. S. (1985). *The Future of Religion: Secularization, Revival, and Cult Formation*. Berkeley: University of California Press.

STOUT, J. L. (1978). "Metaethics and the Death of Meaning: Adams and the Case of the Tantalizing Closing". *Journal of Religious Ethics*, 6/1: 1–18.

—— (1981). *The Flight from Authority: Religion, Morality, and the Quest for Autonomy*. Notre Dame, Ind.: University of Notre Dame Press.

—— (1983). "Holism and Comparative Religious Ethics: A Response to Little". *Journal of Religious Ethics*, 11/2: 301–16.

—— (1992). "Truth, Natural Law, and Ethical Theory". In Robert George (ed.), *Natural Law Theory: Contemporary Essays*. Oxford: Clarendon Press, 71–102.

—— (1993). "On Having a Morality in Common". In Outka and Reeder (1993), 215–32.

—— (1998). "Commitments and Traditions in the Study of Religious Ethics". *Journal of Religious Ethics*, supp. vol. September, 23–56.

STOUT, J. L. (2001[1988]). *Ethics after Babel: The Languages of Morals and their Discontents*, 2nd. edn. with a new Postscript by the author. Princeton: Princeton University Press.

—— (2004). *Democracy and Tradition*. Princeton: Princeton University Press.

TANNER, K. (1997). *Theories of Culture: A Theological Assessment.* Minneapolis: Augsburg Fortress Publishers.

TAYLOR, C. (1995). "A Most Peculiar Institution". In J. E. J. Altham and Ross Harrison (eds.), *World, Mind, and Ethics: Essays on the Ethical Philosophy of Bernard Williams.* Cambridge: Cambridge University Press, 132–55.

WAINWRIGHT, W. J. (2005). *Religion and Morality.* Aldershot: Ashgate Publishing Limited.

WILLIAMS, B. (1985). *Ethics and the Limits of Philosophy.* Cambridge, Mass.: Harvard University Press.

WOLTERSTORFF, N., with R. AUDI (1997). *Religion in the Public Square: The Place of Religious Convictions in Public Debate.* Lanham, Md.: Rowman & Littlefield Publishers, Inc.

YEARLEY, L. H. (1993). "Conflicts among Ideals of Human Flourishing". In Outka and Reeder (1993), 233–53.

SUGGESTED READING

BENAVIDES, G. (1998). "Modernity". In Taylor (1998), 186–204.

BIGGAR, N., and BLACK, R. (eds.) (2000). *The Revival of Natural Law: Philosophical, Theological, and Ethical Responses to the Finnis-Grisez School.* Aldershot: Ashgate Press.

BUNGE, MARIO, and MAHNER, MARTIN (2001). "Function and Functionalism: A Synthetic Perspective". *Philosophy of Science*, 68/1: 75–94.

DE VRIES, HENT (ed.) (2008). *Religion: Beyond A Concept.* New York: Fordham University Press.

FITZGERALD, TIMOTHY (2000). "Experience." In Willi Braun and Russell T. McCutcheon (eds.), *Guide to the Study of Religion.* London: Cassell, 125–139.

FRANKENBERRY, N. K. (ed.) (2002). *Radical Interpretation in Religion.* Cambridge: Cambridge University Press.

GEORGE, R. P. (ed.) (1998). *Natural Law and Moral Inquiry: Ethics, Metaphysics, and Politics in the Work of Germain Grisez.* Washington: Georgetown University Press.

GOOCH, T. A. (2000). *The Numinous and Modernity: An Interpretation of Rudolf Otto's Philosophy of Religion*, Beihefte zur Zeitschrift für die alttestamentliche Wissenschaft, Herausgegeben von Otto Kaisser, Band 293. Berlin: Walter de Gruyter.

GREEN, G. (2002). "The Mirror, the Lamp, and the Lens". *Ars Disputandi*, 2 <http://www.ArsDisputandi.org> ESPR Proceedings Cambridge, UK.

HARVEY, V.A. (1991). "Fuerbach on Religion as Construction". In S. G. Davaney (ed.), *Theology at the End of Modernity: Essays in Honor of Gordon D. Kaufman.* Philadephia: Trinity Press International, 249–68.

HELM, P. (ed.) (1981). *Divine Commands and Morality.* Oxford: Oxford University Press.

IDINOPULOS, T. A., and WILSON, B. C. (eds.) (1998). *What is Religion? Origin, Definition, and Explanation.* London: E. J. Brill.

IDZIAK, J. M. (ed.) (1979). *Divine Command Morality: Historical and Contemporary Readings.* New York and Toronto: Edwin Mellen Press.

Kaufman, Gordon B. (1981). *The Theological Imagination: Constructing the Concept of God.* Philadelphia: Westminster Press.

Kippenberg, H. G. (2002). *Discovering Religious History in the Modern Age,* trans. B. Harshaw. Princeton: Princeton University Press.

Masuzawa, K. (1998). "Culture". In Taylor (1998). 70–93.

Nussbaum, M. (1993). "Non-Relative Virtues: An Aristotelian Approach". In Martha Nussbaum and Amartya Sen (eds.), *The Quality of Life.* Oxford: Clarendon Press, 242–69.

Phillips, D. Z. (ed.) (1996). *Religion and Morality.* New York: St Martin's Press.

Preus, S. (1987). *Explaining Religion: Criticism and Theory from Bodin to Freud.* New Haven: Yale University Press.

Reynolds, F. E., and Schofer, J. W. (2005). "Cosmology". In Schweiker (2005), 120–8.

Rorty R., and Gianni, V. (2005). *The Future of Religion,* ed. Santiago Zabala. New York: Columbia University Press.

Schweiker, W. (ed.) (2005). *The Blackwell Companion to Religious Ethics.* Malden, Mass.: Blackwell Publishing.

Smith, J. Z. (1978). "The Influence of Religions on Social Change". In *idem, Map Is Not Territory.* Leiden: E. J. Brill, 129–46.

—— (1998). "Religion, Religions, Religious". In Taylor (1998), 269–84.

Taylor, Mark C. (ed.) (1998). *Critical Terms for Religious Studies.* Chicago: University of Chicago Press.

Twiss, S. B. (2005). "Comparison in Religious Ethics". In Schweiker (2005), 147–55.

Zagzebski, L. (2005). "Morality and Religion". In William J. Wainwright (ed.), *The Oxford Handbook of Philosophy of Religion.* Also Alles (2001). Oxford: Oxford University Press, 344–65.

CHAPTER 19

THE CONTEMPORARY CONVERGENCE OF ART AND RELIGION

ROBERT WUTHNOW

AT the end of the sixth century, Pope Gregory the Great decreed that music and art would henceforth be carefully monitored. Music used for worship was to include lyrics only from the Bible, and visual art was to depict scenes from biblical stories. The liturgy was thus reformed, but an underground of folk art, ballads, and risqué tales flourished outside the church. Their aim was seldom to focus hearts and minds on God. The church's attempts to control the arts did, however, create the lasting impression that the two spheres are like blood brothers locked in contention and mutual misgiving.

What, then, do we make of the fact that art and religion now so often appear to be cozy co-conspirators? How do we understand Mel Gibson's highly acclaimed—and controversial—big-screen *Passion of the Christ*? Why does a popular vocalist sing about virgins and prayer and call herself "Madonna"? What inspires Oprah Winfrey to baptize her programming with endless discussions of spirituality? Is it just that religion is good for business?

Shift the lens, and churches seem as interested in the arts as the entertainment industry is in religion. Prestonwood Baptist Church in suburban Dallas sponsors its own symphony orchestra. Grace Cathedral in San Francisco periodically adorns its massive sanctuary with huge multi-colored exhibitions of installation art. An evangelical church in Cleveland, Ohio, that until recently condemned dancing and rock music, holds Christian rock concerts on Saturday evenings.

Turn the camera again, and almost invisible traces of artistic creativity linked with spirituality come into focus. A Catholic nun in south Philadelphia teaches homeless children to express themselves in watercolors. At the Graduate Theological Union in Berkeley, California, seminary students practice incorporating dance into the liturgy. An aging Latina in Santa Fe inscribes prayers on the back of her hand-painted *santos*. Are these random examples, or do they form a larger pattern?

Lest one imagine the United States to be unique in these convergences between the arts and religion, one has only to look at other countries. The so-called emerging church currently sweeping Australia attracts young adults by incorporating new contemporary praise music, sometimes composed only hours earlier, into its services. In other contexts one sees similar convergences. When anthropologist Joel Robbins (2004) returned recently to the remote Papua New Guinea village he had studied in the early 1990s, he found the traditional sacred tribal dance being performed to disco music from a portable boom box. In Ghana's burgeoning capital city of Accra, a new genre of music called holy hip hop has become popular (Gifford 2004: 35). Holy hip hop, uniting traditional African music with an updated synthesis of Highlife and Gospel Life music, has generated an industry of performers and broadcasters, and plays to enthusiastic audiences in Ghana's rapidly growing evangelical churches.

Of course none of this is without precedent. Music and art have been connected with religion throughout history. Long before Confucius, ancient Chinese priests inscribed prayers on beautiful metal bells. When Buddhism first spread along the silk road to northern Asia, its monks left a record of their work on delicate murals. One has only to visit the Sistine Chapel or the great cathedrals of Europe to recognize the intersection of art and faith in the history of Christianity.

Yet the overlap between religion and the arts in the past does not explain the convergence evident on so many fronts today. The question is not whether connections between religion and the arts are increasing (although they may be), but why they are as extensive as they are. Even more importantly, what are the social and cultural mechanisms through which religion and the arts are now linked?

Selective Absorption

The place to begin, as is so often the case in sociology of religion, is to look again—and more critically—at the received wisdom about secularization. The richly nuanced contributions of Max Weber, Karl Marx, Émile Durkheim, Ferdinand Tönnies, Ernst Troeltsch, and others that resulted in the so-called secularization paradigm have been reduced in many recent treatments to questions about trends in religious participation. A point that these often tiresome discussions about religion declining or not declining miss concerns the relations among institutions. In modern societies institutions are more complex, and their functions more clearly defined than in earlier societies. The classic example is the proverbial shaman or witch doctor, who serves as resident expert for both religion and medicine. In contemporary London or New York, clergy and doctors are listed in different parts of the phone book and offer quite different services. The secularization of religion in this sense has less to do with declining attendance than with functioning in a more limited sphere. A similar process may be imagined having taken place in religion and the arts. Walk through any major art museum, for instance, and the earliest exhibits suggest a blending of the artistic with magical and religious rites. In contrast, the modern exhibits suggest that "art for art's sake" has become the dominant motif. In short, art and religion have become separate institutional spheres.

There is good reason to think that this process of institutional differentiation might have resulted not in convergence, but in greater distance between religion and the arts. Each is organized separately and enjoys autonomy from the other. Artists set their own standards without worrying much about what clergy (or doctors or politicians) say. When awards are given or paintings are accepted for display, it is a committee of fellow artists which decides, not just anybody from the community. On the religion side, differentiation also works well to curb extraneous influences. The priest or imam decides what to include in a worship service, rather than looking to an artist or musician to make the decision.

Where these arguments falter, though, is in confusing difference with distance. As societies become more specialized, the various specialists actually need to interact more, not less. This was Durkheim's great observation about the social division of labor producing what he termed "organic solidarity" (Durkheim 1947). Clergy contact doctors, and doctors consult clergy. So it is with religion and the arts. When a Baptist church decides to sponsor an orchestra, it does not ask the preacher to conduct the music. It hires a professional musician. The two have specialized functions, but they are also bound by using the same space and having to negotiate with each other about their particular contributions.

If religion and the arts are separate spheres, it might still be supposed that people would opt for one or the other. The training required to become a professional artist, for instance, would preclude someone from also becoming a priest. In reality, though, most people are neither professional artists nor priests. They participate in the arts and religion as consumers, meaning that they can participate in both. Even a professional artist can be religious, and a priest can be interested in the arts.

As avocational participants in religion and the arts, consumers might nevertheless be inclined to choose one instead of the other. The proverbial person who finds it more meaningful to visit a museum or gallery than listen to a sermon would be an example. Data, though, suggest that the trade-off implied is not characteristic of people in general. For instance, by a margin of 28 percent to 23 percent, weekly church-goers in the United States are *more* likely than those who never attend religious services to say that they have visited an art museum or gallery in the past year.[1] Similar data are unavailable for other countries. Yet, other data suggest more congruence than conflict between arts participation and religious involvement. For instance, people who say they are active members of a religious organization are also more likely to say that they are active members of an arts organization, and vice versa. Of course this pattern may be attributable to differences in social class or location, but as a descriptive fact, it belies the notion that people opt to be involved in the arts *or* religion, but not both. It is also a pattern that holds in such diverse contexts as France, Sweden, Ireland, Australia, Russia, Brazil, and Japan.[2] Where data do suggest a modest trade-off between religion and the arts is among professional artists. For instance, a study in the United States showed that fewer artists than non-artists were fundamentalists (17 percent versus 31 percent), that more were non-religious (30 percent versus 11 percent), and that fewer attended religious services weekly (24 percent versus 32 percent). Viewed differently, though, the same results suggest that a large majority (70 percent) of US artists do consider themselves religious, and nearly as many as in the general public participate regularly in religious services (Lewis and Brooks 2005).

To return to the larger question, the more significant difficulty with arguments about institutions becoming more specialized is that descriptions of the process are usually too mechanical. In the standard view, differentiation occurs without people actually making it happen. But people who behave as agents and as decision-makers need to be brought back in. Clergy are sometimes the ones who decide that religious organizations should no longer be involved in government or science or education or counseling (Fenn 1978). By the same token, individuals and committees make decisions about whether a congregation should have an orchestra or put on a Christmas pageant or sponsor an exhibit about the Holocaust.

What can we say about these decisions? The idea that congregations operate a bit like businesses is helpful. I say "a bit like" because Presbyterians and Catholics do not shop as interchangeably at other houses of worship as consumers of Coke and Pepsi do. Still, congregations do compete with one another. Some preach fire and

[1] From my 1999 Arts and Religion Survey conducted among a representative national sample of US adults; for additional detail see Wuthnow (2003).

[2] These results are from my analysis of the World Values Surveys conducted between 1981 and 2000. I found no countries in which positive and statistically significant correlations were not present between being an active member of a religious organization and being an active member of an arts organization.

brimstone to scare people into joining. Some require unusual clothing or conformity to strict moral injunctions. It is more common, though, for congregations to compete by initiating new programs. Going back in history, for instance, congregations in mid-Victorian Britain and North America initiated Sunday schools at a time when weekday schooling was becoming popular among middle-class families but remained out of reach for working-class children. As a result, churches attracted a wider spectrum of the population and grew especially among the poor. Another example occurred in the 1890s, when colleges began shedding their religious auspices to become research universities. Church leaders responded by initiating "Bible institutes", such as the Moody Bible Institute in Chicago, the Gordon Missionary Training Institute in Boston, and the Institute for Home and Foreign Missions in East London (Brereton 1990). With dirt-cheap room and board, free tuition, and opportunities to enter full-time ministry after a few months of training, these institutes attracted thousands of students.

These examples require thinking about secularization in a new way. As traditionally conceived, arguments about secularization emphasize that schools and universities simply became separate institutions beyond the control of religious authorities. In reality, the process was more complex. Church leaders recognized a need, and became part of a wider trend aimed at filling that need. They *selectively absorbed* some of the new ideas about schooling that were emerging and some of the functions of educational institutions, contributed to popularizing these ideas and activities, and found ways to incorporate new educational programs into their ministries (Wuthnow 2003: 14–16).

Selective absorption is one of the important ways in which religious leaders have encouraged closer cooperation with the arts in recent years. Music and art are clearly an important and perhaps increasingly popular aspect of contemporary culture. In the United States, for instance, 70 percent of adults claim to have purchased music on a tape or compact disc in the past year, 35 percent have purchased a painting or sculpture in the past year, and 26 percent have visited an art museum or gallery in the same period. These and other activities are generally more common among younger people than older people, and other data suggest growth in attendance at concerts and plays and consumption of music (Wuthnow 2003: 60–4; see also Walker, Scott-Melnyk, and Sherwood 2002). The same is true in other countries. A study of British 15-year-olds, for instance, found that 73 percent took part in arts activities, and more than a quarter did so two or three times a week (Arts Council England 2005). Religious leaders have selectively absorbed some of this interest in music and art into their own programs. The church in Dallas that sponsors a symphony orchestra is a good example. It has an annual budget of more than $10 million, 100 full-time employees, and a 3,000-seat auditorium. An orchestra fits easily into its overall program, which includes a school, athletic events, a cafeteria, a video library, and several choirs. Many of its members are musicians, and many more enjoy music. Sponsoring an orchestra is simply one of the ways in which its leaders demonstrate to their community that the church is an attractive place to be.

As megachurches like this become more common, their budgets permit them to become important sponsors of arts activities. Yet they are not alone in bridging religion and the arts. Nationally, about half of US church members say that their congregations sponsor musical performances at times other than worship services (Wuthnow 2003: 143). These performances vary considerably in scope and purpose. For instance, even the smallest congregations sponsor an occasional visiting choir or Christmas concert, while larger congregations increasingly hold monthly performances by resident pianists or visiting chamber orchestras, and some host touring rock bands or vocalists. Other artistic events are also fairly common. For instance, about half of members say that their congregation has sponsored a drama or skit in the past year, a third indicate that their congregation holds art festivals or craft fairs, and a fifth belong to congregations that sponsor literature or art discussion groups (Wuthnow 2003: 143).

These recent examples of selective absorption are merely the latest in a long history of religious leaders adapting to the culture by incorporating innovations in art and music. Prominent examples include the Bible regal, an early version of the accordion, which was used widely in European churches in the late Middle Ages, the emerging popularity of the pianoforte for religious services in the eighteenth century, and the displacement of choirs by congregational singing, which did not occur in some American congregations until the end of the nineteenth century (Robert 2003: 124). The most notable example of visual art being adopted where it had previously been proscribed is probably the famous 1941 Warner Sallman "Head of Christ", which adorned thousands of church basements, vestibules, and living rooms (Promey 2001). More recent adaptations include the use of electric guitars in worship services, currently featured in nearly a third of US churches (Chaves 2004: 228).

Democratization

The contemporary convergence of religion and the arts reflects a second process that can best be termed *democratization*. The arts have been democratized through education and communications technology. Classes in vocal music, instrumental music, visual art, and the performing arts have become more common in American public schools over the past century. For children of middle- to upper-income families, extracurricular participation in the arts through ballet classes, summer theater, music camps, and private tutoring have also been popular. Radio, television, cinema, the recording industry, and the Internet have all expanded the opportunities for people of diverse social classes to be exposed to the arts. In recent years, leaders of arts organizations have encouraged further democratization through community arts programs, public television, and grants. Some of these efforts have been driven by public funding opportunities. Officials who may be reluctant to give tax money to a well-heeled gallery lush with private philanthropy, for instance, have less hesitation to fund an arts center in a low-income neighborhood. Democratization is also evident in religion. In most religious traditions, professional clergy remain firmly in charge of worship services and ecclesial politics. Yet the role of laity has in many instances increased. For instance, the Second Vatican Council mandated greater lay participation in worship, opened the liturgy to vernacular languages, and encouraged the use of popularly composed music. Priest shortages have necessitated additional reliance on lay leaders. Among Protestants, the fastest-growing churches worldwide are Pentecostal congregations whose leaders encourage lay participation through speaking in tongues, congregational singing, and purchasing cassettes of popular inspirational music (Meyer 2004). Other churches experiment with laity-led "worship teams", who organize congregational singing and incorporate "praise music" with lyrics that emphasize closeness among believers and with God.

With democratization, boundaries separating religion and the arts become blurred. Democratization authorizes individuals to make their own decisions, to impose their own definitions, and to consider these definitions legitimate. A person who snaps a photograph of a beautiful sunset considers it her right to call the photograph "art" without asking a professional photographer to render an opinion. That same person may "see God" in the sunset, and consider it unnecessary to seek the pastor's permission before describing it in these terms at a weekly prayer fellowship meeting. On a larger scale, the blurring of boundaries in religion is evident in the popularity of "spirituality" as a rubric to describe that which is personally meaningful about one's relationship to the sacred (Roof 1999). Spirituality may or may not be sanctioned by religious authorities. Indeed, it often falls outside the boundaries of religious institutions or religious language, as when a person claims to be inspired by the "Spirit" or "feels spiritual" as a result of doing volunteer work. In the arts, similar difficulties of categorization are sometimes mentioned in discussions of minimalist art, which "becomes art" through the authority of art critics but remains much in doubt even among artists themselves. Folk art raises similar questions, when standards of evaluation may not be widely shared.

Blurred boundaries open possibilities for greater convergence between religion and the arts. A single painting, song, or performance can be sufficiently ambiguous that its inclusion is appropriate in a religious context, an artistic context, or both. For instance, the exterior parish hall wall of a Catholic church in San Francisco is the location of a large mural depicting Aztec and Christian imagery. Is the mural religious because of its imagery and location? Is it art? Does it matter that its location is public rather than inside the church? Ambiguity is conducive to convergence, but also to misunderstanding. In the same neighborhood an art gallery displayed figurines that the owner regarded as art, and thus as morally neutral, but which proved offensive to viewers who saw them as religious icons. Smashed windows were the result.

A more common consequence of democratization has been greater interest among arts leaders and religious leaders in experimenting with partnerships (Walker 2004). Performances and exhibitions move from concert halls and museums to local neighborhoods where churches and synagogues may be the most convenient venues. In one study, 29 percent of US church members said that their church building is sometimes used for musical or theatrical events (Chaves 2004: 233). A congregation-based book club becomes a way to recruit people to attend a play. In the United States, 44 percent of regular church-goers say they sometimes go with church friends to plays, galleries, or concerts.[3] When there is special interest, religious organizations provide a powerful vehicle for mobilizing an audience. Gibson's *Passion of the Christ* sold tickets in large numbers to congregations as well as to individual members of congregations (Duin 2004).

From Creeds to Experience

When people talk candidly about their faith, they usually focus more on personal experience than on creeds. Among US adults, more than four-fifths of whom say they are Christians or Jews, about half say that they trust their own experience for spiritual guidance more than they do the Bible (Wuthnow 2005: 197). It is understandable that people might do this. Experience is *mine*, part of my personal identity, whereas creeds are formulas from the past that may resonate little with the present. The preference for experience over creeds, though, reflects a larger issue in contemporary culture. In a diverse world in which the fact that multiple creeds exist is readily evident, the inevitable question is: which creed is right? Did Jesus really "descend into hell", as Christians assert in reciting the Apostles' Creed? Was Muhammad actually Allah's messenger? I may believe so, but have difficulty persuading someone who thinks differently. If nothing else, arguments persist. In contrast, personal experience is unassailable. If I say "I was touched by an angel", you may disbelieve me, but you cannot credibly challenge my statement. "No you weren't" is easily rebutted by "You weren't there so how would you know?" In short, experience is a good way of dealing with diversity.

[3] Arts and Religion Survey.

Daily life is a constant whir of experience. It is the special moments, though, which convince us that we have been in contact with the sacred—moments of special joy that make us feel in harmony with the universe, times when life seems filled with beauty and wonder, dark moments when we sing the blues. The connections with music and art are evident even in the words we use—harmony, beauty, blues. The most intense moments of transcendence, ecstasy, rapture, despair, cannot be expressed fully in words. We search for metaphors to convey them or turn to music, dance, or art to encapsulate and sharpen them.

Not surprisingly, then, contemporary expressions of spirituality and interest in the arts are closely linked. People conceive of spirituality as a deeply personal, intuitive, and often emotionally charged experience of divine presence, and they consider music and art to be beneficial in seeking and expressing this experience. Of course, some religious traditions encourage thinking in this way more than others. Yet there appears to be widespread agreement about the relevance of art and music to spirituality. Among American Evangelicals, for instance, 54 percent agree that "pictures and images enrich our spiritual lives", the same proportion as among Catholics, and only somewhat fewer than among the 66 percent of mainline Protestants who hold the same view (Wuthnow 2003: 141). In the same study, 46 percent of Evangelicals, 60 percent of mainline Protestants, and 62 percent of Catholics believed that "art can help people to deepen their spirituality".

Research also suggests that many people experience the divine as a result of music and art. Eighty percent of American Evangelicals, 76 percent of mainline Protestants, and 56 percent of Catholics say they have felt close to God from listening to music during a worship service (Wuthnow 2003: 141). Worship is meant to evoke a sense of God's presence. Listening to music in a concert hall or viewing a painting at an art museum would be less likely to inspire the same thoughts. Yet, for a minority of American adults, even art of this kind has spiritual connotations. For instance, 21 percent of evangelicals, 25 percent of mainline Protestants, and 30 percent of Catholics say they have felt close to God while viewing a painting.

The other important connection between the arts and spirituality occurs during times of personal difficulty. When faced with illness, loneliness, or bereavement, people usually turn to their family and friends for support. Three-quarters say that talking with friends is very helpful at such times. A large minority (about four in ten) say that the Bible is helpful as well. In addition, many people find comfort in the arts. For instance, nearly four in ten say that they have found it helpful during times of crisis to paint, sew, or engage in woodworking or similar handicrafts. Almost the same proportion point to music as having been especially helpful. About a fifth mention the help they have received from reading poetry or novels (Wuthnow 2003: 110).

Personal interviews suggest that spirituality and the arts hold a special connection for people who believe that God exists, but are persuaded that God, perhaps by definition, is beyond human comprehension. For them, God is a mystery. Creeds, doctrines, sacred texts, and theological treatises represent efforts—divinely inspired or humanly constructed—to grasp this mystery. Yet the mystery remains. Poets and painters and musicians do not pretend to have comprehended the mystery, either. They merely assist in grappling with it. Art, Paul Tillich (1961: 200) once wrote, "breaks through both the realistic acceptance of the given and the idealistic anticipation of the fulfilled". In so doing, it "reaches into the depth of ultimate reality".

The Rediscovery of Practice

The rub from focusing so much on experience is that it can seem after a while that one is simply running in circles: taking each moment as if nothing had come before. This penchant to live in the moment, though, runs against the grain of all that modern culture teaches about *mastery.* Getting somewhere is important, whether it be in one's work, becoming skilled in athletics, pursuing a hobby, or raising one's children. People speak of wanting to grow as a person and in their spiritual life. Many claim to work at spiritual growth through such activities as prayer and meditation, reading religious texts, and participating in Bible study groups and prayer fellowships.

Practice means something more than mere activity. Dusting a piano is an activity; learning to play the piano is a practice. The defining aspects of a practice are that it involves developing a set of skills, following a set of rules or guidelines, and engaging regularly in activities that make use of these skills and guidelines. Usually there are mentors and definitions of skill levels that help in guiding one's progress. Practices can be performed alone or in the company of others, but they require individual effort, and generally include relationships with other practitioners (Wuthnow 1998).

Spiritual practice has been encouraged in all religious traditions, but there is also at least anecdotal evidence that its importance is being rediscovered. Retreat centers that offer guidance in spiritual practice are sometimes booked months in advance. Seminaries provide new certificate programs in spiritual practice. In interviews, people talk of reading books about spiritual practice, learning to meditate, and joining spiritual support groups. Like the emphasis on experience, practice is a way of dealing with uncertainties about belief. A person may find it difficult to believe in the abstract that God exists, for instance, but through a disciplined regimen of prayer and meditation may come to the conviction that it makes more sense to bet on God's existence than on God's non-existence. A "living prayer" of this kind, sings multiple

Grammy-winner Alison Krauss, provides "a haven from my unbelief" (Krauss 2004). Dedication to a spiritual practice is also a way of settling in, as it were, rather than dabbling with a continuous succession of spiritual fads. Practice is thus a response to the superficiality that many observers associate with consumerism, including the marketplace of self-help programs, angel books, Christian diets, gurus, astrologers, and the like. It involves rejecting the temptation to try everything, and instead emphasizes the value of doing one thing well.

This emphasis on practice is an important point of convergence between contemporary religion and art. Learning to meditate and learning to play the piano are by no means the same. Yet people who meditate, pray, or pursue spiritual growth in other ways often incorporate music and art into their practices. Similarly, artists and musicians frequently indicate that their artistic practices are a form of meditation or discipline that contributes to their sense of spirituality. Lydia Garcia, the Latina woman in Santa Fe who inscribes prayers on the back of her hand-carved *santos*, says her work is like going to Mass or reading the Bible. It quiets her mind, disciplines her emotions, and focuses her attention on God. A concert pianist explains that years of practice have taught him discipline that goes beyond technique. Self and music merge into one. He says he sometimes tastes the eternal (Wuthnow 2001: 116–21).

An important aspect of practice is *repetition.* Practicing the piano requires performing the same finger drills again and again and again. Repetition in one realm (such as sports or the arts) does not lead to mastery in another realm (such as religion). There is, nevertheless, spillover to the extent that a person learns the discipline of doing something repeatedly. It is in this respect that repetition in the arts converges with repetition in religion. Repetition is central to religion, so central in fact that some studies suggest that it alters the brain and becomes memorable less for its content than simply because it is done (Barrett 2004).

Yet practice is much more than subtle reshaping of one's cognitive map. Practice implies a strong personal connection to a tradition. Artists do not master their professions by inventing techniques from whole cloth. Nor do they learn them by participating in a few experiments with wires attached to their brains. The practitioners who take spirituality most seriously usually report that they, too, have learned about God and about life the old-fashioned way. In this, the discipline required to master an art is a metaphor for the spiritual path.

Acts of Transgression

It would be one-sided, though, to emphasize practice without also underlining transgression. Practice implies orderly conformity to the rules: rote learning, playing scales, or shooting baskets until one's muscles are trained to do it automatically. Art is messier than that, and so is religion. It may be, as Peter L. Berger (1967) has argued, that religion is fundamentally concerned with creating order where there was chaos, with *nomizing* the puzzles and disappointments of life. In so doing, religion nevertheless imagines the unimaginable. A mortal person can live forever. A divine being can become human and atone for everyone by leading a perfect life. A god who is universal and unchangeable can be moved by the prayers of a single supplicant. These are all instances of what cognitive psychologists call schema violations (Boyer 2001). They startle and remain memorable because they ascribe abilities that are at once familiar and impossible. Artistry, relying as it does on the imagination, is similarly transgressive. "Sometimes I've believed as many as six impossible things before breakfast", says the White Queen in *Through the Looking Glass.* If not believing strictly in the impossible, artists at least find it necessary to push the envelope, as it were, learning the rules well enough to break them, fashioning something novel in the process.

Though similar in their transgressive potential, art and religion come together most electrically when one breaches the sanctity of the other. Andre Serrano's famous *Piss Christ*—a color photograph of a crucifix immersed in urine—is a prominent recent example. Deeply familiar with Catholic teachings, Serrano knew that the experiment would set off a firestorm of criticism. He was not disappointed. Not only did church officials denounce the work, it was ridiculed on the floor of Congress, and the National Endowment for the Arts' budget was sliced because the NEA had played a small role in funding an exhibit of the work. What the antagonists involved did not immediately foresee, however, is that the debate itself provided a valuable opportunity for public discussion of deeply held values.

As this example suggests, convergence between religion and the arts is not always a harmonious development. Religious leaders are more likely than artists to worry about the sanctity of space, objects, and roles deemed holy. As heads of congregations, they feel obliged to speak out against behavior they consider immoral or indecent. Artists are, comparatively speaking, free spirits. They are less constrained to follow the conventional norms, and for this reason contribute importantly to the larger conversation in which religious leaders are also engaged about the nature of humanity and its deepest responsibilities. "For some people", says master wood-carver David Ellsworth, "there is a meeting of the minds, a gathering together... almost like a church. But I'm the one walking around it in the hills. I think they feel my presence. They know I'm out there" (Wuthnow 2001: 4).

The larger point about transgression is that creativity involves breaking the mold, not for the sake only of violation, but for exploring new insights and new ways of thinking. For the many within religious organizations who feel constrained by the dead hand of the past, the arts are a breath of fresh air. Gender inclusion, explorations of gay and lesbian issues, and concerns about social and environmental justice have all prompted religious communities to experiment with the religious imagination in ways not limited to, but including, the arts.

Conclusion

The contemporary convergence of art and religion does not imply that the two have become indistinguishable. Art is well institutionalized in the special venues where it is learned, practiced, and performed or displayed, and it is judged in terms of aesthetic standards, virtuosity, creativity, and in some instances entertainment value. Religion is expressed through the teachings and rituals of particular faith traditions, is guided by trained clergy and lay leaders, and focuses on its adherents' relationships to the sacred. Although the idea that one can be spiritual without being religious has gained popularity, spirituality continues to be informed by religious teachings, and generally is concerned with a personal sense of relating to God. The distinctions between religion and art mean that practitioners in each realm guard their turf, as it were, and sometimes do so in ways that generate conflict with the other. Professional musicians may decry the selections or quality of singing that takes place in religious congregations, for instance, while clergy may preach against the immorality they fear is conveyed in contemporary art or popular music.

It is nevertheless important to recognize the extent to which religion and the arts overlap. The number of people who actually engage in some kind of choral singing in religious congregations is undoubtedly far larger than the number who do this in any other context. Houses of worship are far more numerous than museums and art galleries, and are important venues for concerts, pageants, plays, and art festivals. Similarly, arts organizations that have no connection with religion are nevertheless significant sources of religious music and displays of religious art. Artists themselves vary considerably in how devoted they are to religion, and yet many—perhaps a majority—are interested in religion and spirituality.

The convergence of art and religion is a phenomenon that deserves greater understanding among social scientists. Sociologists of religion have paid relatively little attention to the role of music and art within religion or to religion's relationships with the arts. In turn, sociologists of culture have largely ignored religion. In their view, religion is somehow a separate field with different emphases that do not inform the broader study of culture, and is at minimum less interesting than studying why people like country music or romance novels. Closer interaction between scholars of religion and scholars of the arts is sorely needed. Both topics are concerned with questions of authenticity and values. Both are concerned with ritual and performance. Both are increasingly influenced by politics. And both are central to understandings of public morality.

Whether social scientists rise to the challenge or not, the convergence of religion and the arts seems destined to continue. In the United States, huge concentrations of resources in megachurches are creating unprecedented opportunities for innovations in religious music and art. The gospel recording industry is flourishing, and evangelical philanthropists seem intent on making greater use of motion pictures.

In Europe, where religious involvement is considerably lower than in the United States, art and religion nevertheless produce periodic clashes, as in the much publicized slaying of Dutch film director Theo Van Gogh. Perhaps most importantly, globalization brings together complex and ever more novel mixtures of indigenous and exogenous religion and art. Holy hip hop—increasingly as popular in Atlanta, as in Accra—is but one example.

References

Arts Council England (2005). "Survey Reveals Participation in Sport and the Arts by Young People". Online at <www.artscouncil.org.uk>.

Barrett, J. L. (2004). *Why Would Anyone Believe in God?* Lanham, Md.: AltaMira Press.

Berger, Peter L. (1967). *The Sacred Canopy: Elements of a Sociological Theory of Religion.* Garden City, NY: Doubleday.

Boyer, Pascal (2001). *Religion Explained: The Human Instincts that Fashion Gods, Spirits and Ancestors.* London: Heinemann.

Brereton, Virginia Lieson (1990). *Training God's Army: The American Bible School, 1880–1940.* Bloomington, Ind.: Indiana University Press.

Chaves, Mark (2004). *Congregations in America.* Cambridge, Mass.: Harvard University Press.

Duin, Julia (2004). "5,000 Pastors Cheer Mel Gibson's 'Passion'". *Washington Times*, 22 Jan.

Durkheim, Émile (1947). *The Division of Labor in Society.* New York: Free Press.

Fenn, Richard K. (1978). *Toward a Theory of Secularization.* Storrs, Conn.: Society for the Scientific Study of Religion Monographs.

Gifford, Paul (2004). *Ghana's New Christianity: Pentecostalism in a Globalizing African Economy.* Bloomington, Ind.: Indiana University Press.

Krauss, Alison (2004). "A Living Prayer". *Lonely Runs Both Ways* (Rounder).

Lewis, Gregory B., and Brooks, Arthur C. (2005). "A Question of Morality: Artists' Values and Public Funding for the Arts". *Public Administration Review*, 65: 8–17.

Meyer, Birgit (2004). "'Praise the Lord': Popular Cinema and Pentecostalite Style in Ghana's New Public Sphere". *American Ethnologist*, 31: 92–110.

Promey, Sally M. (2001). "The Public Display of Religion". In David Morgan and Sally M. Promey (eds.), *The Visual Culture of American Religions.* Berkeley and Los Angeles: University of California Press, 27–48.

Robbins, Joel (2004). *Becoming Sinners: Christianity and Moral Torment in a Papua New Guinea Society.* Berkeley and Los Angeles: University of California Press.

Robert, Dana L. (2003). *Occupy Until I Come: A. T. Pierson and the Evangelization of the World.* Grand Rapids, Mich.: Eerdmans.

Roof, Wade Clark (1999). *Spiritual Marketplace: Baby Boomers and the Remaking of American Religion.* Princeton: Princeton University Press.

Tillich, Paul (1961). "Art and Ultimate Reality". In Joseph Harned and Neil Goodwin (eds.), *Art and the Craftsman: The Best of the Yale Literary Magazine.* New Haven: Yale Literary Magazine, 185–200.

Walker, Chris (2004). *Arts and Non-Arts Partnerships: Opportunities, Challenges, and Strategies.* Washington: Urban Institute.

—— Scott-Melnyk, Stephanie, and Sherwood, Kay (2002). *Reggae to Rachmaninoff: How and Why People Participate in Arts and Culture.* Washington: Urban Institute.

Wuthnow, Robert (1998). *After Heaven: Spirituality in America since the 1950s.* Berkeley and Los Angeles: University of California Press.

—— (2001). *Creative Spirituality: The Way of the Artist.* Berkeley and Los Angeles: University of California Press.

—— (2003). *All In Sync: How Music and Art Are Revitalizing American Religion.* Berkeley and Los Angeles: University of California Press.

—— (2005). *America and the Challenges of Religious Diversity.* Princeton: Princeton University Press.

Suggested Reading

Arthurs, Alberta, and Wallalch, Glenn (eds.) (2001). *Crossroads: Art and Religion in American Life.* New York: New Press.

Morgan, David, and Promey, Sally M. (eds.) (2001). *The Visual Culture of American Religions.* Berkeley and Los Angeles: University of California Press.

Also Chaves (2004); Lewis and Brooks (2005); and Wuthnow (2001, 2003).

CHAPTER 20

THE SOCIAL ROOTS AND MEANING OF TRANCE AND POSSESSION

IOAN M. LEWIS

TRANCE AND ALTERED STATES OF CONSCIOUSNESS

'Altered States of Consciousness' (ASC) is an umbrella term, applied to psychological and sociological phenomena regularly encountered in the study of trance, possession, and shamanism—all of which have significant if problematic links with music. This seminar[1] offers an excellent opportunity to review what is implied in relation to ASC by these terms, which have become commonplace in the anthropological study of religion.

Altered States of Consciousness are most clearly exhibited externally in the form that we commonly call 'trance'. When I think of trance states, apart from my own private experience of rapturous moments and episodes (so-called 'peak-experiences'), I think

[1] An earlier version of this chapter was given at the seminar on 'Music and States of Altered Consciousness: A Still Open Question', Intercultural Studies Institute for Comparative Music, Fondazione Giorgio Cini, Venice, January 2002.

particularly of two dramatic examples, involving others, which I witnessed. The first was at a women's spirit possession séance in the Sudan which I attended with a female colleague who was carrying out anthropological research on the famous *zar* cult in Khartoum. (See Constantinides 1977 and Lewis in Lewis *et al.* 1991.)

The séance took place in a large barn which had become a dancing hall regularly used for spirit ceremonies by the *zar* adherents. There was a large crowd of women, and a few male transvestite homosexuals, dressed in the costumes favoured by their regular spirit partners. The air was heavy with incense and perfume, and the women were dancing to the music, dedicated to the spirits and beaten out on four drums in syncopation and with an increasing tempo. Led by a spirit cult leader (*sheikha*), the women were dancing round a large round stone regularly used for grinding corn. Suddenly one of the women, very obviously pregnant and, as obviously, deeply in trance, began to pound her stomach violently against the grinding stone, thus endangering her baby. Other participants explained that the woman was possessed by a violent southern spirit (associated with the non-Islamic peoples of the southern Sudan). Immediately several other dancing women, with glazed eyes, who appeared also to be in trance, wordlessly sat down on the stone, and thus prevented the frenzied dancer from continuing to beat her body on the stone. It is obvious that these entranced women were not totally oblivious to what was going on round them. Their perception was concentrated on the ritual and the spirits for whom they were dancing, but this did not exclude peripheral attention to other movement in their surroundings.

My other example occurred in a very different and, from some points of view, a more exotic setting, at an international scientific conference on the paranormal held some years ago in a luxury hotel in London (the Hilton). Most of the eighteen participants, well-known figures in this field, were clearly believers, but there were a minority of equally obvious sceptics, including the English specialist on the paranormal, Eric J. Dingwall, the psychological anthropologist, George Devereux and myself. As at a regular European séance, we sat round a large table. At one point in the discussion, as Devereux and I were expressing strongly sceptical views on the reality of ESP, one of the most credulous of the participants, a white South African who claimed to have been initiated as a 'witch doctor' suddenly collapsed in his chair. Several of the participants with medical expertise, including a well-known Italian psychoanalyst who was also a believer in the paranormal, rushed to the witch doctor's side to see if he required medical attention. This, however, soon appeared unnecessary since, in the trance-like state into which our colleague had fallen, he suddenly started speaking—not fully 'in tongues'—but with a strange guttural muttering in which he could be heard saying: 'They are knocking it out of us, they are knocking it all out of us ....'

Devereux and I took this as a defensive reaction to our sceptical and ironical remarks. Everyone, including our psychiatrist colleagues, was embarrassed by this episode from which, after about ten minutes, our witch doctor recovered to resume his normal demeanour, carrying on as if nothing had happened and making no reference to the little drama. In contrast to the Sudanese séance, trance here was an unexpected individual reaction, and there was no musical stimulus, only the pressure of conflict and disbelief to which trance here seemed a significant reaction.

I was also myself recently involved in a much more banal and familiar incident, when someone crashed his car into mine while I was stationary. The driver apologized profusely for his negligence and simply said, rather strikingly in the present context, that 'he was far away, and had not noticed my car'. I took this to mean, and he certainly had a glazed facial expression, that his mind was elsewhere, almost as if he were in trance. While not all degrees of distraction from a person's immediate surroundings imply 'trance' in a serious sense, they can be close to it, as I think we all recognize.

As these examples, like most people's casual personal experience of exalted states of being illustrate, *trance* is appropriately defined as an altered state of consciousness, variable in its intensity, and at its height resembling hypnosis. Along these lines, psychologists define it as a condition of dissociation, characterized by a lack of voluntary movement, and frequently by automatisms in action and thought, illustrated by hypnotic and mediumistic conditions. As our séance examples illustrate, trance also typically involves 'an enhanced internal or external focus of attention' (Overton 1998: 152).

As such, while it is obviously felt as a private, individual experience, particularly in its intense forms, it is also a transpersonal, transcultural condition which can be externally observed and, with some technical difficulty, even measured in variations in brain rhythm, as recorded by EEG tests. Such personal, psychological experiences may, of course, be shared and mutually intensified as in spirit cult séances, evangelical religious services, pop concerts, political rallies, football crowds, etc. The discovery of natural euphoriates (endorphins) in the bloodstream in the early 1970s provided a plausible chemical explanation of trance, and linked it with the effect of psychotropic drugs, thus giving a novel and unexpected meaning to Marx's famous definition of religion as 'the opium of the people'—more accessible and less mysterious than he ever imagined.

Trance Induction

That such neurochemistry is implicated in trance experiences does not invalidate its status as culturally conventionalized behaviour, recognized cross-culturally, and readily observable to the anthropologist who has no means available to test endorphin levels or measure EEGs. Contrary to what the French Tungus specialist

Hamayon (1996) appears to argue, nor does the ultimate involvement of such neurophysical processes reduce the validity of trance as a sociological, as well as a psychological, phenomenon. This is no more the case than it is with sexual orgasm, which is obviously a psychological and social, as well as a physiological, phenomenon with profound cultural colouring and meaning. If women's popular magazines are to be believed, it is, moreover, like trance, subject to artifice and pretence. This does not reduce the value of sexual climax as a symbol of intimacy and transcendence.

More generally, in all known cultures and civilizations, we find essentially two, at first sight contradictory, processes which induce trance. One involves sensory deprivation—trauma, stress, illness, isolation, fasting, and deliberate physical mortification, as in many mystical religious traditions. The other, equally common stimulus involves sensory overloading—with musical and other sonic bombardment (especially monotonous drumming), strobe lighting effects, the ingestion of hallucinogenic drugs, and more mundane procedures like over-breathing and even strenuous exercise such as jogging (which has been shown experimentally to increase endorphin levels (see Banyai 1984; Prince 1982)).

As far as music's role is concerned, the French ethnomusicologist Gilbert Rouget (1985) concludes his magisterial study of music and trance by declaring that 'music's great achievement is to be able to induce trance in the manner that an electric current can set a tuning fork vibrating with the same frequency' (p. 441). But at the same time, he questions those such as Neher who have claimed that drumming induces convulsive effects through its influence on the alpha rhythm of the brain. (More recently, Maxfield (1990) has reported that 'monotonous drumming, characterised cross-culturally by a rhythm with 4–7 beats per second induces a corresponding increase in the so-called theta rhythm in the EEG'.) I do not know whether Rouget would accept this. In any case, he says that music is 'less significant in triggering trance than in sustaining it. It is indispensable for providing the cult member with the means of manifesting identification (with the spirit) and hence externalising trance' (1985: 442). This is so, according to Rouget, because 'music is the only language to speak at once to the head and legs, since it is through music that the group holds up to the individual the mirror in which to behold his borrowed identity' (p. 442). Following this, Rouget is led to pursue what he sees as an analogy between opera in modern culture and the possession séance in traditional cultures; indeed, he calls opera 'lyric possession'.

It seems to me, however, that a more obvious analogy is with ballet; and indeed, it is significant to record here that in Westernized circles in contemporary Egypt, a folkloristic version of the north-east African *zaar* cult has been developed into a new 'Oriental' form of ballet (see the ballet magazine *Arabesque*, 1978; 1983). We must remember, however, that such an embarrassment of riches in the wealth and variety of sensual stimulants, headed by music, is not the only route to trance: sensory deprivation may not be so alluring, but it is equally effective. These contrasting eliciting forces are consistent with the contradictory experiences commonly reported in trance: overwhelming sensations of despair, often associated with images of death and birth, alternating with sensations of ineffable joy. Interestingly here, psychiatrists employing LSD and similar psychotropic drugs in clinical treatment report that drugged female patients often become confused as to whether they are being born or giving birth (see Grof 1977). (More recently, Grof has launched 'Breath-work', in which numbers of subjects lie on mattresses for up to a whole day engaging in deep breathing exercises to a background programme of music culled from the cinema. Most of those involved seem to have trance experiences.)

The opposition of these themes and their resolution is, according to Reichel-Dolmatoff (1971), vividly expressed by the Amazonian Tukano shamans of Columbia. Tukano state that their creator deity, the Sun-father, committed incest with his own daughter at the time of creation. This act produced the hallucinogen (the bannisteriopsis caapi vine) regularly employed by them to achieve ecstatic visions. This trance experience is explicitly comparerd to incestuous sexual intercourse. Hallucination and sexual intercourse, according to Reichel-Dolmatoff, are viewed by the Tukano Indians as equivalent and full of anxiety because of their relation to the idea of incest. The Tukano declare that they take the drug in order to return to the uterus, source and origin of all things, where the individual confronts the tribal divinities, the creation of the universe and of humanity, the first human couple, the creation of the animals, and the establishment of social order with the laws of exogamy. With this example we have broached the question of the meaning of trance (here a transcendent religious experience) and the range of possible interpretations of it in different cultures and sometimes in different contexts in the same culture.

The Interpretation of Trance

Despite its range of sensory modalities and meanings, trance in my view is a universal phenomenon, theoretically and to a certain extent actually, open, as we have seen, to identification and description. Our naturalistic, scientistic definition of trance and dissociation is not unique, and is found in some traditional societies. Amongst the Samburu pastoralists of northern Kenya, for example, trance states are associated with situations of tension and danger, and are regarded as a sign of machismo and self-assertion appropriate to members of the warrior age-grade in this gerontocratic society. Rather similarly, among the Abelan tribe of New Guinea, young bachelors sometimes exhibit similar symptoms which are described as 'deafness'. This is not ascribed to spiritual intervention. Again, among the Tungus reindeer herders of Siberia, who represent the *locus classicus* of shamanism, to which I refer later, hysterical states, involving trembling and the compulsive imitation of words and gestures, do not always signify possession by a spirit. They may simply indicate that those who manifest this behaviour, called *olon*, are in a state of involuntary fear, so that this represents a kind of 'startle' reaction.

The well-known Italian culture complex of tarantism, in its medieval, dancing mania manifestation, represents a more complex phenomenon involving non-mystical and mystical components. The ostensible naturalistic explanation for this compulsion to dance viewed it as a disease, and traced it to the poisonous bite of the tarantula spider. Two cures were favoured: dance therapy to the brisk rhythm of the tarantella played on fife, clarinets, and drums, when, it was believed the poison was expelled as perspiration; and religious exorcism at the shrines of particular saints. However, in his brilliant study, *La Terra del rimorso*, de Martino (1966) decisively demonstrated that the phenomenon was much more complicated, and far from being a simple matter of 'poisoning', as those afflicted appeared to believe. In fact, it involved a form of spirit possession by a hybrid spider–saint (for more recent information on the cult's vestiges in southern Italy today and the continuing significance of its symbolism, see Pizza 1997; 2004). Thus, in Apulia, tarantism and 'pizzicata' music have passed into contemporary folklore and are now a familiar element in local popular culture, with large-scale festivals attracting throngs of tourists in the summer. Tarantism has thus become an important theme in the construction of a new, neo-traditional local identity in Salento—a sub-southern Italian local nationalism. This movement is also associated with the local Greek dialect, which, increasingly, is taught in local schools. So tarantism has been politicized. So, 'Various actors (in Apulia) who live and participate in the practices activated by this programme of revitalisation, tend at times to elaborate it and re-shape it, as the source of an alterative discourse that concieves itself... as radically autonomous and that asserts the impossibility of reducing the lived experience of a taranta music concert or rave party' (Pizza 2004: 221). Clearly this is an entirely new ethnographic context, however much it may seek to ground itself in the rural field situation recorded by de Martino!

In terms of body concepts, in some cultures, trance may be seen as a manifestation of 'soul-loss', as for example among many of the North American Indians. To some extent this is also true of the !Kung bushmen, where in healing dance ceremonies, to a musical accompaniment of hand clapping and singing, men work themselves up into trance states in which the intrinsic 'boiling energy' (or soul) is released from their bodies to fight those evil powers causing illness in others.

But the most common explanation of trance across cultures is that it is a manifestation of the invasion of the human body by an external spirit agent. This may, or may not, be coupled with the idea of soul loss involving the displacement of the host's soul by the alien spirit. As classical tarantism illustrates, we regularly find naturalistic and spiritual explanations of trance competing in the same culture and invoked in different contexts. Possession by an external spiritual force is, of course, a culturally specific explanation of behaviour or of a state of being. It does not necessarily coincide with trance. Indeed, it is often invoked to explain minor maladies (even those as trivial as constipation!), where there is no evidence or expectation of trance. Nevertheless, the two phenomena do coincide at the peak of ecstatic activity—in possession rituals, for example, where members of a possession group are dancing in honour of their possessing spirits (as in our *zar* example), and when the spirit troubling a new victim is being interrogated to establish its identity, so that it can be treated appropriately.

Here we must note that virtually universally, the initial diagnostic treatment of what is often presented as an illness or affliction leads to two opposed possible outcomes. One, aimed at expelling the spirit, is of course, exorcism, with which we are familiar from our own Christian culture and which is equally common in Islam. The other, contrasting treatment, referred to usefully by Luc de Heusch as 'adorcism', instead of seeking to expel the intrusive spirit, endeavours to come to terms with it, reaching an accommodation with it, by paying it cult. Possession then becomes the first step in initiation into a spirit cult. Trance is critical in both cases, since, as has long been noted, it is most marked at the dramatic climax of exorcism as the exorcist wrestles with the intrusive spirit prior to successfully casting it out.

We should note that in male-dominated societies where such women's spirit possession cults flourish, men usually prefer their womenfolk to seek exorcism for their problems rather than induction into such a cult. Hence, in this context exorcism becomes a further implement in the control and subjection of women—as I have argued elsewhere (Lewis 1996). This sociologically significant point is well illustrated in the famous eleventh-century Japanese literary classic, *The Tale of the Genji*, where, as Doris Bargen (1997) has demonstrated, Japanese noblemen sought to control their rebellious 'women's weapon' of spirit possession by insisting on exorcism as the proper treatment. Thus, although exorcism and spirit accommodation ('adorcism') have normally very different outcomes and social implications, they are equally signalled by the coincidence of trance and possession, in a 'peak' experience, one marking an exit, the other the entrance to the routine cult of ecstasy. (In keeping with this common peak experience, it has at once to be acknowledged that this imparts an ambiguity to active (trance) possession which enables some possession cults to masquerade as exorcism. See, e.g., Davis 1980; Lewis 1996; de Heusch 1997; Hell 1999.)

Trance and Sex

These ecstatic cults—secret religions for women and low-status males—have spirit-inspired leaders who graduate from the ranks of the possessed. These cult leaders are empowered by their special relationship (regularly represented explicitly as a marital union) with particular spirits, who become their spirit partners and guides. In Haiti, such spiritual unions may even be formally solemnized in actual marriage certificates (Métraux 1959: 215). As in the myths of ancient Greece and other cultures, such celestial marriages are regularly believed to be blessed with progeny. Thematically, there is an interesting analogy here between possession and pregnancy (cf. Graham, 1976): but possession is not, as some have argued, inherently related to gender through the biological experience of sexual intercourse. Not surprisingly, such spirit unions are seen as standing in contrast to the human marriages of the female devotees concerned, creating rival loyalties and potential conflict. Amongst the Tamils of south India (Nabokov 1997), young brides may succumb to possession by lusty *pey* spirits, which force their prey to elope with them and 'not only sexually enjoy their victims', but incite them to reject their lawful husbands by kicking and biting them (Nabokov 1997: 301). Equally generally, such conjugal spirits are said to ride or 'mount' their human hosts, who, in their turn, in some African cultures, are described as the 'Mares of the Gods'.

On the human side, devotees demonstrate their intimacy with the spirits by going into trance when dancing to their tunes. Those cult members who graduate to become inspired priestesses, behave and practise in the same way as shamans (who are predominantly male) in shamanic religions (cf. Hell 1999: 411 ff.). Such possession cult leaders are often women past menopause and/or widows, who are consequently ascribed male qualities.

Trance, which is sometimes referred to as 'half death' or 'little death', may involve actual sexual orgasm—both, where adorcism is practised, or its opposite, exorcism. In the latter case, for instance, in Christian Sri Lanka, female pilgrims are reported to experience orgasm as they are exorcised at a local shrine, where they rub their genitals on the holy cross and, at the climax, claim they are penetrated by Christ himself (Stirrat 1977; Gombrich and Obeysekere 1988).

The same sexual aura shrouds adorcism in the Christian and Muslim traditions. In the former, Saint Marie of the Incarnation worshipped Jesus as her 'Beloved'. For her part, St Teresa of Avila recorded that in her transports of mystical feeling she had achieved 'spiritual marriage' with Christ. Her most sublime experiences she described as unfolding in three stages: 'union', 'rapture', and the climactic 'wound of love'. As has been pointed out recently (Fales 1996), St Teresa was a member of a family which had been forced to convert from Judaism to Christianity during the religious persecution administered by the Inquisition in fifteenth-century Spain. As a woman, a spinster, and a member of a convert family, despite the latter's wealth, she was in several important respects a marginal figure and, like others in these circumstances in traditional cultures, a strong candidate for spiritual attention. In such a setting, St Teresa appears to have very successfully employed her spiritual intimacy with Christ as a form of personal empowerment, and even political criticism. In similar language, if with less political ambition, the well-known seventh-century Muslim Sufi poet of Basra, Rabi'al-'Adawiyya, expressed her passionate devotion to the Prophet Muhammad in many ardent poems using this conjugal imagery. Similarly, in those North African saints' cults, associated with the former slave populations and known as 'black brotherhoods', ecstatic female dancers explicitly compare their feelings after experiencing trance to those of sexual intercourse (Crapanzano 1973).

These lusty themes are familiar, of course, in the Dionysian cults of ancient Greece, as presented in Euripides' drama the *Bacchae* and in other sources (Dodds 1951; Devereux 1974; Maffesoli 1993). Indeed, in a rather tortuous and not entirely convincing argument, Devereux even claims to distinguish between female followers of Dionysus who experienced true sexual climax in the orgiastic rites and those whose ecstasy took the form of a 'grand hysterical seizure' without actual orgasm. (These, he considers, experienced trance as 'a coitus and orgasm equivalent'. Most women, he adds, 'who have such attacks are vaginally frigid').

This sexual aspect was also strongly emphasized in the earlier tarantist cult and expressed in songs addressed to the hybrid figure of the spider–saint (Paul), as in this invocation sung by female devotees at St Paul's chapel in Galatina (Apulia): 'My St Paul of the Tarantists who pricks the girls in their vaginas; My St Paul of the Serpents who pricks the boys in their testicles' (de Martino 1966: 361).

Trance, as I am arguing, is cross-culturally the most conclusive public demonstration that a human being has been seized by a spirit, and, in the case of those who develop ongoing relationships with spirits, the regular expression of that relationship. Consequently, it is hardly surprising that trance behaviour should be conventionalized and culturally standardized. As a socio-cultural phenomenon, trance necessarily responds and conforms to local expectations: if it did not, it could not be securely recognized as a signal of spiritual intervention in human affairs. Hence, while it is also a cross-culturally recognizable state, regularly induced and sustained by particular musical rhythms, it nevertheless respects the cultural form given it in a particular society. In this it clearly resembles the female sexual climax which, despite its physiological features, is also affected by cultural conventions—to which the vast literature, popular and learned, on the subject testifies.

Trance and Shamanism

We have so far been dealing with trance in the social context of marginal cults involving women and low-status categories of men, where the cult leaders, in my view, exercise a shamanic role. We now come to shamanism proper, where the social context shifts to centre stage and is concerned with public morality and order in the widest sense. Here, in these 'main morality' religions, shamans are typically males, and it is their special relationship with the spirits that is the central issue. As we shall see, however, the same imagery and symbolism is used to describe, and sanctify, shaman–spirit relationships.

The importance of inspirational spirit possession in shamanism disproves the allegedly crucial distinction between these phenomena, promoted by Mircea Eliade (1951), who was himself, of course, not a primary source of ethnographic evidence. On the basis of an inaccurate and partial reading of the primary sources of other scholars, Eliade, as is well known, claimed that the defining feature of shamanism was the shaman's 'mystical flight', in which he experienced 'the ecstasy provoked by the ascension to the sky, or the descent to Hell' (Eliade 1951: 434). This erroneous distinction between possession and shamanism, as essentially separate cultural phenomena, was given a sociological twist and further elaborated rather imaginatively by Luc de Heusch (1962; 1971).

Although the term *shaman* comes originally from the Tungus reindeer herders of Siberia, and is obviously associated there with the local (but externally influenced) cosmology, I do not see the word as limited to that particular ethnological context; nor, despite Eliade's advocacy, does it necessarily exclude possession. As I have argued elsewhere at length, we need a wider understanding of the term (Lewis 1989 [1971], etc.). Thus, I agree with the French Siberian specialist E. Lot-Falck (1973: 2), who writes: 'To be a shaman does not signify professing particular beliefs, but rather refers to a certain mode of communication with the supernatural.'

Many lines of communication are open here, but contrary to Eliade and his eminent Belgian disciple, de Heusch, the crucial one is possession by a spirit or spirits. Shirokogoroff (1935), a medical doctor and our brilliant first-hand source on Tungus shamanism, as it was before and at the beginning of the Russian Revolution, emphasizes how the shaman's ecstatic trance behaviour, signifying the intimacy of his relationship with the spirits, was central to his role. As he puts it himself, the shaman is a master of spirits, and his body is a 'placing', or receptacle, for the invading spirits during the séance. Here, in his classic description:

> The rhythmic music and singing, and later the dancing of the shaman, gradually involve every participant more and more in a collective action. When the audience begins to repeat the refrains together with his assistants, only those who are defective fail to join the chorus. The tempo of the action increases, the shaman with a spirit is no more an ordinary man or relative, but is a 'placing' (i.e. incarnation) of the spirit; the spirit acts together with the audience, and this is felt by everyone. The state of many participants is now near to that of the shaman himself, and only a strong belief that when the shaman is there the spirit may only enter him, restrains the participants from being possessed en masse by the spirit. This is a very important condition of shamanising which does not however reduce mass susceptibility to the suggestion, hallucinations, and unconscious acts produced in a state of ecstasy. When the shaman feels that the audience is with him and follows him he becomes still more active and this effect is transmitted to the audience. (Shirokogoroff 1935: 331)

The contemporary French Tungus specialist, Roberte Hamayon, provides further detailed information on the nature of the shaman's relations with his spirit guides, to whom, as elsewhere, he is bound by marriage. Indeed, here again, the centrality of the marriage alliance between shamans and spirits illuminates the sexual imagery which abounds in shamanic discourse (as is also emphasized by the Italian scholar, Zolla (1986). The séance is of course a drama, and the shaman's 'play acting' in his animal costume, as Hamayon puts it, mimes the act of rutting or coupling with his animal spirit partner. The words employed to describe them clearly demonstrate the sexuality of these actions and gestures that collectively constitute sexual play. In harmony with this strong emphasis on the shaman's séance as a sexual encounter, even the shaman's drum and drumstick, beaten vigorously while he leaps and bounds ritually, are representative of sexual intercourse. This is in keeping with the etymology of the word *shaman* itself, as expounded by Siberian specialists, who stress that the root *sam* signifies the idea of violent movement and of dancing exuberantly, throwing one's body about. Romano Mastromattei (1988) reports that orgasmic seizures occur in the parallel shamanic rituals in Nepal.

Our classical authority, Shirokogoroff, the medical doctor who was such a meticulous observer (in agreement with most other first-hand observers), insisted on the key role of trance as the *sine qua non* of the shaman's séance performance. 'No one', Shirokogoroff reported, 'can be accepted as a shaman unless he can demonstrably experience ecstasy—a half delirious condition "abnormal" in European terms' (Shirokogoroff 1935: 274). Shirokogoroff also gives a vivid impression of the highly charged psychological atmosphere of the séance, and of the emotionally intense interaction between the shaman and his audience as he works himself up into the state he describes as 'ecstasy'.

After shamanising, the audience recollects various moments of the performance, their great psycho-physiological emotion and the hallucinations of sight and hearing which they have experienced. They then have a deep satisfaction—much greater than that from emotions produced by theatrical and musical performances, literature and general artistic phenomena of the European complex, because in shamanising the audience at the same time acts and participates.

(These contrasts could not, of course, be sustained with reference to shamanism and modern Western theatre—nor, indeed, the theatre of Shakespeare's day.) Shirokogoroff also noted the physiological changes in the shaman's comportment during and after ecstasy. During the séance the shaman expended such tremendous energy that, at the end he was covered in perspiration and was unable to move, his pulse weak and slow, his breathing shallow. The ritual drama of the Siberian séance has been elegantly confirmed by the distinguished Finnish specialist on shamanism, Anna-Leena Siikala (1978), who employs the term 'counter roles' for the shaman's spirit guides, which he enacts with such full, ecstatic virtuosity.

In relation to this highly developed drama of the shamanic séance, which is so thoroughly documented, it seems perverse of Roberte Hamayon to claim that the psychological overlay of trance performances invalidates their key significance. All the more so, in that she emphasizes the sexual imagery and symbolism of the shaman's relations with the spirits, which would imply that his trance represents a kind of spiritual sexual climax. Moreover, as we have already noted earlier, sexual intercourse and sexual climax are not merely physiological acts, but also have a complex psychological overlay, and are far from being immune from cultural influence, and even fashion. Such considerations, however, certainly do not reduce their significance cross-culturally as defining particular relationships.

More generally, ritual sexual congress in a number of African cultures is used to signify religious blessing and fertility. In this vein, to take a specific example, amongst the Kikuyu, as Bernardo Bernardi (2001) has shown, the traditional term for the sacred means more colloquially simply human sexual intercourse. Why sexual images and symbolism are so widely utilized in expressing religious feeling is an old problem. I believe that Manning Nash suggests a plausible answer. 'Erotic love', he argues, 'is frequently a template for religious meaning since this form of strenuous play provides a readily available expression of self-transcendence.'

This seems to me to elucidate very well the pervasiveness of eroticism in describing the relations between humans and spirits. More directly to our purposes here, although every instance of trance cannot, of course, be considered an experience of actual orgasm, at their peak, the two seem likely to overlap. In this regard it is suggestive that there are reports from Western ESP contexts of successful mediumistic performances involving actual orgasm on the part of the medium (see Devereux 1974: 50). Sexual congress seems thus to offer a rich store of psychological and physiological experience upon which trance draws, just as the conjugal relationship provides an armoury of powerful symbols to describe and articulate intimate relations between humans and their spirit partners. In this sensual perspective, although the precise modalities of music and trance seem still imprecisely defined, music is nevertheless evidently the food of love.

References

Banyai, E. I. (1984). 'On the Technique of Hypnosis and Ecstasy: An Exceptional Psychophysiological Approach'. In M. Hoppal (ed.), *Shamanism in Eurasia*. Göttingen: Edition Herodot, 174–83.

Bargen, D. G. (1997). *A Woman's Weapon: Spirit Possession in the Tale of the Genji*. Honolulu: University of Hawai Press.

Bernardi, Bernardo (2001). 'La religione dei Kikuyu'. In *idem*, *Nelnome d'Africa*. Milan: Franco Angeli, 26–39.

CONSTANTINIDES, P. (1977). 'Ill at Ease and Sick of Heart: Symbolic Behaviour in a Sudanese Healing Cult'. In I. M. Lewis (ed.), *Symbols and Sentiments*. London: Academic Press, 61–84.

CRAPANZANO, V. (1973). *The Hamadsha: A Study in Moroccan Ethnopsychiatry*. Berkeley: University of California Press.

DE MARTINO, E. (1966). *La Terra del rimorso*. Milan: Feltrinelli.

DEVEREUX, G. (1974). 'Trance and Orgasm in Euripides: Bakchai', In A. Angoff and D. Barth (eds.), *Parapsychology and Anthropology*. New York: Parapsychology Foundation, 36–52.

DAVIS, W. (1980). *Magic and Exorcism in Modern Japan*. Stanford, Calif.: Stanford University Press.

DODDS, E. R. (1951). *The Greeks and the Irrational*. Berkeley: University of California Press.

ELIADE, M. (1951). *Chamanisme et les techniques archaiques de l'extase*. Paris: Payot. English trans.: *Shamanism: Archaic Techniquies of Ecstasy*. Princeton: Princeton University Press, 1974.

ERWIN, F. R., PALMOUR, R. M., MURPHY, B. E. P., PRINCE, R., and SIMONS, R. C. (1988). 'The Psychobiology of Trance: Physiological and Endocrine Correlates'. *Transcultural Psychiatric Research Review*, 25: 267–84.

FALES, E. (1996). 'Scientific Explanations of Mystical Experiences, Part I: The Case of St Teresa'. *Religious Studies*, 32: 143–63. 'Part II: The Challenge of Theism'. *Religious Studies*, 32: 299–313.

GOMBRICH, R., and OBEYSEKERE, G. (1988). *Buddhism Transformed: Religious Change in Sri Lanka*. Princeton: Princeton University Press.

GRAHAM, H. (1976). 'The Social Image of Pregnancy: Pregnancy as Spirit Possession'. *Sociological Review*, (May): 291–308.

GROF, S. (1977). 'The Implications of Psychedelic Research for Anthropology: Observations from LSD Psychotherapy'. In I. M. Lewis (ed.), *Symbols and Sentiments*. London: Academic Press, 141–74.

HAMAYON, R. (1996). 'Pour en finir avec la 'transe' et 'l'extase' dans l'étude du Chamanisme'. In M. I. Beffa and M. D. Even (eds.) (1996). *Variations Chamaniques*, ii. Paris: University of Paris, X, 155–90.

HELL, B. (1999). *Possession et chaminisme: les maîtres du désordre*. Paris: Flammanion.

HEUSCH, L. DE (1962). 'Cultes de possession et religions initiatiques de salut en Afrique'. *Annales du Centre d'études des Religions*, ii. 226–44.

—— (1971). *Pourquoi l'epouser?* Paris: Gallimard.

—— (1997). 'Pour en revenir a la Transe'. Paper read at IVth ISSR Conference on Shamanism, Chantilly.

LEWIS, I. M. (1989[1971]). *Ecstatic Religion*, 2nd edn. London: Routledge.

—— (1996). *Religion in Context*. Cambridge: Cambridge University Press.

—— (1999). *Arguments with Ethnography*. London: Athlone Press.

—— HURREIZ, S., and AL-SAFI, A. (eds.) (1991). *Women's Medicine: the Zar/Bori Cult in Africa and Beyond*. Edinburgh: Edinburgh University Press.

LOT-FALCK, E. (1973). 'Le chamanisme en Sih—'. *Bulletin de l'Asie du Sud-est et monde insult indien*, 4: 1–10.

MAFFESOLI, M. (1993). *The Shadow of Dionysus: A Contribution to the Sociology of the Orgy*. Albany, NY: State University of New York Press.

MASTROMATTEI, R. (1988). *La Terra reale*. Rome: Valerio Levi.

MAXFIELD, M. (1990). 'The Effects of Rhythmic Drumming on EEG and Subjective experience'. (Unpublished dissertation, Institute of Transpersonal Psychology, Menlo Park, Calif.).

MÉTRAUX, A. (1959). *Voodoo in Haiti.* London: Deutsch.

NABOKOV, I. (1997). 'Expel the Lover, Recover the Wife: Symbolic Analysis of a South Indian Exorcism'. *Journal Royal Anthropological Institute,* 3/2: 292–316.

OVERTON, J. A. (1998). 'Shamanism and Clinical Hypnosis: A Brief Comparative Analysis'. *Shaman,* 6/2: 117–50.

PIZZA, G. (1997). 'The Virgin and the Spider: Reconsidering Spirit Possession in Southern Europe'. Unpublished MS, IVth Conference, International Society for Shamanic Research, Chantilly.

—— (2004). 'Tarantism and the Politics of Tradition in Contemporary Salento'. In F. Pine, D. Kaneff, and H. Haukanes (eds.), *Memory, Politics and Religion: The Past Meets the Present in Europe.* Max Plank Institute, Halle Studies in the Anthropology of Eurasia, Lit Verlag, 199–223.

PRINCE, R. (ed.) (1982). 'Shamans and Endorphins'. *Ethos* (special issue), 10.

REICHEL-DOLMATOFF, G. (1971). *Amazonian Cosmos.* Chicago: University of Chicago Press.

ROUGET, G. (1985). *Music and Trance,* rev. English edn. Chicago: University of Chicago Press. Originally pub. as *Lamusique et la trauce.* Paris: Gallimard, 1980.

SHIROKOGOROFF, S. M. (1935). *Psychomental Complex of the Tungus.* London: Kegan Paul.

SIIKALA, A. L. (1978). *The Rite Technique of the Siberian Shaman.* Helsinki: FF Communications, 39, no. 220.

STIRRAT, R. L. (1977). 'Demonic Possession in Roman Catholic Sri Lanka'. *Journal of Anthropological Research,* 33/2: 133–57.

ZOLLA, E. (1986). *L'Amante Invisible: l'erotica sciamanica.* Venice: Marsilio Editori.

SUGGESTED READING

The following are recommended: Lewis (1989[1971]; 1996); Métranx (1959); Rouget (1985); and Prince (1982).

PART IV

RELIGION AND THE STATE, THE NATION, THE LAW

CHAPTER 21

RELIGION AND THE STATE

PHILLIP E. HAMMOND
DAVID W. MACHACEK

Nobody really knows the origins of either religion or the state. One can reasonably speculate, however, about the features of each that must be present if the labels "religion" and "state" are to apply. At a minimum, for example, all religions must have a belief system involving a force or forces believed to be beyond human creation—doctrine—and all religions must have a prescribed set of behaviors toward such force(s)—ritual. While there are many sets of beliefs and behavior, any without doctrine and ritual are not likely to be called religion.

A similar kind of reasoning underlies the concept of a state. Before the label "state" is applied to a set of roles, certain features must exist: methods of controlling violence, of maintaining territorial integrity, of regulating the transmission of property (and thus marriage), and regulating the economy. States may commonly do many more things than these, but unless they do these things, the result is unlikely to be called a state (Pospicil 1971).

From just these two brief sketches, it is obvious why religion and the state are intrinsically related. All religions have a notion of how to live this life. This is as true for so-called other-worldly religions, which call for followers to escape as much as possible from the world, as it is for so-called worldly religions that favor engaging with the world. And all states are invested in policing that life. It is also true, however, that the relationship between religion and the state varies enormously.

This variation comes in two forms, both of great sociological interest. In one form, the variation revolves around the relative power of each sphere—from a theocracy where religion dominates (as in some Middle East countries where ayatollahs serve not just as religious leaders but also as political leaders) to a secular state that would try to stamp out all things religious (as in the case of Communist Russia or China).

The second variation is of a different order; it has to do with the degree of association between religion and the state that is thought to be appropriate. As we shall see in the later sections, changes in the relationship between religion and the state in modern times have had more to do with this second type of variation—what should the relationship be?—rather than with the first type of variation—which has the greater power?

Religions and states are not just ideas, but clusters of roles played by people. They are, as the definitions given above imply, a set of concepts and practices that serve to organize and structure the social reality of a society (Casanova 1994: 15). Again, speculating on the earliest known evidence, the following seems to be suggested: whether nomadic or in stable communities, people reproduce in some fashion and have children. Patterns of authority thus emerge both within families and within collections of families. This authority may be based, for example, on physical strength, age, lineage, or some heroic feat. If this political authority is widely accepted by a population in regular social interaction, then the authority is "legitimate", some kind of stability results, and a "state" may be said to have come into existence.

At the same time, certain questions arise that are not readily answered. Perhaps the greatest of these questions has to do with creation—of people, life and death, the world, the heavens, disasters, and unexpected good fortune. People seek answers from those thought to be wiser, and there emerges a more-or-less coherent set of beliefs, accompanied by rules regarding appropriate behavior surrounding those beliefs. In a way analogous to the emerging legitimate political authority, there emerges a pattern of religious authority.

It is inevitable that these two patterns of authority will be related.

Historical Context

By the time history was being recorded, civilizations had developed empires—large territorial units with elaborate governing mechanisms, made possible by the domestication of horses, metal weaponry, and much else that allowed the world's population to urbanize.

The creation of empires coincides with the birth of the world religions we know today. The emergence of Hinduism around 1500 BCE was followed by Judaism (*c.*1000 BCE), Buddhism (*c.*600 BCE), Confucianism (*c.*500 BCE), Christianity (first century CE), and Islam (seventh century CE). In little more than two millennia, most of the world's population confronted not just political empires but also religious empires. Kings could fight with popes, Czars with metropolitans, Caesars with rabbis. The desire for peaceful coexistence may have been present, but for reasons explained above, the literal separation of state and religion was not possible.

Space does not permit detailed discussion of how each of these world religions is related to the state, but Max Weber (1954[1925]) provided a helpful scheme as a starting point. All religions, he said, indicate how people should live in this world. The result depends upon responses to two unavoidable issues: (1) Should people embrace worldliness, or try to avoid it? (2) Second, should people try to improve the world by shaping it to accord with some ideal, or should they accept this world as they find it? The combination of worldly avoidance and worldly acceptance tends to produce a passive, apolitical outlook, which in turn minimizes conflict between religion and the state. The combination of worldly embrace and a vision of how the world can be improved, by contrast, engenders clashes between religion and the state. In this scheme, therefore, Hinduism, Buddhism, and Confucianism have had relatively peaceful religion–state relations, while Judaism, Christianity, and Islam have had relatively strained religion–state relations.

These are gross generalizations, of course, but they help us understand the history of religion–state relations, especially when we come to the modern period, as empires gave way to nation-states.

It had been in the interest of both imperial rulers and religious authorities to have a mutually satisfying relationship, a pattern that came to be called caesaropapism, in which the realms of religion and state cooperate. This arrangement presupposed a religion authorized and established by a government and a government approved by religion. The emergence of nationalistic fervor disrupted this arrangement, in part because it occurred, at least in Western Europe, with the religious revolt called the Protestant Reformation in the sixteenth century. The Reformation itself was embedded in the intellectual ferment referred to as the Enlightenment. Obviously, this ferment had enormous impact on both states and religions.

Nation-states varied in size, power, and inclination to colonize. Thus Great Britain, France, Germany, the Netherlands, Russia, Belgium, Spain, Portugal, and Italy spread out into all parts of the globe, largely for economic reasons, but also to colonize religiously and culturally. Spain and Portugal, for example, took over all of Latin America, and with their armies came their established church, Roman Catholicism. Spain also conquered the Philippines in the South Pacific, thus putting Catholicism in place there too. Great Britain had the most far-reaching set of colonies—in North America, Asia, and Africa. It was said that the sun never set on this British Empire of colonies, all of which were influenced by Anglicanism, Britain's Established Church. In like fashion, the Dutch exported the Reformed tradition, Russia its Orthodox tradition, and so forth.

The United States, which was "colonized" by dissenters from the Church of England, did not have the usual "establishment" situation when it won its independence late in the eighteenth century. Other colonies around the globe began seeking independence in the nineteenth century. These efforts were largely successful in Latin American by the early twentieth century, but it was during the decades following the Second World War that most of the colonies in Asia and Africa sought and gained independence. Many new nation-states came into existence, and one of their tasks, as they set up constitutions, was to choose a policy on religion–state relations.

Variations in Religion–State Relations

It is worth noting that the world's many constitutions have much in common, in part because a lot of borrowing occurred as the new nations emerged and their constitutions were drafted. Those nations established after the Second World War, furthermore, did so in an era characterized by globalization, and participation in global trade and politics required these states to conform to certain international norms in order to establish their legitimacy not only internally but externally as well. Thus, most constitutions have a preamble, a description of various governmental departments and their duties; and most include an enumeration of citizens' rights and duties.

At the same time, divergence can be maintained, or even increase, in these constitutions' treatment of religion and other cultural practices. Especially is this so among nations that were required to mute their cultural differences under colonial rule, but can now reclaim older cultural identities as a basis of national identity.

Here we examine some of the various patterns of religion–state relations existing in the world today. This task is made easier by a book published in 2003, *Crossing the Gods: World Religions and Worldly Politics*, by N. J. Demerath, III. Demerath analyzes religion–state relations in fourteen radically different situations. Here we give only brief sketches to illustrate some of the main differences.

Brazil and Poland

While Latin America as a whole can be said to be Roman Catholic, and Catholicism has been firmly established historically, three factors have made for change in

Brazil. First, the Catholic tradition of making common cause with an elite regime is being challenged by the more energetic evangelical Protestant appeal to those less well off. Demographers estimate that up to 20 percent of its population is now Protestant.

Second, Liberation Theology, which emerged from the Second Vatican Council (1962–5), challenged the political and economic class structure, aiming to share decision-making power with the poor and rural classes. Some Brazilian bishops, priests, and nuns joined the effort, and, in so doing, played a crucial role in the transition from a repressive national security state to a democratic one. As Casanova points out, however, "the successful transition to democracy and the ensuing institutionalization of political society lead per force to a relative privatization of Catholicism" (1994: 133). With the establishment and consolidation of political society, the church's prominent role as the voice of "the people", in opposition to an authoritarian state, necessarily declined. Waning enthusiasm for political engagement under Pope John Paul II, and now under Pope Benedict XVI, suggests that this pattern of privatization will continue.

Catholicism in Poland is fiercely nationalistic, and the church served as the channel of opposition to the Soviet rulers until the Soviet Union collapsed. That Pope John Paul II was a native, and visited his homeland during his papacy, no doubt gave energy to the Polish crusade, but it appears that it was the people's solidarity, as expressed through their national church, that sustained their resolve.

With the collapse of communism, Poland emerged as a leader among the nations of Central and Eastern Europe in political and economic liberalization. In the process, as happened in Brazil, the church faces challenges to its public political status, the outcome of which remains unclear. On the one hand, there is movement toward the organization "of an autonomous civil society based on the plurality and heterogeneity of norms, values, interests, and forms of life"; on the other hand, the church has been reluctant to give up its role as the nation's keeper (Casanova 1994: 109). The church has found support from the conservative Kaczynski twins, who assumed power in 2005 and 2006, and "produced a political program based on the assumption that Catholic and national values should prevail over permissive liberalism on issues like abortion and gay rights" and distrustful of "the idea that constitutional norms should trump traditional values and majority sentiment" (Rupnik 2007: 13).

Two Islamic Societies: Indonesia and Egypt

Along with Judaism and Christianity, Islam is a religion of "the Book", which, when the text is viewed in a certain way, can give rise to "fundamentalism". Just how fundamentalist is one dimension along which Indonesia and Egypt differ. Another dimension is the degree to which Islamic fundamentalism seeks and/or holds power.

Indonesia, for example, has at once the world's largest Muslim population and a religiously pluralistic population. This dualism no doubt tempers the relations between the state and religion. So, too, does the pledge of allegiance instituted in 1945, called *pancasila*. Designed to be a unifying ideological umbrella, the pledge has five principles: belief in one God, national unity, guided democracy, social justice, and humanitarianism.

Egypt, too, experiences an uneasy peace between secularism and religious ferment. It gained independence from British rule in 1954, when General Gamal Abdul Nasser came to power. Although 90 percent of Egypt's population is Muslim, Nasser was a secularist and fostered socialism, even as he was suspicious of the Muslim Brotherhood (MB), one of Islam's first radical political movements of the twentieth century. Nasser imprisoned most of the MB's senior leadership.

Nasser died in 1970, and was succeeded by Anwar Sadat. With the help of US President Jimmy Carter, Sadat and Israel's Prime Minister Menachem Begin signed the Camp David Accords, and Egypt regained land lost to Israel twelve years earlier in the Six Day War. Sadat and Begin shared a Nobel Peace Prize and much international acclaim, but within two years of the Accords a small group of Muslim terrorists assassinated Sadat.

In 1981 Hosni Mubarak became Egypt's head of state. He has apparently built a political machine that keeps both the secularists and the religionists satisfied—at least enough to keep voting for him.

China

Because China has more Buddhists than members of any other formal religion, it is often grouped with Japan, Thailand, and even India. But China has many Taoists, Confucianists, Catholics, Protestants, and Muslims. This is a society that has been officially secular and atheist since 1949. One might say, then, that the relationship at issue here is that between the Communist-ruled government and all religions.

That statement, however, would be misleading. Taoism and Confucianism are so deeply ingrained in Chinese culture that their suppression is unthinkable. They are folk religions. Buddhism, which arrived in China about the same time as Confucianism, has more "organization" than is typical for a folk religion, but is still less formal than Islam (arriving in the eighth century CE), Catholicism (sixteenth century), or Protestantism (mid-nineteenth century). Repression of all religions was the policy after 1949, but Mao's death in 1976 led to some easing of that policy. Indeed, the 1982 Constitution provides for "freedom of religious belief" and notes that the "state protects legitimate religious activities". However, legitimacy is determined by the state, which recognizes only five religions—Taoism, Buddhism, Islam, Catholicism, and Protestantism—and maintains a watchful eye over them.

Great Britain and the United States

The current religion–state situation in Great Britain starts with the dramatic decision of King Henry VIII to declare himself Head of the Church in England after failing to get Vatican permission to divorce his wife and marry Anne Boleyn. This gesture was ratified in 1559, and the "Church of England" became the Established Church of England. Today that church is the Established Church only of England, but not the rest of Britain. The Church of Scotland, for example, is Presbyterian. Wales disestablished its church in 1920. So entrenched did the Church of England become, however, that for a time, Roman Catholics in England were treated as traitors and their priests were killed.

By the seventeenth and eighteenth centuries, religious freedom expanded, and, while day-to-day religious life in Great Britain resembles that of the pluralistic United States, certain unmistakable signs of Anglican establishment status remain. The monarch must be a Church of England member, for example, and the archbishops of Canterbury and York automatically have seats in the House of Lords. Religious education is mandatory in the public schools of Great Britain, and while an effort is made to teach about the world's religions, Anglican thought and practice still echo.

One huge force for change in the direction of acceptance and toleration of diverse religions came with the breakup of the British Empire. Citizens of any former colony were free to emigrate to Great Britain, and people from India, Pakistan, the Caribbean, and other places poured in. Such people brought not just their religions with them, but also dietary and dress customs. To illustrate, many Hindus found jobs as officials in the transit system, where a dress code required caps. A legal battle ensued over replacing turbans with caps. Hindu and Muslim parents objected to some food offered in state school cafeterias. Compromises had to be worked out.

As we will see in the American case, controversies of this sort are "religious" in a peculiar way. Uniforms are traditional in many occupations, but they are not controversial until foreign immigration makes them so. Parents do not protest their children's lunch diet unless they find themselves required by law to send their children to schools where forbidden food is served.

As great as such problems can be, there appears to be a general acknowledgment by most British people that Hinduism, Islam, etc. *are* religions. That has not been the case with many so-called New Religious Movements, such as the Unification Church or the Church of Scientology. The very status of such perspectives as "religious" is challenged, leading to court cases.

If some cooling down in these instances has occurred—as most students of these matters seem to agree—it may be that Great Britain has not had the experience of the United States since 1980, where the radical political right and the radical evangelical right joined forces (Hammond, Machacek, and Mazur 2004). This collaboration over all manner of "moral" causes has captured the Republican Party in the USA, but nothing at this level has shown up in Great Britain.

Here is the first factor in church–state differences between Great Britain and the United States. The British, too, have an evangelical tradition, perhaps strongest in the Nonconformist traditions, but also present as a segment of Anglicanism. For the most part, however, evangelicalism in Britain has more to do with theological doctrine and styles of worship, rather than politics, as it so clearly has become in the USA, especially since the 1970s.

A second factor in the contrast is found in the levels of "religionists" in the two countries. From 1970 to 1985 there was a 20 percent decline in Church of England membership. This meant only 39 percent of church members were Anglican, compared to 30 percent Roman Catholic and 16 percent Methodist, Presbyterian, or Baptist. The minority position of the "established" Church of England is clear (Lamont 1989: 175). When the civil right to religious tolerance is widespread and the temperature of religious fervor is low, a reasonably placid relationship between the state and religion can be expected.

The society that became the United States was one of England's colonies, but unlike other English colonies, its original "founders" were Dissenters from the Church of England. Moreover, the Puritans were soon followed by other immigrants, including Quakers, Presbyterians, Baptists, Dutch and German Reformed, and Jews, as well as English Anglicans. A single established church, therefore, was unthinkable. Instead, what passed for established religion in the American colonies took the form of tax money paid to a clergyman in each town to teach children, in the belief that good citizenship required moral sensibility.

When, after independence, the time came to write a constitution, the only mention of religion appeared in Article Six: "no religious Test shall ever be required as a Qualification to any office of public trust under the United States." With the addition of the Bill of Rights, the First Amendment read: "Congress shall make no law respecting an establishment of religion, or prohibiting the free exercise thereof." These documents made clear that the purpose was not just to prohibit the kind of established church then widespread in Europe; it was, more daringly, to guarantee the sanctity of individual conscience.

Their first goal was largely achieved; there was never a "national" church, and all the colonies that carried their truncated "establishments" into statehood had done away with them by early in the nineteenth century. The free exercise clause met a different fate because, throughout the nineteenth century and into the twentieth, Americans conceived of themselves as a Protestant Christian nation (Hammond, Machacek, and Mazur 2004). Catholics, Jews, and "others" were tolerated, but only insofar as they accepted and abided by the authority of Protestant moral codes in public life. It was not until 1965, when the US Supreme Court ruled that conscientious objection status should be allowed for an avowed agnostic who had a "faith in a purely ethical creed" (*US v. Seeger*), that conscience, not just participation in and practice of religion, was protected.

It is only in the twentieth century, therefore, that the historically dominant, mainline Protestant denominations fully accepted the legitimacy of constitutional norms as the basis of political legitimacy. Many Americans continue to reject it, however, a sentiment that gave rise to the politically mobilized religious right.

Current Areas of Research

Demerath introduces the book referred to above with the cautionary metaphor of a moth circling a flame. "To many Western ears", he wrote, "the very phrase 'religion and politics' means trouble" (2003: 1). Many of the events that prompted recent interest in the subject by scholars and public alike—the Iranian revolution, the political mobilization of the radical religious right in the United States, Hindu nationalism in India, Muslim terrorists operating across national boundaries in much of the world—would seem to justify such a cautionary perspective.

The association of religion with political absolutism, intolerance, and violent conflict in these cases probably does more to *reinforce* suspicions about mixing religion and politics than it does to *explain* them, however. One can readily point to historical examples where the mixture of religion and politics had more positive outcomes—the Civil Rights movement in the United States and; the role of the Catholic Church in sustaining a civil society in Poland under Communist rule, to name but two.

Among Western scholars, and probably among much of the Western public, the suspicion surrounding the admixture of religion and politics reveals instead deeply rooted assumptions about the modern secular state, and it is helpful, again following Demerath, to note "a critical distinction between religion's relationship to politics and religion's relationship to the state" (2003: 1). Whereas politics involves influence seeking and policymaking, "states involve governing structures" (2003: 2), and specifically those with a monopoly on the legitimate use of coercive force (Weber 1922; Pospicil 1971). From those definitions, it is easy to see why Western audiences, steeped in the liberal tradition of religious freedom, are prone to fear a relationship between religion and the state.

Much confusion has resulted from the failure to make this critical distinction, as is evident in discussions of secularization. Almost all of the literature reviewed for this chapter begins with a discussion of how the resurgence of religion as a political force in the late twentieth century has undermined the notion that religion in the modern world would decline to the point of disappearance, or at least become so privatized as to have little or no public or political consequence. That understanding of secularization still has proponents (Bruce 1996), but the common wisdom among sociologists today is that this represents a misunderstanding of secularization (Casanova 1994), and one that has blinded social scientists to the ways in which religion is likely to remain politically consequential in modern, secularized societies.

Wald and Wilcox (2006) dramatically illustrate this blinding effect among American political scientists. Their search of articles published in the *American Political Science Review* revealed only twenty-five concerned with religion as a significant factor in politics over the course of the journal's 100-year history! Even with the upsurge in religiously based political movements since the 1980s, the journal published just one article on American politics in which religion played a central role in the analysis, and only two such articles on comparative politics (2006: 523–5). Unlike classical European social theorists, such as Marx, Durkheim, and Weber, who "took for granted the political significance of the religious factor", American political scientists "treated religion as part of a traditionalist order destined to be swept away (secularized) or compartmentalized (privatized) by the inexorable march of urbanism, science, and the market economy" (2006: 526).

If one defines the modern state as a differentiated and rationalized state, and if, following Weber, we understand that patterns of differentiation and rationalization in any given society will be influenced by the cultural, including religious, resources present within that society, then we must also recognize that "a great variety of different patterns of modernity of a posttraditional order are likely to develop" (Eisenstadt 1973: 148). Modernization in Europe, according to Weber, was the product of a particular combination of utilitarian concerns, intrinsic values, and ingrained habits. Different combinations of these inputs produce different patterns of relationship between religion and the state. Here, we examine some of the inputs that have been addressed in recent scholarship.

State Regulation and the Vitality of the Religious Sector

Against that background, it is not surprising that much research has been devoted to explaining the vitality of the religious sector in the United States, as opposed to its lethargy in equally modern societies of Western Europe. The so-called supply-side model is, of course, the most important development in such research in recent years.

Advocates of the model argue that when the religious sector, or "market", is relatively unregulated, religious pluralism will thrive, and competition between religious suppliers will make them more responsive to the demands of religious "consumers". Assuming, as these theorists do, that the "demand" for religion remains constant, the result of free competition is a more vital religious sector characterized by relatively high levels of religious participation (or consumption). On the contrary, when the state, through active sponsorship or preferential treatment, allows one or a few religious "firms" to monopolize the market, they become lazy and unresponsive to the demands of consumers, causing atrophy in the religious sector.

The model's predictions about the effect of state regulation of the religious "marketplace" have held up well in empirical research (Froese 2001; 2004; Young 1997; Perl and Olson 2000; Chaves, Schraeder, and Sprindys 1994, for example). While other factors, such as the links between religion and ethnic identity, nationalism, social conflict, and the content of the religion itself, are also important (Bruce 2000), it is clear that the impact of state regulation on the vitality of the religious sector cannot be discounted.

That said, it seems reasonable to think that a certain amount of regulation is required if there is to be free competition in the religious market. A competitive religious marketplace would require prohibitions on the use of coercion to compel adherence, for example. It would require laws protecting religious belief and practice against suppression or discrimination. And it would seem to require some working definition of what "religion" is (Hammond 1998: 48 ff.). That is to say, the state requires some working definition to determine what is and is not "religion", in order to discern when the protections and regulations concerning religion apply. Without these provisions and the existence of a state empowered to enforce them, a competitive religious market could hardly be said to exist.

The Negotiation of Institutional Boundaries

In debates over the boundary between religion and medicine, religion and education, religion and business, religion and the state, one can see the powerful forces of modernity at work—the differentiation of social activities into increasingly distinct institutional spheres, each operating according to its own internal rationale and governed according to distinct laws and regulations. No religious group is immune to these processes, and because the expansion of the authority of one institutional sector involves a loss of authority by the others (as when, for example, medical explanations for mental disease replace religious conceptions of demonic possession), the boundaries are frequently contested, and the state may be called upon to use its regulatory powers to settle them.

Take, for example, a case recently reported in the *New York Times* on "medical bill ministries". Such ministries pool payments by their members to pay medical expenses of participants. The state of Kentucky sued one such ministry, charging that it operated too much like an insurance company to qualify for exemption as a religious ministry from the state's insurance regulations (Henriques 2007). One could readily cite hundreds of examples of such boundary disputes, most so common as to be unremarkable.

The more remarkable examples are well known. Disputes over devotional practices in public schools, for instance, generate newspaper headlines and heated public debate. Clearly, both religion and the state have an interest in the education of children. But the question involves whether injecting devotional practices into state-supported schools represents an improper use of the coercive power of the state to compel religious adherence or practice. Other cases, such as those involving the use of peyote in Native American churches, involve whether the state can justifiably restrain religious activity. Both—establishment and free-exercise cases, respectively—can be seen as attempts to maintain optimal conditions of free competition within the religious sector, as described in the section above.

Globalization

The comments in the above section assume that relations between state and religion occur within nation-state boundaries. While true, this statement is not the whole of the matter. Increasingly, religion–state relations *within* a nation are influenced also by what happens *among* nations, the phenomenon called "globalization". The emergence of an international law regime based on (primarily Western) notions of universal human rights, global markets, international economic institutions, globalized media, and scientific and technological exchange across national boundaries all profoundly influence the ways in which states relate to religion. States that wish to participate in such international institutions face powerful external pressure to implement domestic policies that conform to international standards and norms, and to develop regulatory institutions to administer those policies. This frequently results in challenges to long-standing religious and cultural traditions, and disruption of traditional patterns of authority.

This is most clearly seen in attempts to establish modern administrative states in previously stateless societies (Horton 1971). Attempts at state building may be undertaken for noble purposes such as administering foreign aid to disaster-stricken people or for ignoble ones such as developing new markets or exploiting natural resources. However, when nascent states succeed in disrupting traditional patterns of authority, but fail to establish administrative structures that are self-sustaining and accepted as legitimate by the population, the results can be disastrous. This is the crisis facing so-called weak states (which may exist primarily to administer external aid) and societies where efforts at state building have failed (Nixon 2006).

Fundamentalist religious movements—which assert the authority of religion over all aspects of social and cultural life, and thus actively resist the impact of globalization on their societies—have themselves come to operate across national boundaries, most famously through violent and high-profile acts intended to disrupt and destabilize the powerful forces of these global institutions.

Religious Influence on Political Actions

Considerable research has been done on whether and how individual religious views influence political actions, particularly among voters. Following the Second World War and the refinement of survey research methods, religion has been shown to be a large factor in voting decisions.

Not much systematic research has been done, however, on the question at the leadership level. Much was made of Margaret Thatcher's Nonconformist background and how that weighed in her policymaking. Jimmy Carter declared in his first campaign that he was a born-again Christian, and George W. Bush in his first campaign told Americans that Jesus Christ was the political philosopher who most influenced him. Statements concerning how their religious views affected their leadership, however, have been mainly speculative.

Always interesting to observe at the individual level, when researched at the collective level, major political events can be better understood. Thus the Labour Party in Britain gained political foothold when the Anglican Church ceased to be the "Conservative Party at Prayer". White Southern Baptists in the USA, once loyal Democrats, shifted in a major way to the Republican Party, leading to the election of Ronald Reagan in 1980 and the evolution of "big government conservatism" during the administration of George W. Bush.

It is important to recognize, however, that religiously motivated actors, whether at the level of leadership or at the level of voters, are seldom motivated exclusively by religion. Southern Baptists are not just Southern Baptists, but also farmers, business owners, lawyers, etc. Jews may have great concern for Israel, but also have concerns about health care, the environment, and so on. Bloc voting is a reality, to be sure, but it is wise to keep in mind the metaphor of a kaleidoscope—a modest turn of events can yield a very different picture.

Civil Religion

Although the term was coined by Rousseau, the concept of civil religion developed in the sociology of religion through the work of Émile Durkheim, especially his *The Elementary Forms of Religious Life.* Contemporary sociologists and others who think that Durkheim teaches that societies "need" religion as a means to achieve solidarity, however, frequently misunderstand what Durkheim said.

What Durkheim meant can be captured in five propositions:

1. A population's members *may* have a sufficient mutual identity to be regarded (and regard themselves) as a "people".
2. *Probably* such a "people" will have a "myth of origin" explaining how and why they are a "people" (populations meeting these first two criteria are often called "ethnic groups").

3. *Probably* there will be periodic occasions for a people to assemble and celebrate significant events—both positive and negative—in their history, and these celebrations will become institutionalized and symbolized.
4. Such celebrations are *likely* to be times of great emotional fervor, which Durkheim called "collective effervescence".
5. "It is in the midst of these effervescent moments and out of this effervescence itself that the religious idea seems to be born" (Durkheim 1961 [1912]: 253), and the people's unity is renewed.

In the modern world it is hard to find examples of this Durkheimian phenomenon occurring where religion, as commonly understood, plays a central unifying role. More often it is the state that plays that role: flags, anthems, political holidays, etc. These things may coalesce to form a "civil religion", and to the degree that this occurs, we see another way for the state and religion to relate.

References

Bruce, Steve (1996). *Religion in the Modern World: From Cathedrals to Cults.* Oxford: Oxford University Press.

—— (2000). "The Supply-Side Model of Religion: The Nordic and Baltic States". *Journal for the Scientific Study of Religion,* 39/1: 32–46.

Casanova, José (1994). *Public Religions in the Modern World.* Chicago: University of Chicago Press.

Chaves, Mark, Schraeder, Peter J., and Sprindys, Mario (1994). "State Regulation of Religion and Muslim Religious Vitality in the Industrialized West". *Journal of Politics,* 56/4: 1087–97.

Demerath, N. J. III (2003). *Crossing the Gods: Worldly Religions and Worldly Politics.* New Brunswick, NJ: Rutgers University Press.

Durkheim, Émile (1961[1912]), *The Elementary Forms of Religious Life,* trans. Joseph Swain. New York: Collier.

Eisenstadt, S. N. (1973). "The Implications of Weber's Sociology of Religion for Understanding Processes of Change in Contemporary Non-European Societies and Civilizations". In Charles Y. Glock and Phillip E. Hammond (eds.), *Beyond the Classics: Essays in the Scientific Study of Religion.* New York: Harper & Row, 131–55.

Froese, Paul (2001). "Hungary for Religion: A Supply-Side Interpretation of the Hungarian Religious Revival". *Journal for the Scientific Study of Religion,* 40/2: 251–68.

—— (2004). "After Atheism: An Analysis of Religious Monopolies in the Post-communist World". *Sociology of Religion,* 65/1: 57–75.

Hammond, Phillip E. (1998). *With Liberty for All: Freedom of Religion in the United States.* Louisville, Ky.: Westminster/John Knox Press.

—— Machacek, David W., and Mazur, Eric Michael (2004). *Religion on Trial: How Supreme Court Trends Threaten Freedom of Conscience in America.* Walnut Creek, Calif.: AltaMira Press.

HENRIQUES, DIANA B. (2007). "Regulators Challenge Kentucky Ruling Favoring Religion-Based Health Plan". *New York Times*, 2 Feb.: C4.

HORTON, ROBIN (1971). "Stateless Societies in the History of West Africa". In J. F. A. Ajayi and Michael Crowder (eds.), *History of West Africa*, i. London: Longman, 78–119.

LAMONT, STEWART (1989). *Church and State: Uneasy Alliances*. London: The Bodley Head Ltd.

NIXON, ROD (2006). "The Crisis of Governance in New Subsistence States". *Journal of Contemporary Asia*, 36/1: 75–101.

PERL, PAUL, and OLSON, DANIEL V. A. (2000). "Religious Market Share and Intensity of Church Involvement in Five Denominations". *Journal for the Scientific Study of Religion*, 39/1: 12–31.

POSPICIL, LEOPOLD (1971). *Anthropology of Law*. New York: Harper & Row.

RUPNIK, JACQUES (2007). "Popular Front: Eastern Europe's Turn Right". *New Republic*, (19 and 26 Feb.): 12–14.

WALD, KENNETH D., and WILCOX, CLYDE (2006). "Getting Religion: Has Political Science Rediscovered the Faith Factor?" *American Political Science Review*, 100/4: 523–9.

WEBER, MAX (1954[1925]). *Weber on Law in Economy and Society*, trans. Edward Shils and Max Rheinstein. Cambridge: Cambridge University Press.

YOUNG, LAWRENCE A. (ed.) (1997). *Rational Choice Theory and Religion: Summary and Assessment*. New York: Routledge.

SUGGESTED READING

JELEN, TED GERARD, and WILCOX, CLYDE (eds.) (2002). *Religion and Politics in Comparative Perspective: The One, the Few, and the Many*. Cambridge: Cambridge University Press.

KURTZ, LESTER (1995). *Gods in the Global Village: The World's Religions in Sociological Perspective*. Thousand Oaks, Calif.: Pine Forge Press.

JUERGENSMEYER, MARK (2003). *Terror in the Mind of God: The Global Rise of Religious Violence*, 3rd edn. Berkeley: University of California Press.

LAWRENCE, BRUCE (1989). *Defenders of God: The Fundamentalist Revolt against the Modern Age*. New York: Harper & Row.

MCGRAW, BARBARA A., and FORMICOLA, JO RENEE (eds.) (2005). *Taking Religious Pluralism Seriously: Spiritual Politics on America's Sacred Ground*. Waco, Tex.: Baylor University Press.

SMITH, DONALD E. (ed.) (1974). *Religion and Political Modernization*. New Haven: Yale University Press.

STARK, RODNEY, and BAINBRIDGE, WILLIAM SIMS (1987). *A Theory of Religion*. New Brunswick, NJ: Rutgers University Press.

WALD, KENNETH D. (2003). *Religion and Politics in the United States*, 4th edn. Lanham, Md.: Rowman & Littlefield Publishers, Inc.

Also Bruce (1996); Casanova (1994); Demerath (2003); Pospicil (1971); Young (1997).

CHAPTER 22

RELIGION AND NATIONALISM

CHRISTOPHE JAFFRELOT

FOUNDING fathers of sociology like Durkheim have argued that there is no real distinction between nationality and religion (Durkheim 1994[1912]). Robert Bellah made the same point from a different perspective with his notion of "civil religion", suggesting that national identity cannot be separated from the influence of religion (Bellah 1991[1970]). Similarly, nationalism—which is different from nationality[1]—has often been described as a religion—sometimes to suggest that this ideology alienated the critical mind of its followers, sometimes to argue that, in fact, nationalism fulfilled the same sense of belonging as religious creeds. This approach has been developed by Carlton Hayes, who presented nationalism as "a substitute for, or supplement to, historic, supranatural religion" (Hayes 1960: 176), and Boyd Shaffer, who claimed about modernizing France that "nation and nationalism supplied new gods, new hopes, a means to achieve a good life, at a time of instability, a time when (perhaps more than at any other time) men felt oppressed and ill-adapted to their environment" (Shafer 1964: 163). Such an analysis obviously indulges in a functionalist reading of nationalism, in the sense that it explains its rise by some supposedly commanding need, without any convincing analysis and empirical evidence: why does nationalism meet this need more effectively than any other ideology, for instance?

In the present chapter, we shall study the relationship between religion and nationalism while assuming that they are of a different kind and do not relate

[1] See, on this issue, Jaffrelot (2006).

univocally. There is nothing necessary, automatic, and systematic in the rapport between religion and nationalism. Their relationship has changed over time, and the old never completely disappeared when new configurations emerged. To begin with, nationalism emerged as an emancipatory force, including vis-à-vis religion. But this universalistic brand of nationalism gradually, as is evident in the case of France, had to cohabit with an ethnic one, where religion often played a major role as a key component of the identity in question.

Nationalism as an Anti-Religious Force

Nationalism was born in Western Europe as a subversive, modernizing force. It crystallized first in Britain in the sixteenth century in the garb of an "individualistic civic" set of ideas (Greenfeld 1992: 14) shaped by the emerging bourgeoisie in order to promote an alternative—more egalitarian—socio-political order and, thereby, dislodge the ruling aristocracy from its pinnacle. This ideology was imported into France by the *philosophes*—Montesquieu, Voltaire, Rousseau—who gave a more radical interpretation of its implications in relation to the newly formed Rights of Man. Man being the yardstick of everything, God lost his paramountcy, and society became a collection of citizens. The French Revolution established the nation and democracy in the same breath, the nation being nothing more than the self-governing community of citizens. Further East, contrary to a common prejudice according to which German nationalism is rooted in ethnic—and even primordial—ties, the *Aufklärung* (Enlightenment) invented a form of nationalism also based on individualistic principles. Elie Kedourie convincingly argues that Kant introduced the founding value of nationalism in Germany: that is, self-determination (Kedourie 1960[1985]: 112).

For this school of thought, which developed along with the "Âge des Lumières" (or Enlightenment), nationalism is a by-product of individualism. The autonomy of the subject is the touchstone of the body politic in the making—hence the famous definition of the nation by Ernest Renan, "an everyday plebiscite", and the definition of nationalism by Marcel Mauss: "We regard as forming a nation a society materially and morally integrated, with a stable and permanent centralised political power, well established borders, a relative moral, mental and cultural unity of its inhabitants who consciously adhere to the state and its laws" (Mauss 1953–4[1920]: 588).

There's no room left for religion in this nationalist world; not only because God-oriented doctrines deprive man of his "*libre arbitre*" (self-determination); but also because religious groups form communities with their leaders and identity feelings which virtually compete with those of the nation. Such intermediary bodies have no place in the French version of nationalism, which went further than any other in this direction. For the French, as Louis Dumont underlines, the nation is a collection of individuals, whereas religious world views can give birth only to "communalism" (Dumont 1983; 1991)—not nationalism. (We shall return to this highly problematic viewpoint below.)

The nation-states which took shape in Western Europe as a result of this political philosophy were bound to strive toward the secularization of the public sphere. France, logically enough, went further than any other country in this direction. It nationalized properties of the church and developed a full-fledged secular education system in order to draw youth away from Christianity. This process, which intended to confine religion to the private sphere, culminated in the famous 1905 Act which declared a clear-cut legal separation between the Catholic Church and the (nation-)state. In his most comprehensive study of the Third Republic, Eugen Weber shows to what extent the schoolmasters—as part of the largest civil service—were dispatched across the country to eradicate the influence of ecclesiastical teaching and to build the nation (Weber 1976). As a result, anti-clericalism tended to become part of the official ideology.

Other countries have embarked on a more moderate nation-making process. In Britain, the monarchy continued to patronize religion—probably because Anglicanism was both a religion and a distinctive sign of political identity. In the United States of America, though nationalism was rooted in an emancipatory, anti-colonial, and individualistic agenda, religion retained a strong influence—so much so that the president pledges on the Bible. In India, the first British colony to become independent, in 1947, secularism became one of the official mottos. But secularism did not prevent the state from supporting financially schools established by religious groups, as spelled out in the constitution itself. Indeed, Article 30(1) reads: "All minorities, whether based on religion or language shall have the right to establish and administer educational institutions of their choice."

Certainly the universalistic brand of nationalism has succeeded in promoting Man to the pinnacle, in place of God. In the public domain at least, references to religion have become less frequent and less significant. But the individualistic dimension of this political agenda has not been fully implemented.

Even in France, the state has been obliged gradually to acknowledge the resilience of religious identifies, especially among Muslim immigrants. As a result, Le Conseil Français du Culte Musulman (CFCM) was set up in at the turn of the twenty-first century, almost one century after the famous 1905 Act known as the "Loi de séparation de l'Eglise et de l'Etat" which remains the symbol of French "*laïcité*". Initiated by a socialist Home Minister, Jean-Pierre Chevènement in 1999, it was finalized by Nicolas Sarkozy, who had it passed in 2003. The CFCM is intended to introduce an institutional representation of French Muslims in the public sphere, though in 2005 the forty-three members of its board were elected by only 4,042 persons. These delegates had been designated by the mosques, the number of delegates selected by each mosque depending on the size of the mosque.[2] The Ministry of the Interior became very involved in the election of the president—Dalil Bourbakeur, the imam of the "Grande Mosquée de Paris"—who was formally appointed by the board in 2005. The CFCM is supposed to oversee the building of new mosques, to look after the creation of special zones for Muslims in local cemeteries, to organize religious festivals—including those for which ritual sacrifices have to be observed and, last but not least, to train the imams. The latter mission aimed at reducing the influence of foreign countries like Saudi Arabia, whose input was seen as much too conservative. However, the CFCM has become the stronghold of rather radical movements—so much so that this institution created by the secular Republic explicitly contradicts some of its principles.

To sum up, nationalism was born as a modern ideology dedicated to the emancipation of man against every adverse force, including religion. This enlightened agenda has been implemented by state bureaucracies eager to establish their control over society vis-à-vis church-dominated networks. The universalistic brand of nationalism, therefore, is statist and territorial: it deals, in a top-down manner, with the population situated within the frontiers of the nation-state. Such an agenda was bound to remain unfinished, because of the resilience of religion, even in the most secularized context—especially at a time when migrations increased and brought devotees of foreign religions to the West. But this type of nationalism clearly represents a distinctive socio-political trajectory, different from those which are deliberately constructed according to religious criteria, either in part or fully.

Religion-Based Nationalism

Though the classic contrast between the universalist and the ethnic types of nationalism has been often exaggerated, these ideologies undoubtedly belong to different repertoires (Plamenatz 1973). While the former results from some individualistic mind-set, the latter is rooted in cultural, collective features—including religion. Such a definition of ethnic nationalism does not hark back to any primordialism. Following Edward Shils, Clifford Geertz indulged in a grossly misleading analysis when he claimed that: "The power of the 'givens' of place, tongue, blood, looks, and

[2] However, the representativeness of this institution is reinforced by the fact that there is also a Conseil Régionaux du Culte Musulman in each region.

way-of-life [including religion] to shape an individual's notion of who, at bottom, he is and with whom, indissolubly, he belongs is rooted in the non-rational foundations of personality" (Geertz 1963: 128). National identities are not produced by such primordial ties—were it so, no multicultural society would be in a position to form a nation. But many nationalisms have emerged from the reinterpretation of such material. In some cases languages have been the touchstone of such ideologies; in others religion has played the same role.

How Ethno-Religious Nationalisms Take Shape

Most of the countries where ethno-religious nationalism has developed belong to the non-Western world. This is due to the resilience of religiosity in societies where individualism and materialism are not as pervasive as in the West; but this is also due to the kind of historical encounter that has taken place between these societies and the West. In these new nation-states, too, nationalism is a by-product of the modernization process; but it has crystallized *against* this dominant Other that was the West, as an ideological reaction.

Western expansionism spread over most of the world from the late eighteenth to the early nineteenth century onwards, either through formal colonialism (like the British in India after 1757 and the French in Algeria after 1830) or via forms of imperialism ranging from Perry's policy in Japan to the Concessions in China. Most of the societies impacted in this way were pervaded by religion. Not only ecclesiastical hierarchies exerted a strong influence—as local priests as much as counselors of the rulers, but the whole of life was dominated by religious rituals, festivals, and beliefs. Initially, the level of religiosity found in these milieus—be they Muslim, Buddhist, Hindu, or whatever—was high.

The coming of Westerners to such societies was a major challenge for their elites. The clerical groups and the ruling aristocracies either withdrew into their shells or fought battles with rudimentary means, as evident from the self-defeating 1857 Mutiny of the Cepoys (which, incidentally, was started for religious reasons that included the revolt by Indian soldiers against the introduction of cartridges greased with pig- and cow-made grease).

Members of the intelligentsia of these societies reacted in a very different manner. Ernest Gellner has described the intelligentsia as being "a phenomenon essentially connected with *the* transition [from the traditional societies to the industrial era] ... a class which is alienated from its own society by the very fact of its education" (Gellner 1964: 169–70; 1983). This holds for the initial phase only. To begin with, this group is cut off from its own society because, though it has been socialized in the tradition of its forefathers, it has been trained in a modern, Westernized educational system. This training leads it to look at the tradition in which it used to be immersed as backward and powerless compared to the modern state and Western technology. From this vantage point, this worn-out tradition is suffused with religion. This creed, therefore, is perceived by the intelligentsia as ridden with superstitions and prejudices. This group believes in the Western rationality they have learned in the university, not only because of its intrinsic, emancipatory value, but also because of its effectiveness: it acknowledges in a very pragmatic way that the superiority of the West lies in its scientific mind-set.

Yet, apart from a tiny minority, the intelligentsia is not willing to become Westernized beyond a critical point. It insists on remaining true to its religious tradition. While being fascinated by Western, a-religious modernity, it cannot, nor does it want to, betray its religious tradition and break with it. The solution to this dilemma lies in a reformist strategy.

Reformists do not often look at themselves as innovative. They consider that they bring back tradition in its pristine purity, as evident in the Lutheran Reformation. Similarly, the nineteenth-century intelligentsia of Western-dominated countries reformed their religion by claiming to return to its roots. But in doing so, they invested it with Western, modern features that—they insisted—they had found in the antiquarian forms of their creed. This strategy was obvious in the theological domain. For instance, reformists of polytheist religions insisted that their creed, originally, knew of only one god, for the reason that monotheism was considered more prestigious, given the aura of the Christian rulers. Social and ritual practices were reinterpreted in exactly the same way. For instance, the status of elite groups—castes or tribes—which derived from a hierarchical world view was not justified on the basis of purely traditional beliefs, but by resorting to individualist values such as merit—if the Brahmins, historically, were at the top in India, for example, it was not because of their birth, but because during the old days, this caste included all those who displayed the relevant, personal qualities.

The reformist thus searches for the original religion. Sometimes, scriptural sources are very limited—either because they are scarce or because they do not say much about religious life in ancient time; which leaves great liberty to the exegetes. But even when these sources are rich and dense, those who read them tend to be highly selective. They emphasize only those features which are relevant to their purpose. They argue that most of the rituals denounced by Westerners as superstitious are late accretions and that the ill-treatment of some human beings (women, for instance) are distortions of the original, spiritual meaning of the religious traditions. In fact, such interpretations amount to "inventions of traditions" in the Hobsawm and Ranger (1985) sense of the term.

This detour through a history of religion transforms the reformist into a revivalist, as Anthony Smith has shown in his masterpiece *Theories of Nationalism* (1971). Indeed, while revisiting the initial stages of his religion, the reformist invents a golden age (Smith 1997), a time when his religion was exempt from all the defects arraigned by the dominant other. This evolution takes the reformist's agenda to his logical conclusion: his objective had never been to disown his religion and to severe his links with his community—in contrast to what others (be they occidentalists or assimilationists) tried to do—but to reconcile his tradition with Western modernity. But the invention of a golden age in which the reformist/revivalist "discovers" that the core of his ancestral religion encompasses the very features from which the Westerners draw their pride, restores his own self-esteem. While the reformist had to adopt a defensive attitude vis-à-vis the West—he had to change his religion and society according to Western criteria—the revivalist is not ashamed any more of his traditions. He may eventually hit back. In fact, the very notion of a golden age provides him with an ideological basis that prepares the ground for a nationalist reaction.

The revivalist turns nationalist when he starts arguing that there is no real need to reform anything in his religion because traditions are to be seen as a valuable legacy by virtue of the fact that they shape the country's identity: "My country, right or wrong!", indeed, is the key motto of nationalism. While the reformist/revivalist explains that religion has to be amended in order to be restored to its pristine purity, the nationalist argues that there is no need to change anything because traditions are eternal—without beginning and without end—and, sometimes, even based on sacred text. Religious scriptures can notoriously be interpreted differently, and in the latter case they are used to develop a form of fundamentalism as the platform from which no deviation may be allowed at any cost.

The Specificity of Religion-Based Nationalism

The outcome of this ideological trajectory is nothing other that an ethnic form of nationalism. As noted above, this brand of nationalism may rely on different cultural features. Often it arose from language, and this kind of nationalism displayed a strong resilience even in Europe—as is evident from the situation prevailing today in Spain (with the Basque and the Catalonian issues) and in Belgium (with the Flemish versus the Walloons). But in many other cases it emerged from religion, not so much in Europe—where Ireland may be the last country where religion plays such a role—but everywhere else. British India was partitioned to give birth to the Islamic Republic of Pakistan, and in India, today, Hindu nationalism is a strong and powerful force; the former Yugoslavia has broken into so many parts largely because of growing hostility between Muslims (mostly Bosnians) and Christians (Serbs and Croatians). Lebanon suffers from the growing estrangement between Christians and Muslims. Israel is all the more at pains to solve the Arab issue (to say nothing of the Palestinian issue) as it is an ethnic democracy. Things are even more complicated when linguistic and religious cleavages coincide, as in Sri Lanka, where Hindu Tamils are opposed to Buddhist Sinhalese.

If religion is one of the classic elements of what we call ethnic nationalism, like language, it often plays a more important role than language. Indeed, language-based multiculturalism is easier to maintain than religious-based multiculturalism, as illustrated by the integration of Quebec into Canada and of the Dravidian states into the Indian Union. This is probably due to the fact that federalism can help to defuse tensions more effectively between linguistic groups than between religious communities. But it is also due to the emotional power of religion. Devotees are more ready to mobilize in defense of their religion because of its sacred, hence imperative, character. This argument has been made by those students of nationalism, like Paul Brass, who explain the mobilization of the masses by the manipulation of identity symbols (Brass 1979; 1985). Such a stratagem can certainly operate, but only after a clear-cut ideological discourse has been appropriated by the masses in question. Here religions have undoubtedly a unique quality, as, in many cases, they are the embodiment of full-fledged civilizations commanding all the essential dimensions of life. The very structure of a society—like the caste system in India—sometimes derives from religious considerations.

Yet, religion-based ethnic nationalisms are not permanent and unchanging in either form or content: they change in the course of time according to the context. Many were constructed in relation to a dominant Other in the very specific circumstances of the nineteenth century and the early part of the twentieth century. Since then they have often been deconstructed and reconstructed in different contexts. The Muslim world offers good examples of this phenomenon. Islam has not been such a powerful force. It has not been able to prevent Muslim nations from falling apart: Bangladesh seceded in 1971 from Pakistan, for instance. And none of the projects intended to merge Muslim nation-states have been successful—as evident from the aborted association of Syria and Egypt in 1958–61. More importantly, Islam has not kept its initial role of identity-provider in a number of cases. The growing divide between Shias and Sunnis in Muslim countries like Afghanistan, Pakistan, and of course Iraq challenges the very notion of an Islam-based nationalism. In most of these countries, these developments are analyzed in terms of "sectarianism"; but their mechanisms recall those of the ethnic nationalism of the past. In fact, sectarian groups are ethnic groups who mobilize because they fear the Other—either because that Other is in the majority (Shias in Iraq, Sunnis in Pakistan), or because it benefits from the support of some foreign country (Iran in both cases). This mobilization takes the same route as before: it relies on ideological belief in a golden age based on a rereading of sacred texts and likely to provide the required assertiveness vis-à-vis the so-called threatening other; secondly, it results partly from the instrumentalization of identity symbols endowed with strong emotional potential.

Another reason why Islam-based nationalisms have been reshaped in the course of time can be found in the transnational (and even transcontinental) nature of Islam. In some countries, the frontiers of the nation coincide with those of a religious community—as with Shintoism in Japan—but in others, the religious community is much larger. In the case of Islam, this state of things has been reinforced by the notion of the *Umma*, which de-legitimated the nation-state as a valuable entity. The relevant "unit" could only be "pan-Islamic". All the regional attempts made in this direction during the twentieth century have failed—from the merger of Syria with Egypt to "pan-Turkism". Today, Islamist networks like Al Qaeda try to build a Muslim body politic by going beyond the (Islamic) nation-state. But their ideological building process reproduces key elements of the old brand of ethnic nationalism. For instance, this doctrine crystallizes in reaction to some threatening Other, the West and, more especially, the United States. Anti-Americanism and anti-imperialism are key elements of the Islamic discourse, which, in a way, sounds like an alternative to Guevarism.

Religion-Driven Nationalist Trajectories

In the first part of this essay, I have shown that the initial, universalist brand of nationalism was born against religion—though it was not able to (success)fully secularize society. In the second part, I have examined another brand of nationalism based on religion *as a set of ethnic features* which are not immutable but establish a political identity closed in on itself. One country can harbor both types of nationalism. In France the universalistic type has had to cohabit with an ethnic one, which became dominant after the 1870 defeat by the Germans. For Maurice Barrès and Charles Maurras, the identity of France was primarily rooted in its Catholic culture. In India, secular nationalism à la Nehru developed at the same pace as the Hindutva movement, which equated the nation with the majority community. Louis Dumont refuses to look at the ideology of militant Hinduism as a full-fledged nationalism. He calls it "communalism". But it fulfills all the criteria of ethnic nationalism.

Not only may two kinds of nationalism coexist in one country, but the dominant form of nationalism may transform itself and travel from the universalist pole to the ethno-religious one. Zionism is a point in case. Initially, it was a secular ideology. Theodore Herzl did not want to establish a Jewish state, but a state for the Jews. In his book, *The State of the Jews* he argues: "We shall therefore prevent any theocratic tendencies from coming to the fore on the part of our priesthood....We shall keep our priests within the confines of their temples... they must not interfere in the administration of the State" (Herzl 1946: 100).

Zionism, like many other modern nationalisms, is intended to emancipate "its" people from the influence of all oppressors, including priests. A neutral state has to be built on this very foundation. When Israel was created, however, Zionism gave birth to an officially "Jewish state" and an ethno-democracy in which some citizens were more equal than others. For instance, any Jew who migrates to Israel is given citizenship rights. Keren Hayessod is a national agency raising funds in the Diaspora only for the Jews, to say nothing of the national flag and the very name of the state (Dieckhoff 2003).

Poland followed the same kind of trajectory. At the beginning of the twentieth century, the Polish elite was non church-going and often cultivated anti-clerical ideas. The nationalism of the National Democratic movement was imbued with positivism, and Freemasons exerted a strong influence. Dmowski, one of the leaders of the movement and one of the founders of this first-generation nationalism, wrote in *Thoughts of a Modern Pole* (1902) that "the nation is the product of the state's existence" (cited in Zawadski 2006: 172), without paying any attention to the Catholic culture of society. However, after the Polish state reestablished itself at the impulse of Pilsudski in 1926, the nationalism of the National Democratic movement "Catholicised itself" (Zawadski 2006: 173). In the end, the dominant nationalist discourse equated Poland with Catholicism. This evolution may be explained by the important weight of the "national" minorities—35 percent of the population—which fostered the construction of a strong ethnic identity by the Catholic majority. But Paul Zawadzki suggests another reason, which is not relevant only for Poland: in the end, "the nationalists had to take the popular religiosity into account" (2006: 170).

Here is a parameter that we find at work almost everywhere. So long as politics is the monopoly of limited elite groups, the enlighted intelligentsia can afford to indulge in secular forms of nationalism. But the moment it turns nationalist and attempts to build the nation through popular mobilization, it needs to relate to the masses and energize them. Then religion cannot any longer be ignored. The politicized elite not only needs to identify religious symbols in order to activate people; more immediately, it needs to speak in the same idiom as the masses which have to be transformed into a nation. These masses are so imbued with the religious ethos that it has to be one of the languages of politics. In a way, the intrusion of religion into the nationalist discourse is a by-product of the democratization of politics.

Conclusion

The relations between religion and nationalism are complicated by the ambivalence of both notions. Nationalism is Janus-like. On the one hand, under the garb of its universalist variant, it is a liberating force that contributes to the emancipation of people from all sources of alienation, including religious ideas and hierarchies. On the other hand, in its ethnic incarnation, it is a closed ideology using religion as the mark of an ascriptive identity and as a means of collective mobilization. Interestingly, both versions of nationalism cohabit in most political societies and/or appear in succession in the course of their history. Many of the examples mentioned in this chapter bear testimony to this combination. Most of them also suggest that the classic opposition between universalist and ethnic nationalisms is mitigated by the fact that in both cases a strong secularization process is at work. This is evident so far as the former is concerned, but it is obvious too for the latter, in which religion represents a set of cultural markers within the framework of a power-oriented ideology. Incidentally, most of the theorists of ethno-religious nationalisms were not church (or temple) goers, or even believers—and their knowledge of the sacred scriptures was often either nonexistent or very rudimentary.

Religion is ambivalent too. On the one hand, its communitarian dimension and its doctrinal overtones lend themselves to ethnic nationalism. On the other hand, its spiritual quality makes it open-ended and universalistic. Moreover, there have been examples of universalist nationalisms sustained by a spiritual philosophy. Gandhism is probably the best illustration of the case in point, since the Mahatma associated Indian identity with spirituality, in contrast to that of the materialistic West, and lived his anti-colonial fight as part of his personal salvation quest. Yet it is very difficult to evolve a form of nationalism that is both universalistic and rooted in spirituality, simply because spirituality always draws largely from a particular religious culture: Gandhi could not help but be Hindu—as evident from his reverence for the sacred cow, an attitude which prevented many Indian Muslims from paying allegiance to his leadership. A spiritually oriented universalistic nationalism is probably a contradiction in terms. The very ambivalence of religion-based nationalism makes the whole idea of "religious nationalism"—to use the phrase of Mark Juergensemeyer (1993) and Peter van der Veer (1994)—misleading: there is nothing like "religious nationalism"; there are only ethnic nationalisms relying on religious cultural features.

References

Bellah, R. (1991[1970]). *Beyond Belief: Essays on Religion in a Post-Traditional World.* Berkeley: University of California Press.

Brass P. (1979). "Elite Groups, Symbol Manipulation and Ethnic Identity among the Muslims of South Asia". In D. Taylor and M. Yapp (eds.), *Political Identity of South Asia.* London: Curzon Press, 35–77.

—— (1985). "Ethnic Groups and the State". In *idem* (ed.), *Ethnic Groups and the State.* London and Sidney: Croom Helm, 1–56.

DIECKHOFF, ALAIN (2003). *The Invention of a Nation: Zionist Thought and the Making of Modern Israel.* London: Hurst.

—— and JAFFRELOT, CHRISTOPHE (eds.) (2006). *Revisiting Nationalism: Theories and Processes.* London: Hurst.

DUMONT, L. (1983). *Essai sur l'individualisme: une perspective anthropologique sur l'idéologie moderne.* Paris: Le Seuil.

—— (1991). *L'Idéologie allemande: France-Allemagne et retour.* Paris: Gallimard.

DURKHEIM, E. (1994[1912]). *Les formes élémentaires de la vie religiense.* Paris: PUF.

GEERTZ, C. (1963). "The Integrative Revolution: Primordial Sentiments and Civil Politics in the New States". In *idem* (ed.), *Old Societies and New States.* Glencoe, Ill.: Free Press, 105–57.

GELLNER, E. (1964). *Thought and Change.* London: Weidenfeld & Nicolson.

—— (1983). *Nations and Nationalism.* Oxford: Basil Blackwell.

GREENFELD L. (1992). *Nationalism: Five Roads to Modernity.* Cambridge, Mass.: Harvard University Press.

HAYES, C. H. J. (1960). *Nationalism: A Religion.* New York: The Macmillan Company.

HERZL, T. (1946). *The State of the Jews.* New York: Scopus.

HOBSBAWM, E., and RANGER, T. (eds.) (1985). *The Invention of Tradition.* Cambridge: Cambridge University Press.

JAFFRELOT, C. (2006). "For a Theory of Nationalism". In Dieckhoff and Jaffrelot (2006), 10–61.

JUERGENSMEYER, M. (1993). *The New Cold War? Religious Nationalism Confronts the Secular State.* Berkeley: University of California Press.

KEDOURIE, E. (1985[1960]). *Nationalism,* rev. edn. with Afterword London: Hutchinson University Library.

MAUSS, M. (1953–4[1920]). "La Nation". *L'Année sociologique,* 7–68.

PLAMENATZ, J. (1973). "Two Types of Nationalism". In E. Kamenka (ed.), *Nationalism: The Nature and Evolution of an Idea.* London: Edward Arnold, Ltd., 23–36.

RENAN, E. (1992). *Qn'est ce qu'une nation?* Paris: Press Pocket.

SHAFER B. (1964). *Le Nationalisme, mythe et réalité.* Paris: Payot.

SMITH A. D. (1971). *Theories of Nationalism.* London: Gerald Duckworth & Co. Ltd.

—— (1997). "The 'Golden Age' and National Renewal". In G. Hosking and G. Schöpflin (eds.), *Myth and Nationhood.* London: Hurst, 23–36.

VAN DER VEER, P. (1994). *Religious Nationalism: Hindus and Muslims in India.* Berkeley: University of California Press.

WEBER, E. (1976). *Peasants into Frenchmen: The Modernisation of Rural France, 1870–1914.* Stanford, Calif.: Stanford University Press.

ZAWADSKI, P. (2006). "Nationalism, Democracy and Religion". In Dieckhoff and Jaffrelot (2006), 165–90.

CHAPTER 23

RELIGION AND THE LAW

AN INTERACTIONIST VIEW

JAMES T. RICHARDSON

Religion and law interact in many significant ways in modern societies, a fact overlooked in many sociology of religion treatments of religion in today's world. There was some appreciation of the relationship between law and religion in early works of a few classical theorists such as Max Weber (1952[1921]; 1958[1905]) and Émile Durkheim (1964[1912]). Some contemporary treatments of "cult controversies" also deal with the impact of legal actions on minority faiths (Beckford 1985; Richardson 2004; 2005). However, most sociology of religion textbooks discuss law and legal considerations little, if at all.

This essay will adopt the position that law and religion are inextricably bound together, particularly in modern societies with increasingly pervasive legal systems. Legal systems are usually derived from religious tenets, some very directly. And more powerful religious groups can sometimes manipulate or make use of those legal systems to maintain their position of prominence in a society and promote their own interests. But religions, religious groups, and acts and beliefs defined as religious by individuals are also regulated, via the legal institutions established to enforce the laws of society. This essay will examine significant issues from both perspectives, starting with a discussion treating religion as the independent variable in the equation relating law and religion. That will be followed by a treatment of situations in which law acts as an independent variable with regard to religion.

Religion as Independent Variable

Religion as the Underpinning of Law and Society

Western legal systems derive rather directly from Judeo-Christian tenets taken from the New and Old Testaments of the Bible (Berger 1967). There have been many additions and emendations to the basic ideas found in biblical sources, of course; but at root it is clear that the major source is the Jewish version of morality and law, modified somewhat through development of New Testament ideas of Christianity. The Ten Commandments are well represented in Western legal traditions.

According to some scholars, the Islamic religious tradition has been quite directly transmuted into the normative structure of legal systems in most Islamic countries (Al-Azmeh 1988), although this assertion is denied by others (Gibb and Kramers 1974: 524 ff.). There are extreme examples demonstrating the direct influence of Islam on legal structures and institutions such as Iran in the post-revolutionary period and in some former Soviet-dominated nations. However, even in officially secular nations such as Turkey, Islamic law pervades, in a manner similar to the way in which Judeo-Christian values pervade the legal system of modern-day, officially secular France.

One can find historical and modern examples of virtual theocratic states having been developed within the orbit of both major religious traditions. Contemporary Iran is a case in point within Islam, as was the Taliban regime in Afghanistan. Puritan New England during colonial days exemplifies an effort to build a Puritan state in the "New World". Later in American history the Latter-Day Saints (Mormons) established a theocratic state in the western region around what is now the state of Utah, a situation which involved church courts handling cases of all types (Leone 1979). Although polygamy was the major focus of media attention when controversy erupted between the federal government and the LDS Church, the Church's views concerning theocracy also came under fire and had to be officially abandoned before Utah could become a state. Greece is a modern European example of a state with tendencies toward theocracy, with its stringent laws that criminalize proselytizing parishioners of the Greek Orthodox tradition. Such laws have been a major focus of the European Court of Human Rights, which has ruled against Greece in several cases involving those statutes (Richardson 1995a;

Richardson and Garay 2004). Efforts by Islamic extremists to take over, through violent means if necessary, the political structure of a number of Islamic nations demonstrate that this effort to meld religion and law into a theocratic state is by no means a thing of the past. Some see similar, even if less violent, tendencies within the United States, as fundamentalist Christians attempt to remake society according to basic tenets of their faith.[1]

Religions Constructing and Making Use of Legal Systems

Religious traditions and groups continue to attempt to structure legal systems in ways that will serve their interests, and sometimes they can be very effective players in the dialectic process of legal social constructions (Chambliss and Zatz 1993). The Catholic Church in the USA and elsewhere has been involved for decades in efforts to influence public policy concerning abortion, the death penalty, and other matters of import in its religious tenets. The LDS Church has likewise made efforts to establish legal boundaries over certain behaviors. For example, they joined forces with the Catholic Church in Nevada in the 1980s to help defeat the Equal Rights Amendment to the federal constitution (Richardson 1984).[2] President George W. Bush's effort to establish "faith-based initiatives" to deal with social problems represents the growing influence of fundamentalist Christian values in the USA, and has resulted in billions of tax dollars flowing to religious groups in recent years, in spite of the alleged separation of church and state that is supposed to exist in the USA (Davis 2001).

Former Soviet Union countries, recently liberated from the shackles of communism, show how quickly formerly dominant religious groups can reassert themselves to reconstruct their society's legal system. In Poland, the Catholic Church, which actually gained strength during communist times, quickly tried to assert its values even more into the functioning of Polish society after the fall of communism (Koscianska 2004). It has succeeded in gaining access to schools for religious instruction and getting major changes in laws concerning divorce, abortion, and even the regulation of mass media, precluding thereby criticism of the Church or official government policies. In Russia, the Russian Orthodox Church, an apparently strong supporter of religious freedom in the early 1990s, quickly

[1] For a provocative fictional account of such a development see Margaret Atwood's *The Handmaid's Tale*, published in 1985.

[2] At the time only three more states needed to approve the Equal Rights Amendment for it to become part of the Constitution of the United States. Commentators have noted that it is not accidental that the group of states not approving the amendment were located in the south and in the region around Utah. The amendment failed after thirty-five states had voted to approve it, as it fell just short of the two-thirds required. Clearly religious values played a major role in its defeat.

appeared to redefine the term to mean freedom for the ROC to work its will in the political and social arena of Russia. Its opposition to individual religious freedom and its support for strong "anti-sect and cult" campaigns and legislation that would limit the ability of minority faiths to function has been well documented (Shterin and Richardson 1998; 2000; 2002). New laws criminalizing proselytizing in nations such as Uzbekistan also demonstrate the effort of dominant faiths to reassert themselves even as they themselves are being used by dominant political forces to exert control over the citizenry (Hanks 2004).

Religious groups can also make use of the law, although doing so carries some obligations and risks (Richardson 1998), as well as opportunities to use the law in a manner that may dramatically change the organization (Cote and Richardson 2001). The attempt to make use of the legal arena by a religious group implies that the group will abide by the rules of the legal system and by any judgement rendered by the courts. The obligations and risks for using the legal system are lower for dominant religious groups, of course (see Black 1976; 1999; Richardson 2001), as such entities are what sociologists of law term "repeat players", with experience of using the legal system for their own purposes. Such religious groups also have "friends in high places", in that those in positions of power, including judges and politicians, within a society may share the dominant faith, or at least understand its basic tenets. Smaller faiths seldom have representatives serving in high political office, although this is not unknown. Thus a dominant religion may successfully use the legal system to effect changes in the system, such as changing zoning laws so that it can build new quarters where it desires.

A major battle has been taking place on zoning/land use by religious organizations within the United States over the past decade or so. After an initial major loss on a zoning issue in the US Supreme Court in 1998 (the *Boerne* case; see Richardson 1999*a*), a well-coordinated counterattack was mounted, which has resulted in a new federal law that has since been upheld by the Supreme Court granting religious groups considerable impunity in the area of land use and zoning (Richardson, Chamberlain, and Shoemaker 2006). This example not only shows how a dominant religious group and its allies may make use of the legal system, but it demonstrates as well the power to construct that system in a manner that promotes the interests of more dominant faiths.

Although more rare, some minority faiths have succeeded in using the legal system to defend themselves, or to make changes in the legal system, as well. Examples of the former activity include the Unification Church and other minority faiths defending their right to engage in street solicitation and proselytizing in the USA, as well as Scientology using the legal system to thwart those who would criticize it and also to force governments to grant it recognition as a religion. A notable example of the latter situation concerns Christian Science gaining exemptions from child endangerment laws decades ago, so that the use of "spiritual healing" would not result in criminal charges against the Church (Richardson and DeWitt 1992). These exemptions in state law have been challenged in recent years; but most are still in existence, and have served well to protect the Church and individual members whose children died when illnesses were treated by means of spiritual healing.

Exemptions to drug laws in the United States have been forged in various states with Native American populations involved with the use of peyote in religious ceremonies. The passage of these exemption laws demonstrates that the usual pattern of minority faiths losing in the legal system can be overcome on occasion. Doing so usually involves the intervention of "third party partisans" who become involved in the issue on behalf of the minority faith (Black and Baumgartner 1999; Richardson 2001). This exemption was also a major basis of a recent decision of the US Supreme Court to allow importation and use of a hallucinogenic tea used by a small Brazilian sect in New Mexico (the *Gonzales* case, in 2006).

The *Gonzales* case is a good example of how religious groups can sometimes use the legal system to their advantage, defending their faith and even attacking those who would attack them. Although, as noted, minority faiths rarely win in court, for understandable reasons—they are weak politically and have few people in positions of power who understand them or care about there well-being—on occasion they succeed. The conditions that allow victories for minority faiths to occur usually include the intervention of some more powerful, higher-status parties, acting for whatever reason on behalf of the weaker religious group. Other conditions, such as the presence of an autonomous judiciary staffed by individuals who value religious freedom, are also important, of course (Richardson 2006).

As noted, the concept of third-party partisans is useful in explaining occasional victories for minority religions in court. Examples of effective third-party partisan groups include Amnesty International, which has intervened in various ways on behalf of members of minority faiths, such as with the Falun Gong in China, the American Civil Liberties Union, and the National Council of Churches, which have defended the rights of minority religious groups in the "cult wars" in the USA in recent decades, and even academic scholars and professional academic organizations that also became involved in the "cult wars" (Richardson 1996*b*).

An argument can even be made that some political and judicial organizations can function as third-party partisans in cases involving minority religions, under certain conditions. For instance, the Hungarian parliament in the 1990s was quite supportive of one particular minority religion, the Hare Krishnas, which contributed to its winning a unusual libel action over a major critic (Richardson 1995*b*). That parliament also passed legislation that was helpful to smaller faiths, including a major change in the tax system that resulted in smaller faiths obtaining more direct support from the state. Another example is the European Court of Human Rights, which provides a legal forum for minority faiths to defend themselves against governmental action within the forty-six member states of the Council of Europe. Jehovah's Witnesses have made good use of this forum, as have other minority faiths. The latest example of the import of the ECHR is a 7 April 2007 decision in favor of Scientology against Russia. The Moscow City government had attempted to dissolve Scientology, which fought legal battles over the issue for years, but finally lost within the Russian legal system. However, its appeal to the ECHR was successful. Within the United States, an argument can be made that under the new Chief Justice, John Roberts, the Supreme Court itself may become a crucial third party partisan, as it demonstrated with the *Gonzales* case.

LAW AS INDEPENDENT VARIABLE

Social Control of Religions and Religious Groups

The above discussion of times and situations in which religious groups, especially minority ones, prevailed within the legal system should not leave the impression that this is the usual resolution of such matters. Indeed, such is not the case. Dominant religions can, and usually do, have considerable influence over the outcome of cases involving them. Only in very egregious circumstances, such as the thousands of child sex abuse cases revealed within the Catholic Church in the USA, will a legal system finally take serious action against a dominant religion. Even then, there are ways to avoid serious punishments, such as through declaring bankruptcy, which a number of dioceses in the USA have done. In Russia, the well-known collusion between the Russian Orthodox Church and the Communist regime has been of concern to some, but the idea of the ROC being brought into court to answer for decades of such actions has not been entertained, and instead the church has been allowed, even encouraged, to reclaim its prominent place in the public space of Russia.

The situation with minority faiths in societies around the world is usually more problematic. The theories of Donald Black (1976; 1999) seem well illustrated by predictable outcomes when new or minority religions get involved in legal actions. Such groups typically have low status, few "friends in high places", and little understanding or support from the media and societal political and religious leaders. Those in decision-making positions within the institutional structure of society, including judges and law enforcement personnel, do not usually share personal or cultural "intimacy" with the minority religious group. This lack of intimate contact means that those decision-makers probably do not understand or sanction the beliefs and lifestyles of such groups, and thus tend to act in a normative manner to enforce values and norms of the dominant society. Indeed, as has been the case in Russia (Shterin and Richardson 2000), minority faiths can become pawns in the efforts of dominant faiths and conservative political forces to regain power. In short, the institutional structure of society works in concert to exert social control over, and make use of, religious groups defined as deviant, and the legal system is often at the forefront of such actions. The law can be a formidable social weapon to use against new, and possibly unpopular, minority faiths. And the law can be selective in how it is applied, as considerable discretion exists at all levels of the legal system of any modern society (Richardson 2001).

One key issue concerning minority religions is whether they are in fact considered a religion for legal purposes. Many societies have governmental bureaucracies to deal with religious groups, and most of these have developed an official hierarchy of religious groups (Durham 2000). Such groups range from officially approved state churches to religious groups that are not granted that status but are defined as political or even terrorist organizations. The latter case is illustrated by the approach taken by the Chinese government toward the Falun Gong. China has had since the rise to power of the Communist Party, a two-level official hierarchy of religions. Religious freedom is guaranteed for "normal" churches (a term used in the Chinese Constitution), which means ones established by the state, with leaders selected by the government. When the Falun Gong movement developed, it was initially accepted as an exercise movement, but quickly became defined as an illegal "evil cult" and then, after September 11, 2001, as a terrorist organization (Richardson and Edelman 2004). In Russia, the new 1990 Constitution, modeled after Western ideals concerning religious freedom, defined minority faiths in positive terms. However, groups that had been officially accepted early in the decade of the 1990s quickly became the focus of official attacks, leading to a change of law in 1997 redefining which religious groups were unacceptable, which were acceptable, and which was the most privileged, with the Russia Orthodox Church filling the latter category (Shterin and Richardson 1998, 2000).

A number of Western European nations have established hierarchies of religious groups by law and practice over the years. There is no tradition of separation of church and state in Europe, so this is not an unexpected arrangement. Thus, some churches get major tax concessions, and may also have tax revenues sent directly to them, justified in part because of historical connections, but also by the fact that some dominant churches are involved in delivery of social services to the citizens of the society. In Hungary religion has been allowed to occupy a more prominent place in public space in the post-communist era, and minority faiths have also been granted considerable rights and protections, including even the receipt of tax revenues (Schanda 2004). However, in recent years some Western European nations have moved beyond traditional management of religions, and have declared some newer and smaller faiths to be unacceptable. This has been accomplished in France and Belgium by developing lengthy list of unacceptable "sects and cults". Being placed on such lists has direct negative consequences for those groups and their participants (Richardson and Introvigne 2001). Austria has also approved a hierarchy of religions that makes it much more difficult for minority faiths to function and be accepted in Austrian society.

Even in the United States, the issue of what is and is not a religion is of import. There are no official hierarchies, and no governmental agency, to decide what is and is not an acceptable religion, and where a group claiming status as a religion might fit within that society's hierarchical scheme. However, there is a definite unofficial hierarchy, which does influence governmental policy and the way in which religious organizations are dealt with through the law. This occurs mainly because of the historical situation in the USA (Berger 1967; Richardson 2006), but also in part because of the use of juries in the USA, which means that ordinary citizens with their beliefs, values, and even biases and misinformation, sit on juries that can decide the fate of an individual or an organization in cases involving criminal accusations or civil suits involving minority faiths. Of course, judges and bureaucratic functionaries in governmental agencies are also citizens in the society, influenced by their own views and values, by media treatments, and by the views of significant others within society concerning religious groups that might come before them in their official capacities. Research has shown that ordinary citizens and elites do hold biased views and misinformation about what some religious groups are and how they operate (Pfeiffer 1999; DeWitt, Richardson, and Warner 1997; Richardson 1992; Bromley and Breschel 1992), and those beliefs and biases can be acted out as decisions are made within the legal system.

One major case will illustrate the manner in which these matters are dealt with within the American legal system. In the state of Minnesota a law was passed requiring any group obtaining more than half its operating funds from non-members must register with the state and obtain permission to engage in fund raising. It was clear from testimony when the law was considered that it was directed at the Unification Church. Indeed, one legislator said on the record that the law was not intended to affect the Catholic Church. The UC sued to have the law set aside, and won at trial court level, the intermediate Appeal Court level, and eventually in the US Supreme Court, but only on a five to four vote (*Larsen vs. Valente*, 1982). A minority dissenting opinion penned by Chief Justice Rehnquist raised a question about whether the UC even had standing as a church to bring suit to have the law declared unconstitutional. Although the UC won, it did so barely, and was not pleased to have the Chief Justice of the Court write a dissenting opinion that raised the issue of whether it was a "real religion".

There are several other broad but very important issues in the interaction of law and religion, and in the use of the legal system in social control efforts extended toward minority religions. One concerns who has standing to take legal action against minority faiths; another concerns admissibility of evidence in matters dealing with smaller unpopular faiths. A third important issue concerns the general approach taken toward religion and religious groups within a society. Some societies assume that religion is just another matter to be managed by the state in a "consumer protection", paternalistic mode, while other societies emphasize religious freedom and take a more hands-off posture as far as religion is concerned. Each of these issues will be discussed in turn.

In the United States and many other modern legal systems, a private person or entity cannot sue another person or entity in civil court unless an injury to the plaintiff can be clearly demonstrated. Therefore, religious groups are generally protected from civil actions being filed against them by detractors. In order to sue for damages of any sort, there has to be a legal nexus between the group and the person suing. This would exist if a member or former member wanted to sue for some reason, but the usual rule on legal standing would not allow just anyone to file a legal action. In recent times some nations have allowed such suits on the grounds that doing so furthers the public good. Thus in Russia and in France, for example, people or groups not directly associated with an unpopular religious group are allowed to bring a law suit for damages against a religious group. Also, in these two societies and some others, some private organizations opposed to a religious group or groups may be partially funded by the state. Legal actions which these private plaintiffs take may then be taken over by state authorities and promoted as state policy, as well. Obviously, such an approach to the issue of legal standing and collusion with the state can place minority faiths in considerable jeopardy.

Decisions that courts make on admissibility (or inadmissibility) of evidence can also jeopardize smaller and more vulnerable religious groups. Courts in modern societies often have considerable autonomy, which allows them to exercise discretion on key decisions in this more autonomous circumstance. In turn, that discretion can be used to discriminate against popular groups, as the court exercises its *normative role* in society (Richardson 2000; 2001). A well-known demonstration of the operation of autonomy and discretion to discriminate against minority religions concerns the acceptance for years in the USA, and continuing elsewhere, of claims that those who participated in new religions were "brainwashed" and under "mind control". The scientific basis for this claim is very weak, and should not pass muster on any reasonable application of judicial rules of evidence (Anthony 1990; Richardson 1991; Ginsburg and Richardson 1996). However, such claims were accepted for decades by judges in the USA, and were allowed to be heard by juries, which sometimes acted in very punitive ways toward representatives of minority faiths. Such claims have also served as the basis of governmental action and new statutes in other nations, with France being perhaps the best example (Richardson and Introvigne 2001; Duvert 2004; Richardson 1996*a*), where "mental manipulation" was made a crime in France in 2001.

It is perhaps worth saying that in societies with less autonomous judicial systems, use of the legal system to control unwanted religious groups by whatever institutions are dominant can occur without the operation of judicial discretion. For instance, in Russia, the judicial system lacks autonomy, and is quite dependent on the government for support and even its very existence. The nationalistic government, working in conjunction with the Russia Orthodox Church, has made it very difficult for minority religions to obtain a fair hearing in recent years (Shterin and Richardson 2002). Similarly, Islamic states where there may be strong tendencies toward a theocratic form of government may take direct action against other religions, and do so with impunity because the legal system is dominated by those who share the preferred faith, or who serve at the sufferance of those in power.

A third distinction important for understanding the relationship between law and religion involves the general attitude or stance taken toward religion within society. Some societies are extremely paternalistic, and think the state should have total control of the religious life and even beliefs of citizens. Theocratic states exemplify this type of situation. Such states may by law preclude the operation of other religions within the nation, and make practicing other faiths a criminal offense with harsh penalties. Iran's treatment of the Baha'i is a case in point, as is China's treatment of the Falun Gong. At the other end of the spectrum are states that value individual religious freedom and have legal structures to promote that value, and therefore protect minority faiths, at least to some important degree. The United States fits this category reasonably well, with it religious freedom clause in the US Constitution; but so do some other nations such as Australia which function without a Bill of Rights. These nations recognize the pluralism that exists within their societies and attempt to deal with it in an open manner.

In the middle of this continuum are many nations that define religion as important, but something to be managed, just as any other area of life. This paternalism may derive from historical sources involving severe religious conflicts in the past, as is the case with many European countries, but also other nations such as in Latin and South America. Such nations may have high-level ministries dealing with religion, with authority to determine what is and is not an acceptable faith. These ministries may establish and enforce the hierarchies of religious groups discussed above, and the bureaucracies that develop around this function can be very controlling on occasion, with tendencies to abuse their bureaucratic discretion. If such is the case, the nation will tend toward the controlling end of the spectrum. If more flexibility is allowed in the management of religion, that nation will occupy a place closer to the end where individual religious freedom is valued.

One last area deserving attention in any discussion of social control of religious groups concerns children. Most religious groups involve children, some of them many, as it is a rare religion that does not sanction having children. (The Shakers in early American history come to mind with their abhorrence of sex, but also in more recent times the followers of the Bhagwan Shree Rajneesh were discouraged from having children.) When children are involved, many modern states define those children to varying degrees as wards of the state. Parental authority can be overruled by the state under considerations that are defined in law. Child abuse, especially child sex abuse, is not tolerated in most modern societies, and someone who is willing to claim that abuse of children is taking place in a religious group can cause serious problems for the group (Palmer and Hardman 1999; Richardson

1999*b*). "Best interests of the child" operates to justify intervention, and indeed trumps nearly all laws and constitutional provisions in many societies in today's world (Wah 2001). Assertions of religious freedom concerning how children are to be raised fall by the wayside if someone makes a credible claim that children are being abused within a group. And the abuse claim can be based on anything from sex abuse to material deprivation or home schooling (Richardson 1999*b*). Making a credible claim is made easier if the group is unpopular or relatively unknown, and different from the dominant faith in the society. Even dominant religious groups within a society may find themselves in this circumstance, although it may take much longer, as evidenced by how the Catholic Church scandal concerning child sex abuse by priests has been dealt with in a number of societies.

Conclusion

The interaction of law and religion has been examined from two major perspectives, the first focusing on the impact that religion has had on legal systems, and how religious groups, especially dominant ones, can make use of legal systems, and even help in the construction of them. The other major perspective focuses on how law and legal systems can be used to exert control over religions and religious practitioners. The thrust of this latter section was on control of minority faiths, but even dominant faiths must work within legal systems and sometimes feel the effects of efforts at social control quite directly. Throughout this discussion the interactive nature of the complex relationship between religion and law was stressed, something that has often been overlooked within the Sociology of Religion. It is hoped that this discussion will contribute to the integration of studies of law and religion, and to a more realistic approach to studies of religion in modern societies, most of which have legal systems that play dominant roles, affecting many areas of life, including the religious experiences of citizens and the role that religion and religious groups can play in the public life of society.

References

Al-Azmeh, Aziz (1988). *Islamic Law: Social and Historical Contexts.* London: Routledge.

Anthony, Dick (1990). "Religious Movements and Brainwashing Litigation: Evaluating Key Testimony". In T. Robbins and D. Anthony (eds.), *In Gods We Trust.* New Brunswick, NJ: Transaction Books, 295–344.

Beckford, James (1985). *Cult Controversies.* London: Tavistock.

BERGER, PETER (1967). *The Sacred Canopy.* New York: Doubleday.

BLACK, DONALD (1976). *The Behavior of Law.* New York: Academic Press.

—— (ed.) (1999). *The Social Structure of Right and Wrong.* New York: Academic Press.

—— and BAUMGARTNER, M. P. (1999). "Toward a Theory of the Third Party". In Black (1999), 95–124.

BROMLEY, DAVID, and BRESCHEL, BRUCE (1992). "General Population and Institutional Elite Perceptions of Cults: Evidence from National Survey Data". *Behavioral Sciences and the Law,* 10: 39–52.

CHAMBLISS, WILLIAM, and ZATZ, MARJORIE (1993). *Making Law: The State, the Law, and Structural Contradictions.* Bloomington, Ind.: Indiana University Press.

COTE, PAULINE, and RICHARDSON, JAMES T. (2001). "Disciplined Litigation, Vigilante Litigation, and Deformation: Dramatic Organization Change in Jehovah's Witnesses". *Journal for the Scientific Study of Religion,* 40: 11–26.

DAVIS, DEREK (2001). "President Bush's Office of Faith-Based and Community Initiatives: Boon or Boondoggle?" *Journal of Church and State,* 43: 411–22.

DEWITT, JOHN, RICHARDSON, JAMES, and WARNER, LYLE (1997). "Novel Scientific Evidence and Controversial Cases: A Social-Psychological Analysis". *Law & Psychology Review,* 21: 1–27.

DURHAM, COLE (2000). "The Emerging Legal Environment Faced by Smaller Religious Communities in Central and Eastern Europe". Paper presented at CESNUR/INFORM Conference, London.

DURKHEIM, ÉMILE (1964[1912]). *The Elementary Forms of Religious Life,* trans. J.W. Swain. New York: Macmillan.

DUVERT, CRYILLE (2004). "Anti-Cultism in the French Parliament: Desperate Last Stand or an Opportune Leap Forward? A Critical Analysis of the 12 June 2001 Act". In Richardson (2004), 41–52.

GIBB, H. A. R., and KRAMERS, J. H. (eds.) (1974). "Shari'a". In *Shorter Encyclopedia of Islam.* Leiden: E.J. Brill, 524–9).

GINSBURG, GERALD, and RICHARDSON, JAMES (1996). " 'Brainwashing' Evidence in Light of *Daubert*". In H. Reece (ed.), *Law and Science.* Oxford: Oxford University Press, 265–88.

HANKS, REUEL R. (2004). "Religion and Law in Uzbekistan: Renaissance and Repression in an Authoritarian Context". In Richardson (2004), 319–32.

KOSCIANSKA, AGNIESZKA (2004). "Anti-Cult Movements and Government Reports on 'Sects and Cults': The Case of Poland." In Richardson (2004), 267–78.

LEONE, MARK (1979). *Roots of Modern Mormonism.* Cambridge, Mass.: Harvard University Press.

PALMER, SUSAN, and HARDMAN, CHARLOTTE (eds.) (1999). *Children in New Religions.* New Brunswick, NJ: Rutgers University Press.

PFEIFFER, JEFFREY (1999). "Perceptual Bias and Mock Jury Decision Making: Minority Religions in Court". *Social Justice Research,* 12: 409–20.

RICHARDSON, JAMES T. (1984). "The 'Old Right' in Action: Mormon and Catholic Involvement in an Equal Rights Amendment Referendum". In D. Bromley and A. Shupe (eds.), *New Christian Politics.* Macon, Ga.: Mercer University Press, 213–34.

—— (1991). "Cult/Brainwashing Cases and the Freedom of Religion". *Journal of Church and State,* 33: 55–74.

—— (1992). "Public Opinion and the Tax Evasion Trial of Reverend Moon". *Behavioral Sciences and the Law,* 10: 53–63.

RICHARDSON, JAMES T. (1995*a*). "Minority Religions, Religious Freedom, and the New Pan-European Political and Judicial Institutions". *Journal of Church and State*, 37: 39–60.

—— (1995*b*). "New Religions and Religious Freedom in Eastern and Central Europe: A Sociological Analysis". In I. Borowik and G. Babinski (eds.), *New Religious Phenomena in Central and Eastern Europe*. Krakow: Nomos, 257–82.

—— (1996*a*). "'Brainwashing' Claims and Minority Religions Outside the United States: Cultural Diffusion of a Questionable Legal Concept in the Legal Arena". *Brigham Young University Law Review*, 1996: 873–904.

—— (1996*b*). "Sociology and New Religions: 'Brainwashing,' the Courts and Religious Freedom". In P. Jenkins and S. Kroll-Smith (eds.), *Witnessing for Sociology: Sociologists in Court*. Westport, Conn.: Praeger, 115–34.

—— (1998). "Law and Minority Religions: 'Positive' and 'Negative' Uses of the Legal System". *Nova Religio*, 2: 93–107.

—— (1999*a*). "The Religious Freedom Restoration Act: A Short-Lived Experiment in Religious Freedom". In D. Guinn, C. Barrigar, and K. Young (eds.), *Religion and Law in the Global Village*. Atlanta, Ga.: Scholars Press, 143–64.

—— (1999*b*). "Social Control of New Religions: From 'Brainwashing' Claims to Child Sex Abuse Accusations". In Palmer and Hardman (1999), 172–86.

—— (2000). "Discretion and Discrimination in Legal Cases: Controversial Religious Groups and Allegations of Ritual Abuse". In Rex Ahdar (ed.), *Law and Religion*. Aldershot: Ashgate, 111–32.

—— (2001). "Law, Social Control, and Minority Religions". In Pauline Cote (ed.), *Frontier Religions in Public Space*. Ottawa: University of Ottawa Press, 139–68.

—— (ed.) (2004). *Regulating Religion: Case Studies from around the Globe*. New York: Kluwer.

—— (2005). "Law". In Helen Ebaugh (ed.), *Sociology of Religion and Social Institutions*. New York: Kluwer, 221–34.

—— (2006). "The Sociology of Religious Freedom: A Structural and Socio-Legal Analysis". *Sociology of Religion*, 67: 271–94.

—— and DEWITT, JOHN (1992). "Christian Science Spiritual Healing, the Law, and Public Opinion". *Journal of Church and State*, 34/3: 549–62.

—— and EDELMAN, BRYAN (2004). "Cult Controversies and Legal Developments Concerning New Religions in Japan and China". In Richardson (2004), 359–80.

—— and GARAY, ALAIN (2004). "The European Court of Human Rights and Former Communist States". In I. Borowik (ed.), *Religion and Patterns of Social Transformation*, Krakow: Nomos, 223–34.

—— and INTROVIGNE, MASSIMO (2001). "'Brainwashing' Theories in European Parliamentary and Administrative Reports on 'Cults and Sects'". *Journal for the Scientific Study of Religion*, 40: 143–68.

—— CHAMBERLAIN, JARED, and SHOEMAKER, JENNIFER (2006). "The Future of RFRA: State and Federal Efforts to Promote Religious Freedom in the Wake of *Boerne*". Paper presented at Annual Meeting of the Society for the Scientific Study of Religion, Portland, Oregon.

SCHANDA, BALAZS (2004). "Freedom of Religion and Religious Minorities in Hungary". In Richardson (2004), 279–94.

SHTERIN, MARAT, and RICHARDSON, JAMES (1998). "Local Laws on Religion in Russia: Precursors of Russia's National Law". *Journal of Church and State*, 40: 319–41.

—— —— (2000). "Effects of the Western Anti-Cult Movement on Development of Laws Concerning Religion in Russia". *Journal of Church and State*, 42: 237–46.

—— —— (2002). "The *Yakunin v. Dworkin* Trial and the Emerging Religious Pluralism in Russia". *Religion in Eastern Europe*, 22: 1–38.

WAH, CAROLYN (2001). "Jehovah's Witnesses and Child Custody Cases in the United States 1996–1998". *Review of Religious Research*, 42: 372–86.

WEBER, MAX (1952[1921]). *Ancient Judaism*. New York: Free Press.

—— (1958[1905]). *The Protestant Ethic and the Spirit of Capitalism*, trans. Talcott Parsons. New York: Scribner.

SUGGESTED READING

AHDAR, REX (ed.) (2000). *Law and Religion*. Aldershot: Ashgate.

COTE, PAULINE, and GUNN, JEREMY (eds.) (2006). *The New Religious Question: State Regulation or State Interference?* New York: Peter Lang.

EDGE, PETER (2006). *Religion and Law: An Introduction*. Aldershot: Ashgate.

FETZER, JOEL, and SOPER, CHRISTOPHER (2005). *Muslims and the State in Britain, France, and Germany*. New York: Cambridge University Press.

MADELEY, JOHN T. S., and ENYEDI, ZSOLT (eds.) (2003). *Church and State in Contemporary Europe*. London: Frank Cass.

SAJO, ANDRAS, and AVINERI, SHLOMO (eds.) (1999). *The Law and Religious Identity: Models for Post-Communism*. The Hague: Kluwer.

Also Richardson (2004).

CHAPTER 24

THE SOCIO-CULTURAL AND SOCIO-RELIGIOUS ORIGINS OF HUMAN RIGHTS

ENZO PACE

THE theme of human rights may be considered, to all intents and purposes, a cultural product of modernity. In the specialist literature, which ranges from philosophy to human sciences and from international law to the science of politics and international relations, there is general agreement on the origins of the theme itself. Scholars of these various disciplines believe that there are three main spheres to bear in mind when defining human rights. The first—also in chronological order—is the sphere of *philosophy*; the second that of *politics*, and the third that of *religion*. Enlightenment philosophers such as John Locke, Samuel Pufendorf, Charles de Montesquieu, Jean Jacques Rousseau, and Immanuel Kant were, in fact, the first to reflect on human rights, in the sense of connatural rights of the individual. No political or state authority could damage such rights, since they were deemed the expression of timeless, universal, and innate values belonging to each and every human being, regardless of race, creed, and political orientation (Dufour 1991). From the Enlightenment on, the theme developed to include other disciplines, gravitating more or less around the fields of juridical studies or the science of politics and international relations. This expansion was due to historical and political reasons which are not difficult to understand.

The political origins—and this is the second sphere mentioned above—of human rights is, in fact, linked to the Glorious Revolution in the United Kingdom in 1688 and to the formation of a new nation, the United States of America in 1776 (Declaration of Independence). According to the historical reconstruction proposed by Waldron (1987), at the outset, human rights were nothing but the moral and political flag hoisted by the colonialists of New England against the mother country. They were, therefore, the rights of a minority which felt oppressed fiscally and politically by an authority seen as alien to the economic, productive, and cultural interests of a particular social group.

Similar considerations could be applied to the political origins of the French Revolution. The human rights of which the intellectuals and revolutionaries spoke coincided with the interests and expectations of a new emerging social class, the bourgeoisie, or the third estate. This contingency link between human rights and historically determined political action casts severe doubt over their claim to be universal. This claim was supported by the liberal philosophical thought of the eighteenth century, when the foundations of human rights were traced back to human *nature*, in an inalienable nucleus of values which belong to all human beings in every epoch, regardless of the historical situation. In this connection, it is interesting to note that thinkers of the calibre of Marx, Burke, and Bentham were wont to criticize the claim that human rights are universal, starting from an assessment of the historical situation in England at the time of the Glorious Revolution or, later, the French and American revolutions. Marx, for example, went as far as to state that those who appealed to human rights did so not in the name of universal values, but rather to safeguard their own particular rights, whether of a minority or a social group. Thus, it is a case of particular interest wearing the solemn vestments of the universal, and human rights are nothing more than the ideological cover for the right to egoism (Mendus 1999).

In actual fact, Marx says something a little more complex than this, especially when he tackles the theme of human rights in his celebrated essay *On the Jewish Question* (1844). In this youthful work, Marx approaches the matter through the concept of *emancipation*, in relation to the request advanced by German Jews to have full citizenship recognized. In the opening pages of the essay, he writes:

> The German Jews desire emancipation. What kind of emancipation do they desire? *Civic, political emancipation.* Bruno Bauer replies to them: no one in Germany is politically emancipated. We ourselves are not free. How are we to free you? You Jews are *egoists* if you demand a special emancipation for yourselves as Jews. As German, you have to work for the political emancipation of Germany, and as *human beings*, for the emancipation of mankind, and you should feel the particular kind of your oppression and your shame not as an exception to the rule, but on the contrary as a confirmation of the rule. (Marx 2000[1844]: 5)

Bauer noted that this request by the Jews was a contradiction, since it was addressed to a Christian state, where Christianity was the state religion. In what name, Bauer wondered, do the Jews claim for themselves full human rights and citizenship? In the name of their religion and on the strength of a particular point of view which is in open conflict with the official religion of state? The problem, continues Marx, is not confined to the status of a particular religious minority, but concerns the emancipation of all human beings oppressed by forms of economic and political domination (capitalism and the state). He therefore has no difficulty in saying that:

The most rigid form of opposition between the Jew and Christian is the *religious opposition*. How is an opposition resolved? By making it impossible. How is religious opposition made impossible? By *abolishing religion*. As soon as Jew and Christian recognize that their respective religions are no more than *different stages in the development of the human mind*, different snake skins cast off by *history*, and that man is the snake who sloughed them, the relation of Jew and Christian is no longer religious but is only a critical, *scientific*, and human relation. (Marx 2000[1844]: 9)

Marx concludes his argument by showing that one cannot create political emancipation without its being at the same time human emancipation. Even when the state becomes a *free state*, man is not necessarily a *free man* (Marx 2000 [1844]: 10). What Marx finds unconvincing is the foundation of human rights as natural and universal rights, since in this way the individual (the *real man* of whom Marx speaks in the last lines of his essay) with his living world is still considered an abstraction, an *independent egoist* in that he is a member of a civil society and the holder of public rights in a general sense, in that he is part of the political community. On the other hand, as part of civil society he must be considered a concrete individual, whereas as a member of the political community he is an abstract man. The gap between *man and citizen* cannot be bridged even in liberal states. According to Marx, it will come about only when the former—once fully emancipated—is capable of personally and directly controlling that which takes place in the political sphere as his own social force. He will thus avoid the fiction of being considered a citizen while having no effective power, the formally recognized holder of fundamental rights without any real chance to assert them due to his real human condition. The fact that Marx was not prejudicially hostile to the theme of human rights is also demonstrated by his reference at the end of his essay to a passage from *On The Social Contract*, in which Jean Jacques Rousseau wrote:

Celui qui ose entreprendre d'instituer un peuple doit se sentir en état de changer pour ainsi dire la *nature humaine* de *transformer* chaque individu, qui par lui-même est un tout parfait et solitarie, en partie d'un plus grand tout dont cet individu reçoive en quelque sorte sa vie et son être, de substituer une *existence partielle et morale* à l'existence physique et indépendante. Il faut qu'il ôte à *l'homme ses forces propres* pour lui donner qui lui soient étrangères et dont il ne puisse faire usage sans le secour d'autrui. (Rousseau 2003[1762]: 67)

[Whoever dares undertake to establish a people's institutions must feel himself capable of changing, as it were, *human nature*, of *transforming* each individual, who by himself is a complete and solitary whole, into a part of a larger whole, from which, in a sense, the individual receives his life and his being, of substituting a *limited and mental existence* for the physical and independent existence. He has to take from *man his own powers*, and give him in exchange alien powers which he cannot employ without the help of other men.]

The achievement of the full rights of man coincides for Marx with the idea of the liberation of every human being from every form of subjection and limitation, including religion.

This stance is in sharp contrast with that of those scholars who see in religion the genesis of the rights of man: the third source of human rights, according to our order of explanation. This is the thesis put forward as long ago as 1895 by Jellinek (born in Leipzig in 1851, died in Heidelberg in 1911), a positivist scholar of the theory of the state and author in that year of the work entitled significantly *Die Erklärung der Menschen- und Bürgerrechte* (*The Declaration of the Rights of Man and Citizens*) (Jellinek 1901). In this work, Jellinek theorizes that the first universal declaration of the rights of man was made during the American Revolution, and that it formed the matrix for that of the French Revolution, which owed little in fact to the influence of Rousseau. Consequently, the cultural origins of the declaration are religious in nature. This thesis was taken up not only by jurists and philosophers of law, but also among German sociologists of the same period, such as Ernst Troeltsch and Max Weber.

Ernst Troeltsch, writing on the occasion of Jellinek's death, attributed to him the merit of having linked the origins of the paradigm of human rights to Protestant sects (in particular, Baptists and Quakers, and, in part, other Calvinist formations) (Troeltsch 2002[1923]). Max Weber, on the other hand, though directly interested in the matter of human rights, on several occasions acknowledged his debt to Jellinek in the formulation of his fundamental thesis contained in the work *The Protestant Ethic and the Spirit of Capitalism.* In other words, as Joas (2006) has recently reminded us, within twentieth-century German thought there developed in the sociological and juridical domain a school of thought which traced its origins to Jellinek, who explicitly reflected on the religious origins, Judeo-Christian to be precise, of human rights in open polemic with the anti-religious view (or rather, the stance which opposed the temporal power of the Catholic Church) of the origins of human rights. According to this view, attention is mainly focused on the intellectual climate of the Enlightenment in preparing the Declaration of the Rights of Man drafted by the French revolutionaries.

The debate on the origins of human rights shows us how they came to be the object of sociological enquiry, in particular for the sociology of religion. There are at least two good reasons to support this statement.

First, when we speak of human rights, we are in fact investigating one of the sharpest contradictions in modern society. On the one hand, modern society exalts the primacy and inviolability of individual freedom, and on the other, it expects individuals to recognize and respect the existence of a universal ethical and juridical principle. It is the tension that is part and parcel of modernization, which Touraine (1997) has recently examined, between the pressure to rationalize, which tends to make us all feel equal, and the will to assert our individuality, also expressed as the cultural differences of the group or community of which one feels a part. As can be seen, we come close to the contemporary debate between liberalism and community in so-called multicultural or multi-ethnic societies (Kymlicka 1991). In sociological terms, when we speak of human rights, we ask if something exists at a level higher than particular interests, which can keep individuals together so that they feel they form *society.* To put it another way, we could ask: how is the social order possible without a collective consciousness that makes people believe in the existence of norms that are superior to the will of the individual (Luhmann 2002)? Ultimately, this is what Durkheim, one of the fathers of sociology, was pondering when he thought that he had found the social function of the sacred. The social norms that we ourselves create become in the end something like Olympian gods for us, with lives of their own, independent of our will. This means that every society as such (regardless of the individuals that form it) needs to believe in the existence of a nucleus of values and norms that are shared and universal, a kind of generative grammar of society itself that speaks not the language of utility but that of ethics (Pace 1996; Rosati 2002). The theme of human rights, therefore, becomes—and this is primarily why it is of interest to sociologists of religion—a subject for sociological study because it returns to the question of the relationship between ethics and society, and, to keep faith with the teachings of Durkheim, the relationship between the sacred and society.

The second reason that links the theme of human rights to sociology and the sociology of religion is consequential: human rights may constitute a powerful indicator of a type of conflict which is recurrent in the history of human society and which we can classify as a conflict of values, in that it is not directly linked to interests or the utilitarian dimension of human life, but rather concern acts of *divine will.*

The American Puritans did not expect the state to guarantee their freedom of belief, but rather that the state would not interfere with the plan that God had assigned to them for the creation of a holy community, the kingdom of heaven on earth. This necessarily led them to desire a "light" state, which was not only neutral toward institutional religions (the various confessions that may exist in a pluralist society), but rather respectful of the principle of moral self-determination which each individual requires to achieve higher goals (Viola 1999). When such goals have as their ultimate source the system of religious belief, we understand why the question of human rights is of such interest to religious sociologists; it reveals the internal and external conflicts in the religious field itself: internal conflicts concern the cyclical controversies over defining the genuine message of a particular religion, whereas external conflicts are between religion and other spheres of social life, such as politics, science, the family ethics, bio-ethics, and so on.

We will first analyse the types of socio-religious conflicts that may be traced back to questions of human rights, and then go on to review briefly the main tensions in the great world religions connected to the theme of human rights.

The Law of God and the Laws of Man

The question of human rights arises when a religion presents itself as an all-round system of belief: that is, one which aims at tracing a universal road to salvation, or nirvana (or *moksha*), and at the same time at laying down the principles which are to be the foundation of the social order. In the language of monotheistic religions of Semitic stock, this corresponds to the idea of the law of God, which covers all aspects of human life, be they interior, social, moral, juridical, or political. Law means a higher order laid down by God that human beings cannot disregard, even minimally, unless they wish to run the risk of disobeying his will. This applies, for example, both to Judaism and to Islam—less so to Christianity, since the original message of Jesus of Nazareth, though not starting from open criticism of Judaic law (which he said he wished to observe in spirit), shifts the symbolic confines of the previous rabbinical tradition: thus, it is right to observe the Sabbath (a fundamental precept in Jewish doctrine), but the Sabbath is made for man, not man for the Sabbath. By this phrase, Jesus, a Jew by birth and upbringing, did not intend to demolish the principle of the Law, but to show that the formal observance of precepts is not enough to obey the supreme precept of love. Therefore, if a precept leads to the oppression of man, or is an indirect cause of injustice toward the other who suffers and is in need, it may be overcome by a higher illumination, coming from the commandment to love one's neighbour as one loves oneself, to the extent of loving one's enemy (Flusser 1968).

Judaism, Islam, and, to some extent, the Hindu system of belief are characterized more than other religions by the idea that there exists an immutable, eternal law, dictated by God or preserved in the cosmic order (the dharma for the Hindus is in fact synonymous with law), and that human beings are called upon to obey this law (either because it is revealed directly by God to human beings through the prophets or because it is preserved in the holy scriptures that the first prophets compiled, the Veda for Hindus). This concept has consequences for what sociologists of religion call the type of social action aimed at values. The problems which arise from this are as follows:

a. How is belief in the existence of the law formed? What are the social and historical processes which contribute to forming a corpus of juridical, moral, and social norms, created by human beings and elevated to an eternal and immutable code at some point in the evolution of a system of religious belief?
b. What is the relationship between those who have the authority to preserve and proclaim the content of the law and those who are called upon trustingly to submit to the former and consequently to obey?
c. And finally, what happens when the tension between the freedom to believe, on the one hand, and submission to the principle of obeying the religious authority, the custodian and ultimate interpreter of the law and the cosmic order, on the other, reaches breaking point, when groups and movements of believers dissent in the name of universal human rights?

The first question (a) concerns the complex relationship between the words of a prophet that have inspired a new religious belief and the process of sorting out what these words have announced, a task usually undertaken by his disciples. The passage from the living word of the prophet-founder of a religion to the writing down of what is later regarded as holy scripture is a process which can be measured both by the passing of time and by the difficulties encountered by the community of disciples when they attempt to agree on what the founder-prophet really said and what should be handed down (the tradition). This process is of interest to sociologists of religion as well as historians, because the comparative study of religions shows that the construction of a system of dogmas, norms, and precepts is often the result of complex negotiations, punctuated with conflicts, between various points of view formed within a religious community. The law therefore presents itself as the insuperable boundary, the decisive symbolic border, to define not only the religious identity but also the social one of all those who recognize themselves in a given religious message.

The second question (b) concerns the power relations which are set up in a religion between those who have the authority to control the symbolic borders established by the law (and consequently to mark the border between orthodoxy and heresy) and those who do not. We are dealing here with the division of religious labour between clerics and laymen which is found in many of the great religions: in one part of Christianity (in particular, in the Catholic Church and in the Orthodox Church), in part of Islam (for example, in the Shi'ah), as well as in classical Hinduism, where there is a distinction between the *Brahman* and the lower castes.

Against this background, the third question (c) takes on more obviously sociological aspects. To illustrate them better, I will take an example which concerns the Muslim world, but which, as we shall see, is by no means confined to it.

The Law of God and the Laws of Man: The Case of Islam

When we examine the documents on human rights which were drafted in the Muslim world in the last twenty years of the twentieth century, we get a glimpse of the chief obstacle which seems to prevent a complete and total adhesion by Islam to the modern culture of human rights (Borrmans 1993; Caspar 1983; Redissi 2000; Sahlieh 1994). It is worth mentioning that many so called Muslim countries, including Afghanistan and Iran, were signatories to the UN Declaration of Human Rights (UDHR) in 1948. Only Saudi Arabia abstained from voting. In spite of formal adhesion to the UDHR, some predominantly Muslim countries, like Sudan, Pakistan, and Iran, along with Saudi Arabia, started to criticize the UDHR for its failure to take into account the cultural and religious context of non-Western countries. In 1981 the Iranian representative to the UN, for instance, stressed that the declaration was shaped by the Judeo-Christian approach, and therefore it could not be implemented by Muslims because it doesn't reflect Islamic law. We can understand the context in which both Iran (after the revolution led by Khomeini) and Saudi Arabia promoted the redaction of the Cairo Declaration.

The Cairo Declaration of 1990 is still the most recent and articulate charter of rights issued by countries with a Muslim tradition, grouped together in the organization of the World Islamic Conference. It contains two articles (24 and 25) which leave us in no doubt that if human rights are in conflict with Qur'anic law (*Shari'ah*), the latter prevails. It is a reference to a sort of *Grundnorm* (fundamental and absolute norm) held not to be human, but revealed directly by God. In other words, human rights (*huqûq al-insân*) have no independent foundation, in contrast to the rights of God (*huqûq Allah*). The main reason for this is that, according to Muslim theology, every human being is born with a natural disposition to Islam and to believing in the one God. But the Muslim world has most difficulty over the freedom to change religion. In particular, the possibility of abandoning one's religion of birth (Islam) is not considered a human right, but an abominable evil, listed as an indictable offence. Because those who leave the religion also leave the community of the faithful (*Ummah*), they place themselves against the social and political order that has its meaning and foundation in shared membership of the faith. Therefore, abandoning the faith is, at the same time, both a rejection of divine truth and an act of insubordination toward the powers that be, as was the case with Christianity in medieval Europe, which explains why Thomas Aquinas supported the death penalty for heresy.

The case of apostasy, therefore, together with others, constitutes a good observation point from which to view the difficulties of the Muslim world in fully accepting human rights. However, in many Muslim countries with greater exposure to the free circulation of people and ideas, attention to the theme of human rights has grown, and, until the arrival of the new wave of radical movements, leagues and associations for the defence of human rights had sprung up in countries such as Tunisia, Egypt, Morocco, and Algeria. While civil society still enjoyed a certain freedom in those countries, it was possible to discuss the safeguarding of the fundamental rights of the individual and how to defend human rights violated by political power. The thinking of some Muslims on these issues offers the possibility of accommodating universal human rights to God's law: for example, Khaled Abou el Fadl writes: "the fact that the rights of people take precedence over the rights of God on this earth necessarily means that a claimed right of God may not be used to violate the rights of human beings" (2004: 27–8).

The Declaration of Cairo of 1990, signed by the foreign ministers of the member states of the organization of the Islamic Conference, may therefore be interpreted as a sign of twofold recognition: on the one hand, of the moral authority of the United Nations and, on the other, of the claims of the social movements asserting and defending human rights in many Muslim countries. The declaration represents the endpoint of a long and tortuous journey. It took more than ten years to draft and was the result of much negotiation between the leaders of these member states, those who intransigently defended Qur'anic law (Shari'a) and those more open to a modernist interpretation of it.

Our use of the terms 'intransigently' and 'modernist' in this context refers to the relationship between Qur'anic law and the creation of positive law in modern post-colonial states in the Muslim environment. What distinguishes these two positions is the role assigned to Shari'a and recognized by the constitution in the hierarchy of the sources of law. It is one thing to declare that it is the only, fundamental source, but quite another to consider it one among many possible sources. For example, the recent change in the Egyptian Constitution shifts from the second position to the first. This is a regression to acceptance of the exclusive character of religious law after a long period of building an autonomous sphere dominated by the *Qanûn*, a legacy of the judicial and administrative culture of the Ottoman Empire, and the *Tanzimat* movement (of reforms) which eventually succeeded in secularizing the Turkish state in 1923. This explains why some of the most odious and embarrassing accusations of apostasy against intellectuals and advocates of women's rights have occurred in Egypt recently. Egyptian society, which is modern and open, has had to pay a very high price to limit the growth of Islamic movements, which are ideologically intransigent in wanting a return to the purity and integral nature of Qur'anic law (Babès and Oubrou 2002; Zayd 2000).

In many countries, an apparatus of positive law has grown up alongside norms founded on Shari'a. This has sometimes been accomplished with little publicity and great caution on the part of the governing class, and has enabled them to get around otherwise insuperable problems for running a country they intended to modernize. There are numerous examples of this, but here I will cite just one, to give an idea of the complex challenge that many ruling groups in Muslim countries have had to face, at times successfully. I refer to the norms which in the Muslim juridical and religious tradition are known as the norms of the personal statute derived from Qur'anic law (Mayer 1999).

Historically, the normative nucleus of Qur'anic law derives from a number of sources. According to the juridical school of Al-Shâfi'î (who died in Cairo in 204 AH /820 CE), one of the four main schools recognized by Sunni Muslims, they are the Qur'an, the words and deeds of the Prophet (*Hadith*), the consensus of the community (of the wise), and the rational work of interpretation. Apart from the Qur'an, which in fact contains a limited number of legal precepts (approximately 250 verses of a total of 6,000), the rest come from the mass of words and deeds reordered and tidied up according to the criteria of rigorous authenticity (the credit for this goes to two eleventh-century scholars who reduced the incredible mass of *Hadith* handed down—approximately 60,000!—to a more reasonable 2,000 deemed worthy) and the accumulation in time of consolidated case law. The norms of the personal statute emerged from rational interpretation in the light of the faith, by experts in religion (*'ulama*), jurists (*Fuqaha*), and judges of the courts (*Qadi*), with these experts in religious knowledge subordinate to the political power of the caliphs of the great Muslim empires of the past (Al-Jabri 1996; Laroui 1992; Mernissi 1990; Tozy 1999; Matvejevic´ 2005).

Having established this, let us now turn to the example of polygamy. In 1956 the then undisputed leader of independent Tunisia, Habib Bourghiba, abolished polygamy. Two reasons were given. One was based on his interpretation of the passage in the Qur'an (iv, 3) which mentions polygamy, while the other justifies the choice he made on more practical grounds. Dealing with the first reason, he demonstrates that in fact the Prophet exhorted men to marry only one wife if they are unable to treat them fairly when the number of wives increases to two, three, or a maximum of four. Bourghiba said that now that Tunisia was finally independent and needed to modernize and develop, it was no longer realistic to imagine that anybody is able to respect the Qur'anic precept of equal treatment of more than one wife. Therefore, it being impossible on economic grounds for a man to maintain four wives, the precept may be allowed to lapse. The effect of this historical decision was the start of the emancipation of women in Tunisia, with nothing like it in any other Muslim country. After the abolition of polygamy, the raising of the age of marriage and compulsory schooling for women did the rest. Today, the last obstacle to parity for men and women, at least as far as legislation is concerned (it takes much longer for it to filter through into everyday life), is to overcome the Qur'anic norm which gives women only half the inheritance granted to men.

The example I have cited gives some idea of the basic problem which underlies the relationship between Islam and human rights, and which concerns religious, social, juridical, and political aspects. The problem can be expressed in the following terms. The great difficulty that Islam has in fully accepting the paradigm of human rights, as consolidated by the United Nations, is a structural one, since it concerns the lack of a principle of legitimization of authority (Pace 2004). It may seem paradoxical, but the Islamic belief that the cycle of prophecy ended with Muhammad has unexpected consequences: after the Prophet, no one has the power to interpret the original revelation, at least in principle. At the same time, precisely because history continued after the death of Muhammad in 632, the work of interpretation was carried out for at least three centuries after his death: between the word revealed and the life of the community of believers a bridge was built, which consisted of the law. Between religion and politics (government and society) there stands the law. Without its impressive construction of juridical science, Islam would not have had the driving force to expand which so characterized it up to *c.*1250 CE. This means that a remarkable interpretative tradition exists, which has succeeded in connecting prophetic messages and the regulatory precepts of life in society. If this is so, why, then, does the Muslim world of today show so much resistance to the paradigm of human rights? Could not the door of interpretation be reopened, and reason, illuminated by the faith, be used to develop the humanistic part of the Qur'an and the tradition?

In the final analysis, we have to discover whether there exists a humanistic message in the Qur'an, and if so, why it was compressed by the harshness of Qur'anic law, and, finally, if it is possible, in the light of the debate within the contemporary Muslim world, to liberate the former from the encrustation imposed on it throughout history by political will. This possibility is today sustained by scholars such as Nasr Abû Zayd (1999) and Abdullahi Na'im (1990), as well as by enlightened spiritual leaders such as the Sudanese thinker Mahmoud Taha (1987) (condemned to death for his reformist ideas by the Nimeiri regime in 1985) or by various groups and movements of women engaged in politics, as well as social and academic activities, who for some time have been fighting for radical reform of Qur'anic law (WLUML 2003).

Human Rights and Religious Rights: Sociological Questions

As far as the Muslim world is concerned, the question of rights may be studied from a sociological viewpoint using the violations of, and claims to, rights as indicators and symptoms of social, religious, and political conflicts. A similar approach can also be used in relation to other religions. For example, study of the condition of women within Catholicism (one thinks of the controversy over allowing women into the priesthood, for instance) or in certain ultra-orthodox

Jewish communities may prove fruitful, analysing the types of socio-religious acts carried out by movements and groups that, in the name of fundamental human rights, fight for parity of treatment for women and men in the religious field at all levels. On the other hand, the patriarchal legacy, which is still important in many religions, prevents women from having equal opportunities in the performance of religious functions. From this point of view, a comparative study of the Protestant and Catholic worlds might be an interesting field of enquiry both for historians and sociologists (and not only sociologists of religion). The modern culture of rights has helped to change the conditions for women as regards access to priestly functions. Yet the links between religion and the negation of fundamental rights continue to exist in post-colonial countries where that culture spread only comparatively recently, despite the fact that even in these relatively new nation-states, formed from 1945 to 1960/70, there exist well-organized and active human rights groups and movements.

One example of persistent difficulty in overcoming various forms of gender discrimination, justified on religious grounds, is to be found in the Hindu religious system. It is still based on rigid stratification by caste (*Jati* in Sanskrit), which places individuals unequally on a social scale which has at its apex the *Brahman* and at its base those considered impure, and therefore untouchable, outcasts *par excellence* (the *Avarna* or *Dalit*: literally, those with no colour and oppressed). This system dates back to the second millennium BCE, when it was introduced by the Indo-Aryan invaders. It was later codified and handed down by a certain class of specialists in the sacred (*Brahman*), who, despite the abolition of castes after India gained independence in 1947, still continue to perpetuate the structure, especially in rural and suburban areas of the Indian subcontinent. In the mythology, castes are presented as the result of the dismemberment of the body of a divinity (a rigorously male divinity, thus ensuring that women could not possibly enjoy the same socio-religious status as men): each element corresponds to a caste, and therefore together the various parts correspond to a cosmic order, to a higher law (dharma), divine and immutable (Weber 1967[1917]; Dumont 1966; Singer and Cohn 1968; Bayly 1999; Dirks 2001). Since the religious code prohibits persons of different castes from marrying, mixed marriages have always been considered an affront to supreme divine law. Those who undertake mixed marriages are stigmatized as outcast, the worst situation for a person in Indian society from the social and religious point of view. To try to remedy the situation, the Indian parliament has raised the quota for university access reserved for young people from the lower castes, such as the *Śudra* (belonging to the fourth *Jati*) and the untouchables. Moreover, many of the latter convert to Christianity, which, compared to Hinduism, appears decidedly equalitarian and respectful of human dignity. The outcasts, who are known as *Dalits*, amount to 24 per cent of the Indian population (250 million people). They suffer social discrimination, have neither civil nor political rights, and perform occupations traditionally regarded as the basest, most impure, and degrading (tanners, latrine cleaners, dustmen, gravediggers, executioners, and the like). This remains unchanged, despite Article 17 of the Indian Constitution of 1950 which formally abolished the social position of untouchables. Not only has nothing changed, but those who have been relegated to the status of untouchables have ended up creating their own parallel religious world, with their own temples, rituals, shrines, and so on, thus confirming the socio-religious apartheid in which millions of people are entrapped (Human Rights Watch 1999; Webster 1999; Shah 2001). Likewise, from the strictly Hindu point of view, those who profess a different religious faith and follow other codes of conduct founded on other religions are still considered *barbarians* (*Mleccha* in Sanskrit), especially by politico-religious activists of the new fundamentalist type of Hinduism (Pace and Guolo 2002). This outlook makes relations very difficult between the majority religion (Hinduism) and minority religions, both those which have marked the history of India, such as Islam, and Christian religions which have enjoyed a certain amount of success in recent times.

In a country such as India, therefore, human rights are seen not only in juridical or political terms (i.e., the enforcement of the democratic principles established by the Indian Constitution thanks to Gandhi's and Nehru's efforts to modernize the country), but also from a socio-religious perspective. There are many socio-religious movements active in Indian society today, ranging from neo-Hindu fundamentalists to reformists, and from radical Muslims to groups of *Dalit* fighting for recognition of their fundamental rights, including the freedom to profess a faith other than Hinduism. They provide fertile terrain for an analysis by means of which sociologists of religion may attempt to understand the ongoing socio-religious conflicts, internal divisions in Hinduism itself, religious tensions reflected in politics, and, finally, the dynamic social function of the struggle for human rights, and how all this contributes to the ongoing cultural and social changes in contemporary India (Sen 2004).

Hinduism, like other religions, has developed specific juridical constructions. This applies also, for example, to Judaism, Islam, and the path of the Sikhs. The Catholic Church has its own law, canon law, which regulates the internal life of its *personnel* and the juridical relations of the sacrament of marriage. In present-day multicultural societies, the existence of so many religious laws poses problems of coexistence and recognition by the state (Ferrari 2002), whether the state is rigorously secular (as in the case of France) or willing to acknowledge the public function of churches and religious confessions. In any case, every year for the past few years, the sociology of religion has always had on its agenda a theme which has something to do with human rights. This is the request made by individual religious communities (Hindu, Muslim, Jewish, Sikh) to the public authorities to have their respective religious laws applied, instead of the norms of common public law (Menski 2003; Pearl and Menski 1998).

In sociological terms, the conflict arises when the possible application of a specific rule contained in the religious codes of one community or other is in open contrast not only to the norms of state law, but also to certain fundamental rights (freedom to believe or not to believe, the right to choose one's own partner, the defence of one's own psycho-sexual integrity, and so on). It is also interesting for sociologists of religion to analyse the conflicts which arise in this domain, since it may lead us to a greater understanding of the processes of change currently under way in Europe and generally in countries which are increasingly becoming multi-religious and multi-ethnic societies.

Conclusion

The human rights issue is an object of sociological enquiry, in particular for the sociology of religion, for at least two good reasons, particularly in those societies that are becoming multicultural and multi-religious.

First, when we speak of human rights, we are in fact investigating one of the sharpest contradictions in modern society. On the one hand, modern society exalts the primacy and inviolability of individual freedom, and, on the other, it expects individuals to recognize and respect the existence of a universal ethical and juridical principle. We come close to the contemporary debate between liberalism and community in so-called multicultural or multi-ethnic societies and to the management of the tensions between judging values to be shared by all citizens and the claim to be allowed to observe religious law by a singular community within the state. The same tension arises when in many contemporary societies there is a sharp confrontation between the state and the so-called sects. As Richardson notes (2006*a*; 2006*b*), all these questions could be studied both in sociology of religion and in sociology of law, because the relationship of pluralism to religious freedom concerns not only the socio-legal dimension of the issue, but also the construction of collective identity of a nation, or the social representation of the relation between majority and minorities in religious field (Luca 2004).

This means that every society as such (regardless of the individuals that form it) needs to believe in the existence of a nucleus of values and norms that are shared and universal. Human rights, therefore, become a subject for sociological study because it returns to the question of the relationship between ethics and society, and, to keep faith with the teachings of Durkheim, the relationship between the sacred and society.

The second link between human rights and sociology, and the sociology of religion, is consequential: human rights may constitute a powerful indicator of a type of conflict which is recurrent in the history of human society and which we can classify as a conflict of values, in that it is not directly linked to interests or the utilitarian dimension of human life, but rather concern acts of *divine will.*

References

Al-Jabri, Muhammad (1996). *La Ragione Araba.* Milan: Feltrinelli.

Babès, Leila, and Oubrou, Tariq (2002). *Loi d'Allah, Lois des Hommes.* Paris: Albin Michel.

Bayly, Susan (1999). *Caste, Society and Politics in India from the Eighteenth Century to the Modern Age.* Cambridge: Cambridge University Press.

Borrmans, Maurice (1993). *Islam e Cristianesimo.* Milan: Cinisello Balsamo, Edizioni Paoline.

Caspar, René (1983). 'Les Déclarations des droits de l'homme en Islam depuis dix ans'. *Islamochristiana*, 9: 59–78.

Dirks, Nicholas (2001). *Castes of Mind: Colonialism and the Making of Modern India.* Princeton: Princeton University Press.

Dufour, Alfred (1991). *Droits de l'homme, droit naturel et histoire.* Paris: P.U.F.

Dumont, Louis (1966). *Homo Hierarchicus.* Paris: Gallimard.

El Fadl, Khaled Abou (2004). *Islam and the Challenge of Democracy.* Princeton: Princeton University Press.

Ferrari, Silvio (2002). *Lo Spirito dei Diritti Religiosi: Ebraismo, Cristianesimo e Islam a Confronto.* Bologna: Il Mulino.

Flusser, David (1968). *Jesus.* Reinbeck: Rowohtl Taschenbuch Verlag.

Human Rights Watch (1999). *Broken People: Caste, Violence against India's Untouchables.* New York: Human Rights Watch.

Jellinek, Georg (1901). *The Declaration of the Rights of Man and of Citizens: A Contribution to Modern Constitutional History.* New York: Holt & Co.

Joas, Hans (2006). 'Max Weber and the Origin of Human Rights: A Study on Cultural Innovation'. In Institute for the International Integration Studies Discussion Papers Series, 145, Dublin, 1–22.

Kymlicka, Will (1991). *Liberalism, Community and Culture.* Oxford: Clarendon Press.

Laroui, Abdallah (1992). *Islam e Modernità.* Genua: Marietti.

Luca, Nathalie (2004). *Les Sectes.* Paris: P.U.F.

Luhmann, Niklas (2002). *I Diritti Fondamentali Come Istituzione.* Bari: Dedalo.

Marx, Karl (2000[1844]). *On the Jewish Question.* In *Selected Writings*, ed. David McLellan, 2nd edn. Oxford: Oxford University Press.

Matvejević, Predrag (2005). 'Islam, Laicità e Diritti Umani'. In M. Nordio and G. Vercellin (eds.), *Islam e Diritti Umani: Un (Falso?) Problema.* Reggio Emilia: Diabasis, 96–102.

Mayer, Elizabeth (1999). *Islam and Human Rights.* Boulder, Col.: Westview Press.

Mendus, Susan (1999). *The Politics of Toleration.* Edinburgh: Edinburgh University Press.

Menski, Werner (2003). *Hindu Law: Beyond Tradition and Modernity.* New Delhi: Oxford University Press.

Mernissi, Fatima (1990). *Le Sultane Dimenticate.* Genua: Marietti.

Na'im, Abdullahi (1990). *Toward an Islamic Reformation: Civil Liberties, Human Rights and International Law.* Syracuse, NY: Syracuse University Press.

Pace, Enzo (1996). 'Introduction'. In A. E. Durkheim, *Per una Definizione dei Fenomeni Religiosi.* Rome: Armando, 9–29.

—— (2004). *Sociologia dell'Islam.* Rome: Carocci.

—— and Guolo, Renzo (2002). *I Fondamentalismi.* Rome and Bari: Laterza.

PEARL, DAVID, and MENSKI, WERNER (1998). *Muslim Family Law*. London: Sweet and Maxwell.

REDISSI, HAMADI (2000). 'L'universalità alla Prova delle Culture: Le Dichiarazioni Islamiche dei Diritti dell'Uomo. In P. C. Bori, G. Gilberti, and G. Gozzi (eds.), *La Dichiarazione Universale dei Diritti dell'Uomo Cinquntanni dopo*. Bologna: Cleub, 108–23.

RICHARDSON, JAMES (2006*a*). 'Religion in Public Space: A Theoretical Perspective and Comparison of Russia, Japan, and United States'. *Religion Un, Staat Gesellschaft*, 1: 45–61.

—— (2006*b*). 'The Sociology of Religious Freedom: A Structural and Sociological Analysis'. *Sociology of Religion*, 67/3: 271–94.

ROSATI, MASSIMO (2002). *Solidarietà e Sacro*. Roma and Bari: Laterza.

ROUSSEAU, JEAN JACQUES (2003[1762]). *On the Social Contract*. New York: Dover-Thrift Editions.

SAHLIEH, SAMI ALDEEB ABU (1994). *Les Musulmans face aux droits de L'homme*. Bochum: Winkler.

SINGER, MILTON, and COHN, BERNARD (1968). *Structure and Change in India–Society*. Chicago: Aldine.

SEN, AMARTYA (2004). *La Democrazia degli Altri*. Milan: Mondadori.

SHAH, GHANSHYAM (ed.) (2001). *Dalit Identity and Politics*. New Delhi: Sage.

TAHA, MAHMOUD (1987). *The Second Message of Islam*. Syracuse, NY: Syracuse University Press.

TOURAINE, ALAIN (1997). *Pourrons-Nous Vivre Ensemble?* Paris: Fayard.

TOZY, MUHAMMAD (1999). *Monarchie et islam politique au Maroc*. Paris: Presses de Sciences-Po.

TROELTSCH, ERNST (2002[1923]). *Naturrecht and Humanität in der Weltpolitik*. In *Sehriften zür Politik and Kulturphilosophie (1918–1923)*, Kritische Gesamtausgabe, xv. Berlin, 493–512.

VIOLA, FRANCESCO (1999). *Identità e Comunità: Il Senso Morale della Politica*. Milan: Vita e Pensiero.

WALDRON, JEREMY (ed.) (1987). *Nonsense upon Stilts*. London: Methuen.

WEBER, MAX (1967[1917]). *The Religion of India: The Sociology of Hinduism and Buddhism*. New York: Free Press.

WEBSTER, JOHN (1999). *Religion and Dalit Liberation*. New Delhi: Manohar.

WLUML (Women Living Under Muslim Laws) (2003). *Knowing Our Rights: Women, Family, Laws and Customs in the Muslim World*. New Delhi: Zubaan.

ZAYD, NASR ABÛ(1999). *The Qur'ân: God and Man in Communication*. Leiden: University of Leiden Press.

—— (2000). *Critique du discourse religieux*. Arles: Actes Sud.

SUGGESTED READING

DE LOUBIER, PATRICK (1994). 'Sociology of Human Rights: Religious Forces and Human Rights Policy'. *Labour and Society*, 10: 97–104.

KEOWN, DAMIEN (1992). 'A Bibliography on Buddhism and Human Rights'. *Journal of Buddhist Ethics*, 2: 1–10.

Na'im, Abdullahi (2005). 'Human Rights and Scholarship for Social Change in Islamic Communities'. *Muslim World Journal of Human Rights*, 2/1: 15–26.

—— Jerald, Gort, and Hendrik, Jansen (eds.) (1994). *Human Rights and Religious Values.* Grand Rapids, Mich.: Eerdmans.

Pearce, Tola Olu (2005). 'Human Rights and Sociology: Some Observations from Africa'. *Social Problems*, 48/1: 48–56.

Senturk, Recep (2005). 'Sociology of Rights: I Am Therefore I Am Right: Human Rights in Islam between Universalistic and Communalistic Perspectives'. *Muslim World Journal of Human Rights*, 2/1: 13–24.

Sjoborg, Gideon, Gill, Elizabeth, and Williams, Norma (2001). 'A Sociology of Human Rights'. *Social Problems*, 48/1: 11–47.

Turner, Bryan (1993). 'Outline of a Theory of Human Rights'. *Sociology*, 27/3: 489–512.

—— (2006). *Vulnerability and Human Rights.* Philadelphia: Penn Sylvania State University Press.

—— *et al.* (1995). 'Symposium on Human Rights and the Sociological Project'. *Journal of Sociology*, 31/2: 1–44.

Verschraegen, Gert, and Tinnvelt, Ronald (2006). *Between Cosmopolitan Ideals and State Sovereignty.* Houndmills: Palgrave Mcmillan.

Also Sahlieh (1994); Mayer (1999).

PART V

GLOBALIZATION, FUNDAMENTALISM, MIGRATION, AND RELIGIOUS DIVERSITY

CHAPTER 25

GLOBALIZATION, THEOCRATIZATION, AND POLITICIZED CIVIL RELIGION

ROLAND ROBERTSON

The Argument

In this chapter I argue that one of the most pivotal features of the contemporary global circumstance is the rapidly developing tension between the widespread and disputed quest for explicitly formulated national identities, on the one hand, and the problematic increase in the intra-societal valorization of religious faiths, on the other. This is so in spite—even, in part, because—of the aggressive promotion of ostensibly atheistic and secularistic ideas by prominent intellectuals in the UK and the USA (Dawkins 2006; Dennett 2006; Davis 2007; Hitchens 2007).[1] This tension is embedded in the two major characteristics of globalization itself: increasing

[1] Jones (2007) has maintained in specific reference to Dawkins that "there's an aspiring totalitarianism in Britain which is brilliantly disguised. It's disguised because the would-be dictators—and there are many of them—pretend to be more tolerant than thou. They hide alongside the anti-racists, the anti-homophobes and anti-sexists. But what they are really against is something very different. They... are anti-God, and what they really want is the eradication of religion, and all believers, from the face of the earth." Very strong replies to Dawkins have certainly enhanced the thematization of religion in our time. See, e.g., Ruse 2005; McGrath 2007; Ward 2006; and Robertson 2007*a*.

globe-wide connectivity (or interconnectedness) and increasing global consciousness. An outcome of the tension is, I maintain, a shift in the direction of a *new kind* of theocracy. Such a shift is facilitated by what Pecora has described as "the totalitarian drift of the twentieth century's nation-state... (in) a twilight world where secular rationality rediscovers the putatively religious character of its origins and functions" (Pecora 2006: 129; see also Losurdo 2004; Gray 2007: 74–145). Thus, a principal theme of the present chapter is the link between theodicy and totalitarianism. A somewhat more subdued theme is the rejection of the secularization thesis (Robertson 2007*a*).

My general position has been greatly inspired by Durkheim's thesis concerning the inextricable connection between religion and society and, moreover, relates closely to his more specific claim that religion is the major political institution. His argument in this regard was similar to that of previous French intellectuals, notably Saint-Simon and de Tocqueville (Robertson 1985). Another way of considering the relationship between politics and religion is indicated by Gray (2007: 38) in his recent contention that "modern politics is a chapter in the history of religion". Gray contends that it was partly via the European Enlightenment that utopian ideas were resurrected, remarking that utopian beliefs involved the idea of perfecting human life. This, argues Gray, is an "objective integral to totalitarianism", while maintaining that America is a country founded on utopian ideas.

Gray sees a direct continuity between Margaret Thatcher and Tony Blair with respect to their millennialist optimism about the future, convincingly claiming also that both the second President Bush and Prime Minister Blair "viewed history as the unfolding of a providential design and a feature of their view is that the design is visible to the faithful... if deception is needed to realise the providential design it cannot be truly deceitful" (Gray 2007: 101). For both, human progress was axiomatic, but never to be comprehended solely along secular lines. They came at a peak of ascending utopianism in Western politics, and their goals were "nothing less than the salvation of mankind" (Gray 2007: 105–6).

The emphasis on religious freedom and choice, traditionally so strong in the USA, at first sight clashes with the idea of theocracy. Nevertheless, modern theocracy is manifested in attempts to formulate relatively closed, dogmatic civil religions in the USA, the UK, and elsewhere. The compression of the world as a whole, the squeezing together of nation-states in such a way as to make it seemingly necessary for their political elites to formulate particularly sharp national identities, is largely responsible for this. The result is that the concept of civil religion, influentially heralded by Bellah, mainly in reference to the war in Indochina in the late 1960s, is being rendered in the theocratic—or religio-political—manner that Bellah himself so strongly rejected (Bellah 1967; Bellah and Hammond 1980; Robertson 1978: 148–85).

This chapter concentrates on the UK and the USA, partly because they are interesting test cases, in the particular sense that they are both conventionally regarded as liberal-democratic societies—as societies where one would, perhaps, least expect anything like a theocracy to develop. Having said this, England (as the "core" of the UK), by virtue of its having an established and politically powerful church, has sometimes been described as a "lite" theocracy. Nevertheless, this description certainly has no relevance now. The USA has historically had pockets of theocratic tendencies, such as the Puritan Massachusetts Bay Colony and the short-lived Mormon State of Desert in nineteenth-century Utah; but during the last thirty years or so there has obviously been a theocratic drift in America as a whole (Phillips 2006; Hedges 2007; Sharlet 2006; Smith 2007). Thus, the use of the idea of theocracy is not entirely alien to the either the UK or the USA.

Although Max Weber stated that the only form of pure theocracy had been Llamist Tibet, there have been, and still are, rather a large number of theocracies. Weber himself made a distinction between theocracies and caesaropapist societies, although this is difficult to sustain in modern conditions. For example, is it best to place Saudi Arabia exclusively in one category? In any case, apart from the American and British tendencies mentioned above, one should indicate more clear-cut cases such as Iran, Pakistan, Israel, the Vatican, Andorra, Athos (in Greece), and Methodist Tonga. In the very recent past the Taliban state in Afghanistan also qualified, and may yet, in collaboration with Al Qaeda, return. Various other predominantly Muslim nation-states are borderline, potential cases, notably Indonesia. Nepal is a borderline case in the sense that, historically, it has been virtually a Hindu theocracy but with the militancy of the Maoist movement has precariously moved toward becoming a secular state.

Considering the situation even more historically it is necessary to mention, *inter alia*, Pharaonic Egypt, Calvinist Geneva, late fifteenth-century Florence, Montenegro, Medina, Mecca, Mahdist Sudan, Outer Mongolia, and Swat in the North-West Frontier Province (in that part of India that was to become Pakistan).

A further consideration has to do with the concept of political religion. In this respect it should be noted that President Lincoln stated that the US Constitution constituted a political religion, while various new societies in Africa and Asia have been regarded as having established political religions (Geertz 1963). Other societies with political religions (or theocracies) have included Nazi Germany, contemporary North Korea, and the period of State Shinto in Japan (approximately 1890 until 1945); while China is surely a very prominent contemporary case.

Globalization and National Identity

As has been noted, in contrast to the USA, the UK does have a formally established church, at least in England. The Church of England (Protestant) has, on the other hand, lost many members and much political power in recent decades, and now coexists with an increasing number of non-Christian faiths, although there has recently been an upsurge in Roman Catholicism, due largely to Polish migration in the early twenty-first century. The main non-Christian faiths are Islam, Hinduism, and Sikhism, although the number of adherents to animistic religions—notably those arriving from Africa—is certainly not insubstantial. In contrast, the Jewish population of the UK has been marked by a very high degree of assimilation since the nineteenth century. The overall effect of such diversity has been to disrupt the much heralded cohesiveness of British society, a cohesiveness that has rested largely upon the hierarchical-integrative significance of class and class consciousness in Britain. (Many British people would deny that class is an integrative feature of the UK, but the present author strongly contends that it is.) An additional, complicating factor has been that of devolution, giving much greater power to Scotland and Wales, as well as to Northern Ireland.

Even though, throughout its existence, the American Republic has involved a constitutionally strong separation of church from state, in contrast to the establishment of the Anglican Church in England, it is of the greatest importance to emphasize that in England and Scotland there has been a lengthy and strong secularistic—even atheistic—tradition. Religion has long been a taken-for-granted feature of American *culture*, in spite of the formal separation of church and state. While there have been recurring legal and constitutional disputes concerning the Jeffersonian wall of separation between church and state—ostensibly in order to protect the secular domain from (competing) religious organizations and movements—this has, in fact, served to inhibit the development of a tradition of secularism and, certainly, of atheism.

The globalizing constraint to produce an explicit national identity in the face of such challenges is particularly evident at present in the UK, where a political struggle is centered upon the characterization of Britishness in the face of Scottish and Welsh demands for more devolution, even independence (Robertson 2006*d*; cf. Huntington 2005: 3–33).[2] There is also the problem of Northern Ireland. A consequence of this is that there is a search for a national identity that will simultaneously acknowledge *both diversity and sameness*, not least in the face of

[2] The profound problems associated with attempts to promote national identity and patriotism are becoming very evident. See the article by Shepherd (2007): "What Does Britain Expect?" The subtitle of her article is: "As the curriculum changes to include 'national identity', new research suggests teachers are deeply confused about patriotism in class." It has to be noted that some teachers are protesting that they have, in already mandatory classes on citizenship (nationally required since 2002), been advocating to their students the ideal of *global* citizenship. There was a rapid expansion of the latter in the USA in the 1980s and 1990s, at least in a large number of American states. One now wonders what is destined to happen to the educational meaning of global membership and citizenship in the years ahead, in the face of the rapidly growing focus on *national* identity around the world. As of August 2008, the UK Prime Minister, Gordon Brown, was clearly emphasizing British identity even more intensely than his predecessor, Tony Blair.

the multiple loyalties that have accompanied recent diasporic immigration. This is where the issue of an early twenty-first-century version of theocracy enters the picture in the case of the UK. In a fragile nation-state such as Britain the apparent need for "a religion-beyond-religions" is inevitable, even though in the contemporary political climate it would be suicidal to make such a proposal. Nonetheless, the controversial attempt to invent what I have called a religion-beyond-religions can most appropriately be described as, indeed, a new form of theocracy—particularly when the extent to which the UK has become a surveillance society is taken fully into account, about which more below.

To consider this from a different angle, much of the controversy surrounding British identity—as that in many other countries—revolves around school curricula, and often involves increasing suggestions of the primordial meaning of Britishness. While not resting explicitly on religious or theological considerations, this kind of attempt to formulate national (as well as personal) identities inevitably involves religion in its broadest sense, as opposed to the doctrines of any particular world religion.

The USA does not—at least at the present time—have the same kind of problem concerning internal nations proclaiming their own identity (Robertson 1998; Garreau 1981; Glazer and Moynihan 1970; Glazer 1997; Smelser and Alexander 1999; Portes and Rumbaut 2007). The USA also has a long tradition of explicitly acknowledged multiculturality and/or polyethnicity—particularly since the influential characterization of the USA as a melting pot in the 1920s, inhibiting—but by no means preventing—the kind of problem currently faced in the UK. Since then—and, more particularly, since the publication of *Beyond the Melting Pot* by Glazer and Moynihan (1970)—diversity has been widely (but certainly not consensually) regarded as beneficial to the vitality of American society.[3] There are nonetheless arguments to the effect that the USA is not yet diverse enough (Hollinger 1995). To oversimplify, whereas the USA has a tradition (sometimes contested) of multiculturality, the UK has had a long drawn-out tradition of relatively unproblematic assimilation. This is partly due to the class-deferential, or elitist, character of British society. Nonetheless, the UK has experienced sudden spurts of immigration since the Second World War, resulting in serious moral panics. Such episodes have, of course, occurred in the USA, but these have not often ramified throughout the country.

At the time of writing, both of the societies that are under particular scrutiny in this chapter are in phases of political transition. Even were the Republicans to retain the White House and/or the Congress in 2008 (which is unlikely), there

[3] In the USA there have been modern claims for independence among Native Indian tribes, Hawaiians, and Californian Mexicans. In contrast with the UK, these do not amount to serious challenges to the integralness of the nation-state. But see Garreau 1981. For the UK, see Nairn 1977; Kearney 1989.

would, almost certainly, be a significantly different kind of administration than that of the current President Bush and Vice-President Cheney. In the UK Gordon Brown has recently taken over the premiership from Tony Blair, but at this point it is impossible to tell whether the theocratic tendencies will grow stronger or weaker (for both have shown little embarrassment in invoking religion in their political statements). In any case, the Bush–Blair strategies and policies following 9/11 will be very difficult to unravel.

Increasing connectivity has been much more addressed in the literature on globalization than has the second principal feature, increasing global consciousness. Nevertheless, it is here maintained that they are, in principle, of equal significance. Indeed, they amplify each other empirically. The more that there is connectivity across the world, the more likely it is that there will be greater global consciousness, and vice versa (Robertson 1989; 2002; 2006*a*; 2007*a*; Lechner and Boli 2005). Increasing global connectivity and global consciousness simultaneously challenge national identities *and* promote them.[4]

The Nation-State and Millennialism

In the UK there is, as I have said, a much more explicit enunciation of secularistic and atheistic world views. This, however, is incongruent with a strong advocacy on many points of the political spectrum of the desirability of more faith schools. In conjunction with this, many leading politicians insist that faith schools should emphasize Britishness. There is much controversy, in particular, about Muslim immigration, while the rapid expansion of the Polish-Catholic population is exacerbating the general problem. The latter consists in the tensions among the faith school proposals, the secular-atheistic program, and the search for British identity in the face of national-devolutionist demands. Add to this, among the major political parties, a virtual obsession with the issue of national-social cohesion, and it is quite easy to see the enormity of the problem. While it may be appropriate to talk of a parallel American problem, the taken-for-granted *culture of religion* in the USA makes for a very different circumstance, as does the institutionalized and idealized multiculturality of American society.

Many students of globalization and/or of the contemporary nation-state have argued that the former is undermining the latter. My thesis, however, is that globalization as a process *includes* the nation-state and changes in the nature

[4] Many historical events have undoubtedly raised issues concerning the meaning and potential end of life on earth. The best study of this, in the present author's view, is devoted particularly to the widespread impact of the Lisbon earthquake of 1755: Neiman 2002.

thereof (Robertson 1992: esp. 23–31; Meyer 1980; Boli 1980; Meyer *et al.*, 1997).[5] Indeed, this is a premise of the entirety of the present discussion. Globalization is both challenging the existence of the nation-state as the major "container" of human beings *and* strengthening it. Extensive migration and the increasing proliferation of diasporas and diasporic commitments are loosening the boundaries of nation-states, but at the same time they are provoking societal attempts to homogenize internally their ways of life. Religion is greatly involved in the production and accentuation of this apparent contradiction. On the one hand, religion is frequently the major form of self-identification for migrants, while, on the other hand, intensification and politicization of this increases the tendency for actual or potential political elites to insist upon the formulation of ever sharper, civil-religious national identities for the host country.

Such a focus must inevitably involve attention to the current confusion surrounding everyday, academic, and—not least—political and legal definitions of religion (Lincoln 2006; Pecora 2006). Increasing attention is now being given to this crucial question. In particular, there is much acknowledgment at this time of the heavily constricted nature of canonical definitions of religion in "modern" societies, and also increasing recognition of the, equally canonical, tendency to underestimate the religious aspect of political life (Lincoln 2006; Burleigh 2006; Robertson 2003[1983]).

This matter has a great bearing on the Western academic obsession with the secularization thesis (particularly among sociologists of religion in the USA and the UK), and, indeed, strongly challenges it (Robertson 2007*a*; Vattimo 1992; Caputo and Vattimo 2007). One should add that whereas the preoccupation with the secularization thesis has been manifest more or less neutrally in the USA, sociologists in the UK have, for the most part, eagerly promoted it. In any case, there can be no doubt that "religion" has always been and always will be an "essentially contested" concept, to invoke the famous phrase of Wittgenstein. On the other hand, "religion" is also ongoingly contested in the "real world", in the sense that the demarcations between religion and secularity have been calibrated across the centuries and across the world as a whole in the context of a large variety of cultural and social—as well as international—contingencies (Robertson 1993).

To speak of the world being *in* itself means nothing more than the world being regarded as simply "there". It "just exists" in animate and inanimate respects. In contrast, when we speak of the world becoming *for* itself, we mean that its human inhabitants become increasingly conscious of their (our) being in the same boat, of having a shared fate. Thus, in reference to the contemporary global circumstance, it

[5] Conflicting views on the relationship between globalization and the state—or nation-state—are usefully discussed in Holton 1998. The perspective that includes the nation-state *within* the overall process of globalization is closely related to the emphasis upon its multi-dimensionality, in contrast to the uni-dimensional tendency to reduce globalization simplistically to purely economic factors. See also Robertson and White 2005 and 2007.

is easy to see that there is more and more awareness of the environmental and demographic—as well as health—problems that afflict this planetary world, including issues revolving around global warming, pandemics, and "natural" disasters—or the threat thereof. In essence this means that global consciousness becomes increasingly reflexive (Robertson 2007*a*; 2002; Lechner and Boli 2005), but very conflictful—indeed millennial and apocalyptic (Pearson 2006). Here it is worth mentioning that recent polls show that in the USA about 60 percent of the population believes in the Book of Revelation, and not many less believe that the end of the world is imminent; while in numerous other countries, novels, films, drinking and drug habits, obesity, anorexia—and yet more indicators—strongly support the claim that we live in a highly millennial world.

Thus what I am describing as the global-millennial turn, exemplified in—but not confined to—the "terror war", gives a new twist to the idea of the world being increasingly for itself (Pearson 2006; Wilson 2007).[6] This is so, mainly because many ecological, medical, and other fears of our time are, for the *pre*-millennialists, welcome signs of the "end time". It should be emphasized that pre-millennialism involves the belief that there must and will be messianic intervention prior to the end of the world as we know it. Post-millennialism, on the other hand, insists that the world can and should be perfected prior to the return of "the savior". In maintaining that we are now living in a millennial phase of globalization, it should not be thought that this means that we all live, across the world, in a circumstance of apocalyptic pessimism. Much of modern life operates on the assumption that things are rapidly getting better and better. In particular, scientific, technological, and medical utopianism is an example of a kind of post-millennialism.

As has been intimated, much of the rapidly increasing connectivity in the world directly concerns religion, *and religion is partly generated by such.* On the other hand, global consciousness has clearly involved a strong religious component. Indeed, the rise of the great world religions during the Axial Age had much to do with increasing global consciousness—the placement and fate of humankind in the cosmos (Jaspers 1953; Eisenstadt 2004). We now live in a time when "the clash" of different conceptions of the world as a whole amounts to nothing less than a profound contest concerning what may be called the "definition" of the global situation—something like a *global* civil religion—or, as an Orwellian nightmare, a global theocracy. The latter is, indeed, what some contemporary political religious movements seem to desire. National and civilizational assertions of the latter are in intense rivalry, bordering on nuclear war (Pearson 2006; Barkawi 2006). We have

[6] The recent report of the Intergovernmental Panel on Climate Change has taken the world ever closer to being for itself. As the co-chair of the IPCC has said, "the amount of warming will depend on choices that human beings make" (*The Guardian*, 2 Feb. 2007). This may well be seen in combination with discussions at the 2007 meetings of the American Association for the Advancement of Science, when it was proposed that only global cooperation among nations can effectively deal with the possibility of asteroids colliding with earth. See also Wilson 2007.

arrived at this point through a complex mixture of a rapid intensification of connectivity, on the one hand, and an equally rapid enhancement of our consciousness of the world in its entirety, as well as its place in the cosmos, on the other. This is why I have long argued that such was an almost inevitable phase in the overall globalization process (Robertson 2007*a*; 2007*b*; 2007*c*; 1992: 57–60).

The theocratic temptation is manifest most generally in the way in which the compression of the world puts pressure upon nation-states to identify themselves with more clarity and stipulate their position in the history and future of the world as a whole. This pressure is made especially complex by virtue of a current feature of increasing connectivity and of global flows: namely, extensive migration and the growing significance of transnational identities. This involves a declining willingness of people to conceive of themselves as members of a single nation-state (Altman 2007; Kalra, Kaur, and Hutnyk 2005). In other words, while the nation-state—more specifically, its leaders—attempts, with increasing formality and rigidity, to formulate its identity and criteria of citizenship, this project clashes with the increasing intensity and complexity of migration, as well as with attempts by the nation-state to design forms of multiculturalism (Meyer and Geschiere 2003; Appiah 2006; Modood 2007). In such circumstances the formulation of a single nation-state identity along with multiculturalism becomes ever more difficult. But this also *portends a situation in which the national identity of a state will be centered upon its own particular configuration of multiculturalism—or what is sometimes called polyethnicity.* Closely bound up with this issue is the equally thorny matter of cosmopolitanism, the current literature on which barely mentions religion (e.g. Verovec and Cohen 2002; Beck 2006).

The "War on Terror" and its Implications

The present confrontation between caliphate Islam and "the West" is undoubtedly manifest most dramatically in the so-called war on terror. This politico-religious conflict emerged very clearly in modern times with the Iranian, theocratic revolution of 1979 (Robbins and Robertson 1986; Robertson 1981). It was at that time that the rhetoric about jihadist, caliphate Islam versus the "satanic", imperialist West began firmly to take shape (Esposito 2002; Kepel 2004; Sutton and Vertigans 2005). The attacks on the World Trade Center in 1993 and 2001 have had, of course, enormous consequences, notably after the second President Bush declared a crusade against al-Qaeda. This statement has created much controversy, particularly within the USA, with some claiming that either Bush never said this or that it was of little consequence. Neither of these positions is defensible.

Bush's use of "crusade" received very wide publicity around much of the world, although it seems not to have received anything like the same attention—except, perhaps, within Muslim-American communities—in the USA itself.[7] This was so in spite of Bush's attempt to diminish the strength of his declaration shortly thereafter. The crucial point, nonetheless, is that Bush's words following 11 September 2001, and equally, if not more important, his actions were—and, to some extent, still are—characterized as indicating an intensive and extensive onslaught on Islam per se. This view gained greater momentum after the invasion of Iraq, following the initial incursion into Afghanistan (Modood 2007). The President's description of his policy in Afghanistan and the Middle East as a "crusade", and some of his religio-political allies' description of Islam as (in the Revd Franklin Graham's words on NBC *Nightly News* of 16 November 2001) "wicked, violent and not of the same god", together with the added contention of the late Revd Jerry Falwell, that the Prophet Muhammad was "a terrorist" (on CBS's *60 Minutes* of 6 October 2002), may well account for the plummeting of Muslim-Americans running for public office between 2000 and 2004, from 700 down to 100.

Taken in conjunction with the increasingly conspicuous Muslim presence, notably through much emigration to the UK, the USA, and other Western societies, and the problems sharpened thereby for the "reluctant ideal" of a multicultural society, these developments have shaped not merely world, or international, politics in the early twenty-first century, but have also had a major impact upon national-internal, societal affairs. In fact, there are not many countries in "the West" that have not been affected by Muslim immigration. Many countries in the Caribbean, Latin America, and Western and Central Europe have experienced waves of this kind. In a number of these there is the apparent problem of multiple allegiances to two or more countries, and to religious doctrines and practices outside the domains of Christianity.

[7] Bush's exact phrase, as reported in a White House Press Release of 16 Sept. 2001 was: "This crusade, this war on terrorism is going to take a long while." This was reported in a number of newspapers around the world as, e.g., in *The Christian Science Monitor* of 19 Sept. 2001. In the report in the latter by Peter Ford, entitled "Europe cringes at Bush 'crusade' against terrorists", he summarized reactions from Muslims in Europe and Asia and from France. Ford reported that the Grand Mufti in Marseilles had said that Bush's remark "recalled the barbarous and unjust military operations against the Muslim world", by Christian knights, who launched repeated attempts to capture Jerusalem over the course of several hundred years. See also, Guardian Unlimited: "George Bush: 'God told me to end the tyranny in Iraq'," *The Guardian*, 7 Oct. 2005; <www.guardian.co.uk/usa/story/0,,1586978,00.html-55k->. Very relevant American conceptions of the rhetoric and actions of the Bush administration following 9/11 are explored with respect to different countries in Europe, Asia, and Latin America in Farber 2007.

Theocracy, Civil Religion, and the Totalitarian Drift

The Islamic, theocratic revolution in Iran, the coming to power of the Sandinistan government in Nicaragua, and the breakthrough of the Solidarity movement in Poland in 1979 marked the beginning of the modern tensions between Church and State, and between religion and politics, that have been such a prominent feature of the global situation over the past thirty years or so. Indeed, these tensions have become globalized with increasing rapidity since 1979, not least because religion has become a major vehicle for the expression of national identities (Juergensmeyer 1993; 2000). The last time in modern history that there was such concern with national identity as there is now was during the declining years of the nineteenth and the early years of the twentieth centuries (Robertson 1992: 146–63). Across the Northern Hemisphere, from Washington DC to Tokyo, as well as in much of Latin America, there was a sharp acceleration in what has become known as the invention of tradition, including national identity (Hobsbawm and Ranger 1983). This early twentieth-century development has been, in a sense, repeated—but more globally and "religiously"—about a hundred years later, and can be loosely explained by the global compression of which I spoke earlier, as well as a greatly heightened sense of the destiny of global humanity. At the same time, new questions about religion have recently arisen and given rise to a lot of questioning as to the usefulness of concepts such as secularization and desecularization (Robertson 2007*a*; Pecora 2006; Habermas 2002).

Identification of the national self typically takes place only through identification of *Others*. Thus, for example, it was often remarked at the end of the 1980s that the USA would have to find another Other, to take the place of the Soviet Union. This process—often described as centered upon the phenomenon of alterity—has undoubtedly much to do with the way in which Islam is now seen in much of the USA as the primary Other. It should quickly be added that the onward march—the next Long March—of China may well outflank Islam in this respect, while relations between Putin's Russia and the USA have recently involved resuscitation of elements of the old Cold War (1946–89). In any case, it was almost inevitable that, when confronted by a potential or actual Other that makes no clear-cut distinction between "church" and "state", or between religion and politics, the USA would find its own distinctions hard to maintain.

Another aspect of the globalization of church–state tension quickly developed just before the events in Iran, Nicaragua, and Poland. This was the alliance of convenience between Christian Zionism in the USA and Jewish Zionism in Israel (Robertson and Mouly 1983; Robertson 1988*a*; Lieven 2004). There was a widespread failure, and/or unwillingness, in the media, the academy, and among political elites to register this adequately, even though the alliance between the two Zionisms was by no means secret. Indeed, this has been one of the most egregious analytic oversights of the last fifty years or so. This is not easy to explain, given the fact that the subject was widely addressed in some American Evangelical circles and by *particular* American politicians of the Right (Mead 2006). Undoubtedly, this neglect can partly be attributed to the striking academic tendency of our time to consider religion marginal to *Realpolitik*. There are those who *even now* continue to insist that the current "terror war" is all about oil and geo-politics, that religion is rather like wallpaper with respect to the current crisis. Nevertheless, we are witnessing a significant decline in this manner of thinking, although the latter is a very poor substitute for what sociologists of religion have for long addressed as an ingredient of politics. In any case, the interpenetration of American and Israeli religion has, undoubtedly, been a very significant factor in the relationship between the USA, on the one hand, and much of the Muslim world, on the other.

A crucial premise of the present discussion is that globalization is considered as a *multi-dimensional* (*not* a uni-dimensional, economic) *process*, the major dimensions being the cultural, the social, the political, and, yes, the economic (Robertson and White 2005; 2007). Religion is centered in the cultural dimension, but most definitely has social, political, and economic aspects (Asad 1993). This means that in referring previously to the major, general features of globalization—namely, increasing connectivity (or compression) and increasing global consciousness—I have attended to the fact that compression does not simply have a cultural aspect. It is rather obvious that it has social, political, and economic aspects as well. It should also be said that while, in one sense, cultural globalization transcends national identities—perhaps, in the form of transnational identities—a major feature of globalization in general is that it partly *consists of* the growth of the nation-state. The nation-state is a *crucial feature* of globalization, despite many facile statements to the contrary. At the present time we are undergoing a rapid acceleration of the general process of globalization, but there is very little concrete sign of the end of the nation-state.

This phenomenon can be encapsulated in a simple formula: the *universalization of particularism and the particularization of universalism*. Globalization involves—indeed, encourages and necessitates—the global expression of *particular* identities and loyalties. Viewed in this way, as I think it should be, globalization is often more accurately described as glocalization (Robertson 1995; 2006*c*). Ideas and practices that have been diffused across the world must have had a particular niche to go to; or at least, a niche has had to be created. On the other hand, globalization consists, in and of itself, of the particularization of universalism, which refers to the way in which the world as a whole is increasingly particularized as *a single place*. Moreover, assertion of national identity is interwoven with the recognition of globality (Robertson 2003[1983]; 2006*b*). Nation-states are increasingly constrained to locate their "locality" within the global arena. In some respects this has always been so, but since the rise of *Realpolitik*, this has consistently been neglected, neglected precisely during the period of exponential globalization.

Relativization is central to the overall globalization process and, like many other facets of globalization theory, is greatly significant in any discussion of religion (Campbell 2005). "Relativization" refers to the process in terms of which particular world views, doctrines, ideologies, practices, and so on are rendered precarious and open to challenge when confronted by alternatives. Simply put, relativization involves the potential destabilization of firm attachments to a particular faith. Processes of relativization clearly relate to the matter of Otherness, in the sense that when confronted with another religious doctrine, and associated practices, the adherents of the religion confronting an Other are presented with a number of alternative ways of reacting. These include acceptance of the Other in a pluralistic manner, aggressive rejection of the Other, or, at the other extreme, a retreat into what are thought to be "the fundamentals". The current confrontation between jihadism and the USA and UK (as a minor partner) is a classic example of relativization, particularly when one thinks of the Islamic reaction to the publication in 1988 of Salman Rushdie's *Satanic Verses*. A slightly more subdued reaction was repeated when Rushdie was awarded a British knighthood in June 2007. From the other side, the American fundamentalist fear of having to recognize other ways of life is a more specific example. Such reactions are aspects of a generalized reaction against modernity (and modernism)—as embodied in biblical literalism, Darwinism, and "non-American" immigration—dating back to the late nineteenth century (Marsden 1980; Ruse 2005). It might not be too much of an exaggeration to argue that the new form of theodicy arises in part from processes of relativization.

The development of theocratic tendencies clearly varies in content and speed from one society to another. For example, in some places—most notably the USA—this tendency involves drawing on the majoritarian religious culture and fusing it with the interests of the nations' dominant elite. In others, such as the UK, it involves a relatively overarching invented tradition that includes—but is not confined to—very selective reappropriations of English, Scottish, Welsh, and Irish histories.

Civil Religion, Theocracy, and the Global Arena

My overall thesis has therefore much to do with the significance of *national civil religion in a global context.* Civil religion was re-announced during the 1960s by a small number of sociologists, most notably Robert Bellah. Bellah (1967) argued that the US political and military involvement in the war in Indochina (particularly Vietnam), and the opposition to it, was raising crucial questions concerning "what America really stood for". The answers to such questions could, he argued, be expressed via the concept of civil religion—a religion that stood above and beyond accepted religions of faith, such as the different varieties of Christianity, Judaism, and so on. In the intensive and wide-ranging debate that followed Bellah's original article, it was not infrequently suggested that Bellah's idea of America (i.e., the USA) having a civil religion involved the conflation of church and state. Bellah himself adamantly denied this. Civil religion was conceived as a kind of umbrella indicating the basic themes of American culture, such as its republicanism, its significance in world history, and much that was expressed in the American Constitution (including, of course, the Bill of Rights) and Lincoln's Gettysburg Address of 1863 during the American Civil War.

Even though Bellah agreed that there could be cases of rival civil religions within a particular society, he did not appear to think that such a situation obtained within the USA, although he did speak of the breaking of the American Covenant in the context of the war in Indochina and the Watergate scandal (Bellah 1975). Without speculating as to what Bellah's position might be in the present circumstances, I argue here that since the first period of major debate about civil religion (late 1960s to mid-1980s) a new situation has arisen. Basically, this has involved the intensification of the "culture wars" of which commentators in the USA began to speak fifteen or more years ago. Indeed, the notion of culture war(s)—*Kulturkampf*—can be loosely translated into the idea of rival civil religions. In this connection globalization again appears to be very significant, since it involves the particularization of national identities in a circumstance of considerable global-cultural instability—indeed, of global trauma (cf. Alexander *et al.* 2004). In this circumstance there has been a destabilization of ethical and moral certainties, a consequence being that *fear* has become a paramount globalized emotion of contemporary times. Fear now—more than ever—plays a crucial part in the maintenance of the solidarity and cohesion of nation-states, particularly in the UK and the USA (Moisi 2007; Liptak 2007; Robertson 2006*c*).

In the USA, and elsewhere, it seems essential that, insofar as the idea of civil religion *can* retain its usefulness, we should now think of the *upgrading* of civil religions in the face of new societal and global problems. Along with the process of upgrading, there undoubtedly occur problems of inclusion. Indeed, they are two sides of the same coin. Whereas upgrading refers to the broadening of the "umbrella" of civil religion, inclusion entails the involvement of heretofore excluded groups. At the present time, in many societies—not least in the UK and the USA—the twofold problem of incorporating an increasing variety of ethnic, religious, linguistic, and cultural groups *and* thereby expanding the scope of civil religion increasingly arises.

Both aspects of this problem relate closely to my argument about national particularism and the reassertion of national identities. In the UK there is presently an intense debate about what it means to be British and the degree to, and ways in, which "others", particularly Muslims, should assimilate to Britishness (or resist full incorporation into British society). There is an argument about both the identity of the nation-state and the extent to which "alien" socio-cultural groups should conform to the values and norms of the latter. Needless to say, this raises acute questions concerning "British values"—as it does in the case of American values. However, here there is considerable difference. There seem to be clearer conceptions in the American case of such values and traditions—even though there has been considerable conflict about this—whereas in the British case the conception of national values and traditions is much more implicit or tacit. Thus, when questions are raised about British values, much floundering results. People in Britain—particularly in England—are all too willing to invoke "British values", but have great difficulty in stipulating what they are. "Englishness" does, for the most part, involve images of uncontaminated, "racially pure" Anglo-Saxonism.

Empirically speaking, it seems very doubtful whether such upgrading and inclusion can realistically take place in the present phase of globalization. It is in this manner that we may—we hope, persuasively—speak of new forms of theocracy.

Identities in Flux

Collective memories are frequently contested and fragile, this being magnified by the extensive and intensive processes of globalization that have occurred in recent times. A crucial aspect of contemporary globalization has, of course, been the confrontation between radical, politicized Islam and "the West" (Huntington 1997; Mozaffari 2002; Harris 2004). This has contributed greatly to the destabilization of collective memories and the "invention" of new ones in situations of trauma (Alexander *et al.* 2004). In the face of the relativizing experiences of both "Islam" and "the West", there has been a growing space for the rewriting of national, regional, civilizational, and world histories. Such revisionism is at the heart of much of the current obsession with the formulation of clear-cut national identities. This near-global uncertainty is currently feeding the transition to the new millennial phase of globalization (Robertson 2007*a*).

The great acceleration in migration from one society to others, and the increasingly significant phenomenon of the multiple loyalties of immigrants, as well as emigrants, has led to something of a crisis in the functioning of the nation-state.

In the USA a significant degree of Americanization has been both expected and facilitated as far as immigrants are concerned. This tendency has not been so solidly in place in the UK. In this regard it should be emphasized that the uniqueness of the USA with respect to its being a multicultural society—a land of immigrants—is fast disappearing. Many other countries in the world could now easily be placed in this category or are on the verge of belonging to it. Nonetheless, Fukuyama has made a rather convincing case that multiculturalism in the USA is still more stable than it is in Europe (Fukuyama 2007; cf. Lind 1995: 97–137, 217–388). His argument is that the USA stands out for its having national commemorative and ritualistic events that strongly ameliorate many of the fragmenting effects of multiculturalism—such as the World Series (basketball), the Super Bowl (American football), and other sports championships; as well as Memorial Day, Independence Day, and Thanksgiving, not to speak of slightly less significant "national days" as well as commemorations that link particular identities with national identity such as Columbus Day, St Patrick's Day, and Martin Luther King Day.

All of this has been very much complicated by the trauma of 9/11 (Smelser 2004) and its aftermath, the bombings in Spain, the UK, and elsewhere. The fear, politically manipulated or not, of the Other—or the Stranger—has become virtually institutionalized. In any case, the difficulty of creating a viable civil religion in the face of increasing multiple national loyalties and cultural/ethnic complexity is, to put it mildly, formidable.

Eagerness to establish policies of homeland security has become a central feature of politics in many societies around the world. In connection with this, there have arisen many controversies as to how numerous, canonically accepted, human rights have to be forfeited in the face of problems of national security, this being particularly true of the USA and the UK (Ignatieff 2005; Lieven 2004). Indeed, national security has become such a broad idea that it embraces virtually every aspect of human life, including—not least of all—religious and cultural security (Robertson 2007*a*). The Patriot Act has been at the center of such controversies in the USA, while there has been so much legislation in the UK restricting human liberty that it is not at all unusual to hear the charge made by some in the mainstream media, as opposed to the daily tabloids, that the UK is fast—but "silently"—moving toward a condition of totalitarianism (Robertson 2007*a*). A particular version of this was provided by the Archbishop of York's statement in February 2007 that the UK is on the brink of becoming a police state (<http://news.bbc.co.uk/1/hi/uk/6329815.stm>). All of this runs sharply against the grain of the heretofore, near-conventional, wisdom that the world is becoming increasingly democratic, if not along the lines embedded in the doctrine of American Manifest Destiny (Harrington 1986; Pfaff 2007; Mead 2006; Lefort 2007).

We now find that the nation-state is beginning to monopolize what I would call *the means of being*, while the idea of privacy is rapidly undergoing dissolution (Robertson 2006*d*; 2007*a*). In Western societies generally many people proudly and publicly exhibit what were previously considered to be highly private aspects of their lives, and this has meant that it becomes increasingly difficult to proclaim a right to privacy (Westin 1967; Robertson 2007*a*). In other words, with vast numbers of people eagerly exhibiting their "privacy", how can it then be argued convincingly that privacy is a virtually sacred phenomenon? In the contemporary world one might be tempted to say—with some cynical exaggeration—that the last thing people want to protect is their intimacy. One consequence of this is that modern totalitarianism is, to a not insignificant degree, voluntaristic. In using the term "totalitarianism" in this context, I am rejecting the canard that we should confine this term—much consolidated during the Cold War—to the Stalinist USSR and Hitler's Germany. In any case, the general notion of totalitarianism certainly did not originate in those societies. Indeed, it is often associated with the French Revolution, although it can, of course, be traced back even further (Taylor 2007; Barrell 2007; Groebner 2007).

The irony in all this is that the same kinds of thing that many people in Western societies find objectionable about other—particularly Muslim—societies are to be found in their very "own" societies. Fabled Western values are being undermined only *partly* in response to the fear of the Other. For the strong moves in the direction of totalitarianism have, in significant part, developed indigenously within many Western societies—notably the UK and the USA.

The French Revolution provides an opportunity to return more directly to the link between totalitarian and theocratic trends. At the height of French Revolutionary Terror there were also established various "secular" equivalents of straightforwardly religious festivals and calendrical moments. This well illustrates the phenomenon of "political religions" so characteristic of considerable numbers of all-encompassing dictatorships or highly authoritarian regimes. And at the same time it confronts us with the problem of the difference between theocractic regimes and regimes involving political religions, or whether any worthwhile distinction can be made between them.

The French Revolution occurred at precisely the time when what Barbara Taylor has called "the surveillance culture" was poisoning public life in Britain (Taylor 2007). Barrell (2007) and Taylor attribute the growth of surveillance culture from the mid-eighteenth century largely to religious revivalism and the growing influence of the middle class. The growing middle class sought to tame—indeed, severely constrain—both the libertine lifestyles of notorious aristocrats and the growing challenge of the new working class. This involved a great deal of invasion of privacy, which in effect involved a continuing saga of regulation and repression. As Taylor has said, "the onslaught on the private behaviour of the hoi polloi continued, with increasing middle-class input, throughout the 18th century, until by the outbreak of the French Revolution Britain was swarming with moralists dedicated to policing the personal lives of the poor" (Taylor 2007: 11).[8]

In the contemporary UK there has been extensive comment on the heavy infringement of civil liberties which threatens to make available to many official authorities all manner of information about individuals. This can be summed up in the phrase *the surveillance society.* The attenuation of the right to *habeas corpus* has proceeded apace in both the USA and the UK in recent years, while Guantanamo Bay has been at the center of much parallel legislation and *ex cathedra* presidential pronouncements by government. Perhaps the situation in the USA is best encapsulated in the pronouncement by former member of the Supreme Court, Justice Sandra O'Connor, that the USA is in some danger of degenerating into a dictatorship, with particular reference to political intrusions on the judiciary.

As has been said previously, this "totalitarian drift" cannot quickly be undone, even were there to be Democratic government in the USA and/or the end of Blairism in the UK in the near future. Announcements in both countries of continuing threat—realistic or not—from various other countries or movements amount to *permanent states of emergency.* The latter are not easy to cancel or even significantly reduce. One of the reasons for this is that acceptance of states of emergency has become part and parcel of contemporary conceptions of patriotism based on fear (Robertson 2007*b*). This surely accounts—at least in part—for the widespread acceptance of monitoring of telephone conversations and email communication, and the computerization of what has heretofore been regarded as private information.

As has been said, a central feature of the present Western situation is that of increasing multiculturalism/polyethnicity. On the other hand, some Western societies have also moved in a theocratic, totalitarian direction, and in so doing have incorporated and used as a form of legitimation much of what has been proclaimed in the name of religious freedom, most notably in the USA. However, the latter has led to the encouragement of large-scale migration, very frequently involving immigrants who bring a strong sense of identity with them—or who adapt by developing a distinctive religious identity. Moreover, their "ghettoization" has led—mostly in European countries and, perhaps, particularly in the Netherlands, Sweden, and the UK—to governmental efforts to counter this and strongly encourage what is very often called social cohesion. In addition—and this has particular reference to the USA—the proliferation of religious commitments and of immigrants outside the Judeo-Christian "orthodoxy" has greatly facilitated a counter-move on the part of the latter, majority religious tradition. This has, moreover, led in the recent American past to an alliance between that tradition and the state.

[8] Thus it may be seen that the current idea of the surveillance society can be traced back at least to the eighteenth century. See Robertson 2007*a*; Marx 2007; Lace 2005; Lyon 2003. Cf. Talmon 1952.

Toleration of—indeed, respect for—a variety of religious faith communities has also, ironically, facilitated the state becoming increasingly involved in identity formation. Warnings by a number of public intellectuals, not to speak of "respectable" journals and newspapers, do not seem to be having much effect as yet. One suspects that this is in large part due to what can be called the "present opium of the people" (with no apologies to Karl Marx)—namely, choice. The political celebration of choice, including religious choice—sometimes, very misleadingly, equated with "freedom"—is the central attribute of what we often call consumerism, or the consumer culture. The consumerist aspect of identity is extensive in Western societies, and the cult of consumerism actually involves deeper and deeper penetration of the state into our lives. For this cult has in and of itself involved the offering to the consumer of increasingly intimate aspects of life in contemporary society (Hankiss 2006). But, as this willing acceptance of such penetration proceeds, it opens the way for—indeed, tempts and legitimates—governmental agencies to inspect and control many other aspects of our hitherto private lives.

Summation

The somewhat tiresome issue of secularization (and desecularization) necessarily enters the picture. In a very persuasive piece, entitled "Religion's Return", Sanneh (2006: 13) has insisted on the unavoidable need in an age of globalization to address seriously the return of religion. He argues that in "a religiously awakened world... one can scarcely deny that the ground has shifted, and that the direction of historical inquiry must follow". It is hard to see how anybody can continue to adhere not merely to the secularization thesis but also to the notion that the idea of secularization is of particular interest. However, this kind of question *does* continue to occupy the minds of many sociologists of religion. In discussing the condition of religion in our time, Sanneh draws attention to the various ways in which religion has become a matter of truly global controversy—ranging from, at one extreme, the view that religion will, so to say, save us, and, at the other end of the continuum, to how religion is the cause of all that is bad in the world.

Alongside this global argument there stands the undeniable statistical evidence that Christianity, in particular, is growing rapidly in virtually every part of the world save for much of Europe. Perhaps most significant is the tremendous expansion of Christianity in China. In mainland China alone there are thought to be 7.5 million Catholics (in two different churches), quite apart from a rapidly expanding group of Protestants. In this regard Sanneh quotes Joseph Needham's insistence that, via Marx, China had become "the only truly Christian country in the world ... in spite of its absolute rejection of all religion" (Sanneh 2006: 13–14). It should also be mentioned that when, in 1978, Deng Xiaoping announced a relaxing of the restrictions on religion, he, in effect, opened the floodgates for "the return" of religion. One of the consequences of this has been a remarkable growth of lay Buddhism (Clarke 2006: 319–60).

Sanneh has noted that this return was much influenced by the kind of work on Western societies that had shown that religion had played a crucial role in the rise of capitalism. One might add, in this connection, that in the mid-nineteenth century Latin American "liberal" autocrats attempted to import European Protestantism *well before* the influential writing of such intellectuals as Max Weber and R. H. Tawney, in order to promote the spirit of progress, particularly economic aspects thereof. The Latin American attempts to promote "progress" in this way were largely failures. Similarly, one can, through a strange inversion, predict that so-called Euro-secularists are doomed to a similar lack of success in their apparent eagerness to use the Euoropean Union as a wall against the return of religion. As Sanneh (2006: 14) additionally remarks, within the EU the resistance to religion has involved, "somewhat maladroitly", the promotion of multiculturalism.

Persuasive or not at the time, Bellah's ideal of civil religion has surely been reflexively distorted, so that civil religions across the world have become—one might say, inevitably—subject to virtually endless political manipulation. One of the main sociological phenomena of our time is that the terms of not only societal but also global *order* are basically manipulable. This has placed the religio-cultural dimension of life at the apex of our lives. Whether or not it is helpful to refer, as Sacks does, to "religion as the axial of civilization" may be going too far (Sacks 2003). However, there can be virtually no doubt, in the broadest sense, that the intersection between religious culture and power has been the pivotal aspect of political control.

It is along these lines that there have arisen generalized tensions between the principle of religious freedom and national unity. Since religious freedom is increasingly considered in communal terms, then it is, almost by definition, seen to threaten national unity (or societal cohesion). From a sociological point of view, what is singularly lacking is recognition that only by acknowledging simultaneously the need for the upgrading of societal values and for the enhancing of societal inclusion—in a phrase, making societies genuinely *open*—can we proceed in the direction of a significantly less conflictful world.

As it is, we live increasingly in a world of strangers. A new form of theocracy is the way in which governments are currently attempting to cope with this. The circumstance of multiculturality is currently being greatly exacerbated by the rise of an aggressive form of atheistic secularism in the UK, some proponents of which argue that atheism should be regarded as on an equal footing with religious faiths. Much of the atheistic militancy in the UK is motivated by a form of anti-Americanism, specifically the fear that creationism will increase even more rapidly in the UK than it already has. Hence there is now an increasing clash of fundamentalisms, hidden in small part by the motif of multiculturalism. As fundamentalisms proliferate, so the theocratic temptation grows. However, we find considerable divergence in this regard between the UK and the USA. Whereas Protestant fundamentalism has acquired something like a hegemonic position in the USA (Wills 2006), Protestantism in the UK is in decline. One would be remiss, however, were the "fight back" by the formally established Church of England to be overlooked.

Political religions were, and are, forms of religion that have been, or are, "invented" in order to provide a rallying point of reference for the inhabitants of particular societies. These contrast with Bellah-type civil religions. Whereas the latter provide a standard to which the relevant society has ideally to conform, political religions and theocracies are much more directly manipulable by specific regimes. In Bellah's formulation, the state religion of, for example, Japan—namely, State Shinto—was not a civil religion, precisely because it served the interests of a particular regime. There are, and have been since the late nineteenth century, many examples of political or state religions. One might here add that in Turkey the new regime following the establishment of Turkey as a nation-state in 1923, was influenced by the ideas of Gokalp (1959), who advocated the formulation of an effervescent culture for the new nation, which he called an ethnic family. One of his major sources for this kind of idea was Émile Durkheim. In employing some of the latter's perspectives, Gokalp was well aware that in founding the new Turkish republic, Kemal Atatürk had insisted that it should be strictly secular, along the lines of Western societies, including the USA. And here we come full circle. It was Rousseau, as has been noted, who first used the notion of civil religion in the eighteenth century, and that idea was adopted, in turn, by Durkheim at the beginning of the twentieth century. Bellah was deeply influenced by Durkheim, and thus the history and genealogy of the notion of civil religion has "developed" in complex ways. The missing consideration in the work of Rousseau and Bellah—and, to a lesser extent, Durkheim—has been, or was, globalization. In the Turkish case a continuing and militant "battle" has been fought by the Kemalists against the Islamists, a battle which is very frequently closely balanced.

Thus, if we take Rousseau as the departure point with respect to the growth of ideas concerning solidarity in a modern society, it can readily be seen that the stance of nation-states must involve more complicated ideas than those which have been in place in much of the Western world (and also elsewhere) since the late eighteenth century. In striving for such comprehension, we should be ever mindful of the two different traditions of democratic ideas that have been dominant in the world since that time. The fact that, following the work of Max Weber, a distinction is often made by sociologists between *theocracy* (religion dominating politics) and *caesaropapism* (politics dominating religion) makes no fundamental difference to the centrality of religion, or to the precise nature of the relationship between religion and politics, or, alternatively, church and state.

In any case, when the French Revolution turned into the Terror, it effectively transformed the notion of civil religion into a theocratic form, with all the appurtenances of what might be called a secular-religious nation-state, a kind of national cult (Gray 2007: 146–83; Scurr 2006). This was not what Rousseau apparently envisaged, nor certainly what either Durkheim or Bellah were subsequently to have in mind in invoking the concept of civil religion. However, in spite of Bellah's strenuous attempts to oppose the distortion of civil religion into a theocratic, authoritarian form, it is striking that this is precisely what appears to be happening in many parts of the world, not least in the USA itself. There is some irony in this, since in the years before Bellah published his very influential article on American civil religion in the late 1960s he had been a scholar of Japan. And in speaking of the USA, he emphatically declared American civil religion to be very different from Japanese state religion prior to the Pacific War (which started in 1941, with the USA abolishing State Shinto following the defeat of Japan in 1945). Irony lies in the fact that it is in the USA that one now finds a particular problem of a politicized civil religion with a strong theocratic tinge. In Japan, on the other hand, there are certainly elements of theocracy, but only intermittently do they have a direct effect on politics.

References

Alexander, Jeffrey C., Eyerman, Ron, Giesen, Bernhard, Smelser, Neil J., and Sztempka, Piotr (2004). *Cultural Trauma and Collective Identity.* Berkeley: University of California Press.

Altman, Daniel (2007). "Managing Globalization: The Global Quest for a Second Passport". *International Herald Tribune*, 7 Feb.

Appiah, Kwame A. (2006). *Cosmopolitanism: Ethics in a World of Strangers.* London: Allen Lane.

Asad, Tala (1993). *Genealogies of Religion: Discipline and Reasons of Power in Christianity and Islam.* Baltimore: Johns Hopkins University Press.

Barkawi, Tarak (2006). *Globalization and War.* Lonham, Md.: Rowman & Littlefield.

Barrell, John (2007). *The Spirit of Despotism: Invasions of Privacy in the 1790s.* Oxford: Oxford University Press.

Beck, Ulrich (2006). *Cosmopolitan Vision.* Cambridge: Policy Press.

Bellah, Robert N. (1967). "Civil Religion in America". *Daedalus*, 96 (Winter): 1–27.

—— (1975). *The Broken Covenant: American Civil Religion in Time of Trial.* New York: Seabury.

—— and Hammond, Phillip E. (eds.) (1980). *Varieties of Civil Religion.* San Francisco: Harper & Row.

Boli, John, W. (1980). "Global Integration and the Universal Increase of State Domination". In Albert Bergesen (ed.), *Studies of the Modern World System.* New York: Academic Press, 77–137.

BURLEIGH, MICHAEL (2006). *Sacred Causes: Religion and Politics from the European Dictators to Al Qaeda*. London: HarperPress.

CAMPBELL, GEORGE V. P. (2005). *Everything You Know Seems Wrong: Globalization and the Relativizing of Tradition*. Lanham, Md.: University Press of America.

CAPUTO, JOHN D., and VATTIMO, GIANNI (2007). *After the Death of God*. New York: Columbia University Press.

CLARKE, PETER (2006). *New Religions in Global Perspective*. London: Routledge.

DAVIS, SAM (2007). *Letter to a Christian Nation: A Challenge to the Faith of America*. London: Transworld Publishers.

DAWKINS, RICHARD (2006). *The God Delusion*. London: Bantam.

DENNETT, DANIEL (2006). *Breaking the Spell*. London: Allen Lane.

EISENSTADT, S. N. (2004). "Axial Civilizations and the Axial Age Reconsidered". In J. P. Arnason, S. N. Eisenstadt, and B. Wittrock (eds.), *Axial Civilizations and World History*. Leiden: Brill, 531–64.

ESPOSITO, JOHN L. (2002). *Unholy War: Terror in the Name of Islam*. New York: Oxford University Press.

FARBER, DAVID (ed.) (2007). *What They Think of Us: International Perceptions of the United States since 9/11*. Princeton: Princeton University Press.

FUKUYAMA, FRANCIS (2007). "Identity and Migration". *Prospect*, 139 (Feb.): 26–31.

GARREAU, JOEL (1981). *The Nine Nations of North America*. Boston: Houghton Mifflin.

GEERTZ, CLIFFORD (ed.) (1963). *Old Societies and New States: The Quest for Modernity in Asia and Africa*. New York: Free Press.

GLAZER, NATHAN (1997). *We Are All Multiculturalists Now*. Cambridge, Mass.: Harvard University Press.

—— and MOYNIHAN, DANIEL PATRICK (1970). *Beyond the Melting Pot*. Cambridge, Mass.: MIT Press.

GOKALP, ZIYA (1959). *Turkish Nationalism and Western Civilization*. London: Allen & Unwin.

GRAY, JOHN (2007). *Black Mass: Apocalyptic Religion and the Death of Utopia*. London: Allen Lane.

GROEBNER, VALENTIN (2007). *Who Are You? Identification, Deception, and Surveillance in Early Modern Europe*. New York: Zone Books.

HABERMAS, JÜRGEN (2002). *Religion and Rationality: Essays on Reason, God, and Modernity*. Cambridge, Mass.: MIT Press.

HANKISS, ELMER (2006). *The Toothpaste of Immortality: Self-Construction in the Consumer Age*. Washington: Woodrow Wilson Center Press.

HARRINGTON, MONA (1986). *The Dream of Deliverance in American Politics*. New York: Knopt.

HARRIS, LEE (2004). *Civilization and Its Enemies*. New York: Free Press.

HEDGES, CHRIS (2007). *American Fascists: The Christian Right and the War on America*. New York: Jonathan Cape.

HITCHENS, CHRISTOPHER (2007). *God is Not Great: How Religion Poisons Everything*. New York: Hatchette.

HOBSBAWM, ERIC, and RANGER, TERRENCE (eds.) (1983). *The Invention of Tradition*. Cambridge: Cambridge University Press.

HOLLINGER, DAVID A. (1995). *Postethnic America*. New York: Basic Books.

HOLTON, ROBERT J. (1998). *Globalization and the Nation-State*. Basingstoke: Macmillan.

HUNTINGTON, SAMUEL P. (1997). *The Clash of Civilizations and the Remaking of World Order.* New York: Touchstone.

—— (2005). *Who are We? America's Great Debate.* London: Free Press.

IGNATIEFF, MICHAEL (ed.) (2005). *American Exceptionalism and Human Rights.* Princeton: Princeton University Press.

JASPERS, KARL (1953). *The Origin and Goal of History.* New Haven: Yale University Press.

JONES, TOBIAS (2007). "Secular Fundamentalists are the New Totalitarians". *The Guardian,* 6 Jan., 32.

JUERGENSMEYER, MARK (1993). *The New Cold War? Religious Nationalism Confronts the Secular State.* Berkeley: University of California Press.

—— (2000). *Terror in the Mind of God: The Global Rise of Religious Violence.* Berkeley: University of California Press.

KALRA, VIRINDER S., KAUR, RAMINDER and HUTNYK, JOHN (2005). *Diaspora & Hybridity.* London: Sage.

KEARNEY, HUGH (1989). *The British Isles: A History of Four Nations.* Cambridge: Cambridge University Press.

KEPEL, GILLES (2004). *Jihad: The Trail of Political Islam.* London: I. B. Tauris.

LACE S. (2005). *The Glass Consumer: Life in a Surveillance Society.* Bristol: Policy Press.

LECHNER, FRANK J., and BOLI, JOHN (2005). *World Culture: Origins and Consequences.* Malden, Mass.: Blackwell.

LEFORT, CLAUDE (2007). *Complications: Communism and the Dilemmas of Democracy.* New York: Columbia University Press.

LIEVEN, ANATOL (2004). *America Right or Wrong: An Anatomy of American Nationalism.* London: HarperCollins.

LINCOLN, BRUCE (2006). *Holy Terrors: Thinking about Religion after September 11,* 2nd edn. Chicago: University of Chicago Press.

LIND, MICHAEL (1995). *The Next American Nation.* New York: Free Press.

LIPTAK, ADAM (2007). "Adding to Security but Multiplying the Fears". *New York Times,* 26 Feb.

LOSURDO, DOMENICO (2004). "Towards a Critique of the Category of Totalitarianism". *Historical Materialism,* 12/2: 25–55.

LYON, DAVID (2003). *Surveillance after September 11.* Cambridge: Polity Press.

MARSDEN, GEORGE M. (1980). *Fundamentalism and American Culture: The Shaping of Twentieth-Century Evangelicalism, 1870–1925.* Oxford: Oxford University Press.

MARX, GARY T. (2007). "Desperately Seeking Surveillance Studies: Players in Search of a Field". *Contemporary Sociology,* 36/2: 125–30.

MCGRATH, ALISTER (2007). *The Dawkins Delusion: Atheistic Fundamentalism and the Denial of the Divine.* London: SPCK.

MEAD, WALTER R. (2006). "God's Country". *Foreign Affairs* (Sept.–Oct.): 1–9.

MEYER, BIRGIT, and GESCHIERE, PETER (eds.) (2003). *Globalization and Identity: Dialectics of Flow and Closure.* Oxford: Blackwell.

MEYER, JOHN W. (1980). "The World Polity and the Authority of the Nation-State". In Albert Bergesen (ed.), *Studies of the Modern World System.* New York: Academic Press, 109–37.

—— BOLI, JOHN, THOMAS, GEORGE M., and RAMIREZ, FRANCISCO O. (1997). "World Society and the Nation-State". *American Journal of Sociology,* 103/1: 144–81.

MODOOD, TARIQ (2007). *Multiculturalism: A Civic Idea.* Cambridge: Polity Press.

Moisi, Dominique (2007). "The Clash of Emotions". *Foreign Affairs*, 86/1: 8–12.

Mozaffari, Mehdi (ed.) (2002). *Globalization and Civilizations*. London: Routledge.

Nairn, Tom (1977). *The Break Up of Britain*. London: New Left Books.

Neiman, Susan (2002). *Evil in Modern Thought: An Alternative History of Philosophy*. Princeton: Princeton University Press.

Pearson, Simon (2006). *A Brief History of the End of the World: From Revelation to Eco-Disaster*. London: Robinson.

Pecora, Vincent P. (2006). *Secularization and Cultural Criticism: Religion, Nation, and Modernity*. Chicago: University of Chicago Press.

Pfaff, William (2007). "Manifest Destiny: A New Direction". *New York Review of Books*, 54/2.

Phillips, Kevin (2006). *American Theocracy: The Peril and Politics of Radical Religion, Oil, and Borrowed Money in the 21st Century*. New York: Penguin (USA).

Portes, Alejandro, and Rumbaut, Ruben (2007). *Immigrant America*. Berkeley: University of California Press.

Robbins, Thomas, and Robertson, Roland (eds.) (1986). *Church–State Relations: Tensions and Transitions*. New Brunswick, NJ: Transaction Publishers.

Robertson, Roland (1978). *Meaning and Change: Explorations in the Cultural Sociology of Modern Societies*. Oxford: Blackwell.

—— (1981). "Considerations from within the American Context on the Significance of Church–State in Tension". *Sociological Analysis*, 42 (Fall): 193–208.

—— (1985). "The Development and Implications of the Classical Sociological Perspective on Religion and Revolution". In Bruce Lincoln (ed.), *Religion, Rebellion, Revolution*. London: Macmillan, 236–65.

—— (1987). "From Secularization to Globalization". *Journal of Oriental Studies*, 26/1: 28–32.

—— (1988*a*). "Christian Zionism and Jewish Zionism: Points of Contact". In Anson Shupe and Jeffrey Hadden (eds.), *The Politics of Religion and Social Change*. New York: Paragon House, 239–58.

—— (1988*b*). "Towards the Comparative Genealogy of Religion in Comparative Perspective". *Zen Buddhism Today*, 6 (Nov.), 125–33.

—— (1989). "Globalization, Politics and Religion". In James A. Beckford and Thomas Luckman (eds.), *The Changing Face of Religion*. London: Sage, 10–23.

—— (1992). *Globalization: Social Theory and Global Culture*. London: Sage.

—— (1993). "Community, Society, Globality and the Category of Religion". In Eileen Barker, James A. Beckford, and Karel Dobbelaere (eds.), *Secularization, Rationalism, and Sectarianism: Essays in Honour of Bryan R. Wilson*. Oxford: Clarendon Press, 1–17.

—— (1995). "Glocalization: Time-Space and Homogeneity-Heterogeneity". In Mike Featherstone, Scott Lash, and Roland Robertson (eds.), *Global Modernities*. London: Sage, 25–54.

—— (1998). "Identida nacional y globalizacion: falacias contemporaneas". *Revista Mexicana de Sociologia*, 1 (Jan.–Mar.), 3–19.

—— (2002). "Le Dimensioni Della Cultura Globale". In Elisabetta Batini e Rodolfo Ragionieri (eds.), *Culture e Conflitti Nella Globalizzazione*, Florence: Leo S. Olschki Editore, 17–30.

—— (2003[1983]). "Interpreting Globality". In Roland Robertson and Kathleen E. White (eds.), *Globalization: Basic Concepts in Sociology*, i. London: Routledge, 58–71.

Robertson, Roland (2006*a*). "Global Conciousness". In Roland Robertson and Jan Aart Scholte (eds.), *Encyclopedia of Globalization*, ii. New York: MTM and Routledge, 502–7.

—— (2006*b*). "Globality". In Roland Robertson and Jan Aart Scholte (eds.), *Encyclopedia of Globalization*, ii. New York: MTM and Routledge, 524–6.

—— (2006*c*). "Glocalization". In Roland Robertson and Jan Aart Scholte (eds.), *Encyclopedia of Globalization*, ii. New York: MTM and Routledge, 545–8.

—— (2006*d*). "The Increasing Monopolization of Identity by the State: The Case of the UK and the US". *Nationalism and Ethnic Politics*, 12/3–4: 373–89.

—— (2006*e*). "Nacionalismo e identidade nacional no nosso tempo". In M. V. Cabral, J. L. Garcia, and H. M. Jeronimo (eds.), *Razeo, Tempo e Tecnologa: Estudos em Homenagem a Herminio Martins*. Lisbon: Imprensa de Ciencias Sociais, 105–30.

—— (2007*a*). "Global Millennialism: A Postmortem on Secularization". In Peter Beyer and Lori G. Beaman (eds.), *Religion, Globalization and Culture*. Leiden: Brill, 9–34.

—— (2007*b*). "Globalization, culture and". In George Ritzer (ed.), *Encyclopedia of Sociology*, vi. Malden, Mass.: Blackwell, 1965–70.

—— (2007*c*). "Open Societies, Closed Minds? Exploring the Ubiquity of Suspicion and Voyeurism". *Globalizations*, 4/3: 399–416.

—— and Mouly, Ruth (1983). "Zionism in American Premillenarian Fundamentalism". *American Journal of Theology and Philosophy*, 4/3: 97–109.

—— and White, Kathleen E. (2005). "Globalization: Sociology and Cross-Disciplinarity". In Craig Calhoun, Chris Rojek, and Bryan S. Turner (eds.), *The Sage Handbook of Sociology*. London: Sage, 345–66.

—— —— (2007). "What is Globalization?" In George Ritzer (ed.), *The Blackwell Companion to Globalization*. New York: Blackwell, 53–66.

Ruse, Michael (2005). *The Evolution–Creation Struggle*. Cambridge, Mass.: Harvard University Press.

Sacks, Jonathan (2003). "Global Covenant: A Jewish Perspective on Globalization". In John Dunning (ed.), *Making Globalization Good: The Moral Challenges of Global Capitalism*. Oxford: Oxford University Press, 210–31.

Sanneh, Lamin (2006). "Religion's Return". *Times Literary Supplement*, 5402 (13 Oct.), 13–14.

Scurr, Ruth (2006). *Fatal Purity: Robespierre and the French Revolution*. London: Chatto & Windus.

Sharlet, Jeff (2006). "Through a Glass Darkly: How the Christian Right is Reimagining US History". *Harper's Magazine*, Dec.: 33–43.

Shepherd, Jessica (2007). "What Does Britain Expect?" *The Guardian*, 17 July, E: 1–2.

Smelser, Neil J. (2004). "Epilogue: September 11, 2001, as Cultural Trauma". In Alexander *et al.* (2004), 264–82.

—— and Alexander, Jeffrey C. (eds.) (1999). *Diversity and Its Discontents: Cultural Conflict and Common Ground in Contemporary America*. Princeton: Princeton University Press.

Smith, Tony (2007). *A Pact with the Devil: Washington's Bid for World Supremacy and the Betrayal of the American Promise*. New York: Routledge.

Sutton, Philip W., and Vertigans, Stephen (2005). *Resurgent Islam: A Sociological Approach*. Cambridge: Polity Press.

Talmon, J. L. (1952). *The Origins of Totalitarian Democracy*. London: Seeker & Warburg.

Taylor, Barbara (2007). "Guinea Pigs". *London Review of Books*, 29/3 (Feb.), 10–11.

Vattimo, Gianni (1992). *The Transparent Society.* Baltimore: Johns Hopkins Press.
Verovec, Steven, and Cohen, Robin (eds.) (2002). *Conceiving Cosmopolitanism.* Oxford: Oxford University Press.
Ward, Keith (2006). *Is Religion Dangerous?* Oxford: Lion.
Westin, Alan (1967). *Privacy and Freedom.* New York: Athenaeum.
Wills, Garry (2006). "A Country Ruled by Faith". *New York Review of Books*, 53 (18 Nov.).
Wilson, E. O. (2007). *The Creation: An Appeal to Save Life on Earth.* New York: Norton.

Suggested Reading

Appiah, Kwame A. (2005). *The Ethics of Identity.* Princeton: Princeton University Press.
Assad, Talal (2003). *Formations of the Secular.* Stanford, Calif.: Stanford University Press.
Beyer, Peter (1994). *Religion and Globalization.* London: Sage.
—— (2006). *Religions in Global Society.* London: Routledge.
Casanova, José (1994). *Public Religions in the Modern World.* Chicago: University of Chicago Press.
Chanda, Nayan (2007). *Bound Together: How Traders, Preachers, Adventurers, and Warriors Shaped Globalization.* New Haven: Yale University Press.
Cohen, Robin (2006). Migration and Its Enemies. Aldershot: Ashgate.
Forrester, Duncan B. (2005). *Apocalypse Now? Reflections on Faith in a Time of Terror.* Aldershot: Ashgate.
Juergensmeyer, Mark (ed.) (2006). *The Oxford Handbook of Global Religions.* Oxford: Oxford University Press.
Levey, G.B. and Modood Tariq (eds.) (2007) *Secularism, Religion and Multicultural Citizenship.* Cambridge: Cambridge University Press.
Linker, Damon (2007) *The Theocons: Secular America under Siege.* New York: Random House.
Nussbaum, Martha C. (2007). *The Clash Within: Democracy, Religious Violence and India's Future.* London: Belknap Press of Harvard University Press.
Pappe, Ilan (2006). *The Ethnic Cleansing of Palestine.* Oxford: Oneworld.
Parekh, Bhiku (2008). *A New Politics of Identity: Political Principles for an Interdependent World.* London: Palgrave Macmillan.
Sen, Amartyra (2006). *Identity and Violence: The Illusion of Destiny.* London: Allen Lane.
Taylor, Charles (2007). *A Secular Age.* Cambridge, Mass.: Belknapp Press of Harvard University.
Thomas, Scott M. (2005). *The Global Resurgence of Religion and the Transformation of International Relations.* Basingstoke: Palgrave Macmillan.
Wolin, Sheldon S. (2008). *Democracy Incorporated: Managed Democracy and the Spectre of Inverted Totalitarianism.* Princeton, NJ: Princeton University Press.
Also Huntington (2005).

CHAPTER 26

RELIGIOUS FUNDAMENTALISM

ANSON SHUPE

THE term "religious fundamentalism" has come to be applied to regional, national, and even global developments holding both religious and political dimensions. The conventional wisdom assumes when speaking of causes and movements considered *fundamentalist* that these are inherently opposed to modern, scientific, and secular values. Fundamentalists themselves (as if they were a uniform category) are therefore regarded as atavistic protesters in a rapidly evolving, consolidating world. However, the term represents a much more complex phenomenon.

ORIGIN OF THE TERM "FUNDAMENTALISM"

Fundamentalism as a formal concept began in a single religion, time, and country. As a term it was coined in 1910 from a series of ninety articles by leading conservative American Protestant Christian authors published in twelve volumes starting that year and entitled *The Fundamentals*. The volumes were financed by two businessmen-brothers, Lyman and Milton Stewart. The purpose of the essays was to defend biblical inerrancy; attack the so-called European "higher criticism" that began to examine scriptures from purely philological (historical-linguistic), archaeological, and anthropological perspectives; and refute or counter assorted related threats. Among the latter were the consolidating presences of Roman Catholicism and Mormonism and issues collectively called "modernism", from Darwinian evolution and immigrant-born cultural diversity to urbanization. Within a few years, more than 3 million free copies of *The Fundamentals* were distributed to Protestant pastors, evangelists, and seminary theology students in North America.

The thrust of American Protestant fundamentalism aimed at defending the narrower boundaries of conservative Christian orthodoxy. In so doing the fundamentalist movement became associated with the pre-millennial expectation of Jesus Christ's imminent return to Earth, superpatriotism to the point of xenophobia, rural lifestyles and values, individual piety, a rationalist suspicion of charismatic (or Holy Spirit-filled) enthusiasm characteristic of the emerging Holiness and Pentecostal movements, and anti-intellectualism. Well-known academic fundamentalists of the day included J. Gresham Machen, who abandoned Princeton Theological Seminary because of its alleged liberalness, and founded Westminster Theological Seminary in 1929. Charles Hodge, another conservative Princeton professor, once boasted, "I am not afraid to say that a new idea never originated in this seminary" (Dayton 1976: 12). Such sentiments were also to be found in the popular sermons of early twentieth-century urban evangelists such as Dwight L. Moody and the flamboyant Billy Sunday (Marsden 1978; 1984; McLoughlin 1978; Frank 1986).

So-called modern trends continued throughout the twentieth century, and a gradual liberalness/permissiveness in mass entertainment, public education, and sexual mores /sexual medicine (e.g., contraception, abortion) seemed to inundate North American culture. In response, fundamentalists who had once eschewed social amelioration policies and political involvement in favor of personal piety and spiritual salvation began calling for a "taking back" of the public arena. Mobilized by televangelists and other assiduous users of the mass media, many fundamentalists during the late twentieth century reassumed the older, less stigmatized label "evangelical", and by the early twenty-first century had become a considerable electoral base for conservative politicians in the United States (Henry 1947; Carpenter 1984; Hadden and Shupe 1988).

Expansion of the Fundamentalism Concept

Islamic fundamentalism has existed since the establishment of the Ikwan al Muslimin (Muslim Brotherhood) by Hassan al Banna in Egypt in the late 1920s. Indeed, by the 1930s, similar phenomena had spread to, among other places, Syria and

Lebanon. However, it was during the Iranian revolution of 1979 that much of the Western world heard (and/or took seriously) for the first time the phrase "Islamic fundamentalism" with reference to the Ayatollah Ruhollah Khomeini's militant theocratic attempt to implement the Shar'ia (traditional Islamic law) across all that country's institutions. One long-time observer of Iran succinctly described this specific effort in Islamification thus:

> Unique among the world's major monotheistic faiths, its tenets include laws to govern politics and society as well as a set of spiritual beliefs. It covers business deals and banking, hygiene, marriage and divorce, defense and taxes, penal codes, even family relationships. (Wright 1989: 46)

Various other observers have agreed that Islamic fundamentalism as generally defined seeks a close mixture of faith and state, enshrines patriarchy, pursues a literal scriptural interpretation of social policies and events, and endorses a pan-Islam that must be proselytized abroad in order to create an ideal '*ummah*, or international community of like-minded believers (Esposito 1986; Saiedi 1986; Pipes 1989). Meanwhile, this world view holds to a narrowly monotheistic intolerance of other faiths, rejects historicism and rationalism, and maintains an antagonism toward democratic liberalism and secularization (defined as the loss of religious influence in social, scientific, and socio-political/economic realms). In essence, the agenda of this variety of fundamentalism is for an uncompromisingly authoritarian reconstruction of society in its image of tradition.

Certain resemblances to American Protestant fundamentalism, particularly discomfort with the spread of humanistic values and a "compartmentalized" religious institution, have been apparent in an expanded use of the term. In the latter half of the twentieth century, Islamic fundamentalist movements emerged in Egypt, Lebanon, Sudan, and South Asia/Indonesia. Moreover, there were well under way by the turn of the twenty-first century parallel fundamentalist phenomena in other societies and faith traditions. In a massive five-volume series organized by the Fundamentalist Project in Chicago, the first volume alone contained specialized articles dealing regionally and nationally with currents of "fundamentalisms" in Hinduism and Sikhism, Buddhism of various countries, Japanese Shintoism, and modern Confucianism, notably in countries of non-Occidental traditions experiencing conflicting push–pull reactions to Westernization, industrialization, and their accompanying secularization (Marty and Appleby 1991). Indeed, the latter factor seems the pivotal axis about which all fundamentalisms, Christian, Islamic, or other, can be arranged. Meanwhile, even within the United States, new varieties of Protestant fundamentalism, such as Christian reconstructionism (Barron and Shupe 1992), have continued to develop, along with similar conservative emergences in Roman Catholicism (Dinges 1995) and Mormonism (Krakauer 2003).

Global Fundamentalism

What have been emerging for the past fifty years are social movements that are not simply analogous to conservative Protestantism or in their own discrete ways rigid doctrinaire reactions to social change (whether or not they seek world hegemony). Rather, the current era is experiencing a phenomenon of *global fundamentalism* that represents a pattern of many socio-political movements which share certain characteristics in their responses to a common *globalization process*. The latter is characterized as secularization, in which two contiguous developments are occurring: (1) religion becomes increasingly compartmentalized from (and may even be defined as irrelevant to) other institutional spheres; and (2) the planet is increasingly characterized by economic interdependence among nations through transnational corporations.

What is common to the infrastructure of all fundamentalist movements, therefore, is resistance to the *institutional differentiation process* which progressively relegates religious institutions and beliefs to the periphery of modern society. What is sometimes interpreted as a simple resurgence of nationalism also often accompanies the above resentment at religion being marginalized. Thus, a truly global, and therefore generic, definition of fundamentalism (embracing as well the original Protestant American prototype) sees it *as a proclamation of reclaimed authority over a sacred tradition which is to be reinstated as an antidote for a society perceived to have strayed from its cultural moorings*. Two dimensions are involved in this reclamation of authority: (1) a refutation of the radical differentiation of the sacred from the secular social realms due to modernization; and (2) a plan—no matter how utopian or vaguely conceived—to *de-differentiate* this institutional separation, thus returning religion to center stage as the important factor, not merely as a significantly competing interest constituency, in public policy discussions. Levels of economic development, racial-ethnic traditions, and other aspects of geo-politics may produce on the surface very different forms of global fundamentalism, but they are merely local and regional manifestations of the same underlying phenomenon stirring in the United States, Pakistan, Malaysia, or wherever.

Cases in point are Soka Gakkai/Nichiren Shoshu Buddhism and the post-Second World War neo-nationalist Shinto social movement industry often termed the *Minzokuha* (National Soul School) of contemporary Japan. Both religious movements seek a values transformation of that society and more direct political engagement. Both exalt and promote a form of racial/spiritual folk unity reminiscent of German mysticism (Takayama 1989; Shupe 1991). Such ultra-nationalist groups in Japan range from the "seriously patriotic" to the outright jingoistic. Indeed, Brannen (1968: 51) has argued concerning Soka Gakkai (and Nichiren Shoshu) that due to Buddhism's close relationship(s) to the political culture of various dynasties in Japanese history, "a revival in Buddhism in Japan is tantamount to a recovery of the national identity". But, Brannen fails to add, it is not simply some unifying force like the emperor worship of the 1930s. Such current Japanese movements are fully informed by, and self-consciously located in, transnational economies and a global outreach.

Differences among fundamentalist movements will nevertheless cleave to four dimensions of this genus. First is the *proclamation* by the charismatic prophet or whatever visionary: the cry for a people to return to a tradition lost, to reclaim the values of some earlier, allegedly nobler and more pristine era, as a guidepost for the major realignment to come. Second, there must be the *mythos* of how things went awry and led to the current undesirable state of things, such as a "moral breakdown" or "values corruption", steeped in religious metaphors. Third, the fundamentalist movement must draw *clear continuities* between the tradition lost and itself as the solution for restoration. Fourth, and just as important, while the proposed changes are to be accomplished in the name of the exalted tradition, they are to rely on *modern means*, from military to educational to mass media avenues. The world, of course, is not the same demographically, technologically, economically, or geo-politically as it was during the envisioned golden era; nor are the same mechanisms of opportunity available. Thus, the irony exists that with the justification of traditional values restoration fundamentalist leaders are not merely striving to construct more rigid orthodoxies along the imagined older lines, but are promulgating *new* social orders without actual precedents. The programs and policies of the 1980s Khomeini regime in Iran or of the later Taliban regime in Afghanistan were in actuality not modeled on any working theocratic system in ancient Persia or anywhere else. Neither does the Protestant Christian fundamentalism of recent years accurately reflect the pristine society of a century or more ago as it is thought to have once flourished. Such movements have been largely modern creations for modern times.

The modernity of most variations of fundamentalism can readily be observed in two important (if not always separate) phenomena: fundamentalism's coming to grips with science and its employment of violent means to reach its ends.

Fundamentalism and Science

Rather than portray fundamentalism as anti-scientific or endorsing merely retrograde science, it is more accurate to say that fundamentalisms are *pragmatically selective* in the science they appropriate as an end toward the always paramount mission of theologically realigning society. As Mendelsohn (1993: 23) has observed,

> One of the striking aspects of fundamentalist movements in Judaism, Christianity, and Islam is the open willingness of their members, in many instances, to adopt the instrumentalities and technologies of modernity in order to "reclaim" a society that they believe has been (mis)shaped by the manner in which these modern means have been used by secularists . . . they are . . . careful adaptors to modernity even as they attempt to reinterpret significant elements of the traditional.

To put it bluntly, they do not automatically eschew science, but rather want it solely on their (re-sacralized) terms.

However, the popular, contrary stereotype of religious fundamentalisms as inherently anti-intellectual, anti-science movements was established within a decade of the first publication of *The Fundamentals*. The indisputable watershed event in the United States, and in Western Protestant Christianity, was the 1925 trial of John T. Scopes in Dayton, Tennessee. Scopes, a substitute highschool instructor, taught briefly from a textbook featuring the evolutionary perspective. In so doing, he violated a Tennessee law forbidding mention of any theory "denying the story of the Divine creation of man". In the Scopes "monkey trial" (as it came to be called) the growing Christian fundamentalist movement won a brief victory—Scopes was convicted—but it paid dearly for many years. Agnostic, iconoclastic newspaper editor/pundit H. L. Mencken personally covered the trial proceedings, and succeeded in portraying the prosecuting attorney William Jennings Bryan (a three-time unsuccessful presidential candidate) and fundamentalist supporters generally as splendid economic and educational representatives of America's cultural backwater. Mencken particularly emphasized their smug, small-town know-nothingism, in opposition to "enlightened" rationality, scientific progress, and modernity.

After Scopes, the more aggressive, but increasingly frustrated, fundamentalists withdrew for a time like a defeated army. But they soon regrouped by creating an alternative insulated educational milieu that dispensed with any science that made them spiritually uncomfortable and focused instead on "eternal biblical truths", many of which, it was believed, could literally be taken from scriptures and claimed to be scientifically valid. By 1930, there were at least fifty Bible Colleges and similar schools (many unaccredited), most in major US cities. By 1940, thirty-five more started up, and another sixty schools began during 1940–50 (Hadden and Shupe 1988: 112).

But towards the beginning of the Second World War, a new, more assertive stance maintained that modern scientific facts (rather than theories) were *not* necessarily incompatible with the Bible. All that was needed was a more correct interpretation, which fundamentalist scholars believed they possessed. For example, in 1937 the author of *Modern Science and the Genesis Record* confidently declared: "The entire Bible is able to hold its own in any kind of controversy with human wisdom in any form, and of no part of the Bible is this more true than of the first part of Genesis" (Rimmer 1937). Indeed, "creation science", or "scientific creationism", became a movement within a movement that played well to fundamentalists still seeking some bridge back to the modernity from which they increasingly felt estranged. Groups such as the Religion and Science Association, the Seventh-Day Adventist-based Society for the Study of Deluge Geology and Related Sciences, and the American Scientific Affiliation, while typically short-lived (and virtually shut out from serious consideration by mainstream scientific audiences), kept the belief of a conservative religion–science reconciliation alive.

One benchmark effort, the Creation Science Institute in San Diego, California, headed by hydraulic engineer Henry M. Morris (and aided by refugees from such defunct groups as the old Deluge Geology Society), has continued into the current era. The CSI is a fundamentalist think tank, funded in large part by individual and church contributions and sales of its many creationist publications (such as Morris's classic 1961 *The Genesis Flood* and science textbooks tailored to fundamentalist Bible academies) and subscriptions to its flagship journal *Creation Science Quarterly*.

In more recent years the proposal of an unspecified *intelligent design* behind creation and natural law, minus more explicit biblical references and parallels, has been entered as a competing rival to "improbable" Darwinian ideas such as natural selection. ID maintains that living organisms are so complex that they must have been created by some kind of higher force (though supporters of the idea are rather coy when asked just what such a higher force might be). There are now in the twenty-first century a number of Internet websites, such as those of Access Research Network, the TalkOrigins Archive, IDEA (Intelligent Design and Evolution Awareness Center), the Center for Scientific Creation, and their opponents, such as the NCSE (National Center for Science Education), which serve to keep the debate over ID alive.

However, in recent years fundamentalist proponents of some sort of supernatural, or at least supra-human, agency ordering physical reality seem to have entered into a stalemate with mainstream science. Thus, they have acknowledged evolution as "one possible theory", and have fought with school systems both at local and state levels to have creationism, or some variant thereof, accepted as an "alternative possible theory" paid attention. Promoting this approach, they have met with little ultimate success in courtrooms. In a 1968 ruling in *Epperson v. Arkansas*, for example, an anti-evolution law from the 1920s (similar to ones in some other states) was struck down. As recently as December 2005, in *Kitzmiller v. Dover Area School District*, US District John E. Jones in a Harrisburg, Pennsylvania, courtroom offered a "stinging" attack on the Dover School Board's 2004 decision to insert intelligent design into the school curriculum. Deciding that ID's insertion violated the constitutional separation of church and state, Jones said that there was "overwhelming evidence" that ID "is a religious view, a mere re-labeling of creationism, and not a scientific theory". (Voters subsequently ousted the ID-promoting school board members in the next election and flagged a warning of precedent to attorneys in similar cases in Georgia and Kansas.)

Scholar James Moore (1993: 53) summed up this fundamentalist appropriation of the language and veneer of science:

The dilemma may be put simply thus: *Is creation science religion or science?* In Arkansas and Louisiana the courts replied unequivocally—it is a religion—which is perhaps why, for the first time, fundamentalists have lately begun to realize that selling their cosmology to the American public may require more than scientific prestige, pedagogic ingenuity, and juridicial sophistication.

Thus, in the evolution-versus-creationism example, Protestant Christian fundamentalists have tried to "package" existing facts and patterns to fit their a priori presuppostions, rather than model-testing, experimenting, or predicting new facts and patterns. They fight a rearguard action against biological and geological sciences, to be sure, but in the short run it is apparently sustaining enough, as it continues to produce a literature that nevertheless "preaches" to a limited "choir".

This extended example, unique in some ways to the USA, illustrates the sustaining power—whatever outsiders may think of it—of a fundamentalism's adoption of science that is both creative and derivative. In other nations, political ends and sectarian ethnic identities may play greater roles, driving a more convincing construction of a bridge from religious fundamentalism to "useful" aspects of science. Farhang (1993) found this to be true for Khomeini's Iranian Shi'ite legacy, as well as for Sunni Muslims, as did Tibi (1993), perhaps all the more so in the virtually all-encompassing cultural cocoons of societies where religious fundamentalists are the numerical majority. The Iranian mullahs may resent or even despise the content of Western motion pictures, television programs, videos, and popular music, but they are not about to discard the hardware and technologies which provide the very infrastructure for promulgating their own majoritarian doctrines and values. If the North American promoters of intelligent design seem a bit quixotic, or even hopelessly nostalgic, many religious fundamentalists' relations to the most advanced scientific and engineering technologies in the non-Christian world are not. Consider in this light the morale and propaganda value in the use of videotaped Western prisoners taken by guerrilla groups such as Hezbollah, even the occasional beheadings, and the anti-Western pronouncements by Osama bin Laden, all copied and sagaciously sent to the Al-Arabiya and Al-Jazeera television cable networks for the edification of mostly Muslim audiences. The major Western Powers' concerns in late 2006 and into 2007 about the serious Iranian potential for developing nuclear energy reserves for both peaceful and militaristic uses, coupled with rather militant, apocalyptic rhetoric concerning Islamic *jihad* and the desire to see the end of the state of Israel made by Iranian President Mahmoud Ahmadinejad, were not worst-case idle speculations. Religious fundamentalism ultimately seeks societal structural alignment, which is about power, not merely symbolic victories. Rhetoric aside, twenty-first-century fundamentalists of various religious stripes are cultural products of their own technological era, not of some previous one.

Fundamentalism and Violence

Thus far the argument for the generic fundamentalist complaint has been that institutional differentiation renders religion compartmentalized, robbing it of much of its self-mandated authority to define priorities in private affairs and public policies. This differentiation is often accompanied by increasing cultural diversity through immigration, cross-national employment opportunities, and outside cultural "imperialism" grounded in mass media and high-speed communications, and in some cases some loss of political sovereignty. Together, such perceived collective status declines cultivate frustration, and it is not surprising, therefore, that religion and nationalism serve as two key axes around which searches for relevant values systems and collective pride coalesce.

Fundamentalist movements are more than remedial efforts to restore sacred cultural moorings, however. They perceive themselves as lacking, or barely hanging on to, cultural hegemony, underdogs in a constantly threatening secularist world that wishes them at worst destroyed and at best rendered irrelevant. The often shrill, belligerent pronouncements of their spokespersons fit this context of threat and desperation, and thus the expedient slide from verbal or literary protest into violence is highly probable when other options seem moot. Unlike adversaries in pluralistic democratic societies with large but established countervailing segments of the populace that can exist in nonviolent tension, religious fundamentalists elsewhere are driven to seek and/or maintain a majoritarian position even at the price of eliminating other small pluralities. Violence is the tool of consolidation in the name of reinstating a sacred regime under such conditions. It has become a highly probable, not just optional, strategy of choice.

Thus was violence directed by the Ayatollah Khomeini of Iran, who unflinchingly preached martyrdom, whether against the Great Satan of the Christian West (principally the United States) or other Muslim believers who did not share the same vision of Islamic revolution. He exhorted literally hundreds of thousands of young Iranian men, including adolescents used as human minesweepers, to be slaughtered in human-wave assaults against better-armed Iraqi troops during the 1980s. The carnage was reminiscent of the bloody (and similarly futile) trench warfare in Europe during the First World War. An entire generation of Iranian males was severely decimated in the name of a purifying Muslim holy war. And it was Khomeini who instigated in 1979 the over 200 Iranian "pilgrims" to partake in the annual *hajj* (return) to the Grand Mosque in Mecca, Saudi Arabia. There they fired smuggled-in automatic weapons on a crowd of 40,000 worshipers, briefly taking control of the mosque, and only after nine days of intense house-to-house fighting with Saudi police were all killed or captured.

Meanwhile, during the 1980s Khomeini also decided that the 300,000 Baha'is living in Iran, followers of a Quaker-like universalistic nineteenth-century Persian mystic named Baha'u'llah, threatened to subvert the cultural hegemony of his fundamentalist Islam. Baha'is by the tens of thousands fled Iranian persecution; thousands of those remaining were rounded up, given summary kangaroo court trials, tortured, imprisoned, and then given the choice of conversion to Islam or execution. Wright (1989: 106, 181) relates how more than 400 had been hung or shot by the late 1980s, with the government even coercing families of victims to pay for the firing squads' bullets before letting them claim their loved ones' bodies. Worse, since traditional Islamic law prohibits capital punishment for female virgins, some Baha'i women and girls were reportedly first raped in their prison cells by Iranian soldiers before being executed (Hought 1990: 202).

Many other recent examples of violence in service of re-establishing the presumed "purer" underpinnings of a re-sacralized social order could be cited, given more space, from the Islamic Taliban regime in Afghanistan to Sikh fundamentalist extremists' assassination of India's Prime Minister Indira Gandhi in 1984. One is reminded of French philosopher Blaise Pascal's (2004: 314) pessimistic quip, "Men never do evil so completely and cheerfully as when they do it from religious conviction."

Conclusion

The ultimate cause of global fundamentalism is the "ceiling" eventually reached by globalization culture itself, based on its transnational economic and communications interdependence. A putative interdependent *world system* never successfully evolves, because in moving toward that end, parochial religious traditions and national identities are threatened with becoming irrelevant and subsequently reassert themselves. This globalization "threat" begins the reverse of the process; secular globalization is self-limiting. Instant communications do not simplistically stimulate an automatic sense of planet identity or a cross-national ecumenical consciousness of some kind. They instead foster resentments, rekindle desires for separate identity, and reassert idiosyncratic differences, for not all nations share equally in economic resources and affluence; nor do most faiths consider all others their equals in values or truths. Religion in particular becomes the core set of values around which resentments cluster. Nationalism becomes a frequent accessory after the fact.

At some point, depending on the region and its history, global interconnectedness sets in motion dynamics for searches for ultimate non-scientific meaning, sensitizes challenges to the truth claims of various traditional religions (which are often aligned or identified with particular national powers), and promotes a subsequent rediscovery of national identity. Yet there is a paradox, at least as has been seen so far in the yet-to-be achieved Islamic *ummah* and to a lesser extent in groups such as Buddhist Soka Gakkai with its emphasis on an emerging Third Civilization (of which it claims to be the harbinger): such ideologies' proponents expend more effort on external focuses, to proselytize and to empower cooperative, like-minded allies touching other nation-states, rather than seek internal reform first in their respective "host" societies. It remains to be examined if, when a genuine focus of internal reform is attempted within a society embedded in traditions of religious tolerance such as Great Britain or the United States, the desired internal reform movement inevitably "cools" because of countervailing faith groups, and thereby loses a portion of its external goal directive.

In the end, however, globalization and fundamentalism are two sides of the same dialectic coin. Something akin to the globalization process so often described in recent decades by some global theorists in economics and sociology *is* happening on this planet (Wallerstein 1974); something similar to a worldwide wave of fundamentalist movements with remarkably similar characteristics, claims, and goals is occurring in response (Hadden and Shupe 1988). As this cyclical process occurs in each society, so, at the macro-level, goes the planet.

References

Barron, Bruce, and Shupe, Anson (1992). "Reasons for the Growing Popularity of Christian Reconstructionism: The Determination to Attain Dominion". In Bronislaw Misztal and Anson Shupe (eds.), *Revival of Religious Fundamentalism in East and West*, Religion and Politics in Comparative Perspective Series. Westport, Conn.: Praeger Publishers, 83–96.

Brannen, Noah S. (1968). *Soka Gakkai*. Richmond, Va.: John Knox Press.

Carpenter, Jon (1984). "The Fundamentalist Leaven and the Rise of an Evangelical United Front". In Leonard I. Sweet (ed.), *The Evangelical Tradition in America*. Macon, Ga.: Mercer University Press, 25–88.

Dayton, Donald (1976). *Discovering an Evangelical Heritage*. New York: Harper & Row.

Dinges, William (1995). "Roman Catholic Traditionalism". In Timothy Miller (ed.), *America's Alternative Religions*. Albany, NY: State University of New York Press, 101–7.

Esposito, John L. (1986). "Modern Islamic Sociopolitical Thought". In Jeffrey K. Hadden and Anson Shupe (eds.), *Prophetic Religion and Politics*. New York: Paragon House, 153–72.

Farhang, Rajace (1993). "Islam and Modernity: The Reconstruction of the Alternative Shi'ite Islamic Worldview in Iran". In Marty and Appleby (1993) 103–25.

Frank, Douglas W. (1986). *Less than Conquerors: How Evangelicals Entered the Twentieth Century*. Grand Rapids, Mich.: William B. Eerdmans.

Hadden, Jeffrey K., and Shupe, Anson (1988). *Televangelism: Power and Politics on God's Frontier*. New York: Henry Holt.

Henry, Carl F. H. (1947). *The Uneasy Conscience of Modern Fundamentalism.* Grand Rapids, Mich.: William B. Eerdmans.

Hought, James A. (1990). *Holy Horrors.* Buffalo: Prometheus Books.

Krakauer, Jon (2003). *Under the Banner of Heaven.* New York: Doubleday.

McLoughlin, William G. (1978). *Revivals, Awakenings, and Reform.* Chicago: University of Chicago Press.

Marsden, George M. (1978). *Fundamentalism and American Culture.* New York: Oxford University Press.

—— (1984). *Evangelicals and Modern America.* Grand Rapids, Mich.: William B. Eerdmans.

Marty, Martin E., and Appleby, R. Scott (eds.) (1991). *The Fundamentalist Project,* i. *Fundamentalisms Observed.* Chicago: University of Chicago Press.

—— —— (eds.) (1993). The Fundamentalist Project, ii. *Fundamentalisms and Society: Reclaiming the Sciences, the Family, and Education.* Chicago: University of Chicago Press.

Mendelsohn, Everett (1993). "Religious Fundamentalism and the Sciences". In Marty and Appleby (1993), 23–41.

Moore, James (1993). "The Creationist Cosmos of Protestant Fundamentalism". In Marty and Appleby (1993), 42–72.

Morris, Henry M. (1961). *The Genesis Flood.* San Diego: Creation Science Institute.

Pascal, Blaise (2004). *Thoughts, Letters and Minor Works,* ed. Charles W. Eliot. Harvard Classics Series, 48. Cambridge, Mass.: Harvard University Press.

Pipes, Daniel (1989). "Fundamentalist Muslims in World Politics". In Shupe and Hadden (1989), 123–32.

Rimmer, Harry (1937). *Modern Science and the Genesis Record.* Berne, Ind.: The Berne Witness Company.

Saiedi, Nader (1986). "What Is Islamic Fundamentalism?" In Jeffrey K. Hadden and Anson Shupe (eds.), *Prophetic Religion and Politics.* New York: Paragon House, 173–95.

Shupe, Anson (1991). "Globalization versus Religious Nativism: Japan's Soka Gakkai in the World Arena". In Roland Robertson and William R. Garrett (eds.), *Religion and the Global Order.* New York: Paragon House, 183–99.

—— and Hadden, Jeffrey K. (1989). *Secularization and Fundamentalism Reconsidered.* New York: Paragon House.

Takayama, Peter K. (1989). "The Revitalization Movement of Modern Japanese Civil Religion". *Sociological Analysis,* 48/4: 328–41.

Tibi, Bassam (1993). "The Worldview of Sunni Arab Fundamentalists: Attitudes toward Modern Science and Technology". In Marty and Appleby (1993), 73–102.

Wallerstein, Immanuel (1974). *The Modern World System.* New York: Academic Press.

Wright, Robin (1989). *In the Name of God: The Khomeini Decade.* New York: Simon & Schuster.

Suggested Reading

Ammerman, Nancy Tatom (1987). *Bible Believers: Fundamentalists in the Modern World.* New Brunswick, NJ: Rutgers University Press.

Dobbelaere, Karel (1981). *Secularization: A Multi-Dimensional Concept*, Current Sociology Series, 29. Beverly Hills, Calif.: Sage Publications.

Iaidicola, Peter, and Shupe, Anson (2003). *Violence, Inequality, and Human Freedom*, 2nd edn. New York: Rowman & Littlefield.

Juergensmeyer, Mark (2003). *Terror in the Mind of God: The Global Rise of Religious Violence*, 3rd edn. Berkeley: University of California Press.

Numbers, Ronald L. (1993). *The Creationists: The Evolution of Scientific Creationism*. Berkeley: University of California Press.

Pipes, Daniel (1983). *In the Path of God: Islam and Political Power*. New York: Basic Books.

Wright, Robin (1985). *Sacred Rage: The Wrath of Militant Islam*. New York: Linden Press/Simon & Schuster.

CHAPTER 27

MIGRATION AND THE GLOBALIZATION OF RELIGION

CAROLINE PLÜSS

The Globalization of Religion through Migration

This chapter seeks answers to the question: how do religious practitioners who are migrants engage in processes that globalize their religious beliefs and practices? That is, how do these migrants become carriers of processes of religious globalization? Migrants, including missionaries, engage in processes of globalization of their religious beliefs and practices when they express these beliefs and practices in cultural, social, political, or economic arenas that span several geographical regions. Such transnational arenas are characterized by the fact that the processes taking place in them refer to the characteristics of several geographical regions that these arenas span. Processes taking place in transnational arenas, such as the adaptation of migrants' religion to the migrants' new surroundings, are partly de-territorialized because such processes cannot be explained in terms of the characteristics of one territory alone, such as the new place of residence to which religious beliefs and practices are brought. To attempt to explain such processes in terms of the characteristics of just one territory does not satisfactorily reveal why these beliefs and practices have been acquired, how they are held and performed, and how they explain the ways in which migrants relate to their surroundings. Any explanation of transnational processes needs to account for how such processes reflect the characteristics of several regions that these processes connect. This connecting of the characteristics of several regions explains why processes that take place in transnational arenas are carriers of processes of globalization. A typical example of how religious beliefs and practices become carriers of processes of globalization is when these beliefs and practices express relations with co-religionists and other ethnic groups in a new place of residence, as well as with co-religionists (and possibly other individuals) residing elsewhere.

While trying to understand why and how religious beliefs and practices become embedded in transnational arenas, the underlying interest of this chapter is to analyse whether the expression of religious beliefs and practices in transnational arenas leads to processes that extend cultural homogenization or to processes that create cultural heterogeneity. Cultural homogenization, as an ideal type, occurs when the cultural characteristics from one region are established in another region, without being changed as a consequence of the new cultural surroundings. Cultural heterogenization, on the other hand, occurs when the migration of cultural characteristics from one region to another creates new cultural forms that take on the characteristics of several regions simultaneously, and that create cultural hybridity by combining the cultural characteristics of several regions. The outcome of migrants' transnationalization of religion through processes of cultural homogenization is that co-religionists in different geographical regions come to share very similar religious beliefs and practices. Cultural homogenization, as a form of globalization, rearranges the locations of cultural boundaries by extending these boundaries transnationally. As Lehman suggests, such transnationalization leads to the proliferation of new and reformulated boundaries in the spheres of culture, ethnicity, language, and religion (2002: 311). Although this form of transnationalization of religion changes cultural boundaries by changing the location of a culture, it does not transform the culture's essential substance. One important consequence of such rearranging of cultural boundaries in relation to globalization is that it not only increases the cultural diversity in the place of immigration (with its positive and negative consequences), it also connects individuals transnationally, in that they share very similar religious beliefs and practices that enable them to establish and maintain transnational interactions.

The transnational cultural heterogenization of religious beliefs and practices through migration increases the diversity of existing religious beliefs and practices. It does so by transforming adherents' beliefs and practices when those adherents come into contact with another culture. The concept of cultural hybridization provides useful insights into how religious beliefs and practices may be changed in transnational arenas, because the concept allows us to understand how it is possible to give simultaneous validity to elements from different cultures. Hybridization can be defined as the process by which cultural 'forms become separated from existing practices and recombine with new forms and new practices' (Rowe and Schelling, quoted in Nederveen Pieterse 2004: 64). This definition suggests that selecting, rearranging, and giving new emphases to existing elements of a religious tradition because of contact with another culture may also be considered a form of cultural heterogenization. Adherents of a religion may not only integrate elements from a new culture into their existing religious tradition through some form of assimilation to the new culture in their new place of residence, but may also transform their tradition in less direct ways, such as by rearranging elements of their religion, and by giving these elements different emphases, to increase their differentiation from the new culture. As the term 'world religions' suggests, the history of migration and religion provides us with an example of one of the earliest forms of cultural globalization.

To analyse how migration transforms religious beliefs and practices, it is useful to examine the suggestion that religion becomes transformed by its broader contexts because it expresses concerns that are not religious to begin with (Dirlik 2003: 156). The transnationalization of religion stems not only from the religious projects of individuals and movements, but also from migrants' intention to attain social, economic, and political goals—hence the association of transnational religion with capitalism, colonialism, conquest, and international reconciliation. Differences in access to various resources between geographical regions also influence the directions in which religions may migrate. It is significant that during the time of the Empire, it was Britain that sent the largest number of missionaries abroad, and that today, the largest number of missionaries is sent from the USA. Religion not only spreads with migration, but also, once established in a new region, facilitates the migration of more individuals by providing transnational networks that co-religionists may use to migrate and realize their projects in other places. For example, the Assemblies of God in Zimbabwe, established by Christian missionaries from Britain, became significantly different in relation to the British Christian institutions from which the movement originated. These differences became the more evident once members who had converted to the church in Zimbabwe migrated to London (Lehman 2002: 301–2).

Differences in the religious, economic, cultural, social, and political characteristics of individuals living in different areas explain why there are two fundamentally distinct forms of religious globalization. Reflecting such power differences which underlie the distinction between homogenizing and heterogenizing forms of cultural globalization, Lehman distinguished between fundamentalist and cosmopolitan religious globalization. Fundamentalist religious globalization, which aims to extend cultural homogeneity, may refer to the charisma of a religious leader, or belief in the infallibility of a sacred text, as legitimizations for why religious beliefs and practices need to remain unchanged in a new culture (2002: 299). According to

Lehman, the distinguishing characteristic of fundamentalist religious globalization is that it establishes itself in a new culture without acknowledging this new culture—that is, without theorizing the relations between the culture in which its beliefs and practices have originated and the new culture in which they become embedded (2002: 306). Although even very strongly fundamentalist forms of migrant religions have been observed to integrate references to new cultures in some regards (Clarke 2006: 123), fundamentalist religious globalization indicates strong power differences between the culture in which a religion is rooted and the culture in which it seeks to establish itself, when it comes to defining religious beliefs and practices.

The cosmopolitan type of religious globalization, on the other hand, points towards less accentuated power differences between pre-migration and post-migration cultures. Cosmopolitan religious globalization gives varying degrees of recognition to the characteristics of the cultures into which a religion migrates. As Lehman emphasizes, the most distinguishing feature of cosmopolitan religious globalization is that it generates discourses on the relations between the culture of origin and the culture to which the religion migrates (2002: 302). In other words, cosmopolitan religious globalization theorizes and contextualizes an existing religious discourse in relation to the cultures in which it wishes to establish itself (Lehmann 2002: 305).

Differentiating through Essentializing Migrant Religion

Migrants may use their religion not only as a means to adapt to new surroundings, but also as a means to differentiate themselves from these surroundings through stressing what they understand to be 'the essence' of their religion. Immigrants typically gather around shared religious, linguistic, and regional characteristics, and establish their own religious and cultural communities. Often, religious organizations are the first associations that immigrants set up in a new place of residence. These organizations serve as networks from which the migrants can gain multiple forms of support, and provide symbols of unification of individuals who may otherwise have many different characteristics, such as cultural, economic, and social differences (Levitt 2001: 24; Haller 2003: 76). For example, the first association that Muslim migrants from India formed in Hong Kong in the 1880s, the Trustees of the Islamic Community, represented Muslims from various regions of India, with different languages, customs, and interpretations of Islam, including Sunnis and Shi'ites (Plüss 2006: 662). The association enabled Muslim immigrants to maintain Islamic practices and gave them support to differentiate themselves from non-Muslims in their non-Islamic surroundings. Immigrant religious associations can serve as important channels through which immigrants can articulate, and find support for, the demands they have in relation to living in new surroundings. Religious organizations may campaign for the cultural, social, and economic recognition of the migrants. For example, the United Muslim Association of Hong Kong (UMAH), which was established by Muslim immigrants from Pakistan and India, is one of the oldest established groups in Hong Kong that have appealed to the Hong Kong government to provide more English education in state primary and secondary schools. After the return of Hong Kong to Chinese sovereignty, most state schools have switched from English-language to Cantonese-language teaching, and children of parents who do not speak and read Cantonese have experienced considerable difficulties in succeeding with Cantonese-language teaching. Many of these pupils cannot succeed in Cantonese-language schools. To address this difficulty, the association has opened its own school, which teaches in Cantonese, English, and Urdu.

By providing symbols of unification and support, immigrant religion also works as a conceptual and emotional resource to generate solidarity among co-religionists. For this reason, religion can become a key element in the identities of individuals who migrated for financial, educational, or political reasons, rather than for religious reasons. Migrant religion becomes especially relevant when the immigrants experience little integration into their new surroundings. Religion strengthens their pride in their cultural characteristics, thus ensuring some degree of cultural homogeneity in relation to the characteristics that the immigrants possessed before migrating. Reviving or renewing religious commitment provides migrants with partially de-territorialized, or even extra-territorial, identities that can lessen the impact of uprootedness, alienation, racism, and frustration. This explains why immigrants have been observed to become more religious upon migration. For example, Somali immigrants in Britain and Canada have been observed to combine 'accommodation' to the West with stronger identifications with Islam (McGown 1999: 233). Migrant religion can become a vehicle for expressing immigrants' nostalgia about their way of life before migration, making religion a substitute for the 'homeplace' (Vertovec 2000: 18). Feelings of attachment to a region of origin, expressed through essentialized forms of religiosity, may persist even throughout an extended migration history spanning centuries. For example, Parsis in Hong Kong, despite considerable economic integration and some political integration during Hong Kong's colonial rule, never seriously challenged Zoroastrian rules forbidding exogamy. Such deliberate differentiation was not lessened by the fact that the Parsi community in Hong Kong never counted more than 100 members, and needed to rely on the much larger community in Mumbai to find spouses (Plüss 2005: 209), or by the fact that the Zoroastrians' strong inclination not to accept conversions has accounted for significantly declining numbers of Zoroastrians worldwide.

Maintaining, or reaffirming, religious beliefs and practices upon migration is an important strategy that migrants can use to access cultural, social, economic, or even political resources that are embedded in their relations with co-religionists, whether those co-religionists reside in the same place or elsewhere. Such resources can include information, trust, manpower, work, finance, friends, or even spouses (Haller 2003: 81; Plüss 2005: 209). Silliman observes that Sephardic Jewish traders in Asia with smaller businesses lived and traded almost exclusively among co-religionists, and hardly integrated into majority cultures. Socially and economically, these traders were almost exclusively dependent on their Sephardic diasporic networks in Asia. For example, these merchants needed to undertake long journeys throughout the British Empire in Asia to buy and sell their goods. During these journeys, they resided in each others' houses for extended periods, combining business with meals and the celebration of a shared religious and ethnic identity (Silliman 1998: 57).

My research on Jain diamond traders from India in Hong Kong shows how the sharing of an essentialized Jain religiosity closely intertwines religion and economic pursuits by maintaining and establishing networks of trust, which are crucial for success in the diamond trade. Most Jains in Hong Kong operate, or work in, branches of transnational diamond-trading firms that have their base in India, where the diamonds are mined and cut. For Jains in Hong Kong, sharing essentialized religious identities with co-religionists in Hong Kong, as well as in India and other places, means avoiding any significant degree of assimilation to the Cantonese majority culture, such as, for example, learning the Cantonese language or establishing friendships with Chinese residents. Much of the success of the Jain diamond trade in Hong Kong derives from traders' ability to maintain networks of trust and mutual obligation with diamond-trading co-religionists, so that a trader can find guarantors for the credit he needs to obtain from banks to buy the diamonds. Taking a prominent role in religious activities in the Jain *Sangh* (temple) in Hong Kong signals to other diamond traders that the trader in question is in good business standing. Appearance in the temple, especially since it is linked to moral values enshrined in Jain religiosity, signals to other traders that the person in question has no hesitation about meeting his guarantors, and is therefore worthy of business trust (Plüss 2005: 211). The fact that maintaining essentialized religious identities, and thus differences from surrounding cultures, is essential to Jain identity in Hong Kong is also evidenced by the fact that the Jain *Sangh* hired a priest from India who is fluent in Gujarati and Hindi, but who speaks neither Cantonese nor English.

Another example, that of Sephardic Jews in Hong Kong in the second half of the nineteenth century, illustrates that the promotion of essentialized religious identities helped leading members of that community to obtain access to resources enshrined in their diasporic networks with co-religionists. Despite the fact that during this time period prominent Sephardic traders also made considerable efforts to anglicize their identities in order to increase their acceptance by the British economic and political elites in Hong Kong (and thus to help their trade), these traders were mindful of demonstrated high social status, in the form of religious leadership, among Sephardim in Hong Kong and in the wider diaspora. Maintaining or gaining recognition from co-religionists for being a religious leader provided privileged access to trade, manpower, employment, and authority in the Sephardic diaspora in which religion, family, and business were closely allied. Rivalry over the leadership position in Hong Kong towards the turn of the twentieth century, as evidenced by the competing projects of prominent merchants to construct a synagogue in Hong Kong, led to considerable dispute in the Sephardic community, including a court case (Plüss 2002: 57–60). Promoting essentialized religious identities to increase social prestige in an immigrant community is a process of ethnic differentiation that has also been observed among Hindus living outside India. They give considerable support to revivalist Hinduism in India, and are an important source of the movement's income (Vertovec 2000: 30–2).

From the point of view of migrants, transnational religious connections provide routes for migration that are likely to facilitate movement between places, providing migrants with possible incentives to maintain their religious affiliation. As Levitt observes, the connections between the Catholic Church in Boston and in Ireland provided representation and protection for both Irish immigrants in the United States and for returned migrants from the United States in Ireland. These transnational links even prompted the Irish government to make the Catholic centre in Boston its point of contact with the Irish immigrant community in the United States (Levitt 2004: 7–8). Citing another case, the author also observes that individuals who were once members of a church, and who migrated without keeping their religious affiliation, were not keenly reincorporated by the religious organizations of their place of origin once they returned. This is because church organizations in Europe feared that their former members who had migrated to the United States, where the churches did not have branches, and who then returned, might have converted to another religion and would start proselytizing, might have acquired new ways of thinking that would challenge the churches' authorities, or might have acquired political skills to establish village organizations and labour parties that would challenge the power of the churches (Levitt 2001: 10).

Last, but not least, multicultural policies and policies of ethnic pluralism in places of immigration can also encourage migrants to articulate religious and ethnic identities with strong roots in their previous places of residence. It is, debatable, however, whether such policies alone have a strong impact on the development of transnational religious identifications. Ethnic engineering in the nation-state of Singapore, which classifies Singaporeans into four 'races' with cultural origins partially rooted in other places, appears to foster partly de-territorialized religious identifications when these articulations of ethnicity support the citizens' economic, social, political, or cultural pursuits. For example, promotion of Chinese culture in Singapore, including Confucianism, has been linked to enabling Singaporeans to take advantage of the economic opportunities that opened up in the People's Republic of China after its liberal economic reforms started in the 1980s. Undoubtedly, multicultural policies require people to articulate distinct identities, and such policies encourage immigrants to think about, and become more aware of, what could serve as their distinguishing characteristics. Immigrants' new articulation of their traditions may involve them singling out cultural and religious features from their daily lives, and may transform these features into markers of identity, often making the immigrants religiously more conservative (Van der Veer 2002: 101–2).

Transforming Migrant Religion with Multi-Local Identifications

In so far as religious migrants do not only transfer their religious beliefs and practices from their previous place of residence to the new one, but in one way or another also change them as a consequence of living in a new place, the religious characteristics of the migrants become multi-local. This means that these religions combine characteristics rooted in different regions, and thus become culturally hybrid. As already suggested, even an emphasis on traditionalism in migrant religiosity is likely to denote a degree of adaptation to new circumstances—namely, by denoting differentiation. Emphasizing tradition, therefore, is often not purely a process of cultural homogenization in relation to the characteristics the migrant possessed before migrating. As Van der Veer observes, 'traditional' religions of migrants should not automatically be regarded as being rooted only in the culture preceding migration (2002: 95–101).

Answering questions about living in new surroundings is likely to transform migrants' religion. One question arising for many Muslim immigrants in non-Islamic societies is how they should participate in political and juridical systems whose legitimacy their religion does not recognize. Short of relinquishing their religion, the Muslim immigrants may choose between living in enclaves and avoiding interaction with the dominant cultures (Mattson 2003: 204–11), and finding new ways of thinking about non-Islamic societies in order to engage in selective and restricted cooperation with institutions representing non-Islamic majority cultures. Such involvement is most likely accompanied by formulating new religious identities that partially adopt elements from the dominant culture(s). For example, a few American-Muslim leaders have tried to make the point that

American political concepts are 'authentic' to Islam because the USA allows Muslims to practise and propagate their religion freely (Mattson 2003: 206–8). Increased contact with other cultures, whether because of migration or increased transnational communication, is likely to motivate the adherents of a religious tradition to devise new religious forms. For example, changes in the global financial market, such as the introduction of derivatives, which Muslims may consider to be contradictory to Islamic principles, led Muslims to search for new forms of Islamic banking (Van der Veer 2002: 106).

When religious beliefs and practices strongly contradict moral sentiments or laws in their new place of residence, migrants come under pressure to discard the offending elements. Immigrants can resolve such a conflict of loyalties by developing new interpretations of why some items of religious beliefs and practices have changed, allowing them to keep their religion and maintain the core religious elements they share with co-religionists residing elsewhere (McGown 1999: 230). Assimilation to dominant values in a new place of residence frequently stems from the migrants' wish to improve their access to resources controlled by representatives of the dominant culture(s). For example, ethnically and religiously different Muslims in Hong Kong saw advantages in de-emphasizing their differences in order to access resources provided by the majority culture. The Hong Kong government recognizes only one organization, the Incorporated Trustees of the Islamic Community Fund, to represent Muslims in the territory. The trustees administer land provided by the government for the construction of Muslim cemeteries and mosques. Since the Shi'ites in Hong Kong, who are a much smaller group than the Sunnis, also wish to have a representative among the trustees, and since the Sunnis favour partial inclusion of the Shi'ites, both groups have modified their religious practices. The Shi'ite trustee, who is a Bohra Muslim of Indian origin, performs some prayers in one of the Sunni mosques (Plüss 2006: 668), which is uncommon among Bohras and Sunnis in India.

Adoption of characteristics of majority cultures, even if such cultures are understood to contradict the values and practices of minority immigrant religion, can, despite the implied paradox, work to help the immigrants continue to distinguish their beliefs and practices from those of the majorities. In Hong Kong, it is through learning the Cantonese language that ethnically different Muslims can pool resources to perform a range of religious activities for which many ethnic groups of Muslims alone would not have enough resources. In this sense, assimilation to the majority culture enables Muslims to continue to distinguish themselves from the Cantonese majority culture, because assimilation provides the Muslims with the linguistic means to participate in a larger number of religious activities in Hong Kong (Plüss 2006).

Individuals may adopt new religious beliefs brought to their place of residence through migration, if they perceive that doing so will provide them with a wider range of possibilities to realize their projects. For example, they may perceive that adhering to new religions will allow them to transcend the cultural limitations of their place of residence. One of the reasons why Hong Kong-Chinese residents adopted the doctrines of the Church of Jesus Christ of Latter-Day Saints (Mormons) was that this church offered a path to salvation, which these converts could not find in Chinese culture (Plüss 1999). In addition, a number of younger Chinese residents in Hong Kong joined this church despite significant differences between its doctrines and Chinese culture, and the negative perception of the church among Chinese residents in Hong Kong, because they found that joining could help them to acquire a university education in the USA. The church in Hong Kong offered potential recruits help with learning English by, for example, operating a tutorial college. It also helped Chinese converts gain financial support for studying in the universities it operates in the United States. Co-religionists in the United States helped by providing part-time work for the Hong Kong students. To transcend local limitations, nation-states may deliberately promote the immigration of individuals with characteristics the state in question deems useful, in order to realize its aims in the places the migrants come from. Glick Schiller suggests that the USA supported the immigration of born-again Christians from Haiti so that the migrants would support American foreign policies in Haiti, by giving resources to the 'democratic' opposition in Haiti (2005: 453–4).

Age, gender, ethnicity, region of origin, religious belief, type of religious organization, length of settlement, socio-economic status, aspirations, and characteristics of a host society are factors accounting for why, and how, religious migrants may adapt their religion to their new circumstances. For example, multi-ethnic practices of Islam in Hong Kong were supported by Muslims who have lived in Hong Kong for a considerable length of time. Such practices, most prominently promoted by the Islamic Union of Hong Kong, include Muslims of Chinese, Indian, Pakistani, Indonesian, and mixed ethnic origins. More recent Muslim immigrants, however, strongly link Islam to their experiences in regions where they previously lived, and they interact hardly at all with Muslims from other areas (Plüss 2006: 657). An example of how the characteristics of a new place of residence influence how migrant religion transforms itself are the movements towards privatization and individualization of immigrant religion in Western societies. These processes change the role of immigrant religion from providing collective and stable identifications to supporting the formation of religious identities that have come to be understood as private and personal choices (Van der Veer 2001: 10).

Adapting migrant religion to fit more of the characteristics of the new surroundings may also transform the beliefs and practices of co-religionists residing elsewhere. Allievi finds that the transnational circulation of new discourses on Islam, stemming from Muslims and non-Muslims in countries with Muslim minorities, influences how Islam is thought about by Islamic leaders in the 'heartlands' of Islam, including the leaders' recognition that interpretations of Islam now also stem from places where Muslims are not in the majority (2003: 15–23). Advances in communication and transport technologies increase multi-polar transnational flows between definitions of religious beliefs and practices. For example, Brazilian immigrants who have settled in Massachusetts send recordings of their Portuguese-language Masses to Brazil, where they are broadcast on local television in the area in which the migrants previously lived, and where they have many relatives (Levitt 2004: 1). The flows of missionaries also show potential for cultural heterogenization through the establishment of multi-local identifications. For example, when the International Church of the Four Square Gospel, a Protestant Church formed by Brazilian immigrants in Los Angeles, sent missionaries back to Brazil, the denomination rapidly started to grow in Brazil. Brazilian church members then used links with co-religionists in the United States to migrate to the USA. As the immigrant community of Brazilians in the United States grew, the church in Brazil, in turn, dispatched missionaries to America (Levitt 2004: 9).

Such transnational flows of definitions of religions indicate that analysis of the transformation of religious beliefs and practices through globalization should not use paradigms that take into account only a series of subsequent uni-directional transformations of religious beliefs and practices. Rather, such analysis needs to take into account the fact that religious beliefs and practices become embedded in transnational arenas that need to be understood by their simultaneous and multi-polar references to the characteristics of different geographical regions, while taking into account power differentials enshrined in these regions.

Cosmopolitan or Anti-Cosmopolitan Religious Globalization?

One of the fundamental questions raised by the transnational circulation of religious beliefs, images, practitioners, missionaries, and movements is that of the extent to which such globalization increases cosmopolitanism within a religious tradition—that is, openness towards different cultures, leading to cultural heterogeneity through the integration of characteristics rooted in different geographical regions. When adherents of a religion become concerned that the essence of their faith is becoming diluted or lost, this limits the degree to which they may adopt elements from different cultures. This concern can give rise to schisms, with adherents wanting to save what they perceive to be the essence of their religion. The fact that religion is concerned with salvation makes its adherents likely to be vigilant when it comes to approving changes in their beliefs and practices. The structure linking substantive items of belief, the concepts of access to truth, organizational features, historical legitimacy, and access to social and material resources enshrined in religions can influence how religious practitioners may construct cosmopolitanism upon contact with another culture. A high degree of adaptation to new cultures can lead to the (near) dissolution of an immigrant religion, given that the religion can no longer distinguish itself sufficiently from its surroundings (Clarke 2006: 129).

The Internet and other forms of trans-regional communication can be understood to work towards the democratization of definitions of religious beliefs and practices, at least among individuals who have access to these technologies. The Internet allows individuals to broadcast themselves as 'self-appointed religious specialists' (Van der Veer 2002: 101), and to access this information. The results of the spread of religious messages through global forms of communication are, however, not only democratic. Haller (2003) suggests that Jews and Sindhis in Gibraltar are influenced by how the elites in their communities define the groups' religious identities in relation to how they select images and definitions from transnational circulations of religious identities in the media. Among the Jews, important community positions became filled by orthodox Ashkenazim immigrants, and this change reinforced religious and ethnic boundaries between Jews and Gentiles in Gibraltar. To make these new boundaries visible, community members selected images of Jewish difference from global flows of representations of Jewish identities in the media, such as women wearing wigs. On the other hand, changes in the laws of abode made the leaders of the Sindhi community in Gibraltar more liberal, and this encouraged its members to select symbols indicating the openness of their religious and ethnic boundaries (Haller 2003: 92–3). These examples indicate that individuals who use de-territorialized means of communication also operate in territorial contexts with their own distributions of power. Their appropriation of trans-regional flows of religious images and beliefs, therefore, does not lead only towards increasing cultural heterogenization.

Missionary work is a good example for investigating what kind of cultural hybridizations may be constructed to recruit adherents from other cultures. Religious movements wishing to gain adherents from different cultures often see a need to change their emphasis, so as to respond to the different characteristics of potential members, even if the potential recruits share some of the cultural origins of the religion. For example, when the Vishav Hindu Parishad (VHP), a Hindu revivalist movement originating in India, seeks to recruit new members, it adapts the definitions of its goals to the characteristics of different places. In India, the VHP stresses anti-Muslim politics, whereas in the USA, with its multicultural ethos, the VHP stresses the importance of the family (Van der Veer 2001: 6–7).

Given that the aim of the religion that seeks to incorporate new adherents from another culture is to perpetuate itself, integrating elements from other cultures is unlikely to give such adoptions the same degree of epistemological validity as the elements of the religion's own tradition. Robbins (2004) elaborates this point in an analysis of the spread of Pentecostal-charismatic Christianity, showing how the power differences between the representatives of different cultures are reflected in the discourses by which Pentecostal-charismatic Christianity integrates elements from the cultures in which it seeks to establish itself. Robbins observes that Pentecostal-charismatic Christianity's hybridizations remain essentially anti-syncretic. For example, although the religion incorporates cosmologies from the cultures in which it seeks to establish itself, it does this by denying their validity—that is, by defining these cosmologies as evil. Such cultural hybridization allows Pentecostalism to replicate its existing doctrine, organizational features, and rituals in canonical ways, while adapting itself to new cultures in locally meaningful terms. This means that Pentecostalism operates differently, and means different things, in different places, while maintaining a relatively unchanged core of religious beliefs and practices (Robbins 2004: 117–29). Such anti-syncretic hybridization does make reference to different cultures, but without being significantly open to them. The example of Pentecostal-charismatic Christianity illustrates Beyer's comment on religious globalization suggesting that religious globalization is best understood as a process that establishes local versions of a global model of religious beliefs and practices, and through which religion becomes simultaneously global and local (2003: 379).

With regard to maintaining religious beliefs and practices after migration in relatively unchanged forms, it is relevant to stress that any investigation of the globalization of religion also needs to take into account the fact that its reference to the supernatural, and its emphasis on forming a community of believers, may facilitate transnationalization by motivating extra-territorial identifications. As Levitt stresses, religious migrants can conceive of the possibility that they are not merely the residents of subsequent places but also the inhabitants of a transnational 'third space'—that is, an alternative topography that is determined by their religious 'citizenship' and in which they may see themselves as always 'working for God' in the same religious space (2004: 3).

These claims do not deny that syncretism, hybridization, and cosmopolitanism are essential features in the transnationalization of religion. Yet, given the fact that religions, in most cases, are also ideological communities (however diffuse such ideologies may be), these ideologies by themselves constitute essential elements in religions that hinder the degree to which they can adapt themselves to new values without ceasing to exist. Within these limitations, and as elaborated in this chapter, the transnationalization of religion includes multiple flows and multiple directions by which religious definitions move from one culture to another. Since the transnationalization of religion does not stem from any one centre alone, and involves multiple crossings of cultural boundaries, and thus diversification of religious discourse, the transnationalization of religion works towards an increase in cultural heterogenization, albeit not always in a profoundly cosmopolitan way.

Conclusion

As this chapter has elaborated, the transnationalization of religion through migration is rarely a case of only extending cultural characteristics from one place into another—that is, a process of transnational cultural homogenization. Rather, as Van der Veer suggests, the transnationalization of religion through migration may best be thought of as leading to the formation of diverse localized interpretations of a 'somewhat imprecise "global model" of beliefs, rituals and religious organization' (2001: 6–7). Migrants' religion needs to answer questions about life in changed surroundings, and provide means for adherents to continue to differentiate themselves from their surroundings. Therefore, migrants are likely to change some of their religious beliefs and practices upon migration, while maintaining many definitions of these beliefs and practices as they share them with co-religionists residing elsewhere. Given increasing migration, and the rapid development of transnational forms of communication, embedding religious beliefs and practices in transnational arenas is likely to involve multi-polar processes of transformation of these beliefs and practices, and to involve several centres (or agencies) defining these beliefs and practices.

From the point of view of religious migrants who use religion as a means to relate to their environment, integrating elements from the new surroundings into existing religious beliefs and practices may happen for different reasons. These reasons include the search for rationalizations of changed circumstances; legal and moral opposition to the migrants' religious beliefs and practices; experiences of discrimination in relation to religious, ethnic, or racial characteristics; or increasing interaction with individuals who do not share these beliefs and practices. Religious migrants, given the benefits they can derive from discarding items of religious beliefs and practices that stand in contradiction with the values of a host society, may alternate between holding different values, so that they can engage in identity politics to fit the requirements of different types of social interactions, and experimenting with holding different values while refraining from committing themselves entirely to any one vision. However, since religious beliefs and practices are often closely tied to an individual's affective links with other people, this explains why affective relations with co-religionists, especially those embedded in family life, work as strong forces resisting assimilation of the religious immigrants.

References

Allievi, Stefano (2003). 'Islam in the Public Space: Social Networks, Media and Neo-Communities'. In *idem* and Jorgen S. Nielsen (eds.), *Muslim Networks and Transnational Communities In and Across Europe*. Leiden: Brill, 1–27.

Beyer, Peter (2003). 'De-Centering Religious Singularity: The Globalization of Christianity as a Case in Point'. *Numen*, 50: 357–86.

Clarke, Peter B. (2006). 'Religious Syncretism Japanese Style in Brazil'. In Anton van Harskamp *et al.* (eds.), *Playful Religion: Challenges for the Study of Religion*. Eburon: Delft, 123–35.

Dirlik, Arif (2003). 'Modernity in Question? Culture and Religion in an Age of Global Modernity'. *Diaspora*, 12/2: 147–68.

Glick Schiller, Nina (2005). 'Transnational Social Fields and Imperialism'. *Anthropological Theory*, 5/4: 439–61.

Haller, Dieter (2003). 'Place and Ethnicity in Two Merchant Diasporas: A Comparison of Sindhis and Jews in Gibraltar'. *Global Networks*, 3/1: 75–96.

Lehman, David (2002). 'Religion and Globalization'. In Linda Woodhead, Paul Fletcher, Hiroko Kawanami, and David Smith (eds.), *Religions in the Modern World: Traditions and Transformations*. London: Routledge, 299–315.

Levitt, Peggy (2001). 'Between God, Ethnicity, and Country: An Approach to the Study of Transnational Religion'. Working Paper of the Transnational Communities Programme WPTC-01-13; <http:www.transcomm.ox.ac.uk/working_papers.htm>.

—— (2004). 'Redefining the Boundaries of Belonging: The Institutional Character of Transnational Religious Life'. *Sociology of Religion*, 65/1: 1–18.

Mattson, Ingrid (2003). 'How Muslims Use Islamic Paradigms to Define America'. In Yvonne Yazbeck Haddad, Jane I. Smith, and John L. Esposito (eds.), *Religion and Immigration: Christian, Jewish, and Muslim Experiences in the United States*. Walnut Creek, Calif.: AltaMira Press, 199–215.

McGown, Rima Berns (1999). *Muslims in the Diaspora: The Somali Communities of London and Toronto*. Toronto: University of Toronto Press.

Nedreveen Pieterse, Jan (2004). 'Globalization as Hybridization'. In *idem*, *Globalization and Culture: Global Mélange*. Lanham, Md.: Rowman & Littlefield Publishers, 59–83.

Plüss, Caroline (1999). 'Chinese Participation in the Church of Jesus Christ of Latter-Day Saints (Mormons) in Hong Kong'. *Journal of Contemporary Religion*, 14/1: 63–76.

—— (2002). 'Assimilation versus Idiosyncrasy: Strategic Constructions of Sephardic Identities in Hong Kong'. *Jewish Culture and History*, 5/2: 48–69.

—— (2005). 'Constructing Globalized Ethnicity: Migrants from India in Hong Kong'. *International Sociology*, 20/2: 201–24.

—— (2006). 'Becoming Different while Becoming the Same: Re-territorializing Islamic Identities with Multi-Ethnic Practices in Hong Kong'. *Ethnic and Racial Studies*, 29/4: 656–75.

Robbins, Joel (2004). 'The Globalization of Pentecostal and Charismatic Christianity'. *Annual Review of Anthropology*, 33: 117–43.

Silliman, Jael (1998). 'Crossing Borders, Maintaining Boundaries: The Life and Times of Farah, a Woman of the Baghdadi Jewish Diaspora (1870–1958)'. *Journal of Indo-Judaic Studies*, 1/1: 57–79.

Van der Veer, Peter (2001). 'Transnational Religion'. Working Paper of the Transnational Communities Programme WPTC-01-18; <http:www.transcomm.ox.ac.uk/working_papers.htm>.

—— (2002). 'Transnational Religion: Hindu and Muslim Movements'. *Global Networks*, 2/2: 95–109.

VERTOVEC, STEVEN (2000). 'Religion and Diaspora: New Landscapes of Religion in the West, Oxford'. Working Paper of the Transnational Communities Programme WPTC-01-01; <http:www.transcomm.ox.ac.uk/working_papers.htm>.

Suggested Reading

BEYER, PETER (ed.) (2001). *Religion in the Process of Globalization.* Würzburg: Ergon.

Also Beyer (2003); Clarke (2006); Dirlik (2003); Lehman (2002); Levitt (2004); Robbins (2004); and Van der Veer (2002).

CHAPTER 28

RELIGIOUS DIVERSITY

GARY D. BOUMA

ROD LING

Religious diversity—differences within and between religious groups in a society—has re-entered the sociology of religion in new and powerful ways. Religious difference has become a factor in local and global conflicts and peace building (Appleby 2000; Thomas 2005). The renewed interest in religious diversity follows nearly a century of expectation that religious diversity would decrease as religion itself disappeared in the shadow of science and rational humanism (Wuthnow 2005). In addition, in the West a century of ecumenism had reduced diversity within large Christian groups as they sought to make organizationally real Jesus' injunction 'that they may all be one' (John 17: 11). While the official gaze was on unity, just out of sight until recently, a plethora of new groups sprouted up around ageing Protestant denominations in the United States, Africa, Asia, and Europe. There has also been increased diversity among Catholics, Muslims, Buddhists, and Hindus. The 'new religious movements' of the 1960s and 1970s have morphed into the New Age (Possamai 2005) or familiar religious groups like Scientology, Brahma Kumaris, and the Moonies (Clarke 2006). This increase in diversity and the return of religion to politics (Berger 1999; Thomas 2005) has stimulated debates about the desirability of diversity and its management (Bouma 1999). Whatever, the twenty-first century has begun with bursts of religious diversity, religious conflict, and anything but the withering away of religion from public life.

In our discussion of religious diversity, we distinguish *plurality*, which describes a state of a society, from *pluralism*, which refers to belief and attitudes about diversity. Societies are more or less religiously plural, but may or may not have pluralism—that is, cultures favouring diversity.

Measuring Religious Diversity

Many societies feel more religiously diverse now than they have in the recent past. Western societies have become home to significant Muslim, Buddhist, Hindu, and other Asian religious communities. Similarly, Oriental and African societies have become home to significant communities of Christians. However, religious diversity has been with us for millennia, and it is difficult to say whether there is now more diversity than before. The histories of all the religions of the world show times of ferment, conflict, and diversity, even as the histories of societies rarely depict times of religious homogeneity and stability (Armstrong 1993). For example, the first century CE was a time of prophets and of global religious ferment (Stark 1996; Wilson 1995). The history of the early Christian church is one of conflicting viewpoints, theological creativity, and diversity of practice and periods of repression of diversity. The Protestant Reformation released diversities that had long existed within the Catholic Church. The early nineteenth century spawned diverse movements in Protestant Christianity from Mormons to Brethren to Churches of Christ. That era also saw Baha'i spread from Persia, and movements in Islam, Buddhism, and Hinduism. As a result of theological and liturgical disputes and the migration of national churches to other parts of the world by the mid-nineteenth century, there were myriad Methodists, Baptists, Lutherans, and Presbyterians, some of whom coalesced to form the larger 'mainline' denominations that defined American Protestantism in the twentieth century.

Analysing religious diversity requires choices about categories and classifications. Beckford considers five ways to measure and analyse religious diversity in a social entity such as a nation-state: 'absolute number of separate religious organisations', the number of religious groups with significant membership, the number of 'distinct faith traditions or world religions', 'number of individuals who combine different religious outlooks in their own identity', number of 'internal divisions' 'of unitary faiths' (2003: 74–5). Any attempt to assess religious diversity in a given country requires choice or consideration of these five measures.

When choosing a measure, there is the further issue of choosing an appropriate level of detail. For example, to compare religious diversity in Australia in the 1960s and the present, we might use the first measure, the 'absolute number of separate religions'. At a general level of detail, we could compare the presence of major world religions, Christians, Muslims, Buddhists, Jews, and 'alternative religions'. This analysis might be too general, and we might then disaggregate groups into subgroups. For Christianity we might count Catholic, Protestant, and Orthodox. On a more detailed level we might disaggregate to another level of subgroups. For Orthodox Christianity we include Greek, Ukrainian, Coptic, Russian, Serbian, Romanian, and Ethiopian. We might go even further and include factions and sects. Hence it is difficult to measure religious diversity, whether between periods or countries, and claims that we have more diversity now than in the past are dubious.

The analysis of diversity is also shaped by available information. Aggregates of denominational data only involve those who contribute their data, and will miss emerging forms and groups. Survey data tend to collapse diversity for purposes of analysis and are unable to detect the beliefs and practices of small groups. To identify diversity at detailed levels, systematic measures of religious identification are required, like the Census (Bouma 1995; 2006).

However, religious diversity does seem greater today than in the past, at least the recent past. First, this perception is partly due to twentieth-century efforts to promote unity in Christianity and a strong theological ideology about the unity of the Body of Christ, as opposed to the diversity of the parts of that body (1 Corinthians 12). Second, diversity seems greater today because nineteenth-century Western scholars, writing with colonialist values, constructed the World's Religions as homolithic blocs and papered over substantial and vital differences within these entities (Hinnells 1997: 5).

Third, diversity seems greater today because historical and sociological analysts have assumed low diversity within religious groups (Wilson 1995). For example, mid-twentieth-century religious diversity in the United States could be reduced to Protestant, Catholic, and Jew (Herberg 1955; Lenski 1961). Even if such intra-group diversity is low at some points in time, the degree of intra-group diversity is very likely to vary over time, particularly when groups are in formative or declining stages. Periods of stability within religious organizations are rather shorter than would be expected from a mid-twentieth-century consensualist social theory perspective. Stability is more likely to be a *post hoc* nostalgic (re-)construction of a past which, for those who lived at the time, was not noticeably stable. Like other living organisms, religious organizations are growing, differentiating, struggling to function, or disintegrating.

Religious Diversity Now

The theme of the early twenty-first century appears to be religious diversity and its consequences for social order and public life. Diana Eck (2001) claims that, as a result of recent immigration, the United States is the most religiously diverse country in the world. Australia would lay claim to first or second place and has census data as evidence (Bouma 2006). But diversity is also the order of the day in European states that were formerly more religiously homogeneous due to established official religious monopolies. Diversity is also much more evident now than in the recent past in Pentecostalized Latin America (Martin 2002) and Asia (Barrett 2001).

This increased diversity is in no small part due to the global movement of people and cultures. Religious diversity is no longer 'out there', described to awed locals by travellers to exotic lands. Rather, a plethora of religious practices is encountered in the daily lives of millions—in their homes, as they shop, go to school, and work (Davie 1994; Wuthnow 2005; Tacey 2003; Bouma 2006). The experience of religious diversity is now at first hand, personal and domestic. In a globalizing world it is harder to avoid people whom we once would have seen as 'others' or people outside our social environment. We encounter them on satellite television, the Internet, and in our own markets, schools, and cities. As a result of globalization, 'The societal group now includes everyone' and 'the visage of the devil is becoming increasingly indistinct' (Beyer 1994: 85–6).

Diversity is also encountered within religious groups experiencing significant divisions on theology and practice. For example, internal tensions exist among Muslims about how to live as diasporic communities or how to respond to challenges to develop more liberal and democratic governances and outlooks (Ebaugh and Chafetz 2000; Khatab and Bouma 2007). These tensions threaten to spill into global conflict and local terrorist strikes (Nasr 2006). The Anglican Communion threatens to disintegrate in conflicts over boundary disputes between dioceses, as dioceses, like that of Sydney, export their form of Christianity to others and attempt to impose their policies regarding the suitability for leadership roles of those who happen to be gay or female (Windsor Report 2004; Bates 2004). The early twenty-first century appears to be an age of increased religious diversity and, as a result, increased ferment and the return of religion to public life.

Explanations and Theories of Religious Diversity

There are three primary sources of religious diversity in a society. Religious diversity arises from creative developments within existing groups and the emergence of new religions, from recent social changes involving increased privatization of religion and the rise of consumerism, and from the globalization of religions through new communications technology and the movement of people who take their religion with them as settlers, missionaries, or migrants.

The likelihood of religious diversity emerging in a society is enhanced by social changes that prompt or require new explanatory frameworks and make different forms of spirituality or religion more appealing. Religious diversity arises within religions as they evolve, through theological disagreement, when migration or conquest brings societies into contact (Wilson 1995), and in response to deliberate attempts to spread one religion into a new territory (Montgomery 1996; Wilson 1995). Religious diversity is more likely to emerge where existing organized forms of religion are unable to impose their ways through socialization, surveillance, and legal control. When religion and spirituality slip from the hegemonic control of organized religion, as is the case in the twenty-first century, diversity can be expected to abound (Fenn 2001; Bouma 2006).

New Religious Movements (NRMs) are examples of innovative religious diversity which have proliferated through globalization. In the twentieth century groups such as the Unification Church (the Moonies), ISKON (Hare Krishnas), Falun Gong, and Rastafarianism arose through concerns not just for individual members but also for global humanity—'world transformation as self transformation' (Clarke 2006: 4). NRMs place greater responsibility on their members for their personal affairs, and often allow them to belong to other religious organizations. They view individuals not as essentially sinful, but as beings with potential to develop advanced spiritual enlightenment. NRMs also accept that members can find spiritual answers outside their organizations. In general, NRMs create a religious 'context in which individuals can arrive at their own solutions' (Clarke 2006: 354–5). This empowering of the religious seeker contrasts with the patriarchal, authoritarian approaches of major religious groups, and results in greater religious diversity.

While mid-twentieth-century sociologies presumed stability and order, social and religious reality is probably better seen as a biospace in which diversity is expected and essential to health, change is endemic to living, and contestation for resources the order of the day. The 1960s sociologies of Luckmann (1967) and Berger (1967) strained toward processual thinking while retaining substantial consensualist and integrationist thinking. In their view, religious diversity would undermine social cohesion and reduce the ability of a religion to provide socially integrative meaning. Sacred canopies provide much less shelter than a single overarching integrated meaning system. They were sensitive to the impact of social differentiation on the privatization of religion. Institutional differentiation left religion less connected to other institutions, reducing its social power and ability to influence social change. Privatization would lead and has led, to a proliferation of religions and spiritualities as religious difference comes to make less and less difference to a person's life chances and to social order.

In industrial societies where the role of religion was to support social order and socialize persons motivated to produce, attend to timetables, and cooperate, increases in religious diversity were seen to reduce productivity, threaten social cohesion, and undermine the social significance of religion. However, many societies are now moving to become consumer societies. Privatization, as predicted by Berger and Luckmann, among others, has combined with consumer empowerment in free market religious economies to produce the current resurgence of religion seen in the twenty-first century (Berger 1999; Martin 2002; Thomas 2005). Unregulated religious economies, those in which the state does not support the monopoly power of one religion, are the more effective in supplying the range of services preferred by consumers of religion. Given that consumer preferences are assumed to vary, a single supplier with an undifferentiated product cannot provide for the range of consumer preferences (Starke and Finke 2000: 197–9). With this shift from industrial to post-industrial societies have come different theories of religion and religious diversity.

In a consumer society religious consumers make their choices to increase or maintain their 'social capital' and to enhance 'interpersonal attachments' (Stark and Finke 2000: 280). They choose religions that conserve and enhance their social capital, and they affiliate with individuals with whom they have bonded in their established social networks (2000: 119, 121). Buyers of new religions make choices to increase their social capital through extensions of their current networks. Individuals seeking to extend their social networks are therefore likely to include people who will choose a new religion. Religious groups will be particularly attractive to those who need to make new or re-establish social networks, such as the 'geographically mobile, teenagers and young adults, at marriage, and following a divorce' (2000: 119). By implication, social and geographic mobility facilitates religious diversity as buyers actively seek new choices in their religious economies.

Within unregulated religious markets diversity can also be explained with reference to the degree of tension maintained between religious organizations and their greater social environments (Stark and Finke 2000: 196–9). Greater levels of 'strictness' in religious belief and practice are associated with greater tension between an organization and its society. Consumer preferences for religious organizations holding different levels of tension with society are manifest in a series of market 'niches' that range from preference for lowest tension or strictness, progressing to highest tension or strictness—ultra-liberal, liberal, moderate, conservative, strict, ultra-strict. The distribution of consumers in each group, along this scale, forms a bell curve, where the outer niches, ultra-liberal and ultra-strict have the fewest consumers; and just either side of the centre, moderate and conservative have the highest preferences (2000: 196–7). Religious diversity will be greatest in 'unregulated' religious markets where the state does not support monopoly by one religion.

Within any market, diversity is produced as new religions are born as breakaway sects, usually in a state of high tension with society. If a new religion survives and increases its membership, its level of tension with society will decrease, attracting further members preferring religious participation in groups in lower states of societal tension. However, members committed to the strict beliefs of the group's origins may create an internal sect; or leave to form a new religion, increasing religious diversity (Stark and Finke 2000: 205–6). Religious 'movements' may also secede in the opposite direction to practice less strictly and serve consumers wanting membership of organizations in lower tension with society (2000: 210).

Globalization—the global movement of people, capital, and culture—has profoundly increased the religious diversity of most places. While early analysts feared the McDonaldization of culture as global communications technology and marketing reduced complexity and overwrote local special character (Ritzer 1993), it has become clear that religious diversity has thrived in this context. Although some Christian churches may increasingly be adopting production and service models of 'fast food' (Drane 2006: 121), this style of 'production and service' is inadequate for many parishioners, and significant numbers have left their churches looking for new spaces of religious practice (2006: 121–2). Attempts to rationalize the delivery of religious goods (Stolz 2006) may lead to an increasingly responsive market of religious service-providers. New religious organizations may identify and target market segments based on 'age, education, social class and perhaps gender or sexual preference' and serve religious consumers according to their secular concerns (Wilson 1991: 208), thereby increasing the range of religious organizations and services. Hence increased rationalization leads to greater diversity as new organizations enter religious markets to cater for diverse consumer preferences.

Globalization also creates opportunities for religious diversity by raising the consciousness of global social justice issues that can be addressed through religiously motivated compassion and intervention. Globalization leads to a sense of the world as a 'community' of 'humanity' (Beyer 1994: 129; Robertson and Chirico 1985: 225–8) and increases concern for global, rather than just local, human welfare and human ethics (Clarke 2006: 7). Hence individuals become aware of myriad concerns of the 'human community', such as limits to the development of human potential, the costs of poverty, war, global disease, or the natural environment. Any such theme may be the focus of a new religion (Clarke 2006: 7), bringing together diverse elements of religiosity and spiritual practice.

Globalization in the form of migration also contributes to religious diversity (Ebaugh and Chafetz 2000; Bouma 1995). Since the 1970s, Australia, the United States, Europe, and other parts of the world have accepted migrants and long-term visitors from South-east Asia, Turkey, the Middle East, and Africa. The presence of these new peoples has extended religious diversity significantly, increasing the numbers of practising Hindus, Sikhs, Buddhists, and new forms of Christianity. As they integrate into their new society, migrants enter social networks with those born locally. As they build their communities and religious infrastructure, the visual landscape of cities once dominated by spires changes with the introduction of mosques, temples, gurdwaras, and other religious architecture. Religious diversity in urban areas and towns can facilitate contact between the several religions, allowing for the exchange of religious ideas, practices, and converts. Marriage is the most direct form of contact, which may lead to either partner converting to the religion of another (Badr 2000: 210–13) or the intimate practice of intercultural communication in a religiously mixed marriage. As people move, so do religions.

Consequences of Religious Diversity

There are two sets of views on the social consequences of religious diversity. The first sees diversity leading to a reduction in the authority and power of major religious groups due to competition and to a decrease in cultural integration and social cohesion between religions leading to social conflict. Another set of views holds that religious diversity enables competition, leading to the emergence of a wider range of religious products consistent with the diverse preferences of consumers, and as a result, increasing religious participation and improved capacity to cope with social change. Each set of views is associated with one of the two types of society outlined above: the first relates to a modern production economy, the second to a post-industrial consumer economy.

Religious Diversity and Social Cohesion

In a modern production economy religious diversity has been considered a condition to be rectified, given the belief that such diversity is likely to increase social conflict. Durkheim held that diversity was a generally negative factor for religious faith and social solidarity (1952: 159), as it brings competition and disputes between groups over 'ultimate truths', thus reducing religion's capacity to 'dominate lives', and its role in social solidarity would thus increasingly be provided by the state (Durkheim 1933: 226–7).

The relationship between religious diversity and social cohesion is quite complex. Whether religious diversity undermines existing social order, or whether changing social order brings about religious diversity, is unclear. Religion may appear to support cohesion in a society with a regulated religious economy, where the state supports one religious monopoly, and the principle of 'no freedom to choose' is sustained by lack of diversity. Challenges from alternative religions, or dissident factions within the monopoly religion, are likely to motivate repressive action by the state. The repression of the Falun Gong in China is an example. Alternatively, when the religious economy is unregulated, and the state does not support a religious monopoly, the principle of 'freedom to choose' and diversity are mutually sustaining. Moves by one group to become the monopoly religion in this case are likely to bring resistance from other groups and perhaps the state. The transition of Malaysia from a Muslim minority to Muslim majority country is a case in point.

Finally, since social disruption has not occurred in several multi-religious societies such as the United States, Canada, and Australia, some social forces must be countering religious diversity's expected destabilizing effects. The critical issue facing societies today is whether religious diversity affects how a society sustains and reproduces itself.

Diversity and the Impact of Religion

The extent to which social institutions are affected by changes in religious diversity is related to their degree of secularization. For example, increases in religious diversity will have little direct influence on government systems where religious representatives have no permanent and obligatory role in law making. However, health systems of many countries are less secularized. In many societies hospital patients' religious practices are respected and accommodated. Patients receive food according to their religious dietary laws; hospitals have spaces of worship; religious clerics visit the sick and dying; and some religious organizations own and administer hospitals. An increase in religious diversity may require further styles of care, pressuring hospital administrations and possibly leading patients into conflict over resources. Similarly, the workplace is less secularized, being already subject to the temporal rhythms of the dominant religious group. Increases in religious diversity may require changes to working schedules to accommodate the temporal and holiday patterns of new groups (Bouma *et al.* 2003; Ling 2005; Machacek 2003: 151–7).

The potential for religious diversity to lead to conflict is greater when participation in the impacted institution is compulsory. Religious diversity has led to changes in radio broadcasting, with an increased range of religious-based stations and radio shows. As radio listening is not compulsory, the impact of religious diversity is not likely to generate conflict, as listeners not wishing to hear an unfamiliar religious broadcast have the power to change stations. However, participation in the school system is compulsory in most societies, requiring teachers, students, and parents to deal with issues associated with religious diversity in schools, such as Muslim dress codes, the celebration of non-Christian festivals, and the teaching of minority or new theologies like Creationism (Beckford 2003: 91–4; Machacek 2003: 153–4).

The impact of religious diversity will also depend on the expectations about diversity upheld by the society's religious institution (Bouma 2006; 1998). An increase in religious diversity is more likely to bring conflict when a society expects religious uniformity (Machacek 2003:160). It is also possible for religious diversity to lead to conflict when alternative religions challenge widely held norms. For example, in the context of widely held norms of religious freedom and equality for women, the existence of a minority, alternative religion that discriminates against women, fulfils the first principle while violating the second, and conflict may arise.

The consequences of religious diversity also depend on local social, cultural, and legal contexts. The United States, Australia, and Canada are migrant countries where individuals have a sense of being part of a nation of many different origins. Religious diversity is supported by the belief that society reproduces social solidarity through the freedom to practise 'difference'. However, religious diversity may not be a cohesive force in a society where such 'difference' is viewed negatively.

Religious diversity may also have contingent social effects. On a positive side, religious institutions representing various cultural and ethnic groups may be agents of social integration as public voices and sources of social support. In the context of commerce, religiously diverse societies may provide an advantageous context for learning how to conduct business in a religiously diverse world. Religious diversity is an expression of cosmopolitan life, with various places of worship adding interesting difference to the sight of the landscape and participation by different religions in public events.

On the negative side, religious groups can be unbeneficial, promoting conflict through negative representations of other communities, promoting conflict, dehumanizing the other, encouraging minority separation, or attempting to undermine the social order.

Managing Religious Diversity

The management of religious diversity has become a significant issue in a globalizing world. Migration, travel, and new communications have seen the export of new religions to countries formerly lacking significant diversity. Concern about Islamic terrorism has focused the attention of governments on the management of relations between Muslims and non-Muslims in the United States, Britain, Europe, and Australia. Also the treatment of religious minorities as a human rights issue has underpinned negotiations on free trade and diplomatic relations. The societal management of religious diversity is about limiting consequences that may endanger social solidarity, social cohesion, and national stability. Extreme scenarios of unsuccessful integration of religious minorities include violent tensions between religious groups and growth of religious divisions potentially undermining nations.

All societies manage religious and spiritual activity permissible within society-specific boundaries. The aims of this management vary (Bouma 1999). Following the Treaty of Westphalia in 1648, nation-states have sought a high degree of religious homogeneity to ensure stability. Achieving this aim has always required suppression of difference by force. Examples include the imposition of state churches in Europe, repression of all religion in Maoist China and Stalinist Russia, and the efforts of some Muslim majority states to limit the activities of other religious groups or to reduce Sunni/Shi'a conflict (Richardson 2004; Boyle and Sheen 1997; Nasr 2006). Other societies limit the range of diversity, often citing principles of duty of care for their citizens' well-being. Examples include the current suppression of Scientology in many European states and the use of the state to suppress religious difference which was once prevalent in the West and is not unknown in some Muslim societies.

Finally, there are those societies which take a largely *laissez-faire* approach to religious diversity and intervene only when there are violations of secular criminal codes or direct threats to social order. For example, Australia openly accepts a wide range of religious groups, and provides state support for faith-based education in religious schools including Exclusive Brethren, Muslim, Catholic, and Buddhist (Bouma 2006).

In Western liberal democracies the management of religious diversity has moved from fear of difference, through tolerance of difference, to appreciation of the positive values of difference—sustainability, creative response to change, and productive inclusion of migrants (Bouma 1999; Richardson 2004). This transition has been facilitated in part by changes in the function of religion. In pre-industrial Europe religion and the state were deeply entwined in functions and overall ordering of the society. In industrial societies, religion became differentiated from the state, but only those groups were tolerated that 'pledged allegiance to the state'. The emergence of diversity was permissible so long as the groups socialized into dominant values (Johnson 1961) and took the organizational form of a denomination. Denominations were religiously different, but acceptable to the society because their support for the existing order was assured. Sects were suspect and subject to greater monitoring, due to their tension with the social order.

With the emergence of post-industrial societies, religion is taking a new and different role, one that may demand diversity. In consumer societies, religion becomes something consumed, a product for expressing identity, for showing who one is and differentiating self from other—hence the increases in wearing religious symbols, religious identification, and religious practice. Part of the resurgence of religion (Berger 1999; Thomas 2005) can be attributed to this change in the role of religion. However, there has been an attendant return of religion to the public space not only in matters of identification and dress, but in social policy issues—rights to consume religious products—wearing of hijabs, crosses, or to consume religiously acceptable food—halal, kosher, vegetarian. Religious issues affect the delivery of social and health services, from stem-cell research to contraceptive technology, as individuals and groups ask the meaning and implication of their faith for practice in public life.

Thus, while in the late twentieth century it could have been argued that the privatization of religion into state-supporting denominations would result in the withering away of the effects of religion, the twenty-first century has seen the return of religious difference to the public space, raising issues of the management of this diversity in a new way. Religion is no longer completely contained in easily managed denominational bundles, but is loose in the form of myriad spiritualities and new religious groups, not all of which readily 'pledge their allegiance'. Management of this diversity is much more difficult due, on the one hand, to its fluid nature, and on the other, to the fact that most civil servants have been trained to ignore religion.

While a *laissez-faire* approach seems to suit a free-market model of the religious economy, the pursuit of religious diversity for its own sake may not be without negative aspects. A society with one or only a few religious institutions may have no tendency towards greater diversity, whether the religious market is regulated or not. A focus on diversity for its own sake can also distract from inherent problems like significant imbalances in power between religions, or the potential for religious tensions (Beckford 2003: 81). Further, religious diversity does not necessarily lead to religious tolerance and coexistence. Religious consumers in a diverse religious society may be tightly segmented in insular groups in tense relationships, as was the case in Northern Ireland (Beckford 2003: 81). Unregulated religious competition can also generate anomie, as the free choice of religion leads people to individual rather than group practice, undermining the existence of social solidarity based on religion (Beckford 2003: 96).

Nation-states have attempted to manage religious diversity differently, with some having cultures and laws that prohibit or discourage governments from restricting religious freedoms; others having laws and cultures which place lower restrictions on the prohibition of religious freedoms. The United States and Australia are in the first category, while China and France are in the second. The United States and Australian federal governments have legal obligations to preserve religious freedoms, and their histories and cultures have upheld tolerance between religions, allowing comparatively free entry of new religions into their respective religious markets. Both countries have attempted to manage socially disruptive aspects of religious diversity while not restricting the rights of individuals' religious freedom. The United States government has used taxation and firearms laws to limit the growth of certain 'cults'. The Australian government has carefully negotiated with Muslim communities to facilitate their participation in Australian political and social life while attempting to undermine the spread of Islamist ideologies.

The relationship between religious diversity and freedom of belief, on the one hand, and freedom of conscience and freedom of expression and thought, on the other, is very complex. Insisting on freedom to believe and practise, some groups deny medical treatment to themselves and their children. Recent events in France and China have demonstrated that governments are prepared to impose substantial legal sanctions against religious freedoms. The French have legislated against the wearing in government schools of clothing and adornments associated with religion. The Chinese government has used its more authoritarian power to outlaw the Falun Gong movement and forcibly suppress Muslim separatists in its west.

Finally, it may well be that neither a free market nor a controlled economy approach to religious diversity will avert the social instabilities undermining present cultures and legal powers. The USA and Australia struggle with the tension between prohibiting anti-social and illegal actions by religious groups and preserving religious freedom. When does a religious freedom cross the line and become illegal? The actions of France and China are likely to generate resistance among affected groups whose social solidarity may strengthen. Meanwhile, European nations struggle to come to terms with the facts of their own religious diversity while seeming to retreat to outdated notions of social cohesion requiring uniformity grounded in the necessities of industrial interdependence even as they move toward becoming consumer economies.

Conclusion

Changes in religious diversity and the way societies manage it are part of a complex and changing interrelationship between the social and religion. Changes in religion have had clear impacts on social life, and the ways in which the social is structured impact religious life. Religious diversity and its management provide a window through which to examine these changes (Beckford 2003; Beyer 2006). In some ways the movement of people and religions demonstrates the emergence of a global set of relations between the social and religion. The utility of the nation-state as the primary focus of analysis is reduced by both the diversity of ways in which religions and spiritualities become locally embedded and by their immediate global connection with others through the Internet. The key challenges of current social change for sociology and social analysis become clear in the examination of religious diversity.

References

Appleby, R. Scott (2000). *The Ambivalence of the Sacred: Religion, Violence and Reconciliation.* New York: Rowan & Littlefield.

ARMSTRONG, KAREN (1993). *A History of God: From Abraham to the Present: The 4000-year Quest for God.* London: Heinemann.

BADR, HODA (2000). 'Al-Noor Mosque: Strength through Unity'. In Ebaugh and Chafetz (2000), 210–13.

BARRETT, DAVID (2001). *World Christian Encyclopaedia.* Oxford: Oxford University Press.

BATES, STEPHEN (2004). *A Church at War: Anglicans and Homosexuality.* London: I. B. Tauris.

BECKFORD, JAMES (2003). *Social Theory and Religion.* Cambridge: Cambridge University Press.

—— and WALLISS, JOHN (eds.) (2006). *Theorising Religion: Classical and Contemporary Debates.* Aldershot: Ashgate.

BERGER, PETER (1967). *The Sacred Canopy.* Garden City, NY: Doubleday.

—— (ed.) (1999). *The Desecularisation of the World: Resurgent Religion and World Politics.* Grand Rapids, Mich.: Eerdmans.

BEYER, PETER (1994). *Religion and Globalization.* London: Sage.

—— (2006). *Religions in Global Society.* London: Routledge.

BOUMA, GARY (1995). 'The Emergence of Religious Plurality in Australia, a Multicultural Society'. *Sociology of Religion*, 56: 285–302.

—— (1998). 'Distinguishing Institutions and Organisations in Social Change'. *Journal of Sociology*, 34/3: 232–44.

—— (ed.) (1999). *Managing Religious Diversity: From Threat to Promise.* Special edition of *Australian Religious Studies Review*, 12/2.

—— (2006). *Australian Soul: Religion and Spirituality in the Twenty-First Century.* Cambridge: Cambridge University Press.

—— SMITH, WENDY, HAIDAR, ALI, and NYLAND, CHRIS (2003). 'Work, Religious Diversity and Islam'. *Asia Pacific HRM*, 41: 51–61.

BOYLE, KEVIN, and SHEEN, JULIET (1997). *Freedom of Religion and Belief: A World Report.* London: Routledge.

CLARKE, PETER (2006). *New Religions in Global Perspective.* London: Routledge.

DAVIE, GRACE (1994). *Religion in Britain since 1945: Believing without Belonging.* Oxford: Blackwell.

DRANE, JOHN (2006). 'From Creeds to Burgers: Religious Control, Spiritual Search and the Future of the World'. In Beckford and Walliss (2006), 121.

DURKHEIM, ÉMILE (1933). *The Division of Labour in Society.* London: Macmillan.

—— (1952). *Suicide.* London: Routledge & Kegan Paul.

EBAUGH, HELEN, and CHAFETZ, JANET (eds.) (2000). *Religion and the New Immigrants.* Walnut Creek, Calif.: AltaMira.

ECK, DIANA L. (2001). *A New Religious America: How a 'Christian Country' Has Now Become the World's Most Religiously Diverse Nation.* San Francisco: Harper.

FENN, RICHARD (2001). *Beyond Idols: The Shape of a Secular Society.* Oxford: Oxford University Press.

HERBERG, WILL (1955). *Protestant-Catholic-Jew.* Garden City, NY: Doubleday.

HINNELLS, JOHN (1997). 'Introduction to the First Edition'. In *idem* (ed.), *Handbook of Living Religions.* London: Penguin, 3–8.

JOHNSON, BENTON (1961). 'Do Holiness Groups Socialize into Dominant Values?' *Social Forces*, 39: 309–16.

KHATAB, SAYAD, and BOUMA, GARY D. (2007). *Democracy in Islam.* New York: Routledge.

LENSKI, GERHARD (1961). *The Religious Factor.* Garden City, NY: Doubleday.

LING, ROD (2005). 'Australian Autoworkers in the Early 21st Century: Opportunities for Self-Actualisation and Vocational Development' (Ph.D. dissertation, Monash University).

LUCKMANN, THOMAS (1967). *The Invisible Religion: The Problem of Religion in Modern Society.* New York: Macmillian.

MACHACEK, DAVID W. (2003). 'The Problem of Pluralism'. *Sociology of Religion*, 64/2: 145–61.

MARTIN, DAVID (2002). *Pentecostalism: The World their Parish.* Oxford: Blackwell.

MONTGOMERY, ROBERT (1996). *The Diffusion of Religions: A Sociological Perspective.* New York: New York University Press.

NASR, VALI (2006). *The Shia Revival: How Conflicts in Islam will Shape the Future.* New York: Norton.

POSSAMAI, ADAM (2005). *Religion and Popular Culture: A Hyper-Real Testament.* Brussels: P. I. E. Peter Lang.

RICHARDSON, JAMES (ed.) (2004). *Regulating Religion: Case Studies from Around the Globe.* New York: Kluwer Academic.

RITZER, GEORGE (1993). *The McDonaldization of Society: An Investigation into the Changing Character of Contemporary Social Life.* Newbury Park, Calif.: Pine Forge Press.

ROBERTSON, ROLAND, and CHIRICO, JOANN (1985). 'Humanity, Globalization and Worldwide Religious Resurgence: A Theoretical Exploration'. *Sociological Analysis*, 46/3: 219–42.

STARK, RODNEY (1996). *The Rise of Christianity.* Princeton: Princeton University Press.

—— and FINKE, ROGER (2000). *Acts of Faith.* Berkeley: University of California Press.

STOLZ, JÖRG (2006). 'Salvation Goods and Religious Markets: Integrating Rational Choice and Weberian Perspectives'. *Social Compass*, 53: 13–31.

TACEY, DAVID (2003). *The Spirituality Revolution: The Emergence of Contemporary Spirituality.* Sydney: HarperCollins.

THOMAS, SCOTT (2005). *The Global Resurgence of Religion and the Transformation of International Relations.* New York: Palgrave Macmillan.

WILSON, BRYAN (1991). 'Secularization: Religion in the Modern World'. In Stewart R. Sutherland and Peter B. Clarke (eds.), *The Study of Religion: Traditional and New Religion.* London: Routledge, 195–208.

—— (1995). *Religious Tolerations & Religious Diversity.* Santa Barbara, Calif.: Institute for the Study of American Religion; <http://www.neuereligion.de/ENG/collection/diversity/pointI.htm>, accessed 11 March 2007.

Windsor Report (2004). <http://www.anglicancommunion.org/windsor2004/>.

WUTHNOW, ROBERT (2005). *America and the Challenges of Religious Diversity.* Princeton: Princeton University Press.

SUGGESTED READING

BAUBEROT, J. (1999). 'Laicité, Sects, Societies'. In F. Champion and M. Cohen (eds.), *Sectes et democratie.* Paris: Seuil, 314–30.

BECKFORD, JAMES A. (1985). *Cult Controversies: The Societal Response to New Religious Movements.* London: Tavistock.

Bouma, Gary D., Smith, Wendy, and Vasi, Shiva (2000). 'Japanese Religion in Australia: Mahikari and Zen in a Multicultural Society'. In Peter Clarke (ed.), *Japanese New Religions in the World.* London: Curzon Press, 74–112.

Hunt, Stephen (2003). *Alternative Religions.* Aldershot: Ashgate.

Also Armstrong (1993); Beyer (2006); Bouma (2006); Boyle and Sheen (1997); Clarke (2006); Eck (2001); Richardson (2004); Thomas (2005); and Wuthnow (2005).

PART VI

RELIGIOUS COLLECTIVITIES AND THE STATUS AND ROLE OF THE RELIGIOUS PROFESSIONALS (THE CLERGY)

CHAPTER 29

CHURCH–SECT–CULT

CONSTRUCTING TYPOLOGIES OF RELIGIOUS GROUPS

LORNE L. DAWSON

INTRODUCTION

In 1897 the newspapers in New York mistakenly reported that Mark Twain was dying. A spry and healthy Twain wryly told reporters in England that the rumours of his death were 'grossly exaggerated'. The same can be said of claims that church–sect typology is 'a dead concept, obsolete, sterile, and archaic' (Goode 1967: 77). Certainly a great deal of ink has been spilt criticizing this traditional way of classifying religious organizations, but for better or worse it persists. In part this is because it continues to be useful, in both specific and highly general ways, and because a logical and empirically preferable alternative has yet to be devised. The basic distinctions captured between such groups as churches, denominations, sects, and cults remain plausible and relevant, analytically and pedagogically, in the Western context where most sociologists of religion still ply their trade. In provenance the categories are ethnocentric, and hence their application outside a Christian context is problematic. We need to develop new categories with an awareness of a plurality of religious, historical, and cultural conditions. But few of the scholars associated with the development of this typology ever envisioned its unalloyed application outside the Western context. Bryan Wilson's *Magic and the Millennium* (1973) being a rare but significant exception. There is, however, an appreciation of the ideal or heuristic character of the types, no matter how they are formulated, which duly sustains interest in them as a primary means of identifying, organizing, comparing, and testing social-scientific perceptions and explanations of the nature, development, and interactions of religious groups.

I begin this chapter by briefly surveying the history of church, sect, cult typologies. Second, I survey the chief criticisms advanced against such typologies. Third, I cast some doubt on many of the criticisms by developing a better grasp of the nature and purpose of typologies. Fourth, I examine the relative merits of the two main methodological options used in the creation of typologies: multi- versus unidimensional approaches. Fifth, I argue the merits of using 'the mode of membership' of religious organizations as the primary dimension for a typology, in contrast with 'tension with society' as recently advocated by others.

The Legacy of Church–Sect Theorizing

Sociologists, unlike theologians, historians, and other scholars of religion, have long sought to bring order to the confusing array of forms of religious expression by categorizing different types of religious activity according to their dominant form of social organization. The resultant sets of types of religious groups have been used to facilitate comparative analyses, discuss religious development across time, and assess the impact of different kinds of religious groups on society. This process of categorization has come to be known as church–sect theory after the initial typology framed by Max Weber in *The Protestant Ethic and the Spirit of Capitalism* (1958[1904–5]). The typology is best known, however, in the more elaborate form developed by Weber's friend and colleague Ernst Troeltsch in *The Social Teachings of the Christian Churches* (1931[1911]). The Troeltschian dichotomy of churches and sects has been widely accepted and developed over the years, generating a diverse and often conflicting array of types and subtypes of religious organizations (e.g., Niebuhr 1957[1929]; Wiese and Becker 1932 [1929]; Pope 1942; Yinger 1957; 1970; Wilson 1959; 1970; Robertson 1970; Swatos 1975). Each typology tends to stress one or another set of traits as more fundamental, producing different configurations of primary and secondary features (see, e.g., Knudsen *et al.* 1978). There is, however, an overall polarity of descriptive traits associated with churches and sects that has become part of the standard theoretical repertoire of sociologists.

In terms of membership, churches are organizations into which people are born and baptized as infants. Membership is said to be involuntary, in the sense that most members do not choose their initial affiliation. There are of course converts to these faiths. But in relative terms, it is sects that depend on the conversion of people, frequently as a result of very emotional experiences. If one is born into a sect, then membership depends on submission to special acts of commitment, analogous to a conversion, either as an adolescent or as a young adult. All kinds of people usually can and do belong to churches; they are inclusive, and their membership is heterogeneous. Sects tend to be much more homogeneous in their membership, drawing disproportionately from the underprivileged elements of society, if we restrict ourselves to the classic Western application of the term. This contrast stems in part from the fact that sects are created by schisms within churches, which are aligned with the dominant social structure. The beliefs and practices of sects, then, tend to be more radical and ethically stern than those of churches, and constitute an act of protest against the values of the rest of society. Churches, alternatively, are inclined to accommodate the vagaries of the rest of society in order to maintain their ability to influence, ideally, the whole society. Sects tend to be exclusive; individuals must meet and maintain certain clear ideological and behavioural requirements to belong. Sectarians perceive themselves as an elect, and those who contravene the group's precepts are subject to expulsion much more readily than in churches. The leadership of churches is usually hired or appointed on the basis of special educational qualifications. It operates within hierarchical and impersonal administrative structures. Sectarian leadership tends to be more charismatic in nature, and in line with this feature, sects tend to have smaller, more democratic, and personal organizational structures. In theology and liturgy, churches tend to be more dogmatic and ritualistic. Sects reflect a more inspirational, volatile, and even anti-ritualistic orientation.

There is no special order to this presentation; nor is it exhaustive, because different scholars highlight different features in the name of either reforming the typology or adapting it to the study of a particular case or cases. In fact, Roland Robertson comments that 'Troeltsch's initial typology was, strictly speaking, not a typology at all, but rather a dichotomous classification of religious collectivities in terms of their empirical characteristics' (1970: 115). For pedagogical purposes this is not necessarily problematic. The typology is often introduced to students as a simple descriptive framework, useful in calling attention to such things as the variety of religious groups, and the tensions that exist between them, even within one tradition; how different religious ideas, again even within one tradition, can have diverse consequences for the organization of groups, and hence for their social relations with others; and the reasons why specific kinds of groups are often subject to certain identifiable developmental tendencies.

It is not possible in this context to survey all the many variant typologies devised since Troeltsch's. I will highlight a few well-known developments to illustrate how the typology has been extended, modified, and applied. It bears noting that in each case more elaborate theoretical arguments and empirical descriptions are provided than can be indicated here.

The first significant sociological application and development of Troeltsch's typology was in *The Social Sources of Denominationalism* (Niebuhr 1957[1929]) by the American theologian and historian H. Richard Niebuhr. Niebuhr was the first to apply the typology to the American context, where he used it to explain the proliferation of sects on the American frontier. He also extended the theorizing associated with the typology by proposing a developmental logic, addressed below, and popularizing the term 'denomination' to denote the more pluralistic realities of religious life in America.

Niebuhr's contemporary, the American sociologist Howard Becker (Wiese and Becker 1932 [1929]: 619–44; see Becker 1940: n. 16), proposed alternatively an expanded version of Troeltsch's typology, in terms of what he called four types of 'churches': (1) the ecclesia, (2) the sect, (3) the denomination, and (4) the cult. Ecclesia come in two sub-varieties, international and national, and Becker emphasizes that they are marked primarily by the desire to be large and inclusive, and hence they are closely allied with the interests and values of various dominant social, economic, and political elites. Sects have 'abandoned the attempt to win the whole world over to [their] doctrines'. They have turned inward and are preoccupied with being exclusive, preserving the purity of the true believers. Becker comments that the sect 'appeals to strictly personal trends'. Denominations and cults are extensions of these trends. In Becker's scheme they are more or less transitional types. 'Denominations are simply sects in an advanced stage of development and adjustment to each other and the secular world' (Becker 1940: 36), while 'tendencies toward religion of a strictly private, personal character—tendencies fairly well marked in the sect—come to full fruition in the cult' (1940: 37). Cults are 'very amorphous, loose-textured, uncondensed type[s] of social structure[s]', focused on the 'purely personal ecstatic experience, salvation, comfort, and mental and physical healing' of their participants.

Probably the most influential, even paradigmatic typology of religious groups was framed by the American sociologist J. Milton Yinger (1957). This typology, like Becker's, is Troeltschian in character, but it has the great virtue of identifying more explicitly the criteria for distinguishing between groups, rendering it, in Robertson's reckoning, the first true typology (1970: 119). In order of decreasing inclusiveness (and hence increasing exclusiveness) and decreasing attention to the social integration of members (over against giving increasing attention to the satisfaction of personal needs), Yinger delineated a sixfold typology: the 'universal church' (e.g., the Roman Catholic Church); the 'ecclesia', by which he meant established national churches (e.g., the Church of England, the Russian Orthodox Church); the 'denomination' (e.g., Baptists, Presbyterians); the 'established sect' (e.g., Seventh-Day Adventists, Quakers); the 'sect' (e.g., many Pentecostalists, The Worldwide Church of God); the 'cult' (e.g., The Family, Scientology). Yinger later modified the typology, expanding the parameters from two to three (1970: 251–81) and proposing a further threefold sub-typology of sects (1970: 275–9).

The best-known sub-typology of sects, however, is provided by the British sociologist Bryan R. Wilson (1970). His typology is framed in terms of one of the dominant interpretive thrusts of Weber's sociology of religion (Weber 1963[1922]): that we should make sense of religions in terms of their manifest function, that of offering paths to salvation. Wilson distinguishes sects in terms of the supposedly deviant responses to the world generated by their conception of what we must do to be saved (1970: 36–40). Sects, for example, which view the world and its institutions as evil, and believe that salvation depends on a profound change in one's self, he calls 'conversionist' (e.g., the Salvation Army, Pentecostalists), while sects which 'declare that the world is evil, and that the only prospect of salvation is the overturning of the world by supernatural action', he calls 'revolutionist' (e.g., Jehovah's Witnesses, Christadelphians). In this manner he identifies seven types: conversionist, revolutionist, introversionist, manipulationist, thaumaturgical, reformist, and utopian. Each group utilizes different elements of the Christian tradition, in accordance with the logic of its response to the problem of salvation, and develops a distinctive mode of social organization.

Similar sub-typologies have been devised for cults, using a variety of criteria—ideological, organizational, and attitudinal (e.g., Campbell 1978; Wallis 1984; Stark and Bainbridge 1985: 26–30; Robbins and Anthony 1987). Roy Wallis, for example, extending another well-known Weberian distinction, distinguishes between world-affirming, world-rejecting, and world-accommodating cults (Wallis 1984). But enough has been said to illustrate the relative riches and confusion born of the proliferation of typologies.

Before placing the typologies in critical perspective, we need to note two additional features which they share: the developmental and relative character of the types posited. Niebuhr argued that sects tend to become more church-like with time. As new generations are born and socialized into the sects, and their ways become set, the original impetus to reject the norms and activities of the dominant society wanes. In fact, Niebuhr thought sects largely cease to exist after the passing of the first generation; if they survived, they became denominations. Likewise, as scholars of new religious movements have noted, if a cult is fortunate enough to survive and grow, it will tend to take on the features and the increased stability of a sect (e.g., Nelson 1969; Wallis 1975; Richardson 1979). As sects become churches, and sometimes as cults become more sect-like, a new sect or cult may be spawned out of discontent or loss of interest. We are faced, Stark and Bainbridge (1985: 22–3) observe, with 'an endless cycle of birth, transformation, schism, and rebirth of religious movements'.

Church–sect–cult distinctions are also relative in nature—a point easily and frequently forgotten. A group like the Mormons operates as a sect in most of North America. At the same time, however, it probably warrants being identified as a church, or ecclesia, in the state of Utah, where most of the population is Mormon, and as a denomination in southern Alberta, where about a third of the population is Mormon. In other words, the appropriate classification of this group, like all others, is dependent on the time and the place in question. No single group can necessarily be identified exclusively with any one label.

Criticisms of Church–Sect Theorizing

The attempt to fashion a typology of religious groups has been subject to ample and careful criticism. Broadly speaking, the criticisms can be separated into substantive or empirical concerns and more formal or theoretical concerns.

There are four primary substantive criticisms. First, Troeltsch's typology is too conditioned by the historical context from which it was drawn, pre-eighteenth-century European Christianity (e.g., Wilson 1970: 22–5; Robertson 1970: 116–17, 125–6; Chang 2003: 125–6). This deficiency has distorted most later developments. In the Troeltschian framework the sect is conceptualized too restrictively in terms of its antipathy to a dominant church. This makes sense in terms of the religious life of medieval and Reformation Europe, but is far less relevant to the pluralistic and socially differentiated religious environments of later times, especially in America and even Britain, its Established Church not withstanding. There is no truly dominant church in these societies, and the extension of the political franchise, the separation of church and state, and the diversification of the class structure of modern democratic and industrial states call into question the continued relevance of the Troeltschian presumption that sectarian commitments are motivated by the social protests of the lower classes. In societies where denominationalism has become the norm, sects are 'both less persecuted and, reciprocally, less alienated from the wider society' (Robertson 1970: 117).

Second, the trajectory of sect-to-church development tends to mask a more complex reality. Nelson (1968), Robertson (1970: 118–19, 124), Stark and Bainbridge (1985: 133–8), and Wilson (1993: 55–7), all observe that some cults and sects have survived well beyond their first generation of converts without changing essentially.

Other cults and sects change rapidly for a time, develop some of the features of a church (e.g., bureaucratic administrative structures), but ultimately stabilize as cults or sects (e.g., Scientology, Jehovah's Witnesses). Yinger (1957) framed the new category the 'established sect' to capture this reality, and Robertson refers to 'institutionalized sects' (1970: 124). Similarly, Nelson (1968) and Wallis (1974) talk about 'centralized cults' that act like sects (see Dawson 1997: 376–7), which I call 'established cults' (Dawson 2006: 29). Other developmental trajectories are feasible, but not as well documented.

Third, there is much confusion surrounding 'cult' as a type. Neither Weber nor Troeltsch include such a category in their dichotomies. The type was introduced by Becker and identified in terms of a continuation of the tendency to more personal forms of religiosity. As such, it bears a strong resemblance to a third type of religion called 'mysticism' that Troeltsch discusses later in *The Social Teachings of the Christian Churches.* Until recently, sociologists have neglected this religious phenomenon, which Troeltsch identifies with a kind of 'religious individualism', characterized by an emphasis on subjective experiences and the renunciation of religious communities (Garrett 1975; Daiber 2002). The concept calls to mind such nineteenth- and early twentieth-century metaphysical and esoteric movements as Spiritualism, New Thought, Rosicrucianism, and Theosophy, as well such contemporary phenomena as American Kabbalism, Wicca, and New Age groups (e.g., Stillson 1967; Hanegraaff 1996; Myers 2007).

This delineation of the term was obscured by confusions bred by two pejorative popular usages of the word 'cult'. First, in Christian evangelical circles in the United States in the mid-twentieth century the term was used to denounce various theologically deviant developments within Christianity, such as Christian Science, the Church of Latter-Day Saints, and Jehovah's Witnesses (e.g., Van Baalen 1960). But these groups are probably better classified as sects. Second, the term was later used by both secular and religious anti-cult crusaders to stigmatize new religions like the Children of God/The Family, the Unification Church (i.e., Moonies), the International Society for Krishna Consciousness, and the Church of Scientology. But these large and international movements defy easy classification as cults using the typologies of Troeltsch, Becker, Yinger, and others.

On the one hand, like churches, many of these new groups have developed large and semi-professional bureaucratic administrations. On the other hand, their modes of membership and orientation to the world are more sect-like, while in their origins and many of their beliefs and practices they look like cults. 'Religious individualism', however, is suppressed by the totalism and authoritarianism that mark these groups. It is this ambiguity that prompted the creation of new types, such as the 'established cult'. But the proliferation of types does not really address the underlying problem of finding a more feasible criterion or criteria for placing churches, sects, and cults in a meaningful continuum (Dawson 1997: 370–8).

Fourth, and most obviously, a substantive problem is posed by whether terms derived from the study of Western religious history, and essentially Christianity, can have much explanatory merit outside that context. Does it make sense to speak, even analogously, of Islamic, Hindu, or Buddhist sects (e.g., Bhatt 1968; Hertel 1977; Cook 1999; Sedgwick 2000). Yinger (1970) employs examples from many different religious traditions to illustrate his sixfold typology, but most commentators are very sceptical. Curiously, however, it should be noted that Eister (1967: 88 n. 4) reverses the normal reasoning, arguing: 'The word *sect*... has long applied to groups in Hinduism, Buddhism, Judaism and Islam in ways which make it at best difficult, at worse presumptuous, to try to preempt it for special use in Western Christendom in contradistinction with *church*.'

In truth, the matter has not been explored sufficiently. Few scholars, it seems, have the breadth of knowledge required to tackle this issue—knowledge of both multiple religious traditions and the methodology of sociology. But many of the seemingly substantive problems posed by cross-cultural comparisons actually stem from a lack of sufficient methodological sophistication. Along these lines, Robertson stresses the need to differentiate between cultural and social uses of the typology, and argues that the European origins of the actual terms of reference need not impede the latter use. A focus on the logical elements of the social relations between religious collectivities and their environments can be extended to other cultures, he argues, without fear of ethnocentrism (1970: 120–4). But the lack of alternative labels for the types, ones free of Christian connotations, continues to inhibit the use of the typology—rightly or wrongly.

The formal criticisms of church–sect–cult typologizing stem largely from despair over the applications of this kind of theorizing. Inevitably there are discrepancies between the types framed by scholars and the observations of researchers about specific groups. These discrepancies, as is commonly argued, 'are of the nature of typologies, since it is the variations from the type that stimulate, and guide further research and new exploratory efforts' (Dawson 1997: 369). The problem lies with the way in which many scholars respond to the discovery of discrepancies: they adjust and multiply either the number of types, or the number of traits used to identify a type, or the number of variables used to frame the typology. All three responses tend to make matters worse. Allan Eister (1967), one of the harshest critics of church–sect–cult typologizing, captures the situation well.

First, Eister complains that the seemingly endless search for the right variables or traits may have simply 'side-tracked' scholars from doing more productive 'research on the processes and dynamics of religious movements' (1967: 85; Goode 1967; Chang 2003). Second, he laments that the 'initial clarity that existed in Weber's ideas of church and sect as ideal types has since been lost in a welter of confused and confusing denotations... added by writers who... have not undertaken detailed empirical studies... or who lack the historical erudition of a Weber or a Troeltsch' (1967: 86; Swatos 1976). Third, confusion is sown by the proliferation of different and often contradictory definitions of the sect and its necessary features. 'A survey of what has been said about "the sect" as an analytic concept readily produces a list of more than two dozen distinct dimensions of variables (or of qualitative attributes) assembled in various combinations and presented as "defining traits" or characteristics of "the sect"' (Eister 1967: 86; see also Knudsen *et al.* 1978). Fourth, this proliferation leads to the suspicion that the typologies are 'a priori schemes which are "dreamed up" and never tested, or speculated about and then only illustrated, or—worse yet—used to "explain" other phenomena in a dangerously premature deductive fashion' (Eister 1967: 86–7; Stark and Bainbridge 1985: 20). Fifth, multi-dimensional typologies are particularly problematic, for 'in order to develop any sort of scientifically useful conceptualization, all traits which are to be included in the "type" must be presumed to vary together in some determinable relation or set of relations' (Eister 1967: 88). Yet, Erich Goode argues, there is reason to believe that some 'elements which are often assumed to be correlated... vary quite independently of one another, or sometimes even inversely' (1967: 70). Sixth, this all means that there is a real danger 'of building pseudo-knowledge into the structure of the field.... It can occur, for example, when through repeated though unconfirmed association, two or more characteristics which originally were taken only provisionally or "by definition" to belong together come to belong together "in fact" as parts of church or sect' (Eister 1967: 89; Knudsen *et al.* 1978).

The formal critique, then, is quite damning. The casual use of the typologies has allowed an unwelcome drift towards the reification of these types; yet, ironically, in application most groups defy easy classification, since they constitute mixed types. But it remains an open question whether church–sect–cult typologizing is inherently flawed or simply the victim of bad science. As both Eister (1967) and Goode (1967) imply, many of the problems could be rectified by taking two related steps: (1) returning to the methodological wisdom of Weber's original approach, and (2) breaking down 'the multidimensional conglomerates which presently pass for "sect" or for "church" entirely into their potentially component variables or attributes and... [constructing] empirically-derived clusters of traits, with probabilities of combinations of various characteristics spelled out explicitly on the basis of observed instances of concurrent appearance, or other association, in various historical movements or organizations' (Eister 1967: 86). Others have advocated the first correction as well (e.g., Swatos 1976; Wilson 1982; Dawson 1997). No one, however, has cared to take up the daunting challenge posed by Eister's second recommendation, and careful attention to the first suggestion reduces the need to do so.

The Nature and Purpose of Typologies

Postmodernist discourses have sensitized us to the socially and culturally relative, even the evaluative, character of many of the concepts used in the study of religion (Asad 1993). Few of the sociologists who use the concepts of church, sect, and cult, or various sub-typologies, however, are foolish enough either to reify these constructs or to use them indiscriminately in cross-cultural contexts. Yet, with a few exceptions, most sociologists retain their faith in the pragmatic goals of science, with its regulatory ideals of generalization, theory construction, empiricism, and even prediction. If we keep the truly heuristic nature of typologies in mind, as first expounded by Weber (1949) and later developed by John McKinney (1966), the increased reflexivity stimulated by the criticisms should serve to actually increase the methodological legitimacy of church–sect–cult typologizing,

First, and most fundamentally, as McKinney states, 'the uniformity of nature is a basic assumption of science, and all that science can do is demonstrate specific uniformities that justify keeping the assumption'. This necessitates 'the analytic elimination of the unique, and the *construction* of a *conceptual* order of things wherein the repetitive and the interrelated aspects of phenomena are exposed' (1966: 2).

Second, every form of science uses 'ideal types' (Weber 1949) to create this order, whether we are talking about the frictionless motion or perfect vacuum of physics, or the perfectly mobile factors of supply and demand or rational economic agents of economics, or such conceptions as feudalism or revolution in historical analysis (McKinney 1966: 4).

Third, to be useful, all concepts require precision, which 'can only be given negatively, by setting up limits beyond which the concept has no meaning.... Consequently the very limits that give a concept precision are responsible for some necessary degree of separation of the concept from perceptual experience' (McKinney 1966: 11). In addition, types, as concepts, are delineated by the purposeful 'accentuation' of one or more traits (Weber 1949; McKinney 1966: 11).

Fourth, types should be suited to the task at hand, meaning that they must conform to things already known, logically and empirically.

Fifth, the task at hand inevitably reflects the interests of the researcher creating the typology. There is no avoiding this hermeneutical condition. Therefore, it is important to specify the motivating question and bear it in mind during analyses, since it helps to determine the adequacy of the typology.

Sixth, the value of types rests specifically on their explanatory potential in comparative analyses. They are framed to make 'the experience had in one case, despite its uniqueness,... *reveal with some degree of probability what may be expected in others*' (McKinney 1966: 11–12).

Seventh, unlike other concepts in science, types have a more complex relationship with discovered discrepancies, as McKinney specifies (1966: 12–13):

> The comparison and measurement of empirical approximations reveals nothing but deviations from the construct.... This is not only to be expected, but is to be sought after, for it is the basis of the value of the typological method.... If degree of deviation is to be determined repetitively and comparatively, then the base of measurement (the type) must be held constant.... The type will logically contain within its structure all the essential properties or elements of a concrete structure or course of action, but not necessarily in the exact proportion or relationship pattern of any given empirical occurrence. These properties or elements constitute the variables within the type, and they remain in a fixed invariant relationship with each other for the purpose at hand. The removal of one or more variables, or the alteration of the relations between them, involves the development of a new type. Such removal or alteration may be necessary in the light of empirical requirements.

This last point brings us to the nub of the matter. Eister (1967: 88) complains that the heuristic value of deviations from a particular type cannot be used as an excuse for dismissing criticisms of the type on the grounds of its empirical 'inadequacy'. In other words, questions of 'reliability' intervene as well. The real issue is knowing when the discrepancies discovered by the use of a type or typology warrant replacing it. No one, including Weber, has provided a systematic answer to this question. The problem can be ameliorated, however, with more attention to two methodological issues: (1) the systematically variant qualities of all types and (2) the use of uni- or multi-dimensional typologies.

Becker (1940: 29–39) first stressed the importance of realizing that not all types are the same, and hence that they must be assessed differently. Most rudimentarily he differentiated between the relatively 'undated and non-localized' types used by sociologists and the 'dated and localized' types used by historians, and argued that the criteria of adequacy shift with change in types. McKinney takes this insight further, arguing that all types are constructed around certain persistent variables: '(1) the relation of the type to perceptual experience, (2) the degree of abstraction involved in the types, (3) the purpose of the type, (4) the temporal scope of the type, (5) the spatial scope of the type, and (6) the function required of the type' (1966: 21). He translates these dimensions into six overlapping continua: (1) ideal–extracted; (2) general–specific; (3) scientific–historical; (4) timeless–time-bound; (5) universal–local; and (6) generalizing–individualizing (1966: 20–34). While this approach does not fully resolve the problem of knowing when to retain or replace a type or typology, clearly the more a typology is framed towards the latter end of each continua, the more it is open to empirical testing—in the sense that Eister has in mind. Correspondingly, the more limited is its potential explanatory scope.

In the immediate context of church–sect theorizing this approach stops us from throwing the baby out with the bath water. Too often the substantive limitations of Troeltsch's typology, which is more dated and localized than Weber's and that of others, is used to delegitimate church–sect typologizing per se. Simplifying a complex interpretive problem, Troeltsch framed his more descriptive and multi-variable dichotomy to specifically understand the development of Christianity. Weber's grander concern was to understand how the practical ethic inspired by Protestantism contributed to the spread of modernity, through the progressive disenchantment and rationalization of the world. His conception of the church–sect typology is by design more ideal, general, scientific, timeless, universal, and generalizing. It is also, quite logically, given his task, more uni-dimensional than Troeltsch's typology (see below).

Uni- versus Multi-Dimensional Typologies

Most of the attempts to reform church–sect–cult typologizing have resulted in more precise and elaborate multi-dimensional typologies (e.g., Wiese and Becker 1932[1929]; Yinger 1957; 1970; Robertson 1970; Swatos 1975). If space permitted, it would be intriguing to examine the relative advantages of these typologies. But I am persuaded by Stark and Bainbridge's argument (1985: 19–24) that the only truly scientific approach is uni-dimensional (i.e., to establish a continuum focused on one variable). This view contradicts Robertson's (1970: 115, 119), and builds on the analyses of Benton Johnson (1957; 1963; 1971).

Only a uni-dimensional approach permits us to make meaningful comparative analyses for testing hypotheses about why divisions exist in any one tradition or society, or about the development of specific religious movements. Multi-dimensional typologies create a confusing array of mixed cases, as well as irrelevant null categories (i.e., logical possibilities that match no real instances); and it is rare for the exponents of these typologies to inquire whether the variables they use co-vary consistently (see, e.g., Yinger 1970: 260). Uni-dimensional typologies lay out a single clear axis of variation, which allows us more readily to identify when a change has occurred, and to what degree, thereby facilitating the framing and testing of hypotheses, and hence the generation of potentially more empirically reliable and significant explanations and general theories of development. It is easier, then, as well to tell when a type is relevant or not.

The situation is illustrated succinctly by Stark and Bainbridge (1979: 123; 1985: 22):

> Suppose five correlates are used to define the ideal church, with negative values on the same five defining the ideal sect. Then suppose we treat these criteria as dichotomies. The result is 32 logically possible types (because the defining criteria can vary independently), of which

30 are mixed types. These mixed types cannot be ordered fully. Which is more churchlike, a group possessing characteristics A and B but lacking C, D, and E or one with D and E but not A, B, or C?

'It would humble physicists', they go on to state, 'to try to theorize under such handicaps' (1985: 23). How could we make comparative claims, or track the development over time of any movement or group? The more parsimonious single-variable approach allows us to make unambiguous comparisons. But then the key question is what dimension works best. What one variable allows for clear, easily operationalized, and worthwhile comparisons, especially across cultures?

There is no consensus, but the options available seem to be limited and substantively interrelated. In fact, the three best candidates are probably the three variables that Yinger combines in his well-known later typology (1970: 257): the mode of membership of groups (i.e., the degrees of inclusiveness versus exclusiveness), the nature of the relationship that groups have with the rest of society (i.e., degrees of accommodation versus opposition), and the organizational complexity of groups (i.e., degree of routinization of charisma and institutionalization). No one seems to have pursued the last option, though Yinger's discussion points the way. I have made an initial argument for the first option (Dawson 1997). The second option has been championed by Stark, with Bainbridge and Finke (Stark and Bainbridge 1979; Bainbridge and Stark 1980; Stark and Bainbridge 1985; Stark and Finke 2000).

Benton Johnson (1957; 1963; 1971) was the first to argue explicitly the merits of a uni-dimensional approach, using a single Troeltschian differentia: 'A church is a religious group that accepts the social environment in which it exists. A sect is a religious group that rejects the social environment in which it exists' (1963: 542). Praising Johnson's insight, Stark and Bainbridge operationalized his distinction as 'the degree to which a religious group is in a *state of tension* with its surrounding sociocultural environment' (1985: 23). This is equivalent, they say, to treating sects as instances of 'subcultural deviance', and deviant subcultures are marked by three features: '*difference*, *antagonism*, and *separation*' (1985: 49). Specifying matters this way points to multiple potential measures of the degree of tension between a group and the rest of society, calling on the results of standard social surveys. 'Difference', they propose, can be measured in terms of some aspects of personal behaviour. Some types of behaviour (e.g., drinking alcohol) are characteristically forbidden by deviant subcultures, while other behaviours (e.g., being possessed by the Holy Spirit) are frowned on by society, yet often encouraged by these groups (1985: 51–6). 'Antagonism' can be operationalized in terms of a number of indicators, such as the relative particularism of a group. To what extent do they think that they have the one true path to salvation? How tolerant are they of other religious viewpoints? It is indicated as well by the emphasis placed on actively converting others and defending the faith against other beliefs and criticisms (1985: 56–60). 'Separation' can be measured by the attitudes adopted to social relations with outsiders, and the extent to which people associate with co-religionists. For example, people's attitudes to, and practice of, mixed marriages are indicative of their degree of separation (1985: 60–2). To complete the analysis, Stark and Bainbridge argue, survey data also can be used obversely to measure the degree to which a deviant subculture is rejected by the rest of society (1985: 62–6).

Stark and Bainbridge's argument is persuasive. It is one of the most elaborate attempts to operationalize the church–sect distinction. But the authors are compelled to make an admission that is more problematic than they seem to realize (Bainbridge and Stark 1980: 108; Stark and Bainbridge 1985: 49–50):

> It might be objected that defining subcultural deviance in terms of difference, antagonism, and separation introduces yet another un-ideal collection of disparate variables that defies unambiguous measurement and confident use. But this triad of terms really describes a single concept, and the three are worth distinguishing primarily because they allow us to arrange the indicators of subcultural deviance in a meaningful pattern, thereby rendering them more intelligible and easier to survey.

Are they correct? It is difficult to judge, and in principle their argument applies equally well to many other hypothesized, multi-featured types. Certainly their approach raises the thorny issue of co-variation again, which they do not address directly. Yet co-variation must be demonstrated to establish the hypothesized unity.

However, while their approach is feasible in the modern American context, where researchers have access to a substantial body of relevant survey data, it is less feasible in many other contexts where such data are not available. In the American context, moreover, their approach depends upon a certain circularity. The surveys utilized already incorporate denominational distinctions, and certain presumed attitudinal and behavioural differences, that are indicative of the distinction between churches and sects, and the tensions between them, as commonly understood by both the researchers and the people being questioned.

In other contexts scholars may be forced to fall back upon far more complex and subjective assessments of apparent indicators of difference, antagonism, separation, as well as rejection. Moreover, even within one society the tension between a group and its environment may be highly variable, both in degree and in kind. As a colleague noted in conversation with me once, 'as the Hare Krishna experience has shown in the UK, what constitutes tension with the surrounding society in the village of Letchmore Heath is taken as normal fifty miles away in London'. Judging these situations requires an extensive knowledge of the societies and cultures under study, and their religious histories. This is a daunting requirement, and it introduces further problems for the generation of cross-cultural conclusions. The parsimony of secondary data analysis is replaced by more value-laden assessments of history, doctrines, and behaviours.

Ironically, the focus on tension also carries us back to the first substantive criticism of church–sect theorizing. It tends to re-emphasize a distorting feature of Troeltsch's original formulation: the oppositional and protesting character of sects over against monopolistic churches. As Robertson (1970), Wilson (1982), Chang (2003), and Bruce and Voas (2007) argue, this assumption is less and less relevant in our pluralistic and secularized societies. The rest of society no longer cares much about the differentiation of churches and sects, and the sects themselves no longer think of the churches as their primary 'other'. So a focus on the tension between them may render this typology more dated and localized than is intended.

Likewise, I suspect that the focus on tension fails to provide the explanatory benefits promised by a uni-dimensional approach. Tension is a by-product or symptom of other things. A focus on it does explain why sects form and seek to sustain themselves, so its application is more likely to produce a taxonomy than a typology (i.e., a classification of groups that suggests hypotheses with explanatory value). In fact, both the focus on tension and the untried option of degree of institutionalization are derivative, logically and empirically, of the other option yet to be discussed: the mode of membership of a group (i.e., the degree of exclusivity).

Contrary to the implications of Stark and Bainbridge's argument (1979: 121–2; 1985: 19–20), Weber originally framed a uni-dimensional church–sect typology, one based on an even more parsimonious and relevant variable. Weber reasoned that sects are born of people's desire to have, protect, and promote a 'subjective' foundation for their intense experience of the sacred, over against the persistent tendency for churches to envision themselves as the 'objective' repositories of grace, charged with the duty of bringing even the damned under the laws of God. The conviction of some people that they constitute a 'spiritual aristocracy' gives them a desire to associate strictly with their own kind and be sharply critical of all others (1958[1904–5]: 121–2, 144–5, 254–5). They wish to be what Weber calls 'the believers' church'. Discussing the Baptist sects of post-Reformation Europe, he says this means (1958[1904–5]: 144)

> that the religious community, the visible Church in the language of the Reformation Churches, was no longer looked upon as a sort of trust foundation for supernatural ends, an institution, necessarily including both the just and the unjust, whether for increasing the glory of God (Calvinistic) or as a medium for bringing the means of salvation to men (Catholic and Lutheran), but solely as a community of personal believers of the reborn, and only these. In other words, not as a Church but as a sect.

This is the root religious impulse that Weber and Troeltsch see driving the institutional development of Christianity, reflected in pendulum swings of church-like and sect-like virtuosity, doctrinal developments, and forms of religious association through the centuries. Tension is the incidental outgrowth of the developments born of this dynamic, and its existence and degree are dependent on an array of other social environmental and historical factors.

Even Troeltsch, it is worth noting, did not see tension as essential to the definition of sects (1931[1911]: 331):

> The sects... aspire after personal inward perfection, and they aim at a direct personal fellowship between the members of each group. From the very beginning, therefore, they are forced to organize themselves in small groups, and to renounce the idea of dominating the world. Their attitude towards the world, the State, and Society may be indifferent, tolerant, or hostile, since they have no desire to control and incorporate these forms of social life.

Development of this point, however, requires a more exhaustive analysis than can be managed here.

Focusing on how inclusive or exclusive the mode of membership of an organization is provides a more fundamental and universal criteria for intra- and inter-cultural analyses. It can be operationalized economically in terms of an examination of prescribed and symbolic markers of membership (e.g., adult baptism amongst the Anabaptists) and responses to survey or interview questions about the relative status of insiders and outsiders. The variable, moreover, is explicitly organizational, and hence in keeping with the trans-situational interests of sociology, as opposed to the more problematic tendency to reduce the church–sect distinction to the contrast of accommodative and non-accommodative orientations, or the other 'world view' criteria used by Wilson, Wallis, and others to sort out different types of sects and cults. In addition, use of the mode of membership to distinguish groups brings greater theoretical unity to the theory of religion that Stark has developed with Bainbridge and Finke (Stark and Bainbridge 1985; 1996; Stark and Finke 2000).

First, it conforms with the underlying principle of their cyclical understanding of secularization. Stark and company argue that all large religious organizations are prone to a progressive accommodation to the social values of the surrounding society in ways that stimulate a renewed desire for more subjectively satisfying forms of access to the supernatural or religious experience, which encourages the creation of sects and cults. In other words, their theory of secularization is based on the same dynamic undergirding Weber's and Troeltsch's conceptualization of churches and sects.

Second, the mode of membership criterion conforms with the underlying principle of Stark and Bainbridge's distinction between audience cults, client cults, and cult movements (Stark and Bainbridge 1985: 24–30). These types of cults are differentiated in terms of the operative relationship between religious leaders and their followers, and between the followers. In other words, they are distinguished by their differing modes of membership.

Third, we could achieve an enviable degree of theoretical economy by differentiating between types of religious groups in terms of their modes of membership. One consistent continuum could be used to distinguish between types of religious groups (church, sect, cult), subtypes of the types (e.g., different types of sects), and probably even sub-subtypes (e.g., types of cult movements). I have argued this in detail elsewhere (Dawson 1997: 370–8).

Fourth, the focus on mode of membership conforms with the underlying principle of Stark and Finke's theory of religious group dynamics: levels and types of commitment (2000: 141–50). The rise and decline of religious groups, and many aspects of their internal life and relations with others, is determined, Stark and Finke assert, by differences in the levels of commitment that groups demand. Strong religious organizations make 'exclusive', 'extensive', and 'expensive' demands. But first and foremostly, it is the degree of exclusivity that shapes the nature and future of groups (2000: 141–2), the very criterion I am proposing we measure for differentiating churches, sects, and cults, and all their sub-variants (2000: 141–2).

Thus it seems that use of the mode of membership dimension heightens the integration of several key insights from Stark's influential deductive theory of religion, increasing its utility and that of church–sect typologizing in general, especially in cross-cultural analyses. But more work is needed to make the case.

Conclusion

Scholars are likely to continue to be reluctant to use church–sect–cult typologies to analyse religious groups in non-Western cultures. But our growing global awareness should not be allowed to impair our theoretical judgement in these matters. New, less ethnocentric terminology would help. In the last analysis, however, no mere terminological ingenuity can substitute for a clear grasp of the theoretical dilemmas faced by previous attempts to construct a typology of religious groups. Lessons have been learned that we should not ignore.

To this end, we actually need to engage in more careful analysis of the ideas of Weber and Troeltsch, in the context of a more sophisticated understanding of the methodology of ideal or constructed types, and a more pragmatic grasp of the real but manageable limits of knowledge in the social sciences. I think a renewed effort will demonstrate the superior merits of a uni-dimensional approach, and likely one focused on the distinctly sociological variable of mode of membership. The application is restricted, as Robertson stresses (1970: 122–3), to situations where we are dealing with organized religious collectivities. But I am betting that the concern to strengthen, maintain, or weaken levels of exclusivity is, as Weber (1958[1904–5]), Troeltsch (1931[1911]), and Stark and Finke (2000) suggest, an abiding social outcome of the religious quest for salvation everywhere.

References

Asad, T. (1993). 'The Construction of Religion as an Anthropological Category'. In *idem*, *Genealogies of Religion: Discipline and Reasons of Power in Christianity and Islam.* Baltimore: Johns Hopkins University Press, 27–54.

Bainbridge, W. S., and Stark, R. (1980). 'Sectarian Tension'. *Review of Religious Research*, 22: 105–24.

Becker, H. (1940). 'Constructive Typology in the Social Sciences'. In H. E. Barnes, H. Becker, and F. B. Becker (eds.), *Contemporary Social Theory.* New York: Russell and Russell, 17–46.

Bhatt, G. S. (1968). 'Brahmo Samaj, Arya Samaj, and the Church Sect Typology'. *Journal for the Scientific Study of Religion*, 10: 23–32.

Bruce, S., and Voas, D. (2007). 'Religious Toleration and Organizational Typologies'. *Journal of Contemporary Religion*, 22: 1–17.

Campbell, B. F. (1978). 'A Typology of Cults'. *Sociological Analysis*, 39: 228–40.

Chang, P. M. Y. (2003). 'Escaping the Procrustean Bed: A Critical Analysis of the Study of Religious Organizations, 1930–2001'. In M. Dillon (ed.), *Handbook of the Sociology of Religion.* Cambridge: Cambridge University Press, 123–36.

Cook, M. (1999). 'Weber and Islamic Sects'. In T. E. Huff and W. Schluchter (eds.), *Max Weber and Islam.* New Brunswick, NJ: Transaction Publishers, 273–9.

Daiber, K-F. (2002). 'Mysticism: Troeltsch's Third Type of Religious Collectivities'. *Social Compass*, 49: 329–41.

Dawson, L. L. (1997). 'Constructing Cult Typologies: Some Strategic Considerations'. *Journal of Contemporary Religion*, 12: 363–81.

—— (2006). *Comprehending Cults: The Sociology of New Religious Movements*, 2nd edn. Toronto: Oxford University Press.

Eister, A. W. (1967). 'Toward a Radical Critique of Church–Sect Typology'. *Journal for the Scientific Study of Religion*, 6: 85–90.

Garrett, W. R. (1975). 'Maligned Mysticism: The Maledicted Career of Troeltsch's Third Type'. Sociological Analysis, 36: 205–23.

Goode, E. (1967). 'Some Critical Observations on the Church–Sect Dimension'. *Journal for the Scientific Study of Religion*, 6: 69–77.

Hanegraaff, W. (1996). *New Age Religion and Western Culture.* Leiden: Brill.

Hertel, B. R. (1977). 'Church, Sect, and Congregation in Hinduism: An Examination of Social Structure and Religious Authority'. *Journal for the Scientific Study of Religion*, 16: 15–26.

Johnson, B. (1957). 'A Critical Appraisal of the Church–Sect Typology'. *American Sociological Review*, 22: 88–92.

—— (1963). 'On Church and Sect'. *American* Sociological *Review*, 28: 539–49.

—— (1971). 'Church and Sect Revisited'. *Journal for the Scientific Study of Religion*, 10: 124–87.

Knudsen, D. D., Earle, J. R., and Shriver, D. W. Jr. (1978). 'The Conception of Sectarian Religion: An Effort at Clarification'. *Review of Religious Research*, 20: 44–60.

McKinney, J. C. (1966). *Constructive Typology and Social Theory.* New York: Appleton-Century-Crofts.

Myers, J. (2007). *Kabbalah and the Spiritual Quest: The Kabbalah Centre in America.* Westport, Conn.: Praeger.

Nelson, G. K. (1968). 'The Concept of Cult'. *Sociological Review*, 16: 351–63.

—— (1969). 'The Spiritualist Movement and the Need for a Redefinition of Cult'. *Journal for the Scientific Study of Religion*, 8: 152–60.

Niebuhr, H. R. (1957[1929]). *The Social Sources of Denominationalism.* New York: Henry Holt and Co.

Pope, L. (1942). *Millhands and Preachers.* New Haven: Yale University Press.

Richardson, J. T. (1979). 'From Cult to Sect: Creative Eclecticism in New Religious Movements'. *Pacific Sociological Review*, 22: 139–66.

Robbins, T., and Anthony, D. (1987). 'New Religions and Cults in the United States'. In M. Eliade (ed.), *The Encyclopedia of Religion.* New York: Macmillan, 394–405.

Robertson, R. (1970). *The Sociological Interpretation of Religion.* New York: Schocken Books.

Sedgwick, M. (2000). 'Sects in the Islamic World'. *Nova Religio*, 3: 195–240.

Stark, R., and Bainbridge, W. S. (1979). 'Of Churches, Sects, and Cults: Preliminary Concepts for a Theory of Religious Movements'. *Journal for the Scientific Study of Religion*, 18: 117–33.

—— —— (1985). *The Future of Religion—Secularization, Revival and Cult Formation.* Berkeley: University of California Press.

—— —— (1996). *A Theory of Religion.* New Brunswick, NJ: Rutgers University Press.

—— and Finke, R. (2000). *Acts of Faith: Explaining the Human Side of Religion.* Berkeley: University of California Press.

Stillson, J. J. (1967). *The History and Philosophy of Metaphysical Movements in America.* Philadelphia: Westminster Press.

Swatos, W. H. Jr. (1975). 'Monopolism, Pluralism, Acceptance and Rejection: An Integrated Model for Church–Sect Theory'. *Review of Religious Research*, 16: 174–85.

—— (1976). 'Weber or Troeltsch?: Methodology, Syndrome, and the Development of Church–Sect Theory'. *Journal for the Scientific Study of Religion*, 15: 129–44.

Troeltsch, E. (1931[1911]). *The Social Teachings of the Christian Churches*, i. London: George Allen & Unwin.

Van Baalen, J. K. (1960). *The Chaos of Cults*, 3rd edn. Grand Rapids, Mich.: Eerdmans.

Wallis, R. (1974). 'Ideology, Authority, and the Development of Cultic Movements'. *Social Research*, 41: 299–327.

—— (1975). 'Scientology: Therapeutic Cult to Religious Sect'. *Sociology*, 9: 89–99.

—— (1984). *The Elementary Forms of New Religious Life.* London: Routledge & Kegan Paul.

Weber, M. (1949). 'Objectivity in Social Policy and Social Research'. In *idem*, *The Methodology of the Social Sciences*, trans. and ed. E. A. Shils and H. A. Finch. New York: Free Press, 50–112.

—— (1958[1904–5]). *The Protestant Ethic and the Spirit of Capitalism*, trans. T. Parsons. New York: Charles Scribner's Sons.

—— (1963[1922]). *The Sociology of Religion*, trans. Ephraim Fischoff. Boston: Beacon Press.

Wiese, L. von, and Becker, H. (1932[1929]). *Systematic Sociology.* New York: John Wiley and Sons.

Wilson, B. R. (1959). 'An Analysis of Sect Development'. *American Sociological Review*, 24: 3–15.

—— (1970). *Religious Sects—A Sociological Study.* London: Weidenfeld & Nicolson.

—— (1973). *Magic and the Millennium: A Sociological Study of Religious Movements of Protest among Tribal and Third-World Peoples.* New York: Harper & Row.

—— (1982). 'The Sociology of Sects'. In *idem, Religion in Sociological Perspective.* Oxford: Oxford University Press, 89–120.

Wilson, B. R. (1993). 'Historical Lessons in the Study of Sects and Cults'. In D. G. Bromley and J. K. Hadden (eds.), *The Handbook of Cults and Sects in America*, Part A: *Religion and the Social Order*, iii. Greenwich, Conn.: JAI Press, 53–73.

Yinger, J. M. (1957). *Religion, Society, and the Individual.* New York: Macmillan.

—— (1970). *The Scientific Study of Religion.* New York: Macmillan.

Suggested Reading

The following are recommended: Dawson (1997); Eister (1967); Knudsen, Earle, and Shriver (1978); McKinney (1966); Stark and Bainbridge (1985), 19–30, 48–67; Troeltsch (1931[1911]), 331–43; Wilson (1982); and Yinger (1970), 251–81.

CHAPTER 30

SECTS IN ISLAM

SAMI ZUBAIDA

ISLAM in the modern world is divided principally between the Sunni and Shi'i branches.[1] This broad division hides many other more subtle differences, such as the various Sufi orders and competing doctrines in both. There are also schisms between Sunni groups, notably the Salafi/Wahhabi[2] advocacies against both traditional and reformist trends in current culture and politics. The Sunni branch, with its divisions, comprises the great majority of Muslims in the world, estimated at 85 per cent or more (estimates vary widely) of the estimated one billion or more Muslims in the world. Shi'ism constitutes a minority (estimate, 11–15 per cent of Muslims) with concentrations in certain countries and regions, mainly Iran, Iraq, India/Pakistan, Azerbaijan, Lebanon, and the Gulf.[3]

Sunni Islam is considered, by its adherents and many commentators, as the 'mainstream', the 'church' (though only metaphorically, as there is no equivalent concept or institution in Islam), while the Shi'a and others are 'sects'. Sunnis refer to themselves as *ahlu al-sunna wal-jama'a*, the people of the *sunna*, the correct norm (of the Prophet), and *jama'a*, indicating both the body of believers and their consensus. As against this honorific self-image, the Shi'a are referred to, disparagingly, as *al-rafidha*, the rejectionists—that is, those who have rejected community and consensus. The Shi'a also see themselves as dissidents, but naturally, in favour

[1] A note on terms: Shi'a is the generic plural; Shi'i and Shi'ite are interchangeable terms, nouns and adjectives, referring to persons and attributes.

[2] 'Salafi', meaning the adherence to the doctrines and practices of the ancestors, and 'Wahhabism', the ruling doctrine of the Saudi dynasty, have tended to merge in modern advocacy and propagation, both being literalist and 'fundamentalist'.

[3] See Wikepedia entry 'Demographics of Islam', which sums up various estimates and lists proportions of Sunni/Shi'i populations by country.

of righteousness and legitimacy, holding that rule and leadership belong to the Imam, a divinely inspired, infallible (*ma'sum*) figure, descended from the lineage of the Prophet through Ali and Fatima, but who is currently 'hidden' (for the mainstream *Imami* Shi'a), and will reveal himself in a messianic event to come (Richard 1995: 15–48). There seems, then, to be a tacet agreement that the Shi'a are sectarian, and a discussion of Islamic sectarianism has to be about Shi'ism and its branches. And there are many offshoots from 'mainstream' Shi'ism which are active in the modern world. There may also be an argument for considering Salafis/Wahhabis as Sunni sects. They are sectarian in that they consider all other Muslims to be deficient in their faith and practice, and are actively hostile to Sufism, popular religiosity, such as the visitation of tombs, as well as being fiercely hostile to the Shi'a (Roy 2004: 232–89).

The main Shi'i populations in the modern world are called 'Twelver', or Imami Shi'a, following a line of twelve Imams, the last of whom 'disappeared' in 874 (Richard 1995: 40–3). They have much in common with the Sunnis in terms of belief, ritual, and law. They agree on the text of the Qur'an and on the sanctity of the traditions of the Prophet, though they favour different narrations of these traditions. They agree on the 'five pillars': *tawheed*, affirmation of the unity of God and the prophethood of Muhammad (though the Shi'a add to their call to prayer an affirmation of the friendship of Ali with God); the daily prayers, though the Shi'a allow the reduction of the five prayers to three; the fasting of Ramadan; the giving of alms (with some different categories for the Shi'a); and the obligation of haj, pilgrimage to Mecca. The Shi'a also believe in the merit of pilgrimage to the holy shrines of their Imams, though these are not alternative to the Mecca *haj* and do not rank as equal to it. Shari'a law is common to the practice of both Sunna and Shi'a, with differences in detail relating to ritual, family, and some transactions. We shall note in what follows the major differences between Sunnis and Twelver Shi'a as being ones of authority, culture, philosophy, and ethos.

There are many sects active in the modern world which hold various esoteric doctrines which share a veneration of Ali and his lineage, the best-known example being the Ismailis (Daftary 1990). These differ from both Sunni and Twelver Shi'i Islam in that they do not observe the centrality of the Qur'an and the five pillars, but believe in the sanctity of alternative texts which contain esoteric scriptures, often accessible only to an initiated elite. These are often the religions of isolated communities, many based in remote mountain regions, historically with low levels of literacy. The spread of literacy in the modern world has made conditions more difficult for many of these esoteric religions, such as the Druze in Syria/Lebanon/Palestine, the Alevis in Turkey, and the Ismailis. They have responded by coming forth as ethnic or cultural communities, drawing on religious content mostly for traditions, symbols, and communal leadership.

In what follows I will elaborate on the sociology and politics of some of these groups. These are interwoven with historical narratives.

The Genesis of Shi'ism

The major source of sect formation in Islam is the Shi'ite schism, which is traced by Muslims to their early history. The word 'Shi'a' means 'partisans', in this case of 'Ali bin Abi-Taleb (Ali in what follows), cousin of the Prophet and husband of his daughter Fatima. Their two sons, Hassan and Hussein, were the only male issues from the line of Muhammad. The conflict that gave rise to the dissidence of the Shi'a was the succession to Muhammad at his death in 632.

The Holy Family

The Shi'ite faith revolves around the story of the injustice and suffering that befell *Ahlu al-Bayt*, the people of the House of the Prophet, at the hands of usurpers and tyrants. The story runs as follows.

The Prophet, in the Shi'ite narrative, had designated Ali as his successor, but his wishes were bypassed by his senior companions, who supported one of their number, Abu-Bakr, for the succession, to be followed by 'Umar, then 'Uthman. Ali succeeded as the fourth Caliph only in 656 till his assassination in 661. Ali's Caliphate was troubled by constant challenges from various quarters, culminating in the battle of Siffin with Mu'awiyah, governor of Syria, in 658, in which the latter gained the upper hand and established his rule in Damascus, soon to become the Caliphate of Islam at the death of Ali in 661. Henceforth, in the reckoning of many Muslims, and not just the Shi'ites, Islamic rule became that of dynastic kingdoms, still labelled 'caliphate' (with religious connotations of succession to the Prophet), but in fact a departure from the 'sacred history' of the Rashidun (rightly guided) rule of Muhammad, then of his four Companions.

Mu'awiyah bequeathed the Caliphate to his reportedly dissolute and oppressive son Yazid, a byword for godlessness and tyranny in Muslim history. Yazid had reached an agreement with Ali's elder son Hassan, who, apparently, conceded the Caliphate and led a quiet life in Medina, only, according to the Shi'a, to be poisoned at Yazid's command. The younger son, Hussein, took up the claim to legitimate rule of Muslims, supported by the people of Kufa in Iraq. He travelled in an entourage of his family and retainers from Medina, aiming for Kufa, to lead his followers there, only to be intercepted by Yazid's men, who besieged his party, preventing them from access to the waters of the Euphrates. The tale of this siege, the suffering and thirst of the holy family, especially the infants, the brave fight of the men, and the ultimate martyrdom of Hussein and his male companions, and the capture and humiliation of the women, these tales constitute the legends and symbols of martyrdom constitutive of Shi'a faith and culture, as well as that of many mystics of Islam (Richard 1995: 27–33).

The Sanctity of Ali

The twelve Imams of the mainstream Shi'a start with 'Ali bin Abi-Taleb. His sanctity is the *raison d'être* of Shi'ism and of many of the smaller Alawite sects. Shi'i doctrine rests on the sanctity of the lineage and house of the Prophet, and the belief that Muhammad designated Ali as his successor. Each Imam is believed to have designated his successor, following divine guidance (Richard 1995: 15–48). This doctrine is at odds with the Sunni belief that any righteous and sane Muslim male can be acclaimed as Caliph, with a strong presumption that such a prince should be a descendant from the tribe of Quraysh, that of the Prophet. Seeming Sunni egalitarianism in this respect is made ambiguous by this stipulation, as well as by its acquiescence in dynastic kingdoms.

In addition to the charisma of lineage, 'Ali is credited with superior personal qualities of courage, strength, wisdom, beauty, and righteousness. To mystics, both Sunni and Shi'i, he is the 'Perfect Man'. There are also suggestions of a special relationship to God. The Shi'i call to prayer (*azan*) includes an affirmation that Ali is the friend, *wali*, of God (*ashahdu anna aliyan waliyu allah*). The mystical and less 'orthodox' Shi'a, as well as the other Alawite sects, go much further in the sanctification of Ali. These groups are known as *ghulat*, literally 'exaggerators' or extremists. In many narratives in this vein, Ali is given precedence above Muhammad in his relation to God. Some, such as the Ahli-Haqq sect in Kurdistan are known as *Ali Allahis*: that is, believers in the divinity of Ali (van Bruinessen 2000*a*: 245–65). The Alevis and Bektashis of Turkey and the Balkans appear to postulate a 'trinity' of God, Muhammad, and Ali, as phases or incarnations of the same essence (Shankland 2003: 80–4). These beliefs are denounced as heretical by Twelver Shi'a and their orthodox ulama. However, elements of these beliefs seem to creep into popular legends and mystical speculations. Tales of Ali's affinity to God and of his superlative qualities, such as his incarnation as a lion, are common in popular and mystic beliefs among people who are formally mainstream Twelver Shi'a. These themes lead to accusations of *shirk*, polytheism, levelled at Shi'a by their Sunni opponents, especially in the contemporary demonization of Shi'a by the Salafis/Wahhabis.

The Theology of Imamism

A central belief in mainstream Islam, both Sunni and Shi'i, is that Muhammad was the last Prophet, the 'seal of Prophethood', *khatim al-anbiya*'. They recognize a line of prophets, starting with Adam and continuing with the Old Testament prophets and Jesus, and Muhammad is the last in that line. Any claim to prophethood after Muhammad (and there were many) is considered to be dangerous heresy. Shi'ite Imamism surreptitiously subverts this orthodoxy without acknowledging that it is doing so. Shi'i theology builds the argument from the assumption of God's fundamental justice: he cannot leave mankind without an inspired guide, who is the Imam. God leaves on earth a *hujja*, 'proof' from the lineage of 'Ali through Hassan and Hussein (Watt 1973: 274–5). God delegated to the Imams spiritual rulership over the whole world, which must always have such a guide (Arjomand 1984: 35). The Imamate, then, is part of God's kindness, *lutf*, to believers. The Imam is not, strictly speaking, a prophet. He does, however, enjoy divine inspiration, which makes him free from sin and error, *ma'sum* (Arjomand 1984: 35). Some Shi'ite divines (including Ayatollah Khomeini) have sought inspiration, or illumination, from the Imam, through ascetic exercises, under expert guidance, of fasting, prayer, and continuous wakefulness, culminating in mystic states and dreams (Mottahedeh 1986: 138–44, 182–3). These themes are part of the more philosophical orientation of Shi'ite religious education as compared with its Sunni counterparts. The Sunnis have tended to distrust reasoning and speculation, emphasizing the unfathomable will of God. The Imami Shi'ites adopted *Ijtihad*, or systematic deduction and interpretation of the sacred sources, as part of the profession of the cleric and the jurist, while many Sunnis (not all) have limited or denied the legitimacy of this activity (Zubaida 2003: 24–7). The Shi'i *mujtahid*, therefore, enjoys a greater degree of autonomous authority than the Sunni cleric. In modern times (since the nineteenth century) both Sunni reformists and fundamentalists have declared the validity of *Ijtihad*. But in the Sunni context the opening of *Ijtihad* serves to challenge the authority of traditional ulama in favour of intellectuals and ideologues.

This line of theological reasoning, and the 'technology' that goes with it, are widespread in mystical Islam. Sunni mystics seek illumination through their saints, dead spiritual ancestors in the line of succession of their mystic orders (*tariqa*). They are 'born again' after attaining illumination and can perform miracles (Nicholson 1921: 1–76, 77–142; Zubaida 2003: 35–9). At the intellectual level, mystics seek signs of the Perfect Man, the Pole (*Qutb* or *Wali*), who can merge with manifestations of the Hidden Imam. These beliefs are the points of contact between Shi'ism and some Sufi orders. Many Sufis venerate Ali and the Twelve Imams, as we shall see (Arjomand 1984: 66–84). These beliefs are also at the base of the hostility of mainstream '*ulama*, both Sunni and Shi'i, to mysticism. Not surprisingly, it is seen to infringe the orthodox insistence on the end of prophethood. It also calls into question the authority of the clerics.

Hussein and the Cult of Martyrdom

The narrative of the martyrdom of Hussein at Karbala in 680 is the 'founding myth' of Shi'ite culture, around which many other themes are woven. The martyrdom of Hussein and his entourage is commemorated in the mourning rituals of the month of Muharram, and especially its tenth day, Ashura, the day of Hussein's death. So much of the Shi'i calendar revolves around these events and figures, which distinguish Shi'ite culture and rituals from their Sunni counterparts. The rituals are marked by processions, self-flagellation, and preachers recounting the bloody events and suffering of the holy party, eliciting tears, lamentations, and breast beating. Passion plays of these events are staged in some places. In addition to their mosques, the Shi'a also have 'Husseiniyas', assembly halls dedicated to the rituals of commemoration. Karbala, the location of the martyrdom, thus became a sacred site, a shrine to Hussein. The myth has it that his head was returned to the spot forty days after his death, an occasion for further gatherings and rituals in the shrine, called *al-araba'in*, fortieth day, or *radd al-ras*, the return of the head. Curiously, the Sunni Egyptians hold a counter-myth which asserts that Hussein's head was brought to Cairo and buried at the site of the Mosque of al-Hussein, a central monument in the city to the present day. Hussein became *Sayyid al-Shuhada*', the Prince of Martyrs, not only for Shi'ites, but also for many pious Sunnis. The cult and ritual of his martyrdom, however, is largely confined to the Shi'a, though also celebrated by some Sunni Sufis.

Why did Hussein march to his death in Karbala? As the Imam, with divine inspiration and foreknowledge, should he not have known what awaited him? These are questions asked by Shi'i intellectuals and divines, especially in the modern period, and contrasting answers are indicative of doctrinal positions, with political implications (Enayat 1982: 181–94). The traditional view is that Hussein's martyrdom was predestined, part of a cosmic history with a messianic culmination. Tales relate that at the Creation, Adam, wandering the world, came to the location of Karbala, where a great sadness descended upon him, and he caught his foot on a rock, causing it to bleed. God then revealed to him that the reason for his sadness and injury was the future martyrdom of one of his dear descendants. Adam cries and curses Yazid (Fischer 1980: 26). Hussein, in this conception, is a destined redeemer, like Christ, who died for humanity, for righteousness and against evil and tyranny. Through mourning him, the believers partake in this sacrifice and redemption. Modern(ist) Shi'i thinkers, especially those with political orientations, reject this view in favour of an activist Hussein (Enayat 1982: 181–94). He took up arms, against the odds, in order to set an example in fighting tyranny and evil. As such, he is an inspiration to all reformers and revolutionaries who challenge oppression and injustice. Such was the image of Hussein presented by the radical Ali Shri'ati (d. 1977), whose ideas were to pave the way for the 1979 Iranian Revolution (Richard 1995: 33–4). These are the 'two images of Hussein' in the *imaginaire* of the believers and mourners (Hegland 1983). The image of Hussein the redeemer who intercedes for those who mourn him is the most common and prevalent for much of Shi'ite history. The mourners associate Hussein's suffering with their own, crying for him and for themselves, and urging the saint to intercede for them and ameliorate their suffering. The other image of Hussein is that of the revolutionary exemplar, as we have seen. It is an image which emerges in modern times in the ideological construction of Shi'ism as a revolutionary ideology, as we see in the case of the 1979 Iranian Revolution (Fischer 1980: 12–27).

Sectarian Splits

Disputes over the succession of Imams led to further sectarian splits among the Shi'a. In succession to the fourth Imam, one party followed one Zeyd (d. 740) in preference to Al-Baqer, counted fifth by the Twelvers. This led to Zeydi Shi'ism, which became prominent in Yemen and other parts of Arabia. Zeydi Imams (the succession was not broken) were rulers of Yemen until the mid-twentieth century.

A crucial split was at the succession of the sixth Imam, Ja'far, when one party followed his by then deceased elder son, Isma'il (in effect designating Isma'il's descendants), in preference to the living son, Musa. The Isma'ili sect and its offshoots assumed great importance in the medieval Muslim world. It became a dissident proselytizing group, activist and rebellious, in contrast to the quietism of mainstream Shi'a (Daftary 1990). Arjomand has argued that Ja'far, the sixth Imam, established the mainstream Shi'ites as a quietist sectarian community, participating in the wider society, and even serving the (illegitimate) government, while dissimulating their true beliefs. He did this by formulating a theory of the Imamate in spiritual and philosophical terms, steering it away from political dissent (Arjomand 1984: 35–9). This quietism was later reinforced by the doctrine of the Occultation of the twelfth Imam (more below). The Isma'ilis, by contrast, formed subversive secret societies which threatened the power of the Abbasid Caliphate, then of the Turkic military dynasties which ruled the Middle East. The notorious sect of the Assassins, based in Iran and Syria, was one branch of those Isma'ilis (Lewis 1967, 2003). Most notably, a rival

Isma'ili Caliphate, the Fatimids, assumed power over Egypt and North Africa (969–1171) (Halm 1996). They left their imprint on the architecture of Cairo, including the establishment of Al-Azhar mosque and seminary, which survives to the present day as the foremost academy of Sunni Islam, having been appropriated by the Ayubid Sunnis at the fall of the Fatimids. The triumph of the Ayubids, the famous Salah Eddin or Saladin, initiated persecution of Shi'a in Egypt and Syria. Offshoots of the Isma'ilis survived till our time as sectarian communities, mostly with beliefs and practices considered heterodox and heretical by Sunni and Shi'i Muslims. The Druze of Syria/Lebanon/Palestine are one such offshoot. The most prominent in the modern world are the Agha Khan Isma'ilis.

The doctrines which characterize Isma'ilis and their offshoots are known as *batini*, inner or esoteric. These are similar to Neoplatonic ideas that the external, observable phenomena, as well as the explicit texts (including the Qur'an) are partial or distorted or illusory, and that 'inner' truths can be obtained only by mystical means, and through the special charisma of holy personages. These truths, then, are not accessible to ordinary people, but only to a hierarchy of the learned, the initiates, and those with hereditary charisma, the highest being the Imams. The ultimate truth will be attained only with the messianic manifestation of the last Imam. These doctrines are, naturally, seen by orthodox Muslims, Sunni and Imami Shi'ite, to be heretical and subversive.

Mahdism/Millenarianism

In Shi'ite, and some other Muslim, parlance, the 'Mahdi' is a kind of messiah. His 'return', or manifestation, is expected to usher in a period of supernatural bliss: peace, justice, and prosperity in the world, guided by a divinely inspired messiah. The prospect of a Day of Judgement, the resurrection of the dead and the separation and eternal life of the righteous from the damned, is well attested in the scriptures and traditions of Islam. The idea of the messiah, however, is tenuous, with no clear attestation in the scriptures and different narratives in the traditions. Prophetic narratives (*hadith*) are cited which assert that a Mahdi, from the clan of the Prophet, will appear, in some versions, together or just before, the Christian Jesus, son of Mary. These narratives underpin some Sunni beliefs in a coming Mahdi, but that is distinct from the Shi'ite Mahdi as the revelation of the Hidden Imam, a belief also shared by many Sufis. Ibn Khaldun, the fourteenth-century North African historian and sociologist, in his famous *Muqaddimah*, or Preface to the study of history, reviewed Mahdist narratives at length, and was sceptical about the authenticity of the cited *hadith*. He dismissed messianic ideas, which appealed to the 'stupid masses' (Ibn Khaldun 1958: 156–200). In the Shi'ite tradition, in contrast, the messianic expectation is clearly defined. The Twelfth Imam, Muhammad al-Mahdi, according to the legend, was born in Samarra, the political capital of the Abbasids, where his father, the eleventh Imam, Hassan al-Askari, was imprisoned and later poisoned. Al-Mahdi then disappeared in 874 at the age of 8, in order to be saved from the persecution of the authorities. Yet this disappearance is mystical. He continued to communicate his guidance to the community through agents, *wakil*, until the death of the last of them in 941. The years 874–941 are known as the period of the 'minor occultation', when the Imam still communicated with the community. There followed the greater occultation, which continues to the present. The twelfth Imam is a living, but absent Imam. He is *Imamal-Zaman*, the Imam of all time. He will reveal himself in the fullness of time and bring justice and bliss on earth (Richard 1995: 40–8).

Mahdist Movements

Millenarian movements appeared at various times and places in Islamic history. They were not confined to Shi'i locations. One of the most prominent on the world stage was the Sudanese Mahdi in the nineteenth century (1844–85), which fought British forces and established a Mahdist state till finally overrun. Muhammad Ahmad, believed to be the Mahdi, was a Sufi leader with tribal connections. He modelled his organization, his companions, and the phases of his movement on legends of the Prophet Muhammad and various messianic myths (Holt 1970). There were many minor Mahdist risings in rural Egypt in the nineteenth century. These are examples of Sunni Mahdism, which does not refer to the Shi'ite *Imam al-Zaman*.

The most remarkable effervescence of Mahdism, however, was in nineteenth-century Iran, in a specifically Shi'ite context (Bayat 1982; Arjomand 1984: 253–7). The Qajar state (1779–1925) was weak and decentralized, with wide powers in the hands of local elites, including religious magnates (*mujtahids*). European intrusion, primarily by Britain and Russia, led to dislocations in this fragmented polity. Part of the response consisted of many movements which combined religious ideas with reformist aspirations, often directed against the religious establishment of ulama, seen as reactionary and obscurantist. Some of these movements were secret societies, such as Freemason lodges. Others were religious movements with strong Mahdist elements. The most prominent was the Babi eruption (Cole 1998: 17–48). Sayid Ali Muhammad Shirazi (1819–50), a merchant from Shiraz, declared himself to be the Bab (the gate) to the Mahdi, then declared that he was indeed the Mahdi.

He proclaimed justice and freedom, and attacked the clergy and their religious absolutism. He and his sister also proclaimed liberation of women from traditional bonds. As the Mahdi, he could dispense with the law of the clergy and bring new enactments. This movement found great favour among swathes of the urban population. Predictably, Shirazi was arrested by the authorities and condemned to death by the clergy for heresy. His followers then engaged in violent eruptions in many cities, and he was executed. Clandestine societies of his followers then split into factions, the most successful of which was the Baha'i religion, founded in 1863 by Mirza Hussein Ali Nuri (1817–92), known as Bah'ullah (glory of God). Bah'ullah was eventually exiled to Ottoman Baghdad, where he continued his proselytizing for Babism. He gradually developed his own much more pacific and modernist version of messianism, and declared himself to be the awaited one, falling out with his brother, Subhi-Azal, who headed the remnants of the Babis. The modernity, reformism, pacifism, and ecumenism (he declared the validity and affinity of all religions) of the Baha'i teaching attracted many in Iran and some in Ottoman lands. Baha'ism became a world religion, with communities of followers in the Middle East, India, and the West, but has continued to be persecuted as a heresy in Islamic lands till the present day (Cole 1998: 17–48).

Mahdism has come to prominence in the current politics of the Middle East. We noted the resurgence of Mahdism in the turbulent years of the mid-nineteenth century in Iran and Sudan. The upheavals in Iraq after the American invasion of 2003 have similarly given rise to millenarian aspirations. But millenarian themes also have a function in political calculations. In Iraq, the main conduit of these aspirations and themes is the Mahdi Army of Muqtada al-Sadr (International Crisis Group 2006). This is a populist movement and militia, appealing primarily to poor and disenfranchised urban youth, the second generation of migrants from the most impoverished and isolated region of the marshes of southern Iraq. Their leader, Muqtada al-Sadr, lacks the credentials of the religious establishment, which he challenges, and depends on the charisma of lineage from his father and uncle, both important figures in the political transformation of modern Shi'ism, and both killed by Saddam Hussein. Mahdist themes in this context serve as a position from which Sadr and his supporters can disregard if not dismiss establishment authority. The appeal to the authority of the Mahdi, and the expectation of his imminent reappearance (with hints of special communication), imply that conventional authority of legal and ritual texts is redundant.

Similar political calculations can be discerned behind the Mahdist assertions of Iranian President Ahmedinejad (elected in 2005). His radical populism is disapproved by the state religious establishment of Khamenei, the Supreme Leader, and the conservative clerics. He has no religious authority to challenge them on their own grounds. So his intimations of direct communications from the Hidden Imam and his imminent reappearance allow him to belittle the authorities ranged against him. If you have a direct line to divinely inspired authority, why do you have to bother with earthly clerics?

Sufism and Sectarianism

Sufi beliefs, rituals, and modes of organization are widely diverse. Some are pacific and contemplative, some militant and armed; some are sophisticated intellectual and aesthetic doctrines, others are magical and charismatic; some are 'orthodox' and observant of ritual and legal obligations, others are highly heterodox and syncretistic (the nearest to sectarian Islam). In all cases, however, Sufi orders comprise modes of social organization, authority, and solidarity. In some cases Sufi orders are superimposed on other associations, such as craft guilds and urban quarters. In other cases they act as secret societies and avenues of political intrigue. Generally, Sufi orders are not considered sectarian in themselves, as their adherents are most commonly Sunni Muslims, with some being associated with Twelver Shi'ism or Ismai'ilism. However, many of the formally Sunni orders engaged in beliefs and rituals which were close to Shi'ite and Alawite themes. A notable example is the Bektashi order in the Ottoman world (Birge 1937).

Bektashis and Alevis

There are common religious themes, which include devotion to Ali and his descendants, which feature in many of the heterodox and syncretistic religions of Anatolia, Kurdistan, Central Asia, and the Balkans (what had been called 'the Turko-Iranian world'). They contain elements of Islam, alongside traces of Turkic shamanism, Iranian Manichaeism, and various folk beliefs (van Bruinessen 2000*a*: 245–302). Historically, these syncretistic religions animated the tribal surges which brought both the Ottoman and the Safavid dynasties to power. The armies of the Safavids were known as 'Qizilbash', red heads, on account of the red headgear they sported. This designation has persisted to the present to describe various sectarian Alevi communities, ranging from Afghanistan to Albania and Bulgaria.

Under the Ottomans, the Bektashi Sufi order, mentioned above, was adopted by the Janissaries, a military force that was the mainstay of the Empire in its heyday. Bektashi beliefs were very similar to those of the Qizilbash and the Alevis of Anatolia. They celebrated the cult of Ali, the Twelve Imams, as well as their founding saint Hajji Bektash, to whom they attribute miraculous and almost divine character. Hajji Bektash is an important symbolic figure in the founding myths of the Ottoman dynasty in the fourteenth century. However, the Ottoman sultans soon distanced themselves and their administration from heterodox and charismatic religion in favour of Sunni orthodoxy and its legal apparatus. The heterodox beliefs and practices, however, persisted in the Sufi orders, to which the highest elements of court society belonged for much of their history. The Mevlevi order ('whirling dervishes') was that of the court and high society, while the Bektashi was that of the soldiery. They all had a special place for the passions of Ali, Hassan, Hussein, and Fatima, and many continue to the present day ritually to mourn Hussein and the martyrs at Ashura. Yet, they are all formally Sunnis. Janissary soldiers and generals would engage in ceremonies celebrating the cult of Ali and his descendants, and in mystical exercises involving music, dancing, drink, and drugs (all strongly disapproved of in orthodox Islam, Sunni and Shi'i), but their legal status, in terms of family affairs, inheritance, and property, was that of regular Sunnis.

Alevism is the religion of large numbers of the Turkish population (estimated at 14–20 million, or 20–30 per cent), ethnic Turks and Kurds (van Bruinessen 1996; Shankland 2003). It has close parallels with Bektashis, notably the sanctity and charisma of Hajji Bektash (whose shrine in eastern Anatolia is a site of pilgrimage). Yet, it is clearly a sectarian community, distinct from Sunnis in its beliefs, rituals, and social organization (van Bruinessen 1996). Alevi communities were, for the most part, peasant communities in remote mountain areas, ruled by religious communal leaders who claim esoteric knowledge and scriptures. This is the general pattern of heterodox sectarian communities in the region, which survive to the present, defying the hostility and persecution from Sunni and Shi'i authorities, often by virtue of their mountain isolation, and in some cases of military prowess. The modern world of the nation-state and widespread literacy has made these religions less viable, with the tendency for these sectarians to come forth as ethnic groups with political aspirations.

Sectarianism in Modern Politics

The Iranian Revolution of 1979 raised the question of the political thrust of Shi'ism. It had been argued that the challenge to the legitimacy of worldly rule is inherent in *Welayat-i faqih* (the rule of the jurist) and has manifested itself in the radical ideology of the revolution. We have seen, however, that Shi'ite communities, for much of their existence, were politically quiescent, and had a religious rationale for their quietism. The ideology of the revolution was not Shi'ism as such, but a particular construction of the doctrine in relation to that moment in Iranian history. Indeed, the senior traditional clerics of Shi'ism, in Iran, Iraq, and elsewhere, were sceptical if not openly critical of Khomeini's construction of Shi'ism in his doctrine of *welayat-i faqih*, to the effect that in the absence of the Imam, the Just Jurist is the supreme political as well as religious authority in the community (here identified with the nation-state) (Zubaida 1993: 1–37). This doctrine has provided Iranian clerics with the justification for assuming the commanding powers in the state and the economy. The death of Khomeini in 1989, however, has increasingly deprived this doctrine of his charisma, a charisma lacking in his successors. Many Iranians, especially the younger generations, have come to see this rule as a cynical ploy of power-hungry and corrupt clerics.

Sects and Communal Politics

The politics of sectarianism is not always to do with religion as such, but with the sect as an 'ethnic marker' of communal boundaries and interests. Solidarities and tensions between Sunnis and Shi'is do not always stem from religious similarily or difference, and many 'secular' members of these communities may participate in them. Iranian nationalism, for instance, has Shi'ism as a historical and symbolic component, in distinction and opposition to the Sunni Ottoman world, and subsequently to the predominantly Sunni Arab neighbours. By the same token, the Arab Shi'ites in Iraq and the Gulf are often torn between Arab or Iraqi nationalism and links with Iranian co-religionists, especially after the revolution of 1979. Their national loyalty is often questioned by their Sunni compatriots.

These communal formations and boundaries are constructed in different forms following the political situations in which they occur. A good example is that of Iraq in recent decades. Sunnis and Shi'is did not constitute unitary and antagonistic communities, but each comprised diverse social and regional segments, ranging from rural, tribal peoples to urban intelligentsias and business communities. Many of them, particularly the urban classes, rejected sectarian politics in favour of a national outlook (Jabar 2003: 41–72; Zubaida 1991). Yet, sectarianism was forced upon them by a ruling clique, that of Saddam Hussein and his junta, which rested its power and security on tribal and sectarian solidarities. A series of conflicts, notably the Iran–Iraq War of 1980–8, then the Gulf War of 1990–1 and the uprisings that followed the Iraqi defeat, and finally the American invasion of 2003, all these sharpened the sectarian boundaries, overriding the urban 'national' classes in favour of sectarian populism (Zubaida 2005).

Sectarian politics is also a feature of Syria, where the ruling clique derives some of its power from the solidarity of the Alawi networks, though with more complex links with other elites in army and business.

The formerly fringe Alawi/Alevi[4] sects noted above present interesting political phenomena in various countries. Included in this category are the Druze in Lebanon,

[4] Alawi is Arabic, Alevi the Turkish pronunciation. As it happens, they refer to different groups: Alawis, predominantly in Syria, are also known as Nusairis; Alevis, a different sect, are mainly in Turkey.

Syria, and Palestine/Israel, the Alawis (or Nusairis) of Syria, the Alevis of Turkey, and the Yazidis of Kurdistan (mainly Iraq). We saw that these were mainly esoteric religions, which had departed from mainstream Muslim observances and scriptures, in favour of particular scriptures and rituals which segregated a class of religious virtuosos with access to inner secrets from the common believers who followed them. Typically, the Druze distinguished between a hereditary religious class of *'uqqal*, the wise, and ordinary believers, in turn divided between chiefly families and commoners. This esotericism could not survive general literacy and European intrusion into the inner sanctums. Elements of religious belief and ritual in these religions have lost their importance (barring elements of popular religiosity, saint worship and pilgrimage), in favour of their solidarities as ethnic communities. For the Alawis of Syria this has taken the form of cementing the solidarity of a political and military ruling class, in the form of the Asad family and its networks. In Turkey, the Alevis, mostly of peasant and rural provenance, emerged in modern Turkish politics and society as an ethnic community campaigning for recognition and political participation. Its leaders have been mainly supportive of the official secularism of the Turkish Republic, which they see as protection against Sunni hostility (Shankland 2003). But in reality, the secular Turkish Republic includes an implicit model of the Turkish citizen as a Sunni Muslim (Cagaptay 2006), thus militating against the Alevi quest for equality. The Isma'ili followers of the Aga Khan have benefited from his prominence on the world stage, and have formed a transnational community of wealth and influence, now aided by the fast pace of globalization. One trend among Isma'ilis, supported by their Imam, is the attempt to gain Islamic respectability by gestures of adherence to some elements of mainstream Islam. This trend can also be found among some Alawis and Alevis (van Bruinessen 2000*b*).

Conclusion

Sects in Islam, and the divisions between Sunnis and Shi'ites, are prominent issues on the world stage, entering into regional and international politics, cultures, and conflicts. The Iranian Revolution of 1979 ushered in the Islamic Republic. The politics of that republic and the perception of its actions in other Islamic lands have had contrasting echoes, of Islamic unity on the one side and of its sectarian Shi'ite character on the other. Khomeini issued a clarion call for Islamic unity against the West which found ready response among many radical Sunni Muslims, enthusiastic about the idea of an Islamic revolution. At the same time, the Islamic Republic was unmistakably Shi'ite, its sectarian character merging with Iranian nationalism. This Shi'ite Iranian nationalism was sharpened with the Iran–Iraq War of 1980–8, in which the Iraqi Ba'athist regime appealed to Sunni sectarian sentiments in rallying the predominantly Sunni Arab world. The only Arab ally of Iran was Syria, seen to be ruled by an Alawi sectarian elite, though a predominantly Sunni population. More recently, in the 1990s and 2000s, the success of the Lebanese Shi'ite Hezbollah in standing up to Israel and scoring notable successes, has earned it credit with Sunni Arab nationalists, who also admire Iranian rhetoric against Israel. On the other side, the Sunni Arab governments and many of their peoples are highly antagonistic to what they see as Iranian and Shi'ite threats in their region. The ascendance of Shi'ite parties in the Iraqi government and the sectarian civil war there fuel the hostility. Sunni Arabs fear a Shi'ite Iraq allied to Iran, with the sympathy and support of Shi'ite populations in Arabia and the Gulf, forming a 'Shi'ite crescent' threatening the Sunni world and the Arab nation. This hostility is reinforced by the religious sentiments of Wahhabi/Salafi Muslims, dominant in Saudi Arabia and highly influential throughout the Sunni world, who have always considered the Shi'a to be heretics and enemies of the true Islam. Sectarianism, then, has become a central axis in the geo-politics of the Middle East region. With globalized and transnational Islam, these sentiments and hostilities have spread far and wide, in Europe and elsewhere.

In this chapter we have surveyed the historical evolution of sectarian divisions in Islam and their mutations. These continuing divisions are now reconstructed as important elements in the discourses and politics of government, law, revolution, and geo-political confrontations. We should note, however, as a sociological point, that sectarian boundaries are not 'natural' lines of conflict, emanating from deep historical essences of faith. I hope to have demonstrated here that sectarian divisions, like other religious or communal differences, only become politicized and ideologized under particular conditions, such as the construction of Shi'ism as a radical ideology for the Iranian Revolution.

References

Arjomand, Said Amir (1984). *The Shadow of God and the Hidden Imam: Religion, Political Order and Societal Change in Shi'ite Iran from the Beginning to 1890*. Chicago: University of Chicago Press.

Bayat, Mangol (1982). *Mysticism and Dissent: Socio-religious Thought in Qajar Iran*. Syracuse, NY: Syracuse University Press.

Birge, J. K. (1937). *The Bektashi Order of Dervishes*. London: Luzac.

Cagaptay, Soner (2006). 'Passages to Turkishness: Immigration and Religion in Modern Turkey. In Haldun Gulalp (ed.), *Nationalism and Citizenship*. London: Routledge, 86–111.

Cole, Juan (1998). *Modernity and the Millenium: The Genesis of Baha'i Faith in the Nineteenth Century Middle East.* New York: Columbia University Press.

Daftary, Farhad (1990). *The Ismailis: Their History and Doctrines.* Cambridge: Cambridge University Press.

Enayat, Hamid (1982). *Modern Islamic Political Thought: The Response of Shi'i and Sunni Muslims to the Twentieth Century.* London: Macmillan.

Fischer, M. M. J. (1980). *Iran: From Religious Dispute to Revolution.* Cambridge, Mass.: Harvard University Press.

Halm, Heinz (1996). *The Empire of the Mahdi: The Rise of the Fatimids*, trans. Michael Bonner. Leiden: Brill.

Hegland, Mary (1983). 'Two Images of Hussein: Accommodation and Revolution in an Iranian Village'. In Nikki Keddie (ed.), *Religion and Politics in Iran.* New Haven: Yale University Press, 218–35.

Holt, P. M. (1970). *The Mahdist State in the Sudan, 1881–1898: A Study of its Origins, Development and Overthrow.* Oxford: Oxford University Press.

Ibn Khaldun, Abdul-Rahman bin Muhammad (1958). *The Muqaddimah*, trans. Franz Rosenthal, ii. London: Routledge.

International Crisis Group (2006). *Iraq's Muqtada al-Sadr: Spoiler or Stabilizer?* Middle East Report no. 55. Paris: International Crisis Group.

Jabar, Faleh (2003). *The Shi'ite Movement in Iraq.* London: Saqi.

Lewis, Bernard (1967, 2003), *The Assassins: A Radical Sect in Islam.* London: Phoenix.

Mottahedeh, Roy (1986). *The Mantle of the Prophet: Religion and Politics in Iran.* London: Chatto.

Nicholson, Reynold Alleyne (1921). *Studies in Islamic Mysticism.* Cambridge: Cambridge University Press.

Richard, Yann (1995). *Shiite Islam*, trans. Antonia Nevill. Oxford: Blackwell.

Roy, Olivier (2004). *Globalised Islam: The Search for a New Ummah.* London: Hurst.

Shankland, David (2003). *The Alevis in Turkey: the Emergence of a Secular Islamic Tradition.* London: Routledge Curzon.

van Bruinessen, Martin (1996). 'Kurds, Turks and the Alevi Revival'. *Middle East Report*, 200: 7–10.

—— (2000*a*), *Mullas, Sufis and Heretics: The Role of Religion in Kurdish Society.* Istanbul: Isis Press.

—— (2000*b*). 'Muslims, Minorities and Modernity: The Restructuring of Heterodoxy in the Middle East and South East Asia'. Inaugural Lecture, Utrecht University.

Watt, W. Montgomery (1973). *The Formative Period of Islamic Thought.* Edinburgh: Edinburgh University Press.

Zubaida, Sami (1991). 'Community, Class and Minorities in Iraqi Politics'. In Robert Fernea and Roger Louis (eds.), *The Iraqi Revolution of 1958: The Old Social Classes Revisited.* London: I. B. Tauris, 197–210.

—— (1993). *Islam, the People and the State: Political Ideas and Movements in the Middle East*, 2nd edn. London: I. B. Tauris.

—— (2003). *Law and Power in the Islamic World.* London: I. B. Tauris.

—— (2005). 'Une société traumaise, une société civil anéantie, une économie en ruine'. In Chris Kutschera (ed.), *Le Livre Noir de Saddam Hussein.* Paris: Oh! Editions, 601–28.

Suggested Reading

Nakash, Yithak (2006). *Reaching for Power: The Shi'a in the Modern Arab World.* Princeton: Princeton University Press.

Nasr, Seyyed Vali Reza (2006). *The Shia Revival: How Conflicts within Islam will Shape the Future.* New York: Norton.

Also Enayat (1982); Richard, (1995); Roy (2004); and Zubaida (1993).

CHAPTER 31

CONGREGATIONS

LOCAL, SOCIAL, AND RELIGIOUS

NANCY T. AMMERMAN

Congregations, in their prototypical American form, are locally situated, multigenerational, voluntary organizations of people who identify themselves as a distinct religious group and engage in a broad range of religious activities together. They are usually, but not always, associated with some larger tradition and its affiliated regional and national bodies (i.e., a denomination). The space where they meet may or may not be an identifiably religious building, but congregations do typically have a regular meeting place and regular schedules of religious activities (usually, but not always, at least weekly) (Wuthnow 1994). With well over 300,000 such congregations, more than 80 percent of them Protestant, this American pattern has helped to shape how the term is defined.

While the concept of a congregation is strongly associated with religious practice in the United States, local religious organizations of a similar sort can be found in other parts of the world and long before there was a United States. Something like today's congregations may have originated with the Jews who were scattered into exile in Babylon in 586 BCE. Having left behind the Jerusalem Temple as their center of worship, they may have begun to gather into synagogues to hear the words of their prophets, to pray, and to find community support. Over the next few centuries, synagogues developed the pattern of local, participatory, worshipping communities that subsequently influenced the shape of Christianity and Islam

(Levine 2000). In the centuries since, wherever religious communities are in diaspora, something like a congregation can stand alongside families to sustain a religious tradition that gets little support from the rest of the culture.

In contrast to such diaspora communities, dominant (or monopoly) religions can organize an entire territory into local "parishes". Units of geography are marked off, and all inhabitants are more or less automatically assigned to membership. Groups representing other religious traditions may or may not be welcome to organize on their own. Where there is a legally established religious authority, these local units are likely to absorb a variety of secular functions on behalf of the state—officially recording births, marriages, and deaths, for instance, but also sometimes administering a variety of social services for the population. This arrangement is perhaps most closely associated with the Catholic Church in Europe and Latin America, but it is equally descriptive of various Protestant European countries, as well. It was also the pattern in imperial Japan, where Buddhist temples were often highly regulated by the state, and at some points the entire population was enrolled into temple "parishes" (Horii 2006).

Where religious groupings are legally mandated, individual participation is a matter of citizenship, as well as (or even more than) an expression of religious identification or belief. Nearly 80 percent of the Swedish population, for instance, pays a church tax and is officially Lutheran (Sweden 2005). Although many go to church once or twice a year, on any given Sunday, less than 10 percent of the population can be found in any local congregation for worship. As in much of Europe, local and national religious institutions provide what Grace Davie (2000) calls "vicarious religion" for the Christian population. Congregations are a valued symbolic presence and a point of collective reassurance in times of tragedy. They are supported by collective funds for the good of the whole, but they are significant points of ongoing personal religious engagement for only a fraction of the population.

It is important to note that in much of the world, "religion" has never had the sort of official, separate organizational form that it has assumed in the West (Beyer 2003). People engaged in rites of passage, in healing rituals, in honoring their dead, or in invoking supernatural power—individually and collectively—in ways shaped by the rhythms of daily and seasonal life. Even today, people all over the world gather for collective study, prayer, and ritual in all sorts of forms that make them hard to document in an official or social-scientific survey. Some local religious "organizations" are interwoven with the everyday practices of a whole community or are identified with the followers of a particular healer or prophet. And some gatherings of religious communities take place in cyberspace (Brasher 2001). How people gather will continue to change, continually reshaping how we share religious observances with others; but congregating for spiritual purposes is like to continue.

In a variety of places, local gatherings are defined primarily by what religious professionals do there. There are enclaves of full-time religious virtuosi—monks and nuns, temple priests, and religious students in all their religiously variant forms. Here we find little of the regular oscillation between secular life and sacred duty that characterizes congregations of lay people. Some such Roman Catholic associations are called "congregations", but in common parlance they are more likely to be dubbed "orders", "monasteries", and the like. Congregations—in the usual sense of the term—are places where ordinary people gather.

Sometimes those people gather on something other than a weekly calendar and to perform specific religious rituals with whatever collection of fellow adherents happens to appear. From feasts to seasonal rites to pilgrimages, some religious people gather at a shrine and expect to do nothing more together than accomplish their religious duties (Kurtz 1995). They are devotees or pilgrims, but not members. Their "congregation" is defined by the place and the rituals more than by the relationships among the people who gather there. Nevertheless, this marks another of the ways in which religion is expressed in the local gathering of faithful people. Once settled in a local culture, those gathered at a shrine may, in fact, be more like than unlike, the religious assemblies we usually call congregations.

The Friday prayer service in Muslim territories falls somewhere between the pattern of occasional ritual gathering and settled religious community. Mosques do not routinely have membership rolls and rosters of social programming; the faithful are simply expected to stop (at the nearest mosque or at home or work) when they hear each day's calls to prayer. Communal prayers, however, are highly valued, and the Friday prayers and sermon express both devotion to Allah and the ideals and concerns of the gathered community (Fluehr-Lobban 1994). Being a good Muslim requires these local gathering places for prayer and study, even if in Muslim cultures the faith is sustained by an entire fabric of social institutions beyond the local mosque. Outside Muslim territories, mosques often take on fully "congregational" forms, with imams who function much like other professional clergy (Smith 1999).

There are, in fact, congregation-like gatherings in many of the traditions that are not usually thought of as "congregational". Devotees organize themselves into groups that take on a wider range of religious functions and have a more consistent membership, structure, and calendar. Both the Arya Samaj and the Rashtriya Svayamsevak Sangh (RSS), for instance, are Hindu renewal movements that organize local groups around social, charitable, and political goals, as well as around religious devotion (Gold 1991). And when Hindus move abroad, they are likely to form local societies where families can worship, learn, and teach their children the songs and stories of the tradition (Kurien 1998; R. B. Williams 1988). Whether this form of gathering is a Western (even Protestant) imposition or a more indigenous development, the resulting "congregation" may be expected to share at least some of the social patterns of local religious gatherings elsewhere. As Stephen Warner (1994) has argued, in the United States a "de facto congregationalism" shapes the expectations of all the religious groups that organize themselves there.

The key elements that define congregations, then, are that they are local, social, and religious. Their local character means that even as they may represent some larger tradition, they also reflect the particular culture of the place where they are (even if that "place" is on the Internet). Their social character means that human relationships, in all their richness and complication, are the dynamic force driving the formation, evolution, and structure of congregational life. But congregations are, most fundamentally, religious. They are places where ideas and practices related to "sacred things" are the presumed reason for their existence (as Durkheim's (1964) famous definition of religion would have it). How the local, social, and religious are combined is shaped both by the dictates of religious traditions and by each society's cultural and legal expectations as to how religious organizations are supposed to work—what sociologists might call an "institutional template". In spite of what might seem like an infinite possible array of variation, then, there are some predictable patterns in the local religious gatherings we call congregations.

What Congregations Do

Worship

When sociologist Mark Chaves surveyed a large representative sample of congregations in the USA, he asked some very basic questions about what they do, and the range of activities they reported runs to several pages. Leading the list by a wide margin is some sort of regular gathering for worship (Chaves 2004). My own research demonstrated that same virtually universal pattern. If congregations do nothing else, they provide a way for people to worship (Ammerman 2005*a*). Indeed, even the shape of those worship services is more predictable than one might think: the gathered congregation is very likely to sing together, to read sacred texts, and to listen to some sort of inspirational speech (i.e., a sermon) (Chaves 2004).

What and how they sing may vary enormously, but gathering in a religious congregation is widely expected to include music. The links between religion and music are, of course, long-standing. Much of the world's corpus of published and performed music owes its existence to religious institutions, rituals, and experiences. But beyond the domain of musical professionals, ordinary human beings seem inclined to make music, to make it together, and often to experience those musical events as religious (Clark 1991). Building on the work of ethnomusicologists and psychologists, Stephen Warner (1997) has argued that singing together is a powerful means toward both group cohesion and spiritual transcendence. Rhythms and harmonies created and shared in a group resonate deeply in the consciousness of those who participate, so it is not surprising to find congregations making music together (Bellah 2003). It is not surprising to find immigrant communities gathering to remember and teach the songs of home (Kurien 1998). And it is not surprising that differences over music are so often at the heart of congregational conflicts (Carroll and Roof 2002).

Because worship is (for most traditions) a highly expressive activity, congregations are sites for a wide range of cultural creativity. Beyond music, many worshipers express their religious ideas and experiences in drama and dance, while nearly all religious groups find some sort of visual ways to mark their space as sacred. Even when a religious group uses borrowed "secular" space, special furniture, banners, and table coverings can be brought in for each time of worship. Strict Calvinists and simplicity-minded Quakers have attempted to minimize such visual and artistic display, but the impulse to adorn is strong. For Orthodox Christians, the practice of painting icons is itself a religious devotion; for Muslims piety finds form in calligraphy; and around the globe the architecture and artistry of religious gathering places forms a major part of the world's cultural heritage.

The local and social character of congregational life shapes this religious cultural production, of course. The music and art and architecture of a locale or a cultural group are very likely to be interwoven with what one finds in that group's congregations (Gallagher 2005). Afro-centric themes and colors may characterize a Black Methodist church, while there may be remarkable resonance between a well-to-do Episcopal parish and a symphony hall. "Baby Boomers" may clap and sing as if they were at a rock concert, while the décor of a Mexican parish reflects the origins of its members. The architecture of a rural parish would look odd in an urban neighborhood, because the material expressions of congregational life embody both the local and the religious (P. W. Williams 1997).

Religious Education

Beyond worship, most congregations also exist to pass on religious traditions to the next generation, while encouraging the practices of adults. Tending to children's religious formation is, in fact, a powerful motivation for adult participation (Marler 1995; Brown and Hall 1997). Many congregations sponsor religious day schools for their children (and where religion has an official status in the nation, religious education may also take place in state-sponsored schools); but beyond formal schooling, routine religious socialization takes place in local congregations and in homes. The weekly sermon is usually aimed primarily at adults, but a "Sunday school" and other weekly activities are designed to teach children.

The sermon is normally a part of the weekly worship event, and is thereby both an expressive act and a didactic one. In many congregations, it is no less an artistic performance than are the contributions of the choir. It may be a poetic literary production or a stirring piece of rhetoric or an improvised "call and response" creation (as in many African American churches). Or it may be an unadorned attempt to teach religious principles to the faithful. Catholics typically get a brief exposition on the prescribed scripture readings of the day, while Protestants in the various Reformed churches are likely to get a more extended study of those same biblical texts. Rabbis and imams address different texts, but engage in similar efforts at using sacred texts to teach their members how to live a faithful life. They and other preachers may address ethical issues of the day, while Evangelical Protestants may also use the sermon to call for conversion. Wherever religious people gather in congregations, they are very likely to hear some sort of message or lesson that teaches and encourages them.

For both adults and children, the lessons to be learned in the congregation are likely to take the form of stories. There are certainly doctrines and catechisms to be learned, but congregations are fundamentally about telling stories. Many of those stories are from the scriptures of the tradition and identify the sacred heroes (and anti-heroes) and the exemplary actions that are idealized. Jewish children learn about Moses and Miriam, Esther and Haman. Christian children hear those tales, as well, in addition to learning about Jesus' birth and death, and Paul's missionary journeys. Each tradition reminds its children and adults about the lives of the "saints" of its history—people who have lived and died in the way of the faith. Telling exemplary stories is at the core of what congregations do together.

Because congregations are local, they are likely to add their own chapters to the stock of stories provided by the larger tradition of which they are a part. Not only will they tell the common stories in their own way, they will add stories that express the very particular sacred history of the local group itself (Wind 1990). Stories of their founding, of times of trial or triumph, or of their own local saints are critical to congregational culture. These accounts, like those from sacred scripture, tell the congregation's members who they are, how they should behave, and where they belong in both the worldly and the cosmic schemes of things.

Congregations, in tandem with families, are the primary agents of religious socialization in places where religion has been institutionally separated from an integrated culture that carries religious meanings and practices in the warp and woof of everyone's everyday life. Religious schools may be an important element, as well, but where religion is a voluntary choice, congregations and families are the institutions most likely to be the sites where that choice is supported and given shape. They teach their members the stories, train participants in ritual practice, and develop the ethical guidelines for daily living. Congregations and families are where people learn how to be religious.

Community Formation

Being local and social, as well as religious, means that congregations are a primary form of face-to-face interaction and an important point of identification and belonging. Where membership is officially defined in an established religion, local parishes are likely to be a primary site of civic and cultural activity, in addition to ritual observance. The village or neighborhood church or temple is a place for festivals and celebrations, as well as mourning and exhorting. Part of belonging to the community is belonging to the religious site at its center. Even in the USA, where parishes are not legally established, Catholics often identify their neighborhood by its parish name, rather than by its civic or geographic coordinates (McGreevy 1996), and New England Congregationalists refer to theirs as "The Church in——". For many people, who "we" are is tied to both geography and religious membership.

The more typical experience in the USA, even for Catholics, is choosing one's religious membership, and this means that congregations reflect all the pressures toward homophily (associating with people like oneself) that are present in any other voluntary organization (Emerson and Smith 2000). People know about and feel comfortable in groups of people who are similar. As they move from one place or stage in life to another, they seek out groups whose life experiences are like their own. They may not set out to make a choice based on class and race, but the results are often just that. Denominational traditions themselves have a well-recognized place in the status hierarchy, reflected in everything from architecture to styles of worship (Niebuhr 1929; Davidson *et al.* 1995). Individual members are likely to base their choice of affiliation on both local congregational reputation and pervasive cultural images that suggest to them where they belong. Only the most determined and creative congregations are able to overcome the resulting tendencies toward separation along lines of social class, education, ethnicity, and especially race.

Long described as "the most segregated hour of the week", the worship services of American congregations are, according to Michael Emerson, "hyper-segregated" (Emerson and Woo 2006). He notes that considerably fewer than one in ten congregations has more than 20 percent attendance by any group other than that congregation's dominant ethnic group; and many of those congregations are in transition from one racial dominance to another. Only perhaps 2.5 percent of congregations have a stable, long-term ethnic mix. The most successful multi-ethnic congregations in the USA are urban, young, somewhat upscale (especially in education), and have chosen ethnic diversity for themselves, rather than had it imposed on them by a denominational hierarchy or by necessity. Young second-generation immigrants are more likely to be the core of the ethnic mix than are integrated groups of Black and White Americans. After 200 years of enforced separation, the depth of difference between Black and White religious cultures is exceedingly difficult to bridge, especially when freighted with the differences in power and esteem that still surround race in the USA.

The other side of this story of separation is that congregations are also sites for the preservation and expression of minority cultures (Warner 1999). Black churches are widely regarded as the most central social institution in African American communities (Lincoln and Mamiya 1990). When no other public spaces were open to them, slaves and their descendents gathered in churches for worship and fellowship. The churches and denominations they founded became the backbone of Black civic, and even economic, life. The sacred space of congregational life allowed African Americans opportunities for comfort and self-expression, beyond the reach of White control. Theologian Robert Franklin (1994) describes it as the "safest place on earth", in which all the senses, along with the spirit, could be fully engaged in a supporting community.

Today, immigrant communities find a similar haven in the congregations they form. Familiar languages and holidays and customs can be sustained by a community that gathers for fellowship as much as for worship (Warner and Wittner 1998, Ebaugh and Chafetz 2000). Immigrants joining the majority religious tradition of a country are especially likely to form a congregational identity around their ethnic traditions—what distinguishes their congregation from all the other majority-religion congregations is precisely its immigrant ethnic culture. Immigrants from non-majority religions, on the other hand, form congregations that take their identity first from that religious tradition (Islam or Buddhism, for instance) and may include a variety of immigrant and non-immigrant members (Yang and Ebaugh 2001), as well as immigrants from multiple parts of the world. As second generations come along, the mix of ethnic and religious identities shifts again. Language may decline in importance, and the range of religious expressions may expand, but connections with others who have similar life experiences may keep the adult children of immigrants inside ethnic congregations (Min and Kim 2005).

And everywhere, food expresses cultural and religious identities no less than does the art and architecture, and it binds communities together as powerfully as their singing. Whether Korean *kimchee* or the "gospel bird" (chicken) shared in African American churches (Dodson and Gilkes 1995) or the feasts celebrating Buddhist holidays (Cadge 2005), food says who we are and provides the occasion for creating and building the relationships of the community (Dahm 2004; Orsi 1985). Daniel Sack (2000) has documented the role of food in the history of mainline Protestants in the USA, showing how changes in society have shaped how congregations gather to eat. From rural dinners "on the grounds" to elaborate banquets cooked by church women to food courts in megachurches, people may structure their cooking and eating differently, but they still eat when they come to church. At the most basic level, eating together expresses and creates the bonds of trust and commitment that are essential to congregational life (Warner 1997).

Those bonds of trust and commitment extend, as well, to the mutual caring that is so often apparent in congregations. These are the tangible expression of what Robert Putnam has called "bonding social capital" (Putnam *et al.* 2003). Members care for each other when they are sick, provide comfort in death and tragedy, and supply a variety of material supports to each other. Food, housing, jobs, counseling, and safe haven from violence are among the things that members often know they can expect from their congregations (Nason-Clark 1997). Members often become fictive kin, exchanging obligations and services with people who are part of their religious "family". As Penny Edgell Becker (1999) points out, not all congregations have such expectations for intimacy and exchange. Some are more exclusively focused on worship or on mission activities, but the call for "community" is high on the priority list for many late modern people. Disembedded from tightly knit rural communities and from extended families of blood kin, urban residents have to work harder to establish and maintain their network of relationships (Fischer 1982; Wuthnow 1998). Congregations are among the institutions through which multiple generations come together, where community is constructed, and care is delivered.

Mission

For many congregations, the matter of mutual caring extends beyond their own membership. Most congregations are interested in making a difference in the world. They have a sense that they should do something for others, not just for themselves. The particular goals they pursue are shaped by the theological story they tell about themselves. Each congregation will have some notion about whether the world is likely to change and, if so, what roles they and/or their God might have in the process. Some seek to share material goods with people in need to make earthly life more comfortable. Others share their ideas about God and about how to live, hoping that outsiders will be convinced to change their sinful ways. Still others look for ways to use the organizational clout of the congregation to pursue political and economic change.

In the United States, the impulse toward charitable work is very widespread and crosses theological lines (Ammerman 2005*a*; Chaves and Tsitsos 2001; Cnaan *et al.* 2002). Congregations of all kinds are likely to provide food, clothing, shelter, and many other forms of assistance to people beyond their own membership. Some establish programs with their own resources, but nearly all also provide resources to other community organizations. The nation's congregations are, in fact, important links in the delivery of the services and activities that make their communities a better place in which to live. While mainline Protestant congregations are the most active in service activities in their local communities, nearly all kinds of congregations are at least minimally engaged in charitable outreach. Some Evangelical churches include an appeal for salvation, but even for them service activities are simply part of how American congregations understand their role in the community (Ammerman 2005*b*).

The average congregation provides money, volunteers, space, in-kind donations, and/or staff time to a total of six community outreach organizations (Ammerman 2002). The most common partner organizations are those that provide direct services to people in need, such as food pantries, soup kitchens, shelters for victims of domestic abuse, and hundreds of ministerial alliances that coordinate emergency relief. Other connections support long-term community development or make possible political and social advocacy. These include groups such as Habitat for Humanity, the Urban League, a neighborhood association, Heifer Project, or Bread for the World. Still others help to provide activities that enhance the educational, health, and cultural life of the community, such as daycare centers, scout troops, blood banks, and theatre groups. There are also groups that allow the expression of members' special interests (from hobbies to advocacy) or address areas of personal growth and self-help.

When congregations seek to express their concern for more far-flung needs in the world, they are most likely to work through the denomination of which they are a part (Ammerman 2005*a*). Some denominations (Catholic, Jewish, and mainline Protestant) tend to support economic development projects, work for social justice, health care, and education, often in partnership with indigenous local groups. By working through a denomination, local congregations are able to pool resources to provide assistance to people in many other parts of the world.

The most active global engagement, however, comes from the conservative Protestant sector (Ammerman 2005*a*). Here the work ranges from Bible study to Evangelistic meetings to the same economic development and charitable work that others might do. Both denominational mission agencies and "parachurch" (religious special purpose) groups pool resources, deploy volunteers, and support personnel and projects in every corner of the earth (Hamilton 2000). As a result, members of many local churches have a direct sense of connection to persons and communities around the globe. Global connections are, therefore, religious as much as they are economic and cultural. Evangelical Protestants have long found their place in the world through missionary support and communication (Robert 2002).

That global connection is, of course, simply an extension of the evangelistic impulse that many conservative Protestant churches encourage. Their congregations define "mission" and "outreach" primarily in spiritual terms. They want their members to tell others about the religious truths and the religious way of life promoted by the congregation. Worship services, religious education, and other church activities often have evangelistic goals, as well. These congregations see personal spiritual transformation as the first step toward changing the world. They are not necessarily "other-worldly" in their concerns; but rather than starting with efforts to change social and political structures, they start with individual lives (McRoberts 2003).

As locally organized, socially formed, religious organizations, congregations gather in order to worship, to educate children and adults in the tradition, to create a place of community and belonging, and to do something good for the world. How they worship, what they teach, and what sort of work they try to do in the world are shaped by the dictates of the religious tradition itself. They are also shaped by the place they occupy in the social world. Ethnic and racial groups, people with more and less education or income, people in rural or suburban or urban locations, each shape their worship, outreach, education, and fellowship in ways that draw on the cultural rubrics available to them. Where membership is constrained by law or ecclesial custom, those cultural and social effects may be muted, but the local and social character of congregations is always present alongside their religious purposes.

How Congregations are Organized

Understanding congregations as local and social, as well as religious, means that we should pay attention to *how* they are organized, as well as to what they do. People who gather for religious purposes are as subject to the push and pull of organizational processes as are those who gather to manufacture jet engines, make music, or educate youth. The habits and rules that guide their behavior are products of the particular people who work together, the structures of authority within which they work, the way they exercise and distribute power among their members, and the way they fit into the ecology of organizations as it changes over time. As with *what* they do, *how* they do it is shaped by their own mix of religious tradition and homegrown culture. Some things are predictable in nearly every Roman Catholic parish, for instance, but each of those parishes will put its own stamp on how decisions are made and resources allocated.

That interaction between tradition and local culture is particularly apparent as participants are increasingly mobile across locations and traditions. What sociologists call "switching" involves joining a religious group from a denomination different from the one in which one was raised. It especially refers to movement from one denominational "family" to another—from Catholic to Protestant or from conservative Protestant to mainline Protestant, for example (Sherkat and Wilson 1995). Where the variety of kinds of congregations is small, such switching is obviously less prevalent. But in the sort of open religious "market" present in the United States, it is much more possible and more common. Still, less than a third of the adult population has switched from their denomination of origin, and most of the switching happens among relatively similar denominations—Episcopal to Lutheran or Nazarene to Baptist, for instance (Sherkat 2001).

Given significant levels of geographic mobility and change across a lifetime, the average congregation in the USA includes substantial numbers of members, many of whom are relative newcomers to the particular religious tradition the congregation represents (Ammerman 2005*a*). All religious traditions are affected by the influences being carried from one group to another by this religious mobility. Each congregation and each tradition must decide, then, how membership will be defined and how rigorous the process of joining will be. Where congregations are formed voluntarily, the most basic organizational task is recruiting members and setting the requirements for participation.

Matters of Authority

Making such decisions is not, however, always just a local matter. Some congregations recognize an authority beyond their own membership. In legally established religious systems, the state may be a factor in the congregation's decision making, providing financial resources, perhaps licencing clergy, maintaining buildings, and the like. Within religious traditions themselves, equally centralized and pervasive authorities may be present. Roman Catholic bishops, for instance, can appoint pastors and approve budgets, but may also close a parish entirely (Radin 2006). Since the Second Vatican Council (1962–5), local lay members have been increasingly involved in directing the work of their own parishes, but the limits on their power are still considerable. Some Protestant denominations, most notably the United Methodist Church, have similarly centralized structures of authority (Cantrell *et al.* 1983). Ecclesiastical hierarchies limit the power of local congregations to act as they please.

Other Protestants, as well as most Jewish congregations, have a much looser system of authority. Their "congregational" polity stands in contrast to the hierarchical systems just described. Among groups like Baptists, Congregationalists, and Reform Jews, centralized denominational bodies may provide training for clergy and a variety of programmatic resources, but local congregations are expected to make their own decisions about how they do what they do. Still other congregations have no official denominational connections at all (Thumma 1999). All of these locally autonomous congregations can decide to organize themselves in the first place, to construct a building, or to disband. They can also decide what sort of worship style they will follow, who will lead them, and how they will educate their children. The occasional congregation may stray too far and be "disfellowshiped" by other groups representing the tradition (Ammerman 1990), but the expectation is that local members will take responsibility for their own religious life together.

Between these two poles lies a good deal of territory where outside religious authority is combined with local autonomy. In denominations such as the Presbyterians and Episcopalians, there are official guidelines for the balance between local and central authority, as well as representative assemblies for adjudicating policies.

Theirs is a federated form of association. Even among those with congregational polities, however, the balance between local and external power is complicated. Denominations that are organizationally strong can exercise considerable influence on what happens in local congregations. At its height, for instance, the Southern Baptist Convention provided such comprehensive programmatic support that local congregations from Atlanta to Dallas bore strong resemblance to each other (Ammerman 1990).

Matters of Power

No matter what the external authority structure, every congregation will also have its own ways of getting things done, of distributing power, and of accumulating and disbursing resources (Dudley 1998). Leadership and influence in a congregation may be gained through longevity, high social status, religious wisdom, the investment of energy, or social skill. As social gatherings laced through with the concerns and resources brought to them by their members—along with their particular religious values and goals—congregations have characteristic modes of working. Some look to a clergy leader for primary guidance. Others develop elaborate formal committee structures and rule-books. Still others operate like an extended family or through informal channels and hallway conversations (Becker 1999). Mundane factors ranging from size and location to the educational backgrounds of their members help to account for some of these operational differences. Within the constraints set by the external authorities of their religious tradition, each congregation will bring its own collective history to the task of making decisions.

It will also bring its own store of material and spiritual resources to the task. In order to accomplish its work, a congregation is likely to need money, space, equipment, skills, leadership, and the energy and commitment of its members (McKinney 1998). Its religious vision will define the work that needs to be done. Its social and spiritual capacities will combine to determine whether and how that work happens.

In calling forth the participation and commitment of its members, congregations also provide a social space in which opportunities for leadership are possible. Congregations not only take advantage of the social skills, resources, and connections that their members bring. They also create possibilities for developing new skills and networks. This is especially true for persons who do not otherwise have easy access to places of social influence and civic participation (Verba *et al.* 1995). Both among disadvantaged communities in the USA and among urban migrants in Latin America, observers have noted that the opportunity to organize and run a congregation can provide experience in leadership and democratic participation (Martin 1999).

Matters of Change

As organizations that are local and social, congregations are also units in a constantly changing ecology of other social units (Ammerman 1997; Eiesland 2000). New congregations are often founded in response to population demands, as well as to spiritual excitement. As subsequent neighborhood demographics change, the membership in local congregations may change, as well. As new congregations are formed and old ones decline, the range of choice and competition is altered. Major economic changes—the exodus of southern Black sharecroppers into northern US cities or the emergence of a retirement class that can afford to be "snowbirds"—may shift populations from one place to another. Likewise, new state regulations may make religious participation more or less possible or attractive. Even centuries-old parishes in Europe may once have been Catholic before assuming their current Lutheran or Anglican form.

In most cases, the cycles of change are measured in decades rather than centuries. Congregations situated in urban contexts are very likely to be faced with transient surroundings and populations. The children of today's members rarely remain nearby into adulthood. Every generation or so, congregations have to reinvent themselves or face decline. Those that do not succeed sometimes transfer their property to a new group, merge with another congregation, or otherwise cease to exist (Ammerman 1997).

Sometimes, of course, the changes are less dramatic and obvious. As dynamic human organizations, congregations express the ever-changing values and creativity of their members. New programs and ministries may be added, new space created and renovated, new music performed. New members may join, and new relationships may be forged among those already there. New decision-making strategies may be tried, and new leaders designated and trained. New religious ideas and rituals may emerge, and members may be challenged to adopt new disciplines of life or new campaigns of social reform. As local, social, and religious organizations, congregations are sites of constant transformation.

Summary

Around the world today, people gather locally to express and perpetuate their religious identities. Those gatherings are more and less organized, and more and less voluntary, but they always bear the marks of both the religious tradition they celebrate and the local people doing the celebrating. Where those gatherings take on the form we commonly recognize as a "congregation", they are very likely to include fellowship activities and community outreach alongside their worship and religious education. Congregations are at once both religious and social. How they do their work is shaped both by their place in the social world and by the religious authority they recognize. As populations move across territory and around the globe, congregations may become increasingly common points of communal identification, both locally grounded and religiously connected in webs of transnational affiliation (Levitt 2004). Other populations may eschew organized local connections, in favor of a more amorphous and individual spirituality, but as local, social, and religious institutions, congregations are likely to remain critical players in the fabric of social and religious life.

REFERENCES

AMMERMAN, NANCY T. (1990). *Baptist Battles: Social Change and Religious Conflict in the Southern Baptist Convention.* New Brunswick, NJ: Rutgers University Press.

—— (1997). *Congregation and Community.* New Brunswick, NJ: Rutgers University Press.

—— (2002). "Connecting Mainline Protestant Congregations with Public Life". In R. Wuthnow and J. Evans (eds.), *Quietly Influential: The Public Role of Mainline Protestantism.* Berkeley: University of California Press, 129–58.

—— (2005*a*). *Pillars of Faith: American Congregations and Their Partners.* Berkeley: University of California Press.

—— (2005*b*). "Religious Narratives, Community Service, and Everyday Public Life". In M. J. Bane, B. Coffin, and R. Higgins (eds.), *Taking Faith Seriously.* Cambridge, Mass.: Harvard University Press, 146–74.

BECKER, PENNY EDGELL (1999). *Congregations in Conflict: Cultural Models of Local Religious Life.* Cambridge: Cambridge University Press.

BELLAH, ROBERT N. (2003). "The Ritual Roots of Society and Culture". In M. Dillon (eds.), *Handbook of the Sociology of Religion.* New York: Cambridge University Press, 31–44.

BEYER, PETER (2003). "Social Forms of Religion and Religions in Contemporary Global Society". In M. Dillon (eds.), *Handbook of the Sociology of Religion.* New York: Cambridge University Press, 45–60.

BRASHER, BRENDA (2001). *Give Me That Online Religion.* San Francisco: Jossey Bass.

BROWN, ANNE S., and HALL, DAVID D. (1997). "Family Strategies and Religious Practice: Baptism and the Lord's Supper in Early New England". In D. D. Hall, (ed.), *Lived Religion in America: Toward a History of Practice.* Princeton: Princeton University Press, 41–68.

CADGE, WENDY (2005). *Heartwood: The First Generation of Theravada Buddhism in America.* Chicago: University of Chicago Press.

CANTRELL, R. L., KRILE, J. F., and DONOHUE, G. A. (1983). "Parish Autonomy: Measuring Denominational Differences". *Journal for the Scientific Study of Religion,* 22: 276–87.

CARROLL, JACKSON W., and ROOF, WADE CLARK (2002). *Bridging Divided Worlds.* San Francisco: Jossey Bass.

CHAVES, MARK (2004). *Congregations in America.* Cambridge, Mass.: Harvard University Press.

—— and Tsitsos, William (2001). "Congregations and Social Services: What They Do, How They Do It, and With Whom". *Nonprofit and Voluntary Sector Quarterly*, 30: 660–83.

Church of Sweden (2005). "Church of Sweden Annual Report". Available at <http://www.svenskakyrkan.se/ArticlePages/200508/16/20050816074719_svkhjs928/anuual_report2005.pdf>, accessed 7 Feb., 2007.

Clark, Linda J. (1991). 'Hymn-Singing: The Congregation Making Faith'. In C. S. Dudley, Carroll, W. Jackson, and J. P. Wind (eds.), *Carriers of Faith*. Louisville, K.: Westminster/John Knox Press, 49–64.

Cnaan, Ram A., Boddie, Stephanie C., Handy, Femida, Yancey, Gaynor I., and Schneider, Richard (2002). *The Invisible Caring Hand: American Congregations and the Provision of Welfare*. New York: New York University Press.

Dahm, Charles W., OP (2004). *Parish Ministry in a Hispanic Community*. Mahwah, NJ: Paulist Press.

Davidson, James D., Pyle, Ralph E., and Reyes, David V. (1995). "Persistence and Change in the Protestant Establishment, 1930–1992". *Social Forces*, 74: 157–75.

Davie, Grace (2000). *Religion in Modern Europe: A Memory Mutates*. Oxford: Oxford University Press.

Dodson, Jualynne E., and Gilkes, Cheryl Townsend (1995). "There's Nothing Like Church Food". *Journal of the American Academy of Religion*, 63: 519–38.

Dudley, Carl S. (1998). "Process: Dynamics of Congregational Life". In N. T. Ammerman, J. W. Carroll, C. S. Dudley, and W. McKinney (eds.), *Studying Congregations: A New Handbook*. Nashville: Abingdon Press, 105–31.

Durkheim, Émile (1964). *The Elementary Forms of the Religious Life*, trans J. W. Swain. New York: Free Press.

Ebaugh, Helen Rose, and Chafetz, Janet Saltzman (eds.) (2000). *Religion and the New Immigrants: Continuities and Adaptations in Immigrant Congregations*. Walnut Creek, Calif.: AltaMira Press.

Eiesland, Nancy (2000). *A Particular Place: Urban Restructuring and Religious Ecology*. New Brunswick, NJ: Rutgers University Press.

Emerson, Michael O., and Smith, Christian (2000). *Divided by Faith: Evangelical Religion and the Problem of Race in America*. New York: Oxford University Press.

—— and Woo, Rodney M. (2006). *People of the Dream: Multiracial Congregations in the United States*. Princeton: Princeton University Press.

Fischer, Claude S. (1982). *To Dwell Among Friends: Personal Networks in Town and City*. Chicago: University of Chicago Press.

Fluehr-Lobban, Carolyn (1994). *Islamic Society in Practice*. Gainesville, Fl.: University Press of Florida.

Franklin, Robert Michael (1994). "The Safest Place on Earth: The Culture of Black Congregations". In J. P. Wind and J. W. Lewis (eds.), *American Congregations: New Perspectives in the Study of Congregations*. Chicago: University of Chicago Press, 257–84.

Gallagher, Sally K. (2005). "Building Traditions: Comparing Space, Ritual, and Community in Three Congregations". *Review of Religious Research*, 47: 70–85.

Gold, Daniel (1991). "Organized Hinduisms: From Vedic Truth to Hindu Nation". In M. E. Marty and R. S. Appleby (eds.), *Fundamentalisms Observed*. Chicago: University of Chicago Press, 531–93.

Hamilton, Michael S. (2000). "More Money, More Ministry: The Financing of American Evangelicalism since 1945". In L. Eskridge and M. Noll (eds.), *More Money, More Ministry:*

Money and Evangelicals in Recent North American History. Grand Rapids, Mich.: Eerdmans, 104–38.

Horii, Mitsutoshi (2006). "Deprofessionalisation of Buddhist Priests in Contemporary Japan". Available at <http://www.japanesestudies.org.uk/articles/2006/Horii.html>, accessed 26 Jan., 2007.

Kurien, Prema (1998). "Becoming American by Becoming Hindu: Indian Americans Take Their Place at the Multicultural Table". In Warner and Wittner (1998), 37–70.

Kurtz, Lester (1995). *Gods in the Global Village: The World's Religions in Sociological Perspective.* Thousand Oaks, Calif.: AltaMira Press.

Levine, Lee I. (2000). *The Ancient Synagogue: The First Thousand Years.* New Haven: Yale University Press.

Levitt, Peggy (2004). "Redefining the Boundaries of Belonging: The Institutional Character of Transnational Religious Life". *Sociology of Religion*, 65: 1–18.

Lincoln, C. Eric, and Mamiya, Lawrence H. (1990). *The Black Church in the African American Experience.* Durham, NC: Duke University Press.

Marler, Penny Long (1995). "Lost in the Fifties: The Changing Family and the Nostalgic Church". in N. T. Ammerman and W. C. Roof (eds.), *Work, Family, and Religion in Contemporary Society.* New York: Routledge, 23–60.

Martin, David (1999). "The Evangelical Protestant Upsurge and its Political Implications". In P. L. Berger (eds.), *The Desecularization of the World: Resurgent Religion and World Politics.* Grand Rapids, Mich.: Eerdmans, 37–50.

McGreevy, John T. (1996). *Parish Boundaries: The Catholic Encounter with Race in the Twentieth-Century Urban North.* Chicago: University of Chicago Press.

McKinney, William (1998). "Resources". In N. T. Ammerman, J. W. Carroll, C. S. Dudley, and W. McKinney (eds.), *Studying Congregations: A New Handbook.* Nashville: Abingdon Press, 132–66.

McRoberts, Omar M. (2003). "Worldly or Otherworldly? 'Activism' in an Urban Religious District". In M. Dillon (ed.), *Handbook of the Sociology of Religion.* New York: Cambridge University Press, 412–22.

Min, Pyong Gap, and Kim, Dae Young (2005). "Intergenerational Transmission of Religion and Culture: Korean Protestants in the U.S.". *Sociology of Religion*, 66: 263–82.

Nason-Clark, Nancy (1997). *The Battered Wife: How Christians Confront Family Violence.* Louisville, Ky.: Westminster/John Knox Press.

Niebuhr, H. Richard (1929). *The Social Sources of Denominationalism.* New York: World Publishing.

Orsi, Robert A. (1985). *The Madonna of 115th Street: Faith and Community in Italian Harlem, 1880–1950.* New Haven: Yale University Press.

Putnam, Robert D., Feldstein, Lewis M., and Cohen, Donald J. (2003). *Better Together: Restoring the American Community.* New York: Simon & Schuster.

Radin, Charles A. (2006). "O'Malley to Reveal his Revised Plans to Consolidate Churches". Available at <http://www.boston.com/news/local/articles/2006/11/23/omalley_to_reveal_his_revised_plans_to_consolidate_churches/>, accessed 28 Jan. 2007.

Robert, Dana L. (2002). "The Influence of American Missionary Women on the World Back Home". *Religion and American Culture*, 12: 59–89.

Sack, Daniel (2000). *Whitebread Protestants: Food and Religion in American Culture.* New York: St Martin's Press.

SHERKAT, DARREN (2001). "Tracking the Restructuring of American Religion". *Social Forces*, 79: 1459–93.

—— and WILSON, JOHN (1995). "Preferences, Constraints, and Choices in Religious Markets: An Examination of Religious Switching and Apostasy". *Social Forces*, 73: 993–1026.

SMITH, JANE I. (1999). *Islam in America*. New York: Columbia University Press.

THUMMA, SCOTT (1999). "What God Makes Free is Free Indeed: Nondenominational Church Identity and its Networks of Support". Available at <http://www.hirr.hartsem.edu/bookshelf/thumma_article5.html>.

VERBA, SIDNEY, SCHLOZMAN, KAY LEHMAN, and BRADY, HENRY E. (1995). *Voice and Equality: Civic Voluntarism in American Politics*. Cambridge, Mass.: Harvard University Press.

WARNER, R. STEPHEN (1994). "The Place of the Congregation in the Contemporary American Religious Configuration". In J. Wind and J. Lewis (eds.), *American Congregations: New Perspectives in the Study of Congregations*. Chicago: University of Chicago Press, 54–99.

—— (1997). "Religion, Boundaries, and Bridges". *Sociology of Religion*, 58: 217–38.

—— (1999). "Changes in the Civic Role of Religion". in N. J. Smelser, and J. C. Alexander (eds.), *Diversity and Its Discontents: Cultural Conflict and Common Ground in Contemporary American Society*. Princeton: Princeton University Press, 229–43.

—— and WITTNER, JUDITH G. (eds.) (1998). *Gatherings in Diaspora: Religious Communities and the New Immigration*. Philadelphia: Temple University Press.

WILLIAMS, PETER W. (1997). *Houses of God: Region, Religion, and Architecture in the United States*. Urbana, Ill.: University of Illinois Press.

WILLIAMS, RAYMOND BRADY (1988). *Religions of Immigrants from India and Pakistan: New Threads in the American Tapestry*. Cambridge: Cambridge University Press.

WIND, JAMES P. (1990). *Places of Worship*. Nashville: American Association for State and Local History.

WUTHNOW, ROBERT (1994). *Producing the Sacred*. Urbana, Ill.: University of Illinois Press.

—— (1998). *Loose Connections: Joining Together in America's Fragmented Communities*. Cambridge, Mass.: Harvard University Press.

YANG, FENGGANG, and EBAUGH, HELEN ROSE (2001). "Religion and Ethnicity Among the New Immigrants: The Impact of Majority/Minority Status in Home and Host Countries". *Journal for the Scientific Study of Religion*, 40: 367–78.

SUGGESTED READING

AMMERMAN, NANCY T., CARROLL, JACKSON W., DUDLEY, CARL S., and MCKINNEY, WILLIAM (eds.) (1998). *Studying Congregations: A New Handbook*. Nashville: Abingdon Press.

DOUGLASS, H. PAUL, and BRUNNER, EDMUND DE S. (1935). *The Protestant Church as a Social Institution*. New York: Harper & Row.

WARNER, R. STEPHEN (2005), *A Church of Our Own: Disestablishment and Diversity in American Religion*. New Brunswick, NJ: Rutgers University Press.

Wertheimer, Jack (ed.) (2000). *Jews in the Center: Conservative Synagogues and Their Members.* New Brunswick, NJ: Rutgers University Press.

Wind, James P., and Lewis, James W. (eds.) (1994). *American Congregations: New Perspectives in the Study of Congregations.* Chicago: University of Chicago Press.

—— —— (1994). *American Congregations: Portraits of 12 Religious Communities.* Chicago: University of Chicago Press.

Also Ammerman (1997) and Chaves (2004).

CHAPTER 32

THE SOCIOLOGY OF THE CLERGY

DEAN R. HOGE

THE sociology of the clergy has its roots in the work of Max Weber (1993[1922]), but the bulk of the theory and research was written after 1950, motivated by concrete concerns of churches. This area of research is filled with studies sponsored by religious denominations and organizations hoping to solve practical problems.

Clergy is a profession, yet a unique profession. Like other professionals, clergy are a defined group of trained persons who possess knowledge and skills not accessible to the general public, a group which is relatively autonomous in that the members are entitled to make judgements based on their expertise and are empowered to be largely self-governing. Like other professionals, clergy claim to have authority in their own domain, which gives them status and influence. But, unlike most other professionals, clergy are presumed to be in their positions out of religious motivation, not out of hope for monetary gain or recognition, and their professional expertise is based on traditional sources and texts, not scientific data. In some religious groups such as Roman Catholics, clergy are expected to live an ascetic life apart from the rest of the population. Also, unlike most other professionals, Protestant, Jewish, and Muslim clergy are employed by their constituents, and they need to maintain support from their members if they are to succeed. No other profession is subject to approval by a lay constituency in this way—which makes clergy persons somewhat resemble local politicians. In sum, clergy are professionals, but different from most other professionals.

Should clergy see themselves as professionals? It is commonly argued that the perception of clergy as professionals would add to their social influence and their occupational satisfaction. On the other hand, many ministers and priests ask, "Why be a professional? Was Jesus Christ a professional? Won't this remove us from close identification with our flock?" In Catholic circles there is debate as to whether the priesthood is a profession or rather a religious *vocation* defined theologically (Hoge, Shields, and Griffin 1995). In Evangelical and Pentecostal Protestant circles, clergy are not commonly seen as professionals, partly because many of the preachers do not have seminary training; furthermore, many Evangelicals and Pentecostals do not see such a training as useful. In sum, to analyze clergy as professionals is appropriate only in mainline Protestantism and in most branches of Judaism, but not in Roman Catholicism or Evangelical Protestantism.

Historically, research in this subdiscipline began in the USA with Protestant studies in the 1930s, pioneered by H. Paul Douglass. Catholic research began later, in the 1950s, pioneered by Joseph Fichter (1954; 1961). Studies of Eastern Orthodox priests, Jewish rabbis, Muslim imams, and Buddhist priests have been sparse. For historical overviews of Protestant studies, see Schuller, Strommen, and Brekke (1980), Moberg (1984), Francis and Jones (1996), and Carroll (2006). For overviews of Catholic studies see Fichter (1961) and Hoge and Wenger (2003). The main research topics have been recruitment, training, morale, stress, clarification of roles, and change.

In the United States, a recent research initiative coordinated at Duke University, the "Pulpit and Pew" program, produced seven books, ten reports, and numerous papers on American Protestant and Catholic clergy. These efforts produced the best review of research available today, especially Jackson Carroll's (2006) *God's Potters* (see <www.pulpitandpew.duke.edu>). The clearest way to convey the topics and issues is by proceeding denomination by denomination; thus I will first review the research under the three headings of Protestant, Catholic, and other religions; then I will take up broader theoretical questions.

Research on Protestant Ministers

The Roles of a Minister

The job of Protestant minister calls for the clergy person to perform numerous roles, a requirement which is unusual among learned professions. Clergy need to be preachers, teachers, liturgists, counselors, administrators, managers, community leaders, and more. This breadth of roles leads to overload. For decades ministers have complained that they can't do it all, and they have asked their lay leaders and bishops for a prioritization of roles. Researchers also have devoted much effort to the analysis of roles.

The pioneer research on Protestant ministers' roles was done by Samuel Blizzard in the 1950s (in Blizzard and Blizzard 1985). He identified three levels of ministerial roles: the master role, either theological or functional; integrative roles, identifying the groups and organizations with whom the minister works; and practitioner roles, the six specific tasks of ministry. The six practitioner roles (preacher, pastor, teacher, priest, administrator, and organizer) are a source of stress because they are so varied and difficult. Not only are the skills required too broad, but also the minister's time and energy are too limited to do everything. Most ministers see certain roles as foremost, and see themselves as especially competent in them, but they cannot dedicate themselves to those roles. Blizzard showed how ministers preferred to devote themselves to being pastor, preacher, and teacher, but found themselves forced to spend their time and energy being administrator, pastor, and organizer. The greater the disjunction between roles preferred and roles actually performed, the lower the minister's satisfaction. Later researchers confirmed that ministerial morale was related to how much each person enjoys the specific roles that he or she necessarily performs, with enjoyment of the role of priest and preacher most associated with high morale.

Brunnette-Hill and Finke (1999) carried out a partial replication of Blizzard's pioneer 1955 survey. They found that clergy in 1994 worked fewer hours per week than those in 1955. The main drop was in the number of hours devoted to social interaction with members and potential members, visiting the sick, administration, and involvement with civic leaders. Carroll (2006) replicated this research in 2001, with very similar findings.

Another approach to roles looked at conflicts between ministerial roles and family roles. Ministry is commonly seen as a total way of life, and ministers are not expected (or expect themselves) to have another life in family or leisure time which is distinct from their church work. Carroll, Hargrove, and Lummis (1981) defined this as "role hegemony", indicating that the Protestant ministerial role often takes precedence over all else in a minister's life, so that he or she is on duty twenty-four hours a day, seven days a week. All research has found that ministers complain about this problem.

Stress and Satisfaction

A practical problem which has stimulated Protestant research since the 1970s is occupational stress and satisfaction. A seminal study by Mills and Koval (1971) found that most ministers experience stress, and that it decreases with age. The most commonly reported source of stress was conflict with the congregation, particularly conflict with congregational leaders caused by personal and ideological differences. Later researchers also found high stress. Blanton and Morris (1999) found that the long hours of work in ministry for comparatively low pay is a widely felt difficulty. In addition, families of clergy feel stress because they live a fishbowl existence in which they are expected to demonstrate exemplary family life (see also Schilderman 1998).

Later research on stressors on ministers found that ministers suffer frequent criticism by members and by lay leaders, and this criticism troubles them. A second source of stress, with almost as much impact, is the assumption by lay members that a minister is available any time and can be called upon for help or ministry at short notice. In addition, there is a problem of setting boundaries between ministry and family life, so that ministerial demands intrude too much on family life, including on vacations and family decision making. These problems of family life and marriage are major sources of stress (Carroll 2006). A recent study of Protestant ministers who left local church ministry (Hoge and Wenger 2005) identified seven main reasons for leaving. Three principal reasons were conflict within the congregation, conflict with denominational leaders, and burnout.

Women Ministers

A major theme in Protestant research has been the increase in women ministers. Their numbers were low until 1970 (Lehman 2002), but the 1970s, 1980s, and 1990s were decades of rapid growth. In 2002, women constituted 32 percent of the students enrolled in Master of Divinity programs in US and Canadian theological schools. Today half of the students in some prestigious Protestant seminaries are women.

The suddenness of denominational acceptance of women ministers in the 1960s and 1970s was studied by Chaves (1997). He found that the changed cultural climate after the passage of the 1964 Civil Rights Act in the USA put moral pressure on denominational leaders, since all American institutions were moving toward gender equality. The feminist movement was an additional push. Protestant denominations felt the need to declare gender equality in ordination, and many did so even though the majority of their members did not want it. Tensions have remained in these denominations ever since.

Major research on women ministers began in the 1980s in the USA. Carroll, Hargrove, and Lummis (1981) carried out a survey of the experiences of men and women ministers in nine denominations. They discovered that women found it more difficult than men to get ministerial positions. Three research efforts in the 1980s and 1990s greatly clarified the forces affecting women ministers. Edward Lehman carried out surveys in the USA and England (1993; 2002). Nesbitt (1997) made a study of Episcopalians and Unitarians. Zikmund, Lummis, and Chang (1998) made a cross-denominational study of men and women ministers. The findings of these studies can be summarized briefly.

Women entering ministry after 1970 tended to be older than men. Among them were more "second-career" persons, who were older and more experienced in church life. Their life goals were clearer. The percentage of women who had been divorced was much higher than among men. They came from more educated families than did men.

Evangelical and Pentecostal denominations have offered very few positions to women, even though in principle most affirm women's ordination. Their resistance comes partly from New Testament teachings that women must always be submissive to men. From another theological angle, arguments about sacraments have been influential in the Eastern Orthodox churches, the Episcopal Church, and some Lutheran churches—holding that the human agent presenting the Gospel and the elements of communion represents Christ, and thus must be male (Lehman 2002: 11).

Women have found first placement after ordination more difficult than men. More women have found placements as associate pastors or ministers of education, rather than as senior pastors. Also, in their second or third placements, fewer women find jobs as senior pastors in high-prestige, high-paying churches. These barriers have seemed to recede over time (Nesbitt 1997; Lehman 2002), a result of more formalized hiring practices at the denominational level, which increase fairness in the system and minimize the effects of "good old boy" networks.

Women ministers' salaries are lower than men's. In the Zikmund, Lummis, and Chang study of 1998, women earned about 91 percent as much as men when all other factors such as age, type of position, and size of congregation were held constant. Yet in studies of job satisfaction, women in the 1990s did not express greater dissatisfaction with their salaries. Why not? Carroll, Hargrove, and Lummis (1981) speculated that women entered the ministry with lowered expectations and thus were happier with their placements and salary. Also, a majority of women ministers were married to husbands with good incomes.

Women, more than men, have found themselves in remote communities with small congregations. Men tend to see these churches as temporary stepping stones toward more attractive placements later, and this is often the case. Women, by contrast, find it difficult to move on, and therefore a next step for them entails either getting more education, going into a specialized non-parish ministry, or leaving the ministry altogether.

Several researchers studying resistance to women ministers have developed a "contact hypothesis", which holds that prejudices against unknown persons tend to fall away after personal contact with those persons, provided the contact is non-hierarchical in nature, that is, based on equal status. Research has sustained the hypothesis (Lehman 2002).

The New Seminarians

Protestant seminarians in America have changed in two ways since the 1970s. Most important, the percentage of females has risen, as noted earlier, so that about

35 percent of recent seminary graduates in curricula leading to ordination have been women. Also the seminary students today are older; the average age of incoming students in a 1999 study was 35 years, compared with an average of 26 or 28 in the 1970s. Have standards changed? It is widely believed among seminary leaders today that the current crop of seminarians is less intellectually capable than was true 20 or 40 years ago, and this is bolstered by research on professional preferences of Phi Beta Kappa members. Measured by academic criteria, the standards have dropped, and seminary admissions today are not as competitive as earlier. Wheeler (2001) surveyed seminary students in 1999 to see if men and women were different, and if older students were different from younger ones just out of college. She found that the women performed as well as men in seminary. Older students, in general, came to seminary with lower academic skills and credentials. More of today's seminarians have had practical experience after college, but they have had less intellectual preparation. Fewer come from families in which the parents had graduated from college (Carroll 2006).

Research on Roman Catholic Priests

The Priest Shortage

The main concern motivating research on the Catholic priesthood has been the decline in numbers. After the close of the Second Vatican Council in 1965, a large number of priests resigned, causing alarm in the Catholic leadership. In the USA about 15–17 percent of priests resigned between 1966 and 1975. In 1969 the American Catholic bishops commissioned large studies of the priesthood, studies which were the best research done to date (Greeley 1972; Kennedy and Heckler 1972).

During the 1980s and 1990s, Schoenherr and Young produced definitive studies of the coming priest shortage in the USA. Their main work was *Full Pews, Empty Altars* (Schoenherr and Young 1993). They predicted a 40 percent decline from 1966 to 2005, a prediction which has since been borne out. A few years later Young (1998) updated the projections to 2015, predicting further declines. By the end of the 1990s, American Catholic seminaries were producing ordinations at between 35 and 45 percent of replacement level (i.e., the number needed to replace older priests who retired, resigned, or died). Vilarino found the same decline in Spain (Schoenherr, Young, and Vilarino 1988; Vilarino and Tizon 1998). On similar declines in Italy, see Garelli (2003), and in Germany, see Zulehner (2002).

Why are so few men going to seminary, and why are some priests resigning? Hoge (1987) surveyed Catholic college students in the USA to identify the main deterrents keeping men from becoming priests. He found that the celibacy requirement was the most important single deterrent, and that if celibacy were made optional, the number of seminarians would increase by about four times. He also asked the college students if they would be interested in the priesthood if there were a tour of duty of ten or fifteen years, not a lifetime commitment, and found that many more would be interested. The decline in Catholic seminarians in all the modern industrialized nations since 1965 is explained by the increased perceived costs, relative to rewards, of becoming a priest in the changed social and religious climate. By contrast, in developing nations there is no decline in numbers of seminarians.

Rodney Stark carried out two studies of determinants of priestly vocations in the USA. In the first (1998) he found that in the 171 dioceses, and also in the 50 states, the lower the percentage of Catholics in the population, the more men were ordained priests. This pattern has also been found with financial contributions to churches—that contributions are higher in settings where the denomination is a small minority in the population. For both of these findings, Stark invokes the classic argument of Adam Smith that competition produces vigorous religious organizations, while monopoly produces lazy ones. In the second study, Stark and Finke (2000) found that the more theologically conservative the diocese, as measured by expert ratings, the more men were ordained priests in them. Also, the more a religious community of priests (and nuns) offers an intense level of community life and a sharp separation from secular life, the more members they recruit. Stark and Finke explain these patterns by the stronger social and religious rewards to priests (and nuns) in traditional dioceses and communities, compared with the more liberalized dioceses and communities after the Second Vatican Council. Liberal dioceses and communities have a higher cost–benefit ratio, and therefore attract fewer recruits.

The analysis of cost–benefit ratios in recruiting men to the priesthood continues to be an urgent topic under study, both at the practical and at the theoretical level. Partisan debates are ongoing in Catholicism, asserting either that traditions should be reinstated or that reforms are needed—debates which can be clarified through sociological studies. A topic needing research is the financial cost of a possible shift to optional celibacy for diocesan priests.

The Catholic priest shortage has no counterpart among American Protestant denominations. No Protestant denomination has experienced a large decline in ordinations in recent decades. In overall terms, the supply exceeds the demand in all major denominations except the Lutheran Church–Missouri Synod—which does not ordain women. Young men and women in most Protestant denominations find the rewards of a career of religious leadership to be compelling, and therefore there are plenty of seminary students. The Protestant problem is different. It is the problem of placement. Seminary graduates are typically cosmopolitan in lifestyle, and they refuse to serve small rural churches, thus leaving those churches without ministers, or at least without fully trained ministers. Most US Protestant churches are small, with fewer than 100 regular participants, and thus they cannot afford a full-time pastor. The result is Protestant minister "shortage" in small, marginal churches, while affluent suburban churches have an abundance of candidates (Chang 2004).

Satisfaction and Morale

The landmark 1972 Greeley study of priests devoted much of its attention to priestly satisfaction, priestly identity, and the causes of priestly resignations. The decision to resign was predicted by the desire to marry, loneliness, or modern theological values. Older priests and those feeling satisfied in their work were less likely to resign. Later, Hoge, Shields, and Griffin (1995) replicated the model with data from a 1993 survey of American priests. The predictive model was similar, even though the priests in 1993 were older and felt less desire to marry. Morale was higher in 1993 than in 1970 and 1985, partly because newly ordained priests no longer felt under-utilized.

In 2000, Hoge (2002) interviewed a sample of priests ordained within the past eight years who had already resigned. He found that two conditions are necessary to produce a resignation: (1) the priest must feel lonely or unappreciated; and (2) he either falls in love, rejects celibate living, has a disillusioning experience, or (if he is homosexual) wants a homosexual partner. Unlike the resignees in 1970, almost nobody in the 2000 sample mentioned the difficulty of ministering within the authority structure of the church. Also unlike 1970, the desire by homosexual priests for partners was discussed openly in 2000.

Numerous surveys have asked priests where they get their greatest satisfaction in the priesthood. The surveys have had a consistent outcome. Satisfaction comes most of all from sacramental and liturgical aspects of ministry, and second, from opportunities to be a part of people's lives. Other priestly roles, including social witness, administration, and leadership of the community, are less important sources of satisfaction.

From 1970 to 2001, surveys of American priests have found a shift in the self-identity of priests, from the "servant leader" model current right after the Second Vatican Council to the "cultic" model in the 1990s (Hoge and Wenger 2003). The cultic model, which was dominant in the 1940s and 1950s, sees the liturgical, sacramental, and teaching tasks as central to the priesthood, with emphasis on the holiness and separateness of priests. The servant leader model, by contrast, stresses spiritual leadership of the community, service, and collaboration of priests with laypersons. It was dominant among American priests from the Second Vatican Council until the early 1980s, whereafter the cultic model was again the choice of young priests, a shift which produced a young-versus-old tension among priests today. The reason for the shift to the cultic model beginning in the 1980s has never been adequately explained, though it is somehow associated with the influence of Pope John Paul II and the sharply reduced number of candidates. In England and

Wales, Louden and Francis (2003) surveyed parish priests, with similar results–that the oldest and youngest priests are more traditional in ecclesiology and in their definition of priesthood than the priests ordained in the 1970s and 1980s.

Sexuality and Homosexuality

Interest in the sexuality of priests arises from the vows of celibacy required for the Roman Catholic priesthood, vows which researchers have reported are not being observed by all priests (Wolf 1989; Sipe 2003; Phipps 2004). Sustained study of the situation began only in recent years. The first description of the sexual practices of priests was that of Sipe, based on his decades of practice as a psychoanalyst of American priests. He estimated that about 20 percent of priests at any time are involved in heterosexual relations, and about 25–50 percent have a homosexual orientation, some of whom are active. His conclusions were attacked as being based on non-random samples, yet other Catholic leaders in positions to know the situation have not disagreed with his reports. In the 1980s several other researchers tried to estimate the percentage of American priests who have a homosexual orientation, and came up with numbers ranging between 25 and 55 percent (see Wolf 1989). The impact of homosexuality on the ministry of these priests remains unstudied.

A scandal of priestly abuse of children and youth erupted in the 1980s and 1990s. The scandal to the Catholic community was more in the way the pedophiles and ephebophiles were defended and managed by bishops than in the sexual behavior itself. Two reviews of research on the problem were published by Shupe (1998) and Plante (1999). Later, a Vatican committee published a review of clinical and sociological research on priestly sexual abuse (Hanson, Pfäfflin, and Lütz 2004). New research by John Jay College of Criminal Justice, sponsored by the Catholic bishops, found that 4 percent of priests active in the last five decades had been accused of sexual abuse of minors.

Today a debate is ongoing in the Catholic Church over the possible influence of homosexuality and celibacy on pedophilia. The Vatican review noted above concluded that pedophilia is committed disproportionately by homosexuals, but other church authorities deny this. Any association with celibacy is less clear.

Research on Clergy of Other Religions

Sociological research on other religious leaders is less developed. To my knowledge there is only one published sociological study of Eastern Orthodox priests—done by Schuller, Strommen, and Brekke (1980) as part of a multi-dimensional study of ministerial roles. Orthodox clergy and laity agree that the sacramental-liturgical function is central to the priesthood—similar to the cultic model in Catholicism—and that leadership of the congregation and social involvement are secondary concerns. Most important is that the priest carries out the sacramental duties unerringly, teaches the tradition, and lives an exemplary holy life. But, unlike Catholics, Orthodox secular clergy may marry, and the vast majority are married (Allen 2001).

Sociological research on Jewish rabbis is scant. Not many studies have been published. The main topics of research involving rabbis have been their views of interfaith marriage, Jewish outreach, and Jewish identity. Mayer conducted a 1997 survey of American rabbis on interfaith marriages, in which 36 percent of the rabbis said that they would officiate at an interfaith wedding, but the numbers ranged widely, from zero among the Orthodox and Conservative rabbis to 62 percent of the Reconstructionist rabbis (Mayer 1997).

In organizational terms, Jewish rabbis are similar to free-church Protestant clergy, in that they are directly responsible to a lay board of trustees of the congregation they serve; there is no higher branch (i.e., denominational) authority. Cohen, Kress, and Davidson (2003) surveyed Conservative rabbis and lay leaders, and they asked both groups to rate the importance of different roles a rabbi must play. Both rabbis and lay leaders saw the roles of Jewish educator and pastor as being foremost. They rated managerial and administrative roles as least important. The rabbis reported that they wished they could spend more time in study and in-service training, and less time attending meetings and doing management tasks.

As with Protestant denominations, Jewish branches in America have varied in the degree to which they welcome women rabbis. At present the Orthodox branch has none, the Conservative branch has about 12 percent, the Reform branch about 22 percent, and the Reconstructionist branch, about 47 percent. Women rabbis find placement more difficult than men, a situation which one woman rabbi referred to as the "matzah ceiling".

Japanese Buddhist priests have been studied by Jaffe (2001), Covell (2006), and Horii (2006). Societal change has put pressure on the priests, depriving them of their high occupational status and authority of a century or two ago. Governments have regulated their lives and activities, especially after 1945, and their religious authority in the minds of Japanese young adults has fallen. Their past functions as educators and healers have been taken over by other professionals. Today their main social function is related to funerals.

On Muslim imams the literature is mainly theological and historical. I know of only two sociological studies which include information on imams. The best is a survey of mosques in America by Bagby, Perl, and Froehle (2001). It found that, compared with Christian churches, mosques have fewer staff; 55 percent have no paid full-time staff, and only 10 percent have more than two paid staff. Islam has no doctrinally defined institutional structure, hence the training, legitimation, and deployment of imams vary from nation to nation.

Eighty-one percent of American mosques have an imam, often trained overseas. The rest are led by learned laypersons willing to volunteer. Of all the imams, roughly 50 percent are full-time. An estimated 36 percent of imams have formal Islamic education. A theme in the sociology of mosques is tension between imams trained in the Old World and the values of laity assimilated to American or European individualistic and democratic values (Haddad 2002).

Structurally, the majority of mosques resemble free-church Protestant congregations, in that final decision making rests not with the clergy person but with a lay board of directors. But in 28 percent of the mosques, the imam has final decision-making power. There is no Muslim analog to denominational authority. Most mosques in the United States were established recently, since sizeable Muslim immigration took place only after 1970.

Interpretations of the Role of the Clergy

Trends in clergy and religious leadership can best be understood when research findings are interpreted in terms of broad social change. I will mention four topics in which wider interpretation is crucial.

Egalitarianism and Loss of Authority

Over the centuries, societies have defined clergy in various ways. In ancient Judaism, priests were a separate tribe (Levites) which had legitimation for its teachings and its status. In Hindu culture a separate caste (Brahmans) developed with similar legitimation. In medieval Catholicism, clergy were required to be celibate to avoid development of any dynasties or tribes, and were given special privileges by the secular rulers in return for the support they gave to existing monarchs. During the Protestant Reformation, the special theological status of priests was attacked by the Lutheran doctrine of the "priesthood of all believers", which removed Holy Orders from the list of sacraments and demoted clergy from their elevated theological status. In the French Revolution, political and legal privileges of Catholic priests and bishops were removed. A strong anti-clericalism spread across Europe and strongly influenced the Founding Fathers of the United States.

An attack on clerical authority has been present in Western nations for 300 years, and it continues today. In Protestantism it has been strong since the Reformation, so that Protestant ministers today are perceived to possess limited authority solely by virtue of their ordination. Instead, they need to win personal authority from their flocks through their own actions. In modern nations the Catholic culture is moving in the same direction, decade by decade, with less and less authority being accorded by Catholic laity to priests and bishops. Surveys of American Catholics show a gradual shift toward egalitarianism and withdrawal of ecclesial authority by the laity (D'Antonio *et al.* 2007). In Asia, Buddhist priests are also losing their authority.

If laity accord less and less authority to clergy, how does this change ministry? How does it change the role of the clergy? Is there still a role for a clergy if it has little authority? Probably, with a more educated and autonomous laity in the future, demands and expectations put on clergy will be higher than in the past, and clergy will be less able to fall back on institutionalized status for influence ("Do not forget, I am an ordained minister"). Possibly new forms of religious leadership will arise which are less tied to traditional denominations than in the past (Carroll 2006).

This trend challenges the authority of denominational leaders such as bishops and synods, leading to less hierarchical structures. Denominations in the future will be networks more than powerful hierarchies. In addition, in the USA, non-denominational churches are growing faster than those belonging to denominations. A looming problem in this trend away from denominational authority is possibly inadequate supervision and discipline of clergy, opening the way to scandals and fraud. Therefore the flattening of denominational structures needs to be considered carefully.

The Arrival of Women Ministers

As was mentioned above, the number of women ministers has risen dramatically since the 1970s in many denominations, but not all. Women clergy are still not accepted in the Roman Catholic Church, the Lutheran Church–Missouri Synod, Orthodox Judaism, and a few Evangelical Protestant bodies. The clergy has been slower to accept women than have other comparable professions and occupations, including law, medicine, social work, and academic work. The greater acceptance of women in other learned occupations has put pressure on the remaining denominations which don't accept women—especially the Roman Catholic Church. Broad social trends toward empowerment of women will put pressure on all religious traditions.

Homosexuality

A new issue arose in the 1990s: whether openly homosexual persons should be ordained to the ministry or the priesthood. Is open homosexuality something permitted by the teaching of the Bible? Is this lifestyle an impediment to ministry, or not? Are there special forms of ministry to which homosexuals are suited, even uniquely suited, or not? A fractious dispute has arisen in recent decades in all Christian denominations, a controversy which is beginning to bring schisms and realignments. The topic needs extensive research. Meanwhile, nationwide polls in the USA show increased acceptance of the homosexual lifestyle (Hoge and Wenger 2003: 107). These broader social trends will produce pressures on churches.

Globalization

Today's world has fewer communication barriers and boundaries than ever. Flows of international information and international travel are unprecedented. The Internet has made international contact vastly easier and faster. Contact of Christians with devotees of other world religions is more frequent than ever, and modern national governments are exhorting their citizens to have goodwill toward all religions. The old boundaries between religions are disappearing, and members of specific denominations ask: "What is so important about being a member of ours?"

In a situation of prolonged cross-religious contact, the theological issue of universalism rises higher than ever. How shall one religion relate to others, while keeping its identity? What is the authority of the Bible or the Qur'an in the new circumstances? No longer can a minister preach that those who do not accept Jesus Christ will be sent to hell, since it will occur to everyone that millions of people born in other nations, who have never heard of Jesus Christ, are thus too easily consigned to eternal flames.

The problems of relativism will loom larger than ever in the new globalized society, affecting clergy and laity alike. Denominations will continue to legitimate clergy through their rules and rituals of ordination, but the specific authority of denominations cannot be maintained intact. The authority conferred on clergy through ordination will be weaker, and the amount of loyalty they feel they owe their denominations will be weaker.

Meanwhile, rising educational levels of church members will challenge the opinions of clergy. As one American Catholic priest said in a lecture, "Remember, we have had a learned laity for only one hundred years." Individual laypersons will feel less constrained by family, ethnicity, and heritage when choosing religious communities (such as churches), and will feel entitled to make their own selection or to drop out entirely.

In summary, social and cultural trends are putting new pressures on traditional clerical roles and definitions. The sociological study of clergy needs to prepare everyone for the transitions ahead. We need new research, both in relating its concepts and theories to broader sociological research and in investigating the new social reality.

New research is needed to examine the loss of traditional authority, the more egalitarian relations between clergy and laity, and the diminished roles of clergy in a more differentiated society; gradually some traditional roles are being lost, while other new roles may be gained. Research is needed on the issues of women clergy, homosexual clergy, and clergy outside any denomination. Also, research is needed on religious traditions outside the traditional scope of research—Christianity in the English-speaking nations and Europe. Not many scholars have done sociological studies on Orthodox priests, Muslim imams, Hindu priests, or Buddhist priests. To sum up: future scholars need to relate this subdiscipline better to scholarly work on organizations, professions, political movements, and globalization, and they need to extend it outward to more nations and traditions.

References

Allen, J. J. (ed.) (2001). *Vested in Grace: Priesthood and Marriage in the Christian East.* Brookline, Mass.: Holy Cross Orthodox Press.

Bagby, I., Perl, P. M., and Froehle, B. T. (2001). *The Mosque in America: A National Portrait.* Washington: Council on American–Islamic Relations.

Blanton, P. W., and Morris, M. L. (1999). "Work-Related Predictors of Physical Symptomatology and Emotional Well-Being among Clergy and Spouses". *Review of Religious Research*, 40: 331–48.

Blizzard, S. W., and Blizzard, H. B. (1985). *The Protestant Parish Minister: A Behavioral Science Interpretation.* Storrs, Conn.: Society for the Scientific Study of Religion.

Brunnette-Hill, S., and Finke, R. (1999). "A Time for Every Purpose under Heaven: Updating and Extending Blizzard's Survey on Clergy Time Allocation". *Review of Religious Research*, 41: 48–64.

Carroll, J. W. (2006). *God's Potters: Pastoral Leadership and the Shaping of Congregations.* Grand Rapids, Mich.: Eerdmans.

—— Hargrove, B., and Lummis, A. T. (1981). *Women of the Cloth: A New Opportunity for the Churches.* New York: Harper & Row.

Chang, P. M. Y. (2004). *Assessing the Clergy Supply in the 21st Century.* Durham, NC: Duke Divinity School Pulpit and Pew Project.

Chaves, M. (1997). *Ordaining Women: Culture and Conflict in Religious Organizations.* Cambridge, Mass.: Harvard University Press.

Cohen, S. M., Kress, J. S., and Davidson, A. (2003). "Rating Rabbinic Roles: A Survey of Conservative Congregational Rabbis and Lay Leaders". *Conservative Judaism*, 56: 71–89.

Covell, S. G. (2006). *Japanese Temple Buddhism: Worldliness in a Religion of Renunciation.* Honolulu: University of Hawaii Press.

D'Antonio, W. V., Davidson, J. D., Hoge, D. R., and Gautier, M. L. (2007). *American Catholics Today.* Lanham, Md.: Rowman & Littlefield.

Fichter, J. H. (1954). *Social Relations in the Urban Parish.* Chicago: University of Chicago Press.

—— (1961). *Religion as an Occupation.* Notre Dame, Ind.: University of Notre Dame Press.

Francis, L. J., and Jones, S. H. (ed.) (1996). *Psychological Perspectives on Christian Ministry.* Leominster: Gracewing.

Garelli, F. (ed.) (2003). *Sfide per la Chiesa del Nuovo Secolo: Indagine sul Clero in Italia.* Bologna: Società Editrice il Mulino.

Greeley, A. M. (1972). *The Catholic Priest in the United States: Sociological Investigations.* Washington: United States Catholic Bishops Conference.

Haddad, Y. Y. (2002). *Muslims in the West: From Sojourners to Citizens.* Oxford: Oxford University Press.

Hanson, R. K., Pfäfflin, F., and Lütz, M. (2004). *Sexual Abuse in the Catholic Church: Scientific and Legal Perspectives.* Vatican City: Libreria Editrice Vaticana.

Hoge, D. R. (1987). *The Future of Catholic Leadership: Responses to the Priest Shortage.* Kansas City, Mo.: Sheed and Ward.

—— (2002). *The First Five Years of the Priesthood: A Study of Newly Ordained Catholic Priests.* Collegeville, Minn.: Liturgical Press.

—— and Wenger, J. E. (2003). *Evolving Visions of the Priesthood: Changes from Vatican II to the Turn of the New Century.* Collegeville, Minn.: Liturgical Press.

—— —— (2005). *Pastors in Transition: Why Clergy Leave Local Church Ministry.* Grand Rapids, Mich.: Eerdmans.

—— Shields, J. J., and Griffin, D. L. (1995). "Changes in Satisfaction and Institutional Attitudes of Catholic Priests". *Sociology of Religion,* 56: 195–213.

Horii, M. (2006). "Deprofessionalisation of Buddhist Priests in Contemporary Japan". *Electronic Journal of Contemporary Japanese Studies,* 14 Mar.

Jaffe, R. (2001). *Neither Monk nor Layman: Clerical Marriage in Modern Japanese Buddhism.* Princeton: Princeton University Press.

Kennedy, E. C., and Heckler, V. J. (1972). *The Catholic Priest in the United States: Psychological Investigations.* Washington: United States Catholic Bishops Conference.

Lehman, E. C. (1993). *Gender and Work: The Case of the Clergy.* Albany, NY: State University of New York Press.

—— (2002). *Women's Path into Ministry: Six Major Studies.* Durham, NC: Duke University Pulpit and Pew Project.

Louden, S. H., and Francis, L. J. (2003). *The Naked Parish Priest: What Priests Really Think They're Doing.* London: Continuum.

Mayer, E. (1997). *What Do Rabbis Think and Do about Intermarriage? Highlights of a New Survey of the American Rabbinate.* New York: Jewish Outreach Institute.

Mills, E. W., and Koval, J. P. (1971). *Stress in the Ministry.* Washington: Ministry Studies Board.

Moberg, D. O. (1984). *The Church as a Social Institution,* 2nd edn. Grand Rapids, Mich.: Baker Books.

Nesbitt, P. D. (1997). *Feminization of the Clergy in America: Occupational and Organizational Perspectives.* New York: Oxford University Press.

Phipps, W. E. (2004). *Clerical Celibacy: The Heritage.* New York: Continuum.

Plante, T. G. (ed.) (1999). *Bless Me Father for I Have Sinned: Perspectives on Sexual Abuse Committed by Roman Catholic Priests.* Westport, Conn.: Praeger.

Schilderman, H. (1998). *Pastorale Professionalisering.* Kampen: Kok.

Schoenherr, R. A., and Young, L. A. (1993). *Full Pews and Empty Altars: Demographics of the Priest Shortage in United States Catholic Dioceses.* Madison: University of Wisconsin Press.

SCHOENHERR, R. A., YOUNG, L. A. and VILARINO, J. P. (1988). "Demographic Transitions in Religious Organizations: A Comparative Study of Priest Decline in Roman Catholic Dioceses". *Journal for the Scientific Study of Religion*, 27: 499–523.

SCHULLER, D. S., STROMMEN, M. P., and BREKKE, M. L. (eds.) (1980). *Ministry in America.* San Francisco: Harper & Row.

SHUPE, A. (ed.) (1998). *Wolves within the Fold: Religious Leadership and Abuses of Power.* New Brunswick, NJ: Rutgers University Press.

SIPE, A. W. R. (2003). *Celibacy in Crisis: A Secret World Revisited.* New York: Brunner–Routledge.

STARK, R. (1998). "Catholic Contexts: Competition, Commitment, and Innovation". *Review of Religious Research*, 39: 197–208.

—— and FINKE, R. (2000). "Catholic Religious Vocations: Decline and Revival". *Review of Religious Research*, 42: 125–45.

VILARINO, J. P., and TIZON, J. S. (1998). "The Demographic Transition of the Catholic Priesthood and the End of Clericalism in Spain". *Sociology of Religion*, 59: 25–35.

WEBER, MAX (1993[1922]). *The Sociology of Religion.* Boston: Beacon Press.

WHEELER, B. G. (2001). "Fit for Ministry: A New Profile of Seminanains". *Christian Century*, 11 April, 16–23.

WOLF, J. G. (ed.) (1989). *Gay Priests.* New York: Harper & Row.

YOUNG, L. A. (1998). "Assessing and Updating the Schoenherr–Young Projections of Clergy Decline in the United States Roman Catholic Church". *Sociology of Religion*, 59: 7–23.

ZIKMUND, B. B., LUMMIS, A. T., and CHANG, P. M. Y. (1998). *Clergy Women: An Uphill Calling.* Louisville, Ky.: Westminster/John Knox Press.

ZULEHNER, P. M. (2002). *Priester in Modernisierungsstress.* Ostfildern: Schwabenverlag.

SUGGESTED READING

The following are recommended: Carroll (2006); Chang (2004); Hoge and Wenger (2003); and Zikmund, Lummis, and Chang (1998).

PART VII

SECULARIZATION AND THE REPRODUCTION AND TRANSMISSION OF RELIGION

CHAPTER 33

THE MEANING AND SCOPE OF SECULARIZATION

KAREL DOBBELAERE

THE founding fathers of sociology did not use, or only rarely used, the term 'secularization'. Later generations of sociologists employed the term more frequently, but attached different meanings to it (Shiner 1967). Not until the late 1960s were several sociological *theories* of secularization developed, most prominently by Berger, Luckmann, and Wilson, referring to processes developed by Durkheim (differentiation), Weber (rationalization), and Tönnies (*Gemeinschaft—Gesellschaft*). These theories subsequently led to discussions about their validity and generality. Some sociologists have rejected the term totally, even calling it a 'doctrine' to be carried 'to the graveyard of failed theories' (Stark 1999: 270); others are its staunch defenders (Wallis and Bruce 1992; Wilson 1985; 1998). To understand these contradictory evaluations, one must consider just what different authors mean by secularization. Stark (1999) and also Swatos and Christiano (1999) argue that the prediction of secularization concerned the decline of 'individual piety', citing several authors who have predicted the demise of individual religiosity, and they reject this on the basis of historical and recent empirical data. Wilson, and Wallis and Bruce, to the contrary, stress the macro-level, where religion has lost its social power to regulate the so-called secular subsystems of society, like polity, economy, family, education, and law. But there is still another level of possible changes to analyse: what are the reactions of religious actors? Do they reluctantly accept the changes on the individual and the societal level, or do they react against them and, if so, how? The preceding questions point to three levels of analysis—the societal or macro-level, the organizational or meso-level, and the individual or micro-level—and possible interactions between these levels. Since secularization is perceived as a process of social change on three levels, we need a historical 'baseline' against which to evaluate changes in the social role of religion and also a definition of religion against which to assess religious changes. I will first discuss these preliminary points before elaborating the secularization theory.

As far as changes in the social role of religion are concerned, the baseline may not be the degree of religiousness of the people, since this would involve a comparison of people in different situations: religious compulsion in the past compared to individual freedom at present (Le Bras 1963: 448–9; Delumeau 1975). The level of comparison must be the societal level: the age of religiously prescribed social order, which, in the West, was the age of Innocent III (thirteenth century), when the church controlled 'the formal process of political, juridical, commercial, and social intercourse' (Wilson 1976: 9–10). Consequently, the definition of secularization implies that religious authorities of institutionalized religion have lost control over the other subsystems. Thus, it implies a functional differentiation between religion and the so-called secular subsystems. Concerning the definition of religion, I have argued that for the purpose of studying the process of secularization, we cannot use a functional definition, since any meaning system performing so-called religious functions would be called a religion (Dobbelaere 2002: 49–52). We need, indeed, a substantive, exclusive, and real definition of religion as a baseline, which may read: a unified system of beliefs and practices relative to a supra-empirical, transcendent reality codified by a religious authority that unifies all those who adhere to it in a moral single community. Consequently, we arrive at the following definition of *secularization*: a process, by which overarching and transcendent religious systems of old are confined in modern functionally differentiated societies to a subsystem alongside other subsystems, losing in this process their overarching claims over these other subsystems. This definition refers, of course, to the societal or macro-level, and points out that the religious authorities of institutionalized religion have lost control over the other subsystems like polity, economy, family, education, law, etc.

The Theoretical Background of Secularization Theory

The sociological explanation of secularization starts with the process of functional differentiation: religion becomes a subsystem alongside other subsystems. In fact, secularization is only the consequence of the general process of functional differentiation in the religious subsystem. Indeed, modern societies are primarily *differentiated* along *functional* lines, and have developed different subsystems (e.g., economy, polity, science, and education). These subsystems are similar—since, so to speak, society has equal need of them all—and dissimilar—since they perform their own particular function (production and distribution of goods and services, taking binding decisions, production of valid knowledge, and teaching). Their functional autonomy depends, of course, upon their environment and the communication with other functional systems. To guarantee these functions and to communicate with their environment, organizations have been established (enterprises, political parties, research centres, schools and universities). In each subsystem and in its relations with the environment, communication is based on the medium of the subsystem (money, power, truth, information and know-how). Each organization also functions according to the values of the subsystem (competition and success, separation of powers, reliability and validity, truth) and its specific norms. Regarding religion, these organizations claim their autonomy and reject religiously prescribed rules, i.e. the *autonomization* of the subsystems. For example, the separation of church and state, the development of science as an autonomous secular perspective, the emancipation of education from ecclesiastical authority. Diagnosing the loss of religion's influence on the so-called secular subsystems, members of the religious organizations were the first to talk about secularization, or the emancipation of the secular.

The declining religious authority over the other subsystems—that is, the latter's autonomization—allowed the development of *functional rationality*. The economy lost its religious ethos (Weber 1920: 163–206). Goals and means were evaluated on a cost-efficiency basis. This typical economic attitude, implying observations, evaluations, calculation, and planning—which is based on a belief that the world is calculable, predictable, and controllable (Wilson 1976; 1985)—is not limited to the economic system. The political system was also rationalized, leaving little room for traditional and charismatic authority. Economic production and distribution developed large-scale economic organizations in which the scientific organization of industrial work (Taylorism), which led to the development of the assembly line (Fordism), were extensively applied; and modern states developed their rational administrations. Since these structures needed more and more people who had been trained in science and rational techniques, the educational curriculum changed. A scientific approach to the world and the teaching of technical knowledge increasingly replaced a religious-literary formation. The development of scientifically based techniques also had an impact on everyday life: domestic tasks became increasingly mechanized and computerized. The consequences of these developments were the *disenchantment* of the world and the *societalization* of the subsystems.

First, the disenchantment of the world. The world and the human body being increasingly considered to be calculable and man-made, the result of controlled planning (e.g., by *in vitro* fertilization and through plastic surgery), engendered not only new roles, but also new, basically rational and critical, attitudes and a new cognition. Theses are replaced by hypotheses, the Bible by encyclopaedias, revelation by knowledge. According to Acquaviva (1979), this new form of cognition has been objectified in a new language that changed the image of reality, thus eliminating 'pre-logical', including religious, concepts. The mass media, using this new language, have radicalized this development and made it a social phenomenon. Second, subsystems were also *societalized*, or became more *gesellschaftlich*. The organized world is 'based on impersonal role relationships, the co-ordination of skills, and essentially formal and contractual patterns of behaviour, in which personal virtue, as distinguished from role obligations, is of small consequence' (Wilson 1982: 155). In such systems, according to Wilson, control is no longer based on morals and religion, it has become impersonal, a matter of routine techniques and unknown officials—legal, technical, mechanized, computerized, and electronic—e.g., speed control by unmanned cameras and video control in department stores. Thus religion has lost one of its important latent functions: as long as control was interpersonal, it was founded on religiously based mores and substantive values; but now trust is replaced by credit cards, and sexual mores by condoms.

Societal and Organizational Secularization and Reactions

The process of *manifest* secularization,[1] or 'laicisation' in French, is typical of countries in which the Catholic Church had a near monopoly (Champion 1993: 592–3). The dispute was about clerical guardianship over, among others, the state, culture, education, poor relief, cemeteries, and the registry office. The secularists were vehemently anti-clerical, not necessarily anti-religious. The conflict involved two antagonistic collectivities. In 'la guerre des "deux France"', it was the republican secularists against the 'intégristes'; in Spain the anti-clerical against the clerical; in Belgium the radical liberals and socialists against the Catholics; in Italy the anti-clerical liberals against the church; and in Portugal the secularist forces against the church.

[1] The dichotomy *manifest–latent secularization* refers to Merton's distinction (1957: 51) between manifest and latent consequences of social actions. Manifest consequences are 'intended and recognized'; latent consequences are 'neither intended nor recognized'.

In France, the secularist movement started at the end of the eighteenth century with laws introducing gradually the separation of church and state and elaborating a civil law that did not mention religion: the state, the family, contracts, etc. began to be organized totally independent of the norms of the Catholic Church, and included transfer of the registrars' office from the parish to the municipality, which secularized the certificates of birth, marriage, and death; divesting the church of its medico-religious role; and establishing 'l'École publique laïque'. The state schools were compelled by law to be 'laïque' and 'neutral' towards the different creeds, which were considered to be 'personal, free and varying' (Champion 1993: 593–5). Durkheim was very instrumental in diffusing the 'esprit laïque'. Appointed to the Sorbonne in 1902 in the Science of Education, he lectured to future schoolteachers. Consequently, his ideas were disseminated throughout the state schools of France. According to Lukes (1977: 359–60):

> Durkheim believed that the relation of the science of sociology to education was that of theory and practice; and, in this respect, it [sociology] would become a rational substitute for traditional religion. Teachers should be imbued with the 'sociological point of view' and children should be made to think about the 'nature of society, the family, the State, the principal legal and moral obligations, the way in which these different social phenomena are formed'.

The French case very clearly shows that secularization is not a mechanical process, but is the result of human actions and conflicts (Baubérot 2005). The French republican secularists had gained political control over parliament, enabling them to 'laïcize' important subsystems, resulting on the meso-level in secularized organizations: e.g., in the juridical system, the courts; in the medical system, hospitals; and in the educational system, schools. This example also points to the importance of the educational system: the Durkheimian anti-religious world view shaped the educational personnel, who in turn socialized the younger generation in a secularized world view.

Another interesting case is Belgium, since the attempt manifestly to secularize the country had interesting consequences. After Belgium's independence in 1830, Liberals and Catholics worked together to organize the state. However, after an initial period of cooperation, the radical liberal wing, under the influence of anti-clerical lodges, resented the authoritarian Catholic hierarchy and the guardianship of the priests over culture and poor relief. In the second half of the nineteenth century, under the impact of changing parliamentarian majorities, the radical liberals were able to implement a secularist policy with the help of an emerging socialist party. By law, they reduced the impact of the church in charitable work, in poor relief, and in allocating study grants. The cemeteries were laicized, and ultimately the state schools. This policy was implemented through skilful nomination of governors of the provinces, commissioners of districts, and mayors and aldermen in cities. Here the press played an important role in forming clear-cut opinions and in mobilizing the population, and this often involved street disturbances. The church for its part reacted strongly in sermons, through the confessional, and in refusing the sacraments.

The conflict over schools stimulated Catholic leaders to set up private schools, and this accelerated the establishment of a Catholic pillar. In fact, Catholics reacted to functional differentiation with segmentary differentiation: they established a Catholic pillar by duplicating the services in those sectors that were no longer organized around a Catholic ideology, comprising schools (from kindergarten to university), hospitals, youth and adult organizations, cultural organizations, mass communications, trade unions, sick funds, banks, cooperatives, etc. To institutionalize the pillar, such a corporate channel had to be interlocked with a Christian political party that was able to protect, even to promote, the development of the pillar (Rokkan 1977). Such a development took place not only in Belgium, but also in Austria, Switzerland, and the Netherlands, where a Protestant pillar was also established (Righart 1986).

However, societal and organizational secularization is not always the result of manifest actions. They may also come about as a result of certain actions which *latently* produce a secularizing effect. A good example of this is the introduction of the clock. The development of science, industry, and expanding trade, from the twelfth century on, could no longer be regulated by the time sequence of the monasteries, which was based on bell ringing. One needed a more accurate measure of time which, at the turn of the fourteenth century, was ultimately achieved by the invention of the clock, which imposed a secular time order from the highest tower in the city so that it could be seen by everyone. Canonical time lost its significance, and time was also dissociated from God-given nature, which was provided by the sundial. Once the clock started regulating time, it became controlled by men and dissociated from the religious time cycle. In the nineteenth century, the railroads would impose a strict coordination of time, and later the radio.

The end of the 1950s saw the beginning of another defining change in Christian pillarization. The democratization of secondary education after the Second World War put a heavy financial burden on the Catholic school system. Its financial needs were met by state subsidies (1951), but the law instituted at the same time minimum qualifications for teachers. Priests and religious personnel were no longer sufficiently qualified, on the basis of their studies in theology and philosophy, to teach in certain fields, which resulted in the recruitment of university-trained lay teachers whose reference was no longer the church but their profession. The same was true in Catholic hospitals, where lay nurses replaced religious personnel, who as a result lost control over medical practices. In Catholic hospitals, the specific church ethic concerning abortion, sterilization, artificial insemination, and birth control was increasingly being called into question under the pressure of medical rationality. Medical doctors pointed to the complexity of these problems and the specificity of their field; they sought to solve them by using a broader ethical framework and their specialized knowledge. In other words, the democratization of education and the professionalization of the teaching and medical professions latently promoted the secularization of Catholic institutions. Other factors also played a role (Dobbelaere 1988: 83–90), but the point here is that democratization and professionalization were important factors in *latently* secularizing Catholic institutions (Dobbelaere 1979).

However, secularization is not only 'man-made', it is also reversible. This is very clear in Russia since the collapse of the Communist regime, when an ideological vacuum occurred. Agadjanian (2006: 179) underscores that 'religion was revived from Soviet oblivion, by both religious and secular camps, as a grand narrative believed to be full of strong symbolic content available for collective identity quests (first of all, in the search for a "national idea")'. The same was true in other Eastern Orthodox countries. Borowik (2006: 272) underscores that 'in all the Eastern European cases, religion has probably become more important because it offers a tool for reconstructing political and geopolitical identity in a post-Soviet era when the older 20th-century political identities rooted in the October Revolution are no longer viable'. This use of religion as an identity resource had even more dramatic consequences in former Yougoslavia, where an inter-ethnic war resulted in the creation of three separate states: Orthodox Serbia, Muslim Bosnia, and Catholic Croatia (Voyé 2006*a*: 141–2). However, this desecularization was not only linked to the identity problem; forms of de-differentiation between religion and so-called secular subsystems also occurred. In Romania, for example, the recognized religions are entitled to hold optional classes of religious education in public schools, and an amendment to the Romanian Constitution, approved in an October 2002 referendum, recognizes the right of the churches to set up their own institutions of lay education, allowing for the possibility—but not the obligation—of state financial support for denominational schools (Flora and Szilagyi 2005: 133–4).

Individual Secularization

In the sociological literature from the 1960s, studies on individual secularization began to emerge with works of Aquaviva (1979), Berger (1967), Luckmann (1967), Martin (1978), and Wilson (1969). Luhmann's (1977: 172) statement that the social structure is secularized, but not the individual, is controversial. While most sociologists would not challenge the first part of his statement, some would question the second part: e.g., Norris and Inglehart (2004). However, not Berger (1999), Davie (2002), Martin (2005), and Stark (1999), who would point to the religious fever in the USA—which is contested by other sociologists (e.g., Demerath, 2001)—and in the wider world and reject the universal pattern of individual secularization, while accepting that Europe is to a large extent secularized on the micro-level. For that reason they call Europe the exception, although Davie (2002) relativizes this by pointing out the persistence of religious beliefs and 'religious sensitivity', and by referring to what she calls 'vicarious religion': people drawing on religious capital at crucial times in their individual or collective lives—e.g., for the celebration of rites of passage.

Applying on the individual level the definition given above to societal secularization, I propose that individual secularization means that the *religious authorities* have lost control over the beliefs, practices, and moral principles of individual persons. If one accepts this definition, then individual secularization does not mean religious decline per se, or the decay of individual piety and practices, since central to the definition is the reference to the lost power of the religious authorities of institutionalized religions to control individual religiousness. Consequently, continuing individual religious sensitivity is not a falsification of secularization theory, but confirms it, as do use of the term 'spirituality' in opposition to the term 'religion' and studies using the terms 'religious bricolage', 'pick and choose religiosity', or *religion à la carte*. Indeed, spirituality implies that what is central is not the religious institution but 'me and my experiences'. Spirituality is non-dogmatic, it is flexible; it is a personal search: 'I am on the road'; and God is not the 'radical other' (Otto 1950), not the transcendent, but the immanent, the 'God within' (Voyé 2006*b*). And in a study of religious syncretism, Dobbelaere, Tomasi, and Voyé (2002) found, on the basis of samples taken for the European Religious and Moral Pluralism study (RAMP) in Western and mid-European countries, that no specific pattern of syncretistic beliefs and practices typical of countries, religions, or persons with certain social characteristics, such as men versus women, different generations, or rural versus urban regions, could be detected. The patterns were idiosyncratic: individuals made their own patchworks or bricolages, and their compositions consisted of very heterogeneous elements.

Another aspect of individual secularization is secularization of the mind, or *compartmentalization*. Societal secularization may indeed have had an impact on the way individuals themselves view the relationship between religion and the other spheres of life: the educational, the economical, the juridical, the familial, the medical, the political, and the scientific. The question here is: do people think that institutional religion should inform these so-called profane subsystems, or consider that the latter are autonomous, and that any interference of religion in these subsystems should be rendered void and disallowed? In a survey of 12,342 interviewees in eleven Western and Eastern European countries, the measurement of compartmentalization was based on people's views about the relationship between church and state, law and religion, religion and education, and on their acceptance of financial support for religious schools and religious bodies (Billiet *et al.* 2003: 141–2). The main result of the multi-regression analysis was that people with a high commitment to their church think less in terms of secularization and are much less opposed to the impact of religion on the other subsystems than persons with a low degree of commitment to a church, or none. The latter had the highest degree of compartmentalization, and were more prone to prevent secular institutions from being affected by religious influences. Differences between members of Roman Catholic and Protestant Churches were not found (Billiet *et al.* 2003: 152–3).

How to Explain the Individuation of Religion?

While compartmentalization can be understood as a reflection of societal secularization in the way people think, how can the individuation of religion be explained? We must return to the previously mentioned theory to understand this. The individuation of religion is not the result of an anti-religious attitude, but the outcome of the functional differentiation of society. Luhmann (1977: 232–42) stresses that a functionally differentiated society breaks communal and hierarchical bonds. As a result, 'ascription' becomes dysfunctional, and each person has, in principle, equal access to functions, goods, and services, though not at the same time or in the same fashion. Total inclusion is of course impossible, because people are not all equally competent, nor do they have the same capacity to fill positions; so a professional structure emerges, which, in principle, provides everybody with one and only one profession. In the past, social positions were 'ascribed' on the basis of the social class of the family one was born into, of gender, of age, etc. Today social positions are allocated on the basis of 'achievement'. Examples of this can be found in modern reactions against nepotism and also in the promotion of the emancipation of women. Consequently, total inclusion is possible only if, in all subsystems, there are, besides professional roles, what Luhmann calls *Komplementärrollen*, complementary roles: i.e. a *Publikum*—to wit the position of consumer (in the economy), voter (in the political subsystem), student (in the educational subsystem), etc.—which allows individuals to participate in all subsystems albeit only occasionally and for a limited amount of time. In this way a professional teacher can participate in all other subsystems in complementary roles: as consumer in the economy, as voter in the polity, as plaintiff in the juridical system, as believer in religious bodies, etc.

But between complementary roles functional differentiation needs also to be maintained, otherwise the differentiation between the subsystems would disappear. This means that people cannot be 'compelled' to marry according to their economic position, to have an education depending on the social class of their parents, and to vote in accordance with their church membership. It explains why in modern countries church authorities cannot compel their members to vote for a particular party under the threat that if they do not they will commit a grave sin; in Belgium this happened for the last time in the 1950s. However, is a differentiation of complementary roles possible, and can it be controlled? Luhmann suggests not, and therefore the *privatization of decisions* becomes a functional equivalent. In other words, privatization emerges *structurally* as a consequence of functional differentiation and inclusion, since a strict separation between complementary roles cannot be controlled or enforced. Through the privatization of decisions, a statistical neutralization of role combinations in the complementary roles is aimed at. Such combinations may occur only on the individual level, otherwise they would destroy functional differentiation, and they prevail only for personal motives, and may not be imposed socially. The individual choices in the religious field—decline of involvement, bricolages, idiosyncratic patterns of syncretism and spirituality—are a consequence of the structural changes in modern societies: functional differentiation and inclusion. Indeed, belief becomes a private decision: previously unbelief was a private matter; now belief is. And the insight into such social structural changes, in particular inclusion, also allows us to understand some of the criticisms of some churches: is it possible, given these changes, to limit admission to the clergy on the basis of celibacy, sexual preferences, or gender, and is it acceptable that some churches do not allow their clergy to marry?

The Religious Subsystem: Organizational or Institutional Secularization

Secularization is also present on the organizational level of religions. It represents an adjustment of religion to new conditions evident in, for example, modern trends in ecumenism (Wilson 1969: 168–205). However, organizational secularization, what Luckmann (1967: 36) called 'internal secularization', is not new. The Protestant Reformation can be understood as a powerful re-emergence of precisely those secularizing forces present in the Old Testament that had been 'contained' by Catholicism. 'At the risk of some simplification, it can be said that Protestantism divested itself as much as possible from the three most ancient and most powerful concomitants of the sacred—mystery, miracle, and magic' (Berger 1967: 111). As was previously mentioned, Weber called it the 'disenchantment of the world' (1958: 105). This is an interesting trend, as it clearly shows that reversals of a religious trend are possible. And we see this again in the New Religious Movements (NRMs) that emerged in the latter part of the twentieth century.

Some NRMs, such as the Unification Church, the Family, and ISKCON, seek to re-sacralize the world and its institutions by bringing God back into the different groups operating in different subsystems like the family, the economy, and even the polity. Wallis (1984) has called these 'world-rejecting new religions'. However, the vast majority are of another type, they are 'world-affirming'. They offer their members esoteric means for attaining immediate and automatic recovery, success, heightened spirituality, and a clear mind. Mahikari provides an 'omitama', or amulet; Transcendental Meditation (TM) a personal mantra for meditation; Scientology auditing with an E-meter; Human Potential movements offer therapies, encounter groups, or alternative health and spiritual centres; and Elan Vital offers the knowledge revealed by Maharaji or one of his appointed instructors.

Luckmann (1990) has rightly argued that in many NRMs the level of transcendence has been lowered; they have become 'this-worldly', or mundane. The historical religions, by contrast, are seen as examples of 'great transcendences', referring to something other than everyday reality, notwithstanding the fact that they have been, and continue to be, involved although to a lesser extent in mundane or 'this-worldly' affairs, attested by the pillar structures that they established. However, their reference was always transcendental: e.g. in incantations for healing, for success in examinations or work, or for 'une âme soeur'. Most world-affirming NRMs appear to reach only the level of 'intermediate transcendences'. They bridge time and space, promote intersubjective communication, but remain at the immanent level of everyday reality. Consequently, some, like TM, claim to be spiritual rather than religious movements. What we register in many NRMs is a change in reference: the ultimate has become 'this-worldly'.

The registered change should be conceived as a form of organizational secularization: in these so-called NRMs, the sacred is no longer a 'great transcendence'. It may be objected that this evaluation is based on the substantive definition of religion which I have defended above. However, even when we take a functional definition of religion, we may come to the same conclusion about NRMs. Luhmann (1977: 46) stated that 'the problem of simultaneity of indefiniteness and certainty' is the typical function of religion. Indeed, most of these world-affirming new religions are not concerned with the problems of *simultaneity* of transcendence and immanence, since they focus only on the immanent, on everyday life, on the secular. They are adapted to the secular world, and represent, I would argue, a form of organizational secularization.

However, it is not only reformers of religion who secularize the religious outlook, but also non-professional lay people. An example of latent secularization is given in a study by Voyé of Christmas decorations in a Walloon village in Belgium (Voyé 1998: 299–303). Two decades ago, Isambert (1982: 196) had already underscored the increasing slide from 'the scriptural and liturgical basis of the Nativity, which is altogether oriented towards the Incarnation and Redemption, which it precedes' toward 'the Christ child'. Indeed, the Christ child is placed at the centre of the familial Christmas celebrations and also in the decorations displayed in the cities. In the Walloon village under study, the decorations evoke a further sliding away: signboards, many meters square, erected on the lawns in front of the houses and illuminated in the evening, represented Walt Disney cartoon characters. When Voyé asked why they did not set up a manger scene, the couple who initiated the display and who tried to co-ordinate it, answered: 'some neighbours are thinking about it ... but, we told them "If we put a manger scene, we've got to find among the Disney characters a couple of animals who have a little one. Because we, well we want to stick with the Walt Disney characters"' (Voyé 1998: 300). Here Christmas is not only child-oriented, but, as Voyé rightfully underscores, 'with the Disney characters, we are no longer in History, but in the fairytale and the domain of the marvellous. [Fairytales] peopled with fictive beings' (Voyé 1998: 302). These decorations convey implicitly the idea that Christmas is a marvellous fairy tale far removed from the original Incarnation–Redemption idea that the religious message of Christmas carries. By putting up these decorations, people latently secularize the Christian message.

The Recent Second Wave of Manifest Secularization ('laïcization')

The pluralization of the religious situation in the West is a consequence of the secularization of the population. In all these countries we find the presence of different Christian denominations, be it that the membership in these denominations may differ greatly; but more important is the decline of involvement of the members in their church. Since the late twentieth century, Muslims have become the second largest religious community, due mainly to economic immigration. As a result, there is now a growing number of second-generation Muslims who are national citizens. Sectarian movements and countless NRMs, as we have seen, are also present, although still only a small percentage of the total population. More important, however, is the rapidly growing number of unchurched, especially among the younger generations. Politicians refer to this pluralism to stress the pluralization of the religious and moral outlook of the population, and use this as a motive to change laws that have a typical Christian background. New civil laws were passed in parliaments, e.g. to 'liberalize' divorce (Belgium, France, the Netherlands, and Spain), abortion (Belgium, France, the Netherlands, Portugal, and Spain), and euthanasia (Belgium and the Netherlands), and to institutionalize homosexual marriages (Belgium, the Netherlands, and Spain). These laws concern very sensitive matters for Christian churches, especially the Catholic Church, since they go against fundamental traditional principles of their doctrines and ethics: marriage being an unbreakable union between a man and a woman, and life and death being entirely dependent upon God, and God alone.

Is Secularization a Western Phenomenon?

It is sometimes suggested that secularization is a typically Western phenomenon. A study by Pace (1998) demonstrated that secularization on the societal level is also occurring in the Muslim world. He distinguished two processes: 'secularization from above' and 'secularization from below', and his study allows us to see the interrelationship between the two: each is supportive of the other.

In the first process, the unyoking of politics from religious factors in parts of the Muslim world started at the end of the nineteenth century, and gained momentum from the 1950s on, after the end of colonial domination. There occurred either a complete and traumatic break with the religious tradition—as caused by Kemal Atatürk and the Ba'th party in Syria and Iraq, which provoked the development of strong fundamentalist movements—or a transfer of functions of religion to the field of politics—as in North Africa and the Indian subcontinent. 'A variety of political solutions were adopted.... But they all boil down to the same basic problem of modernity: how to build a modern state with an economy capable of competing in the international market, an independent administrative apparatus (public offices, schools, social services, hospitals etc.), a power basis for the leaderships founded on what is traditionally regarded as "political"' (Pace 1998: 168–9).

In the second process—secularization from below—there is a change in attitudes towards the Islamic tradition. This process is being promoted by four conflicts, which have produced a secularization of customs among the younger generation (Pace 1998: 170–3): first, conflict between country and city, the latter having created new classes, who have a different attitude to religious traditions and who are more willing to accept new choices and values; second, conflict over the patriarchal model contested by sons and daughters, especially in North Africa; third, the access of women to professions, which has weakened 'ancient bonds which limited women's social activity to the confined space of the home or the *hamman* (the public baths)' (Pace 1998: 171); and finally, that arising from emigration, which has affected the Islamic models of family, reproduction, education, society, and religion of both emigrants and those who stayed behind, who compare themselves with their emigrated children, relatives, or friends (Pace 1998: 171–2).

In response to the secularization tendencies in the Muslim world, a wave of Islamic radicalism manifests itself in Europe and South and South-east Asia involving such groups as Tablighi, which is rather pietistic, and Jama'at-I Islami and Hizb ut Tahrir, which also have political aims (Clarke 1998: 9, 13–15). These movements are opposed to the secularization trend among Muslim youth, who may still identify themselves with the Islamic tradition as a source of values giving sense to their lives but, without practising on a regular basis (Cesari 2000: 92–4).

Epilogue

The secularization theory based on functional differentiation explains a trend, but allows for variations, since historical trends cannot fully be explained by one causal factor, even when it is an important one. Martin (1978: 3) has rightfully underscored that the particular cultural complex within which the processes linked to functional differentiation operate also plays an important role. However, to dismiss secularization theory on the basis of counter-examples without taking into account the different levels of functional differentiation of the countries one compares is methodologically unsound.

Not all researchers study individual secularization in the framework of an integrated theory of functional differentiation. A very important study by Norris and Inglehart (2004: 4–5) is a good example: they link the erosion of religious practices, values, and beliefs to the extent to which people have a heightened sense of existential security—i.e., 'the feeling that survival is secure enough that it can be taken for granted'. An important research question emerges here: is the level of existential security linked to the degree of functional differentiation, since more developed countries may have higher degrees of functional differentiation and functional rationalization? It seems, then, that a crucial test to explain individual secularization would be a comparative study of countries with different levels of functional differentiation (Dobbelaere 2007).

Finally, do we expect manifest secularization ('laïcization') to continue? The study of compartmentalization by Billiet *et al.* (2003) may give us an answer. According to this study involving eleven European countries (see above), the level of compartmentalization, secularization of the mind, is related to the commitment of individuals to their churches. Compartmentalization is lowest in the category of nuclear members and increases with declining involvement; the unchurched have the highest degree of compartmentalization. In their chapter comparing individual secularization worldwide, Norris and Inglehart (2004: 72) show convincingly that weekly attendance at religious services, daily prayer, and considering religion 'very important' are highest in agrarian societies and lowest in post-industrial societies, with industrial societies in between. Furthermore, in the European Union, religious participation declined constantly from 1970 to 1998 (Norris and Inglehart 2004: 72). On the basis of these two studies, we may expect that manifest secularization will increase in the European Union in the years to come. There are clear indications of this. In Spain there is an intensive debate on legalizing abortion under certain circumstances, where in certain regions so-called passive euthanasia is already regulated. And in France, the problem of euthanasia is a topic of intense public debate. These are two of a number of fundamental and sacrosanct moral principles once widely regarded as core features of a religious society that are now being challenged even in what were until recently some of the most Catholic countries of Europe. In 'Catholic' Brazil, the legalization of abortion is also keenly debated.

References

Acquaviva, Sabino (1979). *The Decline of the Sacred in Industrial Society.* Oxford: Basil Blackwell.

Agadjanian, Alexander (2006). 'The Search for Privacy and the Return of Grand Narrative: Religion in a Post-Communist Society'. *Social Compass*, 53: 169–84.

Baubérot, Jean (2005). *Histoire de la laïcité en France*, 3rd enlarged edn. Paris: Presses Universitaires de France, Collection *Que sais-je.*

Berger, Peter (1967). *The Sacred Canopy: Elements of a Sociological Theory of Religion.* Garden City, NY: Doubleday and Company.

—— (1999). 'The Desecularization of the World: A Global Overview'. In *idem* (ed.), *The Desecularization of the World: Resurgent Religion and World Politics.* Grand Rapids, Mich.: Eerdmans, 1–18.

Billiet, Jaak, Dobbelaere, Karel, Riis, Ole, Vilaça, Helena, Voyé, Liliane, and Welkenhuysen-Gybels, Jerry (2003). 'Church Commitment and Some Consequences in Western and Central Europe'. In R. Piedmont and D. Moberg (eds.), *Research in the Social Scientific Study of Religion*, xiv. Leiden and Boston: Brill, 129–59.

Borowik, Irena (2006). 'Orthodoxy Confronting the Collapse of Communism in Post-Soviet Countries'. *Social Compass*, 53: 267–78.

Cesari, Jocelyne (2000). 'La querelle des anciens et des modernes: le discours islamique en France'. In F. Dassetto (ed.), *Paroles d'Islam: Individus, sociétés et discours dans l'Islam européen contemporain.* Paris: Maisonneuve et Larose, 87–100.

Champion, Françoise (1993). 'Les rapports Église-État dans les pays européens de tradition protestante et de tradition catholique: essai d'analyse'. *Social Compass*, 40: 589–609.

Clarke, Peter (1998). 'Islam in Western Europe: Present State and Future Trends'. In *idem* (ed.), *New Trends and Developments in the World of Islam.* London: Luzac Oriental, 3–41.

Davie, Grace (2002). *Europe: The Exceptional Case: Parameters of Faith in the Modern World.* London: Darton, Longman and Todd Ltd.

Delumeau, Jean (1975). 'Déchristianisation ou nouveau modèle de christianisme?' *Archives de sciences sociales des religions*, 20: 3–20.

Demerath, Jay III (2001). *Crossing the Gods: World Religions and Worldly Politics.* Brunswick, NJ, and London: Rutgers University Press.

Dobbelaere, Karel (1979). 'Professionalization and Secularization in the Belgian Catholic Pillar'. *Japanese Journal of Religious Studies,* 6: 39–64.

—— (1988). 'Secularization, Pillarization, Religious Involvement, and Religious Change in the Low Countries'. In Thomas Gannon (ed.), *World Catholicism in Transition.* New York and London: Macmillan, 80–115.

—— (2002). *Secularization: An Analysis at Three Levels.* Brussels: P. I. E. Peter Lang.

—— (2007). 'Testing Secularization Theory in Comparative Perspective'. *Nordic Journal of Religion and Society,* 20/2: 137–47.

—— Tomasi, Luigi, and Voyé, Liliane (2002). 'Religious Syncretism'. In R. Piedmont and D. Moberg (eds.), *Research in the Social Scientific Study of Religion,* xiii. Leiden and Boston: Brill, 221–43.

Flora, Gavril, and Szilagyi, Georgina (2005). 'Church, Identity, Politics: Ecclesistical Functions and Expectations toward Churches in Post-1989 Romania'. In Victor Roudemetof, Alexander Agadjanian, and Jerry Pankhurst (eds.), *Eastern Orthodoxy in a Global Age.* Walnut Creek, Calif.: AltaMira Press, 109–43.

Isambert, François-André (1982). *Le Sens du sacré: Fête et religion populaire.* Paris: Alcan.

Le Bras, Gabriel (1963). 'Déchristianisation: mot fallacieux'. *Social Compass,* 10: 445–52.

Luckmann, Thomas (1967). *The Invisible Religion: The Problem of Religion in Modern Society.* New York: Macmillan.

—— (1990). 'Shrinking Transcendence, Expanding Religion'. *Sociological Analysis,* 51: 127–38.

Luhmann, Niklas (1977). *Funktion der Religion.* Frankfurt: Suhrkamp.

Lukes, Steven (1977). *Emile Durkheim, His Life and Work: A Historical and Critical Study.* Harmondsworth: Penguin Book.

Martin, David (1978). *A General Theory of Secularization.* Oxford: Blackwell.

—— (2005). *On Secularization: Towards a Revised General Theory.* Aldershot and Burlington, Vt.: Ashgate.

Merton, Robert K. (1957). *Social Theory and Social Structure,* rev. enlarged edn. Glencoe, Ill.: Free Press.

Norris, Pippa, and Inglehart, Ronald (2004). *Sacred and Secular: Religion and Politics Worldwide.* Cambridge: Cambridge University Press.

Otto, Rudolf (1950). *The Idea of the Holy,* trans. J. Harvey, 2nd edn. London: Oxford University Press.

Pace, Enzo (1998). 'The Helmet and the Turban: Secularization in Islam'. In R. Laermans, B. Wilson, and J. Billiet (eds.), *Secularization and Social Integration.* Leuven: Leuven University Press, 165–75.

Righart, Hans (1986). *De katholieke zuil in Europa: Een vergelijkend onderzoek naar het ontstaan van verzuiling onder katholieken in Oostenrijk, Zwitserland, België en Nederland.* Meppel: Boom.

Rokkan, Stein (1977). 'Towards a Generalised Concept of "Verzuiling": A Preliminary Note'. *Political Studies,* 25: 563–70.

Shiner, Larry (1967). 'The Concept of Secularization in Empirical Research'. *Journal for the Scientific Study of Religion,* 6: 207–20.

Stark, Rodney (1999). 'Secularization, R.I.P.' *Sociology of Religion,* 60: 249–73.

Swatos, William Jr., and Christiano, Kevin (1999). 'Secularization Theory: The Course of a Concept'. *Sociology of Religion,* 60: 209–28.

Voyé, Liliane (1998). 'Death and Christmas Revisited. Beyond Secularization: A Search for Meaning'. In R. Laermans, B. Wilson, and J. Billiet (eds.), *Secularization and Social Integration*. Leuven: Leuven University Press, 287–305.

—— (2006*a*). 'Religion et politique en Europe'. *Sociologie et sociétés*, 38: 139–63.

—— (2006*b*). 'Vers une definition de la spiritualité'. *Working Paper LV1*, ANSO, Université Catholique de Louvain.

Wallis, Roy (1984). *The Elementary Forms of the New Religious Life*. London: Routledge & Kegan Paul.

—— and Bruce, Steve (1992). 'Secularization: The Orthodox Model'. In S. Bruce (ed.), *Religion and Modernization: Sociologists and Historians Debate the Secularization Thesis*. Oxford: Clarendon Press, 8–30.

Weber, Max (1920). *Gesammelte Aufsätze zur Religionssoziologie*. Tübingen: Mohr.

—— (1958). *The Protestant Ethic and the Spirit of Capitalism*. trans. T. Parsons. New York: Charles Scribner's Sons.

Wilson, Bryan (1969). *Religion in Secular Society*. Harmondsworth, Baltimore, and Ringwood: Pelican Books.

—— (1976). *Contemporary Transformations of Religion*. Oxford: Oxford University Press.

—— (1982). *Religion in Sociological Perspective*. Oxford: Oxford University Press.

—— (1985). 'Secularization: The Inherited Model'. In P. Hammond (ed.), *The Sacred in a Secular Age*. Berkeley: University of California Press, 9–20.

—— (1998). 'The Secularization Thesis: Criticisms and Rebuttals'. In R. Laermans, B. Wilson, and J. Billiet (eds.), *Secularization and Social Integration*. Leuven: Leuven University Press, 45–65.

Suggested Reading

The following are recommended: Berger (1967); Dobbelaere (2002); Luckmann (1967); Luhmann (1977); Martin (1978); Norris and Inglehart (2004); and Wilson (1982).

CHAPTER 34

GENERATIONS AND RELIGION

WADE CLARK ROOF

In an unpublished monograph written in 1982 calling upon historians to give more attention to the concept of generations, Anthony Esler quotes Daniel J. Callahan as follows:

> All of us in the process of growing up, sooner or later come to notice that we are part of a generation. The first hints of this often steal upon us by surprise. We may observe in a dim fashion that we do not seem to respond to things the way our elders do, even though we may think we share the same general values and talk the same language. Or we may find that those writers and ideas that enthralled our parents and teachers leave us unmoved . . . at the same time we may gradually come to realize that we are not alone. What seemed a very private response turns out to be a common one. (1965: 3)

Social scientists today have a better sense of the complexities attending the notion of generations, yet Callahan's grasp of the fundamental psychological dynamics is very much on target. Key to understanding and appreciating the concept is recognizing that people see the world and respond to it quite differently than do others who are older, yet also realize that their distinctive views and responses are not just personal and idiosyncratic but are widely shared with others of roughly similar age and social experience. Thus both vertical and horizontal social dimensions come into play in the shaping of generational consciousness—as one gestalt of life experiences take form in relation to another. So conceived, the notion of a generation captures a complex and creative process of social-cultural formation. From the production-of-culture perspective, quite fashionable in sociological circles today, it might be said that generational identities, world views, and values emerge as dynamic constructions, encounters really between a cultural past and a redefined present.

Esler's plea for greater attention to generations in scholarly analysis and commentary met with mixed success. Journalists, novelists, politicians, and public commentators alike make impressionistic use of the notion, and have done so to a considerable extent since the 1960s. "During the generationally turbulent 1960s", he writes, "every newspaper columnist and television commentator, indeed practically every citizen, became his own instant authority on the 'generation gap' " (1982: 2). That something had changed was imprinted on the minds of Europeans in the aftermath of the Second World War, when so many young soldiers were lost and the world awakened to new social and political realities—the generation gap was thus both a demographic and a historical marker. In the United States, the impact of the large post-war Boom Generation reverberated throughout society from the time of their birth, and especially so in the late 1960s and early 1970s when they were identified with a visible, at times quite radical counterculture distinguishing them from older age cohorts; even today, as its members begin to retire, there is much conversation about how in this latest phase of their lives they will redefine the meaning of senior citizenship. Much in the news over the past fifteen years, too, are the Generation Xers, the lesser-known cohort following the Boomers, and more recently those belonging to the Millennial Generation coming of age in the first decade of the twenty-first century. For a variety of reasons, then, much attention has been paid to generations as they relate to social, cultural, and political change over the past seventy-five years; aside from wars having served as major markers, factors such as the expanded role of mass media and the huge influence of television, a greatly expanded global economy, and an increased consumption culture have all contributed to a greater consciousness of distinctive generational cohorts.

Yet, in the scholarly world, the concept of a generation has not received the attention that might have been expected. "There are few terms that have been as frequently invoked—but as little studied—over the last twenty years as the term 'generations' ", wrote Stephen R. Graubard in an issue of *Daedalus* devoted to exploring the concept in 1979 (p. vii). Since then there have been some advances, but the idea of generations remains illusive, and is typically given only passing reference in the scholarly literature; when the concept appears, it is usually for descriptive as opposed to theoretical purposes. Within the social sciences the concept has not achieved the standing comparable, say, with social class, status group, race, or ethnicity. The problem appears to be twofold: first, its lack of conceptual clarity, and second, the difficulties of empirical measurement. Lacking clarity, the concept also has little predictive and/or explanatory power as social scientists see it; yet they keep the term within their vocabulary, as is evident in the discussions of generational patterns relating to a wide range of topics such as cultural styles, media reception, politics and ideology, public opinion, and religion and spirituality scattered throughout the research literature. The concept is invoked, but is treated more as a "quasi-construct" than as a significant notion within the sociological vocabulary. Consequently, it has not received the refinement it deserves, and hence remains somewhat in conceptual limbo.

The second issue is challenging in another way. Can the concept be applied across time and across societies in a comparable manner? This raises questions about how to delimit chronologically a particular generation and how to describe the influences shaping generational outlook and impact upon society. Making the construct even more difficult to apply comparatively, there is also the larger question about modernity and how are we to understand the evolution of "modern society". Can we assume comparable generational dynamics across modern societies? Or does the recent, highly applauded notion of "multiple modernities" preclude such a possibility? Despite unanswered questions like these, there is consensus that generational boundaries have taken on greater significance in modern society: as meritocracy and traditional inheritance of condition and of status have lost force over individual lives, there has arisen greater fluidity in social identities. Peer groups and mass culture have greater impact on individuals and in shaping generational boundaries than in the past. Nor can we overlook the sheer pace of technological innovation in the modern context and the rise of a consumption-oriented culture with its bountiful and seemingly unending supply of social and cultural markers. Within an older, more static society the succession of age groups is mainly, as Annie Kriegel (1979: 25) says, "the replacing of same by same"; but under conditions of greater social and cultural change, that succession becomes "the replacing of same by other, by displacement or by innovative additions". She goes on to observe quite correctly that in this later situation "the distance between age groups then is no longer simply a passage of time... but a sum of changes which impose singularity on a generation by its mores and behavior. A generation is now defined as the generation of electricity, of television, or of blue jeans."

Typically in the social sciences there is scant attention paid to the history of the generational concept. In the interest of broadening dialogue among historians, sociologists, political scientists, and others, the discussion that follows is divided into two parts, one focusing on the evolution of the concept itself and its measurement, and a second looking at generational trends in religious patterns.

Concept and Measurement

Generational thinking dates back to biblical times, when the Psalmists often used the phrase "from generation to generation" and the Preacher in the book of

Ecclesiastes wrote that "a generation goes, and a generation comes, but the earth remains for ever". The notion of a social generation appears in early Western thought—in Homer, in Herodotus, in Plato and Aristotle. Generation as a concept arose in Western thought from its Greek root, *genos*, which is perhaps best defined as "to come into existence". More than simply the marking of biological birth, or even a succession of births, the root implies an ever-shifting threshold in time—of moments when something new in the society or cosmos comes into being. In this sense, *genos* carries a wide scope of meanings, of "life signs" signaling the newness of life in a particular social context. "Like the verb *to be*", writes Laura L. Nash (1979: 2), "generation requires an adjective of context, a predicate of relativity, before it takes on meaning. Used sometimes with complacency ('*my* generation'), sometimes with belligerence ('*your* generation'), and even with affection, as when Telemachus vows his friendship to Peisistratus by reason of their similar ages, generation marks allegiance, time of life, span of years, sameness with one group and otherness from the rest." Commenting on the portrayal of a generation in the *Iliad*, she notes that its meaning extended beyond family as the object of allegiance and basis of social identity to encompass a sense of heroic accomplishment among those of a similar age: a generation was defined largely in terms of its valor and strength as demonstrated on the battlefield. Thus, as far back as these early Greek origins, defining a generation has relied heavily upon extending human qualities to age within particular social settings for its precise meaning.

The distinction between *family generations* and *cohort generations* is crucial to the development of the concept. The cohort generation has no direct linkage to genealogy or lineage, but refers instead to all those individuals brought into being in a given historical period. Greater clarity about this latter notion emerged in the 1800s when social philosophers such as Auguste Comte and John Stuart Mill gave attention to the role of age-based groups in bringing about social change. Younger generations breaking with earlier ones, partly out of rebellion, but also out of the embrace of new values and visions, bring about changes in the life of society; or this latter may be said to have occurred when, as Mill says, a "new set of human beings have been educated, have grown up from childhood, and taken possession of society" (see Strauss and Howe 1991: 438). Similarly, there is the theme which Wilhelm Dilthey articulated so well: that is, the values, beliefs, and attitudes carried by a generation tend both to unite them and to stay with them from early adulthood through old age. In his reflections Dilthey offered an insightful definition of a generation: "a relationship of contemporaneity between individuals, that is, between those who had a common childhood, a common adolescence, and whose years of greatest manly vigor partially overlap. We can say that such men belong to the same generation" (see Strauss and Howe 1991: 438). Again, what is emphasized is the vigor and valor associated with manliness in an age when such qualities were held up as uniting a generation and then remained with them in memory.

Two figures in the twentieth century were especially influential in shaping modern generational theory: José Ortega y Gasset, the Spanish philosopher, and Karl Mannheim, the German sociologist. "A generation", wrote Ortega, "is an integrated manner of existence, or if you prefer, a fashion in living, which fixes itself indelibly on the individual" (quoted in Marias 1970: 19). His emphasis was upon shifting "mentalities" within society and on the power of the bonds linking members sharing a particular world view. In "cumulative" periods these shifts are limited, and a new generation feels itself to a considerable degree as one with the preceding generation; then there are "polemic" periods when, as Julian Marias, one of Ortega's followers, puts it, there are "generations of combat, which sweep away the old and begin new things" (1970: 96). This distinction is a precursor to more recent thinking about the pace of generational change and the fact that some generations leave a far greater impact on society than do others. Whatever the degree of distinctiveness, however, Ortega looks upon each succeeding generation as having the effect of forming a new society. His emphasis is upon neither a handful of influential leaders nor simply the great mass of their followers; rather, he conceives of society as a recurrent social formation resulting from a "dynamic compromise between the mass and individual", and this societal dynamic as the major source "responsible for the movements of historical evolution" (1970: 95). Put simply, he sees energy arising out of the interaction of a new cohort of leaders and the masses, and this new energy as giving direction to changes encompassing the whole of society. Ortega's notions are elusive, and from the standpoint of the contemporary social scientist difficult to pin down empirically; yet his grasp of the ongoing re-creation of culture over time and of continuing shifts in societal centers brought on by ever-emerging generational cohorts is insightful. Something of this same evolutionary dynamic is described by contemporary religious historian Amanda Porterfield (2000: 12) when she writes that "legacies established by earlier generations persist in the lives and ideas of new generations, underpinning and framing everything new, while at the same time, new generations of interpreters constantly create fresh images of the past". Legacies persist, but only to be reclaimed in the newness of the present.

It was the German social philosopher Karl Mannheim who best articulated a sociological conception of a generation and who, more than any other scholar, is cited over the past half-century for advancing a distinct generational theory. Writing early in the twentieth century during a time of much social disruption in Europe, he coined the term *Generationslagerung* ("generation setting"), drawing attention to the social and historical contexts of generations. He spoke of the "problem of generations" (1952), noting not only how they mark sharp breaks in the normative order but also the fact that generations are carriers of distinctive cultures and world views. To cite him more specifically, he spoke of a "social unit": that is, of an age-based constituency that shares "a common location in the historical dimension of the social process" (p. 289) and has a "specific range of potential experience, predisposing it for a certain characteristic mode of thought and experience, and a characteristic type of historically relevant action" (p. 304). He pushed to clarify more carefully the connection between a generation's definition of social reality and its mode of action. Sociologist Robert Wuthnow (1978: 125) offers a systematic description of Mannheim's "social unit", observing that besides (1) a common social historical location, (2) a distinctive mode of thought and experience, and a relevant social action, generations also have (3) a "common destiny", or particular interest, just as that of a socio-economic class, plus (4) an "identity of responses, a certain affinity in the way in which all move with and are formed by their common experiences". He goes on to emphasize what is crucial to understanding the role of generations within society: that being once bound together as a social unit, generations become "vehicle(s) for mobilizing and transmitting change", and as he says, reflecting upon Mannheim's insights, as a "harbinger of discontinuity in the social process".

Several observations regarding Mannheim's definition are in order. One is that an age cohort is transformed into a generation through social interaction among its members and cultivation of a distinctive identity. Generations are "age groups imbedded in a historical-social process", Mannheim wrote (1952: 292), underscoring the importance of the social dynamics peculiar to a particular cohort. A second is that historical events and social developments will not affect all members of a generation in the same way; there are sub-constituencies in every generation which hold contrasting and conflicting views. Social interaction among middle-class college students, for example, was very important in shaping the views of the Baby Boomers (born from 1946 to 1964), and helped to shape the rebellious culture of the late 1960s that was much less embraced—and indeed, was often rejected—by working-class and minority students of the same age. Hence generational identities are contextually variable and ambivalent. Third, in contemporary society generational identities may be assigned from the outside, particularly by the media, often as much if not more than they are self-ascribed by their own members (Williams and Nussbaum 2001: 144–6). Social interaction patterns shaping identities are thus themselves quite complex, involving responses to, and negotiating with, media-based advertising images and messages. This last is obviously a critical component in defining and sustaining generational identities in contemporary, highly developed societies.

Moving beyond conceptual clarification, there are the related challenges involved in applying the category in empirical research. Ortega, for example, argued that generations are born fifteen years apart. But this was hardly an assertion born out of careful systematic research. The real issue is how to delimit chronologically a particular generation in its social and historical context. Typically, historians emphasize the presence of strong leaders, and the span of time they take in shaping a generational ethos and outlook; sociologists, on the other hand, are much more inclined to analyze large bodies of social data in search of empirical patterns, looking for significant shifts in values and lifestyles within the populace as a whole. Some interpreters have gone so far as to suggest that there are cyclical patterns of generational outlook and style—that is, recurring themes that characterize them. William Strauss and Neil Howe (1991), for example, in an ambitious undertaking, read all of American history and indeed into the future as a series of generational cycles, of spiritual awakenings followed by secular crises; they even go so far as to specify for the seventeen completed generations they identify a range in length of exactly 17 to 33 years, or an average of 23.4 years each. But religious and cultural cycles are not so easily identified; nor is it at all clear that the patterns of dominant (idealist) life cycles they identify are necessarily followed by recessive (reactive) life cycles. While some aspects of generational cycles are empirically observable, Strauss and Howe's paradigm is overextended, more imposed on history than arrived at inductively in any rigorous manner.

For empirical researchers, defining the boundaries between generations is hugely problematic, and is probably why many social researchers and commentators make so little use of the concept. First of all, there is no uniform basis even for labeling generations. Within the United States it is common to speak of a "Depression Generation" defined by economic circumstance, a "GI Generation" marked by war; a "Boom Generation" based upon a large bulge in fertility rates, an "X Generation" for lack of a more clearly defining cultural characteristic, and a "Millennial Generation", so named because of the convergence of a cohort's coming into adulthood in the first decade of the new millennium. The Boom Generation is perhaps the easiest to identify empirically, since researchers agree that the birth rate spiraled upward in the years immediately following the second World War; but there is less consensus as to the cutting point in birth years when that generation ended and the so-called X Generation began. But such is the case in defining historical cultural periods generally, and with respect to generations researchers must take a somewhat pragmatic approach to decisions about empirical measurement. The value and utility of the concept in social analysis rest less upon the ease with which boundaries separating generations can be clearly distinguished than on the assumption that a generational identity, even if difficult to define, is discernible in a variety of ways and is important in grasping a cohort's values, outlook, and behavior. Research provides ample evidence for the validity of this assumption: when asked about important social influences in their lives, people generally recall as significant memories events and circumstances during their teens and early twenties. More than just personal and family experiences, they remember national and international events; such memories stemming from the formative years are lasting, involving both cognitive perceptions and emotional, or feeling responses (Schuman and Scott 1989; Roof 1993: 3–5).

Sorting out the influence of generation from that of life cycle and time period is difficult—indeed, impossible in an absolute sense. *Life-cycle* effects refer to those changes associated with stages in the aging pattern; *period* effects refer to influences of a particular moment in time that impact upon all individuals within a society, no matter their age or generation. Thus *generation* effects differ in that they refer specifically to the impact of historical, socializing experiences upon a particular age-based group that become a part of its identity as it ages. Disentangling the three set of influences can only be approximate, yet the distinctions among them should be kept in mind; researchers must be sensitive to these overlapping realities. Especially important, and often overlooked as factors influencing generational identities, are the emotions associated with widely shared, often traumatic experiences such as war, economic collapse, political assassinations, national and technological disasters, death of celebrities: sadness, fear, worries about safety, alienation, awareness of vulnerability, and the like. Memories are lasting not just because they are deeply imprinted but because they are emotionally charged, arising out of a huge frame of generational and personal experiences relating to family life, sexual experiences, gender and lifestyle, politics, prejudice and discrimination, hopes and dreams for the future, and encounters with the sacred. Phrased in this way, the term "generation" refers to a massive, often quite subtle set of influences shaping people's predispositions that they carry with them through life.

Religious Trends

The Post-Second World War Generation

Far more attention has been paid to generational patterns within religion in the United States than elsewhere. Over the past twenty years sociologists have focused especially on the large post-Second World War Boom Generation. Born in the period roughly from 1946 to 1964, this generation called for attention not simply for reasons of its huge numbers and the fact that it remains a trend-setter in the USA, but because its members grew up in a time of so much social and cultural ferment. By now that list of widespread social changes is well known: the youth counterculture, the Civil Rights movement, the Vietnam War protests, the women's movement and gender-role changes, a growing ecological consciousness, and the impact of the assassination of President Kennedy especially upon the older cohort of this generation and of Watergate and the resignation of President Nixon, though less significant, upon the younger cohort. As would be expected, such events and the youth-based movements of this period brought about a great deal of social solidarity and idealistic hopes for a better world; among the older Boomers, levels of trust and confidence in social institutions, especially political but also religious institutions, plummeted and have remained relatively low even as the generation has grown older. Technological advances contributed significantly to a shift in values, outlook, and lifestyles: this was the first generation to grow up with television and to have its perceptions of the world shaped by its daily images; it was the first to have widespread access to safe birth control. The generation came of age in the era of post-war economic expansion, and at very young ages its members were targeted as consumers by marketing firms. Plus, those who were of middle-class parentage entered adulthood having at their disposal a new, more efficient means of making financial transactions: the credit card, which of course radically altered traditional restraints placed upon immediate gratification and opened up new possibilities for self-fulfillment. The world has not been the same since.

Many youths growing up at the time having been reared in a faith tradition defected from churches and synagogues and drifted away from strong belief in God in favor of a more open, exploring, and often agnostic stance regarding religious matters. The San Francisco Bay Area Study, conducted in 1973 in a setting known as a major center of the youth ferment, found that an index of "countercultural involvement" was a better predictor of religious defection than either age or life cycle. The effects of age and life cycle on religion in fact were statistically minimal, which suggests that at a time of intense cultural discontinuities, including widespread rejection of middle-class values, the "generational factor" emerges as particularly significant. Robert Wuthnow (1978: 138–139) concluded from the general population survey that "the current generation gap in religious commitment between the young and the old in the Bay Area appears to be the result of younger people having been more involved in the counterculture than older people, rather than the result of other kinds of differences between the young and the old". His was the first sophisticated statistical analysis of the impact of youth culture on religion, attempting to control for the complex mix of period, life cycle, and generational influences, and thereby gave strong support to the argument about generation as a factor in the study of religion.

Subsequent studies in other parts of the USA uncovered patterns that were less dramatic but which amply supported his interpretation. Based upon my own 1998–9 survey and in-depth interviews in four states—North Carolina, Ohio, California, and Massachusetts—roughly two-thirds of members of this generation reported dropping out of active involvement in church, synagogue, or temple for a period of two years or more at some time while growing up (Roof 1993). We do not know how this compares with other periods of American history; however, considering that nine out of ten people in the survey said that they had attended weekly religious services when they were 8 to 10 years old, the drop-out rate appears to have been quite high. As in Wuthnow's earlier finding, exposure to the countercultural values of the late 1960s and early 1970s proved to be the best predictor of declining religious participation. On related indicators concerning the importance of arriving at one's own beliefs, whether religious attendance is necessary to being a "good" Christian or Jew, and views about the rules of morality within churches and synagogues, there were considerable shifts in outlook for Boomers compared with other cohorts of Americans born prior to the Second World War. But these shifts in institutional religious involvement, values, and outlook should be viewed in their proper social context: older members of this generation were influenced by the conformist, anti-Communist culture during the Cold War of the 1950s and early 1960s. They came into adulthood at a time which might be thought of as an aberration, an uptight era nestled between an earlier, far less tense time—the 1920s—and what would later follow and become known, and is still remembered as, "the 1960s".

The social context encouraged a mix of religious patterns, evident especially as the Boomer Generation grew older. Many of them—about one-quarter—returned to active involvement in religious congregations and other groups once married and raising their own children. Even among those who had not become active again when I and my colleagues interviewed them in the late 1980s and early 1990s, many expressed strong religious interest; when asked whether they would become involved in a congregation again, 70 percent responded by saying that it was "very likely" or "possible". Yet 42 percent remained dropouts. In a second round of interviews with the same people in 1995–6, we found a very diverse set of religious patterns and a somewhat more polarized population (Roof 1999). A slightly larger number reported attending religious services weekly in this later survey, but slightly more reported being not at all religiously involved. Weekly attendance had increased slightly for both evangelical Protestants and mainline Protestants, and remained roughly the same for Roman Catholics. There was little change for Jewish Baby Boomers, which historically have had low levels of communal identification (also see Waxman 2001). Sizeable numbers of mainline Protestants and Catholics had also abandoned the conviction of the exclusive claims of Christianity (also see Presbyterian patterns documented by Hoge, Johnson, and Luidens 1994: 61). But the most significant finding of this later survey was the enormous fluidity in religious styles—which defies simple inferences about either a "religious revival" or a "secular drift" for this generation as of the mid-1990s. Among those who had been identified as returnees in 1988–9, a majority of them claiming a born-again experience, only 43 percent later said that they attended services even as often as once a month; many said they no longer knew what to believe. And among those who in the first survey were classified as dropouts, one-third now said that they attended religious services weekly or more; about half said that they were strong believers. By any institutional measure we had at our disposal, only about a third of those once highly alienated from organized religion—across all major faith traditions—could now be described as dropouts.

Fluidity is expressed as well in the mixing of religious and spiritual themes. Sizeable numbers of the Boomer population reported belief in reincarnation and interest in Eastern and Native American teachings, combining these often with their own inherited faith traditions; roughly 10 percent said that they were "spiritual but not religious". The spiritual culture of the time, quite subjective and protean in character, found expression in "journey" and "recovery" theologies. A majority at the time of the 1988–9 survey indicated a preference "to be alone and to meditate" as opposed "to worship with others", indicative of a highly individualistic, inwardly focused spiritual style. Sixty percent said that they would prefer "to explore many differing teachings", whereas 28 percent said that they preferred "to stick to a faith". By the time of the later survey, the spread in these choices was somewhat less, although there was ample evidence of continuing religious fluidity and of varying identities using both religious and spiritual languages, and of course a mix of the two. Based upon a cross-classification of religious and spiritual identities, we arrived at the following set of major Boomer constituencies in 1995–6: dogmatists, 15 percent; born-again Christians, 33 percent; mainstream believers, 26 percent; metaphysical believers and seekers, 14 percent; and secularists, 12 percent. By "secularists" we refer to those respondents identifying themselves as neither religious nor spiritual. Excluding the latter along with the dogmatists who said that they were not spiritual and the metaphysical believers and seekers who said that they were not religious, the vast majority, or 59 percent, understood their spirituality to be expressed in historic religious forms, and most commonly within established congregations. This fourfold scheme, though obviously simplistic, offers a quite different mapping of the religious–spiritual scene in the United States than the usual denominational or Protestant–Catholic–Jewish breakout of faith communities.

Religious patterns for the post-Second World War generation extend beyond the United States to other Western countries, although tend to be less pronounced. A cross-national study of nine countries—Australia, Britain, France, Germany, the Netherlands, Belgium, Italy, Greece, and the United States—points to a weakening of religious establishments generally, but also suggests two, somewhat opposing trends. Across these countries the evidence indicates that this generation is the "carrier" of more personal, individually tailored modes of religious and spiritual expression; yet for others, though definitely a smaller number of people, we observed a re-energizing of older, traditional patterns of faith and practice. This latter was expressed both as rediscovery of certain traditional themes that were attractive to individuals and as affirmation of belief in new communal structures (see Roof, Carroll, and Roozen 1995). Taken as a whole, five features of the new religious and spiritual scene were identified:

1. a broadly based emphasis upon individual choice and accommodation to personal need arising out of deep psychological and existential concerns;
2. a mixing of codes, or the creation of multi-layered meaning systems drawing from symbols and teachings across various religious and spiritual traditions;
3. bodily expressive trends such as New Age mystical movements, on the one hand, and attraction to conservative, sectarian movements, especially Pentecostal and charismatic movements, on the other;

4. much attention to the experiential aspect of religion and stress upon personal growth and self-actualization; and
5. anti-institutional and anti-hierarchical themes varying somewhat from country to country, but in keeping generally with an emphasis upon the personal, experiential aspects of belief and practice.

Generation X

The succeeding generation carried forward many of the same trends, yet had distinctive characteristics. Born in the years between the mid-1960s and the early 1980s, Generation Xers were bound together in their formative years less by dramatic national or international events than their predecessors. However, they were exposed to greater levels of religious pluralism and family disruption; alternatives in faith tradition and differing family types were taken for granted. Music was a central venue of their experience, its lyrics often giving expression to disharmonious family experiences and to quests for a more distinctive identity; living in the shadow of the Boom Generation that received so much attention, they were supremely conscious of who they were not and sought to assert who they were in contrast. They have grown up within, and are highly dependent upon, an electronic culture: computers, MTV, the Internet, video games. No generation is more "image-heavy", not just in the sense of being exposed to visual imagery but in navigating among images and accommodating to shifting worlds of meaning—"virtual realities" as these have come to be called. More so than preceding generations, they were caught up in what communications analyst Neil Postman describes as the historic transition from a print culture associated with a typographic mind to a visual culture characterized by fleeting imageries and non-linear logics (1986: 30–63). Whereas the first lends itself to the rational, coherent arrangement of ideas, beliefs, and arguments, the latter relies much more upon emotion, imagination, and experiential learning. Thus it is said that "seeing is believing" and "feeling is believing", each taking on the status of an epistemological axiom alongside the more traditional ones of reading and hearing. No doubt the impact of this shift is felt more among educated, middle-class Generation Xers than for others within their generation, which helps to explain their more expansive spiritual consciousness and the ease with which they negotiate among and incorporate differing angles of vision and language when describing who they are religiously and spiritually. In this respect, the notion of an X Generation, or one that is in many ways remains unknown, is an apt description.

Research studies of this generation's religion point to features in keeping with these general characteristics. Not to be overlooked, as Miller and Miller (2000) emphasize, is the immense diversity of popular religious styles, ranging from a generic interest in spirituality to huge numbers with Pentecostal, fundamentalist, and Evangelical Christian commitments. Hybrid forms of spiritual and religious styles are common with fringe constituencies preferring Jesus tattoos and involvement in home churches, Gothic clubs, and gangs. Selective absorption of religious beliefs and practices from traditions other than their own, at least in the early adult years, is looked upon by many of its members as favorable, and often as spiritually rejuvenating. Various researchers note that Generation Xers look for warmth and a sense of community within religious congregations and other kinds of communities, that they attempt to rebuild relationships that for whatever reason were fractured in earlier years, and that generally they are more communally oriented than were the Boomers before them. Generation Xers are drawn to worship services that make use of diverse media and cultivate multi-sensory awareness of the sacred—that is, experiences shaped by music, pop art, and computer-generated designs, videos, and sound tracks. Many inquire into and/or seek to reclaim mystical elements of religious traditions, making use of candles, incense, and chanting, and often creatively incorporating these into modern liturgies. Far more basic still, as both Beaudoin (1998) and Miller and Miller (2000) observe, is a paradigm shift in which an older Enlightenment rationalism separating mind and body has broken down, a situation now giving rise to a burst of creative and experimental energy. The quest is for deeper, transformative experiences of healing with bodily expression and in which the sensual and the spiritual come together in a meaningful whole.

Overview of Three Generations

Several research projects offer descriptive profiles across generations, two such studies in the United States and one in Britain. All three yield findings quite similar with respect to the dominant trends of increased personal religious autonomy and more expressive spiritual styles. D'Antonio, Davidson, Hoge, and Meyer's national telephone survey of American Catholics (2001), for example, shows a downward trend in traditional Catholic views and practices across three generations. The greatest differences they observed are between pre-Vatican II and Vatican II cohorts (roughly, pre-Boomers and Boomers), the former having grown up with a stronger emphasis upon obedience to the "one true Church" and the importance of conforming to church teachings if one is to be a "good" Catholic. Their study documents smaller, yet significant differences between the Vatican II (Boomer) and post-Vatican II (Generation X) cohorts on these same issues. With respect to normative views about Catholic identity, there is a consistent decline across the generations regarding the importance of the sacraments, teachings about Mary as the Mother of God, belonging to a Catholic community, and especially with respect to the teaching authority of the Vatican. "These differences", the researchers say, "indicate a continuing shift from higher to lower levels of community and from compliance with traditional teachings to greater autonomy" (D'Antonio *et al.* 2001: 129). Stressed as well is that many Catholics who hold to the Catholic *faith* are not necessarily highly committed to the institutional *Church*; this holds especially for the younger cohorts (and of course is not restricted just to Catholics). Generation X Catholics do honor certain forms of community within parishes, especially if the bonds uniting them are sensitive to the values, styles, and concerns of their own generation. Catholic parishes holding on to their youth are those that make these accommodations.

A general population survey in North Carolina and southern California carried out by Carroll and Roof (2002) documents increased agreement across the generations on two important items, one being that "an individual should arrive at religious beliefs independent of church groups", and a second that "people who have God in their lives don't need a church or religious group". Within the United States and much of the Western world, personal autonomy in religious and spiritual matters is highly honored and practiced. When asked, "Is it better to explore many religions or focus on the teachings of one faith tradition?", Boomers and even greater numbers of Generation Xers choose the former as compared with pre-Boomers; somewhat surprisingly, and contrary to popular perception, fewer Boomers, and fewer still Generation Xers, identify themselves as evangelical Christians. Compared with pre-Boomers, the two younger generations prefer worship services that are expressive and spiritually uplifting. The latter are also less drawn to congregations making a sharp distinction between the religious and the secular, and somewhat more attracted to those addressing social justice issues. On the whole, cultural and religious differences are greater between pre-Boomers and Boomers. With both Boomers and Generation Xers, quantitative measures of religiosity and spirituality as typically used in research studies fail to capture serious nuances in style and depth of commitment between the two, the major exception being the greater communal orientation of the Generation Xers who are members of, or participants within, churches and synagogues.

A recent British study (Voas and Crockett 2005) finds that generation is a better predictor of a downward trend both in religious belief and belonging than either age of respondent or period effects. As with the early Wuthnow research on youth in the San Francisco area, this is one of very few studies in Britain that attempts to sort out these distinct effects. Unlike studies within the United States, however, this one stresses that the precipitous declines in religious participation began well before the 1960s. Closely associated with the generational changes for any given cohort, they also find, is the strong impact of parental religiosity, or lack thereof. Their data suggest that only about half of parental religiosity as measured using their indicators is successfully transmitted to children, while absence of religion is almost always passed on. The British study is not comparable to those in the United States, since the generational cohorts are reported in ten-year age spans rather than defined culturally or by epoch. Moreover, no data are provided with respect to non-standard religious belief and/or interest in personal spirituality; trends for the latter would likely be very revealing. But not to be missed is the overall message the study conveys, one very much in keeping with other studies cited in this essay, that generational cohorts are significant carriers of religious values and practices, and that the role of parents in passing these on to their children is crucial. Far more systematic research is required for exploring variations in inter-generational transmission of religious patterns cross-nationally.

Generations and Religious Institutions

Similarly, more research is needed with respect to changing forms of religious institutions, and to congregations particularly in relation to generational patterns. Lack of such research is surprising, given the simple fact that religious communities are not static and unchanging, but inevitably adapt as populations, social settings, and cultural values themselves change. Historically, we know that there have been important shifts in voluntary religious communities as found in the United States. Brooks Holifield (1994), for example, points to four major congregational models evolving over various periods of the country's history in response to the changing social and cultural milieus: the *comprehensive congregation* organized for an entire community; the *devotional congregation* offering a distinctive style of worship, music, and liturgy; the *social congregation* providing an array of activities and opportunities for fellowship in addition to worship; and the *participatory congregation* quite common today, emphasizing lay initiative and decision making within the community.

The rise of the participatory model of the religious gathering in the modern era signals the extent to which grass-roots influences can, and increasingly do, impact on religious institutions, and has a particular affinity with the post-Second World War generations. Generally in the period since the mid-twentieth century, voices mounted for greater input by the people in shaping both political and religious agendas, for greater "participatory pluralism" as William R. Hutchison (2003) describes it. In addition to a growing religious pluralism, there is experimentation with religious forms in response to religious and spiritual sensitivities. An example is the "seeker church", one that departs from traditional forms of church to attract a target audience of unchurched people in a post-Christian culture, and especially Baby Boomers (many of whom who were once churchgoers). Christian evangelical churches have led the way in establishing such institutions, making creative use of contemporary music, drama, and film addressing doubt and a questing mood. Preaching in these churches attempts to be non-offensive; worship styles are informal, positively focused, and entertaining. Seeker churches offer a wide range of small groups, with emphasis especially on spiritual journeys and recovery theology. Innovative and seeker-sensitive, such congregations stress personal authenticity and growth, and institutionalize choice in religious style to a greater extent than traditional churches. The churches are popularly known as "mega churches" because of their size (Sargeant 2000), but also as "post-denominational" or "new paradigm" churches (Miller 1997). Though these designations point to some differences in style, generally all such churches are similar in their stress upon the experiential dimensions of faith, small group ministries, contemporary worship, and stress upon bodily and not merely cognitive participation in worship.

Generation X-specific churches and synagogues emerged beginning in the mid-1980s, designed to address particular interests and concerns of this younger generation. They too target unaffiliated members, and even more than seeker churches attempt to blend popular culture with spirituality; some of these congregations go so far as to tout themselves as "generational churches" in what amounts to a major break with historic faith communities. Drawing on music, dance, art, film, computer-generated designs, soundtracks, blogs, and so forth, their worship services try to create multi-sensory, bodily expressive spiritual environments. Worship and social activities are designed to cultivate experiences of intimacy and authenticity. Much emphasis is placed upon personal responsibility and one-to-one relationships as a means of building stronger community. More so than traditional churches, these congregations work at, and often succeed in, forming fellowships that transcend racial and ethnic group divisions—what they call "reconciled faith communities" (Garces-Foley 2007). Ritual and organizational structures tend to be flexible and accommodating, providing, as Shawn Landres (2000: 278) says, "a wide range of human–divine interactions".

As we see, generations are more than simply the carriers of new religious and spiritual styles. More broadly, they are cultural enclaves that give rise to new institutional forms and types of communities. They are yet another source of religion's becoming more diversely structured, more pluralistic in the multicultural sense. Today three major communal structures can be identified: the inherited model of a singular religious community which continues to try to hold generations together by means of custom and tradition; the blended community that is self-consciously designed to appeal across generations but provides generational-based activities within it; and the distinctive generation-specific communities (see Carroll and Roof 2002). Of the three, the blended community is the most common. Beyond variations of this sort, there are the more radical late modern or postmodern institutional innovations which seek to create religious and/or spiritual community in relation to particular lifestyle and experiential constituencies. Increasingly in the United Kingdom and the United States, and to a lesser extent in Australia, New Zealand, and continental Europe, there are the "emerging churches" born out of a movement that deliberately breaks with the older cultural expressions of a now collapsed Christendom (Gibbs and Bolger 2005). These churches attract people who are deeply committed to missional encounters with a post-Christian culture, to new ways of being the faithful church and of cultivating a style of spirituality that is both personally fulfilling and socially engaging. Although the identity of people involved in these churches is more explicitly religious than generational, in very subtle ways church leaders tap deep themes and energies associated with young people. Not to be overlooked, too, are the musical concerts and gatherings of various kinds at retreat centers and elsewhere with spiritual themes, plus the large numbers of young people who journey to places like the Taizé community each year in France in what amounts to a modern-style pilgrimage. In such activities, participants generally seek an intentional religious and spiritual fellowship and celebrate mystery, bonding, compassion, and commitment to social justice.

Conclusion

Research on generations and religion is largely focused upon majority populations in the United States and European countries. Lacking especially are studies of minority and lifestyle populations, and how they differ or are similar to those of the dominant groups. Critically important are the emerging religious patterns of "second-generation" immigrants across countries in the recent era of widespread global movement, about which we know very little at present. Is religion becoming more or less of a cultural marker for generations? In either instance, in what ways is this manifest?

Compared with other social factors such as race, ethnicity, and social class which have long been recognized as crucial to the sociological study of religion, what is striking about the generational concept is its sensitivity to the complexities of cultural change and continuity. Careful analysis of social life calls for attention to both of these fundamental features of human existence. Every generation is distinctive, yet shares much with its forebears; generational identity, values, and outlook are all formed out of processes of cultural exchange and negotiation. Similarly, religion is a source of continuity across generations, as is obvious in the strong hold of custom and tradition upon us, yet its cultural adaptability and myriad of ever-evolving forms, both personal and social, are equally evident. To return to a point emphasized early on in this essay: religion—like culture generally—is socially produced and maintained, and thus reflects both change and continuity in any given moment. So important a nexus as that between generations and religion deserves far more careful attention than it has yet received by sociologists and others who would understand these realities.

References

Beaudoin, Tom (1998). *Virtual Faith: The Irreverent Spiritual Quest of Generation X.* San Francisco: Jossey-Bass.

Callahan, Daniel J. (1965). *Generation of the Third Eye.* New York: Sheed and Ward.

Carroll, Jackson W., and Roof, Wade Clark (2002). *Bridging Divided Worlds: Generational Cultures in Congregations.* San Francisco: Jossey-Bass.

D'Antonio, William V., Davidson, James D., Hoge, Dean R., and Meyer, Katherine (2001). *American Catholics: Gender, Generation, and Commitment.* Walnut Creek, Calif.: AltaMira Press.

Esler, Anthony (1982). "Generations in History: An Introduction to the Concept". Unpublished manuscript.

Garces-Foley, Kathleen (2007). *Crossing the Ethnic Divide: The Multiethnic Church on a Mission.* New York: Oxford University Press.

Gibbs, Eddie, and Bolger, Ryan (2005). *Emerging Churches: Creating Christian Community in Postmodern Cultures.* Grand Rapids, Mich.: Baker Books.

Graubard, Stephen R. (ed.) (1979). *Generations.* New York: W. W. Norton and Company.

Hoge, Dean R., Johnson, Benton, and Luidens, David A. (1994). *Vanishing Boundaries: The Religion of Mainline Protestants Baby Boomers.* Louisville, Ky.: Westminster/John Knox Press.

Holifield, Brooks (1994). "Toward a History of American Congregations". In James P. Wind and James W. Lewis (eds.), *American Congregations*, ii. Chicago: University of Chicago Press, 23–53.

Hutchison, William R. (2003). *Religious Pluralism in America: The Contentious History of a Founding Ideal.* New Haven: Yale University Press.

Kriegel, Annie (1979). "Generational Difference: The History of an Idea". In Graubard (1979), 23–38.

Landres, J. Shawn (2000). "Generation X". In W. C. Roof (ed.), *Contemporary American Religion*, i. New York: Macmillan, 277–8.

Mannheim, Karl (1952). "The Problem of Generations". In P. Kecskemeti (ed.), *Essays on the Sociology of Knowledge.* New York: Oxford University Press, 276–320.

Marias, Julian (1970). *Jose orlega y Gasset/Orlega: Circumstances and Vocation*, trans. Frances M. Lopez-Movillas. Norman, Okla.: University of Oklahoma Press.

Miller, Donald E. (1997). *Reinventing American Protestantism: Christianity in the New Millennialism.* Berkeley: University of California Press.

—— and Miller, Arpi M. (2000). "Understanding Generation X: Values, Politics, and Religious Commitments". In R. Flory and D. Miller (eds.), *Gen X Religion*, New York: Routledge, 1–12.

Nash, Laura A. (1979). "Greek Origins of Generational Thought". In Graubard (1979), 1–21.

Porterfield, Amanda (2000). *The Transformation of American Religion.* New York: Oxford University Press.

Postman, Neil (1986). *Amusing Ourselves to Death: Religious Discourse in the Age of Show Business.* New York: Penguin.

Roof, Wade Clark (1993). *A Generation of Seekers: The Spiritual Journeys of the Baby Boom Generation.* San Francisco: HarperSanFranciso.

Roof, Wade Clark (1999). *Spiritual Marketplace: Baby Boomers and the Remaking of American Religion.* Princeton: Princeton University Press.

—— Carroll, Jackson W., and Roozen, David A. (1995). *The Post-War Generation and Establishment Religion: Cross-Cultural Perspectives.* Boulder, Col.: Westview.

Sargeant, Kimon H. (2000). "Seeker Churches". In W. C. Roof (ed.), *Contemporary American Religion*, ii. New York: Macmillan, 658–9.

Schuman, Havard, and Scott, Jacqueline (1989). 'Generations and Collective Memories'. *American Sociological Review*, 54: 359–81.

Strauss, William, and Howe, Neil (1991). *Generations: The History of America's Future, 1584 to 2069.* New York: William Morrow and Company, Inc.

Voas, David, and Crockett, Alasdair (2005). "Religion in Britain: Neither Believing Nor Belonging". *Sociology*, 39/1: 11–28.

Waxman, Chaim I. (2001). *Jewish Baby Boomers: A Communal Perspective.* Albany, NY: State University of New York Press.

Williams, Angie, and Nussbaum, Jon F. (2001). *Intergenerational Communication across the Life Span.* Mahwah, NJ: Lawrence Erlbaum Associates.

Wuthnow, Robert (1978). *Experimentation in American Religion: The New Mysticisms and Their Implications for the Churches.* Berkeley: University of California Press.

Suggested Reading

The following are recommended: Carroll and Roof (2002); D'Antonio *et al.* (2001); Graubard (1979); Hoge *et al.* (1994); Mannheim (1952); Miller and Miller (2000); Roof (1999); Roof *et al.* (1995); and Waxman (2001).

CHAPTER 35

RELIGION AND FAMILY

PENNY EDGELL

INTRODUCTION

Throughout the history of the United States, religion and family have been intertwined and interdependent institutions, and in this, the present-day United States is no exception (Pankhurst and Houseknecht 2000). Mainstream religious institutions respond to evolving family life and household arrangements by providing new ministries to meet families' needs in an ever-changing social context, and new religious groups and movements—from the Shakers to the Church of Jesus Christ of Latter-Day Saints to feminist spirituality groups—emerge and are organized around alternative understandings of the family. Changes in family life shape how religious institutions are organized, as seen in the Sunday School movement in the early twentieth century and in the new profile of ministries organized around a breadwinner father and stay-at-home mother that emerged in the booming post-war suburbs of the 1950s. Religious institutions depend on families to pass on the rituals and beliefs of a particular faith tradition (Myers 1996).

Religious institutions provide moral guidelines that shape family practices, the organization of family life, and our perceptions of "the good family" (Edgell 2005). Moreover, a person's religiosity, religious practice, and participation in religious institutions have important and wide-ranging effects on both her experiences of family life and on the way she conducts her roles within the family (Sherkat and Ellison 1999). Religious involvement is associated with marital stability, happiness and satisfaction in marital and parenting relations, gender-role ideology, and lower levels of delinquency in adolescence. It also influences how men and women choose to invest their time in home making and financial provision for the family, which can have long-term effects on occupational and status attainment (Glass and Jacobs 2005).

Understanding how religion shapes family life and cultural understandings of the family and how families sustain—and change—religious institutions are central to the sociology of religion, and this is evidenced by the well-developed literatures on religion and relationship quality, religion and adolescent development, how religious institutions retain their youth, and family formation effects on religious involvement (see Sherkat and Ellison 1999). It is also evident in newer work on religion and gender-role ideology and the effect of religion on women's educational and occupational attainment, literatures which have been greatly influenced by the increasing visibility and public involvement of American religious conservatives since the 1980s (Gallagher 2003; Glass and Jacobs 2005). Increasingly, sociologists who study family life and work–family management are paying attention to the effects of religious involvement, whether conceptualized as religious variables that shape family-related outcomes or as religiously based moral frameworks that shape cultural expectations about gender, work, and family (Gerson 2002; Sherkat and Ellison 1999).

Religion and the Cultural Repertoire of Family and Gender

One of the most important religious influences on family life is a cultural one. Religious institutions are social locations for the production and transmission of religious familism, or ideology about what constitutes a family and what a good family should be like. Religious familism varies over time, and differs according to important dimensions of social location like race and class. In the United States, most versions of religious familism have had important elements in common, promoting marital stability and prohibiting divorce and extra-marital sex, emphasizing the centrality of child bearing and rearing to family life, and taking for granted a heterosexual union with a traditionally gendered division of labor (Christiano 2000; Sherkat and Ellison 1999).

Religious familism is an ideology that bridges the public and the private as traditionally understood, because it is fundamentally concerned with defining the public, the private, and the nature of the boundary between the two. Religious familism lends the weight of religious conviction, the power of religious authority, and the rhetoric of ultimate causes to inscribe the family as an embodied, earthly representation of a divine, cosmological order (Friedland 2001). As such, religious familism influences understandings of the private as a separate, feminine-gendered realm, and the state and market as public, male-gendered realms (Lakoff 1996). It encodes citizenship as more fully embodied by those who marry and raise children, providing discourses that justify the provision of public resources to support marriage and child rearing and the exclusion of same-sex couples from the institution of marriage, and linking marriage with ideals of public order (Cott 2002; Hull 2006). Religious familism also shapes individuals' political activism and social movement participation (Ginsburg 1989). The involvement of religious groups on both sides of the same-sex marriage debate is only one recent example of the stakes involved in designating some family forms as morally worthy and of conflating religious and civil understandings of the institutions of marriage and the family. Welfare policies that privilege marriage as a solution to poverty for poor women are another.

In any society there is a cultural repertoire for thinking and talking about family life, a repertoire that includes family schema (or cultural models of what a family is and what a good family is like), family-related discourses, and family-oriented practices. In the United States, and some would argue more widely, religion has a powerful, even a fundamental, influence on the available cultural repertoire of family life (Pankhurst and Houseknecht 2000). Religious family ideology provides cultural frameworks that apportion moral responsibility for financial provision and caretaking within the family, and it systematically links these with understandings of men's and women's innate natures, with what is a public concern and what is private, and with discourses on the good society (Bellah *et al.* 1991).

Questions about how religion shapes our cultural repertoire for thinking about family life are newly relevant after a period of more than thirty years of changes in family life. Since the 1960s, the United States, like most Western Societies, has seen high rates of divorce and an increase in the number of adults who live a substantial portion of their lives without a partner (see tables 35.1, 35.2, 35.3). There has been a large and sustained movement of women into the workforce that spans racial and social class divisions and includes mothers of young children, and the dual-earner couple has emerged as a new, and newly dominant, family form. There has been a shift in gender-role ideology; most Americans now prefer egalitarian relationships between men and women, which is part of a larger transition in which increasing value is placed on freedom and self-expression.

There has also been an increase in the numbers and the visibility of same-sex unions, single-parent families, blended families, and other "alternative" family arrangements that are contested but still far more accepted than they were a few decades ago. Many of the post-1965 wave of immigrants came to the United States with a different understanding of family life, preferring an extended family model and connections with close kin to the dominant nuclear family arrangement they found in the United States. The transition to adulthood is also different now than it was two or three generations ago; the links between education, establishing one's own household, and starting a family have been loosened, and no longer constitute a "package" of markers of adulthood which most young adults undertake to acquire at the same time. We live in an era of pluralism and flexibility regarding family life. Family formation, disruption, and re-formation play a different role in adult lives than used to be the case. There are different cultural understandings of what is normal and desirable in family life, and the families that people form do not all look alike (Coontz 1997; Furstenberg 1999; Skolnick 1991; Treas 1999).

In my work on religion and family, I have concentrated on two interrelated sets of questions that stem from the desire to understand religious familism today. How do religious institutions orient themselves to the wide range of families in our society now? Who do they include and exclude, and do they take an authoritative stance that seeks to define some family forms and arrangements as more appropriate than others? And how do the people who live in and through a diverse and pluralistic set of family arrangements orient themselves to religious institutions? Do they perceive them as relevant? Do they get involved? Or do they find religious communities to be unwelcoming or irrelevant, and seek out other venues for social connection, community involvement, and spiritual expression? This is a set of questions that gets at the fit—or lack of fit—between religion and family today.

Cases

Recently, my research has concentrated on the links between religion and family, based largely on a study of four communities in upstate New York (Edgell 2005), but also including ethnographic work on three urban congregations in the Twin Cities (Edgell and Docka 2007). These studies explored how local congregations produce religious familism through both their rhetoric—what is said in sermons, small group meetings, and echoed in the conversation of members and lay leaders—and through their practices—the practical routines of congregational life, found in both formal programming and in informal ways of doing things.

When scholars study how religion shapes family ideals, they often concentrate on the formal statements of elites—doctrines and position statements on women's roles or same-sex marriage, or the discourse produced by special-purpose groups like Focus on the Family or Promisekeepers. These are important sources of family-oriented discourse, but it is in local congregations that most Americans encounter, interpret, and come to understand the implications of their religion for their family life. There are more than 300,000 local congregations in the United States, and there are strong family formation effects on religious involvement at the local level. Investigating the religion–family link in local religious communities provides a window onto "lived religion" and helps us to understand how official viewpoints and elite discourse shape religion as most people encounter it in their daily lives.

In upstate New York, I investigated the religion–family link by studying congregations and community members in two rural counties, one working-class neighborhood in Syracuse, and one middle-class inner-ring suburb of Syracuse. These communities were largely White (ranging from 76 percent to 95 percent), and they were filled with congregations from mainstream religious denominations—Catholic, mainline Protestant, and Evangelical Protestant (for details see Edgell 2006). These communities are not a "microcosm" of America; they are exemplary of a particular portion of the religious landscape, the religious institutions which comprise the largest and a culturally influential portion of organized religion in the USA. The history and culture of these mainstream religious institutions in the USA has been deeply intertwined with changes in religious familism; these institutions have defined themselves in part through the way that they understand and orient themselves to family life (Bendroth 1993; 2002).

Most of the congregations in these communities, in their rhetoric and programs and routine ways of doing things, took for granted that, though there are many kinds of families, the ideal family is a heterosexual, nuclear family with children in which the father is the breadwinner and the mother is the primary caretaker. That is, most of them upheld the "Ozzie and Harriet" family as ideal. However, they had adapted in incremental and partial ways to some new family realities as well. Although they valued marriage, they were welcoming of single adults, including single parents, and did quite a bit to provide support for the divorced. They had adapted to the reality of dual-earner schedules by holding women's meetings in the evenings, providing baby sitting for many meetings and events, and rearranging the preparation for rituals like confirmation and baptism so that these did not require ten or twelve weeknight meetings. In more liberal Protestant churches, and some progressive Catholic parishes, feminist understandings of women's lives and concerns were expressed, and inclusive language was widely used. Evangelical Protestant churches embraced women's contributions to the community and were the most willing to accommodate the time constraints of dual-earner families with children. These conservative Protestant churches also had active support groups for single parents and members going through a divorce, and their pastors were involved in finding such members, usually women, community-based sources of support as well.

These changes, however, did not displace the emphasis on the importance of an intact family with children, preferably with a male breadwinner, as the ideal family arrangement. This ideal was expressed in part through congregational practices, the programming offered, and informal ways of arranging the daily and weekly life of the congregation. I found that most congregations, liberal and conservative alike, still based most of their programming on a "standard package" of ministries, oriented mostly to women, children, and youth, that emerged as a template during the 1950s post-war religious expansion. Changes to this standard package were incremental and sometimes instituted only after a period of some resistance on the part of the leadership. And in liberal and conservative churches alike, the rhetoric, particularly of pastors and lay leaders, still upheld an Ozzie and Harriet family as ideal.

In conservative churches a neo-patriarchal family ideology was explicit, and was linked to a theology that designates the male as the head of the family as Christ is the head of the church. In these churches, divorce and single parenting were spoken of as forms of "brokenness". Individually, pastors and lay leaders were welcoming and supportive of those who do not fit the two-parents-with-children norm. But in sermons and in informal conversations they upheld a male-headed family with children as a biblically based ideal still relevant today. In mainline Protestant and progressive Catholic parishes, the official rhetoric about the family was progressive and inclusive. But in unofficial discourse—in everyday conversation, in themes that emerged in small group meetings—there was a nostalgia for the Ozzie and Harriet family of the past. This nostalgia was often linked to memories of a 1950s "heyday", when the Sunday school was overflowing, when to be a pastor was to be a respected and even influential member of the community, and when the church ran largely on the volunteer labor of women.

It has become common in the religion and family literature to emphasize the differences between liberal and conservative Christians in family ideology. The family-oriented discourse of conservative Protestants has received particular attention, and this is partly because sociologists who study religion take modernization to be a central problem for their research. Elite conservative Protestant discourse on the family rejects the universalism and egalitarianism that are hallmarks of the transition to modern ways of thought. Rather, it emphasizes the fundamental differences between men's and women's natures, valuing the importance of ascribed characteristics in determining one's status and moral obligations in the world. Conservative Catholic discourse on the family echoes this gender essentialism, but has received less scholarly attention. These differences in official religious discourse were present in the local congregations I studied. Liberal Protestant pastors and progressive Catholic priests never referred to divorce or single parenting as a form of brokenness, and they emphasized the commonalities between men and women, particularly in their parenting roles.

So it is important to understand that, while the elite religious discourse of liberals and conservatives differs a great deal when it comes to what is an ideal family, the congregations I studied, across the liberal/conservative divide, had institutionalized a neo-patriarchal family schema. This points to the importance of balancing our studies of official and elite discourses on the family with analyses of how particular institutional forms become embedded in organizational structure and routines such that they shape and limit an organization's capacity to adapt to change or to express new cultural schemas. Studies of religion and family privilege ideas, beliefs, and official religious discourse and often ignore how institutional forms—like the typical ministry profile of mainstream congregations—are the products of and reproduce cultural models of "the good family".

In the communities included in my study in New York State, about 85 percent of congregations had adapted to some changes in family life (while mostly avoiding more controversial and contested changes like whether to welcome same-sex couples). But they were still operating with a kind of Ozzie and Harriet family ideal regardless of official religious views. This tempered differences based on a left/right ideological divide; evangelical congregations and conservative Catholic parishes in fact welcomed single parents and provided support for those undergoing divorce. Mainline Protestant and progressive Catholic congregations embraced changes in gender roles and the family in theory, while maintaining a considerable nostalgia for an idealized version of the time before these changes occurred (Coontz 1992).

There were some exceptions. About 15 percent of the congregations in these communities were innovators, who had embraced a very different understanding of what the ideal family is like and, attendant to that, a different understanding of the role of the family in the life of the congregation. Innovators were all large congregations with many resources, and they were mostly liberal Protestant, although a few progressive Catholic congregations were innovators, too. Innovators had many programs for people who do not fit the Ozzie and Harriet ideal, and they also had many programs that were not organized around gender and life stage, in which people's family status (married or parent) was not signaled by their participation in a particular activity. These congregations innovated in multiple ways—they had daycare for members, tutoring for youth, and had made some public commitment to welcoming gay and lesbian members and same-sex couples. They also had progressive family rhetoric, with none of the nostalgia for the past found in other congregations. Though only 15 percent of congregations, they comprised over 40 percent of the average Sunday attendance in these communities, and interviews with the pastors and long-term lay leaders suggested that, although they were large and resource-rich before they innovated, they also grew after they decided to do so. These congregations suggest that, particularly in informal programs and practices, but through some formal programs as well, a new family schema is being embodied in daily congregational practice in some parts of the landscape of mainstream American religious institutions.

This new, alternative family schema is largely organized around parenting, but parenting as divorced from either a nuclear family structure or a traditionally gendered division of labor. This schema is also open to same-sex couples. It corresponds most closely to what is called "the nurturing family" (Lakoff 1996). Specific roles and duties are less important than the nurturing and mutual caretaking of members. Innovator congregations, which already privilege practices organized around caretaking, have found caring practices to be a natural way to extend and adapt their model of the family. Informal rhetoric in these congregations is congruent with this nurturing and open approach to the ideal family, emphasizing that God approves of all kinds of families. In these congregations, Ozzie and Harriet belong to the past, and the ideal family is one in which members are loving and committed to one another's well-being.

The Ozzie and Harriet ideal is a very White, middle-class understanding of the family, although as a cultural ideal it has historically been powerful beyond the White middle-class, shaping institutions, as well as popular culture, that affect many other Americans (Meyerowitz 1994). My study of upstate New York was based in communities with an almost exclusively White population. It was unclear how much what I found there was due to the racial composition of the communities and how much was due to fact that the mainstream institutions represented there are themselves pervaded by White, middle-class assumptions, values, and ways of doing things. The research I conducted in the Twin Cities with my colleague Danielle Docka allowed me to begin to investigate whether congregations in a different setting would exhibit a different kind of family-oriented rhetoric and practice (Edgell and Docka 2007). Docka was the lead researcher conducting most of the fieldwork in three urban congregations—a Black church, a parish with a large Hispanic ministry, and a White liberal church active in local justice-oriented ministries. These three congregations were chosen to exemplify those social locations where we would expect considerable distance from the 1950s Ozzie and Harriet ideal.

And these congregations display a range of family ideals wider than the one I found in upstate New York. In the Black church and the Hispanic parish, the extended family was the cultural ideal, and it was supported in a range of practical and symbolic ways that elevate it to near-parity with the nuclear family ideal, including youth-oriented programs that the entire family attends together and mentoring programs that match children and youth with adult, non-familial role models from among the congregational leaders. These congregations did not show incremental variations on an older standard approach; they started from and institutionalized a fundamentally different model of the family. Likewise, the liberal Protestant church was an innovator, particularly in the degree to which it has taken the nuclear family out of the center of congregational rhetoric and practice. At this church people are encountered and embraced as individuals more than as couples or families, and that, too, is based on a different model of what the family is and how the family should and does relate to the religious community.

There is also tension between the more innovative family models that each congregation has developed and that make sense of the lives and experiences of the members, and the Ozzie and Harriet model that most lay and pastoral leaders in these congregations recognize as a preferred one in their particular denomination or faith tradition. This tension comes out particularly in regard to understandings of gender, and was evident in the kinds of boundary maintenance we observed regarding the gender implications of certain family ideals. At the Catholic parish, the affirmation of extended family ties and the support ministries for single parents were things of which the deacon and priest were proud. But when we discussed them in interviews, we were repeatedly told that these should not be taken as an indication of any kind of support for couples living together without marriage. And the rationale for these ministries was firmly rooted in a patriarchal understanding of gender. Both of these pastoral leaders explained that their ministry assumes that women and men have fundamentally different natures, needs, and roles. In the Black church, mentoring programs for African American youth create extended family-like ties while being embedded in a thorough critique of the emasculating conditions that African American men encounter and the forces that undermine their ability to take their rightful place as breadwinners and providers for their families. In both of these congregations, the limits of innovation with regard to family ministry occur whenever a traditional understanding of gender roles could be called into question. These limits are well established, publicly spoken, and often reinforced by the leaders.

One of the implications of this research is the importance of understanding the links between religious familism and the production of other social knowledge and forms of culture. This is especially the case regarding gender. Family ideology is one of the primary ways in which cultural understandings of gender are produced, and religious institutions are a primary location for the production of gender as a social institution (Coontz 1992; Martin 2004). Moreover, many men and women are aware of the messages that religious institutions send about gender and respond to them directly. Religious communities are gendered social spaces in two senses: producing cultural ideals of gender and being locations in which men's and women's religious commitment is expressed in, and means, very different things.

Churchgoing is a gendered activity in all of the congregations I have studied. Men are more likely to become involved as an expression of and to find support for a family-oriented life in a society in which they have few sources of support for decisions to place family and children over work and career. Women, on the other hand, are more likely to seek out religious involvement as a place to express and explore their own faith and spirituality. Heterosexual men understand religion as a family-oriented activity and tend to join when they marry and have children; women are more likely to see religion as a place to express and explore their own faith, and so are more likely to be religiously involved throughout their adult lives. The White, middle-class women I interviewed are more critical of religious institutions and religious authority than are men in the same congregations, and try to teach their children to be the same. Involvement in a local congregation is influenced not only by one's own family structure (married or single, parent or childless), but also by the cultural frameworks through which one interprets the appropriate relationship between religion and family life.

My research has been centrally concerned with how religious institutions produce family-oriented culture—models of the ideal family, symbols and rhetoric through which experiences of family formation and disruption are understood, and forms of programming and daily practices that make it easier for people in some family arrangements to participate in congregational life and harder for others. I have also found that cultural factors shape men's and women's religious involvement. People who interpret participation in a local congregation as an expression of a family and community-oriented lifestyle show different patterns of religious involvement over the course of their lives, and in-depth interviews suggest that the causal relationship between involvement and interpretive frameworks for understanding that involvement may work differently for different people. Some people seek out a religious community when they marry or have children because they already understand this as appropriate, and some people come to view their religious participation as expressive of their family commitments through their experiences in local congregations.

Religion and Family in a Diverse Society

My analyses of the cultural and institutional connections, along with the changes that have occurred in both the family and in religious institutions in the United States, have led me to conclude that our scholarship needs to expand its focus in order to engage with the sociological implications of religion in our society today. To some extent, sociologists who study religion and the family are like the religious leaders I interviewed for my study in upstate New York; we orient our research and ask our questions in a way that is a better fit with the past than with the present. We need to investigate how religious and cultural diversity, transformations of the individual life course, and changing attitudes towards traditional institutions of all kinds are reconfiguring the institutional interdependency between religion and family in our society. And the "we" in those sentences is intentional, because the foci for research that I suggest, below, stem in large part from the awareness of the limits of my own research.

In our studies of religious institutions we need to pay more attention to what feminist scholars term "intersectionality", or how religious familism is embedded within and shapes understandings of race, ethnicity, social class, and gender (Collins 2001). The production of religious familism occurs in real, historically located communities and institutions that vary by race and social class, and in the context of a society that is both hetero-normative and pervasively gendered. Too often our scholarship adopts the voice of neutrality while reproducing taken-for-granted assumptions about what "counts" as a family and what family forms are "good for" society or individual members. The value of maintaining strong institutions in their current form is another common theme, as evident in the characterization of new forms of spiritual expression as flakey or self-indulgent. My own work has not escaped this tendency completely, in part because our community of discourse is pervaded by rhetorical techniques that simultaneously acknowledge that "gender is important" or "race really matters", while proceeding as though that were not the case, and it is quite easy to write in and through that dominant language. But it is crucial to learn how to escape it, because of the growing diversity of the American religious landscape and the increasing unease with which Americans confront traditional institutions of all forms.

One way to change our focus is to understand religious familisms as particular, historically rooted representations of ideals that systematically privilege the interests and experiences of some over others, that justify access to resources and particular social policies, and that have implications for inequality. Research in two different environments, upstate New York and the Twin Cities, though some of it very exploratory, showed that different racial and ethnic groups construct different kinds of religious familism even when they participate in mainstream religious institutions. But it also suggests that mainstream religious institutions are influenced in fundamental ways by neo-patriarchal understandings of gender, and that this is true not only of institutions overtly identified with conservative religious traditions. But we have only just begun to understand the intersection of familism, gender ideology, social class, and race (see, e.g., Read 2003).

The recent scholarly focus on religious conservatives in the United States, particularly conservative Protestants, has led to renewed interest in the links between gender, family, and religion for women and, recently, for men (e.g., Wilcox 2004). Sociologists have concentrated on this part of the religious landscape in part because conservative Protestants seem to be anti-modern in important respects, and modernization is a central sociological problematic. The vitality of conservative Protestantism has provided an impetus for debates about the implications of modernization and privatization for religious authority, religious involvement, and religious institutions. In addition, religious conservatives have been publicly visible and vocal on issues related to gender, sexuality, and the family. But this literature has been largely silent about the intersection between conservative religious familism, racial ideology, and social class location (for an exception, see Heath 2003).

Moreover, American religion is much more diverse than our scholarship reflects, and in ways that bear directly on questions about the link between religion and family. In the Twin Cities, where I now live, we have a large Hmong population which, like many other immigrant communities, values the extended family as a cultural ideal, and maintains strong inter-generational ties that aid in the transmission of resources long after children have reached adulthood. Many immigrant communities form parallel religious institutions, but some are transforming "mainstream" institutions, as Hispanic immigrants are transforming Catholicism in many parts of the United States. Some long-resident non-White populations also value the extended family and have a very different set of expectations than do middle-class Whites about everything, ranging from meaningful styles of worship to whether activities for women, children, and youth should be separate or combined in "families all together" ministries. A focus on White Protestant Christian conservatives is only a partial focus, and does not help us to understand how religious pluralism affects the cultural pluralism surrounding the family which characterizes the USA today.

Other transformations are taking place in how Americans relate to religious institutions. One of the most sociologically significant generational changes in family life is in the loosening of the previously tight connection between completing high school or college, marriage, parenting, and the establishment of one's own family household (Furstenberg 1999). The emergent church movement is just one example of how generational changes are linked to changes in spirituality and the transformation of religious institutions. In addition, there has been a rapid growth of "alternative" religious practices and groups, and the growth of religious seeking or reflexive spirituality. More than 80 percent of Americans now identify as either "spiritual and religious both" or "only spiritual", and estimates of how many

Americans participate in some kind of organized spiritual group or practice range from 20 to 40 percent (Marler and Hadaway 2002; Roof *et al.* 1999).

Scholars embedded within a modernization paradigm have often treated religious "seeking" and exploration of non-Western and non-institutionalized forms of religious and spiritual practice as somewhat flighty, an expression of a form of individualism that is dangerous to community-oriented commitments and troublesome because it undermines healthy institutions (see Marler and Hadaway 2002; Roof *et al.* 1999). This is occasionally true even of some who treat these forms of spirituality sympathetically, because our understanding of what "counts" as religion that is sociologically relevant takes for granted that what matters is structure—organized groups and movements with resources "count" more than loose networks of spiritual practitioners, and individuals who engage seriously with a highly elaborated, rationalized, and historic doctrine are perceived as more rational, in the classic Weberian sense of that word, than those who cast runes, read Tarot, or meditate.

But at least two things are sociologically relevant about these newer, or newly expanded, forms of religious expression. One is their disinterested, even critical, orientation to mainstream religious institutions, which may stem in part from a sense that these institutions are unresponsive to changes in gender roles and family forms. The other is the way in which they provide an entirely different cultural repertoire for thinking about religious authority, commitment, and experience, and how these might relate to family life, gender roles, and gender identity. Both therapeutic discourse and reflexive spirituality provide language for thinking and talking about transcendent meaning in a highly rationalized, individualized society, and as such, they are excellent tools for the project of identity construction in late modernity.

Scholars of religion and the family also need to expand the range of questions they asks when the focus is on the individual and not the religious institution or tradition. Sociologists have understood religious involvement as a straightforward expression of structural location, and have treated family formation as leading to religious involvement in a uniform way, because of the strong statistical relationship between marriage and parenting, on the one hand, and church attendance, on the other (see Edgell 2006 for a review). But that statistical relationship may not be truly linear. Family formation effects on religious involvement may be mediated by cultural understandings of the "fit" between religion and family, understandings that may not be uniformly shared and that may continue to change as men and women confront mainstream religious institutions that have responded only in partial and incremental ways to new family realities.

The relationship between family formation and religious involvement may be fundamentally different for those who identify primarily as "spiritual" and not religious (Hout and Fischer 2002). And for the growing proportion of Americans who identify as neither spiritual or religious, family formation and religion may be disassociated, with other institutional and familial commitments providing the moral socialization of children (Marler and Hadaway 2002). Our scholarship should also focus on the reconfiguration of the life course over the last thirty years in our society by balancing our research on family formation effects on religious involvement with studies of how religious involvement is affected by family disruption, re-formation, and transformation—including the links between religion and family life for same-sex couples and others who are generally treated as exceptional cases and excluded from the kinds of analyses that dominate our field.

Finally, we should do more to understand how religious involvement shapes a broad range of behaviors that have effects on family life. Work has begun on how religion shapes women's labor-force participation, and this is a good beginning. But how does religion influence the work and family life of men, or of working-class Americans, and how do race and ethnicity shape these patterns? How does religiosity influence the inter-generational transfer of resources in populations that value the extended family, and do these dynamics play out in a gendered way, favoring either sons or daughters in patterns of family investment? This overview is not meant to be exhaustive, but rather to share with others how my own experiences of conducting research on religion and family life has made me sensitive to particular ways in which our knowledge is partial, oriented to particular theoretical questions, focusing on particular groups and institutions, and leaving other important questions unaddressed. The society we live in is increasingly diverse and pluralistic in ways that are both transforming our dominant religious institutions and opening up new spaces for religious expression. These transformations are occurring in a society in which religiously based ideologies about good, acceptable, and appropriate forms of family life have public as well as private implications. In such a landscape the institutional link between religion and family is being transformed in ways that call for new questions, new approaches, and a broader scope for our scholarship.

References

Bellah, Robert N., Madsen, Richard, Sullivan, William M., Swidler, Ann, and Tipton, Steven M. (1991). *The Good Society.* New York: Alfred A. Knopf.

Bendroth, Margaret Lamberts (1993). *Fundamentalism and Gender: 1875 to the Present.* New Haven: Yale University Press.

—— (2002). *Growing Up Protestant: Parents, Children, and Mainline Churches.* New Brunswick, NJ: Rutgers University Press.

Christiano, Kevin (2000). "Religion and Family in Modern American Culture". In Pankhurst and Houseknecht (2000), 43–78.

Collins, Patricia Hill (2001). *Black Feminist Thought: Knowledge, Consciousness and the Politics of Empowerment.* Boston: Unwin Hyman.

Coontz, Stephanie (1992). *The Way We Never Were: American Families and the Nostalgia Trap.* New York: Basic Books.

—— (1997). *The Way We Really Are: Coming to Terms with America's Changing Families.* New York: Basic Books.

COTT, NANCY (2002). *Public Vows: A History of Marriage and the Nation.* Cambridge, Mass.: Harvard University Press.

EDGELL, PENNY (2005). *Religion and Family in a Changing Society,* Series on Cultural Sociology, ed. L. DiMaggio, M. Lamont, R. Wuthnow, and V. Zelizer. Princeton: Princeton University Press.

—— and DOCKA, DANIELLE (2007). "Beyond the Nuclear Family? Familism and Gender Ideology in Diverse Religious Communities". *Sociological Forum,* 22: 26–51.

FRIEDLAND, ROGER (2001). "Religious Nationalism and the Problem of Collective Representation". *Annual Review of Sociology,* 27: 125–52.

FURSTENBERG, FRANK (1999). "Family Change and Family Diversity". In S. A. Alexander, *Diversity and its Discontents: Cultural Conflict and Common Ground in Contemporary American Society.* Princeton: Princeton University Press, 147–66.

GALLAGHER, SALLY K. (2003). *Evangelical Identity and Gendered Family Life.* New Brunswick, NJ: Rutgers University Press.

GERSON, KATHLEEN (2002). "Moral Dilemas, Moral Strategies, and the Transformation of Gender: Lessons from Two Generations of Work and Family Change". *Gender and Society,* 16: 8–28.

GINSBURG, FAYE (1989). *Contested Lives: The Abortion Debate in an American Community.* Berkeley: University of California Press.

GLASS, JENNIFER, and JACOBS, JERRY A. (2005). "Childhood Religious Conservatism and Adult Attainment among Black and White Women". *Social Forces,* 84: 555–79.

HEATH, MELANIE (2003). "Soft-Boiled Masculinity: Renegotiating Gender and Racial Ideologies in the Promise Keepers Movement". *Gender & Society,* 17: 423–44.

HOUT, MICHAEL, and FISCHER, CLAUDE (2002). "Americans with 'No Religion': Why Their Numbers are Growing". *American Sociological Review,* 67: 165–90.

HULL, KATHLEEN (2006). *Same-Sex Marriage: The Cultural Politics of Love and Law.* New York: Cambridge University Press.

LAKOFF, GEORGE (1996). *Moral Politics: What Conservatives Know that Liberals Don't.* Chicago: University of Chicago Press.

MARLER, PENNY LONG, and HADAWAY, C. KIRK (2002). "'Being Religious' or 'Being Spiritual' in America: A Zero-Sum Proposition?" *Journal for the Scientific Study of Religion,* 41: 289–300.

MARTIN, PATRICIA YANCEY (2004). "Gender as Social Institution". *Social Forces,* 82: 1249–73.

MEYEROWITZ, JOANNE (1994). *Not June Cleaver: Women and Gender in Postwar America, 1945–1960.* Philadelphia: Temple University Press.

MYERS, SCOTT M. (1996). "An Interactive Model of Religious Inheritance: The Importance of Family Context". *American Sociological Review,* 61: 858–66.

PANKHURST, JERRY G., and HOUSEKNECHT, SHARON H. (eds.) (2000). *Family, Religion, and Social Change in Diverse Societies.* New York: Oxford University Press.

READ, JEN'NAN GHAZAL (2003). "The Sources of Gender Role Attitudes among Christian and Muslim Arab-American Women". *Sociology of Religion,* 64: 207–22.

ROOF, WADE CLARK, PATRICK, ANNE E., GRIMES, RONALD L., and LEONARD, BILL J. (1999). "Forum: American Spirituality". *Religion and American Culture,* 9: 131–57.

SHERKAT, DARREN, and ELLISON, CHRIS (1999). "Recent Developments and Current Controversies in the Sociology of Religion". *Annual Review of Sociology,* 25: 363–94.

SKOLNICK, ARLENE (1991). *Embattled Paradise: The American Family in the Age of Uncertainty.* New York: Basic Books.

TREAS, JUDITH (1999). "Diversity in American Families". In D. D.-M. Phyllis Moen and Henry A. Walker (eds.), *A Nation Divided: Diversity, Inequality, and Community in American Society.* Ithaca, NY: Cornell University Press, 245–59.

WILCOX, W. BRADFORD (2004). *Soft Patriarchs, New Men: How Christianity Shapes Fathers and Husbands.* Chicago: University of Chicago Press.

SUGGESTED READING

The following are recommended: Christiano (2000); Coontz (1992, 1997); Edgell (2005); Furstenberg (1999); Lakoff (1996); and Roof *et al.* (1999).

Table 35.1 Changes in families and households, United States 1950–2000

Household composition +	**1950**	**2000**
Percent (%) of all households comprised of married couples (with or without children)	78	53
Percent (%) of all households comprised of married couples with children under 18	43	25
Percent (%) of all households comprised of single-parent families	11	16
Percent (%) of all *family households*° comprised of single-parent families	8	23
Percent (%) of all households comprised of single adult, living alone	11	31
Family labor force participation*	**1970**	**2000**
Percent (%) of married mothers with children under 6 worked some time during the year	44	68
Percent (%) of married mothers with children under 6 who worked year round, full time	10	33
Percent (%) of families with children under 18 in which both parents had work experience	50	72
Percent (%) of families with children under 6 in which both parents had work experience	44	67
Percent (%) of families with children under 6 in which both parents worked year round, full time	7	28

Sources: + US Bureau of the Census, <http://www.census.gov/population/socdemo/hh-fam/htabHH-1.txt>, accessed 17 Feb. 2004, and <http://www.census.gov/population/socdemo/hh-fam/htabFM-1.txt>, accessed 18 Feb. 2004.

* Figures for 1970 taken from Howard V. Hayghe, and Susan M. Bianchi, "Married Mothers' Work Patterns", *Monthly Labor Review*, June 1994: 24–30. Figures for 2000 taken from <ftp.bls.gov/pub/news.release/History/famee.04192001.news>, accessed 17 Feb. 2004.

Note

° Defined as two or more related persons living together.

Table 35.2 Divorce statistics per 1,000 population

Year	Marriage rate	Divorce rate
1950	11.1	2.6
1970	10.6	3.5
1980	10.6	5.2
1990	9.8	4.7
2000	8.5	4.2

Source: <http://www.census.gov/prod/2004pubs/03statab/vitstat.pdf>

Table 35.3 Marriage, remarriage, and divorce statistics

Year	First marriage rate (per 1,000 women age 15 + yrs)	Remarriage rate (per 1,000 divorced/widowed women 15 + yrs)	Divorce rate (per 1,000 Married Women age 15 + yrs)
1960	87.5	32.7	9.2
1990	57.7	35.8	20.9

Source: Lynne M. Casper and Suzanne M. Bianchi, *Continuity and Change in the American Family*, Thousand Oaks, CA: Sage, p. 28, fig. 1.8, based on National Vital Statistics Reports, various years, produced by the National Center for Health Statistics.

CHAPTER 36

THE REPRODUCTION AND TRANSMISSION OF RELIGION

MATHEW GUEST

The Sociological Legacy

The processes associated with the reproduction and transmission of religion have been at the heart of sociology since its very beginnings. The evolutionist thought that arose in the nineteenth century fashioned narratives of human history that were linear and progressive, assumed to be common to all cultures. Religion was conceived of as an anthropological universal, a mode of thinking and engaging with the world characteristic of a particular stage in cultural development. The implication was, of course, that religion was a thing of the past and represented, at worst, a retarded state out of which humans—at least in the advanced West—had successfully evolved. These assumptions are embedded in Edward B. Tylor's (1871) theory of animism, as well as in James Frazer's famous magnum opus, *The Golden Bough* (1922), which portrayed all civilizations as progressing through developmental stages dominated by magic, religion, and science, each stage superseding the one preceding it. This is echoed in Auguste Comte's slightly earlier argument that all human thought has evolved through three stages: the theological, the metaphysical, and the positive, the latter breaking with earlier quests for origins and essences, and instead seeking laws which explain the correlation between different facts, established on the basis of observation and experiment (Swingewood 2000: 14–19). While this narrative of progress portrays traditional religion as outmoded and primitive, Comte nevertheless recognized the value of religion as a basis for social order. He combined his two key convictions in elevating sociology to the peak of scientific endeavour *and* as a new religion in itself, fulfilling the inbuilt human need to worship or revere something, as well as the collective need for order and social cohesion. In Comte's modernity, humanity is the new God, the focus of a rational, scientific religion for an enlightened people.

Within such models, an understanding of the reproduction and transmission of religion is shaped not so much by careful analysis of cultural forces *in situ*, but by an ideology of human progress. Narratives of human development that exalted Western models of rationality and science were projected on to distant cultures that were often well outside the experience, let alone the research, of their principal advocates. In these early ventures into the sociology of religion, religion was undertheorized and oversimplified, presented as a singular phenomenon with clear-cut boundaries and a preordained place in the history of human development. Its reproduction over time was discussed within the context of ritual, tradition, and institutional change, but the particular significance of these factors was subordinated to the assumptions of an evolutionary paradigm.

Émile Durkheim tackled issues of religious development with far greater subtlety than Tylor, Frazer, and Comte, but nevertheless argued that the ideas and values associated with traditional religion would, in a modern context, be overtaken by more rational, evidence-based, sociologically informed kinds of thinking. Indeed, Durkheim's vision for French education was instrumental in nurturing the laicization that became central to that nation's public identity, not least through his influence over school curricula and the consequent socialization of French school pupils into a secular world view (Lukes 1977). Durkheim's legacy is also important as it marks a shift in the conceptual contours of the sociology of religion, perpetuating evolutionary notions of modernity and progress, while introducing fresh insights into theory and method that shaped subsequent developments in the discipline, not least secularization theory. Indeed, the structural differentiation addressed in Durkheim's *The Division of Labour in Society* (1960) remains axiomatic within contemporary debates about the social significance of religion, demonstrating how the place of religious institutions within the fabric of society, the extent of their integration into wider structures, and their perceived function are all instrumental in determining their power to shape social norms and values. While some sociologists highlighted complicit ideological agendas associated with Marxism and humanism (Martin 1965), the secularization debate nevertheless dominated the sociology of religion throughout much of the twentieth century, thereby helping to perpetuate the linear, progress-oriented understanding of modernity embodied in the work of Comte and his contemporaries. In recent decades, the relative vitality of conservative, anti-modern religious movements—radical Islam and conservative Evangelicalism, for example—has highlighted the limitations of this Paradigm, characteristic of the liberal intellectuals who often dictate the sociological agenda, and has prompted calls for a more complex, dialectical understanding of religious development (Tamney 2002: 258–60).

Such dialectical subtlety is prefigured in the work of Peter Berger (1967; 1969), whose appropriation of insights from phenomenology, particularly the human quest for order and meaning, has engendered a discipline-wide interest in plausibility structures, those shifting social forces that render religious belief more or less meaningful among particular groups within particular cultural contexts. His work demands that we ask precisely how given social conditions relate to the plausibility of religious ideas, and how culturally embedded notions of truth, authority, and meaning affect the power of religious groups to recruit and successfully socialize new members into their existing world view. These questions have preoccupied James Davison Hunter, who has adopted a Bergerian approach to ascertain how effective Evangelical Christians are at reproducing their own value systems within a contemporary Western context. Hunter examines the changing attitudes of North American seminarians and argues that the forces of modernization—characterized by functional rationality, cultural pluralism, and structural pluralism—have penetrated the boundaries of Evangelical religion and initiated a liberalization of its values (Hunter 1983). A weakening of the boundaries of the Evangelical subculture has allowed the importation of notions of tolerance and the elevation of subjective experience popular in late modern American society. Hunter traces a shift away from an understanding of the Bible and Evangelical tradition as external, non-negotiable authorities. Instead, Evangelicals are becoming more tolerant of non-Christians, less rigid in their readings of the scriptures, and more open to possibilities of change within the Evangelical world view (Hunter 1987).

Similar theoretical concerns preoccupy Nancy Ammerman in her book *Bible Believers* (1987), which explores how Southern Baptist Christians in the United States maintain their 'deviant' belief system by defending it against influences from the wider culture. Both studies focus on how the maintenance of effective plausibility structures influences the capacity of religious groups to sustain themselves; how, within a secularizing context, they manage to transmit their values successfully to the next generation. Strategies vary, from attempts to control the socialization of future evangelical leaders, which is a chief focus of Hunter's work, to the development of shared understandings of cosmic order and meaning. For example, Ammerman's study includes a discussion of theodicy, which highlights how fundamentalist Christians make sense of their encounters with misfortune by appealing to a dualistic cosmology, in which Satan has a legitimate place as a persecutor of the righteous (Ammerman 1987: 64). Forces which are inimical to the shared beliefs of the group, such as the temptations of a libertarian lifestyle tantalizingly portrayed by the mass media, are reinterpreted in a way that actually reinforces the dualistic structures that underpin the group's world view: such temptations become proof of Satan's active attempts to undermine God's people. Deviant bodies of belief are successfully reproduced in so far as their advocates are able to negotiate encounters with secular culture in a way that convincingly instils an alternative perspective on the world, often achieved through a subtle control of public discourse alongside the maintenance of close-knit networks of believers.

Studies adopting the sociology of knowledge approach popularized by Peter Berger are frequently used to buttress arguments for secularization, as their tendency to assume a straightforward correlation between the integrity of institutional boundaries and the robustness of religious belief systems is easily translated into a pessimistic prognosis for the future of religion. The fragmentation of communities is a well-documented feature of modernity, and there is a strong sociological tradition going back to Ferdinand Tönnies (1955) and H. Richard Niebuhr (1962) that associates the loosening of traditional, tightly knit bonds of community with the dissipation of social, including religious, values. Religious groups themselves have been vulnerable to the same processes, as population dispersion, increased mobility, and the emergence of a network society (Castells 1998) have undermined the appeal of traditional religious communities based on locality and inherited tradition. As religious values are less firmly embedded in wider social norms, and religious groups lack strong collective structures through which to socialize potential new members, so it becomes increasingly difficult to perpetuate religious traditions successfully (Bruce 2002). Within this context, how can the reproduction of religious values be successfully achieved? Arguments for structural differentiation lead to the same question, and point to the weakening control of religious institutions over processes of education, welfare, and health care, a trend that has, according to many thinkers, engendered a privatization of religion, with the expression of religious ideas and values reserved for the personal or family realm, leaving only very limited space for religion in the public sphere (e.g., Bruce 1995; Wilson 1992).

However, the Bergerian approach has not been without its detractors, from those who question its inbuilt conception of religious identity, which stresses cognitive functions at the expense of more emotional, intuitive, or non-rational motivations, to those critics who call for more detailed analysis of the empirical relationships that shape social structural influences upon patterns of religious belief (Wuthnow *et al.* 1984: 71). Responding to this second problem, some illuminating work has drawn on Arnold Gehlen's concept of secondary institutions, especially as interpreted by Berger, Berger, and Kellner in their seminal work on the social construction of modernity, *The Homeless Mind: Modernization and Consciousness* (1974). Within this analysis, secondary institutions emphasize individual autonomy and interpersonal exchange, and hence offer opportunities for free expression in a world which prizes subjectivity, but are sufficiently institutionalized to provide guidance and structure, hence offering some refuge for what Berger *et al.* called 'homeless minds', and also opportunities for a successful reproduction of shared values (Heelas and Woodhead 2000: 46). In exploring whether secondary institutions are effective carriers of religious meaning, Heelas and Woodhead (2000) point to the phenomenon of the small group meeting, increasingly popular in Evangelical, charismatic, and Pentecostal churches, especially in the USA. Here, the expressive dynamics of the support or encounter group are put to work in the service of Bible study, prayer, and mutual sharing, effectively fostering lay leadership, open expression, and inter-subjectivity as the basis of Christian identity (Miller 1997). It is the latter feature that is the focus of concerns expressed by Robert Wuthnow, who views the tendency of small groups to attribute meaning and truth to statements made by members on the basis of their 'experience' as an invitation to heterodox theologies, a fear heightened by the fact that many of the small groups that Wuthnow analysed in the US context were not monitored by religious specialists like a trained priest (Wuthnow 1994). In so far as the small group movement embodies the subjectivization that is associated with charismatic Christianity and many forms of alternative spirituality, then its power as a secondary institution to reproduce religious meanings may be compromised.

However, other studies of the use of small-scale, alternative community structures by religious groups suggest that a successful perpetuation of core values may be possible. For example, the learnt behaviours associated with prayer and ritualized episodes of charismatic possession often reinforce existing hierarchies and the ideologies they embody, as has been shown within the UK-based house churches of the 1970s and 1980s (Walker 1989), and in Roman Catholic Pentecostal prayer groups (McGuire 1982), also echoing I. M. Lewis's (1986) anthropological work on witchcraft and spirit possession, which highlights how apparently non-rational episodes may serve as vehicles for the reinforcement of existing power relations. Within more self-consciously liberal or culturally accommodating religious communities, such as 'post-Evangelical' or 'post-church' collectives, particularly notable in the UK and Australasia, a common narrative of spiritual progression is infused into internally generated rituals that are typically experimental and practical. These effectively convey a sense of shared identity and shared history among groups that often shy away from liturgical consistency or ideological uniformity (Guest and Taylor 2006; Jamieson 2002).

Contemporary Challenges

More radical challenges to Berger's work have emerged from narratives of late modernity or postmodernity, which have emphasized institutional fragmentation and the breakdown of meta-narratives, drawing attention to 'the moral and ideological frameworks of modernity and their supercession by radical doubt, irony and transitoriness in post-modern conditions' (Beckford 2003: 187). Such accounts pose a challenge to the reproduction of religious values in two major ways. First, the sustainability of collective structures *per se* is called into question. Suspicion towards grand narratives and established authorities, so the story goes, reflects a weakening interest in community, so that individuals are motivated not by past loyalties or enduring affiliations, but by choices made according to personal preference. While most obviously evident in falling membership levels of political parties and trade unions, as well as churches, theorized by some as 'associational disconnection' (Percy 2004: 28), the effects of this shift are more profound. Hence Danielle Hervieu-Léger's (2000[1993]) work examines the phenomenon of 'cultural amnesia', which she sees as central to the transformations of religion in contemporary societies. Discussing the French case, she argues that the fragmentation of traditional institutions, most notably the breakdown of the extended family and connected rituals of parish life, has triggered a loss of collective memory among the population. Those institutions and practices that were once effective carriers of religious identities across generations have been compromised, so that a way of life based on inherited tradition has given way to a more consumer-oriented culture. This trend may be identified across Western Europe and beyond; as choice is elevated as sovereign, so more people, especially the young, are choosing to ignore the religiously infused traditions of the past and feel less obliged to instil their own children with a sense of their importance, preferring to raise them to make their own decisions. This trend is reflected in the findings of the European Values Survey which, in 1990, asked respondents to choose important qualities they felt children should be encouraged to learn in the family home. While 75 per cent—across all participating countries—chose 'tolerance and respect', only 25 per cent placed 'religious faith' in this category (Ashford and Timms 1992: 44, 63). It is against the background of these developments that sociological theorists have adopted the language of reflexive identity construction (Beck 1992; Giddens 1991), stressing individual agency and presenting values and convictions as things to be chosen, rather than inherited or nurtured within an institutional or family context.

This leads us to the second challenge, which concerns the orientation to religious phenomena that so-called postmodern changes foster in people. While some, following Anthony Giddens, have claimed that contemporary Western individualism is incompatible with a commitment to traditional—including religious—bodies of knowledge or values, others observe a change of relationship between religious traditions and the postmodern individuals who engage with them (Beckford 1989; Bauman 1998; Lyon 2000; Mellor 1993). Conceived by some authors as a 'new religious consciousness' (Cohen *et al.* 1984), the argument here is that postmodern changes have not only encouraged a more individualistic, self-driven, perhaps consumerist orientation to religion, but that religious groups have in turn adjusted their own activities to better cater to this more fickle, transient market. Arguments about the so-called pic-'n'-mix nature of New Age or alternative spiritualities are well rehearsed, but there is strong evidence that a comparable development has emerged among more traditional religious groups. For example, many Christian congregations in the UK and the USA promote themselves less as a focus of local identity or lifelong commitment, and more as a spiritual resource at the disposal of the itinerant or upwardly mobile individual, seeking heightened experience, interpersonal affirmation, or temporary fellowship (Coleman 2000; Flory and Miller 2000; Guest 2007*b*). It appears that some religious groups, responding to wider cultural changes, have adjusted their priorities so that the perpetuation of shared values is subsumed within a project that is more episodal, more short-term, and more easily digested by participants whose long-term commitment can no longer be taken for granted.

The underlying process here is the deregulation of religion, the breakdown of tradition and traditional modes of engagement conceived more positively as the freeing up of religious forces from the structures and constraints of the past (Lyon 2000). This phenomenon is not a uniquely postmodern development; indeed, many sociologists have noted the distinctive case of the USA, its First Amendment securing the separation of church and state and thereby establishing a free religious market which has fostered a grass-roots spiritual entrepreneurialism throughout the history of that nation (Hatch 1989). The lack of an established church effectively generated the conditions for a deregulated religious economy, in which religious pluralism was tolerated and religious affiliation accepted as a matter of personal choice (Finke 1990). Addressing the broader, global context, David Lyon places religious deregulation at the heart of the postmodern world, accelerated by the processes of globalization, the dynamics of late capitalism, and time-space compression associated with advanced technology and the growth of the Internet, all of which destabilize inherited traditions and conventional boundaries of identity (Lyon 2000). This constellation of factors has framed much of the current debate about the status of religious phenomena, and while some theorists continue to take the public dimension of religion seriously (e.g., Casanova 1994), the widespread popularity of postmodern narratives describing de-traditionalization, fragmentation, relativization, and multiple identities has emphasized the devolution of power to the individual seeker at the expense of the identity-defining power of collective structures. The diversification of religion in the West, together with the rise of fundamentalism, has exacerbated this imbalance, highlighting both the increasing impotence of established traditions and the power of individual commitment.

Yet institutions and collective structures continue to play an important role in the processes whereby religious identities are transmitted and reproduced. First, they frame wider cultural forces that shape the changing possibilities open to religious groups. Even a market model of contemporary religion needs to take account of processes of production as well as consumption, and the symbolic resources pertinent to the construction of religious identities are made available to individuals via their experience of more immediate interactive contexts, whether a local church or mosque, Wiccan network or web-based spiritualist discussion forum, each embodying wider social trends. Second, they serve as primary contexts in which the reproduction of religious values and identities is steered and managed. The most obvious examples here might be schools, families, and places of worship, institutional contexts that are often sites for the socialization of individuals into a set of moral and religious values, although more innovative analyses might point to new forms of collective identity, such as the 'bund' or 'neo-tribe', which represent attempts to use the resources of postmodernity in the construction of communities based around interest, protest, or enthusiasm (Bromley 1988; Maffesoli 1996). The World Wide Web creates new opportunities here, but novel forms of community have also emerged in less radical contexts, among friendship networks or informal post-church groups, for example (Jamieson 2002). The cultural transitions associated with Western modernization may have altered the form and influence of these collective structures, but they have not entirely undermined their capacity to shape identities and thereby influence processes of religious change. It will be instructive to look at some examples from recent research that illustrate this point.

McDonaldization and Religious Identity

In 1996, George Ritzer published his influential volume *The McDonaldization of Society*, offering a critical analysis of late twentieth-century Western culture in terms derived from the management model associated with the well-known fast food franchise. Picking up on Max Weber's arguments about the rationalization of social processes in the modern age, Ritzer highlights the standardization represented by McDonald's, and uses this to throw into question the assumption that a market-driven global economy ensures a diversity of products and endless consumer choice. What you get at McDonald's is the same the world over, in terms of both service and product. Moreover, the same kind of standardization, so Ritzer argues, can be found in the spheres of education, leisure, politics, health care, and work, in both private businesses and public services. What Ritzer identifies are economically driven policies of working practice that have filtered down into various other cultural contexts, in which they have become normative. He defines McDonaldization in terms of the fourfold model of calculability, efficiency, predictability, and control, key features of the well-honed McDonald's management system designed to maximize profit across a global market (Ritzer 1996).

In showing how 'free' global markets may engender uniformity, rather than variety, Ritzer also highlights how the identity politics of late modernity are constrained by structural factors. Globalization may generate new choices for consumers, but the range of choices on offer is predetermined by unseen economic forces and may actually frustrate, rather than empower, movements of cultural innovation. While it may seem odd to associate religion with McDonald's, the model that Ritzer describes has been wilfully adopted by a range of religious organizations, many of which have embraced McDonaldization as a convenient means of standardizing their processes of promotion and recruitment. Similar notions have filtered into popular understandings of religious identity, and John Drane has referred to the widespread desire for predictability in the spiritual journey (2000: 44), exemplified in the notion of 'stages of faith', and embodied in spiritual retreats and self-help books that reflect a yearning for structural coherence in an otherwise relatively unstable religious economy. In the process, religions are often 'packaged', their message reconfigured into a consumer product so as to be more readily accessible to the late modern individual. Not surprisingly, this trend has appealed most to missionizing groups, for the dynamics of global consumerism are well suited to their proselytizing ambitions. For example, Richard Bartholomew (2006) has studied the expansion of the evangelical publishing industry, arguing that conservative Protestant leaders consolidate their popular appeal, and thereby their evangelistic potential, by acquiring the status of brand names, used in the global marketing of their message.

The most striking example of the McDonaldization of religion is the Alpha Course, the ten-week introduction to Christianity that has been packaged, exported, and promoted with an efficiency that would be the envy of many private businesses. In 1991, there were four churches running Alpha courses; by 1999, the number quoted by its organizers was 11,430, based all over the world, in prisons and universities as well as in local churches. According to Peter Brierley, 'by the end of 2005, 2 million people in the UK and 8 million worldwide had attended an Alpha course' (2006: 229). Holy Trinity, Brompton (HTB), the famous charismatic Evangelical church in London that launched and has continued to be the administrative centre of Alpha, has overseen the development of the course and its carefully managed promotion through an entire industry of accompanying merchandise: books, videos, and CDs, sweatshirts and car-stickers. The Revd Nicky Gumbel's *Questions of Life*, on which the course is based, has now been translated into twenty-eight languages and has sold 500,000 copies (Hunt 2004: 14–15). Critics of Alpha argue that the course reduces Evangelism to a comfortable and predictable process, and in so doing risks trivializing Christian commitment (e.g., Ward 1998). Its carefully controlled presentation of Christianity is also accused of a heavy bias towards a particular form of charismatic Evangelicalism to the exclusion of other avenues of Christian faith, and HTB's application of the principles of calculability, predictability, efficiency, and control has meant that this agenda has been very difficult to challenge. Course materials are produced centrally, cover all possible media, and HTB has affirmed its willingness to invoke copyright law as a way of preventing local adaptations of the Alpha programme, thus pre-empting any grass-roots efforts to adjust its charismatic Evangelical message to reflect better the diversity across the churches.

Alpha's appropriation of fashionable management styles in the service of Christian Evangelism represents an effort to control the reproduction of religious identities in accordance with an Evangelical agenda. However, Stephen Hunt's UK-based research suggests that the course is relatively unsuccessful at securing long-term converts. In his survey of Alpha participants in England and Wales, he discovered that only 8 per cent were non-believers with no church experience; 16.3 per cent were agnostics with some experience of church life; while 74.4 per cent had some connection with the church running the course. Hunt also found that only one in six participants actually converted to Christianity (Hunt 2004: 171, 186). It would appear that, sociologically speaking, the processes of controlled production and delivery associated with McDonaldization need to be distinguished analytically from the engagement of individuals with the ideas and values embedded in those processes. Alpha is perhaps best seen as an attractive channel for the revitalization of Christian identity, rather than an effective means of transmitting religious ideas to the uninitiated. Issues of audience receptiveness are clearly important here, and participation and exposure do not, of course, equate to long-term, or even short-term, commitment. One way of exploring this problem further might appeal to lifestyle affinities. Alpha has often been criticized for presenting Christianity using typically middle-class styles of engagement—a shared meal, public talks, discussion groups—which are likely to alienate many working-class participants. While the destabilization of class identities in late modernity arguably demands a more complex analysis, an examination of how styles of presentation resonate with some social groups more than others reminds us of how the success with which religious ideas are transmitted relates to factors of wealth, occupational networks, or lifestyle. The selective appeal of web-based religion provides an obvious case study (Brasher 2001).

McDonaldization also highlights tendencies that feature in attempts to control expressions of religion in the public sphere. For example, one might point to recent efforts by the UK government to rein in processes of 'radicalization' among the Muslim population as part of an attempt to pre-empt acts of terrorism. A desire to engage with imams and exert influence over processes of teaching in local mosques, madrasahs, and state universities, including the accreditation of professional religious qualifications, reflects attempts by state powers to realign Islamic identity with a particular model of the faith organization, highlighting its function as a source of social cohesion. But while the politicians affirm integration and tolerance, many Muslim leaders fear the dilution of core principles of faith and the imposition of a secular liberal agenda. Here, the micro-management associated with the New Labour Government can be seen to embody some of the forces associated with McDonaldization, which are applied in a quest to delimit the moral-religious landscape and shape the reproduction of religious identities in accordance with its own policies (Birt 2006). Indeed, notions of standardization and control are implicit in government affirmations of religion, which emphasize co-operation, civic responsibility, and tradition, while de-legitimizing expressions of faith that significantly deviate from the 'liberal consensus' or that preach loyalty to minority causes over loyalty to Britain.

The Persistent Importance of the Family

If McDonaldization highlights how economic forces may be filtered through cultural institutions, and thereby shape the reproduction of religious identities, the family presents us with a primary context in which religious values are nurtured under the direction of intimates within the private sphere. While earlier research into secularization paid relatively little attention to the family as a key site for the reproduction of religious ideas, recent studies have reaffirmed its importance. For example, Voas and Crockett have appealed to British survey data in arguing that a child's upbringing has 'an enormous impact on their subsequent propensity to identify with a religion' (Voas and Crockett 2005: 19), further identifying the extent to which parents share religious convictions as crucial to their relative success in transmitting religious values to their children. Moreover, intermarriage—that is, marriage between individuals of different faiths—not only compromises the effective socialization of religion into the next generation; it also adversely affects the capacity of the partners themselves to sustain their original religious identities (Voas 2003). While such analyses illuminate general trends, they do not address the actual processes of value transmission operative within families;

this requires ethnographic observation at a more micro-level, although the comparatively closed nature of family life has often made empirical research both practically and ethically difficult.

In recent years, the work of historian Callum Brown has marked a welcome corrective to this imbalance, his influential book *The Death of Christian Britain* (2001) placing the family at the heart of the secularization process. Appealing to evidence in oral history records, Brown traces the process whereby British Christianity shifted from being 'overwhelmingly discursive' (2001: 195), emphasizing Evangelical themes of purity and virtue, which were conflated with popular notions of respectability, to being associated more with a deliberate commitment to regular churchgoing. He places the axis of this change in the 1960s, arguing that a radical change in the role of women was a key causal factor. For Brown, women had hitherto occupied the role of guardian of the family and its salvation, had maintained a Christian discourse, and had overseen the enforcement of its moral code. With the change in women's roles in the 1960s, triggered by the free availability of the contraceptive pill and changing perceptions of domestic proprieties, these structures were compromised. Children were henceforth no longer socialized as effectively into Christian mores and practices, and subsequent generations ceased to be as articulate in a Christian discourse (Brown 2001: 183). Christianity is transformed into a religion of choice, but suffers from no longer being as intimately enveloped within normal family life.

A rather different configuration of factors is presented in Christian Smith's recent study, *Soul Searching*, which reports on a large-scale empirical investigation into the religious lives of American teenagers. Smith interviewed teenagers with a variety of religious affiliations across the United States, using these conversations to explore the shape and source of their religious identities. His main finding was that most young people are confused and inarticulate about religion, thus raising the question of how effective conventional agents of religious socialization really are. If expressions of religious commitment are confused and unclear, then does this support the argument, advanced by some advocates of secularization, that institutions in the West are no longer capable of successfully transmitting religious values to the younger generations, either because the boundaries of religious traditions are no longer clearly defined or because of the emphasis placed on allowing young people lifestyle choices? Smith's research counts against this argument. He discovered that adults still exert a significant influence over the values of their teenaged children, claiming that the majority of American youths 'faithfully mirror the aspirations, lifestyles, practices, and problems of the adult world into which they are being socialized' and, in addition, seem 'basically content to follow the faith of their families with little questioning' (Smith 2005: 191, 120).

Smith's research raises several challenges pertinent to wider debates about the trajectories of religious development in the contemporary West. First, the fact that the young people he interviewed do not appear to construct their religious identities in rebellion against parents, institutions, or dominant authorities raises the possibility that such patterns do not characterize generational change within the modern period as a whole, but are particular to the cultural experiences of the baby boomers (Roof 1993). Second, Smith finds that very few young people had considered practising other faiths or related to the ideas associated with spiritual seekership (2005: 127–9). In this sense the argument for religious deregulation may be overstated, or at least needs to distinguish between the existence of a religious market and the propensity of such conditions to generate an eclectic or nomadic orientation to religious identity. It also throws into question the issue of choice, and invites further research into the conditions that provoke young people to challenge the ideas and values inherited from their parents. In this case, intergenerational continuity, rather than rebellion, appears to be the norm, not because choice was not held up as an important value, it was; however, most youths *chose* to remain in general conformity with the values of their parents. One might reflect on the role that the cultural conditions of contemporary North America have played in fostering this trend. Indeed, future research faces the intriguing question of how choice and dissent are related in Western democracies. Moreover, why do discourses of religious freedom and individualism so often mask an underlying social conservatism that engenders religious inertia rather than innovation or socio-political engagement?

Finally, the inarticulacy of American youth when it comes to religion is worthy of further note. Smith finds that the vast majority of those he interviewed 'simply could not express themselves on matters of God, faith, religion, or spiritual life' (2005: 133). It appears that parents were successful in transmitting a sense of the significance and authenticity of their religious tradition, but were less so in communicating the precise meaning of its various core doctrines and practices. Instead, young people tended to affirm a more generic set of priorities that Smith summarizes as 'Moralistic Therapeutic Deism', based on (i) the importance of being a good person, pleasant and respectful; (ii) religion conceived as a source of subjective well-being; and (iii) belief in a God who is distant, aside from when he is called upon to help those in need (2005: 162–71). Hence, while Smith's work supports the contention that the family continues to be an important site for the formation of religious identity in the USA, it also highlights the presence of more diffuse constellations of ideas, which are perhaps reflective of a dominant discourse—characterized by a 'soft' individualism—prevalent across the wider culture. Again, macro-level social structural forces influence the reproduction of religious identities in a way that generates patterns closer to standardization than postmodern diversity. Most strikingly, Smith's study highlights how the subjective individualism argued by some to be at the heart of dominant forms of contemporary religion (e.g., Heelas and Woodhead 2005), may engender not creativity and diversity, but stasis and perhaps social conservatism.

Conclusion: The Reproduction and Transmission of Religious Capital

The examples above highlight the limitations of an approach that places too much emphasis on the power of the individual to shape his or her own religious identity, and suggest the need to take institutional factors more seriously. Yet they also highlight a need to move beyond the functionalist approaches of the past (Parsons 1951), the late modern context demanding a more complex theorization of religious identity formation and its relationship to wider social forces. Significant potential may be found in an approach based on a resource mobilization perspective; specifically, a capital-centred perspective, building on the work of Pierre Bourdieu, offers a fruitful approach to understanding the reproduction of religious identities in the contemporary world, and I offer an account of this as a concluding proposal. This approach focuses on the resources associated with religion: their generation, evolution, transmission, and rejection, hence taking account of dynamic processes of reproduction in a way that moves beyond institutions and individual agents. It takes seriously the processes whereby individuals are empowered by religious resources, while framing those resources in relation to the broader social structural conditions that shape their status and distribution. In this sense, it can cope with the heightened sense of agency associated with postmodernity, but insist on a theorization of a broader social field that both facilitates and limits that agency in ways that shape the process whereby religious identities are formed and religious resources reproduced. In proceeding from a metaphor of exchange and circulation, capital theory is especially suited to a deregulated religious landscape, in which religion has become decentred, adrift from its former points of anchorage (Beckford 1989), and available for deployment and reconfiguration in more novel ways.

Ultimately, of course, the theorization of resources as capital derives from the work of Karl Marx, although various developments—for example, human capital, social capital, cultural capital—have emerged in the work of Gary Becker, James Coleman, and Robert Putnam, among others. Some sociologists have applied these theories to the analysis of religious phenomena, as with attempts by Iannacone (1990) and Neuman (1986) to apply Becker's concept of 'human capital' in understanding trends in religious practice, and Andrew Greeley's (1997) application of James Coleman's (1988) work, which analyses religious structures as a source of social capital. Others have sought to acknowledge the peculiar characteristics of religion as a resource by developing a separate theory of religious or spiritual capital, and Pierre Bourdieu has been the most creative thinker within this category. In his articles on religion, Bourdieu is heavily indebted to Max Weber, particularly in adopting an essentially economic model of religious practice (Weber 1978; Bourdieu 1987; 1991).

In keeping with his general theory of capital as a scarce resource within a given social field, Bourdieu identifies the 'resources' at stake in the 'religious field'. These are 'the legitimation of the social order, the sanction of wealth and power, and the sense of meaning that religion brings to people's lives' (Rey 2004: 337). In this sense, networks of power often occupy overlapping social fields, so that a position of dominance in the world of finance, for example, may draw in part from symbolic capital accumulated in the fields of culture or religion. This insight reflects Bourdieu's concern that religious specialists appeal to relations of power in non-religious spheres in order to consolidate their position, just as secular powers appeal to religious language and associations in justifying their own.

While Bourdieu's theory is shaped by a rather heavy-handed Marxism, and owes much to the context of French Roman Catholicism, including a suspicion of the power invested in its priesthood, it has been appropriated and developed in recent studies to great effect. Terry Rey (2004) has adopted Bourdieu's conflict model to illuminate tensions in Haiti, between the Roman Catholic hierarchy and popular voodoo priests. Both parties are locked in a struggle over religious capital, particularly what Bourdieu calls the 'goods of salvation': that is, sacraments, membership of a religious community, and any other condition deemed necessary for salvation. Their attempts to clearly distinguish Roman Catholicism from voodoo represent an effort to control the religious field and vie for the allegiance of a poor lay audience who see the two traditions as intertwined. The transmission of religion is shaped by a continual quest for cultural dominance, and the resources at stake represent distinctive forms of power defined by the social field in which they are operative.

In an attempt to extend the interpretative reach of Bourdieu's theory so as to reflect the complexities of deregulation characteristic of advanced Western cultures, American sociologist Bradford Verter develops the more malleable notion of 'spiritual capital'. Within such contexts, sources of spiritual significance are not restricted by the boundaries of traditional religious hierarchies, as Bourdieu's original argument might suggest, but are more freely available within a complex matrix of exchange (Guest 2007*a*). Verter argues that Bourdieu's categories are 'too rigid to account for the fluidities of today's spiritual marketplace', preferring to speak of 'spiritual capital', 'a more widely diffused commodity, governed by more complex patterns of production, distribution, exchange, and consumption' (Verter 2003: 151, 158). Moreover, critiquing the work of rational choice theorists like Rodney Stark and Roger Finke, who conceive of 'spiritual capital' as a free-floating commodity in an open market of exchange (Stark and Finke 2000), Verter is faithful to Bourdieu's analysis of social power. For Verter, competitors for spiritual capital do not enjoy equal advantages; nor do they accumulate spiritual capital purely on the basis of individual effort. Rather, individuals occupy positions of relative strength or weakness, depending on the capital they possess, and on their relationship to the processes that shape the distribution of that capital. In other words, the relative distribution of spiritual capital is shaped by wider structures of power, highlighting how that capital is fluid and transferable between fields (Swartz 1996: 78).

Verter's development of Bourdieu's theory presents attractive possibilities for the analysis of the reproduction of religious identities. It preserves an account of individual agency, while taking seriously how resources pertinent to religion have become more fluid in late modernity, yet remain caught up in wider structures of power. In this respect it moves beyond a simplistic market model and avoids the problematic instrumentalism of rational choice theory, which presents individuals as driven by calculated self-interest to the exclusion of more altruistic or collective goals. In a study of clergy families co-written by the author, the concept of spiritual capital was used to illuminate processes of value transmission across generations (Davies and Guest 2007). Moving beyond stereotypical images of child conformity and rebellion, we found that the children of senior Anglican clergy in England inherited a fluid spiritual capital which had its origins in their experiences of being raised in a vicarage, but which was deployed in adult life in the service of broader projects of identity construction. Recalled moral exemplars were used to explain current orientations to professional life; a deep-seated sense of moral duty and sacrifice shaped decisions to pursue public service jobs or engage in civic responsibilities; post-sermon family discussions fostered an awareness of religious and moral issues and a confidence in one's own point of view. However, what is externally viewed as spiritual capital can also be experienced as negative, so that a familiarity with priests at an early age can undermine any sense that they embody a spiritual purity. Similarly having a father who is a bishop can diminish one's own sense of religious identity, as outsiders may often measure the child by lofty moral and theological standards.

Three insights emerge from this application, pertinent to wider sociological debates about the reproduction of religion. First, in tracing the processes whereby spiritual capital is acquired, developed, transformed, and transmitted, we arrive at a clearer understanding of the processes of identity construction, both across and between generations. Second, our study highlights how spiritual capital may be applied in a complex analysis of religious leadership, incorporating notions of power that move beyond individual agency and position, and extend to broader networks. Third, our identification of spiritual capital as a resource deployed in the service not merely of personal advancement, but of community building and altruistic expression, highlights possibilities for further critiques of rational choice theory, which preserve a critical understanding of power, while allowing for the coexistence of an emerging social fabric which has the same roots. In other words, the reproduction of religious identities within late modernity may be reconceived so as to address socio-religious power as a potentially constructive, as well as potentially fragmentary, phenomenon. One challenge of future sociological research will be responsibly to disentangle the two.

References

Ammerman, Nancy T. (1987). *Bible Believers: Fundamentalists in the Modern World.* New Brunswick, NJ, and London: Rutgers University Press.

Ashford, Sheena, and Timms, Noel (1992). *What Europe Thinks: A Study of Western European Values.* Aldershot: Dartmouth.

Bartholomew, Richard (2006). 'Publishing, Celebrity and the Globalisation of Conservative Protestantism'. *Journal of Contemporary Religion*, 21/1: 1–13.

Bauman, Zigmunt (1998). 'Postmodern Religion?'. In Paul Heelas (ed.), *Religion, Modernity and Postmodernity.* Oxford and Malden, Mass.: Blackwell, 55–78.

Beck, Ulrich (1992). *Risk Society: Towards a New Modernity.* London: Sage.

Beckford, James A. (1989). *Religion and Advanced Industrial Society.* London: Unwin Hyman.

—— (2003). *Social Theory and Religion.* Cambridge: Cambridge University Press.

Berger, Peter L. (1967). *The Sacred Canopy: Elements of a Sociological Theory of Religion.* Garden City, NY: Doubleday & Company, Inc.

—— (1969). *A Rumour of Angels: Modern Society and the Rediscovery of The Supernatural.* London: Penguin.

—— Berger, Brigitte, and Kellner, Hansfried (1974). *The Homeless Mind: Modernization and Consciousness.* New York: Vintage Books.

Birt, Jonathan (2006). 'Good Imam, Bad Imam: Civic Religion and National Integration in Britain post-9/11'. *The Muslim World*, 96: 687–705.

Bourdieu, Pierre (1987). 'Legitimation and Structured Interests in Weber's Sociology of Religion'. In S. Lash and S. Whimster (eds.), *Max Weber, Rationality and Modernity.* London: Allen & Unwin, 119–36.

—— (1991). 'Genesis and Structure of the Religious Field'. *Comparative Social Research*, 13: 1–44.

Brasher, Brenda (2001). *Give Me That Online Religion.* San Francisco: Jossey-Bass.

Brierley, Peter (2006). *Pulling Out of the Nosedive: A Contemporary Picture of Churchgoing: What the 2005 English Church Census Reveals.* London: Christian Research.

Bromley, D. G. (1988). 'Understanding the Structure of Covenantal and Contractual Social Relations: Implications for the Sociology of Religion'. *Sociological Analysis*, 49: 15–32.

Brown, Callum G. (2001). *The Death of Christian Britain.* London and New York: Routledge.

Bruce, Steve (1995). *Religion in Modern Britain.* Oxford: Oxford University Press.

—— (2002). *God is Dead: Secularization in the West.* Oxford: Blackwell.

Casanova, José (1994). *Public Religions in the Modern World.* Chicago and London: University of Chicago Press.

Castells, Manuel (1998). *The Information Age: Economy, Society And Culture*, iii. *End of Millennium.* Malden, Mass. and Oxford: Blackwell.

Cohen, E., Ben-Yehuda, N., and Aviad, J. (1984). 'Recentring the World: The Quest for "Elective" Centers in a Secularized Universe'. *Sociological Review*, 35/1: 320–46.

Coleman, James (1988). 'Social Capital in the Creation of Human Capital'. *American Journal of Sociology*, 94: 95–120.

Coleman, Simon (2000). *The Globalisation of Charismatic Christianity: Spreading the Gospel of Prosperity.* Cambridge: Cambridge University Press.

Davies, Douglas, and Guest, Mathew (2007). *Bishops, Wives and Children: Spiritual Capital across the Generations*. Aldershot: Ashgate.

Drane, John (2000). *The McDonaldization of the Church: Spirituality, Creativity, and the Future of the Church*. London: Darton, Longman and Todd.

Durkheim, Émile (1960). *The Division of Labour in Society*. Glencoe, Ill.: Free Press.

Finke, Roger (1990). 'Religious Deregulation: Origins and Consequences'. *Journal of Church and State*, 32/3: 609–26.

Flory, Richard W., and Miller, Donald E. (eds.) (2000). *GenX Religion*. New York and London: Routledge.

Frazer, J. G. (1995 [1922]). *The Golden Bough: A Study in Magic and Religion*. London and Basingstoke: Papermac.

Giddens, Anthony (1991). *Modernity and Self-Identity: Self and Society in the Late Modern Age*. Cambridge: Polity.

Greeley, Andrew (1997). 'Coleman Revisited: Religious Structures as a Source of Social Capital'. *American Behavioral Scientist*, 40/5: 587–94.

Guest, Mathew (2007*a*). 'In Search of Spiritual Capital: The Spiritual as a Cultural Resource'. In K. Flanagan and P. Jupp (eds.), *A Sociology of Spirituality*. Aldershot: Ashgate, 181–200.

—— (2007*b*). 'Reconceiving the Congregation as a Source of Authenticity'. In J. Garnett *et al.* (eds.), *Redefining Christian Britain: Post-1945 Perspectives*. London: SCM, 63–72.

—— and Taylor, Steve (2006). 'The Post-Evangelical Emerging Church: Innovations in New Zealand and the UK'. *International Journal for the Study of the Christian Church*, 6/1: 49–64.

Hatch, Nathan (1989). *The Democratization of American Christianity*. New Haven: Yale University Press.

Heelas, Paul, and Woodhead, Linda (2000). 'Homeless Minds Today?' In Linda Woodhead (ed.), *Peter Berger and the Study of Religion*. London and New York: Routledge, 43–72.

—— —— (2005). *The Spiritual Revolution: Why Religion is Giving Way to Spirituality*. Oxford: Blackwell.

Hervieu-Léger, D. (2000[1993]). *Religion as a Chain of Memory*, trans. Simon Lee. Cambridge: Polity.

Hunt, Stephen (2004). *The Alpha Enterprise: Evangelism in a Post-Christian Era*. Aldershot: Ashgate.

Hunter, James D. (1983). *American Evangelicalism: Conservative Religion and the Quandary of Modernity*. New Brunswick, NJ: Rutgers University Press.

—— (1987). *Evangelicalism: The Coming Generation*. Chicago and London: University of Chicago Press.

Iannacone, L. (1990). 'Religious Practice: A Human Capital Approach'. *Journal for the Scientific Study of Religion*, 29/3: 297–314.

Jamieson, Alan (2002). *A Churchless Faith: Faith Journeys beyond the Churches*. London: SPCK.

Lewis, I. M. (1986). *Religion in Context: Cults and Charisma*. Cambridge: Cambridge University Press.

Lukes, Steven (1977). *Emile Durkheim, His Life and Work: A Historical and Critical Study*. Harmondsworth: Penguin.

Lyon, David (2000). *Jesus in Disneyland: Religion in Postmodern Times*. Cambridge: Polity.

MAFFESOLI, MICHEL (1996). *The Time of the Tribes: The Decline of Individualism in Mass Society.* London: Sage.

MARTIN, DAVID (1965). 'Towards Eliminating the Concept of Secularization'. In Julius Gould (ed.), *Penguin Survey of the Social Sciences 1965.* Harmondsworth: Penguin, 169–82.

MCGUIRE, MEREDITH (1982). *Pentecostal Catholics: Power, Charisma, and Order in a Religious Movement.* Philadelphia: Temple University Press.

MELLOR, PHILIP A. (1993). 'Reflexive Traditions: Anthony Giddens, High Modernity, and the Contours of Contemporary Religiosity'. *Religious Studies,* 29: 111–27.

MILLER, DONALD E. (1997). *Reinventing American Protestantism: Christianity in the New Millennium.* Berkeley and Los Angeles: University of California Press.

NEUMAN, S. (1986). 'Religious Observance within a Human Capital Framework: Theory and Application'. *Applied Economics,* 18: 1193–1202.

NIEBUHR, H. RICHARD (1962). *The Social Sources of Denominationalism.* New York: Meridian.

PARSONS, TALCOTT (1951). *The Social System.* New York: Free Press.

PERCY, MARTYN (2004). 'Losing Our Space, Finding Our Place? The Changing Identity of the English Parish Church'. In S. Coleman and P. Collins (eds.), *Religion, Identity and Change: Perspectives on Global Transformations.* Aldershot: Ashgate, 26–41.

REY, T. (2004). 'Marketing the Goods of Salvation: Bourdieu on Religion'. *Religion,* 34/4: 331–43.

RITZER, GEORGE (1996). *The McDonaldization of Society: An Investigation into the Changing Character of Contemporary Social Life.* Thousand Oaks, Calif.: Pine Forge Press.

ROOF, WADE CLARK (1993). *A Generation of Seekers: The Spiritual Journeys of the Baby Boom Generation.* New York: HarperCollins.

SMITH, CHRISTIAN (2005). *Soul Searching: The Religious and Spiritual Lives of American Teenagers.* Oxford: Oxford University Press.

STARK, RODNEY, and FINKE, ROGER (2000). *Acts of Faith: Explaining the Human Side of Religion.* Berkeley: University of California Press.

SWARTZ, D. (1996). 'Bridging the Study of Culture and Religion: Pierre Bourdieu's Political Economy of Symbolic Power'. *Sociology of Religion,* 57/1: 71–85.

SWINGEWOOD, ALAN (2000). *A Short History of Sociological Thought,* 3rd edn. Basingstoke and London: Macmillan.

TAMNEY, JOSEPH B. (2002). *The Resilience of Conservative Religion: The Case of Popular, Conservative Protestant Congregations.* Cambridge: Cambridge University Press.

TÖNNIES, FERDINAND (1955). *Community and Association (Gemeinschaft und Gesellschaft),* trans. and supplemented by Charles P. Loomis. London: Routledge & Kegan Paul Ltd.

TYLOR, EDWARD B. (1903 [1871]). *Primitive Culture.* London: Murray.

VERTER, B. (2003). 'Spiritual Capital: Theorizing Religion with Bourdieu against Bourdieu'. *Sociological Theory,* 21/2: 150–74.

VOAS, DAVID (2003). 'Intermarriage and the Demography of Secularization'. *British Journal of Sociology,* 54/1: 83–108.

—— and CROCKETT, ALISTAIR (2005). 'Religion in Britain: Neither Believing Nor Belonging'. *Sociology,* 39/1: 11–28.

WALKER, ANDREW (1989). *Restoring the Kingdom: The Radical Christianity of the House Church Movement,* 2nd edn. London: Hodder & Stoughton.

WARD, PETE (1998). 'Alpha: The McDonaldization of Religion?' *Anvil,* 15/4: 279–86.

Weber, Max (1978). *Economy and Society.* Berkeley: University of California Press.
Wilson, Bryan R. (1992). 'Reflections on a Many-Sided Controversy'. In S. Bruce (ed.), *Religion and Modernization.* Oxford: Clarendon Press, 195–210.
Wuthnow, Robert (1994). *Sharing the Journey: Support Groups and America's New Quest for Community.* New York, London, Toronto, Sydney, Singapore: The Free Press.
—— *et al.* (1984). *Cultural Analysis: The Work of Peter L. Berger, Mary Douglas, Michel Foucault and Jürgen Habermas.* London, Boston, Melbourne, and Henley: Routledge & Kegan Paul.

Suggested Reading

The following are recommended: Berger (1967); Bourdieu (1987); Brown (2001); Davies and Guest (2007); Smith (2005); and Verter (2003).

CHAPTER 37

RELIGION AND RITUAL: A MULTI-PERSPECTIVAL APPROACH

PETER COLLINS

Preliminaries

The term 'ritual' has been used in various circumstances to describe an extraordinarily wide variety of behaviour, from a Catholic Mass to the chanting of Buddhist monks in the Himalayas, from the apparently cacophonous chaos of Prime Minister's question time in the British House of Commons to the pairing ceremonies of the great crested grebe. The term is used to describe coronations and tea drinking, the initiation of children into adult society, and may describe actions understood as either religious or secular, or both. 'Ritual' can describe certain activities carried out in the workplace by, for example, nurses and sportsmen/women, and the organization of education in schools, pilgrimage, and holidays. And 'ritual' can be public or private. Is there a single property that unites the members of this multifarious category?

The one thing of which we can be certain is that the question 'What is "ritual"?' has kept scholars busy for more than 200 years (Goody 1961; 1977). The short answer is: almost anything you want it to be. It is presented as both process and product, effected by both individual and society. 'Ritual' is so promiscuous in its relation to meaning that I feel compelled to enclose it in scare quotes: 'ritual'. Although this practice might irritate and even annoy some readers, it is a necessary precaution, making explicit, as it does, the danger of assuming a common meaning for what is an extraordinarily slippery term. By 'ritual' I mean all of those references to the term in any context (here or there, now or then, academic or lay, in speech, print, or any other medium).

An early reference of 'ritual', though little used today, was to the book or manual, particularly that relating to Christian liturgy and containing special services for occasional use, such as baptisms, marriages, and visiting the sick. However, 'ritual' is generally conceived in both lay and scholarly discourse as certain kinds of action, as opposed to mental process (such as belief); 'ritual' is communicative, customary, prescribed, playful, stereotypic, secretive, involving the manipulation of objects, formalized, regular; as well as specific acts such as recitation, singing, group processions, dance, sacrifice, and initiation, manipulative of sacred objects; it can be predetermined, meaningless, meaningful, ordered, patterned, sequential, symbolic, and traditional. There is a second group of connotations relating to the desired effects of 'ritual', most obviously connected to magical practices and witchcraft, but also referring to union with a supernatural being or sphere, controlling unpredictable events (such as the weather), actions which open and close meetings, thanking supernatural beings for their help. Such effects might or might not be understood by participants. In psychiatry, 'ritual' is generally used to describe behaviour performed compulsively to relieve anxiety (as, for example, in obsessive–compulsive disorder).

The foregoing strongly suggests that there is no essential property that binds together all of these social phenomena we call 'ritual'—except perhaps their classification as 'ritual' by either observers or participants. An essentialist definition is not necessarily 'wrong', but it is likely to be misleading in its assumption that 'ritual' is characterized by some quality that is ineluctably a part of it, always and everywhere. I will therefore eschew the opportunity to attempt yet another definition of 'ritual' but will, instead, adopt the Wittgensteinian strategy and suggest that 'rituals' share a 'family resemblance' (Wittgenstein 1958). This strategy implies that one might think of any event or action as 'more or less "ritual"', though it may be safer in the long run to abandon the term altogether. So, what did Wittgenstein mean by 'family resemblance' and how might the idea be useful to those wishing to talk about 'ritual'? He asks us, in the *Philosophical Investigations* (§ 66), to consider the enormous variety of 'games':

> What is common to them all? Don't say: 'There must be something common, or they would not be called "games"—but look and see whether there is anything common to all. For if you look at them you will not see something that is common to all, but similarities, relationships, and a whole series of them at that.

Wittgenstein is insistent that the search for the essence of social phenomena is pointless. In relation to games or language or 'ritual', what we actually see, when we bother to stop and look, is a series of 'similarities' and 'relationships'. The point is that different 'rituals' will share some characteristics but not others: there is no single property shared by all. However, 'rituals', like 'games', can be said to share a family resemblance. Perhaps the greatest error that scholars of 'ritual' make is to assume that 'it' has a universal essence, which is then used as the foundation for a general theory.

Theories of 'ritual' have focused primarily on causes and effects, structure, and/or ontology, or on some combination of these. I will review most of the more influential theories of 'ritual'. I will, where appropriate, review these theories with reference to a particular case: the British Quaker meeting for worship. I present this particular case for several reasons. First, it is the 'ritual' with which I am most familiar. Second, it would be considered by most 'ritual' theorists as a very simple 'ritual', suggesting that the elements of 'ritual' will be more obviously apparent; it is sometimes characterized by participants as 'not-ritual', as ontologically continuous with the rest of life, and so spotlights the tension between accounts provided by participants and those by scholars. And finally, here is an opportunity to focus on a contemporary Christian 'ritual', a form that has received relatively little attention from either sociologists or anthropologists. In this instance, instead of the theory remaining constant as the ethnographic cases vary, I will hold the ethnographic case constant and vary the theory.

Liminaries I: 'Ritual' Function

'Ritual' theory has in most cases assumed that 'ritual' has a function and that it is possible to reveal this function. Victorian scholars (Frazer 1890; Robertson-Smith 1889; Tylor 1871; Marrett 1914; Müller 1967[1861]) concerned primarily with 'origins'—the origin of the world, of the human race, and similarly the origin of religion—sought to explain 'ritual' in terms of either evolution or diffusion. They became embroiled in speculative and futile 'chicken-and-egg' arguments. However, such ideas were influential in posing questions which succeeding generations of scholars have continued to puzzle over, including that relating to the relative importance of 'ritual' (action) and belief (thought). For instance, Dandelion (1996) suggests that Quakerism has come to be more about orthopraxy than orthodoxy, since the mid-twentieth century. Furthermore, these early debates prompted the collection of vast quantities of examples, thereby massively increasing the amount of data available for analysis, and eventually prompted a new means of data collection: ethnography.

The majority of accounts of 'ritual' attempt to understand their cause and effect—their function. In the first place, the contemporary form of any 'ritual' is partly a result of its historical trajectory, and Quaker 'ritual' is difficult to comprehend without knowing something of the history of the movement. Men and women, disillusioned with the system of belief and practice of the state church, formed a movement that soon became known as Quakerism during the social, political, and religious turmoil of mid-seventeenth-century England. There was, from the first, a priesthood of all believers, and Quakers in meeting were not distinguished hierarchically. Quakers refused to pay tithes (church taxes) or fines for withholding such payments, to attend church (remember that church attendance was mandatory at this time), to swear oaths of allegiance (or any oath), or to accept the everyday 'rituals' of polite society. Quakers refused, on meeting superiors, to raise their hat, to bow and scrape, and addressed those same superiors as 'thee' and 'thou'—eschewing the polite form, 'you'. This levelling tendency tacitly questioned the hierarchy in society, and until 1700 Quakerism posed not only a religious but a political challenge to the state. The core 'ritual', meeting for worship, involved sitting together in silence, waiting for God (or Christ) to speak through one of those present, and was from the beginning a levelling affair. Both women and men were encouraged to minister (speak). A Marxist commentator might argue that here is another case where threats to those in authority are diffused through the mechanism of religious 'ritual'. Quaker 'ritual' can then be understood as the mute response by one religious group to its own powerlessness in the face of state oppression, *or* as a significant act of resistance by ordinary people to authority. The movement gained a foothold in North America before 1700, primarily because of the large numbers of Quakers who migrated to America, pulled by the availability of large tracts of cheap land and pushed by the persecution they faced at home. While the 'ritual' of Quaker worship remained homogeneous in Britain, it has taken a variety of forms in America, from the unprogrammed form maintained in England to a programmed form of worship facilitated by a paid pastor.

In the nineteenth and early twentieth centuries, American Quaker evangelists from the programmed tradition oversaw the establishment of religion in East Africa, and particularly in Kenya. Kenyan Quaker worship is programmed, but more obviously influenced by vernacular Pentecostalism; a professional pastor conducts proceedings, which include hymns, confessions, public prayer, and sermons. I have heard British Friends (Quakers) question whether Kenyan Quakerism is really Quakerism. 'Ritual' can be mutable, in terms of both time and place, but the outcome of this mutability is likely to cause tensions between traditions. This much we can learn from history.

An important debate in 'ritual' studies revolves around the relative importance of cause and effect, of belief and emotion. Marrett (1914) criticized what he supposed to be the 'intellectualism' of Frazer (1890) and Tylor (1871), argued that 'rituals' performed by early peoples derived from, and gave rise to, emotional states rather than from belief. Ritual was primarily a matter of stepping out of the rational and into the expressive. In recent years John Beattie has made much the same point (1966; 1970), whereas the Tylorean position has been restated by Robin Horton (1968; 1970), who argues that 'ritual' is an attempt to provide rational explanations for confusing natural and social phenomena. If we look at Quaker 'ritual' in the light of this debate, there seems to be some value in each position, enough to doubt the usefulness of the dichotomy. While demonstrations of emotion are rare during meeting for worship (at least in comparison with many 'rituals'), Quakers do sometimes laugh and cry and confirm, when asked, that worship has an expressive quality. Quakers describe a range of emotions stimulated by participating in meeting, including, joy, anger, frustration, and sadness. But it is no less the case that Quaker 'ritual' reflects, and is also constitutive of, a cosmology. The space (meeting room) in which the 'ritual' takes place is empty of religious symbolism—there are no crosses, representations of saints, baptismal fonts, and so on. The chairs on which participants sit are arranged in a circle around a table on which are placed the Bible, copies of *Quaker Faith and Practice* (a semi-canonical text), and usually a vase of flowers: the participants' gaze is inward, not priestward. Outward manifestations of the religious are redundant, since there is 'that of God in everyone': God is immanent. The seating arrangement confirms the non-hierarchical nature of this community. Finally, the windows tend to be large and suggest a continuity, rather than a boundary: Quakers typically believe that the sacred and the profane are one.

As well as 'expressive', 'ritual' has been characterized by several influential scholars as performative (Beattie 1966; 1970; Turner 1974; 1982; 1984; Barth 1975; Tambiah 1985; Schieffelin 1985; Schechner 1993). Tambiah builds his theory of 'ritual' as performance from a few lines of Radcliffe-Brown's only ethnographic study, *The Andaman Islanders* (1964[1922]) referring somewhat obliquely to dance, and particular to its rhythmic nature, which enables people to join together in doing what is manifestly the same thing. Both as expression and as performance, 'ritual' is primarily communicative. Mediated by symbols, 'ritual' communicates its message to both individual participants and significant others, as well as to the group. Characterized in this way, 'ritual' implies a certain playfulness, suggesting a cathartic function. Huizinga (1964; see also Handelman 1999) has argued that play is a crucial part of human life and is likely to be a component of most 'ritual', and Mikhail Bakhtin (1984) suggests as much in his brilliant study of carnival. It is likely that the majority of Quakers would be perplexed by the idea that their core 'ritual' is not only performative but playful. However, while this characterization does not suffice as an interpretation of what goes on in meeting for worship, it is a necessary component. There is sometimes verbal play both within a single spoken ministry and between such ministries. Although play should not be confused with humour, there may also be humour in spoken ministry.

Perhaps the most commonly held reason for meeting for worship among Quakers is the development of 'community'. Quakers meet in a circle, remember, and all participants remain in view of all other participants throughout the 'ritual'. The drive to build community is underlined by the expectation that participants will be available to meet and talk (more or less informally during the time before and after meeting on a Sunday morning). Those who are late or who need to leave early generally excuse themselves with an explanation or apology. Robertson-Smith pointed to the importance of *ritual* for the generation of social cohesion. However, it was Émile Durkheim (1915), 'father of functionalism', who famously defined religious faith and practice firmly in terms of the social: religious 'ritual' is a social fact, which escapes explanation in terms of individual psychology. Primitive people came together, and during moments of communally heightened emotional intensity or effervescence projected that sense of communality on to supernatural beings, thus creating a separate world, which mirrored their own. Religion is a set of ideas and practices by which people sacralize the social structure and bonds of community—whether they are aware of it or not, bonding individuals together to form a community. 'Ritual' plays a key role in constructing religion as 'social glue'. The process which for Marxists amounts to mystification is for Durkheimians entirely a matter of social integration, of positive benefit to individual and society alike. It would be wrong to claim that meeting for worship exhibits 'effervescence', though 'the gathered meeting' is a term used to describe a meeting in which a heightened feeling of togetherness is experienced—at least by some.

This bears on the contrasting interpretations of Durkheim's work provided by Bronislaw Malinowski and A. R. Radcliffe-Brown. While Malinowski (1974) drew on the implicit psychologism in Durkheim's theory, locating religion squarely in the realm of individual psychology and involving personal feelings such as reverential awe, exhilaration, or terror, Radcliffe-Brown (1964[1922]) jettisoned the implicit psychologism in Durkheim, repeating, with increased vigour, that the social could only be understood in terms of the social. Radcliffe-Brown was primarily concerned to understand social order and the way in which social institutions ensured the continuity of that order, that social structure. He argued that 'ritual' (rather than belief or myth) was the more robust vehicle for securing social unity (see also Gluckman 1963; 1970). For Radcliffe-Brown the individual was largely a puppet of social structure and deserved scant attention. It could be argued that during the past two centuries, Quaker 'ritual' has become more explicable in Malinowski's terms, primarily as a result of the steady individualization of Quaker faith and practice—itself a result of the ambient process of modernization.

Maurice Bloch (1979) and in subsequent work (to which we shall return) argued cogently that 'ritual' is, from beginning to end, instrumental, enabling those in positions of power to maintain that power. Bloch argued that 'ritual' is a form of traditional authority using a variety of means to restrain critical thought and action: in 'ritual', actions are prescribed and legitimated by an authority higher than the human experts who direct the ceremony. This is a latent instrumentality, in that participants remain unaware of it: this is 'ritual' as ideology, or 'doxa' (Bourdieu 1977).

Functionalist explanations have also looked to the symbol, as the smallest component of 'ritual' as a means of communicating some idea to the participants, mostly consciously, sometimes unconsciously. The interpretive turn in anthropology owes much to the American scholar Clifford Geertz (1973). Drawing on Weber, he famously proposed that we are suspended in webs of significance that we ourselves have spun; interpretation is the life-blood of human beings—and religion comprises one such web. Turner, especially in his earlier work (e.g., 1969), identifies the symbol as the building block of 'ritual'. Symbols form a system which functions as a code; to crack this code is to arrive at an understanding of 'ritual'. I have myself argued that the meeting for worship is replete with symbolic elements. For instance, it is difficult to account for the presence of the table in the middle of the room. Even if one accepts that it provides a focus on which participants may centre their attention, one is left wondering why, then, a table. If we begin with the historical roots of Quakerism, we see a religious movement playing the *vis-à-vis* with Anglicanism: that is, defining itself *in relation to* the state church (Collins 1996). This opposition continues in residual form in the table at the centre of the meeting room. Now we can think of it as a 'not-altar', a space which frames the very absence of those symbols (the chalice, the plate, the cross) which are central to Anglicanism. While it might be difficult to explain why important messages are made complex in symbols, it seems likely that redundancy might be important in such cases. Asad (1983) criticizes Geertz in particular for emphasizing meaning in religious practice at the expense of power. Drawing on cognitive theory, Sperber (1975) offers a well-argued alternative to Turner and Geertz's cryptological approach. In recent years, a cognitive approach has been developed by Pascal Boyer (1994) and Harvey Whitehouse (2000; Laidlaw and Whitehouse 2004) in particular. Whitehouse, drawing on distinctions made by Durkheim and others, argues that religion diverges into one of two types, one emphasizing the imagistic, the other, the doctrinal. While Hinduism might typically represent the former, Quakerism represents the latter type—though a more exemplary example of the doctrinal type might be Lutheranism, given its biblical focus. 'Ritual', Whitehouse observes, is more likely to be routinized in the doctrinal mode.

Should we assume that 'rituals' have meaning? I have heard Quakers claim that meeting for worship has no meaning: 'It's something I just do!' Inverting the interpretivist perspective, Staal (1975) warns that there is, in such explanations, a tendency to overdetermine the meaning of a 'ritual', to take one's interpretation way further than the participants themselves do. In Staal's view, 'ritual' exists for its own sake. He argues that 'ritual' is primarily the performance of rule-governed action, whose content is irrelevant to its understanding. However, this approach can be subjected to the same criticism which Staal levels at the hermeneuticists—that his theory simply ignores the ability and tendency of participants themselves to interpret 'ritual'. A related approach is proposed in a recent collection of essays edited by Handelman and Lindquist (2004). Contributors to this volume maintain that 'rituals' should be understood, at least in the first instance, 'in their own right'. That is, they should first be analysed in their own terms, and not as epiphenomena of the social order in which they are embedded. Handelman argues cogently that no functional or representational theory can possibly account for all the various members of the 'ritual' family.

Liminaries II: 'Ritual' Structure

If there is a single character of 'ritual' on which scholars broadly agree, it is its threefold structure first identified by Arnold van Gennep (1960[1912]). The first stage, separation, is characterized by acts of purification and references to the loss of one's old identity. The second stage, transition, often involves isolating initiates from the rest of their community, where they remain suspended betwixt and between their old and new identities. This stage is often marked by taboos, quests, trials, and so forth. Leach (1961) argued that one characteristic of this stage is the reversal of time and of quotidian practice. Incorporation, the third stage, is marked by symbolic acts marking the return of the now transformed initiate to the community. The return of initiates to the community with new responsibilities and a new status, they may receive and possibly a new name, new clothes, and insignia, is often marked by a communal meal or some other communal activity. The theory is so prevalent, that there is, increasingly, an assumption that 'ritual' will be structured thus. So widespread is this tendency that we might be forgiven for asking whether 'ritual' has not come to mean any event that has an identifiable threefold structure.

Victor Turner (1969) took up van Gennep's theory and developed it in a number of interesting ways. He accepted the form itself, renaming the stages preliminal, liminal, and postliminal, focusing on van Gennep's second stage and thereby emphasizing the function as well as the structure of 'ritual'. Turner broadened this theory by distinguishing two modes of being, which he called *societas* and *communitas*. *Communitas*, or 'anti-structure', is a form of social solidarity exemplified during the second phase of 'ritual', but involves other similarly heightened states of consciousness and even forms of society: pilgrimage, hippy communes, and so forth. *Societas* is what is left when *communitas* is taken out—the quotidian, humdrum life, daily routine. Turner developed his theory along both analytical and normative lines, suggesting that a balance between these modes of experience was required if people were to thrive. Later, he began to talk about 'liminoid' states, which are transformative for both individuals and communities. Tom Driver (1998) argues that transformation is one of the three core functions of 'ritual' (the other two being order and community). For Driver, the transformative capacity of 'ritual' works at the level of both the individual and the community. Driver goes on to criticize Turner for drifting into a position where he imagined theatre was replacing 'ritual' as the primary liminal space in modern society.

Turning to the Quaker case, it is easy to observe the tripartite structure posited by van Gennep and Turner (Collins 1998). At least, such a structure is obvious if we take 'meeting for worship' to include the time participants spend in the meeting house from the time they arrive to the time they leave (an event which participants often refer to simply as 'meeting'). This has further interest in that the period before and after worship is not normally considered 'religious' by observers, and so begs the question of how scholars are to identify the framing of 'ritual', both in temporal and in spatial terms. Participants typically arrive at the meeting house on Sunday morning from 10 a.m. onwards—let us call this time 'before worship'. Children run, while adults mill around and talk. This 'preliminal phase', marked by noise and movement, is succeeded, as participants settle quietly in the meeting room, by a 'liminal phase'.

During meeting for worship, participants sit in stillness and silence: time is reversed (Leach 1961). The postliminal phase, 'after meeting', is again marked by noise and movement. The extent to which the liminal phase can be characterized as '*communitas*' is open to debate, though a strong argument can be made in favour. The liminal stage is characterized by a marked self-discipline; the norms of everyday life are turned upside down, and it would seem that human agency is held in suspension. This is not quite the case, however, and the participant is faced with a number of decisions on entering the meeting for worship: shall I sit next to A or B? Perhaps I should avoid sitting near X and Y? I like to hear C speak, so I ought to sit near her. I'd like to read a passage from Leviticus this morning—now where is that King James Bible? Such a beautiful day, I'll sit here so that I can look out on to the cherry blossom—and so on and so forth—each decision a part of a longer narrative, and these narratives blur the edges of van Gennep's stages. There is a distinct hexis: participants upright, head bowed, hands resting in lap; but then some slouch, cross their legs, or occasionally lean forward. The intended silence is often far from perfect: children do whisper and chuckle, adults rustle plastic bags, and sometimes cough, sneeze, clear their throats, and occasionally snore. So long as these remain unobtrusive, they are unlikely to provoke reaction. However, a persistent offender is likely to be 'eldered'.

Spoken ministry is couched around with a subtle discipline: speak clearly, for not too long; only speak once; do not enter into conversation with previous speakers; remain still for the duration; and so forth. Until 1923 gifted 'ministers' were officially recorded as such and sat separately, along with elders and overseers. The furniture in some older meeting houses sustains the illusion of that tradition; some meetings have deliberately retained architectural features that memorialize past practices. Certainly, meeting is a means of remembering: meeting is the group memory. Such ministries generally take the form of short homilies, often drawing on a religious text such as the Bible, or on the quasi-canonical *Quaker Faith and Practice*. This is worship at its most obviously communicative: ministry is storied but also moral; it deals with those aspects of social life that involve an 'ought'. After an hour, elders begin to peer clandestinely at their watches until, eventually, 'at the right moment', two bring the meeting for worship to a close with a handshake, followed by handshakes all around. Worship is concluded, but meeting has some way to go. The clerk stands, the hubbub recedes, and the 'notices' are read: the morning collection will go to charity x; there is a meeting of the committee responsible for organizing children's classes on Tuesday evening; a group will met to discuss chapter 18 of *Quaker Faith and Practice* on Thursday evening; and so on. This is an ambiguous phase—is it a part of, or apart from, worship? This ambiguity is reflected in the uncertainty manifested by participants: is it OK to stand and leave, to chat, to interrupt? The notices are concluded after other Friends have been asked to provide information on this or that meeting or event, and then participants drift into the concourse and towards the kitchen for tea. Then more milling around, though a little less frantic than before meeting. Conversations will start afresh or continue from the previous week. Comments will be made regarding the worship just ended: Friends are reminded in the Book of Discipline that they should accept spoken ministry even if it fails to 'speak to one's condition'. As participants leave the meeting room, they return to conversation begun before meeting. Some might reflect on the meeting just held—Quakers do evaluate both meeting for worship as a whole and individual ministry. Sometimes, one who ministered will be congratulated for the delivery, form, or content of their ministry. Very occasionally, one might be gently chastised for speaking too quietly, for too long, or irrelevantly.

Although Turner (1969), as well as Leach (1977) and Douglas (1966), flirted with the French structuralism of Claude Lévi-Strauss (e.g., 1967; 1973), the paradigm they shared was very different from his, tending towards empiricism and realism. Lévi-Strauss focuses his attention on the consequences of the mode of functioning of the human brain, that is, as a binary operator: a device which structures the world in pairs of opposites—nature/culture, male/female, right/left, up/down, raw/cooked, and so forth. For structuralists, the homologization of these pairs is the most important means by which humans make sense of the world and their place in it. Turner, for instance, defines the structure/anti-structure opposition in terms of twenty-three homologous oppositions—the theory seems to work for Quaker 'ritual', which under these terms is clearly a very good example of 'anti-structure' or liminality.

Bloch (1992) also draws heavily on van Gennep in developing earlier work on Merina circumcision 'ritual'. He argues, like Freud (1946[1913]) and Girard (1977), though in this respect only, that violence is the root cause of all and the direct effect of much 'ritual'. Van Gennep believed that, depending on the circumstances, one stage would overshadow the other two, and Bloch draws our attention, unusually, to the third stage—incorporation. He suggests, ingeniously, that during the liminal stage of a 'ritual' the individual sets aside his ordinary vitality, in order to assimilate the extraordinary, supernatural vitality generated by the 'ritual'. This is a 'conquered vitality' drawn from beings outside human society. During the final stage of the 'ritual' the participant moves from Turner's *communitas*, to *societas*, but returns strengthened and empowered by the superhuman vitality given him or her during the 'ritual'. This return is often marked by violence or, more exactly, 'rebounding violence', and Bloch provides a range of examples from diverse cultures, some of which, it must be said, strain to fit his theory. Bloch (1986; 1989) argues that such 'rituals' function to maintain the status hierarchy of a society (it is ideological). The outcome seems right because it merely reinforces a world view already held by people. Furthermore, the 'ritual' reinforces the idea that the violent conquest of inferiors by superiors (elders, priests, or power-holders) is legitimate in that the latter are closer to the gods. Bloch's theory, one of many that claim universality, works better in relation to some 'rituals' (life cycle 'rituals', 'rituals' of rebellion) than others (Christian liturgies).

Mitchell (2004) presents a novel variation of van Gennep's theory, describing how the Maltese *festa* inverts the typical form, in that instead of involving people who are removed from the profane world into the sacred before returning once more to the community, the *festa* involves the movement of the sacred object (the *reffiegha* or holy statue) from its sacred place out into the profane world before returning to the sacrality of its usual resting place. Mitchell further argues that the *festa* is better understood as a public demonstration of the agency and innovatory practice of participants than in terms of Bloch's conservative and over-generalizing theory of rebounding violence (see also Gellner 1999). It is difficult to see how the Quaker meeting for worship might be framed so as to fit Bloch's theory. Early Quakers belonged to a Puritan (anti-Catholic) tradition, which included Anabaptists, the Huguenots, and other more or less heretical groups. It is certainly true to say that radical Protestantism spread from Luther's Germany via the enforced migration of those who were persecuted by civil and religious authorities. To this extent it can be argued that Quaker faith and practice was born of violence, though perhaps not of the 'rebounding' kind.

Liminaries III: 'Ritual' as Practice

In recent years a number of scholars, disillusioned with the limitations of functionalist theory, have turned to practice theory in their accounts of 'ritual' (Asad 1993; Ortner 1978). Catherine Bell (1992) seeks to avoid the kinds of difficulty caused by defining 'ritual' as either a distinctive and essentially different set of paradigmatic activities or as a set of qualities found to some degree in all activity, primarily by diverting our attention from the noun ('ritual') to the verb ('ritualization') and by adopting a practice theory approach. Bell argues that the study of 'ritual' has been beset by a series of unhelpful dichotomies, beginning with the separation of thought and action, where 'ritual' is assumed to equate with action which mediates between the theory and practice of 'ritual'—Geertz on religion, she says, is a prime example of this process. Bell usefully alerts us to the various ways in which the character of 'rituals' themselves affects and legitimates the analyst's methodology. It does happen that a scholar's representation of 'ritual' is simply an artefact of the methodology adopted, which results in the production of a discourse that merely serves to confirm the preconceived hypotheses of the scholar. The fact that 'ritual' can vary 'in every aspect from one instance to another' leads Bell to argue that, from the perspective of practice theory, we can say only that it involves 'ritualization': that is, 'a way of acting that distinguishes itself from other ways of acting in the very way it does what it does' (1997: 81). She introduces the concept 'habitus' from Bourdieu, emphasizing in doing so the embodied character of 'ritualization', and the constitution of 'ritual' space partly by the movement (and in the Quaker case, stillness) of participants. Bell contends that 'ritual' is such by virtue of the intention of participants to frame particular practice as 'ritual'. To the observer, 'ritual' action can look just like 'non-ritual' action; what distinguishes the two is the attitude of participants. Like Bourdieu, she envisages a process that is both structured and structuring, and mostly unconscious. And like Parkin (1992), she emphasizes the spatial aspects of 'ritual'.

This is an issue taken up at considerable length by Lindsay Jones (2000), who emphasizes the dialectical relationship between space and 'ritual', introducing the term 'ritual-architectural event' in order properly to identify and describe it. Practice theory compels the scholar to focus more directly on what people do and how they do it; it subverts the tendency of scholars to commit themselves to some a priori idea of 'ritual'. However, rather like Bourdieu's theory of habitus, Bell's theory of 'ritualization' is in danger of falling into a different trap—that of determinism. She suggests that participants assimilate a kind of 'ritual' habitus comprising unconscious schemes and strategies that after repetition feel entirely natural, requiring no explanation, justification, or legitimization. How, then, can 'rituals' change and develop? Where is human agency here? Can it be that participants are entirely unreflexive of their practice—even their 'ritual' practice?

In stark contrast with the Anglican parish church which towers above it, the meeting house has no tower or spire, no architectural embellishments, no bells, no representations of saints, no stained glass windows. The close proximity of the two buildings invites one to compare two traditions or genres of 'ritual'. Each structure plays the *vis-à-vis* to the other—that is, each is partially defined by the other: the meeting house is just what the parish church is not; while the Quaker building might properly be described as plain, in the Protestant spirit, the neo-Gothic flourishes of the parish church place that building in another genre. Jones (2000) makes clear just how relevant the physical setting of the 'ritual' can be—incorporating it into the 'ritual' itself—'the ritual-architectural event'. There is, in any case, a spatial aspect of 'ritual' in which place and the orientation of the participant can be critically important—in pilgrimage, for instance—where the 'ritual' involves movement from one place to another.

Humphrey and Laidlaw in their analysis of the Jain *puja* 'ritual' (1994) attempt, like Bell, to avoid the perils of defining 'ritual' either in terms of special events or as special characteristics of all events, and like Bell they prefer to talk about 'ritualization'. However, they eschew the opportunity to develop her idea of 'ritual' practice, arguing that thought and action do not need to be separated—action, they aver, necessarily implies purpose. Their argument in full is ingenious, though their central point, whilst controversial, is simple: the pivotal transformation which 'ritualization' effects is to sever the link between the 'ritual' participants' intentions and the identity of the acts they perform. In everyday life, saying something one does not mean is considered a mistake—but 'ritual' action is anything but a mistake: one of the main characteristics of 'ritual' is the consistent displacement of intentional meaning. 'Ritual' is, then, a quality of action. Like Staal, they are proposing that 'ritual' has no intrinsic meaning, but (unlike Bell) that it *is* apprehensible. They seem not to worry about dichotomies, and suggest that the two polar types of 'ritual' are liturgy (e.g., *puja*, the eucharist), in which the key question asked is 'Have we got it right?', and performance (e.g., initiation rites, shamanic 'ritual'), where the key question is 'Has it worked?' The degree of ritualization depends on the degree to which actions are felt to be stipulated. In this sense, *puja*, they suggest, is the prototypical, or *archetypal*, form of 'ritual'. 'Ritual', in this pristine form, consists entirely of a number of stipulated acts, and it is upon the acts rather than their sequence that participants focus their attention. This seems a hasty generalization, however, and is certainly not true of all 'rituals'. They go on to argue that 'ritual' is not dependent on beliefs, ideas, or values, and is typically defined by the commitment, or by the 'acceptance', of participants. The fact that scholars insist on the meaningfulness of 'ritual' is an outcome of asking participants 'What does this mean?' and results, as Lewis (1980) and others have observed, in a mistaken intellectualism. 'Ritual' is a special quality of action, not a quality of belief. While Humphrey and Laidlaw agree that body movement and orientation are often a significant component of ritualization, they do not go as far as Bell or Parkin. They argue, further, that 'ritual' acts are quite distinct from the participants; indeed, they are thought to be natural things, just like trees or turtles, bees or boulders. Individual interpretation is constrained by the quiddity, or 'factness', of each 'ritual' act. 'Ritual' acts are archetypal because they are ontologically and historically prior to actors' own performance of them. 'Ritual' may have socially held purposes, which can be seen as 'cultural models', and such purposes contribute to the shape of 'ritual'. They agree that even when 'rituals' are not underwritten by precise canonical rules, as in the case of Jain *puja* and Quaker worship, they can manifest 'a self-generated, organic unanimity'. While the book contains a great deal of well-observed ethnographic detail relating to Jain 'ritual', there is bound to be a risk in generalizing from a single case. Is it safe to claim from such limiting evidence that Jain *puja* is the prototypical 'ritual'? Jain *puja* manifestly differs from many other 'rituals' in significant ways. For example, there are 'rituals' (Muslim *salat*, for instance) in which participants emphasize the sequence of 'ritual' components. In the case of Quaker worship, the extreme reflexivity of participants ensures that at least some elements of the 'ritual' are carried out self-consciously, even if the rest remain unconscious and largely habitual.

Postliminaries

Despite its apparent plainness or simplicity, Quaker 'ritual' is amenable to a multitude of interpretations, by both participants and scholars. One cause of this multiplicity of meaning is the tendency for interpreters of 'ritual' to overreach themselves by attempting to produce general theories based on their own fieldwork and in doing so often forgetting the particularity of the actions and events and kinds of experience they are describing. I would instead advocate a Geertzian caution here. It might be argued that there continues to be conceptual confusion surrounding 'ritual' which is likely to survive well into the future. This need not be a bad thing, and indeed it might be argued that the term is helpfully imprecise, and that we are confused only in our concern to attain an inappropriate precision in both defining and understanding 'ritual'. Like some other social-scientific terms (think of 'community', 'class', or, nearer home, 'religion'), 'ritual' might well be more hindrance than help in understanding particular social phenomena. On the other hand, attaching a single, unitary definition is likely to stifle the possibility of comparison, and if comparison is undertaken in such circumstances, a very wide variety of social phenomena are likely to be shaped by the analyst in order to make them fit the theory. Equally to be avoided is the temptation to generalize from a single case—a broad, universalizing definition attempting to explain everything will end up explaining nothing. An alternative strategy is to view 'ritual' from as many perspectives as seems reasonable, including those provided by participants themselves. A number of scholars have argued that it is unnecessarily restrictive to apply a single explanation or interpretation to any particular 'ritual'. In her exemplary study of *Chisungu*, the Bemba girls' initiation 'ritual', Richards (1956) makes clear the different levels of analysis that can be applied to any one 'ritual'. These levels do not exist only between various academic analysts, but between those analysts and 'ritual' specialists and ordinary participants. There is no epistemological reason why such levels of analysis should be ranked according to their truth-value—even if this were possible: they are each valid as informed interpretations. This approach is hardly problem-free, however. Clearly, theories do not always share the same ontological, epistemological, or methodological genealogy. Yet subjecting social life to this kind of scrutiny has several benefits. In this way, one that challenges both the over-confidence of universalizers and the under-confidence of particularizers, one pays particular attention to the location of agency and avoids the Scylla of essentialism and Charybdis of determinism.

We are currently enjoying something of a golden age in 'ritual' studies, and that in itself requires investigation—how it relates to the quantity and quality of 'ritual', for instance. What would seem to be, at first sight, merely a jumble of often profoundly different social phenomena manifests what Wittgenstein (1958) called a 'family resemblance'. 'Ritual' has been described and analysed with extraordinary tenacity. Why? Because it informs our understanding of key sociological concepts such as sociality, time, space, and power. Indeed, some have argued that 'ritual' is constitutive of these concepts. As a major component of social life, we are compelled to attempt an understanding of 'ritual', particularly given the continuing significance that religion plays, one way or another, in all our lives. Given its current trajectory, it is likely that 'ritual' will continue to pose interesting and important questions for those interested in religious faith and practice. In recent years there have been a number of imaginative and persuasive attempts to develop earlier interpretations of 'ritual', and this problem-solving approach is likely to continue. Certainly, the perception among scholars (and practitioners) that 'ritual' is a necessary part of the religious life is as true now as it was for Max Müller, writing 150 years ago. Implicit in this chapter is the hope that we will remain open to the insights generated by various scholars and that we should avoid pitching our eggs into one homogenizing basket in the mistaken belief that in doing so we will eventually uncover the one true meaning of 'ritual'. Let our approach be multi-perspectival (Collins 2005).

References

Asad, T. (1983). 'Anthropological Conceptions of Religion: Reflections on Geertz'. *Man* (N.S.) 18: 237–59.

—— (1993). *Genealogies of Religion*. Baltimore: Johns Hopkins University Press.

Bakhtin, M. (1984). *Rabelais and his World*. Bloomington, Ind.: University of Indiana Press.

Barth, F. (1975). *Ritual and Knowledge among the Baktaman of New Guinea*. New Haven: Yale University Press.

Beattie, J. (1966). 'Ritual and Social Change'. *Man* (N.S.) 1: 60–74.

—— (1970). 'On Understanding Ritual'. In B. R. Wilson (ed.), *Rationality*. Oxford: Basil Blackwell, 240–68.

Bell, C. (1992). *Ritual Theory, Ritual Practice*. Oxford: Oxford University Press.

Bell, C. (1997). *Ritual: Perspectives and Dimensions.* Oxford: Oxford University Press.

Bloch, M. (1979). 'The Past and the Present in the Present'. *Man* (N.S.) 13: 591–600.

—— (1986). *From Blessing to Violence.* Cambridge: Cambridge University Press.

—— (1989). *Ritual, History and Power.* London: Athlone.

—— (1992). *Prey into Hunter.* Cambridge: Cambridge University Press.

Bourdieu, P. (1977). *Theory of an Outline of Practice.* Cambridge: Cambridge University Press.

Boyer, P. (1994). *The Naturalness of Religious Ideas: A Cognitive Theory of Religion.* Berkeley: University of California Press.

Britain Yearly Meeting (1995). *Quaker Faith and Practice: The Book of Discipline of the Yearly Meeting of the Religious Society of Friends (Quakers) in Britain.* London: Religious Society of Friends.

Collins, P. (1996). '"Plaining": The Social and Cognitive Practice of Symbolization in the Religious Society of Friends'. *Journal of Contemporary Religion*, 11/3: 277–88.

—— (1998). 'Quaker Worship: An Anthropological Approach'. *Worship*, 72: 501–15.

—— (2005). 'Thirteen Ways of Looking at a Ritual'. *Journal of Contemporary Religion*, 20/3: 323–42.

Dandelion, P. (1996). *A Sociological Analysis of the Theology of Quakers.* Lampeter: Edwin Mellen Press.

Douglas, M. (1966). *Purity and Danger.* London: Routledge & Kegan Paul.

Driver, T. (1998). *Liberating Rites.* Boulder, Col.: Westview Press.

Durkheim, É. (1915). *The Elementary Forms of the Religious Life.* London: Allen & Unwin.

Frazer, J. G. (1890). *The Golden Bough*, 2 vols. London: Macmillan.

Freud, S. (1946[1913]). *Totem and Taboo.* New York: Vintage Books.

Geertz, C. (1973). *The Interpretation of Cultures.* New York: Basic Books.

Gellner, D. (1999). 'Religion, Politics and Ritual: Remarks on Geertz and Bloch'. *Social Anthropology*, 7/2: 135–53.

Girard, R. (1977). *Violence and the Sacred.* Baltimore: Johns Hopkins University Press.

Gluckman, M. (1963). *Order and Rebellion in Tribal Africa.* New York: Free Press.

—— (1970). *Custom and Conflict in Africa.* Oxford: Basil Blackewell.

Goody, J. (1961). 'Religion and Ritual: The Definitional Problem'. *British Journal of Sociology*, 12/2: 142–64.

—— (1977). 'Against Ritual: Loosely Structured Thoughts on a Loosely Defined Topic'. In S. Falk-Moore and B. H. Myerhoff (eds.), *Secular Ritual.* Amsterdam: Van Gorcum, 25–35.

Handelman, D. (1999). 'The Playful Seductions of Neo-Shamanic Ritual'. *History of Religion*, 39: 65–72.

—— and Lindquist, G. (eds.) (2004). *Ritual in its Own Right.* Oxford: Berghahn.

Horton, R. (1968). 'Neo-Tylorianism: A Sound Sense or Sinister Prejudice?' *Man* (N.S.) 3/4: 625–34.

—— (1970). 'African Traditional Thought and Western Science'. In B. R. Wilson (ed.), *Rationality.* Oxford: Basil Blackwell, 131–71.

Huizinga, J. (1964). *Homo Ludens.* Boston: Beacon Press.

Humphrey, C., and Laidlaw, J. (1994). *The Archetypal Actions of Ritual.* Oxford: Clarendon Press.

Jones, L. (2000). *The Hermeneutics of Sacred Architecture*, 2 vols. Cambridge, Mass.: Harvard University Press.

Laidlaw, J., and Whitehouse, H. (2004). *Ritual and History.* Walnut Creek, Calif.: AltaMira Press.

Leach, E. (1961). 'Time and False Noses'. In *idem*, *Rethinking Anthropology*. London: Athlone, 132–6.
—— (1977). *Culture and Communication*. Cambridge: Cambridge University Press.
Lévi-Strauss, C. (1967). *Structural Anthropology*. New York: Basic Books.
—— (1973). *Totemism*. Harmondsworth: Penguin.
Lewis, G. (1980). *Day of Shining Red*. Cambridge: Cambridge University Press.
Malinowski, B. (1974). *Magic, Science and Religion and Other Essays*. Glencoe, Ill.: Free Press.
Marrett, R. R. (1914). *The Threshold of Religion*, 2nd edn. London: Methuen.
Mitchell, J. P. (2004). 'Ritual Structure and Ritual Agency: "Rebounding Violence" and Maltese *festa*'. *Social Anthropology*, 12/1: 57–75.
Müller, F. M. (1967[1861]). *Lectures on the Science of Language*. New York: Scribners.
Ortner, S. B. (1978). *Sherpas through their Rituals*. Cambridge: Cambridge University Press.
Parkin, D. (1992). 'Ritual as Spatial Direction and Bodily Division'. In Daniel de Coppet (ed.), *Understanding Rituals*. London: Routledge & Kegan Paul, 11–25.
Radcliffe-Brown, A. R. (1964[1922]). *The Andaman Islanders: A Study in Social Anthropology*. New York: Free Press.
Richards, A. I. (1956). *Chisungu: A Girls' Initiation Ceremony among the Bemba of Northern Zambia*. London: Faber & Faber.
Robertson-Smith, W. (2002[1889]). *Lectures on the Religion of the Semites*. Edison, NJ: Transaction Publishers.
Schechner, R. (1993). *The Future of Ritual*. London: Routledge.
Schieffelin, E. (1985). 'Performance and the Cultural Construction of Reality'. *American Ethnologist*, 12: 707–24.
Sperber, D. (1975). *Rethinking Symbolism*. Cambridge: Cambridge University Press.
Staal, F. (1975). 'The Meaninglessness of Ritual'. *Numen*, 26: 2–22.
Tambiah, S. J. (1985). 'A Performative Approach to Ritual'. In *idem*, *Culture, Thought and Social Action*. Cambridge, Mass.: Harvard University Press, 123–66.
Turner, V. W. (1967). *The Forest of Symbols*. Ithaca, NY: Cornell University Press.
—— (1969). *The Ritual Process*. Chicago: Aldine de Gruyter.
—— (1974). *Dramas, Fields and Metaphors*. Ithaca, NY: Cornell University Press.
—— (1982). *From Ritual to Theatre*. New York: Performance Arts Journal Publications.
—— (1984). *The Anthropology of Performance*. New York: Performance Arts Journal Publications.
Tylor, E. B. (1871). *Primitive Culture*, 2 vols. New York: Harper.
van Gennep, A. (1960[1912]). *Rites of Passage*. London: Routledge & Kegan Paul.
Whitehouse, H. (2000). *Arguments and Icons: Divergent Modes of Religiosity*. Oxford: Oxford University Press.
Wittgenstein, L. (1958). *Philosophical Investigations*. Oxford: Blackwell.

Suggested Reading

The following are recommended: Bell (1992, 1997), Bloch (1992); Lewis (1980); and Turner (1969).

CHAPTER 38

RELIGION AND THE MEDIA

STEWART M. HOOVER

THE emergence and evolution of the media have raised important challenges to received ways of understanding the world socially. While we like to think of the media as a particular phenomenon of the twentieth century, historical scholarship has demonstrated that many of the trends and capacities of the media age have deep roots. What we know as the media today can in fact be most helpfully traced, in the case of the industrialized West at least, to the development of moveable-type printing in the early modern era. It is telling to reflect on the fact that this was not merely a technological event, but that it also had important economic, structural, and political attributes. Most importantly, the printing revolution led to the development of media industries, autonomous centers of power with the capacity to effect change in existing political and social arrangements.

The effects on religion were profound, as we know. Printing has long been associated with the Protestant Reformation, of course, but it also played a major role in the Counter-Reformation and in subsequent religious evolution. The variety of religious movements that came to be part of what Nathan Hatch (1989) has called the "democratized" religious culture of North America have all relied in one way or another on media technology, and the religious roots of secular American publishing are deep and wide.

Social analysis of the media must take account of the profound and complex relations that have emerged in a range of contexts, from politics to economics to religion, and must also recognize the complex nature of the media themselves. In general, media sociology has focused on three related domains: the institutions of the media, the content of media, and the effects of media. From the mid-twentieth century onward the social sciences have attempted a range of approaches to accounting for the media. What is today the scholarly discipline devoted to media is variously rooted and variously described and understood as "mass communication", "media sociology", "media psychology", and today, more commonly, "media studies". This discipline owes much to its roots in the social sciences of sociology, psychology, and anthropology, and today owes much to increasing interdisciplinary ferment.

Social analysis must take account of fundamental features of the media. First, while technologies are not necessarily or unitarily determinative, the media are fundamentally technological in origin, and technological change plays an important role in their development and evolution. Second, the media are in the main complex institutions with extensive hierarchies and role and task differentiation. Third, the media are important economic forces and are extensively integrated as structures and industries. Fourth, their economic location continues to provide them with a kind of autonomy in relation to other social institutions, and a concomitant range of potential ideological and political implications. Fifth, the media are necessarily translocal. They may be locally based but at the same time can move beyond the local, and today we understand them to be extensively articulated into the processes problematically called "globalization".

As social scientists began to contemplate the media in a more substantive way in the mid-twentieth century, a range of received ideas about the media and their social implications began to emerge. Most of these concentrated on the effects of the media, and owed much to the social and empirical positivism that dominated the social sciences of that era. There is an implicit and tacit logic to the idea that the study of media should be about its measurable "effects". Simply put, we are socialized from an early age to think of ourselves as communicative instrumentalists. It is commonplace to think of communication as something that involves intentions, directionalities, causes, and effects. It is further commonplace to then assume that as interpersonal communication is all about intentions and effects, so mass communication must be the same only writ large. If we can intend to communicate certain unequivocal ideas in interpersonal contexts, then the media can intend to send "messages", and the only question is whether they are effectively "received". And—more importantly to our considerations here—such effects could be clearly and unequivocally measured by the new objective and quantitative techniques emerging in the social sciences.

This received paradigm of media began to come under serious scrutiny in the latter part of the century. This ferment had two sources. First, as social measurement of media effects moved ahead, it became clear that a wide range of media phenomena were not able to be accounted for in this way. Second, and more importantly, emerging intellectual ferment in the disciplines surrounding the media, including linguistics, languages, anthropology, and (increasingly) sociology, led to a rethinking of some fundamental ideas about the way media had been looked at. One of the central articulations of this latter rethinking also had important implications for the social measurement of media relevant to religion. In his essay "Media Rituals", James Carey (1989) laid out a distinction between what he called a "transmission," and a "ritual" view of mass communication.

Carey may have intended merely to raise important questions about the paradigms under which media research was conducted at the time, but for many, he also opened the door to a new and expanded way of looking at the question of ritual, and beyond that, at religion. This was an important shift in that, before that time, relatively little attention had been paid to religion by media scholars. While there are a number of reasons for this relative scholarly inattention, key among them may well have been the underlying assumption of a rather unnuanced reading of theories of secularization (Hoover and Venturelli 1996). It is also likely that many scholars saw the field of religion as complex and nuanced, and concerned with issues beyond the rational, thus beyond the scope of empirical measurement. The assumption was that, as a sector of social and cultural life "in decline", religion was not likely to be an important feature of media evolution. In fact, it was easy to confuse the decline in institutional and formal religion that began in the mid-twentieth century with a decline in religion itself. In this, the fields of media and communication studies were not unique among the social sciences. This assumption was the one most directly confronted by the seeming persistence of religion late in the century, and its increasing presence in popular and public culture. What has more recently emerged as "new paradigm" religious studies (Warner 1993) brought a new focus to the academic study of religion and coincided with a broader scholarly realization that there was much yet to be understood about contemporary religion and religious evolution. At the same time, some media scholars were beginning to argue that the media and processes of modern mediation are an increasingly important context for this religious change.

Scholarship on media and religion has tended to recognize an important distinction: that between the two major faces of mediated public culture, journalism and entertainment. Important early studies of religion and media focused on news, journalists, and news audiences. Landmark works include studies of the religiosity of the journalistic profession (Buddenbaum 1988) and of the reporters who cover religion (Buddenbaum 1986; Dart and Allen 1993; Hoover 1998; Schmalzbaur 2002; Lichter *et al.* 1986). Important questions here involved whether and how reporters' own ideas relate to the way in which religion is represented to news audiences, and implications for public understanding of religion. More recent works have focused on journalistic output as a component of emerging religious cultures and have questioned the role of journalism and journalists in legitimating religious power and prerogatives (Silk 1995; McCloud 2004; Badaracco 2004; Stout and Buddenbaum 1996).

Thus, works on religion journalism have assumed a certain functionalist relationship between media practice and the constitution of religious institutions and religious practices. Consistent with Anglo-American press traditions, this work has looked at and problematized how informed publics are formed and shaped by media practices whose presumed task is to provide that information. Scholarly and lay discourses about media have tended to inscribe a bright line between the supposedly purposive practice of journalism and the seemingly more trivial realm of entertainment media. With the exception of a prodigious literature focused on the social effects of children's television, non-news media have tended to be studied as a lesser form of media practice. This implicit Calvinism has been particularly active in relation to questions of religion, where it has been easy to assume a gulf between media and normative ideals of "the religious".

This distinction was even more present in consideration of the phenomenon that, more than any other, occasioned the emergence of the study of media and religion: televangelism. Religion has long been a feature of American broadcasting. Religious programs were among the first to appear in the early days of radio, and throughout the twentieth century, the trope of the "radio preacher" came to be a standard feature of American culture. With the emergence of commercial television in the 1950s, religion also migrated there, and the first landmark study of religion and electronic media was published (Parker, Barry, and Smythe 1955). But the relationship between the formal mainstream media and religion remained problematic and somewhat controversial, and a sea-change in the relationship in the 1970s led to an explosion in attention to religion and media. That change was brought about by technological innovation: the development of satellite broadcasting and the satellite-based distribution of programming to the growing cable television industry. This enabled the emergence of a series of religiously based television "networks", of which Pat Robertson's *700 Club* was the most prominent (and long-lived).

The results of this development moved in a number of directions. Concerns were raised by religious institutions over the competition that "media religion" might pose to "conventional religion", including a potential struggle over financial resources. More nuanced concerns were also expressed. As the majority of these new "TV ministries" were rooted in conservative, Evangelical, and Pentecostal movements, the possibility existed that they might well advantage the conservative side of American religion (Hadden and Swann 1981; Schultze 1990). Their potential political implications emerged somewhat later, but have come to be an important element in the Evangelical surge into American politics in the latter decades of the century (Hadden and Shupe 1988; Hunter 1992).

Social analysis of media and religion looked at a range of issues surrounding these ministries. Institutional studies investigated their histories, sources, and structures (Horsfield 1984; Bruce 1990; Frankl 1987). Research on their effects on audiences found that some of the early concerns were misplaced, with the media's significance lying in their ability to build identity and solidarity among the already committed their most important implication (Hoover 1988; Gerbner *et al.* 1986). More recent studies have focused on the cultural meanings of religious broadcasting, identifying it as an important element in the construction of contemporary religious consciousness (Mitchell 1999; Hangen 2002; Peck 1993). Recent historical work has accounted for religious broadcasting in the context of mainstream broadcasting (Rosenthal 2002).

In general, though, social analysis of televangelism continued to address the notion of a "bright line" existing between media and religion. Consistent with a Durkheimian view of religion as authentic and authentically rooted as a generative source of society, it was easy to assume that the media, as technologies and institutions, would operate at a level of some remove from mechanical solidarity, and that the way to look at media would be in terms of their "threats" or at least "effects" on religion. Some of this work (cf. Hoover 1988; Peck 1993) began to question this received idea; but as televangelism has to an extent faded as a public concern, work on media and religion has moved on.

Carey's essay on ritual played an important role in undermining the easy assumptions about relations between media and religion. For many, it opened the possibility of seeing media and the process we might call "mediation" in a new way: as a source or center of religious practice or insight. This is somewhat distinct from claims, such as those of McLuhan, which center media in the transformation of ways of seeing and knowing. Rather, the scholarly sensibility which has emerged is one that is much more social in its orientation, using social theory and social methodologies to look for religion in contexts—specifically mediated contexts—outside the bounds of tradition and institutional structure. This work has also shared with thought in fields such as sociology the assumption that "media" and "mediation" extend beyond the boundaries of the media industries to the whole sphere of commodified cultural practices which center on the media sphere (cf. Ritzer 1996; Giddens 1991; Gergen 1991).

Thus contemporary work on media and religion has moved beyond questions of instrumentalism (the ways in which the media might affect or be affected by religion) to questions of the role that media and "mediation" might play at the center of the construction, reconstruction, maintenance, or decline of the range of institutional, collective, individual, and interactive practices that might be labeled "religion". A valence of this shift that is also implied by the germinal work of James Carey and others (cf. Rothenbuhler 1993; Couldry 2003; Rothenbuhler and Coman 2005) is the notion that the media might be assuming a role at the center of the culture, being the location for both large and small rituals of what Robert Bellah (1992) once called the "civil religion". There is much cause to see such a role for the media in such things as the commemorations of the Kennedy assassination (Zelizer 1993), the death of Princess Diana, and the experience of the 9/11 attacks and their aftermath (Zelizer and Allen 2002; Hoover 2006).

But, the range of ways in which the media are involved in the contemporary sociology of religion is not limited to journalism, large and small social and cultural rituals, or to the ways in which the media are instrumentally related to broader religious processes and practices. As noted earlier, the whole broad sphere of entertainment media in a wide variety of sources, channels, and guises and interconnected with commercial and commodity culture has the capacity to support and encourage the development of new and reconstructed religious forms.

For media scholars who look at religion, work has increasingly focused in the third area of traditional media analysis: audiences and their reception of media messages and participation in mediated experiences of "the religious". The significant exception to this has been the important emerging discourse about religion in digital media, where a good deal of attention has been paid to the content of digital media, including websites, blogs, online communities, and gaming.

Much of the momentum of social analysis of media and religion has derived from trends in the fields of religious studies and media studies that have allowed scholarship to contemplate a convergence between these fields and the emergence of the mediated religious social marketplace. In religious studies, these trends have been driven by an increasing interest in the evolution of religious and spiritual exploration. Rooted in the work of scholars such as Wade Clark Roof (1999) and Robert Wuthnow (1998), this approach to the sociology of religion has been articulated by Stephen Warner (1993) within the larger framework of a "new paradigm" in the social analysis of religion. Fundamental to this paradigm shift, according to Warner, is a reorientation from religion "as ascribed" to religion "as acheived". There is a range of research under this paradigm which has substantially broadened the field of study of the sociology of religion.

This shift recognizes a rather fundamental change in the nature of American religion, away from being institutionally focused toward being more determined by the practices of religion. The rise of what has been called "autonomy" in matters of religion (Hammond 1992) has led to the development of a faith sensibility that has been called "seeking" or "questing" (Wuthnow 1998; Roof 1999), meaning that more and more of the authority over faith and spirituality is now in the hands of the individual. This has implications important to the study of the media. First, it means that authority has shifted from the received doctrines and institutions of religion to individuals as they work to perfect the "self" in late modernity (Giddens 1991). The second important implication is that with the withdrawal of institutional authority over which symbolic and other resources may be used in the making of religious meaning and identity, religion today can be sought and found well outside the boundaries of tradition, thus opening up the whole field of media culture and media commodities as potentially significant to the religious quest.

This evolution in sociology of religion has coincided with the further development of trends in media studies toward greater attention to audience practice and audience reception. In the same way as the shift in orientation away from institutional prerogatives has changed the way we think about where religion might be found and made, so media scholarship increasingly sees that what matters is not what media industries or producers intend through their productions, but instead what audiences make of, and do with, these messages (Gauntlett and Hill 1999). The shift away from media instrumentalism, then, means that, regardless of media channel, genre, or form, the goal of the social study of media should move to the way that these things are used, interpreted, and made sense of by audiences. In a way reminiscent of Warner above, the shift is from what is ascribed to media consumption to what is achieved in that process.

There is thus an emerging convergence between the scholarships of religion and of media. As it is rooted in an implicit turn toward culture, this convergence of course shares much in common with Alexander's (Alexander and Smith 2002) call for a "strong program" in cultural sociology. At the same time, though, this scholarship contemplates a situation in which actually existing media and religion are converging as well. The reason for this convergence on the ground is largely technological in origin. An increasing proliferation of channels has proceeded apace since the latter twentieth century, with cable and satellite television, as well as home videos providing a prodigious array of media sources. The gradual digitalization of the media has further accelerated these trends, with an emerging media marketplace now typified by a level of diversity and choice that is nearly overwhelming in its breadth.

This has meant that within this diversity of sources, a surprising diversity of content is possible. For religion, this means that whereas once the formal media of the culture might have exercised various kinds of control over the kind of religion that might be broadcast (Rosenthal 2002), today there is much more of an open marketplace of media sources of religion. These sources include both formally "religious" ones and ones that might traditionally have been called "para-church" or "secular".

This emerging religious media marketplace thus replicates in important ways the nature of American religion as a "democratic" (Hatch 1989) public sphere. As sociologists of religion now understand it, contemporary religion extends the tendency for religion and spirituality to be largely a function of choice within a range of "marketplaces", both material and conceptual (Finke and Stark 1993). These derive some of their force and significance from histories that saw American Protestantism (in particular) as a kind of free marketplace of religious supply from the colonial period onward, lending legitimacy to the "seeking" sensibility that has only gained momentum in the new century. An emergent media marketplace that includes a supply of religious and spiritual symbols and resources thus articulates with emergent modes of practice and reception, resulting in an ever more significant role for mediation in the individual, private, and autonomous practices of religion and spirituality. The social and institutional autonomy of the media sphere can thus be said to constitute a location for the making of religion that is in many ways independent from religious doctrine, institution, and history.

In this view, *mediation* means something beyond the mere instrumental role that the various media might play in conveying religious ideas or doctrines (Martin-Barbero 1997). Even printing during the Reformation was more integral to the structural changes under way than that, but today the tendency for the media to constitute an autonomous and independent force is even more profound and far-reaching (Hoover 2006). For scholars who wish to look at these issues, this means that there is a large array of media, contexts, practices, and forms that may be significant for social analysis. The range of scholarship at the intersection of media and religion demonstrates this, and derives from the histories, contexts, and practices that define this situation today. The question "How is religion or spirituality mediated today?" is answered in a variety of ways, across a variety of contexts, and through a variety of practices. The kind of work that has emerged heretofore is not exhaustive, and any taxonomy will necessarily account for these things only in formation, and should be taken only as indicative, not as exhaustive. There follows an account of key efforts, works, and approaches.

It is important to recognize that what has now developed in the way of mediated religion in the American context has deep roots in national religious history. The phenomenon of religious broadcasting was discussed earlier, and in many ways set the stage for what we know today as the specifically religious use of media, both radio and television (Hadden and Swann 1981; Gaddy and Pritchard 1985; Rosenthal 2002). This history has left the legacy of both a set of social understandings about the class and religious location of such broadcasting, and sets of religiously defined cohorts for whom the use of media for religious ends is relatively unproblematic (Schultze 1987).

There is another legacy of history, though, and this has to do with the prodigious mediation of American religion undertaken by religious organizations and interests from the mid-twentieth century onward. For example, there is good reason to see the rise of what came to be called "neo-Evangelicalism" as a phenomenon of mass mediation. The historian George Marsden (1983), for instance, has argued that the iconic role of Billy Graham at the center of this movement resulted from conscious efforts on the part of Evangelical leaders to craft a modern face for the movement, and from the self-conscious assessment that that face needed to be a media-savvy one. Graham was, therefore, both a religious and a media figure who, from the very beginning of his ministry, carefully built a media organization and became known as a media figure.

The Graham organization expanded this media orientation through extensive production work in a variety of media, from books to film to television. Heather Hendershot (2004) has shown that these efforts by Graham and other media-oriented organizations had important implications for the Evangelical movement and for American religion in general. Not only did these products enter religious discourse as important sources of ideas and symbols about religion and religious identity, they also developed increasingly sophisticated religious media "taste cultures", which have formed the basis for increasingly sophisticated religious productions, such as the recently successful children's series *Veggie Tales* (Warren 2005).

It can also be argued that the involvement of Evangelicalism in popular mediation has led to an acceptance, among members of that community, of the notion that the media industries themselves are an important context for the expression of religious interests and motivations. While for some groups, such as Catholics, the question of whether one can work in the media and hold onto one's soul is not settled (Schmalzbaur 2002), for others, including Evangelicals, there is an assumption that the media can be turned to "the good" through the efforts of committed religionists in positions of power (Lindsay 2006). The prodigious production efforts of the Evangelical community raise yet another important question: that of the relative importance of "religious" and "secular" contexts for the presentation of religious and spiritual material. A wide range of media, from print to electronic to popular music, are produced and distributed as specifically "religious". In addition to the Evangelical broadcasting already discussed, examples include the extensive outputs of the Christian Booksellers Association (Borden 2007) and so-called "Contemporary Christian Music" (Hendershot 2004). Specifically, there is the question of whether it is possible for either producers or audiences to "cross over" from the secular to the religious side, or vice versa. While such crossing over has been widely anticipated and noted, there is some reason to doubt whether it happens very often (Hendershot 2004; Hoover 2006).

As has been noted, research and scholarship on media and religion have tended to focus in recent years on the reception of religion as much as on institutional or content studies. The new paradigms in media and religion scholarship have militated in the direction of understanding the achievement of religion and spirituality through media commodities, at the expense of more substantive studies of issues such as power and social structure. In general, the objective of much of this work has been understanding of religious *identity* as an important conceptual (and methodological) marker of relations between the realms of religion and the media sphere (Clark 2003; Hoover 2006).

Just as the introduction of satellite broadcasting in the 1970s introduced new religious and spiritual media, practices, and products, so the more recent evolution of the digital age has rearranged the analytical field of research on religion and media. The Internet, World-Wide Web, and the personal digital media have introduced entirely new questions and contexts of analysis in two important ways. First, they introduce a whole set of new phenomena worthy of analysis. Second, they can be claimed to represent, in themselves, the larger picture of the evolving relationship between media and religion. In doing so, they also invoke important questions of authority and authenticity. Christopher Helland (2000) has introduced a valuable analytic distinction, that between "religion online", and "online religion". The former describes the use of the digital realm by formal religious bodies and institutions, or by individuals for more or less conventional religious purposes. It is media-as-instrument to a great extent. In fact, recent research has suggested that this is the predominant religious use of digital media

(Hoover, Clark, and Rainie 2004). The notion of *online religion* contemplates the idea that the digital realm might be forming the basis of whole new ways of being and doing religion. A range of scholars have pursued research on this (O'Leary 1996; Zaleski 1997; Brasher 2001), having recognized that the Internet and the Web in particular offer a wide range of content and other resources that seem to contemplate just such new formations and meanings (Brasher 2001; Hoover and Park 2002). In short, there is a way in which the structuration and interactivity of digital media fit well with the notion of the "seeking" religious subject (Helland 2004; Campbell 2005).

Scholarship on digital religion is only one of a number of emerging fields, contexts, and literatures significant to the sociology of media and religion. Important scholarship has also been undertaken within the frameworks of material culture and visual culture. The former focuses on the practices of religion and spirituality, and looks at ways in which those practices are lodged in material contexts, including objects, built environments, and geographies (McDannell 1995; Chidester and Linenthal 1995; Schmidt 1995; Williams 1997). The material culture of religion is, to this way of thinking, a "found" culture, rather radically focusing on the notion of "religion as achieved", to use Warner's category, described earlier. This work necessarily assumes that it matters less which institutions and histories provide legitimation to religious and spiritual practice, than what those practices make in the way of meaning and identity. Research in this direction necessarily verges toward the boundary between the marketplaces of religious and spiritual commodities and of the media.

Work in the area of visual culture necessarily centers more directly on the media and mediation. David Morgan (1998; 1999; 2005; 2007) has in many ways pioneered a field that focuses on the ways in which American religion (in particular) has been visually represented and experienced. Breaking with established traditions in art history, he has argued that popular consumption of visual imagery is at the center of American piety. Because such visual practice necessarily involves mediation (that is, production and reproduction of such images are a media function), this work in visual culture is necessarily also work about media and religion. Introducing the notion of popular practice also has important consequences for the way in which this work contributes to understandings about the role of media and mediation in contemporary religion. Like much of this work, it focuses on practices that are necessarily in tension with institutional and doctrinal authority. In the area of both visual culture (Morgan 1999) and material culture (McDannell 1995) this tension is rooted in those authorities' derogation of these objects and practices as imperfect resources to faith and spirituality. Questions of the power of religious structures and institutions are therefore again at the center of considerations of mediation.

Material and visual culture studies also fit within a larger context that we've seen as significant in a number of ways: the extent to which mediation takes place largely in the context of commercial, material, and cultural marketplaces. As noted earlier, there is a long and significant history of commodification in American religion (Moore 1994). In the case of religious mediation, this is particularly profound, with the histories of American religious and secular publishing linked, and linked *commercially* (Underwood 2002; Nord 2004; Borden 2007). At the same time, there is a growing literature that looks at the ways in which markets and marketing are increasingly important loci of religious practice in the contemporary West (Belk, Wallendorf, and Sherry 1989). Looking at religion and spirituality in terms of markets also expands the boundaries of what is meant by "religion" and "spirituality". For example, the so-called New Age spiritualities can be said to have been particularly located in markets of various kinds, and to have been less concerned than more traditional faiths with questions of authority and authenticity. As these sensibilities have continued to develop, new mediations have also developed, and new religious media markets (particularly in publishing) have emerged (Emerich 2006; Einstein 2007).

Generational differences and specificities also form the basis of important work on the mediation of religion. Simply put, there are significant differences in media consumption patterns and practices of reception between the generations. Most work in this area has focused on youth and youth cultures, places where the intersection between media and religion seems to be particularly significant. Youth are relatively heavier users of media and relatively less interested in religion than others, but at the same time, much religiously based media have been directed at the youth market (Clark 2003; Hendershot 2004). This opens two streams of inquiry: first, into the way in which religious media directed at youth might be succeeding in increasing interest and participation in religion; second, of how "secular" media might be being read in religious and spiritual ways by younger audiences. This latter direction is consistent, obviously, with the general theme we've been looking at here: the way in which the media context is an important framework for the construction and reconstruction of religious meaning and identity. Lynn Schofield Clark (2003), for example, has shown how youth audiences encounter and decode spiritually—and religiously—oriented media content in particular ways, potentially leading to the formation of new kinds and locations of identity.

The media as a field of inquiry also necessarily leads research in international and global directions. The ongoing processes of globalization are in many ways media phenomena. The speed and breadth of international communication have led to a situation in which social, cultural, economic, and political relations are increasingly translocal and transnational. In addition, the global context that is thus constructed has led to a situation such that formerly distinct cultural and social dimensions and contexts are elided and new landscapes of culture are formed (Ginsburg, Abu-Lughod, and Larkin 2002; Appadurai 1990). Within this context, further, the mediation of religion is increasingly important to social research and scholarship. First and foremost, the media provide the most obvious context for global religious representation, understanding, and conflict. The way in which religion is portrayed in international journalism, for example, is the primary way in which religions are understood within and outside their national contexts. This was most obvious in the events surrounding the 9/11 attacks and their consequences.

But there are other emerging scholarships focusing on religion and media in the global context. Certainly, much has changed since 9/11, with a seeming global boom in representations of religion in the media and in the production of media by religious interests of various kinds. The particular case of Islam is, of course, the most obvious. Scholars have looked at the representation of Islam in various contexts, including the Internet and the Web, as well as the use of digital media by Muslim organizations and interests. A more provocative area of research, however, is the emerging interest in how mediation in the Muslim world may be leading to a remaking of Islam in the global context (Kraidy 2002). Nabil Echchaibi (2007), for example, has argued that the emergence of new satellite networks in the Middle East has stimulated cultural ferment within the Muslim world, leading to the development and expression of newer, more media-oriented forms of Islam. This may well lead to more profound shifts as Islam, through its mediation, comes to a different position in global public discourse and global representations.

A range of studies have begun as well to look at the mediation of religion and culture in specific local contexts (Ginsburg, Abu-Lughod, and Larkin 2002). Against what was the dominant view of the relationship of media to local cultures, a variety of scholars are demonstrating that, rather than dominating local culture, those local cultures are increasingly in negotiation and dialogue with the global, leading to new media forms, and to new practices and identities (Meyer and Moors 2005). Examples range from indigenous identity practices in rural Australia (Ginsburg 2006), to popular religious practices in Egypt (Hirschkind 2006), to women's reception there (Abu-Lughod 2002), to the reception of Hindi film in India (Dwyer 2006). In these, there is a continued concordance with the overall theme that has marked the evolution of research in media and religion: a turn away from purely "instrumentalist" ways of understanding the relationship, toward more nuanced and complex analyses of ways in which religion and media are increasingly integrated.

As noted, the events of 9/11, as well as the Bali bombings, the Madrid train bombings, and the 2005 London Underground bombings, have moved issues of religion to the center of media discourse and media scholarship. We may never again face the situation where the sociological study of media can take place without reference to the question of religion. In the same way, religion scholarship is increasingly cognizant of the media, media symbolism, and the process of mediation. Yet there is much to be done. There is a range of contexts and phenomena remaining to be studied before a more substantive and comprehensive account of the role of media in the sociology of religion can be made.

References

Abu-Lughod, Lila (2002). "Egyptian Melodrama: Technology of the Modern Subject?" In Faye Ginsburg, Lila Abu-Lughod, and Brian Larkin (eds.), *Media Worlds: Anthropology on New Terrain.* Berkeley: University of California Press, 1–38.

Alexander, Jeffrey, and Smith, Philip (2002). "The Strong Program in Cultural Theory". In Jonathan H. Turner (ed.), *Handbook of Sociological Theory.* New York: Kluwer Academic/Plenum Publishers, 135–50.

Appadurai, Arjun (1990). "Disjuncture and Difference in the Global Cultural Economy". *Public Culture,* 2/2: 1–24.

Badaracco, Claire (2004). *Quoting God: How Media Shape Ideas about Religion and Culture.* Waco, Tex.: Baylor University Press.

Belk, Russell W., Wallendorf, Melanie, and Sherry, John F. Jr. (1989). "The Sacred and the Profane in Consumer Behavior: Theodicy on the Odyssey". *Journal of Consumer Research: An Interdisciplinary Quarterly,* 16: 1–38.

Bellah, Robert (1992). *The Broken Covenant: American Civil Religion in a Time of Trial.* Boston: Beacon Press.

Borden, Anne (2007). "What Would Jesus Buy? Christian Booksellers Negotiate Ministry and Markets". In Lynn Schofield Clark (ed.), *Religion, Media, and the Marketplace.* New Brunswick, NJ: Rutgers University Press, 67–89.

Brasher, Brenda (2001). *Give Me That Online Religion.* San Francisco: Jossey-Bass.

Bruce, Steve (1990). *Pray TV: Televangelism in America.* New York: Routledge.

Buddenbaum, Judith M. (1986). "Analysis of Religion News Coverage in Three Major Newspapers". *Journalism Quarterly,* 63: 600–6.

—— (1988). "The Religion Beat at Daily Newspapers". *Newspaper Research Journal,* 9: 57–69.

Campbell, Heidi (2005). *Exploring Religious Community Online: We Are One in the Network.* London: Peter Lang.

Carey, James (1989). "Media Rituals". Repr. in *idem, Communication as Culture: Essays on Media and Society.* Boston: Unwin-Hyman, 13–36.

Chidester, David, and Linenthal, Edward Tabor (eds.) (1995). *American Sacred Space.* Bloomington, Ind.: Indiana University Press.

Clark, Lynn Schofield (2003). *From Angels to Aliens: Teenagers, the Media, and the Supernatural.* New York: Oxford University Press.

Couldry, Nick (2003). *Media Rituals: A Critical Approach.* London: Routledge.

Dart, John, and Allen, Jimmy (1993). *Bridging the Gap: Religion and the News Media.* Published report of the Freedom Forum First Amendment Center, Vanderbilt University.

Dawson, Lorne, and Cowan, Douglas (eds.) (2004). *Religion Online/Online Religion: Finding Faith on the Internet.* New York: Routledge.

Dwyer, Rachel (2006). *Filming the Gods: Religion and Indian Cinema.* London: Routledge.

Echchaibi, Nabil (2007). "From the Pulpit to the Studio: Islam's Internal Battle". *Media Development,* 1: 16–19.

Einstein, Mara (2007). *Brands of Faith: Marketing Religion in a Commercial Age.* London: Routledge.

EMERICH, MONICA (2006). "The Spirituality of Sustainability: Healing the Self to Heal the World Through Healthy Living Media" (Ph.D. dissertation, University of Colorado).

FINKE, ROGER, and STARK, RODNEY (1993). *The Churching of America, 1776–1990: Winners and Losers in Our Religious Economy.* New Brunswick, NJ: Rutgers University Press.

FRANKL, RAZEELLE (1987). *Televangelism: The Marketing of Popular Religion.* Carbondale, Ill.: Southern Illinois University Press.

GADDY, GARY, and PRITCHARD, DAVID (1985). "When Watching Religious TV is like Attending Church". *Journal of Communication*, 35/1: 123–31.

GAUNTLETT, DAVID, and HILL, ANNETTE (1999). *TV Living: Television, Culture, and Everyday Life.* London: Routledge.

GERBNER, GEORGE, GROSS, LARRY, HOOVER, STEWART, MORGAN, MICHAEL, SIGNORIELLI, NANCY, WUTHNOW, ROBERT, and COTUGNO, HARRY (1986). *Religion and Television: The Annenberg–Gallup Study of Religious Broadcasting.* Philadelphia: The Annenberg School of Communications.

GERGEN, KENNETH (1991). *The Saturated Self: Dilemmas of Identity in Contemporary Life.* New York: Basic Books.

GIDDENS, ANTHONY (1991). *Modernity and Self-Identity: Self and Society in the Late Modern Age.* Stanford, Calif.: Stanford University Press.

GINSBURG, FAYE (2006). "Rethinking the Digital Age". Paper presented to the Conference on Media Change and Social Theory, Oxford University, 7 September.

—— ABU-LUGHOD, LILA, and LARKIN, BRIAN (2002). "Introduction". In *eadem* (eds.), *Media Worlds: Anthropology on New Terrain.* Berkeley: University of California Press, 1–38.

HADDEN, JEFFREY K., and SHUPE, ANSON (1988). *Televangelism: Power and Politics on God's Frontier.* New York: Henry Holt and Co.

—— and SWANN, CHARLES (1981). *Prime-Time Preachers: The Growing Power of Televangelism.* Reading, Mass.: Addison-Wesley.

HAMMOND, PHILLIP E. (1992). *Religion and Personal Autonomy: The Third Disestablishment in America.* Columbia, SC: University of South Carolina Press.

HANGEN, TONA (2002). *Redeeming the Dial: Radio, Religion, and Popular Culture in America.* Chapel Hill, NC: University of North Carolina Press.

HATCH, NATHAN O. (1989). *The Democratization of American Christianity.* New Haven: Yale University Press.

HELLAND, CHRISTOPHER (2000). "Online-Religion / Religion-Online and Virtual Communitas". In Jeffrey K. Hadden and Douglas E. Cowan (eds.), *Religion on the Internet: Research Prospects and Promises.* New York: JAI Press, 205–23.

—— (2004). "Popular Religion and the World Wide Web: A Match Made in [Cyber] Heaven". In Dawson and Cowan (2004), 23–35.

HENDERSHOT, HEATHER (2004). *Shaking the World for Jesus: Media and Conservative Evangelical Culture.* Chicago: University of Chicago Press.

HIRSCHKIND, CHARLES (2006). *The Ethical Soundscape: Cassette Sermons and Islamic Counterpublics.* New York: Columbia University Press.

HOOVER, STEWART M. (1988). *Mass Media Religion: The Social Sources of the Electronic Church.* Newbury Park, Calif.: Sage.

—— (1998). *Religion in the News: Faith and Journalism in American Public Discourse.* Newbury Park, Calif.: Sage.

Hoover, Stewart M. (2006). *Religion in the Media Age*. London: Routledge.

—— and Park, Jin Kyu (2002). "Religion and Meaning in the Digital Age: Field Research on Internet/Web Religion". Paper presented to the Association of Internet Researchers, 3.0, Maastricht.

—— and Venturelli, Shalini (1996). "The Category of the Religious: The Blindspot of Contemporary Media Theory?" *Cultural Studies in Mass Communication*, 13: 251–65.

—— Clark, Lynn Schofied, and Rainie, Lee (2004). *Faith Online: A Report of the Pew Internet in American Life Project*. Arlington, Va.: Pew Internet in American Life Project.

Horsfield, Peter (1984). *Religious Television: The American Experience*. New York: Longman Press.

Hunter, James D. (1992). *Culture Wars: The Struggle to Define America*. New York: Basic Books.

Kraidy, Marwan (2002). "Arab Satellite Television: Between Regionalization and Globalization". *Global Media Journal*, 11 available at <http://lass.calumet.perdue.edu/cca/gmj/fa02/gmj-kraidy.htm>.

Lichter, S., Rober, Rothman, Stanley, and Lichter, Linda S. (1986). *The Media Elite*. Baltimore: Adler and Adler.

Lindsay, Michael (2006). "Faith in the Corridors of Power: Religious Identity and Public Leadership" (Ph.D. dissertation, Princeton University).

Marsden, George (1983). "Preachers of Paradox: The Religious New Right in Historical Perspective". In M. Douglas and S. Tipton (eds.), *Religion and America*. Boston: Beacon Press, 150–68.

Martin-Barbero, Jesus (1997). "Mass Media as a Site of Resacralization of Contemporary Cultures". In Stewart M. Hoover, and Knut Lundby (eds.), *Rethinking Media, Religion and Culture*. Beverly Hills, Calif.: Sage, 102–16.

McCloud, Sean (2004). "Popular Culture Fandoms, the Boundaries of Religious Studies, and the Project of the Self". *Culture and Religion*, 4/2: 187–206.

McDannell, Colleen (1995). *Material Christianity: Religion and Popular Culture in America*. New Haven: Yale University Press.

Meyer, Birgit, and Moors, Annelies (2005). "Introduction". In *eadem* (eds.), *Religion, Media, and the Public Sphere*. Bloomington, Ind.: Indiana University Press, 1–28.

Mitchell, Jolyon (1999). *Visually Speaking: Radio and the Renaissance of Preaching*. Edinburgh: T & T Clark.

Moore, Lawrence (1994). *Selling God: American Religion in the Marketplace of Culture*. New York: Oxford University Press.

Morgan, David (1998). *Visual Piety: A History and Theory of Popular Religious Images*. Berkeley: University of California Press.

—— (1999). *Protestants and Pictures: Religion, Visual Culture, and the Age of American Mass Production*. New York: Oxford University Press.

—— (2005). *The Sacred Gaze: Religious Visual Culture in Theory and Practice*. Berkeley: University of California Press.

—— (2007). *The Lure of Images: A History of Religion and Visual Media in the United States*. London: Routledge.

Nord, David Paul (2004). *Faith in Reading: Religious Publishing and the Birth of Mass Media in America, 1790–1860*. New York: Oxford University Press.

O'Leary, Stephen D. (1996). "Cyberspace as Sacred Space: Communicating Religion on Computer Networks". *Journal of the American Academy of Religion*, 64/4: 781–808.

PARKER, EVERETT, BARRY, DAVID, and SMYTHE, DALLAS (1955). *The Television–Radio Audience and Religion.* New York: Harper.

PECK, JANICE (1993). *The Gods of Televangelism.* Cresskill, NJ: Hampton Press.

RITZER, GEORGE (1996). *The McDonaldization of Society: An Investigation into the Changing Character of Contemporary Social Life.* Thousand Oaks, Calif.: Pine Forge Press.

ROOF, WADE CLARK (1999). *Spiritual Marketplace: Baby Boomers and the Remaking of American Religion.* Princeton: Princeton University Press.

ROSENTHAL, MICHELLE (2002). "Turn it Off: TV Criticism in Christian Century Magazine, 1946–1960". In Stewart M. Hoover and Lynn Schofield Clark (eds.), *Practicing Religion in the Age of the Media: Explorations in Media, Religion, and Culture.* New York: Columbia University Press, 138–62.

ROTHENBUHLER, ERIC (1993). *Ritual Communication: From Everyday Conversation to Mediated Ceremony.* Newbury Park, Calif.: Sage.

—— and COMAN, MIHAI (2005). *Media Anthropology.* Newbury Park, Calif.: Sage.

SCHMALZBAUR, JOHN (2002). "Between Objectivity and Moral Vision: Catholics and Evangelicals in American Journalism". In Stewart M. Hoover and Lynn Schofield Clark (eds.), *Practicing Religion in the Age of the Media: Explorations in Media, Religion, and Culture.* New York: Columbia University Press, 165–87.

SCHMIDT, LEIGH ERIC (1995). *Consumer Rites: The Buying and Selling of American Holidays.* Princeton: Princeton University Press.

SCHULTZE, QUENTIN (1987). "The Mythos of the Electronic Church". *Critical Studies in Mass Communication*, 4/3: 245–61.

—— (ed.) (1990). *American Evangelicals and the Mass Media.* Grand Rapids, Mich.: Academie Press.

SILK, MARK (1995). *Unsecular Media: Marking News of Religion in America.* Urbana, Ill.: University of Illinois Press.

STOUT, DANIEL, and BUDDENBAUM, JUDITH (eds.) (1996). *Religion and Mass Media: Audiences and Adaptations.* Thousand Oaks, Calif.: Sage.

—— —— (eds.) (2001). *Religion and Popular Culture: Studies on the Interaction of Worldviews.* Ames, Ia.: Iowa State University Press.

UNDERWOOD, DOUG (2002). *From Yahweh to Yahoo!: The Religious Roots of the Secular Press.* Urbana, Ill.: University of Illinois Press.

WARNER, R. STEPHEN (1993). "Work in Progress toward a New Paradigm for the Study of Religion in the United States". *American Journal of Sociology*, 98/5: 1044–93.

WARREN, HILLARY (2005). *There's Never Been a Show Like Veggie Tales: Sacred Messages in a Secular Market.* Walnut Creek, Calif.: AltaMira Press.

WILLIAMS, PETER (1997). *Houses of God: Region, Religion, and Architecture in the United States.* Urbana, Ill.: University of Illinois Press.

WUTHNOW, ROBERT (1998). *After Heaven: Spirituality in America since the 1950s.* Berkeley: University of California Press.

ZALESKI, JEFFREY (1997). *The Soul of Cyberspace: How New Technology is Changing our Spiritual Lives.* New York: Harper Collins.

ZELIZER, BARBIE (1993). *Covering the Body: The Kennedy Assassination, the Media, and the Shaping of Collective Memory.* Chicago: University of Chicago Press.

—— and ALLEN, STUART (2002). *Journalism after September 11.* New York: Routledge.

Suggested Reading

The following are recommended: Clark (2003); Ginsburg, Abu-Lughod, and Larkin (2002); Hendershot (2004); Hoover (2006); Lynch (2005); Meyer and Moors (2006); Morgan (2007); Rothenbuhler and Coman (2005); and Underwood (2002).

CHAPTER 39

RELIGION AND THE INTERNET

GARY R. BUNT

Introduction

Studying religions on the Internet requires a synthesis of conventional religious studies methodologies, combined with knowledge and awareness of disparate fields associated with technology and cyber cultures. The study of this field was met by scepticism in its early period by some involved in the study of religions, but that antipathy and dismissal have been dissipated to an extent by recognition that, for many aspects of the study of religion, the Internet is now a crucial area for the understanding of contemporary religious issues. However, there are dangers in overemphasizing the transformative powers of the Internet in the area of religion, and clearly each case must be assessed on its own merit. Exploring religions through cyberspace provides new opportunities for exposure to religious ideas, but also introduces significant new theoretical and methodological questions associated with contemporary phenomenology. The subject is an appropriate one for diverse perspectives and interpretations, especially in terms of how content is gathered and analysed.

The Internet, within and between its different elements and forms, holds transformative potential for religions, in terms of representation, networking, by adherents, and application as a proselytizing tool. As access intensifies and technology

I am grateful to Dr Wendy Dossett (Lampeter) and Tony Fox for their comments on aspects of this work during its preparation.

becomes cheaper, those well placed in the information marketplace will reap potential 'benefits' of access. Even the most reluctant or technophobic agents of diverse forms of religious belief and expression in diverse cultures have found a place online. Some strands of belief may now be dependent on search engine ratings and placement to acquire and maintain an impact or profile, especially towards those areas of technologically literate populations with access and inclination to utilize the Net as a primary source of knowledge about religions and their adherents.

There are many dynamic and interactive elements of religion and the Internet to consider, centring on a variety of belief perspectives. These raise a number of provocative issues, some of which still need to be addressed by academics. These include the ways in which Internet media are applied to represent spiritual and religious interests online. Levels of interactivity are particularly significant, with some sites offering specific 'religious experiences' via their pages. Others endeavour to present sacred texts, either to existing believers and/or to outsiders, for example, in the case of proselytizing religions and/or apologists for a belief.

Contemporary approaches to 'mapping the sacred' encompass diverse approaches to understanding religious world views and practices, and can now in many cases incorporate an Internet element. Religious organizations, platforms, and individuals can increasingly be seen as media and service providers. This introduces specific marketplace issues—for example, as some websites become commercial hubs, as well as self-contained environments for religious activities in varied forms. Organizations and platforms associated with beliefs can operate as broadcast channels, news providers, and multimedia concerns. There is a commercial edge to the Internet and religion, as part of the wider electronic media footprint associated with some forms of religious expression.

Into this equation, one should also consider the religious content of conventional 'mainstream' broadcasters and the evolving media distribution models that are changing the nature of global broadcasting. This introduces the issue of media saturation, with multi-channel choices extended within and between religious concerns too. This may allow individuals to engage with perspectives outside narrow, culture-centric traditional approaches, and to exchange views through forums. In some cases, this can have a profound effect on individuals. The Web has certainly offered wider exposure for certain strands of belief, and a sense of 'connectivity' within and between small networks. Web content and interaction can, according to some observers, contribute to increases in participation within diverse religiously oriented activities generated and represented online. The extent to which this translates into affiliation and membership, if relevant, is open to question. The spiritual supermarket now has an online checkout, where surfers may shop for the religious concepts and artefacts that appeal to them. The Internet has also provided opportunities for religious organizations to acquire data about their own adherents and/or those with an interest (altruistic or otherwise) in their beliefs. However, as much as being an agent of change, religious expression on the

Internet may also engender conformity and tradition, especially within specific micro-areas of religious interests, driven by notions of membership.

Content associated with religion can also be viewed as 'entertainment'. Service providers may be competing to provide entertaining religious content. External channels may be highlighting aspects of religion that are seen as humorous or voyeuristically appealing (to some), or facilitating social networks to create new forms of religious space. Specific challenges of the nature of content emerge: poorly considered or designed content will not reach readers in the same way as technologically slick and regularly refreshed sites, which create a sense of ownership. It may also alienate 'traditionalists'. In cyberspace, one can observe shifting models of religious organizations and authorities increasingly being challenged by 'smaller' players and individuals. They are unable to match sharp reactive content and focus (or control it), especially when it is generated through forums, blogs, tagging, and/or social networking tools.

Specific questions emerge on the social reach of computer-mediated religious material, which also impacts on the inherent social divisions within content production and consumption models (Cowan and Dawson 2004). The Internet and computer access continue to grow, although it should be kept in mind that in many contexts Internet access remains in the hands of an elite. This 'digital divide' influences the nature of religious materials on the Web, in terms of the type of audiences it may have and also in terms of who is providing the content.

Studying Religions through Cyberspace

In approaching this field, consideration should be given to the substantial amount of research undertaken on the sociology of cyberspace in general. McLuhan anticipated many issues in his seminal works (McLuhan 1967; McLuhan and Fiore 1967; 1968). A number of ground-breaking studies informed the academic and developmental models associated with cyber studies (Castells 1996; 2000; 2004; Negroponte 1995; Rheingold 1993; Turkle 1995). Whilst religion was referred to in some of these works, a specific early analysis of virtual rituals emerged from O'Leary (1996). Contributions within Hadden and Cowan's edited volume (2000) suggested theoretical frameworks for the study of religions in cyberspace. Substantial work has subsequently been undertaken in a variety of areas associated with specific religions in (and of) cyberspace (discussed below).

Some works have related specifically to disciplinary frameworks associated with studying aspects of religions and the media. Others involved in the contemporary study of religions have integrated consideration of cyber frameworks as part of their analysis. This recognizes the potential impact of the Internet on aspects of the knowledge flow, religious authority, and religious identity. Not all works are published in print form: websites and blogs have emerged as study resources in their own right, some managed by academics and/or supported by scholarly bodies and institutions. Many journalistic contributions have also added to the volume of knowledge and resources associated with this area of study.

Those intending to study religion in cyberspace may do so from a number of diverse disciplinary perspectives, including specialization in a specific religious belief framework. The study of religions in cyberspace has become a subject for study in its own right, with several universities offering degree-level courses on the subject, and postgraduate research degrees being awarded on associated themes, such as the research, development, and management of digitized texts. Those seeking to undertake such studies need to develop sustained awareness of contemporary information-technological trends and innovation.

For those from technically literate generations, brought up in the Internet age, such familiarity may already exist or be easier to develop. Such literacy goes beyond the operation of computers and information technology, towards a developed awareness of the language and technical development issues associated with Internet cultures. Knowledge of the etiquette of chat-rooms and mailing lists, the construction of web pages, the delivery of content through different formats, and the construction of online identities are all significant strands of knowledge that need to be cultivated. Familiarity with filtering technology and censorship issues is also important. Added to this should be the study of the development of computers and the Internet, and familiarity with diverse methodological and disciplinary theories associated with computer-mediated communications, both in general and in specifically religious spheres. This may be integrated with an appreciation of studies associated with the study of religions and the media.

Those who have studied religions (whether insiders or outsiders) in recent times are likely to have recognized the potential of the Internet as a research resource, and to have knowledge of the architecture and system flows of Internet knowledge. Training is required on the systems which need to be put in place for continual monitoring and archiving of site changes relating to research areas, including news feeds, blogs, social networking sites, portals, and forums. A degree of training in determining the origins and 'reliability' of such information can also be relevant. Different notions of fieldwork, interaction, and data capture can be applicable in cyberspace, although familiarity with 'real world' practices remains necessary. Students of religion and the Internet need to develop appropriate methodologies for the capture, recording, and storage of data; this can include the backing up of materials, given the potential for computer systems failure realized to the cost of some early pioneers in the field. Above all, there is a need to adapt and react to evolving and mutating cyber environments that cannot always be systemized in a scientific, rigid, or hierarchical fashion.

Developing maps of the relationships between religions and the Internet is not just a textual exercise; such activities can involve diverse software, recording techniques, and media. It may require the integration of different search engine models and methodologies, including the 'deep searching' of Web areas not covered by conventional search engines, as well as utilizing techniques for making optimum academic use of these resources.

The Internet has also become a repository of information about religions, some of it previously obscure, such as where adherents and/or scholars have placed precious information such as manuscripts or archives online. This may expose marginalized or difficult-to-locate documents to a wider audience. However, within the shifting landscape of the Net, one can only conjecture how much content on or about religions has been lost, trashed, or closed to view. It may not be archived appropriately, or available for general access, given the personal and ephemeral nature of some content. Much may be lost, whilst the sheer quantity of data introduces difficulties in the management and observation of even relative micro-areas associated with religions in cyberspace. The Internet spectrum is a complex and ever-changing phenomenon in relation to religion. Its intricacy is engendered not only by the diversity of frequently changing and evolving materials in many languages, but also by the changing nature of technology. Tools such as blogs, podcasts, and social networking sites combine with technological innovations, such as webcams and MP3–4 players, to impact on how scholars explore and interpret religions and the Internet.

Questions that have a specific Internet edge have emerged in relation to the study of religion: these include the textual impact of sacred texts as searchable objects, whose content can be rapidly mined for key words and concepts. This may be dependent on the interface dynamics and design impact, as well as considerations of content ownership, editing, data input accuracy, provision, and design. Texts are reduced to data bytes. Hyperlinks may possess a 'value' as religious object, whilst the symbolism and iconography of religion can require a phenomenological assessment of whether computer-mediated religion and ritual are legitimate in the eyes of its practitioners and a religion's authorities. Religious expression on the Internet may in some cases be read in conjunction with questions associated with objectives such as conversion, networking, and spiritual enhancement. Some sites may be closed and secured for members only, and seek to maintain a low profile. Nuanced models of readers and content apply in any interpretation. Into the equation, factors such as censorship, the financial cost and availability of access, and users' IT knowledge and education can create barriers and restrictions to access. Some online materials may receive a relatively small audience, but that may be substantial compared with pre-digital equivalents.

Versions of religious texts can be found online, some of them benefiting from scholarly interpretations. Critiques of such materials also receive an online airing. Heightened familiarity of these issues is relevant not just for those studying this field, but for those whose research requires reference to, or application of, the Internet and digital materials. There are specific issues of the observation of such sites, but also the ethical concerns associated with researcher identity, the use of avatars, and anonymity. There is also a need to identify patterns of Internet use by different sectors of society, reflected in the many ways in which site content is presented by organizations and individuals, or fragmented for consumption by different audiences. Organizations linked to many religions have chosen to place their own 'official' sites online, including sects and subgroups. The ways in which on-screen information is read, processed, and distributed can differ from conventional information distribution, and there can be inherent difficulties of information overload to address on many sites. Users of such materials may be faced with similar challenges, with 'Internet addiction' occurring in religious spheres as much as in other areas.

For many subjects associated with religion in the contemporary world, the appropriate application and study of resources are imperative within research projects, and indeed the medium itself has become the focus of attention. For those with access, the Net is the primary resource and can create a critical first impression about a religion and its adherents. It is a natural phenomenon for those seeking information about a religion, from whatever background, to search for it using the Internet. The ways in which Google or other search engines are used, and the parameters of the search, are influential. A site's rating in Google has been based in part on meta-data contained within its HTML coding, on the popularity of hyperlinks from other websites that link to it, and its PageRank. Surfers may choose to visit the top-ranked site, or one that appears in online advertisements such as a GoogleAd, rather than take a deep search beyond the first page of results. The typology of information available from websites can differ substantially, especially between 'popular' and 'academic' sites, although there can be considerable cross-over between and within these two phenomena. Major search engines such as Windows Live Search, Yahoo! Search, and Google produce different results, based on their algorithms and other search criteria.

Google was the most prominent searching tool (at the time of writing) and relevant for some academic activities. However, there is little point simply putting 'God' into Google. The results are non-specific and confusing. The number of hits is almost infinite. Refined surfing will allow a more sophisticated, research-oriented approach to develop. Deep searching, using tools which go beyond Google (which only searches a relatively small proportion of the World-Wide Web), can add extra layers of understanding to the quest for knowledge online. As with all search engines, it is imperative that care is taken when entering search phrases, and options of alternative terms and spellings (especially in relation to transliterated words) should be considered. When working in a language other than English, there will be appropriate alternative search engines to integrate into data-mining activities. It must also be considered that there is a substantial 'invisible web' of data, which cannot be located through conventional channels. A certain level of lateral thinking is essential, including the application of portals and specialized digital channels of research. Computer searching should combine with human interaction, drawing on the appropriate expertise of subject librarians and academics, especially in a micro-field of study associated with the study of religion.

It can be necessary to determine the origins of a site, in terms of its ideological-theological approach to a religious belief, but also in relation to affiliated organizations and its geographical location. Some sites are apparently transparent about their location and origin, providing a postal address and telephone contact numbers together with e-mail addresses, which may or may not be genuine. In some cases, however, this information is not immediately available. The reasons for this can vary: a site may be presenting a 'controversial' view, and personal data on its authors and origins could compromise the site and the safety of its affiliates. Its authors may be at risk of censorship or imprisonment for their beliefs. Clearly, there are some important academic and ethical issues at stake, when attempts are made to 'track down' the authors. Governmental agencies (and others) may have access to sophisticated electronic tools to determine the origins and ownership of a site. Those are not the tools that are under discussion here, however, but rather the generic tools which are publicly available for any Internet user to find out more about a site. These tools have many applications: in some cases, they can be utilized to determine the origins of 'spam' mail; they can be used to track the source of 'offensive' Web content. It has to be said, in both cases, that there are many ways to avoid being tracked in this fashion.

Some Internet companies have been accused of collaborating in varying degrees with state agencies to develop specific censorship and filtering protocols, in some cases leading to the persecution of 'transgressors', including those associated with specific religious views. Filtering technology uses a complex of algorithms to determine and remove terms that its program deems as contentious. The parameters of such filtering can be adjusted, but standard packages may filter out some 'religious' content. Some religious perspectives have been subject to filtering technology. For example, pagan sites were incorporated into a 'ban' by one filtering package under the umbrella of 'Satanic/cult' beliefs. Another package filtered out an Understanding Islam site, the Quakers, and a Holocaust Remembrance site. A study found that the Saudi Arabian government reportedly applied filtering technology to prevent access to sites containing content on a variety of religions: 'For example, we found blocking of at least 246 pages indexed by Yahoo as Religion (including 67 about Christianity, 45 about Islam, 22 about Paganism, 20 about Judaism, and 12 about Hinduism)' (Zittrain and Edelman 2002). There is evidence of other governments filtering out 'religious' (and other) content. There are a number of organizations and individuals monitoring such censorship, and it is also a theme in a number of chat-rooms (Reporters Sans Frontières).

A glimpse into the ways in which religions and the Internet might effectively be studied, if specific financial and human resources are available, has been presented in the field of 'terrorism studies'. Clearly, the objectives of the following example are very different from those generally present in the study of religions; but it does demonstrate how sustained technical and human resources *could* be applied in a quantitative approach to an aspect of political-religious expression on the Internet. The University of Arizona's Artificial Intelligence Lab (henceforth AI Lab) benefited from sustained investment in content analysis of '*jihadi*' materials online, including a comprehensive archive of content harvested and catalogued from the Internet. Certain aspects of the methodologies and resources applied there cannot always be realistically envisaged as being applied to other, relatively more mundane and under-funded areas associated with the study of religions and the Internet. AI Lab draws upon the utilization of a mass of appropriate technology, a team of highly trained researchers in computer science and subject specific fields, and a sustained plan of future research. There are elements that might be useful in determining parameters for work on the study of religion and the Internet.

Members of the AI Lab applied automated Web harvesting technology, including analysis of backlinks (the external hyperlinks linking into a site) as a means of exploring *jihadi* cyberspace. These tools focus on key players, primarily at an organizational level, which is one part of a more complex picture: they are not necessarily useful in picking up the finer details and nuanced statements on cyberspace, including the output of those sites which are not focused on generating substantial numbers of hits for a mass market, but are more concerned with reaching or creating a specific, small group of adherents to a specific political-cultural-religious interpretation. The organizational emphasis does not leave room for our understanding of individuals or small groups, perhaps working autonomously without a direct link to a specific organizational platform. The number of links or hits is only one indicator of influence; a closed site may have more impact on community and society. As with any study of cyberspace, a machine-generated analysis is a snapshot of a particular space at a certain time, which can evolve and change rapidly. Automatic information retrieval has been applied, including indexing algorithms, as a means of retrieving key conceptual data from vast numbers of materials. AI Lab has also approached *jihadi* cyberspace through the development of visual software, intended to enable a reader to understand the (on- and offline) interconnectivity between *jihadi* organizations (Chen *et al.* 2005). There is certainly room for a variety of approaches to such subject material; the *modus operandi* of the AI Lab was not the same as that of an academic concerned with the study of religion; but the two approaches may have much to gain from each other. In AI Lab's case, working with one criteria for analysis being an understanding of a 'threat level' clouds understanding of other aspects of the cyber environment, and it may be that a holistic understanding of all aspects of beliefs as placed online would offer more granulated and complex interpretative opportunities.

It must be recognized that analysis of cyber materials still remains one aspect of a more complex picture of real-world activities, albeit one that is integrated into the world views of many people. This raises issues associated with the capture and analysis of data in relation to religion and the Internet, whether the information be randomly acquired (perhaps derived from the intuition of a reader, a tip, or hyperlink from another site, forum or portal, or a search engine), or the product of a systemized 'scientific' trawl.

The ever-changing face of the World-Wide Web means that sites evolve, change content, and at times disappear or relocate. Unlike print content, there may not be a 'hard copy' of a particular site. This can be problematic, particularly if it is referred to in a textbook. In extreme circumstances, hacking and other disruptive activities can also alter a site's appearance and content. There is no formal archiving of the Internet, raising specific methodological concerns for those students of religion seeking to interpret the historical impact of, for example, specific websites for religious interests. In order to interpret religion on the Internet from a contemporary perspective, data management and archiving skills have to combine with the ability to process a broad range of ever-changing pages and information. There are some online options regarding archived Web materials. The Internet Archive, established by Alexa in 1996, has been 'crawling' and preserving a broad range of sites in a resource which is publicly available. It is possible to create specific searches based on thematic or site parameters. Although comprehensive, the Internet Archive crawls sites only on a bi-monthly basis, and does not necessarily reach all areas of the Web. Some sites prevent their content from being crawled. Others request its deletion, or have been deleted because of their 'contentious' content, and a proportion of sites do not necessarily get visited at all. The Internet Archive (1996) and similar services do present enormous opportunities for scholars engaged in the study of religion on the Internet.

Research of this nature also requires clarification of site ownership, determined through a number of different tools, which provide a variety of technical data and related data, based on the input of an IP (Internet Protocol) address. This is the unique numeric code that each computer and website has. On some occasions, this code is cloaked or obscured from monitoring. Further information about a site can be gleaned from determining who is hyperlinked to it. This can include supporters and opponents who have chosen to incorporate a site's URL (Uniform Resource Locator) into their own pages. They may have blogged and commented on the site, or interpreted the data in a way that is of research interest. Checking a site's affiliations, through application of a generic tool such as SamSpade.org, is particularly useful when exploring 'minority' perspectives, which cannot be located through conventional searching methods.

Many religious platforms now utilize diverse media such as television, radio, print, and recordings in conjunction with the Internet. These diverse media interact with the Internet too—for example, in making archived broadcasts available online. Examples could include evangelical sermons or religious performances, archived for a (potential) global audience. Exactly who uses such content is open to question: the counters that record page visits are not necessarily a useful indicator of how a site is being used. For example, one person might download a sermon, and then print it out and copy it hundreds of times for a local audience, burn it on CD-ROM or DVD, or re-present it on another website. The potentially high degrees of anonymity in cyberspace also make realistic assessment of visitor profiles problematic.

Representing Religions in Cyberspace

The motivation for placing religious material on the Web can vary considerably. For some, it is an attempt to digitally distil a religious experience and place it online, although whether such transference is successful is clearly in the eye of the beholder. Degrees of 'ritual' may appear or be represented online for many purposes: to explain to outsiders a belief practice, to encourage new adherents, to engender a sense of identity amongst existing practitioners, and/or to reflect and relate to offline social processes and interactions. The concept of a specific online religion or belief, with no offline equivalent (at least at its developmental stage), has been a key innovation; whether there is any measure or criterion through which the 'success' of such ventures can be measured is open to discussion. The development and innovation of religious practices and concepts online might range from the opinions articulated by scholars in response to readers' questions on existing religious practices, to entirely new religious frameworks and ideas.

The formulation and exploration of faith identities through discussion forums is one example of such concepts, explored by a number of scholars. It may not be feasible to replicate offline religious facilities and resources online, but that may not be the intention: a critical issue is online representation. In order to 'prove' their existence to the wider world, religious beliefs may require a virtual presence, although that is not always a desirable objective for some religious organizations and individuals. If they are to publicize their online existence, it may be as simple as presenting a URL on a sign outside a religious building, alongside the times of services. Rather than being an innovation, a virtual presence has become a standard requirement for many religious beliefs. Significantly, it is the nature of that representation which is more important. In some religious societal contexts, the Internet offers an opportunity for members to maintain and enhance their religious beliefs and identities through online interaction.

The virtual representation of a belief system may take many forms, ranging from the purely textual to the multimedia. The popularity of Second Life saw a further development requiring the monitoring of scholars. Second Life is a virtual world, where participants can create their own digital avatar according to their personal wishes; the avatar can travel, in pictorial form, through a variety of landscapes and settings, meeting other avatars in the process. There is the possibility of events and activities that go beyond simple 'chat'; inevitably, there are commercial ramifications to some of these elements, with the establishment of Second Life representation of online shops. Religions have been establishing virtual places of worship, such as churches, a synagogue, and a mosque (Islam 2007; Second Life 2003–).

A further critical consideration is how one can measure the effectiveness of the presentation of an online message associated with religion, in comparison with other formats. Surfing a page can be a different experience from reading the printed page, especially if the reader is scanning for key words, hyperlinks, multimedia, and other elements such as advertising links. The motivation for surfing a page can be varied: it may, for example, emerge from a search engine, from advertising, or from a link to another site. A reader may perform a quick search of a page, to determine its relevance, before moving on to another site. Site designers may build a variety of possible reader models into their sites, whilst also ensuring that content is picked up effectively through search engines. Reader experiences of the computer-mediated site content can also be substantially different, and one cannot make assumptions about audiences/readers, infrastructures, content delivery models, and/or equipment availability/accessibility. Visiting religious material online can be part of a wider surfing pattern, integrating other areas of the Web, not all of which could be classified within the 'religious' genre.

In developing an initial typology of religious content online, a variety of models emerge, ranging from central sites, portals, and authority models to offshoots in the forms of critiques, hubs, and diverse belief interests. The model is further nuanced through consideration of multimedia content, forums, social networking sites, and integrated streaming/download/podcast media approaches. The emergence of a variety of content-delivery platforms outside the personal computer is also important: Web Assisted Phones, Personal Digital Assistants, and Internet-enabled television (through entertainment centres) have opened up new audiences to material and required content providers to adapt their content provision. Operating systems have increasingly been refined to provide personal integrated media hubs, linked to personal computers. Shifts in access patterns and formats of materials also influence how religion is read online, such as RSS feeds, blogs, podcasts, and video-blogs.[1] Whether this is a shift away from the printed word, or supplementary to it, is open to question, especially as there is potential for many new audiences to be exposed to such materials via the Net. Individuals may read

[1] RSS refers to formats of feeds derived from the Web, including Really Simple Syndication, Rich Site Summary, and RDF (Resource Description Framework) Site Summary. These can be applied in blogs, podcasts, and regularly updated Web content such as news sites. See Wikipedia, 'RSS', <http://en.wikipedia.org/wiki/RSS_(file_format)>.

fewer books, may read them differently, and may also access different books as the Internet extends choice of possible purchases and enhances potential academic dialogues and interactions through forums, e-mail listings, and blogs. This is analogous to the Long Tail of Internet economics, a concept introduced by Chris Anderson (2004): 'The Long Tail equation is simple: 1) The lower the cost of distribution, the more you can economically offer without having to predict demand. 2) The more you can offer, the greater the chance that you will be able to tap latent demand for minority tastes that was unreachable through traditional retail. 3) Aggregate enough minority taste, and you'll often find [you] get a big new market.' 'The Long Tail' can relate equally to concepts associated with religions and the Internet, with 'minority tastes' being served via the Internet.

The Internet may offer greater access to source materials through bibliographical databases, retailers, and file exchange, presenting a cost-effective model for diffusion of opinions. For some, a sense of an online religious community or identity can be enhanced through the Internet, in particular websites operating religious 'product' placements, special elements for subscribers, interaction with fellow adherents, and an interface with other forms of religious media. For students working to find out more about religion, the answer may be Internet-driven—for example, searching for information on a specific belief or even using an essay bank(!) Bibliographical databases may lead to other materials: the provision of digital books, with key content providers such as Amazon and Google developing in this area, is likely to increase further and shift perceptions and methods of knowledge retrieval in association with the study of religions. Online collaboratively edited resources such as Wikipedia can be another significant source; such sources may not be academically refereed, and can contain content that, in some cases, has been deemed contentious or inaccurate by critics. But this has not stopped Wikipedia being cited in academic discourse.

Conventional print publishers have shifted content of their reference works into cyberspace, as adjuncts or in some cases replacements of print editions. They are effectively competing with resources specifically developed for online use from outside the publishing sphere, often with volunteer input: Project Gutenberg (1971–) and the Internet Sacred Texts Archive (1999–) have both endeavoured to make copies of significant texts available for study and use. Again, specialist sites have emerged, focusing on the texts of specific belief orientations or interests, such as ancient religious beliefs (*Encyclopedia Mythica* 1995–). Other specific hubs and search pages present the human interfaces of their authors and opportunities for interaction, rather than being driven by data-management logarithms. Academic expertise on the study of religions may be found on the Web in many forms, including blogs and podcasts on academic subjects. The fresh perspectives and alternatives contained through social networking tools have an impact on perceptions of religion for a wider population, if not in academic discourse.

A Template for Future Study

Shifts in the study of religions and the Internet have been observed. It is no longer necessary to explain (basic) information technology to academic and other readers. Some readers may still be technophobic to a degree, but awareness of the implications of information culture and computer-mediated communication has heightened. Conversely, when discussing Internet developments, it may be necessary to explain to younger readers the relative limitations of equipment and services in the past. These include file-size issues, slow download times, poor connections, slow equipment, text-only browsers, early alternative browsers, and the development of ARPANET.

Site observation requires new skills (and academic infrastructure), including awareness of design, XML, HTML, Flash, Macromedia, RSS, site management, technological knowledge, deep searching techniques, site tracking analysis, and information management. Studying religions on the Internet can be labour-intensive to a major level, requiring constant recording, observation, file backup, user-impact analysis, and awareness of technological shifts. Content analysis includes determining design considerations, evaluating hyperlinks, tracking content, and observing the refresh rate of new materials. Undertaking such studies can require regular harvesting of site data; this introduces a complex number of issues associated with the archiving of digital data, its storage and preservation, and associated concerns relating to format issues and degradable content. Data can be vulnerable, especially if there are viruses in the system or proactive hackers/crackers can access the database. Academic libraries are not necessarily geared to facilitate high levels of digital storage and archiving.

A key question is what snatches of electronic conversation and digital pages will be preserved for future scholars? Much is lost: e-mail evaporates, databases crash, personal content not intended for public consumption is hidden on hard drives, which may be wiped or destroyed. The ephemeral nature of the Net, the mundane nature of content, and the sheer volume of material raise specific issues for those analysing the relationships between religions and the Internet. Scholars in this area should have the facility to adapt, think, and react immediately to shifting content, technology, and service provision. These issues affect any researcher whose work brings them into contact with religions and the Internet, even marginally, indicating that this is a significant area of training for new scholars. A number of institutions associated with the study of religions offer such training (Bunt 2005; Institute for Textual Scholarship and Electronic Editing 2005–).

Knowledge of the *Zeitgeist* surrounding specific online manifestations of religious understanding is particularly relevant. It brings in specific issues associated with user knowledge and profiles. It also has implications in terms of fieldwork: users may be anonymous or unwilling to divulge details of their surfing habits. Their personal security may be threatened; activities in the name of religion may be clandestine; users may fear that their movements are being tracked and recorded by security organizations. Attempts to cover their tracks can inhibit research. It is problematic to attempt to acquire a representative sample of surfing habits in specific religious-cultural groups; claims of religious activities online may mask or interact with other surfing activities, including shopping, interaction with popular culture, and social networking.

References

Anderson, Chris (2004). 'The Long Tail'. *Wired*, 12/10; <http://www.wired.com/wired/archive/12.10/tail.html>.

Artificial Intelligence Lab, 'Dark Web Terrorism Research', <http://ai.arizona.edu/research/terror/index.htm>, accessed 10 Sept. 2005.

Beckerlegge, Gwilym (2001). *From Sacred Text to Internet*. Aldershot and Burlington, Vt.: Ashgate and Open University.

Brasher, Brenda E. (2001). *Give Me That Online Religion*. San Francisco: Jossey-Bass.

Bunt, Gary R. (2000). *Virtually Islamic: Computer-Mediated Communication and Cyber Islamic Environments*. Cardiff: University of Wales Press.

—— (2001). *The Good Web Guide to World Religions*. London: Good Web Guide.

—— (2003). *Islam in the Digital Age: E-Jihad, Online Fatwas and Cyber Islamic Environments*. London: Pluto Press.

—— (2005). *MA Module: Studying Religion on the Internet*. Lampeter: University of Wales.

Campbell, Heidi (2005). *Exploring Religious Community Online: We Are One in the Network*. New York: P. Lang.

Careaga, Andrew (2001). *Eministry: Connecting with the Net Generation*. Grand Rapids, Mich.: Kregel Publications.

Castells, Manuel (1996). *The Rise of the Network Society*. Malden, Mass.: Blackwell Publishers.

—— (2000). *End of Millennium*. Oxford and Malden, Mass.: Blackwell Publishers.

—— (2004). *The Power of Identity*. Malden, Mass.: Blackwell Publishers.

Chen, Hsinchun, Qin, Jialun, Reid, Edna, Chung, Wingyan, Zhou, Yilu, Xi, Wei, Lai, Guanpi, Bonillas, Alfonso A., and Sageman, Marc (2005). 'The Dark Web Portal: Collecting and Analyzing the Presence of Domestic and International Terrorist Groups on the Web'. *IEEE Intelligent Systems Archive*, 20/5: 44–51; <http://ai.arizona.edu/research/terror/publications/ITCS_Dark_Web_submission.pdf>.

Cowan, Douglas E. (2004). *Cyberhenge: Modern Pagans on the Internet*. New York: Routledge.

—— and Dawson, Lorne L. (eds.) (2004). *Religion Online: Finding Faith on the Internet*. New York: Routledge.

Encyclopedia Mythica (1995–). <http://www.pantheon.org>, accessed 9 Jan. 2007.

Hadden, Jeffrey K., and Cowan, Douglas E. (eds.) (2000). *Religion on the Internet: Research Prospects and Promises*. New York: Elsevier Science.

Højsgaard, Morten T., and Warburg, Margit (eds.) (2005). *Religion and Cyberspace.* London: Routledge.

Hoover, Stewart M., and Clark, Lynn Schofield (eds.) (2002). *Practicing Religion in the Age of the Media: Explorations in Media, Religion, and Culture.* New York: Columbia University Press.

Institute for Textual Scholarship and Electronic Editing (2005–). *MA Editing Texts in Religion.* Birmingham: University of Birmingham.

Internet Archive Wayback Machine (1996–). <http://www.archive.org>, accessed 9 Oct. 2006.

Internet Sacred Texts Archive (1999–). <http://www.sacred-texts.com>, accessed 9 Oct. 2006.

Karaflogka, Anastasia (2007). *E-Religion: A Critical Appraisal of Religious Discourse on the World Wide Web.* London: Equinox.

Larsson, Göran (ed.) (2007). *Religious Communities on the Internet.* Stockholm: Swedish Science Press.

Lawrence, Bruce B. (1999). *The Complete Idiot's Guide to Religions Online.* Indianapolis: Alpha Books.

McLuhan, Marshall (1967). *Understanding Media: The Extensions of Man.* London: Sphere Books.

——and Fiore, Quentin (1967). *The Medium is the Massage.* New York: Random House.

———— (1968). *War and Peace in the Global Village.* New York: McGraw-Hill.

Negroponte, Nicholas (1995). *Being Digital.* New York: Knopf.

O'Leary, Stephen (1996). 'Cyberspace as Sacred Space: Communicating Religion on Computer Networks'. *Journal of the American Academy of Religion,* 64: 781–808.

Project Gutenberg (1971–). <http://www.gutenberg.org/wiki/Main_Page>, accessed 6 Feb. 2007.

Reporters Sans Frontières <http://www.rsf.org>, accessed 30 Jan. 2007.

Rheingold, Howard (1993). *The Virtual Community: Homesteading on the Electronic Frontier.* Reading, Mass.: Addison-Wesley.

Second Life (2003–). <http://secondlife.com>, accessed 10 March 2007.

Taher, Mohamed (2006). *Cyber Worship in Multifaith Perspectives.* Lanham, Md.: Scarecrow Press.

Turkle, Sherry (1995). *Life on the Screen: Identity in the Age of the Internet.* New York: Simon & Schuster.

Universität Heidelberg Institut für Religionswissenschaft (2005–). *Online - Heidelberg Journal of Religions on the Internet.* Heidelberg: Institut für Religionswissenschaft, Universität Heidelberg, <http://online.uni-hd.de>.

Zittrain, Jonathan, and Edelman, Benjamin (2002). 'Documentation of Internet Filtering in Saudi Arabia'. Berkman Center for Internet & Society, Harvard Law School; <http://cyber.law.harvard.edu/filtering/saudiarabia>, accessed 5 April 2003.

Suggested Reading

The key text in the field is Hadden and Cowan (2000), which introduced a number of scholarly approaches to the subject area from scholars. This was followed by three significant edited collections of associated studies: Cowan and Dawson 2004; Højsgaard and Warburg 2005;

Larsson 2007. These volumes refined approaches to the field, the latter two emerging from the findings of international academic conferences. These can be seen in conjunction with Karaflogka's (2007) study of online religion/religion online. There are a number of texts in associated subject areas: Lawrence (1999) and Bunt (2001) are guides to online resources associated with religions and cyberspace. Beckerlegge (2001) wrote an overview of issues associated with computer-mediated religion. It includes a summary on 'religious hate' sites, as well as a discussion of various 'virtual communities'. Hoover and Clark (2002) can be read in conjunction with Beckerlegge, in order to assist in the development of a theoretical construct for studying religion online. It will become clear from reading this, and also Cowan and Dawson's (2004) sociological approach to data online, that there are several approaches to this kind of activity. This can be compared with the phenomenological (and highly personal) survey provided by Brasher (2001), in which she develops an understanding of the significance of 'sacred time' and 'virtual pilgrimage' within her analysis of a broad range of religious content. She takes this further, looking at 'virtual shrines' and 'virtual prophets'. Taher (2006) has discussed the nature of religious experiences online. The University of Heidelberg started the production of a Journal of Religions on the Internet in 2005. Detailed studies of specific religions, and the diversity of sacred (and other) online phenomena within them, include Campbell's (2005) study of Christian communities online, my writings on Islam and the Internet (Bunt 2000; 2003), and Cowan's (2004) analysis of cyber-paganism. A number of texts advocating methodologies for e-ministry from confessional perspectives should also be explored (Careaga 2001).

PART VIII

RELIGIOUS CHANGE: NEW RELIGIONS AND NEW SPIRITUALITIES, ESOTERICISM AND IMPLICIT RELIGION

CHAPTER 40

NEW RELIGIONS AS A SPECIALIST FIELD OF STUDY

DAVID G. BROMLEY

THE study of new religious movements (NRMs) is emerging as a new area of specialization within the study of religion. New Religions Studies (NRS) has its roots in a variety of disciplines: anthropology, history, psychology, religious studies, and sociology. NRS arose in response to the appearance of a cohort of NRMs during the 1960s and 1970s and to the existence of a cohort of scholars with more sophisticated theoretical and methodological tools for studying the movements, a combination that did not previously exist. NRS has produced a substantial corpus of scholarship on the NRMs that became so visible and controversial in the West beginning in the early 1970s (Bainbridge 2007; Bromley and Hadden 1993; Dawson 2006; J. R. Lewis 2004; Robbins 1988; Saliba 1990); there has been less work connecting the contemporary expressions of new religion to other historical periods or cultural contexts (Jenkins 2000; Clarke 2006). Therefore, the analysis presented here is based on the contemporary cohorts of NRMs in the West.

Given the proliferation of scholarship on NRMs, it is not surprising that the question of the significance that these movements have for the study of religion has been raised. Indeed, it might be, and has been, argued that NRMs are of relatively little significance. Most have not achieved substantial size relative either to mainline religious groups or to a number of new religious movements in other parts of the world. No group in the current cohort of movements appears poised to become a major force in the religious economy of any Western society. The movements have drawn converts largely from young, well-educated, middle- and upper-middle-class individuals; other segments of the population have been much less responsive to their appeals. Even among young adults, only a small minority of individuals actually experimented with any NRM, and in the vast majority of cases these periods of experimentation were quite brief. NRMs have had their greatest success in urban rather than rural communities; in the United States this has been primarily in cities on the East and West coasts. Elsewhere their impact has been relatively minor. Further, the time period during which most NRMs drew substantial numbers of converts was limited and linked to specific socio-historical events.

If NRS is not to be simply the study of religious exotica, the study of NRMs must be linked to the larger project of understanding religion as a social and cultural form. It is equally true that the study of religion cannot be simply the study of established religion that has become accommodated and institutionalized. The study of new religion constitutes a means of illuminating the origination of religious groups and the dynamics of their development. Two major points of connection between the study of religion and the study of new religion are what the study of new religions can reveal about the larger social order and what the study of NRMs can reveal about the origination of religion. There has been considerable discussion and debate on the first issue, principally around the relevance of NRMs for understanding macro-social processes, most notably secularization and globalization (Beckford 1992; Beyer 1994; Dawson 1998; 2004; Robertson 1985). While NRMs do provide some clues about those two macro-processes, it is unlikely that data on these groups will resolve either debate. The case for NRS needs to be made in terms of what the study of NRMs itself can contribute to the study of religion. In this essay, therefore, I shall address the less explored issue of the importance of the study of NRMs for understanding the origination of religious organization.

All contemporary religions were new religions at some time, and NRMs are significant with respect to religion because they offer insight into how new forms of religion emerge and develop. The vast majority of scholarship on religion centers on religious traditions that originated centuries or millennia ago, making it problematic to ascertain how these traditions survived and developed during their early histories, before they successfully became integral parts of their respective social orders. Contemporary NRMs offer the opportunity to observe the social construction of religion as it is occurring. I shall argue that NRS contributes to the understanding of religion in several ways: illuminating the distinguishing characteristics of various types of new religion, connecting the emergence of new religion to various types of social dislocation, providing a more complex and nuanced understanding of religious conversion, identifying the challenges attending the formation of new religious groups, and clarifying the role of oppositional groups in the survival and development of new religious groups.

Conceptualizing New Religion

The issue of how to define and identify different forms of religious organization is one that has been central to the study of religion. Dating to the work of Weber (1949), Troeltsch (1931), and Niebuhr (1929), and followed by the work of Johnson (1963; 1971), Yinger (1970), and Stark and Bainbridge (1979), among others, the most influential distinction has been between church and sect, with the later additions of denomination and cult. This distinction has been problematic for religion scholars for some time, both theoretically and empirically, but the church–sect typology continues to be widely employed in discussions of different types of religious organizations. Scholars in NRS have not found this classificatory system helpful in defining new religions, as none of these terms captures either the commonality or the diversity of NRMs. In particular, neither the concept sect nor cult, either in its sociological or popular culture usage, corresponds to the characteristics of NRMs. As a result, the study of NRMs offers an occasion for rethinking types of religious organization and delineating their characteristics. While the primary focus has been on defining NRMs, there are broader implications for conceptualizing other types of religious organizations as well.

Several scholars have offered perspectives on how NRMs might best be delineated. Two different approaches have been adopted. Barker (2004) argues for social characteristics that NRMs exhibit: movement members are first-generation, that is converts; converts produce a high level of enthusiasm and radicalism within the movement; movements appeal to individuals in specific locations within the social order, rather than having general appeal; movements are organized around a leader with charismatic authority; movements are typically regarded as deviant, or even dangerous, by the host society; and movements typically undergo constant and rapid change during their early histories.

Melton (2004) and I (Bromley 2005) both take a more relational approach, focusing on the religious group–societal relationship, which also incorporates other religious group forms in a comparative framework. Melton defines new religions as those that are "unacceptably different" from the established religious bodies and identifies a number of characteristics (aggressive proselytization, rejection of core theological tenets of established religious groups, non-conventional sexual practices, illegal conduct, violence, alternative health and healing practices) that are likely to lead to assessments of unacceptability. I divide religious groups into four types based on their degree of social and cultural alignment with the dominant religious groups in the social order under analysis. From this perspective denominations are those socially "settled" (Swidler 1986) or priestly (Bromley 1997*a*) religious groups that are socially and culturally aligned with other established institutions and are accepted as legitimate representations of the dominant religious tradition(s). Sects are religious groups that lay claim to and are recognized as deriving from the dominant religious tradition culturally, but have established independent, prophetic organizational auspices. Ethnic churches are priestly religious groups that are socially settled and accommodative to established religious groups but represent other cultural traditions. New religious movements are neither socially nor culturally aligned with the established traditions; their mythic systems and organizational forms both challenge established religion. It is this latter group that has been the primary focus of NRS and that provides unique insight into the formation of new religion by virtue of creating both cultural and social forms *de novo*. The characteristics that Barker enumerates are consistent with new groups that have no cultural or social ties to established religious groups.

Conceptualizing religious groups in this way both expands the number of types to include ethnic religious groups and creates a single axis (alignment) for relating the various types. Although the characteristics of each type have yet to be delineated, each is likely to be distinctive. For example, sectarian groups typically recruit adults from the parent tradition, while at least the current cohort of new religions has drawn more broadly from an array of religious traditions. Ethnic churches usually reflect the parent religious tradition culturally and the ethnic community socially. This expanded typology also broadens the traditional sociological conception of cult so that cults become one possible form of new religion. Once the range of religious forms is acknowledged, it becomes possible to understand better the different factors that lead to their formation. The origination of sectarian groups tracks most directly to tensions within established churches, which, in turn, may reflect specific organizational tensions or tensions with the larger social order. To the extent that the latter is the case, sectarian cohorts can be the focus of analysis. The emergence of ethnic churches is clearly linked to the existence and size of ethnic populations, and hence to factors such as immigration, governmental regulation of religion, and cultural homogeneity. New religions appear to be the product of social dislocation that results in individuals distancing themselves from existing social and cultural arrangements and becoming available for recruitment to alternative religious auspices. If the conditions that produce new forms of religion vary, it follows that the numbers of each type of religion group appearing at any given time will also fluctuate. The current debate over whether there are periods of greater and lesser formation of new religious movements, for example, may be partially resolvable by distinguishing and counting different types of groups. There is no particular logic to arguing for or against the appearance of new religion overall when the factors leading to different types of new religion may be quite distinct. Finally, distinguishing types of religious groups is compatible with the widely accepted assertion that churches are groups in low tension and sects are groups in high tension with the prevailing social order (Johnson 1971; Stark and Bainbridge 1979), but allows greater specification of the kind and level of tension. In modern, Western societies, at least, ethnic religious groups typically do not arouse organized opposition so long as they remain within their ethnic community niches. It is the attempt to extend their influence outside these boundaries that is most likely to produce a control response. Sectarian religious groups are most likely to engender tension with their parent tradition, but may also precipitate conflict with other major institutions to the extent that their educational practices, child-rearing practices, and medical practices clash with those of established institutional norms.

The issue of how to conceptualize different forms of religious organization has been a seminal one in sociology and religious studies. The traditional church–sect typology acknowledged only one type of new religion. The addition of the concept "cult" did not adequately incorporate the range of non-sectarian alternatives. Reconceptualizing the concepts of church and sect, adding ethnic religious groups and the broader category of new religious groups, and linking them through a single dimension provides one way of addressing the long-standing conceptual challenges.

NRMs and Social Dislocation

The study of when NRMs emerge contributes to an understanding of the relationship between religion and the larger social order. Religion constitutes a means of constructing transcendent meaning systems that authorize activities and relationships in the everyday world and create for adherents a sense of empowerment and control. The kind of stability to which established religion contributes is most likely in a society in which the institutional order possesses cultural legitimacy and institutional effectiveness (Lipset 2003). For some period of time societies may endure conditions in which institutional solutions to life problems are effective even if they lack a legitimating cultural framework or if they possess legitimacy while lacking effectiveness in dealing with those problems. Ultimately, however, the erosion of either legitimacy or effectiveness undermines societal stability. New religious groups offer insight into the conditions under which legitimacy and effectiveness have eroded and new systems of meaning and social organization are sought.

In attempting to account for the emergence of new religious groups, one of the most common explanations is "some acute and distinctively modern dislocation which is said to be producing some mode of alienation, anomie or deprivation" that in turn leads to individuals "responding by searching for new structures of meaning and community" (Robbins 1988: 60). There appears to be general agreement on the historical dislocation that gave rise to the current cohort of NRMs. A major structural transition was under way as the burgeoning opportunities for professional/managerial employment in rapidly expanding governmental and corporate organizations following the Second World War led to the increased necessity of both educational credentialing in the middle classes and constraining rational/legal bureaucratic organization of those occupational opportunities. Beginning in the 1950s youth began encountering problems of making the transition from childhood to adulthood. There was also growing disillusionment with racism in the United States and the sometimes violent resistance to the Civil Rights movement (Friedenberg 1965; Gitlin 1987; Kenniston 1971). Opposition to increasingly regimented higher education, restrictive drug laws, systemic racism and sexism, and, most significantly, the Vietnam War fueled the emergence of the youth counterculture and protest movements. The rapid growth of the Baby Boom Generation on college campuses provided the recruitment base for those social movements. However, while the counterculture served as a means of distancing oneself from conventional society, it never offered a viable long-term way of life for its supporters, and also met with determined resistance from established institutions. As countercultural cohesiveness began to decline, particularly when the Vietnam War no longer served as a catalyst for protest, experimentation with NRMs became one avenue through which some members of the counterculture continued the protest (Kent 2001).

Theoretical approaches to understanding dislocations during this historical period have emphasized either its cultural dimension or its social dimension. Robert Bellah (1976) and his student, Stephen Tipton (1982), are representative of the cultural perspective. They argue that the moral crisis during this era involved a repudiation of the two dominant elements of American culture through which individuals constructed moral meaning: utilitarian individualism and biblical religion. Bellah argues that the American civil religious myth has been eroded, leading to a crisis of moral meaning and a variety of attempts to create new mythic systems. Tipton argues that youthful protesters have rejected utilitarian culture and its central values (power, money, technology) in favor of expressive culture values (self-actualization, interpersonal love, and intimacy). By joining NRMs, young adults resolved the historic tension between utilitarian and expressive culture by combining religious moral authority with the project of individual self-development.

One of the most developed statements of social dislocation has been formulated by James Hunter (1981). Drawing on the work of Peter Berger (1967), Hunter regards NRMs as a protest against modernity. There has been an erosion of traditional social order, he asserts, with the contemporary world becoming divided into public and private spheres. The public sphere (governmental, legal, corporate institutions) is highly rationalized, impersonal, and bureaucratically organized, which undermines any sense of personal uniqueness and increases the individual's sense of vulnerability and expendability. By contrast, the private sphere (intimate, friendship, familial, and spiritual relationships) has been progressively de-institutionalized. The result is that the most central emotional relationships in people's lives have become unstructured, leaving individuals confronted with an overwhelming array of choices. New religious groups reduce the corrosive feelings of uncertainty and anxiety and offer their members a heightened sense of psychological stability and well-being by grounding their identities in a sacred order.

Arguments based on some concept related to social dislocation present a number of theoretical and empirical problems and are often criticized. There is a variety of related terms—contradiction, tension, social/cultural turbulence, crisis, upheaval, malaise, and anomie—that are often freely invoked in a global fashion without empirical connections to the emergence of new movements and without reference to the different theoretical traditions from which these concepts derive. Used in this way, arguments based on these concepts are difficult either to prove or to disprove. If social dislocation is defined in structural terms, some type of dislocation can virtually always be identified, which makes disconfirmation problematic. It is equally hard to confirm dislocation arguments given the difficulty of convincingly creating a macro–micro link that connects structural conditions and individual-level responses. As a result, dislocation-based arguments often appear to be a convenient way to avoid incisive theoretical analysis.

At the same time, dislocation arguments appear to be integral to explanations of the emergence and nature of new religion (Barkun 1974; Cohn 1961; Eister 1974; I. Lewis 1971; McFarland 1967; Wallace 1956). For example, in addition to theories of NRM origination reviewed previously, explanations of the distinctive qualities of NRM myths are often linked to narrative innovation that addresses the failure of existing narratives to provide individuals with a meaningful symbolic orientation. One characteristic of charismatic authority that is typical of NRMs is the capacity of the charismatic leader to address the sense of dislocation that adherents are experiencing and provide authorization for an alternative path. Influential theories of conversion also stress the importance of some type of dislocation as precipitating the process of shifting loyalty from one social network to another and as creating a pool of available recruits. Most ethnographies of NRMs implicitly or explicitly reference some dislocation as a starting point in accounting for NRM formation and appeal.

Given the importance of theories of dislocation in accounting for the origination of NRMs, it becomes important to provide more adequate empirical anchors to ground the argument. Analysis of contemporary NRMs suggests means of identifying such empirical anchors. These include describing the religious economy in which NRMs appear, specifying the temporal markers that frame the designated historical period, and linking factors leading to the emergence of NRMs to related changes in established institutions.

A successful dislocation argument must incorporate a full description of the religious economy in which NRMs emerge: that is, the demand, supply, and control components of the historical situation. To begin, the argument must specify the identity and location of those open or motivated to reorganize identities and loyalties. The literature on NRM formation has not only identified young adults as the general population most receptive to NRMs, but has also noted gender variation in the appeal of various groups within the young adult population, age gradations among young adults by group (communal groups drawing younger individuals prior to labor market entry and New Age therapeutic groups drawing somewhat older individuals), and specific historical events that were the source of NRM appeal for young adults. Of course, demand was increased by virtue of the exceptionally large pool of young adults that coincided with the period of dislocation. With respect to supply-side issues, the available evidence indicates that the concept of "new religion" must be interpreted flexibly in understanding the relationship between dislocation and NRM formation. In the case at hand, entirely new groups were formed during a period of dislocation, but it was also the case that preexisting groups suddenly gained popularity as a result of recruit availability, immigrant groups that arrived for unrelated reasons gained popularity in part because they offered a critique of the dominant culture, and an array of other groups (communes, intentional communities, and quasi-religious groups) broadened the range of available outlets for disenchanted young adults. In other words, a variety of groups not only formed directly in response to the dislocation but also became responses to it and therefore became part of the NRM cohort. Finally, the argument must identify social control mechanisms that may or may not be available to contain the formation of new groups. NRM research has emphasized the importance of immigration law changes in producing the influx of Asian religious groups, the demise of the *in loco parentis* principle by which colleges and universities had extended familial control during the transition from adolescence to adulthood, legal and constitutional constraints on governmental control of religious groups, and the tension facing families as they attempted to maintain family solidarity while simultaneously encouraging individual autonomy, voluntarism, and self-directedness for young adults. All of these factors suggest a complex, mediated model of dislocation-religious movement formation.

An empirical anchor for the temporal dimension of a dislocation argument also needs to be established. The historical events marking both the beginning and the ending points of the dislocation period must be identified. In the case of contemporary NRMs, the beginning point has been reasonably well tracked in terms of the simultaneous increase in the number of available religious groups and potential recruits as well as a decline in the availability and attractiveness of corresponding political groups. The ending point, at least of high growth rates, has been linked to the decline of countercultural activity. The findings on this point are rather dramatic as groups for which the most complete information is available, and particularly the communally organized groups, began to experience a sharp decline in recruitment rates by the late 1970s.

A particularly important way of supporting the dislocation argument is to demonstrate alternative responses to the same structural conditions. NRMs have responded to an increasingly modern, secular environment by resisting these structural changes, on the one hand, or accommodating them, on the other hand. For example, Wallis's (1984) influential movement typology juxtaposes "world-affirming" and "world-rejecting" movements, with both types constituting responses to the same social "world". In a similar vein, I (Bromley 1997*c*) treat adaptive religious movements and transformative religious movements as alternative responses to historically rooted tensions between contractual and covenantal forms of social relations. In analogous fashion, the dislocations giving rise to NRMs can be linked to corresponding trends in established religious groups. There is considerable evidence that liberal mainline churches have contributed to increasing individual autonomy by reducing their moral authority and adopting a voluntary, service-provider orientation (Hammond 1992). A number of NRMs, most notably New Age groups, have gone even further in that same direction by sacralizing selfhood. At the other end of the spectrum, a number of evangelical and fundamentalist Christian churches have resisted the advance of modern, secular society by attempting to build collective strength through strengthening family–church ties. In parallel fashion, a number of collectivist NRMs have sought even stronger collective strength by creating communally organized spiritual families. In this sense, both established religious groups and NRMs are reacting in comparable ways to the same structural forces.

Conversion

By far the largest body of work on NRMs has been on conversion of individuals to specific movements (Saliba 1990; Snow and Machalek 1984). The outpouring of research on conversion was precipitated both by social scientists' acceptance of the secularization thesis, which rendered the conversion of well-educated young adults anomalous, and the cult controversy, which involved attempts to discredit the authenticity of conversions to NRMs. However, theory and research on conversion in NRS have produced a more complex, sophisticated understanding of the transformation of religious identity and involvement generally. The process is now understood to be multi-dimensional and to involve identity and social network transformations, some combination of individual agency and group influence, various modes of connection between individuals and movements, and conversion careers.

One important distinction that has been drawn on the basis of research on conversion to NRMs is between the symbolic and social dimensions of conversion. Snow and Machalek (1984) emphasize the reconstruction of individual identity through a process of biographical reconstruction; adoption of a "master attributional scheme" that offers a single, all-encompassing source of explanation; the replacement of metaphorical with more literal reasoning that treats group ideology as ultimate truth; and embracing a convert identity so that individual and movement interests coincide. Lofland and Stark (1965) focus on the change in social network alliances through a sequence of problem-solving activity on the part of the convert. They identify a set of "predisposing conditions" (tension that derives from dissatisfaction with current life circumstances, defining that tension as having religious meaning, and dissatisfaction with one's current religious affiliation or available conventional alternatives) and "situational contingencies" (reaching a turning point in life when current lines of action are perceived to be ineffective, building affective bonds with the new group, weakening affective bonds outside the new group, and intensifying behavioral involvement in the group). Distinguishing the social and symbolic dimensions of conversion is important, since it raises the possibility that individuals may connect on one or both dimensions, creating variable types and levels of individual commitment.

A second distinction concerns the source of the impetus and influence in the conversion process. Both Snow and Machalek (1984) and Lofland and Stark (1965) emphasize agency on the part of the convert, although both also acknowledge group influence. However, it is clear that NRM membership is the product of both individual agency and group socialization (Long and Hadden 1983; Straus 1979). With respect to group influence, one of the most elaborate analyses is Kanter's work on communal groups (1972; see also Coser 1974; Lalich 2004). She identifies a number of sources of organizational power that are employed both to shape individual identity and embed individuals in a closely controlled social environment. These consist of three types of commitment mechanisms (instrumental, affective, and moral), each of which has a corresponding set of practices (sacrifice and investment, renunciation and communion, and mortification and transcendence) that promote collective over individual interests.

A third distinction involves the mode of connection between individuals and movements. Lofland and Skonovd (1981; see also Kilbourne and Richardson 1988;

Travisano 1970) identify six themes that characterize these different types of connection (intellectual, mystical, experimental, affective, revivalist, and coercive). Each, in turn, reflects a different combination of factors (social pressure, temporal duration, affective arousal, affective content, and ordering of belief and group involvement). Although specific types of conversion may predominate in individual movements, the implication is that movements are likely to be populated by individuals with diverse kinds of relationships to the group. This observation builds on the distinction between social and symbolic identity change in illuminating the difficulty in creating organizational cohesiveness and membership commitment when the basis for ongoing individual involvement is quite variable.

A fourth distinction emphasizes the difference between a conversion and a conversion career. Since conversion historically was regarded as a transformative spiritual experience and a "change of heart", it did not easily incorporate the notion of exit. Indeed, the primary corresponding concepts, such as "falling from the faith" and apostasy, have a negative connotation. What NRM research has demonstrated is that conversion theory needs to conceptualize a larger process that incorporates what is potentially an affiliation–disaffiliation sequence (Richardson 1978; Bromley 1997*b*). In fact, research indicates that contemporary NRMs have extremely high rates of membership turnover (Barker 1988; Bird and Reimer 1982; Galanter 1989; Wright 1987; 1988). Analogous to the affiliation process, the disaffiliation process can involve several modes of disconnection. The severing of bonds with a movement may involve cognitive disillusionment with the group's beliefs, practices, leadership, or potential for success; erosion of emotional energy, attachment, belongingness, and solidarity; or organizational isolation or separation. Severing group ties cognitively, emotionally, morally, or physically increases the attractiveness of alternative personal, domestic, and occupational opportunities (Wright 1988; Jacobs 1989; Skonovd 1983).

The study of conversions to NRMs has essentially problematized the concept of conversion. What emerges from the study of conversion in NRMs is that it is a multi-dimensional process in which both individual and group have some degree of influence, individuals and groups connect in diverse ways, personal transformation may be symbolic and/or social, and involvements may be short- or long-term. This multi-dimensional conception of conversion moves theorizing away from traditional religious/spiritual interpretations and toward a socio-political process of shifting individual alliances and social network identification. The study of conversion to NRMs is also revealing about the process of movement development. Given the mixture of types and levels of involvement, it is clear that movement organizations are much less stable or monolithic than they might appear. A major problem for developing movements is finding a means of channeling those diverse types of involvement. Particularly if movement attractiveness is related to sociocultural crisis, movements may founder if they rely simply on a temporary supply of potential recruits and a heightened level of motivation. Sustained development requires developing an institutionalized context for continued membership, a solution that has eluded many NRMs.

The Development of New Religious Movements

NRS is uniquely positioned to develop theories concerning the development of new religious groups. Previous work has identified some issues confronting religious organizations as they institutionalize (O'Dea 1983: 38–64), and church–sect theory is premised on the tendency of religious groups to settle and accommodate. However, there has not been systematic study on either the process of new religious group formation and development or the various organizational challenges that new groups must resolve, such as prophetic failure, death of the founder/leader, and managing charismatic authority.

Rodney Stark (1999; see also Bromley and Hammond 1987) has articulated the most complete model of initial NRM development. He argues that revelations tend to occur in a supportive cultural tradition when recipients have role models on whom they can draw; there are countless anomalous experiences occurring at all times, and some of these may be interpreted as spiritual in nature and attributed to supernatural origin; such revelatory experiences are most likely to originate during periods of dislocation and with individuals who are exceptionally sensitive or creative and for whom conventional faith traditions have become unsatisfying. Once individuals have revelatory experiences, their confidence in them increases with acceptance, and acceptance produces further, more detailed and novel revelations. The revelatory period is limited, however, as over time group pressure mounts to curtail and control revelations in order to create greater life stability and predictability. Stark (1996) has also created a model for NRM success, which identifies the kinds of problems that new groups must solve if they are to become a major force in the religious economy. He argues that movements are more likely to be successful if they occur within a non-hostile socio-cultural environment, maintain a moderate level of tension with dominant institutions in the host social order, have continuity with established traditions in the host social order, and compete with weak conventional groups. Internal movement factors that increase the probability of success include non-falsifiable doctrines, effective and legitimate leadership, highly motivated membership, and a level of fertility sufficient to insure membership replacement.

A number of other scholars have identified other problems that must be resolved between the initial period of movement development and the later stages of institutionalization. Two such issues confronting many groups are prophetic failures and the death of the movement's founder/leader. There is reason to expect that disconfirmation of predictions of supernatural intervention that are central to movement myths may be the occasion for loss of faith by members and loss of legitimacy for leadership. However, there is now considerable research to demonstrate that prophetic failure is not catastrophic for movements, and identifying the variety of account construction techniques that groups employ to neutralize potentially discrediting prediction failures (Stone 2000). There is also reason to expect that the death of a founder/leader who often personally embodies a movement could leave a movement unraveling organizationally. Again, however, a number of studies conclude that most religious movements are able to survive that moment and create new forms of leadership that allow the movement to continue, and not infrequently to prosper (Miller 1991).

Finally, movements face the challenge of managing charismatic leadership. It is not simply failed prophecies and founder/leader passings that threaten stable leadership patterns; charismatic authority presents a continuing challenge to new movements. The identity of the charismatic founder/leader and the group are often inextricably bound together during the early stages of NRM history. It is not uncommon for charismatic leaders to formulate revelations that incorporate both their own personal biographies and events that are occurring in the socio-cultural environment. Leaders have to find a means of generalizing their own individual experiences so that they have broader relevance to potential recruits. They also have to find a means to forge a connection between the social order that they are rejecting and the new future that they envision. The genius of these charismatic leaders is that they blend new and old in innovative ways that re-establish a sense of empowerment and control for their adherents. Movement leaders teach that traditional goals are achievable through new means, and that new goals can be achieved through the old means (Swallow 1982). These leaders must also manage their own charismatic authority. Dawson (2002) documents four ongoing charismatic management problems: protecting the leader's charismatic persona against erosion, preventing followers from over-identification and zealotry, negotiating a satisfactory routinization of charisma as the group develops, and achieving new successes to sustain the leader's charismatic resources. Charismatic leaders must also defend their authority against challenges from their inner-circle confidants, the emerging ranks of bureaucratic leaders, and grass-roots followers (Bromley and Bobbitt, forthcoming). The available evidence suggests that the success that leaders achieve in managing charisma is quite variable. Most leaders appear to survive these challenges, but the challenges remain a constant threat and, in some cases, result in the collapse of leadership authority.

Opposition to New Religious Movements

The survival and growth of new religious groups is not simply the product of the previously discussed socio-cultural, environmental conditions and internal movement dynamics. One of the key factors in the early development of many new religious groups is opposition that they encounter. While the extent of opposition varies, it is highly likely that opposition will emerge given that NRMs challenge the established order socially and culturally. In order fully to understand how new forms of religion develop, therefore, it is important to construct theories that incorporate both movements and the forces that oppose them. There is a substantial literature on certain aspects of nineteenth-century opposition to religious minorities (Billington 1974; Davis 1960; Moore 1986). However, the research on contemporary NRMs has produced more systematic analysis of movement–opposition interaction as it has occurred. The focal point here is the movement–counter-movement relationship, but clearly any adequate theory needs to incorporate other components, notably movement–state and movement–media relationships (Richardson 2004; Richardson and van Driel 1997).

Theory and research on opposition to NRMs strongly suggest that the developmental problems confronting oppositional groups are roughly equivalent to those facing NRMs. Like NRMs, oppositional groups must develop mythic/ritual systems, organizational units, and external alliances that will produce convergence around their respective causes. In the contemporary case, oppositional groups were confronted by protest movements that were sacralizing their protest in terms of freedom of religious expression. In order to legitimate the control that they wished to exercise, oppositional groups fashioned a mythic system around the equally sacralized concept of free will. The various versions of anti-cult ideology (brainwashing, mind control, coercive persuasion) served to de-legitimate NRM affiliations by denying their voluntarism. The corresponding ritual system involved a variety of practices (de-programming, strategic intervention, exit counseling) designed to reorient the loyalties of NRM members to their families of orientation and to conventional lifestyles and commitments. This interactive, symbiotic relationship between movement and counter-movement has produced a kind of mirror imagery in their respective ideologies.

Oppositional movements also faced many of the same recruitment and organizational development problems confronting NRMs. The anti-cult movement emerged as a set of independent groups supported primarily by families of NRM converts. These groups faced the problem of maintaining organizational commitment, as participants were likely to disaffiliate once they had resolved their own family situations, and were never able to broaden their constituency base substantially beyond directly aggrieved families. More significantly, the anti-cult movement was never able to forge alliances with professional associations and governmental agencies, which ultimately limited its capacity to implement its social control agenda. Anti-cult mythic and ritual systems raised a host of legal and constitutional issues for the state, challenged the knowledge-base claims of several academic disciplines and professions, and raised concerns about the broader extension of control over religion. They were more successful in gaining an alliance with the media and in influencing public opinion by drawing on popular culture conceptions of cults and brainwashing.

NRS scholars have begun to develop theoretical models that capture the movement–counter-movement relationship. Two models have proved particularly useful: moral panics and counter-movements. The former focuses primarily on the reaction to NRMs and illuminates how a combination of governmental, media, and oppositional groups combine to "demonize" NRMs as "folk devils". The counter-movement model focuses on how oppositional groups construct the myths, rituals, and organizational structures that allow them to pursue their social control objectives. Both models clearly indicate that the developmental trajectory of NRMs has been significantly influenced by varying types and levels of governmental constraint, hostile media coverage, direct interventions that have increased NRM isolation and radicalism, and widespread public mistrust. The incorporation of movement–counter-movement interaction in the development of new forms of religion represents an important contribution to understanding the developmental trajectory of NRMs.

Conclusions

NRS is a newly emerging area of study that is the product of the recent cohort of NRMs and a cohort of theoretically and methodologically sophisticated scholars available to study the movements. The proliferation of new movements and the availability of interested scholars has made possible the rapid and unprecedented accumulation of knowledge about NRMs. However, the impressive corpus of scholarship on NRMs also raises questions about the ultimate significance of that knowledge. One answer has been that research on NRMs contributes to the ongoing debates concerning secularization and globalization. Without disputing that possibility, I have argued that the more important contribution of NRS is in providing greater insight into the ways in which religious groups originate and develop. Among the issues that NRS is particularly well positioned to address are the diverse types of religious groups, the socio-cultural conditions under which new forms of religion emerge, the nature and dynamics of conversion, the developmental challenges that new religious groups face, and the role that organized opposition to new religion plays in the trajectory of religious group development. In a broader sense, the argument developed here is that NRS complements and provides balance to the study of the dominant forms of religion that have been the primary representation of religion among academic scholars. If a larger challenge awaits NRS, it is to transcend the focus on NRMs in the USA and Europe and to increase and integrate knowledge about the much larger number of NRMs in Asia, Africa, and Eastern Europe.

References

Bainbridge, W. (2007). "Teaching New Religious Movements: A Bibliographic Essay". In D. G. Bromley (ed.), *Teaching New Religious Movements.* New York: Oxford University Press, 331–56.

Barker, E. (1988). "Defection from the Unification Church: Some Statistics and Distinctions". In D. G. Bromley (ed.), *Falling from the Faith.* Newbury Park, Calif.: Sage, 166–84.

—— (2004). "What Are We Studying? A Sociological Case for Keeping the Nova". *Nova Religio,* 8: 88–102.

Barkun, M. (1974). *Disaster and the Millennium.* New Haven: Yale University Press.

Beckford, J. (1992). "Religion, Modernity and Post-modernity". In B. Wilson (ed.), *Religion: Contemporary Issues.* London: Bellew, 11–23.

Bellah, R. (1976). "New Religious Consciousness and the Crisis of Modernity". In C. Glock and R. Bellah (eds.), *The New Religious Consciousness.* Berkeley: University of California Press, 333–52.

Berger, P. L. (1967). *The Sacred Canopy.* Garden City, NY: Anchor Books.

Beyer, P. (1994). *Religion and Globalization.* Thousand Oaks, Calif.: Sage.

Billington, R. (1974). *The Origins of Nativism in the United States, 1800–1844.* New York: Arno Press.

Bird, F., and Reimer, W. (1982). "Participation Rates in New Religious Movements and Para-religious Movements". *Journal for the Scientific Study of Religion,* 21: 1–14.

Bromley, D. G. (1997*a*). "Constructing Apocalypticism: Social and Cultural Elements of Radical Organization". In T. Robbins and S. Palmer (eds.), *Millennium, Messiah, and Mayhem.* New York: Routledge, 31–46.

—— (1997*b*). "The Process of Exiting New Religious Movements". In W. Shaffir and M. B. Lev (eds.), *Leaving Patterns of Religious Life: Cross Cultural Perspectives.* Greenwich, Conn.: Association for the Sociology of Religion and JAI Press, 31–60.

—— (1997*c*). "A Sociological Narrative of Crisis Episodes, Collective Action, Culture Workers, and Countermovements". *Sociology of Religion,* 58: 105–40.

—— (2005). "Whither New Religious Studies: Defining and Shaping a New Area of Study". *Nova Religio,* 9: 83–97.

—— and Bobbitt, R. (forthcoming). "Challenges to Charismatic Leadership". In J. Lewis (ed.), *Sacred Schisms.* New York: Oxford University Press.

—— and HADDEN, J. K. (eds.) (1993). *The Handbook on Cults and Sects in America*, 2 vols. Greenwich, Conn.: Association for the Sociology of Religion and JAI Press.

—— and HAMMOND, P. (eds.) (1987). *The Future of New Religious Movements.* Macon, Ga.: Mercer University Press.

CLARKE, P. (2006). *New Religious Movements in Global Perspective: A Study of Religious Change in the Modern World.* London: Routledge.

COHN, N. (1961). *The Pursuit of the Millennium.* New York: Harper.

COSER, L. (1974). *Greedy Institutions*, Glencoe, Ill.: Free Press.

DAVIS, D. (1960). "Some Themes of Counter-Subversion: An Analysis of Anti-Masonic, Anti-Catholic, and Anti-Mormon Literature". *Mississippi Valley Historical Review*, 47: 205–22.

DAWSON, L. (1998). "Anti-Modernism, Modernism, and Postmodernism: Struggling with the Cultural Significance of New Religious Movements". *Sociology of Religion*, 59: 131–56.

—— (2002). "Crises of Charismatic Legitimacy and Violent Behavior in New Religions". In D. G. Bromley and J. G. Melton (eds.), *Cults, Religion and Violence.* New York: Cambridge University Press, 80–101.

—— (2004) "The Sociocultural Significance of Modern New Religious Movements". In Lewis (2004), 68–98.

—— (2006). *Comprehending Cults: The Sociology of New Religious Movements*, 2nd edn. Oxford and New York: Oxford University Press.

EISTER, A. (1974). "Culture Crises and New Religious Movements: A Paradigmatic Statement of a Theory of Cults". In I. Zaretsky and M. Leone (eds.), *Religious Movements in Contemporary America.* Princeton: Princeton University Press, 612–27.

FRIEDENBERG, E. (1965). *Coming of Age in America.* New York: Random House.

GALANTER, M. (1989). *Cults: Faith, Healing and Coercion.* New York: Oxford University Press.

GITLIN, T. (1987). *The Sixties: Years of Hope, Days of Rage.* New York: Bantam.

HAMMOND, P. (1992). *Religion and Personal Autonomy: The Third Disestablishment in America.* Columbia, SC: University of South Carolina Press.

HUNTER, J. D. (1981). 'The New Religions: Demodernization and the Protest against Modernity'. In B. Wilson (ed.), *The Social Impact of the New Religious Movements.* New York: The Rose of Sharon Press, 1–19.

JACOBS, J. (1989). *Divine Disenchantment: Deconverting from New Religions.* Bloomington, Ind.: Indiana University Press.

JENKINS, P. (2000). *Mystics and Messiahs: Cults and New Religions in American History.* New York: Oxford University Press.

JOHNSON, B. (1963). "On Church and Sect". *American Sociological Review*, 28: 539–49.

—— (1971). "Church and Sect Revisited". *Journal for the Scientific Study of Religion*, 10: 124–37.

KANTER, R. (1972). *Commitment and Community.* Cambridge, Mass.: Harvard University Press.

KENNISTON, K. (1971). *Youth and Dissent: The Rise of a New Opposition.* New York: Harcourt Brace Jovanovich.

KENT, S. (2001). *From Slogans to Mantras: Social Protest and Religious Conversion in the Late Vietnam War Era.* Syracuse, NY: Syracuse University Press.

KILBOURNE, B., and RICHARDSON, J. (1988). "Paradigm Conflict, Types of Conversion and Conversion Theories". *Sociological Analysis*, 50: 1–21.

Lalich, J. (2004). *Bounded Choice: True Believers and Charismatic Cults.* Berkeley: University of California Press.

Lewis, I. (1971). *Ecstatic Religion.* Baltimore: Penguin.

Lewis, J. R. (ed.) (2004). *The Oxford Handbook of New Religious Movements.* New York: Oxford University Press.

Lipset, S. (2003). *The First New Nation.* Somerset, NJ: Transaction.

Lofland, J., and Skonovd, N. (1981). "Conversion Motifs". *Journal for the Scientific Study of Religion,* 20: 373–85.

—— and Stark, R. (1965). "Becoming a World-Saver: A Theory of Conversion to a Deviant Perspective". *American Sociological Review,* 30: 863–74.

Long, T., and Hadden, J. (1983). "Religious Conversion and the Concept of Socialization: Integrating the Brainwashing and Drift Models". *Journal for the Scientific Study of Religion,* 22: 1–14.

McFarland, H. N. (1967). *The Rush Hour of the Gods.* New York: Macmillan.

Melton, J. G. (2004). "Toward a Definition of 'New Religion'". *Nova Religio,* 8: 73–87.

Miller, T. (ed.) (1991). *When Prophets Die: The Postcharismatic Fate of New Religious Movements.* Albany, NY: State University of New York Press.

Moore, R. L. (1986). *Religious Outsiders and the Making of Americans.* New York: Oxford University Press.

Niebuhr, H. R. (1929). *The Social Sources of Denominationalism.* New York: Henry Holt.

O'Dea, T. (1983). *The Sociology of Religion.* Englewood Cliffs, NJ: Prentice-Hall.

Richardson, J. (ed.) (1978). *Conversion Careers: In and Out of the New Religions.* Beverly Hills, Calif.: Sage.

—— (ed.) (2004). *Regulating Religion: Case Studies from around the Globe.* New York: Kluwer /Plenum.

—— and van Driel, B. (1997). "Journalists' Attitudes toward New Religious Movements". *Review of Religious Research,* 39: 116–36.

Robbins, T. (1988). *Cults, Converts and Charisma.* London: Sage.

Robertson, R. (1985). "The Relativization of Societies, Modern Religion, and Globalization". In T. Robbins, W. Shephard, and J. McBride (eds.), *Cults, Culture, and the Law,* Chico, Calif.: Scholars Press, 31–42.

Saliba, J. (1990). *Social Science and the Cults: An Annotated Bibliography.* New York: Garland Publishing.

Skonovd, L. N. (1983). "Leaving the Cultic Religious Milieu". In D. G. Bromley and J. T. Richardson (eds.), *The Brainwashing/Deprogramming Controversy.* New York: Edwin Mellen, 91–105.

Snow, D., and Machalek, R. (1984). "The Sociology of Conversion". *Annual Review of Sociology,* 10: 167–90.

Stark, R. (1996). "Why Religious Movements Succeed or Fail: A Revised General Model". *Journal of Contemporary Religion,* 11: 133–46.

—— (1999). "A Theory of Revelations". *Journal for the Scientific Study of Religion,* 38: 287–308.

—— and Bainbridge, W. (1979). "Of Churches, Sects and Cults: Preliminary Concepts for a Theory of Religious Movements". *Journal for the Scientific Study of Religion,* 18: 119–21.

Stone, J. (2000). *Expecting Armageddon: Essential Readings in Failed Prophecy.* New York: Routledge.

STRAUS, R. (1979). "Religious Conversion as a Personal and Collective Accomplishment". *Sociological Analysis*, 40: 158–65.

SWALLOW, D. (1982), "Ashes and Powers: Myth, Rite and Miracle in an Indian God-man's Cult". *Modern Asian Studies*, 16: 123–58.

SWIDLER, A. (1986). "Culture in Action: Symbols and Strategies". *American Sociological Review*, 51: 273–86.

TIPTON, S. (1982). *Getting Saved from the Sixties*. Berkeley: University of California Press.

TRAVISANO, R. (1970). "Alternation and Conversion as Qualitatively Different Transformations". In G. Stone and H. Faberman (eds.), *Social Psychology through Symbolic Interaction*. Waltham, Mass.: Ginn-Blaisdell, 594–606.

TROELTSCH, E. (1931). *The Social Teachings of the Christian Churches*, 2 vols. New York: Macmillan.

WALLACE, A. F. C. (1956). "Revitalization Movements". *American Anthropologist*, 58: 264–81.

WALLIS, R. (1984). *The Elementary Forms of the New Religious Life*. London: Routledge & Kegan Paul.

WEBER, M. (1949). *The Methodology of the Social Sciences*. New York: Free Press.

WRIGHT, S. (1987). *Leaving Cults: The Dynamics of Defection*. Washington: Society for the Scientific Study of Religion.

—— (1988). "Leaving New Religious Movements: Issues, Theory and Research". In D. G. BROMLEY (ed.), *Falling from the Faith*. Newbury Park, Calif.: Sage, 143–65.

YINGER, J. M. (1970). *The Scientific Study of Religion*. New York: Macmillan.

SUGGESTED READING

The following are recommended: Clarke (2006); Dawson (1998; 2006); and Robertson (1985).

CHAPTER 41

UNCHURCHED SPIRITUALITY

EVA M. HAMBERG

One of the main questions debated by sociologists of religion has been the development of religion in modern societies. Is religion doomed to lose its importance, or can we expect religion to survive, either in the traditional forms or in new forms? This debate has largely focused on the situation in Western Europe, where the religious development since 1750 has been described as 'the decline of Christendom' (McLeod 2003).

During the second half of the twentieth century, many European countries experienced a decline in churched religion. In particular, declining church attendance was an important aspect of this process, and a characteristic of the development that has been described as the secularization process. For a relatively long time many scholars have assumed that this decline of churched religion was equivalent to a decline of religion per se. Moreover, it was often assumed that this development, although it was particularly evident in Europe, would not remain unique to Europe but would become a characteristic of modern societies in general. Religion, some researchers maintained, would necessarily lose ground as a consequence of economic development, the spread of education, and modernization.

Other scholars, however, have maintained that the decline in organized religion that is evident in many parts of Europe has not implied a decline in religion as such. Instead, there are indications that other forms of religion—for example, unorganized religion or spirituality outside the churches—have gained ground.

Thus, a crucial question would seem to be this: does the decline in some aspects of religious adherence, notably church attendance, imply that religion per se is declining? Or, should this development perhaps be seen as a zero-sum game, where a decline in some forms of religion is accompanied by an increase in other forms? A discussion of this question is complicated by the fact that certain concepts that are central for the discussion, in particular the concepts 'religion' and 'spirituality', can be defined in various ways. Moreover, the choice of definitions will, at least to some extent, determine what answer scholars give to this question.

Sociological studies of individual, unchurched religion or spirituality have often focused on European conditions (McGuire 2000: 108). One reason for this is that scholars have been interested in the question of possible relationships between traditional religious adherence and spirituality outside the churches. This question is of particular interest with regard to Europe because of the decline in church adherence in many European countries during the past century. However, individual religion or spirituality in North America has also been the topic of important studies. Needless to say, unorganized individual religion or spirituality in various forms exists in other parts of the world as well, but this essay will focus on the European and American context.

Definitions of 'Spirituality'

In the academic world, the term 'spirituality' has been used to denote several different, but interrelated, concepts. In studies of the history of Christianity and other religions the term has for a long time been used to denote forms of piety that are associated with mystical and monastic traditions. Spirituality in this sense is still an important field of research, notably among church historians, but also among scholars in other fields, e.g. theology, history of religions, and the psychology of religion. In this use of the term, spirituality stands for a form of religiosity with a strong emphasis on the individual's (or a group's) relation to God or a transcendent reality, in which spiritual exercises such as prayer, meditation, and fasting are often important elements. Spirituality in this sense is not a phenomenon that exists independently of or outside traditional religious institutions. Rather, it can be seen as one aspect of institutional religion, e.g. of traditional Christianity, although the degree to which a person's religiosity can be described as 'spiritual' in this sense will differ between individual believers.

More recently, however, the term 'spirituality' has increasingly come to be used to denote forms of religiosity that exist *outside* traditional religious institutions, and in particular—since the focus has been on Europe and North America—outside the Christian churches. Among sociologists of religion this use of the term 'spirituality' is now common.

To give a survey of the scholarly literature on spirituality is an undertaking that is complicated by the fact that the term 'spirituality' is extremely ambiguous. Although the word is widely used, both by the general public, by religious professionals, and by scholars, it is often used without a definition or with definitions that are not sufficiently precise. To be sure, attempts have been made to clarify the various ways in which the term is used, but it has also been pointed out that the concept is obscure, vague, and 'fuzzy' (e.g. Zinnbauer *et al.* 1997; Rose 2001).

Hence, an essay on (unchurched) spirituality must necessarily contain a brief overview of how the term has been used. Obviously, such an overview will be far from comprehensive; rather, the aim is to give some examples of the various ways in which the term is used among sociologists of religion. The emphasis will be on how the term has been used by scholars, but I will begin with a short presentation of the findings of a few studies of how the term 'spirituality' is used among the general public and among religious professionals, respectively.

Not only is 'spirituality' defined in very diverse ways both among religious professionals and among scholars (see below), but there is also considerable variation in the way in which the term is understood and used among the general public (see, e.g., Roof 1999: 34–5). However, sociologists of religion have paid relatively little attention to the ways in which the general public understand and use the term (Zinnbauer *et al.* 1997: 551). This is surprising, considering that an understanding of the development and prevalence of contemporary spirituality and of the relationship between religion and spirituality requires studies of how people interpret survey questions related to the concept 'spirituality'.

In a study of how different groups of Americans from a wide range of religious backgrounds understood the terms 'spiritual' and 'religious', Zinnbauer *et al.* found evidence of both convergence and divergence in the understandings of these concepts. While 93 per cent of the respondents identified themselves as spiritual, and 78 per cent identified themselves as religious, there were variations in the definitions of these terms. Zinnbauer *et al.* point out that the findings of their study 'illustrate the necessity for researchers to recognize the many meanings attributed to religiousness and spirituality by different religious and cultural groups, and the different ways in which these groups consider themselves religious and/or spiritual' (1997: 562). This study was not based on random samples, however, but on samples drawn from institutions where people where more likely to be religiously involved than Americans in general.

More recently, data from various surveys investigating the relationship between being 'religious' and being 'spiritual' have been compared and discussed by Marler and Hadaway (2002). This study demonstrates how different ways of sampling (e.g., random samples as opposed to convenience samples) and different formulations of survey questions affect the results of surveys and make comparisons between different surveys hazardous. The authors found that the question as to whether Americans have become 'more spiritual' and 'less religious' could not be answered definitively, since there were important differences between surveys with regard to questions, wording, and methods of sampling. However, they concluded that the relationship between 'being religious' and 'being spiritual' is not a zero-sum proposition. Instead, 'the most significant finding about the relationship between "being religious" and "being spiritual" is that most Americans see themselves as both' (Marler and Hadaway 2002: 297). A similar conclusion can be drawn from Wade Clark Roof's study of the Boomer Generation, in which he found a substantial overlap between those who described themselves as 'religious' and those who described themselves as 'spiritual': 74 per cent said they were 'religious', and 73 per cent said they were 'spiritual'. Of those who described themselves as religious, 79 per cent also claimed to be spiritual. However, there were also people who claimed to be spiritual but not religious, or religious but not spiritual (Roof 1999: 173).

In a study of how the term was used among professionals from the five major religious traditions, Rose found that while considerable differences in the understanding of the term existed, there was also evidence of a basic set of characteristics. In particular, three criteria for the appropriate use of the term 'spirituality' seemed to be agreed upon by many of the respondents: 'some form of continuous religious or comparable experience, particular maintained effort or practice, and the experience of love' (Rose 2001: 193). Rose concluded that the term 'spirituality', as it was used by the religious professionals in his study, had a much more specific meaning than it has in current usage and was used to denote in part the same aspects as the term 'religion'. While the overall view among the respondents seemed to be that the two terms have similar meanings, the term 'spirituality' was understood as being 'more expansive' (pp. 193, 205).

The Concept 'Spirituality' in Sociology of Religion

To what extent can spirituality be regarded as a modern, or perhaps even postmodern, phenomenon? Scholars differ in their answers to that question. While some see spirituality as something that has increasingly characterized Western societies during the past half-century, others emphasize the similarities between contemporary forms of spirituality and the characteristics of popular religion, not only in its contemporary but also in its pre-modern forms (McGuire 2000). These different views are related to different definitions of the concept 'spirituality'. In the following, I will give a few examples of the different ways in which sociologists of religion nowadays use the term 'spirituality'.

Stark, Hamberg, and Miller (2005: 7) note that 'recently, discussions of popular religion have been dominated by spirituality, a label which is applied to an immense variety of beliefs, feelings, and practices concerned with things of the spirit as opposed to the material'. Although the concept is seldom defined in any precise way, 'all forms of *spirituality* assume the *existence of the supernatural* (*whether Gods or essences*) and that *benefits can be gained from supernatural sources.* The term also connotes that these beliefs are *not necessarily associated with organized congregations* and *often do not constitute creeds*, for all that exponents often freely pick and choose from an array of creedlike bodies of doctrine.' Since the forms of spirituality that are discussed in this essay are usually not associated with organized congregations, the term 'unchurched spirituality' may be used to distinguish them from other forms of spirituality, e.g. in the monastic tradition. However, the terms 'spirituality' and 'unchurched spirituality' will often be used synonymously in the following, since this reflects the way in which the term 'spirituality' is used among sociologists of religion.

In a discussion of individual religion in a social and historical context, Meredith McGuire (2000) argues for the need to pay attention to 'the personal beliefs and practices by which individual spiritual lives are shaped and transformed, expressed and experienced, over time'. In McGuire's use of the concept, spirituality is 'a way of conceptualizing individual involvement in religion that allows for the considerable diversity of meanings and ritual practices which ordinary people use in their everyday lives' (2000: 99). She stresses the parallels between contemporary forms of spirituality and popular religion (2000: 103). With this understanding of the concept, contemporary spirituality has many characteristics in common with folk religion or popular religion, and is understood as a phenomenon that can be traced many centuries back, even though its expressions may vary over time.

The definitions of spirituality cited above are wide. For instance, as mentioned, spirituality has characteristics in common with folk religion, and it is not seen as a modern phenomenon only. An example of a different understanding of 'spirituality' is found in the work of Paul Heelas (2002: 358), in which 'religion' is defined 'in terms of obedience to a transcendent God and a tradition which mediates his authority', and 'spirituality' is defined as 'experience of the divine as immanent in life'. According to Heelas, the following key characteristics have come to be associated with 'spirituality': it 'has to do with the personal; that which is interior or immanent; that which is one's experienced relationship with the sacred; and that wisdom or knowledge which derives from such experiences. At heart, spirituality has come to mean "life".'

Spirituality and Religion—Changes in the Use of the Concepts?

The literature concerning spirituality shows that there are great differences between scholars with regard to the views held of the relationships that may exist between religion and spirituality, both historically and with regard to the contemporary situation. These diverging views can at least in part be ascribed to the fact that the concept 'spirituality' is defined in different ways—or, indeed, sometimes not defined at all. Moreover, not only 'spirituality' but also 'religion' can be defined in various ways, and there have been changes over time in the use of both concepts (see, e.g., Zinnbauer *et al.* 1997).

Sociologists of religion have traditionally used either substantive or functional definitions of religiousness (see, e.g., Berger 1969: 175–7). Substantive definitions are narrower and more specific than functional definitions. They are more explicit about the content of religion and define what religion *is*. They focus on the beliefs and practices of individuals in relation to a higher power or divine being. Functional definitions are usually broader and emphasize what religion *does* for the individual and for the social group. They focus on the function that religion serves in the life of the individual (McGuire 1992: 11–15; Zinnbauer *et al.* 1997: 550).

Functional definitions tend to include all that substantive definitions identify as religion, but are usually much broader (McGuire 1992: 14). It is pointed out by Zinnbauer *et al.* (1997: 551), however, that both these types of definitions have been 'broad enough to subsume the "spiritual" as well as both individual and institutional beliefs and activities. As spirituality has become differentiated from religiousness, however, it has taken with it some of the elements formally (*sic*!) included within religiousness. Therefore, recent definitions of religiousness have become more narrow and less inclusive.'

In contemporary sociology of religion there is, of course, great variation among scholars regarding the definitions of religion and religiousness that are chosen. However, Zinnbauer *et al.* may be right in their claim that there has been a shift in the way the terms 'religiousness' and 'spirituality' are used. This is worth noting, since it may have implications for the assessment of hypotheses and assertions about contemporary trends of secularization and the future of religion in modern societies. For instance, the question of whether or not 'religiousness' has declined in Europe in recent decades can be answered in different ways, depending on how 'religiousness' is defined.

Secularization is a concept that has been defined in various ways, but it is usually understood as 'a historical development by which religion has lost (or is losing) a presumed central place in society' (McGuire 1992: 249). One aspect of this process is a decline in the social power of religious institutions, which has undoubtedly taken place in Europe; but often this process has also been understood to imply a decline in personal piety (Stark and Finke 2000: 59–60).

If 'secularization' is defined as a decline in 'religiousness', where religiousness is narrowly understood as adherence to traditional Christian beliefs and practices, many European countries have undoubtedly become more secularized in recent decades. With such a definition of religiousness, recent developments may be seen as evidence for the assertion that the secularization process is well under way in Europe.

With a wider definition of religion or religiousness, however, the development in Europe would be interpreted differently. An example of this is given by Stark and Iannaccone (1994: 232), who define religion as 'any system of beliefs and practices concerned with ultimate meaning that assumes the existence of the supernatural'. With the use of this definition, not only church-oriented forms of religion, but also much of what might be denoted as unchurched spirituality, falls within the boundaries of religion, and it would be misleading to draw a sharp distinction between religion and (unchurched) spirituality. Hence, it is not surprising that Stark and Iannaccone do not find evidence for the secularization of Europe; indeed, they suggest that 'the concept of secularization be dropped for lack of cases to which it could apply' (p. 230), and conclude that 'the evolutionary future of religion is not extinction. The empirical evidence is that the vitality of religious firms can fluctuate greatly over time, rising as well as falling, although subjective religiousness seems to vary far less' (p. 249).

Thus, if we use a narrow definition of religion, where 'religion' is understood as equivalent to traditional church-oriented religion, we may conclude that religion has declined in many European countries, while (unchurched) spirituality has increased. If we use a wider definition of religion, however, we may instead conclude that there is no evidence of a long-term decline of religion, even though the forms of religiousness have changed over time, and traditional forms of religion have been partly replaced by the phenomena that are often referred to as 'spirituality'. The question of religious change in Europe can thus be answered in different ways, depending on our definitions.

Characteristics of Contemporary Unchurched Spirituality

Since the term 'spirituality' is used in different senses, descriptions of its main characteristics also vary to some extent. Nevertheless, descriptions of spirituality tend to have important themes in common.

Some scholars point to characteristics that contemporary spirituality has in common with popular religion. According to McGuire (2000: 103), important features of contemporary spirituality include 'holism, autonomy, eclecticism, tolerance, this-worldly activism and pragmatism, appreciation of materiality, and blurring of boundaries between sacred and profane'. It has also been pointed out that much that is now called 'spirituality' is not religion but magic, as in the case of, e.g., astrology, crystals, tarot, intuitive medicine, bio-rhythms, numerology, and telepathy. Other forms of spirituality involve religion, with or without belief in gods, but they often lack congregations or creeds, and sometimes both (Stark, Hamberg, and Miller 2005: 7).

Scholars who see contemporary spirituality as a modern phenomenon often stress individualism, a focus on the 'self'; subjectivism, an emphasis on quest and personal experience; and changes in the attitudes to religious institutions as important aspects of spirituality. Obviously these themes are closely related.

Heelas (2002) uses the concept 'spiritualities of life', and distinguishes between New Age spiritualities of life and theistic spiritualities of life. The New Age spiritualities of life 'equate spirituality with the life which we are born with, and all the potentials which this is experienced as possessing' (p. 375). The theistic spiritualities of life combine components of traditional Christian beliefs with elements from New Age spiritualities of life (p. 366). They stand for forms of religious activity which 'combine use of tradition with reliance on what the Holy Spirit (or similar inspirers or transformers) have to offer with regard to the salvation of life in the here-and-now' (p. 375). According to Heelas (p. 370), both New Age and theistic spiritualities of life involve 'a remarkably similar dynamic', since they both promise release from the wrong kind of selfhood in the present life, 'the here and now'.

Heelas argues (2002: 363–9) that New Age spiritualities of life are no longer confined to New Age—that is, to those who are willing to accept this label—but are a growing force in mainstream culture. He also argues that theistic spiritualities of life are a growing force within institutionalized traditional religion, and sees this as evidence that a shift from religion to spirituality, in his words 'a spiritual revolution', is taking place even within religion. In particular, this is seen in the increased importance ascribed to the Holy Spirit relative to tradition. Heelas stresses the subjective, emotional aspects of these theistic forms of spirituality. Small groups of believers, whose participants discuss scripture and share insights on the basis of their own life experiences, play an important role. Personal conviction is seen as more important than theological doctrines, and personal experience of the sacred and of the guidance of the Holy Spirit in daily life is emphasized.

It might be argued, however, that some of the characteristics that Heelas regards as typical of theistic spiritualities of life have also characterized many Christian groups in history. Christian revival movements have often had strong emotional elements, and they have often stressed the importance of personal experience of the guidance of the Holy Spirit. So a spirituality in which these elements are central is not necessarily a new phenomenon that has developed in modern societies. Rather, such forms of theistic spirituality may have a long historical record. On the other hand, it can perhaps be argued that the very strong focus on the individual in contemporary spirituality is a new element that may distinguish contemporary theistic spirituality from earlier forms of Christian spirituality. While in traditional

Christian spirituality the relationship between God and man was strongly centred on God, the focus in contemporary theistic spirituality seems to have shifted towards the human person.

Wade Clark Roof (1999) discusses religious change in the United States with a focus on the generation born after the Second World War, the 'Baby Boomers', whom he sees as the principal carriers of 'an emerging spiritual quest culture' (p. 49). Like Heelas, Roof emphasizes experience as an important characteristic of contemporary spirituality: 'Generally, primacy is placed not on reason or inherited faith, but on experience, or anticipation of experience, engaging the whole person and activating, or reactivating, individual as well as collective energies' (p. 469).

Roof sees spirituality as encompassing four 'big' themes: 'a source of values and meaning beyond oneself, a way of understanding, inner awareness, and personal integration'. What is at stake is a viable conception of the 'self'. 'Contemporary quests for spirituality are really yearnings for a reconstructed interior life, deliberate and formative efforts aimed at forging an integrated self and transcending the limits of the given' (Roof 1999: 35).

Roof (1999) also found evidence of an emerging boundary definition of social and psychological consequence: namely, defining oneself as primarily 'spiritual' or 'religious'. 'More often than we expected, we encountered people who spoke with conviction about their discoveries of the spiritual and how it had changed their lives—including rescue "from religion" that was too limiting' (p. 137). He concludes that in American religious life, there is a tension 'between personal religious experience and its institutional expression; between "religiously based spirituality" as found within the religious establishment and the less-structured styles of "free-floating spirituality" outside of it' (p. 143).

The relationship between contemporary spirituality and participation in organized religion is a crucial question, and an important aspect of contemporary spirituality has been described as 'believing without belonging' (Davie 1994). The phenomenon of people who are 'believers but not belongers' has been discussed both in the American and in the European context (Roof and Mc Kinney 1987: 52; Davie 1990; 1994; Lambert 2004; Glendinning 2006), and recent data indicate that the share of the population who are believers but not belongers is increasing in Europe (Lambert 2004).

In Scandinavia, the reverse situation can be said to exist. Since a large share of the population belong to the Lutheran churches but do not share the beliefs of the church, they might be described as 'belongers but not believers', if belonging is defined as formal membership (Hamberg 1990: 39). However, the definition of 'belonging' is crucial. In the Scandinavian countries the percentage of the population who believe in God is considerably higher than the percentage who attend worship services (Lambert 2003: 69–73). Hence, if 'belongers' are defined as persons who have regular contacts with their church, many Scandinavians can indeed be defined as 'believers but not belongers', and various forms of unchurched spirituality are widely diffused among them.

Individualism, a focus on the 'self', has often been noted as an aspect of contemporary spirituality. It is possible that there is a relationship between the importance attached to the 'self' and a strong focus on health that has been found in Swedish studies (Hamberg 2003). Survey data indicate that among Swedes health now is a dominant value in life, more important than family and friends or material values. Several factors may contribute to this emphasis on health, but an important factor is probably an increasing individualism, which includes such themes as self-expression, self-realization, and personal autonomy, which tend to bestow a sacred status upon the individual (Luckmann 1990). Illness and death being the ultimate threat to the individual's existence, the increasing importance accorded to self-realization and personal autonomy may well lead to a growing concern for preserving or improving one's health.

Religion and Unchurched Spirituality—Future Developments?

We may safely assume that the decline in church-oriented religion that has been notable in parts of Europe during the twentieth century has led to an increase in spirituality outside the churches. When a churched religion has passed through several generations of non-participants, religious socialization becomes ineffective, and the religion assumes the characteristics of a folk religion (Stark, Hamberg, and Miller 2005). Hence, if participation in institutional religion should continue to decline, we can expect unchurched spirituality to become even more prevalent than it is today.

What assumptions can we make about the future of religion in the Western world, and more particularly in Europe? Will organized religion in its present forms continue to decline, and if so, will it be replaced by other forms of religion and unchurched spirituality?

The decline in adherence to Christian beliefs and practices in Europe during the past half-century has often led to the assumption that this is part of a long-term decline in churched religion that will continue into the future. However, this assumption can be questioned. For instance, recent survey data indicate a possible trend-break that has been described by Yves Lambert (2004: 42) as a 'religious mutation in Europe'. While the 1981 and 1990 European Values Study surveys indicated increasing secularization in Western Europe, the survey in 1999 revealed significant changes. Lambert finds evidence both for a Christian renewal and for the development of religiosity without belonging. These tendencies were especially notable among young people. In all countries, young people who declared themselves Christian seemed to be more religious in 1999 than in 1981 and 1990. '*À la carte* Christianity' that, together with uncertainty of beliefs and relativism, was previously spreading among Christians, in particular among the young, a trend that was considered typical of late modernity, remains dominant, but it is in slight decline among the young. Lambert concludes that 'from a religious point of view, Europe is at a turning point, particularly if we look at the last 30–40 years: the tendency of religious decline that was clearly dominant, particularly among young people, is brought into question by the development of Christian renewal and autonomous spirituality' (p. 42). Whether or not this is a break in long-term trends and an indication of 'de-secularization' can be judged only on the basis of further research. For instance, analyses of data from the World Values Surveys have indicated that awareness of existential concerns seem to have increased over the previous decades (Norris and Inglehart 2004: 75), and that church-oriented religious involvement has demonstrated rather country-specific patterns of both increases, decreases, and overall stability (Pettersson 2006).

In a discussion of possible future developments we also need to consider the impact of immigration, which is now an important factor in both Europe and North America. There is strong evidence that religious pluralism has an impact on religious participation in a society, and the lack of religious pluralism has been seen as an important explanation of the low levels of religious participation in Europe today (Stark and Iannaccone 1994). At present, the religious landscape in many European countries is changing because of immigration, and during the past few decades Islam has emerged as Europe's second largest religion. In some countries where religious pluralism used to be very low, it is now increasing, and religion is becoming more visible in society. In a long-term perspective, immigration may well be a factor that counteracts the past trend of decline in organized religion.

Some Methodological Issues in Studies of Spirituality

Methodological questions are an important issue that requires more attention from scholars studying spirituality. As pointed out by McGuire (2000), the methods used for the study of unchurched spirituality need to be further developed. In McGuire's view, both the quantitative and the qualitative methods usually employed by scholars in this area are inadequate: not only are surveys and other quantitative methods not well suited to this purpose, but 'much qualitative research is far too unsystematic and imprecise and shallow' (p. 109).

Obviously, survey data are of limited use in studies of spirituality. For instance, the interpretation of survey data presents various problems. One of the most serious is that respondents may interpret questions in very diverse ways. Hence, we run the risk of drawing the wrong conclusions if we assume that the respondents interpret the questions in the way we expect them to. However, this and other problems with regard to survey data can often be solved at least partially if surveys are supplemented by interviews, in which respondents are asked about their interpretation of questions. This can diminish the risk of misinterpretations and help to improve the future formulation of questions. Thus, surveys used in combination with interviews can help to elucidate important aspects of individual religion. An example of this is a nation-wide study of world views and value systems carried out in Sweden in 1986, in which interviews including both closed and open-ended questions were combined with a questionnaire, which the respondents were asked to fill in immediately after the interview (Hamberg 1990; 2003). This combination turned out to be fruitful in several respects: for example, by providing information about the divergent ways in which respondents interpreted the formulation of some questions. It also shed light on another important issue: namely, the great variation between individuals in the degree of personal commitment with which beliefs and values are held. Surveys that ask about religious beliefs often lack questions that might provide us with information about the salience of such beliefs. Survey questions need to be designed with this problem in mind—for example, by asking respondents to estimate how important their religious beliefs or practices are to them. In order to achieve a deeper understanding of the salience of individual religion, however, we need to combine the use of survey data with qualitative methods.

Survey data are, of course, necessary for many purposes—for example, in studies of the prevalence of religious beliefs and practices in a population. Longitudinal studies based on surveys are also needed in order to discover developments that are too subtle to be detected by other methods. For instance, new trends can be discovered by comparing data from surveys undertaken at intervals, such as the European Values Study (EVS) or the International Social Survey Programme (ISSP). This is exemplified by the recent tendencies in the European religious development that are described by Yves Lambert as a 'religious mutation in Europe' (Lambert 2004: 42). Lambert discovered these new tendencies by analyses of data from the European Values Study in 1981, 1990, and 1999.

However, surveys alone usually do not provide the information needed to arrive at a deeper understanding of the factors underlying such changes. For instance, Lambert poses the question of whether there is a link between a return of belief in life after death and a new, more pessimistic view of modernity. He regards this as plausible, but points out that we lack the support of a thorough study of the subject. In particular, we lack interview studies that might shed light on this question. He concludes that in order to 'understand better what is happening now, it would be necessary to collect new data via in-depth interviews, notably biographies . . . to update survey questions and to contextualise findings—on the theoretical level—from the perspective of a long-term evolution of modernity' (Lambert 2004: 44).

Thus, while surveys alone are of limited use in studies of spirituality, studies that combine survey data with qualitative data from personal interviews can shed light on important aspects of individual religion. A good example of this is provided in the above-mentioned study by Wade Clark Roof (1999), in which the analysis builds on a combination of survey data, in-depth interviews, and field observations. This project was built on a panel study, where the same persons were followed over a period of eight to nine years. The participants were initially contacted in a telephone survey, which was followed up by telephone and face-to-face interviews. After some years they were contacted in a new telephone survey and in some instances also interviewed again (pp. 10–11, 315–16). The material obtained in the panel study was combined with other material, such as interviews with religious and spiritual leaders and field observations. Roof describes the aim and methodology of the study in these words:

> My aim is to link people's life histories and stories with information gleaned from large-scale surveys. Personal narratives are rich in meaning and nuance, a means of exploring the many webs of cultural meaning that people spin. Surveys allow for generalizations, absolutely indispensable for describing social trends. Combining the two methods makes for a balanced approach for understanding what is happening to religion 'on the ground,' to its meaning and function in everyday life. (Roof 1999: 11)

Combinations of quantitative and qualitative methods are indeed necessary in order to improve our understanding of contemporary individual religion or spirituality.

Some Suggestions for Future Research

Spirituality outside the churches will probably continue to be an important issue in the sociology of religion for the foreseeable future. Both the development and the prevalence of contemporary spirituality are fields where much remains to be done. Another issue where more research is needed concerns the relationship between traditional churched religion and unchurched spirituality. To what extent has the secularization process that is going on in many European countries been accompanied by a growth of spirituality outside the churches?

In order to shed light on such questions, we must, of course, use empirical methods, and, as was observed above, the methodological problems involved in such studies require more attention than they have hitherto been given. Moreover, a crucial issue is how to define the concepts used. As pointed out above, the term 'spirituality' is very ambiguous. Although it is widely used, by the general public, by religious professionals, and by scholars, it is often used without a definition or with definitions that are not sufficiently precise. The divergent views that can be found among scholars regarding such issues as the historical development of spirituality outside the churches can at least in part be ascribed to the use of different definitions of the concept. Of course, the fact that different definitions are used is not necessarily a problem, but it is necessary for the scholarly debate that definitions are stated explicitly and that they are formulated with sufficient precision.

An issue that also merits attention, is the impact—or lack of impact—of unchurched spirituality in defining and sustaining the moral order. It has been observed that religions or spirituality without congregations cannot exert social pressure on adherents to observe the moral order. Hence, 'the sociological "law" that "religion functions to sustain the moral order" is limited to churched religions' (Stark, Hamberg, and Miller 2005: 19). This is an issue that needs to be explored further. Another issue that deserves more attention is the impact of unchurched spirituality on attitudes towards science. Unchurched religions, and especially those engaged in spirituality, tend to reject commitment to rationality, and often condemn the very idea that there are rules of logic and evidence (Houtman and Mascini 2002). Expressions of scepticism, and even hostility, to science are also common on Internet spirituality sites. In contrast, several studies have indicated that churched religion offers 'a very substantial barrier to belief in magic and various forms of "pseudo"-science—it even seems to be far more supportive of conventional science than education' (Stark, Hamberg, and Miller 2005: 20). Hence, the attitudes towards science among those who embrace unchurched spirituality deserve to be explored further in future studies. More generally, the social and cultural effects of an increase in the prevalence of unchurched spirituality would seem to be an important field for future research.

References

BERGER, PETER L. (1969). *The Sacred Canopy: Elements of a Sociological Theory of Religion.* Garden City, NY: Doubleday & Company, Inc., Anchor Books.

DAVIE, GRACE (1990). 'Believing without Belonging: Is This the Future of Religion in Britain?' *Social Compass*, 37/4: 455–69.

—— (1994). *Religion in Britain since 1945: Believing without Belonging.* Oxford: Blackwell.

GLENDINNING, TONY (2006). 'Religious Involvement, Conventional Christian, and Unconventional Nonmaterialist Beliefs'. *Journal for the Scientific Study of Religion*, 45/4: 585–95.

HAMBERG, EVA M. (1990). *Studies in the Prevalence of Religious Beliefs and Religious Practice in Contemporary Sweden.* Uppsala: Acta Universitatis Upsaliensis.

HAMBERG, EVA M. (2003). 'Christendom in Decline: The Swedish Case'. In Hugh McLeod and Werner Ustorf (eds.), *The Decline of Christendom in Western Europe, 1750–2000*. Cambridge: Cambridge University Press, 47–62.

HEELAS, PAUL (2002). 'The Spiritual Revolution: From "Religion" to "Spirituality"'. In Linda Woodhead, Paul Fletcher, Hiroko Kawanami, and David Smith (eds.), *Religions in the Modern World: Traditions and Transformations*. London and New York: Routledge, 357–77.

HOUTMAN, DICK, and MASCINI, PETER (2002). 'Why Do Churches Become Empty, while New Age Grows? Secularization and Religious Change in the Netherlands'. *Journal for the Scientific Study of Religion*, 41/3: 455–73.

LAMBERT, YVES (2003). 'New Christianity, Indifference and Diffused Spirituality'. In Hugh McLeod and Werner Ustorf (eds.), *The Decline of Christendom in Western Europe, 1750–2000*. Cambridge: Cambridge University Press, 63–78.

—— (2004). 'A Turning Point in Religious Evolution in Europe'. *Journal of Contemporary Religion*, 19/1: 29–45.

LUCKMANN, THOMAS (1990). 'Shrinking Transcendence, Expanding Religion?'. *Sociological Analysis*, 50/2: 127–38.

MARLER, PENNY LONG, and HADAWAY, C. KIRK (2002). '"Being Religious" or "Being Spiritual" in America: A Zero-Sum Proposition'. *Journal for the Scientific Study of Religion*, 41/2: 289–300.

MCGUIRE, MEREDITH B. (1992). *Religion: The Social Context*, 3rd edn. Belmont, Calif.: Wadsworth Publishing Company.

—— (2000). 'Toward a Sociology of Spirituality: Individual Religion in Social/Historical Context'. *Tidskrift for Kirke, Religion og Samfunn*, 13/2: 99–111.

MCLEOD, HUGH (2003). 'Introduction'. In Hugh McLeod and Werner Ustorf (eds.), *The Decline of Christendom in Western Europe, 1750–2000*. Cambridge: Cambridge University Press, 1–26.

NORRIS, PIPPA, and INGLEHART, RONALD (2004). *Sacred and Secular: Religion and Politics Worldwide*. Cambridge: Cambridge University Press.

PETTERSSON, THORLEIF (2006). 'Religion in Contemporary Society: Eroded by Human Well-being, Supported by Cultural Diversity'. *Comparative Sociology*, 5/2–3: 231–57.

ROOF, WADE CLARK (1999). *Spiritual Marketplace: Baby Boomers and the Remaking of American Religion*. Princeton: Princeton University Press.

—— and MCKINNEY, WILLIAM (1987). *American Mainline Religion: Its Changing Shape and Future*. New Brunswick, NJ: Rutgers University Press.

ROSE, STUART (2001). 'Is the Term "Spirituality" a Word that Everyone Uses, But Nobody Knows What Anyone Means by It?' *Journal of Contemporary Religion*, 16/2: 193–207.

STARK, RODNEY, and FINKE, ROGER (2000). *Acts of Faith: Explaining the Human Side of Religion*. Berkeley: University of California Press.

—— and IANNACCONE, LAURENCE R. (1994). 'A Supply-Side Reinterpretation of the "Secularization" of Europe'. *Journal for the Scientific Study of Religion*, 33/3: 230–52.

—— HAMBERG, EVA, and MILLER, ALAN (2005). 'Exploring Spirituality and Unchurched Religions in America, Sweden, and Japan'. *Journal of Contemporary Religion*, 20/1: 3–23.

ZINNBAUER, BRIAN J., PARGAMENT, KENNETH I., COLE, BRENDA, RYE, MARK S., BUTTER, ERIC M., BELAVICH, TIMOTHY G., HIPP, KATHLEEN M., SCOTT, ALLIE B., and KADAR, JILL L. (1997). 'Religion and Spirituality: Unfuzzying the Fuzzy'. *Journal for the Scientific Study of Religion*, 36/4: 549–64.

Suggested Reading

Bellah, Robert N., Madsen, Richard, Sullivan, William N., Swidler, Ann, and Tipton, Steven M. (1985). *Habits of the Heart: Individualism and Commitment in American Life.* Berkeley: University of California Press.

Heelas, Paul, and Woodhead, Linda, with Seel, Benjamin, Szerszynski, Bronislaw, and Tusting, Karin (2005). *The Spiritual Revolution: Why Religion is Giving Way to Spirituality.* Malden, Mass.: Blackwell.

Hervieu-Léger, Danièle (2000). *Religion as a Chain of Memory.* Cambridge: Polity Press.

Luckmann, Thomas (1967). *The Invisible Religion: The Problem of Religion in Modern Society.* New York: Macmillan.

McLeod, Hugh, and Ustorf, Werner (eds.) (2003). *The Decline of Christendom in Western Europe, 1750–2000.* Cambridge: Cambridge University Press.

Roof, Wade Clark (1993). *A Generation of Seekers: The Spiritual Journeys of the Baby Boom Generation.* San Francisco: Harper.

Wuthnow, Robert (1998). *After Heaven: Spirituality in America since the 1950s.* Berkeley: University of California Press.

Also Roof (1999); Stark and Finke (2000); and Stark *et al.* (2005).

CHAPTER 42

SPIRITUALITIES OF LIFE

PAUL HEELAS

During recent decades, the language of spirituality has come into its own. A wealth of evidence supports this appraisal. Church-attending Christians frequently refer to spirituality. Terms like 'spiritual' have largely replaced terms like 'mystical'. Expressions like 'mind–body–spirit' have entered popular consciousness, especially among those looking for alternatives apart from Christianity. Increasingly, the language of spirituality is used to mark a break with what is taken to be harmful or meaningless 'religion'.

Within the academy, researchers and teachers are gradually, sometimes hesitantly, taking on board the study of spirituality. Some suggest that the sociology of religion should be renamed the sociology of religion and spirituality. The more radical argue that the sociology of spirituality should be a research and teaching enterprise with its own priorities.

At the same time, it has become a commonplace to state that the meaning of the term spirituality is 'vague', 'fuzzy', 'obscure', or extremely 'ambiguous'. Those who study spirituality might well be disturbed for two reasons. First, it is implied that they do not really know what they are studying. And second, it is more than implied that their investigations to date have not got very far in that most preliminary of tasks: ascertaining the characteristics of spirituality, or, more exactly, spiritualities.

Thanks are due to Charlotte Hardman, Dick Houtman, Stefania Palmisano, and Deborah Sawyer for their most helpful suggestions and material.

Spiritualities of Life in Context

Criticizing the fuzzy claim, a claim popularized by Brian Zinnbauer and associates (1997), one of the most obvious meanings found in the discourses of spirituality has to do with life itself. It is the force, energy, or vitality that sustains us. It has to do with our natural goodness and wisdom. It is the life we are born with—basic attributes, capacities, capabilities, potentialities. Once experienced, spirituality flows through our lives to heal, to empower, and to inspire creativity and wisdom, change ill-being into well-being, enable us to become truly 'alive'. A great range of activities, including reiki, meditation, spiritual forms of psychotherapy or reflexology, and the most popular, yoga, it is said, enable participants to 'get in touch with' what they are by nature—spiritual beings. Accordingly, the inner life of spirituality is held to provide the key to human flourishing: most immediately in connection with the transformation of the quality of the interior life; more expressively in connection with the transformation of the quality of relationships with the world, its inhabitants, institutions, and environment. All in all, bringing 'life' to life.

Involving as it does inner sources of authority and significance, taking away the transcendent God of theism leaves the heart of spiritualities of life intact. In contrast, to remove the transcendent God of religious tradition means that there is little left of Christianity or any other theistic teaching. And this includes Christian forms of spirituality. Whether it be transcendent spirituality (a spirituality of experiencing the God-on-High), holy spirituality (a spirituality of experiencing the indwelling Holy Spirit), the spirituality of theistic humanism (a spirituality of experiencing relationships between God's creations), or immanent spirituality (a spirituality of experiencing God's gift of the 'spark' within), all ultimately depends on a source existing over and above what we are by virtue of 'mere' nature.

Analytically speaking, it is thus perfectly easy to distinguish between five forms of spirituality. And on the ground, it is just as easy to identify all those people who adhere predominantly to one or another of these varieties. There is nothing obscure or fuzzy about this. At least in considerable measure, ideal types match empirical evidence.[1]

Evolving Debates

The widespread and relatively rapid adoption of the language and practices of inner-life spirituality during recent decades means that academic inquiry has

[1] The 'only religious', 'only spiritual', 'religious and spiritual' literature stimulated by Zinnbauer *et al.*'s (1997) article does not focus on the matter to hand.

tended to lag behind developments on the ground. Consequently, claims have often been made on the basis of inadequate evidence. There is thus plenty of opportunity for divergent, often contradictory, points of view to flourish.

The Numerical Significance Debate

According to Steve Bruce (1996), in Britain 'the number of people who have shown any interest in alternative religions is minute' (p. 273). Even if we limit ourselves to those actively participating in inner-life activities, as of 2001 slightly over 900,000 inhabitants of Great Britain were involved on a weekly basis in associational activities regarded as spiritually significant by practitioners (Heelas and Woodhead 2005: 53). This figure includes some 146,000 spiritual practitioners. These figures are hardly 'minute'—unless one is happy to apply this term, for example, to the number of GPs (37,352) in Britain in 2004. In the United States, recent survey-based data show that around 28 million practice yoga—some, it is true, as an adjunct to Christianity; others, it is equally true, with much more of an inner-life focus; and over 60 per cent of fitness clubs provide yoga instruction (Page 2007; Schmidt 2004).

Or consider personal beliefs. In Britain, a recent survey found that 37 per cent of the population agree with the statement, 'God is something within each person, rather than something out there'. In Sweden, the figure rises slightly, to 39 per cent; in Denmark, it drops slightly, to 35 per cent. Across eleven European countries, the average is around 30 per cent. If evidence of this variety is anything to go by, belief in the sacred of the inner life is widespread: indeed, more popular than belief in the sacred of transcendent, 'personal God' theism, where the figure for Britain is 23 per cent (Heelas 2007*b*).

Given popular belief, it is hardly surprising that spiritualities of life are now firmly at home in the mainstream of Western society. For many people, they serve to provide something akin to a 'sacred canopy' within popular culture. Certainly, inner-life spirituality has sprung up within influential mainstream fields of the culture, such as the press and women's magazines. It has also entered 'nooks and crannies', specific sites like bed-and-breakfast establishments, the Sports Centre of Lancaster University, private gardens, veterinary practices, even the Los Angeles zoo and Rentokil (both using feng shui). More generally, the expression 'mind–body–spirit' has entered the realm of cultural slogans; so has the term 'holistic', encountered in numerous contexts, including that new addition, medispas; so too has the central theme of 'going deeper', as with the Imedeen advert, 'Beautiful skin begins within'. Subjective well-being culture—where explicit attention is devoted to quality-of-life concerns—is replete with holistic provisions and services, from all the books promising to enhance personal experience incorporating mind, body, and spirit, to all the ways in which holistic spiritualities of life have entered the workplace. Going deeper to reach the parts that other aspects of life cannot reach, to feel good *about* oneself.

Looking briefly at the workplace, by 2001 almost half the general practices of England were providing access to CAM activities, those complementary and alternative forms of healing which frequently incorporate inner-life spirituality (Dobson 2003). Almost one-third of CAM activities are provided in-house. Within hospitals an increasing number of nurses have been attracted by what holistic approaches promise (Heelas 2006*b*). Within hospices, holistic spiritual counselling of a 'life'-focused nature has probably become the norm. In line with Ofsted's definition of spirituality, referring as it does to 'inner life' and the importance of 'valuing a non-material dimension to life' (1994: 86), interest is increasingly shown by teachers, especially in primary schools.

Then there is the mainstream of capitalism. Management trainings and consultancies, publications, specialized journals, workshops, and conferences have proliferated since the 1960s. In their *A Spiritual Audit of Corporate America* (1999), Ian Mitroff and Elizabeth Denton note that the majority of interviewees 'take it for granted as a fact that everyone is a spiritual being and that spirituality is an integral part of humankind's basic makeup' (p. 41). In Britain, courses and experiential activities provided by a number of business and management schools indicate the state of play.

Although a great deal more (challenging) research needs to be done to establish the numerical significance of spiritualities of life in settings like hospitals, let alone among the population at large, it is now quite clear that the debate over numbers has been settled in favour of those who draw attention to the numerical importance of what is in evidence beyond traditional theism.

A great deal more research also needs to be done to get a better idea of the numerical significance of a zone of activity which lies between the 'congregational domain' and the 'holistic milieu'. To explain, for the purposes of the Kendal Project (a local study of forms of the sacred, 2000–2002) we defined the former as the realm of associational activities, run by Christians, and meeting in designated places of worship. We defined the latter as the realm of associational activities, run by spiritual holistic practitioners, and meeting in a variety of places. With the Kendal Project set up in this way, we did not really know what to do with activities, like networks and small groups populated by spiritual seekers, which retained elements of theistic religion, did not take place in designated places of worship, and also incorporated elements of inner-life spirituality. Rather clumsily, we allocated betwixt-and-between activities of this kind to the holistic milieu, omitting one small group altogether on the grounds that it was impossible to decide whether it was predominantly theistic or of an inner-life nature.

I am now firmly convinced that the either–or approach of the Kendal Project was something of an unavoidable mistake. Thinking of Britain as a whole, let alone Kendal in particular, it is perfectly clear that considerable numbers of people are active in what can be thought of as 'dual source' activities. That is to say, despite the logical incoherence of doing so, participants experience two 'absolute', but radically different, sources of authority and significance: that provided by the theistic God of their Christian faith and that provided by their inherent inner-life spiritual resources. If we had deployed it, a third zone—neither one nor the other of the categories we used—would have included some of the activities we ended up allocating to the holistic milieu. Accordingly, to have worked with a 'dual source' zone would have diminished the numerical importance of the milieu. Furthermore, by ignoring the 'twin star' zone (as it could also be called) we missed the opportunity to contribute to the exploration of a form of the sacred which is growing in Britain, as well as in other Western countries—for instance, to examine the relevance of terms like 'pantheism' (for which God and the universe are identical, thereby implying the denial of the transcendence and personality of God) and 'panentheism' (for which God includes the world as part of his being, thereby leaving more room or scope for transcendent theism).

Reflecting on the numerical significance of personal beliefs, a great deal more thought is required to tackle the exceedingly tricky matter of addressing the fact that beliefs are often far from determinate—frequently not really being (propositional) 'beliefs' at all. Ethnographic inquiry suggests that people are often unclear about what they 'believe', change their minds over time, combine apparently incompatible beliefs, prefer to avoid the language of belief by using expressions like 'I simply don't feel as though I'm only a mind and a body'. The Soul of Britain survey found that 23 per cent agree with the statement 'There is something there' (Heald 2000); and across Europe, it can be added, it looks as though around a third of the adult population think that 'there is something [after death], but I don't know what'. It could well be the case that we will never be able to determine the 'exact' number of those who believe that life is sacred (Heelas 2007*b*; 2008). The goal is to try.

The Spiritual Significance Debate

So far as I know, no one has claimed that spiritualities of life are in decline. Neither does anyone dismiss the fact that whereas 1960s inner-life spirituality was seen by 'straights' as a weird aspect of the lives of 'hippies', primary school teachers, nurses, and upper-level managers are now among those who might be practising yoga or reading about inner-life Sufism.

However, it is argued that growth and establishment are more apparent than real, that much of what is growing is not 'really' about spirituality, that we are witnessing a 'fag ending' of the sacred. Of the various strands of this controversial argument, perhaps the most fundamental is that inner-life spirituality is 'actually' secular. Discussing findings from the Kendal Project, David Voas and Steve Bruce (2007) write: 'the descriptions of spirituality given by Kendal [holistic] respondents seem to have little to do with the supernatural or even the sacred' (p. 51). For Voas and Bruce, the descriptions take the form of 'pseudo-science' (p. 51). In much the same vein, Wouter Hanegraaff (1998) argues that the 'foundations' of the 'New Age' consist of an already thoroughly secularized esotericism' (p. 523), elsewhere writing of 'the emergence of *secular spiritualities*' (1999: 152).

An argument against claims of this variety is that holistic participants typically speak of spirituality in ways which transgress the scientific frame of reference. Spirituality cannot be observed; it cannot be measured; it belongs to another dimension; the spiritual dimension is taken to be immaterial, incorporeal, intangible; the 'magical' powers often ascribed to spiritual experience or spiritual well-being are not the powers found by science; the 'natural goodness' found in human nature is not likely to be accepted by the sociobiologist (or secular ethicist); an absolutely central Kendal Project finding—that a little over 80 per cent of holistic milieu participants agree with the statement that 'some sort of spirit or life force pervades all that lives' Heelas and Woodhead 2005: 25)—concerns a state of affairs which is unlikely to be accepted by scientists, now or in the future; in and of itself, spirituality is mysterious—that is, it cannot be adequately captured in words, let alone by measuring tools. To draw on the title of M. H. Abrams's (1973) magisterial study of that great precursor of contemporary spiritualities of life, the 'spirit' of Romanticism, we are in the territory of 'natural supernaturalism': a spirituality which transcends the naturalism of science but which nevertheless belongs to the natural order; a spirituality which is metaphysical, if the physical is defined scientifically, but which is nevertheless 'natural', to be experienced as 'flowing' through the 'dimensions' of the body and mind; a spirituality which is not taken to be a form of 'brain training'.

The fact remains, though, that we do not have a very clear idea of the extent to which the language of spirituality refers to the spirituality of life in the here-and-now rather than being used in other—albeit somewhat related—ways. In context, it is clear what Wordsworth had in mind (better, 'in experience') when he wrote:

> While with an eye made quiet by the power
> Of harmony, and the deep power of joy,
> We see into the life of things.

It is much less clear what people mean today when they use terms like 'spirit', 'spiritual', and 'spirituality' to refer to what could be 'just' aesthetic experiences or profound affectivities; to what James Leuba (1950) describes as 'the higher reaches of the mental life' (p. 4 n.); to what the influential British educationalist David Bell refers to when he opines that 'spirituality has come into its own as encapsulating those very qualities that make us human' (cited by Smithers 2004).[2]

Another way of dismissing growth as more apparent than real is to draw attention to the this-worldly orientation of practices. 'In much New Age spirituality', writes

[2] Although some of the terms of the language of spirituality are used in (relatively) secular contexts, it is reasonable to suppose that the sacralization of life implied by 'God within' findings (e.g.) refers to an ontology which goes beyond the secular. See Heelas 2008 for further discussion.

Bruce (2002: 85), 'therapy is the manifest, not latent, function. Good health, self-confidence, prosperity and warm supportive relationships are no longer the accidental by-product of worshipping God; they are the goals sought after through the spiritual activity.' To the extent that spirituality is about secular ends, the argument runs, then to that extent inner-life spirituality is secularized. Of the points which could be made in objection, one is that on a global scale the sacred frequently and primarily functions as a means to the end of this-worldly necessities and/or ambitions—with enlightenment, even 'next-worldly' heavenly salvation, widely taking second place. If spiritualities of life are to be treated as secularized by virtue of their this-worldly thrust, then so does an implausibly large sector or dimension of the sacred in general. Another objection is that it is not as though the ends sought by holistic participants need remain secular. From their perspective, health or well-being, for example, become sacralized by virtue of the fact that spirituality is experienced as suffusing these aspects of their lives. Yet another objection is that it is very unlikely that 'beliefs' of the '*God* within but not without' variety refer to the secular.

Then there is the closely related argument that the growth of holistic activities can be explained away by reducing them to acts of consumption, to acts of interior decoration. It has become positively fashionable among academics to argue that holistic activities are nothing (much) more than vehicles for the hedonistic, self-absorbed, self-interested, selfish gratification of desire; vehicles for me so that what is carried results in a 'me-to-me': an argument which was set in train by Christopher Lasch (1980; 1987), and which has since been advanced by, among others, Zygmunt Bauman (1988), Jeremy Carrette and Richard King (2005), Kimberly Lau (2000), and Graham Ward (2006).

Making a stand against this fashion, I have recently completed a volume, *Spiritualities of Life* (2008), which develops a battery of arguments against the 'consuming capitalism' idea: against the idea that capitalism, in consumer culture mode, uses spirituality to encourage consumption—in that holistic activities are consumed by capitalism. Accepting that holistic well-being provisions, services, or activities—like those provided by almost all upmarket spas—can function as ways of indulgently pleasuring the self, the argument is that this is most emphatically not the whole story. The key objection is that holistic activities and most holistic publications, for instance, are bound up with humanistic and expressivistic values: values which it is ridiculous to reduce to consumption. It does not make sense to treat values like equality, or valued states of being like authenticity, as states of affairs which can be consumed, that is 'taken in' and 'used up'—without giving anything back. From the point of view of in house authors (most of whom are practitioners), and many participants, these values and valued ways of being are spiritually suffused; are sacred in the Durkheimian sense of standing over and above 'mere' utilitarian considerations, such as satisfying those desires which happen to have been stimulated by the devices of secular consumer culture.

The Debate over Efficacy

When spiritually suffused, expressive-cum-humanistic ethicality is in evidence, inner-life spirituality can contribute to making a stand against the acquisitive, self-centred self of capitalism and can encourage a form of the 'good life'. For Bruce (2000: 234), 'while some elements of the New Age are tangentially radical, its fundamental principles are those of modern capitalism'. Clearly, there is not much scope for making a stand here. The argument against Bruce is that the values of spiritualities of life are in fact able to make a difference. To illustrate by reference to the heartlands of capitalism itself, some people aim to introduce inner-life spirituality to nourish virtues such as trust, honesty, openness, accommodating others, responsiveness, a sense of collective responsibility, co-operation, and (positive) co-dependence; the values of what the Dalai Lama, with his concern for business life, calls 'basic spirituality': the 'basic human qualities of goodness, kindness, compassion, caring' (Dalai Lama and Cutler 1998: 258), including the exercise of corporate responsibility. In contrast to the competitive, combative, stressful, dysfunctional, blinkered individualism which, it is claimed, can so readily be generated by the contemporary obsession with target achievement, values of the kind under consideration are taken to serve as a counterweight. Furthermore, as Durkheim argued in *The Division of Labour in Society* (1984[1893]), values and moral sentiments of a humanistic, relational, trustworthy kind are vital for productivity. Continually to police the exercise of self-responsibility or agreements is too costly to be other than counter-productive. In addition, humanistic (and expressivistic) values are vital for the quality of life within companies: getting on with others, feeling good about oneself, rather than simply dissipating energies: becoming isolated, getting depressed or anxious by continually having to monitor progress by reference to the criteria of performance management. The overall goal is to bring life back to work, to develop a form of 'participatory "capitalism"' to serve the life of employees—and productivity itself.

To broaden the argument, Bruce's (2002) claim that spiritualities of life have 'little social impact' (p. 91) is undermined by the consideration that well-being has profound significance for those in employment, as well as others like the retired. The Leader of the British Conservative Party, David Cameron, was widely reported when he recently stated: 'It is time we focused not just on GDP but on GWB, general well-being'. The underlying assumption, it is fair to say, is that GDP depends in part on GWP. Absentee rates, tax revenues spent on long-term disability benefits, sluggish performance at work due to depression, erratic performance due to anxiety, the effects of alcohol: all count against the GDP. In line with this way of thinking, the Office for National Statistics has recently set out to measure 'societal well-being', in particular the well-being productivity, for patients, of the National Health Service. The influential government advisor, Lord Layard, recommends deploying 10,000 NHS psychologists to tackle depressive illness (Gould 2007: 24): Aristotelian *eudaimonia* as an all-round good.

What have spiritualities of life to do with this? Evidence provided in the House of Lords Sixth Report (2000), together with numerous articles in journals like *Complementary Therapies in Medicine*, show that CAM activities, often incorporating a spiritual dimension, are widely associated with an enhanced sense of well-being. The claims of holistic, mind–body–spirituality practitioners to 'lift the spirit' or to reduce stress, for example, are also supported by the fact that such activities are increasingly popular. If participants did not experience positive benefits, they would stop participating; and general practices, one assumes, would stop encouraging participation. It need not matter whether 'placebos' (as many scientists might call them), releasing opiates (as very recent research demonstrates), are involved—so long, that is, as participants experience benefit (House of Lords 2000: 3.32).

Serving as adjuncts to mainstream companies—that is, with holistic participation taking place after work, during lunch breaks, or during trainings—mind–body spirituality can play a (as yet modest) role in contributing to the vitality and well-being required for successful target performance—and the general ethical 'health' of the company. Beyond the capitalistic workplace, an increasing number of primary schools provide yoga, tai chi, and other activities to contribute to the educational goals of developing the 'whole child' in a 'child-centred' way—with humanistic and expressivistic values well in evidence. Among those being nursed, the retired and those in hospices, spiritualities of life contribute to the restoration or 'completion' of life. *Contra* Bruce, 'social impact' is surely in evidence; so too is significance for the person. And *contra* Woodhead's (1997) Chesterton-like claim, it can be added, it is surely misguided to write that the 'reduction' of God to the god within is 'downright dangerous' (p. 208). What is urgently required, though, is systematic and qualitative research. After all, in Britain, governmental policy to do with how to teach 'religion' in schools is at issue; as is, for example, the relationship between CAM provisions and NHS expenditure.

The Matter of 'Identity'

According to Linda Woodhead, 'many of the holistic practices we witnessed [during the Kendal Project] had to do with *basic* identity construction' (2007*b*: 122; my emphasis). Bearing in mind the fact that spiritual participants understood themselves to be revealing (expressing, developing, transforming) aspects of themselves on the *basis* of what they take to be experiential, inspirational, authentic selfhood rather than engaging in 'construction', 'identity' is not an especially appropriate word for grasping the meaning of what takes place within holistic circles. Holistic activities have a great deal to do with broadening horizons, opening up new possibilities in life beyond the confines of any particular 'identity'. Caring for oneself is primarily a matter of 'health and fitness' (Heelas and Woodhead 2005: 91): no doubt one can say that assertions like 'I am a healthy person' is a form of identity statement, but it is highly doubtful that this captures what it is to feel healthy or experience vitality whilst one sets about one's daily round. That the language of holistic activities often revolves around the theme of the true, authentic self should not be taken to entail that the 'true self' has any kind of 'role-identity'—certainly not of the circumvented type found when someone asserts, 'I *am* a bank manager, and I'm proud of *it*'. From the perspective of most of those interviewed during the Kendal Project, who referred to the matter, the 'true self' is a self which is ever in the process of being 'realized' rather than undergoing the process of being 'foreclosed'; ever in the process of being ever more profoundly experienced rather than being confined to what can be obtained from a determinate essence. (The pragmatism of Dewey or Rorty.) To the extent that activities are efficacious, 'new' experiences, 'transformed' feelings or emotions, 'deeper' comprehension, more profound sentiments, 'being' a 'free spirit', are at 'issue' (in both senses of the word)—not the rigidities of essentialized 'identity' or 'role' as these terms are commonly used in connection with everyday, secular life. 'Everything is movement', writes Gurli Linden (1998: 12) of that great precursor, spiritual artist Hilma af Klint.

To take participants seriously is to acknowledge that the 'true self' exists in experience—not in an 'identity' belonging to the realm of propositional belief. Indeed, 'de-identification' or cognates are frequently used in the primary literature—appropriately so, for the art of the liberated life. Thinking of Judith Butler's *Gender Trouble* (2007[1990]), that highly influential contribution to 'third wave' feminism, it is not going too far to say that many holistic participants are something akin to 'indigenous Butlerians'. Few are second wave, 'essential difference' feminists (to draw on the title of the critical volume edited by Naomi Schor and Elizabeth Weed (1994). There is certainly not much evidence of participants thinking or acting in forceful binary terms, constructing essentialized, 'reactive' identities to oppose men, thereby becoming implicated in, and constricted by, what is opposed (as Butler argues in criticism of the second wave). Holism, unitary humanism, the harmonization of life, the strongly emphasized inclusivism of possibility—to a degree which Butler would probably not allow—count against, or temper (radical) essentialized feminism or oppositionality—to the extent of the post-gendered (often) coming into evidence (Hardman, forthcoming). Butler's 2004 book title, *Undoing Gender*, says a great deal: the undoing of 'normative restriction', including the restrictions of gender identities themselves, to 'aim' for 'greater livability' (p. 1). It thus comes as no surprise to find so many holistic participants, as something akin to indigenous Butlerians, valuing freedom. Just as freedom is central to what Butler means by 'performativity', so is it central to what holistic practitioners mean by 'becoming' through expression, especially during holistic activities. Through performativity—as manifestation through action—the authentic self of the person comes into the 'being' (cf. Hardman, forthcoming; Heelas 2008). *Contra* Woodhead's (2007*a*) claim that 'identity' is 'discovered from within' (p. 576), it is true that the person who says at a dinner party (for example) 'I'm a spiritual person' might well be taken to be making an identity statement by her fellow diners. But if the person under consideration is an adept, it is highly likely that she will know only too well that what lies within is ultimately mysterious, flowing through (all) the aspects of her unique life in ways which far 'transcend' reduction to identity statements of all bar the most non-specific kind; perhaps of any kind.

Birthright Spirituality Abroad

Leaving Britain and other Western countries to consider what is happening elsewhere, spiritualities of life are being called upon to do a number of jobs. In Eastern contexts, spiritualities of life provide indigenous or quasi-indigenous resources which are being drawn upon for various purposes. In a range of countries, from Pakistan to Indonesia, spiritual leaders, politicians, educationalists, local NGO personnel, and others belonging to the ranks of the liberal intelligentsia are actively promoting inner-life, universalistic forms of the Sufi wing of Islam, non-theistic/partially theistic forms of Buddhism and Hinduism, or universalistic syntheses. Whether fuelled by poverty, exclusivistic forms of religious tradition, or—as is frequently the case—a combination of the two, the aim is to handle potential or actual conflict.

Typically infusing humanistic values with spirituality, spiritualities of life can be thought of as forms of birthright spirituality. That is to say, humans, by virtue of their very nature, are taken to be born with an essentially shared, value-laden spirituality: values which provide the foundation for their entitlements, their human rights; values which correspondingly inform the moral sentiments of the ethic of humanity—responding to the distress of others, for example. Thus in Pakistan, President Musharraf sees inner-life Sufism as a way of providing a sacralized rendering of the ethic of humanity. His aim is to bring Sufism to bear, especially through education, to help unite the nation. When it is couched in the quasi-secular terms of the Constitution of Pakistan, the ethic of humanity, including its human rights, is deeply unpopular among religious conservatives. The plan is that this aversion—due in no small measure to the ethic being associated with Western empire-building—can be circumvented by grounding the ethic in forms of Sufism found in even the most conservative territories of the country. Sacred lives: what better foundation for the values of the golden triangle of the ethic of humanity, the values ascribed to life, equality, and freedom, in such a 'religious' country? To provide another illustration from Pakistan, one of the primary aims of the world-renowned Orangi Project, orchestrated by Sufi Akhtar Hameed Khan (2005), has been to diminish tension and conflict in a large, impoverished area of Karachi by way of Sufi-inspired 'context setting'.

Engaged inner-life Islam (more widely, Buddhism, Hinduism, etc.): how such will fare in the confrontation with the forces of exclusivistic conservatism is open to question. From the perspective of academic inquiry, the important thing is to study unfolding initiatives, and thereby contribute to vital political debate and policy making. Equally, it is important to study how 'indigenous' forms of healing and empowerment are faring: CAM, as it would be called in the West, is currently being attacked by a major sector of the Chinese medical establishment (led by Zhang Gongyao), supported by the governments of several central and eastern African countries, and (apparently) by the Pakistan government as a service running parallel to the officially secular government-funded hospital system.

Explaining Growth and the Role of Women

To date, there have been few attempts to explain the growth of holistic spiritualities of life. In *The Spiritual Revolution* (Heelas and Woodhead 2005), we argued the case for the subjectivization thesis. Stemming from the widely canvassed theory that the assumptions, beliefs, and values of the autonomous self have a detrimental effect on forms of religion which devalue autonomy, the simple, albeit critical, explanatory move was to apply the 'ideology' of the autonomous self to explain the growth of spiritualities of life. More specifically, the aim was to explore the idea that cultural themes of the 'It is my life, and I won't be told how to live it' or 'Be yourself, only better' variety are at work. More specifically still, the aim was to explore the idea that subjective life, so important for autonomous selves who, by definition, can only exercise what they take to be their autonomy from within, provides the key explanatory tool.

The argument is that among the progressively increasing numbers of those who value their own unique subjective lives as their primary source of authority and significance, the values and expectations, potentialities and vulnerabilities of subjective life are best served by forms of the sacred which enable participants to exercise their freedom to develop and express their valued subjectivities and to transform their negativities. If those who prioritize the quality of their 'interior' life per se are involved with the sacred, or become involved, it is thus highly likely that it will be with spiritualities of life. For with spirituality experienced at first hand from the heart of one's life, the uniqueness, growth, and expressivity of one's own life are assured.

But is the subjectivization thesis able to handle the fact that around 80 per cent of those participating in holistic activities are women? That growth is primarily in the hands of women? 'With hindsight', writes Linda Woodhead (2007*b*) of *The Spiritual Revolution* (Heelas and Woodhead 2005), 'it is clear that our struggle over the "puzzle" of women's disproportionate involvement in the holistic milieu of Kendal was generated by the *failure* of the sociological theory [the subjectivization thesis] on which we depended to take issues of gender seriously' (p. 124; my emphasis). The 'puzzle' to which she refers first struck me after hearing a conference presentation by Dick Houtman and Peter Mascini (2003; and see Houtman and Mascini 2002: 464–8), a presentation which contained passing reference to the fact that 'moral individualism'—a crucial index for identifying those who prioritize their subjective life as a source of significance—is evenly dispersed between women and men. Hence the puzzle: how is one to explain the 80 : 20 ratio in favour of women among holistic participants when the ratio among those most likely to become involved is 50 : 50? The 50 : 50 ratio obviously demonstrates that the subjectivization thesis is not 'gender-blind', as Woodhead would have it (2007*b*: 115). As is equally obvious, though, the thesis was to demonstrate and explain the (no more or less 'gender-blind') 80 : 20 ratio found among holistic participants.

And this is what we sought to do in *The Spiritual Revolution.* Moral individualism or autonomous selfhood, we argued, is best thought of in terms of two ideal types: individuated and relational forms of subjectivism. In Western cultures, and possibly elsewhere, men tend to approximate to the former, women to the latter. (For very recent data, see Mike Savage's analysis of British Household Panel Surveys; reported by Smith 2007). Having refined the basic subjectivization thesis in this way, the task was to explain why holistic activities mainly attract women of a relational disposition.[3] Without going into all the arguments here, one was that holistic activities often attract women who work, or who have worked, in relational jobs: careers which are person-centred; careers where the theme of developing with, through, and for others is important; careers which emphasize helping others to change or come to terms with their personal lives; careers which emphasize responsiveness. Especially for those who find that their attempts at work to make relational contributions are thwarted by narrow, blinkered efficiency targets, bureaucratic procedures, and so on (the nurse in the ward standing by a living person in an instrumentalized bed in the 'iron cage' of the ward), holistic activities beckon as a way of 'truly' relating and experiencing what it is to *enable* others (generally speaking a much more appropriate expression than 'caring for', with its connotation of passivity, let alone 'mothering', with its exclusivism); in the process contributing to one's own development in one's vocation.

[3] What is argued in *The Spiritual Revolution* (Heelas and Woodhead 2005) makes it difficult to understand Woodhead's more recent claim that we 'treat[ed] male experience as a universal experience' (2007*b*: 117).

Dick Houtman and Stef Aupers (2008) concentrate on personal beliefs rather than activities, and offer a somewhat different explanation. Providing evidence for the fact that 'men and women do not differ with regard to post-traditionalism', logic demands that higher levels of ('post-traditional') New Age affinity among women 'cannot simply be attributed to a high[er] level of post-traditionalism' (p. 109). The 'gender puzzle' is then tackled by focusing on the ways in which women experience de-traditionalization. Houtman and Aupers's argument is that although de-traditionalization—the loss of faith in traditional ways of doing things and the commensurate value which is accorded to individual autonomy or choice—'creates tensions and anxieties for men and women alike', 'women are substantially more likely to become caught up in new webs of contradiction and ambiguity' (p. 110). For a variety of reasons, most significantly those to do with the meaning of home work, paid work, and the way these two spheres relate, 'post-traditional women are... more likely than post-traditional men to be haunted by the questions of meaning and identity that are evoked by detraditionalization and that stimulates late-modern individuals to explore the depths of their souls' (p. 110). Accordingly, 'post-traditional women are more likely than post-traditional men to embark on a spiritual quest and sacralize their selves' (p. 110). And, it should be emphasized, are more likely to turn to spiritual guidance, found through practices, to help them make decisions within the context of 'contradiction and ambiguity'.

Like Hontman and Aupers in this regard, Woodhead (2007*b*) also emphasizes the role played by the 'iron cage'—or more exactly, iron cages. We read that: 'If the iron cage' of the world of paid work 'had proved an inadequate container for the aspirations of men's fulfilment, it was even less likely to prove adequate for female fulfilment' (pp. 117–18). We also read that 'Post-traditional women, by contrast [to "post-traditional" man], have to struggle against the constrictions not only of a work role but, more importantly, of traditional women's roles—as dutiful wife and mother—which are likely to leave even less scope for subjective expression and fulfilment' (p. 119). Unable to express themselves satisfactorily at work, and 'above all... trying to cope with difficulties relating to roles of care and responsibility for others and not least the difficulty of being "over-powered" by others at the expense of their own self-development' (pp. 121–2), their unique subjective life tends to be suffocated rather than developed and expressed, and fails to provide much of a sense of 'true' autonomous identity or to live up to expectations to do with quality.

When women are so inclined and have the opportunity, holistic activities can come into play. In the words of Woodhead (2007*b*), 'to a greater extent than had been anticipated, our [Kendal Project] data reveal that holistic spirituality was often being used as a safe space in which women (and some men) were able to recognise and deal with a sense of worthlessness and low self-esteem related to the subordination of their own needs to those of others, and to the use and abuse of the self by (male) others' (p. 122). I must say that much of this is news to me. It is true that recently completed analysis of key questionnaire data shows that a significant percentage of holistic participants report 'problems' to do with caring for the illnesses of close family members (for example); and although the data are not determinate on the point, it is also likely that some get 'landed' with having to look after others. However, despite the popularity of the term (low) 'self-esteem' in the widespread cultural lexicon of well-being, none of the respondents use it (or the term 'worthless'); neither do practitioners make play of terms like these in their publicity; neither is 'emotional support'—which might be expected to be well in evidence on Woodhead's interpretation—of significance as a factor encouraging participation (Heelas and Woodhead 2005: 91); and only one questionnaire respondent refers to 'space' (or anything like it), writing of the difficulty of 'find[ing] enough space for myself'. Furthermore, apart from a few reporting issues deriving from childhood, nothing of significance supports the contention that women understand their more recent experiential circumstances to involve 'abuse of the self by (*male*) others' (my emphasis). (And what about men bullied by other men, or by women, losing their self-esteem accordingly?) Yet again, given the socio-economic and cultural circumstances of many holistic participants, it is highly likely that a significant number are self-assured; and practitioners are experts at their craft, exercising their 'autonomous' skills to respond to and engage with discerning participants (Heelas 2008).

As we noted in *The Spiritual Revolution* (2005), the 'caring for others at the expense of oneself so let's concentrate on me' argument has a role to play in explaining the appeal of holistic activities (p. 104). But bearing in mind the relationality, the expressive and humanistic ethicality of these activities, it is highly likely that the more important theme is learning or experiencing better ways of *enabling* others by looking after or cultivating oneself as well (Heelas 2008); as with the hospice spiritual counsellor, developing herself not so much for herself *per se*, but for herself as someone working *with* others—whilst developing through that commensurately. Sheila Larson, the young nurse made famous by Robert Bellah *et al.*'s *Habits of the Heart* (1985), defines her 'own Sheilaism' as 'just try[ing] to love yourself' (p. 221); and who 'had the experience that "if she looked in the mirror" she "would see Jesus Christ"' (p. 235) whilst caring for a dying woman. It is nonsense to suppose that people like this nurse—and it seems that there are many of this outlook participating in holistic activities—more or less give up deeply rooted habits of the heart to dwell on themselves *per se* (or, for that matter, flee from one identity to construct another basic one).

The L'Oréal slogan 'Because You're Worth It'—presumably to change to 'Because it's worth it' now that the company has entered India!—is cited by Woodhead (2007*b*: 121) in connection with her argument that holistic participation serves to compensate for low self-esteem: compensating by finding a 'new and *stronger* sense of self', by performing 'act[s] of self-assertion', by 'gaining . . . control', by developing 'self-worth', by learning how to 'hold your own power' (pp. 122–3; my emphasis). Maybe for some. But the language of L'Oréal signals a capitalistic,

'I've earned it', Rodney Stark-like 'this is *my* reward' form of '"holistic" fulfilment' (p. 121); signals the theme of narcissistically compensating for low self-esteem to bask in one's own self-empowered glory—quite possibly at the expense of others. Priceless! As a generalization—which is how Woodhead seems to present it—this picture does grave injustice to people like Sheila, belittles all those intent on 'extending' their 'own' or 'autonomous' growth to inform 'deeper', more considerate, modest relationality, and demeans those like Sheila who already value what their lives have to offer (Heelas 2008; compare Woodhead 2008).[4]

As for Woodhead's iron cage theme, from the Romantics onward, many have argued that the subjective turn of modern culture is in measure generated by iron cage experiences. However, Woodhead does not provide convincing evidence that the iron cage is widely and significantly experienced in the home life of the (typically) professional or ex-professional, middle-class and middle-aged (or older) women who are attracted by holistic activities. Overall, Woodhead's use of deprivation compensation theory (with sacred power compensating for the 'real' thing) suffers from the standard criticisms of this kind of theorizing: basically, that it is only too easy to apply the theory, only too difficult to verify it, even harder to render applications falsifiable. At the very least, we need to have much more evidence to indicate that significant numbers of holistic participants are 'disempowered' within the workplace of paid employment, and, for that matter, by '"traditional" female roles based around domestic labour' (2007*a*: 576). And where is the *evidence* that *significant* numbers prioritize the 'quest' for power to deal with their supposedly oppressed circumstances?[5]

[4] The extent to which Woodhead emphasizes power is attested by what she asserts in another recent article (2007*a*). 'Self-spirituality' is classified as a 'questing' form of 'religion', one which is 'marginal' and 'confirmatory' (pp. 570, 575). The category has to do with 'us[ing] sacred power in ways which aim at... transformation and movement towards a position of *greater advantage* within the existing gender order'; to 'improve one's position' within this order; not infrequently, 'to maximise her advantage within it' (p. 575; my emphasis). Female participants, it seems, draw on sacred power to compete more successfully with men (with 'coping' somehow entering the picture as well (p. 576)). Leaving aside the fact that this ignores the 'counter-cultural' aspects of many holistic 'teachings' (Heelas 2008), and also leaving aside the fact that many activities do *not* focus on women *qua* women (i.e., as comprising some sort of essentialized entity/identity of the kind criticized earlier in this essay), Woodhead grossly exaggerates the theme of making 'use of sacred power to try to achieve a more favourable position within the existing gender order' (when that order is largely controlled by men) (p. 578). Apart from the obvious point that the 'gender order' with which many participants are involved, when in paid employment, is predominantly populated by women (as in primary schools or nursing, for example), in the (great) majority of holistic participants and activities, the theme of instrumentalized empowerment is nowhere nearly as significant as other life orientations (Heelas 2008). Power hungry? Maybe for some, say among feminist 'seekers' in Brazil. But this most certainly does not amount to anything approaching the whole story for the holistic in all its modes.

[5] Among other things, Woodhead's argument fails to take into consideration the facts that, (i) most of those participating in the holistic activities of Kendal and environs are happy with their home (and work) lives; (ii) only around 20 per cent have children under the age of 18 living at home;

The primary value clash is surely between the values of 'life', in expressivistic-cum-humanistic form, and the values of 'life' in the specified, delimited mode of those 'human resources' which count towards efficiency and economic productivity. Life values of the first mode are bound up with becoming more truly or authentically human at work, and are often positively encouraged; whereas the latter, which are typically encouraged much more, are bound up with all those constraints or disciplines which are taken to be necessary for focusing, disciplining the self so that 'it' can obtain measurable, productive targets.

In many work environments, the values of the expressive life exist in very considerable tension with the values of the instrumentalized life. Consider the caring professions. Given that women are numerically more significant than men, it is not surprising that tensions or value clashes affect more women than men. Women in the caring professions, finding self-fulfilment by helping others—then running slap bang into that culture of targets which undermines holistic self-fulfilment by 'constructing' the self in that narrowly defined way which is required to meet economic objectives of a quantifiable kind. It is precisely this clash which could very well help explain why nurses sometimes turn to holistic activities: if they can, within the workplace, to make a stand against the pressure to engage in 'positivistic' nursing; if not, outside the workplace to help them return to work more inspired to attend to patients' 'spiritual needs' (Heelas 2006*b*). And much the same argument can be applied to primary school teachers (who are largely women), those working in the area of human resource development (frequently women), the increasing number of women in management consultancy, and so on. Furthermore, as Aupers and Houtman (2006) show, it is this clash which explains why senior businesspeople (female and male) not infrequently leave the 'fast lane'. This is positivism in action—that is, the measurable, the testable at work—to explaining why businesspeople retreat from the world of fragmented quantities to down-size, perhaps finding new careers as practitioners.

(iii) approaching 30 per cent live alone; and (iv) around 20 per cent are retired. More generally, the holistic participants of Britain tend to be drawn from the 2 million couples who are in committed relationships but live separately (Bennett, 2007) and the 6.5 plus million adults who live alone. Participants are also drawn from the ever-increasing numbers who are affluent enough to 'dine out' (Rozenberg and Duncan 2006). Contrary to Woodhead's argument, and taking the mid-life and older factor into account, the broad picture is of women participating in holistic activities once home life becomes rather less challenging. Furthermore, on the 'iron cage' for women theme, Kendal and environs data shows that almost 30 per cent of all participants (80 per cent of whom are women) are in part-time employment, a quarter are self-employed, and only 30 per cent work full-time: data which suggest that whatever 'iron cage' effect employment might have (and value clashes within the workplace obviously disrupt whatever 'cages' might be in evidence), it is not as significant as all that—including the pressures it might put on home life. This is not to say, however, that iron cage features of employment within the mainstream do not play an important role in encouraging people to down size, perhaps taking up holistic activities in the process.

Further Considerations

An enormous amount of tricky research is required for the sociological (etc.) study of inner-life spirituality to arrive at a satisfactory account of its growth—in particular the role played by life in the mainstream of work, and even more particularly, for we know so little about it, the role played by life at home. Even the most obsessional of people have multiple motivations, with multiple expectations, fears, and concerns. We would have to study what activities have to offer to people living through different circumstances, ranging from pregnant women, to the retired, to those in the process of dying (for example); how activities are perceived by those attracted to them. We would have to look at the experienced 'benefits' which ensure that numbers of those attracted remain for considerable lengths of time ('benefits' which include 'letting me be me', spiritual well-being, the opportunity to reflect on, and engage with, life dilemmas, the 'opening up' of new possibilities in life, feeling more at home with oneself, feeling more spiritually inspired to serve as a 'force for good'). And to be sound sociologists of spirituality, we surely have to take inspiration from the great pioneers of the study of spirituality, most recently Steven Tipton (1984), to go as deeply as we can into how general and particular 'structural' and cultural formations contribute to those *specific* aspirations, motivations, etc. which inform the appeal of holistic activities. *Contra* those like Woodhead who veer towards essentialized, all-absorbing, arguably reductionistic 'mono-explanations', it is my view that a myriad of dynamics have to be incorporated to arrive at more general explanations of growth.

Rooted in sophisticated socio-cultural theorizing, with Georg Simmel (1997) of primary significance, and now supported by a considerable amount of evidence (see, e.g., Houtman and Aupers 2007), the subjectivization thesis works. It is *how* it works—that is, in connection with *which* socio-cultural (and personal) circumstances—that requires further attention. What attracts a primary school teacher to adopt inner-life spirituality in her child-centred work is unlikely to involve the same detailed considerations as what attracts a senior manager of an oil company, or a retired person who feels homeless at home, with too much time on her hands, too many memories to incorporate, and an urge to find ways of catching up with 'life' lost whilst previously at work in the paid sector. It seems likely, however, that generalizations will emerge—for example, patterns to do with those whose life focus lies in professional employment, those who attend to the quality of life of close kin, those (retired) who are primarily concerned with caring for themselves, those who find the (so-called) work–life balance a matter of pressing concern, and so on.

As things stand, the information bearing on these more specific (and general) dynamics is not, in the main, especially 'rich' (and that includes material from the Kendal Project). The call has to be for qualitative-cum-quantitative research focused on specific sites or topics of inquiry: for example, the ways in which NHS general practices are contributing to growth; the role of Hindu temples; the role played by relatively secular subjective well-being culture (Heelas and

Woodhead 2005: 83–94); the role played by directives provided by the NHS and Ofsted; the role played by mundane ill-being problems, such as back pains; and the role played by the $57 billion anti-ageing industry.[6]

Of particular note, a great deal more (predominantly ethnographic) research is required to gauge the relative significance of the 'flight from caring' culminating with the narcissism of 'I'm worth it', on the one hand, and the 'true self' as 'the relational self' on the other. On occasion, no doubt, the turn within is to address 'issues' to do with low (or overweening) esteem. It is highly likely, though, that the turn within typically takes place in the context of the values of expressive humanism (Heelas 2008). What is basically at stake here is exploring the 'balance' which participants strike between autonomy and relationality; the integration; the extent to which the celebration, the expression, of autonomy takes the form of celebrating the self *qua* the self.[7] In related vein, what is at stake is exploring whether individuals are exercising their authority as consumers to indulge, expand, and wave the 'all about me' flag (Crompton 2007) or are striving to self-actualize life with, through, and for others (Heelas and Woodhead 2005; Heelas 2008).

Assistance is at hand, though. Cognate or overlapping fields of inquiry—for example CAM research (which has provided a number of quantitatively grounded explanations of growth), health and fitness studies (including the investigation of gender differentials), and the growing amount of research into subjective well-being—have much to offer.

Explaining 'Belief'

There is relatively sound evidence that most of those who come to participate in holistic activities are already convinced, or partially convinced, of the truth of at

[6] The increasingly important role played by advice received within general practices, the increasing importance of inner-life spirituality within other more mainstream health contexts, the increasing significance of spirituality within the realms of sport, Hinduism, colleges of further education, and so on: the 80 : 20 ratio is probably changing in the direction of more males. This clearly has implications for explaining growth.

[7] As a rough guide to where the balance lies, in answer to the open-ended question 'What would you say are the three most important problems facing you, personally, these days?', the most frequent answers given by the holistic participants of Kendal and environs have to do with relationships (including the lack of them, namely loneliness), with the emphasis lying on 'making a contribution' as one respondent puts it, health and ageing, and employment-related issues (financial, time pressures, etc.). The state of society and the world comes next. If low self-esteem is present, it is best described in the language of respondents—for example, in connection with being 'lonely'. There is no questionnaire evidence to suggest that the problem is failing to engage in self-celebration. However limited in scope this kind of evidence from the Kendal Project might be, it cannot be ignored.

least the basics of inner-life spirituality. (If this were not the case, it is reasonable to suppose that not so many would become participants.) And so to the matter of explaining 'belief'.

Recalling the rather extraordinary 'God within, not without' percentages presented earlier, why have so many come to believe—if that is the right word—in the sacrality of the inner life? The general subjectivization thesis has a role to play (see Houtman and Aupers 2007). But the 'gendered' applications of the thesis, emphasizing the role played by women and used to explain the growth of holistic activities, are of limited value. For it appears to be the case that as many men 'believe' in inner-life spirituality as women (Barker 2004: 36). In addition, the gap between what Gallup and Jones call 'believing' and 'belonging' in the religious sphere (1989: 100) is very considerable in the inner-life spirituality context. (In Britain, whereas the gap in the religious sphere is provided by the difference between the 23 per cent of believers in the personal God of theistic religion and the 7.9 per cent of regular church attendees, the gap in connection with inner-life sacrality is at least indicated by the difference between the 37 per cent 'God within, not without' believers and the 1.6 per cent figure for holistic, mind–body spirituality participants.) And this means that participation in holistic activities cannot account for the 'beliefs' of many people.

The multi-million dollar question facing the sociology of spirituality—explaining the growth of 'belief'—remains the most poorly researched and theorized matter of all (Heelas, in preparation).

The Debate over the Future

Bruce argues that alternative, 'New Age' spiritualities 'will decline' (2002: 79). The reason is that their organizational and cultural arrangements are too fragile to fare at all well in the future. Bruce discerns radical individualism among participants—an individualism, the argument goes, which results in every participant calling her or his own tune rather than agreeing on what is required to serve as a 'solid base' for the future (p. 101), or, indeed, as a confirmatory plausibility system for the present. Of the many objections which can be directed at this analysis, the most obvious is that the growth to date becomes virtually if not entirely inexplicable. Other objections, stemming from the role played by the *lingua franca* that is in fact widely abroad in inner-spirituality circles, or stemming from the role played by the values embedded in activities (of the 'you have to be honest "about" yourself for this to work' variety), are now being canvassed, for instance by Stef Aupers and Dick Houtman (2006; see also Heelas 2006*a*; 2008).

No doubt this debate is set to run. However, the evidence currently available strongly suggests that the future is rosy. Holistic activities appear to be remarkably adept at handling one of the great dilemmas of life in the contemporary West: the tension, if not clash, between key values of the ethic of humanity itself—values to do with freedom, autonomy, and self-expression, on the one hand, and values to do with equality, respect, and dignity, on the other. Holistic activities, in other words, serve as a 'model' of how to marry (experienced) self-expressivity with (experienced) equality of relationality; how to marry autonomy with sharing life with others. In addition, the further that Western cultures move in the direction of prioritizing equality over freedom, the greater the restrictions on freedom—that is, when the exercise of freedom generates inequality by way of exclusivism. The more that freedom is threatened or curtailed, however, the more it is valued. Frequently catering for the subjectivities of those who want to be 'free spirits', the future of holistic activities looks promising. Furthermore, the cultural emphasis on equality is catered for: participants are encouraged to experience equality as 'natural' rather than imposed. In considerable measure, holistic activities work well with particular key values of the times.

Much depends, though, on younger people. Although the number of those in their twenties (and younger) who are participating in activities like yoga are growing, it remains relatively small. This does not appear to augur too well for for the future. Significantly, though, considerably larger numbers of younger people appear to have an inner-life outlook or orientation. Evidence is provided by Eileen Barker's (2004) analysis of RAMP (Religions and Moral Pluralism) survey data, William Kay's (2006) analysis of school survey data from England and Wales, Yves Lambert's (2004) discussion of 'autonomous spirituality' in Europe (p. 42), Dick Houtman's and Peter Mascini's (2002) analysis of data from the World Values Survey data, and my own re-analysis of data found in Christian Smith and Melinda Denton's *Soul Searching: The Religion and Spiritual Lives of American Teenagers* (2005; Heelas 2007*a*). All this—and more—suggests that spiritualities of life are not a cultural flash in the pan. But, as with so many of the topics introduced in this essay, more research is urgently required.

Conclusion

The sociology of spirituality is coming into its own at a time of glorious opportunity. For a spiritual revolution—which is surely what developments are amounting to in a number of Western countries—is taking place right under our noses. Unless change is studied now, it will be too late for critical first-hand research.

References

Abrams, M. H. (1973). *Natural Supernaturalism.* London: W. W. Norton.

Aupers, Stef, and Houtman, Dick (2006). 'Beyond the Spiritual Marketplace: The Social and Public Significance of New Age Spirituality'. *Journal of Contemporary Religion*, 21/2: 201–22.

Barker, Eileen (2004). 'The Church Without and the God Within: Religiosity and/or Spirituality'. In Dinka Marinovic Jerolimov, Sinisa Zrinscak, and Irena Borowik (eds.), *Religion and Patterns of Social Transformation.* Zagreb: Institute for Social Research, 23–47.

Bauman, Zygmunt (1988). 'Postmodern Religion?'. In Paul Heelas, Scott Lash, and Paul Morris (eds.), *Religion, Modernity and Postmodernity.* Oxford: Blackwell, 55–78.

Bell, Daniel (1976). *The Cultural Contradictions of Capitalism.* London: Heinemann.

Bellah, Robert N., Madsen, Richard, Sullivan, William M., Swidler, Ann, and Tipton, Steven M. (1985). *Habits of the Heart.* Berkeley: University of California Press.

Bennett, Rosemary (2007). 'Couples that Live Apart... Stay Together'. *The Times*, 12 May, 37.

Bruce, Steve (1996). 'Religion in Britain at the Close of the 20th Century: A Challenge to the Silver Lining Perspective'. *Journal of Contemporary Religion*, 11/3: 261–75.

—— (2000). 'The New Age and Secularisation'. In Steven Sutcliffe and Marion Bowman (eds.), *Beyond New Age.* Edinburgh: Edinburgh University Press, 220–36.

—— (2002). *God is Dead.* Oxford: Blackwell.

Butler, Judith (2004). *Undoing Gender.* London: Routledge.

—— (2007[1990]). *Gender Trouble.* London: Routledge.

Carrette, Jeremy, and King, Richard (2005). *Selling Spirituality.* London: Routledge.

Crompton, Simon (2007). *All About Me: Loving a Narcissist.* London: Collins.

Dalai Lama, and Cutler, Howard (1998). *The Art of Happiness.* London: Hodder & Stoughton.

Dobson, R. (2003). 'Half of General Practices Offer Patients Complementary Medicine'. *British Medical Journal*, 327: 1250.

Durkheim, Émile (1984[1893]). *The Division of Labour in Society.* Basingstoke: Macmillan.

Gallup, George Jr., and Jones, Sarah (1989). *100 Questions and Answers: Religion in America.* Princeton: Princeton Religion Research Center.

Gould, Mark (2007). 'In Pursuit of Happiness'. *Health Service Journal*, 10 May, 22–4.

Hanegraaff, Wouter J. (1998). *New Age Religion and Western Culture.* Albany, NY: State University of New York Press.

—— (1999). 'New Age Spirituality as Secular Religion'. *Social Compass*, 46/2: 145–60.

Hardman, Charlotte (forthcoming). 'Shamanism, Neo-Shamanism and Gender'.

Heald, Gordon (2000). *Soul of Britain.* London: The Opinion Research Business.

Heelas, Paul (2006*a*). 'The Infirmity Debate: On the Viability of New Age Spiritualities of Life'. *Journal of Contemporary Religion*, 21/2: 223–40.

—— (2006*b*). 'Nursing Spirituality'. *Spirituality and Health International*, 7: 8–23.

—— (2007*a*). 'The Holistic Milieu and Spirituality: Reflections on Voas and Bruce'. In Kieran Flanagan and Peter Jupp (eds.), *A Sociology of Spirituality.* Aldershot: Ashgate, 63–80.

—— (2007*b*). 'The Spiritual Revolution of Northern Europe: Personal Beliefs', *Nordic Journal of Religion and Society*, 20/1: 1–28.

HEELAS, PAUL (2008). *Spiritualities of Life: New Age Romanticism and Consumptive Capitalism.* Oxford: Blackwell.

—— (in preparation). 'Explaining the Popularity of "the God Within"'.

—— and WOODHEAD, LINDA (2005). *The Spiritual Revolution.* Oxford: Blackwell.

House of Lords (2000). *Science and Technology, Sixth Report.* <www.Parliament.the-stationery-office.co.uk>.

HOUTMAN, DICK, and AUPERS, STEF (2007). 'The Spiritual Turn and the Decline of Tradition: The Spread of Post-Christian Spirituality in Fourteen Western Countries (1981–2000)'. *Journal for the Scientific Study of Religion,* 46/3: 305–20.

—— —— (2008). 'The Spiritual Revolution and the New Age Gender Puzzle: The Sacralization of the Self in Late Modernity (1980–2000)'. In Kristin Aune, Sonya Sharma, and Giselle Vincett (eds.), *Women and Religion in the West: Challenging Secularisation.* Aldershot: Ashgate, 99–118.

—— and MASCINI, PETER (2002). 'Why do Churches become Empty, while New Age Grows? Secularization and Religious Change in the Netherlands'. *Journal for the Scientific Study of Religion,* 41/3: 455–73.

—— —— (2003), 'Why do Churches become Empty, while New Age Grows? Secularization and Religious Change in the Netherlands'. paper presented at the Alternative Spiritualities and New Age Studies Conference, May–June, The Open University, Milton Keynes.

KAY, WILLIAM K. (2006). 'England and Wales: Open Theism and Materialism'. In Hans-Georg Ziebert and William K. Kay (eds.), *Youth in Europe,* ii. Berlin: Lit Verlag, 81–103.

Kendal Project. <www.kendalproject.org.uk>.

KHAN, AKHTAR HAMEED (2005). *Orangi Pilot Project.* Karachi: Oxford University Press.

LAMBERT, YVES (2004). 'A Turning Point in Religious Evolution in Europe'. *Journal of Contemporary Religion,* 19/1: 29–46.

LASCH, CHRISTOPHER (1980). *The Culture of Narcissism.* London: Picador.

—— (1987). 'Soul of a New Age'. *Omni,* Oct., 78–80, 82, 84–5.

LAU, KIMBERLY J. (2000). *New Age Capitalism.* Philadelphia: University of Pennsylvania Press.

LEUBA, JAMES H. (1950). *The Reformation of the Churches.* Boston: Beacon Press.

LINDEN, GURLI (1998). *I Describe the Way and Meanwhile I am Proceeding Along It.* Stockholm: Rosengardens Forlag.

MITROFF, IAN, and DENTON, ELIZABETH (1999). *A Spiritual Audit of Corporate America.* San Francisco: Jossey-Bass.

Ofsted (2004). 'Promoting and Evaluating Pupils' Spiritual, Moral, Social and Cultural Development'. <www.ofsted.gov.uk/publications>.

PAGE, JEREMY (2007). 'American Attempts to Patent Yoga Puts Indians in a Twist'. *The Times,* 31 May, 47.

ROZENBERG, GABRIEL, and DUNCAN, GARY (2006). 'Dining Out Replaces Eating In as Nation's Spending at Table Soars'. *The Times,* 19 Aug. 9.

SCHMIDT, JULIA (2004). 'Big Business Lunges for a Piece of Fat Yoga Profits'. *USA Today,* 30 Aug.

SCHOR, NAOMI, and WEED, ELIZABETH (eds.) (1994). *The Essential Difference.* Bloomington, Ind.: Indiana University Press.

SIMMEL, GEORG (1997). *Essays on Religion.* New Haven: Yale University Press.

Smith, Christian, with Denton, Melinda Lundquist (2005). *Soul Searching: The Religious and Spiritual Lives of American Teenagers.* Oxford: Oxford University Press.
Smith, Lewis (2007). 'A Friend is Loyal, Kind, True . . . and Probably a Woman'. *The Times*, 8 Mar., 5.
Smithers, Rebecca (2004). 'Ofsted Chief says Scrap Law on Worship'. *The Guardian*, 22 Apr., 6.
Tipton, Steven M. (1984). *Getting Saved from the Sixties.* Berkeley: University of California Press.
Voas, David, and Bruce, Steve (2007). 'The Spiritual Revolution: Another False Dawn for the Sacred'. In K. Flanagan and P. Jupp (eds.), *A Sociology of Spirituality.* Aldershot: Ashgale, 43–61.
Ward, Graham (2006). 'The Future of Religion'. *Journal of the American Academy of Religion*, 74/1: 179–86.
Woodhead, Linda (1997). 'Spiritualising the Sacred: A Critique of Feminist Theology'. *Modern Theology*, 13/2: 191–212.
—— (2007*a*). 'Gender Differences in Religions Practice and Significance'. In James A. Bechford and N. J. Demerath III (eds.), *The Sage Handbook of the Sociology of Religion.* London: Sage, 566–86.
—— (2007*b*). 'Why so Many Women in Holistic Spirituality? A Puzzle Revisited'. In Kieran Flanagan and Peter Jupp (eds.), *A Sociology of Spirituality.* Aldershot: Ashgate, 115–25.
—— (2008). '"Because I'm Worth it": Religion and Women's Changing Lives in the West'. In Kristin Aune, Sonya Sharma, and Giselle Vincett (eds.), *Women and Religion in the West: Challenging Secularisation.* Aldershot: Ashgate, 147–61.
Zinnbauer, J., *et al.* (1997). 'Religion and Spirituality: Unfuzzying the Fuzzy'. *Journal for the Scientific Study of Religion*, 36/4: 549–64.

Suggested Reading

Beckerlegge, Gwilym (2004). 'Iconographic Representations of Renunciation and Activism in the Ramakrishna Math and Mission and the Rashtriya Swayamsevak Sangh'. *Journal of Contemporary Religion*, 19/1: 47–66.
Clarke, Peter (2006). *New Religions in Global Perspective.* London: Routledge.
Costea, Bogdan, and Crump, Norman (2007). 'Managerialism and "Infinite Human Resourcefulness": A Commentary on the "Therapeutic Habitus", "Derecognition of Finitude" and the Modern Sense of Self'. *Journal of Cultural Research*, 11/3: 245–64.
Flanagan, Kieran, and Jupp Peter, (eds.) (2007). *A Sociology of Spirituality.* Aldershot: Ashgate.
Frembgen, Jurgen Wasim (2006). *The Friends of God: Sufi Saints in Islam.* Oxford: Oxford University Press.
Hunt, Kate (2003). 'Understanding the Spirituality of People Who Do Not Go to Church'. In Grace Davie, Paul Heelas, and Linda Woodhead (eds), *Predicting Religion.* Aldershot: Ashgate, 159–69.
King, Michael, Jones, Louise, Barnes, Kelly, Low, Joseph, Walker, Carl, Wilkinson, Susie, Mason, Christina, Sutherland, Juliette, and Tookman, Adrian (2006). 'Meas-

uring Spiritual Belief: Development and Standardization of a Beliefs and Values Scale'. *Psychological Medicine*, 36: 417–25.

KRAUT, RICHARD (2007). *What is Good and Why: The Ethics of Well-Being*. Cambridge, Mass.: Harvard University Press.

NUSSBAUM, MARTHA C. (2007). *The Clash Within: Democracy, Religious Violence, and India's Future*. Cambridge, Mass.: Harvard University Press.

PARTRIDGE, CHRISTOPHER (2004, 2005). *The Re-Enchantment of the West*, 2 vols. London: T & T Clark.

RAMSTEDT, MARTIN (2007). 'Transforming Notions of Mercy at Work'. In Peter Jan Margry and Herman Roodenburg (eds.), *Reframing Dutch Culture*. Aldershot: Ashgate.

SCHNEIDERS, SANDRA M. (2003). 'Religion vs. Spirituality: A Contemporary Conundrum'. *Spiritus*, 3: 163–85.

SHARMA, URSULA (2002). 'Integrated Medicine: An Examination of GP–Complementary Practitioner Collaboration'. In Gillian Bendelow, Mick Carpenter, Caroline Vautier, and Simon Williams (eds.), *Gender, Health and Healing*. London: Routledge, 212–35.

WALSH, KIRI, KING, MICHAEL, JONES, LOUISE, TOOKMAN, ADRIAN, and BLIZARD, ROBERT (2002). 'Spiritual Beliefs may Affect Outcome of Bereavement'. *British Medical Journal*, 324 (June): 1551–5.

WERBNER, PNINA (2004). *Pilgrims of Love: The Anthropology of a Global Sufi Cult*. Bloomington, Ind.: Indiana University Press.

WHITE, GILLIAN (2006). *Talking about Spirituality in Health Care Practice*. London: Jessica Kingsley.

WULFF, DAVID M. (2003). 'A Field in Crisis: Is it Time for the Psychology of Religion to Start Over?' In Peter H. M. P. Roelofsma, Jozef M. T. Corveleyn, and Joke W. Van Saane (eds.), *One Hundred Years of Psychology and Religion*. Amsterdam: VU University Press, 11–32.

ZINNBAUER, B. J., PARGAMENT, K. I., and SCOTT, A. B. (1997). 'The Emerging Meanings of Religiousness and Spirituality: Problems and Prospects'. *Journal of Personality*, 67: 889–919.

CHAPTER 43

THE SOCIOLOGY OF ESOTERICISM

KENNET GRANHOLM

Introduction

At the turn of the millennium Wouter J. Hanegraaff wrote that the study of Western esotericism 'finds itself in the middle of a process of academic professionalization and institutionalization' (Hanegraaff 2001: 5). In the years since Hanegraaff's statement, the amount of research conducted in the field has grown, and the area is increasingly being recognized as a proper subdiscipline of the scientific study of religion. However, most research in the field has had a historical focus, and sociological viewpoints have largely been neglected. There have been studies of esoteric religiosity conducted in the field of the sociology of religion, but a sociology of Western esotericism proper has not yet been developed. A sociology of esotericism which takes into account historical factors and pays heed to the historical research conducted on the matter can greatly enhance the understanding of both contemporary and historical esotericism.

This chapter is not to be understood as the definitive account of the sociology of esotericism. The aim, rather, is to point to paths on which the researcher interested in doing sociological research on esotericism can venture.

What is Esotericism?

A prerequisite for serious academic treatment of a subject is some degree of academic consensus concerning the definition of the subject. In other words, it is important that we are all talking about the same thing. This naturally applies to esotericism as well, and definitions will thus form the starting point of the present discussion. There have been several attempts to delineate and define esotericism, and I will present and discuss some of these here.

In 1964, Frances Yates presented 'the Hermetic Tradition' as a neglected, but important and influential, counterculture to both science and religion. She proposed that this 'tradition', although in itself non-progressive in character, had been the driving force behind the Scientific Revolution. Yates's thesis, and the large body of research influenced by it, is infused with two major problems. First, it appears somewhat problematic to establish causal links between modern science and esoteric philosophies and practices and at the same time argue for oppositional relations between the two. Furthermore, as Wouter J. Hanegraaff notes, Yates's approach is characterized by 'modernist narratives of secular progress' (Hanegraaff 2001: 16). Secondly, presenting esotericism (in this case termed Hermeticism) as a self-contained 'tradition' unduly simplifies and homogenizes the subject matter. This easily causes the researcher to neglect the complex history and large diversity of different esoteric traditions (see Hanegraaff 2001: 13–18 for a discussion of the 'Yates Paradigm').

In the 1970s the idea of counterculture was repeated in attempts to define esotericism and occultism in sociological terms. Marcello Truzzi (1974: 245) treats occultism as a 'wastebasket for deviant knowledge', simply comprising knowledge not accepted in mainstream religion, science, or culture. A consequential problem with this definition is that its subject matter lacks any independent substance; the occult stops being occult when enough people accept it (see Hanegraaff 1998: 40–2 for a critique). Edward Tiryakian (1974: 265) defines esoteric knowledge as 'secret knowledge of the reality of things ... to a relatively small number of persons'. Tiryakian's focus on the 'secret' and 'select' nature of the esoteric is in line with common dictionary definitions of the term (see Hammer 2004). The major problem with the typological definitions of esotericism common from the 1960s to the late 1980s is that they oppose esotericism to both science and religion, portraying it as fundamentally countercultural in nature and homogeneous in character. The great variety of esoteric manifestations, in their societal, cultural, and doctrinal dimensions, is neglected. Furthermore, these definitions tend to overlook historical factors and favour structural ones.

The type of definition which has become prevalent in the academic study of Western esotericism since the 1990s views esotericism as a historically related set of currents and notions in Western culture (hence *Western* esotericism), which can be identified according to a set of characteristics. The typology presented by Antoine Faivre in his *L'Esoterisme* of 1992 (see Faivre 1993; 1994 for English dissemination of the typology) has been adopted by many current scholars of esotericism (see Hanegraaff 1996; 1998; 2001; 2004; 2005*a*; Hammer 2001; Bogdan 2007; Granholm 2005). In Faivre's research, Western esotericism is defined as 'an ensemble of spiritual currents in modern and contemporary Western history which share a certain *air de famille*, as well as the form of thought which is its common denominator' (Faivre 1998: 2), and is seen as comprised of four intrinsic and two secondary characteristics. The four intrinsic characteristics are:

1. The idea of correspondences, in which invisible linkages are thought to exist in the cosmos. Through these linkages everything affects everything else, and it is, in effect, possible to influence the physical world by seemingly non-causal means.
2. The idea of a living nature, in which the divine force is immanent.
3. The central role of imagination and mediation in the acquisition of spiritual knowledge. Imagination, which Hanegraaff called an 'organ of the soul' (1996: 398), is thought to provide knowledge that the rational mind cannot provide.
4. The idea of transmutation. The esotericist is on a journey of progress, in which he or she strives to attain higher and higher stages of spiritual development.

The secondary characteristics, the presence of which are common, but not necessary, are:

1. The idea of concordance, that some, most, or all religions are based on a common inner kernel of truth. In the Renaissance the idea of concordance became a major theme in the search for *philosophia perennis*, the ancient and unifying origin of all religion (Faivre 1994: 114–15).
2. Specific forms of transmission, in which the esoteric knowledge is divulged to the adept through established channels and in successive stages.

Faivre further views Western esotericism as consisting of currents, corresponding to movements, schools, and traditions—e.g., Rosicrucianism and Paracelsism—and notions, corresponding to spiritual attitudes and practices—e.g., Gnosis. Some of these, e.g. alchemy and magic, are both notions and currents (Faivre 1998: 3–10).

Faivre's definition has been criticized on at least two major counts. First, it has been claimed that Faivre's typology is concerned only with 'Christian esotericism in the early modern period' (Stuckrad 2005: 83; see also Hanegraaff 1998: 46–7). Secondly, due to Faivre construing his definition in rather strict historical and religious contexts, his schemata does not really take into account the transformation of esotericism over time (see Hanegraaff 1998: 46–7; 2003).

Kocku von Stuckrad (2005) argues that the view of esotericism as a structural element in Western culture should be favoured over the approach of historical currents, and suggests a discursive model of esotericism. This model would take into account both the change of esotericism through time and pluralism in the esoteric field, thus addressing the problems in Faivre's typology. Stuckrad's account focuses on discourses of 'claims of higher knowledge'—basically claims of knowledge which surpasses all 'common knowledge' and which might even make 'common knowledge' obsolete—and 'ways of accessing higher knowledge', including mediation of knowledge from 'higher' or alien beings and the perquisite of individual experience in gaining knowledge. He also views ontological monism as a general base of many esoteric world views (Stuckrad 2005: 93). As the approach suggested by Stuckrad does not focus strictly on historical relations, it might also be possible to include non-Western traditions, such as certain forms of Hindu and Buddhist Tantra, under the umbrella term of esotericism. Stuckrad does not, however, directly suggest this.

I do not regard Faivre's and Stuckrad's approaches to be in opposition, and they can be used to supplement each other. While Stuckrad's approach opens up the field to a wider range of phenomena, Faivre's schema nonetheless describes central ingredients in esoteric world views.

It should be noted that while esotericism can often be identified as religious, and always has a spiritual dimension to it, it should not be approached as religious automatically. Looking at esotericism as a form of thought, or as a structural element, one finds esoteric traits in seemingly non-religious phenomena. For example, in its early history experimental science was as good as indistinguishable from esoteric methodology (see, e.g., Dobbs 1975). Furthermore, esoteric qualities can be found in certain interpretations of contemporary natural science as well, both in popular science and in the sentiments of certain natural scientists. Stuckrad (2005: 91) gives the example of genetics, which at times is treated fairly esoterically ('the unlocking of the human genome will give us the answers to everything'). Rather than being a 'third tradition' opposed to religion and science, esotericism is a recurrent theme in Western history that can be found in both science and religion.

Contemporary Esotericism and the Sociology of Religion

The historical study of Western esotericism has been focused almost exclusively on the inner workings of specific esoteric traditions and on prominent figures in esotericism (see, e.g., Godwin 1994; Chanel, Deveney, and Godwin 1995; Barnes 2006). According to Malcolm Hamilton (2001: 2), the sociology of religion studies the role of religion in society, the significance and impact of religion upon society, and seeks to understand the social forces and influences that shape religion. Both religious organizations and individuals should be studied (see Konieczny and Riesebrodt 2005: 139–40). A sociology of esotericism would therefore have to take a different form from the one dominant in the current academic study of Western esotericism. Sociological studies have been conducted on religious organizations that can be identified as esoteric, mainly on the New Age movement and neo-paganism (see, e.g., York 1995; Heelas 1996). However, few studies have analysed the movements specifically as esotericism.

A researcher interested in doing sociological studies on esotericism does well to bear in mind that the esotericism of academic research is a scholarly construct; in Hanegraaff's words, it is 'not "discovered" but *produced*' (Hanegraaff 1998: 16). The researcher should not make the mistake of searching for 'the true essence' of esotericism; there simply is not one. It is the choices and delineations of the researcher that construe the field, not the other way around (Hanegraaff 1998: 13–18; 2004: 489–91). This is, of course, the nature of all scholarly definitions.

Whether one chooses to employ the definition of esotericism *à la* Faivre or to use the discursive approach of Stuckrad, one faces the same problem. Esotericism presents itself as an extremely amorphous and diverse phenomenon. While the similarities between, let us say, contemporary Wicca and eighteenth-century Rosicrucianism are sufficient for them both to be analysed as esotericism, there are still major differences. It might be useful to talk of a sociology of esotericism*s* rather than a sociology of esotericism.

The difficulties that a sociologist of esotericism is faced with are largely the same as those the sociologist of new religious movements (NRMs) encounters. The number of esoterically inclined organizations and individuals is almost impossible to assess. Also, similar to NRMs, the rate of turnover, as well as instances of double membership, is large (see Barker 1999).

Aspects of Esotericism

With a starting point in Meredith McGuire's *Religion: The Social Context* (2002), I will try to highlight a few areas where sociological perspectives on esotericism might be useful, and show how the use of esotericism as an analytical category might benefit the study. McGuire discusses certain dimensions of religion which are central in sociological studies. These are naturally of importance when doing sociological research on esotericism as well. I will discuss the aspects of belief, ritual, religious experience, and community.

Belief

Belief is the cognitive aspect of religion and defines what adherents know about the world. It forms the basis for action and shapes ritual activity (McGuire 2002: 15–17).

Beliefs have been studied to a great extent in historically inclined researches on esotericism. The ways in which beliefs affect the lives of believers, however, have not been given much consideration. This is consistent with historical grand-scale research where 'the big picture' is sought. Sociological studies, by contrast, need to get down to a more intimate level and ask the question: 'How do specific beliefs held by individuals and communities influence their decisions and everyday lives?' The norms, values, ethics, attitudes, etc. of individuals are strongly shaped by the content of their beliefs.

Let us take a look at neo-pagan spirituality through the lenses of definitions of esotericism and sociological perspective. The belief content of most neo-paganism fits Faivre's characteristics of esotericism (Faivre 1994: 10–15). Invisible linkages in existence are experienced (concordance), and nature is approached as a living force (living nature). A natural outcome of this view of the external world is that it no longer seems so external. What happens to the environment is experienced as more or less directly happening to the Self, and ecological concerns easily become major issues. In her Ph.D. thesis, Galina Lindquist discusses the fervent involvement of the Swedish neo-shaman community in the opposition to a planned residential construction project which would have levelled large areas of forest (Lindquist 1997: pp. vii–x). The esoteric focus on mediating symbols, the fostering of imagination (imagination and mediation), and the goal to evolve the self (transmutation) is a fertile breeding ground for individualism and the search for personally inspired rules of ethical conduct (see Bauman 1996 on 'postmodern ethics').

When adopting a discursive approach to esotericism, the same conclusions can be drawn. The discourses of higher knowledge and of ways of accessing this knowledge foster individualism and personal ethics. A world view of ontological monism fosters ecological concerns.

We have another example in the so-called New Age movement. The 'movement' is something which scholars of alternative spirituality agree is very real, but which no one so far has been able to define in a satisfactory manner (see Sutcliffe 2003: 21–5; Granholm 2005: 90–2; Granholm 2008). The focus on self-betterment (transmutation), as well as the esoteric world view of correspondences and a union of body and spirit, has spawned numerous self-help manuals, alternative therapies, and forms of holistic medicine. The focus on imagination and mediation as the primary devices for gaining spiritual knowledge, often viewed as surpassing the limited knowledge of traditional science and medicine, have fostered the popularity of the standard form of gaining knowledge in New Age spirituality—channelling. The esoteric imperative, with its focus on the individual actor, combined with the enterprise centeredness of capitalist philosophy, has played an important role in the commodification of spirituality.

Ritual

McGuire (2002: 17) identifies ritual as the 'enactment of religious meaning', and considers it to be closely intertwined with the dimension of belief. Ritual activity strengthens and reaffirms the belief systems of any particular group of believers. Furthermore, rituals symbolize and contribute to group unity. For the sociologist, the primary perspective on ritual is not on the content of the act but on the symbolic meaning attached to it by participants. It is this meaning which makes it a ritual act (McGuire 2002: 17–18).

The organizational and doctrinal systems of esoteric movements are frequently centred on initiatory structures in and through which the member advances from lower to higher stages of membership and knowledge step by step. This is part of both the extrinsic characteristic of transmutation and the non-intrinsic one of transmission in Faivre's schema. Initiations in esoteric movements are surrounded by highly ritualized acts which often constitute the main forms of activity in the movement. Through initiations the participant links his or her self-identity and spiritual progress to the movement and to other members of the movement. Although members of esoteric and occult movements may express sentiments of loyalty towards the ritual rather than the organization—for example, towards the practice of magic rather than the movement in which the magic is practised (Granholm 2005: 175), many of them nonetheless display a level of commitment to the organization which far surpasses their expressed loyalty.

The ritual activity in esotericism follows a participatory model. This means that the participant in an esoteric ritual plays an active part in it, rather than a passive one, as is the case in, for example, regular church attendance. This active stance, combined with the fact that many esoteric movements are fairly small in membership, will most probably facilitate integration of the belief structures in the practitioner's self-image.

I will discuss the aspect of ritual by giving examples from the Church of Scientology. The doctrine of Scientology is infused with the notion of higher knowledge as well as unorthodox ways of acquiring this knowledge (compatible with Stuckrad's discursive take on esotericism). The goal for the Scientologist is to evolve on a spiritual level, and this is done by advancing through a succession of levels (Chryssides 1999: 283–6; Christensen 2005). The practice of auditing, in which the auditor seeks to help the client gain freedom from restricting 'engrams' with the help of an E-meter, is a ritual act. It is not the act of auditing in itself, which could be compared to other forms of therapy—traditional as well as alternative—that is particularly religious (or esoteric), but rather the religious meaning systems which are invoked in the practice. The auditing, with the reading of the E-meter, is set in a discursive reality in which the client has engrams (obstacles to becoming clear) from his or her earlier life experience hindering his or her spiritual emancipation. Through the auditing rituals infused in the belief systems of Scientology, the client attains the state of 'clear'—in which his or her earlier engrams have been resolved. The Scientologist can then move onward through different 'Operating Thetan' levels (Chryssides 1999: 285–9; Christensen 2005). The rhetoric of Scientology is set in a secular, scientific language, but the presuppositions and underlying discourse set it apart from traditional science. The use of scientific or pseudo-scientific lingo is a common feature in much contemporary esotericism (see Hammer 2001), and can be traced back to the transformation of esotericism in a disenchanted and secular world (see Hanegraaff 1996: 421–42; 2003; 2005*b*).

Religious Experience

An important dimension of religion is that of experience. Religious experiences, even collective ones, have an individual dimension, and are often highly subjective. They are, however, based on culturally acquired models and communicated in fairly standard sets of discourses. The cognitive belief systems of a movement, which are realized in symbolic fashion in ritual activity, combined with earlier experiences of other practitioners, shape the experience of the individual. These experiences, in turn, shape the future experiences of other individuals. Thus even personal experiences become collective material (McGuire 2002: 18–20).

The characteristic of imagination and mediation, or in Stuckrad's discursive model, the discourse of ways of acquiring higher knowledge, inherent in esotericism effectively shapes the possible and probable forms of experiencing in esoteric movements. The standard ways of gaining knowledge in esotericism, as identified by Stuckrad, are mediation by higher beings and individual experience. Both of these methods entail the active participation of the individual, and thus intense religious experiences are frequently encountered in esoteric settings.

An aspect of religious experience is altered states of consciousness, or peak experiences. These entail situations in which the practitioner's consciousness is 'relatively remote from the sphere of everyday reality' (McGuire 2002: 19–20). McGuire (2002: 20) considers peak experiences to be one extreme in the continuum of religious experience, and thus not as the primary form of religious experience. In esotericism altered states of consciousness are, however, sought actively. This is deeply connected to the focus on initiation and active participation in ritual settings (see above). The prerogative of individual experience also paves the way for intense and direct religious experiences, or at least the discourse of intense religious experience. In the case of mediated higher knowledge, such as channelling in New Age spirituality, this mediation can be performed by any individual without the need for mediating religious authorities.

Community

Religious community signifies the awareness of belonging to a group of believers. According to McGuire, religious groups are 'communities of memory' (2002: 20), meaning that they hold important collective memories and exist through the continuity of these memories. The shared experiences and ritual activity of the group reproduce and transmit the collective sense of identity and belonging (McGuire 2002: 20–2).

Esotericism presents a wide display of diverse forms of organization. At one end of the continuum we find spiritualities that lack traditional forms of organization, such as the New Age movement, and at the other end we find spiritualities with highly developed forms of organization and administration, such as Freemasonry. Consequently, the aspect of community takes many different forms in esotericism. Community in the more organized esoteric movements naturally resembles that of traditional religion. In organized esotericism shared religious experiences are important in strengthening group identity as well as the individual's self-identification as a member of the group. Shared experiences could consist of, for example, a shamanic drum journey by a neo-shaman group or a magic ceremony conducted by the Ordo Templi Orientis. In a group experience individual experiences are communicated and discursively negotiated until group consensus is achieved. For example, in the magic order Dragon Rouge it is common that experiences are shared and discussed after a collective ritual (Granholm 2005: 236).

Community does exist even in the most individualized forms of esotericism. The community of New Age spirituality mirrors the characteristics of the milieu; it is not so much community of a geographically and socially tight-knit group, as a loosely bound transnational community of spiritual kinship. This community is reproduced through literary productions, New Age fairs, feng shui home furnishing, and other kinds of New Age activities. Individuals in remote locations share a sense of community in the knowledge that there are many other individuals pursuing the same, or similar, spiritual interests.

A distinct trait of esotericism is that of imagined community. As per the non-intrinsic characteristic of concordance (Faivre 1994: 15), an esoteric history of humanity is constructed, and through this imagined history a cross-cultural and cross-historical community of esotericists is created. This imagined community grants the esotericist a feeling of belonging, even though he or she might be the only esotericist in his or her community, lacking any contacts with other living practitioners.

As has become apparent from the above discussion, these four integral components of religion, or in this case of esotericism, are deeply intertwined. Belief is communicated in ritual, which in turn conveys religious experiences, which in turn are communicated in a social setting, which in turn strengthens and shapes belief. No one dimension can be considered to be more fundamental than an other, or as the primary source and origin of religion.

Demography

Issues not really raised in the historical study of Western esotericism are those of demography: the age, gender, social class, etc. of people involved in esotericism.

Esotericism and occultism, in particular in the form of Satanism and Black Magic, have generally been regarded as adolescent phenomena. This is closely connected with the view of esotericism as counterculture, and as being rebellious and anomalous in character. In a study of Satanism, James R. Lewis (2001) found that the average Satanist is 26 years of age and has been a Satanist for eight years. The age of Lewis's informants ranged from 14 to 56. This would hardly qualify Satanism as an adolescent, or even purely a youth, phenomenon. I found the same when studying the magic order Dragon Rouge. The average age of active members was about 25–35 in Sweden and 25–40 for members outside Sweden (Granholm 2005: 172). Furthermore, the average age of members in the order seems to be on the rise, with the most active and leading members being about 35. Discarding the view of occultism as something anomalous and instead focusing on the continuity of this 'form of thought' or 'structural element' in the Western history of ideas, certain preconceived assumptions can be discarded.

With regard to gender, esotericism is a diverse field. Traditional Freemasonry admits only men (Haywood 1980: 209), whereas certain Wicca and goddess worship groups admit only women (see, e.g., Chryssides 1999: 338). New Age spirituality appeals mostly to white, middle-aged women (Hammer 1997: 283), whereas occultist magic orders appear to be more appealing to men than women. A sociologist of esotericism will have to make a thorough examination of the factors underlying these differences of appeal, but for the sake of demonstration I will make some crude generalizations based on forms of organization, objectives, rhetorical strategies, and projected image.

Organization

Whereas esotericism in general focuses the attention on the individual, the individualism of New Age spirituality is taken to an extreme level. This individualism effectively counteracts the forming of regular organization (see Hanegraaff 2004: 499). This lack of organizational hierarchy might provide the feeling of empowerment for women who, due to issues of structural gender inequality, experience frustration in social hierarchies.

Modern and contemporary magic orders are often organized in initiatory structures with hierarchical implications for membership. This form of organizational hierarchy creates situations where members can approach spirituality in terms of career, and gain a feeling of achievement and advancement.

Objectives

New Age spiritualities are often concerned with holistic healing, from a personal to a societal level (Lewis 1992: 7). Their techniques help the practitioner make sense of and overcome difficulties in life, and thus grant the practitioner a feeling belonging in her world of existence.

Magic is often concerned with the attainment of, mostly personal, power (see, e.g., Granholm 2005: 124–5). Its techniques help the practitioner overcome difficulties in life by granting him the feeling of control over his world of existence.

Rhetorical Strategies and Projected Image

In New Age spirituality the focus is on 'the New', as in novel scientific theories and new alternative therapies (Hammer 2001: 502–3). New Age spiritualities use the rhetoric of 'light', 'progress', and 'good', and project a corresponding image (York 1995: 159–60). These strategies might be appealing to individuals whose concerns are focused on the self in relation to others.

Tradition, claiming existence in a lineage of 'True spirituality', is often emphasized in magic orders. Consequently, the focus is on 'the Old', as in ancient forms of spiritual practice (see, e.g., Grant 1994*a*; 1994*b*). Magic orders generally use rhetoric of 'emerging from darkness' and spiritual transformation, and project an image of mysticism (see, e.g., Granholm 2005). These strategies may be appealing to individuals whose personal concerns are focused on the Self and their place in social hierarchies.

New Age exists in a lineage of esotericism, building on older traditions, and magic orders do incorporate novel elements. Thus, the focus on the new and the old are to be seen as primarily rhetorical strategies.

The above discussion is of course grossly oversimplified, in regards to both the forms of esotericism discussed and gender issues. My aim is not to reproduce a stereotypical view of gender, or to argue for some essential nature of men and women. I merely suggest that through cultural factors and socialization certain discourses are generally more appealing to men, and others to women.

The question of the social class of people involved in esotericism is as yet relatively unstudied. There are indications that New Age spirituality mainly involves middle-class people, whereas Freemasonry seems to attract more people from the upper middle class and above. There are also indications that working-class people are not as involved in esotericism as the middle and upper classes, but all of this might be disproved as more research is conducted.

Western Esotericism and Sociological Perspectives—Some Areas of Research

In this section I will discuss a few themes current in the sociology of religion and how they relate to esotericism.

Alternative Spirituality, New Religious Movements, and Esotericism

Through the lens of Western esotericism, religiosity which might seem extremely novel and strange is given a background in the history of ideas. For example, studies of the New Age movement commonly see the North American counterculture (Lewis and Melton 1992: p. xi) and New England metaphysical tradition (York 1995: 33) as roots of the movement. These influences are of course very important, but taking into consideration the history of esotericism/esoteric discourse, a deeper insight can be gained, and clearer linkages between seemingly dissimilar spiritualities can be construed. Definitions of New Age spirituality are often cumbersome in that they provide a long list of possible characteristics through which almost any spirituality could be termed New Age (see Lewis 1992: 8; Hammer 1997: 18–19). By utilizing esotericism as an analytical tool, this problem is quite effectively side-stepped.

Many of the new religious movements display esoteric characteristics, and can thus be defined as esotericism. This does not mean that all esotericism is 'new religiosity'.

Christianity and Esotericism

The question of the relationship between Christianity and esotericism is a contested area. Issues have been raised concerning whether esotericism and Christianity are incompatible (see Neugebauer-Wölk 2003; discussed in Stuckrad 2005: 83–4), and, as stated earlier, Faivre's view of esotericism has been criticized for focusing in a rather limited fashion on Christian forms of esotericism. In the research inspired by Frances Yates, from the 1960s to the late 1980s, esotericism was generally perceived as a sort of counterculture in opposition to both science and Christianity (Hanegraaff 2001: 15–16). However, it seems to be the case that esotericists in general identified themselves as Christians far into the nineteenth century. It was with the process of secularization and the ideology of rationalism that this began to change (Hanegraaff 2004: 497–9). Thus, when approaching esotericism as a form of thought, or as a discursive complex, both Christian and non-Christian esotericisms can be identified. The Christian status of many pre-Enlightenment esotericists could, of course, be contested from orthodox and theological positions, but the fact remains that these people identified themselves as Christians and operated with Christian terminology and symbolism. An example of a contemporary movement with esoteric ingredients and Christian self-identification is the Church of Jesus Christ of Latter-Day Saints (Mormonism).

Paul Heelas's notion of 'theistic spiritualities of life' is, although perhaps not entirely beyond criticism, of interest to a scholar researching Christianity and esotericism. Heelas (2002) describes 'theistic spiritualities of life' as spirituality set in traditional contexts, i.e. churches, and whose adherents position authority not only in scripture but in personal religious experience.

Secularization and Esotericism

As said earlier, esotericism was closely linked to Christianity well into the nineteenth century. With the diminishing influence of Christianity during the Enlightenment, this began to change. The imperative of scientific rationality broke the hegemony of the Church and opened up the religious field to greater pluralism. The impact of secularization upon esotericism was profound, causing several fundamental transformations. In general, esotericists where quick to abandon religious parlance and to adopt scientific vocabulary and rhetoric (see Hanegraaff 1996; 2001; Hammer 2001). Instead of manipulating an animated nature, esotericists more and more frequently operated with invisible fluids and magnetism. Since the early twentieth century, psychological discourse has dominated the rhetorical strategies of esotericists. Influences from oriental religions, mainly Hinduism and Buddhism, came to compete for attention with the earlier Christian sources. For example, the Theosophical Society adopted concepts of reincarnation and karma from Indian religion. Scientific ideologies were adopted in evolutionary models of spiritual progress, in which both humans and the world as such where viewed as evolving to more perfected states of being. Hanegraaff calls these 'attempts to come to terms with a disenchanted world' occultism (Hanegraaff 1996: 422; 2005*b*: 888). Although Hanegraaff's general thesis is accepted, the use of the term 'occultism' with this specific meaning is contested, and alternative terms such as 'post-Enlightenment esotericism' have been suggested (Faivre 2005: 6781; Hammer 2001: 5–7).

The transformation of esotericism is, of course, an ongoing process. In late modernity spiritual matters have become important and influential anew, although assuming very different roles from those dominant in pre-Enlightenment Europe (see Heelas 2002). In many Western societies, traditional religion is losing influence (see, e.g., Sundback 2000: 47–8), while alternative spirituality is gaining popularity. Disenchantment with the post-Enlightenment world seems to have lost its fervour, and we are now experiencing something of a re-enchantment of the world. The emergence of post-secular esotericism can be argued. This post-secular esotericism bears traits of both pre- and post-Enlightenment esotericism, but emerges as different in character. Rather than viewing science and religion as being in opposition, it views them as complementary models of existence. In some cases post-secular esotericists operate in a 'postmodern' fashion, combining contradictory models of explanation without experiencing this as a problem. The natural world is viewed as both adhering to the natural laws of science and imbued with living forces. This take on esotericism can be found, for example, in many Left-Hand Path spiritualities, such as the magic order Dragon Rouge (see Granholm 2005).

There are, of course, several other important aspects of esotericism that it would be fruitful to study from a sociological perspective. Due to space constraints I can only mention a few of these.

Esotericism is fairly prominent in contemporary popular culture. TV series, films, comic books, and music with esoteric themes and/or drawing inspiration from esoteric spirituality are produced in increasing number. For example, the TV series *Buffy the Vampire Slayer* (1997–2003), *Charmed* (1998–2006), and *Carnivàle* (2003–5); the films *Constantine* (Warner Bros., 2005), *Practical Magic* (Warner Bros., 1998), and *Hellboy* (Columbia Pictures, 2004); the comic books *Sandman* (DC comics/Vertigo, 1988–96), *Lucifer* (DC Comics/Vertigo, 1999–2006), and *Hellblazer* (DC Comics/Vertigo, 1988–) display obvious esoteric influences. Hard rock and heavy metal music have throughout their history been infused with esoteric themes, and these themes seem to grow in popularity in cross-over music as well (e.g., the Finnish band HIM).

Esotericism is showing a lively existence on the Internet. The Internet is a meeting place for many neo-pagans, in particular Wiccans, who otherwise might not be able to communicate with other believers. There are even Wicca covens that exist solely on the web (Arthur 2002; Lövheim 2003). A contemporary incarnation of the Hermetic Order of the Golden Dawn conducts its initiations on the Internet. The Web has made it easier for many small esoteric groups to spread their message to the larger population. For example, the magic order Dragon Rouge attributes great importance to the Internet as a tool for attracting members outside the order's country of origin (Granholm 2005: 168–9). The Internet also plays a role in the creation of community in many esoteric movements. For example, due to the transnational character of many relatively small magic orders, the situation arises where a member of the order is the only one is his or her region. Internet chat-rooms and e-mail thus become arenas for meeting other members and achieving a feeling of community.

Conclusion

Wouter J. Hanegraaff (1998: 41) writes that a sociology of esotericism has to be compatible with the historical approach, and I agree. The historical study of Western esotericism has provided important insights and will continue to do so. However, by applying sociological perspectives to the subject matter, more comprehensive insights can be gained. Through employing coherent definitions of esotericism, based on the historical approach of Antoine Faivre and supplemented by Hanegraaff's thoughts regarding the change of esotericism through time, or by applying the recent discursive model of Kocku von Stuckrad, esotericism can be properly contextualized in sociological studies. For the sociologist it might be useful to make further distinctions of subcategories of esotericism in order analytically to reach certain social differences of different esotericisms.

Although esotericism displays considerable diversity, there are nonetheless certain features in the different dimensions of religion that one is more likely than not to find in esoteric movements. Beliefs in esoteric movements tend to build on ontological monism (Stuckrad 2005). Ritual activity in esoteric movements is often based on initiation and successive advancement through a degree structure, although this system might be fairly transparent. Religious experiences tend to be more immediate, due to the focus on individual experience and active participation. Communal forms and demographic factors vary to a great degree. We find movements with all male participants, and other with all female participants. Some movements attract mainly young adults, and others attract mainly senior members. We find movements that are extremely active in propagating their doctrines, and movements that are extremely selective in their membership. We find movements that have very rigid organizations, and movements that operate through very loose networks. Through the common feature of the search for the *philosophia perennis*, however, even the most solitary esotericists experience at least imagined community.

The historical study of Western esotericism would be greatly enriched by sociological studies, and sociological studies of New Age spirituality, neo-paganism, contemporary magic, New Religious Movements, and so forth, would be greatly enriched by making use of the insights gained in the historical study of Western esotericism.

References

Arthur, S. (2002). 'Technophilia and Nature Religion: The Growth of a Paradox'. *Religion*, 32: 303–14.

Barker, E. (1999). 'New Religious Movements: Their Incidence and Significance'. In J. Cresswell and B. Wilson (eds.), *New Religious Movements: Challenge and Response.* London: Routledge, 15–31.

Barnes, K. (2006). *The Higher Self in Christopher Brennan's Poems: Esotericism, Romanticism, Symbolism.* Leiden: Brill.

Bauman, Z. (1996). *Postmodern Ethics.* Oxford: Blackwell.

Bogdan, H. (2007). *Western Esotericism and Rituals of Initiation.* Albany, NY: State University of New York Press.

Chanel, C., Deveney, J. P., and Godwin, J. (1995). *The Hermetic Brotherhood of Luxor: Initiatic and Historical Documents of and Order of Practical Occultism.* York Beach: Samuel Weiser.

Christensen, D. Refslund (2005). 'Scientology'. In W. J. Hanegraaff with J-P. Brach, R. van den Broek, and A. Faivre (eds.), *Dictionary of Gnosis and Western Esotericism.* Leiden: Brill, 1046–50.

Chryssides, G. D. (1999). *Exploring New Religions.* London: Cassell.

Dobbs, B. J. T. (1975). *The Foundations of Newton's Alchemy or 'The Hunting of the Greene Lyon'.* Cambridge: Cambridge University Press.

Faivre, A. (1992). *L'Esoterisme.* Paris: Presses Universitaires de France.

—— (1993). 'Introduction I'. In A. Faivre and J. Needleman (eds.), *Modern Esoteric Spirituality.* New York: Crossroad, pp. xi–xxii.

—— (1994). *Access to Western Esotericism.* Albany, NY: State University of New York Press.

—— (1998). 'Questions of Terminology Proper to the Study of Esoteric Currents in Modern and Contemporary Europe'. In A. Faivre and W. J. Hanegraaff (eds.), *Western Esotericism and the Science of Religion.* Leuven: Peeters, 1–10.

—— (2005). 'Occultism'. In L. Jones (ed.), *Encyclopedia of Religion*, 2nd edn. Detroit: Macmillan, 6780–3.

Godwin, J. (1994). *Theosophical Enlightenment.* Albany, NY: State University of New York Press.

Granholm, K. (2005). *Embracing the Dark: The Magic Order of Dragon Rouge—Its Practice in Dark Magic and Meaning Making.* Åbo: Åbo Akademi University Press.

—— (2008). 'New Age *or* the Mass-Popularization of Esotenic Discourse: Some Preliminary Reflections on the Reconceptualization of the New Age'. Torino: CESNUR. Online: http://www.cesnur.org/2008/london_granholm.htm.

Grant, K. (1994*a*). *Cults of the Shadow.* London: Skoob.

—— (1994*b*). *Nightside of Eden.* London. Skoob.

Hamilton, M. (2001). *The Sociology of Religion: Theoretical and Comparative Perspectives*, 2nd edn. London: Routledge.

Hammer, O. (1997). *På spaning efter helheten: New Age—en ny folktro?* Stockholm: Wahlström & Widstrand.

—— (2001). *Claiming Knowledge: Strategies of Epistemology from Theosophy to the New Age.* Leiden: Brill.

—— (2004). 'Esotericism in New Religious Movements'. In J. R. Lewis (ed.), *Oxford Handbook of New Religious Movements.* Oxford: Oxford University Press, 445–65.

Hanegraaff, W. J. (1996). *New Age Religion and Western Culture: Esotericism in the Mirror of Secular Thought.* Leiden: Brill.

—— (1998). 'On the Construction of "Esoteric Traditions"'. In A. Faivre and W. J. Hanegraaff (eds.), *Western Esotericism and the Science of Religion.* Leuven: Peeters, 11–61.

—— (2001). 'Beyond the Yates Paradigm: The Study of Western Esotericism between Counterculture and New Complexity'. *Aries*, 1: 5–37.

—— (2003). 'How Magic Survived the Disenchantment of the World'. *Religion*, 33: 357–80.

—— (2004). 'The Study of Western Esotericism: New Approaches to Christian and Secular Culture'. In P. Antes, A. Geertz, and R. Warne (eds.), *New Approaches to the Study of Religion*, i. New York: Walter de Gruyter, 489–519.

—— (2005*a*). 'Esotericism'. In W. J. Hanegraaff with J-P. Brach, R. van den Broek, and A. Faivre (eds.), *Dictionary of Gnosis and Western Esotericism*. Leiden: Brill, 336–40.

—— (2005*b*). 'Occult/Occultism'. In W. J. Hanegraaff with J-P. Brach, R. van den Broek, and A. Faivre (eds.), *Dictionary of Gnosis and Western Esotericism*. Leiden: Brill, 884–9.

Haywood, H. L. (1980). *More about Freemasonry*, rev. edn. Richmond: Macoy Publishing & Masonic Supply Co., Inc.

Heelas, P. (1996). *The New Age Movement: The Celebration of the Self and the Sacralization of Modernity*. Oxford: Blackwell.

—— (2002). 'The Spiritual Revolution: From "Religion" to "Spirituality"'. In P. Fletcher, H. Kawanami, and L. Woodhead (eds.), *Religion in the Modern World: Traditions and Transformations*. London: Routledge, 357–77.

Konieczny, M. E., and Riesebrodt, M. (2005). 'Sociology of Religion'. In J. R. Hinnells (ed.), *The Routledge Companion to the Study of Religion*. London: Routledge, 125–43.

Lewis, J. R. (1992). 'Approaches to the Study of the New Age Movement'. In J. R. Lewis and J. G. Melton (eds.), *Perspectives on the New Age*. Albany, NY: State University of New York Press, 1–12.

—— (2001). 'Who Serves Satan? A Demographic and Ideological Profile'. *Marburg Journal of Religion*, 6/2; <http://web.uni-marburg.de/religionswissenschaft/journal/mjr/pdf/2001/lewis2001.pdf>.

—— and Melton, J. G. (1992). 'Introduction'. In *eadem* (eds.), *Perspectives on the New Age*. Albany, NY State University of New York Press, pp. ix–xii.

Lindquist, G. (1997). *Shamanic Performances on the Urban Scene: Neo-Shamanism in Contemporary Sweden*. Stockholm: Stockholm University Press.

Lövheim, M. (2003). 'Religiös identitet på Internet'. In G. Larsson (ed.), *Talande tro. Ungdomar, religion och identitet*. Lund: Studentlitteratur, 119–41.

McGuire, M. B. (2002). *Religion: The Social Context*, 5th edn. Belmont, Calif.: Wadsworth.

Neugebauer-Wölk, M. (2003). 'Esoterik und Christentum vor 1800: Prolegomena zu einer Bestimmung ihrer Differenz'. *Aries*, 3: 127–65.

Stuckrad, K. von (2005). 'Western Esotericism: Towards an Integrative Model of Interpretation'. *Religion*, 35: 78–97.

Sundback, S. (2000). 'Medlemskap i de lutherska kyrkorna i Norden'. In G. Gustafsson and T. Pettersson (eds.), *Folkkyrkor och religiös pluralism—den nordiska religiösa modellen*. Stockholm: Verbum förlag, 34–73.

Sutcliffe, S. J. (2003). *Children of the New Age: A History of Spiritual Practices*. London: Routledge.

Tiryakian, E. A. (1974). 'Towards the Sociology of Esoteric Culture'. In *idem* (ed.), *On the Margin of the Visible: Sociology, the Esoteric, and the Occult*. New York: John Wiley & Sons, 257–280. (Originally published in *American Journal of Sociology*, 78 (1972).)

Truzzi, M. (1974). 'Definition and Dimensions of the Occult: Towards a Sociological Perspective'. In E. Tiryakian (ed.), *On the Margin of the Visible: Sociology, the Esoteric, and the Occult*. New York: John Wiley & Sons, 243–55. (Originally published in *Journal of Popular Culture*, 5/3 (1971).)

YATES, F. A. (1964). *Giordano Bruno and the Hermetic Tradition*. London: Routledge & Keegan Paul.

YORK, M. (1995). *The Emerging Network: A Sociology of the New Age and Neopagan Movements*. Oxford: Rowman & Littlefield.

SUGGESTED READING

FAIVRE, A., and HANEGRAAFF, W. J. (eds.) (1998). *Western Esotericism and the Science of Religion*. Leuven: Peeters.

—— and NEEDLEMAN, J. (eds.) (1993). *Modern Esoteric Spirituality*. New York: Crossroad.

HANEGRAAFF, W. J., with BRACH, J. P., BROEK, R. VAN DEN, and FAIVRE, A. (eds.) (2005). *Dictionary of Gnosis and Western Esotericism*. Leiden: Brill.

—— and BROEK, R. VAN DEN (eds.) (1998). *Gnosis and Hermeticism from Antiquity to Modern Times*. Albany, NY: State University of New York Press.

Partridge, C. (2004). *The Re-Enchantment of the West: Alternative Spiritualities, Sacralization, Popular Culture, and Occulture. Volume 1*. London: T & T Clark International.

—— (2005). *The Re-Enchantment of the West: Alternative Spiritualities, Sacralization, Popular Culture, and Occulture. Volume 2*. London: T & T Clark International.

STUCKRAD, K. VON (2005). *Western Esotericism: A Brief History of Secret Knowledge*. London: Equinox.

—— (2010). *Locations of Knowledge in Medieval and Early Modern Europe: Esoteric Discourse and Western Identities*. Leiden: Brill.

VERSLUIS, A. (2001). *The Esoteric Origins of the American Renaissance*. Oxford: Oxford University Press.

CHAPTER 44

IMPLICIT RELIGION

EDWARD BAILEY

THE meaning of implicit religion can be identified, first, through its most commonly accepted definitions; secondly, through comparison with its nearest synonyms (as they appear in some classic background texts); and thirdly, by way of contrast with some cousins that might be confused with it. Then, some criticisms of the basic concept, and some limitations of this way of verbalizing it, can be considered. Forms taken by its study will then be listed, to indicate the directions that have been pursued so far. Finally, contingent factors, present within the context of its formulation and application, will be considered, along with benefits arising from its use, some questions to which it gives rise, and its possible future development.

DEFINITIONS

Although three definitions of implicit religion have usually been suggested together,[1] the first of them has received most attention, possibly because it is the shortest and simplest: 'Commitment(s)'. This description of its meaning directs

[1] e.g., in Bailey 1983; 1990*b*; 1990*c*; 2000.

attention to the whole hierarchy of layers of consciousness that, in any particular instance, can fall within the purview of the expression: it recognizes that the commitment may be at the sub- or pre-conscious level, or at the unconscious or conscious level, or at the self- or (as self-conscious experiences of transcendence might be termed) sur-conscious level.

The second definition is 'integrating foci'. As 'commitment(s)' draws attention to the whole hierarchy of levels of consciousness, so this description directs attention to the whole width of possible forms of sociality. It invites consideration of the intra- and inter-individual, the familial and small group, the community and organizational, the social and societal, the gender and the ethnic, the species and the cosmic. Again, its plural form anticipates the likelihood (subject to contrary evidence in particular instances) that the various foci (or commitments) may themselves be imperfectly integrated: they may be logically inconsistent, emotionally incoherent, or conatively conflicting, even if they are not consciously in dispute.

The third standard definition is 'intensive concerns with extensive effects'. This description draws upon the study of religion, rather than of psychology or of social psychology and sociology. It emphasizes the criterion by which the data become relevant, the restrictive measure that is required to balance the holistic approach. It makes plain that the commitment suggested by attendance at a football match on Saturday afternoon is assessed less by decibels, or even *angst* or *camaraderie*, than by the influence it has upon the rest of the week, or by the influence borne upon it by what lies outside that particular activity. It recognizes that if the 'sacred' is to be more than a hobby (or hobby-horse), a mere 'superstition', it must actively interface with the remainder of experience, with the 'ordinary'. Conversely, what is unimportant of itself, perhaps, may yet be significant as the tip of an iceberg, a revelation of, or handle upon, underlying realities.

Near Synonyms

The expression 'implicit religion', and these descriptions of its intended referent, may prompt a question as to how it differs from Tillich's 'ultimate concern' (1965). It may, indeed, be seen as a development of the latter, albeit unconsciously. 'Development', because 'ultimate concern' appears to anticipate a single (overriding, underlying, *all-pervading*) concern, however numerous and diluted the forms of its expression, while 'implicit religion' is seen as a general noun, covering a multiplicity of implicit religions within any single body (whether an individual or a social body). There is also a difference of nuance: just as 'ultimate' may be excessively ambitious, so 'concern' smacks of the verbal earnestness associated with students' seminars. However, most of life, for most people, tends to be somewhat less cerebral and serious.

Luckmann's 'invisible religion' (1967) obviously differs from 'implicit religion' in the choice of sense organ (the eye, rather than the ear or the mouth) as the metaphor for the typology. The most substantial difference, however, is simply the chronology of the two terms' use. Luckmann's profound and comprehensive theory was followed, a generation later, upon his retirement from his main professional career, by observation and analysis of various German families' table-talk. 'Implicit religion', on the other hand, having been posited as a phenomenon (or a hermeneutic) was tested empirically from the beginning, simultaneously with the development of its conceptualization.

A third near-synonym for 'implicit religion' is 'civil religion'. Attentive reading of Bellah's great but succinct essay (1967) dispenses with most of the criticisms with which it was met. However, the title Bellah borrowed from Rousseau displays the limitations of its origin: concerned primarily with 'civic theology', it only scratches at the surface of 'civil religion' itself. Perhaps it was this initial limitation to the verbal, and formal, and mainly societal, that led one of Bellah's main collaborators to remark (both publicly and privately) how much 'richer' (more comprehensive, presumably) he found the term 'implicit religion'.

Non-Synonyms

Those familiar with Roman Catholic writing, sometimes enquire as to the relationship between Karl Rahner's 'anonymous Christians' (1972) and 'implicit religion'. The question is sometimes fraught, as Rahner is felt to have indulged in a supreme (Christian) form of 'orientalism', in finding that others were 'Christian' although (like M. Baudrillard speaking prose) they 'did not know it'. However, in this case, there is no suggestion that whatever form(s) of implicit religion may be discovered in any particular context will bear any resemblance whatsoever to any form of ('explicit') religion that has so far been named (as 'Christian', or anything else). Indeed, not only is there no desire to label anything as Christian: there is also no desire either to presuppose that 'everyone has a religion' or that 'religion' is 'a good thing'—or even to insist upon the use of the word 'religion', should 'world view' or 'life stance' (etc.) be found less offensive.

On the other hand, it would not be surprising if the 'implicit religion', or even the 'secular religion', of a society which has had centuries of exposure to a particular explicit religion, was found to bear some resemblance (positive or negative), to that named tradition. However, whether that resemblance is historical or developmental, phenomenological or epiphenomenal, psychological or spiritual, sociological or political, moral or cultural, is open to question in each particular case; as is the question, which is the chicken, and which is the egg? Instead of implicit religion being 'like' religion (a 'quasi-religion', to use a 1960s term), it could be that 'explicit religion' is 'like' the implicit religion to which real allegiance is given (Bailey 1997*b*).

Others sometimes enquire as to the relationship between 'folk religion' and 'implicit religion'. Understood as the 'natural' or ethnic religion of the *Volk*, until as recently as a millennium or so ago in Scandinavia for instance, this must indeed be a major causal factor in whatever forms of implicit religion (or explicit religion) might be present in those or neighbouring countries. However, it is a closer cousin to civil religion than to implicit religion, for, at a less self-conscious and contrived level, it is necessarily limited in the first instance to societal, or at least social, life, whereas implicit religion covers both the individual and the social, equally.

In North American contexts, 'folk religion' is sometimes used in an 'orientalist', even 'survivalist' (or 'revivalist') manner: on a par with folk dancing, folk costume, folk custom, and so on. While such secular hobbies can become all-consuming (and therefore can become instances of implicit religion), it is doubtful whether any form of folk religion, in this 'folksy' sense, can become so all-embracing (unless the various forms of paganism be judged to qualify for consideration, and, in some cases, to be sufficiently influential to qualify).

In (English-language) Japanese religious studies 'folk religion' refers to a congeries of individual or familial religious practices (e.g., to do with departed relatives), which appears to be seen as lying somewhere between the 'named' or 'recognized' religions, and the perennial world of 'private' superstition(s) (Miyake 1972). This usage is exemplary in its neutrality. It is also salutary in suggesting that out of such concerns, with such practices, upon such foundations, the 'organized' or 'global' religions must be built, if they are not to become irrelevant (mere hobbies, themselves). Not even in the Japanese context, however, does this use of 'folk religion' refer to the core of what is meant by implicit religion: generally (if not always specifically), the effort and trust put into such activities probably pales beside the striving and perceived benefits associated with work, for instance. Explicit religion may indeed fully express the deepest implicit religion; but in this case, although it is a real form of implicit religion, it seems on the whole to be of secondary importance.

Among Anglican clergy in England (and perhaps others), 'folk religion' used to be used in the 1970s (the situation had changed by the end of the century) to describe the 'use' (meaning, 'abuse') of the churches' *rites de passage*, by those who took little other part in the church's life, and whose usage of them was therefore considered 'insincere'. The suggestion was that they were engaging in at best a familial (or, at worst, a superstitious) *practice* (cf. Japan), which was somewhat of a *pretence* (cf. North America), in order to *conform* (cf. Scandinavia) with a merely external tradition. However, such *pre*-judgement of individual motivation (always a mystery, even to the individual him or her self, if they are wise) demonstrates the precise opposite of what the concept of implicit religion seeks to develop; such a supercilious attitude towards the other may be seen as even more reprehensible than the idolization of religion itself. Certainly, it prevents proper investigation (and precludes appropriate discernment).

The 'popular religion' that sometimes seems to be associated with warmer countries may also be linked with 'implicit religion'. (Japanese scholars speak of both 'folk' and 'popular' religion.) Where leisure time is more often spent out of doors, as in many Roman Catholic, Muslim, Hindu, and Buddhist societies, then religious types of group activity also 'spill out of' the churches, mosques, and temples (or should we say, 'return to' the people, where they actually are and live and have their being?). In urban settings these activities tend to be called 'popular', and in rural areas 'folk', religion. In either case, as indications of continuing commitments, they are obviously grist to the mill for the student of religion, both implicit and explicit. However, they are not, therefore, the *particular* concern of implicit religion: that concept is intended to concentrate upon (without excluding other commitments) those ordinary, continuous commitments that are, still, in danger of being overlooked; which is why it was originally termed 'secular religion'.

Criticisms

The most obvious criticism that can be made of the concept of implicit religion is a practical one. If its study requires the study of whatever a person or group may 'happen' to be committed to, at some particular time, how can a librarian or bookseller (or the architect of a course of study) know what study materials to provide, or how they should be catalogued and shelved?

The question may be real, but it is neither unique, nor insuperable. For 'implicit religion' is not the only concept whose precise application fluctuates from group to group, generation to generation, or even from time to time within the life of an individual. If we were to deprive ourselves of the benefit of hindsight, and to forget how rapidly we adjust our world views and expectations, we might find our (1950, say) selves bemused by the suggestion (if it came our way) that international diplomacy would involve itself with cricket (or ping-pong), that politics at every level would be involved with childcare, that medicine would include cosmetic surgery, that exhibitions of art should display a soup tin or an unmade bed. That such unexpected turns should occur, and be taken seriously, is a tribute to the capacity of the human sciences to follow where 'the [human] spirit blows'. It would be ironic indeed, if the only laggards in this respect were the sciences of religion, claiming to know in advance of their studies exactly what it is they were studying (cf. Bianchi 1975).

Fortunately the problem is not difficult to solve in practice, once our thinking adjusts itself. As items are published on sporting sanctions, as childcare at work (including in the House of Commons) is costed in national and commercial budgets, as the 'right' to breast implants or smoking cures is argued, as the meaning of 'art' is widened (or restored) to 'how' any sort of art-ifice is achieved by any kind of art-isan, so the range of applications is broadened—and so *the common thread becomes clearer.* In the same way, adding further languages and/or 'babytalk' to Language Studies will call for additional study materials and a certain mental readjustment, but it can enrich and clarify the understanding of language and linguistics.

However, the most common criticism (if that is not too grand a word) of the concept of 'implicit religion' is not that perfectly comprehensible practical one. Rather, it takes the form (whatever its psychological origin may be), of a complaint, which is without logical or empirical foundation. For the concept hypothesizes that, in advance of empirical study, it is not possible to state what form the implicit religion of any individual or group may take. As anthropologists have long said, it seems that anything may be (found to be) religious or sacred, in some context or other. But presumably this 'law' of anthropology has not impinged upon some of those engaged in other social sciences; for the riposte is sometimes thrown down, 'But if everything is religious, the word is meaningless'. 'Riposte' seems to be the apt description of a response or 'reply' to what has not been either said or suggested. Indeed, to hypothesize that 'anything may [in the course of investigation be found to] be religious' is so far away from any such (nonsensical) claim as saying 'everything is religious', as to call for self-scrutiny on the part of any tempted to such confusion. It would be comparable to saying that everything is (or will become, or should be) secular.

Limitations

The offer of three definitions, and the inability to select a single one at the expense of the other two, was initially seen as a limitation upon the viability of them all. Subsequently, it was seen as confirming that each and every one was pointing towards a real phenomenon; perhaps only abstract constructs are capable of actual and precise definition, *tout simple.* Where the real and especially the human is concerned, to look for 'descriptions' and 'pointers' may be more appropriate. While other descriptions might be or have been suggested (e.g., 'human depths'), three are sufficient to give confirmation, demonstrate overlap, and provide a point of intersection.

However, even a multiplicity of descriptions of the term's meaning cannot altogether save the original conceptualization from the limitations inherent in language's attempt to express human intuition. Each of the two words involved in 'implicit religion' suffers from imprecision, to the point of potential contradiction.

A literalist reading of 'implicit' would suggest that the study of 'implicit religion' is concerned only with non-verbal behaviour. In fact, it is meant to convey (and it usually succeeds in conveying) that it is its characterization as religious which is implicit, rather than the behaviour itself (which may be very articulate). But that still leaves the problem of (for instance) the articulate secularist who, far from being unconscious of the parallelism in his passionate stance against religion, nevertheless wishes to deny that his secularism is indeed itself a kind of religion, and may resent the appellation. To this there is a threefold response.

First, a more acceptable term may happily be found, such as philosophy or world view or value system or tradition or even community of faith. Secondly, the student of implicit religion may still wish to retain his original concept in his own reflection, on the ground that it raises a greater variety of questions, which together make for a more holistic and profound understanding of the other. Thirdly, the observer may insist that he or she has as much right to his or her interpretation as the actors have to theirs, and indeed may welcome the debate that such diversity invites. In the same way, adherents of the recognized traditions have learnt to welcome the insights into (say) the Councils of the Early Church that have been provided by secular historians, economists, and psychologists. If 'secular' approaches to 'religious' affairs can be fruitful, so might 'religious' approaches to secular life. Each can gain in its self-understanding through the application of concepts deriving from elsewhere.

If 'implicit' is not altogether a clear adjective, 'religion' might be expected to be an even more uncomfortable noun. Is it now generally agreed that 'religion' is one of Wittgenstein's 'family resemblance' concepts, reminiscent of Augustine's comments on time: although we cannot say exactly what it means, we understand approximately what others mean and would have to invent it if we did not have it (as African, Indian, and now Chinese, and even possibly Muslim, experience seems to indicate). Certainly, the absence of unanimity, or of exactitude, does not prevent its formal and informal use by, say, Departments of Religious Studies.

It may be suggested, however, that the concept of implicit religion offers a precision to the meaning of 'religion', and therefore a coherence to 'religious studies', that is simultaneously in keeping with both its historical origin and its popular usage. For the *philosophes*' derivation of *religio* from classical Latin was akin to their landed cousins finding ancestors in ancient Rome. It paved the way for a concordat, between a secular 'ministry [*sic*] of cults' and a vaunted ecclesiastical monopoly of the sacraments and of the sacramental or sacred, as though worship lacked wider ramifications, and as though its symbols were not, by their very nature, simultaneously both sacred and ordinary (hence much of their power). For, at least as far as British English is concerned, the historical origin of *religio* must be monastic—just as the current ordinary meaning of 'religious' is (to use monastic terms) regular (yet voluntary), habit-ual (yet deliberate), professed (*and* practised). For, 'I read the papers [or 'clean my shoes' etc., etc.,] religiously' is the popular, and phenomenologically identical, meaning of the (medieval) canonical usage, which, of course, is also still current.

So, to describe parish churches or denominations, church attendance or prayer, as 'religious' is itself somewhat metaphorical. Its original (and continuing) meaning is 'monastic', and only generally ecclesiastical by extension (just as 'manufacture', 'hand-made', was extended first to include, and then to actually suggest, 'machine-made'). (Some of us, today, are properly known as 'secular clergy', because we live according to the long-term rule of the world, as in the economist's 'secular trends', and not according to the Rule of St Benedict, for instance.) So it is not that monks are 'super-churchgoers'; rather, that churchgoers are 'mini-monks'. Thus 'implicit religion' is, on the one hand, a further extension of the meaning of 'religion' itself; while at the same time, on the other hand, curiously, it both returns it to its original meaning—and makes 'common sense' with the public use of the term.

Therefore the concept of *implicit religion*, by taking commitment as its core concern, offers a criterion, first, for gauging degrees of religiousness; secondly, it makes the study of religion a prototype, for reflecting upon the specifically human attribute of intentionality; and, thirdly, it leapfrogs over the porous, shifting, disputed, and ultimately 'arbitrary' (i.e., unpredictable, to the outsider, but natural, to the insider) division between, on the one hand, the twin poles of the sacred and the profane (properly so called: i.e., the abominable), and, on the other hand, the ordinary that lies between the two. Of course it requires the use of subjectivity, but every human attribute is required in furthering our understanding of the human: and, once articulated, at least it is available for debate.

The Study of Implicit Religion

Although the phrase 'implicit religion' has been found in one earlier publication (Hoult 1958), its sustained use and systematic study began in 1968. Having concluded, during my first lived experience of an ordinary worshipping congregation, that, at least for some people, their (explicit) religion was a causal, not an epiphenomenal, factor in their lives, I surmised that neither could some people's secular lives be understood, without positing the existence of some comparable phenomenon; and was invited by the Africanist F. B. Welbourn[2] to test my hypothesis. This led to a trio of trials: a hundred interviews, with such open-ended stimuli as the initial, 'What do you enjoy most in life?', and the concluding, 'Who are you?'; a hundred four-hour sessions working as a barman in a public house; and thirty-six years' 'observant participation' in the life of a local community.[3]

[2] F. B. Welbourn's far-sightedness is proverbial; see esp. Welbourn 1960; 1969.

[3] For reports on all three studies, see Bailey 1976, which formed the basis for 1997*a*, and further works in 1998 and 2002*a*.

The first step in the wider dispersion of the concept was taken in 1978. This took the form of the first of a series of annual residential academic conferences with this concern (which have profited, however, from contributions made on the basis of practical as well as academic experience). In 1983 the academic gatherings (which became known as the Denton Conferences[4]) gave rise to short courses for religious educationists, and study days for church people. Papers were also given in academic contexts,[5] and in some RE and church groups, and a number of written items of mine were published.[6] A number of relevant volumes were also published by scholars, including of course some who were not associated with the developing 'network for the study of implicit religion' (NSIR).

A second stream of activities began in 1983 when Trinity [theological] College in Bristol offered a diploma in implicit religion, and a doctoral programme validated by the (then) CNAA (Council for National Academic Awards). Subsequently, in 1997, at Ninian Smart's suggestion, Middlesex University invited the Centre for the Study of Implicit Religion and Contemporary Spirituality (CSIRCS), which had developed alongside the Network, to its White Hart Lane campus, and established a research programme. However, upon the virtual closure of Religious Studies there, and simultaneous downsizing of Social Studies (which could have provided an alternative home), the other locations for the study of implicit religion became the heirs, rather than companions, of the Middlesex location.

They included the Centre for Advanced Religious and Theological Studies (CARTS), in the Faculty of Divinity at Cambridge (with an endowed senior post); and shorter-term posts at the College of the Ascension (now, The Queen's Foundation) in Birmingham, the University of Wales at Bangor, and the University of Leiden in the Netherlands, where a Chair in Non-institutional Religion was established in 2006. At the time of writing (2007), further associated developments seem likely, particularly at Staffordshire University, Leeds Metropolitan University, and Ripon [theological] College, Cuddesdon (Oxford), and the United Theological College in Bangalore, and at the University of Quebec at Montreal (UQàM), focusing upon contemporary culture and public life, management studies and leisure, health and ageing, and professional application and practical theology.

[4] Individuals' papers read at these meetings have been published in various journals and collections. A group of eight, however, were edited and translated into French (Bailey and Menard 1996). A further twenty were published in Bailey 2002*b*. Others are regularly made available to a wider public through *Implicit Religion: Journal of the Centre for the Study of Implicit Religion and Contemporary Spirituality* (London: Equinox, 1997–); <www.equinoxpub.com>.

[5] Including IAHR and AAR, the SSSR, SISR, and World Congress of Sociology, and courses of lectures at the universities of Middlesex, Bristol, and California (Santa Barbara), as well as individual lectures at universities in England, Wales, Scotland, Sweden, Denmark, Canada, the United States, New Zealand, and Hong Kong.

[6] The more notable among these articles have been published in *Religion: Journal of Religion and Religions*, 1983; in *Focus: Quarterly Journal of the North Central Sociological Association*, 1990*b*; in *Social Compass*, 1990*a*, *c*; in *Modern Believing*, 1997; and in *Ultimate Reality & Meaning: Interdisciplinary Studies in the Philosophy of Understanding*, 2000.

The two streams (of conferences and publications, and of research and teaching) obviously overlap, but they most clearly combine in the publication since 1998 of a refereed journal, called simply *Implicit Religion.* Its contents illustrate, and its editorial policies epitomize, the concerns and approach that are involved in the study of implicit religion.[7] While particularly interested in secular life, it is as much an approach or hermeneutic as an area of study, so it also welcomes studies of explicit religion if they demonstrate commitments (however conscious or not, and however they may be labelled). Its (*un*-hidden) agenda is a deeper understanding of persons as intentional beings; its (similarly explicit) assumption is that categories originating within the framework of Religious Studies may assist in the process of developing understanding of such behaviour, including 'secular' behaviour.

The Context

Modernism may have found liberating truth in general formulas. However, 'late modernity' may coincide with religious traditions in finding specificity of time and place a qualification rather than a bar to the value of insights and suggestions. So the particular origin of the concept of implicit religion may be confessed: it was, first, a reaction to the view that (what is usually seen as) religion is an epiphenomenon, a reaction which arose from observing and weighing the known lives of at least some individuals in an actual worshipping congregation. Then it was, secondly, the extension of this empirically driven conclusion, to those who took little or no part in such activities (and in some cases affirmed their dissociation from them): they too had their own beliefs and values, practices and commitments—in a word, their own religion, albeit a secular one.

The hunch or hypothesis, intuition or insight, was indeed a product of its time (the late 1960s) and place (the 'Western' world). (How else can anything be?) In forty years, times have changed, even in the (relatively) slow-moving 'West'. For instance, during the 1960s, 'pastoral' ceased to be a purely ecclesiastical word, and

[7] Amongst the theoretical considerations of the concept are: Smart 1998; Pye and Roberts 1999; Swatos 1999; Homan 2000; Dupré 2001; Hamilton 2001; Menard 2001; Swatos 2001; Thomas 2001; Austin 2002; Hills and Argyle 2002; Dupré 2003; Gollnick 2003 (and Grainger 2004); Hay 2003; and Schnell 2003; Borg 2004; Hunter 2004; Menard 2004; Stahl and Stenmark 2004; Dupré 2005; Lord 2006; Dupré 2007; Lewis 2007, and Sundback 2007.

Amongst the empirical applications of the concept, are French 1998; Bellamy *et al.* 1999; Nathanson 1999; Papadopoulos 1999; Portman 1999; Badertscher 2000; Brown 2000; Grimshaw 2000; Schmied 2000; Schnell 2000; Ustorf 2000; Campbell 2001; Lowe 2001; Allcock 2004; Amoah 2004; Francis and Robbins 2004 (and Davie 2004); Gelder 2004; Gollnick 2004; Heddendorf 2004; Johnson 2004; Lamb 2004; Smith 2004; Brierley 2005; Gauthier 2005; Gollnick 2005; Grainger 2005; Jenkins 2005; Menard 2005; Moss 2005; Sharpe 2005; Solyom 2005; Tyers 2005; Borgman *et al.* 2006; Connor 2006; Francis *et al.* 2006; Hanson 2006; (Kelso 2006; Nolan 2006; Pärna 2006; Swatos 2006; Campana 2007; Hanson 2007; Johnson 2007; Macdonald 2007; Wender 2007; Bullivant, forthcoming.

was adopted in education; but the suggestion that 'spiritual' might be added to the aims of the New Education Fellowship, at its Annual General Meeting in 1966, led male members in their thirties and forties to threaten resignation ('You'll want to add "religious" next'). Then, in the 1974 General Election, the Labour Party advertised itself as 'the Party with a Soul', and during that decade 'mission statements' became *de rigueur* for every kind of organization, while by its end two different publishers began publishing series of 'classics' in spirituality, including volumes of North American Indian and Secular Spirituality.

The tide had turned. By the 1990s in England even local churches (irony of ironies?) had to have a mission statement attached to their annual reports and accounts; and courses in Christian and other forms of spirituality proliferated at universities. Indeed, spirituality had become so popular a concept that, according to one survey, 300 out of the 500 management courses available in the UK also had a 'spirituality' component within them. Likewise, the 'spiritual' aim of education in the 1944 Act, which (when it had even been noticed) had been universally dismissed as meaningless in the 1960s, was ordered to be both developed and delivered. Paradoxically (or, perhaps, logically) it was a government whose leader had unguardedly but famously said, 'There's no such thing as society' (and hence spirituality?[8]), which decreed that spiritual development must be measured. It also tended to be the religious who denied its possibility, despite a tradition of spiritual direction and of criteria for its measurement that, in the case of Christianity, went back to the Epistles (e.g., Jas 2: 14–26) and Gospels (e.g., Matt. 7: 15–23, 25: 31–45) themselves.

Such 'spirituality' overlaps with 'implicit religion', without being identical with it. However the word is understood (and, by its nature, although it may be incapable of definition, it nevertheless has signs and evidences and consequences, as well as roots and causes and influences), it may be generally agreed as referring, first, to the 'how' of human behaviour, and only secondly to specific forms of behaviour that are intended to assist in the development of such qualitative dimensions. Its super- or sub-quantitative character can lead to its being confused with the emotional, just as it used to be dismissed as being 'unreal' because it was subjective. Now, though, intellectuals mostly recognize the wisdom of the populace (especially the female and the elderly), who never ceased being capable of 'sussing out' 'the look in the eye', and the other body language of individuals, or the 'attitude' of groups, and the 'atmosphere' of places.

However, the concept of 'implicit religion' invites wider comparison than that of 'spirituality'. It inevitably and immediately raises questions to do with group solidarities, organizational institutions, ritual behaviours, inter-entity relationships, cosmological myths, assumed ontologies, sacral foci, heroic pioneers, diabolical personages, canonical scriptures, beliefs, and norms, etc., which 'spirituality'

[8] For this contrary view, cp. Durkheim 1961[1915] and Taylor 1973.

may not necessarily suggest. So, just as talk of 'culture' has led the way to recognition of the spiritual, so interest in spirituality opens the door to implicit religion, of which it is part (as the spiritual is part of any human behaviour), but only a part[9].

The opening of the way towards concern with implicit religion in the West is by no means a rehearsal of what must happen anywhere else, let alone everywhere else. Thus, members of an academic inter-faith gathering in South India in 2005 could hardly conceive at any time of a 'secular' vacuum in Indian life (Hindu or Muslim), which would be available for the study of its 'implicit religion'. Yet the meeting was in Bangalore, and even when all the forms of 'Sanskritization', extending to the use of IT, have been acknowledged, an absolutely totally coherent pattern of life, there as elsewhere, still seems more likely to be 'a consummation devoutly to be desired' than a current empirical reality.

The spread of mutually exclusive religious labels (rather than of religious typologies), so that people are assumed to be *either* Hindu *or* Muslim (etc.), has unfortunately been accompanied by a globalization of the assumptions of 'an over-realized eschatology', such as St Paul certainly did not recognize: he recognized a life-long conflict of religions within himself. To be totally integrated, to have a single identity, must be to be uniquely unique.

In Future

'Choice' works, as a political goal, and 'programmed', as a human metaphor, because of increasing awareness (and, probably, experience) of at least a constant, and probably a constantly increasing, degree of freedom in what, indeed, is sometimes called the human 'project'. However, to choose is to commit, and thus to demonstrate commitment. Choice necessitates criteria (even if only of commitment to acting on whim). Implicit religion, as a hypothesis or study project, suggests that we bring to bear upon this increasingly common experience, not only all that we can glean from the (secular) human sciences, but also all that we can gain from the religious sciences (including the experiential wisdom of the religious traditions themselves), to assist in our understanding of this most human of phenomena.

There is no need to labour either the practical value, or the sheer interest, of such studies: 9/11 and soap operas, alone, are sufficient evidence. It may place the study of the religious, and of religion, at the leading edge of consideration of what it means to be human (and therefore sub-human and inhuman). But that is for others to do what they will with: the aim of the study of implicit religion is the empirically based understanding of human being, 'religious' or 'secular'.

[9] This typology of historical and bibliographical context, and of human consciousness and religious experience, as shifting between the sacred, the holy, and the human, was further developed in Bailey 2002*a*.

References

Allcock, J. B. (2004). 'Infinite Justice: Implicitly Religious Responses to the International Criminal Tribunal for the Former Yugoslavia'. *Implicit Religion*, 7/1: 76–93.

Amoah, M. (2004). 'Christian Musical Worship and Hostility to the Body: The Medieval Influence versus the Pentecostal Revolution'. *Implicit Religion*, 7/4: 59–75.

Austin, M. (2002). 'Derrida's Kind of Salvation'. *Implicit Religion*, 5/1: 49–59.

Badertscher, J. (2000). 'Northern Lights: Canadian Studies in Implicit Religion'. *Implicit Religion*, 3/1: 15–29.

Bailey, E. I. (1976). *Emergent Mandalas: An Enquiry into the Implicit Religion of Contemporary Society* (Ph.D. thesis, accessible from the author, or from Bristol University Library, where it is catalogued as *The Religion of a Secular Society*).

—— (1983). 'The Implicit Religion of Contemporary Society: An Orientation and Plea for its Study'. *Religion: Journal of Religion and Religions*, 8: 69–83.

—— (1990*a*). 'Implicit Religion: A Bibliographical Introduction'. *Social Compass*, 37: 483–98.

—— (1990*b*). 'The Implicit Religion Concept as a Tool for Ministry'. *Focus: Quarterly Journal of the North Central Sociological Association*, 23: 203–17.

—— (1990*c*). 'The Implicit Religion of Contemporary Society: Some Studies and Reflections'. *Social Compass*, 37: 499–509.

—— (1997*a*). *Implicit Religion in Contemporary Society*. Den Haag: Kok Pharos; repr. Leuven: Peeters, 2002, 2006.

—— (1997*b*). 'Religion and Implicit Religion: Which is the Analogy?' *Modern Believing*, n.s., 30–6.

—— (1998). *Implicit Religion: An Introduction*. London: Middlesex University Press. Trans. with Introduction by Guy Menard as *La religion implicite: une introduction*. Montreal: Liber, 2006.

—— (2000). 'The Sacred, the Holy and the Human, as Tripartite Symbols of Ultimate Reality and Meaning'. *Ultimate Reality & Meaning: Interdisciplinary Studies in the Philosophy of Understanding*, 23: 277–84.

—— (2002*a*). *The Secular Faith Controversy: Religion in Three Dimensions*. London: Continuum.

—— (ed.) (2002*b*). *The Secular Quest for Meaning in Life: Denton Papers in Implicit Religion*. Lampeter: Edwin Mellen.

—— and Menard, G. (eds.) (1996). 'Religion Implicite'. *Religiologiques: sciences humaines et religion*, 14: 5–168, 199–211.

Bellah, R. N. (1967). 'Civil Religion in America'. *Daedalus: Journal of the American Academy of Arts & Sciences*, 96/4: 1–21.

Bellamy, J., Black, A., and Hughes, P. (1999). 'Responses among Australians to the Death and Funeral of Princess Diana: The Spiritual Dimension'. *Implicit Religion*, 2/2: 89–100.

Bianchi, U. (1975). *The History of Religion*. Leiden: Brill.

Borg, M. B. ter (2004). 'Some Ideas on Wild Religion'. *Implicit Religion*, 7/2: 108–19.

Borgman, E., Drongelen, H. van, and Meijknecht, T. (2006). 'Pastoral Work: Search for a Common Language'. *Implicit Religion*, 9/1: 90–104.

Brierley, P. (2005). 'Implicit Religion: 72% Christian, 8% Attendance'. *Implicit Religion*, 8/2: 178–94.

Brown, E. (2000). 'How Long Is the Future?: Working with Life-Limited and Life-Threatened Children'. *Implicit Religion*, 3/1: 5–13.

Bullivant, S. (forthcoming). 'Introducing Irreligious Experiences'. *Implicit Religion*, 11/1.

Campana, Daniel (2007). 'Civil Religion at the Hearth: Current Trends in American Civil Religion from the Perspective of Domtestic Arrangement'. *Implicit Religion*, 10/2: 146–60.

Campbell, R. A. (2001). 'When Implicit Religion Becomes Explicit: The Case of the Boy Scouts in Canada'. *Implicit Religion*, 4/1: 15–25.

Connor, K. R. (2006). 'The Fifth Corner: Hip Hop's New Geometry of Adolescent Religiosity'. *Implicit Religion*, 9/1: 7–28.

Davie, G. (2004). 'A Reply to Francis & Robbins'. *Implicit Religion*, 7/1: 55–8.

Dupré, W. (2001). 'Difficulties in Discerning Religious Phenomena'. *Implicit Religion*, 4/2: 73–85.

—— (2003). 'The Critical Potential of the Concept of Implicit Religion'. *Implicit Religion*, 6/1: 5–16.

—— (2005). 'The Quest for Myth as a Key to Implicit Religion'. *Implicit Religion*, 8/2: 147–65.

—— (2007). 'Why (and When) Should We Speak of Implicit Religion?' *Implicit Religion*, 10/2: 128–47.

Durkheim, E. (1961[1915]). *The Elementary Forms of Religious Life*, trans. Joseph W. Swain. Glencoe, Ill.: Free Press; New York: Collier.

Francis, L. J., and Robbins, M. (2004). 'Belonging without Believing: A Study in the Social Significance of Anglican Identity and Implicit Religion among 13–15-Year-Old Males'. *Implicit Religion*, 7/1: 37–54.

—— —— and Williams, Emyr (2006). 'Believing and Implicit Religion beyond the Churches: Religion, Superstition, Luck and Fear among 13–15 Year-Old Girls in Wales'. *Implicit Religion*, 9/1: 74–89.

French, H. W. (1998). 'The Victorian Broad Church, Seedbed of Twentieth-Century Religious Pluralism and Implicit Religion: An Historical Perspective'. *Implicit Religion*, 1: 55–67.

Gauthier, F. (2005). 'Orpheus and the Underground: Raves and Implicit Religion from Interpretation to Critique'. *Implicit Religion*, 8/3: 217–65.

Gelder, L. van (2004). 'At the Confluence of Paradox: Implicit Religion and the Wild'. *Implicit Religion*, 7/3: 207–27.

Gollnick, J. (2003). 'Is Implicit Religion Spirituality in Disguise?' *Implicit Religion*, 6/2–3: 146–60.

—— (2004). 'Religion, Spirituality and Implicit Religion in Psychotherapy'. *Implicit Religion*, 7/1: 120–41.

—— (2005). 'Implicit Religion in Dreams'. *Implicit Religion*, 8/3: 281–98.

Grainger, R. B. (2002). *Health Care and Implicit Religion*. London: Middlesex University Press.

—— (2004). 'A Reply to Gollnick: Implicit Religion isn't Spirituality in Disguise'. *Implicit Religion*, 7/3: 276–8.

—— (2005). 'The Faith of Actors: Implicit Religion and Acting'. *Implicit Religion*, 8/2: 166–77.

Grimshaw, M. (2000). 'I Can't Believe My Eyes: The Religious Aesthetics of Sport as Postmodern Salvific Moments'. *Implicit Religion*, 3/2: 87–99.

Hamilton, M. (2001). 'Implicit Religion and Related Concepts: Seeking Precision'. *Implicit Religion*, 4/1: 5–13.

Hammond, Philip (2007). 'Implicit Religion from Below'. *Implicit Religion*, 10/3: 273–81.

Hanson, S. (2006). 'Law as Implicit Religion'. *Implicit Religion*, 9/2: 136–65.

—— (2007). 'The Sacred Paradox of English Law'. *Implicit Religion*, 10/1: 8–36.

HAY, D. (2003). 'Why is Implicit Religion Implicit?' *Implicit Religion*, 6/1: 17–40.

HEDDENDORF, R. (2004). 'From Faith to Fun: The Role of Humor in a Secular World'. *Implicit Religion*, 7/2: 142–51.

HILLS, P., and ARGYLE, M. (2002). 'A Psychological Dimension to Implicit Religion'. *Implicit Religion*, 5/2: 69–80.

HOMAN, R. (2000). 'The Marginality of the Implicit'. *Implicit Religion*, 3/2: 101–9.

HOULT, T. F. (1958). *The Sociology of Religion*. New York: Holt, Rinehart & Winston.

HUNTER, R. J. (2004). 'Implicit Religion as Commitment Process: Insights from Brickman and Bailey'. *Implicit Religion*, 7/1: 20–36.

JENKINS, T. D. (2005). 'Sacred Persons in Contemporary Culture'. *Implicit Religion*, 8/2: 133–46.

JOHNSON, S. M. (2004). 'American Civic Tradition after 9/11: Protestant, Catholic, Jewish, & African-American Resources for Healthier National Faith and Community'. *Implicit Religion*, 7/3: 228–45.

—— (2007). 'Faith, Facts, and Fidelity: H. Richard Niebuhr's Anonymous God'. *Implicit Religion*, 10/1: 65–89.

KELSO, T. (2006). 'Viewing Advertising through the Lens of Faith: Finding God in Images of Mammon'. *Implicit Religion*, 9/1: 29–53.

LAMB, C. J. (2004). 'The Implicit Religion of Love'. *Implicit Religion*, 7/1: 7–19.

LEWIS, KEVIN (2007). '"Religion" in the Middle East: Implicit and/or Invisible'. *Implicit Religion*, 10/1: 52–64.

LORD, K. (2006). 'Implicit Religion: Definition and Application'. *Implicit Religion*, 9/2: 205–20.

LOWE, B. M. (2001). 'Animal Rights as a Quasi-Religion'. *Implicit Religion*, 4/1: 41–60.

LUCKMANN, T. (1967). *The Invisible Religion: The Problem of Religion in Modern Society*. London: MacMillan.

MACDONALD, A. (2007). 'The Implicit Religion of Organs: Transformative Experience, Enduring Connections, and Sensuous Nations'. *Implicit Religion*, 10/1: 37–51.

MENARD, G. (2001). 'Religion, Implicit or Post-Modern?'. *Implicit Religion*, 4/2: 87–95.

—— (2004). 'The Moods of Marianne: Of *Hijabs*, Nikes, Implicit Religion and Postmodernity'. *Implicit Religion*, 7/3: 246–55.

—— (2005). 'O Come All Ye Faithful: Contemporary Sexuality, Transcendence and Implicit Religion'. *Implicit Religion*, 8/3: 266–80.

MIYAKE, HITOSHI (1972). 'Folk Religion'. In Ichiro Hori *et al.* (eds.), *Japanese Religion: A Survey by the Agency for Cultural Affairs*. Tokyo: Kodanska International Ltd., 121–43.

MOSS, B. (2005). 'Thinking Outside the Box: Religion and Spirituality in Social Work Education and Practice'. *Implicit Religion*, 8/1: 40–52.

NATHANSON, P. (1999). 'I Feel, Therefore I Am: The Princess of Passion and the Implicit Religion of our Time'. *Implicit Religion*, 2/2: 59–87.

NOLAN, P. (2006). 'Spirituality: A Healthcare Perspective'. *Implicit Religion*, 9/3: 272–82.

PAPADOPOULOS, I. (1999). 'Spirituality and Holistic Caring: An Exploration of the Literature'. *Implicit Religion*, 2/2: 101–7.

PÄRNA, K. (2006). 'Believe in the Net: The Construction of the Sacred in Utopian Tales of the Internet'. *Implicit Religion*, 9/2: 180–204.

PORTMANN, A. (1999). 'Friends at Table: Cooking and Eating as Religious Practices'. *Implicit Religion*, 2/1: 39–49.

PYE, M., and ROBERTS, R. (1999). 'Implicit Religion in Inter-faith Perspective: Focusing the Issues'. *Implicit Religion*, 2/2: 109–11, 111–12.

RAHNER, K. (1972). 'Atheism and Christianity'. *Theological Investigations*, 9: 145–64.

SCHMIED, G. (2000). 'Why Celebrate Christmas with the Deceased?' *Implicit Religion*, 3/2: 123–8.

SCHNELL, T. (2000). 'I Believe in Love'. *Implicit Religion*, 3/2: 111–22.

—— (2003). 'A Framework for the Study of Implicit Religion'. *Implicit Religion*, 6/2–3: 86–104.

SHARPE, K. (2005). 'The Pursuit of Happiness: Evolutionary Origins, Psychological Research and Implications for Implicit Religion'. *Implicit Religion*, 8/2: 118–32.

SMART, N. (1998). 'Implicit Religion across Culture'. *Implicit Religion*, 1: 23–6.

SMITH, G. (2004). 'Implicit Religion and Faith-based Urban Regeneration'. *Implicit Religion*, 7/2: 152–82.

SOLYOM, A. E. (2005). 'The Internal Morality of Medicine in the Contexts of Implicit Religion and Spirituality'. *Implicit Religion*, 8/1: 7–21.

STAHL, W. A., and STENMARK, L. L. (2004). 'Stories that Matter: A Normative Approach to Implicit Religion'. *Implicit Religion*, 7/3: 256–75.

SUNDBACH, SUSAN (2007). 'Membership of Nordic "National" Churches as a "Civil Religious" Phenomenon'. *Implicit Religion*, 10/3: 254–72.

SWATOS, W. H. Jr. (1999). 'Re-visiting the Sacred'. *Implicit Religion*, 2/1: 33–8.

—— (2001). 'Meaning and Contradiction'. *Implicit Religion*, 4/1: 97–106.

—— (2006). 'Implicit Religious Assumptions within the Resurgence of Civil Religion in the USA since 9/11'. *Implicit Religion*, 9/2: 166–79.

TAYLOR, J. V. (1973). *The Go-between God: The Holy Spirit and Christian Mission*. London: SCM Press.

THOMAS, D. G. (2001). 'Walter Benjamin's Aura: A Key Concept for Implicit Religion'. *Implicit Religion*, 4/2: 113–23.

TILLICH, P. (1965). *Ultimate Concern: Dialogues with Students*, ed. D. M. Brown. London: SCM Press.

TYERS, P. (2005). 'Engaging with the Religion of Those Who Do Not Attend Public Worship'. *Implicit Religion*, 8/1: 53–63.

USTORF, W. (2000). 'Championing the Dead: A Reflection on Funeral Theologies and "Primal" Religion'. *Implicit Religion*, 3/1: 51–61.

WELBOURN, F. B. (1960). 'Towards a Definition of Religion'. *Makerere Journal*, 4.

—— (1969). 'Towards Eliminating the Concept of Religion'. Paper presented at Second Lancaster Colloquium on Religion, December.

WENDER, ANDREW (2007). 'State Paver as a Vehicle for the Expression and Propagation of Implicit Religion: The Case Study of the "War on Terrorism"'. *Implicit Religion*, 10/3: 236–53.

SUGGESTED READING

The following are recommended: Bailey (1997*a* and for a basic, wider reading list, 1998: 98–100); Bellah (1967); Grainger (2002); Luckmann (1967); and the journal *Implicit Religion* (cf. n. 4).

PART IX

RELIGION AND ECOLOGY, HEALTH, SOCIAL ISSUES, AND VIOLENCE

CHAPTER 45

RELIGION AND ECOLOGY

MARY EVELYN TUCKER

Background

The environmental crisis has been well documented in its various interconnected aspects of resource depletion and species extinction, pollution growth and climate change, population explosion and over-consumption. It is increasingly evident that human attitudes and decisions, values and behavior, will be crucial for the survival and flourishing of numerous life forms on Earth. Indeed, the formulation of viable human–Earth relations is of central concern for a sustainable future for the planet. Along with such fields as the natural sciences and social sciences, and in concert with ecological design and technology, religion, ethics, and spirituality are contributing to the shaping of such viable relations. Moreover, a more comprehensive cosmological world view of the interdependence of life is being articulated along with an ethical responsiveness to care for life for future generations.

The Role of Religions: Cosmologies, Symbols, Rituals, and Ethics

The emerging field of religion and ecology is playing a role in this.[1] This is because world religions are being recognized in their great variety as more than simply

[1] Parts of this essay have appeared in earlier forms as the field has developed.

beliefs in a transcendent deity or means to an afterlife. Rather, religions are seen as providing a broad orientation to the cosmos and to human roles therein. Attitudes toward nature have thus been significantly, although not exclusively, shaped by religious views for millennia in cultures around the globe.

In this context, then, religions can be understood in their largest sense as a means whereby humans, recognizing the limitations of phenomenal reality, undertake specific practices to effect self-transformation and community cohesion within a cosmological context. Religions thus refer to those cosmological stories, symbol systems, ritual practices, ethical norms, historical processes, and institutional structures that transmit a view of the human as embedded in a world of meaning and responsibility, transformation and celebration. Religions connect humans with a divine presence or numinous force. They bond human communities, and assist in forging intimate relations with the broader Earth community. In summary, religions link humans to the larger matrix of indeterminacy and mystery from which life arises and unfolds, and in which it flourishes.

Certain distinctions need to be made here between the particularized expressions of religion identified with institutional or denominational forms of religion and those broader world views that animate such expressions. By world views I mean those ways of knowing, embedded in symbols and stories, which find lived expression, consciously and unconsciously, in the life of particular cultures. In this sense, world views arise from and are formed by human interactions with natural systems or ecologies. Consequently, one of the principal concerns of religions in many communities is to describe in story form the emergence of the local geography as a realm of the sacred. World view generates rituals and ethics, ways of acting, which guide human behavior in personal, communal, and ecological exchanges. Exploration of world views as they are both constructed and lived by religious communities is critical, because it is here that we discover formative attitudes regarding nature, habitat, and our place in the world. In the contemporary period, to re-situate human–Earth relations in a more balanced mode will require both a re-evaluation of sustainable world views and a formulation of viable environmental ethics.

A culture's world views are contained in religious cosmologies and expressed through rituals and symbols. Religious cosmologies describe the experience of origination and change in relation to the natural world. Religious rituals and symbols arise out of cosmologies and are grounded in the dynamics of nature. They provide rich resources for encouraging spiritual and ethical transformation in human life. This is true, for example, in Buddhism, which sees change in nature and the cosmos as a potential source of suffering for the human. Confucianism and Daoism, on the other hand, affirm nature's changes as the source of the Dao (Way). In addition, the death–rebirth cycle of nature serves as an inspiring mirror for human life, especially in the Western monotheistic traditions of Judaism, Christianity, and Islam. Religions have also helped to celebrate the gifts of nature such as air, water, and food that sustain life.

The creative tensions between humans seeking to transcend this world and yearning to be embedded in it are part of the dynamics of world religions. Christianity, for example, holds the promise of salvation in the next life as well as celebrating the incarnation of Christ as a human in the world. Similarly, Hinduism holds up a goal of *moksha*, of liberation from the world of *samsara* (cycle of rebirth), while also highlighting the ideal of the god Krishna acting in the world.

This realization of creative tensions leads to a more balanced understanding of the possibilities and limitations of religions regarding environmental concerns. Many religions retain other-worldly orientations toward personal salvation outside this world; at the same time they can, and have, fostered commitments to social justice, peace, and ecological integrity in the world. A key component that has been missing in much environmental discourse is how to identify and tap into the cosmologies, symbols, rituals, and ethics that inspire changes of attitudes and actions for creating a sustainable future within this world. Historically, religions have contributed to social change in areas such as the Abolitionist and Civil Rights movements. There are new alliances emerging now that are joining social justice with environmental justice.

In alignment with these "eco-justice" concerns, religions are encouraging values and ethics of reverence, respect, redistribution, and responsibility for formulating a broader environmental ethics that includes humans, ecosystems, and other species. With the help of religions, humans are now advocating a reverence for the Earth and its long evolutionary unfolding, respect for the myriad species of flora and fauna, restraint in the use of natural resources on which all life depends, equitable distribution of wealth, and recognition of responsibility of humans for the continuity of life into future generations.

Clearly religions have a central role to play in the formulation of world views that orient humans to the natural world and the articulation of rituals and ethics that guide human behavior. In addition, they have institutional capacity to affect millions of people around the world. Religions of the world, however, cannot act alone with regard to new attitudes toward environmental protection and sustainability. The size and complexity of the problems we face require collaborative efforts both among the religions and in dialogue with other key domains of human endeavor, such as science, economics, and public policy.

Call for the Participation of Religions

Religions were acknowledged by scientists in the early 1990s as having an important role to play in re-visioning a sustainable future. Scientists recognized the importance of religions as key repositories of deep civilizational values and as indispensable motivators in moral transformation around consumption, energy use, and environmental protection. Two important documents were issued by scientists calling for collaboration with religious leaders, laypersons, and institutions.

One is the statement of scientists entitled "Preserving the Earth: An Appeal for Joint Commitment in Science and Religion", which was signed at the Global Forum meeting in Moscow in January 1990. It states:

> The environmental crisis requires radical changes not only in public policy, but in individual behavior. The historical record makes clear that religious teaching, example, and leadership are powerfully able to influence personal conduct and commitment. As scientists, many of us have had profound experiences of awe and reverence before the universe. We understand that what is regarded as sacred is more likely to be treated with care and respect. Our planetary home should be so regarded. Efforts to safeguard and cherish the environment need to be infused with a vision of the sacred.

A second document is called "World Scientists' Warning to Humanity". This was produced by the Union of Concerned Scientists in 1992 and signed by more than 2,000 scientists, including more than 200 Nobel laureates. The document also suggests that the planet is facing a severe environmental crisis, and will require the assistance and commitment of those in the religious community. It states:

> A new ethic is required—a new attitude towards discharging our responsibilities for caring for ourselves and for the Earth. We must recognize the Earth's limited capacity to provide for us. We must recognize its fragility. We must no longer allow it to be ravaged. This ethic must motivate a great movement, convincing reluctant leaders and reluctant governments and reluctant peoples themselves to effect the needed changes.

Response of Religious Leaders and Communities

The response to these appeals was slow at first, but is rapidly growing. It might be noted that there were some strong voices advocating a religious response more than half a century ago. These included Walter Lowdermilk, who in 1940 called for an Eleventh Commandment of land stewardship, and Joseph Sittler, who in 1954 wrote an essay entitled "A Theology for the Earth". Likewise, the Islamic scholar Seyyed Hossein Nasr has been calling since the late 1960s for a renewed sense of the sacred in nature, drawing on perennial philosophy. Lynn White's essay in 1967 on "The Historical Roots of our Ecologic Crisis" sparked controversy over his assertion that the Judeo-Christian tradition has contributed to the environmental crisis by devaluing nature. In 1972 the theologian John Cobb published a prescient book entitled *Is It Too Late?*

Over the last two decades some key movements have taken place among religious communities that have shown growing levels of concern and commitment regarding alleviating the environmental crisis. These include the interreligious gatherings on the environment in Assisi under the sponsorship of the World Wildlife Fund (WWF) in 1984 and under the auspices of the Vatican in 1986. The Parliament of World Religions held in Chicago in 1993 and in Cape Town, South Africa, in 1999 issued major statements on global ethics embracing human rights and environmental issues. The 1993 statement on global ethics was formulated by the Catholic theologian Hans Kung, who continues to pursue efforts in this regard through his institute in Germany. The 1999 Parliament in Cape Town issued a challenge to lead institutions (educational, economic, political) to participate in the transformation toward a sustainable future.

The Global Forum of Spiritual and Parliamentary Leaders held international meetings which had the environment as a major focus in Oxford in 1988, Moscow in 1990, Rio in 1992, and Kyoto in 1993. Since 1995 a critical Alliance of Religion and Conservation (ARC) has been active in England and in Asia for environmental protection and restoration. Similarly, the National Religious Partnership for the Environment (NRPE) has organized Jewish and Christian groups on this issue in the United States. The Coalition on Environment and Jewish Life (COEJL) has activated American Jewish participation in environmental issues. In August 2000 a historic gathering of more than 2,000 religious leaders took place at the United Nations during the Millennium World Peace Summit of Religious and Spiritual Leaders, where the environment was one of four major themes discussed.

Several major international religious leaders have emerged as strong spokespersons for the importance of care for the environment. The Tibetan Buddhist leader, the Dalai Lama, and the Vietnamese Buddhist monk Thich Nhat Hanh have spoken out for many years about the universal responsibility of the human community for the environment and toward all sentient species. Church leaders, such as the Anglican Archbishop Rowan Williams and Robert Edgar, former President of the National Council of Churches, USA, are pointing to environmental problems, such as resource use and climate change, as major ethical challenges. The Greek Orthodox Patriarch Bartholomew has sponsored a series of "symposia at sea" that have brought together scientists, religious leaders, civil servants, and journalists to highlight the problems of marine pollution and fisheries depletion. These have included symposia on the Mediterranean, the Black Sea, the Adriatic, and the Baltic, as well as the Danube River and Greenland. The symposium on the Adriatic concluded in Venice with a joint statement signed by both the Patriarch and Pope John Paul II on the urgent need for environmental protection and care of nature's resources.

It is now the case that most of the world's religions have issued statements on the need to care for the Earth and to take responsibility for future generations. These statements range from various positions within the Western monotheistic traditions to the different sectors within Asian traditions of Buddhism and Daoism. By no means monolithic, they draw on different theological perspectives and ethical concerns across a wide spectrum. They reflect originality of thought in bringing religious traditions into conversation with modern environmental problems, such as climate change, pollution, and loss of biodiversity. Within the various denominations of Christianity, for example, the Protestant-based World Council of Churches has published treatises on "justice, peace, and the integrity of creation"; the Greek Orthodox Patriarch Bartholomew has issued statements on destruction of the environment as "ecological sin"; the Evangelical community has published letters and position papers calling for care of creation; the Catholic Bishops of the Philippines issued a pastoral letter on the environment; and the American Catholic Bishops have published several statements on ecology, including a letter on the Columbia River bioregion. These statements are being used as a moral call to engage in further action on behalf of the environment. Many of them can be viewed on the Harvard website <www.environment.harvard.edu/religion/>.

Intellectual Influences on Religion and Ecology

It is within this global context that the field of religion and ecology has emerged within academia over the last decade. While it is still a relatively new field that is in the process of defining its scope, the academic study of religion and ecology is drawing on other disciplines and thinkers to develop theoretical, historical, ethical, cultural, and engaged dimensions. Among many thinkers, some of the theoretical and historical foundations have been laid by key philosophers. These include Clarence Glacken, who developed a study of nature in Western culture, and Arne Naess, who drew on Baruch Spinoza and South Asian thought to elaborate a theory of deep ecology emphasizing the primacy of the natural world over human prerogatives. Other philosophers and ethicists such as Baird Callicott and Holmes Rolston have helped to develop the field of environmental ethics. The cultural dimensions are influenced by the work of anthropologists, such as Julian Steward, who coined the term "cultural ecology" to describe the relations between the environment and the economic and technological aspects of society. Furthermore, anthropologist Roy Rappaport extended cultural understanding of the ways in which ritual sustains social life in specific bioregions. The geographers David Soper and Yi Fu Tuan have investigated the spatial and ecological characteristics of religion.

Historians such as Thomas Berry and William McNeill have provided a perspective from world history for understanding the mutual influences involved in human interactions with ecosystems. Theologians such as John Cobb and Gordon Kaufman have brought together theoretical and engaged perspectives by suggesting ways in which Christian beliefs can be more effectively expressed theologically and in environmental action. Eco-feminists such as Rosemary Ruether, Sallie McFague, and Heather Eaton have illustrated the contested nature of the treatment of the Earth and the exploitation of women. Eco-justice writers such as Robert Bullard, Dieter Hessel, Mark Wallace, and Roger Gottlieb have also made important contributions to understanding the linkages between social injustice and environmental pollution. For many of these thinkers the theoretical, historical, ethical, cultural and engaged perspectives are not separate, but mutually inclusive. It is appropriate, however, to distinguish these approaches as they are currently informing the emerging field of religion and ecology.

These approaches are animated by several key questions. Theoretically, how has the interpretation and use of religious texts and traditions contributed to human attitudes regarding the environment? Ethically, how do humans value nature and thus create moral grounds for protecting the Earth for future generations. Historically, how have human relations with nature changed over time, and how has this change been shaped by religions? Culturally, how has nature been perceived and constructed by humans, and conversely, how has the natural world affected the formation of human culture? From an engaged perspective, in what ways do the values and practices of a particular religion activate mutually enhancing human–Earth relations? What are the contributions of eco-feminist or eco-justice perspectives to a sustainable future? These questions and others have been raised by individuals and groups as the field has begun to take shape over the last decade.

The Emerging Academic Field of Religion and Ecology

The emergence of an academic field of religion and ecology over the last decade has been marked by a number of key efforts of individuals and groups. These include conferences organized, forums created, websites constructed, books published, courses taught, and undergraduate and graduate programs that have been created. All of this can be seen within the larger context of the humanities, which are now making significant contributions to environmental studies.

Harvard Conference Series

A three-year international conference series took place at Harvard University's Center for the Study of World Religions from 1996 to 1998. The goal was to examine the various ways in which human–Earth relations have been conceived in the world's religions. The project was launched to provide a broad survey that would help to ground a new field of study in religion and ecology. It was not intended to be exhaustive, but rather to be suggestive of the wide variety of resources—intellectual and engaged—to be drawn on from the world's religious traditions. Recognizing that religions are key shapers of people's world views and formulators of their most cherished values, this research project uncovered a wealth of attitudes and practices toward nature sanctioned by religious traditions.

Acknowledging the gap between ancient texts and traditions and modern environmental challenges, it drew on a broad method of retrieval, re-evaluation, and reconstruction. The intention was to avoid simplistic eco-friendly or apologetic readings of scriptures written in vastly different times and circumstances. The scholars were engaged in critically retrieving aspects of the religious traditions for re-examination and re-evaluation in the contemporary context. This has been part of the dynamic unfolding of religions historically, as they have struggled to balance orthodoxy with the urgencies of adapting to new circumstances or cultures. Religious traditions have never been monolithic, but rather have embraced a broad range of interpretive positions ranging from orthodox to reform. Discerning appropriate change and the abiding value of tradition has been an important part of the life of religious teachers for centuries. Jewish rabbis, Christian theologians, Islamic imans in the West and Hindu pundits, Buddhist monks, and Confucian scholars in Asia have all been involved in interpretation of their respective traditions over time. The Harvard project drew on that ongoing process of discernment so as to move toward a constructive phase. In the constructive phase the scholars of the various religions could point toward actual or potential sources of ecological awareness and action from within the particular traditions.

The Harvard conferences were also designed to foster interdisciplinary conversations drawing on the synergy of historians, theologians, ethicists, and scientists as well as on the work of grass-roots environmentalists. This synergy proved to be indispensable, as it provided a dynamic open space for fresh conversations. An awareness emerged that religion and ecology was a new field of study that was being created in both dialogue and in an ongoing network of exchange. The openness of the discussions was enhanced by the fact that there were no "experts", as participants were discovering new approaches together. A spirit of collaborative scholarship, rather than individualistic research, emerged naturally in the conferences. This was in part because participants realized that there was not one way forward, but multiple possibilities that each of the religions might contribute. Moreover, there arose a remarkable sense that cooperative efforts with regard to the future of the planet were more valuable than claims to a superior perspective from one tradition or by one scholar. Individual traditions, scholars, and projects were seen as part of larger, long-term efforts aimed at the flourishing of life on the planet for future generations.

With this spirit of engagement, from 1996 to 1998, more than 800 scholars participated in a series of ten conferences examining the traditions of Judaism,

Christianity, Islam, Hinduism, Jainism, Buddhism, Daoism, Confucianism, Shinto, and Indigenous religions. The conferences were organized by John Grim and myself with a team of area specialists in the world's religions. Each of the conferences was designed to include a spectrum of positions ranging, for example, from Orthodox, Conservative, and Reform in Judaism, from Catholic, Protestant, Orthodox, and Evangelical in Christianity, and from Theravada, Mahayana, and Vajrayana in Buddhism. The conferences were also intended to embrace both historians and scholars of the traditions along with religious spokespersons for them. Moreover, scientists, environmentalists, and activists, as well as graduate and undergraduate students, were invited. Each conference included plenary sessions for a broader public. A wide range of funders insured that participants could be brought from around the world. This attempt at breadth and inclusivity resulted in some remarkable gatherings and some inevitable challenges. The Indigenous conference had representatives from every continent and from numerous ethnic groups. The Shinto conference was the largest gathering of Shinto priests and practioners ever to occur outside Japan. The Islam conference, with representatives from across the Islamic world, fostered lively discussions over differences between Sunni and Shi'ite interpretations of jurisprudence.

The edited papers from these conferences have been published in ten volumes by the Harvard Center for the Study of World Religions and distributed by Harvard University Press.

The purposes of the conferences and books were:

- To examine various attitudes toward nature from the religions of the world, with attention to the complexity of history and culture.
- To contribute to the articulation of functional environmental ethics grounded in religious traditions and inspired by broad ecological perspectives.
- To stimulate the interest and concern of religious leaders and lay people as well as students and professors of religion in seminaries, colleges, and universities.

This research project assumed that religions could contribute toward a more sustainable future, but that multi-disciplinary approaches were needed. With this assumption in mind, three culminating interdisciplinary conferences were held in the fall of 1998 at the American Academy of Arts and Science in Cambridge, Massachusetts, and at the United Nations and the American Museum of Natural History in New York. These conferences included scientists, economists, educators, and policymakers as well as scholars from the various world religions. The journalist Bill Moyers interviewed the religious scholars to highlight the insights from their particular perspectives for a sustainable future. Maurice Strong, Secretary-General of the Stockholm and Rio UN environmental conference, and Timothy Wirth, Director of the United Nations Foundation, participated in the conferences. Other participants included from the field of science Jane Lubchenco, past president of the AAAS, from economics and policy, Ismail Serageldin, of the World Bank, from higher education, George Rupp, President of Columbia University. The cultural historian, Thomas Berry, and the cosmologist, Brian Swimme, spoke from the perspective of the evolutionary story of the universe and our current environmental crisis.

Forums

In October 1998 at the United Nations conference, the formation of the Forum on Religion and Ecology was announced. It had three objectives: to continue the research in the area of religion and ecology, to foster the development of teaching in this area, to encourage outreach within academia to interdisciplinary environmental studies programs and outside academia to religious and policy groups. It has since grown into a global network of some 5,000 people and is coordinated by John Grim and myself.

Since the initial Harvard conferences, the Forum has continued its research agenda by organizing several other Harvard conferences on World Religions and Animals (resulting in a volume entitled *Communion of Subjects*, Columbia University Press, 2006), on the Ecological Imagination with leading nature writers, and on World Religions and Climate Change that resulted in a *Daedalus* volume (2001) which is available online at <www.amacad.org/publications/fall2001/fall2001.aspx>.

Internationally, the Forum has encouraged outreach by organizing panels at the Parliament of World Religions in Capetown and Barcelona, as well as at environmental conferences in Asia, Europe, and the Middle East. It has participated in the symposiums on the Aegean and the Baltic seas convened by the Greek Orthodox Patriarch Bartholomew. It has worked with the United Nations Environmental Programme on various projects, and participated in two symposia that it organized in Iran. It has also been involved in the Earth Charter movement through workshops in North America and international conferences in South America and in Europe. I was a member of the Earth Charter International Drafting Committee and am now a member of the Earth Charter International Council.

In 2003 a group of Canadian scholars, including Heather Eaton, James Miller, Anne Marie Dalton, and Stephen Scharper, formed a Canadian Forum on Religion and Ecology (CFORE). They have been active in Canada in developing the field of study, as well as in sponsoring talks and workshops and participating in public forums and radio discussions (<www.cfore.org>). They are sponsoring a book series on religion and ecology from the University of Toronto Press.

Websites

A website was created by the Forum on Religion and Ecology under the Harvard Center for the Environment (<www.environment.harvard.edu/religion>) to assist in fostering research, education and outreach in the area of religion and ecology. To encourage research, there are annotated bibliographies of the literature on the world religions along with selections from sacred texts and environmental statements from the world's religious communities. There are posted examples of some 100 grass-roots religiously inspired environmental movements around the world that illustrate engaged practices in this area.

To enhance teaching, the website contains introductory essays to each of the world's religious traditions and their environmental contributions. It posts syllabuses and lists audiovisual resources. It links to the highschool teacher's website in this area: Religious Studies in Secondary Schools, <www.rsiss.net>.

To illustrate the importance of interdisciplinary dialogue in partnership with science, economics, and policy, the website contains introductory sections on each of these areas. An annotated bibliography of the evolutionary and ecological sciences is posted, along with bibliographies of ecological economics and ecological ethics.

Publications

The academic literature has been growing rapidly, and interest among students at both the secondary and collegiate level has been robust. The ten-volume Harvard series on World Religions and Ecology edited by John Grim and myself was published between 1997 and 2003. This involved key area specialists in the world religions and hundreds of scholars and environmentalists. Two years later another major multi-year project was completed, with the publication of the two-volume *Encyclopedia of Religion and Nature* edited by Bron Taylor. This has been years in production, has involved hundreds of scholars, and makes an invaluable contribution in identifying the many approaches, topics, and movements included in religion and ecology. In addition, a peer reviewed journal entitled *Worldview: Global Religions, Culture and Ecology* has been published for more than a decade.

Challenges to Religion and Ecology

As the field of religion and ecology emerges within academia and beyond, it is clear that religions offer both promise and problems for ameliorating environmental issues. Religions have sustained human aspirations and energies for centuries, but they have also contributed to intolerance, violence, and fundamentalist views of various kinds. The world's religions may thus be seen as necessary but not sufficient for ecological solutions. Religions have their problematic and dogmatic tendencies and have been late in coming to recognize the scale and scope of the global environmental crisis.

There are limits, then, to what religions may contribute to solving environmental problems. One example of these limits concerns the issue of population. Some of the religious traditions have presented recurring obstacles to open discussion of certain kinds of birth control at UN population conferences. These religious groups are associated largely with Islam, Roman Catholicism, and evangelical Christianity. However, there is an alternative research project identifying a more plural approach to population control among world religions. Led by Daniel Maguire at Marquette University, this project is called the "Religious Consultation on Population, Reproductive Health and Ethics".

Hence, while noting that religions may at times be problematic, there is also recognition that religions may bring a broadened ethical perspective to environmental issues. There is a felt need for creative humanistic and religious initiatives so as to formulate more interdisciplinary approaches to environmental science, policies, law, and economics. The directors of many environmental studies programs at leading universities in the United States are understanding this and exploring ways to integrate religion and ethics into traditional science- and policy-based programs. At the same time these directors of environmental programs are trying to define the parameters of scholarship and public service. Should environmental programs be simply centers of research? To what extent should they be arenas for debating public policy or even advocating certain environmental policy approaches?

Analogous questions are arising in the field of religion and ecology as it begins to define itself and seeks to be in dialogue with science and policy. Should religion and ecology simply be a scholarly field of historical or theoretical research apart from contemporary issues? How should it relate to science and policy concerns? Should it pursue engaged scholarship such as eco-justice? What, if any, is the role of advocacy within academia? Can academics be engaged scholars or public intellectuals in the environmental field within academia and beyond? These are potentially creative and healthy tensions that have emerged in the field of religion and ecology.

The pressing nature of the environmental crisis is urging some scholars within academia to become public intellectuals who are contributing to the understanding of environmental problems and pointing toward possible solutions. This debate on the role of academics engaged in environmental studies and policy making crosses the disciplines from the sciences and social sciences to the humanities. Many people are calling on higher education and research universities to make a larger contribution to the solution of environmental problems. It is at this lively intersection between theoretical, historical, and cultural research and engaged scholarship that the field of religion and ecology is growing.

The Limits of Science and Policy

The field of religion and ecology is becoming well situated to make a contribution to interdisciplinary environmental studies within academia as well as to be in conversation with scientists and policymakers outside academia. In analyzing the current global environmental situation, leaders from both science and policy fields are wondering why we have not made more progress in solving environmental problems. Over the last fifty years, the enormous contributions of science to our understanding of many aspects of environmental problems, both global and local, is being fully recognized.

However, while thousands of scientific studies have been published and then translated into policy reports, many experts have concluded that we have not made sufficient progress in stemming the losses of ecosystems and species. We are stymied by a range of obstacles, from lack of political will to unchanging human habits. For many environmentalists there is a growing realization that a broader sense of vision and values is missing.

Scientists are noting that dire facts about environmental problems, as overwhelming as they may be, have not altered the kinds of human behavior that are rapaciously exploiting nature. Nor have such facts affected human habits of addictive consumption, especially in the richer nations. Moreover, policy experts are realizing that legislative or managerial approaches to nature are proving insufficient for the complex environmental challenges at hand. One cannot simply legislate change or manage human nature.

In short, environmentalists are observing that while science and policy approaches are necessary, they are not sufficient to assist in transforming human consciousness and behavior for a sustainable future. They are suggesting instead that values and ethics, religion and spirituality, are important factors in this transformation. This is being articulated in conferences, in books and articles, and in policy institutes like Worldwatch. Here is where the field of religion and ecology is beginning to make an important contribution both to environmental studies within the academy and to policy initiatives outside the academy.

Response of Policy Groups and Scientists

One such initiative has been promoted by the United Nations Environment Programme (UNEP), which has established an Interfaith Partnership for the Environment that for some twenty years has distributed thousands of booklets on *Earth and Faith* for use in local congregations and communities. It has encouraged the participation of religious leaders, scholars, and lay people in conferences that it has organized. Klaus Toepfer, the former executive director, has called for environmental ethics and spiritual values to be integrated more actively into environmental protection. He draws on Hans Jonas's principle of responsibility as crucial for future generations. He notes that legal and compliance mechanisms are indispensable, but that a more holistic approach to environmental issues is needed. He has suggested, for example, that resources such as water should be seen not as simply economically important for human use but also as spiritually valuable. In this light, he cites the need to develop indicators for assessing not just market values but spiritual and ethical values as well. Toepfer has been instrumental in encouraging this broader ethical approach in many international conferences. These include two conferences that UNEP organized in Tehran in cooperation with the Islamic Republic of Iran in June 2001 and May 2005.

A conference in Lyon in 2001 chaired by Mikhail Gorbachev also reflected this search for broader ethical approaches to environmental problems. Its title was "Earth Dialogues: Is Ethics the Missing Link?" This Earth Dialogue conference was followed by another in Barcelona in 2004, at which religious and ethical issues were also prominent. While not looking for quick solutions or easy answers, many thoughtful people are observing that human motivation, values, and action are critical in making the transition to a sustainable future.

Think tanks such as the Worldwatch Institute in Washington DC are also realizing that statistics and alarming reports are not enough to initiate the changes needed for an ecologically sustainable world. In the final chapter of the Worldwatch *State of the World 2003* report, senior researcher, Gary Gardner, wrote of the growing role of religions in shaping attitudes and action for a broader commitment to environmental protection and restoration. His essay received significant attention, and the larger version of the chapter is published in a separate Worldwatch Paper (#164) entitled "Invoking the Spirit: Religion and Spirituality in the Quest for a Sustainable World".

There are several prominent scientists and policymakers who are recognizing that human values and ethical perspectives need to be part of the equation in environmental discussions. They are noting that arguments from "sound science" and computer models that draw on reams of data and statistics do not necessarily move people to action. The Harvard biologist E. O. Wilson, in his 2003 book *The Future of Life*, observes the potential power of religious beliefs and institutions to mobilize large numbers of people for ecological protection. In this vein, James Gustave Speth, Dean of Yale's School of Forestry and Environmental Studies, in his 2004 book *Red Sky at Morning*, acknowledges that ethics and values will need to play a larger role in environmental discussions. Moreover, Speth has encouraged the development of a graduate program in religion and ecology at Yale by the School of Forestry and Environmental Studies and the Divinity School. This is now emerging under the leadership of Steven Kellert along with John Grim, Willis Jenkins, and myself.

The Stanford biologist Paul Ehrlich voiced similar concerns in an address to the Ecological Society of America in Portland in August 2004. He observed that "for the first time in human history, global civilization is threatened with collapse".

Thus, he suggests: "The world therefore needs an ongoing discussion of key ethical issues related to the human predicament in order to help generate the urgently required response." He observed that the Millennium Ecosystem Assessment Report was undertaking an evaluation of the conditions of the world's ecosystems. He noted, however, that "there is no parallel effort to examine and air what is known about how human cultures, and especially ethics, change, and what kinds of changes might be instigated to lessen the chances of a catastrophic global collapse". He called for the establishment of a Millennium Assessment of Human Behavior (MAHB) to address these problems.

In the thirty-year anniversary edition of *Limits to Growth* in 2004, Dennis Meadows and his colleagues observe that we need new "Tools for the Transition to Sustainability". The authors admit:

> In our search for ways to encourage the peaceful restructuring of a system that naturally resists its own transformation we have tried many tools. The obvious ones are—rational analysis, data systems thinking, computer modeling, and the clearest words we can find. Those are tools that anyone trained in science and economics would automatically grasp. Like recycling, they are useful, necessary, and they are not enough. (Meadows *et al.* 2004: 269)

Instead, they suggest qualities beyond the usual frame of environmental science and policy in mapping the road toward sustainability: namely, in planning for a future that will sustain the life needs of humans and other species. The qualities for ensuring such a future include visioning, networking, truth telling, learning, and loving. These qualities indicate a major shift for social planners and policy-oriented environmentalists. The authors identified the importance of such "soft tools" in 1992, but now feel that they are not simply optional but rather essential for the transition to sustainability.

Conclusion

It is becoming increasingly clear that environmental changes will be assisted by a variety of disciplines in very specific ways. Scientific analysis will be critical to understanding nature's ecology; educational awareness will be indispensable to creating modes of sustainable life; economic incentives will be central to adequate distribution of resources; public policy recommendations will be invaluable in shaping national and international priorities; and moral and spiritual values will be crucial for the transformations, both personal and communal, required for the flourishing of Earth's many ecosystems. All of these disciplines and approaches are needed. In this way, the various values, incentives, and knowledge that motivate human activity can be more effectively channeled toward long-term sustainable life on the planet. It is in this nexus that the field of religion and ecology is making important contributions, within academia and beyond.

References

MEADOWS, DONELLA, RANDERS, JORGEN, and MEADOWS, DENNIS (2004). *Limits to Growth: The 30-Year Update.* London: Earthscan Publications Ltd.

SPETH, JAMES GUSTAVE (2006). *Red Sky at Morning: America and the Crisis of the Global Environment.* New Haven: Yale University Press.

TAYLOR, BRON (ed.) (2005). *Encyclopedia of Religion and Nature,* 2 vols. London: Thoemmes Continuum.

WILSON, E. O. (2002). *The Future of Life.* New York: Alfred A. Knopf–Random House.

Worldwatch Institute (2003). *State of the World 2003: A Worldwatch Institute Report on Progress toward a Sustainable Society.* New York: W.W. Norton & Co.

Suggested Reading

The Harvard Series on World Religions and Ecology

All these volumes were published by The Harvard Center for the Study of World Religions in Cambridge, Mass.

CHAPPLE, CHRISTOPHER KEY (ed.) (2002). *Jainism and Ecology: Nonviolence in the Web of Life.*

—— and TUCKER, MARY EVELYN (eds.) (2000). *Hinduism and Ecology: The Intersection of Earth, Sky, and Water.*

FOLTZ, RICHARD C., DENNY, FREDERICK M., and BAHARUDDIN, AZIZAN (eds.) (2003). *Islam and Ecology: A Bestowed Trust.*

GIRARDOT, NORMAN J., MILLER, JAMES, and LIU, XIAOGAN (eds.) (2001). *Daoism and Ecology: Ways within a Cosmic Landscape.*

GRIM, JOHN A. (ed.) (2001). *Indigenous Traditions and Ecology: The Interbeing of Cosmology and Community.*

HESSEL, DIETER T., and RUETHER, ROSEMARY RADFORD (eds.) (2000). *Christianity and Ecology: Seeking the Well-Being of Earth and Humans.*

SAMULESON, HAVA TIROSH (ed.) (2003). *Judaism and Ecology: Created World and Revealed Word.*

TUCKER, MARY EVELYN, and WILLIAMS, DUNCAN RYUKEN (eds.) (1997). *Buddhism and Ecology: The Interconnection of Dharma and Deeds.*

—— and BERTHRONG, JOHN (eds.) (1998). *Confucianism and Ecology: The Interrelation of Heaven, Earth, and Humans.*

Other Works

American Academy of Arts and Sciences (Fall 2001). "Religion and Ecology: Can the Climate Change?" *Daedalus: The Journal of the American Academy of Arts and Sciences,* 130/4.

BERRY, THOMAS (2006). *Dream of the Earth,* 2nd edn. San Francisco: Sierra Club Books.

FOLTZ, RICHARD C. (ed.) (2002). *Worldviews, Religion, and the Environment: A Global Anthology.* Belmont, Calif.: Wadsworth-Thomson Learning.

GOTTLIEB, ROGER (2003). *This Sacred Earth: Religion, Nature, and Environment,* 2nd edn. London: Routledge.

SWIMME, BRIAN (1994). *The Universe Story: From the Primordial Flaring Forth to the Ecozoic Era—A Celebration of the Unfolding of the Cosmos.* New York: HarperOne-HarperCollins.

TUCKER, MARY EVELYN (2003). *Worldly Wonder: Religions Enter their Ecological Phase.* Chicago: Open Court.

—— and GRIM, JOHN (eds.) (2003). *Worldviews and Ecology: Religion, Philosophy, and the Environment.* Maryknoll, NY: Orbis Books.

WALDAU, PAUL, and PATTON, KIMBERLY (eds.) (2006). *A Communion of Subjects: Animals in Religion, Science, and Ethics.* New York: Columbia University Press.

CHAPTER 46

RELIGION, SPIRITUALITY, AND HEALTH

AN INSTITUTIONAL APPROACH

WENDY CADGE

"Dear Lord," a woman named Emma wrote recently on a fluorescent pink post-it note stuck to a prayer board in an urban hospital chapel, "Please watch over and protect my loving husband as he undergoes his surgery and recovery. Thank you for all the gifts you've given us." Emma's prayer was one of fifty stuck to this board, and one of others offered silently and aloud in the hospital by chaplains, patients, families, and staff. Outside this hospital, prayers and rituals for healing take place regularly at churches, temples, and mosques in the city, in general services and specific healing gatherings throughout the calendar year. Recent national surveys show that more than half of Americans pray regularly for their own health or the health of their family members. More than three-quarters of Americans believe

Research for this article was supported by the Robert Wood Johnson Foundation Scholars in Health Policy Research Program at Harvard University and by the Theodore and Jane Norman Fund for Faculty Research at Brandeis University. Many thanks to Brian Fair and Jennifer Dillinger for research assistance. Thanks also to Courtney Bender and Lance Laird for comments on earlier drafts.

that prayer can have a positive effect on people who are ill, and close to three-quarters believe that God can cure people given no chance of survival by medical science.[1]

Recent national headlines in the United States, "Religion and Health: The Prayer Cure", "Faith and Health", and "Mixing Prayer, Health", in the *Wall Street Journal*, *Newsweek*, and the *Houston Chronicle* respectively, bring into national view questions about the efficacy of prayers for healing and related studies of intercessory prayer. These headlines join a broader national conversation about the relationships between religion, spirituality, and health taking place amongst politicians, health-care workers, religious leaders, proponents of complementary and alternative medicine, and millions of Americans. A *Time* magazine cover asks "Can Spirituality Promote Health?", and books with titles like *A Spiritual Journey through Breast Cancer* and *Fasting for Spiritual Breakthrough* fill bookstore shelves. Recent debates about health-care workers' rights to conscience focus on whether pharmacists can refuse to dispense birth control and morning-after pills based on personal religious convictions, whether religious healers can freely dispense their wares, and whether physicians should pray with patients.

The relationships between religion, spirituality, health, and healing occupy a consistent but shifting position historically in American public and private life. Historians, religious studies scholars, medical researchers, and social scientists address these issues in steadily expanding bodies of research. Scholars in religious studies, for example, tend to focus on questions about religious healing and the historical and contemporary approaches to health and medicine in explicitly religious contexts (e.g., Numbers and Amundsen 1986;. Barnes and Sered 2005; Porterfield 2005). Medical research has paid increased attention to questions about religion and spirituality in recent years; the number of articles catalogued in PubMed, the main biomedical search engine, with religion or spirituality and health in the title or abstract more than doubled between 1980 and the present. Much of this research focuses on whether individuals' religions or spiritualities, measured in terms of their identities, beliefs, and/or practices, influence their health, both physical and mental. These studies, described in several review articles, tend to focus on individuals as the units of analysis, outside their familial, religious, or other institutional contexts (Sherkat and Ellison 1999; Chatters 2000; Koenig, McCullough, and Larson 2001).[2]

Social scientists, sociologists in particular, have also made important contributions to current thinking about the relationship between religion, spirituality, and health at the individual level. Most of this work, however, has considered individual behaviors apart from the multiple institutional contexts in which these behaviors

[1] Data from a survey conducted by *Newsweek*, dated 1 Nov. 2003; available through Polling the Nation.

[2] See also reviews of the field at <http://www.metanexus.net/tarp/>.

become meaningful. I respond in this article by shifting the unit of analysis from individuals to institutions. I focus specifically on how questions about religion, spirituality, and health are currently present and addressed in medical and religious institutions in the United States.

The chapter proceeds in three sections. First, I briefly review the relationship between religious and bio-medical institutions in American history with particular attention to the role of religion in the creation of the nation's first hospitals. Second, I focus on one set of bio-medical institutions, hospitals, to examine the presence of religion and spirituality and how they are addressed. I concentrate on the evolution of related guidelines from the Joint Commission for the Accreditation of Healthcare Organizations (JCAHO), the work of hospital chaplains, and the role of religion in the work of hospital staff, particularly doctors and nurses. Third, I briefly consider how local American religious organizations address health and bio-medicine with particular attention to healing services and bio-medical health care services offered through some religious organizations.

While recognizing the diversity of religious and spiritual forms of expression, I concentrate here on the largest and most institutionalized religious traditions in the United States.[3] The words "religion" and "spirituality" are not used in consistent ways in existing research literature. The word "religion" tends to be used to refer to religious institutions, and the word "spirituality" to describe personal beliefs and practices. I attempt to use them accordingly, but the distinctions between them are complex and worthy of an article of its own.[4] I also focus almost exclusively on current bio-medical conceptions of health and bio-medical institutions (for other approaches to health and healing, see (Gevitz 1988; Hufford 1988; McGuire 1988; Barnes and Sered 2005). I draw materials selectively from across the disciplines to argue that religious and bio-medical institutions play central roles in shaping (a) individuals' private experiences of religion/spirituality and health; (b) the current relationships between the organizations themselves; and (c) broader public dialogue about a range of related issues. While I focus primarily on hospitals and local religious centers, similar questions need to be asked about other health care and religious institutions, including nursing homes, rehabilitation centers, hospices, para-church organizations, religious health care, and social service organizations. Rather than continuing to focus on individuals outside their institutional contexts, I encourage sociologists to bring organizations and institutions into research and broader public conversations about religion, spirituality, and health along the axes modeled here.

[3] This approach leads me not to address Christian Scientists, Seventh-Day Adventists, and a range of other religious/spiritual groups that have existed historically in some tension with bio-medicine. For additional information, see, e.g., DesAutels *et al.* 1999; Numbers 1992). I also do not address the development and institutionalization of alternative/complementary medicine as described by Ruggie (2004) and others.

[4] See, e.g., <http://religion.ssrc.org/reforum/Bender/>.

Brief Historical Considerations

Conceptions of "holiness" and "healing" share an etymology rooted in notions of wholeness, often understood through shifting distinctions between the body and the soul, mind, or spirit (Turner 1987). In the Christian context a dualistic cosmology operated historically that ennobled the soul while degrading the body. People of faith were to offer charity to those in need, most especially the sick, through hospitals that emerged during the Middle Ages from houses of Christian charity (Mollat 1986). These medieval hospitals, which provided more solace and shelter than treatment, first institutionalized public care for the sick, which expanded dramatically in eighteenth- and nineteenth-century England and through related European, North American, and overseas Christian missions (Porter 1993; Risse 1999). Started as what some called "houses of God", it was not religious or spiritual concerns but bio-medicine that was new to hospitals as they developed in the modern context (Lee 2002).

The model of the physician that emerged from the ecclesiastical form and content of higher education based in the Middle Ages has developed over subsequent centuries. Scientifically trained physicians evolved from physicians trained in religious universities, as physicians and religious leaders gradually mapped out separate spheres (Porter 1993). In the early American colonies, clergy provided much of the medical care, particularly in New England, as did some clergy in Britain and parts of Europe. This changed in the nineteenth century as scientific medicine and medical education emerged, and states enacted laws prohibiting clergy without medical training from practicing medicine (Numbers and Sawyer 1982). Formal training for nurses emerged in the United States in the late nineteenth century following much informal nursing done by women in the home. Orders of religious or vowed nurses were also gradually replaced by secular nurses over the next century (Numbers and Sawyer 1982; Reverby 1987; Coburn and Smith 1999; Nelson 2001).

Early American hospitals were charity institutions for the poor, the gravely ill, and the desperate; everyone else was cared for in their homes (Starr 1982; Rosenberg 1987; Kauffman 1995). When hospitals began to develop and expand numerically in the mid nineteenth century, religion influenced the process. Catholic and Jewish hospitals were started for patients not treated well in other facilities, and for doctors and nurses who could not find work in them (Vogel 1980; Rosenberg 1987; Lazarus 1991). Catholic hospitals in New York, for example, opened largely to care for poor immigrants in the languages and cultures with which they were familiar (McCauley 2005). Catholic hospitals offered not only ethnic identity, but also the privilege of being treated as a paying patient rather than a charity case in another hospital (Rosenberg 1987). Similarly, Jewish hospitals were started by members of the Jewish community to meet the needs of Jewish patients (Levitan 1964; Sarna 1987). Mount Sinai and then Beth Israel hospitals in Boston, for example, had kosher food and Yiddish-speaking physicians (Linenthal 1990). Religious-affiliated hospitals were open to everyone and, until the mid-twentieth century cared for more than one-quarter of all hospitalized patients (Numbers and Sawyer 1982).

In the past century and a half, the formal distance between religion and biomedical organizations has increased. Professional sectarian battles have resulted in the increased scientific and technological foci of medicine (Starr 1982; Stevens 1989).[5] Church ownership of hospitals has become less common, and where religious connections remain, distinctions between religious and secular hospitals are apparent primarily in sexual and reproductive services (Numbers and Sawyer 1982; Uttley 2000; McCauley 2005).[6] Such differences are particularly contested when secular and religious hospitals consider mergers (Joyce 2002). Despite the institutional secularization of medical care, some religiously based health care organizations remain, and new ones continue to emerge. Post-1965 immigrants, for example, have started medical centers in a range of traditions. A Cambodian Buddhist temple began to offer Western counseling services supported by Buddhist healing practices in the 1980s, and in the 1990s the University Muslim Medical Association (UMMA) Free Clinic was established in Los Angeles offering free health care to all, in the Muslim tradition of compassion (Orr and May 2000). Buddhist hospices founded by largely White converts to Buddhism have also opened, and many Christian congregations have started parish nursing programs (Garces-Foley 2003). In light of these and other developments, the secularization of medical institutions is not complete. These institutions continue in diverse ways to address the religions and spiritualities of the decidedly non-secular people who work, are treated, and pass through them regularly.

Medical Institutions: Hospitals

Hospitals across the United States currently acknowledge and respond to religion and spirituality in a wide range of ways. Though fewer hospitals are religiously

[5] Interestingly, however, the American Medical Association established a Committee on Medicine and Religion in the mid-1960s, which also included a column in the *Journal of the American Medical Association* (*JAMA*) to facilitate work between physicians and religious leaders (Rhoads 1967; O'Donnell 1970). *JAMA* has continued to address questions about religion and medicine, though they are clearly peripheral to the journal's other emphases (Rosner 2001).

[6] A small body of research considers other differences between Catholic and non Catholic hospitals in terms of compassionate care, services available, etc. (White and Begun 1998–9; K. R. White 2000; White *et al.* 2006; Prince 1994).

affiliated than in the past, many continue to make space for religion and spirituality in hospital chapels or meditation rooms. Such spaces range from small, closet-sized rooms in out-of-the-way places to larger gathering places equipped with movable altars, meditation cushions, Muslim prayer rugs, texts from multiple religious traditions, and other objects required for practice in a range of traditions. A study of hospital chapels in large academic medical centers demonstrated wide variation in usage. Some chapels were rarely visited, while others were frequented daily by hundreds of people who were looking for quiet places to sit or meditate, formal services, spaces for large family meetings, and other things (Cadge and Dillinger 2007). Further variation in the presence and importance of religion and spirituality in hospitals is evident in the number of hospital chaplains and their degree of integration, the kinds of religious items for sale in hospital gift shops, the questions about religion and spirituality that patients are asked on admission to hospital, and in the ways in which staff respond to religion and spirituality professionally and personally in their work.

Joint Commission for the Accreditation of Healthcare Organizations (JCAHO)

At the macro-level, hospital responses to religion are shaped through evolving policies of the Joint Commission for the Accreditation of Healthcare Organizations (JCAHO). Started in 1910, JCAHO establishes guidelines to ensure the provision of safe quality care at health care organizations across the United States.[7] Concerning spirituality, JCAHO guidelines in 2005 stated that: "Each patient has a right to have his or her cultural, psychosocial, spiritual, and personal values, beliefs, and preferences respected", and that hospitals accommodate the "right to pastoral and other spiritual services for patients". JCAHO provided additional guidelines regarding religion and spirituality in relation to dietary options, pain concerns, resolving dilemmas about patient care issues, end-of-life issues, and the treatment and responsibilities of staff.

The Joint Commission first addressed religion in hospitals in 1969 with a focus on patient care: "Patients' spiritual needs may be met through hospital resources and/or through an arrangement with appropriate individuals from the community." During the 1980s, this guideline was expanded to state that religion had to be assessed in patients being treated for alcoholism and drug dependence. In the 1990s, issues around religion and spirituality were reframed in the guidelines as a "right" treated primarily under the heading of "Patients Rights". The Commission replaced the language of "religion" with the more inclusive language of "spirituality" and

[7] For more information see <http://www.jointcommission.org/AboutUs/joint_commission_history.htm>.

expanded the range of topics for which spirituality could be relevant to include end-of-life issues. In 1995 the guidelines incorporated the rights of hospital staff related to spirituality and religion by directing hospitals to address conflicts between staff members' cultural or religious beliefs and their work.

The 1990s also saw discussion and transition in the Joint Commission's standards about what the spiritual care of patients should be called and who, specifically, might provide it. In 1996, the Joint Commission stated that hospitals were to demonstrate respect for "pastoral counseling", a phrase replaced by "pastoral care and other spiritual services" in 1999, after leaders in hospital chaplaincy argued that this phrase better reflects what they do. While the Joint Commission has not established specific guidelines or licensing requirements as to who should or can provide spiritual care, they mentioned pastoral services departments and pastoral personnel from outside the facility in the 1999 standards as possibilities. As examples, small hospitals could "maintain a list of clergy who have consented to be available to the hospital's patients in addition to visiting their own parishioners", while larger hospitals could "employ qualified chaplains who have graduated from an accredited Master of Divinity degree program". Following similar discussions in the medical and nursing literatures, the Joint Commission also currently describes "spiritual assessments" which, in the words of JCAHO's Associate Director of Standards Interpretation, "determine how a patient's religion or spiritual outlook might affect the care he or she receives.... At minimum the spiritual assessment should determine the patient's religious denomination, beliefs, and what spiritual practices are important to the patient" (Staten 2003).

Little to no research examines how hospitals have responded to changing JCAHO policies regarding religion and spirituality and whether or how spiritual assessments take place in hospitals across the country. While health care providers have developed a range of templates for conducting spiritual assessments and gathering spiritual histories, little is known about how they are actually used and responded to by health care providers and patients (Maugans 1996; Chambers and Curtis 2001; LaPierre 2003; Carson and Koenig 2004; Hodge 2006).

Hospital Chaplaincy

At some hospitals, religious and spiritual issues are addressed primarily by hospital chaplains (Cadge *et al.* 2008). Data collected by the American Hospital Association in its annual survey of hospitals suggests that between 54 percent and 64 percent of hospitals had chaplaincy services between 1980 and 2003, with no systematic trend during the period. As in smaller studies, larger hospitals, those in more urban areas, and hospitals that are church affiliated were more likely to have chaplains in 1993 and 2003 than others (Flannelly *et al.* 2004; Cadge and Dillinger 2007). Researchers estimate that there are more than 10,000 hospital chaplains in the United States, many of whom belong to professional organizations, including the Association of Professional Chaplains, the National Association of Catholic Chaplains, the National Association of Jewish Chaplains, and/or the Association of Clinical Pastoral Education (Weaver *et al.* 2004). Chaplains include women and men who are lay people as well as ordained leaders in their religious traditions.

While a broad history of hospital chaplaincy remains to be written, scholars agree that hospital chaplaincy developed in the late nineteenth and early twentieth centuries through the work of Richard Cabot, Anton T. Boisen, Helen Flanders Dunbar, and others. It developed in parallel with Clinical Pastoral Education (CPE), an initially Protestant-based movement, designed to train theological students in the work of bedside ministry (Hall 1992). Clinical Pastoral Education remains a central part of clerical training in several religious traditions, and is currently offered in Clinical Pastoral Education Programs at hospitals and in a range of other settings (for descriptions see Lee 2002; Angrosino 2006).[8] CPE students likely provide a fair amount of the religious and spiritual care available to patients at some of the hospitals where they are trained because, as a form of graduate medical education, federal Medicare funds will reimburse hospitals for a fraction of the students' work (McSherry and Nelson 1987; Lee 2002; L. White 2003).

What hospital chaplains do and how they are understood varies across hospitals. They are organizationally integrated into hospitals in a wide range of ways (VandeCreek *et al.* 2001). At some hospitals, chaplains are employed directly by the hospital, a cost the hospital meets out of its bottom line, because chaplaincy services are not reimbursed by health insurance companies (for more on financing, see VandeCreek and Lyon 1995). At other hospitals, chaplains are exclusively volunteers or are employed by local Catholic dioceses, churches, or Jewish social service organizations. In some cases, particularly in New York City through the work of the Healthcare Chaplaincy, hospital chaplains are hired and supervised by outside organizations (Flannelly *et al.* 2003).

The daily work of chaplains at individual hospitals may include providing emotional, practical, ritual, and crisis intervention services to patients, families, and staff individually or as members of health care teams (Carey 1973; Bassett 1976; Barrows 1993; Rodrigues *et al.* 2000; Flannelly *et al.* 2005; Sakurai 2005). Increasingly, hospitals work on multi- or interfaith models where individual chaplains work with people across traditions rather than only with those who share their religious backgrounds. In a study of chaplains working at Memorial Sloan-Kettering Cancer Center, researchers found that chaplains worked with family members and friends in addition to patients, received referrals particularly from nurses, and spent more time with patients after surgeries than before (Flannelly *et al.* 2003). At a

[8] For more information see <http://Www.Acpe.Edu/Cpehistory.Htm>.

community hospital, chaplains were most often called for patients with anxiety, depression, or pregnancy loss (Fogg *et al.* 2004). Various hospital constituencies perceive chaplains' roles and importance differently, with the largest number of referrals to chaplains often coming from nurses and social workers (Bryant 1993; Thiel and Robinson 1997; Fogg *et al.* 2004). First-person descriptions of life as a chaplain published in the *Journal of Pastoral Care and Counseling* and the *Journal of Healthcare Chaplaincy* provide the best overviews of daily work.

As a group, hospital chaplains have become increasingly professionalized in recent years. In 2000, leading hospital chaplaincy organizations prepared a document, "A White Paper. Professional Chaplaincy: Its Role and Importance in Healthcare", that emphasized the distinct aspects of spiritual care provided by clinically trained hospital chaplains who work across disciplinary boundaries in hospitals (Association of Professional Chaplains *et al.* 2001). A newly developed certification process outlines the criteria for "board certification" which include the certification of a faith tradition, a graduate-level theological degree, and four units of Clinical Pastoral Education.[9]

In the spirit of evidence-based medicine, studies of hospital chaplains have also begun to assess the relationship between patients' visits with hospital chaplains and patient satisfaction with the overall hospital experience (Parkum 1985; VandeCreek and Connell 1991; VandeCreek and Lyon 1997; Clark *et al.* 2003). Studies have also begun to describe how chaplains work differently with different populations, depending on the age of the patient, severity of illness, religious/spiritual tradition, presence of family, availability of local clergy, etc. (VandeCreek and Lyon 1997).

Religion and Spirituality among Nurses and Doctors

In addition to their work with patients and families, hospital chaplains work with hospital staff who themselves attend to religion and spirituality both professionally and personally in their work. Medical staff confront such issues directly in conversations with patients and families and indirectly in their own experiences of the sacred and profane (R. Fox 1988). Zane Robinson Wolf's (1988) descriptions of nursing rituals around postmortem care, medication administration, bathing patients, and end-of-shift reports, and other researchers' descriptions in more recent ethnographic considerations of hospitals, provide numerous examples of these indirect explorations independent of organized religious values (van der Geest and Finkler 2004; van der Geest 2005).

In addition to hospital chaplains, nurses have provided, and continue to provide, spiritual care for patients. Some nurses were themselves trained in religious

[9] For more information, see <http://www.acpe.edu/acroread/Common%20Standards%20for%20Professional%20Chaplaincy%20Revised%20March%202005.pdf>.

institutions, and studies of nursing textbooks and curricula show that discussions of religion and spirituality appear regularly, if tangentially, in general and more specific courses (Brittain and Boozer 1987; Groer *et al.* 1996; Lemmer 2002; McEwen 2004). A recent survey of nurses at a large academic medical center found that 91 percent consider themselves spiritual, and more than 80 percent think that there is something spiritual about the care they provide. Almost none believe promoting spirituality is at odds with medicine (Cavendish *et al.* 2004; Grant *et al.* 2004). Professional nursing associations have also developed diagnostic guidelines for evaluating patients' "spiritual distress", and for providing spiritual care/intervention (Emblen and Halstead 1993; Grant 2004; Ross 2006).

Amongst physicians, religion and spirituality are a newer addition to medical school curricula, considered in courses on compassionate care or spirituality and medicine that emphasize communication, patients' beliefs, spiritual history taking, the work of chaplaincy, etc. (Kelly *et al.* 1996; Levin *et al.* 1997; Puchalski and Larson 1998; Graves *et al.* 2002; Barnes 2006).[10] Overall, these courses tend to focus on religion and spirituality amongst patients and families rather than among health care providers, despite the fact that just over half of physicians reported in a recent survey that their religious or spiritual beliefs influence their practice of medicine (Curlin *et al.* 2005*a*). Physicians describe the connections between their religion or spirituality and work in a range of ways. For some they are private, while for others they are addressed with like-minded colleagues, as evident in an ethnography of a scripture-based group in an academic medical center (Caitlin *et al.* 2001; Messikomer and De Craemer 2002; Carson and Koenig 2004; Cadge and Catlin 2006).[11]

Studies of the relationship between religion and decision making amongst physicians deal with similar themes. A recent study found that religiously committed doctors are less likely than others to believe that physicians must refer patients or disclose information about medical procedures that the physician opposes for moral reasons (Curlin *et al.* 2007). In studies about the withdrawal of life support, abortion, and other issues, religion has also been associated with physicians' decisions (Imber 1986; Aiyer *et al.* 1999; Abdel-Aziz *et al.* 2004). In a study of Pennsylvania internists, for example, after controlling for other independent variables, Catholic and Jewish physicians were less willing than others to withdraw life support (Christakis and Asch 1995). When religion-related conflicts arise for patients in their decision making, a small interview study showed that physicians tried to balance respect for patient autonomy with efforts to persuade them to follow medical recommendations (Curlin *et al.* 2005*b*).

[10] A very few hospitals and medical schools have adapted chaplaincy training programs for health-care providers who want to learn more about providing spiritual care (Todres *et al.* 2005).

[11] Demographically, recent surveys show that physicians are more likely to belong to minority religious traditions than members of the general public and to consider themselves spiritual but not religious (Curlin *et al.* 2005*a*).

Apart from decision making, research about religion raises questions as to how comfortable physicians are talking about religion or spirituality directly with patients. Studies show wide variation, depending on physician and patient populations (e.g., Wilson *et al.* 2000; Chibnall and Brooks 2001; Siegel *et al.* 2002; Armbruster *et al.* 2003; Luckhaupt *et al.* 2005). A significant percentage of physicians are uncomfortable addressing religion or spirituality with patients, a finding that makes ironic broader public debates about whether physicians should pray with patients (Koenig *et al.* 1989; Post *et al.* 2000). Patients tend to welcome personal inquiries about their religion or spirituality in the contexts of more serious illness and/or if the issues are personally relevant to them (Daaleman and Nease 1994; Ehman *et al.* 1999; MacLean *et al.* 2003). When asked directly whether they believe that religion influences health, physicians in a small interview study said that it does. They emphasize that it provides a framework for patients' understandings and decision-making processes and is often a source of community support. Religion or spirituality was viewed as harmful by the physicians in this study if it led to psychological conflict or conflicted with medical advice (Curlin *et al.* 2005*c*).

Small studies that describe religion and spirituality amongst physicians, nurses, patients, and families suggest that religion and spirituality is often more important to patients and families than to staff, perhaps leading to gaps in understandings and care (Koenig *et al.* 1991). Among staff, religion and spirituality are addressed more consistently in the literature, and probably in practice, around end-of-life issues than as related to other aspects of the content of their work or the institutional contexts in which they work.

Local Religious Institutions

Apart from bio-medical institutions, local religious centers have long been viewed as sites of healing through services and gatherings, connections facilitated with relevant resources, and through the many forms of social support created and nurtured therein. I focus attention here on health and healing in local religious services and on the kinds of networks that some religious centers are developing with bio-medical health providers, particularly through parish nursing programs and other preventative health efforts. The multiple ways in which local religious gatherings influence individual behaviors, provide social interaction and emotional support, and foster instrumental connections that may influence individual health outcomes are important and described in other reviews (Sherkat and Ellison 1999; Chatters 2000; Koenig *et al.* 2001).

Healing Services

Individual communities of faith respond to health and illness in a broad range of ways. Many regularly address health and healing in communal gatherings. A primary prayer for spiritual healing and physical cure in Judaism, the *Mi Sheberakh*, for example, is often recited in a synagogue by an individual or a family member of an ailing individual. Similarly in many Christian groups, sick individuals are publicly named during prayers and rituals in the context of weekly services.

In addition to addressing health concerns in weekly services, some religious centers have separate gatherings for healing. In a study of healing services in Episcopal congregations, Jennifer Hollis (2005) found that they take place in many different ways and include practices such as anointing with oil, laying on of hands, and prayer. These services create community around people who are ill, Hollis argues, allowing them to speak publicly about their illness and offering them sensory experiences of beauty, touch, and scent in the rituals. Participants described healing in the context of these services as emotional, spiritual, and physical, and not limited to the body. Similar kinds of rituals take place in many African American churches and in a wide range of other contexts in the contemporary United States (Jacobs 2005; Barnes and Sered 2005).

Individuals in some religious traditions also conduct rituals for healing privately with religious leaders. Some Thai Buddhist monks in the United States, for example, offer chants, amulets, and herbal remedies intended to effect magical cures. Others encourage practitioners to obtain a treatment and diagnosis plan from a physician and then work with the individual around meditation and other trainings for the mind that, in the words of one monk, make it easier to follow the doctor's instructions (Numrich 2005). Some of these actions take place in religious centers, while other rituals are brought to individuals at home or in hospital when they are ill. All of these services supplement the regular visiting and counseling that many religious leaders do with congregants (Moran *et al.* 2005).

Religious–Bio-Medical Health Linkages

In addition to working with individuals in their religious communities, some religious leaders and organizations facilitate relationships between individuals and bio-medical health programs and organizations. Individuals often seek such assistance from religious leaders, who then refer congregants to health-care providers (Daaleman and Frey 1998). Religious leaders also bring health care services to religious centers in the form of information, public health screenings, health promotion efforts, and religiously based health centers (Djupe and Westberg 1995; Chatters *et al.* 1998; 'Engaging Faith Communities' 1999). A smoking cessation program facilitated through local congregations in Baltimore, for example, proved more successful than self-help models (Voorhees *et al.* 1996). Blood pressure screenings, blood drives, and healthy eating and exercise programs also regularly take place in religious centers. A range of Christian dieting programs described by R. Marie Griffith in *Born Again Bodies: Flesh and Spirit in American Christianity* (2004) have been supported in part through local congregations.

Health efforts in African American religious communities have been the subject of particular attention (Chatters *et al.* 1998). Studies point to the importance of fostering relationships between Black churches and a wide range of physical and mental health providers (Caldwell *et al.* 1995; Adksion-Bradley *et al.* 2005). Clergy are often a first contact point for African Americans, particularly for people with mental health concerns (Neighbors *et al.* 1998). Substantial numbers of African American congregations also have programs that offer assistance with family, health, or social service needs (Taylor *et al.* 2000). The size of a congregation and the educational attainment of its clergy were found to be the most significant predictors of whether it has church-sponsored community health outreach programs (Thomas *et al.* 1994).

Parish nursing is another way in which religious organizations address public health issues. Started by Granger Westberg in the mid-1980s, parish nursing programs in Protestant and Catholic contexts attempt to combine the work of physicians, nurses, and religious leaders by providing limited health care services to people through their local congregations. The first parish nurses were employed at Lutheran General Hospital in Chicago and also began to care for people at local churches. Today parish nurses are employed or volunteer within local churches or hospitals to provide health care services ranging from routine screenings and immunizations to more involved medical follow-up and coordination. The American Nursing Association recognized parish nursing as a specialty in the late 1990s. Additional research is needed to study its history, demographics, practices, organizational models, and training in spiritual development (Solari-Twadell and McDermott 1999; Orr and May 2000; Vandecreek and Monney 2002).

Conclusions

Following the examples of Paul DiMaggio, Walter Powell, Robert Wuthnow, and other institutionally oriented sociologists, this chapter steps back from individually oriented research about religion and health to consider the institutional contexts in which questions about religion, spirituality, and health are addressed (DiMaggio and Powell 1991). Rather than continuing to focus on individuals and the extent to which religion and spirituality influence individual health and wellness, I encourage sociologists to consider how religion and spirituality are addressed in bio-medical organizations, how bio-medicine is addressed in religious organizations, and what the relationship is between these sets of organizations historically and in the present. Religious and bio-medical institutions play central roles in shaping individuals' private experiences with religion, spirituality, and health, and broader public dialogue about a range of related issues.

Methodologically, such institutionally oriented studies might start with the organizations in question, as outlined here, examining their histories, policy contexts, and the ways in which bio-medicine and religion are understood and intersect through their leadership, staff, mission statements, etc. Such studies might focus on religious or bio-medical organizations or might consider how issues related to religion and bio-medicine interact in other institutions such as public schools, childcare centers, workplaces, or social and community organizations. Alternatively, such studies might begin with individuals who themselves draw from and combine spiritual or religious and medical teachings, discourses, and beliefs. Glimpses of such relationships are evidence in ethnographic studies (e.g. R. C. Fox 1959; Rapp 1999; Kaufman 2005), but need to be interrogated to better understand the relationships that people endorse between faith in medicine or science and faith in spirituality or religion as shaped in a wide range of settings. Such studies would also investigate empirically and nuance theoretically claims about faith in medicine replacing faith in spirituality or religion in the modern era.

It is only by paying attention to the organizations and institutions in which individuals grapple with questions of spirituality, religion, health, and medicine that sociologists can enlarge their conceptual approach to this research area and the range of questions they attempt to address. Existing research about the possible effects of religion and spirituality on individual health is one piece of this puzzle, but it is not the only way of thinking about the relationships between religion, spirituality, and health. Future researchers can contribute to broader academic and public conversations by paying attention to institutions. They may thus provide helpful contextual frames for ongoing public conversations about related topics, such as health care workers' religious and moral obligations, spiritually oriented alternative medical approaches, spiritual and medical interventions at the end of life, and the extent to which individuals want their physicians and religious leaders involved in their decisions about medical care in coming decades.

References

Abdel-Aziz, E., Arch, B., and Al-Taher, H. (2004). "The Influence of Religious Beliefs on General Practitioners' Attitudes towards Termination of Pregnancy—A Pilot Study". *Journal of Obstetrics and Gynaecology*, 24: 557–61.

ADKSION-BRADLEY, C., JOHNSON, D., SANDERS, J. L., DUNCAN, L., and HOLCOMB-MCCOY, C. (2005). "Forging a Collaborative Relationship between the Black Church and the Counseling Profession". *Counseling and Values*, 49: 147–54.

AIYER, A., RUIZ, G., STEINMAN, A., and HO, G. (1999). "Influence of Physician Attitudes on Willingness to Perform Abortion". *Journal of Obstetrics and Gynaecology*, 93: 576–80.

ANGROSINO, M. (2006). *Blessed with Enough Foolishness: Pastoral Care in a Modern Hospital.* West Conshohocken, Pa.: Infinity Publishing.

ARMBRUSTER, C. A., CHIBNALL, J. T., and LEGETT, S. (2003). "Pediatrician Beliefs about Spirituality and Religion in Medicine: Associations with Clinical Practice". *Pediatrics*, 111: 227–35.

Association of Professional Chaplains, Association for Clinical Pastoral Education, Canadian Association for Pastoral Practice and Education, National Association of Catholic Chaplains, and National Association of Jewish Chaplains (2001). "A White Paper. Professional Chaplaincy: Its Role and Importance in Healthcare". *Journal of Pastoral Care*, 55: 81–97.

BARNES, L. L. (2006). "A Medical School Curriculum on Religion and Healing". In L. L. Barnes and I. M. Talamantez (eds.), *Teaching Religion and Healing.* New York: Oxford University Press, 307–25.

—— and SERED, S. S. (eds.) (2005). *Religion and Healing in America.* New York: Oxford University Press.

BARROWS, D. C. (1993). *"A Whole Different Thing"—The Hospital Chaplaincy: The Emergence of the Occupation and the Work of the Chaplain* (unpublished dissertation, University of California, San Francisco).

BASSETT, S. D. (1976). *Public Religious Services in the Hospital.* Springfield, Ill.: Charles C. Thomas.

BRITTAIN, J. N., and BOOZER, J. (1987). "Spiritual Care: Integration into a Collegiate Nursing Curriculum". *Journal of Nursing Education*, 26: 155–60.

BRYANT, C. (1993). "Role Clarification: A Quality Improvement Survey of Hospital Chaplain Customers". *Journal for Healthcare Quality*, 15: 18–20.

CADGE, W., and CATLIN, E. A. (2006). "Making Sense of Suffering and Death: How Health Care Providers Construct Meanings in a Neonatal Intensive Care Unit". *Journal of Religion and Health*, 45: 248–63.

—— and DILLINGER, J. (2007). "The Content and Function of Hospital Chapels: An Overview". Working Paper, Department of Sociology, Brandeis University.

—— with FREESE, J., and CHRISTAKIS, N. (2008). "Hospital Chaplaincy in the United States: A National Overview". *Southern Medical Journal*, 101(6): 626–30.

CAITLIN, E. A., GUILLEMIN, J. H., THIEL, M. M., HAMMOND, S., WANG, M., and O'DONNELL, J. (2001). "Spiritual and Religious Components of Patient Care in the Neonatal Intensive Care Unit: Sacred Themes in a Secular Setting". *Journal of Perinatology*, 21: 426–30.

CALDWELL, C. H., CHATTERS, L. M., and BILLINGSLEY, A. T. R. J. (1995). "Church-Based Support Programs for Elderly Black Adults: Congregational and Clergy Statistics". In M. Kimble, S. H. McFadden, J. W. Ellor, and J. J. Seeber (eds.), *Aging, Spirituality and Religion.* Minneapolis: Fortress Press, 306–24.

CAREY, R. G. (1973). "Chaplaincy: Component of Total Patient Care?" *Hospitals: The Journal of the American Hospital Association*, 47: 166–72.

Carson, V. B., and Koenig, H. G. (eds.) (2004). *Spiritual Caregiving: Healthcare as a Ministry.* Philadelphia: Templeton Foundation Press.

Cavendish, R., Luise, B. K., Russo, D., Mitzeliotis, C., Bauer, M., Bajo, M. A. M., Calvino, C. H. K., and Medefindt, J. (2004). "Spiritual Perspectives of Nurses in the United States Relevant for Education and Practice". *Western Journal of Nursing Research,* 26: 196–212.

Chambers, N., and Curtis, J. R. (2001). "The Interface of Technology and Spirituality in the ICU". In J. R. Curtis and G. D. Rubenfeld (eds.), *Managing Death in the ICU: The Transition from Cure to Comfort.* New York: Oxford University Press, 193–205.

Chatters, L. M. (2000). "Religion and Health: Public Health Research and Practice". *Annual Review of Public Health,* 21: 335–67.

—— Levin, J. S., and Ellison, C. G. (1998). "Public Health and Health Education in Faith Communities". *Health Education & Behavior,* 25: 689–99.

Chibnall, J. T., and Brooks, C. A. (2001). "Religion in the Clinic: The Role of Physician Beliefs". *Southern Medical Journal,* 94: 374–9.

Christakis, N. A., and Asch, D. A. (1995). "Physician Characteristics Associated with Decisions to Withdraw Life Support". *American Journal of Public Health,* 85: 367–72.

Clark, P. A., Drain, M., and Malone, M. P. (2003). "Addressing Patients' Emotional and Spiritual Needs". *Joint Commission Journal on Quality and Safety,* 29: 659–70.

Coburn, C. K., and Smith, M. (1999). *Spirited Lives: How Nuns Shaped Catholic Culture and American Life, 1836–1920.* Chapel Hill, NC: University of North Carolina Press.

Curlin, F. A., Lantos, J. D., Roach, C. J., Sellergren, S. A., and Chin, M. H. (2005*a*). "Religious Characteristics of U.S. Physicians". *Journal of General Internal Medicine,* 20: 629–34.

—— Lawrence, R. E., Chin, M. H., and Lantos, J. (2007). "Religion, Conscience, and Controversial Clinical Practices". *New England Journal of Medicine,* 356: 593–600.

—— Roach, C., Gorawara-Bhat, R., Lantos, J. D., and Chin, M. H. (2005*b*). "When Patients Choose Faith over Medicine: Physician Perspectives on Religiously Related Conflict in the Medical Encounter". *Archives of Internal Medicine,* 165: 88–91.

—— —— —— —— —— (2005*c*). "How are Religion and Spirituality Related to Health? A Study of Physicians' Perspectives". *Southern Medical Journal,* 98: 761–6.

Daaleman, T. P., and Frey, B. (1998). "Prevalence and Patterns of Physician Referral to Clergy and Pastoral Care". *Archives of Family Medicine,* 7: 548–53.

—— and Nease, D. (1994). "Patient Attitudes Regarding Physician Inquiry into Spiritual and Religious Issues". *Journal of Family Practice,* 39: 564–8.

DesAutels, P., Battin, M. P., and May, L. (1999). *Praying for a Cure: When Medical and Religious Practices Conflict.* New York: Rowman & Littlefield Publishers, Inc.

DiMaggio, P., and Powell, W. (1991). "The Iron Cage Revisited: Institutional Isomorphism and Collective Rationality in Organizational Fields". In *eadem* (eds.), *The New Institutionalism in Organizational Analysis.* Chicago: University of Chicago Press, 63–82.

Djupe, A. M., and Westberg, G. (1995). "Congregation-Based Health Programs". In M. Kimble, S. H. McFadden, J. W. Ellor, and J. J. Seeber (eds.), *Aging, Spirituality and Religion.* Minneapolis: Fortress Pres, 325–34.

Ehman, J. W., Ott, B. B., Short, T. H., Ciampa, R. C., and Hansen-Flaschen, J. (1999). "Do Patients Want Physicians to Inquire about their Spiritual or Religious Beliefs if they Become Gravely Ill?" *Archives of Internal Medicine,* 159: 1803–6.

EMBLEN, J. D., and HALSTEAD, L. (1993). "Spiritual Needs and Interventions: Comparing the Views of Patients, Nurses and Chaplains". *Clinical Nurse Specialist*, 7: 175–82.

"Engaging Faith Communities as Partners in Improving Community Health" (1999). Centers for Disease Control and Prevention, Public Health Practice Program Office.

FLANNELLY, K. J., HANDZO, G. F., and WEAVER, A. J. (2004). "Factors Affecting Healthcare Chaplaincy and the Provision of Pastoral Care in the United States". *Journal of Pastoral Care & Counseling*, 58/1–2: 127–30.

—— —— —— and SMITH, W. J. (2005). "A National Survey of Health Care Administrators' Views on the Importance of Various Chaplain Roles". *Journal of Pastoral Care & Counseling*, 59: 87–96.

—— WEAVER, A., and HANDZO, G. (2003). "A Three-Year Study of Chaplains' Professional Activities at Memorical Sloan-Kettering Cancer Center in New York City". *Psychooncology*, 12: 760–80.

FOGG, S. L., WEAVER, A. J., FLANNELLY, K. J., and HANDZO, G. F. (2004). "An Analysis of Referrals to Chaplains in a Community Hospital in New York Over a Seven-Year Period". *Journal of Pastoral Care and Counseling*, 58: 225–35.

FOX, R. (1988). "The Human Condition of Health Professionals". In *idem* (ed.), *Essays in Medical Sociology: Journeys into the Field.* New Brunswick, NJ: Transaction Books, 572–87.

FOX, R. C. (1959). *Experiment Perilous: Physicians and Patients Facing the Unknown.* Glencoe, Ill.: Free Press.

GARCES-FOLEY, K. (2003). "Buddhism, Hospice, and the American Way of Dying". *Review of Religious Research*, 44: 341–53.

GEVITZ, N. (ed.) (1988). *Other Healers: Unorthodox Medicine in America.* Baltimore: Johns Hopkins University Press.

GRANT, D. (2004). "Spiritual Interventions: Why, How, and When Nurses Use Them". *Holistic Nursing Practice*, 18: 36–41.

—— O'NEIL, K., and STEPHENS, L. (2004). "Spirituality in the Workplace: New Empirical Directions in the Study of the Sacred". *Sociology of Religion*, 65: 265–83.

GRAVES, D. L., SHUE, C. K., and ARNOLD, L. (2002). "The Role of Spirituality in Patient Care: Incorporating Spirituality Training into the Medical School Curriculum". *Academic Medicine*, 77: 1167.

GRIFFITH, R. M. (2004). *Born Again Bodies: Flesh and Spirit in American Christianity.* Berkeley: University of California Press.

GROER, M. W., O'CONNOR, B., and DROPPLEMAN, P. (1996). "A Course in Health Care Spirituality". *Journal of Nursing Education*, 35: 375–81.

HALL, C. (1992). *Head and Heart: The Story of the Clinical Pastoral Education Movement.* Decatur, Ga.: Journal of Pastoral Care Publications.

HODGE, D. R. (2006). "A Template for Spiritual Assessment: A Review of the JCAHO Requirements and Guidelines for Implementation". *Social Work*, 51/4: 317–26.

HOLLIS, J. L. (2005). "Healing into Wholeness in the Episcopal Church". In Barnes and Sered (2005), 89–102.

HUFFORD, D. (1988). "Contemporary Folk Medicine". In Gevitz (1988), 228–64.

IMBER, J. B. (1986). *Abortion and the Private Practice of Medicine.* New Haven: Yale University Press.

JACOBS, C. F. (2005). "Rituals of Healing in African American Spiritual Churches". In Barnes and Sered (2005), 333–41.

Joyce, K. M. (2002). "The Evil of Abortion and the Greater Good of the Faith: Negotiating Catholic Survival in the Twentieth-Century American Health Care System". *Religion and American Culture: A Journal of Interpretation*, 12/1: 91–121.

Kauffman, C. J. (1995). *Ministry and Meaning: A Religious History of Catholic Health Care in the United States.* New York: Crossroad.

Kaufman, S. R. (2005). *And a Time to Die: How American Hospitals Shape the End of Life.* New York: Scribner.

Kelly, M., Olive, K., Harvill, L., and Maddry, H. (1996). "Spiritual and Religious Issues in Clinical Care: An Elective Course for Medical Students". *Annals of Behavioral Science and Medical Education*, 4: 29–35.

Koenig, H. G., Bearon, L. B. and Dayringer, R. (1989). "Physician Perspectives on the Role of Religion in the Physician–Older Person Patient Relationship". *Journal of Family Practice*, 28: 441–8.

—— —— and Hover, M. (1991). "Religious Perspectives of Doctors, Nurses, Patients and Families". *Journal of Pastoral Care*, 45: 254–67.

—— McCullough, M. E., and Larson, D. B. (eds.) (2001). *Handbook of Religion and Health.* New York: Oxford University Press.

LaPierre, L. I. (2003). "JCAHO Safeguards Spiritual Care". *Holistic Nurse Practitioner*, 17: 219.

Lazarus, B. (1991). "The Practice of Medicine and Prejudice in a New England Town: The Founding of Mount Sinai Hospital, Hartford, Connecticut". *Journal of American Ethnic History*, 10: 21–42.

Lee, S. J. C. (2002). "In a Secular Spirit: Strategies of Clinical Pastoral Education". *Health Care Analysis*, 10: 339–56.

Lemmer, S. C. (2002). "Teaching the Spiritual Dimension of Nursing Care: A Survey of U.S. Baccalaureate Nursing Programs". *Journal of Nursing Education*, 41: 482–90.

Levin, J. S., Larson, D. B., and Puchalski, C. M. (1997). "Religion and Spirituality in Medicine: Research and Education". *Journal of the American Medical Association*, 278: 782–93.

Levitan, T. (1964). *Islands of Compassion: A History of the Jewish Hospitals of New York.* New York: Twayne Publishers, Inc.

Linenthal, A. J. (1990). *First a Dream: The History of Boston's Jewish Hospitals: 1896–1928.* Boston: Beth Israel Hospital in association with the Francis A. Countway Library of Medicine.

Luckhaupt, S., Yi, M., Mueller, C., Mrus, J., Peterman, A., Puchalski, C., and Tsevat, J. (2005). "Beliefs of Primary Care Residents Regarding Spirituality and Religion in Clinical Encounters with Patients: A Study at a Midwestern U.S. Teaching Institution". *Academic Medicine*, 80: 560–70.

MacLean, C., Susi, Beth, Phifer, N., Schultz, L., Bynum, D., Franco, M., Klioze, A., Monroe, M., Garrett, J., and Cyert, S. (2003). "Patient Preference for Physician Discussion and Practice of Spirituality". *Journal of General Internal Medicine*, 18: 38–43.

Maugans, T. A. (1996). "The Spiritual History". *Archives of Family Medicine*, 5: 11–16.

McCauley, B. (2005). *Who Shall Take Care of Our Sick? Roman Catholic Sisters and the Development of Catholic Hospitals in New York City.* Baltimore: Johns Hopkins University Press.

McEwen, M. (2004). "Analysis of Spirituality Content in Nursing Textbooks". *Journal of Nursing Education*, 43: 20–30.

McGuire, M. B. (1988). *Ritual Healing in Suburban America.* New Brunswick, NJ: Rutgers University Press.

McSherry, E., and Nelson, W. A. (1987). "The DRG Era: A Major Opportunity for Increased Pastoral Care Impact or a Crisis for Survival". *Journal of Pastoral Care,* 41: 201–11.

Messikomer, C. M., and De Craemer, W. (2002). "The Spirituality of Academic Physicians: An Ethnography of a Scripture-Based Group in an Academic Medical Center". *Academic Medicine,* 77: 562–73.

Mollat, M. (1986). *The Poor in the Middle Ages: An Essay in Social History,* trans. Arthur Goldhammer. New Haven: Yale University Press.

Moran, M., Flannelly, K. J., Weaver, A. J., Overvold, J. A., Hess, W., and Wilson, J. C. (2005). "A Study of Pastoral Care, Referral, and Consultation Practices among Clergy in Four Settings in the New York City Area". *Pastoral Psychology,* 53: 253–64.

Neighbors, H. W., Musick, M. A., and Williams, D. R. (1998). "The African American Minister as a Source of Help for Serious Personal Crises: Bridge or Barrier to Mental Health Care?" *Health Education and Behavior,* 25: 759–77.

Nelson, S. (2001). *Say Little, Do Much: Nurses, Nuns and Hospitals in the Nineteenth Century.* Philadelphia: University of Pennsylvania Press.

Numbers, R. L. (1992). *Prophetess of Health: Ellen G. White and the Origins of Seventh-Day Adventist Health Reform.* Knoxville, Tenn.: University of Tennessee Press.

—— and Amundsen, D. (1986). *Caring and Curing: Health and Medicine in the Western Religious Traditions.* Baltimore: Johns Hopkins University Press.

—— and Sawyer, R. C. (1982). "Medicine and Christianity in the Modern World". In M. E. Marty and K. L. Vaux (eds.), *Health/Medicine and the Faith Traditions.* Philadelphia: Fortress, 133–60.

Numrich, P. D. (2005). "Complementary and Alternative Medicine in America's 'Two Buddhisms'". In Barnes and Sered (2005), 343–58.

O'Donnell, T. J. (1970). "Medicine and Religion: An Overview". *Journal of the American Medical Association,* 211: 815–17.

Orr, J., and May, S. (2000). *Religion and Health Services in Los Angeles: Reconfiguring the Terrain.* Los Angeles: USC Center for Religion and Civic Culture.

Parkum, K. H. (1985). "The Impact of Chaplaincy Services in Selected Hospitals in the Eastern United States". *Journal of Pastoral Care,* 39: 262–9.

Porter, R. (1993). "Religion and Medicine". In W. F. Bynum and R. Porter (eds.), *Companion Encyclopedia of the History of Medicine.* New York: Routledge, 1449–68.

Porterfield, A. (2005). *Healing in the History of Christianity.* New York: Oxford University Press.

Post, S., Puchalski, C., and Larson, D. B. (2000). "Physicians and Patient Spirituality: Professional Boundaries, Competency, and Ethics". *Annals of Internal Medicine,* 132: 578–83.

Prince, T. R. (1994). "Assessing Catholic Community Hospitals versus Nonprofit Community Hospitals, 1989–1992". *Health Care Management Review,* 19: 25–37.

Puchalski, C., and Larson, D. (1998). "Developing Curricula in Spirituality and Medicine". *Academic Medicine,* 73: 970–4.

Rapp, R. (1999). *Testing Women, Testing the Fetus: The Social Impact of Amniocentesis in America.* New York: Routledge.

Reverby, S. M. (1987). *Ordered to Care: The Dilemma of American Nursing, 1850–1945.* Cambridge: Cambridge University Press.

Rhoads, P. (1967). "Medicine and Religion: A New Journal Department". *Journal of the American Medical Association,* 200: 172.

Risse, G. B. (1999). *Mending Bodies, Saving Souls: A History of Hospitals.* New York: Oxford University Press.

Rodrigues, B., Rodrigues, D., and Casy, D. L. (2000). *Spiritual Needs & Chaplaincy Services: A National Empirical Study on Chaplaincy Encounters in Health Care Settings.* Medford, Oreg.: Providence Health System.

Rosenberg, C. E. (1987). *The Care of Strangers: The Rise of America's Hospital System.* New York: Basic Books.

Rosner, F. (2001). "Religion and Medicine". *Archives of Internal Medicine,* 161/15: 1811–12.

Ross, L. (2006). "Spiritual Care in Nursing: An Overview of the Research to Date". *Journal of Clinical Nursing,* 15: 852–62.

Ruggie, M. (2004). *Marginal to Mainstream: Alternative Medicine in America.* Cambridge: Cambridge University Press.

Sakurai, M. L. (2005). "Ministry of Presence: Naming What Chaplains Do at the Bedside". (unpublished dissertation, San Francisco Theological Seminary).

Sarna, J. D. (1987). "The Impact of Nineteenth-Century Christian Missions on American Jews". In T. M. Endelman (ed.), *Jewish Apostasy in the Modern World.* New York: Holmes and Meier Publishers, 232–54.

Sherkat, D., and Ellison, C. (1999). "Recent Developments and Current Controversies in the Sociology of Religion". *Annual Review of Sociology,* 25: 363–94.

Siegel, B., Tenenbaum, A. J., Jamanka, A., Barnes, L., Hubbard, C., and Zuckerman, B. (2002). "Faculty and Resident Attitudes about Spirituality and Religion in the Provision of Pediatric Health Care". *Ambulatory Pediatrics,* 2: 5–10.

Solari-Twadell, P. A., and McDermott, M. A. (1999). *Parish Nursing: Promoting Whole Person Health within Faith Communities.* Thousand Oaks, Calif.: Sage Publications.

Starr, P. L. (1982). *The Social Transformation of American Medicine.* New York: Basic Books.

Staten, P. (2003). "Spiritual Assessment Required in All Settings". *Hospital Peer Review,* 28/4: 55–6.

Stevens, R. (1989). *In Sickness and in Wealth: American Hospitals in the Twentieth Century.* Baltimore: Johns Hopkins University Press.

Taylor, R. J., Ellison, C. G., Chatters, L. M., Levin, J. S., and Lincoln, K. D. (2000). "Mental Health Services in Faith Communities: The Role of Clergy in Black Churches". *Social Work,* 45: 73–87.

Thiel, M. M., and Robinson, M. R. (1997). "Physicians' Collaborations with Chaplains: Difficulties and Benefits". *Journal of Clinical Ethics,* 8: 94–103.

Thomas, S., Quinn, S., Billingsley, A., and Caldwell, C. (1994). "The Characteristics of Northern Black Churches with Community Health Outreach Programs". *American Journal of Public Health,* 84: 575–9.

Todres, I. D., Catlin, E. A., and Thiel, M. M. (2005). "The Intensivist in a Spiritual Care Training Program Adapted for Clinicians". *Critical Care Medicine,* 33: 2733–6.

Turner, B. S. (1987). *Medical Power and Social Knowledge.* London: Sage Publications.

Uttley, L. J. (2000). "How Merging Religious and Secular Hospitals Can Threaten Health Care Services". *Social Policy,* 30/4: 4–13.

VANDECREEK, L., and CONNELL, L. (1991). "Evaluation of the Hospital Chaplain's Pastoral Care: Catholic and Protestant Differences". *Journal of Pastoral Care*, 45/3: 289–95.

—— and LYON, M. A. (1995). "The General Hospital Chaplain's Ministry: Analysis of Productivity, Quality and Cost". *Caregiver Journal*, 11: 3–10.

—— —— (1997). *Ministry of Hospital Chaplains: Patient Satisfaction*. New York: Haworth Press.

—— and MONNEY, S. E. (2002). *Parish Nurses, Health Care Chaplains, and Community Clergy: Navigating the Maze of Professional Relationships*. New York: Haworth Press.

—— SIEGEL, K., GOREY, E., BROWN, S., and TOPERZER, R. (2001). "How Many Chaplains per 100 Inpatients? Benchmarks of Health Care Chaplaincy Departments". *Journal of Pastoral Care*, 55: 289–301.

VAN DER GEEST, S. (2005). " 'Sacraments' in the Hospital: Exploring the Magic and Religion of Recovery". *Anthropology & Medicine*, 12: 135–50.

—— and FINKLER, K. (2004). "Hospital Ethnography: Introduction". *Social Science & Medicine*, 59: 1995–2001.

VOGEL, M. J. (1980). *The Invention of the Modern Hospital: Boston 1870–1930*. Chicago: University of Chicago Press.

VOORHEES, C. C., STILLMAN, F. A., SWANK, R. T., HEAGERTY, P. J., LEVINE, D. M., and BAKER, D. M. (1996). "Heart, Body, and Soul: Impact of Church-Based Smoking Cessation Interventions on Readiness to Quit". *Preventative Medicine*, 25: 277–85.

WEAVER, A. J., KOENIG, H. G., FLANNELLY, K. J., and SMITH, F. D. (2004). "A Review of Research on Chaplains and Community-Based Clergy in the *Journal of the American Medical Association*, *Lancet*, and the *New England Journal of Medicine*: 1998–2000". *Journal of Pastoral Care & Counseling*, 58: 343–50.

WHITE, K. R. (2000). "Hospitals Sponsored by the Roman Catholic Church: Separate, Equal, and Distinct?" *Milbank Quarterly*, 78/2: 213.

—— and BEGUN, J. W. (1998–9). "How Does Catholic Sponsorship Affect Services Provided?" *Inquiry*, 35: 398–407.

—— —— and TIAN, W. (2006). "Hospital Service Offerings: Does Catholic Ownership Matter?" *Health Care Management Review*, 31: 99–108.

WHITE, L. (2003). "Federal Funding Preserved for CPE Programs". *ACPE Webpage*.

WILSON, K., LIPSCOMB, L. D., WARD, K., REPLOGLE, W. H., and HILL, K. (2000). "Prayer in Medicine: A Survey of Primary Care Physicians". *Journal of the Mississippi State Medical Association*, 41: 817–22.

WOLF, Z. R. (1988). *Nurses' Work, the Sacred and the Profane*. Philadelphia: University of Pennsylvania Press.

SUGGESTED READING

The following are recommended: Angrosino (2006); Barnes and Sered (2005); Chatters (2000); Chatters, Levin, and Ellison (1998); and Rosenberg (1987).

CHAPTER 47

THE ROLE OF RELIGIOUS INSTITUTIONS IN RESPONDING TO CRIME AND DELINQUENCY

BYRON R. JOHNSON

INTRODUCTION

There is no shortage of academic scholarship addressing the various dimensions and consequences of crime and delinquency. To state that crime is an important topic closely monitored and debated by government officials, decision-makers, and the public at large would be a gross understatement. It comes as no surprise, therefore, that the latest trends in criminal activity, as well as efforts to control crime, remain a top priority for scholars and politicians alike. At the same time, evidenced-based approaches to government have gained wide support in recent years even among political foes. Thus, increasing importance is obviously being attached to scientific evaluations and ongoing research of best practices in confronting social problems like crime, gang violence, teen drug abuse, or post-release recidivism rates for former prisoners.

In a similar vein, there is no shortage of research on the topics of religion, spirituality, religious practices, and belief. Though most of this research quite naturally focuses on samples of Christian populations, this is does not mean that other religions are irrelevant to these discussions. Indeed, in years to come it is hoped that we will begin to compare and contrast the relative efficacy of interventions by different religious groups, traditions, and faith communities. However, this chapter largely focuses on the extant research which happens to be based largely on Christian samples. Beyond the many historical, theological, or philosophical studies of religion, in recent years there has been a great deal of interest in the role of religious institutions and faith-based organizations in confronting social ills and in the provision of social services to those most in need in contemporary society. From studies of social capital to spiritual capital, scholars are interested in understanding how religion may be linked, if at all, to civic engagement, volunteerism, and altruistic behavior more generally.

In light of the fact that crime and religion receive so much independent attention from the academic community as well as the popular media, it is an interesting observation that we do not have an extensive or well-developed research literature that addresses the relationship of religion to crime, or vice versa, though this would seem like a natural line of inquiry for social scientists who have begun to address the religion–crime nexus in meaningful way over the last several decades. This is an unfortunate oversight, because, as we shall see shortly, the religiosity–crime relationship is a robust and important one that carries with it considerable implications at both the theoretical and the public policy levels.

In order to understand better the past, present, and future role of religion and religious institutions in addressing matters related to crime, delinquency, offender treatment, rehabilitation programs, and even the transition of prisoners back into society, this chapter reviews the existing literature in a systematic fashion that will make it possible to assess the benefit or harm that religious influences may bring to each of these important areas. It therefore examines and summarizes the current state of our knowledge regarding the relationship between religion and crime, as well as the current and potential role of religion and religious institutions in crime reduction, offender rehabilitation, and offender aftercare.

Examining the Relationship between Religion and Crime: A Systematic Review of the Literature

Over the last five or six decades there has been an interest in discovering if religion decreases, increases, or has no relationship to criminal behavior. Contemporary research on the religion–crime nexus can be traced to Hirschi and Stark's classic "Hellfire and Delinquency" study (1969). Hirschi and Stark surprised many when they discovered that no relationship existed between levels of religious commitment among youth and measures of delinquency. Subsequent replications both supported (Burkett and White 1974) and refuted (Albrecht *et al.* 1977; Higgins and Albrecht 1977; Jensen and Erickson 1979) Hirschi and Stark's original finding. Stark and colleagues later suggested that these contradictory findings were the result of the moral makeup of the community being studied. Stark, Kent, and Doyle (1982) suggested that areas with high church membership and attendance rates represented "moral communities", while areas with low church membership typified "secularized communities". Stark's moral communities hypothesis, therefore, predicted an inverse relationship between religiosity and delinquency in moral communities as well as the expectation that there will be little or no effect of religiosity on individuals in secularized communities. This theoretical perspective provided an important framework for understanding why some studies of delinquency had yielded an inverse relationship between religious commitment measures and delinquency, while others failed to generate the inverse relationship (Stark 1996; Stark *et al.* 1982).

Empirical evidence suggests that the effects of religiosity remain significant even in communities typified by decay, poverty, disadvantage, and disorganization (Freeman 1986; Jang and Johnson 2001; Johnson *et al.* 2000*a*; 2000*b*). For example, I and my colleagues (2000*b*) found that individual religiosity helped at-risk youths such as those living in poor inner-city areas (e.g., Boston, Chicago, and Philadelphia) to escape from drug use and other illegal activities. Further, results from a series of multi-level analyses indicate that church attendance (the frequency of attending religious services) has significant inverse effects on illegal activities, drug use, and drug selling among disadvantaged youths (Johnson *et al.* 2000*a*).

There is also increasing evidence that religious involvement may lower the risks of a broad range of delinquent behaviors, including both minor and serious forms of criminal behavior (Evans *et al.* 1996). Aided by a steady stream of important delinquency studies and several systematic reviews of this literature, it has become increasingly clear that the relevant literature may not be inconclusive, as some scholars continue to assert (Baier and Wright 2001; Johnson *et al.* 2000*c*; Johnson 2002). In a meta-analysis of forty studies that focus on the relationship between religion and delinquency, I and my colleagues (2000*c*) found that most of these studies reported an inverse relationship between measures of religiosity and delinquency. Several studies found no relationship or were inconclusive, and only one found a positive link between greater religiosity and increasing delinquency. Interestingly, they found among those studies with the most sophisticated research design, the stronger the likelihood that increasing religiosity is linked to decreases in delinquency. Conversely, those studies reporting inconclusive results tended to be less methodologically rigorous. In a second meta-analysis, Baier and Wright (2001) reviewed sixty studies in the religiosity–delinquency literature and reached much the same conclusion as the previous study by me and my colleagues (2000*c*). They found that studies using larger and more representative datasets are more likely to find significant inverse effects (i.e., increasing religiosity and decreasing delinquency) than studies that utilize smaller, regional, or convenient samples. In a third meta-analysis, I (Johnson 2002) reviewed studies examining religion and multiple outcome areas including several that are relevant to our current discussion (i.e., alcohol abuse, drug use/abuse, and crime/delinquency). Among the ninety-seven alcohol studies reviewed, only two found religiosity to be associated with deleterious outcomes. Another ten studies reported inconclusive findings, while eighty-five studies found an inverse relationship, indicating that increasing religiosity was associated with a lowered likelihood of alcohol abuse. I also found a similar pattern among the fifty-four studies reviewed examining drug use or abuse. Fifty of those studies found increasing religiousness linked to decreasing drug use or abuse, while only one study found a positive relationship. Finally, I reviewed another forty-six studies within the crime and delinquency literature that examined the influence of religion, and the same trend was obvious—increasing religiosity was associated with lowered likelihood of criminal or delinquent behavior (thirty-seven studies), while religiosity was positively related to delinquency in only one study.

In sum, these meta-analyses confirm the consistent and mounting evidence that suggests that heightened religious commitment or involvement helps protect youth from delinquent behavior and deviant activities. Simply stated, these three reviews or meta-analyses document that increasing religiosity is associated with a lowered likelihood of committing delinquent or criminal acts. But are these research findings consistent with the more recent research literature on religion and crime? In order to answer this question, I report findings from a new systematic review of the relevant research literature on religion and crime.

This comprehensive review covers studies published between 1944 and 2007, with a majority of these published over the last several decades. In this systematic review, I examine the type of study (e.g., cross-sectional, prospective cohort, retrospective, clinical trial, experimental, case control, descriptive, case report, or qualitative), the sampling method (e.g., random, probability, systematic sampling, convenience/purposive sample), the number of subjects in the sample population (e.g., children, adolescents, highschool students, college students, community-dwelling adults, elderly, church members, religious or clergy, gender, and race), location, religious variables included in the analysis (e.g., religious attendance, scripture study, subjective religiosity, religious commitment, intrinsic religiosity, extrinsic religiosity, etc.), controls, and findings (e.g., no association, mixed evidence, beneficial association with outcome, or harmful association with outcome).

In total, 109 studies were reviewed, and the results of this current review confirm that the vast majority of the studies report a beneficial relationship between measures of religion or religious commitment and various crime and delinquency measures or outcomes. As can be seen in Table 49.1, approximately 89 percent of the studies (97/109) find an inverse or beneficial relationship between religion and some measure of crime or delinquency (i.e., increasing religiosity is associated with lower crime/delinquency). Only eleven studies found no association or reported mixed findings, and only one study from this exhaustive literature review found that religion was associated with a harmful outcome.

Researchers over the last several decades have made steady contributions to this emerging religiosity–crime literature; yet, until recently, there was a lack of consensus about the nature of this relationship between religion and crime. Stated differently, in studies utilizing vastly different methods, samples, and research designs, increasing religiosity (religiousness, religious activities, or participation) is consistently linked with decreases in various measures of crime or delinquency. These findings are particularly pronounced among the more methodologically and statistically sophisticated studies that rely upon nationally representative samples (Johnson *et al.* 2000*c*). Religion is a robust variable that tends to be associated with the lowered likelihood of crime or delinquency or recidivism and, as such, should no longer be overlooked by criminologists or social scientists. In fact, failure to consider religion variables will cause researchers to be needlessly shortsighted in estimating models designed to explain its direct and indirect influences on crime and delinquency.

How and Why Religion Matters: Protective Factors and Pro-social Behavior

As we have seen from the current systematic review of the research literature, there is clear and compelling empirical evidence that religious commitment is linked with crime and delinquency reduction.[1] In short, we know that religion matters;

[1] See Koenig *et al.* 2001 and Johnson 2002 for a systematic review of the research literature documenting the protective role of religion in depression, suicide, mortality, promiscuous sex, alcohol abuse, and drug use/abuse.

Table 49.1. A Systematic Review of the Religion and Crime Literature

Investigators	Type	Method	N	Population	Location	Religious Variable	Control	Findings
Albrecht (1977)	CS	C	244	Mormon teenagers	Utah, Idaho, LA	SR, ORA	MC	B
Allen (1967)	CS	S	179	M (16–18) B, W	HS & youth fac.	D, ORA, SR	MC	B
Avtar (1979)	CS	C	54/59	CA/HS	Ottawa, Can	SR	N	B
Bainbridge (1989)								
Barrett (1988)	PC	S	326	Mex-Am clients	Texas	ORA	MC	B
Benda (1995)	CS	S	> 1,000	HS	Arkansas & MD	ORA, SR	MC	B
Benda (1997)	CS	S	724	HS (9th–12th graders)	Arkansas & OK	ORA, SR	MC	B
Benda (1997b)	CS	R	1,093	HS	5 US cities	ORA, SR	MC	B
Benda (2002)	CS	C	326	M (15–24) R, B	Arkansas	SR	SC	B
Benson P (1989)	CS	R	> 12,000	HS	National US	SR	MC	B
Burkett (1974)	CS	C	855	HS	Pacific NW US	ORA	SC	B
Burkett (1993)	CS	R	612 & 428	HS	Pacific NW US	Pot smoking is sin	MC	B
Carr-Saunders (1944)	CC	C	276 vs. 551	Delinquents	London, England	ORA	N	B
Chadwick (1993)	CS	R	2,143	Ad (Mormons)	Eastern US	ORA	MC	B
Clear (2002)	PC	S	769	M, Prisoners	DE, TX, IN, MS	SR, D	SC	B
Cochran (1989)	CS	R	3,065	Ad	Midwest US	ORA, SR, D	MC	B
Cochran (1991)	CS	R	3,065	Ad	Midwest US	ORA, SR, D	MC	B
Cochran (1994)	CS	C	1,600	HS	Oklahoma	ORA, SR	MC	NA
Cohen (1987)	PC	S	976	Mothers/caretakers	New York	ORA	MC	B
Cretacci (2003)	CS	R	6,500	Ad, youth	National	SR, ORA, RCm, D	MC	B
Dennis (2005)	Q	SCD	1,725	(15–21) 79% W	National	SR	SC	B
Dudley (1987)	CS	R	801	SDA Youth	National	ORA, NORA, CM	SC	B

Elifson (1983)	CS	R	600	Ad, public HS	Atlanta, GA	RB, SR, NORA	SC	NA
Ellison (1999)					National US	ORA	MC	B
Ellison (2001)					National US	ORA	MC	B
Ellison (2007)	CS	P	3,144/3,666	M, W	National US	ORA	MC	B
Ellis (????)	P	C	11,000	CS, R	US & Canada	D		B
Ellis (1995)	CS	R	17,226	CDA	Industrial nation	16 variables		B
Engs (1999)	CS	C	4,150/3,117	CS help professions	Scotland	D, SR	N	B
Evans (1995)	CS	S	477	CDA, 100% W	Midwest US	OR, SR, RB, D	MC	B
Evans (1996)	CS	R	263	HS	Midwest City	ORA, SR, peer RC	SC	B
Fernquist (1995)	CS	–	180	CS	–	ORA, NORA	N	B
Forliti (1986)	CS	C	8,165/10,467	Ad/parents, CM	United States	RB, ORA, SR	NS	B
Free (1994)	CS	C	916	College	SW & Midwest	ORA, SR	N	B
Freeman (1986)	CS	R/R	2,358/4,961	Young BM/WM	Boston, Chi, Phil	ORA	MC	B
Grasmick (1991)	CS	R	304	CDA	Oklahoma City	D, ORA, SR	SC	B
Grasmick (1991)	CS	R	285	Adults	Oklahoma City	D, SR	MC	B
Hadaway (1984)	CS	R	600	AD, HS, W, F	Atlanta	ORA, SR, NORA, O	SC	B
Hardert (1994)	CS	C	1,234	HS, CS	Arizona	ORA, SR	MC	B
Hardesty (1995)	CS	C	475	HS, CS (16–19)	Midwest US	Family religiosity	SC	B
Hater (1984)	CS	S	1,174	PP (opiate addicts)	National US	ORA, SR	MC	NA
Hercik (2004)	PC	C	413	Prisoners	Florida	Religious Program	MC	B
Higgins (1977)	CS	R	1,410	HS (10th grade)	Atlanta, GA	ORA	SC	B
Hirschi (1969)	CS	R	4,077	HS	Northern CA	ORA	N	NA

(continued)

Table 49.1. (continued)

Investigators	Type	Method	N	Population	Location	Religious Variable	Control	Findings
Jang (2001)	PC	R	1,087	Youth (13–22)	National US	ORA, SR	MC	B
Jang (2003)	CS	R	2,107	BM/BF	National US	ORA, NORA, SR	MC	B
Jang (2004)	CS	R	2,107	BM/BF	National US	ORA, NORA, SR	MC	B
Jang (2005)	CS	R	2,107	BM/BF	National US	ORA, NORA, SR	MC	B
Jang (2007)								
Johnson B (1987)	RS	S	782	Former prisoners	Florida	ORA, SR	MC	NA
Johnson B (1997)	CC	S	201 vs. 201	Prisoners/X prisoners	New York	ORA, NORA	MC	B
Johnson B (2000)	CS	R/R	2,358/4,961	Young BM/WM	Boston, Chi, Phil	ORA	MC	B
Johnson B (2000b)	PC	R	226	Ad, B	National US	ORA	MC	B
Johnson B (2001)	PC	R	1,725	Youth	National US	ORA, SR	MC	B
Johnson B (2002)	CC	S	148 vs. 247	Former prisoners	Brazil	Religious program	SC	B
Johnson B (2003)	PC	C	177 vs. 177	Former Prisoners	Texas	Religious program	MC	B
Johnson B (2004)	CC	S	201 vs. 201	Former prisoners	New York	ORA, NORA	MC	B
Kerley (2005)							MC	B
Kerley (2005b)							MC	B
Kerley (2006)							MC	B
Kvaraceus (1944)	CS	S	700 +	Ad	New Jersey	ORA	N	NA
Lee (2004)								
Lee (2004)								
Lee (2006)								
Middleton (1962)	CS	–	554	CS	California, FL	RB, ORA, SR	N	B
Montgomery (1996)	CS	–	392	HS (Catholic), F	Great Britain	NORA	SC	B
Morris (1981)	CS	C	134	CS	Tennessee	IR, ER	N	B

Study	Type	Method	N	Population	Location	Religious Variables	Controls	Findings
Parfrey (1976)	CS	R	444	CS	Ireland	ORA, RB	N	B
Peek (1985)	PC	–	817	HS, M	National US	religiosity	MC	M
Pettersson (1991)	CS	R	118	Police districts	Sweden	ORA	SC	B
Powell (1997)	CS	S	521	HS high risk, B	Birmingham, AL	ORA, SR	MC	B
Regnerus (2003)	PC	R	11,890	Ad, Parents	National US	ORA, RC, D	MC	B
Regnerus (2003)								
Resnick (1997)	CS	R	12,118	Ad	National US	SR	MC	NA
Rhodes (1970)	CS	R	21,720	HS	Tennessee	ORA, D, Misc.	MC	B
Rohrbaugh (1975)	CS	C	475/221	HS/CS	Colorado	ORA, RB, RE	N	B
Shcoll (1964)	CC	C	52 vs. 28 Cs	Ad delinquents	Illinois	RB, RE	N	H
Sinha (2007)	CS	R	2,004	Ad	National US	ORA, SR	MC	B
Sloane (1986)	CS	R	1,121	HS	National US	ORA, SR	MC	B
Stark (1982)	CS	R	1,799	Ad M	National US	RB, SR, ORA	N	B
Stark (1996)	CS	R	11,955	Ad	National US	D, ORA	SC	B
Travers ()								
Tittle (1983)								
Wallace J (1998)	CS	R	5,000	HS	National US	D, ORA, SR	MC	B
Wattenburg (1950)	CS	S	2,137	Delinquent boys	Detroit, MI	ORA	N	B
Wickerstrom (1983)	CS	C	130	CS (Christian)	4 states	IR, ER	MC	B
Wright (1971)	CS	C	3,850/1,574	CS	England	RB, ORA, Misc.	N	B
Zhang (1994)	CS	C	1,026	CS	China,Taiwan, US	SR, NORA, ORA	MC	B

Type: CS cross-sectional; PC prospective cohort; RS retrospective; CT clinical trial; Exp experimental; CC case control; D descriptive; CR case report; Q qualitative. **Method** (sampling): R random; probability, or population-based sample; S systematic sampling; C convenience/purposive sample. **N:** number of subjects in sample; Cs controls. **Population**: C children; Ad adolescents; HS high school students; CS college students; CDA community dwelling adults; E elderly; CM church members; R religious or clergy; F female; M male; B black; W white. **Location:** city, state, or country. **Religious Variables:** ORA organizational religious activities (religious attendance and related activities); NORA (scripture study); SR subjective religiosity; RC religious commitment; IR intrinsic religiosity; ER extrinsic religiosity; Q quest; SWB spiritual well being; R religious coping; M mysticism; O orthodoxy; RB religious belief; RE religious experience; CM church membership; I FBO intervention; D denomination; SDA Seventh Day Adventist. **Controls:** N No controls; SC some controls; MC multiple controls. **Findings:** NA no association; M mixed evidence; B beneficial association with outcome; H harmful association with outcome.

but researchers have spent far less time considering how or why measures of religion, religious institutions, or religiosity measures are inversely related to crime and delinquency. In this section I turn my attention to considering how and why various religious variables matters in reducing crime and delinquency.

Linking Religion to Protective Factors

There is growing evidence that religion, individual religious commitment, or religious congregations have the potential to help prevent high-risk urban youths from engaging in delinquent behavior (Johnson *et al.* 2000*a*; 2001). I and my colleagues (Johnson *et al.* 2000*b*) estimate a series of regression models and find that (1) the effects of neighborhood disorder (i.e., high-crime neighborhoods) on crime was partly mediated by an individual's frequency of church attendance,[2] and (2) involvement of African American youth in religious institutions significantly buffers the effects of neighborhood disorder on crime and, in particular, serious crime. We conclude that the African American Church has the potential to be an important agency of local social control, and researchers should not overlook the important role that these religious congregations may play in the lives of disadvantaged youth.

Preliminary evidence suggests that youth who have continued religious involvement or participation throughout adolescence may be the beneficiaries of a cumulative religiosity effect that lessens the risk of illicit drug use (Jang and Johnson 2001). This finding suggests that youth who continue to attend and participate in religious activities are less likely to commit crimes or delinquent acts. Indeed, I (2000) found that church-attending youth from disadvantaged communities are less likely to use illicit drugs than youth from suburban communities who attend church less frequently or not at all.

Recent research helps to confirm that there is growing evidence that religious commitment and involvement help protect youth (and adults) from delinquent behavior and deviant activities (Baier and Wright 2001; Jang and Johnson 2003; 2004; 2005; Johnson *et al.* 2000*c*). Recent evidence also suggests that such effects persist even if there is not a strong prevailing social control against delinquent behavior in the surrounding community (Johnson *et al.* 2000*a*). Stated differently, youth from "bad places" can still turn out to be "good kids" if religious beliefs and practices are regular and important in their lives. There is additional evidence that religious involvement may lower the risks of a broad range of delinquent behaviors, ranging from minor to serious forms of criminal behavior (Evans *et al.* 1996; Regnerus 2003; Wallace and Ferman 1998). Preliminary research findings also

[2] See also Clarke 2001.

indicate that religious involvement may have a cumulative effect throughout adolescence and thus may significantly lessen the risk of later adult criminality (Jang and Johnson 2001; Jang, Bader, and Johnson, forthcoming). Whereas criminologists have tended to focus on the effects of community disadvantage on predisposing youth to delinquent behavior, we are now beginning to understand the effects that religion or religious institutions may play in providing communities of "advantage" for youth. In other words, uninterrupted and regular church attendance may further inoculate or insulate youth from crime and delinquency.

In a similar vein, preliminary research has examined intergenerational religious influence and found that parental religious devotion protects girls from delinquency (Regnerus 2003). There is additional research documenting that religion can be used as a tool to help prevent especially difficult populations, like high-risk urban youths, from engaging in delinquent behavior (Johnson *et al.* 2000*b*; 2001). For example, youth living in poverty tracts in urban environments, or what criminologists call "disadvantaged communities", are at elevated risk for a number of problem behaviors, including poor school performance, drug use, and other delinquent activities (Johnson *et al.* 2000*a*; 2000). However, youth from these same disorganized communities who participate in religious activities are significantly less likely to be involved in deviant activities. In this way, religiously committed youth are "resilient" to, and protected from, the negative consequences of living in impoverished communities.

Confirmed in previous meta-analyses as well as the current systematic review of the crime and religion literature reported in this chapter, we now have solid empirical evidence demonstrating that religion is a protective factor that may buffer or shield youth as well as adults from delinquency, crime, and recidivism. Youth exposure to religious and spiritual activities, in conjunction with other environmental factors, is a powerful inhibitor of juvenile delinquency and youth violence. For example, youth who attend church frequently are less likely to engage in a variety of delinquent behaviors, including drug use, skipping school, fighting, and violent and nonviolent crimes. The fact that these findings hold even in disadvantaged communities provides additional evidence of the connection between religiousness and resilience. Stated differently, the role of religion and religious institutions is especially critical in communities where crime and delinquency are most prevalent.

In sum, a review of the research on religious practices or commitments and deviant behavior indicates that, in general, higher levels of religious involvement are associated with lower rates of crime and delinquency. The empirical evidence demonstrates that those who are most involved in religious activities are less likely to commit criminal or delinquent acts. Thus, aided by systematic reviews of the relevant literature, it is accurate to state that religiosity is now beginning to be acknowledged as a key protective factor that buffers or shields youth from criminal and delinquency outcomes.

Religion Promotes Pro-Social Behavior

Criminologists have for several centuries studied factors thought to be linked to the causes of crime and delinquency. Books, journals, and thousands of studies have been dedicated to examining the many characteristics of offenders and communities, as well as the antecedents to criminal behavior, in order to predict future criminal or delinquent behavior more accurately. Quite naturally, a great deal of criminological research can best be understood as attempting to answer these two central questions. Why do people commit crime? And how can we prevent it? As a result, voluminous research literatures have emerged that examine the deleterious effects of poverty and disadvantage, lack of education and unemployment, to mention just a few, in causing or contributing to crime and deviant behavior. Indeed, many criminology course curricula in academic institutions are literally devoted to the study of crime causation.

Social scientists and criminologists have much less often asked another equally important question. Why is it that people do not commit crime? Social control theorists like Travis Hirschi (1969) have provided a unique and important perspective, arguing that there are very important reasons why people do not commit crime or engage in delinquent behavior. Studying and emphasizing factors that essentially keep people from breaking the law, control theorists reason, ultimately advances our understanding of how to pursue crime prevention. Religion, therefore, is but one of many factors that control theorists might argue "bond" an individual to society and conventional or normative behavior. Indeed, it is easy to see how religion may play a central "bonding" role between each of Hirschi's four elements at the heart of social control theory: attachments, commitments, involvements, and beliefs (1969).[3]

As we have demonstrated from a systematic review of the extant research literature, increasing religiosity is a well-documented protective factor that buffers or insulates youth and even adults from crime and delinquency. In this way, religion helps youth to be resilient and to avoid delinquent paths in spite of characteristics and factors that would otherwise seem to predict a deviant behavioral trajectory. We now pose another equally important though understudied question: Why is it that people do good things?

Less commonly acknowledged by researchers is the contribution of religious belief and practice in fostering positive or normative behavior. I argue here that it is

[3] Social control theory is not unique in its theoretical relevance for the role of religion in reducing or preventing crime and delinquency. Social disorganization, labeling, differential association, life course perspective, rational choice, and strain are but a few of the theoretical perspectives within criminology that easily allow the introduction of religious variables and influences within existing frameworks. These lines of inquiry make it possible for researchers to generate and test hypotheses of direct and indirect contributions of religion variables in explaining any number of outcomes relevant to criminology and delinquency studies.

at least as important to understand why people turn into good citizens as to understand why they go bad. In essence, we have probably spent too much time asking: why people do bad things, like commit crime?

In addition to documenting the protective factor that religion can play, scholars have also discovered that at-risk youth from disadvantaged communities who exhibit higher levels of religiousness not only are less likely to commit crimes than their disadvantaged counterparts, they are also more likely to stay in school, make better grades, and find and retain steady employment (Freeman 1986; Johnson *et al.* 2000*a*).

Clearly, not enough scholarship has focused on the pro-social side of the equation. Scholars need to do a much better job of documenting the factors and conditions that motivate, cause, support, and sustain positive or pro-social behavior. It is important to note that when discussing pro-social behavior there is much more involved here than merely obeying the law and desisting from criminal behavior. We need to know why people do admirable things. For example, why do people do such things as support charities, volunteer work, return lost valuables or participate in civic activities?

A number of studies have been published in recent years documenting the relationship between increasing religiosity and higher levels of pro-social behavior. This body of research consistently finds that religious commitment promotes or enhances beneficial outcomes like well-being (Blazer and Palmore 1976; Graney 1975; Markides 1983; Musick 1996; Tix and Frazier 1997; Willits and Crider 1988), hope, meaning and purpose (Sethi and Seligman 1993), self-esteem (Ellison and George 1994; Bradley 1995; Koenig *et al.* 1999), and even educational attainment (Regnerus 2000; 2001; Johnson *et al.* 2000*a*; Jeynes 2007). Indeed, the more actively religious are more likely to give to charities (both religious and non-religious) and to volunteer time for civic purposes (Brooks 2006). The review of a large number of studies across multiple disciplines, with diverse samples and methodologies, leaves one with the robust conclusion that the empirically documented effect of religion on physical and mental health outcomes is remarkably positive (Koenig *et al.* 2001).

Studies also suggest that being involved in or exposed to altruistic or pro-social activities and attitudes—something that many churches and other faith-based organizations reportedly have as intrinsic aspects of their mission—appears to reduce the risk of youth violence. A proper understanding of the mechanisms associated with pro-social behavior will assist in the development of future prevention and intervention strategies. Unraveling the role of religiousness, religiosity, religious institutions and congregations, as well as religious practices and beliefs, in promoting pro-social behavior among youth should be a priority for academic researchers.

Just as the studies reviewed earlier document that religious commitment is a protective factor that buffers individuals from various harmful outcomes (e.g., hypertension, depression, suicide, and delinquency), so there is mounting empirical evidence to suggest that religious commitment is also a source for promoting or enhancing beneficial outcomes (e.g., well-being, hope, meaning and purpose, educational attainment, and charitable giving). This review of a large number of diverse studies concludes that, in general, the effect of religion on physical and mental health outcomes is remarkably positive (Koenig *et al.* 2001; Johnson 2002). These findings have led some religious health-care practitioners to conclude that further collaboration between religious organizations and health services may be desirable (Miller 1987; Olson 1988; Levin 1984). According to Peterson (1983):

> These phenomena combined point to the church as having powerful potential to affect the health of half the population.... We are convinced that a church with a vigorous life of worship, education, and personal support together with the promotion of wellness has more of an impact on the health of a community than an addition to the hospital or another doctor in town. Right now this is a hunch; in five years, we'll have the data to prove it.

This enthusiasm notwithstanding, more research utilizing longitudinal and experimental designs is needed further to address important causal linkages between religion and myriad pro-social outcomes.

Religious involvement may provide networks of support that help adolescents internalize values that encourage behavior that emphasizes concern for others' welfare. Such processes may contribute to the acquisition of positive attributes that give adolescents a greater sense of empathy toward others, which in turn makes them less likely to commit acts that harm others. Recent research confirms that religiosity can help youth to be resilient even in the midst of poverty, crime, and other social ills commonly linked to deleterious outcomes.

Frequent participation in religious activities may help adolescents learn values that give them a greater sense of empathy toward others, thereby decreasing the likelihood of committing acts that harm other people. Similarly, once individuals become involved in deviant behavior, it is possible that participation in specific kinds of religious activity can help steer them back to a course of less deviant behavior and, more important, away from potential career criminal paths. For example, preliminary empirical studies addressing faith-based approaches to prison treatment have shown that inmates who regularly participate in volunteer-led Bible studies or who complete a faith-based program are less likely to commit institutional infractions (Hercik 2004) or commit new crimes following release from prison (Johnson *et al.* 1997; Johnson 2004). In the first major evaluation study a faith-based prison launched in 1997 in Houston, Texas, Larson and I (Johnson and Larson 2003) found that inmates completing the InnerChange Freedom Initiative, an 18–24-month-length faith-based prison program operated by Prison Fellowship (a Christian prison ministry), were significantly less likely to be arrested than a matched group of prisoners not subject to this religious intervention (8 percent versus 20 percent respectively) during a two-year post-release period. Similar results were reported in a study comparing former prisoners in two Brazil prisons, one a faith-based prison program[4] and the other a model prison based on a vocational model[5] in Brazil (Johnson 2002).

Utilizing a meta-analytic approach, we have demonstrated from a systematic and objective assessment of the research literature that individual religious commitment or religiosity as well as religious congregations can have a significant buffering or protective effect that lessens the likelihood of delinquent or criminal behavior among youth as well as adults. In a separate review of the research literature we also document that increasing measures of religiousness are associated with an array of pro-social outcomes. In this way, we can argue that religion not only protects from deleterious outcomes like crime and delinquency; it promotes pro-social or beneficial outcomes that are considered normative and necessary for a productive society.

Conclusions

This study confirms that religious influences do impact the behavior of many adolescents in multiple settings such as family, peers, and school. The vast majority of studies document the importance of religious influences in protecting youth from harmful outcomes as well as promoting beneficial and pro-social outcomes. The beneficial relationship between religion and health behaviors and outcomes is not simply a function of religion's constraining function or what it discourages—drug use or delinquent behavior—but also through what it encourages—behaviors that can enhance purpose, well-being, or educational attainment.

Although some researchers have identified low religiosity as a risk factor for adolescent health risk behaviors, religion measures are not routinely included in adolescent research, and research that explicitly examines religion and health among young people remains rare. Future research on adolescent health and social outcomes should include multiple measures of religious practices and beliefs. It is time for researchers and federal funding agencies to discontinue the pattern of overlooking this important line of policy-relevant research. New research will allow us more fully to understand the ways in which religion directly and indirectly impacts health and social outcomes. Churches, synagogues, mosques, inner-city blessing stations, and other houses of worship are among the few institutions that remain within close proximity of most adolescents, their families, and their peers.

[4] Based on a Catholic model, the faith-based prison went by the name Humaita.

[5] In 2000, the Braganca prison was widely promoted as an exemplar and a model for future prisons in Brazil.

Research now confirms that these religious institutions can play an important role in promoting the health and well-being of those they serve.

As policymakers consider strategies to reduce delinquency, gang activity, and crime, it is essential for such deliberations seriously and intentionally to consider the role of religion and religious institutions in implementing, developing, and sustaining multi-faceted approaches. From after-school programs for disadvantaged youth to public/private partnerships that bring together secular and religious groups to tackle social problems like the prisoner reentry crisis, it is apparent that any strategy will be needlessly incomplete unless religious communities are integrally involved.

References

Albrecht, S. L., Chadwick, B. A., and Alcorn, D. (1977). "Religiosity and Deviance: Application of an Attitude–Behavior Contingent Consistency Model". *Journal for the Scientific Study of Religion*, 16: 263–74.

Baier, C., and Wright, B. (2001). "If You Love Me, Keep My Commandments: A Meta-analysis of the Effect of Religion on Crime". *Journal of Research in Crime and Delinquency*, 38: 3–21.

Blazer, D. G., and Palmore, E. (1976). "Religion and Aging in a Longitudinal Panel". *Gerontologist*, 16: 82–5.

Bradley, D. E. (1995). "Religious Involvement and Social Resources: Evidence from the Data Set 'Americans' Changing Lives' ". *Journal for the Scientific Study of Religion*, 34: 259–67.

Brooks, A. C. (2006). *Who Really Cares: The Surprising Truth about Compassionate Conservatism.* New York: Basic Books.

Burkett, S., and White, M. (1974). "Hellfire and Delinquency: Another Look". *Journal for the Scientific Study of Religion*, 13/4: 455–62.

Clarke, P. (2001). "Buddhism, Humanism and Catholic Culture in Brazil". In D. Machacek and B. Wilson (eds.), *Global Citizens.* Oxford: Oxford University Press, 326–48.

Ellison, C., and George, L. K. (1994). "Religious Involvement, Social Ties, and Social Support in a Southeastern Community". *Journal for the Scientific Study of Religion*, 33: 46–61.

Evans, D., Cullen, F., Burton, V., Dunaway, R. G., Payne, G., and Kethineni, S. (1996). "Religion, Social Bonds, and Delinquency". *Deviant Behavior*, 17: 43–70.

Freeman, R. B. (1986). "Who Escapes? The Relation of Church going and Other Background Factors to the Socioeconomic Performance of Black Male Youths from Inner-City Tracts". In R. B. Freeman and H. J. Holzer (eds.), *The Black Youth Employment Crisis.* Chicago: University of Chicago Press, 353–76.

Graney, M. J. (1975). "Happiness and Social Participation in Aging". *Journal of Gerontology*, 30: 701–6.

Hercik, J. (2004). *Navigating a New Horizon: Promising Pathways to Prisoner Reintegration.* Caliber Associates.

Higgins, P., and Albrecht, G. (1977). "Hellfire and Delinquency Revisited". *Social Forces*, 55/4: 952–8.

Hirschi, T. (1969). *Causes of Delinquency.* Berkeley: University of California Press.

—— and Stark, R. (1969). "Hellfire and Delinquency". *Social Problems*, 17: 202–13.

Jang, S. J., and Johnson, B. R. (2001). "Neighborhood Disorder, Individual Religiosity, and Adolescent Use of Illicit Drugs: A Test of Multilevel Hypotheses". *Criminology*, 39: 109–44.

—— —— (2003). "Strain, Negative Emotions, and Deviant Coping among African Americans: A Test of General Strain Theory and the Buffering Effects of Religiosity". *Journal of Quantitative Criminology*, 19: 79–105.

—— —— (2004). "Explaining Religious Effects on Distress among African Americans". *Journal for the Scientific Study of Religion*, 43: 239–60.

—— —— (2005). "Gender, Religiosity, and Reactions to Strain among African Americans". *Sociological Quarterly*, 46: 323–58.

—— —— and Bader, C. (forthcoming). "The Cumulative Effect of Religiosity in Crime Desistance". *Journal of Drug Issues.*

Jensen, G., and Erickson, M. (1979). "The Religious Factor and Delinquency: Another Look at the Hellfire Hypothesis". In Robert Wuthnow (ed.), *The Religious Dimension.* New York: Academic Press, 157–77.

Jeynes, W. H. (2007). *American Educational History: School, Society, and the Common Good.* Thousand Oaks, Calif.: Sage.

Johnson, B. R. (2000). "A Better Kind of High: How Religious Commitment Reduces Drug Use". *CRRUCS Report*, University of Pennsylvania.

—— and Larson, D. B. (2003). "The Inner Change Freedom Initiative: A Preliminary Evaluation of a Faith-Based Prison Program". ISR Research Report, Baylor University.

—— (2002). "Assessing the Impact of Religious Programs and Prison Industry on Recidivism: An Exploratory Study". *Texas Journal of Corrections*, 28: 7–11.

—— (2004). "Religious Programs and Recidivism among Former Inmates in Prison Fellowship Programs: A Long-Term Follow-Up Study". *Justice Quarterly*, 21: 329–54.

—— (2006). *A Better Kind of High: How Religious Commitment Reduces Drug Use.* ISR Research Report, Institute for Studies of Religion, Baylor University.

—— Jang, S. J., Larson, D. B., and Li, S. D. (2001). "Does Adolescent Religious Commitment Matter? A Reexamination of the Effects of Religiosity on Delinquency". *Journal of Research in Crime and Delinquency*, 38: 22–44.

—— Larson D. B., and Pitts, T. (1997). "Religious Programming, Institutional Adjustment and Recidivism among Former Inmates in Prison Fellowship Programs". *Justice Quarterly*, 14/1: 145–66.

—— —— Li, S. D., and Jang, S. J. (2000*a*). "Escaping from the Crime of Inner Cities: Church Attendance and Religious Salience among Disadvantaged Youth". *Justice Quarterly*, 17: 377–91.

—— —— Jang, S. J., and Li, S. D. (2000*b*). "The "Invisible Institution" and Black Youth Crime: The Church as an Agency of Local Social Control". *Journal of Youth and Adolescence*, 29: 479–98.

—— Li, S. D., Larson, D. B., and McCullough, M. (2000*c*). "Religion and Delinquency: A Systematic Review of the Literature". *Journal of Contemporary Criminal Justice*, 16: 32–52.

Koenig, H., McCullough, M., and Larson, D. B. (2001). *The Handbook of Religion and Health.* Oxford: Oxford University Press.

Koenig, H., McCullough, M., and Larson, D. B. Hays, J., Larson, D., George, L., Cohen, H., McCullough, M., Meador, K., and Blazer, D. (1999). "Does Religious Attendance Prolong Survival?: A Six-Year Follow-up Study of 3,968 Older Adults". *Journal of Gerontology*, 54A/7: 370–6.

Levin, J. S. (1984). "The Role of the Black Church in Community Medicine". *Journal of the National Medical Association*, 76: 477–83.

Markides, K. S. (1983). "Aging, Religiosity, and Adjustment: A Longitudinal Analysis". *Journal of Gerontology*, 38: 621–5.

Miller, J. (1987). "Wellness Programs through the Church". *Health Values*, 11/5: 3–6.

Musick, M. A. (1996). "Religion and Subjective Health among Black and White Elders". *Journal of Health and Social Behavior*, 37: 221–37.

Olson, L. (1988). "The Religious Community as a Partner in Health Care". *Journal of Community Health*, 13: 249–57.

Peterson, B. (1983). "Renewing the Church's Health Ministries: Reflections on Ten Years' Experience". *Journal of Religion and the Applied Behavioral Sciences*, 4: 16–22.

Regnerus, M. (2000). "Shaping Schooling Success: Religious Socialization and Educational Outcomes in Metropolitan Public Schools". *Journal for the Scientific Study of Religion*, 39: 363–70.

—— (2001). "Making the Grade: The Influence of Religion upon the Academic Performance of Youth in Disadvantaged Communities". *CRRUCS Report* 2001–3, University of Pennsylvania.

—— (2003). "Linked Lives, Faith, and Behavior: Intergenerational Religious Influence on Adolescent Delinquency". *Journal for the Scientific Study of Religion*, 42/2: 189–203.

Sethi, S., and Seligman, M. (1993). "The Hope of Fundamentalists". *Psychological Science*, 5: 58.

Stark, R. (1996). "Religion as Context: Hellfire and Delinquency One More Time". *Sociology of Religion*, 57: 163–73.

—— Kent, L., and Doyle, D. P. (1982). "Religion and Delinquency: The Ecology of a Lost Relationship". *Journal of Research in Crime and Delinquency*, 19: 4–24.

Tix, A. P., and Frazier, P. A. (1997). "The Use of Religious Coping during Stressful Life Events: Main Effects, Moderation, and Medication". *Journal of Consulting and Clinical Psychology*, 66: 411–22.

Wallace, J. M., and Ferman, T. A. (1998). "Religion's Role in Promoting Health and Reducing Risk among American Youth". *Health Education and Behavior*, 25: 721–41.

Willits, F. K., and Crider, D. M. (1988). "Religion and Well-being: Men and Women in the Middle Years". *Review of Religious Research*, 29: 281–94.

Suggested Reading

Johnson, Byron, with Thompkins, Brett, and Webb, Derek (2002). "Objective Hope—Assessing the Effectiveness of Religion and Faith-Based Organizations: A Systematic Review of the Literature". Institute for Studies of Religion (ISR Research Report), Baylor University, Tex.

—— (2003). "The InnerChange Freedom Initiative: A Preliminary Evaluation of a Faith-Based Prison Program". Institute for Studies of Religion (ISR Research Report), Baylor University, Tex.

Regnerus, Mark D. (2006). "Adolescent Delinquency". In Helen Rose Ebaugh (ed.), *Handbook of Religion and Social Institutions*. Springer: New York, 265–82.

—— (2007). *Forbidden Fruit: Sex and Religion in the Lives of American Teenagers*. Oxford: Oxford University Press.

Stark, Rodney, and Bainbridge, William Sims (1997). *Religion, Deviance, and Social Control*. New York: Routledge.

CHAPTER 48

RELIGION AND ALTRUISM

KEISHIN INABA
KATE LOEWENTHAL

Religious traditions normatively prescribe caring for others as one of the central platforms of religious teaching. Initial research, however, gave a rather unclear picture of the relationship between religion and altruism. It remains a leading-edge question in social science: are religious people nicer people? (Duriez 2004). We will attempt explore the relationship between religion and altruism using three sources. First, we will examine religious teachings and prescriptions about altruism. Second, we will examine social-scientific definitions and explanations of altruism and altruistic behaviour. Finally, we will examine the research evidence on the relationship between religion and altruism, and attempt to draw conclusions.

What is religion, and what is altruism? We will take as a preliminary working definition of religion a set of (complex) systems of shared beliefs and behaviours about spiritual reality, God, morality, and purpose, with methods for communicating and endorsing these (Loewenthal 2000: 3). The further complexities of the definition and measurement of religion are beyond the scope of this article. For altruism, we will take as a starting point Comte's (1875) view of altruism as unselfish regard for the welfare of others. Later, we will explore some refinements of this definition.

Religious Teachings, Prescriptions, and Beliefs about Altruism

'Love your neighbour as yourself' (Lev. 19: 18) has been a core teaching of Judeo-Christian religious traditions, expressed in varying forms. We will examine a selection of teachings and beliefs in different religious traditions, and some social-scientific views and findings.

Is altruism a religious value in itself, or simply a means to ultimate reward or punishment? For instance, religion has been always concerned with soteriology: what shall we do to be saved? The meanings of salvation differ from one religion to another, and so do the ways of attaining it. Altruistic acts of religious people may be motivated by the quest for salvation. Weber notes 'a quest for salvation in any religious group had the strongest chance of exerting practical influences when there has arisen, out of religious motivations, a systematization of practical conduct resulting from an orientation to certain integral values' (1978: 528).

If the ministry of Jesus was a paradigm of altruism, his death, as interpreted by his followers, was its ultimate manifestation. For Christians, Novak (1992: 9) states, 'Jesus is the altruistic man who died for others as he had lived for them'. '*Agapē*', or 'love', is usually used instead of 'altruism' in Christianity. Browning (1992: 422) remarks that 'Agapē, the Greek word most often used to refer to the rule or law of love in the New Testament, is defined in many Protestant sources as entailing primarily impartial, self-sacrificial action on behalf of the other and without regard to oneself'. However, only 'the religious virtuosi' can achieve the extreme self-sacrificial demands of the Christian concept of love that exclude all self-regarding motives. Weber (1978: 539) remarks that 'not everyone possesses the charisma that makes possible the continuous maintenance in everyday life of the distinctive religious mood which assures the lasting certainty of grace'. The extreme self-sacrificial demands of the Christian concept of love may be too hard for 'the average person' to practice. Consequently, as Browning (1992: 423) points out, in stark contrast to the initial goals, extreme self-sacrificial demands may fail to extend natural kin altruism to the wider community, or may rather function to diminish wider altruism. Nevertheless, for at least some, 'salvation may be viewed as the distinctive gift of active ethical behavior performed in the awareness that God directs this behavior, i.e., that the actor is an instrument of God' (Weber 1978: 541). Weber calls this type of attitude 'ascetic'.

In the Jewish tradition, the practice of altruism is regarded as potentially achievable by all. Charitable activity may be practised in a habitual manner, and this can accord with natural kindly inclination. This is spiritually valuable, and achieves cosmologically beneficial effects. But self-sacrifice, involving efforts directed to the overcoming of natural habit and inclination, is a universal potential and can achieve more permanently beneficial effects (Shneur Zalman of Liadi 1973 [1796]: 236).

In the case of Buddhism, the doctrine of karma may relate to altruistic beliefs and practices. The doctrine of karma is the most complete formal solution of the problem of theodicy. Weber presents the doctrine of karma as follows:

> This world is viewed as completely connected and self-contained cosmos of ethical retribution. Guilt and merit within this world are unfailingly compensated by fate in the successive lives of the soul, which may be reincarnated innumerable times in animal, human, or even divine forms. Ethical merits in this life can make possible rebirth into life in heaven, but that life can last only until one's credit balance of merits has been completely used up. The finiteness of earthly life is the consequence of the finiteness of good or evil deeds in the previous life of a particular soul. What may appear from the viewpoint of retribution as unjust suffering in the present life of a person should be regarded as atonement for sin in a previous existence. Each individual forges his own destiny exclusively, and in the strictest sense of the word. (Weber 1978: 524–5)

Inaba's (2004) work examined the meanings and constructions placed on altruism by individual Christians and Buddhists. Christians' altruistic activities aimed to help people not so much in practical ways as in spiritual ways. Altruism is to exalt people other than oneself and to seek the welfare of others rather than one's own. When they talked about altruism, some Christians referred to reward. They believed that God would reward their altruistic acts—but their altruistic deeds towards others are ultimately directed to God. Buddhists pointed out that it is more important to give what others need rather than what one thinks they should have. For them, however, altruism is not solely oriented towards other people: altruism is seen as both personally rewarding as well as helpful to other people. It was emphasized that people who perform altruistic acts should also take their own spiritual and material well-being into account.

It can be seen that the practice of helpful and altruistic behaviour has been endorsed and encouraged in a range of religious traditions, as one very important aspect of the practice of goodness. There is some distinction made between more natural forms of helpfulness—such as kin altruism—and truly disinterested and self-sacrificial altruism. The latter may not be achieved by all, but there is some indication that it is an ideal to be emulated and attempted. The practice of goodness has been linked to other important features of religious teachings—notably existential purpose, soteriology, and theodicy.

This elaborate intellectual system varies in some details between religious traditions, and indeed between denominations of the same tradition, cultures, and individuals. Nevertheless, common features can be seen. Altruistic acts may be motivated by a single factor—the hope of salvation, for example—and/or are part of a system in which concern and care for others are embedded in a network of beliefs about spirituality and purpose in life.

Social-Scientific Definitions and Explanations of Altruism

As mentioned, Comte used altruism to denote unselfish regard for the welfare of others, or a devotion to the interests of others as an action-guiding principle. The term 'altruism' was coined by Comte (1798–1857), and came into the English language in 1853 in translation. The original French term 'altruisme' was suggested by the French legal phrase 'le bien d'autrui' (the good of others), and was formed from the Italian equivalent, 'altrui', itself a derivative of the Latin 'alter', or 'other'. Altruism is precisely 'other-ism': the effort or actual ability to act in the interest of others (Novak 1992: 2). Comte (1875) considered that within the individual were two distinct motives: one was egoistic, and the other was altruistic. Comte acknowledged that human beings had self-serving motives even if they were helping others, and called the motivation to seek self-benefit 'egoism'. On the other hand, there are some kinds of social behaviour that come from an unselfish desire to help others, and Comte called this type of motivation 'altruism'. Since Comte's proposals, altruism has been an analytical concept in the social sciences.

It is important to bear in mind that the term 'altruism', as Novak (1992: 3) notes, has the advantage of not being rooted in a specific religious linguistic tradition and serves as a general term that captures an important family resemblance among the world's diverse ethical vocabularies.

Turning to subsequent social-scientific attempts to understand altruism, these attempts have been clearly influenced by the question as to whether pure selflessness is possible, and whether and when helpfulness can go further than 'natural' kin and own-group helpfulness. In parallel, there have been related efforts to identify the factors that motivate helpful and altruistic behaviour. What factors might motivate altruism?

Apart from external forces such as increased status, social desirability, or social approval, it has also been pointed out that feelings of guilt can motivate altruism and that feelings of guilt seek compensation that can be achieved through altruistic acts (Carlsmith and Gross 1968: Regan *et al.* 1972). If altruism is defined, however, as the willingness to help others without normative obligation and without expecting benefits at a later time, we would rarely find actions that are altruistically motivated. Macaulay and Berkowitz (1970: 3) defined altruism as 'behavior carried out to benefit another without anticipation of rewards from external sources'. Regarding this definition, Rushton and Sorrentino noted:

> [This definition] includes both the altruist's intentions and his or her behaviour. It does, however, exclude such rewards from internal sources as self esteem, self praise for one's action and relief from empathetic distress, alleviation of feelings of guilt. Such an exclusion

has the practical advantage of avoiding both unobservable variables as well as the philosophical issue of whether there can ever be a truly unselfish act. (1981: 426)

Rushton's view is that 'the primary focus of research attention should be on altruistic behavior, and that postulated motivators such as "empathy" and "norms of social responsibility" are hypothetical constructs, to be added only if they can account for the behavioral regularities more thoroughly' (Rushton and Sorrentino 1981: 427). Moreover, Montada and Bierhoff (1991: 18) defined altruism as 'behaviour that aims at a termination or reduction of an emergency, a neediness, or disadvantage of others and that primarily does not aim at the fulfillment of own interests', adding that 'the behaviour has to be carried out voluntarily'. This behavioural definition of Montada and Bierhoff may be the most appropriate for the social-scientific understanding of altruism.

Rushton and Sorrentino (1981) provide a historical perspective on altruism. They argue that there have been three main views on altruism. The first is that humans are innately evil or bad (e.g., selfish, sinful, aggressive, and non-social), and that socialization is required to make them social and altruistic. According to Rushton and Sorrentino, many writers of the Bible, the Sophists (fifth and fourth century BCE), Chinese Confucian philosopher Xun zi (third century BCE), Machiavelli (1469–1527), Hobbes (1588–1679), and Freud (1856–1939) held this first view. The second view is that humans are basically good and that they can be improved or perverted by social conditions. Socrates (fifth century BCE), Chinese Confucian philosopher Meng zi (fourth century BCE), Aristotle (384–322 BCE), Rousseau (1712–78), Maslow (1908–70), and Rogers (1902–87) held this view. The third is that humans are neutral: basically neither good nor bad. Plato (427–374 BCE), Epicurus (341–270 BCE), Locke (1632–1704), Marx (1818–83), Watson (1878–1958), and Skinner (1904–90) held this third view.

Whether altruism is innate or acquired is another issue. Allport (1897–1967), Kohlberg (1927–87), and Rushton (1980: 10) provided abundant evidence in support of the theory that altruism can be learned and developed by social learning. On the other hand, Novak (1992: 28–32) points out three obstacles to the development of altruism. First is the neural factor: significant moral progress is difficult or impossible because of the structure of the human brain. A second obstacle to altruistic transformation is psychological. Each human being born into this world wishes to be a unique centre of importance and value. The very behaviour, dispositions, and attitudes that help people emerge from childhood as relatively autonomous individuals become to some extent psychological barriers to the emergence of altruism. The human being's natural quest for selfhood creates psychological habit patterns which are difficult to alter. A third obstacle is the sociological or social. The social groupings to which people belong implicitly reinforce an ingrown and out-group mentality which at best sets limits to the growth of altruism and at worst is antithetical to it. However, Krebs and Van Hesteren (1992) contend that individuals normally acquire the capacity to perform increasingly adequate types of altruism as they develop, and that individual differences in altruism stem from the interaction between the stage of their development and the opportunities and demands of the social contexts they create and encounter.

The proposed link between empathy and altruism has been carefully examined. Empathy means identifying with and feeling sympathy for another person. Sympathy is a similar concept, but carries connotations of being on someone's side. People can empathize with their enemies—but may not sympathize. There is an abundant literature on 'the empathy–altruism hypothesis', emphasizing that sympathy or empathy for the needy is the motive for altruistic activities. One feels sorry for homeless people or people in need, and wishes to reduce their distress. Some people feel compassion for those who are suffering, and reach out to those suffering people. On the other hand, some feel empathetic distress themselves when they feel sorry for those who are suffering. Their distress arises from the unpleasant emotions which they feel as a result of seeing homeless people or people in need. Alternatively, their distress may arise from emotions of guilt or shame they anticipate if they do not help. In any case, they feel sorry for people in need and carry out acts to help them. Their altruistic acts also relieve them from their own empathetic distress (Inaba 2004).

It has also been suggested that rational choice underlies altruism. According to Schmidtz (1995), rational choice consists in maximizing one's utility subject to a budget constraint. In recent times theorists have taken the term 'utility' to mean something related to or identical to preference satisfaction. In some cases there are reasons to embrace and nurture one's concern for others, and the reasons have to do with what is conducive to one's utility. It is rational to be peaceful and productive in order to create a secure place for oneself in society, which requires one to have a regard for the interests of others. People have self-regarding reasons to internalize other-regarding concerns. On the other hand, one seeks not only to earn the respect and concern of others, but also to earn one's own respect and concern. Moreover, a person of principles inspires more respect than a person driven by mere expedience (Schmidtz 1995: 110).

Related to the rational-choice explanation of altruism is the link between altruism and positive emotional states. Not only are happier people more likely to be charitable, true, or 'authentic', but happiness has been suggested as a consequence of altruistic behaviour (Seligman 2002; Joseph *et al.* 2006). Wuthnow (1995: 67) points out that individual happiness and the good of others are not incompatible, but in fact linked. In his survey (Wuthnow 1991), many people reported that helping others made them feel good and was a good way of gaining a sense of satisfaction and fulfilment for themselves. Gaining fulfilment for oneself and feeling good can be considered as compensation for the time and energy invested. Some religious people regard altruism as giving from a purer part of them to something bigger. Schmidtz (1995: 112) regards this kind of attitude as rational: 'we give ourselves more to live for by becoming important parts of something bigger than ourselves. A principled character lets us pursue this wider integration without losing our own identity.'

Some people's motivations for altruism may involve rational choice in the sense that they calculate the benefits they will receive later. However, we have seen much to indicate that one's own benefit is not inevitably a primary objective of altruism.

Sorokin's early work on the positive aspects of human nature identifies altruism as an important feature. Noting that in the early twentieth century the social sciences cultivated disciplines for the study of negative aspects of humanity, such as crime and insanity, Sorokin (1889–1968) pointed out that 'Western social science has paid scant attention to positive types of human beings' (1950: 4). Sorokin carried out sociological studies of good neighbours and Christian saints, focusing on the characteristics of altruistic persons and how people become altruistic. He found that most of those in this category professed to be religious in some sense; the majority were female, and there seemed to be no relationship between intelligence and altruism. Self-reports concerning the motivation for altruism showed factors such as parental training, life experience, religion, and education to be particularly relevant (Sorokin 1950). Since his research, positive aspects of human nature, such as altruism, have been increasingly taken as the subject of further inquiry in social sciences (Seligman 2002; Joseph *et al.* 2006). We have seen that the social-scientific understanding of altruism has been dominated by the testing of motivational explanations of altruism, with underlying questions about true selflessness.

Religion has been a theme quite prevalent in the literature on altruism. We now turn to the examination of altruism in relation to religion, and particularly the question of whether religion fosters altruism.

The Relationship between Religion and Altruism: Empirical Evidence and Interpretations

There has been considerable research into the correlation between altruism and religion. Research into altruism has usually considered questions such as: why and under what conditions do people sacrifice their lives for the sake of others? When and under what conditions do people reach out to help somebody in need or distress? And under what conditions is a person more likely or less likely to help others?

In studying altruism, a range of techniques have been used: experimental and observational methods, questionnaires and psychometric measures, and interviews. All have advantages and disadvantages, but together they help to develop understanding of altruism in relation to religion. In recent years, improvement in the qualitative analysis of interview material and other discourse has entailed a decreased reliance solely on survey and questionnaire material, and has improved understanding and interpretation of the research material available.

Early research on religion and altruism showed unclear relations between religion and altruism. There were some findings that religion related positively to altruistic behaviour. In 1973, the American Institute of Public Opinion conducted a survey of 1502 respondents, which included the question, 'How often do you feel that you follow your religious beliefs and take concrete action on behalf of others?' This survey showed that church attendees perceived themselves as more helpful to others than non-church attendees (Langford and Langford 1974). A study by Nelson and Dynes (1976) in southwest USA eight months after a city had been struck by a damaging tornado studied men's helping behaviour following the tornado. The researchers assessed a number of indices of religiosity: self-rated religious devotion, frequency of private prayer and of church attendance, and importance of prayer. Helping behaviour related to the aftermath of the tornado studied was: giving money and/or goods to tornado victims and performing voluntany disaster services. 'Routine' helping behaviour, unrelated to the disaster, was also assessed, such as picking up hitchhikers, doing voluntary work, and contributing money or goods to social service agencies. Both types of helping—post-disaster and routine—were positively related to all the indices of religiosity.

On the other hand, some research showed that religiosity was unrelated to offering help to others. Cline and Richards (1965) conducted a survey in the Salt Lake area of the USA and found no relationship between religiosity factors (as measured by frequency of church attendance, frequency of prayer, and contribution of money) and such variables as 'having love and compassion for one's fellow man' and 'being a Good Samaritan'. In another study, no relationship was found between religiosity and volunteering to help people (Smith *et al.* 1975). Moreover, Rokeach (1969) noted that those who rated high on church attendance were more likely to be insensitive and unconcerned for disadvantaged groups.

One explanation for such disparity in the results of the studies in the 1960s and the 1970s is that altruistic behaviour at that time might have been be so much a part of organized religion, and organized religion so normative in society, that respondents failed to answer self-report inventories honestly. On the other hand, religious people might be more likely to answer questionnaires honestly, because of their belief that 'a Supreme Being knows people's thoughts and acts in all situations'. Methodological problems such as the measurement of altruism, the measurement of religiosity, and the amount of respondent diversity might contribute to the mixed results.

Since the 1980s, various studies have indicated more clearly that religion promotes altruism. An analysis based on findings from a questionnaire survey of 300 undergraduate students in the USA indicated that religious persons were more likely to carry out altruistic acts (Zook 1982). Lynn and Smith (1991) reported that those who did voluntary work in the UK gave religion as one of the main reasons for their participation.

A study by Yablo (1990) contrasted native-born Thai and US citizens on the relationship between religion and altruistic behaviour. The results showed that people in Thailand, where 95 per cent of the population is Buddhist, displayed a stronger orientation towards altruistic behaviour than US citizens. Interview results revealed qualitative differences in philosophies and rationale regarding altruistic behaviour. The Thai interviewees were influenced by Buddhist doctrine, while the USA interviewees reported being influenced less by religion and more by pragmatic considerations. The findings of this study suggest a relationship between cultural and/or religious values and altruistic behaviour.

Research by Perkins (1992) examined the relationship between Judeo-Christian religiosity and humanitarianism. The study was based on data collected during 1978–9 at five diverse colleges and universities in England and the USA and data collected during 1988–90 at the same institutions. This study shows that religiosity was most salient in directly promoting humanitarian compassion and that the influence of other socio-demographic factors failed to attain any level of significance. Perkins concluded: 'these data suggest that the nature of one's religious commitment might remain one of the few important influences on humanitarianism for young persons in the college setting cross-nationally' (1992: 359).

Regarding the contribution of religion to voluntary work, Wilson and Janoski (1995) analysed data derived from the three-wave Youth–Parent Socialization panel study by the University of Michigan. The results indicate that the relationship between religion and voluntary work is complex and that caution is called for in generalizing about the connection. However, regarding American giving to charitable organizations, Regnerus *et al.* (1998) found an association with religiosity by analysing the data from the 1996 Religious Identity and Influence Survey. The 13 per cent of the American population which considered itself non-religious gave less money to charitable organizations than did the rest of the population which held religious beliefs. Moreover, the results showed that 'which religious tradition a person professes and practices is less important than the fact that they practice one' (Regnerus *et al.* 1998: 490).

Analysing various surveys such as British Social Attitudes, the Gallup Poll, and the British Household Panel Survey, Gill concluded:

> There is a great deal of evidence showing that churchgoers are relatively, yet significantly, different from nonchurchgoers. On average they have higher levels of Christian belief (which is hardly surprising), but, in addition, they usually have a stronger sense of moral and civic order and tend to be significantly more altruistic than nonchurchgoers. (1999: 261)

Other research has examined the processes and factors involved in altruistic behaviour, linking them to religion. Based on interviews with young people involved in community service, as well as data from national surveys in the United States, Wuthnow (1995) contends that caring is not innate, but learned, in part from the spontaneous warmth of family life and in part from finding the right kind of volunteer work. He also argues that the best environment to nurture the helping impulse is the religious setting.

Recent work has examined altruism in the context of new religious movements (Inaba 2004; Neusner and Chilton 2005; Habito and Inaba 2006). For example, Inaba (2004) reported a study of Buddhist and Christian new religions involving interview, participant observation, and questionnaires. Altruism was developed not so much (or not primarily) by studying teachings as by relationships between members in the two new religions. The two religions changed members' attitudes positively towards altruism through a combination of relationships between members, ethical teachings, and practices.

Three factors—namely, teachings and practices, role models, and socialization in religions—seem to be significant factors in the development of altruism. People may mention religious practices such as prayer and meditation when they talk about the underlying reasons for development of their altruism. Others may claim that teachings promote their altruism (Inaba 2004). Love is one of the core teachings of Judaism and Christianity. The love commandments, 'You shall love the Lord your God with all your heart, with all your soul, and with all your mind' (Deut. 6: 5), 'You shall love your neighbour as yourself' (Lev. 19: 18), are seen as central. There are variations on the theme of these love commandment in the New Testament (e.g., Matt. 19: 19, 22: 39; Mark 12: 31, 12: 33; Luke 10: 27). Altruism stems not only from these teachings, but from practical examples set by religious role models. In Wuthnow's research on caring (1995), many regarded Mother Teresa as the most compassionate person in the world, although a few admitted that they could not relate to her because she was celibate or too dedicated. For others, role models are close at hand in religious communities.

In Buddhism, some people cultivate their altruism through meditation practice. Meditation may give some sort of peacefulness, enabling or leading to greater altruism. Other Buddhists mention the teachings when they talk about their altruism. In Buddhist texts, there is an emphasis on four states of mind: '*metta*' (lovingkindness: bringing joy and happiness to others), '*karuna*' (compassion: relieving the suffering of others), '*mudita*' (joy at the joy of others), and '*upekkha*' (equanimity). '*Metta*' and '*karuna*' are comparable to '*agapē*' in Christianity.

Newcomers start to form friendships within their religious communities. In the socialization of religious converts, some may experience tension and anxieties in accepting rules and participating in activities in their new religious life. However, because of involvement in practices and activities of their religious communities, they have greater opportunities to share their problems and interact with one another, and may thus find the support, stability, and security. In such circumstances, relationships based on the same faith may result in greater altruism.

In his pioneering qualitative study of religious change, Starbuck suggested that the process of religious conversion and change initiated a more altruistic and selfless perspective. Starbuck (1899: 49–51) listed eight categories for the motives and forces leading to conversion: (1) fear of death or hell; (2) other self-regarding motives; (3) altruistic motives; (4) following out a moral ideal; (5) remorse and conviction for sin; (6) response to teaching; (7) example and imitation; and (8) urging and other forms of social pressure. The representative instances given by Starbuck in the category of altruistic motives are 'I wanted to exert the right influence over my pupils at school', 'I felt I must be better and do more good in the world', and 'It was love for God who had done so much for me' (p. 50). The findings of his survey are notable. Starbuck wrote:

> Only 5 per cent are altruistic motives; and if we select from these the ones who mention love of God or Christ as leading them to a higher life, we find only 2 per cent. This is significant in view of the fact that love of God is a point of great emphasis in Christian ethics. It is of interest to compare fear of hell and conviction for sin, which are prominent, with hope of heaven and love of Christ and God, which are almost absent. (p. 53)

By contrast, with regard to the new life after conversion, Starbuck (p. 126) stated that 'there is clearly bound up in the process a self-forgetfulness, a sympathetic outgoing which apparently exactly contradicts the exaltation of self'. Starbuck (p. 127) offers instances of what the respondents said:

- 'I was no longer self-centred. The change was not complete, but there was a deep undercurrent of unselfishness.'
- 'The change made me very affectionate, while before I was cold to my parents.'
- 'My motive to chase worldly riches was changed to that of saving others.'

Starbuck concluded (p. 128) that in a number of cases 'an immediate result of conversion is to call the person out from himself into active sympathy with the world outside'. Starbuck went on to argue that the outcrops of self-appreciation and of altruism were two aspects of the same thing:

> The heightened worth of self and the altruistic impulses in conversion are closely bound up together, and the differences between them lie simply in the different content of consciousness, determined by the direction in which it is turned. The central fact underlying both is the formation of a new ego, a fresh point of reference for mental states ... in conversion the element which is most fundamental from the standpoint of priority is the wakening of self-consciousness, while the essential factor from the standpoint of development is the process of unselfing. (pp. 129–30)

Thus, Starbuck thought that in conversion the most fundamental aspect was the awakening of self-consciousness, and that the essential factor from the standpoint of development was the process of 'unselfing'.

Other work on religion and altruism has examined the possibility that the altruistic and helpful behaviour reported and observed in religious people is the result of social desirability effects, the wish to 'seem good' (e.g., Darley and Batson 1973; Loewenthal 2000; Duriez 2002; Saroglou *et al.* 2005; Pichon *et al.* 2006). Careful survey and experimental work has established that altruistic and helping behaviour is likely to be an intrinsic aspect of (social) identity among religious people. For example in a Belgian study, Pichon *et al.* found that religious concepts acted at the unconscious level (i.e., after brief exposures too short for conscious recognition) to activate pro-social behavioural schemas. Thus social desirability does not explain the links between religion and pro-social and altruistic behaviour.

In this section, we have examined work indicating general associations between religious involvement and helpful and altruistic behaviour. Although earlier work gave a rather unclear picture, as research methodologies have improved, we can now conclude with more confidence that the links between religion and altruistic behaviour are genuinely causal. Religions can and do promote altruistic behaviour by encouraging the study, socialization, and practice of values including altruism. Altruism is linked to feelings of self-worth, purpose, spirituality, and religious identity.

Summary and Conclusions

This review has indicated the importance of altruism as a core value and ideal in religious teachings, embedded in a network of beliefs about spirituality, soteriology, and purpose in life. Social-scientific concern with altruism, identified and initiated by Weber, has explored the definitions and explanations for helping, pro-social, and altruistic behaviour. The role of religion in promoting altruistic values and behaviour has been a long-standing concern. Although early research offered a rather muddled picture of the role of religion in promoting altruism, research since the 1980s has indicated more clearly that religion is likely to play a causal role in promoting altruism. Across a range of religious traditions, religious teachings and role models are the likely routes by which these effects are achieved.

References

Browning, Don (1992). 'Altruism and Christian Love'. *Zygon*, 27: 421–36.

Carlsmith, J., and Gross, A. (1968). 'Some Effects of Guilt on Compliance'. *Journal of Personality and Social Psychology*, 11: 232–9.

Cline, V. B., and Richards, J. M. Jr. (1965). 'A Factor-Analytic Study of Religious Belief and Behavior'. *Journal of Personality and Social Psychology*, 1: 569–78.

Comte, Auguste (1875). *System of Positive Polity*, i. London: Longmans, Green & Co.

Darley, J. M., and Batson, C. D. (1973). 'From Jerusalem to Jericho: A Study of Situational and Dispositional Variables in Helping Behavior'. *Journal of Personality and Social Psychology*, 27: 100–8.

Duriez, Bart (2004). 'Are Religious People Nicer People? Taking a Closer Look at the Religion–Empathy Relationship'. *Mental Health, Religion and Culture*, 7: 249–54.

Gill, Robin (1999). *Churchgoing and Christian Ethics*. Cambridge: Cambridge University Press.

Habito, R., and Inaba, K. (eds.) (2006). *The Practice of Altruism: Caring and Religion in Global Perspective*. Cambridge: Cambridge Scholars Press.

Inaba, Keishin (2004). *Altruism in New Religious Movements: The Jesus Army and the Friends of the Western Buddhist Order in Britain*. Okayama: University Education Press.

Joseph, S., Linley, A., and Maltby, J. (eds.) (2006). *Mental Health, Religion and Culture*. Special issue of Positive Psychology and Religion.

Krebs, Dennis L., and Van Hesteren, Frank (1992). 'The Development of Altruistic Personality'. In P. M. Oliner and S. P. Oliner (eds.), *Embracing the Other: Philosophical, Psychological, and Historical Perspectives on Altruism*. New York: New York University Press, 142–69.

Langford, B., and Langford, C. (1974). 'Review of the Polls: Church Attendance and Self-Perceived Altruism'. *Journal for the Scientific Study of Religion*, 13: 221–2.

Loewenthal, K. M. (2000). *A Short Introduction to the Psychology of Religion*. Oxford: Oneworld.

Lynn, P., and Smith, H. (1991). *Voluntary Action Research*. London: The Volunteer Centre.

Macaulay, J. R., and Berkowitz, L. (eds.) (1970). *Altruism and Helping Behavior: Social Psychological Studies of some Antecedents and Consequences*. New York: Academic Press.

Montada, Leo, and Bierhoff, Hans Werner (1991). 'Studying Prosocial Behavior in Social Systems'. In *eadem* (eds.), *Altruism in Social Systems*. New York: Hogrefe & Huber Publishers, 1–26.

Nelson, L., and Dynes, R. (1976). 'The Impact of Devotionalism and Attendance on Ordinary and Emergency Helping Behavior'. *Journal for the Scientific Study of Religion*, 15: 47–59.

Neusner, J., and Chilton, B. (eds.) (2005). *Altruism in World Religions*. Washington: Georgetown University Press.

Novak, Philip (1992). *Religion and Altruism*. Petaluna, Calif.: Institute of Noetic Sciences.

Perkins, H. Wesley (1992). 'Student Religiosity and Social Justice Concerns in England and the United States: Are They Still Related?' *Journal for the Scientific Study of Religion*, 31: 353–60.

Pichon, I., Boccatto, G., and Saroglou, V. (2006). 'Nonconscious Influences of Religion on Prosociality'. *European Journal of Social Psychology*, 36: 1–14.

Regan, D. T., Williams, S., and Sparling, S. (1972). 'Voluntary Expiation of Guilt: A Field Study'. *Journal of Personality and Social Psychology*, 24: 42–5.

Regnerus, M., Smith, C., and Sikkink, D. (1998). 'Who Gives to the Poor? The Influence of Religious Tradition and Political Location on the Personal Generosity of Americans toward the Poor'. *Journal for the Scientific Study of Religion*, 37: 481–93.

Rokeach, Milton (1969). 'Religious Values and Social Compassion'. *Review of Religious Research*, 2: 24–39.

RUSHTON, J. PHILIPPE (1980). *Altruism, Socialization, and Society.* Englewood Cliffs, NJ: Prentice-Hall.

—— and SORRENTINO, RICHARD M. (eds.) (1981). *Altruism and Helping Behavior: Social, Personality, and Developmental Perspectives.* Hillsdale, NJ: Lawrence Erlbaum Associates.

SAROGLOU, V., PICHON, I., TROMPETTE, L., VERSCHUEREN, M., and DERNELLE, R. (2005). 'Prosocial Behaviour and Religion: New Evidence Based on Projective Measures and Peer Ratings'. *Journal for the Scientific Study of Religion*, 44: 323–48.

SCHMIDTZ, DAVID (1995). *Rational Choice and Moral Agency.* Princeton: Princeton University Press.

SELIGMAN, MARTIN (2002). *Authentic Happiness.* New York: Free Press.

SHNEUR ZALMAN of LIADI (1973[1796]). *Likkutei Amarim—Tanya*, bilingual edn., trans. N. Mindel, N. Mandel, Z. Posner, and J. I. Shochet. London: Kehot.

SMITH, RONALD E., WHEELER, GREGORY, and DIENER, EDWARD (1975). 'Faith without Works: Jesus people, Resistance to Temptation, and Altruism'. *Journal of Applied Social Psychology*, 5: 320–330.

SOROKIN, PITIRIM A. (1950). *Altruistic Love: A Study of American 'Good Neighbors' and Christian Saints.* Boston: Beacon Press.

STARBUCK, EDWIN D. (1899). *The Psychology of Religion: An Empirical Study of the Growth of Religious Consciousness.* New York: Scribner.

WEBER, MAX (1978). *Economy and Society*, ed. G. Roth and C. Wittich. Berkeley: University of California Press. Originally published in 1921–2 in 2 vols.

WILSON, JOHN, and JANOSKI, THOMAS (1995). 'The Contribution of Religion to Volunteer Work'. *Sociology of Religion*, 56: 137–52.

WUTHNOW, ROBERT (1991). *Acts of Compassion: Caring for Others and Helping Ourselves.* Princeton: Princeton University Press.

—— (1995). *Learning to Care: Elementary Kindness in an Age of Indifference.* Oxford: Oxford University Press.

YABLO, PAUL DAVID (1990). 'A Cross-cultural Examination of Altruism and Helping Behaviour: Thailand and the United States' (Ph.D. thesis: California School of Professional Psychology).

ZOOK, AVEY (1982). 'Religion, Altruism, and Kinship: A Study of Sociobiological Theory'. *Journal of Psychology and Christianity*, 1/2.

SUGGESTED READING

GRANT, COLIN (2001). *Altruism and Christian Ethics.* Cambridge: Cambridge University Press.

POST, STEPHEN, *et al.* (2002). *Altruism and Altruistic Love: Science, Philosophy, & Religion in Dialogue.* Oxford: Oxford University Press.

SEGLOW, JONATHAN (ed.) (2004). *The Ethics of Altruism.* London: Frank Cass.

Also Gill (1999); Habito and Inaba (2006); Inaba (2004); Seligman (2002); Sorokin (1950); and Wuthnow (1995).

CHAPTER 49

RELIGIOUS VIOLENCE

MARK JUERGENSMEYER

Religion is not entirely about violence, of course. Sacred teachings present the most profound images of peaceful existence to be found anywhere, and the idea of nonviolence is central to most religious traditions—it supplies, for instance, the very name of Islam—a word that is cognate with *salaam,* meaning "peace". The ethical principles of religion allow the taking of human life for none but the most extreme reasons, such as defending one's very existence or protecting the faith. Yet the images in the news in the post-Cold War world are often of a great range of violent acts perpetrated in the name of religion. The slaughter of Sunni families in Baghdad by Shi'ite death squads, the strident voices of Jewish settlers aimed at cleansing their territories of Arab occupants, the attacks on abortion clinics by Christian militia in the USA, the anger of Buddhist monks in Sri Lanka towards Tamil separatists and the government that seeks to reconcile with them—how can all of these militant postures be justified in religious terms?

In fact, virtually every religious tradition contains images of violence and instances of social violence that are legitimized by what is imagined to be divine will. The relationship of violence and the sacred clouds the histories of every tradition and has fascinated some of the keenest theorists of religion. Visions of destruction are ubiquitous in religious symbols, mythology, and rituals, and the histories of most religions have left a trail of blood. It is a source of great scholarly fascination to understand why this is so—why violence is essential to religious language and images, how violence is justified in religious ethics, and when religion may be employed to justify acts of social conflict.

At the outset, though, we need to clarify what we mean by "religious violence". As one can see from the illustrations in the first paragraph of this chapter, the term can refer to everything from blood sacrifice in ancient Egypt to the terrorist attacks of September 11; from the Crusades to ethnic fratricide in Sri Lanka; from the epic wars of the Mahabharata to the release of nerve gas in a Tokyo subway. The principal variables are these: are we talking about symbolic images or actual acts of violence? Are we looking at protracted warfare or single terrorist events? Are we referring to contemporary incidents or historical memories? Are we viewing solely religious images and events, or are we seeing how religion is used in incidents that are largely for social or political purposes?

In this chapter, we will be talking about all of these. It would, of course, be conceptually easier if we could focus on one or other of these dichotomies. Given the rise of a certain kind of religious violence in the first decade of the twenty-first century, my preference would be to limit our discussion to something like "contemporary acts of terrorism undertaken for religious motives". But—as if the world were determined to make life difficult for social analysis—the reality is not so simple. Events of religious violence today often cut across our attempts to categorize them. As indicated by the last instructions given to the nineteen men who hijacked airlines and crashed them into the Pentagon and the World Trade Center on September 11, 2001, their act was performed in the pattern of religious ritual. Their commitment touched religious depths, and their *jihadi* ideology was suffused with the images and ideas of their religious history (Lincoln 2006).

Was the bombing of the World Trade Center a religious act or a political one? It can be said to be either or both, for it is apparent that one of the most significant features of contemporary religious activism is that it entails not only the politicization of religion, but the religionization of politics. By the latter term I mean the way in which political life has been encompassed by the religious imagination, and how social and political struggles have been drawn into the realm of cosmic drama. Ordinary fights between political opponents have become charged with spiritual force, so that those engaged in combat are opposing what they imagine to be not just a despicable opponent but a satanic foe—as Hamas has characterized both the State of Israel and, at times, the secular Palestinian leadership that does not share its vision of Palestine as a religious state. A foe of such evil proportions is dehumanized to the extent that it is no longer a person: it is an evil thing, and any form of force is warranted in subduing it.

Because today's events of religious violence defy any easy categorization, they invite the explanations of theories as varied as the dimensions of religious violence that these incidents contain: theories relating to symbolic and real violence, warfare and terrorism, contemporary and historical events, religious and socio-political motivations. The authors of these theories come from fields as multiple as the topics: from literary theory, psychology, anthropology, sociology, political science, and theology. As we shall see, each set of theorists presents its own theoretical solace to the Job-like plague of religious violence in our contemporary life.

Sacrificial Violence: Anthropology and Early Sociology

In many theories about religion, symbols of religious violence occupy a prominent place—just as they do in religion itself. The martyrdom of Husain in Shi'ite Islam, the crucifixion of Jesus in Christianity, the savage death of Guru Tegh Bahadur in Sikhism, the bloody conquests in the Hebrew Bible, the terrible battles celebrated in Hindu epics, and the religious wars described in the Sinhalese Buddhist chronicles are all testimony to the significance of violence in religious myth and history. The visibility of such symbols as the Christians' cross, the Muslims' sword, and the Sikhs' saber witnesses to their power.

Perhaps the most common symbol of violence—one that is ubiquitous in all ancient traditions—is sacrifice. The domestication of sacrifice in evolved forms of religious practice—such as the Christian ritual of the eucharist—belies the real acts of violence that were present in the ancient acts: a real animal (in some cases a human) offered its life on a sacred chopping block, an altar. The Vedic Agnicayana ritual—some 3,000 years old and probably the most ancient ritual still performed today—involves the construction of an elaborate altar for sacrificial ritual, originally an animal sacrifice. Some say it involved human sacrifice (Staal 1983). This was said to be so at the other side of the world, at the time of the ancient Aztec empire. Literary accounts describe situations in which conquered soldiers were treated royally in preparation for sacrifice—and their still-beating hearts would then be ripped from their chests and offered to Huitzilopochtli and other gods, eventually to be eaten by the faithful, their faces skinned to make ritual masks. In the Hebrew Bible, sacred to Jews, Christians, and Muslims, the book of Leviticus gives detailed guides for preparing animals for sacrificial slaughter, and the very architecture of ancient Israeli temples reflects the centrality of the sacrificial act.

Because of its centrality, some of the earliest scholarly theories of religious violence begin with sacrifice. In the nineteenth century, E. B. Tylor (1870) posited that primitive sacrifice was an attempt to bribe the gods; as religion evolved, Tylor explained, sacrifice became internalized in the form of self-renunciation. W. Robertson-Smith (1889) saw sacrifice as a ritual meal, its destructiveness leading to a covenantal bond. In *The Golden Bough*, James G. Frazer (1900) identified sacrifice as the key element of religion: the killing of kings and holy men allowed the gods to be rejuvenated, and the symbolic sacrifice of modern religion Frazer saw as an extension of this ancient magic.

The concept of sacrifice was also important to the notion of religion advanced by Émile Durkheim. Perhaps the most expressive statement from a Durkheimian perspective was the study of sacrifice prepared by sociologists Henri Hubert and Marcel Mauss (1899). They regarded sacrifice as the seminal religious act, since it provided a mediation between the sacred and profane realms of reality: the sacrificer offered life—the sacrificed animal—to the eternal being, who in turn bestowed life to the giver. Killing the sacrificed animal was a way of communicating with the divine. According to these anthropologists, the sacrificial act of mediation between the sacred and the profane is what gives religious communities their transcendent character and what makes possible the sacred legitimation for political authority and social order.

Hubert and Mauss's Durkheimian theory continued to be used by a great number of anthropologists and other scholars throughout the twentieth century, including anthropologist E. E. Evans-Pritchard in his famous study of Nuer sacrifice (Evans-Pritchard 1956). It has come under criticism, however, for being overly dependent on Vedic, Jewish, and Christian examples. Scholars of Greek and African cultures have revised Hubert and Mauss to fit their own cases. One of the sharpest critics has been the classicist Marcel Detienne (1979), who accepts the Durkheimian notion of sacrifice as mediation, but focuses on the act of cooking and eating the sacrificed animal as an element equal to, or more important than, the act of killing it.

One of the most interesting of the recent theories of religious violence in the Durkheimian tradition—and the most relevant for our contemporary situation—comes from an anthropologist, Maurice Bloch. Bloch has accepted Detienne's critique of Hubert and Mauss, providing a revised theory of sacrifice that relates symbolic acts of violence to acts of warfare and conquest in the real world. In his book, *Prey into Hunter* (1992), Bloch shows how sacrificial ritual in many societies is an empowering act: it is a way of identifying with a victim in order to surmount the fear of victimization and become a conquering warrior and hunter.

Although Bloch's references are to tribal societies, one could relate Bloch's ideas to contemporary acts of terrorism, and suggest that they too are symbolic attempts at empowerment. In the case of Islamic militants in Algeria and Egypt, their use of terrorism may be a symbolic attempt by disenfranchised groups to gain a sense of the power that has been denied them at the ballot box. But more than that, as indicated in Bloch's theory, they may hope that the confidence built through such acts will lead to the reality of power. This symbolic transformation from powerlessness to real power was precisely what was prescribed by Franz Fanon, author of *The Wretched of the Earth* (1963), who wrote about an earlier period of political conflict in Algeria, its colonial struggle against the French. According to Fanon's philosophy of terrorism, a symbolic act of violence can impart a feeling of empowerment to the masses, and thus spark a real revolution. In reality, however, such acts of catalytic violence are often counterproductive. To the terrorists' dismay, the masses are often repelled rather than empowered by such acts, and the strategy may alienate potential supporters of the cause as much as it attracts them.

Displaced Violence: Literary Theory and Psychology

Is symbolic violence empowering? Or does it conduce to social harmony? Another strand of intellectual thought—also focusing on sacrifice—argues that symbolic acts of violence, such as sacrificial rituals, diffuse violence and lead to social bonding. A body of psychological and literary analyses in the twentieth century has attempted to show that such symbols as sacrifice are culturally useful precisely because they defuse violent urges between people and thus allay real acts of violence.

Many of the ideas relating to this understanding of the violent symbols of religion can be traced to the pioneering psychological theories of Sigmund Freud. Freud advanced a theory of religious violence that by extension accounts for virtually all forms of culture. In *Totem and Taboo* (1918), Freud explained that the destructive instinct in human nature would tear apart a family, tribe, or civil society if it were not symbolically displaced and directed toward a sacrificial foe. Freud regarded the myth of Oedipus—in which a man desires to kill his father and seduce his mother—as the prototype of all myth.

Although many aspects of Freud's theories are now discredited, the major theme—that symbolic violence can reduce the threat of real acts of violence—has survived. Ernst Becker (1973; 1975), for instance, accepts that the purpose of violence in religion is to sublimate the violence of real life, and ultimately to deny the reality of death. Weston La Barre (1970) argues that all religion—like the Ghost Dance religion of the Plains Indians—is an attempt to escape the horrors of cultural and physical destruction, and to appeal for support from immortal forces. Writing in the same vein, but employing semiotic analyses of sacrifice by Jean-Pierre Vernant and Marcel Detienne, and biological studies of aggression by Konrad Lorenz, Walter Burkert (1972) concludes that the bloody myths and sacrificial rituals of ancient Greece and other societies allow a group collectively to confront the reality of death and the power of violence, to increase inner-group solidarity, and to give the group a biological advantage for survival (see also Kitts 2005).

The role of sacrifice in allaying both violence and the fear of sexuality—a theme that is prominent in Freud—is revived by an American psychologist, Eli Sagan (1972), in psychoanalytic studies of Greek myth and cannibalism, relying on both historical and anthropological accounts. In a vastly different way, this combination is also evoked by the French literary theorist Georges Bataille (1973), who mixes sex, religion, violence, and modern capitalism in a curious mélange (and with a writing style that some may find to be excessively self-indulgent). Although Bataille regards Durkheim as his intellectual forebear, he borrows as much from Freud and Foucault as he does from Durkheim in a theory that tries to explain external conquests and acts of control as attempts to reclaim the shattered self.

In America, the most influential attempt to resuscitate Freud's ideas on religious violence—and one that has been used to explain contemporary terrorist acts—comes from a French literary theorist, René Girard, who teaches at Stanford. In *Violence and the Sacred* (1972), Girard accepts the Freudian point that religion's symbols and rituals of violence evoke, and thereby vent, violent impulses and allow those who embrace them to release their feelings of hostility towards members of their own communities. Parting company with Freud, however, Girard rejects the notion that aggressive instincts are the motor that drives the sacrificial act, and identifies instead the basic impulse as "mimetic desire"—the urge to imitate and better one's rival, and to desire what one's rival desires.

Like other literary theorists and psychologists, Girard generally avoids the problem of real acts of religious violence, such as the terrorism that has gripped many parts of the contemporary world. After all, according to Girard's theories (and, for that matter, the theories of Freud), the proper enactment of the symbols and rituals of religion should conduce to nonviolence and social harmony, not to terrorism and social disruption. From Girard's and Freud's points of view, symbolic expressions of violence in myths and rituals should alleviate the desire for violent acts.

Girard's theories—and Girard himself—have been put to the test by a number of critics, including a working committee of the Harry Frank Guggenheim Foundation. The Guggenheim project was an encounter between Girard and a group of social scientists who have studied contemporary aspects of religious violence. I was privileged to chair the committee and participate in the project, which resulted in a volume, *Violence and the Sacred in the Modern World* (Juergensmeyer 1991), that contains both critiques of Girard and attempts to apply his theories to the contemporary situation. The volume concludes with a response from Girard.

In the Guggenheim volume several authors find Girard's insights to be usefully applied to the contemporary situation. A modern historian of Islam, Emmanuel Sivan (1991), describes a kind of mimesis—the ideological rivalry between Islamic and Jewish militants in the Middle East—as a central component in the conflict. A political scientist, Ehud Sprinzak (1991*b*), sees Rabbi Meir Kahane's envy of the Gentiles as a prime factor in the feelings of vengeance that have propelled the

Rabbi's anti-Arab ideology. A Middle East studies scholar, Martin Kramer (1991), takes a close look at the members of the Hezbollah and Amal terrorist groups who were selected as the suicide bombers in attacks on Israeli and American military. Kramer finds that these young people bear many of the characteristics of sacrificial victims in traditional religion. Moreover, he sees something of a sacrificial rivalry between Hezbollah and Amal, each trying to outdo the other in acts of martyrdom.

Perhaps the most controversial essay in the book was written by a colleague of Girard's, Mark Anspach (1991), who utilizes Girardian theories to explain why, in his frame of reference, Islam is more prone to violence than other traditions. He argues that this allegation is true in part because the Muslim tradition lacks a sufficient ritual apparatus to diffuse violent urges, and instead violence is "channeled outward against the infidels" as a "ritual requirement in Islam". Christianity, on the other hand, is alleged by Anspach to be more pacifist in its outlook, not only because it has sufficient rituals to act out, and thereby prevent, violence, but also because Christianity is alone among the world's religions in portraying its God—in the person of Christ—as a sacrificial victim. Critics of Anspach's theories about the alleged violent character of Islam and the pacifist character of Christianity cite evidence to show that Christianity has been an even greater instigator of international and internal conflict throughout history than Islam. One can contest these historical examples on both sides by challenging what constitutes an incident of conflict and what can be attributed to religious rather than political instigation. The point remains that the theoretical analysis of an assumed fact is as valid as the assumption on which it rests. For this reason analytical perspectives drawn primarily from historical and literary examples are often applied to contemporary cases with a certain amount of controversy.

Strategies of Violence: Sociologists and Political Scientists

Other social scientists have approached the matter of religious violence quite differently. Rather than beginning with sacrifice and other artifacts of religion, they begin with the social and political contexts that give rise to religious images and acts. Here the theoretical roots lie in the ideas of two great theorists of society, Max Weber and Karl Marx. Weber saw religious values as affecting social patterns, and vice versa; the case of the "Protestant ethic" both shaping and being informed by "the spirit of capitalism" is Weber's (1930) best-known example. Marx (1960), on the other hand, took religion to be both a tool of the social situation and an expression of it: both an "opiate" and a "sigh of the oppressed". In this context

Marx thought of violence—in the form of class conflict—as being endemic to the social role that religion played as an instrument of exploitation.

Although few modern sociologists and political scientists hew closely to Weberian or Marxist formulas, they, like their famous forebears, tend to see religion as an expression of social structure, and religious violence as an instrument of social or political forces. They are primarily interested in real acts of violence in the world, and less interested in the symbolic and ritualized depictions of it. For that reason, some social scientists who study political conflict and terrorism find nothing intrinsically special about religious forms of public violence. There is no category for "religious terrorism" in Walter Laqueur's encyclopedic study, *The Age of Terrorism* (1987), for example.

Along similar lines, Martha Crenshaw, a political scientist who specializes in the study of theories of terrorism, finds no special theoretical approach to the study of religious terrorist movements. Rather, she distinguishes between "instrumental" and "organizational" approaches to the subject. The former focus on the instrumental results that a terrorist group hopes to achieve by using its strategy of violence, and the latter look at the organizational context of the group itself: the schisms, power plays, and internal conflicts that may lead to acts of bravado meant more to impress or intimidate wayward members of their own group than to achieve strategic victory against their external opponents (Crenshaw 1988; 1995).

But although most social scientists are concerned with the matter of how religious activists behave in political and social ways—and not with their religious motivations—some social scientists have returned to Weber's challenge of trying to understand the interaction of values and social structure, and see how religious beliefs may have a social impact. A political scientist, David C. Rapoport, for example, finds that terrorist strategies are evoked by religious activists especially in times of messianic expectation, when their acts may be justified by apocalyptic images of a radical transformation of history and society (Rapoport 1988; 1991). Another political scientist, Ehud Sprinzak, describes the "catastrophic messianism" that can emerge in Israeli society in times of weak authority structures and an unbridled ideology of democracy (Sprinzak 1988; 1991*a*). Martin Riesebrodt (1993), a sociologist of religion at the University of Chicago, has compared the implicit violence of Christian fundamentalists in the United States and Islamic revolutionaries in Iran, and cited the respective traditions' propensities for shoring up patriarchal patterns of religious and secular authority.

In my own book, *Global Rebellion: Religious Challenges to the Secular State* (Juergensmeyer 2008), I put the current rise of religious violence in the context of geo-politics and the historical decline of the intellectual hegemony of what Jürgen Habermas (1975) calls "the Enlightenment project". The resulting loss of faith in secular nationalism in various parts of the world, I argue, has spawned new attempts to secure the moral footings of public life in the traditional ethics of religious traditions. I see these movements for religious nationalism as historically new inventions; for in some cases they merge the values of traditional community with the modern artifice of the nation-state, providing a religious legitimization for nationalism at a time of global political insecurity. In other cases their visions are transnational, and aim at alternatives to the Western-oriented forms of economic and cultural globalization. The violence of these movements is understandable, I assert, for they challenge the established political order at its theoretical roots.

In a chapter of my book devoted specifically to the issue of violence, I observe that the religious character of new nationalist movements gives a particularly violent tinge to the encounter, since religion gives moral justification for undertaking violent acts. As Max Weber once observed, the power of the state rests in large part on its monopoly over morally sanctioned violence, which it uses primarily for police protection and military defense. Religious authority is the only entity that can challenge that monopoly (Weber 1946: 78). For that reason, I regard acts of religious violence as revolutionary: the symbolic potency of religion is potentially a resource for political as well as spiritual empowerment.

Theological Justifications for Religious Violence

The idea of religious violence as empowerment, a theme central to many social scientists who have written about the subject, is a motif that is sometimes also adopted by those writing from within religious traditions. Sacrificial rituals, for instance, can be spiritually interpreted as acts of renewal and regeneration. In this, as in many related areas, theological and social-scientific points of view converge.

Often theological writings will describe symbolic images of destruction as acts of purification and transformation, and as expressions of the quest for social harmony, in ways that are not that dissimilar from the insights of the psychologists, literary theorists, and social scientists mentioned above. The writings of René Girard, for instance, have attracted a great deal of attention from Christian theologians. A leading Latin American theologian has published a volume of essays mining Girard's ideas for their utility in liberation theology (Assmann 1991).

Theologians and other religious thinkers have written thoughtfully not only about these symbolic acts of violence but also about real ones. In a sense they have no choice. The violence perpetrated in the name of religion during the present age and over the centuries requires some sort of religious response, either to condemn it or give it moral justification.

Christianity

The controversy over whether Christianity sanctions violence has hounded the church from its very beginning. Some have argued that Christians were expected to follow Jesus' example of selfless love (*agapē*), and "love your enemies and pray for those who persecute you" (Matt. 5: 44). Those who took the other side have referred to the incident in which Jesus drove the money changers from the Temple, and to his enigmatic statement: "Do not think that I have come to bring peace on earth; I have not come to bring peace but a sword" (Matt. 10: 34; cf. also Luke 12: 51–2). The early Church Fathers, including Tertullian and Origen, asserted that Christians were constrained from taking human life, a principle that prevented Christians from serving in the Roman army.

When Christianity was vaulted into the status of state religion by Constantine in the fourth century CE, it began to reject pacifism and accept the doctrine of just war, an idea first stated by Cicero and later developed by Ambrose and Augustine. The abuse of the concept in justifying military adventures and violent persecutions of heretical and minority groups led Thomas Aquinas, in the thirteenth century, to reaffirm that war is always sinful, even if it is occasionally waged for a just cause. Remarkably, the just war theory still stands today as the centerpiece of Christian understanding about the moral use of violence (see, e.g., Ramsay 1968; Potter 1969). Some Christian theologians have adapted the theory of just war to liberation theology, arguing that the church can embrace a "just revolution" (Brown 1987; Gutierrez 1988).

An American Protestant theologian, Reinhold Niebuhr, showed the relevance of the just war theory to contemporary social struggles by relating it to the Christian requirement to fulfill social justice. When violence is employed for the sake of justice, Niebuhr explained, it must be used as swiftly and skillfully "as a surgeon's knife" (Niebuhr 1932: 134). In a famous essay answering the question, "why the Christian Church is not pacifist", Niebuhr—who had himself been a pacifist earlier in his career—built his case on Augustine's understanding of original sin. Because of the sinful nature of humanity, Niebuhr argued, righteous force was sometimes necessary to extirpate injustice and subdue evil within a sinful world (Niebuhr 1940).

Islam

Other religious traditions have also found ways of justifying violence—either for defense of the faith or to maintain social order. In Islam, for instance, violence is required within the tradition for purposes of punishment, and in Muslim contacts outside the tradition violence is sometimes deemed necessary in order to defend the faith. In the "world of conflict" (*dar al harb*) outside the Muslim world, force is a means of cultural survival. In such contexts, maintaining the purity of religious existence is sometimes a matter of *jihad*, a word that literally means "striving", and is often translated as "holy war" (Peters 1979; Martin 1969). This concept has sometimes been used by Muslim warriors to justify the expansion of political control into non-Muslim regions. But Islamic law does not allow *jihad* to be used arbitrarily, for personal gain or to justify forcible conversion to the faith; the only conversions regarded as valid are those that come about nonviolently, through rational persuasion and a change of heart.

In recent years Muslim political activists have employed the notion of *jihad* to justify militant political acts, implicitly a defense of the faith in a secular—and therefore presumably hostile—world. According to an Egyptian author, Abd al-Salam Faraj, one of the thinkers behind the group implicated in the assassination of Sadat, *jihad* has been a "neglected duty" (Jansen 1986). It is one nonetheless incumbent on all true Muslims, who are urged by Faraj to defend the faith—violently if necessary—in the hostile social and political spheres of the modern world. An early twentieth-century Pakistani thinker, Sayid Abul Ala Maududi, has been influential in the thinking of Faraj and many other radical Sunni Muslims, and has helped them to understand the necessity of appropriating violent means in the political defense of the faith (Adams 1966; Jansen 1986). Ideas about religious revolution and the righteous use of violent power expressed by the Ayatollah Khomeini (1981) have also had a seminal influence—especially on Shi'ite Muslims in Iran, but also on Muslims of all persuasions throughout the world. From Khomeini's perspective, the Islamic world has been captive to Western—especially American—cultural and economic control, and must free itself not only for purposes of political liberation but also for spiritual freedom as well.

Judaism

In the Jewish tradition, some of the earliest images are the most violent. "The Lord is a warrior," proclaims Exodus 15: 3, and the first books of the Hebrew Bible include scenes of utter desolation caused by divine intervention. Rabbinic Judaism, despite several militant clashes with the Romans—including the Maccabean Revolt (166–164 BCE) and the revolt at Masada (73 CE)—is largely nonviolent. At the level of statecraft, however, the rabbis did sanction warfare, but distinguished between "religious" war and "optional" war (Biale 1987; Baron *et al.* 1977). The former they required as a moral or spiritual obligation: to protect the faith or defeat enemies of the Lord. These they contrasted with wars waged primarily for reasons of political expediency.

In modern Israel, religious writings have emerged that support warfare in the cause of Israeli irridentism, and justify force used against the Arabs. The most influential of these are the writings of Rabbi Abraham Isaac Kuk (also spelled

Kook) and his son (Metzger 1968; Agus 1946; Biale 1983), with their notions of messianic Zionism. Following Kuk's train of thought, Rabbi Meir Kahane developed his own distinctive "catastrophic Messianism", as Ehud Sprinzak (1991*b*) has called it (see also Kahane 1978; 1981). One of the dark features of Kahane's logic is what he regarded as the theological necessity of eradicating Arabs from biblical Israel (including the West Bank)—a position that caused some observers to dub him "Israel's Ayatollah" (Mergui and Simonnot 1985; and Kotler 1986). His posturing has left a legacy of violence—including his own assassination in 1990 at the hands of the Muslim group in New York City implicated in the 1993 bombing of the World Trade Center and the 1994 massacre at the Cave of the Patriarchs by Dr Baruch Goldstein, one of Kahane's followers.

Hinduism

In India's ancient Vedic times, warriors called on the gods to participate in their struggles, thus merging the sacred and worldly realms, and providing a divine basis for warfare. In the later development of Hinduism, the Bhagavad Gita gives several reasons why killing in warfare is permissible, including the argument that the soul can never really be killed: "he who slays, slays not; he who is slain, is not slain" (Bhagavad Gita 2: 19). Another position given in the Gita is based on dharma (moral obligation): duties of a member of the *ksatriya* (warrior) caste by definition involved killing, so it was justified in the very maintenance of social order. Mohandas Gandhi (1960), like many other modern Hindus who revere the Gita, regarded its warfare as an allegorical reference to the eternal conflict between good and evil. Gandhi, who ordinarily subscribed to nonviolence, allowed for an exception to his general rule of pacificism when a small, strategic act of violence would defuse a greater violence (see Juergensmeyer 2005). The rise of Hindu nationalism has been the occasion for new justifications of Hindu militancy and a fair amount of Hindu violence. In the anti-colonial struggle against the British, militant Bengali Hindus were inspired by Kali, goddess of destruction. The use of force in more recent versions of Hindu nationalist ideology is justified by V. D. Savarkar and other leaders of the militant Rashtriya Swyamsevak Sangh (National Service Organization), which is one of the precursors to the hugely successful Hindu nationalist political organization, the Bharatiya Janata Party (Savarkar 1969; Andersen and Damle 1987; van der Veer 1994).

Sikhism

Like the Hindu tradition, to which it is historically related, Sikhism contains precepts that are basically peaceful, yet allow enough exceptions that recent militant activists can utilize these ideas to justify violent acts. Guru Nanak, the sixteenth-century spiritual master regarded as the Sikhs' founder, is portrayed in literature and hagiography as a gentle soul. But the movement in time came to be led by members of a militant tribal group, the Jats, and Sikhs have periodically clashed with Mughals, the British, and other Indian rulers (McLeod 1976). The core of the Sikh community is known as "the army of the faithful" (*Dal Khalsa*), and their symbol is a double-edged sword. The conquests of the great nineteenth-century ruler Maharaja Ranjit Singh and the violent exhortations of the twentieth-century militant, Jarnail Singh Bhindranwale, are both justified by the Sikh doctrine of *miri-piri*: the idea that religion is to be victorious in both the spiritual and worldly realms (Bhindranwale 1999). Bhindranwale was killed on 5 June 1984, when the Indian Prime Minister, Indira Gandhi, sent troops into the Sikhs' Golden Temple where the militant leader was ensconced. Later that year Mrs Gandhi herself was savagely killed by her own Sikh bodyguards in retaliation for Bhindranwale's death and the invasion of the Temple, which was regarded by many Sikhs as an act of desecration that warranted revenge.

Buddhism

One might expect that the Buddhist doctrine of *ahimsa*—nonviolence—would make it immune from religiously justified acts of violence. But even traditional Buddhist teachings allow for exceptions to the rule, and require that five conditions be satisfied in order to prove that an act of violence has indeed taken place: (1) something living must have been killed; (2) the killer must have known that it was alive; (3) the killer must have intended to kill it; (4) an actual act of killing must have taken place; and (5) the person or animal attacked must, in fact, have died (Saddhatissa 1970). It is the absence of the third condition—the intention to kill—that typically allows for some mitigation of the rule of nonviolence. For instance, many Buddhists will eat meat as long as they have not themselves intended that the animal be killed or been involved in the act of slaughtering it. Armed defense—even warfare—has been justified on the grounds that such violence has been in the nature of response, not intent. To use violence nondefensively—for the purpose of political expansion, for example—would be prohibited under Buddhist rules (Saddhatissa 1970; Tambiah 1987; 1992).

In modern political struggles in Buddhist societies such as Sri Lanka, Buddhism has been bent to fit the revolutionary goals and motives of nationalist ideologies. When I asked a Buddhist monk in Sri Lanka how, in light of the Buddhist subscription to *ahimsa*, he justified support for a militant movement implicated in hundreds of deaths, including assassination attempts on political leaders, he resorted again to Buddhist concepts: "We live in an adhammic [immoral] world," he said, implying that, like Christian, Muslim, and Jewish thinkers, the immorality of this sinful world drives the religious person to acts of violence for justice, survival, and defense of the faith (Juergensmeyer 2008).

Comparative Studies of Religious Violence

Although each of these justifications and explanations for religious violence is enlightening, taken together the differences in their emphases and the contradictions between their conclusions can be vexing. This is especially so when one attempts to apply these insights to contemporary acts of violence committed in the name of religion. The conundrum of religious violence is puzzling in large part because it involves an attempt to explain not only why bad things happen, but also why bad things happen for reasons purported by their perpetrators to be good. Since we are products of an intellectually self-confident age, we are not content to let explanations for such religious violence reside entirely in the mind of God.

Yet it is helpful to attempt to understand religious violence from the point of view of the nature of religion itself—not only from the perspective of particular theological positions, but from the reference point of the religious imagination in general. Several of the schools of theory that I have discussed have tried to do just that: to locate the justification for violence within a comprehensive understanding of religion, an approach that is also taken by philosophers from Kant to Derrida (de Vries 2001). Durkheimians, for instance, have seen conflict as part of a quest for order lying behind the sacrificial interaction between sacred and profane; Freudians view the role of symbolic violence in the mediation of conflict and efforts to produce social harmony; other social scientists see violence as part of the symbolic expression of social conflict and cooperation; and theologians of all stripes see the violence in religion as a dimension of transcendence itself and part of a broad spiritual understanding of sacred history and material life.

The field of religious studies—the academic study of religion also known as "comparative religion", "the history of religions", and "the phenomenology of religions", and to German-speaking scholars as *Religionswissenschaft*—places its discussions of religious violence within this totalistic perspective. Following the pioneers in this field, such as Joachim Wach and Mircea Eliade, scholars of religious studies attempt, as Jacques Waardenburg (1978: 94) put it, to "reconstruct religious meanings". Wilfred Cantwell Smith (1959: 37) has described it as an understanding of "the religious life" of a community that knits together the various literary, social, and psychological ways in which that life is manifest.

In line with the religious studies school of thought, one of Eliade's students, Bruce Lincoln, has brought the Hubert and Mauss thesis on sacrifice into a broad analysis, and envisioned violent acts as part of a "master discourse" intended to link together the cosmos, the human body, and society (Lincoln 1991). At Santa Barbara, Roger Friedland and Richard Hecht (1996), in combining sociological with religious studies perspectives, have regarded sacred centrality (divine axes in both space and time) as primary to the religious world view. In their study of the conflict between Jews, Muslims, and Christians over the sacred sites in Jerusalem, they show how such conflicting views of sacrality can easily lead to violence.

My own contribution to an understanding of religious violence comes from the intersection of religious studies and the sociology of religion, in my discussion of the concept of cosmic war (Juergensmeyer 2003). It seems to me that what unites symbolic and real acts of religious violence is a fundamental religious impulse, the quest for order. Underlying the savage imagery of cosmic war is an orderly perception of the world, a world divided into warring camps and knit together in a scenario of warfare that will ultimately lead to a triumphant and peaceful end. The conceptual template of cosmic war is able to embrace apparent social anomalies—such as the persistent control of societies by alien forces or the sudden destruction of major buildings in a modern urban center—and provide a framework in which these anomalies make sense. The images of cosmic war do what religion in general does well: provide a deep framework of order that gives meaning to life's contradictions and hope that counters despair.

This way of thinking about religion—as ultimate order—is not wholly new; it is one that has been enunciated in various interpretations by social theorists in the Durkheimian school and by theologians such as Paul Tillich and David Tracy (Tracy 1975). It seems to me that religious violence, in both its symbolic and its real forms, illuminates this basic characteristic of religion. Acts of religious violence fit into large religious programs of cosmic order. These paradigms of order provide ways of thinking about the world as caught between secular and transcendent histories, the latter offering a world that is regarded by the faithful as eventually moving beyond the state of worldly violence to a stage of being that is harmonious and just. It is this paradox—that violence is perceived as a pathway to peace—that is central, I believe, both to religious violence and to religion in general. Those of us who work in this field are still groping towards a general theory of religion that will allow us to understand how the religious impulse of humanity is always a yearning for transcendence and tranquility, even when it fuels the most vicious aspects of human imagination. In the mind of God, if not in humans' reckoning, we are convinced that there is a link between violence and nonviolence, between worldly disorder and transcendent order. Understanding this link may help us moderate the most savage effects of religious violence and give greater force to the nonviolent aspects of religious teachings.

In the early years of the Ayatollah Khomeini's rise to power, one of my colleagues, an Islamicist, was bold enough to compare the Ayatollah to Mahatma

Gandhi. In almost every way, she explained, the two were similar: both condemned the vacuousness of modern secular society; both envisioned a moral politics built on traditional values; and both conceived the transition to be a time of struggle in which worldly order would be disrupted so that Godly order could intervene. They both led mass movements that were mobilized by socially adept religious leaders. The only difference, she said, was that Khomeini allowed for violent means, whereas Gandhi did not.

In a sense my colleague was wrong; for there is a world of difference between an approach to social change that justifies violence and one that does not. In another sense, however, she was correct: both Khomeini and Gandhi were concerned with the generation of social and spiritual power through religion, and how it can be morally justified and applied. The headlines in today's newspapers graphically show how potent a force religion is. The question that remains is how we can understand the relationship between this power and the religious goals of harmony and peace.

References

Adams, Charles (1966). "The Ideology of Mawlana Mawdudi". In Donald E. Smith (ed.), *South Asian Politics and Religion.* Princeton: Princeton University Press, 371–84.

Agus, Jacob B. (1946). *Banner of Jerusalem: The Life, Times, and Thought of Rabbi Abraham Isaac Kuk.* New York: Bloch.

Andersen, Walter K., and Shridhar, D. Damle (1987). *The Brotherhood in Saffron: The Rashtriya Swayamsevak Sangh and Hindu Revivalism.* Boulder, Col.: Westview Press.

Anspach, Mark R. (1991). "Violence Against Violence: Islam in Comparative Context". In Juergensmeyer (1991), 24–32.

Assmann, Hugo (ed.) (1991). *Sobre idolos y sacrificios: Rene Girard con teologos de la liberación.* San Jose, Costa Rica: Editorial Departamento de Investigaciones.

Baron, Salo, Wise, George S., and Goodman, Lenn (eds.) (1977). *Violence and Defense in the Jewish Experience.* Philadelphia: Jewish Publication Society of America.

Bataille, Georges (1973). *Théorie de la Religion.* Paris: Éditions Gallimard. English trans. by Robert Hurley: *Theory of Religion.* New York: Zone Books, 1992.

Becker, Ernest (1973). *The Denial of Death.* New York: Free Press.

—— (1975). *Escape from Evil.* New York: Free Press.

Bhindranwale, Sant Jarnail Singh Khalsa (1999). *Struggle for Justice: Speeches and Conversations of Sant Jarnail Singh Khalsa Bhindranwale,* trans. Ranbir Singh Sandhu. Dublin, Ohio: Sikh Educational and Religious Foundation.

Biale, David J. (1983). "Mysticism and Politics in Modern Israel: The Messianic Ideology of Abraham Isaac Ha-Cohen Kook". In Peter H. Merki and Ninian Smart (eds.), *Religion and Politics in the Modern World.* New York: York University Press, 191–202.

—— (1987). *Power and Powerlessness in Jewish History.* New York: Schocken Books.

Bloch, Maurice (1992). *Prey into Hunter: The Politics of Religious Experience.* Cambridge: Cambridge University Press.

Brown, Robert McAfee (1987). *Religion and Violence*, 2nd edn. Philadelphia: Westminster Press.

Burkert, Walter (1972). *Homo Necans*. Berlin: Walter de Gruyter and Co. English trans. by Peter Bing: *Homo Necans: The Anthropology of Ancient Greek Sacrificial Ritual and Myth*. Berkeley: University of California Press, 1983.

Crenshaw, Martha (1988). "Theories of Terrorism". In David C. Rapoport (ed.), *Inside Terrorist Organizations*. London: Frank Cass and Company, 13–31.

—— (1995). *Terrorism in Context*. University Park, Pa.: Pennsylvania State University Press.

Detienne, Marcel (1979). "Culinary Practices and the Spirit of Sacrifice". In Marcel Detienne and Jean-Pierre Vernant (eds.), *The Cuisine of Sacrifice among the Greeks*. English trans. by Paula Wissing. Chicago: University of Chicago Press, 1989. Originally published in French as *La cuisine du sacrifice en pays grec*. Paris: editions Gallimard, 1979.

de Vries, Hent (2001). *Religion and Violence: Philosophical Perspectives from Kant to Derrida*. Baltimore: Johns Hopkins University Press.

Evans-Pritchard, E. E. (1956). *Nuer Religion*. Oxford: Oxford University Press.

Fanon, Franz (1963). *The Wretched of the Earth*. New York: Grove Press.

Frazer, James G. (1900). *The Golden Bough: A Study in Magic and Religion*, rev. edn. London: Macmillan.

Freud, Sigmund (1918). *Totem and Taboo: Resemblances between the Psychic Lives of Savages and Neurotics*, trans. A. A. Brill. New York: Moffat, Yard, and Co.

Friedland, Roger, and Hecht, Richard D. (1996). "Divisions at the Center: The Organization of Political Violence at Jerusalem's Temple Mount/al-Haram al-Sharif—1929 and 1990". In Paul Brass (ed.), *Riots and Pograms: The Nation-State and Violence*. New York: Macmillan, 114–53.

Gandhi, Mohandas (1960). *Discourses on the Gita*, trans. from the original Gujarati edition by V. G. Desai. Ahmedabad: Navajivan Publishing House.

Girard, René (1972). *La violence et le sacre*. Paris: Éditions Bernard Grasset. English trans. by Patrick Gregory: *Violence and the Sacred*. Baltimore: Johns Hopkins University Press, 1977.

Gutierrez, Gustavo (1988). *A Theology of Liberation: History, Politics, and Salvation*, rev. edn. Maryknoll, NY: Orbis Books.

Habermas, Jürgen (1975). *Legitimation Crisis*, trans. Thomas McCarthy. Boston: Beacon Press.

Hubert, Henri, and Mauss, Marcel (1899). *Essai sur la nature et la function du sacrifice*; repr. in M. Mauss, *Oeuvres*, i. Paris: Éditions de Minuit, 1968. English trans. by W. D. Halls: *Sacrifice: Its Nature and Function*. Chicago: University of Chicago Press, 1964.

Jansen, Johannes J. G. (1986). *The Neglected Duty: The Creed of Sadat's Assassins and Islamic Resurgence in the Middle East*. New York: Macmillan.

Juergensmeyer, Mark (ed.) (1991). *Violence and the Sacred in the Modern World*. London: Frank Cass.

—— (2003). *Terror in the Mind of God: The Global Rise of Religious Violence*, rev. edn. Berkeley: University of California Press.

—— (2005). *Gandhi's Way: A Handbook of Conflict Resolution*, rev. edn. Berkeley: University of California Press.

—— (2008). *Global Rebellion: Religious Challenges to the Secular State*. Berkeley: University of California Press.

Kahane, Meir (1978). *Listen World, Listen Jew*. Jerusalem: Institute of the Jewish Idea.

Kahane, Meir (1981). *They Must Go.* Jerusalem: Institute of the Jewish Idea.

Khomeini, Imam [Ayatollah] (1981). *Islam and Revolution: Writings and Declarations*, trans. and annotated by Hamid Algar. Berkeley: Mizan Press.

Kitts, Margo (2005). *Sanctified Violence in Homeric Society: Oath-Making Rituals and Narratives in the Iliad.* Cambridge: Cambridge University Press.

Kotler, Yair (1986). *Heil Kahane.* New York: Adama Book.

Kramer, Martin (1991). "Sacrifice and Fratricide in Shiite Lebanon". In Juergensmeyer (1991), 71–81.

La Barre, Weston (1970). *The Ghost Dance: The Origins of Religion.* Garden City, NY: Doubleday.

Laqueur, Walter (1987). *The Age of Terrorism.* Boston: Little, Brown and Company.

Lincoln, Bruce (1991). *Death, War, and Sacrifice: Studies in Ideology and Practice.* Chicago: University of Chicago Press.

—— (2006). *Holy Terrors: Thinking about Religion after September 11*, 2nd edn. Chicago: University of Chicago Press.

Martin, Richard C. (1969). "Religious Violence in Islam: Towards an Understanding of the Discourse on Jihad in Modern Egypt". In Paul Wilkinson and A. M. Stewart (eds.), *Contemporary Research on Terrorism.* Aberdeen: Aberdeen University Press, 55–71.

Marx, Karl (1960). "Excerpts from 'The German Ideology' ". In *K. Marx and F. Engels on Religion.* Moscow: Foreign Language Publishing House, 192–203.

McLeod, W. H. (1976). *Evolution of the Sikh Community.* Oxford: Clarendon Press.

Mergui, Raphael, and Simonnot, Philippe (1985). *Meir Kahane: Le rabbin qui fait peur aux juifs.* Lausanne: Éditions Pierre-Marcel Favre. English trans.: *Israel's Ayatollahs: Meir Kahane and the Far Right in Israel.* London: Saqi Books, 1987.

Metzger, Alter B. Z. (1968). *Rabbi Kook's Philosophy of Repentance: A Translation of "Orot Ha-Teshuvah".* Studies in Torah Judaism, 11. New York: Yeshiva University Press.

Niebuhr, Reinhold (1932). *Moral Man and Immoral Society.* New York: Charles Scribner's Sons.

—— (1940). *Why the Christian Church is Not Pacifist*, 2nd edn. London: SCM Press.

Peters, Rudolph (1979). *Islam and Colonialism: The Doctrine of Jihad in Modern History.* The Hague: Mouton.

Potter, Ralph (1969). *War and Moral Discourse.* Richmond, Va.: John Knox Press.

Ramsey, Paul (1968). *The Just War: Force and Political Responsibility.* New York: Charles Scribner's Sons.

Rapoport, David C. (1988). "Messianic Sanctions for Terror". *Comparative Politics*, 20/2: 195–213.

—— (1991). "Some General Observations on Religion and Violence". In Juergensmeyer (1991), 118–40.

Riesebrodt, Martin (1993). *Pious Passion: The Emergence of Modern Fundamentalism in the United States and Iran*, trans. Don Reneau. Berkeley: University of California Press.

Robertson-Smith, William (1889). *Lectures on the Religion of the Semites.* New York: Appleton.

Saddhatissa, H. (1970). *Buddhist Ethics.* London: George Allen & Unwin.

Sagan, Eli (1972). *Cannibalism: Human Aggression and Cultural Form.* New York: Psychohistory Press.

Savarkar, V. D. (1969). *Hindutva: Who is a Hindu?* Bombay: Veer Savarkar Prakashan.

Sivan, Emmanuel (1991). "The Mythologies of Religious Radicalism: Judaism and Islam". In Juergensmeyer (1991), 71–81.

Smith, Wilfred Cantwell (1959). "Comparative Religion: Whither—and Why?". In Mircea Eliade and Joseph Kitagawa (eds.), *History of Religions: Essays in Methodology*, Chicago: University of Chicago Press, 31–58.

Sprinzak, Ehud (1988). "From Messianic Pioneering to Vigilante Terrorism: The Case of the Gush Emunim Underground". In D. C. Rapoport (ed.), *Inside Terrorist Organizations*. London: Frank Cass and Company, 194–216.

—— (1991*a*). *The Ascendence of Israel's Radical Right*. New York: Oxford University Press.

—— (1991*b*). "Violence and Catastrophe in the Theology of Rabbi Meir Kahane: The Ideologization of Mimetic Desire". In Juergensmeyer (1991), 48–70.

Staal, J. Frits (1983). *Agni: The Vedic Ritual of the Fire Altar*. Berkeley: Asian Humanities Press.

Tambiah, Stanley J. (1987). *World Conqueror and World Renouncer*. Cambridge: Cambridge University Press.

—— (1992). *Buddhism Betrayed? Religion, Politics and Violence in Sri Lanka*. Chicago: University of Chicago Press.

Tracy, David (1975). *Blessed Rage for Order: New Pluralism in Theology*. New York: Seabury Press.

Tylor, Edward Burnett (1870). *Primitive Culture: Researches into the Development of Mythology, Philosophy, Religion, Language, Art, and Custom*, 2nd edn. London: J. Murray.

Van der Veer, Peter (1994). *Religious Nationalism: Hindus and Muslims in Modern India*. Berkeley: University of California Press.

Waardenburg, Jacques (1978). *Reflections on the Study of Religion*. The Hague: Mouton.

Weber, Max (1930). *Protestant Ethic and the Spirit of Capitalism*, trans. Talcott Parsons. London: G. Allen & Unwin.

—— (1946). "Politics as a Vocation". In Hans H. Gerth and C. Wright Mills (eds.), *From Max Weber: Essays in Sociology*. New York: Oxford University Press, 77–128.

Suggested Reading

Appleby, R. Scott (1999). *The Ambivalence of the Sacred: Religion, Violence, and Reconciliation*. Lanham, Md.: Rowman & Littlefield Publishers.

Burkert, Walter, Rene Girard, and Jonathan Z. Smith; Robert Hamerton-Kelly (eds.) (1988). *Violent Origins: Ritual Killing and Cultural Formation*. Stanford, Calif.: Stanford University Press.

Juergensmeyer, Mark, and Margo Kitts, (eds.) (2008). *The Princeton Reader on Religious Violence*. Princeton: Princeton University Press.

Lawrence, Bruce B., and Karim, Aisha (2007). *On Violence: A Reader*. Durham, NC: Duke University Press.

Steffan, Lloyd (2003). *The Demonic Turn: The Power of Religion to Inspire or Restrain Violence*. Cleveland: Pilgrim Press.

Also de Vries (2001).

CHAPTER 50

GIRARD, RELIGION, VIOLENCE, AND MODERN MARTYRDOM

MICHAEL KIRWAN

Introduction

In an interview in *Le Monde* (6 November 2001), the French-American cultural theorist René Girard was asked to comment on the terrorist atrocities of September 11, and specifically whether his 'mimetic theory' could be applied to these terrible events. His interpretation differs from those of other commentators, who saw the attacks in terms of a clash of civilizations, religious fundamentalism, or imperfect secularization.

> The error is always to reason within categories of 'difference' when the root of all conflicts is rather 'competition', mimetic rivalry between persons, countries, cultures. Competition is the desire to imitate the other in order to obtain the same thing he or she has, by violence if need be. No doubt terrorism is bound to a world 'different' from ours, but what gives rise to terrorism does not lie in that 'difference' which removes it further from us and makes it inconceivable to us. On the contrary, it lies in an exacerbated desire for convergence and resemblance. Human relations are essentially relations of imitation, of rivalry. What is experienced now is a form of mimetic rivalry on a planetary scale. (Girard 2001)

Girard has elsewhere spoken of his obsession with violence as 'a subtle destroyer of the differential meaning it seems to inflate'; in other words, the paradox that the more rivals try to emphasize their distinctiveness from each other by antagonistic or even violent gestures, the more alike they become—even to the point of becoming mirror images of each other's hatred. He sees this form of desire as the 'gravitational' force which draws the West and its self-declared enemies closer together, while simultaneously forcing them apart. It is 'a dimension that transcends Islam, a dimension of the entire planet' (Girard 2001). On the one hand, the perpetrators are the losers: Third World victims, trying and failing to keep up with the developed world. On the other hand, in their sophisticated choice of means and symbolic targets, the bombers were, in a sense, 'American'. Figures like Osama Bin Laden, who after all are hardly materially dispossessed, are nevertheless consumed by mimetic 'contagion', imitating the hated West and adopting its values. 'These competitive relations are excellent if you come out of it as the winner, but if the winners are always the same then, one day or the other, the losers overturn the game table (Girard 2001).'

There have been many attempts to account for the shocking 'violent return of religion', made iconic for us in the destruction of the Twin Towers. Girard sees here a crisis not of 'difference', but of its opposite: the collapse of difference and 'an exacerbated desire for convergence and resemblance'. However, it would be a disservice both to the facts and to René Girard to think that mimetic theory offers an exhaustive explanation of the phenomenon of religious-inspired violence. There are, of course, other views: Samuel Huntington's notion of a 'clash of civilizations' has dominated thinking since the early 1990s; Richard Dawkins and Terry Eagleton (albeit from very different positions) insist that religion has always manifested destructive potential; Jürgen Habermas sees fundamentalist violence as a modern phenomenon which should be attributed to imperfect processes of secularization.

These authors differ in their sympathy towards religious belief; each has his own understanding of how, if at all, the specific conditions of modernity are responsible for the present crisis; all are writing against an increasingly widespread recognition of the limitations of the secularization thesis as the 'master model' of sociological inquiry. Only Girard offers a committed 'insider's' response from within a faith tradition, that of Christianity. Girard's account of the relationship between religion, violence, and culture comprises three elements: first, the claim that 'desire is mimetic'; secondly, a social anthropological account of 'the sacred', as the means by which a society's mimetic rivalry and its consequent aggression are contained and channelled on to victims or 'scapegoats' (Girard 1977[1972]); and lastly, an increasingly explicit avowal of the ways in which these two 'home truths' about human beings—the mimetic structure of our desire, and our propensity for scapegoating violence—are revealed by the Judeo-Christian scriptures, above all in the life, death, and resurrection of Christ. Paul Dumouchel, a philosopher, describes the impact of these ideas:

> Beginning from literary criticism and ending up with a general theory of culture, through an explanation of the role of religion in primitive societies and a radical interpretation of Christianity, René Girard has completely modified the landscape of the social sciences. Ethnology, history of religion, philosophy, psychoanalysis, psychology and literary criticism are explicitly mobilised in this enterprise. Theology, economics and political sciences, history and sociology—in short, all the social sciences, and those that used to be called the moral sciences—are influenced by it. (Dumouchel 1988[1985]: 23)

Girard has made clear that this 'discovery' is inseparable from the religious conversion which accompanied it in the spring of 1959. His work on five European novelists (Girard 1966 [1961]) had convinced him of the Christian 'undertow' to the moments of aesthetic and moral insight to be found in writers such as Flaubert, Proust, and Dostoevsky. This evangelical spirit has permeated his writing ever since—to the perplexity of many of his critics. Jean-Marie Domenach refers to his work as 'a voyage to the end of the sciences of man'; reason, 'having completed its ravages', turns back from the abyss, and towards the domain of the Word of God (1988[1985]: 159). This reversal permits us 'to be, in a single motion, scientists and believers', though there is a need for caution and misgivings. Girard's ideas have met with a fair amount of resistance, not least in his large anthropological claims about the origins of pre-state societies and religion in terms of victimization and scapegoating processes. In this respect, his closeness to Freud's theory as set out in *Totem and Taboo* arouses discomfort in many. Nevertheless, as indicated above, Girard's ideas have generated enormous excitement, and a considered judgement may be that 'we are still a long way from the point when anyone will have measured the scope of the question Girard has raised' (Fleming 2004: 164).

With regard to the present theme, I am proposing that Girard is invaluable as a reflector upon specifically modern configurations of culture and violence, and that his contribution to the discussion of the nature and meaning of martyrdom in the present age is twofold. First, he offers a commentary on two of the philosophical architects of the modern world—specifically, an analysis of Hegel's struggle for 'recognition', but more relevant to this study, the notion of '*ressentiment*' (Nietzsche). Secondly, Girard's own Christian faith and sympathetic readings of the Judeo-Christian scriptures and tradition allow for a powerful, post-secularization hermeneutic to account for the unexpected, and too often violent, return of religion.

Girard's contribution to our understanding of martyrdom will become apparent after a sociological overview of the phenomenon, and a consideration of martyrdom as classically understood within the three main monotheistic faith traditions; some degree of historical background is useful for an adequate appraisal of contemporary martyrdom. The final section will attempt to draw the strands together, with attention to the distinctiveness of Jewish, Christian, and Islamic doctrines of martyrdom, and also to the importance of modern philosophies of recognition and resentment in addressing religious violence.

The Martyr's Conviction

In *The Martyr's Conviction: A Sociological Analysis*, Eugene and Anita Weiner (1990) trace the classical and Judeo-Christian core of the traditional concept of martyrdom, while also exploring contemporary and secular usage. Theirs is one of the few attempts at a comprehensive sociological analysis. They are clear that the martyr ideal includes elements of *choice, suffering, and conviction*, that it involves active and passive attitudes towards death, and that the term may cover both those who articulate their convictions and those who do not. Beyond this, however, basic questions appear at every turn.

> It is not at all clear who or what actually makes the martyr. Is it a matter of personal intention, dramatic circumstances, agonizing experiences or merely clever propaganda? Does the martyr primarily make himself or herself? Is the martyr created by the persecutor and the oppressor? In other words, are martyrs created through particular external circumstances, or through the unique force of their internal convictions? (Weiner and Weiner 1990: 9)

They decide upon three basic elements: *the martyrological confrontation* (a structured confrontation in which the martyr confronts his or her persecutor), *the martyr's motive* (a disposition on the part of the martyr to self-sacrifice for conviction), and *the martyrological narrative* (a literary tradition that immortalizes the martyr's story). This last point is too easily neglected: for a narrative to emerge, a martyrologist must be there to chronicle the raw occurrences and render them events of social significance, a narrative which is shaped by the oral and literary traditions of the culture: for example, the tragic or liturgical.

> The martyr seems to touch deeply some basic human need, but the source of this potency is unclear. We may choose to situate it in the psychic makeup of the individual, some biologically determined altruistic process, or some social need necessary to the functioning of the group. But is it deeply encoded in cultural traditions, the result of some need for the dramatization of human purposes? Or is martyrdom a name given to disparate things only loosely connected, or a historically limited expression of human behaviour from which no broad generalisations can be made? (Weiner and Weiner 1990: 24–5)

As a rich symbol, martyrdom condenses many meanings into one act, connoting purity of motive, conviction, commitment, selfless sacrifice, surety of reward beyond this life, courage in the face of agony, dramatic gesture, sincerity, and so on. Martyrdom represents not just an individual action: it is also a social construction in which many kinds of social actors participate, an act that comes to be legitimized and celebrated in a narrative. The Weiners consider the martyr as a social type (cf. Alastair McIntyre), located between the innocent hero and the suicidal zealot: 'The martyr will be seen as a member of a suppressed group who, when given the opportunity to renounce aspects of his or her group's code, willingly submits to suffering and death rather than forsake a conviction' (Weiner and Weiner 1990: 10).

Martyrdom 'raises a serious challenge to those who claim there are intrinsic limitations to the socialisation of individuals. When reading the martyrological literature, one does not find those unconscious areas of the human psyche that are totally resistant to group socialisation' (Weiner and Weiner 1990: 75). Another aspect of the Weiners' analysis which we should note here is a psychoanalytical theory of group formation (one which nods in the direction of René Girard's *La Violence et le sacré*), according to which a martyr's dramatic strengthening of the group bond is due to the primal link between birth and sacrifice (Weiner and Weiner 1990: 54–5). There is a need for gestures of placation, submission, and single-minded devotion, in order to offset the pride and intoxication associated with creating something new. Just at the moment of creative fulfilment, there seems to be a mythic, unconscious requirement that part of the creation—the best part—be sacrificed in order to ensure the remainder. The martyr's sacrifice, as a fundamental conflict strategy which emerges under specific historical circumstances, has therefore a specific relation to the origins of social movements and to moments of social crisis.

A sociology of the martyr, such as the one offered by Eugene and Anita Weiner, sees him or her as the contestant in an arena; he or she fights a universal fight, around a culture either in the early stages of creation or in the process of revitalization. Martyrs expose themselves to the universal struggle between two formidable forces: the basic drive for biological survival and man's deep need for a life of conviction. No culture, group, or grand idea can do without a martyr to make it plausible. Despite the preference of the modern mind for a 'conviction against conviction' and for programmes of radical doubt, 'we are our convictions'. They explore what links the creation of culture, the building of symbolic realms of meaning, and the fear of mortality: 'The martyr serves as a key to understanding the problem of making culture plausible within the human condition' (Weiner and Weiner 1990: 52).

The Weiners' sociological account is invaluable, but limited. They eschew the search for 'unfathomable' psychological motivation by defining motive as 'the way in which the self and others perceive and organise the action of social actors, in order to make that action more understandable'. This is effectively done, but gives us little sense of how martyrs themselves—and martyrologists—within different faith traditions articulate their beliefs. For this we need to turn to the faith traditions themselves, and to their formal reflection (theology) upon the practice of martyrdom.

It will also become increasingly evident that Girard's hypothesis relating religion and violence does not fit squarely into this approach. For Girard, the (limited) effectiveness of sacrificial thinking and processes is due to a misunderstanding, *méconnaisance.* The expulsion or extermination of a victim will indeed bring stability and order to a turbulent group, but only insofar as the members of that group are unaware of what they are doing. Girard cites Jesus on the cross, 'Father forgive them, they know not what they do!' To the objection that any explanation is problematic which overrides the self-understanding and intentions of the actors themselves, Girard replies that this is exactly what we do with, for example, the transcripts of medieval witch trials. All the participants may be convinced that witchcraft activity has been taking place (perhaps the accused has even attempted necromancy), and yet we routinely refuse to believe any of it. Our scepticism toward such texts is supreme: but how can we possibly justify such confidence? Girard insists that we have no choice. We must either 'do violence to the text' or allow the text to continue to do violence to victims.

Martyrdom in Christian and Jewish Traditions

For the Christian, the question 'What is a martyr?' must be reframed etymologically: at what point do the terms *martus* and *marturia* cease to mean simply 'witness'—whether in a formal legal setting or metaphorically for all kinds of observation and attestation—and take on the specialized technical sense of a death endured after a confession of faith? Though this linguistic transition clearly occurs in the New Testament period (specifically, the Johannine literature of late first century CE), W. H. C. Frend begins the story earlier, with the Maccabean struggles from the mid-second century BCE. Martyrdom as such is a 'personal witness to the truth of the Law against the forces of heathenism, involving the suffering and even death of the witness' (Frend 1965: 44). At stake, still, is the issue broached by Frend forty years ago, when he distinguished two streams of opinion: scholars who emphasize the originality of the Christian sense (thereby playing down the debt to Judaism) and others who attempt to derive the Christian from the Jewish ideal. Semantically, the former case seems to be stronger, since the actual term *marturia* does not seem to be applied by Jewish writers to describe those who have died for Torah, though there are plenty of Jewish examples.

Different theologies of martyrdom emerged in different parts of the Roman Empire. In the East, a positive evaluation of Greek philosophy and an optimistic view of man's destiny and place in the world held sway, to the detriment of martyrdom theology. In the West, however, the legacy of the Maccabean wars, and of the distinctively Jewish attitude towards the pagan power, meant that 'the problem which the Christians posed to the Empire was fundamentally the same as that posed by Judaism, namely the reconciliation of the claims of a theocracy with those of a world empire' (Frend 1965: 22).

G. W. Bowerstock, in *Martyrdom and Rome* (1995), contests this account, not least by denying that the notion of martyrdom has strictly Jewish roots at all. 'The written record suggests that, like the very word "martyr" itself, martyrdom had nothing to do with Judaism or Palestine. It had everything to do with the Graeco-Roman world, its traditions, its language, and its cultural tastes' (Bowerstock 1995: 28). Martyrdom was 'solidly anchored in the civic life of the Graeco-Roman world of the Roman empire. It ran its course in the great urban spaces of the agora and the amphitheatre, the principal settings for public discourse and for public spectacle. It depended upon the urban rituals of the imperial cult and the interrogation protocols of local and provincial magistrates' (Bowerstock 1995: 54).

Frend is clear about where we are to look for the genesis of the Christian martyr ideal: namely, in the militant resistance of Jews refusing to assimilate. 'In point of time, the Maccabean revolt against Hellenism, whether Syrian or Jewish, was the obvious beginning. Here was the first great revolutionary outbreak against what became the values of the Greco-Roman world' (Frend 1965: p. xiii). However, as we have seen, there is no clear consensus in favour of the Jewish origins of martyrdom: Bowersock insists that its origins are to be found in a Roman milieu rather than a Jewish one, and that the Maccabean paradigm is in fact dependent on Christian sources, rather than the other way round. A judicious compromise, perhaps, would be to acknowledge both continuity and discontinuity. Van Henten (1995) urges us to think of 'analogies without an interdependency', with similar ideas emerging independently in different groups.

Why is this important? Aetiology is of limited but nevertheless real value in clarifying terms and concepts. A decision regarding the respective strengths of martyrdom's Jewish, Christian, and pagan provenance will help to determine how widely or narrowly the category should be allowed to stretch. If the martyr is a direct descendant of the Maccabean freedom fighter, then there is legitimate scope for militant versions of the martyr ideal. If the martyr is basically the supreme exponent of the *imitatio Christi*, then a passive endurance of suffering is the key element, and martyrdom is incompatible with military resistance. In each case, as Bowersock and Frend both make clear, there is complex interaction with the political, cultural, and philosophical environment of the Greek and Roman empires, in which the martyrdom of Christians served as both catalyst and mirror.

It is interesting to note that the element of political confrontation which is common to both Jewish and Christian understandings has been prominent in contemporary re-evaluations of the doctrine of martyrdom. Van Henten sees continuity in the early Christian's search for distinctive identity, which is expressed in Jewish and pagan *topoi* of patriotism. For both Jews and Christians, the martyrs are 'heroes' of a unique nation. In a modern application of this, a political theologian, William T. Cavanaugh (1998) aligns martyrology with a new configuration of the ancient problematic of church and state.

> For the church itself, martyrdom disciplines the community and helps it to claim its identity... martyrdom recalls into being a people, the people of God, and makes their life visible to themselves and to the world. They remember Christ and become Christ's members in the Eucharist, re-enacting the body of Christ, its passion and its conflict with the forces of (dis)order.... The body of the martyr is thus the battleground for a larger contest of rival imaginations, that of the state and that of the church. A crucial difference in these imaginations is that the imagination of the church is essentially eschatological; the church is not a rival *polis* but points to an alternative time and space, a mingling of heaven and earth. (Cavanaugh 1998: 64–5)

Cavanaugh's account is part of a wider case study of the Roman Catholic Church in the early stages of the Pinochet regime in Chile in the 1970s, so his urging of the visibility of the martyr and of the believing community is especially poignant. 'The effect of the regime's strategy [of torture and disappearances] was to produce not martyrs but victims. Martyrs by their public witness build up the body of Christ in opposition to the state' (Cavanaugh 1998: 66). A similar pattern is most evident in a number of liberation theologians, principally from Latin America, but also from other countries of the 'South', whose 'crucified peoples' use the conceptuality of martyrdom to articulate their struggle for political and economic justice.

The late Jesuit theologian Karl Rahner gives this an important theological rendition (Rahner 2006[1983]). He considers the possibilities for expanding the traditional theology of Christian martyrdom, which has always explicitly excluded death endured in active combat. Rahner asks whether this judgement is unrevisable. In contrast to the tradition, he rejects any 'precise conceptual and verbal apartheid' between the two kinds of death, active and passive, since death always involves an inward and outward powerlessness, even death in battle. Just like the passive martyr in the traditional sense, the Christian warrior imitates Christ in his helplessness before evil. It is here, in the explicit reflections of political and liberation theology, that we come closest to the possibility of a transformed understanding of Christian martyrdom—one which would edge closer towards the militant *jihadi* understanding which has come to the fore in Islamism.

Martyrdom Traditions in Islam

The all-inclusiveness of Islam precludes isolating the concept of *shahada* (martyrdom) from those of *jihad* (holy struggle) and of Islam itself, rooted in *salama*, and meaning a wholesome, peaceful submission to the will of Allah. The martyr ideal is present from the beginning of Islam, as the celebration of those who had died in the struggle to establish and expand Islam. Nevertheless, the status before God of those commemorated in this way is broadly identical with that of the Jewish martyrs in the Maccabean tradition.

As with the Greek word itself, the technical terms for martyr (*shahid*) and martyrdom (*shahada*) connote eyewitness, or legal testimony. This is clearly related to truth (*haqq*), and the martyr's readiness to recognize and declare it, as well as struggle and die for it. It may be that the association of 'witness' and 'death on behalf of the faith' is taken over from Syrian Christianity. Early Islamic martyrdom is for the most part exemplified in military prowess, in contrast to the passive endurance of suffering which is a marked, even a defining feature of Jewish and certainly of Christian martyrologies.

Closely related is the necessity of human guidance to the truth, which is provided by the model or paradigm of truthful living, not just for Muslims but for all. This task, which defines the Islamic notion of prophethood, is fulfilled above all by Muhammad, the best model of Islam. For Shi'ism, this guiding function is distinctive in the understanding of leadership, or the Imamate. The death of the Prophet's grandson Imam Husayn on Ashura, 680 CE, at Karbala in Iraq, is the defining event, transforming the martyr ideal and giving it a central place in the worship and self-understanding of Shi'ism. The martyr's death is no longer seen as an individual contribution to *jihad*, but rather as a deliberate redemptive act of cosmic importance. Its inspirational significance is reflected in the slogan that 'every day is "Ashura", and every place is "Karbala"'.

Even so, a greater diversity regarding the value of martyrdom is to be found among Muslim scholars than among early Christian theologians. The category of acceptable death is expanded, to include drowning, death by plague, and death in childbirth. The pains of those who suffer unrequited or undeclared love are noted as a form of martyrdom, and there is due recognition (in accordance with Clement of Alexandria's praise of painstaking scholarship) of the '*jihad* of the pen'. Within Sufism, the tragedy of the mystic lover who dies because of his inordinate love of the Divine is a rarefied spiritual application of the martyr ideal. In the medieval period, we find a spiritualization and internalization of the martyr ideal.

With the modern period there seems to be a reversal of this sublimation, and a revival of the earlier, more militant ideas of martyrdom. Most strikingly, the founder of the Muslim Brotherhood, Hasan al-Banna, exhorts the *umma* to be 'skilled in the practice of death'. *Jihad* and a readiness to die are regarded as a duty for every Muslim, a valorization of martyrdom which is highlighted by modern Shi'ite authorities. Modern political contexts have heightened this 'militant tendency' in at least three ways: Islamic resistance to colonialism; a reformulation of *jihad* in terms of recognition of the state's right to self-defence; finally, the possible influence of nineteenth-century anarchist or nihilist movements in radicalizing understanding.

One other scholarly discussion requires attention here: namely, the question of *naskh*, or 'abrogation' (Wicker 2006: 2–3). This refers to a way of adjudicating a potential difference of meaning between two Qur'anic verses; for some exegetes, this means that an earlier verse is held to be superseded, or 'abrogated'. This has been fateful where militant readings of the later, so-called Medinan 'sword verse' are favoured over earlier pacific ones (see Afsaruddin 2006). Because of this, the more violent understandings of *jihad* and *shahid* have come to hold sway. Scholars maintain that unless the doctrine of *naskh* is modified by Muslims, the Qur'an will continue to be used to resource terrorist ideology. However, given the lack of a central doctrinal authority in Islam, it is not easy to see how the older tradition can be rehabilitated against more modern 'hardline' positions.

One factor at least should be made clear: both Christianity and Islam have always distanced themselves from self-killing, so any attempt to align so-called suicide bombers with religious motivation must be highly suspect. It is true that a suicidal impulse is never entirely distinguishable from the more enthusiastic endorsements of martyrdom, but this has always been marginal, and firmly condemned. Where, then, does the glorification of suicide come from? Nineteenth-century anarchist traditions would seem to play a significant part here. We should note David Rapoport's argument for a continuity between four 'waves' of terrorism: 'anarchist', 'anti-colonial', 'new left', and the present 'religious' wave, each having a life span of roughly forty years. To the 'Russian' experience of the 1880s we owe 'the development of a doctrine or strategy for terror, an inheritance for successors to use, improve and transmit' (Rapoport 2002: 3), as well as the apotheosis of the terrorist as 'noble, terrible, irresistibly fascinating, uniting the two sublimities of human grandeur, the martyr and the hero' (Rapoport 2002: 4) For Andrew McKenna, Fyodor Dostoyevsky is the indispensable guide, in *The Devils* and especially in the self-tormenting narrator of *Notes from Underground*, 'debating violence and desire as issues for our self-understanding' (McKenna 2002: 2).

McKenna interprets the 'mimetic contagion' of which Girard speaks in his *Le Monde* article by referring us to the hellish existence of the Underground Man in *Notes from Underground*, and beyond this, to the pathology observed by Nietzsche: resentment as the basis of moral valuation (in the *Genealogy of Morals*). He concludes that Islamist terrorism is not medieval, and in fact, is not even Islamic. 'It does not obey Koranic imperatives but the laws of desire, as explored by Dostoyevsky, which... resentment inhabits more intimately than the worm does the apple' (McKenna 2002: 23; see Regensburger 2002 and Juergensmeyer 1991, for other articles on mimetic rivalry and terrorism).

Girardian Conclusions

One of the most distressing features of our contemporary crisis has been the discovery that, as in the cases of the bombings in Oklahoma and in London (July

2005), our would-be killers are not foreign or exotic, but home-grown. Girard's exhortation to look not for 'difference' but for an 'exacerbated desire for convergence' should prepare us for this shattering realization. He and McKenna (reading Dostoyevsky) insist that 'resentment's sacralizing isolation' is the basis of modern consciousness, and can be redeemed only by something akin to a religious conversion: hence the title of Girard's study of the Russian novelist, *Resurrection from the Underground* (1996[1963]). For Girard, the *imitatio Christi* which underpins the Christian doctrine of martyrdom is entirely free of the nihilistic contagion that Dostoyevsky portrays so powerfully.

We considered at length the work of Eugene and Anita Weiner, one of the few extensive sociological treatments of martyrdom, in which

> the search for motive is not conducted among the hidden springs and impulses which cause action. It is rather an analysis of how actors in the midst of action seek explanations, assign meanings and differentiate themes; how these actors decide what is happening to themselves and others; whether these explanations are persuasive in social interaction; and how effective they are in advancing interests and making people feel they understand what is going on. (Weiner and Weiner 1990: 66–7)

I have also made clear where Girard's hypothesis differs from this, insofar as (like Freud and Marx) he sees social interactions unfolding as a result of the misunderstanding (*méconnaisance*) of the agents concerned. At the heart of mimetic theory is a distinction between *myth* and *gospel*, between two rival descriptions of these social processes. Myth is the 'cover story' by which a community, newly reconciled to itself by the ecstatic expulsion or extermination of a victim, disguises its violence from itself—even though clues remain embedded in the narrative, like fossils. Similarly, prohibitions and rituals are mechanisms for maintaining a safe distance between a community and its aggression. This, for Girard, is the origin of religion, expressed in his *dictum* that 'violence is the heart and secret soul of the sacred'.

But it is precisely this state of affairs that is exposed and rendered ineffective by the gospel revelation. Through much of *Le bouc émissaire* (*The Scapegoat*), Girard points up the contrast between the way we read the Oedipus legends and how we read a medieval persecution text, one in which Jews are superstitiously blamed for the plague. We bring to the latter an attitude of total disbelief regarding the alleged guilt of the Jews, 'interrogating' the text with questions which never occur to us to ask of the Oedipus narrative. As we have seen, for Girard the choice is clear: 'ou bien on fait violence au texte ou bien on laisse se perpétuer la violence du texte contre des victimes innocents' (Girard 1982: 16).

For Girard it is the Christian gospel which makes possible this stridency. Our knowledge of what happened to Christ, the innocent Lamb of God, empowers us to decode similar attempts at persecution—even when these are carried out in the name of Christianity, such as the hunting of witches or heretics. The argument is analogous to that of Rodney Stark (2004), who alerts us to the shaping influence of monotheism in the early modern period, not least in its contribution to the rise of science. 'The scientific spirit cannot come first,' Girard concurs, in the concluding chapter of *Le bouc émissaire* (Girard 1982: 291–311). Only when communities no longer hunt witches are they liberated to explore alternative explanations for the disasters which afflict them.

Girard follows through the implications of this grand theory of history for the doctrine of martyrdom. The Christian martyrologies are tales of persecution, but they are not 'myths' in the sense described above. We see in them the semblance of a scapegoating event; however, the perspective which prevails is not that of the oppressing community, but that of the oppressed victim. Only with Christian apologists such as Lactantius and Tertullian does the Latin legal term *persecui* come to have a negative connotation of 'injustice', just as the Greek term *martyr* once meant, neutrally, a legal witness, but through Christian usage came to denote a persecuted and innocent victim. The outrageous charges levelled against the first Christians, such as cannibalism, incest, atheism, and so on, indicate the irrational frenzy of the mob gathering against them, while the selection of women and slaves as victims is typical of the scapegoating process. Yet there is little hint in these stories of a sacralizing 'double transference' (Girard 1982: 293), except in isolated exceptions such as St Sebastian and medieval saints' lives. The violence of these stories remains entirely on the human and social plane. The glorification of martyrs through official canonization is not the same as sacralization.

It is of course the passion of Christ which serves as model for the Christian martyr. This is not simply pious rhetoric, but the beginning of the critique of *les représentations persécutrices*. We should not be misled by the partisan tendency of Christians to value and defend only their own victims; this partiality is certainly there, but it is a secondary characteristic. What is primary is the formidable revolution which is taking place: throughout Occidental history, persecutory representations (myths) are losing their effectiveness. For Girard, our contemporary recognition of the victim's innocence (even where this leads to excesses of political correctness) is ultimately a radicalized intensification of our solidarity with the martyrs—which in turn derives from our immersion in the story of Christ's passion. Girard cites the parable of the Last Judgement, the separation of the sheep from the goats in Matthew 25, to emphasize Christ's identification with the weak and vulnerable. It is on their ability to discern Christ in the innocent victim, not on their formal religious allegiance, that Christians will ultimately be judged.

Girard's robustly Christian account is problematic for many, not least for the apparent superiority it affords the Judeo-Christian revelation in the face of multicultural and pluralist instincts. This charge has been put to Girard, and he has noted it, though curiously enough the central theological problem raised here may also provide the resource for moving forward. What is argued in *The Scapegoat*, and in mimetic theory in general, may be described as a kind of 'supersessionism'. This term is controversial, because it is usually taken to mean the doctrine by which Christianity has 'superseded', rendered null or made redundant, the religious dispensation of the Jewish people. This assertion of superiority, it is claimed, has historically facilitated centuries of Christian antagonism towards the Jews, and, ultimately, the Holocaust. By contrast, what Girard describes and celebrates is the annulment of the 'violent sacred', the false transcendence which underpins and justifies the actions of the scapegoating mob. The realization that we are, after all, 'butchers pretending to be sacrificers' (Girard cites Shakespeare's *Julius Caesar*) is a fruit of a gospel encounter with the genuine sacred, who is the Lamb of God, and not a projection of collective frenzy.

This is indeed 'supersessionist', but precisely *not* in a way that privileges any group or faith community over others. It may be fanciful to draw a parallel here with the problem of supersession which presents itself in Islam, and which was explored briefly above: namely, the question of *naskh*, or 'abrogation'. I noted how the struggle for pacific rather than militant versions of Islam depends upon a modification of this doctrine, so that it is not used to prioritize violent interpretations. I have noted some of the obstacles that stand in the way of such a modification, not least the lack of a single interpretative authority in Islam. Nevertheless, it may be argued that the discussion about *naskh* opens up a precious hermeneutical space, a recognition that there is in fact scope for interpretation where too often we are told there is none. The challenge, as Wicker points out, is not to change the meaning of *naskh*, but to restore its original sense and 'to get the alternative, non-violent message heard amidst the cacophony of violent discourse which has dominated discussion on both sides' (Wicker 2006: 4).

This is entirely familiar to Girardian analysis. It is a supersession not of one group or faith tradition by another, but the 'abrogation' of the false and violent sacred, to be replaced by a transcendence which is truly merciful. Contestation of terms such as *jihad* and *shahid* is precisely analogous to the history and meaning of the words 'sacrifice' and 'martyr' in Christianity. Ultimately, it is the history and meaning of 'the sacred' itself.

References

Afsaruddin, Asma (2006). 'Competing Perspectives on *Jihad* and "Martyrdom" in Early Islamic Sources'. In Wicker (2006), 15–31.

Bowersock, G. W. (1995). *Martyrdom and Rome.* Cambridge: Cambridge University Press.

Cavanaugh, William T. (1998). *Torture and Eucharist.* Oxford: Blackwell.

Domenach, Jean-Marie (1988[1985]). 'Voyage to the End of the Sciences of Man'. In Dumouchel (1988[1985]), 152–9.

Dumouchel, Paul (ed.) (1988[1985]). *Violence and Truth: On the Work of René Girard.* London: Athlone Press. [*Violence et Vérité: autour de René Girard: Proceedings of Colloque de Cerisy on R. Girard.* Grasset, Paris]

Fleming, Chris (2004). *René Girard: Violence and Mimesis.* Cambridge: Polity Press.

Frend, W. H. C. (1965). *Martyrdom and Persecution in the Early Church: A Study of a Conflict from the Maccabees to Donatus.* Oxford: Oxford University Press.

Freud, Sigmund (1955[1913–14]). *Totem and Taboo.* In *Complete Psychological Works of Sigmund Freud.* London: Hogarth press.

Girard, René (1966[1961]). *Deceit, Desire and the Novel: Self and Other in Literary Structure.* Baltimore: Johns Hopkins University Press. [*Mensonge romantique et vérité romanesque.* Paris: Grasset].

—— (1977[1972]). *Violence and the Sacred.* London: Athlone Press. [*La violence et le sacré.* Paris: Grasset].

—— (1985[1982]). *The Scapegoat.* London: Athlone Press. [*Le bouc émissaire.* Paris: Grasset].

—— (1996[1963]). *Resurrection from the Underground.* New York: Crossroad. [*Dostoievski: Du double a l'unité.* Paris: Plon].

—— (2001). 'What we are Witnessing is Mimetic Rivalry on a Planetary Scale'. *Le Monde*, 6 Nov.; at <http://www.media.euro.apple.com/en/livepage/>.

Henten, J. W. van (1995). 'The Martyrs as Heroes of the Christian People'. In M. Lamberigts and P. van Denn (eds.), *Martyrium in Multidisciplinary Perspective.* Leuven: Leuven University Press, 303–22.

Juergensmeyer, Mark (ed.) (1991). Violence and *the Sacred in the Modern World.* London: Frank Cass & Co.

McKenna, Andrew (2002). 'Scandal, Resentment, Idolatry: The Underground Psychology of Terrorism'. *Anthropoetics*, 8/1 (Spring/Summer), posted 1 June at <http://www.anthropoetics.ucla.edu/ap0801/resent.htm>.

Nietzsche, Friedrich (1994[1887]). *On the Genealogy of Morals*, trans. Carol Diethe. Cambridge: Cambridge University Press.

Rahner, Karl (2006[1983]). 'Broadening the Concept of Martyrdom'. In Wicker (2006), 147–50.

Rapoport, David (2002). 'The Four Waves of Rebel Terror and September 11'. *Anthropoetics*, 8/1 (Spring/Summer), posted 1 June at <http://www.anthropoetics.ucla.edu/ap0801/terror.htm>, accessed 19 Feb. 2006.

Regensburger, Dietmar (ed.) (2002). Colloquium on Violence and Religion (COV&R), critical commentaries and articles on *Terrorism, Mimetic Rivalry and War* at <http://theol.uibk.ac.at/cover/war_against_terrorism.html>.

Stark, Rodney (2004). *For the Glory of God: How Monotheism Led to Reformations, Science, Witch-Hunts, and the End of Slavery.* Princeton: Princeton University Press.

Weiner, Eugene, and Weiner, Anita (1990). *The Martyr's Conviction: A Sociological Analysis.* Brown Judaic Studies, 203. Atlanta, Ga.: Scholar's Press, Brown University.

Wicker, Brian (ed.) (2006). *Witnesses to Faith? Martyrdom in Christianity and Islam.* Aldershot: Ashgate.

Suggested Reading

Cormack, Margaret (2002). *Sacrificing the Self: Perspectives on Martyrdom and Religion.* Oxford: Oxford University Press.

Eagleton, Terry (2005). *Holy Terror.* Oxford: Oxford University Press.

Juergersmeyer, Mark (2000), *Terror in the Mind of God: The Global Rise of Religious Violence.* Berkeley: University of California Press.

Kirwan, Michael (2004). *Discovering Girard.* London: Darton, Longman and Todd.

McTernan, Oliver (2003). *Violence in God's Name: Religion in an Age of Conflict.* London: Darton, Longman and Todd.

Also Cormack (2002); Fleming (2004); Girard (1985[1982]); Juergensmeyer (1991); Kirwan (2004); and Wicker (2006).

CHAPTER 51

RELIGION AND SOCIAL PROBLEMS

A NEW THEORETICAL PERSPECTIVE

TITUS HJELM

Sociology of religion and the social-scientific study of social problems are both well-established fields of scholarship, but interestingly enough the intersection between the two remains mostly an unexplored area. True, some recent influential studies do discuss religion in a broader context of social capital and social problems (e.g., Putnam 2000: 65–79), but few sociologists of religion have been aware of the developments in social problems theory proper. And vice versa, social problems textbooks usually mention religion only when it is relevant as an 'impact factor' in assessing a particular social problem. While this chapter falls short of a comprehensive survey of research into the issue at hand, it aims to provide a fresh theoretical view of the relationship between religion and social problems, and how the intersection between the two could be studied from a sociological perspective.

I am of course not claiming that I'm treading on completely unmapped territory. Already in 1980 Jeffrey Hadden wrote some tentative ideas on religion and social

Parts of the section on religion as a social problem were reworked from an earlier published article (Hjelm 2006*b*). Used with kind permission of Nordicom.

problems, using Spector and Kitsuse's *Constructing Social Problems* (2001), a modern classic of social problems theory originally published in 1977. Despite Hadden's plea for a fuller theoretical examination of the relationship between religion and social problems, his paper did not strike a chord in the sociology of religion community at the time and did not lead to further theoretical elaboration, except in limited form among scholars of new religions (see below). In 1989, James A. Beckford's presidential address to the Association for the Sociology of Religion was entitled 'The Sociology of Religion and Social Problems' (Beckford 1990), and although important in many ways, it did not discuss religion in the framework of social problems theory per se, but rather from a broader theoretical perspective.

In the field of sociology of religion, social problems theory has had—perhaps not surprisingly—most impact on the study of new religious movements, or 'cults'. The often negative public reaction provoked by new religions has created a whole subfield of study that examines the social processes whereby religious groups become labeled as deviant—that is, how religion becomes a social problem in itself (e.g., Beckford 1985; Robbins 1985; 1988; Swanson 2002). Research on the Satanism scare that gripped the USA in the late 1980s and early 1990s (Richardson *et al.* 1991) has most explicitly anchored itself in contemporary social problems theory. Among the contributors to this work was Joel Best, one of the leading figures in the sociology of social problems (see Best 1991).

Nevertheless, in spite of a budding interest, a systematic overview of the intersection of the sociology of social problems and the sociology of religion has not surfaced to date. The aim of this chapter is to discuss how social problems theory has been and could be effectively used in the study of religion and also how studying religion can broaden the study of social problems. I admit that the examples I'm using have a definite Western bias, but the theoretical discussion should provide a basis for the application of social problems theory in the study of religion in a wider context too. I will first provide a brief outline of the development of social problems theory and then discuss three possible approaches to the study of religion and social problems: namely, the effects of religion on social problems, how religion is socially constructed as a cure to social problems, and how religion is constructed as a social problem itself. Lastly, I will discuss the methodological questions that the issue poses and examine how the study of religion and social problems ties in with wider interests in the sociology of religion.

What is a Social Problem?

The sociology of social problems has probably produced as many definitions of a social problem as sociology of religion has produced definitions of religion. The definition by sociologists Richard Fuller and Richard Myers, however, catches best the varied aspects of social problems, and although almost seventy years old, is still very useful:

> A social problem is a condition which is defined by a considerable number of persons as a deviation from some social norm which they cherish. Every social problem thus consists of an objective condition and subjective definition. The objective condition is a verifiable situation which can be checked as to existence and magnitude (proportion) by impartial and trained observers, e.g. the state of our national defense, trends in the birth rate, unemployment, etc. The subjective definition is the awareness of certain individuals that the condition is a threat to certain cherished values. (Fuller and Myers 1941: 320)

Here Fuller and Myers explicate the two features that every social problem has: an *objective condition* and a *subjective definition.* As theory building developed, the focus of the study of social problems also shifted. The early sociologists were interested in the objective conditions, and firmly believed that they were the 'impartial and trained observers' capable of measuring whether or not a condition was a social problem. Later generations, however, were increasingly interested in the subjective definition part of Fuller and Myers's classic formulation.

A definitive break from earlier sociology of social problems occurred in the 1960s with several important publications endorsing a completely revised approach that became known as 'labeling theory'. Howard Becker, often quoted as one of the main representatives of the approach, wrote in his influential book *Outsiders*:

> *Social groups create deviance by making the rules whose infraction constitutes deviance*, and by applying those rules to particular people and labeling them as outsiders. From this point of view, deviance is *not* a quality of the act the person commits, but rather a consequence of the application by others of rules and sanctions to an 'offender'. (Becker 1991[1963]: 9; emphases original)

Becker's definition was clearly different from the prevailing understanding of deviance, and for a while research based on the labeling perspective supplanted the older approaches and became the hegemonic 'theory' in the sociology of deviance (see Becker 1991[1963]: 178).

Some opponents of the labeling approach based their critiques on the older tradition of the study of deviance and went on conducting research that focused on the objective conditions, stating that the labeling approach was simply not adequately supported by empirical facts (e.g., Akers 2000: 126–8). Another strand of criticism, however, was inspired by the labeling approach but wanted to take it further. This strand of criticism eventually evolved into what is now known as the social constructionist perspective on social problems (Rubington and Weinberg 1995: 287–92).

Constructing Social Problems

The first and most influential flag-bearers of the social constructionist approach were John I. Kitsuse and Malcolm Spector, who wrote two important articles (Kitsuse and Spector 1973; Spector and Kitsuse 1973) that redefined the study of social problems in the early 1970s. They later compiled their ideas into a book entitled *Constructing Social Problems* (Spector and Kitsuse 2001[1977]), which soon became the definitive work on the constructionist perspective.

Spector and Kitsuse's argument was that although the labeling approach had rightly emphasized subjective definitions over objective conditions, Becker and others did not take the approach to its logical conclusion. Even if the labeling process was the focus of the labeling approach, it still presupposed an objective act that was considered deviant according to norms that were similarly considered objective (Kitsuse and Spector 1975: 584–5). For example, using cannabis became labeled deviant because people *were* smoking marijuana and it *was* against the norms and values of society, and therefore was later criminalized. In turn, marijuana smokers adopted a deviant identity because of the labeling, and so the deviant behavior was strengthened. Most of the studies of labeling tried, after all, to explain how *persons* really—that is, in the objective sense—become deviant.

Spector and Kitsuse's radical reformulation was that deviance was important only insofar as people recognized an act as deviant. According to them, a proper sociology of social problems did not even exist (Spector and Kitsuse 2001[1977]: 1). They argued that for a proper sociology of social problems the only important thing was the process whereby an act or a situation became defined as a problem, *regardless of the objective condition.* Following this line of thought, marijuana is not a social problem because some people are smoking it, but because some people are concerned about others smoking it.

Spector and Kitsuse's approach radically subjectivized the study of social problems. Their definition of social problems makes clear that objective conditions play little role in their study: 'Thus, we define social problems as *the activities of individuals or groups making assertions of grievances and claims with respect to some putative conditions*' (Spector and Kitsuse 2001[1977]: 75; emphasis original). The important word here is 'putative':

> We use the word [putative] to emphasize that any given claim or complaint is about a condition *alleged* to exist, rather than about a condition that we, as sociologists, are willing to verify or certify. That is, in focusing the attention to the claims-making process we set aside the question whether those claims are true or false. (Spector and Kitsuse 2001[1977]: 76; emphasis original)

In effect, Spector and Kitsuse take a completely disinterested stance towards any claims regarding the reality of the phenomenon in question. What matters is the public reaction, and this is what sociologists should study. Therefore, the process of *claims making* becomes the focus of constructionist study of social problems. Social problems are social movements in themselves, because they would not exist without people who make claims about them (Mauss 1975). This radical approach became widely used in the study of social problems, but also ignited a critical discussion that continues to date (see Holstein and Miller 2003; Miller and Holstein 1993). A more moderate version, usually referred to as *contextual constructionism*, reads Spector and Kitsuse in less strict terms, allowing that although the claims-making process remains the focus of constructionist research, it is framed by a social and cultural context which influences and limits the forms and expressions that claims making can take (Best 1993). It is this kind of constructionism that I am referring to when I talk about the construction of religion as a solution to social problems and the construction of religion as a social problem in itself. But first I will look at more traditional ways of analyzing the intersection of religion and social problems.

Religion and Social Problems: The 'Traditional' Approach

How does religion figure in the study social problems, then? Overall—and this is obvious from the small number of studies mentioned above and also noted by other scholars (Stark and Bainbridge 1996: 149–55; Beckford 1990: 3–4)—religion has played little role in theorizing about social problems and deviance. In this sense the study of social problems seems to follow more general patterns in sociology (e.g., Beckford 2003: 1; Hamilton 2001: p. vii). The question of whether this is the outcome of the explicit secular outlook of the profession, as some suggest (Stark *et al.* 1996) is beyond the scope of this chapter; but it is relevant to note that the centrifugal effect that religion has had in sociology is not confined to social problems theory alone.

When religion *has* played a role in the study of social problems, it has usually been in the form of a variable in quantitative assessments. Titles such as 'The Impact of Religion on...' and 'The Effects of Religion on...' sometimes occur in studies that measure different variables affecting the emergence of and solution to social problems. This is what I refer to as the 'traditional' approach to religion and social problems. It should be noted that 'traditional' in this sense is not an evaluative assessment. The reason I'm calling it 'traditional' is that, first, it was the earliest approach to studying religion and social problems, and, second, it has so far also been the most popular one.

The 'father' of this type of inquiry is of course Émile Durkheim. In his *Suicide* (1897) Durkheim compared statistical data from different European countries in order to analyze the impact of social and cultural factors on the voluntary taking of one's life. Many consider this Durkheim's most important work, and many of the concepts he created in the study—for example, *anomie*—have become parts of standard social-science vocabulary. From the perspective of religion and social problems, the most relevant part of Durkheim's argument was that Protestants were more prone to commit suicide than followers of other confessions in all of the countries he compared (Durkheim 1979[1897]: 154). This notion became very influential, to the extent that eminent sociologist Robert K. Merton 'credited Emile Durkheim with having discovered sociology's first and thus far its only scientific "law"' (Stark and Bainbridge 1996: 31).

In an ardent critique of Durkheim, Rodney Stark and William Sims Bainbridge show, however, that Durkheim's data and methods were deeply flawed. Because Durkheim more or less equated religion with social integration, religion was in fact relegated to the status of an epiphenomenon (Stark and Bainbridge 1996: 30). Stark and Bainbridge's studies (1996 and 1985) have shown that religion does have an effect on suicide and other individual and social problems independently of social integration. The problem, however, is that sociologists often continue to follow the original example set by Durkheim, thus distorting the impact of religion on social problems such as suicide (Stark and Bainbridge 1996: 50–1). This is of course not to say—especially when no comprehensive reviews of the literature discussing the impact of religion on social problems other than suicide exist—that all of the 'traditional' perspectives are plagued by Durkheim's shadow. There is a growing number of empirical studies of the effects of religion on a variety of issues (e.g., Evans *et al.* 1995; Johnson *et al.* 2001; Shields *et al.* 2007) which show that the 'traditional' perspective remains the most significant approach to religion and social problems, and that the approach is continuously evolving.

Constructing Religion as a Solution to Social Problems

A quick database search of 'religion and social problems', 'religion and deviance', or 'religion and crime', for example, reveals that the field has not perhaps been as quiescent as Stark and Bainbridge noted in 1996. An emerging corpus of empirical (quantitative) studies (see above) discuss the impact of religion on the above-mentioned issues. If, however, we look at the connection between religion and social problems from another perspective, little headway has been made in reference to contemporary social problems theory in particular. What I want to do here is to discuss how religion figures and could figure in the constructionist theory of social problems, outlined above. This is partly because of my own theoretical leanings, but also because constructionism is a major strand in the contemporary study of social problems.

As already noted, from a constructionist point of view 'a social problem does not exist unless it is recognized by the society to exist' (Blumer 1971: 302). The process of claims making, which ideally results in social recognition of a problematic condition, has to point out the moral reprehensibleness of a condition, name the villains and victims, and, preferably, what should be done about the condition (Loseke 1999: 103). In doing so, the claims-makers and their claims-making activities form a social movement in itself (Mauss 1975). The focus here is on how religious communities and movements have contributed to the construction of social problems and what solutions they have offered.

First of all, it is worth reiterating here the more or less obvious fact that religious groups have been throughout time major claims-makers in social problems issues. From early Christians to Gandhi and the Civil Rights movement, religious groups and individuals have been in the forefront to point out issues of social injustice. Contemporary protests against perceived social evils, such as war, the death penalty, and abortion, for example, have often been initiated and led by religious groups. The claims and organizing efforts of religious communities have led to changes in legislation and, longer term, in culture. The social movements that have grown out of the will to change perceived social problems have often been led by religious leaders and driven by religious motivations.

In many cases the scope of the problems is such that religious communities and movements themselves can only point out the problem and bring it out in the open—in other words, 'make it real' by public construction. This is obviously the case for issues where legislative changes are needed in order to remedy the problem, for example. Sometimes, however, religious communities and movements aim to change perceived problematic conditions by more direct action, constructing solutions by themselves. Some of these solutions are alternatives to other social welfare initiatives, others specific to religions. A very general typology can be created about the claims that religious communities and movements make. In ascending order of abstraction, the claims can be *material*, *communal*, or *spiritual*.

Material Claims

Religious communities have throughout time provided people in need with material resources, including food and shelter, for example. The advent of the centralized nation-state and the subsequent transition of social welfare from the private to the public sphere has made this connection more problematic—especially so in countries such as the United States, where 'church' and state are constitutionally separated (Wuthnow 2006). Despite the emergence of the modern welfare state (in its diverse forms), religious communities have retained their material charity functions in many cases. Where the modern state has been unable to provide adequate social services, the ideology of 'loving your neighbor' (again, in many of its forms) has prompted direct action in the form of material help. Although many religions and religious communities still aim to affect public policy through claims making, among the claims is that the community itself should take care of the less well-off. This has manifested itself in a myriad of forms, ranging from food distribution to providing housing, employment, and educational resources.

There are differences in the social arrangement of these material solutions. First, the religious communities may benefit from direct support by the state. This is the case in Finland, for example, where the state collects revenues from church members in the form of a 'church tax' and distributes it directly to the two constitutionally recognized religious bodies, the Evangelical Lutheran Church of Finland and the Orthodox Church. In this arrangement these religious organizations function effectively as state welfare agencies, despite the occasional reference to them as 'third sector' actors. Second, similar to the above but in a more contested sense, the state may support the material services of religious organizations through direct budgetary allocations. In the United States, President George W. Bush initiated an expansion of existing Charitable Choice programs to include faith-based organizations and set up the Office of Faith-Based and Community Initiatives in his first month in office. While religious organizations had received federal funding before, these actions and the bills introduced in the House and the Senate to implement the President's proposals incited an unprecedented public discussion on the role of religion in state affairs (Ebaugh *et al.* 2003). Unlike the constitutionally enshrined arrangements such as those in Finland, this material support policy is much more dependent on the current ideological atmosphere in the administrative and legislative bodies. Finally, material support for social problems work is gained through voluntary work, whether in the form of private donations or actual labor (see Ch. 52 below). This type of material solution overlaps most of the time with public funding schemes, but is also often the only source of alleviating social problems for religious communities and movements.

Claims of Community

Durkheim might have been mistaken in equating religion and sense of community, but his ideas echo in the claims that religious groups make about the beneficial effects of belonging to a (spiritual) community. Community claims overlap both material claims and spiritual claims, but as a form of discourse they are quite unique and important in the claims-making process. Using social-scientific knowledge reflexively (sometimes explicitly, sometimes implicitly), religious groups can claim that they provide not only the material framework for decent living but also *people* to relate to, thus making individuals tackling social problems part of a wider community tackling the same problems. This is especially important in the case of youth who are in the crucial phase of socialization, and even more so for youth in danger of being marginalized (see Smith and Denton 2005; Bainbridge 1997: 276–80; Stark and Bainbridge 1996: 81–99).

Spiritual Claims

On the most abstract level, the feature that sets religious communities apart from all other actors in the social problems field is the claim of spiritual community. When one accepts baptism, for example, one becomes part of a cosmic community, in which the material world is in close interaction with the spiritual (Berger 1973: 34). There is huge variation between religions and within specific religious traditions as to how the spiritual level is believed to affect coping with social life, and social problems in particular. First, there is difference as to whether solutions to problems can be found in this life through pious action, or only in an afterlife. For example, the prong of Karl Marx's famous dictum '[religion] is the opium of the people' was aimed against religious beliefs which promise relief from suffering in an afterlife and in so doing in fact perpetuate inequality by diminishing people's will to change society themselves. Second, even if the transcendent is considered to have an effect on everyday lives, there are differences in the interpretation of the intensity of divine influence. Whereas a liberal Protestant might see narratives of miracles and divine intervention as metaphorical (although psychologically or existentially useful), in an Evangelical understanding the human world is in continuous interaction with the spirit world, mirroring the eternal struggle between born-again Christians and the hordes of Satan (Fenn 2006). Therefore, in Evangelicalism 'spiritual warfare' (Arnold 1997) is as important as finding material solutions to social problems.

Constructing Religion as a Social Problem

It is perhaps intuitively obvious that religious communities have for a long time been central in raising awareness about social problems and offering solutions to them. What has been less obvious—at least until September 11, 2001—is that religion can be, and has been, constructed as a social problem in itself. While nowadays the traditions referred to as 'world religions' are also increasingly regarded as the *source* of social problems (Juergensmeyer 2001; 2004; Lincoln 2003), this is a perspective already familiar to scholars of new religious movements (see above, and Robbins 1988: 201–2).

The public arenas in which religion is constructed as a social problem are very much the same as those in the process of constructing awareness and solutions to social problems: news media, politics, and the court system (Loseke 1999: 40). Of these, the arena of the courts is perhaps the best researched (see Richardson 2003). Whereas the research on constitutional battles over religion in the United States Supreme Court (see Hammond 1998), for example, is a well-established field of study, research on the importance of the media in the public construction of religions is somewhat lagging behind (for some notable exceptions, see Said 1981; Silk 1998; Beckford 1999; Hjelm 2006*b*; McCloud 2004). Although individual studies of the different arenas of contestation exist, very little research has been done to chart all of the above aspects in specific cases.

Regardless of the arena, there are several recurring types of claims or discourses in which religion is constructed as a social problem, just as with the claims of religion as solutions to social problems. I have named the discourses *ethics*, *healthiness*, *heresy*, *rationality*, and *pseudo-religion*. The typology is drawn from empirical research in Finland (Rikkinen 2002; Hjelm 2006*b*), and as such represents only one possible typification. However, I believe that the above claims represent a fairly comprehensive sample of accounts of 'bad religion'. What is contextually dependent is the priority of the different discourses. For example, in the American 'Bible belt' a small rural newspaper might be more prone to report fundamentalist Christian views as expert testimony of 'Satanic cults' engaging in criminal activities—the credibility of the claim from a law enforcement perspective notwithstanding. The relative silence of national newspapers on occult issues, on the other hand, most likely reflects a less shared sense of 'us', a context where explicitly fundamentalist Christian claims might be considered offensive, trivial, or absurd (Lowe and Cavender 1991; Shupe and Bromley 1980). Although the objectives (implicit or explicit) of the claims might be the same, the context shapes their final form.

Ethics

The discourse on the (un)ethicality of a religion or its practices is almost self-evident, since all claims of deviance are eventually moral claims (Loseke 1999: 55). To claim that a religion is deviant and that its practices constitute a social problem is to say that what it does is wrong, and that it should be restricted, or even prohibited. The 'problem' with this kind of argumentation is that in contemporary multicultural and religiously plural societies, explicitly moralistic claims can be seen as problematic. For example, the mainstream media tend to present news as neutral communication, and in this genre explicit moral claims are often eschewed. Therefore, significant variation exists according to whether a moral claim is made explicitly or implicitly. The old 'journalist as a moralist' (see Einstadter 1994; Buddenbaum 1998: 91–2; Buddenbaum and Mason 2000: p. xix) has in most cases given way to the silent 'compiler of facts'. Implicitly, however, religions can be, and are, constructed as a social problem by using experts that confirm the unethicality of a religious practice. Although the experts may be biased themselves (as the 'cult controversies' have shown), their testimonies fade the journalist's voice into the background, thus making the news more 'objective'. Furthermore, it depends on the legitimacy of the religion in question whether it is publicly denounced as 'bad religion' in the substantive sense—that is, claiming that the religion itself is deviant—or whether only a particular practice of the religion is condemned. For example, in many cases Scientology is represented as controversial, without much detail about what exactly makes it problematic. On the other hand, Islam, as a world religion, is in general recognized as legitimate, but incites controversy on the ethics of specific practices, such as veiling and ritual slaughter.

Healthiness

In their ground-breaking book *Deviance and Medicalization: From Badness to Sickness*, Peter Conrad and Joseph Schneider (1980) coined the influential term *medicalization.* In short, medicalization refers to the transformation whereby 'deviant behaviors that were once defined as immoral, sinful, or criminal have been given medical meanings' (Conrad and Schneider 1980: 1). In the public discussion on religion, this process is manifested in a significant change from explicitly moral language to an appreciation of religion and religious practices according to their healthiness or unhealthiness. The argument first gained credence in the debate concerning alleged cult 'brainwashing' (Bromley and Shupe 1981; Beckford 1985; Robbins 1988; cf. Zablocki and Robbins 2001). Later, it has become increasingly prominent in describing religion and religious practice of all kinds. Its appeal lies in the scientific aura it emanates and the sense of objectivity it conveys. In this respect, medicalized arguments are much more difficult to challenge than explicitly moral ones. Through medicalization, deviant religious practices become *technical* problems which can be technically solved by suggesting the removal of the practice without taking into account the possible moral problems involved in dismissing tradition and orthodox belief and practice (see Gusfield 1980: p. vii). This is in line with what Gusfield calls the *depoliticization* of social problems: 'The medicalization of social problems depoliticizes them and diminishes the recognition of differences in moral choices that they represent' (Gusfield 1980: p. viii).

Heresy

For a long time arguments against other religions, especially the evil 'cults', were made on explicitly religious grounds (Jenkins 2000: 10–12; McCloud 2004). Religions other than whatever was considered 'good religion' in a given context were condemned on the basis of their deviance from the prevailing religious culture—that is, as heresy. Since the advent of multiculturalism and religious pluralism in the West, this kind of language has become increasingly rare in public discourse, but re-emerges sometimes in times of crisis. The terrorist attacks of 9/11 were condemned in America in explicitly religious terms by prominent commentators, such as Jerry Falwell and Ann Coulter. Although most certainly dismissed as bigotry by many Americans, this kind of *crisis religion* achieved unprecedented coverage exactly because of a crisis situation. What I have termed 'crisis religion' refers to the process where by religious discourse achieves a significant status in explaining certain social phenomena that are perceived as problematic and threatening (Hjelm 2006*b*). Why the extraordinary situation was crucial to the emergence of openly religious public statements can be summed up in Durkheimian tones: 'One of the surest ways to confirm an identity, for communities as well as for individuals, is to find some way of measuring what one is *not*' (Erikson 1966: 64; emphasis original).

Rationality

One type of discourse which falls somewhat outside the circle of moral claims is rationality discourse. It is of course a good question whether religion can (or should) ever be portrayed as rational; but this type of discourse explicitly trivializes religious beliefs and practices by presenting them as irrational, and thus funny, foolish, or as a waste of time. In general, recent bestsellers such as Richard Dawkins's *The God Delusion* (2006) have incited public debate over the rationality of religious beliefs. Claims that construct religion as a social problem from a rationality perspective are probably unlikely to affect those who are part of a steady religious community that keeps the plausibility structure (Berger 1973: 54–7) of religion alive. However, in contexts where (traditional) religion is treated with increasing indifference, this type of discourse may have a further alienating effect. Furthermore, the rise of alternative spiritualities (sometimes grouped under the label 'New Age'; see Heelas 1996; Heelas and Woodhead 2005), often operating in the well-being market of contemporary Western societies, has prompted replies from skeptics eager to demonstrate the irrationality of such beliefs. The boundary drawn between religion and science has the consequence that some forms of alternative medicine, for example, may be defined as deviant and problematic precisely *because* they are 'religious', or are based on views and beliefs not supported by Western allopathic medicine.

Pseudo-religion

The last type of discourse in my typology concerns the definition of religion. Almost diametrically opposed to the religion/science discussion mentioned above in conjunction with the rationality discourse, claiming something as pseudo-religious makes religion problematic because it is actually not 'really' a religion. This all has to do with the legitimacy of particular religions in specific social contexts and is particularly important in the case of alternative religions (Hjelm 2007), which often do not have the legitimacy that more established religions possess (Melton 2003; Lewis 2003). In Finland, for example, practising any religion is allowed. However, registering as an officially registered religious community gives a group certain benefits and, most of all, a certain aura of legitimacy. The Finnish Ministry of Education's decision to deny the Finnish Free Wicca Association the status of a religious community certainly had an effect on the public understanding of Wicca as a non-*bona fide* religion, but also, perhaps more importantly, on the drawing of boundaries of belief and practice within the movement (Hjelm 2006*a*; 2007).

Studying Religion and Social Problems: Brief Methodological Considerations

After considering the application of social problems theory to the study of religion, it seems appropriate to discuss briefly what methodological implications the above approaches have. Again, we can take Fuller and Myers's (1941) definition of social problems as a starting point. Although whether we are focusing on the objective conditions or the subjective definitions does not necessarily dictate the choice of method, it does make some choices more feasible than others. As shown above, most of the studies of objective conditions have used quantitative methods, exemplified in Stark and Bainbridge's well-known studies (1996; 1985). However, the history of social problems research shows that the choice of quantitative methods is not inevitable: for example, many of the sociologists of the famous 'Chicago School' used ethnographic methods in studying street gangs and social inequality in city settings (e.g., Park *et al.* 1967).

The situation with claims making is a bit different. By its nature, public discourse is less easily converted into numbers (although quantitative content analysis is used in media research, for example), therefore making qualitative methods usually a primary choice. By calling the claims presented above—both those of religion as a solution and those of religion as a problem—*discourses*, I have already hinted at one possibility of analysis. The constructionist tradition in American sociology has not been very explicit about the methods of studying claims making, but I have found the developments in European discourse theory helpful in this sense. Little used in sociology of religion so far (Spickard 2007), discourse analysis focuses on the use of language as an element of social interaction (Fairclough 2003: 2–3). There are many approaches to discourse analysis, and many other approaches close to it (such as conversation analysis), but the main focus overall is on how discourses—in our case, claims referring to social problems and religion—on the one hand draw from social practices and on the other hand shape these social practices. Put differently, the analysis asks how the social world is constructed in discourse.

Conclusion: Religion and Social Problems as a Sociological Prism

Much more could be said about the interface between sociology of religion and the study of social problems. It is also clear that the examples presented above are by no means the only way to approach the subject. What is offered as 'new' here is the focus on social problems as claims-making activity and how, on the one hand, religions construct solutions to social problems and, on the other hand, how religion is constructed as a social problem in itself. What I find most interesting and important is that in addition to being a solid field of inquiry in itself, the study of religion and social problems also works as a prism through which many other central problems in sociology of religion—and sociology in general—can be examined. For example, first, the role of religious communities in alleviating social problems raises crucial questions about the function and performance of religion in the contemporary world (Beyer 1994). That is, is religion losing its unique status as a spiritual institution by concentrating on 'profane' issues such as social problems? Second, the construction of religion as a social problem tells us a lot not only about 'bad religion', but also about the image of what 'good religion' (or '*our* religion') is. In Clifford's (1986: 23) words: 'It has become clear that every version of an "other", wherever found, is also a construction of the "self".' This too has implications for other issues, such as multiculturalism and religious pluralism, that, although not necessarily directly related to social problems, explore the question of interaction between cultures and religious traditions. Many other examples could be added, which only goes to show that the emerging field has a lot to offer—both in empirical study and theoretical refinement—for the sociological study of religion in the contemporary world.

References

Akers, R. (2000). *Criminological Theories: Introduction, Evaluation, and Application*, 3rd edn. Los Angeles: Roxbury.

Arnold, C. (1997). *Spiritual Warfare.* London: Marshall Pickering.

Bainbridge, W. S. (1997). *The Sociology of Religious Movements.* New York: Routledge.

Becker, H. S. (1991[1963]). *Outsiders: Studies in the Sociology of Deviance.* New York: The Free Press of Glencoe.

Beckford, J. A. (1985). *Cult Controversies: The Societal Response to the New Religious Movements.* London: Tavistock.

—— (1990). "The Sociology of Religion and Social Problems". *Sociological Analysis,* 51/1: 1–14.

—— (1999). "The Mass Media and New Religious Movements". In B. Wilson and J. Cresswell (eds.), *New Religious Movements: Challenge and Response.* London: Routledge, 102–19.

—— (2003). *Social Theory and Religion.* Cambridge: Cambridge University Press.

Berger, P. L. (1973). *The Social Reality of Religion.* Harmondsworth: Penguin. (Originally published in 1967 as *The Sacred Canopy.*)

Best, J. (1991). "Endangered Children and Antisatanist Rhetoric". In Richardson *et al.* (1991), 95–106.

—— (1993). "But Seriously Folks: The Limitations of the Strict Constructionist Interpretation of Social Problems". In Miller and Holstein (1993), 109–27.

Beyer, P. (1994). *Religion and Globalization.* London: Sage.

Blumer, H. (1971). "Social Problems as Collective Behavior". *Social Problems,* 18 (Winter): 298–306.

Bromley, D. G., and Shupe, A. D. (1981). *Strange Gods: The Great American Cult Scare.* Boston: Beacon Press.

Buddenbaum, J. M. (1998). *Reporting News about Religion.* Ames, Ia.: Iowa State University Press.

—— and Mason, D. L. (2000). *Readings on Religion as News.* Ames, Ia.: Iowa State University Press.

Clifford, J. (1986). "Introduction: Partial Truths". In J. Clifford and G. Marcus (eds.), *Writing Culture.* Berkeley: University of California Press, 1–26.

CONRAD, P., and SCHNEIDER, J. W. (1980). *Deviance and Medicalization: From Badness to Sickness*. St Louis, Mo.: The C.V. Mosby Company.

DAWKINS, R. (2006). *The God Delusion*. London: Bantam.

DURKHEIM, E. (1979[1897]). *Suicide*. New York: The Free Press.

EBAUGH, H. R., & PIPES, P. F., SALTZMAN CHAFETZ, J., and DANIELS, M. (2003). "Where's the Religion? Distinguishing Faith-Based from Secular Social Service Agencies". *Journal for the Scientific Study of Religion*, 42/3: 411–26.

EINSTADTER, W. J. (1994). "Crime News in the Old West". In G. Barak (ed.), *Media, Process, and the Social Construction of Crime*. New York: Garland Publishing, 49–67.

ERIKSON, K. T. (1966). *The Wayward Puritans: A Study in the Sociology of Deviance*. New York: John Wiley & Sons.

EVANS, D. T., CULLEN, F. T., DUNAWAY, R. G., and BURTON, V. S. (1995). "Religion and Crime Reexamined: The Impact of Religion, Secular Controls, and Social Ecology on Adult Criminality". *Criminology*, 33/2: 195–224.

FAIRCLOUGH, N. (2003). *Analysing Discourse: Textual Analysis for Social Research*. London: Routledge.

FENN, R. K. (2006). *Dreams of Glory: The Sources of Apocalyptic Terror*. Aldershot: Ashgate.

FULLER, R. C., and MYERS, R. R. (1941). "The Natural History of a Social Problem". *American Sociological Review*, 6/3: 320–8.

GUSFIELD, J. R. (1980). "Foreword". In Conrad and Schneider (1980), pp. v–x.

HADDEN, JEFFREY K. (1980). "Religion and the Construction of Social Problems". *Sociological Analysis*, 41/2: 99–108.

HAMILTON, M. B. (2001). *The Sociology of Religion: Theoretical and Comparative Perspectives*, 2nd edn. London: Routledge.

HAMMOND, P. (1998). *With Liberty for All: Freedom of Religion in the United States*. Louisville, Ky.: Westminster/John Knox Press.

HEELAS, P. (1996). *The New Age Movement*. Oxford: Blackwell.

—— and WOODHEAD, L. (2005). *The Spiritual Revolution*. Oxford: Blackwell.

HJELM, T. (2006*a*). "Between Satan and Harry Potter: Legitimating Wicca in Finland". *Journal of Contemporary Religion*, 21/1: 39–58.

—— (2006*b*). "News of the Unholy: Constructing Religion as a Social Problem in the News Media". In R. Salokangas and J. Sumiala-Seppänen (eds.), *Implications of the Sacred in (Post)modern Media*. Gothenburg: Nordicom, 63–76.

—— (2007). "United in Diversity, Divided from Within: The Dynamics of Legitimation in Contemporary Witchcraft". In O. Hammer and K. von Stuckrad (eds.), *Polemical Encounters: Esoteric Discourse and Its Others*. Leiden: Brill, 291–309.

HOLSTEIN, J. A., and MILLER, G. (eds.) (2003). *Challenges & Choices: Constructionist Perspectives on Social Problems*. New York: Aldine deGruyter.

JENKINS, P. (2000). *Mystics and Messiahs: Cults and New Religions in American History*. Oxford: Oxford University Press.

JOHNSON, B. R., JANG, S. J., LARSON, D. B., and DE LI, S. (2001). "Does Adolescent Religious Commitment Matter? A Reexamination of the Effects of Religiosity on Delinquency". *Journal of Research in Crime and Delinquency*, 38/1: 22–44.

JUERGENSMEYER, M. (2001). *Terror in the Mind of God*, updated edn. Berkeley: University of California Press.

—— (2004). "Thinking about Religion after September 11". *Journal of the American Academy of Religion*, 72/1: 221–34.

Kitsuse, J. I., and Spector, M. (1973). "Toward a Sociology of Social Problems: Social Conditions, Value Judgments and Social Problems". *Social Problems*, 20/4: 407–19.

—— —— (1975). "Social Problems and Deviance: Some Parallels". *Social Problems*, 22/5: 584–94.

Lewis, J. R. (2003). *Legitimating New Religions*. New Brunswick, NJ: Rutgers University Press.

Lincoln, B. (2003). *Holy Terrors*. Chicago: University of Chicago Press.

Loseke, D. R. (1999). *Thinking about Social Problems: An Introduction to Constructionist Perspectives*. New York: Aldine De Gruyter.

Lowe, L., and Cavender, G. (1991). "Cauldrons Bubble, Satan's Trouble, but Witches Are Okay: Media Constructions of Satanism and Witchcraft". In Richardson *et al.* (1991), 263–75.

Mauss, A. L. (1975). *Social Problems as Social Movements*. Philadelphia: Lippincott.

McCloud, S. (2004). *Making the American Religious Fringe: Exotics, Subversives, & Journalists, 1955–1993*. Chapel Hill, NC: University of North Carolina Press.

Melton, J. G. (2003). "Perspective: Toward a Definition of 'New Religion'". *Nova Religio*, 8/1: 73–87.

Miller, G., and Holstein, J. A. (eds.) (1993). *Constructionist Controversies: Issues in Social Problems Theory*. New York: Aldine deGruyter.

Park, R. E., Burgess, E. W., and McKenzie, R. D. (1967). *The City*. Chicago: University of Chicago Press.

Putnam, R. D. (2000). *Bowling Alone: The Collapse and Revival of American Community*. New York: Simon & Schuster.

Richardson, J. T. (ed.) (2003). *Regulating Religion: Case Studies from Around the World*. Dordrecht: Kluwer.

—— Best, J., and Bromley, D. G. (eds.) (1991). *The Satanism Scare*. New York: Aldine deGruyter.

Rikkinen, M. (2002). *Yhteisön nimeen: Kirkon identifikaatioprosessi uususkonto-keskusteluissa*. Helsinki: Department of Comparative Religion, University of Helsinki.

Robbins, T. (1985). "Nuts, Sluts, and Converts: Studying Religious Groups as Social Problems". *Sociological Analysis*, 46/2: 171–8.

—— (1988). *Cults, Converts and Charisma: The Sociology of New Religious Movements*. London: Sage.

Rubington, E., and Weinberg, M. S. (eds.) (1995). *The Study of Social Problems: Seven Perspectives*. New York and Oxford: Oxford University Press.

Said, E. W. (1981). *Covering Islam*. London: Routledge & Kegan Paul.

Shields, J., Broome, K. M., Delany, P. J., Fletcher, B. W., and Flynn, P. M. (2007). "Religion and Substance Abuse Treatment: Individual and Program Effects". *Journal for the Scientific Study of Religion*, 46/3: 355–71.

Shupe, A. D., and Bromley, D. G. (1980). *The New Vigilantes*. Beverly Hills, Calif.: Sage.

Silk, M. (1998). *Unsecular Media: Making News of Religion in America*. Urbana, Ill., and Chicago: University of Illinois Press.

Smith, C., and Denton, M. (2005). *Soul Searching: The Religious and Spiritual Lives of American Teens*. New York: Oxford University Press.

Spector, M., and Kitsuse, J. I. (1973). "Social Problems: A Reformulation". *Social Problems*, 21/2: 145–59.

Spector, M., and Kitsuse, J. I. (2001[1977]). *Constructing Social Problems*. New Brunswick, NJ: Transaction Publishers.

Spickard, J. V. (2007). "Micro/Qualitative Approaches to the Sociology of Religion: Phenomenologies, Interviews, Narratives, and Ethnographies". In J. Beckford and J. N. Demerath (eds.), *The Sage Handbook of the Sociology of Religion*. London: Sage, 121–43.

Stark, R., and Bainbridge, W. S. (1985). *The Future of Religion: Secularization, Revival, and Cult Fermation*. Berkeley: University of California Press.

—— —— (1996). *Religion, Deviance, and Social Control*. New York: Routledge.

—— Iannaccone, L. R., and Finke, R. (1996). "Religion, Science, and Rationality". *American Economic Review*, 86/2: 433–7.

Swanson, P. L. (2002). "Religion as a Social Problem". *Bulletin of the Nanzan Insitute for the Study of Religion & Culture*, 26: 8–18.

Wuthnow, R. (2006). *Saving America? Faith-Based Services and the Future of Civil Society*. Princeton: Princeton University Press.

Zablocki, B., and Robbins, T. (2001). *Misunderstanding Cults*. Toronto: University of Toronto Press.

Suggested Reading

The following are recommended: Beckford (2003); Loseke (1999); Rubington and Weinberg (1995); Spector and Kitsuse (2001[1977]); and Stark and Bainbridge (1996).

CHAPTER 52

RELIGION AND SOCIAL PROBLEMS

INDIVIDUAL AND INSTITUTIONAL RESPONSES

ANNE BIRGITTA PESSI

This chapter brings the sociological viewpoints on social problems and religion into a dialogue by illustrating a few of the more central theoretical notions by reference to recent empirical material. The focus is on *responses*, both at the individual level and in terms of religious institutions, and on the search for *holism*. The chapter begins with a consideration of the concept of a social problem, followed by a brief overview of the role of religion in social problems. The text is then divided into three empirically oriented sections: first, on the role of religion in the search for a holistic, happier life; second, on individuals' responses to social problems; and third, on institutional responses to social problems. The article concludes with a section that reflects on future developments and the possible role of religion in

The author wishes to thank warmly Professor Peter B. Clarke and Professor Grace Davie for very valuable comments on this chapter.

solidarity and 'horizons of significance'. An important limitation must be acknowledged: this is all very contextual. This chapter considers only Christianity, and (almost exclusively) in the form of Western European majority churches, particularly the Nordic ones. The context of this chapter, Europe, is a secularized context in which religion has only rather recently re-entered the public arena.

Understanding the Concept of a Social Problem

How should we understand the concept of a 'social problem' in today's sociological discourse? Are we dealing with a crystal-clear sociological concept to be used for a particular empirical phenomenon, or an all-compassing, extremely imprecise description of practically all present-day phenomena? A sociologist may even ask what 'non-social problems' might be. The answer also depends on the way we perceive our time; are we longing for 'the lost time of communality, simple days, days of caring'? Or do we view late modernity as the golden era of novel independent opportunities, or something in between? Furthermore, as Rubington and Weinberg (2003: 3) have pointed out, some sociological observers view modern society as producing more social problems than previous societies. Additionally, some see our era as producing more and more solutions, while others consider that our society actually over-produces so-called solutions.

The idea that there are social problems about which something should be done is actually fairly recent, since a consciousness of social problems arose only during the latter part of the eighteenth century (Green 1975). Social problems have been, and continue to be, at the heart of sociological analysis; in fact, sociology has dominated the study of social problems. Sociology developed during an era of radical social change; moreover, its central focus is social relations, as is that of social problems (Rubington and Weinberg 2003: 3).

Social problems may be defined as 'an alleged situation that is incompatible with the values of a significant number of people who agree that action is needed to alter the situation' (Rubington and Weinberg 2003: 4). Similarly, for Loseke (2003: 7), social problems are 'a condition evaluated as wrong, widespread, and changeable—[it] is a category for conditions we believe *should* be changed'. The perspectives on social problems cover the range from the 'objective viewpoint' (problems are about measurable conditions; this is the perspective of most social problems text books) to 'subjective worry' (Loseke 2003).

The sociological study of social problems has developed through six stages, particularly in the Northern American tradition, where social problems have been one of the central topics of sociology, much more so than in Europe (see Rubington and Weinberg 2003). At the outset, the field developed from the perspective of social pathology (as in Gillin 1939) to that of social disorganization (e.g., Cooley 1927), followed by the value conflict perspective that synthesized European and American classical theories of conflict (such as Fuller and Myers 1941). The succeeding stages centred around studies of deviant behaviour (e.g., Cohen 1955) and of labelling (e.g., Becker 1963), building on G. H. Mead and A. Schutz. Research on social problems then experienced the rise of the Marx-inspired, Frankfurt School-oriented critical perspective. The most recent development includes social constructionism (e.g., Kitsuse and Spector 1973); as Loseke (2003: 14) has put it, 'a social problem does not exist until it is defined as such'.

Something is shared, though—a common 'enemy'. One central source of problems (direct or indirect) that lies in practically all theoreticians' viewpoints on social problems, whether they are more related to industrialization, urbanization, or any other grand narrative of our field, concerns networks and communality, and particularly concern about weakening cohesion and togetherness. Mediated or indirect social relations have growing in importance, and thus communities lack visibility and unity (Delanty 2005). This leads to a more individualized way of life. Yet this discourse is one-sided; individuals are far from being entirely free. Recent societal changes do not necessarily imply dramatic internal transitions (see Grow 2002; Castells 2004). The present-day societal context deeply underscores the question of how the individual can become both more free, more of an individual, yet more closely linked to society and networks—as well as underscoring old and new social problems. Religion is deeply interwoven into these processes, as we will see in the next section.

Religion—Cause or Solution?

During the 1970s and 1980s there were scholars (e.g., Hadden 1980) who already understood what most sociologists of religion now understand: the role of religion in defining and resolving social problems continues to be central and to become even more urgent (see Beckford 1990). Religion plays various roles in both defining and resolving—and indeed causing—social problems. Various of these positive and negative contributions also reflect larger issues and debates; for instance, that over women priests and bishops concerns the broader issues of gender roles.

Religion demands reactions to social problems, as well as legitimizing them. In the Christian way of understanding life, 'living well' and the 'good life' are inseparable; an individual can neither be happy nor lead a good life without morally good actions (Hallamaa 1999*a*; 1999*b*; Kuula 2004) such as engaging in altruism. Even if many studies (mostly by theologians) still present Christianity as 'the main source of the modern altruism concept' (Grant 2000: 167), views emphasizing altruism are not typical only of the Christian faith; there is a strong obligation of giving and helping in the Jewish tradition, in Islam, and in various Oriental religions (e.g., Neusner and Chilton 2005).

While this link between religions and altruism is self-evident, it is also very problematic (see Monroe 1996: 122–3; Post *et al.* 2003; Yeung 2004*a*; also Oord 2003; Johnson *et al.* 2003). Let me point out just one dilemma. Blackmore has suggested in *The Meme Machine* (1999), based on Dawkins's *The Selfish Gene* (1976), that religious institutions may use altruism and welfare activities as a gimmick; people respect individuals and institutions who help, and at the same time they spread their cultural memes; people believe in their dogmas and spread their teachings. Blackmore sees Christianity as utilizing the human genetic-cultural inclination for altruistic acts and attitudes. Christianity is one of 'the viruses of the mind' which spread as a 'parasite' carried by the altruistic operation practised by the religious communities (Blackmore 1999; also Goodenough 1995). Church workers may actually be aware of this dilemma; one vicar I interviewed wondered, alluding to biblical notions: 'When your left hand is helping others, your right hand should not know about it.'

The role of religion in relation to social problems has recently become more crucial for several reasons, two of which will be noted here. First, secularization, rather than reducing the role of religion and churches in relation to social problems, has had the reverse effect. Looking at the churches and states of differentiated Western societies, most often there is at least a latent tension between the two. Religious institutions are not under an obligation to uphold the *status quo*, and being autonomous, the churches enjoy new opportunities in relation to social problems and the freedom to criticize the state (Hadden 1980: 100). Beckford has noted, in relation to Simmel, that differentiated institutions can retain power by 'becoming "autonomous" in the sense of drifting apart from the matrix of practices, interests, and institutions in which they were originally encased' (Beckford 1990: 11). The churches of today are empowered; the situation has opened them up to various novel public roles—for instance, via welfare activities (Casanova 1994; Yeung 2003).

Second, contemporary society, no matter how differentiated and fragmented, seeks holism and holistic experience. Issues such as happiness, welfare, and the good life are high on everyone's agenda. For instance, as distinct from the pre-Second World War era issues such as the labour movement and political parties, contemporary social movements are increasingly about holistic issues of quality, sustainability, self-fulfilment, and dignity (Beckford 1990). As a result, there is also greater scope for religious contributions to such movements, as we see in the fact that human rights and peace movements have been 'a perennial component of many industrial societies, and they have more often than not had religious origins and inspiration' (Beckford 1990: 7–8).

However—perhaps ironically—the factors that explain the growing relevance of religion in relation to social problems are the very same reasons why religions are becoming increasingly problematic. Additionally, religious forms in their new arenas are also more available for co-operation with, or even hijacking by, secular forces and groups (Beckford 1990: 12). Religion has the capacity to promote both violence and welfare, solidarity and conflict. Religious institutions may encourage selflessness, generosity, and altruism, but also attitudes and acts of animosity and violence. This dilemma is deepened by the fact that religion easily captures wider perspectives, including global ones; examples range from peace movements to the Catholic movement, opus Dei, and from the theology of the poor to various forms of utopianism, extremists groups, and fundamentalism. In most of its extreme modes, religion is becoming more of a social problem *in its own right.*

Thus, religion and social problems can be—and have been—approached from two directions: religion solving (or, at least aiming or claiming to solve) social problems (for studies, see, e.g., Jules-Rosette 1989; McBride *et al.* 1994; Bäckström 2005) and religion being constructed as a social problem and/or causing social problems (for studies, see, e.g., Kramer 1983; Moxon-Browne 1983; C. Smith 1996). Still, as Beckford (1990: 3) has pointed out, there has been too little inducement for sociologists of religion to regard social problems as a high priority on their agendas. To take an example, we have research both on welfare in Europe and on European religiosity, yet still little research that would bring these together. This Handbook offers important insights to religion and social problems in topics related to, for instance, delinquency (Chapter 47), human rights (Chapter 24), fundamentalism (Chapter 26) and violence (Chapter 49; see also Chapter 51).

As previously mentioned, this chapter aims to bring the sociological viewpoint regarding social problems and the theme of religion into a dialogue and to illustrate some of the more central theoretical notions with recent empirical material.[1] Much social-scientific research into social problems has focused on issues that are assumed to be problematic. Similarly, in the few texts in which the relationship between religious and social problems has been examined, there has been a tendency to focus on only the problematic aspects of religion (Beckford 1990: 3).

[1] The first-hand empirical material referred to here comes from Finland, a country which is quite a textbook example of a Nordic country in which membership of the Lutheran majority church is still relatively high (83 per cent of Finns being members), yet the religious scene is very privatized (e.g., high indications of prayer, very low church service participation). From an international perspective, the Finnish system of congregational church social work is an interesting subject, owing to its uniqueness; social work in the church includes a large group of paid workers and has a central position in canon law and church organization as a whole. The forms of activity in Finnish church social work now range from food banks to counselling, from home visits to various camps, from financial assistance to support groups, etc.

However, Spector and Kitsuse in their classic work on social problems have defined social problems as 'the activities of individuals or groups making assertions of grievances and claims with respect to some putative conditions' (1977: 75). The essence thus concerns responses. This is the viewpoint on social problems and religion taken in this chapter: *responses*, both at the individual level and in terms of religious institutions. Second, the search for *holism*, and the scope for religion noted above in this search, relates to the fact that most responses carry the inherent sense of aiming for a better life and well-being. But, as only belatedly have churches and religions begun to actively engage with the health and wholeness of the individual and the planet, the focus on holism here concerns only the search for the good life from the perspective of the particular case of happiness.

All in all, this chapter, rather than focusing on religion *as* a social problem, *illustrates theoretical notions of religion and social problems with empirical material that deals with two angles: responses to social problems and the search for a holistic, happier life*. I begin with the latter.

Seeking Holism: The Case of Happiness

Happiness studies are a particularly challenging endeavour. There are countless international studies indicating that people report their happiness as relatively high (i.e., over 5 on a 1–10 scale) (e.g., Diener and Diener 1996; Hirvonen and Mangeloja 2006). However, people do tend to overestimate their personal happiness. Present-day individualism-oriented culture may even put additional pressure on providing such answers. What, then, makes us happy? No single factor predominates. Most international research (such as Layard 2005) indicates that the most crucial elements are health, family, and human relations, as well as spirituality. Frey and Stutzer (2002) concluded that happiness is grounded in three sets of factors: contextual (health, family, relations, job), personality (high self-esteem, self-control, optimism, extroversion), and institutional (religion, opportunity to exert influence, and freedom).

Religiosity, measured (as in Hirvonen and Mangeloja 2006) as religious activity, faith in religious teachings, and importance of faith, indeed has a positive relationship to experienced happiness. The effect of religion on happiness is found even after controlling for variables such as education, age, and occupation (Argyle 2001: 164; Witter *et al.* 1985; see also Francis *et al.* 2000). For instance, Helliwell (2002; 2005) has indicated that in fifty-seven countries subjective well-being and religiosity share a strong connection. Inglehart's (1990) study on fourteen

European countries also reported a positive correlation between churchgoing and life satisfaction. Similarly, new Finnish survey data[2] looking at the interconnection between happiness (e.g., 'How content are you with your life as a whole?') and religiosity ('I am a religious person') reveal clearly that the more religious a person is, the more content he or she is with life as a whole. This picture breaks down only with the most *non*-religious, who are approximately as happy as the moderately religious. However, when asking what makes people happy, Finns underscore the role of family, health, and love, putting least emphasis on the role of communal activities and religiosity. Thus, even if the statistical analysis clearly indicates that the more religious an individual is, the happier she or he is, individuals themselves do not seem to experience (or admit, or consider) this connection (Yeung 2007*a*; Torvi and Kiljunen 2005). Related to this, another dilemma concerns the question of whether the link *is* genuinely there, since a critic may ask whether members of religious institutions are just too strongly socialized into repeating the story of 'how happy religion makes me'.

Still, even the critic has to ask the question: as religion seems to set at ease individuals and support them in the face of various social problems, how is this connection to be explained? Argyle (2001[1986]: 165–8) has suggested four possibilities. First, a cohesive, supportive church community plays a central role by providing social networks. Second, belief in higher powers, and particularly experienced closeness to God, sets an individual at ease (see also Pollner 1989; Ellison *et al.* 1989). Third, firm beliefs and faith that support personal identity also play a definite role. The effect of church attendance and private devotions on well-being is reported to be via beliefs (see Ellison 1991; Ellison *et al.* 1989). Fourth, what may be called 'spiritual well-being' (Paloutzian and Ellison 1982) also has its positive effect; this includes having both a satisfying relationship with God ('religious well-being'; close to the belief in higher powers noted above) and life satisfaction and purpose ('existential well-being').[3]

In addition to such direct effects, religion may be influential more indirectly. Religious norms may protect individuals; values may become more family- and health-oriented; life may be more meaningful; and so on. Furthermore, religious activities offer positive emotional as well as communal experiences. Faith may also increase self-esteem, lower stress, and provide a buffer against negative experiences (Hirvonen and Mangeloja 2006; Yeung 2007*a*).

[2] A random sample survey of Finns on experiences of altruism, good life, and religiosity, N = 1040, collected in 2006. The data are representative of Finnish citizens; only statistically significant results are reported in this chapter. The survey material was enhanced by twenty-five interviews with respondents; the interviewees were chosen to represent various age-groups, localities, and relations to religiosity, as well as both sexes. The same data (both quantitative and qualitative) are used in several sections of this text.

[3] In addition to these four links between happiness and religiosity, other studies such as Poloma and Pendleton (1991) and Maltby *et al.* (1999) have also reported on the strong influence of peak experiences, and particularly prayer, on well-being.

Furthermore, the fact that religious norms may shift the individual's attention more in the direction of fellow human beings may actually be closely linked to the happiness–religiosity link. My preliminary findings with qualitative data (Yeung 2007*a*; on data, see n. 2) underscore the role of altruism in mediating the happiness–religiosity connection. In other words, how, and particularly why, individuals become engaged with the social problems of others may explain this link, at least in part. Interview material has identified five elements. First, putting faith and values into concrete action brings 'results' such as joy. This is supported, second, by a personal relationship to God, as well as, third, the role of institutions (home, congregations, etc.) which offer individuals notions of how to live and how to treat others. Fourth, communal support in the congregations and social networks of the church reciprocally support altruism, and thus happiness as well. Fifth, even individuals who described themselves as very passive church members and non-affiliated individuals underscore the role of religious texts such as the Bible in their basic values, particularly the religious teachings about how to treat fellow human beings. To borrow the words of a non-affiliated woman in her late twenties: 'I consider the doctrines of the church as sort of general norms, rules of behaviour—principles like do to others what you would want them do to you, and so on, they are so absolutely good and I would like to follow them too—good guidelines' (Yeung 2007*a*).

In recent times, religion has become increasingly *visible*; spirituality 'that favours synoptic, holistic, and global perspectives on issues transcending the privatized self and the individual state' are increasingly relevant, as Beckford (1990: 8–9) has noted. We are surrounded by various networks, campaigns, and movements that are characterized by a problem-oriented, pragmatic, global outlook and ones that often build on symbols from various religious sources. Religion indeed may play a productive role here: a role that may be used *and* misused by both individuals and institutions.

Individual Responses to Social Problems

In this section I look at how individuals face social problems. Three particular questions form the core of this section. Do individuals have altruistic attitudes, and if so, are these related to their religiosity? Of which institutions do they have particular expectations? What are their expectations of the church?

Notwithstanding the rise of individualistic values, the values of solidarity and altruism continue to play an important role in the European values landscape. This is echoed in the country investigated in this article, Finland, where the majority

(67 per cent) regard helping others as personally important or very important, only a third agreeing with the claim that 'everyone should primarily care for themselves'. These values are also reflected in actions (or at least, peoples' *reports* of their actions), since responses to the question 'Have you helped the following groups during the last two years' showed that a clear majority have helped their relatives (84.8 per cent), friends (91.1 per cent), as well someone or some individuals unknown to themselves (85.7 per cent) (Yeung 2007*a*). Does religion play a role here? The figures do indeed indicate that the more important a person considers Christian values and the more that religion is part of one's reported, identity, the more likely she or he is to consider helping others important. Can a similar connection be found in terms of deeds? Christian values show no differential when it comes to helping family members and friends. Helping neighbours, however, starts to bring differences. Moreover, even more demanding, further-reaching acts of helping reveal clearer statistical differences in that the more Christian the set of values one has, the greater the likelihood that she or he has donated money or committed him or herself to a longer-term aid project (Yeung 2007*a*).

This connection is not that surprising, since much research provides evidence of the link between religiosity and volunteerism (see Bernt 1989; Greeley 1997; Lam 2002; Uslaner 1997; Yeung 2004*b*). However, the link is a complex one if we wish to *explain* these findings. As Monroe has put it, 'the overall influence of religion [on altruism] was much more complex and subtle than has been thought' (1996: 122–3). In the previous section I already pondered the possible connections between altruism, happiness, and religiosity. How do individuals themselves explain their altruism? In this survey (Yeung 2007*a*; on data, see n. 2), we offered an alternative: 'I want to put Christian love for one's neighbour into action.' This theme divides the respondents, two out of five thinking that this claim does not describe them, and two out of three—in fact, a surprisingly big group—considering it to fit them at least to some extent. Further on this dilemma, previous research on motives for volunteering (Yeung 2004*a*) yielded conceptualizations of both 'religious altruism' (whose basis is activities and helping, with faith as an additional aspect) and 'altruistic religiosity' (whose basis is faith, helping being its manifestation). Furthermore, previous study (Yeung 2004*b*) concluded that different congregational structures promote communal spirit and altruism differently: smaller, minority religious groups support, and probably demand, closer social ties, more intimate altruistic links, and more hours of volunteering within their own circles. However, the same study also indicated through survey material that religiosity (specifically, churchgoing and the importance of God) has a positive correlation not only with church volunteering but also with non-church volunteering. In other words, the church as an institution may support individual altruistic motivation even though these acts are not always directed at church activities but are part of the battle against wider social problems, via wider arenas.

Many issues arise in relation to the motivational depths of the triangle of altruism, religiosity, and social problems. I will note just one: namely, whether religion promotes altruism at all, or rather self-interest. In other words, are religious institutions and/or individuals particularly challenging in relation to the 'pureness of the gift'? In all major religions, selfless action for others produces benefits for the doer; e.g., in Christianity a place in heaven, in Hinduism, rewards in the karmic system.

Who should the churches assist and who in particular should they assist? In our recent survey (Yeung 2007*a*), we tested various cases of need: a distressed, a lonely, a poor, a physically and a mentally ill person, as well as a 'person in need of economic support who wants at the same time to talk about his/her worries'. Overall, the strongest expectations are directed towards the public sector in all cases. This is typical of Western Europe, but different from, for instance, the USA. In the cases of the physically and mentally ill and the poor, people also direct strong expectations to the person's immediate circles, such as family. In the case of the mentally ill and those in distress, the expectations of the church are high. The case of lonely people proves a particularly interesting case: the expectations of the public sector, together with the third sector (e.g., welfare associations), are the lowest, but the expectations of one's immediate circles and the church run high. Furthermore, in the case of the 'person in need of economic support who wants at the same time to talk about his/her worries', people's expectations of the church also continue to be high. The majority also demand that 'Church should both do spiritual work and help the needy, and sometimes helping is even more important' (80.7 per cent of Finns agree), and 'the Church should participate vigorously in public discussions on such things as fairness' (89.9 per cent) (Yeung 2007*a*).

Looking at people's expectations with qualitative data (Yeung 2006*a*; 2006*b*), however, reveals some differences.[4] On the one hand are those who consider welfare activities an integral part of church life, like an elderly man of my data (see n. 4) who put it: 'Without welfare work the church would be like a barren cow. Sorry for this simile! But without social work the church could not produce spiritual benefits.' On the other hand, others feel that the church's role is not—or should not have to be—in actual social work. Nevertheless, a clear majority consider that the ideal role of the church is actually in maintaining societal and individual morality, ethics, and specifically the spirit of caring for one's neighbours. Thus, contributing to the public welfare debate is considered at the heart of

[4] For the international WREP (Welfare and Religion 2003) research project, I have conducted a small survey (N = 100), twenty-nine interviews with the church representatives (four elected officials and twenty-five employees, mostly priests and church workers), ten interviews with municipal authorities, and six group interviews with the local citizens in Lahti, a middle-sized town in southern Finland. The aim of the data collection was to document how representatives of the local church see the organization and development of welfare and the role of the churches in it. For overall findings on Finland, see Yeung 2006*a*; 2006*b*, and on the wider European perspective of the project WREP, see Yeung *et al.* 2006; Pettersson 2006; 2007.

the church's responsibility for social problems. As a middle-aged man in the same data pondered: 'The church must be the conscience of our society. It must dare to be in opposition. It should walk in the frontline and wave the flag—they should dare to oppose the clichés in the words and statements made by local authorities' (Yeung 2006*a*: 183). The church is not let off easily; it is expected to be the voice and vanguard of love and caring.

Institutional Responses to Social Problems

I will now discuss when, why, and how religious institutions are to become engaged in social problems, if at all. More particularly, are there variables that are particular and unique to religious institutions? Such institutions may bring various resources to confronting social problems: economic, leadership, manpower, and powers which confer legitimacy. More importantly, this potential concerns *both* the activities pursued *and* the definition of certain phenomena as problems, and others as not (Hadden 1980: 103–5). Organizational strength (i.e., position *vis-à-vis* other institutions and society), structure, and doctrinal value consensus also affect the question of whether and how a religious institution becomes involved in social problems. Linking social and doctrinal values may increase the freedom to engage in social problems (Hadden 1980: 105; also Wood 1975). All this determines the role of the church in relation to the welfare system; it may resemble the role of vanguard, improver, value guardian, or service provider, to borrow Kramer's (1981) notion.

Religious institutions not only affect social problems as institutions, but have also fundamentally affected the establishment and development of larger social structures, such as institutions of social policy. For instance, the dominant religious institutions have had an impact on the construction of the present organization of welfare (Bäckström 2005), such as the European system of the welfare state. In contrast, the USA has never had such a comprehensive welfare state, and (perhaps in part due to this) local religious organizations have retained a vigour not apparent in many European contexts (Ammerman 2005*b*: 21–2). Religious organizations in the USA are involved in very substantial ways in care, both through informal partnerships and their own programmes. Since 1996, churches and faith-based initiatives have been receiving more and more funds from the state for services, according to 'Charitable Choice' (Ammerman 2005*a*; 2005*c*; Chaves 2004; Cnaan *et al.* 2002; Sherman 2000). This development seems to be welcomed by citizens: half of Americans approve of providing public funds to faith-based groups, while a third objects (American Religious Landscapes 2004).

Still, during recent decades, both European and American churches have ever increasingly become welfare agents. This also applies to statements concerning social policy dealing with social problems. Still, the roles vary. In Western Europe, there is Germany at one end of the continuum, where the social functions of the majority churches (both Protestant and Catholic) are part of the basic organization of the welfare system (Leis 2006), and England at the other, where the most active voluntary agents in social welfare tend to be smaller churches, not the Church of England (Middlemiss 2006). The Nordic countries, where the church seems to offer services complementary to the public sector, fall in between (Pettersson 2006; 2007; Yeung *et al.* 2006). Overall, however, these activities are appreciated by society: citizens all over Europe support the idea of religious actors battling social problems. This is particularly so at times of crisis (see, e.g., Pettersson 2003), the churches being the quintessential place for most people, both physically and figuratively, of mourning, both collective and individual.

The reality is more complex at the grass-roots and national levels. Empirical research with the employees of the Finnish Church reveals varying, contradictory ideals on church and social problems (Yeung 2006*a*). Such questions arise as: Is assisting with social problems more or less important than evangelism? In other words, what is the actual mission of the church institution? Is it primarily or even entirely preaching dogma and evangelizing, or is it, rather, concentration on putting dogma into action? Furthermore, how visible should the church be, in the media, in debating social issues? That is, what is the ideal concerning the church's societal visibility—to be in the middle of the social action, acting and commenting loud and clear, or behaving as a silent, reliable background agent?

In relation to these questions, all in all, analysis of this Finnish qualitative data (Yeung 2006*a*; 2006*b*; on data, see no. 4) led to the conclusion that some church employees emphasize evangelizing and spirituality, thinking that the church should ideally incorporate less welfare activities. Many—most in fact—are much more positive regarding welfare activities, but consider that the practical social work activities of the church should only be temporary. Still others emphasize that the church must incorporate both spiritual and social work equally; a few even noted that in some instances the social work should take precedence over spiritual activities. Similarly, Greg Smith (2004), on the basis of a UK study, concluded that in faith-based organizations there are values and theologies which contradict the values of social work and social inclusion, an implicit dualism separating the spiritual and material realms. Recent empirical research on eight European countries has further indicated that there is a tension between the spiritual identity and the public social role of the churches: their spiritual nature should be kept hidden when acting as social agents providing welfare services (Pettersson 2007; 2006). Such a dualism also naturally informs the relationship between religious institutions and the larger society; as Hadden (1980: 104) put it, the greater the gulf between the religious institution's transcendental precepts and the values and ideals of the society (which in the third millennium are in itself hugely varied), the greater the resources that must be invested in protection of transcendence—protection in either a defensive or offensive moder.

What about the public sector and the role of the church in social problems? Local authorities interviewed in Finland clearly consider that the church has a role to play in the construction of welfare and in combating social problems, *both* in providing services *and* in reminding people of their responsibilities for others' well-being. The church should keep up the voice of the weaker as well as the shared spirit of not leaving your pal who is in need behind (Yeung 2006*a*). Similar voices can be heard throughout Europe (Pettersson 2007; 2006)—which in relation to the history of welfare state is rather surprising and very novel. The role of the churches is underscored particularly in psycho-social services, crisis help, and work with special groups and the weakest. Church representatives share this view, many noting that the invisible misery which the society and municipal aid channels do not reach, that is our field (see Yeung *et al.* 2006). This all reflects expectations that Harris (1998: 156, 159) has called the 'care catalyst' functions of churches: being able to identity people in need of care and to disseminate the information.

Why these fields of welfare precisely? The public authorities in Finland consider that church representatives have special welfare know-how related to, first, spirituality and values particularly (the values of caring and communality especially), and second, the ability to encounter people better than other agents. There is clearly a sense of idealism even in the way in which the welfare services of the churches are pictured; social problem activities by the church are seen as motivated by 'spirituality, love, voluntarism'. Church representatives themselves also share this view, their welfare being seen as qualitatively different—better, encountering the individual more—even if they offer similar forms of work as other agents.[5]

Such idealism raises the question of whether help from the churches is easier or more difficult to accept. All gifts are binding according to classical sociological studies on altruism and gift-giving. Along these lines, a USA-based study has concluded that welfare services provided by a public agency may be easier to receive than those from faith-based agents; they are provided under professional aegis, and people do not have to feel obliged. Congregations, according to this American study, may send the message: 'Please reform your ways and demonstrate values and attitudes that are in line with social responsibility' through their social work (Cnaan *et al.* 2002: 292–3). The findings for Finland, however, in part contradict this view. People see the church work as based on free will; as a middle-aged woman I interviewed put it: 'The help is very easy to accept—They help me simply because they want to. They are not obliged.'

[5] Here too, a similar picture emerges from various European case studies (see Pettersson 2007), concerning both church representatives and public authorities pondering the role of the church.

Towards Solidarity and Horizons of Significance

In the midst of all the sociological discourse on postmodernity, it is often easier to observe and pinpoint changes than continuities. Let us return to a classic text on the role of values in social problems by American sociologist W. Waller (1936), who considered that there is a fundamental tension between organizational mores (i.e., basic mores upon which the social order is founded, such as private property) and humanitarian mores, and that people make value judgements on the basis of the latter. However, people are constrained in wanting to eliminate social problems because that would entail a change in the organizational mores. Thus, social problems are not solved because people do not really want to solve them or to do anything about them. Describing this as 'lots of words, no deeds' is appropriate to the ethos of the present-day individualistic risk society.

Thus, considering the future of social problems, two matters seem highly relevant. First is a sense of solidarity. Whether we conduct sociological analysis in relation to the concepts of social capital or altruism, or put our efforts into analysing matters such as migration, identity, cohesion, cultural change, or the future of European politics, the notion of solidarity is at the heart of the debate. In terms of both praxis and analysis, solidarities are transforming. To take just one example, the informal care produced by families and associational communities has become the target of political thinking (Julkunen 2006: 259). Yet this scenario is fragile, as there is no certainty that the networks of individuals and communities are going to shoulder the task of increasing care. Possible sources of conflict, inequality, and exclusion may be increasing.

Second are the horizons of significance. Taylor's insightful analysis of our times (1992) discusses the 'three malaises' of modernity: individualism, primacy of 'instrumental reason' (including a focus on efficiency), and the rise of industrial-technological bureaucracy. Together these have consequences such as moral subjectivism and an extreme emphasis on subjective seeking of authenticity. Taylor is not a supporter or an opponent of individualism. His point is that after extreme freedom, all choices remain relativistic; we lack the meaningful moral horizons that self-choice always needs. Ideals cannot stand alone.[6] Where are such horizons to be found? Horizons to be 'used' as a perspective into which we place (or compare, link, or even just separate oneself from, etc.) our own choices? I would strongly argue that religious institutions, particularly through their role in fighting social

[6] Taylor formulates this beautifully: 'Only if I exist in a world in which history, or the demands of nature, or the needs of my fellow human beings, or the duties of citizenship, or the call of God, or something else of this order *matters* crucially, can I define an identity for myself that is not trivial' (Taylor 1992: 40–1).

problems, may be such 'institutions of authenticity'. Through their words and deeds they may offer trustworthy horizons of significance, where words and deeds speak the same language, even in the context of privatized faith and ideological frames. This is not to say that some other agents (such as the human rights movement) may not fulfil the same role. Indeed, there are numerous examples of altruistic behaviour also in Europe—at the level of both individuals and institutions—where the churches have been numerically weak. Moreover, there surely are examples in every sphere of the field of social problems where the secular world has taken the initiative in these matters and continues to do so.

Religious institutions always have the special asset of their own in spirituality, however, offering the horizon of transcendence. There are strong empirical indications that religious institutions may indeed be playing an enhanced role in promoting the values of solidarity through their welfare activities and media visibility regarding the issues of care and equality, throughout Europe—at least when it comes to citizens' expectations.[7] However, in future, it must be both contemplated and studied. Whose solidarity are the churches aiming to contribute to? Are they agents of shared societal cohesion, or of the cohesion of a smaller group (thus an agent of possible conflict, an agent of division)?

Interestingly, this signifies a positive cycle for religious institutions, in that the more they speak about and act to alleviate social problems, the more they are trusted and viewed positively. Such trust, then, improves their image further. The culture of trust always needs its moral institutional frame(s). Such a frame may be constructed by solidarity, a sense of loyalty, as well as by principles of fairness, keeping one's word, and keeping one's faith (Offe 1999; Ilmonen and Jokinen 2002). Furthermore, trust needs 'points of touch'—and these the welfare activities of the church can indeed offer. As institutions are becoming increasingly fragmented, fluid, and porous, the societal weight of the welfare activities of religious institutions may actually increase.

It could be argued against this that in moving towards social problems and welfare, religious institutions may be moving away from their 'pure communication' function, to use Luhmannian terminology. Are they becoming internally secularized? The answer depends on one's perspective—both that of the analyst and that of the religious institutions themselves. Are the activities which confront social problems intrinsically linked to theological positions and other church activities?[8] Overall, the way in which a religious institution faces contemporary social problems is precisely where the teachings of the institution are given flesh and blood as a lived reality. It is the way in which the teaching of the institution

[7] For empirical illustrations and analysis of Western Europe, see Pettersson 2007; 2006; Yeung *et al.* 2006.

[8] For most observers they certainly seem to be; for instance, just to mention one example, for Finns the most important reason for belonging to the Lutheran Church is church ceremonies and church welfare activities.

may become familiar, even to people who do not participate in church activities—the group that expands in the era of privatized religion.

Still, the situation challenges religious institutions. They are *both* at the crossroads in relation to their agendas and visions *and* on the 'borderline' of societal structure; they are no longer majority institutions shared by most, but neither are they just one institution among many. Most European majority churches still seem to find their place between the public and private and/or third sectors (see Casanova 1994), and in relation to the expectations of both the people and public authorities. European majority churches continue to function as an intermediate structure between individual and collective levels of society, especially through their welfare activities. Religion may thus be seen as a 'public good' even in today's Europe. Healthy civil society is one with diversity. Critical questions remain, however: for instance, are churches' welfare activities used to reduce taxes and tax benefits? Furthermore, if the level of participation in church life continues to decrease, can the high level of trust and appreciation of welfare activities of churches (alone) maintain Europe's religious heritage?

Overall, we see the development of an *enhanced social role* for the majority churches in the public sphere simultaneously with their *decreasing role in the privatized* sphere (Pettersson 2007; Yeung 2006*b*; 2007*b*). Might these processes even be mutually enhancing? To return to the point noted by Blackmore, do churches use welfare as a 'gimmick' to retain power and popularity? Other questions too remain to be researched. Will the role vis-à-vis social problems of religious institutions in the future be one of the supporting, assisting agent, or more in the contesting, prophetic role of a radicalist aiming for structural change? Do religious institutions dare to oppose the public sector? And what happens if they take positions which are further from the prevailing political opinions? The ever-increasingly colourful religious scenes throughout the world only make these questions more and more fascinating.

References

American Religious Landscapes and Political Attitudes 2004. The Pew Forum on Religion and Public Life, Surveys, September 2004; <http://pewforum.org/>.

Ammerman, Nancy T. (2005*a*), *Pillars of Faith: American Congregations and their Partners.* Berkeley: University of California Press.

—— (2005*b*). 'Religion, the State and the Common Good: Shifting Boundaries in Europe and the United States'. In Bäckström (2005), 21–34.

—— (2005*c*). 'Religious Identities and Religious Institutions'. In Michele Dillon (ed.), *Handbook of the Sociology of Religion.* Cambridge: Cambridge University Press, 207–24.

Argyle, Michael (2001[1986]). *The Psychology of Happiness*, 2nd edn. London: Routledge.

Bäckström, Anders (ed.) (2005). *Welfare and Religion*. Uppsala: Diakoniavetenskapliga Institutet.

Becker, Howard S. (1963). *Outsiders: Studies in the Sociology of Deviance*. New York: Free Press.

Beckford, James A. (1990). 'The Sociology of Religion and Social Problems'. Presidential Address, 1989. *Sociological Analysis*, 51/1: 1–14.

Bernt, F. M. (1989). 'Being Religious and Being Altruistic: A Study of College Service Volunteers'. *Personality and Individual Differences*, 10: 663–9.

Blackmore, Susan (1999). *The Meme Machine*. Oxford: Oxford University Press.

Casanova, José (1994). *Public Religions in the Modern World*. Chicago: University of Chicago Press.

Castells, Manuel (2004). *The Power of Identity*, 2nd edn. Oxford: Blackwell.

Chaves, Mark (2004). *Congregations in America*. Cambridge, Mass.: Harvard University Press.

Cnaan, Ram A., *et al.* (2002). *The Invisible Caring Hand: American Congregations and the Provision of Welfare*. New York: New York University Press.

Cohen, Albert K. (1955). *Delinquent Boys: The Culture of the Gang*. Glencoe, Ill.: Free Press.

Cooley, Charles Horton (1927). *Social Organization: A Study of the Larger Mind*. New York: Scribner.

Dawkins, Richard (1976). *The Selfish Gene*. Oxford: Oxford University Press.

Delanty, Gerard (2005). *Community*. London: Routledge.

Diener, E., and Diener, C. (1996). 'Most People Are Happy'. *Psychological Science*, 7/3: 181–5.

Ellison, Christopher G. (1991). 'Religious Involvement and Subjective Well-Being'. *Journal of Health & Social Behavior*, 32: 80–99.

—— Gay, David A., and Glass, Thomas A. (1989). 'Does Religious Commitment Contribute to Individual Life Satisfaction?' *Social Forces*, 68: 100–23.

Francis, Leslie J., Jones, Susan H., and Wilcox, Carolyn (2000). 'Religiosity and Happiness: During Adolescence, Young Adulthood and Later Life'. *Journal of Psychology and Christianity*, 19: 245–57.

Frey, B., and Stutzer, A. (2002). *Happiness and Economics*. Princeton: Princeton University Press.

Fuller, Richard C., and Myers, Richard (1941). 'Some Aspects of a Theory of Social Problems'. *American Sociological Review*, 6/3: 320–8.

Gillin, John (1939). *Social Pathology*. New York: Appleton-Century.

Goodenough, Oliver R. (1995). 'Mind Viruses—Culture, Evolution, and the Puzzle of Altruism'. *Social Science Information*, 34/2: 287–320.

Grant, Colin (2000). *Altruism and Christian Ethics*. Cambridge: Cambridge University Press.

Greeley, A. (1997). 'The Other Civic America: Religion and Social Capital'. *American Prospect*, 32: 68–73.

Green, Arnold (1975). *Social Problems: Arena of Conflict*. New York: McGraw-Hill.

Grow, G. (2002). *Social Solidarities*. Buckingham: Open University Press.

Hadden, Jeffrey K. (1980). 'Religion and the Construction of Social Problems'. *Sociological Analysis*, 41/2: 99–108.

Hallamaa, Jaana (1999*a*). 'Ihmisen elämän tarkoitus ja Jumalan valtakunta [Purpose of Life and God's Kingdom]. In *idem* (ed.), *Rahan teologia ja Euroopan kirkot [Theology of Money and the Churches of Europe]*. Jyväskylä: Atena, 155–78.

—— (1999*b*). 'Tarvitaanko Euroopan ymmärtämiseksi Kristinuskoa?' [Do we Need Christianity in Order to Understand Europe?]. In *idem* (ed.), *Rahan teologia ja Euroopan kirkot [Theology of Money and the Churches of Europe]*. Jyväskylä: Atena, 140–54.

Harris, Margaret (1998). *Organizing God's Work: Challenges for Churches and Synagogues*. London: Macmillan.

Helliwell, J. (2002). *How's Life? Combining Individual and National Variables to Explain Subjective Well-being*. National Bureau of Economic Research, Working Paper Series, WP no. 10896. Cambridge: National Bureau of Economic Research.

—— (2005). *Well-being, Social Capital and Public Policy: What's New?* National Bureau of Economic Research, Working Paper Series, WP no. 11807. Cambridge: National Bureau of Economic Research.

Hirvonen, Tatu, and Mangeloja, Esa (2006). *Miksi kolmas hampurilainen ei tee onnelliseksi? [Why a Third Hamburger Does Not Make One Happy?]*. Jyväskylä: Atena.

Ilmonen, Kaj, and Jokinen, Kimmo (2002). *Luottamus modernissa maailmassa [Trust in the Modern World]*. Jyväksylä: Sophi.

Inglehart, Ronald (1990). *Culture Shift in Advanced Industrial Society*. Princeton: Princeton University Press.

Johnson, Byron, *et al.* (2003). 'Social Science Research on Altruism, Spirituality, and Unlimited Love' In Stephen G. Post *et al.* (eds.), *Research on Altruism & Love: An Annotated Bibliography of Major Studies in Psychology, Sociology, Evolutionary Biology & Theology*. Philadelphia: Templeton Foundation Press, 62–116.

Jules-Rosette, B. (1989). 'The Sacred in African New Religions'. In J. A Beckford and T. Luckmann (eds.), *The Changing Face of Religion*. London: Sage, 147–62.

Julkunen, Raija (2006). *Kuka vastaa? Hyvinvointivaltion rajat ja julkinen vastuu [Who Takes Responsibility? The Limits of the Welfare State and the Public Responsibility]*. Helsinki: Gummerus.

Kitsuse, John I., and Spector, Malcolm (1973). 'Toward a Sociology of Social Problems: Social Conditions, Value Judgments, and Social Problems'. *Social Problems*, 20/4: 407–19.

Kramer, Fred (1983). 'Cult Members as Victimizers and Victims'. In Donald MacNamara and Andrew Karmer (eds.), *Deviants: Victims and Victimizers, Annual Review of Studies of Deviance*, vii. 163–82.

Kramer, Ralph M. (1981). *Voluntary Agencies in the Welfare State*. Berkeley: University of California Press.

Kuula, Kari (2004). *Hyvä, paha ja synti: Johdatus Raamatun etiikkaan [Good, Bad and Sin: Introduction to the Ethics of the Bible]*. Helsinki: Kirjapaja.

Lam, P. (2002). 'As the Flocks Gather: How Religion Affects Voluntary Association Participation'. *Journal for the Scientific Study of Religion*, 41: 405–22.

Layard, R. (2005). *Happiness: Lessons from a New Science*. New York: Penguin.

Leis-Peters, Annette (2006). 'Protestant Agents of Welfare in Germany'. In Yeung *et al.* (2006), 56–122.

Loseke, Donileen R. (2003[1999]). *Thinking about Social Problems: An Introduction to Constructionist Perspectives*, 2nd edn. New York: Aldine DeGruyter.

Maltby, J., Lewis, C. A., and Day, L. (1999). 'Religious Orientation and Psychological Well-being: The Role of the Frequency of Personal Prayer'. *British Journal of Health Psychology*, 4: 363–78.

McBride, Duane C., *et al.* (1994). 'Religious Institutions as Sources of AIDs Information for Street Injection Drug Users'. *Review of Religious Research*, 35/4: 324–34.

Middlemiss, Martha (2006). 'The Anglican Church as an Agent of Welfare'. In Yeung *et al.* (2006), 1–55.

Monroe, Kristen Renwick (1996). *The Heart of Altruism—Perceptions of a Common Humanity*. Princeton: Princeton University Press.

Moxon-Browne, E. (1983). *Nation, Class and Creed in Northern Ireland*. Aldershot: Gower.

Neusner, Jacob, and Chilton, Bruce D. (eds.) (2005). *Altruism in World Religions*. Washington: Georgetown University Press.

Offe, C. (1999). 'How Can We Trust Our Fellow Citizens?' In M. Warren (ed.), *Democracy & Trust*. Cambridge: Cambridge University Press, 42–87.

Oord, Thomas Jay (2003). 'Religious Love at the Interface with Science'. In Stephen G. Post *et al.* (eds.), *Research on Altruism & Love: An Annotated Bibliography of Major Studies in Psychology, Sociology, Evolutionary Biology & Theology*. Philadelphia: Templeton Foundation Press, 215–87.

Paloutzian, R. F., and Ellison, C. W. (1982). 'Loneliness, Spiritual Well-being, and the Quality of Life'. In L. A. Peplau and D. Perlman (eds.), *Loneliness: A Sourcebook of Current Theory*. New York: Wiley, 224–37.

Pettersson, Per (2003). 'The Estonia Disaster: The Church of Sweden as Public Service Provider of Rituals'. In P. Post, A. Nugteren, *et al.* (eds.), *Disaster Ritual: Explorations of an Emerging Ritual Repertoire*, Liturgia condenda 15. Leuven: Peeters, 187–99.

—— (2006). 'The Role of Religion as an Agent of Welfare in Modern Europe: A Sociological Analysis. Presentation in XVI ISA World Congress of Sociology, Durban, July.

—— (2007). 'Welfare and Religion in Europe: Sociological Analysis at Three Levels (Manuscript).

Pollner, M. (1989). 'Divine Relations, Social Relations, and Well-being'. *Journal of Health and Social Behavior*, 30: 92–104.

Poloma, M. M., and Pendleton, B. F. (1991). *Exploring Neglected Dimensions of Religion in Quality of Life Research*. Lewiston, NY: Edwin Mellen.

Post, Stephen G., *et al.* (eds.) (2003). *Altruism & Altruistic Love: Science, Philosophy & Religion in Dialogue*. Oxford: Oxford University Press.

Rubington, Earl, and Weinberg, Martin S. (2003). 'Social Problems and Sociology'. In *eadem* (eds.), *The Study of Social Problems: Seven Perspectives*, 6th edn. New York: Oxford University Press, 3–15.

Sherman, Amy (2000). 'Churches as Government Partners: Navigating "Charitable Choice"'. *Christian Century*, 117: 716–21.

Smith, Christian (1996). *Disruptive Religion: The Force of Faith in Social Movement Activism*. New York: Routledge.

Smith, Greg (2004). 'Implicit Religion and Faith-Based Urban Regeneration'. *Implicit Religion*, 7/2: 152–82.

Spector, Malcolm, and Kitsuse, John I. (1977). *Constructing Social Problems*. Menlo Park, Calif.: Cummings.

Taylor, Charles (1992). *The Ethics of Authenticity*. Cambridge, Mass.: Harvard University Press.

Torvi, Kai, and Kiljunen, Pentti (2005). *Onnellisuuden vaikea yhtälö [Difficult Formula of happiness]*. Helsinki: EVA.

Uslaner, Eric (1997). 'Faith, Hope and Charity: Social Capital, Trust and Collective Action. MS, Department of Government and Politics, University of Maryland.

Waller, Willard (1936). 'Social Problems and the Mores'. *American Sociological Review*, 1/6: 922–33.

Witter, Robert A., *et al.* (eds.) (1985). 'Religion and Subjective Well-being in Adulthood: A Quantitative Synthesis'. *Review of Religious Research*, 26/4: 332–42.

Welfare and Religion (2003). Welfare and Religion in European Perspective, Project Description. Uppsala: Uppsala Institute for Diaconal and Social Studies.

Wood, James R. (1975). 'Legitimate Control and "Organisational Transcendence"'. *Social Forces*, 54: 199–211.

Yeung, Anne Birgitta (2003). 'The Re-emergence of the Church in Finnish Public Life? Christian Social Work as an Indicator of the Public Status of the Church'. *Journal of Contemporary Religion*, 18/2: 197–211.

—— (2004*a*). *Individually Together. Volunteering in Late Modernity: Social Work in the Finnish Church*. Helsinki: Finnish Federation for Social Welfare and Health.

—— (2004*b*). 'An Intricate Triangle: Religiosity, Volunteering, Social Capital. European Perspective—the Case of Finland'. *Nonprofit and Voluntary Sector Quarterly*, 33/3: 401–23.

—— (2006*a*). 'The Finnish Lutheran Church as a Welfare Agent: The Case of Lahti'. In Yeung *et al.* (2006), 142–203.

—— (2006*b*). 'A Trusted Institution of Altruism: The Social Engagement of the Scandinavian Churches'. In Ruben L. F. Habito and Keishin Inaba (eds.), *The Practice of Altruism: Caring and Religion in Global Perspective*. Cambridge: Cambridge Scholars Press, 99–124.

—— 2007*a*. 'The Circle of Good Life? Research on the Inter-relations between Happiness, Altruism, and Spirituality'.

—— (2007*b*). 'Servant of Solidarity, Institution of Authenticity: The Dilemma of Welfare in the Church of Finland'. *Nordic Journal of Religion and Society*, 2.

—— *et al.* (eds.) (2006). *Churches in Europe as Agents of Welfare*. Working papers 2:1 and 2:2 from the Project Welfare and Religion in a European Perspective. Uppsala: Uppsala Institute for Diaconal and Social Studies.

Suggested Reading

Cole, William E. (1965). *Social Problems—A Sociological Interpretation*. New York: David McKay.

Etzioni, Amitai (1976). *Social Problems*. Englewood Cliffs, NJ: Prentice Hall.

Knudsen, Dean D. (1978). 'Virtues, Values and Victims: Toward a Theory of Social Problems'. *Sociological Focus*, 11/3: 173–84.

Miller, Gale, and Holstein, James A. (1997). *Social Problems in Everyday Life: Studies of Social Problems Work*. Greenwich, Conn.: KAI Press.

Also Ammerman (2005*a*); Beckford (1990); Hadden (1980); Harris (1998); and Loseke (2003).

PART X

TEACHING THE SOCIOLOGY OF RELIGION

CHAPTER 53

THE TEACHER OF RELIGION AS ETHNOGRAPHER

ELEANOR NESBITT

Introduction

The designation 'teacher of religion' refers to practitioners of many backgrounds and intents, including individuals of commitment to particular interpretations of particular faiths as well as to scholars professionally engaged in theology and the social sciences. Teaching of religion may be confessional (whether in home, synagogue, madrasah, or seminary) or non-confessional; the students may be children or adults; and the context may be private homes, faith-specific centres such as churches, or state-funded educational institutions. In this chapter 'student' subsumes 'pupil', the term that is used more specifically for students of school-going age.

For the 'insider' of a faith community teachers of religion will almost certainly include parents and other elders who pass on the tradition both consciously and unconsciously as role models (Furseth and Repstad 2006: 114–17). Socialization includes 'formal nurture' by volunteer teachers in Sunday schools and comparable supplementary classes, such as the Hindu classes studied by Joanna Dwyer (Brear 1992), Jackson and Nesbitt (1993: 147–65), and Pocock (1976). In addition to locally based functionaries such as imams and rabbis, Roman Catholic or Orthodox priests and Protestant ministers, the late twentieth century saw the rise of intercontinentally itinerant preachers and evangelists, including Sikh *sants* (charismatic spiritual masters) (Tatla 1992) and Hindu gurus (Nesbitt 1999).

In higher-education institutions in many countries the twentieth century saw the emergence of religious studies, a multi-disciplinary field committed, like the social sciences more generally, to the pursuit of truth independently of any religious perspective (see Capp 1995; Corrywright and Morgan 2006; Ford, Quash, and Soskice 2005; Nicholson 2003). From the viewpoint of scholars in religious studies, the relationship of religious studies with the longer-established discipline of (usually Christian) theology has been uneven and uneasy (Cunningham 1990). In the view of Anglican theologian David Ford (2006), relationships between religious studies and theology result from argument and negotiation, and new challenges (from new religions, political and financial stakeholders) may shift the relationship further; moreover, the degree to which religious studies and theology have integrated and combined in UK universities is unusual. By contrast, in the United States, there is a stronger divide between private institutions, often with religious roots, where theology may be taught, and state-supported institutions with departments of religious studies from which it is excluded (Ford 2006).

The argument of the present chapter developed in the field of scholarly debates regarding primarily neither confessional teaching (for whatever clientele) nor religion in higher education, but religious education, the statutory curriculum subject in publicly funded schools in England and Wales. In England and Wales (and the situation is similar in Sweden, Norway, Denmark, the Netherlands, and some German *Länder*, as well as South Africa) religious education is 'a subject that is non-confessional (i.e. it should not try to convert pupils to any particular religion), multi-faith (i.e. it should involve learning about a number of religions) and respectful of non-religious ways of life (i.e. it is not just about religions)' (Stern 2006: 3).

Denise Cush (1999) distinguishes the non-confessional approach to religious education (as in state schools in the UK) from its understanding in confessional terms in the USA. She proceeds to argue that religious education is a distillation of the higher-education subject of religious studies, rather than a watered-down version, and to point out that in religious education, unlike religious studies, learning *from* religions is an integral part, no less than learning *about* them is (see also Corrywright and Morgan 2006). These aims (of both learning about religion and learning from it) owe their formulation to Michael Grimmitt and G. T. Read (Grimmitt 2000: 34–7) and characterize the 'instrumental' approach whereby religious education is taught in such a way that 'pupils become informed about religious beliefs and values and are able to use them as instruments for the critical evaluation of their own beliefs and values' (Grimmitt 1987: 141).

An ethnographic approach too, this chapter contends, encourages a distinctive type of 'learning from' which additionally involves raising students' awareness of their religious, cultural, and ethical assumptions, and the roots of these in, for example, media portrayals of communities and ideas. This sharpening of critical reflection meshes with the transition in twentieth-century ethnography from (simply) portraying societies to a more critical reflection on the methods and data. Indeed, it is successive ethnographic studies, conducted over two decades in the Institute of Education at the University of Warwick (Nesbitt 2001; 2004), of young people's religious socialization within faith communities, and increasingly critical reflection on these studies, that provide the basis for the argument of this chapter.

There is a particular historical affinity between ethnography and religious studies (insofar as it is an interdisciplinary field embracing the anthropology and sociology of religion), and—thanks to the 'interpretive approach to religious education' advocated by the 'Warwick school' (notably the work of Robert Jackson and myself)—the relationship between ethnography and religious education has gained prominence in religious education discourse (see, e.g., Jackson 1997; Cush 2001: 5; Nesbitt 2004). The contention of this chapter, moreover, is that ethnography also has a contribution to make in the more confessional environments of theology and of religious instruction and nurture. Importantly for all concerned, I will propose that ethnographic approaches dissolve the distinction between teaching and learning and between teacher and learner—and herein is a particular challenge for some authoritarian religious understandings of knowledge and of teaching.

In the present chapter a necessarily summary reference to relevant preoccupations in ethnography (as methodological context) prefaces a consideration of today's plural society (as social context). Discussion will shift to the value to both teachers and students of religious education and religious studies of (a) engaging with published ethnographic studies of, for example, specific faith communities and (b) appropriating an ethnographic perspective (and trying out ethnographic methods), concerning both their 'subject' (i.e. religion) and also the character of the teaching event. Albeit briefly, attention is paid to inducting students into an ethnographic role and finally to the application of ethnography in faith-based higher education courses.

At each stage reference to relevant selected literature will be integral to the discussion. The most influential contribution to the argument for teachers of religions to develop ethnographic awareness—if not competence—remains Robert Jackson's *Religious Education: An Interpretive Approach* (1997), and Jackson's ideas have been imaginatively reworked and applied in increasingly diverse national contexts (see Jackson, forthcoming). Jackson drew on methodological ideas from social anthropology and other sources to argue the 'inner diversity, fuzzy edgedness and contested nature of religious traditions as well as the complexity of cultural expression and change from social and individual perspectives' (Jackson and O'Grady 2007). 'Individuals are seen as unique, but the group tied nature of religion is recognized, as is the role of the wider religious traditions in providing identity markers and reference points' (Jackson and O'Grady 2007).

Ethnography

Disaggregating ethnographic awareness and skill requires consideration of ethnography's origins and non-quantitative character, the role of time scale and physical location, and the ethnographer's tools, notably participant observation. This in its turn involves attention to issues of engagement: the insider/outsider debate, power imbalances between researcher and 'subject' or 'participant', reflexivity and transparency.

Martin Stringer, in his introduction to his studies of worship in four UK Christian congregations, usefully distinguishes ethnography as currently practised in disciplines such as sociology, social psychology, media studies, and cultural studies (and we may add religious studies) from the 'ideal' ethnographic methods of anthropology (1999: 42–3). He identifies three expectations of ethnography in the work of the acclaimed father of anthropology, Bronisław Malinowski. These are that ethnography requires immersion over a period of years rather than months (let alone weeks or days); that it is holistic inasmuch as it is takes account of everything happening within a specific community and provides a holistic understanding of this; and lastly, that the ethnographer tries to understand what is happening from 'the native's point of view'.

The present chapter is not contending that teachers of religion should (all) engage in carrying out ethnography on this scale, but that the more widely accessible enterprise to which the designation of 'ethnography' is now frequently applied is one in which they can participate, and that such participation will enhance their competence. For one reason, debates arising within ethnography, regarding, for example, reflexivity, highlight issues (such as identity formation) that are of key concern to the teacher and student of religion.

Social scientists have tended to define ethnography in distinction from the quantitative and experimental methods which came to dominate the social sciences during the twentieth century (Hammersley and Atkinson 1983: 1). Thus ethnography exemplifies naturalism, as contrasted with positivism (Hammersley and Atkinson 1983: 10), and it is inductive, with hypotheses emerging continuously from data analysis rather than providing the launching pad for an investigation (Glaser and Strauss 1967). As for its characteristics, ethnography describes (and does so in depth), rather than pre-defining, in contrast with the more quantitative approaches of many sociologists. So, using the example of church attendance, the anthropologist and theologian Timothy Jenkins points out that, by contrast with ethnographic exploration, the recording and analysis of attendance figures say 'nothing about how the people so recorded regard attending' (1999: 31). Jenkins quotes the sociologist of religion, Steve Bruce, in identifying two failures of the survey method: namely, that 'views about complex but important matters can rarely be expressed sensibly by picking one of four choices in answer to a question asked of us by a complete stranger' and that surveys 'treat all respondents as if they were of equal importance... they investigate the typical.' (1999: 33–4).

Despite broad agreement on the potential qualitative depth of ethnography, there is also 'diversity in prescription and practice' (Hammersley and Atkinson 1983: 1). For Hammersley and Atkinson ethnography is synonymous with participant observation. For Fetterman (1989: 11): 'ethnography is the art and science of describing a group or culture', seeking out the usual and the predictable. The fact that the first definition is couched in terms of method and the second primarily in terms of outcome, should not, however, obscure the fact that the authors agree fundamentally on the nature of the enterprise. Primary school teacher Jon Swain's encapsulation of ethnography comprises both elements: 'the qualitative, empirical interpretation of the practices of a specific culture in their "natural" setting over a sustained period' (2006: 206). Informing the present chapter is the understanding that the purpose of ethnography is 'to understand human behaviour at ever increasing depth, from the point of view of those studied, and to communicate this deepening understanding sensitively to others' (Nesbitt, cited by Stern 2006: 96).

For the ethnographic researcher technological progress continues to influence the means of recording and reporting, but the underlying methods remain those of observation—for which also read 'listening' (Nesbitt 2000*b*)—and interviewing. Related to the (oral) interview in a variety of ways is the written interview, including the (more or less structured) questionnaire. E-mail exchanges increasingly provide the medium, with resultant blurring between questionnaire and interview (Markham 2005). Diaries too are potential sources of data, whether journalling by participants at the researcher's request or the researcher's logs of methodological reflection, as well as sequences of field notes and analytic memos. Complementing these types of primary data are documentary sources, including ephemera such as programmes for festival events and newsletters for congregations. Increasingly, the Internet provides both subject matter and communication tools, as ethnography merges with cyber-ethnography, and the focus of investigation (for example, a particular faith community's use of cyberspace) is simultaneously at home and worldwide (Markham 2005; Bunt 2006).

Swain, like Stringer, mentions time scale, and one marked difference between diverse exemplars and definitions of ethnography is certainly time span. The fieldwork of contemporary ethnographers is often of shorter duration (if full-time) or more intermittent (if carried out alongside other duties) than that of those pioneers who spent years overseas, usually in locations colonized by European powers. Even leaving aside the virtual, online aspect of faith communities, today's ethnographic studies are also, in the majority of cases, conducted much closer to home—often within the ethnographer's own locality and in many instances in his or her own social context (such as place of work or interest group). This closeness to home has made the imperative of 'making the familiar strange' at least as important as 'making the strange familiar', to repeat a phrase beloved in ethnography no less than in semiotics (Chandler 2001), and has increased the dangers of 'observer blindness'. However, it also makes first-hand engagement in field work a possibility for the teacher.

Settings close at hand to the ethnographer have included schools (e.g., Bullivant 1978; Burgess 1983; Bhatti 1999; Scholefield 2004), in addition to congregations (e.g., Heilman 1976 on a US synagogue; Stringer 1999 on four UK churches) and local faith communities in other contexts (e.g., Meyerhoff 1978, on Jewish elderly in southern California) as well as studies of young people (Gillespie 1995; Hall 2002). Among the latter are studies of religious socialization (e.g., Jackson and Nesbitt 1993, on young Hindus in Coventry, and Nesbitt 2000*a* on their Sikh counterparts). Studies of religious socialization often focus on the 'formal nurture' that occurs in supplementary classes (e.g., Brear 1992; Gent 2006; Pocock 1976). As secondary school head of religious education, Kevin O'Grady, points out (2007), ethnographic study of religious education in the school setting is scant. To date it has been conducted by religious educationists, notably Ipgrave (1998; 2005) and O'Grady (2003) in England, and Norwegian religious educationist, Heid Leganger-Krogstad, who 'combined ethnographic field studies with action research, carrying out experiments together with my students' (Jackson 2004: 112). To the subject of the teacher of religion as action researcher we will be returning.

The 'participant observation' which Hammersley and Atkinson identified with ethnography subsumes a spectrum of possible balances that the researcher may reach, from complete participation—for example, as a teacher or student in a religion class which he or she is also studying as ethnographer, on the one hand—to complete observation, as a 'fly on the wall' who does not intervene in any circumstances, on the other.

Clearly, when religions and institutions provide the field and focus, this tactical decision making is influenced by the extent to which the researcher is an 'insider' (such as Heilman in his synagogue congregation) or an 'outsider', as in the case of Jackson and Nesbitt (1993) and Malory Nye (1995) in relation to their local Hindu communities. The energetic debates surrounding the issue of whether and how research into religion may be conducted by insiders or outsiders (see Arweck and Stringer 2002) include arguments both for and against researchers as insiders and as outsiders to the community concerned (McCutcheon 1999; Stringer 2002: 2), and concerned scholars list the relative merits and demerits of the resultant ethnographies. Importantly too, scholars increasingly problematize any over-easy dichotomizing of insider and outsider (Stringer 2002). Individuals' plural and situational identities compound the complexity. Raj (2003) and Chaudhry (1997) suggest that other members of the ethnographer's religio-ethnic group are not unproblematically her or his 'nation of birth'. Bilal Sambur points out that 'there are many Muslims today who approach the study of Islam by looking through the eyes of Western social scientific theory, which is considered an outsider's perspective within the broader Muslim community' (2002: 27). Additionally, while (*qua* researcher) all ethnographers are outsiders, at the same time (*qua* humans with a spectrum of characteristics) all are in some way insiders. The degree to which one is insider or outsider will also alter during fieldwork, not least if one undergoes ritual initiation (see Brown 1991: 11) or marriage into a community. Moreover, Pink Dandelion, a Quaker sociologist, provides a useful fourfold typology in which (a) covert insider research is distinguished from overt insider researcher and (b) being an insider to a particular group (such as the congregation of a particular church) is distinguished from being a member of the wider context (for example, belonging to the same Christian denomination) (Dandelion 1996: 37–50).

In fact, discourse on researcher positioning, and on the awareness of all concerned (the researcher herself, participants, readers) of this is of particular relevance to the teacher of religion. Additionally, reflection on whether (perceived) 'stance' and 'positioning' are metaphors for individuals' personal journeys is essential to ethnographers (Nesbitt 2002: 146–8) and is pertinent to both students and teachers of religion, if 'them and us' dichotomies are to be avoided. Indeed, O'Grady, as religious educationist reporting his ethnographically informed classroom-based action research, reminds us (2006: 109) of the ethnographer James Clifford's designation of the 'research field' as 'an itinerary rather than a bounded site—a series of encounters and translations' (1997: 11). In Clifford's view the 'researcher's movement in and out of the field is constitutive of the field of study' (1997: 66–8; cited in O'Grady 2006: 119). For teachers and students alike, this unsettling of all too easily assumed positioning can prompt realization of the continuous, interactive global society in which no individual or group is totally 'other', and attitudes and ideas develop in human interactions. The challenge of the multi-faith classroom or lecture theatre to teachers' positioning is likely to predispose some practitioners to these ethnographic debates.

Jackson (notably 1997) has called for religious educators to apply anthropology's interpretive approach to the teaching of their subject. In addition to reflexive awareness (entailing iterative connections between one's own experience and that of the community being studied), this means making connections between the constituent 'parts' of the faith that one is studying and teaching. For example, the teacher may suggest deliberate connections between, say, a passage of scripture or a 'membership group' (such as a Christian denomination or a Hindu *sampradaya*) and the 'whole' (in this case Hindus' or Christians' 'cumulative tradition') and will encourage pupils to do so. Such an approach endorses the multi-layered, 'thick' description advocated by anthropologist Clifford Geertz (1973), in which an event is explained within its context, and seeks out the 'grammar' of faith traditions—their structure and patterning—rather than isolating phenomena for examination.

Under the influence of Edward Said (e.g., Said 1989) and others, the latter half of the twentieth century saw scholars increasingly conscious of the imbalance of power between those who represent (in writing or film) and those (the other) who are represented and—in the process—distanced, exoticized, romanticized, or orientalized. Acknowledgement too of the ethnographer's tendency towards bias spurred a call for transparency in reporting. In recognition of the interactive nature of ethnographic research, scholars advocated attention to reflexivity: that is, attentiveness to 'the fact that it [social research] is part of the social world it studies' (Hammersley and Atkinson 1983: 10). In fact, the emphasis on reflexivity and transparency marks a challenge to positivist assumptions about the desirability—and the possibility—of achieving objective knowledge and a confident break from twentieth-century endeavour among sociologists to project and protect their 'scientific' credentials by the use of quantitative methodology. When a teacher of religion reflects upon, let us say, ways in which the content of belief in one faith tradition influences those who identify with a different faith or none, and on ways in which the enquirer's questions affect the thinking and self-presentation of adherents, that teacher is likely to represent 'world religions' as less firmly bounded, homogeneous, and static and to be aware that his or her teaching is contributing to pupils' evolving values, beliefs, and identities.

Sensitivity to the feelings of groups and individuals (within the faith tradition and within the classroom) is fundamental to this application of ethnographic insight (Nesbitt 2000*b*), the more compellingly so when groupings of pupils intersect in multiple ways with the constellation of religious communities and philosophical assumptions under consideration in class.

Social Context

The context for this discussion of 'the teacher of religion as ethnographer' is early twenty-first-century society: that is, human populations globally in all their national, ethnic, and religious diversity. Now, arguably to an unprecedented degree, teachers' and students' understanding of society depends upon attention to aspects that ethnography is honed to disclose: the fine grain of complex groups as well as the dynamics at work. The ideas under discussion have evolved in a particular Western social context, and principally in the UK, a national setting which illustrates both 'traditional plurality' and 'modern plurality'. When Harvard anthropologist of religion Diana Eck describes the 'marbling' of contemporary society (2000), she is evoking what the Norwegian religious educationist Geir Skeie (2002) and British religious educationist Robert Jackson (2004) term 'modern plurality'. 'Modern plurality' designates the 'variegated intellectual climate of late modernity or postmodernity' (Jackson 2004: 8) in which individuals, whatever their background in terms of faith, ethnicity, or ancestral tradition, are influenced by exposure to ideas from culturally diverse sources.

To take some examples of evidence of this modern plurality, many Europeans are aware of, or receptive to, assumptions concerning the reincarnation of the human 'soul' after death (e.g., Waterhouse 1999). They encounter this idea through film and other media, through religious education lessons (on Hinduism, for example) in their schools, and in other ways. Or, to take another example, the attitudes of Hindus—certainly those living in the UK—towards food and fasting demonstrate a multitude of both contradictory and mutually reinforcing influences (Nesbitt 2004: 21–34). 'Traditional plurality', by contrast, designates the social diversity that arises from the coexistence in a particular locality of communities with different ancestries. This jigsaw of culturally diverse groups usually stems from successive migrations, impelled by economic push and pull. Indeed, economic factors are often implicated in that other precipitator of migration: aggression—notably war. For war may involve the relocation and settlement of victors, the more or less forcible conversion of and intermarriage with the defeated, or the influx of refugees from areas of conflict. Over time, traditional plurality merges into modern plurality as contact and interaction, including marriages, between initially more distinct communities increase and language barriers come down.

Not only society's pluralities but also other processes that are under way strengthen the argument that this chapter presents for ethnography to inform the teaching of religion. Crucial to grasping the nature of religion currently is some understanding of (1) the shifting balance between secularization and religiosity, in relation to (2) a continuum from apathy to 'extremism', 'fundamentalism', and violence, or conceived of as (3) the simultaneous decline of religion (exemplified in the case of religious organizations with diminishing membership and attendance) and (4) both the rise of 'new' religions and the resurgence of older traditions and movements. No less important is a critical awareness of (5) the elusive relationship between 'spirituality' (with its many definitions and guises) and religion. The fallacy of equating (as many sociologists once did) modernity with secularization is now admitted by most (Berger 2002: 292). In Ford's words, UK society 'is complexly and simultaneously both religious and secular with intense debates about how this dual reality should be defined, described, explained and responded to' (2006).

Not only is social diversity the *backdrop* to religion and the teaching of it, but also, as a driver of pluralism (an affirmative response to diversity coupled with commitment to social harmony), it provides a *motivation and a rationale* for much teaching of religion. In fact, ethnographic interviews by two teacher trainers with trainee teachers of religious education in England revealed that the most frequent reason that trainee teachers of religious education give for their choice of career is promoting understanding between faith communities (Everington and Sikes 2001). The urgency of this aspiration relates to the increasing perception that religious teachings and their interpretations can fuel conflict (Bowker 1997: pp. xxii–xxiii) and can underpin social segregation. Given that 'anthropological tradition and the fieldwork experience have always been represented as an effort to meet other people, to explore, document and interpret widely different lives' (Gobbo 2004: 3), religious educators can reasonably look to ethnography for tried and tested methods. In religious education a shift in focus occurred from racism as a moral issue to emphasis in the 1970s on 'promoting an understanding of different cultures and peoples through the "phenomenological" study of 'world religions' (Everington and Sikes 2001: 181, citing earlier authors). Astley *et al.* (1997: 183) reported teachers rating highest as outcomes/ aims for religious education 'respecting other people's rights to hold beliefs different from their own' and 'becoming more tolerant of other religions and world-views' (cited in Everington and Sikes 2001: 183).

Hence religious educationist Andrew Wright's concern (1993) that the religious education profession was selling out to 'social engineers' in order to justify the place of religious education in the curriculum. The promotion of religious education as an essential tool in the construction of a harmonious multicultural society had, Wright maintained, been achieved at the cost of misrepresenting religions—as equally agreeable, valid, and socially functional—and of denying pupils the opportunity to recognize and evaluate competing truth claims (Everington and Sikes 2001: 182). In fact, the educationist Michael Hand's argument concerning the 'connection between the study of religion and the acquisition of values appropriate to a multicultural society' (2006: 12) accords with Wright's view of religious education as equipping pupils with critical, informed 'religious literacy'. In Hand's view, while religious education has the capacity to develop in pupils 'positive regard for religious traditions other than their own' and works strongly in favour of civic friendship across religious divides, this positive regard is grounded in the fact that religions are worthy of respect because they address important questions seriously, rather than needing to be respected because a cohesive society depends upon the exercise of such mutual respect, or on the basis of ethnographically grounded understanding of religious communities (2006: 14).

Wright, Hand, and Sikes and Everington write in the context of post (or late) modernity, a period of both rapid globalization and a sometimes resultant ethnocentrism (Hargreaves 1994, cited in O'Grady 2007). O'Grady (2007) accordingly reformulates religious education's twin aims of learning about and learning from religion as teaching for citizenship and teaching for identity. As indicated already, ethnography provides tools for an understanding of diversity, and this in turn is a foundation for both responsible citizenship and informed identity formation. Thus social anthropologist Jessica Jacobson's (1998) analysis of young British Muslims' levels of identification and religious educationist Sissel Østberg's (2003) discussion of the 'integrated plural identity' of young Norwegian Pakistanis provide models for teachers not only in presenting the dynamics of a diasporic Muslim community but also in interacting with students whose own sense of who they are is developing. These ethnographies have a place in the representation of Islam, complementing as they do historical and theological introductions to Islam.

In its opening up of the diversity of individuals within any group, ethnographic training can contribute to students' education for citizenship. Indeed, Østberg (2003: 107) sees an 'important role for RE [religious education] as providing an inter-cultural recognition of diversity as the foundation of a meaningful citizenship', in line with Martin Stringer's statement of ethnography's purpose as being 'to highlight the diversity and complexity of real life, where simplistic theories no longer apply' (1999: 49). The fact that citizenship education is increasingly integral to the role of the religious education teacher (for example, in many UK secondary schools since Citizenship became statutory in 2002) further strengthens the case for both teachers and pupils developing ethnographic skills.

Imaging Religion and Culture

For all engaged in the study and teaching of religion, whether they are deliberately ethnographic or not in their approach, one way of understanding the extent and aspects of religion is through attentiveness to its 'dimensions'. Those postulated by the eminent phenomenologist Ninian Smart (1996) have been particularly formative for generations of students of religious studies: his seven dimensions are 'the practical and ritual', 'experiential and emotional', 'narrative or mythical', 'doctrinal and philosophical', 'social and institutional', 'ethical and legal', and 'material', in which he included art, architecture, and sacred places. The anthropologist, Roger Ballard's (1994) dimensions, drawn from his study of experience and expression of religion in Punjab, distinguish the body of people with a shared religious commitment; religion as explanation of otherwise inexplicable human predicament and provider of its antidote; morality; and *qaum*, or people with an enhanced sense of solidarity to advance collective, often political intentions.

Ethnographic awareness involves the teacher in making explicit to him or herself what his or her picture of religion (and of *a* religion) is. It therefore entails challenging the too easily taken for granted equation of religion with 'belief' and 'practice', categories that have long characterized accounts of Christianity. Uncritically, other faith traditions have been reduced to the same two categories, despite the fact that 'there is something distinct about the Christian idea of belief that is not found in other religions' (Pouillon, in Stringer 2002: 12), and that 'belief' may not have the same degree of significance (e.g., as historically a feared test of 'orthodoxy') in some non-Christian communities. Teachers of a critical religious education and religious studies must be able to contest the categories established by textbooks and syllabuses, and ethnographic insights provide support for challenging such categorizations, even while preparing students to meet the requirements of examiners.

Stringer's distinction between 'culture' and 'faith' too is salutary, with culture as 'part of a discourse that is undertaken by dominant groups as part of their domination of the other' and faith as 'part of a discourse undertaken by the dominated, the threatened, in order to retain their distance, their identity and their distinctiveness' (2002: 14). Once again, an awareness of ethnographic discussion serves to sharpen analysis of one's assumptions as teacher of religion. Importantly, ethnographic awareness unsettles the paradigm, long established in UK religious education, of 'world religions' as unproblematically distinct and relatively homogeneous entities (Geaves 1998) and alerts practitioners to the dangers of political naïveté (Searle-Chatterjee 2000).

The Teacher of Religion as Ethnographer

The following possibilities for professional practice relate to ethnographic studies of faith communities, to relationship with students, to pedagogies, and to the class of students as itself an ethnographic field.

A religion teacher's attentiveness to others' ethnographic studies of faith communities in her or his own country and beyond complements (without substituting for) textual and theological investigation and presentations of the faith by both adherents and others. The teacher's engagement in fieldwork (for example, as a postgraduate student) raises more compellingly issues of representation as it highlights the internal diversity of faith traditions and the gap between curricular representations of 'faiths' and the experience of individuals (including pupils) who identify with the tradition concerned (Nesbitt 1998). The experience, whether first-hand or vicarious, supports adoption of an interpretive pedagogy, and at least affects one's use of language. Generalizations of the 'Hindus believe...' order give way to 'Some Hindus...', 'many Orthodox Christians', 'some young Muslims in Europe...'. Such a teacher's unwillingness to essentialize 'religions', and alertness to stereotypes and to the rhetoric of 'leaders' and spokespeople, translates into enabling students to take note of diversity within supposed communities, and to distinguish principles from practice. Reading reports such as Ron Geaves's (1998) of devotional practice in north Indian communities—and listening and observing among local groups—is likely to generate a realization of the contested nature of boundaries between, for example, Hinduism and Sikhism, and so foster suspicion of simplistic definitions and presuppositions in 'world religions'-based syllabuses and curriculum material.

The ethnographically insightful teacher is alert to straddlers of supposedly distinct faith boundaries and to the presence of new religious movements and groupings within and without 'world religions', and is attuned to dynamics of change and continuity at the level of individuals, 'membership groups' (see Jackson 1997: 65–9), and wider tradition, as well as vigilant in noting the role of gender and whether voices are those of leaders or laity.

At the same time, the teacher's multiple roles and positioning (Swain 2006) emerge from the writing of teacher ethnographers, whether Marie Gillespie (1995) among her Punjabi secondary school pupils' families in Southall, Ipgrave (2005) facilitating pupil-to-pupil dialogue for her (mainly Muslim) Leicester primary school pupils, or O'Grady (2007) investigating the roots of motivation in his Sheffield secondary school by action research that involved interviews with his religious education students. Action research, as advocated by O'Grady, requires cycles of planning, teaching, observation, and reflection which helps shape the next cycle. It is ethnographic in its attention to in-depth observation and only lightly structured group interviews. Action research coheres strongly with educational philosophies of empowerment—for example, Paulo Freire's principles of humanization, conscientization, and praxis (O'Grady 2007: 80)—as it does also with liberation theology as applied in the base Christian communities that have evolved for motivational Christian nurture (Reeve 2006).

The teacher–student relationship has ethical implications which are more complex when the teacher is also conducting a field study of the class or of a community to which members of the class or their families belong, or is involving the students in cycles of teaching, observation, reflection, and intervention in action research. The fact that the principal aim may well be educationally sound—for example, increasing students' motivation—does not reduce the questions to be asked regarding the creation of knowledge when the same person is teacher, observer, interpreter of data, and decision-maker regarding subsequent modifications to teaching content and strategy.

Students as Ethnographers

'All teachers know the value of first hand encounter with the traditions. This is one of the strengths of the Warwick RE Project's concept of children as ethnographers' (Cush 1999: 138). At the same time a teacher's ethnographic commitment helps young people to become aware of their own cultural conditioning (e.g., *re* secularism, the relativity of all cultural expressions, and the importance of individual autonomy), the concern of Norcross (1989) cited by Everington and Sikes (2001: 193). In a break from the tenets of classical phenomenology, students are encouraged not to try to 'bracket out' their own opinions but to engage in active dialogue regarding their own ideas, beliefs, and experience in relation to another's. Here Jackson provides guidelines for an interpretive interaction with people, texts, and religious events. While for the teacher-ethnographer, students may constitute a 'field' (or offer individual extensions of fields), they are also potential co-ethnographers. Roles meld and merge, for a pedagogy which allows the teacher to present her or his own case (for example, as a Hindu or a Pentecostal) as a case study, and in which pupils may interview each other and/or 'outsiders', such as a member of staff ready to share experience of Eid, having a Jewish marriage, or responding to ethical dilemmas as a Mormon.

Students need exercises to skill them as ethnographers, notably exercises in heightening their awareness of their own presuppositions. In the context of religious studies in higher education, Ram-Prasad (2001: 6) calls for effort to make apparent

> the unquestioned 'Western' mental maps of British students.... By 'folk Westernism' I mean an unexamined ideology that takes as normal and normative certain behaviours, values, and interpretive paradigms drawn from conventional characterization of an imagined 'Western society'... The skill of concerned lecturers consists in gently drawing out these assumptions.

The Martian exercise in making the familiar strange (Jackson 1989: 5) has been adapted creatively by teachers. For example, Julia Ipgrave asked her (mainly Muslim) primary school pupils to view a video of *haj* (pilgrimage to Mecca) as if they were visitors from another planet, so picking out the elements that they would find particularly strange and listing questions that they might ask (2005: 41).

In order to develop some skill in interviewing and representing others, students may be asked to interview each other on, for example, how they identify themselves or on a significant event in their lives or on a topical dilemma or controversy. Following this by inviting the interviewers to report back, and then eliciting their interviewees' reactions to how they had been represented, can alert students to pitfalls in questioning, recording, and interpreting.

The concern to relay 'multiple voices' in one's 'quest for meanings' (Livezey 2002: 159–60), suggests a classroom practice that encourages pupils to research in pairs or collectively, to investigate as a team, and to learn through dialogue. Ipgrave (2005) demonstrates ways in which the teacher takes a facilitating role, developing pupils' skills in dialogue on the basis of her own ethnographic understanding. Students can be encouraged to draw in parallel on diverse sources, including, for example, life story (possibly from interviewing a local person). Examining a textbook account of the Passover meal, listening to a Jewish speaker's memories, watching a *seder* on DVD, participating in a partial re-enactment provide sources for triangulation, as the teacher guides pupils in attentive comparisons. Ethnographic research among Muslims in East Anglia provided religious educationist Sarah Smalley with transcripts of women sharing the reasons why they and close relatives had decided for or against assuming the hijab (Stern 2006: 100). In listening to diverse experiences and standpoints, students' stereotypes of all Muslim women as oppressed victims dissolve. With skilled teaching they develop interpretive skills in connecting the individual voice with the wider context woven of Islamic and non-Islamic particularities.

> Pedagogically, the approach develops skills of interpretation and provides opportunities for critical reflection in which pupils make a constructive critique of the material studied at a distance, re-assess their understanding of their own way of life in the light of their studies and review their own methods of learning. (Jackson and O'Grady 2007: 182)

As O'Grady argues, ethnography can be 'equalizing' because it moves away from education as 'banking' of information in children towards empowering them, and so is a more democratic approach, with both teacher and pupil as researchers together (2006: 87). Moreover, developing students' ethnographic awareness and skills may heighten critical as well as empathetic awareness of both the subject matter (religion) and the teacher's performance.

Confessional Teaching and Ethnography

As noted above, confessional teaching too can draw upon ethnographic research (Reeve 2006). For teachers of religion in confessional settings, 'context' has become a key concern. In the decades since Bruce Malina (1981) and others advocated anthropological contextualization of text, attention has turned to introducing students in faith-specific higher education to ethnographic study of the context(s) provided by their faith communities. (See, e.g., the emphasis on 'Ethnography of Jews and Judaism' in The Rabbi Donald A. Tam Institute for Jewish Studies, available at <http://www.jsemory.edu/currentofferings/F04grad.html>.) As Reeve pointed out, 'all bible study is contextualised and therefore examination of local contextual issues is key in bible-based nurture' (2006: 4). Joyce Mercer's (2005) discussion of 'a congregational studies pedagogy for contextual education' makes a strong case for inducting theological seminary students into study of a particular congregation (in this case a Korean congregation in San Francisco and a multicultural one in Oakland) in which they not only serve as 'guest teachers' but also interview, observe, and participate in order to learn the theology, practices, and dynamics of the congregation, as well as something of what members do with the rest of their time. Students operated within a framework of congregational studies outlined by Ammerman *et al.* (1998), based on the five 'lenses' of culture, process, resources, ecology, and theology. Ethnography is thus invoked to bridge the gap between seminary and the student's post-graduation congregation, with a view too to enhancing the teaching that the graduate will provide and (as in Reeve's case with villagers in Mozambique) increasing their motivation.

But the respect for diversity inherent in ethnography, the acknowledgement of change, and the collapse of boundaries between priest and lay, or between student and teacher, are at odds with certain religious orthodoxies. It will then be for the sociologist of religion to investigate the denominational extent of applied ethnography in confessional contexts. It seems likely that the readiness of teachers of religious studies to engage with ethnography will extend to increasing numbers of religious educationists and into the vocational training of some ministers of religion. But in the confessional setting, ethnography will at best only be called in to support the pastor's task of transmitting spiritual faith and promoting religious culture.

In Conclusion

An ethnographic approach to the teaching and study of religions reduces the risk of assuming religions to be bounded, static, internally homogeneous, depersonalized entities, and of presenting them in this reified and essentialized way. Instead, both teacher and student engage with the dynamics of individuals in their various interpenetrating groupings, and their own self-understanding develops through this engagement. Boundaries between oneself and others are unsettled, and teacher and student progress together along paths of continuing discovery and relearning. Such an approach to the study of religion, originating as it does in the discipline of anthropology, is preferably integrated with approaches informed by other disciplines such as philosophy and history. (Dialogue and interaction are salutary, not only between insiders and outsiders to faith communities, but also between theoretical and pedagogical approaches and their exponents.) Exploring faith communities in fieldworker mode can be refreshingly motivational, whilst also unsettling the received 'world religions' frameworks and stereotypical definitions which some examination syllabuses presuppose. Herein lies a challenge for the teacher in higher education as well as in schools.

Given the scholarly roots of ethnography and the capacity of ethnographic exploration to set 'authorities' in a wider context and expose them to inquiry, it is unsurprising that in most confessional settings neither leaders nor devotees have encountered, let alone embraced, its methods. In the confessional context of perpetuating a particular faith, ethnographic methods are most likely to be used instrumentally—for example, in equipping ministers for congregational ministry. The truly reflexive practitioner who is teaching in more secular settings may well reflect upon the point at which commitment to an ethnographic approach, and to liberal inquiry more generally, itself becomes confessional or evangelical.

Future research could well examine the applications of aspects of ethnography in teaching/training in Christian and Jewish institutions of vocational and higher education. The contribution of the Internet, and of online ethnography in particular, to religion teachers' understandings and representations of religions and to their pedagogy invites examination. Meanwhile, as concern mounts to educate pupils effectively for active citizenship in diverse societies, empirical studies of teachers' strategies—including the development of pupils' skills in listening, observation, interpretation, and reflexive discussion—can inform debate on intercultural education.

References

Ammerman, N. T., Carroll, J. W., Dudley, C. S., and McKinney, W. (1998). *Studying Congregations: A New Handbook.* Nashville: Abingdon.

Arweck, E., and Stringer, M. D. (2002). *Theorizing Faith: The Insider/Outsider Problem in the Study of Ritual.* Birmingham: University of Birmingham Press.

Astley, J., Francis, L. J., Burton, L., and Wilcox, C. (1997). 'Distinguishing between Aims and Methods in RE: A Study among Secondary RE Teachers'. *British Journal of Religions Education,* 19/3: 171–85.

Ballard, R. (1994). 'Panth Kismet Dharm te Qaum: Continuity and Change in Four Dimensions of Punjabi Religion'. In P. Singh and S. S. Thandi (eds.), *Punjabi Identity in a Global Context.* New Delhi: Oxford University Press, 7–38.

Berger, P. (2002). 'Secularization and De-Secularization'. In L. Woodhead, P. Fletcher, H. Kawanami, and D. Smith (eds.), *Religions in the Modern World: Traditions and Transformations.* London, Routledge: 291–8.

Bhatti, G. (1999). *Asian Children at Home and at School: An Ethnographic Study.* London: Routledge.

Bowker, J. (ed.) (1997). *The Oxford Dictionary of World Religions.* Oxford: Oxford University Press.

Brear, D. (1992). 'Transmission of a Swaminarayan Hindu Scripture in the British East Midlands'. In R. B.Williams (ed.), *A Sacred Thread: Modern Transmission of Hindu Traditions in India and Abroad.* Chambersburg: Anima, 209–27.

Brown, K. M. (1991). *Mama Lola: A Vodou Priestess in Brooklyn.* Berkeley: University of California Press.

Bullivant, B. M. (1978). *The Way of Tradition: Life in an Orthodox Jewish School.* Hawthorn: Australian Council for Educational Research.

Bunt, G. (2006). 'Virtually Islamic: Research and News about Islam in the Digital Age'; available at <http://www.virtuallyislamic.com>.

Burgess, R. G. (1983). *Experiencing Comprehensive Education: A Study of Bishop McGregor School.* London: Methuen.

Capp, W. H. (1995). *Religious Studies: The Making of a Discipline.* Minneapolis: Fortress Press.

Chandler, D. (2001) 'Semiotics for Beginners'; available at <http://www.aber.ac.uk/media/Docments/S4B/sem11.html>, accessed 28 Dec. 2006.

Chaudhry, L. N. (1997). 'Researching "My People", Researching Myself: Fragments of a Reflexive Tale'. *Qualitative Studies in Education*, 19/4: 441–53.

Clifford, J. (1997). *Routes: Travel and Translation in the Late Twentieth Century.* Cambridge, Mass.: Harvard University Press.

Corrywright, D., and Morgan, P. (2006). *Get Set for Religious Studies.* Edinburgh: Edinburgh University Press.

Cunningham, A. (1990). 'Religious Studies in the Universities: England'. in U. King (ed.), *Turning Points in Religious Studies: Essays in Honour of Geoffrey Parrinder.* Edinburgh: T & T Clark, 21–31.

Cush, D. (1999). 'The Relationship between Religious Studies, Religious Education and Theology: Big Brother, Little Sister and the Clerical Uncle?' *British Journal of Religious Education*, 21/5: 137–46.

—— (2001). 'The Mutual Influence of Religious Education in Schools and Religious Studies/Theology in Universities in the English Context'. *Spotlight on Teaching*, American Academy of Religion, 16/3: 5–6.

Dandelion, P. (1996). *A Sociological Analysis of the Theology of Quakers.* Lampeter: Edwin Mellen.

Eck, D. (2000). 'Dialogue and Method: Reconstructing the Study of Religion'. In K. Paten and B. Ray (eds.), *A Magic Still Dwells: Comparative Religion in the Postmodern Age.* Berkeley: University of California Press, 131–49.

Everington, J., and Sikes, P. (2001). '"I Want to Change the World": The Beginning RE Teacher, the Reduction of Prejudice and the Pursuit of Intercultural Understanding and Respect'. In H-G. Heimbrock, C. T. Scheilke, and P. Schreiner (eds.), *Towards Religious Competence: Diversity as a Challenge for Education in Europe.* Münster: Lit Verlag, 180–202.

Fetterman, D. M. (1989). *Ethnography Step by Step.* London: Sage.

Ford, D. (2006). 'Theology and Religious Studies for a Multifaith and Secular Society'. Paper presented at conference on Theology *and* Religious Studies or Theology *vs* Religious Studies, St Anne's College, University of Oxford, July.

—— Quash, B., and Soskice, J. (eds.) (2005). *Fields of Faith, Theology and Religious Studies for the Twenty-First Century.* Cambridge: Cambridge University Press.

Furseth, I., and Repstad, P. (2006). *An Introduction to Sociology of Religion: Classical and Contemporary Perspectives.* Aldershot: Ashgate.

Geaves, R. (1998). 'The Borders between Religions: A Challenge to the World Religions Approach to Religious Education'. *British Journal of Religious Education*, 21/1: 20–31.

Geertz, C. (1973). 'Thick Description: Toward an Interpretive Theory of Culture'. In *The Interpretation of Cultures.* New York: Basic Books, 5–6, 9–10.

GENT, W. (2006). 'Muslim Supplementary Classes and their Place within the Wider Learning Community: A Redbridge-Based Study' (unpublished Ed.D. thesis, University of Warwick).

GILLESPIE, M. (1995). *Television, Ethnicity and Cultural Change.* London: Routledge.

GLASER, B. G., and STRAUSS, A. L. (1967). *The Discovery of Grounded Theory.* Chicago: Aldine.

GOBBO, F. (2004). 'Ethnographic Research as a Re/Source of Intercultural Education'; available at <http://www.inst.at/trans/15Nr/08_1/gobbo15.htm>.

GRIMMITT, M. (1987). *Religious Education and Human Development.* Great Wakering: McCrimmons.

—— (ed.) (2000). *Pedagogies of Religious Education: Case Studies in the Research and Development of Good Pedagogic Practice in RE.* Great Wakering: McCrimmons.

HALL, K. D. (2002). *Lives in Translation: Sikh Youth as British Citizens.* Philadelphia: University of Pennsylvania Press.

HAMMERSLEY, M., and ATKINSON, P. (1983). *Ethnography Principles in Practice.* London: Routledge.

HAND, M. (2006). 'Answers for a Troubled World'. *Report,* the magazine from the Association of Teachers and Lecturers, January; available at <www.atl.org.uk>.

HARGREAVES, A. (1994). *Changing Teachers, Changing Times: Teachers' Work and Culture in the Postmodern Age.* London: Cassell.

HEILMAN, S. (1976). *Synagogue Life: A Study in Symbolic Interaction.* Chicago: University of Chicago Press.

IPGRAVE, J. (1998). 'Issues in the Delivery of Religious Education to Muslim Pupils: Perspectives from the Classroom'. *British Journal of Religious Education,* 21/3: 146–57.

—— (2005). 'Pupil-to-Pupil Dialogue in the Classroom as a Tool for Religious Education'. In R. Jackson and U. McKenna (eds.), *Intercultural Education and Religious Plurality.* Oslo: The Oslo Coalition on Freedom of Religion or Belief, 39–42.

JACKSON, R. (1989). *Religions through Festivals: Hinduism.* Harlow: Longman.

—— (1997). *Religious Education: An Interpretive Approach.* London: Hodder & Stoughton.

—— (2004). *Rethinking Religious Education and Plurality: Issues in Diversity and Pedagogy.* London: RoutledgeFalmer.

—— (forthcoming). *Education and Diversity: The Interpretive Approach in an International Context.* Münster: Waxmann.

—— and NESBITT, E. (1993). *Hindu Children in Britain.* Stoke on Trent: Trentham.

—— and O'GRADY, K. (2007). 'Religions and Education in England: Social Plurality, Civil Religion and Religious Education Pedagogy'. In R. Jackson, S. Miedema, W. Weisse, and J. P. Willaime (eds.), *Religion and Education in Europe: Developments, Contexts and Debates.* Münster: Waxmann, 181–202.

JACOBSON, J. (1998). *Islam in Transition: Religion and Identity among British Pakistani Youth.* London: Routledge.

JENKINS, T. (1999). *Religion in English Everyday Life: An Ethnographic Approach.* New York: Berghahn Books.

LIVEZEY, L.W. (2002). 'Epilogue: The Ethnographer and the Quest for Meanings'. In Arweck and Stringer (2002), 155–66.

MALINA, B. J. (1981). *The New Testament World: Insights from Cultural Anthropology.* London: SCM Press.

Markham, A. N. (2005). 'The Methods, Politics and Ethics of Online Ethnography'. In N. K. Denzin and Y. S. Lincoln (eds.), *The Sage Handbook of Qualitative Research.* Thousand Oaks, Calif.: Sage, 793–820.

McCutcheon, R. (ed.) (1999). *The Insider/Outsider Problem in the Study of Religion.* London: Cassell.

Mercer, J. A. (2005). 'Teaching the Bible in Congregations: A Congregational Studies Pedagogy for Contextual Education'. *Religious Education,* 100/3: 280–95.

Meyerhoff, B. (1978). *Number our Days.* New York: Simon & Schuster.

Nesbitt, E. (1998). 'Bridging the Gap between Young People's Experience of their Religious Tradition at Home and at School: The Contribution of Ethnographic Research'. *British Journal of Religious Education,* 20/2: 98–110.

—— (1999). 'The Impact of Morari Bapu's *Kathas* on Britain's Young Hindus'. *Scottish Journal of Religious Studies,* 20/2: 177–92.

—— (2000*a*). *The Religious Lives of Sikh Children: A Coventry Based Study.* Leeds: Department of Theology and Religious Studies, University of Leeds.

—— (2000*b*). 'Researching 8–13 Year Olds' Perspectives on their Experience of Religion'. In A. Lewis and G. Lindsay (eds.), *Researching Children's Perspectives.* Buckingham: Open University Press, 135–49.

—— (2001). 'Ethnographic Research at Warwick: Some Methodological Issues'. *British Journal of Religious Education,* 23/3: 144–55.

—— (2002). 'Quaker Ethnographers: A Reflexive Approach'. In Arweck and Stringer (2002), 133–54.

—— (2004). *Intercultural Education: Ethnographic and Religious Approaches.* Brighton: Sussex Academic Press.

Nicholson, E. (ed.) (2003). *A Century of Theology and Religious Studies in Britain.* Oxford: Oxford University Press.

Norcross, P. (1989). 'The Effects of Cultural Conditioning on Multi-Faith Education in a Monocultural Primary School'. *British Journal of Religious Education,* 11/2: 87–91.

Nye, M. (1995). *A Place for our Gods: The Construction of an Edinburgh Hindu Temple Community.* London: Curzon.

O'Grady, K. (2003). 'Motivation in Religious Education: A Collaborative Investigation with Year Eight Students'. *British Journal of Religious Education,* 25/3: 214–25.

—— (2007). 'Motivation in Secondary Religious Education' (unpublished Ph.D. thesis, University of Warwick).

Østberg, S. (2003). *Pakistani Children in Norway: Islamic Nurture in a Secular Context.* Leeds: Department of Theology and Religious Studies, University of Leeds.

Pocock, D. (1976). 'Preservation of the Religious Life: Hindu Immigrants in England'. *Contributions to Indian Sociology,* N.S. 10/2: 341–65.

Raj, D. S. (2003). *Where Are You From? Middle-Class Migrants in the Modern World.* Berkeley: University of California Press.

Ram-Prasad, C. (2001). 'Teaching South Asian Religions in Britain'. *Spotlight on Teaching,* American Academy of Religion, 16/3: 3 and 6.

Reeve, R. (2006). *Action Research Towards the Provision of Motivational Christian Nurture in Base Communities, Maputo, Mozambique* (unpublished M.A. dissertation in Religious Education, University of Warwick).

Said, E. (1989). 'Representing the Colonised: Anthropology's Interlocutors'. *Critical Enquiry,* 15/2: 205–25.

Sambur, B. (2002). 'From the Dichotomy of Spiritualism/Ritualism to the Dichotomy of Insider/Outsider'. In Arweck and Stringer (2002), 21–34.

Scholefield, L. (2004). 'Bagels, Schnitzels and McDonald's: "Fuzzy Frontiers" of Jewish Identity in an English Jewish Secondary School'. *British Journal of Religious Education*, 26/3: 237–48.

Searle-Chatterjee, M. (2000). '"World Religions" and "Ethnic Groups": Do these Paradigms Lend themselves to the Cause of Hindu Nationalism?' *Ethnic and Racial Studies*, 23/3: 497–515.

Skeie, G. (2002). 'The Concept of Plurality and its Meaning for Religious Education'. *British Journal of Religious Education*, 25/1: 47–59.

Smart, N. (1996). *Dimensions of the Sacred: An Anatomy of the World's Beliefs*. London: HarperCollins.

Stern, J. (2006). *Teaching Religious Education*. London: Continuum.

Stringer, M. D. (1999). *On the Perception of Worship: The Ethnography of Worship in Four Christian Congregations in Manchester*. Birmingham: University of Birmingham Press.

—— (2002). 'Introduction: Theorizing Faith'. In Arweck and Stringer (2002), 1–20.

Swain, J. (2006). 'An Ethnographic Approach to Researching Children in Junior School'. *International Journal of Social Research Methodology*, 9/3: 199–213.

Tatla, D. S. (1992). 'Nurturing the Faithful: The Role of the Sant among Britain's Sikhs'. *Religion*, 22/4: 349–74.

Waterhouse, H. (1999). 'Reincarnation Belief in Britain: New Age Orientation or Mainstream Option?' *Journal of Contemporary Religion*, 14/1: 97–109.

Wright, A. (1993). *Religious Education in the Secondary School: Prospects for Religious Literacy*. London: David Fulton.

Suggested Reading

The following are recommended: Gobbo (2004); Jackson (1997); Mercer (2005); and Nesbitt (2004).

CHAPTER 54

ETHNOGRAPHY/ RELIGION

EXPLORATIONS IN FIELD AND CLASSROOM

JAMES V. SPICKARD

It should not be news that ethnography has undergone a sea-change in the last twenty years. Scholars' increasing realization of the epistemological limitations of top-down research—alongside its potential misuse by political and economic elites—has produced a serious rethinking of the ethnographic enterprise. Nor has the pedagogical revolution of the last generation failed to attract attention, at least in the United States. Though still prominent, professor-centered teaching is less universal than formerly, especially in the humanities and social sciences. Even undergraduate university students are now encouraged to direct their own learning.

The connection between these two phenomena is not generally noticed. On inspection, their parallel emergence at the end of the twentieth century and their growth in the early twenty-first marks a culture transformation. Not surprisingly, there is evidence of a similar shift in the religious sphere. This chapter summarizes these three shifts, with special attention to the sociology of religion—methodologically, pedagogically, and theoretically.

Reshaping Ethnography

As a research method, ethnography is used by both anthropologists and sociologists. Unlike other qualitative methods, such as surveys or in-depth interviews, it calls for long-term participant observation in a target community. The ethnographer lives with her study subjects, often for years, getting a detailed and nuanced sense of their lives. She must learn how they conceive of themselves—the classic hermeneutic task—but she must also learn to see the life patterns of which they are unaware. Ethnography thus works from two directions, inside and outside. The inside movement attempts to understand the 'natives' as they understand themselves. The outside movement attempts to understand them as only an outsider can. Both are essential—and they take time. Done right, ethnography is one of the most labor-intensive methods, far more so than most other kinds of social research.

There are many published guides to the fieldwork part of ethnography, among them Fetterman (1998), Lofland *et al.* (2005), and Schensul and LeCompte's seven-volume *Ethnographer's Toolkit* series (1999). Technique is not, however, where the sea-change has occurred. The most significant change is that ethnographers are now more sensitive than before to their own role in ethnographic encounters. Whereas ethnographers used to present their studies as objective portrayals of their target peoples, they now admit that their views are limited by the information their social location lets them see. This goes beyond the obvious fact that male ethnographers are often denied access to women's worlds, and vice versa. It also involves the relative socio-political power of ethnographers and their subjects, and the (often unconscious) attitudes this engenders.

A bit of disciplinary history helps underscore the problem. Anthropological ethnography is an outgrowth of Euro-American colonialism (Asad 1973; Hymes 1969). The British and American governments both sponsored early ethnographic expeditions, in part to gain clues about how to rule their disparate subjects. The equivalent French, German, and Russian bureaucrats did likewise. Their understandings and representations of their subjects were colored by this colonial interest.

Two examples will do. The Bureau of American Ethnography (BAE) famously enlisted James Mooney (1896) to investigate the Plains Indian Ghost Dance and similar religious outbursts, so as to understand Native American religious revivalism and to avoid a repeat of the 1890 Wounded Knee massacre (D. Brown 1970). On the British side, E. E. Evans-Pritchard (1940) was sent to learn how leadership works in the south of Sudan—a society with no formal governance—in part because the British system of co-opting native governments did not work there. Both ethnographers produced classic work, because they went beyond their original charge and sought to understand native society on its own terms. But they did give their sponsors what they had asked for; indeed, Evans-Pritchard came to understand Nuer governance well enough to organize their raids against the Italians at the start of the Second World War (Geertz 1988).

Once political control was established, both British and American ethnography shifted, with ethnographers imagining themselves to be recording so-called vanishing ways of life. This was itself a colonial conceit, misunderstanding as much as it revealed. One need only recall the story of We'wha, the Zuni "princess" brought to Washington DC by the BAE's Matilda Stevenson. We'wha was in fact no salvaged female trophy but a *berdache*—a cross-dressing male—and, more importantly, an ethnographer in reverse, who had come to the center of White power to learn how to resist colonial encroachment (McFeely 2001). Stevenson never did understand the implications of this event, though the Zuni learned a lot about their colonial masters. One does not need the sensibility of an Edward Said (1978; 1985; 1993) to realize the vacuity of the ethnographers' claim to know the natives better than they know themselves.

The first American sociological ethnographers were no less politically implicated, though their situation was more subtle. Working out of the well-known "Chicago School" (America's first academic department of sociology at the University of Chicago), they were influenced by Jane Addams's work with immigrant slum dwellers (Deegan 1986). Their studies[1] showed that social problems in these poor neighborhoods were not the result of moral defects of the inhabitants; instead, ignorance, disease, and crime were the result of economic desperation. With Addams, they argued that, if afforded a decent education, adequate living conditions, and reliable income, any person could become a productive member of society.

One can, and perhaps should, put this more crudely: the poor could become "just like us"—middle-class—with the right combination of soap and schooling. Firmly grounded in the urban intelligentsia, the scholars of the Chicago School treated their own class position as normative. American sociological ethnography has thus typically explored the lives of deviants (Whyte 1943; Liebow 1967; Spradley 2000[1970]), the lower classes (e.g., Komarovsky 1964; Kotlowitz 1991), or rural folk (Pope 1958; Vidich and Bensman 1968)—albeit usually with great sympathy. With some exceptions (e.g., Seeley *et al.* 1956), few ethnographers have gazed at the educated middle class, much less at the powerful.[2]

[1] Early urban ethnographers associated with the Chicago School included Robert Park (Park *et al.* 1925), John Dollard (1937), W. F. Whyte (1943), St. Clair Drake (Drake and Cayton 1945), and W. Lloyd Warner (the Yankee City series, 5 vols. beginning with Warner and Lunt 1941).

[2] American anthropological ethnography of the same era was more influenced by Franz Boas at Columbia. He and his students emphasized the separateness of various cultures and the importance of recording their "vanishing" knowledge. Field notes from his Northwest Coast Indian projects contain some wonderful blueberry pie recipes.

On the one hand, the sympathetic portrayals of "others" as potential "us" made the strange familiar, to use the old saw. This undercut America's accustomed emphasis on the poor's moral failings, and planted sociology firmly in the liberal political camp. On the other hand, even the most respectful ethnographies (e.g., Liebow 1993) sustained the normativity of middle-class life. Sociological ethnographies have seldom questioned the American ideology of social uplift, even as they moved its emphasis from moral to structural factors.

Religious ethnographies are no exception to this pattern, at least in the United States. Though more Americans attend denominational churches—both Protestant and Catholic—than attend sectarian ones, ethnographers have spent much more effort on the latter. For every study of a mainline Protestant congregation (Warner 1988; Davie 1995), we find half a dozen about sectarian groups (Aho 1990; Ammerman 1987; Beckford 1975; Birckhead 1997; 2002; Brasher 1998; Ingersoll 2003), immigrant religions (K. Brown 2001; McAlister 2002; Levitt 2001; Tweed 1997; Warner and Wittner 1998; Woldemikael 1989), or new religions (Barker 1984; Chancellor 2000; Goldman 1999; Lofland 1966; Rochford 1985; Tipton 1982). More studies of African American religion focus on Black Pentecostals than on non-Pentecostal AME (African Methodist Episcopal) or Baptists (Baer 1984; Kostarelos 1995; Nelson 2004). Ethnographies of Catholics less often cover mainstream parishes (Fichter 1951) than charismatics (Neitz 1987), saints' devotees (Orsi 1996), or base Christian communities (Adriance 1995). The same is true of studies of Jewish groups (Davidman 1991; Feder 1998; Shaffir 1974). Are mainstream, middle-class congregations apparently too normal to be worth investigating? Or has the notion of social uplift of deviants been repeated in the religious sphere?

The ethnographic revolution of the last twenty years has uncovered such ideological assumptions and the ways in which they become embedded in ethnographic texts. As Clifford Geertz (1998: 72) put it, socially conscious anthropology now finds that "poking into the lives of people who are not in a position to poke into yours [is] something of a colonial relic". One response has been for anthropologists to poke into our own society's root beliefs about the world. This can be both humorous and enlightening, as with Van Maanen and Laurent's (1993) study of the different cultural meanings of Disneyland for Americans and for Japanese.[3] But it is serious, as well. Contemporary anthropology recognizes that its own activity is as much a cultural product as are the cargo cults of the South Seas. Why do "we"—members of the educated middle class—want to know about these particular peoples' lives? What does this tell us about our society and about ourselves?

Most importantly for this Handbook, how do the cultural presumptions that have so far been embedded in the ethnographic project prevent us from fully

[3] Their close analysis of the structure of the Disney theme parks in the two countries shows how Americans believe that everyone is, at root, just like themselves—albeit with different "ethnic" clothing and foods—while Japanese believe in their own cultural uniqueness.

understanding the 'others' who are the subjects of our investigations? How does ethnography's historic position, as the educated West gazing at the 'underdeveloped' Rest, keep us from understanding that Rest correctly? Old-style ethnography claimed a 'missionary position': as supposedly knowledgeable scientists investigating supposedly less knowledgeable subalterns.[4] Contemporary anthropological ethnographers reverse this; they listen as the Empire talks back. They would take We'wha seriously, recognizing the truth of her/his implicit critique of the colonial system. Despite all her knowledge of Zuni life, Matilda Stevenson missed this, and thus misunderstood her subjects. Today's ethnographers do not wish to repeat this mistake.

Representation

What does it take to 'get the picture right' in a postcolonial era? Anthropologists have lately focused their attention on the ethnographic encounter. If we can understand what happens there, and see how it limits our knowledge, then we can (perhaps) correct for these limitations. We can at least be clear about what we do and do not know.

A good part of this reflection has been on the problem of representation. This includes not only how the ethnographer represents herself to her informants (her role, loyalties, etc.) and how the informants represent themselves to her (which has always been part of ethnographic reporting). Most significantly, it also includes how she represents her informants' lives in the products of her research: in film or in print. Writing and other forms of representation are important because, to use Geertz's (1973) famous phrase, ethnography is "thick description". It involves sorting out the webs of significance that one finds in one's field site and conveying these significances to one's readers. The ethnographer must not only express her understanding of her informants' lives, while communicating their humanity to readers who are not necessarily accustomed to treating cargo cultists (Bateson 1958), Pentecostals (Coleman 2000), or Fundamentalists (Harding 2000) as fully human. She must also communicate her own standpoint—including its limitations—so that the reader can evaluate her presentation (Clifford and Marcus 1986; Behar and Gordon 1995; James *et al.* 1997).

[4] The term is Antonio Gramsci's (1992[1949]), who used it to refer to groups that sit outside the established structures of political representation. Gayatri Spivak and other postcolonial theorists have popularized it to refer to marginalized groups and the lower classes in general, especially in non-Western societies. Without taking on her intellectual baggage, Spivak's (1988) essay, "Can the Subaltern Speak?" is relevant to ethnography's current self-examination.

J. Shawn Landres (2002) expands this discussion by noting that there are at least eight levels of representation embedded in every ethnographic encounter, each of which shapes our knowledge. His first two levels arise during the first days of fieldwork. In his listing (p. 106):

1. "I the Anthropologist" represent myself and people like me (i.e., anthropologists and ethnographers, even academic scholars as a group) to the "Others".
2. The "Others" represent me to themselves. They decide for themselves who I really am and why I am among them.

Ethnographers typically try to control the first; what ethnographer has not worried about how to present herself to her potential informants? The second may be more powerful, however, and we have less leverage over it. For example, at various times in my work with religious social activists I have been seen as a college professor (and thus a potential source of status and legitimation), as a religious seeker (and thus a potential convert), as an experienced social activist (and thus someone who can help with strategies), as a nosy male reporter (who is suspect because "men cannot understand us"). All of these are true, of course, but that is not the point. The point is that the information I get is shaped by—and limited by—these informants' representations. Different attributed identities produce different ethnographic knowledge.

Landres's next two levels of representation are also beyond our control (p. 107):

3. The "Others" represent themselves within their own groups.
4. The "Others" represent themselves to me and to people like me.

As Landres notes, the first of these is something which ethnographers typically study: how people conceive of and represent themselves, in their own terms. This is part of what we are supposed to convey to our readers. Too many ethnographers, though, forget that they are themselves part of the action. They are not just watching others' actions; they are an audience for those actions, and the "Others" know it. In Landres's words (p. 107), "the fieldworker becomes what Neil Jarman calls a 'watched watcher', the spectator who is the object of their performance and thus a part of it.... Often [the informants] are quite consciously... stag[ing] a brilliant performance of the identity they wish to claim." Unless the ethnographer realizes this, she will take the informants' self-presentations as "real"—as did the Zuni We'wha's interlocutors. Not seeing others' acts as performances, she will miss much of what is really going on.

The fifth level of representation (p. 108) focuses on another side of the interaction between ethnographer and informant: the co-construction of the former's identity.

5. The 'Others' represent me to myself.

This reminds us that our identities, too, are influenced by those around us. For example, Susan Harding (1987) reports being told by her Fundamentalist informants that she was not, in fact, an academic researcher but a "seeker" whom God was leading toward conversion. This was more than just a matter of how the informants identify the ethnographer to each other (level 2 above)—though it was that as well. It was also an attempt to convince Harding to take on the role that the informants had created for her. The fact that they did this told her something important about them, but it also limited the kinds of information that they would share with her. Not only would her informants not tell her anything inappropriate to her role (level 2), but they actively encouraged her to act the "seeker's" part, rewarding her with confidences when she did so. Was the information she gained thus shaped by the identity into which they were trying to push her? Certainly! The point is that ethnographers need to notice this, at the cost of inaccurate reporting.

Landres's next two levels of representation (p. 109) involve ethnographic writing; they are the topic of the previously cited work by Clifford and Marcus (1986), Behar and Gordon (1995), and James *et al.* (1997).

6. "I the Anthropologist" represent the "Other" to fellow anthropologists, as well as to the public.
7. "I the Anthropologist" represent the "Other" to themselves.

Ethnographic writing does not "create" its informants in any metaphysical sense. It does, however, create a public representation of those informants, and different ethnographers notoriously create different such representations. The best-known case is the contrast between Robert Redfield's *Tepoztlán* (1930) and Oscar Lewis's *Life in a Mexican Village* (1951), both of which were written about the same community, but a generation apart. Elizabeth Marshall Thomas (1959; 2006) and Marjorie Shostak (1983) have similarly disparate depictions of the !Kung people of the Kalahari (see Konner 2007). Such cases remind us that ethnographers produce at best partial representations of their informants' lives.

In addition, unlike in the colonial period, today's 'natives' read our ethnographies and sometimes quarrel with the images they find. Anthony Appiah (2000) reports, for example, that some Ik were so upset with the picture that Colin Turnbull painted of them in *The Mountain People* (1972) that they tried to figure out how to sue him. Arthur Vidich and Joseph Bensman were hanged in effigy for their book about an upstate New York town. More than a few ethnographers have found their field sites closed to them, once their informants have read their work. This does not mean that they were inaccurate; it merely highlights the conflicting representations possible.

Finally, says Landres (p. 110),

8. "I the Anthropologist" represent "the Ethnographer" not only to the public, but also to my fellow anthropologists.

By this, he means that ethnographies do not just represent the people about whom they are written; they represent the writer as well. Each ethnography produces an implicit image of what it means to do ethnographic work, how ethnographers ought to do that work, and how they ought to structure their reports about it. As texts, ethnographies are thus prescriptive as well as descriptive. Perhaps this is why graduate training for anthropologists now asks students to read hundreds of them, whereas graduate training for sociologists still focuses on techniques (field entrée, interview skills, etc.). The former opens one to the representational possibilities. The latter leads one to ignore representation as a core part of the ethnographic process.

What is the underlying issue here? Simply put, it is that each of these levels of representation shapes the knowledge that we, as ethnographers, produce. On the data-gathering side, what we know depends on how we present ourselves to our informants and how they, in turn, read our presentations. It depends on how they present themselves, both to each other and to us as outsiders. And it depends on how they change us, as people, in their representations to us of what we are doing. On the writing side, we represent "Others" and ourselves to our various audiences as accurately as we can, recognizing that all such representations are partial. Each level of representation could be done differently; the net outcome would be a different ethnography and different knowledge. This makes good ethnography as much an art as a science, but this is not an excuse for anything goes. There are still "better" and "worse" ethnographies, or—perhaps more accurately—more and less insightful ones. The more that ethnographers take these various levels of representation into account, the more insightful they can be.

Anthropological ethnographers generally recognize that these eight levels of representation shape knowledge. Sociologists, on the other hand, more often imagine that the knowledge they produce is epistemologically secure. Here I have to side with the anthropologists; as a reflexive ethnographer—one who recognizes that I, too, am part of the social scene that I am studying—I must be aware of these various kinds of representation if I am to recognize the limits of my work. This is what "getting it right" means in a post-colonial era: to be aware of the limits of one's own knowledge; to be aware of the social and political patterns that have structured that knowledge and of the biases that are presumed by it; to bring those patterns and biases to the surface in one's writing, so that one's readers can account for them; to write so as to see past the distortions that such patterns and biases inevitably bring.

The point is not just that all knowledge is partial—a throw-up-your-hands attitude that abandons the field at the first sign of adversity. The point is to foreground this partiality: to learn its shape and texture, then to use that learning to bring into focus what we heretofore have not seen. Our present critique of early ethnographers as the unconscious servants of the Empire or of the ascendant middle classes allows us to do better ethnography, because we can guard against the things they did not see. Learning about Matilda Stevenson's work, both the good (her detailed field notes) and the bad (her unconscious imperial presumptions) helps us copy the former and abandon the latter. Reflexive ethnography consistently seeks to expand its self-understanding.

Regulative Ideals

For a more formal look at the epistemological issues involved here, it helps to turn to the work of Charles Sanders Peirce (1877; 1955). Peirce argues that every science is a communal activity, dedicated to seeking "truth". This truth is not, however, conceived of as something preexisting—that is, as facts that can be discovered once and forever. Instead, to use Peirce's (rather opaque) phrasing:

> Truth is that concordance of abstract statement with the ideal limit towards which endless investigation would tend to bring scientific belief, which concordance the abstract statement may possess by virtue of the confession of its inaccuracy and one-sidedness, and this confession is an essential ingredient of truth. (Peirce 1934[1902]: 565–6)

To use more contemporary language, "truth" is not achieved by basing one's work on some secure theoretical or methodological foundation. Such foundations are temporary; each intellectual generation demonstrates the flaws in its predecessors' foundations, producing scientific revolutions in the process (Kuhn 1970; Feyerabend 1975). Science involves more than just the accumulation of facts; it involves the continual rethinking of basic concepts and relationships. Truth is therefore always something just out of reach.

The growth of knowledge, however, depends on the *idea* of "truth", even if that truth is unspecifiable. It is possible only because the community of scientists knows that whatever it now believes to be true is not the whole truth, but instead needs correction. Scientists test their current beliefs against whatever the scientific community at that historical moment thinks is "reality", to determine whether the beliefs hold up to experience. Those that do are affirmed—provisionally. Those that do not are discarded. Science is the process of progressively discarding past "truths" for the sake of "better", yet provisional ones. It lives in faith that, if this process continues long enough, we will comprehend the world. We do not have to choose between Redfield's or Lewis's Tepoztlán, or between Thomas's or Shostak's !Kung; by recognizing the various representations that shaped each study, we can identify at least some of their limitations. We can then triangulate to an understanding that surpasses them all.

Peirce's point is that this whole process depends on the *concept* of "truth", even though the truth-as-a-reality can never be achieved with any certitude. "Truth", here, is not an object; it is a *regulative ideal.* This is an idea that, while undemonstrable in itself, makes inquiry possible. Holding "truth" as the ideal toward which they strive gives scholars something to aim at, while reminding them that all human endeavors fall short of their aims. But it is a *communal* aim, one that, precisely because it is shared, allows scholars to build upon each other's work.[5]

In this sense, ethnography is firmly grounded in the sciences. Ethnography does seek to "get it right"; the community of ethnographers does recognize that some partial views are better than others. Contemporary anthropological ethnographers recognize the flaws in the old imperial way of doing things. Current standards dictate that ethnographers take Landres's eight levels of representation into account, for we have learned that failing to do so produces an inaccurate picture of informants' social worlds.

There is a further turn of the screw here, however. Implicit in our account of these various levels of representation is a claim that ethnographers do not live on a higher plane than their subjects. In place of knowledgeable ethnographers studying less knowledgeable subalterns, we have various sets of people—ethnographers, informants, and reading publics—all representing to themselves and each other what they and the others are doing. There is no metaphysical distinction between the representations that ethnographers make about themselves to their informants and the representations that the informants make of themselves to the ethnographer (levels 1 and 4). There is similarly no metaphysical distinction between the representations the ethnographer makes of her informants to the reading public and the representations the informants make of the ethnographer to their friends and co-workers (levels 6 and 2). Aside from the publishing industry and its products, these representations are equivalent—and we all know that putting something in print does not make it "true".

This implies a fundamental equality between ethnographer and informant, based on the metaphysical equivalence of their representations. Realizing this equality makes for *better* ethnographies than not doing so. Framed negatively, *not* understanding the dynamics of representation leads ethnographers to imagine that their picture of "native" life trumps the natives' own. While this may be true in some cases, the validity of such a claim rests not on the supposedly superior outside vantage-point of the educated scholar but on the care with which evidence is collected and the reasoning that accompanies its collection. There is no a priori reason to assume that ethnographers get this right more often than natives do. There is, however, every reason to assume that both ethnographers and natives have only partial access to multi-faceted social reality.

[5] For a more detailed discussion of the notion of "regulative ideals", see Spickard (2002; 2006*b*). In brief, were social science to lack the notion of "truth" as a regulative ideal, it would be impossible for anyone to fault a particular piece of research. "Truth" as an ideal provides the possibility of such critique—even if that truth is not itself known but only specifiable eschatologically. Anyone who points out flaws, or even gaps, in research implicitly judges that research as inadequate—and upholds the idea that adequate research is possible.

Contemporary ethnography has responded to this situation by instituting a *de facto* second regulative ideal governing ethnographic reports. This is the sense that one must treat one's informants as equals. This is not to say that "natives" know exactly the same things as do scholars. They do know things that scholars do not, however, and their points of view need to be given their due weight. Not only can these informants have deep insights into their own lives; their insights into the ethnographic encounter itself deserve being taken seriously. A whole series of recent ethnographic biographies (K. Brown 2001; Crapanzano 1980; Herzfeld 1998) charts such "native" insights in the context of the ethnographer's charting of their social milieus.

Contemporary ethnographers have discovered that assuming such equality produces better work. It provides a truer picture of "native" life than does the old imperial ethnography. This assumption functions much like science's primary regulative ideal—"truth"—in that "equality", too, is an unprovable starting point that makes research possible. The recognition that the ethnographer's representations have the same metaphysical status as the natives', and that both affect what we can know, produces better ethnography than the old presumption that outsiders can know insiders better than the latter know themselves. "Equality" as a regulative ideal moves research in the right direction.

There are, of course, religious ethnographies that do treat their subjects as equals. Two recent books do a masterful job of representing new middle-class religion. Wendy Cadge (2005) compares two Theravada Buddhist communities, one made up of Thai immigrants and the other of upper-middle-class White meditators. Courtney Bender (2003) explores the religious life of volunteers at a New York meal program for AIDS patients. Both depict religions as lived by relatively elite populations; like Jodie Davie's (1995) study of Presbyterian women or Wade Clarke Roof's (1993; 1999) work with Baby Boomers, their informants' education and social status make it impossible to take the imperial position.

Too few sociological ethnographies are fully reflexive, however. Too few dissolve the glass wall that separates the research subjects (on one side) from the ethnographer and the audience (on the other). Such work is hard to write, and even harder to get published. Karen Brown (2001) succeeded with *Mama Lola*, in part because she is an anthropologist (where reflexivity is now *de rigeur*) who teaches in a department of religious studies (where taking religious people seriously is more of a cultural norm). The book's topic is, however, a selling point: one can almost hear book-buyers saying "Voodoo in Brooklyn? I've got to read about that!" This is not to question Brown's integrity—she has lots—but rather highlights the cultural proclivities of the contemporary public.[6] The ethnographic push for equality

[6] I have written about this elsewhere (Spickard 2003), as a ninth level of ethnographic representation. Figuring out what attracts readers to particular books and how they receive them tells us a lot about our own culture's fascinations—an important part of the reflexive ethnographic enterprise. This level of representation does not, however, shape our ethnographic knowledge in precisely the same way as the others, except to the degree that writing about a socially attractive topic gets our work published at all.

produces a truer picture of "native" lives, but the wider culture still buys books to satisfy its cultural voyeurism. Treating our informants as attractive exotics is no better than treating them as deviant "Others". Only equality will do.

The Student-Centered Classroom

University undergraduate-level pedagogy in the United States has also undergone a sea-change in recent years, though this one is easier to miss because of the pillarized nature of American higher education (Calhoun 1999). Leaving aside new education programs for working adults, American universities are of two types. On the one hand, there are the large research universities, dedicated to the production of new knowledge and little interested in undergraduate teaching. Some of these schools, in fact, now value faculty grantsmanship even more than scholarly publications—most likely because grant overhead payments fund an increasing share of university expenses. On the other hand, smaller "liberal arts" colleges and universities emphasize the quality of their undergraduate education and the attention that students get, even from full professors. Much more of their money comes from tuition, so schools compete to attract worthy, bill-paying students. They emphasize a new form of teaching to do so.

I have elsewhere described the affect that this bi-modal educational structure has on the transmission of sociological knowledge in textbooks, particularly those texts' picture of the sociology of religion (Spickard 1994). The recent growth of online publishing, increasing concentration in the publishing industry, and the growing efficiency of the used textbook market have only accentuated course standardization at the research university level. So has the increasing piece-work nature of the faculty job market: only about one-quarter of new faculty appointments are to full-time, tenure-track positions (Finkelstein 2003), and temporary job-holders typically lack the freedom for pedagogical creativity.[7]

[7] There is even a term, "freeway flyers", for those faculty who teach part-time at several schools (at pittance wages), rushing from one to another so that they can teach enough classes to pay their bills. They use textbooks as a matter of survival; creative class design requires more hours than they can devote to any one course.

This is not to say that teaching is completely ignored in American research universities, several of which have established teaching centers to train their graduate students. Nor is it ignored by institutional sociology, as the presence of such journals as *Teaching Sociology* and the American Sociological Association's frequent teaching workshops and numerous teaching guides demonstrates.

However, the reward structure for faculty promotion at research universities and among institutionally oriented sociologists makes it clear that teaching is not valued very highly in such places, while scholarly publication and grant winning are.

The situation is different at liberal arts universities. Not only is teaching rewarded; it is also talked about differently. In place of the transmission of knowledge, liberal arts ideology focuses on teaching critical thinking (Paul 1999), developing learning communities (Baker 1999), inculcating responsibility-centered learning (Aldrich and Lillijord 1999), and connecting knowledge to the "real world" (Newman 1999). Innovations go beyond seminar-style discussion to—among other things—cooperative learning groups (Rau and Heyl 1990), structured faculty vulnerability (Brookfield 1999), and attention to student personality profiles (Powers 1999). The new pedagogical ideology emphasizes such notions as "active learning" (Neal 1996) and "student-centered learning" (Stuart 1997), which it contrasts with traditional "teacher-centered" approaches. Lecture is out; discussion is *de rigeur.* As James Renfield (n.d.), a professor with the University of Chicago's Committee on Social Thought, remarks, "If you find a sentence in *Newsweek* that begins, 'Such and such a college is a place where professors do not lecture, but . . .', it really doesn't matter much what comes after the dots. You're sure it's superior to lecturing." Renfield notes that not all students welcome class discussions, which often put them on the spot—not a comfortable place to be when one has not done one's homework. The current call for student-centered teaching is, in fact, teacher-driven. In his words,

> I think our belief about how much better it is to have a discussion class involves, among other things, our rooted objection to hierarchy, which is one of the good things about us. One of the great discoveries of post-classical civilization is that every soul is valuable; everyone has something to say; everyone deserves to be heard. We talk about this when we talk about learning from our students. This is one of the things we teachers say, always with a tone of self-satisfaction.

This comment uncovers the values behind the whole movement. If traditional lecturing is a listen-to-your-superiors-tell-you-how-it-is kind of experience, then discussion, active learning, etc. are votes for equality. The same value claimed by contemporary ethnographers as the key to accurate ethnographic reporting is also claimed by student-centered teachers as the necessary key to learning. Yes, teachers know more than students—or at least know more about what they are trying to get across in the classroom.[8] But students learn best, so the story goes, when they take responsibility for their own education and when teachers treat them as younger equals. Malcolm Knowles' (1984) "andragogy"—originally developed as a theory of mature adult learning—has been relocated to undergraduate life.

Sociologically speaking, this makes a certain class sense. American mass education was originally developed to prepare an immigrant working class for factory labor. Teacher-directed schooling taught students to "show up, sit up, and shut up"—exactly the skills they would need in a hierarchical workplace. The middle-class

[8] Listening last year to a group of my students sing the words to every tune played by a disk jockey during a five-hour stint in an Australian Outback bar convinced me that American students know quite a bit, even if they do not read all the course material.

"organization man" (Whyte 1956) continued those skills at the university level, using them to survive a corporation life that was just as hierarchical as the factory floor. The research university's hidden curriculum (Snyder 1973) still trains the mass of students for this life; its aversion to involved teaching plays a "useful" social role.

There have, however, been two major shifts in the American class system since the Second World War. The first of these created a new middle class of college-educated workers (Bensman and Vidich 1971)—ones that staffed the big corporations. The second hollowed out that middle class, making its position less secure (Ehrenreich 1989; 2005). Well-paid working-class jobs are also in decline, as is lifetime employment in all industries. As Beth Rubin (1995) notes, labor has been forced to become "flexible". Those workers who know how to retrain themselves—the "dynamically flexible"—can create several new careers over a lifetime and can maintain their class status; the "statically flexible" lack such skills, so are vulnerable to falling.

"Student-directed learning" teaches precisely those skills needed for dynamic flexibility. It explicitly teaches self-management, individual initiative, teamwork, and responsibility for one's own education. These are also the skills used by high-status self-directed professionals—doctors, lawyers, and, yes, college teachers. With the outsourcing of more and more mid-level management jobs to independent consultants, plus the need for mid-career retraining, even among the already educated, the market for these skills has grown. "Training for lifelong learning" is the new educational mantra.

The very brightest undergraduates can direct their own education wherever they are—even in the largest universities. Liberal arts schools appeal to the merely bright, to those who do not do so well in impersonal crowds, and to those who need extra attention to succeed. American middle-class parents are willing to "buy" their sons and daughters such future work skills by paying the high tuition fees that such teaching schools demand. "Student-directed" pedagogical ideology produces an education for independence that meets students' future employment profiles, though that was never quite the ideologues' intention.

Contemporary ethnographers' commitment to equality with their informants serves as a *de facto* regulative ideal that ensures solid knowledge. Contemporary liberal arts education is similarly committed to student–teacher equality because "every soul is valuable" and "everyone has something to say" (Renfield, n.d.). Are these commitments really functional, or are they part of a common cultural trend?

A Religious Parallel

It seems a bit odd to turn to religion for evidence on this matter. After all, mainstream sociology—embedded in its secularization paradigm—notoriously considers religion *passé*. What possible help could a look at religions bring?

As I have written elsewhere (Spickard 2006*a*; 2006*c*), sociologists of religion tell six different stories about what is happening to religion in the modern era. Secularization theorists say that it is declining; observers of the new Christian Right and radical Islam say that it is becoming more political; market theorists say that it is changing shape in responding to market forces; and so on. Among these six narratives is a story about religious individualism. Put briefly, this story focuses on the power shift from clergy to laity in Euro-American religions—a shift from hierarchy toward equality in the religious sphere. As McGuire and I phrased it,

> The story goes like this. In the past, religions centered around church life. People's membership in one or another church pretty much predicted their beliefs and actions, in part because they had been socialized into their church's institutional package of beliefs and practices. . . . Now, however, . . . religious diversity has grown, not just between churches but within them. *Where once most individuals accepted what their leaders told them, today they demand the right to decide for themselves: their core beliefs as well as the details.* And they do not feel compelled to switch religious communities when their religious views change. Official and unofficial religiosity are thus out of synch, with the latter growing in importance. (Spickard and McGuire 2002: 292; emphasis added)

Tracking this at the denominational level, Roof and McKinney (1987) refer to an American "new voluntarism", by which individuals demand the right to make their own religious choices. Roof (1993) and Roof and Gesch (1995) further explored that theme among American Baby Boomers. Hervieu-Léger (1999 196 ff.) showed how European church members now practice "religion *à la carte*", paying less and less attention to organizational authorities. Riis (1994) saw a similar emphasis on individual autonomy in "secularized" Scandinavia. Orsi (2005) notes that the popular distinction in the USA between "spiritual" and "religious" involves just the assignment of "good" individual choice to the former and "bad" organizational authoritarianism to the latter.

The point here is that religion seems to have been infected with the same equalitarian values that have shaped recent ethnographic and pedagogical thinking—at least in the accounts of one group of sociologists of religion examining certain European and American religious trends. Moreover, those shown to favor individual religious choices belong to the same social strata as those advocating ethnographic and pedagogical equality: the educated, relatively elite, politically liberal, and anti-authoritarian new middle classes (Hout and Fischer 2002). Fundamentalists do not advocate student-centered pedagogy; nor do they embrace cultural relativism. Quite the contrary: they seek a return to the authority of (often imagined) tradition as a source of social and moral stability. Nor do *jihadists* insist on personal religious or pedagogical choice[9] (though we have no idea how they might practice ethnography, were they to do so).

[9] On the other hand, both Peter Clarke (2006: ch. 7) and Olivier Roy (2004) argue that Islamists, like liberals, emphasize the importance of individual reasoning.

Is it not possible that all three equalitarian urges—ethnographic, pedagogical, and religious—are fed by the same cultural forces? Perhaps; though a Peircian philosophy of science would remind us that a culturally induced equalitarianism does not make equality-oriented ethnography wrong. But Matilda Stevenson did not think her ethnography wrong, either, despite our now clear vision of its time-bound parochial concerns. It is easy—and a bit cheap—to point out how American it is for rational-choice sociology to treat religions in terms of markets, thus imagining that our own world is the measure of the universe as firmly as nineteenth-century imperialists imagined themselves to be the pinnacle of social development. It is a bit harder—but no less accurate—to recognize how our ethnographic 'science' is shaped by our own commitment to equality. Are we any different from the ethnographers of the Chicago School, who sought to remake poor immigrants into reflections of themselves? Much contemporary ethnographic thinking imagines that only imperial ethnographers fail to escape their own unacknowledged cultural prejudices. Too bad.

References

ADRIANCE, MADELEINE COUSINEAU (1995). *Promised Land: Base Christian Communities and the Struggle for the Amazon.* Albany, NY: State University of New York Press.

AHO, JAMES A. (1990). *The Politics of Righteousness: Idaho Christian Patriotism.* Seattle: University of Washington Press.

ALDRICH, HOWARD, and LILLIJORD, SOLVE (1999). "Stop Making Sense! Why Aren't Universities Better at Promoting Innovative Teaching?" In B. A. Pescosolido and R. Aminzade (eds.), *The Social Worlds of Higher Education: Handbook for Teaching in a New Century.* Thousand Oaks, Calif.: Pine Forge Press, 301–8.

AMMERMAN, NANCY T. (1987). *Bible Believers: Fundamentalists in the Modern World.* New Brunswick, NJ: Rutgers University Press.

APPIAH, KWAME ANTHONY (2000). "Dancing with the Moon: A Review of *In the Arms of Africa: The Life of Colin M. Turnbull* by Richard Grinker". *New York Review of Books*, 16 Nov., 55–9.

ASAD, TALAL (ed.) (1973). *Anthropology and the Colonial Encounter.* London: Ithaca Press.

BAER, HANS A. (1984). *The Black Spiritual Movement: A Religious Response to Racism.* Knoxville, Tenn.: University of Tennessee Press.

BAKER, PAUL (1999). "Creating Learning Communities: The Unfinished Agenda". In B. A. Pescosolido and R. Aminzade (eds.), *The Social Worlds of Higher Education: Handbook for Teaching in a New Century.* Thousand Oaks, Calif.: Pine Forge Press, 95–109.

BARKER, EILEEN (1984). *The Making of a Moonie: Choice or Brainwashing?* Oxford: Blackwell Publishers.

BATESON, GREGORY (1958). *Naven.* Palo Alto, Calif.: Stanford University Press.

BECKFORD, JAMES A. (1975). *The Trumpet of Prophecy: A Sociological Study of Jehovah's Witnesses.* New York: John Wiley & Sons.

BEHAR, RUTH, and GORDON, DEBORAH (eds.) (1995). *Women Writing Culture.* Berkeley: University of California Press.

BENDER, COURTNEY (2003). *Heaven's Kitchen: Living Religion as God's Love We Deliver.* Chicago: University of Chicago Press.

BENSMAN, JOSEPH, and VIDICH, ARTHUR J. (1971). *The New American Society: The Revolution of the Middle Class.* Chicago: Quadrangle Books.

BIRCKHEAD, JIM (1997). "Reading 'Snake Handling'. Critical Reflections". In S. D. Glazier (ed.), *Anthropology of Religion: A Handbook,* Westport, Conn.: Greenwood Press, 19–84.

—— (2002). " 'There's Power in the Blood': Writing Serpent Handling as Everyday Life". In J. V. Spickard, J. S. Landres, and Meredith B. McGuire (eds.), *Personal Knowledge and Beyond: Reshaping the Ethnography of Religion.* New York: New York University Press, 134–45.

BRASHER, BRENDA (1998). *Godly Women: Fundamentalism and Female Power.* New Brunswick, NJ: Rutgers University Press.

BROOKFIELD, STEPHEN (1999). "Building Trust with Students". In B. A. Pescosolido and R. Aminzade (eds.), *The Social Worlds of Higher Education: Handbook for Teaching in a New Century.* Thousand Oaks, Calif.: Pine Forge Press, 447–54.

BROWN, DEE (1970). *Bury My Heart at Wounded Knee: An Indian History of the American West.* New York: Holt, Rinehart & Winston.

BROWN, KAREN MCCARTHY (2001). *Mama Lola: A Vodou Priestess in Brooklyn,* updated and expanded edn. Berkeley: University of California Press.

CADGE, WENDY (2005). *Heartwood: The First Generation of Theravada Buddhism in America.* Chicago: University of Chicago Press.

CALHOUN, CRAIG (1999). "The Changing Character of College: Institutional Transformation in American Higher Education". In B. A. Pescosolido and R. Aminzade (eds.), *The Social Worlds of Higher Education: Handbook for Teaching in a New Century.* Thousand Oaks, Calif.: Pine Forge Press, 9–31.

CHANCELLOR, JAMES D. (2000). *Life in the Family: An Oral History of the Children of God.* Syracuse, NY: Syracuse University Press.

CLARKE, PETER (2006). *New Religions in Global Perspective.* London: Routledge.

CLIFFORD, JAMES, and MARCUS, GEORGE E. (eds.) (1986). *Writing Culture: The Poetics and Politics of Ethnography.* Berkeley: University of California Press.

COLEMAN, SIMON (2000). *The Globalisation of Charismatic Christianity: Spreading the Gospel of Prosperity.* Cambridge: Cambridge University Press.

CRAPANZANO, VINCENT (1980). *Tuhami: Portrait of a Moroccan.* Chicago: University of Chicago Press.

DAVIDMAN, LYNN (1991). *Tradition in a Rootless World: Women Turn to Orthodox Judaism.* Berkeley: University of California Press.

DAVIE, JODIE SHAPIRO (1995). *Women in the Presence: Constructing Community and Seeking Spirituality in Mainline Protestantism.* Philadelphia: University of Pennsylvania Press.

DEEGAN, MARY JO (1986). *Jane Addams and the Men of the Chicago School, 1892–1918.* New Brunswick, NJ: Transaction Publishers.

DOLLARD, JOHN (1957[1937]), *Caste and Class in a Southern Town.* New York: Doubleday.

DRAKE, ST. CLAIR, and CAYTON, HORACE R. (1945). *Black Metropolis: A Study of Negro Life in a Northern City.* New York: Harcourt Brace and Company.

EHRENREICH, BARBARA (1989). *Fear of Falling: The Inner Life of the Middle Class.* New York: Pantheon Books.

—— (2005). *Bait and Switch: The (Futile) Pursuit of the American Dream.* New York: Metropolitan Books.

EVANS-PRITCHARD, EDWARD E. (1969[1940]), *The Nuer.* New York: Oxford University Press.

FEDER, SHOSHANAH (1998). *Passing Over Easter: Constructing the Boundaries of Messianic Judaism.* Walnut Creek, Calif.: AltaMira Press.

FETTERMAN, DAVID M. (1998). *Ethnography Step by Step*, 2nd edn., Applied Social Research Methods Series, 17. Newbury Park, Calif.: Sage Publications.

FEYERABEND, PAUL (1975). *Against Method.* London: Verso.

FICHTER, JOSEPH (1951). *Dynamics of a City Church.* Chicago: University of Chicago Press.

FINKELSTEIN, MARTIN (2003). "The Morphing of the American Academic Profession". *Liberal Education*, 89/4: 6–15.

GEERTZ, CLIFFORD (1973). "Thick Description: Towards an Interpretive Theory of Culture". In *idem* (ed.), *The Interpretation of Cultures: Selected Essays.* New York: Basic Books, 3–30.

—— (1988). *Works and Lives: The Anthropologist as Author.* Stanford, Calif.: Stanford University Press.

—— (1998). "Deep Hanging Out". *New York Review of Books*, 22 Oct., 69–72.

GOLDMAN, MARION S. (1999). *Passionate Journeys: Why Successful Women Joined a Cult.* Ann Arbor: University of Michigan Press.

GRAMSCI, ANTONIO (1992[1949]), *The Prison Notebooks*, trans. J. A. Buttigieg and A. Callari. New York: Columbia University Press.

HARDING, SUSAN FRIEND (1987). "Convicted by the Holy Spirit: The Rhetoric of Fundamental Baptist Conversion". *American Ethnologist*, 14/1: 167–81.

—— (2000). *The Book of Jerry Falwell: Fundamentalist Language and Politics.* Princeton: Princeton University Press.

HERVIEU-LÉGER, DANIÈLE (1999). *Le Pèlerin et le Converti: La Religion en Mouvement.* Paris: Flammarion.

HERZFELD, MICHAEL (1998). *Portrait of a Greek Imagination: An Ethnographic Biography of Andreas Nenedakis.* Chicago: University of Chicago Press.

HOUT, MICHAEL, and FISCHER, CLAUDE S. (2002). "Why More Americans Have No Religious Preference: Politics and Generations". *American Sociological Review*, 67 (April): 165–90.

HYMES, DELL (ed.) (1969). *Reinventing Anthropology.* New York: Random House.

INGERSOLL, JULIE (2003). *Evangelical Christian Women: War Stories in the Gender Battles.* New York: New York University Press.

JAMES, ALLISON, HOCKEY, JENNY, and DAWSON, ANDREW (eds.) (1997). *After Writing Culture: Epistemology and Praxis in Contemporary Anthropology.* New York: Routledge.

KNOWLES, MALCOLM (1984). *Andragogy in Action.* San Francisco: Jossey-Bass.

KOMAROVSKY, MIRRA (1964). *Blue-Collar Marriage.* New York: Random House.

KONNER, MELVIN (2007). "Dim Beginnings". *New York Review of Books*, 1 Mar., 26–9.

KOSTARELOS, FRANCES (1995). *Feeling the Spirit: Faith and Hope in an Evangelical Black Storefront Church.* Columbia, SC: University of South Carolina Press.

KOTLOWITZ, ALEX (1991). *There Are No Children Here: The Story of Two Boys Growing Up in the Other America.* New York: Doubleday.

KUHN, THOMAS S. (1970). *The Structure of Scientific Revolutions*, 2nd edn., enlarged. Chicago: University of Chicago Press.

LANDRES, J. SHAWN (2002). "Being (in) the Field: Defining Ethnography in Southern California and Central Slovakia". In J. V. Spickard, J. S. Landres, and Meredith B. McGuire (eds.), *Personal Knowledge and Beyond: Reshaping the Ethnography of Religion.* New York: New York University Press, 100–12.

Levitt, Peggy (2001). *The Transnational Villagers.* Berkeley: University of California Press.

Lewis, Oscar (1951). *Life in a Mexican Village: Tepoztlán Restudied.* Urbana, Ill.: University of Illinois Press.

Liebow, Elliot (1967). *Tally's Corner: A Study of Negro Streetcorner Men.* Boston: Little, Brown & Company.

—— (1993). *Tell Them Who I Am: The Lives of Homeless Women.* New York: Free Press.

Lofland, John (1966). *Doomsday Cult: A Study of Conversion, Proselytization, and Maintenance of Faith.* Englewood Cliffs, NJ: Prentice-Hall.

—— Snow, David, Anderson, Leon, and Lofland, Lyn H. (2005). *Analyzing Social Settings: A Guide to Qualitative Observation and Analysis,* 4th edn. Belmont, Calif.: Wadsworth Publishing Company.

McAlister, Elizabeth (2002). *Rara!: Vodou, Power, and Performance in Haiti and its Diaspora.* Berkeley: University of California Press.

McFeely, Eliza (2001). *Zuni and the American Imagination.* New York: Hill and Wang.

Mooney, James (1896). *The Ghost Dance Religion and the Sioux Outbreak of 1890.* Technical Report 14, II. Washington: Bureau of American Ethnology.

Neal, Ed (1996). "Active Learning Beyond the Classroom". *POD Network Teaching Excellence Essay Series.* University of Chicago Center for Teaching and Learning; <http://teaching.uchicago.edu/pod/neal.html>; retrieved Feb. 26 2007.

Neitz, Mary Jo (1987). *Charisma and Community: A Study of Religious Commitment within the Catholic Charismatic Renewal.* New Brunswick, NJ: Transaction Publishers.

Nelson, Timothy J. (2004). *Every Time I Feel the Spirit: Religious Experience and Ritual in an African American Church.* New York: New York University Press.

Newman, David M. (1999). "Three Faces of Relevance: Connecting Disciplinary Knowledge to the 'Real World' ". In B. A. Pescosolido and R. Aminzade (eds.), *The Social Worlds of Higher Education: Handbook for Teaching in a New Century.* Thousand Oaks, Calif.: Pine Forge Press, 309–17.

Orsi, Robert A. (1996). *Thank You St. Jude: Women's Devotion to the Patron Saint of Hopeless Causes.* New Haven: Yale University Press.

—— (2005). "Snakes Alive: Religious Studies between Heaven and Earth". In *Between Heaven and Earth: The Religious Worlds People Make and the Scholars Who Study Them.* Princeton: Princeton University Press, 177–204.

Park, Robert Ezra, McKenzie, R. D., and Burgess, Ernest (1925). *The City: Suggestions for the Study of Human Nature in the Urban Environment.* Chicago: University of Chicago Press.

Paul, Richard (1999). "Critical Thinking, Moral Integrity, and Citizenship: Teaching for Intellectual Virtues". In B. A. Pescosolido and R. Aminzade (eds.), *The Social Worlds of Higher Education: Handbook for Teaching in a New Century.* Thousand Oaks, Calif.: Pine Forge Press, 128–36.

Peirce, Charles Sanders (1877). "The Fixation of Belief". *Popular Science Monthly,* 12 (Nov.): 1–15.

—— (1934[1902]). "Truth and Falsity and Error". In *Collected Papers of Charles Sanders Peirce,* v, ed. C. Hartshorne and P. Weiss, Cambridge, Mass.: Harvard University Press, 565–73.

—— (1955). *Philosophical Writings of Peirce*, ed. J. Buchler. New York: Dover Publications, Inc.

POPE, LISTON (1958). *Millhands and Preachers: A Study of Gastonia.* Oxford: Oxford University Press.

POWERS, GERALD T. (1999). "Teaching and Learning: A Matter of Style?" In B. A. Pescosolido and R. Aminzade (eds.), *The Social Worlds of Higher Education: Handbook for Teaching in a New Century.* Thousand Oaks, Calif.: Pine Forge Press, 435–46.

RAU, WILLIAM, and HEYL, BARBARA (1990). "Humanizing the Classroom: Collaborative Learning and Social Organization among Students". *Teaching Sociology*, 18: 141–55.

REDFIELD, ROBERT (1930). *Tepoztlan, a Mexican Village: A Study of Folk Life.* Chicago: University of Chicago Press.

RENFIELD, JAMES (n.d.). "On the Discussion Class". University of Chicago Center for Teaching and Learning; <http://teaching.uchicago.edu/tutorial/renfield.shtml>; retrieved 26 Feb. 2007.

RIIS, OLE (1994). "Patterns of Secularisation in Scandinavia". In T. Pettersson and O. Riis (eds.), *Scandinavian Values.* Uppsala: Acta Universitatis Upsaliensis, 99–128.

ROCHFORD, E. BURKE JR. (1985). *Hare Krishna in America.* New Brunswick, NJ: Rutgers University Press.

ROOF, WADE CLARK (1993). *A Generation of Seekers: The Spiritual Journeys of the Baby Boom Generation.* San Francisco: Harper.

—— (1999). *Spiritual Marketplace: Baby Boomers and the Remaking of American Religion.* Princeton: Princeton University Press.

—— and GESCH, LYN (1995). "Boomers and the Culture of Choice: Changing Patterns of Work, Family, and Religion". In N. T. Ammerman and W. C. Roof (eds.), *Work, Family, and Religion in Contemporary Society.* New York: Routledge, 61–80.

—— and MCKINNEY, WILLIAM (1987). *American Mainline Religion: Its Changing Shape and Future.* New Brunswick, NJ: Rutgers University Press.

ROY, OLIVIER (2004). *Globalized Islam: The Search for a New Ummah.* New York: Columbia University Press.

RUBIN, BETH (1995). *Shifts in the Social Contract: Understanding Change in American Society.* Thousand Oaks, Calif.: Pine Forge Press.

SAID, EDWARD W. (1978). *Orientalism.* New York: Pantheon Books.

—— (1985). "Orientalism Reconsidered". In F. Barker, P. Hulme, M. Iversen, and D. Loxley (eds.), *Europe and Its Others*, i. Colchester: University of Essex, 14–27.

—— (1993). *Culture and Imperialism.* New York: Alfred A. Knopf.

SCHENSUL, JEAN J., and LECOMPTE, MARGARET D. (eds.) (1999). *Ethnographer's Toolkit*, 7 vols. Lanham, Md.: Altamira Press.

SEELEY, JOHN R., SIM, ALEXANDER, and LOOSELY, ELIZABETH W. (1956). *Crestwood Heights: A Study of the Culture of Suburban Life.* New York: Basic Books.

SHAFFIR, WILLIAM B. (1974). *Life in a Religious Community: Lubavitcher Chassidim in Montreal.* Toronto: Holt, Rinehart & Winston.

SHOSTAK, MARJORIE (1983). *Nisa: The Life and Words of a !Kung Woman.* New York: Vintage Books.

SNYDER, BENSON R. (1973). *The Hidden Curriculum.* Cambridge, Mass.: MIT Press.

SPICKARD, JAMES V. (1994). "Texts and Contexts: Recent Trends in the Sociology of Religion as Reflected in American Textbooks". *Social Compass*, 41/3: 313–28.

SPICKARD, JAMES V. (2002). "On the Epistemology of Post-Colonial Ethnography". In J. V. Spickard, S. Landres, and M. B. McGuire (eds.), *Personal Knowledge and Beyond: Reshaping the Ethnography of Religion*. New York: New York University Press, 237–52.

—— (2003). "Slow Journalism? Ethnography as a Means of Understanding Religious Social Activism". PPRES Working Papers 36; <http://www.wcfiareligionproject.org/rsrchpapsum.asp?ID=721>; retrieved 26 Feb. 2007.

—— (2006*a*). "Narrative Versus Theory in the Sociology of Religion: Five Stories of Religion's Place in the Late Modern World". In J. A. Beckford and J. Walliss (eds.), *Religion and Social Theory: Classical and Contemporary Debates*. London: Ashgate Publishers, 163–75.

—— (2006*b*). "Post-Colonial or After Colonialism? Reflections on the Politics and Faiths of Social-Scientific Theorizing". Conference paper presented 29 July at the World Congress of Sociology, Durban, South Africa. Conference Proceedings (CD-ROM) available from the International Sociological Association,

—— (2006*c*). "What is Happening to Religion? Six Visions of Religion's Future". *Nordic Journal of Religion and Society*, 19/1: 13–28.

—— and McGuire, Meredith B. (2002). "Four Narratives in the Sociology of Religion". In M. B. MCGUIRE (ed.), *Religion: The Social Context*. Belmont, Calif.: Wadsworth, 285–300.

SPIVAK, GAYATRI CHAKRAVORTY (1988). "Can the Subaltern Speak?" In C. Nelson and L. Grossberg (eds.), *Marxism and the Interpretation of Culture*. Champaign, Ill.: University of Illinois Press, 271–316.

SPRADLEY, JAMES P. (2000[1970]). *You Owe Yourself a Drunk: An Ethnography of Urban Nomads*. Prospect Heights, Ill.: Waveland Press.

STUART, A. (1997). "Student-Centered Learning". *Learning*, 26 (Sept./Oct.): 53–6.

THOMAS, ELIZABETH MARSHALL (1959). *The Harmless People*. New York: Vintage Books.

—— (2006). *The Old Way: A Story of the First People*. New York: Farrar, Straus and Giroux.

TIPTON, STEVEN M. (1982). *Getting Saved From the Sixties: Moral Meaning in Conversion and Cultural Change*. Berkeley: University of California Press.

TURNBULL, COLIN (1972). *The Mountain People*. New York: Simon & Schuster.

TWEED, THOMAS A. (1997). *Our Lady of the Exile: Diasporic Religion at a Cuban Catholic Shrine in Miami*. Oxford: Oxford University Press.

VAN MAANEN, JOHN, and LAURENT, ANDRÉ (1993). "The Flow of Culture: Some Notes on Globalization and the Multinational Corporation". In S. Ghoshal and D. E. Westney (eds.), *Organization Theory and the Multinational Corporation*. New York: St Martin's Press, 275–312.

VIDICH, ARTHUR J., and BENSMAN, JOSEPH (1968). *Small Town in a Mass Society: Class, Power, and Religion in a Rural Community*, rev. edn. Princeton: Princeton University Press.

WARNER, R. STEPHEN (1988). *New Wine in Old Wineskins: Evangelicals and Liberals in a Small-Town Church*. Berkeley: University of California Press.

—— and WITTNER, JUDITH G. (eds.) (1998). *Gatherings in Diaspora: Religious Communities and the New Immigration*. Philadelphia: Temple University Press.

WARNER, W. LLOYD, and LUNT, PAUL S. (1941). *The Social Life of a Modern Community*. New Haven: Yale University Press.

WHYTE, WILLIAM FOOTE (1943). *Street Corner Society: The Social Structure of an Italian Slum*. Chicago: University of Chicago Press.

Whyte, William H. (1956). *The Organization Man.* New York: Simon & Schuster.
Woldemikael, Tekle Mariam (1989). *Becoming Black American: Haitians and American Institutions in Evanston, Illinois.* New York: AMS Press.

Suggested Reading

McGuire, Meredith B. (2007). *Lived Religion.* New York: Oxford University Press.
Pescosolido, Bernice A., and Aminzade, Ronald (eds.) (1999). *The Social Worlds of Higher Education.* Thousand Oaks, Calif.: Pine Forge Press.
Spickard, James V., Landres, J. Shawn, and McGuire, Meredith B. (eds.) (2002). *Personal Knowledge and Beyond: Reshaping the Ethnography of Religion.* New York: New York University Press.
Van Maanen, John (1988). *Tales of the Field: On Writing Ethnography.* Chicago: University of Chicago Press.
Also Asad (1973); Behar and Gordon (1995); Birckhead (1997); Clifford and Marcus (1986); Geertz (1988); Hervieu-Léger (1999); James *et al.* (1997); and Roof (1999).

Index